D0079513

# HOLOCAUST LITERATURE

## A Handbook of Critical, Historical, and Literary Writings

*Edited by* SAUL S. FRIEDMAN

*Foreword by* DENNIS KLEIN

**GREENWOOD PRESS**
Westport, Connecticut • London

**Library of Congress Cataloging-in-Publication Data**

Holocaust literature : a handbook of critical, historical, and
  literary writings / edited by Saul S. Friedman ;  foreword by Dennis
  Klein.
        p.  cm.
    Includes bibliographical references and index.
    ISBN 0–313–26221–7
    1. Holocaust, Jewish (1939–1945)  I. Friedman, Saul S.
D804.3.H35  1993
940.53′18—dc20        92–24135

British Library Cataloguing in Publication Data is available.

Library of Congress Catalog Card Number: 92–24135
ISBN: 0–313–26221–7

First published in 1993

Greenwood Press, 88 Post Road West, Westport, CT 06881
An imprint of Greenwood Publishing Group, Inc.

Printed in the United States of America

The paper used in this book complies with the
Permanent Paper Standard issued by the National
Information Standards Organization (Z39.48–1984).
10 9 8 7 6 5 4 3 2 1

For Nora Levin and Earl Friedman,
scholars who left us too soon

# Contents

Foreword: The Fate of Holocaust Literature

        DENNIS KLEIN          xiii

Preface          xix

**Part I: Conceptual Approaches to the Holocaust**      1

1. The Major Texts of the Holocaust

    ANNETTE EL-HAYEK          3

2. The Rise and Development of National Socialism in Germany

    REYNOLD KOPPEL          21

3. Selected Biographies and Interpretations of Hitler

    ROBERT H. WHEALEY          39

4. The Concentration Camps and Killing Centers of the Third Reich

    CHARLES W. SYDNOR, JR.          74

5. Asking Unanswerable Questions: A Bibliographic Study of Post-Holocaust Jewish Philosophies

    STEVEN H. ADAMS          106

6. The Church and the Holocaust

    DAVID A. RAUSCH          121

7.  The Righteous Gentiles
    LEON W. WELLS                                           140

8.  Understanding Motivations in the Holocaust
    EVA FOGELMAN                                            161

9.  Jewish Women in the Holocaust Resistance
    BEA STADTLER                                            176

10. The Relationship of Genocide to Holocaust Studies
    NORA LEVIN                                              194


Part II:  Holocaust Area Studies                           201

11. Relations Between Jews and Poles During the Holocaust:
    New and Old Approaches in Polish Historiography
    SHMUEL KRAKOWSKI                                        203

12. The Last Tragedy of the Shoah: The Jews of Hungary
    ASHER COHEN                                             216

13. The Holocaust in Czechoslovakia: A Survey of the Literature
    SAUL S. FRIEDMAN                                        249

14. The Ukrainian Halychyna Division: A Case Study of
    Historical Revisionism
    SOL LITTMAN                                             279

15. Approaches to the Study of the Holocaust in the Balkans
    ALEXANDER KITROEFF                                      301

16. The Holocaust in France
    SANFORD GUTMAN                                          321

17. Holland and the Holocaust
    EARL M. FRIEDMAN                                        364

18. Italy and the Holocaust
    ALAN CASSELS                                            380

19. The Holocaust in Spain
    JOHN AXE                                                408

20. Switzerland and the Holocaust
    HERBERT HOCHHAUSER                                      430

21.  Great Britain and the Holocaust
     MONTY NOAM PENKOWER                                    439

22.  The Politics of Collaboration: A Historiography of Arab-
     German Relations, 1933–1945
     JONATHAN C. FRIEDMAN                                   459

23.  American Response to the Holocaust, 1933–1945
     JACK FISCHEL                                           470

Part III:   The Holocaust in Education and the Arts         479

24.  The Holocaust in the School Textbooks of the Federal
     Republic of Germany
     WALTER RENN                                            481

25.  Holocaust Diaries and Memoirs
     LAURENCE KUTLER                                        521

26.  The Holocaust in Fiction
     HARRY JAMES CARGAS                                     533

27.  The Poetry of the Holocaust
     GLORIA YOUNG                                           547

28.  Juvenile and Youth Books About the Holocaust
     BEA STADTLER                                           575

29.  The Holocaust in Art
     NELLY TOLL                                             582

30.  Music of the Holocaust
     IRENE HESKES                                           591

31.  The Holocaust as Seen in the Movies
     MORRIS ZYRL AND SAUL S. FRIEDMAN                       604

32.  Resources for Holocaust Study
     SAUL S. FRIEDMAN                                       623

Author/Title Index                                          633

Subject Index                                               655

About the Contributors                                      673

# Foreword: The Fate of Holocaust Literature

*Dennis Klein*

I last visited Berlin in 1987. That was two years before the Wall came down; two years before the end of German history as we knew it. The Wall was the most visible symbol of Germany's troubled past, a reminder of the calculated Nazi destruction of European Jewry and other ''undesirables.'' It was a reminder of Germany's self-destruction as well, for hatred, as James Baldwin observed, ''never failed to destroy the man who hated.''

I remember, in particular, two places that seemed to freeze the past in time. One was Potsdamer Platz, site of the former Reich Chancellory and adjacent to the former headquarters of the Gestapo, SS, and SD.

Further east was a burial ground for Jews, much smaller than the better known Weissensee Jewish cemetery. Like Potsdamer Platz, it stands as a historical relic. Except for forgettable explanatory plaques, nothing conferred on these two sites a sense of how they interact with the present, the way the original but damaged Gedaechtniskirche, the famous church built in the nineteenth century, is flanked (and dwarfed) by two postwar buildings. Although Potsdamer Platz attracted many visitors, to get to either site was not easy.

At least these two places could evoke a more distant past. In fact, they had the remarkable effect of coaxing me to the 1920s, when Potsdamer Platz prevailed as the cultural and political center of Berlin. I was able to imagine the coffee houses, the Haus Vaterland among them, which drew the literati of Weimar Germany; the world's first traffic light signaling the excitement and effervescence of the city; the home of the UFA, the German film industry signifying not only a creative energy but also the status Berlin once had as a *Weltstadt*, a world city.

A flood of like visions filled the vacant spaces of the cemetery as well—not of the particular lives whose names appeared on the tombstones, but of the life of an entire community. Here I could also imagine Jews walking, as I did, down the cemetery's dark and quiet paths, thinking innocently (as I could not) about death as a natural, if unhappy, event. It occurred to me that I had come to mourn not a single life, and not only the life of Jews who once lived and prospered in Berlin. I was mourning a lost assumption about a way of life, the belief (to which Jews had clung) that, despite disagreements and self-doubts, a people could feel perfectly at home. German Jews felt at home in Germany.

That same frame of mind set the mood for me as I recalled the rest of Germany. Here, beside Potsdamer Platz where I stood, used to be a people who knew they were a part of something special, something world-historical. For them, there were no limits to what they could achieve on behalf of mankind—always on behalf of mankind—in politics, research, music, art, film, and technology. Let there be no doubt about it, Germans had felt every bit as insecure as Jews did. They may never have had to prove their worth to their compatriots, but, having had just lost a war and losing control in the volatile 1920s over their economic fortunes, they worried a great deal about their self-worth. Still, neither Germans nor German Jews felt hopelessly defeated. They did not feel desperate. Not yet.

With the unification of the two Germanys just a few years ago, even memories of events that predated World War II and the misery and defeat that followed seemed to vanish with the Wall. In that extraordinary year Germans were determined to declare a second *Stunde Null*, a second "zero hour" (the first was in 1945), when nothing before then could possibly count as much as the present and future. Potsdamer Platz would literally disappear. The Jewish burial ground could easily disappear as well, if not from "urban renewal," which threatens Jewish cemeteries all over Germany, then from persistent local neglect. Although I didn't fully realize it during my visit, an assault on German history was already well under way. The year before, German historian Ernst Nolte wrote a controversial article for the *Frankfurter Allegemeine Zeitung*. He titled it, "The Past That Will Not Go Away." Nolte's impatience was soon to be rewarded.

It's fair to say that the rest of the Western world was, and is, running out of patience too. To say that people can bear only so much agony (to paraphrase T. S. Eliot) is only part of the reason. Some people are downright tired of the subject—too many docudramas, too many movies. The most recent pulse-taking of American opinion on this subject—Harris and Roper surveys in 1986—indicated that almost half the respondents were weary of discussions about the Holocaust. All this suggests that memories can inundate just as easily as illuminate.

Today there is a kind of backlash *against* the Holocaust. I interpret this as partly anti-Semitic and partly neoconservative. On the one-hand, historical "revisionists," a pseudo-intellectual cabal if there ever was one (they claim the Holocaust never happened), want to rob Jews of the political capital they think is gained from talk about the Holocaust (they believe Jews use the Holocaust to

justify the new state of Israel or to curry special favors). The vague perception
that the Holocaust is a "Jewish subject" and is not penetrable by non-Jews (an
observation historian Lucy S. Dawidowicz made in 1976) fuels their suspicion
that the emphasis given to it by Jews is self-serving (read: conspiratorial).

More corrosive is a popular belief that America is in decline, weakened from
within by competing group claims for attention. Subjects that were, before the
1960s, declasse—women's, blacks', and Hispanics' rights, Third World cultures,
the Holocaust—now contend for overdue consideration. The "silent majority"
is appalled. To them, the erosion of American hegemony and the insinuation
into the mainstream of traditionally marginal and insignificant social concerns
are not coincidental.

I believe many educators unintentionally contribute to the denaturing of the
subject. I refer to the constant temptation to glean something relevant or to draw
poignant lessons from past events, especially, I might add, from the Holocaust
years. In all my years in teaching and writing about the Holocaust, I never
understood why it isn't obvious that the subject stands on its own. What is more
dramatic than survivor memoirs, stories about rescuing Jews from the terror, the
puzzle of how Europe "took" to racial beliefs—enthusiastically and so insidiously? What is more compelling than an event whose occurrence shattered forever
the world's innocent faith in state government and national leaders, in reason
and compromise, or in the inexorable progress of human civilization?

This, however, does not describe the state of the art today. The Holocaust,
we're told, is worth teaching because it serves to warn us about the power and
deadly consequences of prejudice. It causes us to redouble our commitment to
core American democratic values. We are asked to imagine ourselves in Nazi
Germany: How would we react to the abduction of our neighbors or the incin-
eration of homes and synagogues? Wouldn't we steel ourselves, no matter the
personal risks, to save others (even strangers) in distress? Repudiate indifference!
Get involved!

Never mind the anti-historical approach students are urged to adopt when
studying the Holocaust this way. It's enough just to wonder if the Holocaust
will even exist much longer as a subject of legitimate study. If all students are
asked to explore is its relevance, if the subject is nothing more than a *pretext*
for honing values and civic awareness, it loses its intrinsic value and becomes
merely one of many possible subjects for discussion. Eventually a consensus
might emerge that the Holocaust is really *less* relevant, less didactic, than other
calamities, such as the tragedy of Native Americans, the historical enslavement
of American blacks, or the devastation of inner cities.

Fortunately, we're not there yet. Although they appear more serious than
before, revisionists are no more persuasive. The Holocaust and other nontraditional subjects, on the other hand, have gained a foothold in American
education. The task that lies ahead is a matter of strategy, not principle; that is,
finding ways to incorporate discrete subjects into a new synthesis of American
and world history. To be sure, the Holocaust stands on its own, but that doesn't

mean it should stand alone. It didn't when it happened (contrary to the misguided belief that Auschwitz was a historical accident), and we should acknowledge that fact whenever we teach about it.

Nor has the subject withered. Directly and indirectly, the Holocaust was a theme that dominated the 1992 National Book Critics Circle awards competition. The subject, despite its strategic flaws, proliferates in American schools. Glimmers of interest, demonstrated by the creation of Germany's first Holocaust resource center (in Frankfurt) and the magnificent exhibit in Berlin on Jewish life and culture, resist the urge over there to lay the subject to rest. It's true just as the German historian said: The past refuses to go away.

We've witnessed periods of historical amnesia before. In the 1950s and 1960s, only a handful of memoirs and studies served to recall and record the Holocaust. The subject was virtually taboo, a consequence of the first and universally affirmed *Stunde Null*. Self-exonerating national myths, making cases for ignorance (an American predilection) or helplessness (Austrians and the French regarded themselves as victims), postponed the day of self-examination.

As the present bibliographic anthology amply illustrates, the past fifteen to twenty years reversed the tendency to forget or obfuscate history. Educators established a beachhead in West German schools (see the essay by Walter Renn); writers charted new thematic frontiers (e.g., Wells, Fogelman, and Stadtler); historians anchored the subject in specific, national contexts (see part II); subcultures began to crystallize in literature, art, music, and film (e.g. Cargas, Young, Toll, Heskes, Zyrl, and Friedman); indeed, Holocaust studies emerged as a distinctive field of inquiry (Levin).

In my opinion, the essays included in this impressive volume represent something more than a chronicle of cumulative reflection on the Holocaust years. Taken together, it is, itself, a testament. The *Handbook* comes at a time of renewed skepticism and cynicism over a subject that deserves much more. Its inventory of knowledge will not, of course, stem the tide. It will do nothing, for example, to relieve the weariness and impatience of those who have had enough. It will not help emancipate the subject from the academic ghetto it finds itself in. I'd like to believe it will dilute the revisionist denials of history.

Even its raison d'etre—a review of sources—might be taken as a sort of swan song, a eulogy for a period of intellectual ferment that is no more, a summary statement that, like Potsdamer Platz, freezes the past in time. I don't accept this point of view. After all, a volume like this could have the opposite effect. It could stimulate new recall or set the stage for new courses and new lines of investigation. I believe this is the *Handbook*'s signal contribution precisely because, page after page, it keeps the subject in focus. No pretensions to intellectual self-importance here. Not a hint of "comparative suffering" (Levin does, however, offer useful distinctions).

Most refreshing of all is this volume's avoidance of drawing moral lessons from the Holocaust. On the contrary, it shows us that the subject's significance is in its details: the evolution of the Nazi party (Koppel, Whealey), the role of the Church (Rausch), the formation of killing centers (Sydnor), the multiple national paths to murder (part II), and the postwar struggles to bear witness (Kutler, Hayek, Adams).

The *Handbook* is less interested in the meaning or implications of survival and rescue as it is the question of why the odds against survival and rescue were greater in some countries than in others. Its tone is appropriately critical, not sermonic. It affirms specificity and context over abstraction and timeless, really vacuous relevance. It is a scholarly corrective, not "politically correct."

At a time when the subject is victim to ideological warfare and, for that reason, threatens to vaporize completely, the publication of these thirty-two bibliographic essays is noteworthy. The editor's intention to "sift the wheat from the chaff" is exactly what's needed to reconstitute a subject that thoroughly documents a critical part of our history.

# Preface

## FOUNDATIONS OF HOLOCAUST HISTORIOGRAPHY

Holocaust is a Greek word meaning a burnt offering. It probably derives from the Hebrew *oleh* (a going up), the kind of sacrifice practiced by priests in the ancient temple of Jerusalem. Over the past forty years the term *Holocaust* has come to represent the deliberate campaign of extermination of Jews by the Nazis in Germany's Third Reich. Among Jews there are disputes over whether the deaths of so many people may be regarded as a *churban* (sacrifice) or *shoah* (destruction). Historians differ as to the proper starting date for discussing this tragic period of history. Some favor 1933; others favor 1938, 1939, or 1919. While scholars debate the extent of Nazi genocide, self-proclaimed revisionists contest whether "It" ever occurred, and other oppressed peoples assert that they actually suffered more than the Jews.

The fact that Auschwitz and Dachau were realities for many people still living, Jews and non-Jews, explains why the field of Holocaust studies is an evolving phenomenon. Until 1967 (when the prospect of a slaughter of Jews in Israel sparked renewed interest in the subject), few academic institutions beyond professional seminaries offered course work in Jewish history, let alone Holocaust.

In the time between the end of World War II and the Six-Day War, three foreign-born scholars—Elia Tcherikover, Philip Friedman, and Jacob Robinson—were responsible for preserving documents and nurturing studies in the United States. Together, these men helped make YIVO (the Institute for Jewish Research) into the foremost center of Yiddish studies in the world.

YIVO was founded in Berlin in 1925 by several historians, including Tcherikover, Simon Dubnow, and Max Weinreich. Its original center was Vilna, the city known as the Jerusalem of Poland. At the height of Nazi power in 1939–40, Tcherikover and aides (including the much-maligned Zosa Szajkowski) managed to flee Europe, bringing with them boxes of Russian, German, and Polish files. Since then, the American branch of YIVO, located in New York City, has published annual yearbooks and bilingual translations of writers such as I. L. Peretz and Sholom Aleichem, convened seminars on topics ranging from economics to psychology, and rendered assistance to numerous researchers in its library.

Jacob Robinson joined Tcherikover in New York in 1940. A onetime diplomat in Lithuania, Robinson was instrumental in setting up the Institute for Jewish Affairs during the war and served as an advisor to Chief Allied Prosecutor Robert Jackson at the Nuremberg trials. Appointed to the UN Human Rights Commission, he helped coordinate the 1952 reparations agreement between Israel and West Germany. At the same time, Robinson served as coordinator of research publications for YIVO, working closely with Philip Friedman, a Polish-born scholar who survived the Holocaust in hiding. Responsible for organizing the Jewish Historical Institute in Warsaw, Friedman came to New York after the displaced persons' camps in Germany were closed. A teacher at Columbia University, he published two of the most readable books on the Holocaust, *Martyrs and Fighters: The Epic of the Warsaw Ghetto* in 1954 and *Their Brothers' Keepers* in 1957. Together, Robinson and Friedman edited the *Guide to Jewish History Under Nazi Impact* (1960), which was soon supplemented with Robinson and Friedman's *Bibliography of Books in Hebrew on the Jewish Catastrophe and Heroism in Europe* (1960) and Friedman and W. J. Gar's *Bibliography of Books in Yiddish on the Jewish Catastrophe and Heroism* (1962). Along with Robinson's *The Holocaust and After: Sources and Literature in English* (1973) and Friedman's essay on problems of research in *The Catastrophe of European Jewry: Antecedents, History, Reflections* (Jerusalem: Yad Vashem, 1976), these tracts stand as the fundamental bibliographic texts on the Holocaust, and no student should begin work without first consulting them.

Because there were no established schools of thought or interpretation on the subject of deliberate human extermination, those who committed themselves to the study of the Holocaust had to develop their own guidelines. In one sense, the recent nature of the subject offered opportunities to a number of female scholars, such as Nora Levin, Lucy Dawidowicz, Hannah Arendt, Leni Yahil, Marie Syrkin, Miriam Novitch, and Deborah Lipstadt, who were not constrained by strictures or prejudices in more traditional academic fields. Generally, however, within Holocaust studies, conservative conventions prevailed. As late as the 1970s potential researchers were advised that insufficient time had lapsed for historians to reach thoughtful conclusions about Nazi genocide. Jewish historians were told not to deal with a subject that was certain to evoke emotional, rather than objective, responses. Creative writers were lectured for their "purplish prose." Scholars who honored the 2,200-year-old instruction from Polybius that history must have utility saw their work denigrated as "political." For all but the most daring in the field of Holocaust studies, it was as if the curious sigillographer from Anatole France's *Penguin Island* were still dictating to the neophyte historian when he cynically admonished: "Historians copy from one another. Thus they spare themselves trouble and avoid the appearance of presumption. An original historian is the object of distrust, contempt, and loathing from everybody."[1]

Over the past four decades, only a handful of books dealing with the Holocaust have been greeted with general accolades, among them Lucy Dawidowicz's *The War Against the Jews*, Terrence Des Pres's *The Survivor*, Walter Laqueur's *The Terrible Secret*, David Wyman's *The Abandonment of the Jews*, and Michael Marrus's *The Holocaust in History*. A better short list might include Nora Levin's *The Holocaust*, Arthur Morse's *While Six Million Died*, Stanley Milgram's *Obedience to Authority*, David Szonyi's *The Holocaust: An Annotated Bibliography and Resource Guide*, Gerhard Schoenberner's *The Yellow Star*, and Andre Schwarz-Bart's incomparable *The Last of the Just*. Each of these books has its peculiar strengths and flaws, but once a work is accepted as definitive, those who take issue with conventional icons risk being branded as heretics.

Not surprisingly, since the liberation of the death camps, the veneration of images has become extremely important in Holocaust observances and studies. Some of these are deserved, others questionable. There is no debate, for example, over the moral courage of Dr. Henryk Goldszmit (Janusz Korczak), the Warsaw Jewish physician who accompanied 190 orphans to their deaths in Treblinka, or the 120,000 Jews, including 5 unnamed babies, murdered at Babi Yar. Not everyone who lived through that period, however, merits deification. They were people: some did extraordinary things like fighting with homemade bombs against tanks, others risked their lives as smugglers or teachers, women tried to protect their children and parents, and others were simple victims of panic or fear. As more and more information becomes available, especially from German and East European archives, scholars have an obligation to try to understand the perpetrators, bystanders, rescuers, or victims not as saints or demons but as individuals. To those who suggest that such a task is impossible, who teach that the Holocaust was inenarrable, "metahistory," bigger than history and thus impossible to comprehend, another teacher from the Warsaw ghetto, Genia Silkes, comments:

All the time people in the United States are making *reboyne shel oylem* [literally ruler of the world, the most important thing in the world] out of the Holocaust. God, God, God. Where was God? There was no God. God was not in the ghettos. God was not in the camps. People in Israel, at the Yad Vashem and the Ghetto Fighters Museum, they laugh at Holocaust historiography in the United States. Holocaust was no mystery, no Chasidism like [people] make it. It was a horrible, historical fact.[2]

## The Revisionist Threat

The professional historian is obliged to analyze facts, make observations, and, where necessary, explode myths. Well-intended iconoclasm can be a troublesome thing if carried too far. Take, for example, the question of the numbers of Jews killed during the Holocaust. In speeches, documents, and deed, the Nazis made it clear that they intended to rid Europe of what they regarded as a pestilence. During World War II special units of the German police and military carried out mass roundups and executions of Jews. The objects of a conference held at Interpol headquarters located in the Berlin suburb of Wannsee on January 23, 1942, Jews were deported to concentration camps where large numbers perished. By the time World War II ended, entire Jewish communities in Europe had been obliterated. Studies done by the Anglo-American Committee of Inquiry, the American Jewish Congress, Leon Poliakov (author of *Harvest of Hate*, one of the first texts on the Holocaust), and others put the number of dead at close to six million, a statistic accepted by most scholars. Others believe that this figure is too high. Raul Hilberg, in *The Destruction of the European Jews,* argues that five million is more likely. He is joined in this by Israeli Yehuda Bauer, author of *A History of the Holocaust*, who recently disputed the estimate of two million Jews murdered in Auschwitz.

Academic squabbles such as these, it seems to me, merely embolden those who care little for Jews. If only five million died, why not four million or three million, or even, as some have suggested, five hundred thousand to six hundred thousand? There have always been apologists for Hitler and the Third Reich. Less popular in the postwar years when images of Dachau and Belsen were more immediate, less potent in Germany where their publishing rights have been circumscribed, old-fashioned anti-Semitic elements have revived in the United States. In the past decade, the Institute for Historical Review, a pseudoacademic front created by Willis Carto, publisher of *The Liberty Lobby*, has won some unwitting converts. In conferences, broadcasts, and journal articles, the institute (feigning continuity with the likes of Harry Elmer Barnes and Sidney Fay, reputable critics of America's involvement in World War I) contests whether the Holocaust ever happened. In this telling, the death camps of Treblinka and Sobibor were no more than detention centers like the ones created by the Roosevelt government for Japanese at Manzanar. *Sonderbehandlung,* normally interpreted as a euphemism for annihilation of Jews, really meant special care by Germans for their Jewish internees. Revisionists have employed ''experts'' on gas chambers to suggest that gas chambers in concentration camps functioned solely for the purpose of delousing clothes. If Jews died, they aver, they died alongside others—Germans, Slavs, or Greeks—victims of the normal exigencies of warfare, bombardment, disease, and food shortages, and not as a result of a deliberate program of murder. The Holocaust, therefore, was a postwar invention of Zionists, who schemed to win sympathy and money for Israel, their intruder state in the Middle East that continues to sap the economic life of Western democracies.

The IHR has repeatedly been debunked, as in a 1981 Los Angeles court suit brought by survivor Mel Mermelstein; in a 1991 Massachusetts court where its authority on gas chambers was shown to hold a degree neither in engineering, history, nor chemistry; and in academic meetings from Boston to Seattle where the credentials and methodology of its principal spokespersons, such as Arthur Butts and Paul Rassinier, have been exposed. Nothing, it seems, can totally dispel the indecent claims of the revisionists. Those who labor in Holocaust studies can bear witness to the effectiveness of the Big Lie. What Leon Bloy once taught and Joseph Goebbels practiced holds true:

To say to the man in the street, even to the shabbiest specimen of a rottenness beyond hope: "These perfidious Hebrews who bespatter you with mud, they have stolen all your money. Get it back from them, O Egyptian! Beat them up, if you have any guts, and chase them into the Red Sea!"—to keep on saying this, to say it everywhere, to bellow it in books and in newspapers, and even now and then to fight a duel, so that the idea will echo nobly over the hills and dales, and above all never to speak of anything else, that is the prescription and the mystification, the established tactics of the big guns which will ensure a triumphant success. No one—God help us!—can resist all that.[3]

Despite the efforts of conscientious historians, the IHR and its offspring flourish. In 1991–92, in the interest of free speech, student newspapers at Northwestern, Cornell, Duke, Ohio State, and Michigan universities published advertisements submitted by the Committee for Open Debate on the Holocaust. Libraries continue to order their publications. A growing number of naive readers in the United States and abroad believe their claims that Hitler was not, after all, so different from other leaders in history who committed excesses out of nationalistic zeal.

Some of these relativist arguments have been embraced by reputable scholars. In *Der Europäische Bürgerkrieg* (1987), Ernst Nolte of the Free University of Berlin claimed that Nazism was a response to Soviet communism and that everything Hitler did had a precedent in Stalin's Gulag. The relativist assertion that "genocide" must be understood within the context of total war has also recently been adopted by Princeton's Arno Mayer in his controversial *Why Did The Heavens Not Darken?*

Part of the problem, it seems to me, stems from the scope of the Holocaust. Apart from the astonishing number of victims—two of every three European Jews died; three million Polish Jews were reduced to six thousand in one generation—these deeds were perpetrated by a nation that had enriched civilization with Bach, Beethoven, and Kant. The Holocaust took place in the heart of the most cultured continent, and it happened yesterday, not a thousand years ago. Unlike previous massacres where Jews were offered the option of converting by religious zealots, every last Jewish man, woman, and child was condemned to die for the crime of being alive. That certain death sentence is what distinguished the fate of the Jews from that of Yugoslavs selected to be killed in reprisals or Polish kapos sent to Auschwitz as lawbreakers or German Communists detained at Buchenwald or even the feebleminded and insane who were murdered as part of the Nazis' provisional euthanasia scheme that was halted by protests of German

bishops in 1941. The only other group that shared the fate of the Jews was the
Gypsies, five hundred thousand of whom were murdered in a similar scheme of
genocide. As Emil Fackenheim has aptly noted, "The Holocaust was a unique
descent into Hell."[4]


## Comparative Pain

Sensing that non-Jews may be sated with talk, books, films, and docudramas
dealing with Jewish suffering, some Jewish scholars have tried to impute universal relevance to the Holocaust by making reference to all innocent victims
of Nazism, whether in or out of concentration camps. Once again, indeterminate
numbers have been bandied about: five million, six million Gentiles. They include
the victims of bombings in Warsaw, Coventry, and Rotterdam and, by illogical
extension, the Germans of Hamburg and Dresden. They include Ukrainians who
died alongside Jews and Germans in Dachau. They include the villagers of
Ouradour in France or Lidice in Czechoslovakia, most of whom were killed in
reprisal.

To a certain extent, this attempt to equate all human suffering has been
counterproductive. It has even pitted victims against victims in a kind of contest
of comparative pain. Austria, which contributed the likes of Hitler, Adolf Eichmann, Reichskommissar Arthur Seyss-Inquart, and Terezín commandants Siegfried Seidl, Hans Rahm, and Anton Burger as well as Kurt Waldheim to the
Nazi movement, has rewritten history to make itself out to be the first victim of
Nazism. Poland, which did not hesitate to snatch Silesian coalfields from Czechoslovakia after the Munich Conference of October 1938, promotes its image as
the pristine object of Nazi aggression. Ukrainian nationalists gloss over their
own participation in cleansing ghettos and guarding death camps and point instead
to the seven, eight, or even ten million claimed dead in the Stalin-orchestrated
famines of the 1930s. Conveniently ignoring the Molotov-Ribbentrop Pact that
paved the way for Hitler's aggression against Poland, Leonid Brezhnev used to
resurrect the image of twenty million Russian dead in the "Great Patriotic War."

The most extreme example of another oppressed people preempting the dubious distinction of greatest genocide in history is the claim by some African-
Americans that one hundred million blacks perished in the transatlantic slave
trade. Historians who have researched the subject say otherwise, noting that 10
percent of the eight to twenty-five million Africans transported to America perished in transit. That is horrible enough, but many American blacks refer to the
slave trade as "the most heinous Holocaust in history" and subscribe to the
fanciful notion uttered by Louis Farrakhan and Leonard Jeffries that "a small
clique" of Jews was responsible for "the ships that brought our fathers into
slavery."[5]

It is as if people who have been oppressed resent attention given to Jews and
feel a compulsion to show how much more they have suffered. If vulnerable

minorities seek compassion, they should not fabricate or inflate their tales of woe. They must also be sensitive to the pain of others. As Nora Levin points out in her essay on genocide in this volume, each of these sagas has its own configuration and must not be ignored. The study of other tragedies in history is necessary for anyone seeking an understanding of the Holocaust. Similarly, an appreciation of the Holocaust is necessary for people seeking to understand the horror of chattel slavery or racism. What happened to Armenians at Deir-ez-Zor in 1916, Jews at Proskurov in 1919, the Kulaks of Kamenetz-Podolsk in 1931, Ugandans under Idi Amin, or Cambodians under the Khmer Rouge is instructive and humbling for those who believe in the infinite goodness of man.

## Bitburg and Forgiveness

Such study is especially obligatory as we move further from the terrible events of 1944 and 1945. In an imperfect world people continue to starve and die from poison gas and bombs. New tragedies blur the impact of older ones. As survivors of the Holocaust age and die out, whatever guilt or responsibility the onlookers may have felt in 1945 also dissipates. In some instances specific perpetrators like Kurt Rascher, who conducted hypothermia experiments upon unwilling subjects at Dachau, and Arthur Rudolph, once a production director at the slave camp of Dora and subsequently a key figure in the U.S. Apollo project that landed men on the moon, have been rehabiliated, even vindicated. Elsewhere, as at Bitburg in 1985, posthumous blessings have been bestowed upon whole ranks of SS men.

Jews have even had responsibility for the Holocaust turned back upon themselves. The most outrageous example of renewed victimization of the victims is contained in George Steiner's *The Portage to San Cristobal of A.H.*, which is literary fantasy, not history. Steiner's work tells of the capture by Israelis of an aged Adolf Hitler, living in the Amazon forest. In the climactic sequence, a leering Hitler finally speaks, giving vent to every anti-Semitic canard from the charge that Judaism is nothing but an economic contract between Jehovah and man to implicit Jewish responsibility for communism through "Rabbi Marx." Worse, Steiner's toothless Nazi caricature justifies the Final Solution by prattling: "But I learned. From you. Everything. To set a race apart. To keep it from defilement. To hold before it a promised land. To scour that land of its inhabitants or place them in servitude. . . . My racism was a parody of yours, a hungry imitation. What is a thousand-year *Reich* compared with the eternity of Zion? Perhaps I was the false Messiah sent before. Judge me and you must judge yourselves . . . chosen ones!"[6]

If the president of the United States lays a wreath before a monument to an organization declared by an international military tribunal in 1945 to be criminal, if the writings of a George Steiner can be saluted by Anthony Burgess and reviewers at the Washington *Post* as "a work of literature . . . an astonishing book" and an exceptional book that "more than succeeds—it triumphs!" how can anyone be surprised by a resurgence of anti-Semitism in America? Even before the Bitburg gaffe, the Anti-Defamation League had reported a disturbing rise in neo-Nazi groups in the United States. The Reagan years were also the years of Richard Butler's Aryan Nation, Richard Metzger's White Aryan Resistance, Robert Matthews's Order, Willis Carto's National Alliance, the Posse Comitatus, the Covenant, the Sword and Arm of the Lord, skinheads, and sundry Klansmen, all of whom raged against the "Zionist Occupation Government" in Washington. Some of these extremist groups counted only a few dozen members, but there are others that have since taken on a disturbing air of respectability, among them the followers of Libertarian Lyndon LaRouche, the Populist party, and David Duke. They appeal to a wide spectrum of disgruntled Americans with their call for tax reduction, cutbacks in social welfare and affirmative action, and even isolationism. No political analyst can accurately gauge how many blue- and white-collar Americans sitting in family-room armchairs may be nodding in agreement with respectable bigots.[7]

The situation is even gloomier in Europe, where, for the first time in nearly half a century, nationalist movements are able to express themselves freely. Because there were the Bermans in Poland, Leon Trotsky and Grigory Zinoviev in Russia, Anna Pauker in Romania, and Rudolph Slansky in Czechoslovakia (Communist leaders who were born Jewish but renounced any attachment to their people), some ethnic leaders have chosen to pluck the string of anti-Semitism that runs deep in Eastern European culture. In the former Soviet Union members of Pamiat have tried to revive publication of the Protocols of the Elders of Zion, the hoary libel that purports to tell of a Jewish scheme for world domination. In Romania onetime members of the Fascist Iron Guard serve as leaders of the National Peasants party. In Poland supporters of Lech Walesa deride his rivals within Solidarity as Jews. Reactionaries in Czechoslovakia, Arrow Cross veterans in Hungary, and Republicans in West Germany publicly blame the woes of their nations upon the Jews. This anti-Semitism without Jews seems to validate the sad judgment of Elie Wiesel, who has commented, "We wrote words, we made books. And we failed."[8] That may be too harsh a judgment, but the outbreak of war with Iraq in January 1991 demonstrated that a considerable portion of the world could remain mute when Holocaust survivors and their families in Israel, along with refugees from the Soviet bloc and the Arab world, were compelled to don gas masks in the face of threats of annihilation from another petty Haman. The persistence of "ethnic cleansing" in Bosnia in spite of cries of indignation also demonstrates the lack of world resolve to confront racism.

## THE SCOPE AND PURPOSE OF THIS VOLUME

Jews generally mark their Holocaust memorials around the world with the word "zachor" (remember). I prefer the inscription left by Kent State University president Michael Schwartz on the May 4, 1970, Memorial on that campus. It reads: "Think. Learn. Reflect." Whether in the United States, the Russian republics, or Israel, Jews can only hope that a world community that endorses the doctrine of self-determination will stand by its commitment made to the Jewish people. As I. L. Peretz wrote more than eighty years ago: "We Jews have not suffered these thousands of years in order now to forget our own civilization. We want to and we have to continue our way of life, so that we may later unite with the company of mankind as equal partners with equal rights and equal shares."[9]

This volume is intended to help those who seek an understanding of the Holocaust and who wish to apply its lessons to our present world. It is not intended as an encyclopedia. Readers who seek such a comprehensive work might consult the *Encyclopedia of the Holocaust* (1989), or Louis Snyder's *Encyclopedia of the Third Reich* (1989). Also helpful is a series of bibliographies published in 1985-86. Harry James Cargas's *The Holocaust: An Annotated Bibliography* offers paragraph-long analyses of several hundred volumes. Abraham and Herschel Edelheit's *Bibliography on Holocaust Literature* contains more citations, but is less detailed and was not professionally printed. Overall, David Szonyi's *The Holocaust: An Annotated Bibliography and Resource Guide* (1985) is the best of these bibliographies.

This volume is addressed to researchers, teachers, and students, primarily in the English-speaking world, who need to grasp the dimensions of the Holocaust in depth and who want to know which books on specific subjects come highly recommended and which should be avoided. For convenience, I have divided the chapters into three sections: (1) those that follow a conceptual approach covering a philosophical question (such as the theological implications of the Holocaust, the role of the onlooker, books on Nazism); (2) area studies focusing upon a particular country (Italy, France, Holland) or region (the Balkans, the Middle East); and (3) analyses that deal with the Holocaust in the arts (poetry, children's books, music, and film). I have tried to be as comprehensive as possible, but there are admitted gaps. These are immensely challenging subjects, and the pool of experts is limited. After years of trying to assign additional chapters while having contributors keep their submitted materials up to date, this editor finally decided that the time had come for publication.

I have asked that all contributors conform to a uniform pattern in their chapters, offering first a clear synopsis of the issue, then justifying their selections of recommended and not-recommended texts. Despite these guidelines, there are many different approaches in and among the chapters. That is unavoidable in a compendium that draws upon the talents of contributors from three continents. Some, like Monty Noam Penkower (Great Britain), Asher Cohen (Hungary), Sanford Gutman (France), and John Axe (Spain), have emphasized factual developments, supplementing their respective chapters with bibliographic commentaries. Others, like Robert Whealey (interpretations of Hitler), Walter Renn (contemporary German texts), Annette el-Hayek (major Holocaust texts), Alan Cassels (Italy), Alexander Kitroeff (the Balkans), and Shmuel Krakowski (Po-

land), have opted for a more theoretical approach. Several chapters are certain
to arouse emotions. The behavior of onlookers is questioned by survivors Leon
Wells (righteous Gentiles) and Nelly Toll (Holocaust art). That of perpetrators
is investigated by Charles Sydnor (concentration camps) and Sol Littman (the
Ukrainian Halychyna Division). The role of collaborators is explored by Earl
Friedman (Holland); that of resistance fighters by Bea Stadtler (Jewish women
in the resistance) and Eva Fogelman (understanding motivations). Perhaps the
most perplexing issue to emerge from the Holocaust, the relationship of man
and God, is discussed thoroughly by David Rausch (the church and the Holocaust)
and Rabbi Steven Adams (post-Holocaust Jewish philosophies).

Where I have deemed it necessary for continuity, I have supplemented chapters
with a list of additional readings, noting that these are my own suggestions. As
one who has experienced the emendation of his own essays in print, my intention
from the start was to offer contributors the widest latitude possible in the hope
that readers who pick up this volume will find it interesting and useful. Because
new books are appearing daily on the subject of the Holocaust, the recommendations offered here can never be complete. Readers may also be disappointed
'o find personal favorites missing. No one list of recommended books can be
definitive.

I believe that I speak for all the contributors when I say that this volume is
intended to stimulate discussion, pique curiosity, and encourage people to learn
from one another. One example should suffice. For years, I assigned John
Hersey's *The Wall* as a supplement for my class on the Holocaust at Kent State
University. About ten years ago I substituted Schwarz-Bart's *The Last of the
Just*. The reaction from students was incredible. I received book reviews that
went beyond the normal classroom response. Some wrote of feeling despair,
anger, some of weeping while they read this novel of a little boy's trauma in
Nazi Germany. Some spoke of walking about the campus, sensing the loss of
a friend in Ernie Levy. It was obvious that Schwarz-Bart had tapped a well of
human emotions with his immortal protagonist. Since then, I have assigned *The
Last of the Just* as a supplement. Professional historians may also learn from
their students.

Finally, a personal word of thanks to every individual who made this work
possible. They include the secretarial staff at Youngstown State's History Department headed by Mary Bellotto with Paula Burke, Janet McLain, and Denise
Mangine; a large group of student aides who tracked down bibliographic la-
cunae—Jim Allgren, Tom Darland, Jim Dull, Lisa Ellis, Ray Fenstermaker, Jim
Fowler, Elizabeth Glasgow, Marc Hall, Omar Jadue, Patrick McClendon, Tom
Molocea, Patrick Pacalo, Carmen Rodriguez, Laura Rothermel, Allison Ruggles,
Shirley Shemunovich, Marcelle Wilson, and Andrew Zibrik; four selfless and
invaluable research assistants, Jonathan Friedman, Dirk Hermance, James Guy,
and Joe Alessi; the professional staff at Greenwood Press, especially Marilyn
Brownstein, Maureen Melino, Charles Eberline, Alicia S. Merritt, and Andrew
Schub; and the corps of essayists who have enriched us all through their writings.

My thoughts especially go out toward two scholar/teachers—Earl Friedman and Nora Levin—who passed away while the handbook was taking form. This book is dedicated to their memory.

## NOTES

1. Anatole France, *Penguin Island* (New Haven: Leete's Island Books, n.d.), p. vii.

2. Genia Silkes, quoted in Saul S. Friedman, *Amcha: An Oral Testament of the Holocaust* (Washington, D.C.: University Press of America, 1979), p. 146.

3. Malcolm Hay, *Europe and the Jews* (Boston: Beacon Press, 1960), p. 187.

4. Emil Fackenheim, *The Jewish Return into History* (New York: Schocken Books, 1978), p. 27.

5. For an elaboration of remarks made by Farrakhan and Jeffries and factual refutation found in the works of historians Philip Curtin, Herbert Klein, James Rawley, Roger Anstey, David Eltis, and Colin Palmer, see Saul Friedman, "An Old/New Libel: The Role of Jews in the Transatlantic Slave Trade," *Midstream* 37 (October–November 1991), pp. 12–14.

6. George Steiner, *The Portage to San Cristobal of A.H.* (New York: Washington Square Press, 1979), p. 182.

7. Anti-Defamation League, *Hate Groups in America* (New York: ADL, 1988).

8. "The Long Shadow," *Newsweek* 115 (May 7, 1990): 44.

9. I. L. Peretz, *Peretz*, ed. and trans. Sol Liptzin (New York: YIVO, 1947), p. 336.

## SELECT BIBLIOGRAPHY

Anti-Defamation League. *Hate Groups in America*. New York: ADL, 1988.

Cargas, Harry James. *The Holocaust: An Annotated Bibliography*. Chicago and London: American Library Association, 1985.

Dawidowicz, Lucy. *The War Against the Jews, 1933–1945*. New York: Holt, Rinehart and Winston, 1975.

Des Pres, Terrence. *The Survivor: An Anatomy of Life in the Death Camps*. New York: Oxford University Press, 1976.

Edelheit, Abraham J., and Herschel Edelheit. *Bibliography on Holocaust Literature*. Boulder, Colo.: Westview Press, 1986.

*Encyclopedia of the Holocaust*. Edited by Yisrael Gutman. New York: Macmillan, 1989.

Fackenheim, Emil. *The Jewish Return into History*. New York: Schocken Books, 1978.

France, Anatole. *Penguin Island*. New Haven: Leete's Island Books, n.d.

Friedman, Philip. *Martyrs and Fighters: The Epic of the Warsaw Ghetto*. New York: Praeger, 1954.

———. *Their Brothers' Keepers*. New York: Crown, 1957.

Friedman, Philip, and W. J. Gar. *Bibliography of Books in Yiddish on the Jewish Catastrophe and Heroism*. New York: YIVO, 1962.

Friedman, Saul S. *Amcha: An Oral Testament of the Holocaust*. Washington, D.C.: University Press of America, 1979.

———. "The Holocaust and Its Historiography." In *Handbook of American-Jewish Literature*, edited by Lewis Fried, pp. 441–70. Westport, Conn.: Greenwood Press, 1988.

Hay, Malcolm. *Europe and the Jews*. Boston: Beacon Press, 1960.

Hilberg, Raul. *The Destruction of the European Jews*. New York: Quadrangle, 1951.

Laqueur, Walter. *The Terrible Secret*. Boston: Little, Brown, 1981.

Levin, Nora. *The Holocaust*. New York: Crowell, 1968.

Marrus, Michael. *The Holocaust in History*. Hanover, N.H.: University Press of New England, 1987.

Mayer, Arno. *Why Did the Heavens Not Darken?* New York: Pantheon, 1988.

Milgram, Stanley. *Obedience to Authority*. New York: Harper and Row, 1974.

Morse, Arthur. *While Six Million Died*. New York: Random House, 1967.

Nolte, Ernst. *Der Europäische Bürgerkrieg*. Munich: Desch, 1968.

Peretz, I. L. *Peretz*. Edited and translated by Sol Liptzin. New York: YIVO, 1947.

Poliakov, Leon. *Harvest of Hate*. Syracuse, N.Y.: Syracuse University Press, 1954.

Reitlinger, Gerald. *The Final Solution*. London: Beechhurst Press, 1953.

Robinson, Jacob. *The Holocaust and After: Sources and Literature in English*. Jerusalem: Israel Universities Press, 1973.

Robinson, Jacob and Philip Friedman. *Bibliography of Books in Hebrew on the Jewish Catastrophe and Heroism in Europe*. New York: YIVO, 1960.

———. *Guide to Jewish History Under Nazi Impact*. New York: YIVO, 1960.

Schoenberner, Gerhard. *The Yellow Star*. New York: Bantam, 1973.

Schwarz-Bart, Andre. *The Last of the Just*. New York: Atheneum, 1960.

Snyder, Louis L. *Encyclopedia of the Third Reich*. New York: Paragon House, 1989.

Steiner, George. *The Portage to San Cristobal of A.H.* New York: Washington Square Press, 1979.

Szonyi, David. *The Holocaust: An Annotated Bibliography and Resource Guide*. New York: Ktav, 1985.

Wyman, David. *The Abandonment of the Jews*. New York: Pantheon, 1984.

# Part I

## Conceptual Approaches to the Holocaust

# Chapter 1

# The Major Texts of the Holocaust

## Annette El-Hayek

A wide variety of literature has appeared on various aspects of the Holocaust. Survivors have given personal accounts of the tragedy. Some of the victims have left behind valuable diaries, and others who were directly or indirectly involved in the machinations of the Nazi regime have given their own accounts of the subject. Ronald Sanders, reviewing the latest addition to the general texts, Leni Yahil's *The Holocaust* (English edition, 1990), questions the validity of yet another book on the tragedy, which "has been thoroughly covered in literature."[1] Thoroughly covered, perhaps, but certainly not exhaustively, for in actual fact there are only a few books presenting an overall study of the topic, and in the future these may be in danger of being outnumbered by the revisionist version of Holocaust history.

The major nonrevisionist texts have received much acclaim and are valuable contributions to Holocaust history in their own right. While these texts expose most of the important events prior to and during the actual calamity, each study is a unique contribution. The authors' treatments of the numerous debates concerning victims, perpetrators, collaborators, bystanders, extermination, or resistance and rescue vary according to their viewpoints. Which work, therefore, gives the most complete, unbiased depiction of this tragedy, and what purpose does each serve in its understanding? An attempt to answer this question will be made in the following historiographic analysis of the first six major texts together with Yahil's contribution and another by Martin Gilbert.

The works examined are the most recent editions by the authors in question: Frenchman Leon Poliakov's 1979 revised and augmented *Harvest of Hate* (originally *Bréviaire de la haine,* 1951); works by two British authors, Gerald Reitlinger's 1968 second revised and augmented edition of *The Final Solution* (1953) and Martin Gilbert's *The Holocaust* (1985); works by three Americans, Raul Hilberg's 1985 student edition of *The Destruction of the European Jews* (1961), Nora Levin's 1974 edition of *The Holocaust* (1968), and Lucy Dawidowicz's *The War Against the Jews* (1975); and finally, two works by Israelis, Yehuda Bauer's *A History of the Holocaust* (1982) and Leni Yahil's *The Holocaust* (1990). Each will be analyzed according to the subdivisions mentioned in the preceding paragraph.

## VICTIMS

Hannah Arendt's 1963 treatise on the Eichmann trial created a stir in the Jewish community.[2] The author reproached the Jewish Councils for assisting the Nazis. Arendt's accusation has been interpreted by some as inferring that the Jews therefore allowed themselves to be "led like sheep to the slaughter." A passionate debate has since ensued among historians of the subject, and varying degrees of acceptance or rejection of Arendt's thesis are evident in the comprehensive general texts on the Holocaust.

The first of these texts to appear were initially written in the early 1950s. It is conceivable that they were revised and augmented in response to Arendt and in order to include other information that was diffused during the trial. According to Poliakov, the victims responded to their Jewishness. Unlike Arendt, however, the French author believes that the Jews were duped into submission.[3] While Reitlinger would agree on this latter point, he would most certainly disagree with Arendt. Reitlinger, more than any other author cited here, stresses the role of both passive and active resistance once the Jews realized their impending fate.

Another respected historian who discounts the Arendt charge is Nora Levin. Besides numerous references throughout her work, her chapter on the Brand mission to save Hungary's Jews with the cooperation of Eichmann is particularly important in outlining that the Jews tried everything humanly possible to prevent their annihilation.[4] Indeed, Levin's work is unique in its compassionate portrayal of victims throughout the entire work. Gilbert, the only other author to continuously bear in mind the victims' plight, allows eyewitnesses to speak for themselves. He appears cold, however, compared to Levin, who identifies with the subject.

Lucy Dawidowicz explains the response in terms of a "hold on, hold out" reaction innate to the Jews because of their past experience,[5] which again can be perceived as a reaction to their Jewishness. This also is Yehuda Bauer's opinion. The Israeli scholar, like most of the others, effectively outlines the persecution of the Jews prior to the Nazi regime. However, he traces this further back in Jewish history to the roots of his people's forced migration to Europe, where they continued their fateful destiny.

Hilberg fluctuates from offering valid reasons for compliance[6] to accusing the victims of having assisted, through inaction, in their own extermination.[7] He is the only author of the eight to condemn the leaders of Jewish Councils for their actions. Surprisingly, however, most of the authors suggest past history as an explanation of the Jews' response. None of these authors, with the exception of Yahil, seems capable of discarding his or her own Jewishness in order to ask if Christians, Muslims, or others would respond in the same way. Of course, no other tragedy can be compared to one on such a scale as this. The Jews were hostages, and as with hostages today, they complied when threatened.

Such a response is the normal human reaction. After all, it appears better to live in fear of losing one's life than to risk immediate death through defiance. Compliance and accommodation with a hostile environment is not necessarily a Jewish phenomenon. Have not the Copts in Egypt and Christians in Iran and Lebanon been obliged to adapt to their hostile Muslim surroundings? Would not the Nazis also have complied had the roles been reversed? Yahil certainly saw no difference between the reactions of Russian POWs and Jews sent off to the gas chambers.[8] Peter Michael Lingens describes an encounter between an SS man, brought into the War Crimes Division of the U.S. forces in Germany, and Simon Wiesenthal:

The image of the Teutonic superman who, equipped with power over life and death, commands fate rather than obeys it, was still so deeply ingrained in Wiesenthal that he found it difficult to recognize him in that bundle of fear.

Then Wiesenthal himself described the incident:

It was as if a hare was expected to grasp that the huntsman is afraid of it. It took me a long time to understand how much alike people are in certain situations. He had the same fear as one of us Jews would have when the SS found him in his hideout.[9]

Indeed, another survivor, writing under the pen name Martin Gray, was able to put this thesis to the test.[10] After escaping from several camps and ghettos, Gray volunteered to join the Russian army on its march to Berlin. At first, his mission was restricted to Poland, where he was engaged in weeding out collaborators who had assisted in handling the ''Jewish question.'' After finding one particularly odious Jew-baiter, Gray was obliged to intervene on his behalf to save him from the wrath of a fellow survivor. He refused to allow his friend to stoop to the level of a former persecutor.[11] In another incident Gray unsuccessfully attempted to rescue SS prisoners from being burned to death in an abandoned bus at the hands of Russian soldiers. He empathized with them:

I understood the looks the SS men were exchanging. I could imagine their terror. I was seized by fear too, an anguish in my throat. I could have ordered my driver to leave and avoid looking. But I wanted to see, see how far men can go when war deforms them.[12]

Gray was finally allowed to join the Russian occupation of Germany, and as he witnessed the resignation of the German population, he realized that they too might have complied as the Jews did. To prove his point, he had posters printed requiring all Germans in Dramsburg over sixteen years of age to wear an armband with a swastika on their right arm.[13] Ironically, the next morning he had to intervene on behalf of a number of townspeople who had been rounded up and risked execution at the hand of the Russians for daring to sport Hitler's insignia. A friend of Gray's named Durek seemed relieved and vindicated: "You copied the ghetto and they wore them. Like us they wore them."[14]

## PERPETRATORS

That ordinary men are capable of monstrous acts in a perverse environment such as Nazi Germany or Nazi-occupied Europe has been scientifically demonstrated in Stanley Milgram's psychological study *Obedience to Authority*.[15] Most of the authors considered in this chapter would agree with Milgram's thesis. They posit that those involved in the destruction process were ordinary people fulfilling their jobs. While some conscientiously performed their odious tasks, others were content merely to comply with minimum efforts.

Gilbert's perpetrators, seen through the eyes of those who survived the tortures, can only be perceived as monsters. Hilberg, who gives the best overall analysis of the men behind the horrors, would disagree: "These men were in no sense hoodlums, delinquents, common criminals or sex maniacs. Most were intellectuals.[16] By and large they were in their thirties, and undoubtedly they wanted a certain measure of power, fame and success."[17]

Reitlinger broaches the theory that many who took part in the notorious *Einsatzgruppen* did so to get away from the front or to procure extra food rations. Others preferred participation as an alternative to punishment for various military misdemeanors, including desertion. Once they had agreed, it was difficult to back out.[18]

The actual implementation of the Final Solution was not as carefully planned as some would suggest. Bauer and Poliakov particularly stress this point and suggest that "progress," like any normal job undertaken by ordinary men, was reached through trial and error. According to Poliakov, only fanatics like Julius Streicher and Reinhard Heydrich had dreams of total destruction of the Jews from the beginning,[19] whereas in Dawidowicz's view, without Hitler there could have been no Final Solution.[20]

Of course, the perpetrators need not have carried out their gruesome tasks. Citing refusals by German SS men such as Herz Jost, Erwin Schulz, Rudolf Diels, and Graf Faber Castel, Reitlinger demonstrates that noncompliance in atrocities generally led to neither punishment nor admonishment.[21] To this list Gilbert and Yahil add, among others, the name of Anton Schmidt. This German sergeant, responsible for rounding up stray German soldiers, used means at his disposal to hide and transport Jews fleeing toward White Russia.[22] Thus, as in Milgram's experiments, some men were unwilling to participate. Others, according to Hilberg, were overly conscientious in their zeal,[23] but most of the authors agree that without collaboration, the "successes" of the Nazi plan would have been much more difficult.

## COLLABORATORS

Levin's and Yahil's works give the most complete and fairest assessments of collaboration by Jewish leaders. Their country-by-country examinations of the Holocaust analyzes thoroughly the role of compliance with Nazi policy. Hilberg appears bitter in his reproach of railroad employees who not only "played a critical role in concentration," but also "a decisive one in the deportations."[24] He sharply condemns Jewish leadership:

Thus the Jewish leadership both saved and destroyed its people, saving some Jews and destroying others, saving the Jews at one moment and destroying them in the next. Some leaders refused to keep this power, others became intoxicated with it.[25]

Dawidowicz views the Jewish leaders from another perspective. She claims that they can not be branded as collaborators since none of them at any time wished ultimate victory for the Nazis.[26] Reitlinger also absolves those who cooperated with the Nazis.[27]

Concerning the role of the army, most of the authors render a critical verdict and deplore in particular those soldiers who acted on their own initiative in some instances. Hilberg's general discussion of collaboration, however, is incomplete. In his abridged work there is no mention of collaboration in countries other than Poland and Russia.

Neither Poliakov nor Reitlinger give an adequate interpretation of French collaboration. The latter goes so far as to suggest that Pierre Laval was largely responsible for saving most of France's Jews.[28] Obviously those who ordered the French premier's execution felt that Laval was guilty of collaboration. Poliakov's negligence is understandable; writing as a French Jew, he was cautious about inspiring the wrath of his countrymen. He most certainly was aware, at the time, that French authorities were unwilling to reveal their dubious past. Reitlinger's omission is inexcusable, but may be explained by his respect for his French colleague, who assisted him with research in Paris.

But perhaps collaboration had a positive outcome in some instances. After all, resistance, even when actively pursued by an entire nation, did not always reap positive rewards. A nation such as the Netherlands lost the majority of its Jews, whereas France through collaboration lost mainly the foreign element among them.

From descriptions of life in the ghettos, well defined in most of the works considered, it can be concluded that collaboration by Jewish leaders allowed more longevity. Poliakov offers such a thesis in his depiction of the Lodz and Kovno ghettos, which were liquidated only as the Germans retreated from Russian advances in 1944.[29] Chaim Rumkowski, dubbed one of the most villainous

Jewish collaborators due to his complete domination over his subjects, was able to keep his Lodz ghetto in operation longer than most. According to Poliakov, Rumkowski's sincerity in doing his utmost to preserve life exonerates him.[30] Yahil would agree, as she herself reached a similar conclusion regarding Mark Alten of Lublin's Judenrat.[31] The answer to compliance by Jewish Councils was, as Gilbert points out, a divided debate. On the one hand, the rabbi in Kovno, after consulting his religious texts, reached the conclusion that a Jewish community's leaders were obliged to save as many people as possible when all were in danger.[32] Yet in Vilna rabbis condemned those who complied. Referring to Maimonides, they stated that it would be better for all to be killed than to surrender one soul of Israel.[33] Of course, the debate on collaboration will continue. Collaboration was, nonetheless, certainly effective in some instances.

## BYSTANDERS

Another hotly discussed debate questions the role of bystanders. Lucy Dawidowicz and Leni Yahil obviously attach little importance to this issue, for they make only brief reference to it in their works. In Hilberg's view, however, the Nazis followed closely the reactions of the outside world and adapted Nazi policy accordingly in a deliberate ploy to drag the Allied powers into the plot as passive but willing accomplices.[34]

Once again Nora Levin's account far outshines the others in its almost exhaustive treatment of this topic. No one escapes criticism: the populations of Germany, most of occupied Europe, the Allies, the churches (both Catholic and Protestant), and, astonishingly, the International Red Cross. Reitlinger overlooks the shortcomings of the latter, preferring instead to linger on one of its rare rescue missions in Romania during the final collapse of the Reich.[35]

Poliakov introduces a unique concept for explaining the passivity of the German people. The population in general benefitted on a scale ranging from small to large from the confiscation of Jewish property. Thus millions of Germans became "direct accomplices in the major crime of genocide."[36] The Frenchman also attacks the Catholic church for blindly following dogma, which had devastating consequences for the persecuted Jews.[37]

However valid these criticisms are, none is more important than the one made against the Allies. They alone, besides the Nazis, had the power to avert the destruction as early as 1938. Levin points this out in her chapter devoted to the failed Evian Conference.[38] Bauer, Dawidowicz, Reitlinger, Poliakov, and Yahil make brief reference to this, but it is omitted in Gilbert's history and also Hilberg's abridged edition.

The Allies were wrong not to call the Nazi bluff by allowing the Jews sanctuary. Of course, it is not certain that the Germans would have permitted orderly emigration in any case. Poliakov is the only author to make this logical point.[39] He cites a 1939 declaration from the Ministry of Foreign Affairs that affirmed that the removal of Jews from German soil would still not solve the Jewish question.[40]

While Reitlinger accuses many bystanders, he downplays Britain's role, which often moved from passive to active in hindering attempts to find havens for those Jews who succeeded in dodging their execution. His rendering of the Brand mission ignores the British sabotage of Eichmann's "Jews for trucks" offer, which is clearly documented in Levin's accounts. Nor does this British author mention his country's policies in Palestine or its refusal to bomb gas chambers and railway lines leading to the extermination centers. Yahil, too, says little against Britain but praises its efforts for taking in Jewish children.[41]

It would be unfair to reprimand the world in general. Even today have we as Jews, Christians, and others not also participated through inaction in the needless slaughter of innocent people by the Khmer Rouge in Cambodia and in the starvation of millions of Africans? During the Holocaust, as well, there were only a few "just men" willing to speak out or risk their lives to offer assistance to their fellow humans. But before pursuing the topic of resistance, we must first consider the extermination process itself.

## EXTERMINATION

Most writers prove that the Nazis were not the well-organized technocrats in their implementation of the Holocaust that commentators in newsreels or liberators of the camps would have us believe. Although all the texts include an adequate description of the extermination process, Hilberg's depiction far outshines the others in portraying the process and its actors. However, Levin's and Gilbert's versions keep the victims themselves in mind through all aspects of the killing procedures. Poliakov gives an excellent account of the development stages and of the methods used in the implementation of the Final Solution. Dawidowicz is weaker in this area. All agree that efficiency was achieved through trial and error.

Poliakov describes the three main stages: *Einsatzgruppen* actions in 1941, the use of gas vans and primitive centers such as Chelmno (Kulmhof), and finally the intensification when the remaining Jewish laborers were replaced by Polish Aryans.[42] Bauer, Levin, Poliakov, Reitlinger, Gilbert, and Yahil all point out that the gassing program was perfected by already scientifically tested methods used in euthanasia experiments that had to be halted due to pressure from the families of victims, the church, and the population in general.[43] Reitlinger also reveals that personnel from the euthanasia program, (doctors, nurses, and others) were then conveniently transferred to share their expertise in the killing centers. He, Levin, Bauer, Gilbert, and Yahil also give a detailed account of Kurt Gerstein, the chief disinfection officer in charge of Zyklon B.[44] Gerstein warned several foreign dignitaries of the true nature of the Final Solution. He also sabotaged several shipments of the gas, probably saving many Jews from death.[45] Reitlinger, however, is the only one to report the use of some form of gas chamber in every German concentration camp. These unsophisticated chambers were not used to exterminate, per se, but to get rid of weak Russian and Jewish inmates no longer able to work.[46]

It was easier to dispose of people by the use of gas than by the mass shootings performed by *Einsatzgruppen*. The gas chambers masked the reality of the fate that awaited the victims. Most of the victims believed that they were really going for a shower. Their actual fate was not evident, as it was in the shooting operations where victims could see the bodies of those disposed of before them lying in ditches. Sometimes they had to witness other exterminations as they awaited their turn. Of course, the Nazis did not arrange the "progress" to gassing operations for the benefit of the victims, but rather to make their own job easier and to lessen the psychological side effects felt by the exterminators involved. After all, it is easier to kill when one does not have to look the victim in the eye or experience the event at close range. The gas technique indeed seemed a valuable "asset" in the process, but there were other obstacles to confront as the world realized what was happening. Rescue and resistance increased, particularly when it became evident that Germany was losing the war.

## RESISTANCE AND RESCUE

All the works provide a depiction of the famous uprising in the Warsaw ghetto that was symbolic in its bravery and hopelessness. What could a few guns do against tanks and well-armed troops? Those who participated realized that they had no other alternative. According to Reitlinger and Poliakov, it was difficult to resist when families were rounded up in units.[47] It was also not an easy task to do so in such a totally hostile environment. Without the support of the local population, resistance was practically impossible.[48]

Favorable geographic conditions were also necessary. In the Netherlands the population was sympathetic, but the flat land was not conducive to partisan activity. Denmark's proximity to Sweden, a neutral country, made success more likely.[49]

Hilberg's student edition of his work does not review the Jewish situation in countries outside of Eastern Europe. Coverage of resistance and rescue is therefore incomplete. Reitlinger, on the other hand, tends to overdo emphasis on resistance efforts. One wonders how so many could have perished when so much resistance was present. Indeed, Reitlinger questions the total death figure, which, according to most traditionalist historians, approaches six million.[50] However, he exposes incidents downplayed or omitted by others.

In 1941, when Jews in Germany were forced to wear the star, many Germans also did so in support. The population was even more disgusted by the roundups, and the Nazi party was obliged to issue anti-Jewish pamphlets and threaten reprisals to those offering assistance.[51] In 1943 the evacuation of a home for aged Jews was temporarily halted after German crowds protested.[52] As late as

May 1943, eighteen thousand Berlin Jews had escaped roundups by blending in with the Aryan population.[53]

Apart from Hilberg, most of the authors give some account of the Italian effort. Until the fall of Mussolini, Jews in Italy and the Italian-occupied territory in France were spared the fate of their brethren elsewhere. These authors also point out that although Bulgaria gave up foreign Jews and assisted in the deportation of Jews from Greece and Yugoslavia, the Bulgarian populace demonstrated against the government and was able to save its own Jews.

In addition to these incidents, rescue attempts by Raoul Wallenberg, Kurt Gerstein, members of the clergy, and even Nazis who offered "Jews for sale" propositions in Hungary, Romania, and Slovakia are depicted. Only Levin and Dawidowicz broach the subject of the Neumann mission to the Evian Conference in 1938, which is outlined in Hans Habe's novel *The Mission*.[54]

Also mentioned is Belgium's rescue of its Jews, championed by Queen Elizabeth and supported by railroad workers who sabotaged numerous transportations. However, Bauer claims that the queen's pleas for the most part were ignored despite Nazi promises to the contrary. This is corroborated by the fact that only 1,276 of the 25,437 who were deported from Malines in July 1944 returned.[55]

Bauer, Gilbert, and Yahil also offer new contributions to the list of rescuers. Obviously the Israelis' proximity to abundant archives on the subject and their access to more Holocaust survivors than most has been fruitful in bringing these to light. The most remarkable revelation concerns the Japanese consul at Kovno, Senpo Sugihara, who, before he was forced to leave on August 31, 1940, issued visas for 3,600 Jews. All were able to reach safe haven in the Western Hemisphere and Shanghai.[56] In Shanghai Jews who had difficulty extending visas could, according to Yahil, count on another Japanese dignitary, Professor Sitzuso Kotsuji, for help.[57] Others, like German factory chief Otto Busse in Bialystok and Anna Shimaite, a Lithuanian, offered rescue from unexpected sources. Paul Grüninger, a Swiss policeman lost both his job and his pension when it was discovered that he had been deliberately disobeying his country's orders and allowing Jews to cross freely into the Helvetic state.[58] Aristedes da Sousa Mendes, Portuguese consul in Bordeaux, defied his government by issuing transit visas to thousands in what is perhaps the largest single rescue operation recorded.[59]

Both Gilbert and Yahil even praise the pope, who has been accused by many of inaction. These recent accounts claim that he intervened personally on behalf of Hungary's Jews.[60] Gilbert also contends that the pope himself ordered the Vatican clergy to open sanctuaries to all "non-Aryans" in need of rescue and offered gold to meet ransom demands.[61]

While numerous other rescuers not previously credited for their efforts in other works are venerated in the two latest contributions to general histories of the Holocaust, only in Gilbert's work is it evident that the efforts were too little, too late. To counter every rescue by the clergy, certain members of the Wehrmacht and the SS, ordinary people in many lands, or remarkable individuals like Mayor Lukos Karrer of Zante,[62] Ernst von Rath's father,[63] Dr. Petras Baubles,[64] or the incredible villagers of Chambon-sur-Lignon,[65] Gilbert cites the innumerable other cases that ended in doom for the Jews.

## HARVEST OF HATE

This first major attempt at a general history of the Holocaust was the culmination of research drawn from the archives of the Nuremberg trials and a few other primary sources housed in the Center for Contemporary Jewish Documentation in Paris. Leon Poliakov has made a commendable contribution considering the lack of documents at his disposal compared to those available to more recent historians. In spite of this obvious handicap, the French author has succeeded in encompassing most of the major issues analyzed in later works.

This short rendition traces the progression of the Holocaust from its base in Nazi anti-Semitism to the killing centers via the euthanasia programs and *Einsatzgruppen* actions. It also describes the plight of the Jews during the period in their own countries, countries of so-called sanctuary, ghettos, camps, and extermination centers. This is also the first work to attempt analyses of the perpetrators, bystanders, and rescuers. The work could have been enhanced with the inclusion of maps and pictures. However, as one of the pioneers in the field, Poliakov's work has probably served as a model for expansion and improvement in works by later researchers.

## THE FINAL SOLUTION

Gerald Reitlinger acknowledges Poliakov's contribution and concedes that the latter provided him with most of the materials necessary for his research. The British author's book appeared two years after his mentor's original French version and since both had access to the same sources, it is no wonder that there are similarities in the exposition of the various topics treated. However, Reitlinger's analyses of these topics are more thorough. Not only does he raise the same issues regarding the victims, perpetrators, bystanders, collaborators, and rescuers, but he also expands the descriptions offered by Poliakov in most instances and certainly gives rescuers more credit than most who have analyzed this era. This is also the only work taken into account here that outlines the fate of many of the perpetrators.

However, there are a few minor flaws. Reitlinger's statistics regarding those exterminated by various means appear to overwhelm him. The danger in this lies in analyzing the numbers, which he claims to be nearer 4.5 million. While the total figures are not important to this extent, revisionist historians may make use of the confusion to corroborate their own theories.

## *THE DESTRUCTION OF EUROPE'S JEWS*

The abridged student edition of Raul Hilberg's three-volume opus falls short in many ways. First of all, in this version the title is a misnomer since nothing is said about the Jews outside Eastern Europe. Its emphasis is Poland. The publishers have deliberately omitted notes, which are indispensable in any scholarly work and especially one particularly aimed at college students, and refer readers to the larger work. Most of the topics included in the other major texts are missing in Hilberg's student edition.

However, his description, complete with maps and charts, of camps and ghettos and the progression of various stages of the extermination far outshines those of the other texts. Besides defining the role of the technocrats in the implementation of the Final Solution, Hilberg also includes some criticism of those he accuses of passively assisting in this horror through inaction. He fails, as have others, to portray a compassionate account of the victims themselves. In spite of the flaws, this work is still more accessible to a larger audience than the more voluminous three-volume version.

## NORA LEVIN'S *THE HOLOCAUST*

This work also covers the areas considered in most of the major texts. It gives a detailed account of the response to the atrocities in the various occupied, neutral, or Axis countries of Europe and the degree of hindrance or help offered in each. Levin points out the difficulty in assessing the final death toll, as those spared in one country became part of the fatalities in another.

Throughout the work, no matter what the main focus is, the plight of the Jews is outlined. The specific ordeals of Jewish men, women, and children in the various camps and ghettos throughout Europe are exposed. The interrelation between victims and perpetrators, together with the ruses used by the latter to dupe their innocent ''prey,'' is also well described. Levin defends collaborators in the Jewish Councils because they succeeded, at the price of their self-esteem, in preventing or impeding numerous deportations. She also mentions how the Vichy regime and Fascist Italy were successful in saving most of their Jewish nationals, whereas the Netherlands, due to defiance, lost most of its Jewish population. However, she is critical of bystanders.

The author includes pictures and maps to familiarize the reader with the participants and locations. She gives a well-rounded version of this episode in history and includes a chapter on the fate of the surviving Jews after liberation from the camps, a topic that is omitted in most renditions. She appears to be the only one to give credit to Hans Habe's claim of a secret mission to offer Austria's Jews for ransom at the Evian Conference. However, in the index, she confuses Neumann the physician who was supposedly charged with this mission with Neumann the Wehrmacht officer.

Another technical error on Levin's part appears on page 138 when she writes,

"On the same date three other ships limped into Beirut, Syria" instead of Beirut, Lebanon. On page 144 the same error is repeated. Apart from these petty criticisms the work is outstanding in its almost comprehensive appraisal of the Holocaust and merits more recognition from scholars familiar with this field.

## THE WAR AGAINST THE JEWS, 1933-1945

Lucy Dawidowicz's work focuses on the same time frame as Levin's work. Like Levin, Dawidowicz analyzes the anti-Semitic legislation within the Reich and later its extension through Nazi foreign policy into the countries annexed by, occupied by, or allied with Germany. She also attempts to explain the reasons for such brutal anti-Semitism.

In the section devoted to the Holocaust, the author depicts life among German Jews between 1933 and 1938 and contrasts this with the later period of ghettoization. The role of the many Jewish organizations and their help or unintentional hindrance of the Jewish cause is also outlined. She ends the section with an analysis of Jewish behavior during the crisis, but her rendition, like those of others, is impersonal.

The country-by-country account of the fate of Europe's Jews is not given thorough investigation and indeed is included only in the appendix. Dawidowicz also fails to credit Denmark fully or even recognize Sweden for their contribution to rescue efforts. She does, however, give an excellent explanation of the role of Eastern European countries, and her sources are extremely well documented.

Besides this, the book appears to have been written in haste, without much feeling. Too much valuable space is devoted to Himmler's biography. Practically no mention is made of the bystanders who failed to speak up against the atrocities. Yet in spite of these flaws, the work has been praised by many of the historian's peers and received the Anisfield-Wolf Prize in 1976.

## A HISTORY OF THE HOLOCAUST

Another well-written, relatively short rendition of the Holocaust is Yehuda Bauer's depiction of this tragedy. The Israeli author traces the origins of anti-Semitism in Europe and the migration of Jews there. He points out the fact that in many places the Jews were there before those who would later claim to be nationals.

Bauer also encompasses much of the information on the various aspects of this period included in the other major works. He devotes more space to the Weimar Republic, whose failure resulted in the rise of the Nazis, and his criticism of bystanders is not as bitter. As a Jew he is hesitant to criticize adherents of another religion for their failure to make an all-out effort to stop the atrocities. He cites many cases of aid offered by church officials and nuns and is the first to mention the Vatican's intervention (although he does not contend that it was the pope's), albeit after the Allied invasion of Italy, on behalf of Hungarian Jews. New names are added to the list of rescuers mentioned in other works, sometimes from unexpected sources such as the SS men themselves, Japanese, or officials from neutral countries.

Research material for this work appears to be mainly obtained from secondary sources. This is disappointing in view of the primary sources and eyewitnesses available in the author's homeland. He also cites his own works on various aspects of the Holocaust a bit too often. However, in spite of these flaws, the work remains a valuable contribution.

## MARTIN GILBERT'S *THE HOLOCAUST*

From the "Notes and Sources" in this recent addition to Holocaust history, it is evident that Gilbert's research was based mainly on primary sources and interviews with survivors. The British author allows the latter to speak for themselves and offers little in the way of analyses of the facts.

The book is treated chronologically. For this reason there is no false impression of lengthy periods of respite, as is given in works that jump around in time frame. Nor is there any doubt that the mass murder started earlier than the period of the invasion of Russia in 1941 claimed by most. Gilbert points out that as early as 1939, after the invasion of Poland, Jews were taken from the ghettos or rounded up in the street to be shot in designated spots nearby. This method was used to hasten the slower, deliberate annihilation from starvation and disease. While there was a lull in the process for some, it is obvious that the process was continued somewhere else.

Besides the well-known concentration or extermination camps and ghettos, Gilbert familiarizes his readers with others omitted in other works. He is the only one to broach the subject of camp brothels but does not mention anything about their inmates or clientele.

Gilbert's work, although not innovative in the field of literature,[66] certainly is so in its approach to treating a general history of the Holocaust. In no other work is the reader forced to absorb the vividly depicted atrocities against the Jews on such a scale. Almost every page of the voluminous work includes a gory account of the sadism inflicted by the Nazis and their henchmen. Reading this work, a psychologically harrowing experience, is definitely not for everyone. But who, after completing such a task, could dare question the authenticity of such crimes against humanity?

## LENI YAHIL'S *THE HOLOCAUST*

This latest work on Holocaust history has not only benefitted from other secondary sources but also numerous primary materials housed at Yad Vashem in Israel. In spite of this, however, the author does not have much to add to other works already available. Besides a few more names to the list of those who offered assistance, Yahil mentions the fate of two relatively unknown groups of Jews in the Crimea, the Karaites and the Krimchaks. The former, not being considered racial Jews and having enjoyed exemption from pogroms in the past, were spared the fate of most of their brethren. The Krimchaks, who spoke a Tartar language, suffered the same fate as their Ashkenazic cousins. Yahil also acquaints us with the Jews in Upper Silesia who benefitted from special privileges granted by the Geneva agreement in 1922. In 1933 they were threatened by the Nazi racial laws. Through the Bernheim petition they succeeded in obtaining a reprieve until 1937, when their special privileges expired.

Although Yahil has attempted a comprehensive look at all aspects of the Holocaust, she does not trace anti-Semitism back further than 1932. At times, too, as she jumps from country to country, ghetto to ghetto, or camp to camp, the trials and tribulations of the Jews appear not too serious.

While Yahil is adamant that the Jews did not allow themselves to be "led like sheep to the slaughter," she does not fully expand on the debate of rescue and faith that, according to Yahil, made resistance by the Orthodox Jews more difficult. In her analyses of rescue from the neutral countries' standpoints, she omits Turkey and Portugal after giving the impression that all would be included. A large map of the various types of camps is included, but no explanation of the difference, if any, between "death" and "murder" camps is given. Another technical error is her mention of Saône-sur-Chalon in the book and its index when in fact she surely means the French town of Chalon-sur-Saône. This work, which certainly is not the definitive source for a general history of the Holocaust, is nevertheless a valid addition to the other nonrevisionist works already in existence.

## CONCLUSION

All the works cited have contributed to an understanding of one of the world's greatest historical tragedies. Poliakov's and Bauer's short, well-rounded renditions make them particularly well suited as Holocaust reading supplements for high-school or undergraduate classes in almost any twentieth-century European history course. Hilberg's book, which has probably been shortened to make it more attractive for use in such classes, unfortunately does not give an overall view of the Holocaust. It also lacks notes on sources, which the author states can be verified in the unabridged original volumes. Nevertheless, this student edition still delivers the best account of the extermination process and its orchestrators.

The works by Reitlinger and Dawidowicz, while offering some interesting theses on the subject, do not give a well-balanced account. Reitlinger's statistics are overwhelming, and the author himself appears to have difficulty analyzing the data. Dawidowicz skims over many areas that would have been better had they been given a more complete analysis.

Gilbert's work, a valuable account where the victims are not merely nameless statistics, is nevertheless not one that "must be read and reread," as Elie Wiesel suggests on its cover. While it personalizes the tragedy with testimonials not previously cited in other works, the vivid and often-gory depiction given throughout the entire work makes even a first reading painful. However, it would make a considerable contribution as a reference source for specific aspects of the Holocaust.

The latest contribution by Yahil is, as Sanders suggests in his previously mentioned review, quite difficult to describe as the definitive work on the subject. Apart from an interesting analysis of the role of neutral and occupied countries, it offers little in addition to the works already available.

Nora Levin's account, although lengthy, is by far the best of the eight. It would be indispensable for any course dealing primarily with the Holocaust itself. Her fair, well-researched assessment of all aspects also takes into account the many debates that have surfaced on the subject. However, hers is certainly not the definitive account.

All of the writers mentioned are Jewish, and in the future, when there are no survivors left to quell the doubts of those who would believe the revisionist historians' versions, the works of non-Jewish authors, more apt to be believed as unbiased observers, would be a welcome addition. Of course, Jewish historians should also continue with this passionate subject, for there is certainly much more to explore in this area.

## NOTES

1. Ronald Sanders, review of *The Holocaust*, by Leni Yahil, *New York Times Book Review*, November 22, 1990, p. 7.

2. Hannah Arendt, *Eichmann in Jerusalem* (New York: Viking Press, 1963). Arendt claimed that the leaders of the Jewish community actually allowed the Holocaust to take place through compliance. Had they resisted instead of allowing themselves to be exterminated, according to Arendt, the Holocaust would not have taken place.

3. Leon Poliakov, *Harvest of Hate* (*Bréviaire de la haine*, Paris: Calmann-Lévy, 1951; English revised and expanded edition, New York: Walden Press, 1979), p. 302.

4. Nora Levin, *The Holocaust* (New York: Schocken Books, 1973; 1st ed., 1968, pp. 619–37.

5. Lucy Dawidowicz, *The War Against the Jews, 1933–1945* (New York: Holt, Rinehart and Winston, 1975), pp. 344–46.

6. Raul Hilberg, *The Destruction of the European Jews*, student edition (New York: Holmes and Meier, 1985), p. 126.

7. Ibid., pp. 624–25 and 662–69.

8. Leni Yahil, *The Holocaust*, translated from the Hebrew by Ira Friedman and Haya Galai (New York: Oxford University Press, 1990), p. 478.

9. Simon Wiesenthal, *Justice, Not Vengeance*, translated from the German by Ewald Osers (New York: Grove Weidenfeld, 1988), p. 13.

10. Martin Gray, *For Those I Loved*, translated from the French by Anthony White (Boston: Little, Brown, 1972; translation of *Au nom de tous les miens*, Paris: Editions Robert Laffont, 1971).

11. Ibid., p. 240.

12. Ibid., p. 241.

13. Ibid., p. 243.

14. Ibid.

15. Stanley Milgram, *Obedience to Authority* (New York: Harper and Row, 1974). Milgram conducted a lab experiment where volunteers were told to administer increasing voltages of electric shock (not really administered) to other volunteers (in reality actors who would scream out in pain) when they failed to make a correct reply to various questions. The tests were conducted from various angles, and in almost all the cases the volunteers did as they were told although most realized that high voltage could be fatal. All the participants were provided with psychological counseling after they realized what they were capable of doing. Ironically, one of the volunteers who refused to participate was a German nurse who remembered her country's past history.

16. In Milgram's experiment, too, it was observed that intellectuals complied more than others.

17. Hilberg, *Destruction of the European Jews*, p. 105.

18. Gerald Reitlinger, *The Final Solution*, revised and augmented edition (New York: Thomas Yoseloff, 1968), p. 224.

19. Poliakov, *Harvest of Hate*, pp. 2–3.

20. Dawidowicz, *War Against the Jews*, p. 163.

21. Reitlinger, *Final Solution*, pp. 204–5.

22. Martin Gilbert, *The Holocaust* (New York: Holt, Rinehart and Winston, 1985), p. 238; Yahil, *Holocaust*, p. 279.

23. Hilberg, *Destruction of the European Jews*, p. 271.

24. Ibid., p. 70.

25. Ibid., p. 76.

26. Dawidowicz, *War Against the Jews*, p. 348.

27. Reitlinger, *Final Solution*, p. 68.

28. Ibid., p. 106.

29. Poliakov, *Harvest of Hate*, p. 103.

30. Ibid., p. 106.

31. Yahil, *Holocaust*, p. 200.

32. Gilbert, *Holocaust*, p. 223.

33. Ibid., pp. 227–28.

34. Hilberg, *Destruction of the European Jews*, p. 159.

35. Reitlinger, *Final Solution*, p. 438.

36. Poliakov, *Harvest of Hate*, p. 82.

37. Ibid., p. 298.

38. Levin, *Holocaust*, pp. 74–94.

39. Poliakov, *Harvest of Hate*, p. 26.

40. Ibid., p. 28.

41. Yahil, *Holocaust*, p. 118.

42. Poliakov, *Harvest of Hate*, pp. 111–16.

43. Yehuda Bauer, *A History of the Holocaust* (New York: Franklin Watts, 1982), pp. 135–36, 209; Reitlinger, *Final Solution*, pp. 132–40; Poliakov, *Harvest of Hate*, pp. 183–91; Levin, *Holocaust*, pp. 301–16; Gilbert, *Holocaust*, pp. 426–28, 439; Yahil, *Holocaust*, pp. 307–11.

44. Also depicted as one of the main heroes in Rolf Hochhuth's *The Deputy*, trans. Richard and Clara Winston (New York: Grove Press, 1964).

45. Bauer, *History of the Holocaust*, pp. 307–17; Reitlinger, *Final Solution*, pp. 161–64; Levin, *Holocaust*, pp. 493–501, 686.

46. Reitlinger, *Final Solution*, pp. 141–42.

47. Ibid., p. 220; Poliakov, *Harvest of Hate*, p. 102.

48. Reitlinger, *Final Solution*, pp. 287–88; Gilbert, *Holocaust*, p. 827.

49. Reitlinger, *Final Solution*, pp. 374–75.

50. Poliakov criticizes Reitlinger for this but attributes it to understatement, typical of most Britons; *Harvest of Hate*, p. 336.

51. Reitlinger, *Final Solution*, p. 46.

52. Ibid., p. 176.

53. Ibid., p. 177.

54. Hans Habe, *The Mission* (New York: Coward-McCann, 1966). In this work Habe outlines Heinrich von Benda's (alias Heinrich von Neumann, world famous aurist) mission to present a diabolical scheme by the Viennese Gestapo to offer its Jews for ransom at $250 per head, $1,000 per family.

55. Bauer, *History of the Holocaust*, p. 340.

56. Ibid., p. 289; Gilbert, *Holocaust*, pp. 117–18; Yahil, *Holocaust*, pp. 616–17.

57. Yahil, *Holocaust*, p. 617.

58. Bauer, *History of the Holocaust*, pp. 288–89.

59. Ibid., p. 228.

60. Yahil, *Holocaust*, pp. 514, 640; Gilbert, *Holocaust*, p. 701.

61. Gilbert, *Holocaust*, pp. 662–63.

62. Ibid., pp. 683–84.

63. Ibid., p. 117.

64. Ibid., pp. 230–31.

65. Ibid., pp. 403–4. This remarkable village has now been officially recognized by Yad Vashem. Recently an honor grove of trees was planted there to commemorate the rescue of Jews.

66. Peter Weiss has written a play based purely on testimonials from the Nuremberg trials, *Die Ermittlung* (Frankfurt: RoRoRo, 1969).

## SELECT BIBLIOGRAPHY

Bauer, Yehuda. *A History of the Holocaust*. New York: Franklin Watts, 1982.

Dawidowicz, Lucy. *The War Against the Jews, 1933–1945*. New York: Holt, Rinehart and Winston, 1975.

Gilbert, Martin. *The Holocaust*. New York: Holt, Rinehart and Winston, 1985.

Hilberg, Raul. *The Destruction of the European Jews*. Student edition. New York: Holmes and Meier, 1985.

Levin, Nora. *The Holocaust*. New York: Schocken Books, 1968.

Poliakov, Leon. *Harvest of Hate*. Revised and expanded edition. Boston: Little, Brown, 1972. (Originally *Bréviaire de la haine*. Paris: Calmann-Lévy, 1951.)

Reitlinger, Gerald. *The Final Solution*. Revised and augmented edition. New York: T. Yoseloff, 1968.

Sanders, Ronald. Review of *The Holocaust*, by Leni Yahil. *New York Times Book Review*, November 22, 1990.

Wiesenthal, Simon. *Justice, Not Vengeance*. Translated from the German by Ewald Osers. New York: Grove Weidenfeld, 1988.

Yahil, Leni. *The Holocaust*. Translated from the Hebrew by Ina Friedman and Haya Galai. New York: Oxford University Press, 1990.

# Chapter 2

# The Rise and Development of National Socialism in Germany

## *Reynold Koppel*

In selecting works dealing with the rise and development of national socialism in Germany, one is faced with the challenge of the sheer quantity of the books written on the subject, particularly since the early 1970s. There are hundreds of so-called "biographies" of Adolf Hitler and other leading Nazi personalities, a large number of studies covering the rise of national socialism and the policies of the Third Reich from beginning to end, and thousands of monographs dealing with a variety of political, social, cultural, economic, and psychological themes. Trying to compose a selective, yet broadly based bibliography from this vast quantity of materials presents a serious problem, and perusers of the following survey will, no doubt, find omissions.

An older, general work that covers the entire period of German history from the end of World War I to 1945 was written by Hannah Vogt, *The Burden of Guilt*.[1] The author's purpose is not merely to present a straight narrative of the key developments of the period, particularly those that promoted the rise of national socialism, but to attack many of the popular myths and the consequent self-justification still prevalent among a large segment of the postwar West German populace. This work was originally composed as a guide for German students at the upper gymnasium and university levels. Despite its comparative brevity, it is far superior to and much less biased than the popular best-seller by William L. Shirer, *The Rise and Fall of the Third Reich* (New York: Simon and Schuster, 1960). Although Shirer begins by emphasizing that he intends to present a straightforward, unbiased account, his text is riddled with name-calling, preconceptions, and popular prejudices. However, in Shirer's favor one must point out that he is able to provide excellent character descriptions of many of the leading personalities of the Third Reich, including Adolf Hitler himself, whom Shirer met and interviewed while serving as a foreign correspondent in Berlin during the late 1930s. His work was also one of the first to try to cover the entire gamut of the rise and fall of national socialism in Germany. An earlier work whose author tried to achieve the same goal, though in the guise of a biography, is Alan L. C. Bullock's *Hitler: A Study in Tyranny*. Although Professor Bullock's work was written at a time when much of the archival material used by later scholars was not yet available, it still remains one of the most popular narratives about the period because of its clarity and its unpretentious analysis of the personality, goals, strengths, and weaknesses of Adolf Hitler and his movement.

In looking at works dealing with the era of the Weimar Republic, the period during which the National Socialist German Workers' party (NSDAP) rose from a tiny localized Bavarian right-wing splinter group to become the largest political party in Germany, the reader who wishes to have a broad, yet highly scholarly, analytical survey of the entire period should consult the two-volume work by Erich Eyck, *A History of the Weimar Republic*.[2] While the author's emphasis is primarily centered on the political trends of the Weimar era, he also provides a clear insight into popular sentiments after World War I, while showing that these, at least prior to the end of the 1920s, contributed little to the growth of the Nazi movement. A similar argument in regard to the growth of the Nazi party is made in the first volume of the two-volume work by Dietrich Orlow, *The History of the Nazi Party, 1919-1945*. Orlow's work is, to date, the most extensive examination of every aspect of the NSDAP and its organization, auxiliaries, key personalities, regional strengths and weaknesses, and goals. In his second volume, which deals with the party after the Nazi takeover in 1933, the author discusses the problems faced by the leadership in transforming the rank-and-file members of a movement out of power to the responsibilities of being in power. A more recent analysis of the socioeconomic background of the leaders and rank and file of the NSDAP is the work of Michael Kater, *The Nazi Party: A Social Profile of Members and Leaders, 1919–1945*. A valuable brief documentary source for the pre-1933 period is Hajo Holborn's *Republic to Reich: The Making of the Nazi Revolution*.

If one wants to gain a clearer understanding about the local conditions in and around Munich during the year following the end of World War I and how these helped gain popularity for a group such as the German Workers' party, a highly readable and entertaining work is Richard M. Watt's *The Kings Depart*. Although the author covers the general political situation in and around Munich in 1918–19 and mentions the Nazi party only in passing, he provides a lucid picture of the political vacuum and general instability created by the end of the *ancien régime*, not only in Bavaria but throughout Germany.

Among the many studies concerned specifically with the Nazi party prior to 1933 that provide a deeper insight into the types who joined the movement, its early ideology, and its growing strength are Geoffrey Pridham's *Hitler's Rise* to *Power: The National Socialist Movement in Bavaria, 1923–33*, Eugene Davidson's *The Making of Adolf Hitler: The Birth and Rise of Nazism*, Harold J. Gordon, Jr.,'s *Hitler and the Beer Hall Putsch*, and the documentary collection compiled and edited by Barbara Miller Lane and Leila J. Rupp, *Nazi Ideology Before 1933*. One may also find an interesting discussion on Nazi attempts to win the support of the urban workers during this period in a book by Max H. Kele, *Nazis and Workers, 1919–1933*.

There are literally hundreds of so-called "biographies" of Adolf Hitler. Most of them, however, are not primarily biographical in nature, nor is the Führer necessarily the central figure in them. This is probably due to the fact that very little is actually known about Hitler's private life, other than what the Führer has revealed about his youth in *Mein Kampf*. Hitler, even after 1933, guarded his privacy carefully, and only a few of his closest associates, including his doctors, Albert Speer, and his secretaries were able, after his death, to shed a limited amount of light on his personal life.

Among these general histories of Hitler and the Third Reich, some of the best have been written by persons who were not originally professional historians. Yet many of these works have been painstakingly documented and go beyond the narrative stage to a careful, frequently intriguing analysis. Outstanding in this category is the book by Joachim C. Fest, *Hitler*.[3] This work is especially informative about Hitler's Vienna period, challenging many of the assertions that Hitler made in *Mein Kampf* about his life in the Austro-Hungarian capital. Also of considerable value, although somewhat less analytical, is John Toland's *Adolf Hitler*. The modern German historian who has concentrated more heavily on Adolf Hitler and the Third Reich than most of his contemporaries is Werner Maser. He limits himself more to the person and policies of the Führer than do the writers mentioned earlier. Probably his two most noted works are *Adolf Hitler: Legend, Myth, and Reality*[4] and *Adolf Hitler: Das Ende der Führer-Legende*. Maser not only destroys many of the legends that Hitler created about himself in *Mein Kampf*, but also the popular image of the Führer as one totally dedicated to the public weal. A further effort to destroy the Hitler legend is to be found in Ian Kershaw's work *The "Hitler Myth": Image and Reality in the Third Reich*.[5] A more favorable picture of Hitler is presented in Richard Pemsel's *Hitler: Revolutionär, Staatsmann, Verbrecher*. Here, however, the main thrust of the author appears to be to place most of the failures and crimes of the Third Reich on Hitler's shoulders and, conversely, to exonerate the rest of Germany.[6] Another work that tries to rationalize, if not excuse, Hitler's policies by placing them in the context of the 1930s is Hans Bernd Gisevius's *Adolf Hitler: Versuch einer Deutung*. An interesting, though not always reliable, account of Hitler's early years in Linz and Vienna is to be found in the work of his boyhood friend, August Kubizek, *The Young Hitler I Knew*.[7] An early work about Adolf Hitler in the 1920s and early 1930s was written by Konrad Heiden, a onetime supporter of national socialism and the Führer, who later broke with him and fled, *Der Führer: Hitler's Rise to Power*.[8] While strongly biased, Heiden gives the reader a deeper insight into Hitler, the man and the politician, than he or she can get from many later, more scholarly sources.

In recent decades Adolf Hitler has become a favorite subject of the psycho-historians, who have attempted to take a closer look at the forces, particularly those of his childhood and early family environment, that may help to explain his later ideas and policies. The first effort in this direction was made during the last years of World War II in the work by Walter C. Langer, *The Mind of Adolf Hitler*, in response to a request by the U.S. Office of Strategic Services. Although it contains a number of errors, it does attempt to offer some explanations for the Führer's "hangups." More recently, there have been two authors who have tried to offer a psychohistorical interpretation of Adolf Hitler, Rudolph Binion, *Hitler Among the Germans*, and Robert G. L. Waite, *The Psychopathic God: Adolf Hitler*. While the reader may find some new ideas and interpretations in works using the psychohistorical approach, he or she should realize that the authors are merely suggesting possible interpretations, not any final explanations of Hitler's thoughts and actions. One work about Hitler that was popular for many years was Robert P. S. Payne's *The Life and Death of Adolf Hitler*. However, although it is written in the flowing style that characterizes the other biographies by this author, it is not presented in a scholarly manner and lacks documentation. This is particularly distressing since Payne introduces new "facts" into his narrative about Hitler, data that are not found in the works of other authors. For example, he claims, without listing any sources, that Hitler spent several months in England in 1911, visiting his elder stepbrother, and from this time on developed a strong respect for British might.

Two former Nazis who briefly were close associates of Hitler but later broke with him were Hermann Rauschning and Otto Wagener. Both had conversations with the Führer and were part of his entourage during the three or four years prior to his appointment as chancellor. The record of their experiences provides a more intimate picture of Hitler than do many of the more scholarly works. Rauschning's book was a sensation when it appeared in the United States under the title *The Voice of Destruction*.[9] Wagener's recollections about his association with Hitler during the period 1929–32 were edited by Henry Ashby Turner, Jr., as *Hitler: Memoirs of a Confidant*.[10] As both works were written by "renegades" of the Nazi movement, some of their assertions are suspect, but overall they are of value for the unique insights that they offer into Hitler's thoughts. Another work of the same genre, but giving us a more intimate view of Hitler as a private person, was written by Henriette von Schirach, the widow of the former Reich [Hitler] Youth leader, *Anekdoten um Hitler: Geschichten aus einem halben Jahr-hundert*. Not only was she a part of Hitler's inner circle during the Third Reich, but as the daughter of Heinrich Hoffmann, the Führer's personal photographer, she first met him as an eight-year-old girl in 1921 and saw him frequently thereafter during the next few years when he was a visitor at the Hoffmann apartment in Munich.[11] Finally, a brief incisive analysis of Hitler, his career, philosophy, strengths, and weaknesses, a work that may also serve as a desirable college textbook, was written by William Carr, *Hitler: A Study in Personality and Politics*. An additional useful feature of this book is its annotated bibliography. An excellent, concise discussion and analysis of the Führer's ideas on a wide range of topics are presented in a book by Eberhard Jäckel, *Hitler's World View: A Blueprint for Power.*[12]

Relatively few biographies have appeared about other leading National Socialists, and most of these have been in German. An exception is Hermann Göring, about whom stories abounded both during and after the end of the Third Reich, most of them apocryphal. These largely stemmed from Göring's public humor and bonhomie, qualities singularly lacking in Hitler and most of the other leading party members. Most of his biographers have tried to show that, in fact, Göring's actions were quite different from his public image, and that he was one of the most ruthless and dedicated, if also most corrupt, followers of Hitler. One such biography is R. J. Overy's *Goering, the "Iron Man."* A more favorable view of Göring is presented by the pseudorevisionist British writer David Irving, *Göring: A Biography.*

Probably the best known of Hitler's closest associates is Albert Speer, if only because he produced several works, partly of an autobiographical nature, after his release from Spandau Prison in 1965. These include *Inside the Third Reich*[13] and *Spandau: The Secret Diaries.*[14] While both of these books are highly readable and provide some supplementary information, particularly about Hitler, they must be read with care, since the principal aim of the author is to exonerate himself, at least from the worst excesses of the Nazi regime. An attempt to place Albert Speer in a more objective light has been made by Adelbert Reif in *Albert Speer: Kontroversen um ein deutsches Phänomen.*[15] A biography of limited value about Propaganda Minister Joseph Goebbels was written by Helmut Heiber, *Goebbels.*[16] A more in-depth analytical picture is presented by Viktor Reimann, *Goebbels.*[17] A recent, somewhat exculpatory biography of Deputy Führer Rudolf Hess was written by Wulf Schwarzwäller, *Rudolf Hess, the Last Nazi.*[18]

Until very recently the only works of value about Reichsführer SS Heinrich Himmler were one by Roger Manvell and Heinrich Fraenkel, *Himmler*, and one that presents a perceptive analysis of his early development, written by Bradley Smith, *Heinrich Himmler: A Nazi in the Making, 1900–1926*. During 1991 two highly incisive works using several new sources appeared. They are Richard Breitman's *The Architect of Genocide: Himmler and the Final Solution* and the biography by the naval historian Peter Padfield, *Himmler*.

There are a number of works about Himmler's second-in-command, Reinhard Heydrich; most noteworthy are Günther Deschner's *Reinhard Heydrich: Statthalter der totalen Macht* and the biography by Edouard Calic, *Reinhard Heydrich: The Chilling Story of the Man Who Masterminded the Nazi Death Camps*. A work based on unpublished British and Czech archives and dealing with the conception and execution of the plot to assassinate Heydrich has been written by Callum MacDonald, *The Killing of SS Obergruppenführer Reinhard Heydrich*. An analytical biography of Heydrich's successor, Ernst Kaltenbrunner, was written by Peter R. Black, *Ernst Kaltenbrunner: Ideological Soldier of the Third Reich*.

The only noteworthy work about the man who exercised considerable power during the last years of the Reich because he controlled access to Hitler has been written by Jochen von Lang and Claus Sibyll, *The Secretary: Martin Bormann, the Man Who Manipulated Hitler*.[19]

Although not primarily intended as a biography, the very popular, if controversial, work on Adolf Eichmann by Hannah Arendt is worthy of mention, *Eichmann in Jerusalem: A Report on the Banality of Evil*.

To many experts on the Third Reich the most truly offensive personality was the Gauleiter of Franconia and publisher of *Der Stürmer*, a virulent anti-Semitic newspaper, as well as of many anti-Semitic books and pamphlets, Julius Streicher. Surprisingly, few scholars have attempted to write about him. An exception is the biographical work by Randall L. Bytwerk, *Julius Streicher: The Man Who Persuaded a Nation to Hate Jews*. The author explains the reasons why and to what segment of the German public the *Stürmer* materials had an appeal, and he includes many excerpts and illustrations.

There are several exculpatory autobiographies by some of the men who were close to Hitler during one or several phases of his career. These works are mainly worthy of citation because they provide a closer look at the Führer and the source of his attraction than are to be found in secondary biographies. These include a "tear-jerker" account of the career of Reich Youth leader Baldur von Schirach, *Ich glaubte an Hitler*; the posthumously published reminiscences of the head of the Generalgouvernement in Poland, Hans Frank, *Im Angesicht des Galgens: Deutung Hitlers und seiner Zeit auf Grund eigener Erlebnisse und Erkenntnisse*; and an entertaining, but rather cursory, look back by Ernst "Putzi" Hanfstaengl, the Harvard University graduate who was a close friend of Hitler prior to 1933, *Fünfzehn Jahre mit Hitler: Zwischen Weissem und Braunem Haus*.

Finally, there are a number of books that provide brief accounts of the character and roles of various Nazi leaders. The best of these, authored by Joachim C. Fest, *The Face of the Third Reich*, presents a series of short biographical essays on all of the previously mentioned personalities, as well as Ernst Röhm, Franz von Papen, Alfred Rosenberg, Joachim von Ribbentrop, Rudolf Hoess, and others.[20]

There are many general studies of the era of the Third Reich in its entirety, as well as, more recently, monographs concerned with more limited political, social, and economic aspects of the period. Among the older but more pervasive analyses of the political and socioeconomic structure of the Nazi state is the work by Karl-Dietrich Bracher, *The German Dictatorship: The Origins, Structure, and Effects of National Socialism*.[21] A brilliant interpretive study of the inner conflicts that characterized the Third Reich, the tensions between the party and the state and between the inherited institutions, based on the rule of law, and the arbitrary activities of the Gestapo and other organizations created after 1933, is to be found in the work by Martin Broszat, *The Hitler State: The*

*Foundation and Development of the Internal Structure of the Third Reich.*[22] Writing in a somewhat similar vein, but with greater stress on how and why conflict within the political structure of the Hitler state was an essential characteristic, is Edward N. Peterson in *The Limits of Hitler's Power*. The author's main thrust is to demonstrate that the Führer encouraged competition and rivalry among his subordinates, as well as among various institutions of his regime, in order to strengthen his own position as unquestioned leader and to deter any ambitious subordinate from attempting to replace him. A highly ambitious effort regarding both the external and internal policies of the Hitler state is to be found in the book edited by Robert E. Herzstein, *Adolf Hitler and the Third Reich*. The work is both documentary and analytical, drawing upon excerpts from the writings of several respected historians, as well as of key personalities of the era, on various aspects of Nazi foreign relations, the Reich at war, and some of the groups and institutions of Nazi society. A more strictly documentary collection on various internal and external aspects of the Third Reich is to be found in a work by the historian Reinhard Kühnl, *Der deutsche Faschismus in Quellen und Dokumenten*. Although the documents themselves are of considerable value to the student of the period, the strongly biased interpretations of the author necessitate that the work be used with care.[23] A more conservative view of the rise and chief characteristics of the Nazi state is to be found in the older work by Walther Hofer, *Die Diktatur Hitlers bis zum Beginn des zweiten Weltkrieges*. A series of interesting analytical essays on what Hitler's followers liked to call his "seizure of power" has been edited by Peter D. Stachura, *The Nazi Machtergreifung*. A useful brief summary of the Nazi era, its role in German history, and its legacy, as well as an analysis of recent scholarship on various aspects of the period, is to be found in a work by Klaus Hildebrand, *The Third Reich*.[24]

Turning to books that deal with particular aspects of the Nazi state and its society, both before and after the outbreak of World War II, we find a number of valuable studies on German foreign policy. These include a recent work on the role of the German Foreign Ministry and its bureaucracy in implementing, as well as hampering, the Führer's goals by Hans-Jürgen Döscher, *Das Auswärtige Amt im Dritten Reich*. Another valuable analysis of early Nazi foreign policy is to be found in a work by John L. Heineman that, despite its title, is not primarily biographical, *Hitler's First Foreign Minister*. In the same category is an earlier work by Gerhard L. Weinberg, *The Foreign Policy of Hitler's Germany*. Vol. 1, *Diplomatic Revolution in Europe, 1933–1936*. For a study of German foreign policy under Joachim von Ribbentrop, one will find *The Ribbentrop Memoirs* of considerable value, especially for the introductory section by Alan L. C. Bullock.[25]

One may get some valuable insights into the new direction of German foreign policy, as well as the tactics of prewar Nazi diplomacy, in the memoirs of a foreign diplomat in Germany in the 1930s, André François-Poncet's *The Fateful Years: Memoirs of a French Ambassador in Berlin, 1933–1938*.[26] An in-depth analysis of the relationship of Nazi ideology and institutions to Hitler's immediate and long-term foreign policy goals is to be found in a two-volume work by Norman Rich, *Hitler's War Aims*.[27] German foreign policy and the preparation for war is also the theme of a work by the popular British author David Irving, *The War Path: Hitler's Germany, 1933–1939*. However, as is the case with some other works by the same author, his information about German foreign policy is not always reliable, and he is generally, though without providing logical justification, sympathetic to the Führer's goals.

In the area of internal developments during the Third Reich, there are several broad studies on the impact of the advent of national socialism on German society as a whole as well as on particular segments of the German population. These include a scholarly analysis by David Schoenbaum, *Hitler's Social Revolution*, and a broad, highly readable work by Richard Grunberger, *The 12-Year Reich: A Social History of Nazi Germany*. To this should be added the study of a respected German historian who is sympathetic to many Nazi developments and goals, if not to those who provided the leadership during this period, George L. Mosse, who has edited a work providing an overview of various aspects of German society during the Third Reich under the title *Nazi Culture*. Into this general category on the impact of national socialism on German society also fall a large number of works that have appeared in the Federal Republic of Germany and, in translation, abroad in recent years. Some of these do not pretend to be scholarly.[28] One of the better discussions on the subject is to be found in Bernt Engelmann's *Hitler's Germany: Everyday Life in the Third Reich*,[29] which, while partly autobiographical, covers a wide range of topics without any attempts to find excuses for what happened. Another valuable work in this area consists of a series of analytical essays about various aspects of German life by several noted German and foreign historians, edited by Detlev Peukert and Jürgen Peukert, *Alltag im Nationalsozialismus*. An interesting series of essays by a number of historians on how the Nazi regime affected the life of various segments of German society has been edited by Richard Bessel, *Life in the Third Reich*. Although it is rare to find diary entries by ordinary people published in book form, one such valuable source, expressing reflections on contemporary events during the second half of the Third Reich and the immediate postwar period, has been edited by Heinrich Breloer, *Mein Tagebuch: Geschichten vom Überleben, 1939–1947*. There is no attempt to analyze these entries, some of which are quite long and cover several years, but this makes them all the more unique and valuable. Included also are caricatures, some highly critical of the regime, drawn by the contributors and an extensive collection of contemporary photographs.

Finally, there is a short series of essays edited by Otis C. Mitchell, *Nazism and the Common Man*, although the title of this book is somewhat misleading. While it includes essays on youth and workers in the Third Reich, it discusses them not in terms of their responses as individuals, but as members of organizations (Hitler Youth and ''Strength through Joy'') created by the regime. Other essays deal with the Sturmabteilung (SA), the police, and letters to Streicher's *Stürmer*.

In the category of the role of women in the Third Reich, the most complete discussion and analysis is presented by Claudia Koonz in *Mothers in the Fatherland: Women, the Family, and Nazi Politics*. The author deals at length with the place of women in the Weimar Republic as well as in Nazi Germany, especially in terms of women's organizations that were formed during these periods. While Koonz has a tendency to imbue German women of the 1920s and 1930s with the same feelings about their role in society that members of the American women's liberation movement have today, she does cover every aspect of women's roles in the aforesaid periods. Her work is especially valuable for the insights the reader gets from her interviews of Gertrud Scholtz-Klink, the unrepentant former Reichsfrauenführerin of women's affairs. She also provides the reader with an extensive bibliography of primary and secondary sources. A somewhat less analytical, yet interesting, study that discusses in more detail the relationship between gender and social role in Nazi Germany is to be found in a book by Hans Peter Bleuel, *Sex and Society in Nazi Germany*.[30]

Much has been written about the role and education of German youth in the Third Reich. The most thorough discussion of the Hitler Youth and other contemporary youth organizations, the extent to which German youth understood and promoted the goals of Nazism, and the impact of World War II on Germany's youth is to be found in a work by H. W. Koch, *The Hitler Youth*. A more recent work on the role of young people in the Reich, not only those who were enthusiastic supporters of the regime, but also those who, for a variety of reasons, bedevilled the authorities, has been written by Gerhard Rempel, *Hitler's Children: The Hitler Youth and the SS*.

There are several shorter monographs dealing with the activities of youth during the Third Reich. While these are somewhat less scholarly than the studies mentioned earlier, they are fairly well written and provide the reader with information not found in other works on the subject. Among the more incisive ones in this genre are Alfons Heck's *A Child of Hitler: Germany in the Days When God Wore a Swastika*[31] and Hans Siemsen's *Die Geschichte des Hitler Jungen Adolf Goers*.[32]

Some interesting work has been done on various aspects of formal education in the Third Reich. Especially noteworthy is a study undertaken by a working committee of the Pedagogical Museum of Hamburg under the direction of Norbert Franck, *Heil Hitler, Herr Lehrer: Volksschule im 3. Reich: 1933–1945, Das Beispiel Berlin*. In addition to providing a description of the daily activities in the types of schools attended by most children in the Third Reich, the book includes many documents and pictures not found in other works on this subject. An interesting survey of a variety of educational institutions, including Jewish schools, in the Third Reich, based on interviews with former pupils and containing a rich collection of documents, has been produced by a ninth-grade class of the Gerhart Hauptmann–Schule in Kassel under the direction of its teacher, Geert Platner, *Schule im Dritten Reich: Erziehung zum Tod*. A more scholarly, analytical coverage of this topic may be found in the work by Gilmer W. Blackburn, *Education in the Third Reich*.

A very well documented presentation and analysis of the various types of literature written expressly for German children in order to reinforce Nazi ideals is to be found in a work by Christa Kamenetsky, *Children's Literature in Hitler's Germany: The Cultural Policy of National Socialism*. In a related category is the monograph by Fred Hahn, *Lieber Stürmer*, a study of a series of letters on various topics written by children to Julius Streicher. While it is difficult to draw conclusions from these letters, since they were clearly written under supervision, they do demonstrate the values and ideals that were being inculcated into children in Nazi Germany.

There are several studies concerning public opinion in various periods of the Nazi era and/or in specific regions of Germany. One highly interesting analytical discussion of the reaction to Nazi policies by various segments of Bavaria's population is to be found in Ian Kershaw's *Popular Opinion and Political Dissent in the Third Reich: Bavaria, 1933–1945* A survey of public opinion and popular responses to Germany's changing fortunes during World War II may be found in a work by Marlis G. Steinert, *Hitler's War and the Germans*.[33] Much of German public opinion was, of course, molded by what people read in newspapers. The role of the press in Hitler's Germany has been studied and analyzed in a work by Oron J. Hale, *The Captive Press in the Third Reich*. An interesting discussion of the impact of various propaganda efforts by the government and the party may also be found in a brief survey by Z. A. B. Zeman, *Nazi Propaganda*.

Concerning the two major paramilitary organizations that played a key role in the rise and development of the National Socialist party and state, the Sturmabteilung (SA) and the Schutzstaffel (SS), surprisingly little has been produced in book form on the former organization, either in German or English. The only work worth mentioning deals primarily with the purge of the SA and its leadership in 1934 and was written by Max Gallo, *The Night of the Long Knives*.[34] Far more extensive and in-depth studies are available on the SS and on its rise, development, organization, and changing role. One of the earliest, works on this subject, but still highly respected, was written by Gerald Reitlinger, *The SS, Alibi of a Nation*, which surveys the multifarious activities of the SS both prior to and during the war. A few years later, a more in-depth examination of the SS was produced as a joint effort by the German historians Helmut Krausnick and Martin Broszat, *Anatomy of the SS State*.[35] In addition to a discussion of the role of the SS in the implementation of the Holocaust, the work includes an analysis of the SS as an organization, its relationship to the regular police, its administration of the concentration- and extermination-camp system, and a study of the ''SS mentality.'' Although it was published more than twenty years ago, the most complete analytical survey of the SS and of its leadership, activities, goals, and policies is the work by Heinz Höhne, *The Order of the Death's Head*.[36] A more detailed study of one branch of the SS, the Waffen-SS, and of its origins, key functionaries, and activities may be found in George H. Stein's *The Waffen SS*.

In subsequent chapters of this volume, books on the background and highlights of the Holocaust will be discussed in detail. Therefore, I will here mention only a few works concerning anti-Semitism, in theory and in practice, and its role as an integral feature of national socialism and the Third Reich. An older work, first published in 1941 and revised in 1961 and 1965, is Peter Viereck's *Metapolitics: The Roots of the Nazi Mind*. Although the author analyzes various Nazi concepts, most of his study deals with the Nazi racial doctrines and their origin, as well as a brief history of anti-Semitism in modern Germany since the Thirty Years' War. His relaxed, fluent style does not detract from the scholarly analyses embodied in the presentation. A more recent monograph, written in a similar vein, but concentrating exclusively on the history of racial anti-Semitism, including its ties to more traditional forms of religious anti-Semitism, is George L. Mosse's *Toward the Final Solution: A History of European Racism*. A well-documented, analytical discussion of the history of anti-Semitism in Germany after 1870, the role of anti-Semitism in the rise of Hitler and the Nazi party, and the effectiveness of propaganda in the promotion of anti-Semitism before and after 1933, as well as public support for, and opposition to, the treatment of the Jews in the Third Reich, is the subject of a recent book by Sarah Gordon, *Hitler, Germany, and the Jewish Question*.

Much scholarly work on a variety of topics dealing with anti-Semitism in modern Germany has been done under the auspices of the Leo Baeck Institute in New York, including many of its yearbooks, which cover Jewish life and challenges during several stages of this period. One of its more recent publications consists of a series of papers presented at a conference held in Berlin in 1985. The theme of the conference was "Self-Assertion in Adversity: The Jewish in National Socialist Germany, 1933–1939." Included in this volume are presentations by German and American scholars on Jewry in Weimar as well as in Nazi Germany. Some of the papers go beyond 1939 to 1943, the year of the last deportation of Jews from Germany. The papers are representative of some of the finest work dealing with the story of the response of the Jews to their changing environment, both in the Weimar era and in the Third Reich. The collection was edited by Arnold Paucker, Sylvia Gilchrist, and Barbara Suchy under the joint title *Die Juden im Nationalsozialistischen Deutschland: The Jews in Nazi Germany, 1933–1943*.

Finally, there are three collections, consisting mainly of primary source materials, that should be included in this bibliographic survey. All provide extensive and, in the case of the third work, unusual documentation on almost every aspect of the rise of national socialism during the Weimar era and its development in the Third Reich. The first is a three-volume compilation of original documents by Jeremy Noakes and Geoffrey Pridham, *Nazism, 1919–1945: A Documentary*

*Reader.*[37] The second work, by Michael Freeman, *Atlas of Nazi Germany*, provides a large number of detailed maps and charts dealing with such matters as the development and early distribution of the NSDAP, the economy, and the chains of command of various state and party organizations.

The third book falls into a completely different genre of source materials. It consists primarily of a collection of photographs, caricatures, drawings, and so on, many of which are not to be found in other books of this type, gathered by Frederic V. Grunfeld, *The Hitler File: A Social History of Germany and the Nazis.* Each section of the book, dealing with a period of modern German history between 1918 and 1945, has a brief, at times perceptive commentary, but it is the pictures themselves, many of them unique, that provide the reader with a detailed representative view of life in Germany during the Weimar and Nazi eras.

## NOTES

1. Translated by Herbert Strauss from the original German edition, Hannah Vogt, *Schuld oder Verhängnis? Zwölf Fragen an Deutschlands jüngste Vergangenheit* (Frankfurt am Main: Verlag Moritz Diesterweg, 1961).

2. Translated by H. P. Hanson and Robert G. L. Waite from the original German edition, Erich Eyck, *Geschichte der Weimarer Republik*, 2 vols. (Zürich: Fintenau Verlag, 1956).

3. Translated by Richard and Clara Winston from the original German edition, Joachim C. Fest, *Hitler, Eine Biographie* (Frankfurt am Main and Berlin: Ullstein Verlag, 1973).

4. Original German edition, Werner Maser, *Adolf Hitler: Legende, Mythos, Wirklichkeit* (Munich and Esslingen: Bechtle Verlag, 1971).

5. Translated by Richard Barry from the original German edition, Ian Kershaw, *Der Hitler-Mythos: Volksmeinung und Propaganda im Dritten Reich* (Stuttgart: Deutsche Verlags-Anstalt, 1980).

6. Although not officially recognized as such, Grabert Verlag, the publisher of Pemsel's book, must be classified as a "revisionist" publishing house. It has published the memoirs of a number of unrepentant former Nazi officials of middle and higher rank, including the autobiography of Gertrud Scholtz-Klink, the former Reichsfrauenführerin of the NS Frauenschaft und Frauenwerk.

7. Translated by George Kern from the original German edition, August Kubizek, *Adolf Hitler, mein Jugendfreund* (Graz and Göttingen: Styria Verlag, 1953).

8. Translated by Ralph Manheim and Norbert Guterman from the original German edition, Konrad Heiden, *Der Führer: Hitlers Aufstieg zur Macht* (Berlin: Rohwolt Verlag, 1931).

9. Rauschning's work was originally published as *Hitler m'a dit* (Paris, 1939), as well as *Hitler Speaks* (London: Thornton Butterworth, 1939). A year later it appeared as *Gespräche mit Hitler* (Zürich: Europa Verlag, 1940).

10. Translated by Ruth Hein from the original German edition, Otto Wagener, *Hitler aus nächster Nähe: Aufzeichnungen eines Vertrauten* (Frankfurt am Main: Ullstein Verlag, 1978).

11. Here Hitler also met Hoffmann's assistant, Eva Braun.

12. Translated by Herbert Arnold from the original German edition, Eberhard Jäckel, *Hitlers Weltanschauung: Entwurf einer Herrschaft* (Tübingen: Rainer Wunderlich Verlag Hermann Leins, 1969).

13. Translated by Richard Barry from the original German edition, Albert Speer, *Erinnerungen* (Frankfurt am Main and Berlin: Ullstein Verlag, 1969).

14. Translated by Richard and Clara Winston from the original German edition, Albert Speer, *Spandauer Tagebücher* (Frankfurt am Main and Berlin: Ullstein Verlag, 1975).

15. A critique of Speer's allegations, demonstrating that he deliberately falsified some of his wartime diaries and other personal documents, may be found in a well-documented work by the historian Matthias Schmidt, *Albert Speer: Das Ende eines Mythos* (Bern and Munich: Scherz Verlag, 1982).

16. Translated by John K. Dickinson from the original German edition, Helmut Heiber, *Joseph Goebbels* (Berlin: Colloquium Verlag Otto Hess, 1962).

17. Translated by Stephen Wendt from the original German edition, Viktor Reiman, *Dr. Joseph Goebbels* (Stuttgart: Molden Verlag, 1971).

18. Edited and translated from the original German edition, Wulf Schwarzwäller, *Rudolf Hess, der Letzte von Spandau* (Vienna: Molden Taschenbuch, 1974).

19. Translated by Christa Armstrong and Peter White from the original German edition, Jochen von Lang and Claus Sibyll, *Der Sekretär: Martin Bormann, der Mann der Hitler beherrschte* (Stuttgart: Deutsche Verlags-Anstalt, 1977).

20. Translated by Michael Bullock from the original German edition, Joachim C. Fest, *Das Gesicht des Dritten Reiches* (Munich: R. Piper, 1963).

21. Translated by Jean Steinberg from the original German edition, Karl Dietrich Bracher, *Die deutsche Diktatur: Entstenhung, Struktur, Folgen des Nationalsozialismus* (Cologne: Kiepenheuer und Witsch, 1969).

22. Translated by John W. Hiden from the original German edition, Martin Broszat, *Der Staat Hitlers* (Munich: Deutscher Taschenbuch Verlag, 1969).

23. Reinhard Kühnl, professor of history at the University of Marburg, is considered a leader among German socialist historians. Generally, these comprise the majority among the younger scholars of the Third Reich in the Federal Republic of Germany. They view the rise and development of Nazism as the inevitable outgrowth of the inner conflicts of modern capitalism and imperialism, and not as something uniquely German. One characteristic of these scholars is that they shy away from the term "national socialism," not only because some might take it to mean that it was a German form of socialism, but because it is associated only with Germany. Thus they generally substitute for it the term "German fascism."

24. Translated by P. S. Falla from the original German edition, Klaus Hildebrand, *Das Dritte Reich* (Munich: R. Oldenbourg Verlag, 1979).

25. Translated by Oliver Watson from the original German edition, Joachim von Ribbentrop, *Joachim von Ribbentrop: Erinnerungen* (Zürich and Vienna, 1953).

26. Translated by Jacques Leclerq from the original French edition (unpublished), André François-Poncet, *Les Ans à Berlin*.

27. The subtitle of volume 1 is *Ideology, the Nazi State, and the Course of Expansion*, while that of volume 2 is *The Establishment of the New Order*.

28. During the late 1970s and early 1980s the government of the Federal Republic of Germany sponsored a series of annual middle- and upper-school-level contests on the theme of everyday life in the Third Reich. Students developed some very insightful

conclusions on the basis of interviews of survivors, although they were given little direction on how to evaluate these interviews. To this writer, however, it appears that the principal aim of these contests has been to portray the ordinary German as an innocent bystander during the period or even as an opponent.

29. The original German edition of Bernt Engelmann's work appeared in two volumes. The first was titled *Im Gleichschritt marsch: Wie wir die Nazizeit erlebten, 1933–1939*; the second, *Bis alles in Scherben fällt: Wie wir die Nazizeit erlebten, 1939–1945* (Cologne: Verlag Kiepenheuer und Witsch, 1983).

30. Translated by J. M. Brownjohn from the original German edition, Hans Peter Bleuel, *Das saubere Reich* (Bern and Munich: Scherz Verlag, 1972).

31. Another work on this subject by the same author, but one in which he tends to ramble, is Alfons Heck, *The Burden of Hitler's Legacy* (Frederick, Colo.: Renaissance House, 1988).

32. The original, shorter edition appeared in English, Hans Siemsen, *Hitler Youth* (London: Drummond, 1940).

33. Edited and translated by Thomas E. J. DeWitt from the original German version, Marlis G. Steinert, *Hitlers Krieg und die Deutschen* (Düsseldorf: Econ Verlagsgruppe, 1976).

34. Translated by Lily Emmet from the original French edition, Max Gallo, *La Nuit des longs couteaux* (Paris: R. Laffont, 1971).

35. Translated by Richard Barry et al. from the original German edition, Helmut Krausnick, Hans Buchheim, Martin Broszat, and Hans-Adolf Jacobsen, *Anatomie des SS-Staates* (Olten and Freiburg im Breisgau: Walter Verlag AG, 1965).

36. Translated by Richard Barry from the original German edition, Heinz Höhne, *Der Orden unter dem Totenkopf* (Hamburg: Verlag Der Spiegel; Gutersloh, Sigbert Mohn Verlag, 1967).

37. The documents are arranged as follows: volume 1, *The Rise to Power, 1919–1934*; volume 2, *State, Economy, and Society, 1933–1939*; volume 3, *Foreign Policy, War, and Racial Extermination, 1933–1945*.

## SELECT BIBLIOGRAPHY

### Works in English or English Translation

Arendt, Hannah. *Eichmann in Jerusalem: A Report on the Banality of Evil*. New York: Viking Press, 1963.

Bessel, Richard, ed. *Life in the Third Reich*. Oxford: Oxford University Press, 1987.

Binion, Rudolph. *Hitler Among the Germans*. New York: Elsevier, 1976.

Black, Peter R. *Ernst Kaltenbrunner: Ideological Soldier of the Third Reich*. Princeton, N.J.: Princeton University Press, 1984.

Blackburn, Gilmer W. *Education in the Third Reich*. Albany: State University of New York Press, 1985.

Bleuel, Hans Peter. *Sex and Society in Nazi Germany*. Philadelphia and New York: Lippincott, 1973.

Bracher, Karl-Dietrich. *The German Dictatorship: The Origins, Structure, and Effects of National Socialism*. New York: Praeger, 1970.

Breitman, Richard. *The Architect of Genocide: Himmler and the Final Solution.* New York: Knopf, 1991.

Broszat, Martin. *The Hitler State: The Foundation and Development of the Internal Structure of the Third Reich.* London and New York: Longman, 1981.

Bullock, Alan L. C. *Hitler: A Study in Tyranny.* New York: Harper and Row, 1962.

Bytwerk, Randall L. *Julius Streicher: The Man Who Persuaded a Nation to Hate Jews.* New York: Dorset Press, 1983.

Calic, Edouard. *Reinhard Heydrich: The Chilling Story of the Man Who Masterminded the Nazi Death Camps.* New York: Hippocrene Books, 1988.

Carr, William. *Hitler: a Study in Personality and Politics.* London and Baltimore: Edward Arnold, 1978.

Davidson, Eugene. *The Making of Adolf Hitler: The Birth and Rise of Nazism.* New York: Macmillan, 1977.

Engelmann, Bernt. *Hitler's Germany: Everyday Life in the Third Reich.* New York: Pantheon Books, 1986.

Eyck, Erich. *A History of the Weimar Republic.* 2 vols. Cambridge, Mass.: Harvard University Press, 1967.

Fest, Joachim C. *The Face of the Third Reich.* New York: Pantheon Books, 1970.

———. *Hitler.* New York: Random House, 1975.

François-Poncet, André. *The Fateful Years: Memoirs of a French Ambassador in Berlin, 1933–1938.* New York: Howard Fertig, 1949.

Freeman, Michael. *Atlas of Nazi Germany.* London and Sydney: Croom Helm, 1987.

Gallo, Max. *The Night of the Long Knives.* New York: Harper and Row, 1972.

Gordon, Harold J., Jr. *Hitler and the Beer Hall Putsch.* Princeton, N.J.: Princeton University Press, 1972.

Gordon, Sarah. *Hitler, Germany and the Jewish Question.* Princeton, N.J.: Princeton University Press, 1984.

Grunberger, Richard. *The 12-Year Reich: A Social History of Nazi Germany.* New York: Holt, Rinehart and Winston, 1971.

Grunfeld, Frederic V. *The Hitler File: A Social History of Germany and the Nazis.* London: Weidenfeld and Nicolson, 1974.

Hale, Oron J. *The Captive Press in the Third Reich.* Princeton, N.J.: Princeton University Press, 1964.

Heck, Alfons. *A Child of Hitler: Germany in the Days When God Wore a Swastika.* Frederick, Colo.: Renaissance House, 1981.

Heiber, Helmut. *Goebbels.* New York: Hawthorn Books, 1972.

Heiden, Konrad. *Der Führer: Hitler's Rise to Power.* Boston: Houghton-Mifflin, 1944.

Heineman, John L. *Hitler's First Foreign Minister.* Berkeley: University of California Press, 1979.

Herzstein, Robert E., ed. *Adolf Hitler and the Third Reich.* Boston: Houghton Mifflin, 1971.

Hildebrand, Klaus. *The Third Reich.* London: Allen and Unwin, 1984.

Höhne, Heinz. *The Order of the Death's Head.* New York: Coward-McCann, 1970.

Holborn, Hajo. *Republic to Reich: The Making of the Nazi Revolution.* New York: Vintage Books, 1972.

Irving, David. *Göring: A Biography.* New York: William Morrow, 1989.

———. *The War Path: Hitler's Germany, 1933–1939.* New York: Viking Press, 1978.

Jäckel, Eberhard. *Hitler's World View: A Blueprint for Power*. Middletown, Conn.: Wesleyan University Press, 1972.

Kamenetsky, Christa. *Children's Literature in Hitler's Germany: The Cultural Policy of National Socialism*. Athens: Ohio University Press, 1984.

Kater, Michael. *The Nazi Party: A Social Profile of Members and Leaders, 1919–1945*. Cambridge, Mass.: Harvard University Press, 1983.

Kele, Max H. *Nazis and Workers, 1919–1933*. Chapel Hill: University of North Carolina Press, 1972.

Kershaw, Ian. *The "Hitler Myth": Image and Reality in the Third Reich*. Oxford: Clarendon Press, 1987.

————. *Popular Opinion and Political Dissent in the Third Reich: Bavaria, 1933–1945*. Oxford: Clarendon Press, 1983.

Koch, H. W. *The Hitler Youth*. New York: Stein and Day, 1975.

Koonz, Claudia. *Mothers in the Fatherland: Women, the Family, and Nazi Politics*. New York: St. Martin's Press, 1987.

Krausnick, Helmut, and Martin Broszat. *Anatomy of the SS State*. Cambridge, England: William Collins Sons, 1968.

Kubizek, August. *The Young Hitler I Knew*. Boston: Houghton Mifflin, 1955.

Lane, Barbara Miller, and Leila J. Rupp. *Nazi Ideology Before 1933*. Austin: University of Texas Press, 1978.

Lang, J. V., and Claus Sibyll. *The Secretary: Martin Bormann, the Man Who Manipulated Hitler*. Athens: Ohio University Press, 1978.

Langer, Walter C. *The Mind of Adolf Hitler*. Reprint. New York: Basic Books, 1972.

MacDonald, Callum. *The Killing of SS Obergruppenführer Reinhard Heydrich*. London: Odhams, 1962.

Manvell, Roger, and Heinrich Fraenkel. *Himmler*. New York: Putnam, 1965.

Maser, Werner. *Adolf Hitler: Legend, Myth, and Reality*. London and New York: Allen Lane, 1973

Mitchell, Otis C., ed. *Nazism and the Common Man*. Minneapolis: Burgess Publishing, 1972.

Mosse, George L. *Nazi Culture*. New York: Grosset and Dunlap, 1966.

————. *Toward the Final Solution: A History of European Racism*. New York: Howard Fertig, 1978.

Noakes, Jeremy, and Geoffrey Pridham, eds. *Nazism, 1919-1945: A Documentary Reader*. 3 vols. Exeter and London: A. Wheaton, 1984–87.

Orlow, Dietrich. *The History of the Nazi Party, 1919–1945*. 2 vols. Pittsburgh: University of Pittsburgh Press, 1969–73.

Overy, R. J. *Goering, the "Iron Man."* London: Routledge and Kegan Paul, 1984.

Padfield, Peter. *Himmler*. New York: Henry Holt, 1991.

Paucker, Arnold, et al., eds. *Die Juden im Nationalsozialistischen Deutschland* [*The Jews in Nazi Germany, 1933–1943*]. New York and Tübingen: Leo Baeck Institute and J. C. B. Mohr (Paul Siebeck), 1986.

Payne, Robert P. S. *The Life and Death of Adolf Hitler*. New York: Praeger, 1973.

Peterson, Edward N. *The Limits of Hitler's Power*. Princeton, N.J.: Princeton University Press, 1969.

Pridham, Geoffrey. *Hitler's Rise to Power: The National Socialist Movement in Bavaria, 1923–1933*. New York: Harper and Row, 1974.

Rauschning, Hermann. *The Voice of Destruction*. New York: Putnam, 1940.

Reiman, Viktor. *Goebbels*. Garden City, N.Y.: Doubleday, 1976.

Reitlinger, Gerald. *The SS, Alibi of a Nation*. London: William Heinemann, 1956.

Ribbentrop, Joachim von. *The Ribbentrop Memoirs*. London: William Heinemann, 1956.

Rich, Norman. *Hitler's War Aims*. 2 vols. New York: Norton, 1972.

Schoenbaum, David. *Hitler's Social Revolution*. Garden City, N.Y.: Doubleday, 1966.

Smith, Bradley. *Heinrich Himmler: A Nazi in the Making, 1900–1926*. Stanford, Calif.: Hoover Institution Press, 1971.

Speer, Albert. *Inside the Third Reich*. New York: Macmillan, 1970.

————. *Spandau: the Secret Diaries*. New York: Macmillan, 1976.

Stachura, Peter D., ed. *The Nazi Machtergreifung*. Winchester, Mass.: Unwin Hyman, 1983.

Stein, George H. *The Waffen SS*. Ithaca, N.Y.: Cornell University Press, 1966.

Steinert, Marlis G. *Hitler's War and the Germans*. Athens: Ohio University Press, 1977.

Toland, John. *Adolf Hitler*. New York: Ballantine Books, 1976.

Viereck, Peter. *Metapolitics: The Roots of the Nazi Mind*. New York: Capricorn Books, 1941 (revised editions, 1961, 1965).

Vogt, Hannah. *The Burden of Guilt*. New York: Oxford University Press, 1964.

Wagener, Otto. *Hitler: Memoirs of a Confidant*. Edited by Henry Ashby Turner, Jr. New Haven, Conn. and London: Yale University Press, 1985.

Waite, Robert G. L. *The Psychopathic God: Adolf Hitler*. New York: Basic Books, 1977.

Watt, Richard M. *The Kings Depart*. New York: Simon and Schuster, 1968.

Weinberg, Gerhard L. *The Foreign Policy of Hitler's Germany*. Vol. 1, *Diplmatic Revolution in Europe, 1933–1936*. Chicago: University of Chicago Press, 1970.

Zeman, Z. A. B. *Nazi Propaganda*. London: Oxford University Press, 1964.

## Works in German

Breloer, Heinrich. *Mein Tagebuch: Geschichten vom Überleben, 1939–1947*. Cologne: Verlagsgesellschaft Schulfernsehn, 1984.

Deschner, Günther. *Reinhard Heydrich: Statthalter der totalen Macht*. Esslingen am Neckar: Bechtle Verlag, 1977.

Döscher, Hans-Jürgen. *Das Auswärtige Amt im Dritten Reiche*. Munich: Siedler Verlag, 1986.

Franck, Norbert, ed. *Heil Hitler, Herr Lehrer: Volksschule im 3. Reich, 1933–1945: Das Beispiel Berlin*. Reinbek bei Hamburg: Rowohlt Verlag, 1983.

Frank, Hans. *Im Angesicht des Galgens: Deutung Hitlers und seiner Zeit auf Grund eigener Erlebnisse und Erkenntnisse*. Neuhaus bei Schliersee: B. Frank, 1955.

Gisevius, Hans Bernd. *Adolf Hitler: Versuch einer Deutung*. Munich and Zurich: Droemer Knaur, 1967.

Hahn, Fred. *Lieber Stürmer*. Stuttgart: Seewald Verlag, 1978.

Hanfstaengl, Ernst. *Fünfzehn Jahre mit Hitler: Zwischen Weissem und Braunem Haus*. Munich: Piper Verlag, 1980.

Hofer, Waltner. *Die Diktatur Hitlers bis zum Beginn des zweiten Weltkrieges*. Bonn: Akademische Verlagsgesellschaft Athenaion, 1960.

Kühnl, Reinhard. *Der deutsche Faschismus in Quellen und Dokumenten*. Cologne: Pahl-Rugenstein Verlag, 1975.

Maser, Werner. *Adolf Hitler: Das Ende der Führer-Legende.* Düsseldorf: Econ Verlag, 1980.

Pemsel, Richard. *Hitler: Revolutionär, Staatsmann, Verbrecher.* Tübingen: Grabert Verlag, 1986.

Peukert, Detlev, and Jürgen Peukert, eds. Alltag im Nationalsozialismus. Wuppertal: Peter Hammer Verlag, 1981.

Platner, Geert. *Schule im Dritten Reich: Erziehung zum Tod.* Cologne: Pahl-Rugenstein Verlag, 1988.

Reif, Adelbert. *Albert Speer: Kontroversen um ein deutsches Phänomen.* Munich: Bernard und Graefe Verlag, 1978.

Schirach, Baldur von. *Ich glaubte an Hitler.* Hamburg: Mosaik Verlag, 1970.

Schirach, Henriette von. *Anekdoten um Hitler: Geschichten aus einem halben Jahrhundert.* Munich: Turmer Verlag, 1980.

Siemsen, Hans. *Die Geschichte des Hitler Jungen Adolf Goers.* Berlin: LitPol Verlagsgesellschaft, 1981.

# Chapter 3

# Selected Biographies and Interpretations of Hitler

## Robert H. Whealey

### PRIMARY SOURCES

Hitler's own words are published in his famous *Mein Kampf* (Munich: F. Eher, 1925) with editing and collaboration by his deputy Rudolf Hess. The standard unabridged English translation by Ralph Manheim (Boston: Houghton Mifflin, 1943) is considered the definitive version in English. Hans Staudinger's *The Inner Nazi: A Critical Analysis of Mein Kampf* (Baton Rouge: Louisiana State University Press, 1981) was written by a German Socialist who fled to New York in 1933. His book was written in 1941–43, and the author died in 1980. Hitler's text is examined by Michael D. McGuire, "Mythic Rhetoric: A Case Study of Adolf Hitler's *Mein Kampf* " (Ph.D. diss., University of Iowa, 1975) and "Mythic Rhetoric in *Mein Kampf:* A Structuralist Critique," *Quarterly Journal of Speech* 63 (February 1977): 1–13. See also James J. Barnes et al., "An English Translation of Hitler's Mein Kampf, Printed in Germany, ca. 1940," *Papers of the Bibliography Society of America* 80 (1986): 374–77. After World War II, Gerhard L. Weinberg of the University of North Carolina discovered in the captured German records a second volume by Hitler, never published during the Führer's lifetime. It is translated as *Hitler's Secret Book*, introduction by Hugh R. Trevor-Roper (New York: Grove Press, 1962).

Early in World War II, when Hitler thought that he was winning the war, his secretaries took notes on his private monologues on every subject on the face of the earth, from dogs to medicine. These have been published in German as *Hitlers Tischgespräche im Führerhauptquartier, 1941–1942*, edited by Henry Picker et al. (Stuttgart: Seewald, 1965). The standard English version is *Hitler's Table Talk*, introduction by Hugh R. Trevor-Roper (London: Weidenfeld and

Nicolson, 1953). A second and less complete American version appeared as *Hitler's Secret Conversations* (New York: New American Library, 1961).

The relationship between Hitler and his Nationalist reactionary allies in 1933–34 is clarified by the publication of *Akten der Reichskanzlei: Regierung Hitler, 1933–1938: Die Regierung Hitler*, Part 1, *1933/34*, vols. 1–2, edited by Karl-Heinz Minuth (Boppard am Rhein: Harald Boldt Verlag, 1983). See the review of these documents by Dietrich Orlow, *Journal of Modern History* 58 (March 1986): 370–74.

Extracts of major speeches are edited and translated by Norman H. Baynes, *The Speeches of Adolf Hitler, April 1922–August 1939*, 2 vols. (London: Oxford University Press, 1942). A more complete but still selective German edition of his speeches is Max Domarus, ed., *Hitler: Reden und Proklamationen*, 2 vols. (Neustadt a. d. Aisch: Verlagsdruckerei Schmidt, 1962). Werner Maser, as editor, published early Hitler material in *Hitler's Letters and Notes*, translated by Arnold Pomerans (New York: Harper and Row, 1974). Contemporary compilations of Hitler's speeches are Otto von Kursell, *Adolf Hitlers Reden* (Munich: Deutscher Volksverlag, 1925); Ernst Boepple, ed., *Adolf Hitlers Reden* (Munich: Deutscher Volksverlag, 1934); Heinz Preiss, ed., *Adolf Hitler in Franken: Reden aus der Kampfzeit* (Nuremberg: Verlag der Stürmer, 1939); Raoul de Roussy de Sales, ed., *Adolf Hitler: My New Order* (New York: Reynal and Hitchcock, 1941). Gordon Prange of the University of Maryland edited *Hitler's Words* (Washington, D.C.: American Council on Public Affairs, 1944); see also *The Testament of Adolf Hitler: The Hitler-Bormann Documents to April 1945*, edited by François Genoud, introduction by Hugh R. Trevor-Roper (London: Cassell, 1960).

There have been a number of short documentary collections edited in Hitler's name to record his career as warrior. They were mostly written by General Wilhelm Keitel of the Oberkommando der Wehrmacht (OKW), with notations by the Führer. See *Hitler Directs His War*, ed. by Felix Gilbert (New York: Oxford University Press, 1950); Hugh R. Trevor-Roper, ed., *Hitler's War Directives* (London: Sidgwick and Jackson, 1964); Helmut Greiner and Percy Schramm, eds., *Kriegstagebuch des Oberkommandos der Wehrmacht, 1940–1945*, 4 vols. (Frankfurt am Main: Bernard und Graefe, 1961– ); *Lagebesprechungen im Führerhauptquartier: Protokollfragmente aus Hitlers militärischen Konferenzen, 1942–1945*, edited by Helmut Heiber (Munich: Deutscher Taschenbuch Verlag, 1963); Thilo Vogelsang, "Hitlers Rede an die Generäle, 3 Februar 1933," *Vierteljahrshefte für Zeitgeschichte* 2 (1954): 434ff.; "Führer Conferences on Matters Dealing with the German Navy, 1939–1945," 2 vols. (Washington, D.C.: U.S. Department of the Navy, 1947, Mimeographed).

Other specialized, political documentary collections edited in Hitler's name are Werner Jochmann, ed., *Im Kampf um die Macht: Hitlers Rede vor dem Hamburger Nationalklub von 1919* (Frankfurt am Main: Europäische Verlagsanstalt, 1960); Reginald H. Phelps, ed., "Hitler als Parteiredner im Jahre 1920," *Vierteljahrshefte für Zeitgeschichte* 11 (July 1963): 274–330; *The Hitler*

*Trial Before the People's Court in Munich*, translated by Francis Freniere et al., 3 vols. (Frederick, Md.: University Publications of America, 1976); Ernst Deuerlein, ed., *Der Hitler-Putsch: Bayerische Dokumente zum 8./9. November 1923* (Stuttgart: Deutsche Verlags-Anstalt, 1962); Wilhelm Treue, ed., "Hitlers Denkschrift zum Vierjahresplan 1936," *Vierteljahrshefte für Zeitgeschichte* 3 (April 1955): 184–210; *Reichsführer! Briefe an und von Himmler*, edited by Helmut Heiber (Stuttgart: Deutsche Verlags-Anstalt, 1968); *Es spricht der Führer: Sieben exemplarische Hitler-Reden*, ed. by Hildegard von Kotze and Helmut Krausnick (Gütersloh: Mohn, 1966); Richard W. Alsfeld, "Adolf Hitler's Letter to the Editor: A Note on Hitler's Message to *The Nation*" (document), *International Social Science Review* 61 (Summer 1986): 123–27; unpublished Hitler calendar (January 1, 1934–June 12, 1943), "Sekretär des Führers, Führers Tagebuch" (Washington, D.C.: Library of Congress, n.d.) (see also the important Mussolini-Hitler correspondence cited in the section "Hitler and Foreign Policy"); Elek Karsai, ed., "The Meeting of Gömbos and Hitler in 1933," *New Hungarian Quarterly* 3 (1962): 170–96; Miklos Szinai and László Szücs, "Horthy's Secret Correspondence with Hitler," *New Hungarian Quarterly* 4 (1963): 174–91; Gerhard L. Weinberg, "Hitler's Private Testament of May 2, 1938," *Journal of Modern History* 27 (December 1955): 415–19; *Staatsmänner und Diplomaten bei Hitler: Vertrauliche Aufzeichnungen über Unterredungen mit Vertretern des Auslandes, 1939–1941*, edited and commentary by Andreas Hillgruber (Frankfurt: Bernard und Graefe Verlag für Wehrwesen, 1967). On foreign affairs in general, see the introduction to *Documents on German Foreign Policy*, series D, vol. 1 (Washington, D.C.: U.S. Government Printing Office, 1949).

The complete diaries of Hitler's propagandist Joseph Goebbels are now in the process of being published. They shed light on Hitler. See Elke Fröhlich, "Joseph Goebbels und sein Tagebuch: Zu den handschriftlichen Aufzeichnungen von 1924 bis 1941," *Vierteljahrshefte für Zeitgeschichte* 35 (October 1987): 489–522. According to John Lukacs, Hitler's reputation as an intellectual will be raised, while that of his propaganda minister will decline as scholars digest Goebbels's complete multivolume work. See "In Love with Hitler," *New York Review of Books*, July 21, 1988, p. 14.

The biographies of Hitler cited in the next section have long lists of memoirs of people who met the Führer. An additional work needs mention here: Otto Wagener, *Hitler: Memoirs of a Confidante*, edited by Henry Ashby Turner, Jr. (New Haven, Conn.: Yale University Press, 1985). Wagener was chief of staff for the Nazi Brownshirt militia, the Sturmabteilung (SA), 1929–32.

## BIOGRAPHIES

We now turn from documents to secondary sources. Oxford scholar Alan Bullock, *Hitler: A Study in Tyranny*, 2d ed. (Harmondsworth, England: Penguin Books, 1962), is still the best general biography of the Führer and Reich chancellor, despite the "Hitler wave" of the 1970s and 1980s. Because of Bullock's work, Hitler is far better understood than the secretive Joseph Stalin or Francisco Franco, and possibly even than the flamboyant Benito Mussolini. The second standard biography, originally published in West Germany in 1973, is Joachim C. Fest, *Hitler*, translated from the German (New York: Random House, 1975), which is a later account and has a more up-to-date bibliography. For Fest's later amendments see the article Jarausch cited in the section "Bibliographies and Reviews." Yet for American readers, Bullock is preferable. His is a liberal and rationalistic interpretation. The two books are comparable in size: 808 pages of text and notes for Bullock and 816 for Fest. Bullock has a table of contents designed for historians; Fest, for general readers. Bullock's index is outstanding, whereas Fest has only an index of persons. Bullock clearly understands economics better than Fest and puts more emphasis on both the army and the navy. The English historian is also better on foreign affairs generally, particularly on Japan, Spain, and the smaller Eastern European countries. The treatment of Britain and the Soviet Union by Bullock and Fest is about equal, although Fest could not resist making the obiter dictum that Stalin was as bad as Hitler. Generally Fest avoids national bias, but on page 653 he slips and refers to the French as "the enemy." The one area in which Fest is clearly superior is that of Hitler's early youth when his ideas and ideology were being molded. Certainly Hitler had a strongly irrational side, which Fest's interpretation stresses more than Bullock's. Fest imaginatively compares the Führer with Genghis Khan, Julius Caesar, Alexander the Great, and Al Capone.

Professional journalist John Toland's two-volume *Adolf Hitler* (Garden City, N.Y.: Doubleday, 1976), adds 130 interviewees to the bibliography, but in style his book is basically a popular account. This is Toland's fourth book dealing with aspects of World War II. It is the thickest of the Hitler biographies, with 1,052 pages in two volumes of text and notes. Its index is better than Fest's but not as good as Bullock's. Toland also has many more photos and maps than the other two. The bibliography is longer than Fest's but, like the German biographer's, ignores the economic dimension. Toland seeks out the colorful and personal, and his biography boasts a quick pace. His Hitler is cocky and self-assured. He takes liberty with hindsight information for dramatic effect. To be sure, this may be a quarrel of a historian arguing with a journalist about footnotes, because Toland's basic thesis is sound.

Biographies of Hitler written before the Bullock biography (1962) can be ignored here. Many are listed in the bibliographies of Bullock, Fest, and Toland.

In addition to Bullock, Fest, and Toland, there have been a few other attempts at comprehensive biographies, including Karl-Dietrich Bracher, *Adolf Hitler* (Bern: Scherz Verlag, 1964), and Rainer Zitelmann, *Hitler: Selbstverständis eines Revolutionärs* (Hamburg: Berg, 1987). His *Adolf Hitler: Eine politische Biographie* (Göttingen and Zürich: Muster-Schmidt Verlag, 1989) is a condensed version. George Stein edited a short textbook, *Hitler* (Englewood Cliffs, N.J.: Prentice-Hall, 1968) with selections from Bullock, Trevor-Roper's *The Last Days of Hitler* (see the section "The Final Six Weeks"), and other well-known commentators. It constitutes a brief, 179-page collection of essays. Noteworthy among these is Stein's own short bibliographical essay on the Führer. Also see William Carr, *Hitler: A Study in Personality and Politics* (London: Edward Arnold, 1978), and "Historians and the Hitler Phenomenon," *German Life and Letters* 34 (January 1981): 260–72. Carr still finds Bullock the best biography, with Fest as runner-up. He discusses the controversial ideas of Binion and Waite (cited later in this section). A handy list of many biographies of Hitler can be found in John Hiden and John Farquharson, *Explaining Hitler's Germany: Historians and the Third Reich* (Totowa, N.J.: Barnes and Noble, 1983).

Brief biographies in English for beginning students include Joseph P. Stern, *Hitler: The Führer and the People* (Glasgow: Fontana, 1975), and Helmut Heiber, *Adolf Hitler: A Short Biography*, trans. from the German (New York: St. Martin's Press, 1972). A more recent brief, comprehensive biography is Norman Stone, *Hitler* (Boston: Little, Brown, 1980). This 181-page book is too thin for the scholar, and the Cambridge University historian confesses that it can not serve as a replacement for Bullock and Fest. He ignores Toland. It is hard to justify the publication of this book, even though it reads well, except as an account for lay people. It adds a short bibliography, including some new material on Hitler's views on economics.

Robert Payne, popular biographer of such diverse people as André Malraux and Mao Tse-tung, has published over forty books, including the popular *The Life and Death of Adolf Hitler* (New York: Praeger, 1973). This was good for beginning students in its day, but in light of so much serious scholarship only deserves mention since its use is widespread. Michael Katur (cited later in the section "Bibliographies and Reviews") points out that Payne's account of Hitler's visit to England is definitely false.

Sebastian Haffner, *The Meaning of Hitler* (New York: Macmillan, 1979), is a short essay written by a journalist born in Germany and educated in England. He makes the bizarre comment that Hitler was closer to Stalin than he was to Mussolini. Historians would have to look at characteristics other than cruelty to come to such a judgment. Ronald Lewin has written an insightful essay, *Hitler's Mistakes* (New York: William Morrow, 1984), which focuses on the military and on psychology. This "biography" is highly selective and suits its author's personal tastes. He lists some thirty-five mistakes by the German dictator in the index. They range from the Führer's treatment of the Catholic church to his North African campaign.

Eberhard Jäckel's *Hitler's World View: A Blueprint for Power,* translated from the German (Middletown, Conn.: Wesleyan University Press, 1972), argues that Bullock and Fest emphasized Hitler's opportunism too much and underestimated his ideological determination. Jäckel, in addition, has produced two more volumes, *Hitler in History* (Hanover, N.H.: University Press of New England, 1984) and *Hitlers Herrschaft: Vollzug einer Weltanschauung* (Stuttgart: Deutsche Verlags-Anstalt, 1986), which advance the same line.

The recent book by Ian Kershaw, *The "Hitler Myth": Image and Reality in the Third Reich* (Oxford: Clarendon Press, 1987), concentrates on how the press, his party associates, and the general public viewed Hitler, and therefore is not a general biography. See also Kershaw, "Hitler and the Germans," in Richard Bessel, ed., *Life in the Third Reich* (New York: Oxford University Press, 1987).

Rudolph Binion, *Hitler Among the Germans* (New York: Elsevier, 1976), is not a complete biography but an interpretative survey of Hitler's anti-Semitism. The book should be compared with Robert G. L. Waite, *The Psychopathic God: Adolf Hitler* (New York: Basic Books, 1977). Both add some new material on Adolf Hitler's early youth, and Waite includes results of new research on the death of Hitler.

Waite's book is well documented and scholarly but has been treated with caution by other historians because he takes a Freudian point of view. It is the second major monograph by the mature scholar from Williams College. He argues that Hitler's sexual maladjustments from puberty were at the root of his irrational sentiments toward the Jews that shaped his actions throughout his life. Sensational for Americans was his reiteration of information (becoming known in the mid-1970s although Soviet historians had known about it since 1968) that Hitler died with only one testicle. Waite basically questions the Führer's sanity. His thesis is unoriginal and borrows from an earlier psychiatric study done for the Office of Strategic Services (OSS) by Dr. Walter C. Langer (brother of a more famous historian, William L. Langer). The Langer report was written during World War II but was published as *The Mind of Adolf Hitler: The Secret Wartime Report*, afterword by Robert Waite (New York: Basic Books, 1972). Waite also utilizes articles by Peter Lowenberg, "Psychohistorical Perspectives on Modern German History," *Journal of Modern History* 47 (1975): 229–79, by a psychohistorian at UCLA, and Hans Gatzke, "Hitler and Psychohistory," *American Historical Review* 78 (1973): 394–401. Waite shows why Hitler stubbornly clung to anti-Semitism until the end, and how he was able to exploit the fears of people around him: Hermann Göring, Joseph Goebbels, Ernst Röhm, and even foreigners like Neville Chamberlain, Georges Bonnet, and Joseph Stalin.

But then one could argue that these leaders were all, like Hitler himself, misfits shaped by World War I and its consequent social upheavals. This does not require sexual explanation. In any case, during the period from 1923 to 1943 Hitler obviously could master economic, military, and diplomatic details. Hitler demonstrated ruthlessness but also a shrewd and flexible talent for political decision. In his 582-page book Waite hardly mentions Admiral Erich Raeder or even France, much less the German conquest of Paris. However, he does have more space than Bullock or Fest, for example, to discuss Hitler's views on cancer, anti-Semitism, and Catholicism. In the last few months of the war Hitler did revert to the suicidal fantasies of storm and stress so evident in his youth. The Waite thesis is most convincing in showing the molding of Hitler's mind up to 1923, when the alienated young Austrian artist was searching for roots. Hitler ultimately found those roots in romantic German social Darwinism. Richard Wagner, rather than Jesus, portrayed Hitler's gods. The Jew represented his devil.

Binion, a professor at Brandeis University, rejects Waite's view that fear of sexual acts was basic to Hitler's Judeophobia. He argues that it was rather the Führer's fear of poison gas and cancer that motivated him. According to Binion, Hitler regarded the Jews as a group as the source of "blood contamination."

For Waite, Hitler blamed a Jewish doctor for the death by cancer of his mother, who was the object of Hitler's supposed incestuous infatuation, while he hated his cruel father. The missing testicle, along with hypochondria and his consistent surrounding of himself with medical quacks until his death, intensified his emotional or supranormal Freudian oedipal feelings. Hitler's fanatic will to dominate and his attachment to the music of Richard Wagner were compensations for sexual impotence.

For Binion, Hitler's fear was an irrational confusion between his mother's death and the horror of the World War I trenches. In both cases the Jews became the scapegoat or devil substitute to explain evil and to preserve Hitler's self-esteem in his own eyes after many early failures.

An interesting account of Hitler's private life and early years was written by Werner Maser, translated from the German, *Adolf Hitler: Legend, Myth, and Reality* (New York: Harper and Row, 1973). He asserted that Hitler as a World War I soldier fathered an illegitimate son with a Frenchwoman. He also claims that the Russians autopsied the wrong corpse, which Waite flatly denies.

Donald M. McKale, *Hitler, the Survival of a Myth* (New York: Stein and Day, 1981), is the best book yet on Hitler's death. He confirms Waite on the missing testicle and rejects Maser's hypothesis about Hitler's supposed illegitimate son. Milan Hauner's bibliography (cited later in the section "Bibliographies and Reviews") has a total of seven works by Maser, but strangely he leaves out McKale. On the effects of drugs on Hitler's health, see Leonard Heston and Renate Heston, *The Medical Casebook of Adolf Hitler* (New York: Stein and Day, 1980).

Hitler actually was a mad genius. He was mad in his ultimate objective of *Lebensraum* and the extermination of Europe's Jews, Gypsies, and Slavic elites on the basis of alleged racial inferiority. Hitler was a genius in propaganda, and he was occasionally an inspired diplomatic and military leader. Even as late as December 1944 Hitler was winning the Battle of the Ardennes Forest (the Bulge) because he correctly believed that the Allies had tapped the German radio codes, a fact his generals never suspected. On the tricky theme of anti-Semitism, it is clear that Hitler did not all by himself lead an innocent Europe to the death camps. Hitler gave direction and outlet to Judeophobic sentiments at the grass roots (see the section "Hitler and the Jews" later in this chapter).

Desmond Seward, an English popular writer, has published *Napoleon and Hitler: A Comparative Biography* (New York: Viking, 1988). This is a 300-page essay with twenty-nine footnotes from English-language sources. Seward took an idea suggested by Pieter Geyl of the University of Utrecht in 1941 and elaborated on it. The links between the two men are Clausewitz, Russia, England, Egypt, and, most important, a psychological tendency toward megalomania. The various nations of Europe were slow in both situations to perceive the inner character of the two dictators. Seward could have said something about the theme of revolution and counterrevolution in both cases, but missed the opportunity. This British writer knows more about Napoleon than about Hitler.

The latest wrinkle is a book originally published in German by Wulf Schwarzwäller, *The Unknown Hitler: His Private Life and Fortune* (Bethesda, Md.: National Press Books, 1988). The German author was born in 1928 and is a professional journalist. The bibliography is a short list of books, and there are no footnotes. He presents the thesis that Hitler died a multimillionaire and that all the previous biographies are incorrect in assessments of Hitler's wealth. The Führer's fortune was made in publishing propaganda—not altogether a new discovery. According to Schwarzwäller, Hitler was not ascetic; that was a myth that the Führer cultivated about himself. Schwarzwäller takes a paragraph from Bullock and expands it into a book of 221 pages. Unique is the amount of space given to Hitler's relationship to his publishers, Max Amann and Franz Eher. If the author wants the American scholarly community to take his book seriously, he needs a second edition with footnotes.

## BIBLIOGRAPHIES AND REVIEWS

An extensive German biographical and bibliographical comment is Gerhard Schreiber, *Hitler Interpretationen, 1923–1983: Ergebnisse, Methoden, und Probleme der Forschung* (Darmstadt: Wissenschaftlische, 1984). This book attempts to analyze 1,500 titles. See also W. Wippermann, ed., *Kontroversen um Hitler* (Frankfurt: Suhrkamp, 1986). To supplement scholarly findings on Hitler, one should also consult Michaelis Meir, "World Power Status or World Dominion? A Survey of Literature on Hitler's Plan of World Dominion, 1936–1970," *Historical Journal* 15 (June 1972): 331–60; James Joll, "Under an Evil Star," *Times Literary Supplement*, July 26, 1974, p. 780; Geoffrey Barraclough, "Farewell to Hitler," *New York Review of Books*, April 3, 1975, pp. 13–17; Rudolf Binion, "Foam on the Hitler Wave," *Journal of Modern History* 46 (September 1974): 522–28; Reginald H. Phelps, "Hitler in Recent Perspective: . . . ," in *Proceedings of the Citadel Symposium on Hitler and the National Socialist Era, 24–25 April 1980*, edited by Michael B. Barrett (Charleston, S.C.: The Citadel Development Foundation, 1982), pp. 1–9; Michael Kater, "Hitler in a Social Context," *Central European History* 14 (September 1981): 243–74; and chapter 1 in John Hiden and John Farquharson, *Explaining Hitler's Germany* (cited earlier in the section "Biographies").

There are numerous general annotated bibliographies of Germany and Nazism that put Hitler in perspective. Among these one should check Frederic M. Messick, comp., *Primary Sources in European Diplomacy, 1914–1945: A Bibli-*

*ography of Published Memoirs and Diaries* (Westport, Conn.: Greenwood Press, 1987); Philip Rees, *Fascism and Pre-Fascism in Europe, 1890–1945: A Bibliography of the Extreme Right* (Totowa, N.J.: Barnes and Noble, 1984), in which general theory is covered in pages 1–25 and Germany in pages 233–316; Helen Kehr and Janet Langmaid, *The Nazi Era, 1919–1945* (London: Mansell Publishers, 1982); Gail Schlachter, *The Third Reich, 1933–1939: A Historical Bibliography* (Santa Barbara, Calif.: ABC-Clio Research Guide, 1984); Louis L. Snyder, ed., *The Third Reich, 1933–1945: A Bibliographical Guide to German National Socialism* (New York: Garland, 1987), and "National Socialism in Germany," *Canadian Review Studies in Nationalism* 13 (1986): 1–76; and Peter D. Stachura, *The Weimar Era and Hitler, 1918–1933* (Oxford: Clio, 1977). The American Historical Association's (AHA) journal, *Recently Published Articles*, should be consulted for works since 1988; and the *Vierteljahrshefte für Zeitgeschichte* should be consulted by those who read German.

*Hitler: A Chronology of His Life and Time* (New York: St. Martin's Press, 1983) by Milan Hauner is a book that does exactly what the subtitle says. It is a 203-page chronology based on primary sources and would be valuable for any future biographer. The problem with the chronology is that it is incomplete and unclear as to the criteria of selection. Hauner's three-page bibliographical note lists additional German sources not mentioned in this chapter. The bibliography contains twenty-one items published since 1976 that would supplement Toland's biography. The book, however, fails in its attempt at a comprehensive bibliography in six pages.

Scholarship on the German dictator is caught in a dilemma. On the one hand, we have in English the three solid biographies by Bullock, Fest, and Toland. On the other hand, a vast collection of supplemental bibliography and essays has accumulated in the past fifteen years. In addition, the research on the complex society of the Third Reich keeps growing, further discouraging first-rate historians from compiling a new, comprehensive biography that could replace the big three. The sources outlined in the previous three paragraphs will lead the scholar to a vast bibliography in German. It is to be hoped that Lord Bullock will complete an updated edition of his classic biography.

Konrad H. Jarausch, in "Removing the Nazi Stain? The Quarrel of the German Historians," *German Studies Review* 11 (May 1988): 285–302, discusses not Hitler's personality, but rather the continuing debate among West German historians about German nationalism and the legacy of Nazi crimes, 1933–45. One aspect of the current debate is led by Ernst Nolte, intellectual historian at the Freie Universität of Berlin, on the right, and Jürgen Habermas, philosopher at Frankfurt, on the left. Both grant that the Führer's career was criminal or at least a tragic mistake. Nolte, however, argues that Hitler was primarily motivated by anticommunism, and thus, by implication, his war with the USSR was justified. Habermas argues that anticommunism was a mere cover for the more fundamental anti-Semitism and was no excuse for attacking the USSR. Jarausch outlines the many nuances of more than a dozen National Socialist experts in

West Germany on this theme. See also Richard J. Evans, "The New Nationalism and the Old History: Perspectives on the West German Historikerstreit," *Journal of Modern History* 59 (December 1987): 761–97, and his *In Hitler's Shadow: West German Historians and the Attempt to Escape from the Nazi Past* (New York: Pantheon Books, 1989). Evans is sharply critical of Nolte and his allies. See also Roger Fletcher, "History from Below Comes to Germany: The New History Movement in the Federal Republic of Germany," *Journal of Modern History* 60 (September 1988): 555–68; Charles S. Maier, *The Unmasterable Past: History, Holocaust, and German National Identity* (Cambridge, Mass.: Harvard University Press, 1988); and H. U. Wehler, *Entsorgung der deutschen Vergangenheit? Ein polemischer Essay zum "Historikerstreit"* (Munich: Beck, 1988).

## HITLER'S EARLY LIFE, 1889–1923

Turning away from general biographies, bibliographies, and essays, we must now evaluate monographs that enlighten us on political, as opposed to psychological, impacts on the Führer's views of the world. His career divides into four periods: the first, from his birth in April 1889 to November 1923, when he made his first attempt to overthrow the Weimar Republic; the second, from 1923 to his nomination as chancellor in 1933; the third, from his accession to power to 1939, the outbreak of World War II; and finally, as warrior to his death in 1945.

Before the 1923 Munich Beer Hall Putsch, German and Austrian history greatly influenced Hitler. The abortive 1923 coup d'état and the subsequent trial (see Harold J. Gordon, Jr., *Hitler and the Beer Hall Putsch* [Princeton, N.J.: Princeton University Press, 1972]) gave the hitherto-obscure lance corporal from World War I a nationwide audience in Germany. See Sydney J. Jones, *Hitler in Vienna, 1907–13* (London: Bond and Briggs, 1983).

Charles Bracelen Flood's *Hitler: The Path to Power* (Boston: Houghton Mifflin, 1989) is the author's tenth book. He is a popular American Southern writer and biographer who had previously written a book on Robert E. Lee. He uses German but is dependent on a university language teacher to do some of his research. He acknowledges the help of Toland, whose notes are cited in his book and in that by Hauner. Flood's book contains 658 pages with a bibliography and notes. One weakness is that he has no chapter titles, and therefore the book is aimed at the casual reader, not the researcher. He emphasizes party politics and tries to avoid economics. "Path to power" means up to 1924 and Hitler's writing of *Mein Kampf*. The book should be compared with that by Harold Gordon.

## HITLER AND WEIMAR, 1923–1933

During the second period, from the trial on, Hitler began to impact history directly in a major way. From 1923 to 1929 Hitler devoted himself to building the National Socialist German Workers' party (NSDAP), the Nazi party. On the early Nazi party there is Dietrich Orlow, *The History of the Nazi Party, 1919–1945*, 2 vols. (Pittsburgh: University of Pittsburgh Press, 1969–73), and Michael H. Kater, *The Nazi Party: A Social Profile of Members and Leaders, 1919–1945* (Cambridge, Mass.: Harvard University Press, 1983). From 1930 to 1933 Hitler concentrated on persuading the German traditional elites to make him chancellor. His relationship with his lieutenants changed during the second period. Hermann Göring, Alfred Rosenberg, Gregor Strasser, Ernst Röhm, and Rudolf Hess had mostly influenced him from 1919 to 1923; thereafter, the Nazi Führer dominated them. By the mid-1920s he added Joseph Goebbels and Heinrich Himmler to the inner circle.

In 1928 the Nazi party held 12 seats in the Reichstag (out of a total of 491) and 2.6 percent of the popular vote. After the global stock-market crash of October 1929, the German economy fell into depression and unemployment. The Nazi vote grew so that by September 1930 the NSDAP became the second most important party. In July 1932 Nazi party power increased further when the National Socialists received one-third of the vote among the seven major parties in the dying Weimar Republic. President von Hindenburg nominated Hitler as Reich chancellor in January 1933, and with that, the second period of Hitler's life came to an end. See Thomas Childers, *The Nazi Voter: The Social Foundations of Fascism in Germany, 1919–1933* (Chapel Hill: University of North Carolina Press, 1986); Rudy Koshar, *Social Life, Local Politics, and Nazism: Marburg, 1880–1935* (Chapel Hill: University of North Carolina Press, 1986); Martin Broszat, *Hitler and the Collapse of Weimar Germany*, translated from the German (Leamington Spa, N.Y.: Berg, 1987); and Peter D. Stachura, ed., *The Nazi Machtergreifung* (London: Allen and Unwin, 1983).

On foreign policy during this second period, see the book by Geoffrey Stoakes, *Hitler and the Quest for World Dominion: Nazi Ideology and Foreign Policy in the 1920s* (Leamington Spa, N.Y.: Berg, 1986), and the earlier but better German work by Jochen Thies, *Architekt der Weltherrschaft* (Düsseldorf: Droste, 1976).

## HITLER AND THE ECONOMY

From 1933 to 1939, during this third period, Hitler had two prime concerns: creating full employment in Germany while tipping the balance of power in favor of the Third Reich through coercion, diplomacy, and occasional military action, thus weakening the other great powers. On the subject of Hitler and the economy, not much clearly thought-out literature exists. One key problem is the failure by historians to define adequately the concept of the economy. Hitler was a contemporary of the influential economist Lord John Maynard Keynes, who pointed out, among other things, that as a result of World War I, the world economy underwent a great upheaval. The extent of that war's economic effects is not fully understood to this day.

Too often economic writing overloads the mind with ideology, philosophy, or mathematics. These persistent tendencies of economists can confuse the real issues, namely, decision making on how to utilize land, labor, and capital in order to maximize production and consumption for all. Whether economic and social decisions are made in corporate boardrooms or in bureaucratic offices is perhaps less important than the Marxists, Keynesians, and advocates of laissez-faire assume. Economic literature often is fragmentary, concentrating on certain specialized periods and topics while ignoring others. Thus historians and economists tend to tell us more about their own economic ideas than about those of Hitler and his Nazis.

Before 1914 the world was governed by two contradictory eighteenth-century economic ideas. The mercantile idea promoted state regulation of the economy for the increased welfare of that state or nation; laissez-faire (the economics of Adam Smith) advocated that the state allow individual households, or individual entrepreneurs as opposed to corporations, maximum freedom to produce desired and needed goods and services. By the time of World War I large multinational corporations and cartels had in practice partially undermined the idea of the household economy and the unregulated marketplace. Besides, Marxist critics pointed out the injustice of banks and corporations determining economic decision making at the expense of wage and salaried workers, consumers, and farmers. The Russians subsequently attempted, in a very distorted way, to apply Marx's ideas to their multinational empire. World War I also pushed Russia into a vast social revolution that ultimately created the USSR in 1922, leading first to Leninism and then to Stalinism.

Also, in Western Europe Democratic Socialist and Marxist movements may have peaked as an ideological force by 1914, although after the war the Left gained votes in Scandinavia, England, France, the Weimar Republic, and some other democratic countries. The war economy of World War I led to a wild inflation in Germany by 1923, followed, after a short recovery, by the greatest global depression of all time, 1929–33. To remedy these circumstances, Keynes invented a new branch of economics. Welfare economics, or neomercantilism, advocated that the state intervene in the marketplace for the sake of creating full employment. Franklin D. Roosevelt, whose 1933–45 administration in the United States happened to cover the same years as Hitler's, attempted a kind of Keynesianism in the New Deal. Despite the ideological differences of Hitler and Roosevelt, John A. Garraty made the comparison administratively between the two regimes in "The New Deal, National Socialism, and the Great Depression," *American Historical Review* 78 (October 1973): 907–44.

Hitler was never trained in academic economics. Yet as a postcard salesman in Vienna before the Great War, and as Führer of a bizarre party making his living in the 1920s by selling political propaganda, he had an intuitive understanding of economics. His decisions were to have profound economic consequences for the world. Moreover, through Hess he picked up Karl Haushofer's idea of geopolitics. Combined with German racism, this gave Hitler the belief in the early 1920s that Germany should seize the natural resources of the Ukraine to create a Reich that would last a thousand years—the idea of *Lebensraum*.

Most historians have jumped to the conclusion that this crazy idea ends further economic discussion and that no more investigating need be done. Hitler's ideas, however, went beyond mere *Lebensraum*. From 1933 to 1939, in fact, Hitler was also devoted to the goal of creating full employment for "pure" Germans.

National differences among the victors of World War II (Americans, Russians, British, and French) have further distorted the record of Hitler's economics. The urge of West Germans to ingratiate themselves with Americans and the still greater need for East Germans to butter up the Soviet authorities have obscured economic issues. Marxist theories about economic and social contradictions in society led Soviet and East German historians into a procrustean research that tried to prove that Nazism was the last stronghold of decadent, laissez-faire, corporate capitalism. Despite their ideological prejudices, the East Germans did inherit many of the corporate archives, so footnotes cited in East German historiography are important. East German works have been wrongly dismissed by too many Western scholars on general anti-Communist ideological grounds. In the United States, East German sources were generally ignored until Andreas Dorpalen published *German History in Marxist Perspective: The East German Approach* (Detroit: Wayne State University Press, 1985). But Dorpalen, the late professor at Ohio State University, was a Rankean political historian with a bias against economics.

In the West the arms race with the Soviet Union likewise obscured the Hitler story. It produced a literature that seemed to assume that arms production creates more and better jobs than alternative investments in civilian products. This may have been naively believable in America in the 1950s, but West Germany and Japan since the 1960s have disproven the thesis. Some have declared Hitler a "military Keynesian" and a precursor to the American military-industrial complex. Others consider that Hitler, because he was an ideological fanatic, had no understanding of economics. This view narrowly defines economics as laissez-faire economics or Mussolini's corporate economics. The real, pragmatic Hitler did not live up to the myth of totalitarianism in the field of economics. His appointments showed a shrewd insight into managing short-range economic problems, despite his moral madness. He had some definite ideas, and when he intervened, he intervened decisively. Nevertheless, on a day-to-day basis, he allowed the badly divided Nazi party, traditional corporate leaders, and the inherited bureaucracy of the Weimar Republic considerable room to jockey for position. Hitler thus was more pragmatic about the economy than his anti-Fascist opposition gave him credit for being.

The date 1939 is important because on either side of that watershed, the rules of economics drastically changed. Biographers of Hitler have yet to outline the role Hitler actually played in the economy of two eras, first within the Third Reich, from 1933 to 1939, and then on a global stage, from 1939 to 1945.

There is an attempt at a comprehensive look at Hitler's ideas about the economy, at least in the prewar period, in an article by John Heyl, "Hitler's Economic Theory: A Reappraisal," *Central European Review* 6 (March 1973): 83–96.

Heyl makes a modest beginning in recording the contradictions in the literature, but he does not come to a conclusion other than the simple point that Hitler did indeed have some workable economic ideas. See also Heyl's 1971 dissertation "Economic Policy and Political Leadership in the German Depression, 1930–1936" (Washington University, 1971).

With hindsight, it is clear that Hitler could be regarded as a neomercantilist, but that he was neither a liberal nor a libertine, as suggested by Harold James and his reviewer Peter Hayes, *American Historical Review* 93 (February 1988): 177 (James is cited later in this section, on the topic of production). The National Socialist party (leaning toward state socialism) had little use for laissez-faire and saw itself as an answer to "the international Jewish Marxists." Liberals, Social Democrats, Leninists, and Stalinists were all lumped together as internationalists by Hitler and were emotionally rejected. In the early years of Hitler's rule, the German manual and salaried workers admired their leader for providing job opportunities along quasi-socialist lines.

The NSDAP actually was deeply divided within from 1919 to 1933, and to some extent it remained so to the very end. The division was between the socialistic and populist-leaning Gregor Strasser wing and Hermann Göring's social conservative wing, which aped the aristocracy and admired the great industrialists. Hitler listened to the economic arguments of both groups and made various ad hoc political-economic decisions that became important policies. The nonideological nature of many of these decisions has been downplayed by Hitler's biographers.

In 1928, under the influence of Göring, Hitler decided for electoral reasons to ally the Nazis with the conservative Nationalists of Alfred Hugenberg. Hugenberg was a press lord and director of the Krupp corporation, so Hitler at that point deemphasized the socialistic elements of the party's twenty-five-point platform and assured corporate leaders that they would have little to fear from him if he ever came to power. This secret decision effectively contradicted his public devotion to socialism, which Hitler may have originally absorbed in part through a party hack, Gottfried Feder, whom Hitler met in 1919 and mentioned in *Mein Kampf*. Certainly Feder had less influence after 1928. See Albrecht Tyrell, "Gottfried Feder and the NSDAP," in *The Shaping of the Nazi State*, edited by Peter D. Stachura (London: Croom Helm, 1978), pp. 48–87. Also see Feder's three published works cited in Henry Ashby Turner, *German Big Business and the Rise of Hitler* (discussed later in this section), and Oran J. Hale, "Gottfried Feder Calls Hitler to Order," *Journal of Modern History* 30 (December 1958): 358–62. Also enlightening on the socialist side of Hitler is Peter D. Stachura, *Gregor Strasser and the Rise of Nazism* (London: Allen and Unwin, 1983).

Another of the missing links in describing Hitler's economics is the role of Wilhelm Keppler (see the work of Eckart Teichert cited later in this section), who succeeded Feder as an important advisor to the Reich chancellor. Keppler was influential from about 1930 until at least 1937, when he was shunted into a less important job in the Foreign Ministry. More research is necessary on both

Feder and Keppler, as well as on Robert Ley of the National Socialist Labor Front and Walther Darré, minister of agriculture. A scholarly look needs to be taken at how Hitler balanced his socialistic inclinations with his need to satisfy the industrialists in order to utilize their capacity for war production.

Soon after Hitler became chancellor in 1933, he made the important decision to reappoint Hjalmar Schacht as Reichsbank president. Schacht had held the post from 1925 to 1929. In fact, the Führer expanded Schacht's role in 1934 by making him minister of economics as well. Schacht's idea of economics, as a friend of banks and corporations, was that Germany had been drained of gold and foreign exchange by the Versailles Powers, particularly the United States. Schacht set up two standards of payment to avoid transferring any more gold to foreigners. In essence, he declared a trade war on Britain, the United States, and France. Foreign exchange was rationed. Germany bartered its manufactured goods for the raw materials of Latin America, the Balkans, and the USSR. Germany forced American investors to reinvest the short-term profits from their long-term investments in the German war machine. Schacht financed, with disguised deficit spending, the rearmament of the Third Reich from 1933 to 1937. During that period Nazi Germany also did better at solving unemployment than any other capitalist nation.

Meanwhile, by August 1936 Hitler and Göring became dissatisfied with the slow pace of rearmament administered by Schacht, and the two set up a new party organization known as the Four-Year Plan to have Germany economically ready for a major war within four years. Schacht, although he hung on to his office as Reichsbank president until January 1939, gradually lost influence after mid-1936. Eckart Teichert, *Autarkie und Grossraumwirtschaft in Deutschland, 1930–1939: Aussenwirtschaftspolitische Konzeptionen zwischen Wirtschaftskrise und zweitem Weltkrieg* (Munich: Oldenbourg, 1984), has an extensive bibliography on the debates about the economy. Also see René Erbe, *Die nationalsozialistiche Wirtschaftspolitik 1933–1939 im Lichte der modernen Theorie* (Zürich: Polygraphischer Verlag, 1958). Dieter Petzina, *Autarkiepolitik im Dritten Reich: Der Nationalsozialistische Vierjahresplan* (Stuttgart: Deutsche Verlags-Anstalt, 1968), has been for many years a standard work on the National Socialist Four-Year Plan. Petzina highlights his major points in an article in English, "Germany and the Great Depression," *Journal of Contemporary History* 4 (1969): 59–74.

The struggle between Göring and Schacht is outlined by Berenice Carroll of the University of Illinois, *Design for Total War: Arms and Economics in the Third Reich* (The Hague: Mouton, 1968), in my view the best general book in English on Nazi economics (1933–39). She used the archives of the Four-Year Plan, the Krupp and I. G. Farben combines, and the Reich War Ministry to come up with hard statistics. Carroll concludes that from 1936 to 1939 Göring gradually stole economic bureaucrats from Schacht and from private corporations for military mobilization. The demand for arms provided the lower classes with new jobs.

Amos Simpson, "The Struggle for Control of the German Economy," *Journal of Modern History* 31 (March 1959): 37–45, gives a briefer and earlier account of the Schacht-Göring conflict. Walther Hubatsch, *Entstehung und Entwicklung des Reichswirtschaftsministeriums* (Berlin: Duncker und Humblot, 1978), also adds to Carroll's work. Ingeborg Esenwein-Rothe, *Die Wirtschaftsverbände von 1933 bis 1945* (Berlin: Duncker und Humblot, 1965), deals with business organizations and associations that interacted with the NSDAP.

The many biographies of Göring stress his role with the Luftwaffe and underplay his economic importance. It was Hermann Göring who, in a 1935 speech, coined the famous economic slogan that people must choose between "guns or butter." The first biographer of Göring who took economics seriously was Richard J. Overy, *Goering, the "Iron Man"* (London: Routledge and Kegan Paul, 1984). See also his article, "Unemployment in the Third Reich," *Business History* 29 (July 1987): 253–84, and his dissertation, "The Luftwaffe in the German Economy" (Cambridge University, 1956). Other biographies include Stefan Martens, *Hermann Göring: "Erster Paladin des Führers" und "Zweiter Mann im Reich"* (Paderborn: Schöningh, 1985); Alfred Kube, *Pour le Mérite und Hakenkreuz: Hermann Göring im Dritten Reich* (Munich: Oldenbourg, 1986); David Irving, *Göring* (New York: Morrow, 1989); his state secretary for economic affairs, Erich Gritzbach, *Hermann Goering, Werk und Mensch*, 2d ed. (Munich: Eher, 1938); and Gerhard Meinck, *Hitler und die deutsche Aufrüstung, 1933–1937* (Wiesbaden: Steiner, 1959), and "Der Reichsverteidigungsrat," *Wehrwissenschaftliche Rundschau* 6 (August 1956): 411–22. Robert H. Whealey, *Hitler and Spain: The Nazi Role in the Spanish Civil War, 1936–1939* (Lexington: University Press of Kentucky, 1989), stresses the importance of Göring in the German economy. Göring was more important than Feder or Keppler, but was later demoted by Hitler and superseded by Speer.

Hjalmar Horace Greeley Schacht, who had many friends in America, published his side of the story in several memoirs: *Account Settled* (London: Weidenfeld and Nicolson, 1949), *Confessions of The Old Wizard* (Boston: Houghton Mifflin, 1956), and *My First Seventy-Six Years* (London: Wingate, 1955). There are also three biographies in English: Edward N. Peterson, *Hjalmar Schacht: For and Against Hitler: A Political-Economic Study of Germany, 1923–1945* (Boston: Christopher Publishing, 1954); Amos E. Simpson, *Hjalmar Schacht in Perspective* (The Hague: Mouton, 1969); and Earl Beck, *Verdict on Schacht: A Study in the Problem of Political Guilt* (Tallahassee: Florida State University Press, 1955).

Although he was allied with the conservative Schacht and Göring, Hitler still was enough of a "socialist" to set up subsidies administered through Ley, who used the National Socialist Labor Front to replace labor unions and welfare offices. See Max H. Kele, *Nazis and Workers* (Chapel Hill: University of North Carolina Press, 1972). Hitler, who struggled through the inflation of 1923 and the depression of 1929 to 1933, translated the unemployment lines into votes for the NSDAP. The Nazi dictator remained an avid reader of both the Communist and Social Democratic press. Over the objections of both Göring and Schacht,

Hitler protected working conditions of the German working class from 1933 to 1936, and the Third Reich led Britain, France, and the United States in the search for full employment. Hitler handed out welfare checks to the poor in amounts greater than the Weimar Republic had paid in 1932. Also on the economy of the National Socialist regime, Timothy W. Mason, "Labour in the Third Reich, 1933–1939," *Past and Present*, April 1966, pp. 112–41, has some material on Ley. Mason, as a critic of Hitler's make-work program, published *Arbeiterklasse und Volksgemeinschaft: Dokumente und Materialien zur deutschen Arbeiterpolitik, 1936–1939* (Opladen: Westdeutscher Verlag, 1975) and "Women in Germany, 1925–1940: Family, Welfare, and Work," *History Workshop* 1 (Spring 1976): 92–93. See also Werner Sörgel, *Metallindustrie und Nationalsozialismus* (Frankfurt am Main, 1965); Günther Hase, *Der Werdegang des Arbeitsdienstes* (Berlin and Leipzig, 1940). On Robert Ley, see his own *Deutschland ist schöner geworden* (Munich: Eher, 1940); Ronald Smelser, *Robert Ley: Hitler's Labor Front Leader* (New York: Berg, 1988); and Anson G. Rabinbach, "The Aesthetics of Production in the Third Reich," *Journal of Contemporary History* 11 (October 1976): 43–74, on the beautification campaign within the Nazi labor program.

Hitler also took care of farmers through subsidies controlled by Walther Darré, minister of agriculture. On Darré, see Heinz Haushofer, "Richard Walther Darré," *Neue Deutsche Biographie* (Berlin: Duncker und Humblot, 1957), p. 517; Teichert, *Autarkie und Grossraumwirtschaft in Deutschland* (cited earlier in this section); Joachim Petzold and Wolfgang Schumann, "Der faschistische Reichsnährstand," *Zeitschrift für Geschichtswissenschaft* (East Berlin) (May 1962): 1046; Anna Bramwell, *Blood and Soil: Richard Walther Darre and Hitler's Green Party* (Bourne End, Buckinghamshire: Kensal, 1985). See also Joachim Petzold, "Grossgrundbesitzer Bauern: NSDAP zu ideologischen Auseinandersetzungen und die Agrarpolitik der faschistischen Partei, 1932," *Zeitschrift für Geschichtswissenschaft* (September 1981): 1128–39; Frieda Wunderlich, *Farm Labor in Germany, 1810–1945* (Princeton, N.J.: Princeton University Press, 1961). What emerges from the economic zigzags is that the party had more of a monopoly voice in agriculture than in industry.

The biggest remaining gap concerns Walther Funk, minister of economics, who has been dismissed as unimportant by all recent scholarship. See Paul Oestreich, *Walther Funk: Ein Leben für die Wirtschaft* (Munich: Eher, 1940).

If Hitler had been assassinated in 1939, he could have gone down in history as a great economic leader. The Jews, of course, were excluded from the programs that improved the general welfare, as is discussed later in this section. Hitler's steering of the economy from 1933 to 1939 is quite significant in helping to explain the Führer's popularity on the eve of World War II. Yet he lived to see that the arms race that he had initiated was destroying Germany by 1945 and had thus undermined any good his full-employment and welfare policies may have done during an earlier period. Since the end of World War II he has been judged as an ultimate economic failure. Hitler's economic success of 1939 was completely ruined by his return to a primitive form of warfare economics, the outright theft of land. He invaded Poland in 1939 and the USSR in 1941 on the basis of *Lebensraum*. Diverting his attention from economics, the coming of war caused Göring, Schacht, Darré, and Ley all to decline in influence with Hitler.

Albert Speer inherited various economic subagencies that were incorporated into a newly created Ministry of Armaments in February 1942, while Göring went into eclipse as an economic administrator. See Albert Speer, *Inside the Third Reich* (New York: Avon, 1971) and *Spandau: The Secret Diaries* (New York: Pocket Books, 1977). Besides these two memoirs there is Gregor Janssen, *Das Ministerium Speer: Deutschlands Rüstung im Krieg* (Berlin: Ullstein-Verlag, 1968). Although slave laborers and Jews caught in the German war machine did not see it that way, Speer proved to be an efficient leader of war production. Speer, among all of Hitler's inner circle of friends, was the only one admired to the end by the Führer. Speer's predecessor in the armaments office, an official working for Göring's Four-Year Plan, was the engineer Fritz Todt, famous for building the autobahns. See F. W. Seidler, *Fritz Todt: Baumeister des Dritten Reiches* (Munich: Herbig, 1986).

Burton Klein, *German Economic Preparations for War* (Cambridge, Mass.: Harvard University Press, 1959) uses the U.S. bombing records on the destruction of German industry to show that Hitler's rearmament plans were inefficient compared with those of the British. A book greatly expanded with better sources is by Alan S. Milward of the University of Manchester, *The German Economy at War* (London: University of London, Athlone Press, 1965).

Despite the sensational title and obscure publisher, Charles Higham's *Trading with the Enemy: An Exposé of the Nazi-American Money Plot, 1933–1949* (New York: Delacorte Press, 1983) has a good bibliography on the economic connections between the capitalists of America and Hitler's Reich. Higham is an American journalist who does not employ German sources. He has only visited the National Archives. The 1949 date is an error, for the story ends with Hitler's death in 1945.

If we turn from economic planning to production, we find that other groups of historians have concentrated their attention on aspects of this topic. Harold James's *The German Slump: Politics and Economics, 1924–1936* (Oxford: Clarendon Press, 1986) does not add much to the Hitler story. Writing in the spirit of the laissez-faire school of economics, James is mostly concerned with explaining the German depression of 1929–33.

On private corporations, there have been four attempts in English to write the I. G. Farben story, largely because the company directors were put on trial at Nuremberg at the end of the war. Josiah DuBois, *The Devil's Chemists* (Boston: Beacon Press, 1952) was the first. The other three are cited in Turner, *German Big Business and the Rise of Hitler* (discussed later in this section). There are also three books on the Krupp Corporation, which handled Germany's steel and heavy arms industry. See Norbert Mühlen, *The Incredible Krupps* (New York:

Holt, 1959); popular historian William Manchester's *The Arms of Krupp* (Boston: Little, Brown, 1968); and Peter Batty, *The House of Krupp* (London: Secker and Warburg, 1966). In German there is Jörg-Johannes Jäger, *Die wirtschaftliche Abhängigkeit des Dritten Reiches vom Ausland dargestellt am Beispiel der Stahlindustrie* (Berlin: Berlin Verlag, 1969). The directors of Krupp, like Farben, were put on trial and their records assembled and partly published. Turner also lists a number of published studies of AEG, Siemens, the Deutsche Bank, Alfred Hugenberg, banker Kurt von Schröder, the Flick Steel Company, Fritz Thyssen, Otto Wolff, and other companies and businessmen with extensive Nazi contacts. H. Pohl et al., *Die Daimler-Benz AG in den Jahren 1933 bis 1945*, edited by the Gesellschaft für Unternehmensgeschichte (Stuttgart: Steiner, 1986), is a recent work illustrating the industrial organization of Hitler's Germany.

On oil, see Wolfgang Birkenfeld, *Der synthetische Treibstoff, 1933–1945: Ein Beitrag zur nationalsozialistischen Wirtschafts- und Rüstungspolitik* (Göttingen: Musterschmidt, 1964); Philippe Marguérat, *Le IIIe Reich et le pétrole roumain* (Leiden: A. W. Sijthoff, 1977); and Wilhelm Meier-Dörnberg, *Die Ölversorgung der Kriegsmarine, 1935 bis 1945* (Freiburg: Verlag Rombach, 1973). The German struggle to obtain petroleum revealed the limits of national self-sufficiency or autarky, a favorite Nazi principle; eventually imperialistic adventures were undertaken to take over desired resources, including oil.

There are mimeographed books in English on Germany's four major banks during the Nazi era, the Reichsbank, the Dresdener Bank, the Deutsche Bank, and the Commerzbank. Unfortunately these are only published in typescript form and in limited editions. The authors were Americans working for the Office of Military Government of the United States who completed their work in 1946–47. The OMGUS records from the U.S. military occupation of Germany are in the National Archives at the branch in Suitland, Maryland. There are dozens of other histories of corporations in an even more fragile form; several are limited to a few copies tucked away in these archives. These records were partly released in 1972, and my screening of them was completed in 1981, at which time some minor files were not yet declassified. For a short guide to these resources, see the bibliographical note in Robert Whealey, *Hitler and Spain*, cited earlier in this section.

For most German Jews there was little difference between Hitler's pre-1939 and post-1939 economic programs. They had already been treated as "economic parasites" and plundered since the passage of the Nuremberg Laws in 1935. From an economic standpoint, the fate of the Jews became a precursor to what later happened to the Czechoslovaks, Poles, and Soviets from 1939 to 1943. See Helmut Genschel, *Die Verdrängung der Juden aus der Wirtschaft im Dritten Reich* (Göttingen: Musterschmidt, 1967), and Edward Homze, *Foreign Labor in Nazi Germany* (Princeton, N.J.: Princeton University Press, 1967). Heinrich Himmler's SS ran factories for the German war effort. See Klaus Drobisch, "Der Freundeskreis Himmler," *Zeitschrift für Geschichtswissenschaft* 8 (1960): 304–28; and Michael Kater, "Heinrich Himmler's Circle of Friends, 1931–

1945," *MARAB: A Review* (University of Maryland Abroad) 2 (Winter 1965–66): 74–93. (For more details on Hitler's general treatment of the Jews, see the section "Hitler and the Jews").

Henry Ashby Turner, master of archives and professor of history at Yale University, in *German Big Business and the Rise of Hitler* (New York: Oxford University Press, 1985), states that in the period 1930 to 1932 Hitler received little financial support from heavy industry. Turner defends the reputation of large corporations rather than focusing on what Hitler was doing. Turner's main point is that it was not "big" business that financed Hitler, but that the Führer was financed by medium-sized, provincial bankers and corporate directors. Turner's real field is corporations in Weimar Germany, rather than in the Nazi era, yet his extensive bibliography goes beyond 1933. He cites, among other opponents, East Germans who disagree with his thesis. The Yale historian then picks an acrimonious quarrel with socialist-leaning David Abraham, who undoubtedly made archival errors in his Ph.D. dissertation published in 1981 as *Collapse of the Weimar Republic: Political Economy and Crisis*. Abraham tried to show that Hitler's party did receive financial support from big capitalists as a second alternative in case their preferred party, the Nationalists, failed. This first edition was originally panned by most critics, who sided with Turner, but Abraham published a second corrected version of the book (New York: Holmes and Meier, 1986). Abraham deals with the problem of big business by discussing classes and structures, but not individuals.

The facts are that after January 1933, when Hitler came to power, many of the biggest German corporations donated to the Nazi party, excluded Jews from corporate boards, and put Nazi party members on their boards. This means that the Turner-Abraham dispute about what happened from September 1930 to December 1932 was much ado about rather small points. Turner presents a short but coherent sketch of Hitler and economics on pages 71–83. The problem is that he underestimates Hitler because he perceives the Nazi dictator as untrained in economics and surrounded by crackpots, as seen by the three orthodox schools (liberals, socialists, and mercantilists) of 1932. But such a dismissal fails to explain how Hitler achieved full employment by 1939, something underplayed by the British, French, and Americans. Turner's portrayal misses the importance of Ley, Darré, Göring, Schacht, and Keppler, although some light is shed on Keppler elsewhere in his well-documented book.

The Turner-Abraham dispute also illuminates the passionate ideological concepts about economics and sociology that influence what kind of research gets done. Both authors assume that Hitler's shrewd and daring flexibility in matters of politics indicates economic stupidity. Despite the downplaying of economics from 1933 to 1939, Turner ironically turns out to be right (that Hitler was a fool)—if the historian goes all the way to 1945 and shows that the Führer's military failures undermined his pragmatic economics of the 1930s. Willi A. Boelcke, *Die Kosten von Hitlers Krieg: Kriegsfinanzierung und finanzielles Kriegserbe in Deutschland, 1933–1948* (Paderborn: Ferdinand Schöningh,

1985), shows how Hitler fooled most of the Germans by financing rearmament through disguised deficits to be paid for in the late 1940s and 1950s.

## HITLER AND THE SOCIAL CRISIS

From September 1930 to January 1933, when Hitler became chancellor, Germany suffered a severe social crisis. The Communists on the Left were demanding revolution, the Social Democrats were demanding that Prussian estates be shared with the unemployed, and the Nazis were demanding dictatorship. The traditional rightist and centerist parties allied in the Reichstag to keep Hitler out of power for a while. But these parties failed to solve the unemployment question, which eventually helped persuade President von Hindenburg to name the former Austrian lance corporal as chancellor.

British and American scholarship on the social question was based at first on the views of the Social Democrats. Franz Neumann, exiled Social Democrat, published *Behemoth: The Structure and Practice of National Socialism, 1933–1941* (London: Victor Gollancz, 1942), which had tremendous influence in the United States until the mid-1950s, after which anti-Marxist bias led laissez-faire-minded historians to ignore the work. During the 1930s and through the war others followed in Neumann's tradition. Robert Brady, *The Spirit and Structure of German Fascism* (London: Gollancz, 1937) was written in the Social Democratic spirit. Additional examples are works by an exiled German Jewish Social Democrat, George W. F. Hallgarten, *Hitler, Reichswehr, und Industrie* (Frankfurt: Europäische Verlagsanstalt, 1955), *Why Dictators?* (New York: Macmillan, 1954), and "Adolf Hitler and German Heavy Industry, 1931–1933," *Journal of Economic History* 12 (1952): 222–46. Hallgarten was also a critic of capitalism. See also Claude W. Guillebaud, *The Economic Recovery of Germany* (New York: Macmillan, 1939), and *The Social Policy of Nazi Germany* (Cambridge, England: Cambridge University Press, 1941); Ernest K. Bramsted, *Aristocracy and the Middle-Classes in Germany* (Chicago: University of Chicago Press, 1964); and Hans Speier, *German White-Collar Workers and the Rise of Hitler* (New Haven, Conn.: Yale University Press, 1986). Arthur Schweitzer, economics professor at Indiana University, in *Big Business in the Third Reich* (Bloomington: Indiana University Press, 1964), takes a socialist, anticorporate view. See also his "The Nazification of the Lower Middle Classes and Peasantry in the Third Reich," in *The Third Reich*, published under the auspices of the International Council for Philosophy and Humanistic Studies and with the assistance of UNESCO (London: Weidenfeld and Nicolson, 1955). Schweitzer is strong on ideology and weak on exploring the archives of corporations and bureaucrats to see how they actually functioned. Toning down this leftist picture are the latest works by Childers, Koshar, and Broszat cited in the section "Hitler and Weiman, 1923–1933."

David Schoenbaum of the University of Iowa did a seminal social, rather than economic, history entitled *Hitler's Social Revolution: Class and Status in Nazi*

*Germany, 1933–1939* (Garden City, N.Y.: Doubleday, 1966). His argument is that the parties of the Weimar Republic, rigidly organized around class interests, gave the NSDAP a great opportunity after the 1929–32 crash. The Nazis, more than any other political group in the Weimar Republic, were open to talented people seeking careers, although these had to be "Aryans." The National Socialists made a social revolution that was muffled under a barrage of reactionary ideological talk. It was "a revolution carried out under a blanket." Schoenbaum challenged the thesis of Neumann's *Behemoth*, which led to the further decline of socialist and liberal thinking about the Nazi phenomenon. Zitelmann's *Hitler* (cited in the section "Biographies") adds details to this theme. The leading edge of historical research is now examining each of many German professions and the relationship they had to the Nazi party. The earlier concept of class struggle, while not wrong, appears too general under twentieth-century conditions. The best social historian of the Nazi era writing in English today is Michael Kater (see the section "Bibliographies and Reviews"). His thesis is that Hitler, in order to appeal to all classes, deliberately kept his own class origins obscure, anonymous, and classless. Toward the nobility and higher officer corps he sometimes voiced his rage while secretly admiring and aping them. There was a reciprocal relationship between the masses and the mass leader.

## HITLER AND FOREIGN POLICY

When one turns from controversial economics and sociology to foreign policy, a rich and well-defined literature, rather less debatable, is available. For Hitler's second period, 1923–33, see Geoffrey Stoakes, *Hitler and the Quest for World Dominion*, cited in the section "Hitler and Weimar, 1923–1933."

From 1933 to 1939, during Hitler's third and expansionist period, France, the USSR, and Britain were his ultimate rivals. Italy and Japan were won over as allies. During this dynamic period, the Führer added Joachim von Ribbentrop to his National Socialist entourage. An encyclopedic work, based on many years of archival research and covering the 1930s in foreign policy, is Gerhard L. Weinberg, *The Foreign Policy of Hitler's Germany*, vol. 1, *Diplomatic Revolution in Europe, 1933–36*; vol. 2, *Starting World War II, 1937–39* (Chicago: University of Chicago Press, 1970, 1980). Hans-Adolf Jacobsen, *Nationalsozialistische Aussenpolitik, 1933–1938* (Frankfurt: Alfred Metzner Verlag, 1968), is the standard work on foreign policy among the West Germans, with more emphasis on the role of the NSDAP and ideology and less on the diplomats. Esmonde M. Robertson, *Hitler's Pre-War Policy and Military Plans, 1933–1939* (London: Longmans, 1963), has the virtue of brevity. On bibliography, Christop M. Kimmich has edited *German Foreign Policy, 1918–1945: A Guide to Research and Research Materials* (Wilmington, Del.: Scholarly Resources, 1981).

A. J. P. Taylor, former don at Oxford, is in my opinion the greatest diplomatic historian of the twentieth century. He has mastered the archives for the period

1848 to 1918 and also had a hobby in political journalism. It should be emphasized that his book *The Origins of the Second World War* (New York: Atheneum, 1961) was a provocative essay, not a work of scholarship. His aim was not to raise or lower the reputation of Hitler or the German people, but to attack Anglo-American historiography from 1945 to 1961 for taking too seriously the "great man" theory of history. Taylor assumed that Hitler was even unconsciously glorified by historians who hated Hitler, but who used the Führer's demonic character as an excuse for not doing serious work in the archives. Taylor's point was that his friend Alan Bullock, also at Oxford, had already done the great biography of Hitler. What needed to be done in 1961 was to look into the British, American, French, German, Italian, Japanese, and Soviet archives to discover the complex, multicausal origins of World War II. Unfortunately, narrow-minded historians concentrated on picking holes in Taylor's sensational statements. They made ad hominem attacks on the pacifist-inclined historian. Lacking any sense of humor, they mistook a historiographic essay, written in a journalistic way for a mass audience, for seriously researched diplomatic history about Germany and Hitler. The book does not and was not really intended to shed new light on the character of Hitler. It was written mostly by taking old book reviews, which had been well received at the time, and combining, condensing, and jazzing them up a bit to create a best-seller. *The Origins of the Second World War* is still useful for M.A. history students for its shock appeal. What Taylor understood better than his critics is that works of history, like journalism, soon go out of date. But it takes twenty or thirty years, rather than a year, to undermine an established academic reputation. See also Taylor, *The Second World War* (The Creighton Memorial Lecture on History), (London: University of London, 1973) and *1939 Revisited* (1981 Annual Lecture in the German History Institute of London) (London: German Institute, 1981). See also Gordon Martel, ed., *The Origins of the Second World War Reconsidered: The A. J. P. Taylor Debate After Twenty-Five Years* (Boston: Allen and Unwin, 1986), for a critical view of the whole episode. Taylor asked for research; Weinberg, Jacobsen, and Norman Rich in *Hitler's War Aims* (cited in the section "Hitler and the Military") have done it and have provided many answers about Hitler's road to World War II.

When we look at the diplomacy of Hitler during the third stage of his life, 1933–39, Italy, Japan, Britain, France, and the USSR were the key nations in the balance-of-power system. They were offered temporary deals or truces as long as they deferred to the Führer's immediate objects and long-range plans to master Europe.

Hitler's relations with Mussolini and Italy were, at least in the early period, the most important of all his foreign connections. The Fascist dictator had come to power first, in 1922, promoting the ideas of fascism internationally, which burgeoned into prominence throughout Europe in the 1930s. In addition to agreeing with Hitler on an anti-Communist and antidemocratic stance, the Duce proved useful to the Führer because Italy's geographic location served as an anti-French factor in the balance of power. In light of Italy's importance to Hitler over a long period of time, scholars should check primary collections of documents for the Axis tie; see *Les Lettres secrètes échangées par Hitler et Mussolini*, edited by André François-Poncet (Paris: Editions du Pavois, 1946). An important overall work is Denis Mack Smith, *Mussolini* (New York: Knopf, 1982). For earlier standard works, see Alan Cassels, *Mussolini's Early Diplomacy* (Princeton, N.J.: Princeton University Press, 1971); Renzo De Felice, *Mussolini e Hitler: I rapporti segreti, 1922–1933* (Florence: Le Monnier, 1975), an essay with edited documents included; MacGregor Knox, *Mussolini Unleashed, 1939–41: Politics and Strategy, Fascist Italy's Last War* (New York: Cambridge University Press, 1982), and "Conquest, Foreign and Domestic, in Fascist Italy and Nazi Germany," *Journal of Modern History* 56 (March 1984): 1–57; Mario Toscano, *The Origins of the Pact of Steel*, translated from the Italian (Baltimore: Johns Hopkins University Press, 1967); and Elizabeth Wiskemann, *The Rome-Berlin Axis* (New York: Oxford University Press, 1949). In German, there are Ferdinand Siebert, *Italiens Weg in den Zweiten Weltkrieg* (Bonn: Athenäum, 1962); Jens Petersen, *Hitler, Mussolini: Die Entstehung der Achse Berlin-Rom, 1933–1936* (Tübingen: Max Niemeyer Verlag, 1973); and Gerhard Schreiber, *Revisionismus und Weltmachtstreben: Marineführung und deutsch-italienische Beziehungen, 1919 bis 1944* (Stuttgart: Deutsche Verlagsanstalt, 1978). There is an extended note in the bibliography of F. W. Deakin, *The Brutal Friendship: Mussolini, Hitler, and the Fall of Italian Fascism* (New York: Harper and Bros., 1962), that focuses on the World War II period. Deakin's title catches the essence of the Axis relationship and how Hitler dealt with his fellow Fascist, Benito Mussolini.

Geography explains the Führer's relatively good relations with Japan. Both had an interest in allying against the USSR; both propagated fanatic anti-Communist ideology; both allied themselves with Italy; and all three were aggressive empires in a hurry. Hitler met with Japanese negotiators in mid-1936, and their Anti-Comintern Pact was signed that November. About the same time the Rome-Berlin Axis was forged, with Mussolini officially joining the Anti-Comintern Pact the following year.

Hitler's "friendship" with the other two dictatorships was characteristically exploitive. On the Japanese connection, see Frank Iklé, *German-Japanese Relations, 1936–1940* (New York: Bookman, 1956); Ernst L. Presseisen, *Germany and Japan: A Study in Totalitarian Diplomacy, 1933–1941* (The Hague: Nijhoff, 1958); Johanna Meskill, *Hitler and Japan: The Hollow Alliance* (New York: Atherton, 1966); James W. Morley, ed., *Deterrent Diplomacy: Japan, Germany, and the USSR, 1935–1940*, translated by Hans H. Baerwald (New York: Columbia University Press, 1976); and Gerhard L. Weinberg, "German Recognition of Manchoukuo," *World Affairs Quarterly* 28 (July 1957): 149–64. The standard German source for Hitler's connection with Japan is Theo Sommer, *Deutschland und Japan zwischen den Mächten, 1935–1940, vom Antikominternpakt zum Dreimächtepakt* (Tübingen: J. C. B. Mohr, 1962). J. P. Fox,

*Germany and the Far Eastern Question, 1931–1938* (Oxford: Clarendon Press, 1982), is more up-to-date. In September 1940 Hitler turned the trilateral Anti-Comintern Pact into a military alliance directed against the United States.

On Nazi Germany's relations with China, see Lloyd E. Eastman, "Fascism in Kuomintang China: The Blue Shirts," *China Quarterly* 49 (January–March 1972): 1–31; William C. Kirby, *Germany and Republican China* (Stanford, Calif.: Stanford University Press, 1984); Joachim Peck, *Kolonialismus ohne Kolonien: Der deutsche Imperialismus und China, 1937* (East Berlin: Akademie Verlag, 1961). The Far Eastern question became the back door to war for the Americans, although it was Hitler who, honoring his September 1940 pact with Japan, declared war on the United States on 11 December 1941.

The postwar West Germans were more interested in researching the Anglo-German relationship than the British were in examining their bilateral connection with Germany. The British were obsessed not with Hitler but with debating appeasement and the Chamberlain government, 1937–40. Therefore, the best sources on the Anglo-German relationship are Josef Henke, *England in Hitlers politischem Kalkül, 1935–1939* (Boppard: Harald Boldt, 1973), and Dietrich Aigner, *Das Ringen um England: Das deutsch-britische Verhältnis, Die öffentliche Meinung, 1933–1939: Tragödie zweier Völker* (Munich: Bechtle, 1969). Although somewhat thin and limited to secondary sources, in English there is Martin Gilbert, *Britain and Germany Between the Wars* (London: Longmans, 1964).

On France, which was on the defensive from 1933 to 1945, there is Eberhard Jäckel, *Frankreich in Hitlers Europa* (Stuttgart: Deutsche Verlags-Anstalt, 1966), and William E. Scott, *Alliance Against Hitler: The Origins of the Franco-Soviet Pact* (Durham, N.C.: Duke University Press, 1962). There have been some fifteen annual academic symposia published in West Germany that cover, among other things, French relations with the Third Reich. The Deutsches Historisches Institut (Paris/Munich) has put out a special yearbook since 1973, *Francia: Beihefte* (published in both French and German).

On the great dictator's relations with the USSR, see an important memoir, Peter Kleist, *Zwischen Hitler und Stalin, 1939–1945* (Bonn: Athenäum, 1950). Covering the Nazi-Soviet Pact era are Gerhard L. Weinberg, *Germany and the Soviet Union, 1939–1941* (Leiden: E. J. Brill, 1954); Barry A. Leach, *German Strategy Against Russia, 1939–1941* (New York: Oxford University Press, 1973); and Anthony Read and David Fisher, two journalists, who have written the latest scholarly version of a story now well known in *The Deadly Embrace: Hitler, Stalin, and Nazi-Soviet Relations, 1939–1941* (New York: Norton, 1988).

For the World War II period, Alexander Dallin, *German Rule in Russia, 1941–1945* (London: Macmillan), first published in 1957, has become a classic. It was last revised in 1981. A longer time span is covered in Gerald Reitlinger, *The House Built on Sand: The Conflicts of German Policy in Russia, 1939–1945* (New York: Viking Press, 1960); Paul Carell, *Hitler's War on Russia: The Story of the German Defeat in the East* (London: Harrap, 1964), and *Scorched Earth*

(Boston: Little, Brown, 1970); Earl F. Ziemke, *Stalingrad to Berlin: The German Defeat in the East* (New York: Columbia University Press, 1968); and Earl F. Ziemke and Magna E. Bauer, *Moscow to Stalingrad: Decision in the East* (Washington, D.C.: Center of Military History, U.S. Army, 1987). *Geschichte des Grossen Vaterländischen Krieges der Sowjetunion*, vol. 1, *Die Vorbereitung und Entfesselung des Zweiten Weltkrieges durch die imperialistischen Mächte* (East Berlin: Deutscher Militär-Verlag, 1962) is an official Soviet history of World War II in a German edition. See also Lionel Kochan, ''Russia and Germany, 1935-1937: A Note,'' *Slavonic and East European Review* 40 (1962): 518–20; Karlheinz Niclauss, *Die Sowjetunion und Hitlers Machtergreifung: Eine Studie über die deutsch-russischen Beziehungen der Jahre 1929 bis 1935* (Bonn: Röhrscheid, 1966); Hermann Teske, *General Ernst Köstring, Der militärische Mittler zwischen dem Deutschen Reich und der Sowjetunion, 1921–1941* (Frankfurt: Mittler, 1966); Barton Whaley, *Codeword Barbarossa* (Cambridge, Mass.: MIT Press, 1973); John Erickson, *The Road to Stalingrad* (London: Weidenfeld and Nicolson, 1975); Albert Seaton, *The Russo-German War, 1941–45* (London: Barker, 1971); Timothy Patrick Mulligan, *The Politics of Illusion and Empire: German Occupation Policy in the Soviet Union, 1942–1943* (New York: Praeger, 1988); Geoffrey Jukes, *Hitler's Stalingrad Decisions* (Berkeley: University of California Press, 1985); H. W. Koch, ''Operation Barbarossa—The Current State of the Debate,'' *Historical Journal* 31 (June 1988): 377–90; and Louis Rotundo, ''Stalin and the Outbreak of War in 1941,'' *Journal of Contemporary History* 24 (April 1989): 277–300.

Despite this lengthy German-Soviet bibliography, the Holocaust tragedy, also played out primarily in Eastern Europe, is much better known than Alfred Rosenberg's and Wilhelm Keitel's war against the Soviet Union. On the Soviet theme, Toland is strangely weaker than either Bullock or Fest. Toland is more interested in what Hitler and his generals thought about the battles than in the Soviets' efforts and sacrifices while driving Hitler's army back out of Eastern Europe.

The outstanding book on the Führer's dealings with the United States, important to Hitler only after the Pearl Harbor attack on December 7, 1941, is by Saul Friedländer. He is an Israeli historian who treats the United States with a certain detachment in *Prelude to Downfall: Hitler and the United States, 1939–41* (New York: Knopf, 1967). Friedländer shows that Hitler, remembering the U.S. role in World War I, tried with considerable patience to keep America neutral in the period 1939 to 1941. Arnold A. Offner, a historian at Boston University, reading history from 1945 back to the 1930s, presents a pro-Roosevelt, anti-Hitler point of view in *American Appeasement: United States Foreign Policy and Germany, 1933–1938* (Cambridge, Mass.: Harvard University Press, 1969). His protests against Chamberlain's position and his defense of Roosevelt's seem unnecessary by now, but he captures very well the spirit in Washington at that time. Patrick J. Hearnden, *Roosevelt Confronts Hitler: America's Entry into World War II* (Dekalb: Northern Illinois University Press,

1987), emphasizes that economic competition pressed the Roosevelt adminis-
tration toward war. See also James V. Compton, *The Swastika and the Eagle:
Hitler, the United States, and the Origins of World War II* (Boston: Houghton
Mifflin, 1967); Paul Schroeder, *The Axis Alliance and Japanese-American Relations, 1941* (Ithaca, N.Y.: Cornell University Press, 1958); Hans Trefousse,
"Germany and Pearl Harbor," *Far Eastern Quarterly* 2 (1951): 35–50; Andreas
Hillgruber, "Der Faktor Amerika in Hitlers Strategie, 1938–1941," *Aus Politik
und Zeitsgeschichte* 13 (1966): 3–21; Gerhard L. Weinberg, "Hitler's Image of
the United States," *American Historical Review* 69 (July 1964): 1006–21; and
Waldo Heinrichs, *Threshold of War: Franklin D. Roosevelt and American Entry
into World War II* (New York: Oxford University Press, 1988).

## HITLER AND THE MILITARY

In 1939 the Führer entered the fourth period of his life, becoming the number
one warlord of Europe until his death in the Berlin bunker in April 1945. General
works dealing with this topic include Percy Ernst Schramm, *Hitler: The Man
and the Military Leader*, translated by Donald Detwiler (Chicago: Quadrangle
Books, 1971); Harold C. Deutsch, *Hitler and His Generals: The Hidden Crisis,
January–June 1938* (Minneapolis: University of Minnesota Press, 1973), and
"Military Planning and Foreign Policy: German Overtures in Two World Wars,"
in *Military Planning in the Twentieth Century*, edited by Henry R. Borowski
(Washington, D.C.: Office of Air Force History, 1986); Michael Geyer, *Auf-
rüstung oder Sicherheit: Die Reichswehr in der Krise der Machtpolitik, 1924–
1936* (Wiesbaden: Steiner, 1980); Michael Geyer, "German Strategy in the Age
of Machine Warfare, 1914–1945," in *Makers of Modern Strategy*, edited by
Peter Paret, 2d ed. (Princeton, N.J.: Princeton University Press, 1986); Andreas
Hillgruber, *Germany and the Two World Wars*, translated by William C. Kirby
(Cambridge, Mass.: Harvard University Press, 1980); Klaus-Jürgen Müller, *The
Army, Politics, and Society in Germany, 1933–1945* (New York: St. Martin's
Press, 1987); and Albert Seaton, *The German Army, 1933–45* (London: Wei-
denfeld and Nicolson, 1982). See also Robert O'Neill, *The German Army and
the Nazi Party, 1933–39* (London: Cassell, 1966); Andreas Dorpalen, "Hitler,
the Nazi Party, and the Wehrmacht in World War II," in *Total War and Cold
War: Problems in Civilian Control of the Military*, edited by Harry L. Coles
(Columbus: Ohio State University Press, 1962), pp. 69–90; Telford Taylor,
*Sword and Swastika: Generals and Nazis in the Third Reich* (Chicago: Quadrangle, 1969); Volker Berghahn and Martin Kitchen, eds., *Germany in the Age
of Total War* (London: Croom Helm, 1981); and Trevor N. Dupuy, *A Genius
for War: The German Army and General Staff, 1807–1945* (Englewood Cliffs,
N.J.: Prentice-Hall, 1979).

Hitler as military man was a paradox. His early experience as a lance corporal
in World War I somehow provided him with a minimum understanding of
Clausewitz, whom he mentioned in *Mein Kampf*. P. M. Baldwin, "Clausewitz

in Nazi Germany,'' *Journal of Contemporary History* 16 (January 1981): 5–26, showed that since the 1920s Hitler had gradually come to use Clausewitz. Moreover, the Führer demonstrated an amazing talent in dealing with the Rhineland crisis, the Spanish civil war, Czechoslovakia, and Operation White (Poland, 1939) to Operation Marita (Yugoslavia, March 1941). The Third Reich won a dozen early campaigns.

On the other hand, militarily his invasion of the USSR in 1941, more than any other event, brought him to ruin. He bit off more than he could chew. At this point, a fanatic attitude toward Jews and communism led to his downfall among many of his generals. As a psychological gambler he could not brook retreat. The German people, as a nation and as a state, were sacrificed by Hitler starting with the Battle of Kursk in July 1943, when Hitler probably realized that he could not win the war. From July 1943 to the last campaign, the Battle of Berlin in April 1945, the stubborn Hitler fought a losing battle. At this stage he manipulated his people for the sake of his own chauvinistic dreams. Any insight he had that war is an instrument of politics, which he seemed to understand so well from July 1936 (when he first intervened in Spain) to November 1942 (the beginning of the Battle of Stalingrad), was lost. Hitler as warrior became drunk on his early successes. Holding firm to Schopenhauer's faith that willpower can triumph over all, Hitler after mid-1943 weltered in a state of administrative quasi-paralysis. On the importance of the Führer's grand strategy as opposed to technological warfare, see Norman Rich, *Hitler's War Aims,* 2 vols. (New York: Norton, 1972). For naval aspects of the war, see Cajus Bekker, *Hitler's Naval War* (London: Macdonald and Jane's, 1974); Keith W. Bird, *German Naval History: A Guide to the Literature* (New York: Garland Reference Library of Social Science, 1985); and Holger H. Herwig, ''The Failure of German Sea Power, 1914–1945: Mahan, Tirpitz, and Raeder Reconsidered,'' *International History Review* (February 1988): 68–105. For aviation, see Edward L. Homze, *German Military Aviation: A Guide to the Literature* (New York: Garland Publications, 1984); Williamson Murray, *Luftwaffe* (Baltimore, Md.: Nautical and Aviation Publishing Company of America, 1985); and R. J. Overy, ''Hitler and Air Strategy,'' *Journal of Contemporary History* 15 (July 1980): 405–21.

With regard to the costs of war, both financial and human, Hitler brought suffering and death not only to Germany but to the world. Strangely, none of the three standard biographies—Bullock, Fest, and Toland—does an adequate job on the military. The battle statistics they put in occasionally are mostly for color. The next biography needs a table summing up Hitler's some dozen wars, beginning in Spain in 1936, moving to Poland in 1939, to Yugoslavia and Greece in March 1941, and then to the gigantic Operation Barbarossa in the USSR. Also included should be Hitler's war and extermination policy against the Jews, listed as a separate campaign. Future historians should add the costs of the wars of liberation from 1943 to 1945, with particular attention paid to the Germans themselves. The air wars and sea wars need to be covered, with the casualties suffered on both sides.

Martin K. Sorge, *The Other Price of Hitler's War: German Military and Civilian Losses Resulting from World War II* (Westport, Conn.: Greenwood Press, 1986), seems to indicate the beginning of a new line of research, but it does not constitute a definitive work. It contains many statistics, and the questions he raises are good. Unfortunately, this high-school teacher and author sometimes has not provided adequate notes for his complex material. Also, he is more concerned with the deaths of Germans than of their victims.

## HITLER AND THE JEWS

The single most important motivator throughout Hitler's life was the so-called "Jewish question." From his teenage years to his last will and testament, the fanatic and paranoid Hitler consistently hated all Jews, whom he regarded as a race rather than a religion, economic group, or nationality. Heinrich Himmler, Reichsführer of the SS, was Hitler's chief agent against the Jews. The costs of Himmler's war against the Jews—the Final Solution or the Holocaust—are touched upon by the three biographers. With each succeeding copyright date (Bullock, 1962; Fest, 1973; and Toland, 1976) they have raised the figures on the death toll. Toland devotes the most space to the extermination of the European Jews because he had more basic monographs available than the others. In the recent Habermas-Nolte debate (see Jarausch, "Removing the Nazi Stain?" cited in the section "Bibliographies and Reviews"), I side with Habermas. Judeophobia was more important to the great dictator than anticommunism. Hitler exploited the national, economic, and religious prejudices of very many Gentiles who despised Jews for various reasons. (See the works of Binion and Waite cited under "Biographies" on the ideological dimensions.) A more general picture is given in Peter G. J. Pulzer, *The Rise of Anti-Semitism in Germany and Austria in the Nineteenth Century*, 2d ed. (Cambridge, Mass.: Harvard University Press, 1988). See also George Mosse, *Germans and Jews* (New York: Grosset and Dunlap, 1970).

For the operations of the SS and the concentration camps, there are several classics: Gerald Reitlinger, *The Final Solution* (London: Beechhurst Press, 1953), and *The SS, Alibi of a Nation* (London: Heinemann, 1956); also Raul Hilberg, *The Destruction of the European Jews*, 1st ed. (New York: Quadrangle, 1951); 2d ed., expanded, 3 vols. (New York: Holmes and Meier, 1985), with the review article by Jeffrey M. Masson, "Hilberg's Holocaust," *Midstream* 32 (April 1986): 51–55. Hilberg wrote a new essay, "The Bureaucracy of Annihilation," in *Unanswered Questions: Nazi Germany and the Genocide of the Jews*, edited by François Furet (New York: Schocken, 1989). See also Homze, *Foreign Labor in Nazi Germany*, and Christopher R. Browning, *Fateful Months: Essays on the Emergence of the Final Solution* (New York: Holmes and Meier, 1985). Other syntheses in a growing field of research include Michael Marrus, *The Holocaust in History* (Hanover, N.H.: University Press of New England, 1987), and his review article, "The History of the Holocaust: A Survey of Written Literature,"

*Journal of Modern History* 59 (March 1987): 114–60; Sarah Gordon, *Hitler, Germany, and the Jewish Question* (Princeton, N.J.: Princeton University Press, 1984); Gerhard Hirschfeld, ed., *The Policies of Genocide: Jews and Soviet Prisoners of War in Nazi Germany* (London: Allen and Unwin, 1986). Noteworthy in Hirschfeld are key essays bringing out the full barbarity of the Wehrmacht in the Soviet war and in Hitler's war against the Jews. Also see Omer Bartov, *The Eastern Front, 1941–45: German Troops and the Barbarization of Warfare* (London: Macmillan, 1986). Too much other past research has concentrated on the SS, thereby letting the army off its legal and moral responsibilities.

The subject of the Holocaust is so important that a special yearbook, *Simon Wiesenthal Center Annual*, edited by Henry Friedlander and Sybil Milton, which began in 1983, keeps historians up-to-date. The AHA convention in Washington, D.C., in December 1987 featured a panel, "Origins of the Final Solution of the Jewish Question," with papers by Charles Sydnor, Richard Breitman, and Christopher R. Browning and commentary by Robert Wolfe. This was followed by another conference on the same theme with some of the same people at Northwestern University on November 11–13, 1989.

The central issue of the present debate concerns the date when Hitler's fantastic idea of killing all the Jews became a national policy of the Third Reich. The term *final solution* has not been pinned down to a specific order in the sense that Operation Barbarossa was a military plan. As early as 1920 Hitler had vague intentions to do away with the Jews, but the actual "solution" evolved with Hitler's wartime successes. As of September 1939, with the war on Poland, the plan was to expel Jews from Germany and western Poland to the Lublin zone of eastern Poland. There they would be worked to death as slave laborers. The SS implemented the plan by forced ghettoization, accompanied by starvation, disease, and work. In June 1940 Hitler and his henchmen toyed with the idea of expelling Jews to the French colony of Madagascar. When Operation Sea Lion against Britain was shelved by Hitler, the Madagascar plan was dropped. In February 1941, before the invasion of Russia, the Nazis' plan was to wipe out Soviet Jews by shooting. Hitler decided in July 1941 that Europe's surviving Jews would eventually be gassed. By January 1942 at the Wannsee Conference genocide was clearly national policy. See David Bankier, "Hitler and the Policy Making Process on the Jewish Question," *Holocaust and Genocide Studies* 3, no. 1 (1980): 1–20.

David Irving, an Irishman with an anti-English bias, in 1963 publicized the Anglo-American firebombing of Dresden. His book on this 1945 war atrocity is basically sound. Later he made a career of rehabilitating Nazis, publishing *Hitler's War* (New York: Viking Press, 1977) and *The War Path: Hitler's Germany, 1933–1939* (New York: Viking Press, 1978). Irving is a free-lance, privately funded scholar who annotates his material. The 1977 book is unique among serious historians (we can ignore yellow journalists) in trying to argue that Hitler did not order the "Final Solution." Irving himself has claimed that he wrote these books as if he were Hitler writing his memoirs. No other scholar who uses archives accepts the thesis. Irving discovered a real problem, however: Hitler did not put the operation known as the Final Solution down on paper. He apparently gave the order orally in March–June 1941 as part of the planning for Operation Barbarossa, the invasion of the USSR. Receiving the order were Himmler, head of the SS, and Martin Bormann, the party deputy who succeeded Hess after the original head of the party bureaucracy fled to Britain in May 1941. Thus Irving makes a legalistic defense of Hitler, namely, that there are no documents linking Hitler to extermination.

Almost all the rest of the vast scholarship considers oral testimony as historically acceptable. In particular, Gerald Fleming, *Hitler and the Final Solution* (Berkeley: University of California Press, 1984) refuted the Irving thesis by going over the archives and Raul Hilberg's and Gerald Reitlinger's now-classic works (cited earlier in this section). Moreover, the order for the Final Solution was interpreted by the rank-and-file SS men in such a loose way that it could mean either immediate extermination by gas or shooting, or slave labor followed by premature death from disease, malnutrition, and overwork.

The most recent controversial and imaginative accounts are by Arno Mayer, *Why Did the Heavens Not Darken? The "Final Solution" in History* (New York: Pantheon, 1988), and Charles Maier, *The Unmasterable Past* (cited under "Bibliographies and Reviews"). See also Israel Charny, *Genocide: A Critical Bibliographic Review* (London: Mansell, 1988).

## HITLER AND COMMUNISM

Hitler's attitude toward communism first developed from 1919 to 1923 when the constitutional future of Germany was in doubt, and the Soviet regime was solidifying its power in Russia. Classics for this period are Werner T. Angress, *Stillborn Revolution: The Communist Bid for Power in Germany, 1921–1923* (Princeton, N.J.: Princeton University Press, 1963); Allan Mitchell, *Revolution in Bavaria, 1918–1919: The Eisner Regime and the Soviet Republic* (Princeton, N.J.: Princeton University Press, 1965); Robert Waite, *Vanguard of Nazism: The Free Corps Movement in Germany, 1918–1923* (Cambridge, Mass.: Harvard University Press, 1952); Charles B. Burdick and A. J. Ryder, eds., *The Political Institutions of the German Revolution, 1918–1919* (New York: Praeger, 1966); and A. J. Ryder, *The German Revolution of 1918: A Study of German Socialism in War and Revolt* (Cambridge, England: Cambridge University Press, 1967). See the more recent work on the eve of Hitler's coming to power by Eve Rosenhaft, *Beating the Fascists? The German Communists and Political Violence, 1929–1933* (Cambridge, England: Cambridge University Press, 1983). Again, during the unemployment crisis from 1929 to 1933, anticommunism became useful to propagandize the frightened German people into giving Hitler dictatorial power. From 1933 to the summer of 1939, Hitler worked to convince leaders of conservative and Fascist movements in Europe and Japan to ally with him against the so-called "Bolshevik menace." We have seen that anticommunism was important in forging his deals with Mussolini and the Japanese generals.

The Reich dictator astounded the world on August 23, 1939 by making a nonaggression pact with Joseph Stalin, thus isolating Poland militarily. The Poles were immediately attacked on September 1 by Hitler. The world was less surprised when the German dictator betrayed Stalin by invading the Soviet Union in June 1941.

Ever since meeting the Baltic journalist Alfred Rosenberg and his poet friend Dietrich Eckart about 1920, Hitler had taken up their emotional formula "Communism is Jewish." For Hitler the Jew was the real enemy and "communism" only one of his disguises. This formula came back again in June 1941 when Hitler justified the extermination of the Jewish people in the USSR first and then throughout occupied Europe as part of his war against "international communism." See Jarausch's "Removing the Nazi Stain?" (cited under "Bibliographies and Reviews") on the Nolte debate about the nature of communism; also see Whealey on Hitler's anticommunism in *Hitler and Spain* (cited under "Hitler and the Economy").

## HITLER AND OTHER PHILOSOPHIES, IDEOLOGIES, AND RELIGIONS

For Hitler's attitude toward liberalism, democratic socialism, Protestantism, and Catholicism, the bibliographies of Schreiber, Rees, and Snyder (see "Bibliographies and Reviews") cite the relevant literature. To Hitler, these groups were only fools to be manipulated with propaganda. During the decisive year of 1933, as the Nazis revolutionized the German government by systematic, "legal" decrees, German liberals, socialists, Catholics, and Protestants chose either to collaborate with the Nazis, flee, or go into a mostly passive dissidence. Hitler's attitudes on these themes are better developed in Waite than in Bullock or Fest, although Waite does not cover the churches and clergy. These traditionalist opponents are covered in great detail by the authors mentioned in the next section.

## RESISTANCE IN GERMANY

The topic of resistance to Hitler and his regime is perhaps overdone by historians in the Bundesrepublik. Resistance did not really surface until the famous plot on the Führer's life of July 1944. Despite moral earnestness, dissidents to Nazism failed in their immediate political objectives. See the bibliographies of Schreiber, Rees, Snyder, and other major biographers for a vast literature. According to Gerhard Weinberg, Peter Hoffmann, *German Resistance to Hitler*, translated by Richard Barry (Cambridge, Mass.: Harvard University Press, 1988), originally published in German in 1979, is the best survey of this topic.

See also Harold C. Deutsch, *Hitler and His Generals* (cited in the section "Hitler and the Military"), which centers on this theme, as does his *The Conspiracy Against Hitler in the Twilight War* (Minneapolis: University of Minnesota Press, 1968), and Herbert Mason, *To Kill The Devil: The Attempts on the Life of Adolf Hitler* (London: Joseph, 1979). A more generalized recent social history focusing on the German resistance is Michael Balfour, *Withstanding Hitler in Germany, 1933–45* (London: Routledge, 1988).

## THE FINAL SIX WEEKS

Hitler's last days, from March 22, 1945, when he decided on suicide for himself and his party, found the Führer clearly becoming psychotic. At approximately midnight of April 29–30, the German dictator and his mistress, as well as Goebbels and his family, destroyed themselves. This frantic time is covered in great detail by Hugh Trevor-Roper in *The Last Days of Hitler* (New York: Macmillan, 1947). At the end of the war, the Soviet government was circulating the fiction that Hitler was still alive. The Soviets wanted to maintain suspicion and fear to keep the anti-Fascist national liberation front idea alive as long as possible. Trevor-Roper, a scholar of sixteenth-century British history, was commissioned by British intelligence to discover, through interviewing the last people who saw Hitler alive, the details of the dictator's death. The result was Trevor-Roper's colorful popular essay depicting the weird ends of the Nazi leaders. Gerhard Boldt has a German memoir that adds to the story, *Hitler: The Last Ten Days: An Eye Witness Account*, translated from the 1947 original (New York: Coward, 1973). In 1968 the Soviet Union released the autopsy of Hitler's body, which shaped the new interpretations like those of Robert Waite, *Psychopathic God*, and Donald McKale, *Hitler* (cited under "Biographies").

## EPILOGUE

There are dozens of other books on such specialized aspects of the great dictator's life as Hitler and his party, Hitler and Roosevelt, Hitler and women, or Hitler and Hungary. These can be checked in the standard bibliographies of Gerhard Schreiber, Philip Rees, or Louis Snyder on the Führer and the Third Reich.

## NOTE

This chapter is written primarily from the point of view of English-language readers. Scholars may also wish to consult the German originals of some of the English translations mentioned here. I have intentionally left out foreign-language material unless there is nothing in English. I also wish to acknowledge the criticisms of professors Konrad Jarausch of the University of North Carolina and Walther Kirchner of the University of Delaware.

## SELECT BIBLIOGRAPHY

Abraham, David. *Collapse of the Weimar Republic: Political Economy and Crisis*. Princeton, N.J.: Princeton University Press, 1981.

Balfour, Michael. *Withstanding Hitler in Germany, 1933–45*. London: Routledge, 1988.

Bartov, Omer. *The Eastern Front, 1941–45: German Troops and the Barbarization of Warfare*. London: Macmillan, 1986.

Baynes, Norman, ed. and trans. *The Speeches of Adolf Hitler, April 1922–August 1939*. 2 vols. London: Oxford University Press, 1942.

Berghahn, Volker, and Martin Kitchen, eds. *Germany in the Age of Total War*. London: Croom Helm, 1981.

Binion, Rudolph. *Hitler Among the Germans*. New York: Elsevier, 1976.

Broszat, Martin. *Hitler and the Collapse of Weimar Germany*. Leamington Spa, N.Y.: Berg, 1987.

Bullock, Alan. *Hitler: A Study in Tyranny*. Harmondsworth, England: Penguin Books, 1962.

————. *Hitler and Stalin: Parallel Lives*. Toronto: McClelland and Stewart 1991.

Childers, Thomas. *The Nazi Voter: The Social Foundations of Fascism in Germany*. Chapel Hill: University of North Carolina Press, 1986.

Dallin, Alexander. *German Rule in Russia, 1941–1945*. London: Macmillan, 1957, 1981.

Deutsch, Harold C. *Hitler and His Generals: The Hidden Crisis, January–June 1938*. Minneapolis: University of Minnesota Press, 1973.

Dorpalen, Andreas. *German History in Marxist Perspective: The East German Approach*. Detroit: Wayne State University Press, 1985.

DuBois, Josiah. *The Devil's Chemists*. Boston: Beacon Press, 1952.

Evans, Richard. *In Hitler's Shadow*. New York: Pantheon, 1989.

Fest, Joachim C. *Hitler*. New York: Random House, 1975.

Fleming, Gerald. *Hitler and the Final Solution*. Berkeley: University of California Press, 1984.

Friedländer, Saul. *Prelude to the Downfall: Hitler and the United States, 1939–1941*. New York: Knopf, 1967.

Gordon, Sarah. *Hitler, Germany, and the Jewish Question*. Princeton, N.J.: Princeton University Press, 1984.

Hiden, John, and John Farquharson. *Explaining Hitler's Germany: Historians and the Third Reich*. Totowa, N.J.: Barnes and Noble, 1983.

Hillgruber, Andreas. *Germany and the Two World Wars*. Translated by William C. Kirby. Cambridge, Mass.: Harvard University Press, 1980.

Hirschfeld, Gerhard, ed. *The Politics of Genocide: Jews and Soviet Prisoners of War in Nazi Germany*. London: Allen and Unwin, 1986.

Hitler, Adolf. *Mein Kampf*. Translated by Ralph Manheim. Boston: Houghton Mifflin, 1943.

Hoffmann, Peter. *German Resistance to Hitler*. Cambridge, Mass.: Harvard University Press, 1988.

Jäckel, Eberhard. *Hitler in History*. Hanover, N.H.: University Press of New England, 1984.

————. *Hitler's World View: A Blueprint for Power*. Middletown, Conn.: Wesleyan University Press, 1972.

Kater, Michael H. *The Nazi Party: A Social Profile of Members and Leaders, 1919–1945*. Cambridge, Mass.: Harvard University Press, 1983.

Kershaw, Ian. *The ''Hitler Myth'': Image and Reality in the Third Reich*. Oxford: Clarendon Press, 1987.

Kranzler, David. *Japanese, Nazis, Jews*. New York: Yeshiva University, 1976.

Langer, Walter C. *The Mind of Adolf Hitler: The Secret Wartime Report*. New York: Basic Books, 1972.

Maier, Charles S. *The Unmasterable Past: History, Holocaust, and German National Identity*. Cambridge, Mass.: Harvard University Press, 1988.

Milward, Alan S. *The German Economy at War*. London: University of London, Athlone Press, 1965.

Mosse, George. *Germans and Jews*. New York: Grosset and Dunlap, 1970.

Orlow, Dietrich. *The History of the Nazi Party, 1919–1945*. 2 vols. Pittsburgh: University of Pittsburgh Press, 1969–73.

Picker, Henry et al., eds. *Hitler's Table Talk*. London: Weidenfeld and Nicolson, 1953.

Pulzer, Peter G. J. *The Rise of Anti-Semitism in Germany and Austria in the Nineteenth Century*. Cambridge, Mass.: Harvard University Press, 1988.

Read, Anthony, and David Fisher. *The Deadly Embrace: Hitler, Stalin, and Nazi-Soviet Relations, 1939–1941*. New York: Norton, 1988.

Reitlinger, Gerald. *The House Built on Sand: The Conflicts of German Policy in Russia, 1939–1945*. New York: Viking Press, 1960.

———. *The SS, Alibi of a Nation*. London: Heinemann, 1956.

Rich, Norman. *Hitler's War Aims*. 2 vols. New York: Norton, 1972.

Schleunes, Karl. *The Twisted Road to Auschwitz*. Urbana: University of Illinois Press, 1970.

Schoenbaum, David. *Hitler's Social Revolution: Class and Status in Nazi Germany, 1933–1939*. Garden City, N.Y.: Doubleday, 1966.

Snyder, Louis L., ed. *The Third Reich, 1933–1945: A Bibliographical Guide to German National Socialism*. New York: Garland, 1987.

Taylor, A. J. P. *The Origins of the Second World War*. New York: Atheneum, 1961.

Toland, John. *Adolf Hitler*. 2 vols. Garden City, N.Y.: Doubleday, 1976.

Trevor-Roper, H. R., ed. *Hitler's War Directives*. London: Sidgwick and Jackson, 1964.

Turner, Henry Ashby. *German Big Business and the Rise of Hitler*. New York: Oxford University Press, 1985.

Waite, Robert G. L. *The Psychopathic God: Adolf Hitler*. New York: Basic Books, 1977.

Weinberg, Gerhard. *The Foreign Policy of Hitler's Germany*. 2 vols. Chicago: University of Chicago Press, 1970, 1980.

# Chapter 4

# The Concentration Camps and Killing Centers of the Third Reich

## *Charles W. Sydnor, Jr.*

Over the last thirty years, one of the most important developments in contemporary scholarship has been the growth of historical research and writing devoted to the Holocaust. Defined as Nazi Germany's systematic extermination of the European Jews, the Holocaust has become the subject of a vast literature in a variety of languages. The immense, worldwide interest in the subject will continue to grow; in many respects it is only just beginning.

Much of what is now known of the history of the Holocaust has come through knowledge gained from research into the rational and organized determination of the Nazi perpetrators to exterminate all of those who became their victims. As a phenomenon unique to the social and political order that was Hitlerian Germany, the Holocaust was ideological, territorial, and functional.

For the general reader or the interested student, one introductory approach to the Holocaust involves specific reading in the most reliable works devoted to the institutions of mass murder: the concentration camps and the extermination centers. This focus embraces the ideological, the territorial, and the functional dimensions of the Holocaust itself.

To comprehend how the Germans were able to organize history's greatest campaign of systematic slaughter, and to understand why they succeeded in making the Holocaust a trans-European phenomenon, uprooting, transporting, and obliterating millions of human beings—to fathom the basics of this gigantic process, one simply has to know something about the places of industrialized extermination that were the Nazi death camps. In short, to grasp the enormity of what the Germans attempted and achieved in the Holocaust, learning about the places where they murdered helps to explain why and how they were so successful at it.

This approach suggests an additional assignment. The Holocaust was the invention of an empirical culture. From beginning to end, the extermination of the European Jews was bureaucratic genocide, depending at each step and through every stage of the killing process upon the organizational experience and the technical capabilities of a great, modern industrial state. The Nazi and SS leaders who initiated and directed it, the hundreds of thousands of German bureaucrats, officials, and workers in the ministries and agencies of the Reich who organized its every detail and kept it running on a daily basis, and the thousands of SS perpetrators who guarded, operated, repaired, maintained, and expanded the machinery of death all drew upon experience and precedent.

These functionaries applied their pragmatic and practical managerial skills to devise useful adaptations or to invent new and more efficient refinements in the killing process throughout the vast machinery of death. This was especially true in the extermination camps of German-occupied Eastern Europe. All of these facilities operated, to some extent and in varying degrees, on the basis of the organizational precedents established earlier in their prototypes, the prewar SS concentration camps that had been built within the borders of Nazi Germany. The Germans would not have succeeded in the Holocaust without these killing facilities, which, in turn, could not have existed or operated without the experience the Nazis had gained in and from the concentration camps that preceeded them.[1] Consequently, as an introduction to suggested readings in English in this important area of the history of the Holocaust, it is necessary to establish the connections and to link the institutions—concentration camps and extermination centers—in a brief review detailing how the development of policies of brutalization in the former influenced the operations of mass murder in the latter.

The essential prerequisite for establishing a revolutionary and totalitarian order is an effective system of terror. The movement or force seeking to grasp power must have the means to intimidate, silence, apprehend, brutalize, and finally destroy its critics, opponents, and enemies, real and imagined. This was the major purpose of concentration camps in prewar Nazi Germany. The camps became the foundation upon which the entire system of institutional Hitlerian and SS terror was built.

The Nazi concentration camps became so successful, and the system of terror they served so effective, because from the outset the camps were organized outside the law. Since Hitler came to power in a civilized state, with laws and institutions framed in some semblance of constitutional order, the development and operation of the Nazi system of terror had to be immune to the force of legality. The concentration camps had to be beyond the reach or jurisdiction of normal civil regulations or the ability of traditional authorities to interfere with the acts of terror that took place within them.[2]

The solution was simple and ingenious. Beginning in March 1933, the first concentration camps, most notably Dachau, were placed under the authority of agencies of the Nazi party. They were never subordinated to the competent authorities of the individual German states in which they were located. From the first, the brown-shirted Storm Troopers, or *Sturmabteilung* (SA), and then the black-uniformed units of the Protective Guard, or *Schutzstaffel* (SS), guarded and brutalized the prisoners thrown into the camps.[3]

The legal precedents for establishing concentration camps in Nazi Germany were accomplished just as easily. Two emergency laws and a series of administrative decrees and regulations were all that Hitler required. The first measure was the Law for the Protection of the People and the State, or the so-called Reichstag Fire Decree. This emergency measure was promulgated by Reichs President Paul von Hindenburg on February 28, 1933, in response to Hitler's demand, as chancellor, for emergency authority to deal with what the Nazis claimed was an imminent threat of Communist revolution. The great fire that had destroyed the Reichstag in the heart of Berlin the previous day allegedly was the signal for a political onslaught from the Left.[4]

President von Hindenburg signed the measure, as he was legally entitled to do, under the provisions for emergency presidential powers enumerated in article 48 of the Constitution of the Weimar Republic. This presidential decree empowered Hitler's new government, and the auxiliary police forces it created from the ranks of the SA and SS, to suspend or disregard most of the guarantees of civil liberty and individual freedom contained in the Weimar constitution, including the freedom from unwarranted search and seizure and the right to judicial due process.

The measure legitimized the Nazi reign of terror that began immediately with mass arrests. The decree was, in fact, never rescinded, and the state of emergency it created throughout Germany lasted until the very end of the Third Reich.

The second measure was even more important for the permanent establishment of concentration camps to hold the throngs of political opponents rounded up by the police and the SA and SS. This was the Enabling Act, passed on March 23, 1933, as the single and final item of business by the last multiparty Reichstag elected in the Weimar Republic. The law altered the constitution by giving Hitler full executive and legislative power to govern the country by decree for a period of four years. Armed with this enormous legal authority, Hitler and the Nazi party rapidly and systematically abolished or destroyed almost every vestige of institutional independence and political, social, and cultural pluralism in Germany. During the remaining months in 1933 the Nazi party used these new laws to seize control of the governments of all the German states, to outlaw all other political parties and the nation's trade unions, to close down or take over the country's independent newspapers and publishing industry, and effectively to suppress or silence all opposition.[5]

These two laws, the Hindenburg decree and the Enabling Act—the one legalizing mass arrests of people to be detained indefinitely, and the second legitimizing Hitler's authority to establish concentration camps by merely signing a decree—became the twin foundation blocks upon which the Hitlerian dictatorship and the system of SS concentration camps were built. The mortar needed to bond these foundation blocks was mixed and applied through two related steps that were begun in 1933 and culminated in 1939: the drafting and expansion of the protective-custody (*Schutzhaft*) regulations for seizing individuals and placing them in the Nazi concentration camps, and the centralization and incorporation of the entire German police system into the SS.

The von Hindenburg presidential decree of February 28, 1933, created the extralegal provisions for *Schutzhaft*, or protective custody. This law empowered the regular police and their Nazi auxiliaries to arrest and to place in protective custody any person judged in any way to constitute a threat to the state or to civil order. Though the law did not specify incarceration in concentration camps for those arrested on the basis of protective custody, the vast majority of those caught in the roundups of March and April 1933 were thrown into the makeshift concentration camps hastily established at that time by the SA and the SS.

One year later, in April 1934, the Nazi Ministry of the Interior promulgated standard regulations to be used in protective-custody arrests throughout Germany. These decrees clearly stipulated that *Schutzhaft* be used as grounds to arrest people engaged in political rather than criminal activities, specifically any individual who "by his behavior directly endangers the public safety and order, particularly by activity hostile to the state." Protective-custody arrests were to be carried out by the Gestapo (the Secret State Police) without any participation or interference by the courts and absent any legal recourse by the arrestee. Equally important, the duration of *Schutzhaft* was to be indefinite, or "for as long as its purpose demands."[6]

Over the course of the next four years, from 1934 to 1938, the use of protective-custody arrests was constantly expanded to include not only those engaged in active political opposition, but also individuals "presumed" to be "likely" opponents of the Nazi regime. By 1935 protective-custody arrests were being applied also to men and women whose activities were not political, but could be considered "potentially harmful" to the National Socialist state. These categories included clergymen, Jews, Jehovah's Witnesses, German emigrants returning to the country, the chronically unemployed, and individuals considered to be "asocial"—that is, "beggars, vagabonds, Gypsies, tramps, loafers, prostitutes, complainers, psychopaths, and the mentally ill." Under the political-police provisions of *Schutzhaft*, virtually everyone arrested in any of these categories landed in a concentration camp for indefinite detention.[7]

Early in 1938 the SS and police system of terror tightened its grip even further. The Reich Ministry of the Interior drafted a whole new set of regulations governing the use of protective custody. From this point on, the procedure could be imposed upon any individuals who "by their behavior endanger the safety and survival of the German people and state." For the first time the Gestapo was given the specific and exclusive authority, in all instances, to impose Schutzhaft and to decide whether or not to release persons from protective custody. Most important, this decree explicitly defined protective custody as indefinite, long-term detention and expressly stipulated that all persons in protective custody were to be confined only in concentration camps.[8]

During the same years that protective custody became an all-purpose provision for the Gestapo to use in funneling the victims of Nazism into the concentration camps, what remained of the professional independence of the police forces and agencies throughout Germany and of the restraints upon their powers was systematically dismantled by the Nazi regime. In a process that began in the spring of 1933 and was completed just after the outbreak of war in September 1939, two of Hitler's closest and most trusted subordinates, Heinrich Himmler and Reinhard Heydrich, directed the centralization and incorporation of the police into the structure of the SS as an agency of the Nazi party.[9]

In the summer of 1934, Hitler moved decisively to break the power of the brown-shirted Storm Troopers, or SA, by ordering the murder of the SA chief of staff, Ernst Röhm, and his closest confederates. Himmler and Heydrich directed the murders and widespread arrests, which were carried out by Gestapo and SS units, including a detachment of SS guards from the Dachau concentration camp. The man then serving as commandant at Dachau, SS General Theodor Eicke, personally shot Röhm to death in the Munich prison cell where he had been confined.

In the aftermath of this bloody purge, the SS was granted independent status from the SA, to which it had been subordinated since the first SS units had been organized in 1925 as bodyguards and armed escorts for Hitler. As Reich leader of the SS (Reichsführer SS), Heinrich Himmler now became Hitler's direct subordinate, with a new mandate to gain control of the agencies that could impose order and security and to make them directly responsive to his and to Hitler's will. One of the first steps Himmler completed was that of eliminating finally the remaining vestiges of SA control over the concentration camps. In July 1934 all of the then-existing concentration camps came fully under SS control with the creation of a new central office in the SS, inspector-general of concentration camps and commander of SS guard units. Himmler placed Theodor Eicke in this critically important post, with orders to proceed in building a centralized system of SS concentration camps for the Third Reich. As inspector-general, Eicke became Himmler's direct subordinate, immediately responsible to the Reichsführer SS for the administration and operation of all concentration camps.[10]

Simultaneously, Himmler and Heydrich moved to gain direct and complete control of all of the police and internal security forces in Germany. This process took less than two years. On June 17, 1936, Hitler signed a decree investing Heinrich Himmler with a new title and the enormous powers that reflected the merger of the German police with the SS. Himmler received the official title Reich leader of the SS and chief of the German police (Reichsführer SS und Chef der Deutschen Polizei). Himmler's Nazi party and official state functions were combined, and from June 1936 until the collapse of the Third Reich he worked as the chief of all German police within his capacity as Reich leader of the SS. At the same time, Heydrich carried out the first in a series of reorganizations of SS and police agencies that would increase his own powers immensely and, three years later, complete the merger of the police with the SS. In the summer of 1936 Heydrich was promoted from chief of the Gestapo to the new post of chief of the security police and the SD. This step combined three separate SS and police institutions into one new and enormously powerful security apparatus. The Secret State Police, or Gestapo, merged with the German Criminal Police and with the Security Service of the SS (the *Sicherheitsdienst* or SD) to become the Security Police and the SD.[11]

In late 1937 all of the offices of the German Order Police, whose chief was SS General Kurt Daluege, were merged into the SS, and a new reorganization was begun. Within two years this process was completed, and a larger and even more powerful SS and police bureaucracy emerged as World War II began. The new creation, the Reich Security Main Office, more generally known by its acronym, the RSHA, became the institutional overseer of all police and terror activities within Germany and throughout Nazi-occupied Europe until the end of the war. From 1939 until his assassination by Czech partisans in May 1942, Heydrich served as head of the RSHA, extending the power of the SS and police into the conquered regions overrun by German armies and directing the policies of exploitation, enslavement, and mass murder initiated by Hitler and Himmler among the captive populations all across the continent. Above all, it was Heydrich, acting upon the directives and guidelines formulated by Hitler and Himmler, who organized and deployed the manpower, resources, and experience of the RSHA to plan, prepare, and carry out the systematic destruction of the European Jews.[12]

What Heydrich and the RSHA lacked was the infrastructure for genocide— the methods by which to destroy and dispose of the victims and the places in which to accomplish the killings. Once the war with Russia began, special mobile SS units roamed the areas behind the advancing German armies conducting organized massacres of Jewish communities wherever they were found. The logistical, psychological, and public-relations difficulties involved in attempting to shoot so many defenseless people of all ages soon confirmed what had become obvious. The assignment simply was too gigantic for such methods; the murder machinery had to be drastically expanded to accommodate the volume. The only precedent, the sole possibility, for making the Final Solution really final lay in building larger variations of the existing concentration camps and adapting them to operate as factories for extermination. The experience in adaptation rapidly revealed just how effectively the SS concentration camps had been developed as prototypes in industrialized human destruction.

The sole architect and the chief construction engineer who designed and built the SS concentration camps was Theodor Eicke. The prototypes that were later adapted into the wartime extermination camps were his creation. His role in developing the functional machinery of destruction was unique; retrospectively, he must be viewed as a figure of early and enormous importance in the history of the Holocaust. Eicke served as inspector-general of concentration camps from July 1934 until September 1939, when he left the camp system to become commander of one of the first armed SS (Waffen-SS) divisions, the SS Death's Head Division, which drew most of its original personnel from three strengthened regiments of SS guards and officers from the prewar concentration camps.

When Himmler appointed Eicke inspector-general in 1934, his new assignment carried an agenda of three items: establishing SS control over all the widely scattered ad hoc concentration camps throughout Germany; centralizing them into a smaller number of larger and permanent camps; and creating uniform administrative procedures and disciplinary regulations in all the concentration camps that would enable the SS to deal effectively with all of the enemies of national socialism confined in the facilities. Within four years Eicke succeeded on all counts far beyond even Himmler's most optimistic expectations.

In fact, at the time Himmler gave him the camp inspectorate, Eicke had already succeeded in creating an impressive, prototypical concentration camp upon which a whole system could be, and subsequently was, modeled. The Reichsführer SS had sent Eicke to Dachau in March 1933 as commandant with express directives to create order, stability, and proper procedures in one of the earliest and most important, but also most violent and chaotic, of the Nazi concentration camps. Within one year Eicke managed to transform Dachau into what the entire Nazi hierarchy, including Hitler, admiringly pointed to as "the model concentration camp." During the fifteen months he served as commandant at Dachau, Eicke created all of the elements of form and substance history has come to identify with the Nazi concentration camps. When he moved from Dachau to the command of all the camps, he saw to it that all of the features of concentration-camp life at Dachau became the operating rules for the new system. The disciplinary and punishment regulations he drafted at Dachau for abusing, degrading, beating, torturing, and even killing the inmates became standard procedures for the SS guards throughout the camp system after July 1934 and seven years later were introduced into the new camps in France, Holland, and Poland on an even larger and more terrible scale.[13]

The administrative and organizational structure of all of these SS facilities, the concentration camps and the extermination centers, was patterned on the "Dachau model" Eicke had developed between the spring of 1933 and the summer of 1934. The whole system of enforced slave labor, which utilized inmate productivity in economic and industrial concerns important to the SS in wartime, had its origins in the successful enterprises Eicke created in the prisoner workshops at Dachau in 1934. Even the physical structure of the camps, within Germany and throughout Nazi-occupied Europe, with modifications and alterations, was patterned on the original design and layout that Eicke had ordered at Dachau during his tenure as commandant. The security zones, the electrified wires, the guard towers with machine guns, the system of prisoner roll calls, the isolation cells and interrogation bunkers, and the arrangement and construction of inmate barracks were all features of Auschwitz, Mauthausen, and Stutthof in 1944 as they had been originally at Dachau in 1934.

One of the most vivid remaining symbols linking the prewar concentration camps with the wartime extermination centers is the motto cast in iron letters above the entrance gates at both Dachau and the original Auschwitz camp: "Arbeit macht frei" (work will make you free). This cynical exhortation and warning to all prisoners entering the camps was first written by Eicke and installed at Dachau in 1933. In differing forms it adorned the entrances to all the German concentration camps after 1934.[14]

Equally important as a measure of Eicke's definitive influence upon the camps was the ethos of mistreatment he established through the training programs and the Service Regulations and Code of Conduct for the SS guards. These procedures, which combined racial and ideological indoctrination with military training, were systematically applied and practiced throughout all the SS Death's Head formations guarding and administering the German concentration camps before the war and were introduced and followed after 1940 in the facilities built in the East for slave labor and extermination. SS guards were constantly drilled in the notion that concentration-camp inmates were the most dangerous enemies of the Nazi state and the German people—unscrupulous and lethal subhuman adversaries who had to be guarded closely and treated harshly, without the slightest trace of compassion, pity, or mercy.[15]

In Eicke's phrase, all concentration-camp inmates, and most especially Jews, were "enemies behind the wire." The SS camp guards were taught to be ruthlessly correct in any dealings with prisoners. The brutalities they inflicted were devised by Eicke to be administered impersonally. The regulations and code of conduct created a system of prescribed, institutional SS cruelties in the camps that helped to deaden or desensitize the guards to the inhumane mistreatment of prisoners. Even the most horrible punishments were imposed by stipulation, according to orders. In creating this climate, this environment of formalized brutality, which he imposed upon the SS guard units in the system through the individual camp commandants who were his direct subordinates, Theodor Eicke left a legacy indispensable to the conduct of the mass murder that began well after he departed the camp inspectorate: Eicke succeeded in creating new and closed worlds where inhumanity was routine, barbarism was the norm, and helpless inmates, reduced to the level of filthy and diseased animals in the consciousness of their SS guards and masters, were brought to the very brink of destruction—the next and logically the final procedure to which the SS would subject them. Theodor Eicke did not invent, design, or build the wartime extermination camps, but in the most important sense he did survey and clear the roadbed and lay upon it the tracks that led to the doors of the gas chambers.[16]

The administrative and organizational development of the camp system during and after Eicke's service as inspector-general evolved systematically to increase the institutional power of the SS within the Nazi state, to intensify the role of the camps within the SS network of terror, and to reduce to utter helplessness all those arrested and thrown into the concentration camps. Shortly after Eicke established the headquarters of the new Concentration Camp Inspectorate in Berlin in October 1934, he took steps to bring the small, temporary, and widely scattered camps and detention facilities for political prisoners throughout Germany under his direct control. At this juncture there was no effective opposition, or even objection, from within the Nazi party or its agencies, or from the traditional state bureaucracy.[17] The major difficulties were logistical. Eicke had to close the independent, ad hoc facilities while making arrangements to transfer inmate records, usable materials, weapons, and foodstuffs, and all the prisoners into larger and better-constructed camps. By March 1935 he had managed to centralize everything into the first version of a concentration-camp system. At that time the inspectorate controlled seven complete concentration camps containing just over 9,000 prisoners. These camps of the first system included Dachau, Esterwegen, Lichtenburg, Sachsenburg, Columbia Haus, in the city of Berlin, Oranienburg, just north of Berlin, and the Fehlsbüttel camp in northwestern Germany near Hamburg.

Eicke intended to operate this first group of seven camps only temporarily, as an interim step leading to the construction of a handful of much larger and permanent concentration camps. Within a year he had substantially worked out a general plan for reorganization and had either completed or had under construction the new camps for the permanent system. In February 1936 the original camp at Oranienburg, one of the first organized by the Nazis in March 1933, was shut down and relocated nearby as the Sachsenhausen concentration camp. Five months later Eicke closed Fehlsbüttel, Esterwegen, and the Columbia Haus detention center in Berlin and transferred all the prisoners from these facilities to Sachsenhausen, where they joined the inmates relocated from Oranienburg.[18] During these same months new construction, the expansion of the SS barracks and support facilities, and a significant strengthening of the system of electrified wires, guard towers, and escape obstacles completed the transformation of Dachau. With only minor, additional modifications, this first "model camp" remained in operation until the very end of World War II.

In the summer of 1937 Eicke completed the new camp system while simultaneously directing its first expansion. In July the Sachsenburg camp was closed, the handful of small facilities that remained were dissolved, and the Gestapo swept out of the regular prisons any holdover detainees deemed suited for the concentration camps. All of these prisoners were then transferred to the new Buchenwald concentration camp, which Eicke had ordered built months earlier near the city of Weimar in Saxony. Another new concentration camp for women, Lichtenburg, was finished and opened that same summer.

In the two years that remained before the German invasion of Poland, these four concentration camps—Dachau, Sachsenhausen, Buchenwald, and Lichtenburg—were the foundation of the system. Hitler's growing aggressiveness externally and the tightening Nazi repression internally combined to prompt another increase in the number of concentration camps, a process of expansion that was to continue without interruption once war began. After the *Anschluss* in March 1938, Himmler authorized Eicke to build and open a permanent concentration camp in Austria, based on the established German facilities. During the spring of 1938 Eicke traveled extensively through the newly incorporated Ostmark and selected a site near the village of Mauthausen, adjacent to a huge stone quarry on a bluff above the Danube east of Linz. The construction of the camp was finished in July, and Mauthausen received its first influx of inmates. Mauthausen gained a deserved reputation as one of the most horrible of all the Nazi camps and was the last to be liberated by Allied troops, one week after the collapse of the Third Reich in 1945.

Even before Mauthausen opened officially, Eicke was busy with plans for additional concentration camps. The growing numbers of women seized by the Gestapo on various pretexts created such overcrowding in Lichtenburg that another new camp became an urgent necessity. In the autumn of 1938 Eicke opened the second concentration camp for women at Ravensbrück, some fifty miles north of Berlin.

Following the invasion and conquest of Poland and the German defeat of France and the Low Countries, additional thousands of foreign nationals considered to be enemies, asocials, or potential resistance leaders or generally viewed as dangerous undesirables were rounded up and deported to the German concentration-camp system. The war and German expansion therefore required the construction of even more concentration camps. Between the invasion of Poland and the defeat of France, new camps were constructed and opened to receive the constant and growing stream of prisoners and to expand the number and scope of economic enterprises and war industries utilizing the camp inmates as slave labor. They included Flossenburg in northeast Bavaria, Neuengamme near the Elbe River southeast of Hamburg, Natzweiler near Strasbourg in the region of Alsace annexed from France, Gross Rosen in the region of Upper Silesia taken from Poland, and Stutthof in the marshy plain east of Danzig, just inland off the Baltic Sea.

Finally, in late June 1940, Himmler directed the establishment of a new concentration camp in Silesia in a collection of brick buildings that had served until 1939 as a barracks complex for an artillery regiment of the Polish army. The new camp was to house Polish political prisoners and other undesirables and was given the Germanicized name of the Polish town it adjoined, Auschwitz. Its first commandant, handpicked by Himmler, was one of Theodor Eicke's longtime subordinates in the prewar concentration-camp system, Rudolf Hoess. Hoess began as an SS guard at Dachau in 1934 and was to end, by his own evaluation, as commandant of the greatest facility for mass murder in the history of humankind.[19]

Rudolf Hoess was but one among many important operatives of mass extermination who had served under and been trained by Theodor Eicke. Hoess, like the others, had been hardened into a condition of professional specialization and suitability for mass murder. Among the other products of Eicke's tutelage was Adolf Eichmann, who began his SS career as a guard at Dachau in 1934, transferred from the concentration camps to the Gestapo, served with the SS Office for Jewish Emigration in Vienna in 1938 and 1939, and then moved to the RSHA to become Heydrich's principal subordinate in the Gestapo office of the RSHA that handled the operation of the entire Final Solution.

In addition to Hoess, the two main camps at Auschwitz, Auschwitz I and Auschwitz II (Birkenau), were under the command of Eicke's protégés for most of the five years they were in operation. Karl Fritsch, who began as a guard at Dachau in 1933 and was steadily promoted and advanced under Eicke's supervision, went to Auschwitz I as deputy commandant in 1940 and remained until the construction of the Birkenau extermination camp was completed in August 1942. Richard Baer, who replaced Arthur Liebehenschel as commandant of the Auschwitz camps in May 1944 and stayed until Auschwitz was evacuated and closed in January 1945, first served in the camps as a guard at Dachau in 1933 and was promoted and transferred to Columbia Haus and thence to command as an officer in the SS Death's Head units. After frontline service, he was transferred in November 1942 as deputy to SS General Oswald Pohl in the SS Main Economic and Administrative Office in Berlin, the central SS office that controlled all the concentration camps after 1942. With Pohl's enthusiastic recommendation, Baer moved to Auschwitz.

Friedrich Hartjenstein, commandant successively of the Birkenau extermination camp and then the Natzweiler concentration camp in France, had served in the camps before the war and had been a battalion commander under Eicke in the SS Death's Head Division. Paul-Werner Hoppe, posted briefly as commander of an SS guard detachment at Auschwitz, was promoted to commandant of the Stutthof concentration camp nearby in August 1942. For years Hoppe had been among Eicke's most trusted subordinates, both as staff officer in the Concentration Camp Inspectorate and then as Eicke's adjutant in the SS Death's Head Division.[20]

Karl Koch, the notorious commandant of Buchenwald, who was executed on Himmler's orders early in 1945 after an extensive SS investigation into corruption at Buchenwald, was among the very first group of Eicke's SS officers at Dachau in 1933. Koch had performed exceptionally to Eicke's standards in the prewar camps and in staff assignments with the Concentration Camp Inspectorate. After the first investigation began at Buchenwald in the autumn of 1941, Koch was transferred as commandant to Majdanek to begin the expansion of the facility for mass extermination.

Koch's longtime deputy at Buchenwald, who was also highly regarded by Eicke, was Arthur Rödel. Rödel had served at Dachau in 1934 under Eicke and had worked in both the Sachsenburg and Lichtenburg camps before being promoted to Buchenwald in 1938 as Koch's deputy. Untainted by the scandal that brought down Koch, Rödel was promoted in October 1942 to serve as commandant of the Gross Rosen camp in Silesia, where he remained until October

1943. Rödel was succeeded as commandant by Johannes Hassebröck, himself a longtime veteran of the concentration-camp system and a man whose SS career had been advanced through Eicke's esteem and favor. Hassebröck remained at Gross Rosen until the camp was disbanded and the prisoners and SS guards evacuated to escape the advancing Red Army in early 1945.[21]

Among Eicke's pupils and the SS alumni of the Dachau guard units, Max Kögel became one of the most accomplished operatives in mass extermination. From an SS officer commanding guards at Dachau in 1934, Kögel was promoted in rank to Columbia Haus and thence to Sachsenhausen before returning to Dachau in 1937 as deputy commandant of the Protective Custody Camp. Eicke considered him such a model camp officer that he promoted Kögel in 1938 to serve as the first commandant of the new women's concentration camp at Ravensbrück. At Ravensbrück Kögel did so well by the SS standards for the camps that in April 1942 Himmler personally approved his transfer to Majdanek to relieve the compromised Karl Koch and to complete the expansion of the camp into a mass-murder facility. Kögel remained commandant at Majdanek from April 1942 until December 1943, a tenure that spanned Majdanek's peak operation as an extermination camp.[22]

Perhaps none of Eicke's protégés in concentration-camp administration became more immediately or extensively identified with the horrors of the death camps in the imagination of the postwar world than the unshaven, menacing figure of Josef Kramer, the last commandant of Bergen-Belsen. Eicke had spotted Kramer early in 1934, when he was a Death's Head guard posted at Dachau, as a man with great natural ability and real potential for advancement in concentration-camp work. Between 1935 and 1938 Eicke promoted Kramer steadily and followed his career closely as an SS staff officer at Esterwegen, Dachau, and then Sachsenhausen.

By August 1938 Eicke judged Kramer to be well prepared for larger tasks and dispatched him with a promotion to the rank of SS captain to serve as adjutant to Franz Ziereis (another Eicke disciple), who was the commandant at the then newly opened camp at Mauthausen. By Eicke's standards, Kramer performed admirably at Mauthausen, developing a reputation in the camp administration and with the Concentration Camp Inspectorate as a solid and capable specialist, particularly adept in handling the demands associated with running a new concentration camp with a growing number of prisoners. In the summer of 1940 Kramer was promoted again, from Mauthausen to the new camp at Auschwitz to serve as adjutant to Rudolf Hoess.[23]

After a year at Auschwitz, the Concentration Camp Inspectorate detailed Kramer to a special training course at Dachau for SS Death's Head officers judged to be on a fast track to promotion as camp commandants. From Dachau Kramer was promoted to command of the protective-custody camp at Natzweiler in Alsace, and shortly thereafter, in July 1942, Himmler approved his appointment as commandant of Natzweiler.

Kramer remained commandant at Natzweiler until late April 1944, when his abilities and experience as one of the most senior of the SS camp administrators placed him in line for a larger and even more important assignment. On May 5, 1944, with the rank of SS major, Josef Kramer became commandant of Auschwitz II (Birkenau), a move timed to place him in charge of the planned extermination of the Hungarian Jews in that gigantic killing facility. Between Kramer's arrival at Birkenau on May 5, 1944, and his transfer to Bergen-Belsen the following November, over 400,000 Hungarian and other European Jews were gassed and their corpses incinerated under his command and supervision at Auschwitz-Birkenau.[24] The worldwide publicity attending the liberation of Bergen-Belsen in April 1945 and the extensive film and photographic documentation of the indescribable conditions and horrors in the camp, juxtaposed against the brutish and revolting image Kramer presented when displayed to the press by his British captors, initially overshadowed the even greater criminal record Josef Kramer had accumulated through a decade of command in the concentration camps and extermination complexes of the Third Reich.

The careers of Max Kögel and Josef Kramer illustrate another aspect of SS policy in adapting the experiences of the concentration camp to the requirements of the extermination complex. The SS men chosen to run the machinery of murder had to be experienced enough in brutality and killing to be morally impervious to the daily routine of extermination and at the same time skilled or capable enough to adapt to the demands for improvising in an endeavor that had no precedent. What they had to manage was the equivalent of an industrial revolution in human destruction.

The physical requirements for annihilating so many millions of intended Jewish victims were so great as to surpass the projected capabilities of Auschwitz and Majdanek and the SS personnel drawn from the concentration camps to staff the work of mass murder. Additional people and more efficient methods were needed; both evolved as key elements in the plans completed in January 1942.

By the spring of 1942 all the infrastructure requirements were in place to proceed with the Final Solution to the Jewish Question. The policy decisions had been taken, the German bureaucracy had been ordered into action, the SS personnel had been selected and organized, and the experiments in mass killing with poison gas had been completed to the satisfaction of the SS experts involved. The mass extermination of the European Jews was to be carried out primarily in six killing facilities, all located within the German-annexed or -occupied regions of Poland.

Though organized and built to serve the same general purpose, the SS extermination camps were of two different types. The Auschwitz camps, including the huge killing machinery at Birkenau, and the Majdanek camp, built in the suburbs of Lublin, were permanently constructed facilities designed for both mass murder and slave labor. These camps retained a substantial population of prisoners for labor—inmates drawn from the continuous influx of Gestapo arrestees and arriving transports of Jews from all over Europe. Those spared for slave labor were reprieved only temporarily; the appalling sanitary conditions, disease, exposure, starvation, maltreatment, and exhaustion killed off all but the strongest within a matter of months.[25]

The other four camps were built and run exclusively as extermination centers; virtually all of the arriving Jewish victims crammed into each of the transports were gassed immediately upon arrival. In addition, and from the first, these four death camps were never intended to be permanent facilities. They were temporary, single-purpose institutions. When the work of mass murder was done, their SS operatives tried to destroy them completely and to erase even the slightest hint that they had ever existed.

These four extermination camps were Chelmno, north of Lodz in the incorporated region the Nazis called the Wartheland; Treblinka, some seventy miles northeast of Warsaw along the main railroad line to Bialystok; and the camps at Sobibor and Belzec, near the Bug River in eastern Poland in the district of Lublin. Administrative jurisdiction over all the concentration and extermination camps in the occupied East was divided three ways within the SS power structure. Auschwitz, Gross Rosen, Stutthof, and Majdanek were subordinated to the Inspectorate of Concentration Camps and the SS Main Economic and Administrative Office in Berlin; Chelmno came under the jurisdiction of the SS and police authority in the Wartheland; and Belzec, Sobibor, and Treblinka were directly controlled by SS General Odilo Globocnik, the SS and police leader in the Lublin District, who operated from June 1942 under Himmler's immediate supervision as commander of Operation Reinhard, the SS code name for the extermination of the three and one-half million Polish Jews. Between early December 1941, when the first gassings were carried out at Chelmno, and late November 1944, when the last transports of victims were liquidated at Auschwitz-Birkenau, more than five million human beings, men, women, and children, Jews, Gypsies, and political, social, cultural, and religious prisoners of every European nationality, were murdered in the concentration and extermination camps throughout Nazi-dominated and German-occupied Europe.

Several of the leading Holocaust scholars have pointed to the absence of a large, published literature on the concentration camps as both a reflection of the difficulties confronting the historian and an indication of the tremendous work yet to be done in this field.[26] To a large degree, forty-five years after the liberation of the last camps, the best works about them remain the memoir accounts of survivors. The concentration camps may well become the one area in which the most important works as yet unwritten in the history of the Holocaust will appear: of all the regions currently being explored, it contains some of the least familiar terrain.

One successful approach to an understanding of the role of the camps within the experience of the Holocaust lies through the broader, preliminary step of studying the significance of the Holocaust in human events. Placing the larger questions in perspective first can strengthen an appreciation for the central and inseparable place of the camps in the development of the Third Reich and in the evolution of the Final Solution to the Jewish Question.

The serious student may begin by consulting Michael R. Marrus, *The Holocaust in History*, an excellent, superbly crafted study.[27] As a historical survey of the Holocaust, it is organized and written to inform without confusing or overwhelming any reader uninitiated in the subject. There is something in it for virtually any reader at every level of knowledge: a useful, general narrative; an examination, chapter by chapter, of all the important historical and moral issues, as reflected in the historiography of the Holocaust to date; an expertly crafted synthesis relating all of these questions to each other and to the larger subject of the Holocaust itself; and notes and a bibliography that point the reader to further and more specialized studies in every aspect of the Holocaust.

To complement Marrus' book, and to move toward a more extensive and detailed examination of the extermination camps, the reader should examine carefully and thoroughly Raul Hilberg, *The Destruction of the European Jews*. The new, revised, and definitive three-volume edition published by Holmes and Meier is also available in a one-volume, paperback, student version, specifically adapted for college and university classroom use. The student edition is an excellent summary of the most important chapters in the larger, three-volume work.[28] Since the appearance of the first edition in 1961, Hilberg's book has come, I believe, to be regarded generally as the standard work on the Holocaust. The new, enlarged edition incorporates the results of scholarship over the last two decades, but changes little in the interpretations and conclusions originally drawn.

Few details in the vast and horrible panoply of Nazi extermination have escaped Hilberg's scrutiny, the various threads weaving together in his narrative as a process moving ever more clearly and rapidly toward destruction. Hilberg guides the reader logically and chronologically through the development of Nazi anti-Jewish policy—the stages of the destruction process codified in the laborious accumulation of prewar anti-Semitic laws and regulations. When the wartime German bureaucracy was ready to implement the final phase, destruction, anti-Jewish measures had become so commonplace that lower-level administrative edicts replaced what earlier only the Führer's orders or ministerial directives had accomplished. In one sense, the destruction of the European Jews succeeded because it had become but another form of German administrative routine.

With unfailing attention and accuracy, Hilberg depicts a German bureaucracy and SS technicians time and again ingeniously improvising, cleverly circumventing and skillfully resolving or surmounting the problems, barriers, and impediments that lay in the path of their Final Solution. These volumes follow the trail of destruction step by step, year by year, and country by country, based upon a knowledge of the sources and records left by the Nazi perpetrators and a familiarity with the experiences of those who perished and those who survived that are unrivalled by any other living historian.

In addition to Hilberg's classic, there are other, single-volume general histories of the Holocaust that can also be highly recommended, not only because of their literary quality and scholarly authenticity, but also because they each treat in a major way and as a central focus the concentration and extermination camps. From these works the reader can turn directly to the only book currently in print in English that deals comprehensively with all of the Nazi concentration and extermination camps: Konnilyn G. Feig, *Hitler's Death Camps: The Sanity of Madness*. Among the many admirable qualities that should recommend this book to students of the Holocaust are special efforts the author incorporated into her research. Professor Feig writes about all the camps with unusually strong conviction and authenticity because she traveled throughout Europe and visited the site or memorial and archives of every single concentration camp or extermination center described in the volume. Among the appendixes in the book to assist the reader, Feig has also included precise travel directions for anyone seeking to find and visit the current sites and memorials of the former camps.

In the opening section of her study, Feig sketches the background details in the history of the Third Reich that explain how and why the camps became such important institutions in the Hitlerian New Order. This is then followed by the real introduction to the history of the concentration camps, a chapter analyzing the early role and continuing importance of Dachau as the model facility upon which the entire system of camps was patterned administratively, organizationally, and functionally.

The great majority of the book, about four hundred pages, is divided into individual chapters of varying length that narrate the history of each concentration and extermination camp. Professor Feig has arranged the organization of her chapters to parallel the process by which the camps evolved chronologically and territorially: the German camps in the order of their development, followed by the camps in the countries annexed by Germany and then those in the territories conquered by the Wehrmacht. The longest, most important, and best chapters are those devoted to each of the extermination camps built by the SS in Poland.

In addition, the notes and the bibliography are arranged chapter by chapter, so that the interested reader has a ready guide to further literature available on each camp. The author does not lay claim to a definitive or exhaustive bibliography of manuscript materials and published works; she has included the most important studies that are most readily available to readers in English-speaking countries. Feig also includes descriptive citations of the most important sources of published documents on the concentration camps and the most useful bibliographical guides to further reading in the history of the Holocaust.

To complement Feig's study, there is an excellent summary in English of the organizational and administrative development of the concentration camps from the first months of the Third Reich through the point of their wartime expansion into economic and genocidal enterprises. This is the long chapter by Martin Broszat, ''The Concentration Camps, 1933–1945,'' in Helmut Krausnick and Martin Broszat, *Anatomy of the SS State*. The chapters in this collaborative work were first written as contextual and background information for the German courts hearing the trials of former SS guards at Auschwitz in the early 1960s. The text was then revised and first published in a two-volume German edition in 1965. The English translation, with an introduction by Elizabeth Wiskemann, appeared in 1968. Though now long out of print, this book, in either the German or the English edition, remains the most complete, the most important, the most incisive, the clearest, and the most understandable study of the entire collection of SS institutions that has yet appeared.

Broszat's meticulously researched, densely packed chapter on the history of the concentration camps condenses into just over one hundred pages a three-dimensional portrait of the system as the indispensable basis upon which the entire Hitlerian system of permanent police terror and repression rested. The chapter details the consolidation of SS control over the early camps as extralegal institutions under the control of an agency of the Nazi party and beyond the authority or the competence of the traditional offices and ministries of government to interfere with the activities and the mistreatment of the prisoners thrown into the camps. Broszat describes the enormous importance that the "Dachau model" had upon the development of the camp system and the crucial role of Theodor Eicke in building a network of administrative terror totally responsive to the will of Hitler and Himmler.

In like manner, the narrative proceeds carefully through the stages by which the development of "protective custody" arrests became an all-purpose, unchecked method for the SS-controlled police to incarcerate indefinitely in concentration camps anyone even remotely suspected of the slightest offense against or opposition to Hitler's regime. The serious student who reads and reflects upon this chapter cannot fail to understand how the concentration-camp system developed before World War II and why it was so admirably suited for expansion and utilization in executing the racial and ideological objectives Hitler delegated to Himmler and Heydrich for the conquered regions of Europe. One of the major areas in the history of the camps Professor Broszat's chapter does not explore involves the parallel wartime development of the temporary, exclusive-purpose extermination camps that were built in Poland and were not under the command or control of the Concentration Camp Inspectorate, but remained under the jurisdiction of the SS and the police leader in the Lublin District, SS General Odilo Globocnik, who reported directly to Himmler. This gap in our knowledge of how and where so many victims of the Holocaust perished has now been filled by the book to which the student of the subject should next turn.

This is the work by the distinguished Israeli scholar and director of the Yad Vashem Memorial and Archives, Yitzhak Arad, *Belzec, Sobibor, Treblinka: The Operation Reinhard Death Camps*. It is a seminal study, an indispensable work of reference, and a compelling and unforgettable exploration of the least known and innermost workings of the physical machinery of destruction. By relying upon three general and critical categories of source materials as no other scholar has, Arad has been able to reconstruct an exhaustive and terrifying picture of how the SS carried out the murder of millions of Polish and other European Jews at the death camps at Belzec, Sobibor, and Treblinka between the spring of 1942 and the late autumn of 1943. These sources are the contemporary documents and materials of the SS and the Nazi agencies involved, the trial records and evidence amassed in the postwar proceedings against the perpetrators, and the first-person accounts left at the time or compiled after the war by the victims and the survivors of Operation Reinhard, in particular the Jewish and Russian prisoners who helped to organize and carry out the revolts and mass escapes from Treblinka in August 1943 and from Sobibor two months later.

By drawing upon this vast array of sources, Arad creates a straightforward but gripping narrative, leading the reader through the stages of SS planning and organization of the machinery of destruction in Poland. He details the construction of the camps at Sobibor and then at Treblinka, describes the logistical and transport problems that had to be mastered to ship the victims to the two extermination centers on schedule, and reconstructs in nearly relentless detail the daily routine of unloading, stripping, shaving, and gassing the victims and plundering both their corpses and their belongings.

In a brief but powerful interim section in the middle of the volume, Arad paints compelling portraits of the main SS figures, both in the direction of Operation Reinhard and in the administration of Sobibor and Treblinka. In one of the most extraordinary and original contributions to the history of the Holocaust, the author re-creates the atmosphere and routine of daily life endured by the Jewish and Russian laborers, artisans, and body-disposal squads kept alive by the SS and supervised by the Ukrainian auxiliaries who operated the gassing machinery in both camps. Perhaps the finest chapters in this remarkable book are those describing the uprisings and attempted mass escapes from Treblinka on August 2, 1943, and from Sobibor on October 14, scarcely two months later.

In the aftermath, as the author documents extensively, the fate of many who survived the breakouts and made it to the forests or other places of temporary shelter was not the destiny of fellow sufferers given sanctuary by the oppressed Poles. Some were killed by various Polish resistance groups, others were murdered individually by local inhabitants, and still others were betrayed to the Germans. Though the uprisings failed to shut down the machinery of murder in both camps, they hardened Himmler's resolve to accelerate and achieve the complete extermination of Polish Jewry and to dismantle and destroy all traces of Sobibor and Treblinka as rapidly as possible. For Himmler, the strategic reversal of the war and the growing possibility of German collapse and defeat made the erasure of all traces of the crime as important a priority as the complete extermination of the European Jews. With the advance of the Red Army, Sobibor and Treblinka were dismantled, and considerable effort was undertaken to disguise completely the very existence of the two camps.

For those wishing to undertake more specific research in the Nazi and SS agenda of destruction, there are several types of works available in English. Many of these may be found in the notes and bibliographies of the works previously cited. Others may be located as sources and recommended readings in the books and publications cited in the notes to this chapter. In general, these works may be classified into four broad categories: the histories of individual concentration camps; the memoirs or accounts of the camps written by survivors; the memoirs and testimony of the SS perpetrators; and major published reference sources and guides for further reading and research. The remainder of this chapter will cite, as illustrations, individual works in each category that are important both as contributions to the historiography of the concentration camps and extermination centers and as introductory examples for additional reading in each category.

Among the major problems confronting English-language readers interested in the camps, one must count the scarcity, or inaccessibility in translation, of individual histories of the concentration camps. This difficulty is now receding as important books and documentary histories of specific concentration camps become available in English. In particular, there are three works that deserve specific mention and recommendation.

The work by Paul Berben, *Dachau, 1933–1945: The Official History,* published in a revised and expanded edition in London by the Norfolk Press in 1975, makes available in translation an important work first published in French in 1968.[29] Since Dachau was the model upon which the entire camp system was built after 1934, this volume is critical to any understanding of what the first permanent concentration camp was like, and how it guided the creation and development of all the other SS camps. After introductory chapters that describe the organization of the camp and its administration and the mentality of the SS guards recruited to become concentration-camp specialists, the book deals with virtually every important aspect in the history of Dachau: the prisoners' daily struggle for survival, the special persecution of clergy confined at Dachau, the medical experiments conducted on inmates, the camp's relationship to the killings in the euthanasia program, and the murders systematically conducted by the SS during the twelve years of Dachau's operation. In addition, the author deals extensively with the postwar trials of SS figures responsible for the administration of the camp and includes both a bibliography of sources and suggestions for further reading, as well as a catalog of works about the camp deposited in the archives at the Dachau museum and memorial.

In some respects, Mauthausen may have been the worst of all the concentration camps. It was built near Linz in the summer of 1938, after the *Anschluss.* Theodor Eicke and his staff from the Concentration Camp Inspectorate had selected a site on a bluff above the Danube and the village of Mauthausen and adjacent to a huge stone quarry. The prisoners at Mauthausen were to serve as slave laborers in the quarry, cutting and removing stone for shipment to the Reich, ostensibly to construct the great buildings and monuments to the Nazi Millennium at Nuremberg and Berlin. During the six years of the camp's existence, many thousands of prisoners labored in the quarry, carrying huge stones up "the Stairs of Death." Many thousands died from the brutal labor, and thousands more were murdered by the SS in the quarry.

From the first, the lethal working conditions and the extraordinarily harsh treatment to which the prisoners were subjected, even by SS standards, made confinement at Mauthausen a virtual sentence of death. These conditions were codified by Himmler and Heydrich early in 1941.[30] All the then-existing concentration camps were divided into categories determined by the presumed danger of the prisoners confined in them and the corresponding severity of the treatment they received as a formal and regulated matter of camp policy. Mauthausen was the only concentration camp designated as category III (the harshest and worst). Official SS policy assumed that no prisoner sent to Mauthausen would ever emerge from the camp alive. Those who did survive lived only by accident, by luck, by the circumstance of transfer to one of the subcamps of Mauthausen utilizing slave labor for war production, or as a result of their own individual resourcefulness and will to live.

Moreover, beginning in 1942, Mauthausen served sporadically and selectively as a killing center in the Nazi program of mass murder. Though the camp was never designated an extermination center or modified to destroy human life on the scale of the facilities in the occupied East, a small gas chamber was built to liquidate inmates too sick to work or prisoners charged with infractions of camp regulations. In addition, between the autumn of 1941 and the liberation of Mauthausen by the U.S. Army in early May 1945, uncounted thousands of Soviet prisoners of war, captured Allied airmen, political prisoners and Jews from all over Europe, Gypsies, and Catholic and Protestant clergymen were murdered outright or gradually worked to death in the stone quarry at Mauthausen.

In a work as thorough and absorbing in narrative as it is astounding for its wealth of specific factual detail, the history of Mauthausen is recorded in the kind of volume that could well serve as a model for the future histories of other camps—studies that badly need to be written. Hans Maršálek, who was a political prisoner and survivor of Mauthausen and who worked in the records office of the camp administration, began assembling information, retrieving documents, conducting interviews, and compiling the vast array of materials that made it possible for him to devote a lifetime to the writing of this extraordinary history. His work, *Die Geschichte des Konzentrationslagers Mauthausen*, published in a second, revised edition in Vienna in 1980, is available in copies in various languages in the bookstore of the Mauthausen concentration-camp memorial in Austria. The book is published under the auspices of the Austrian Committee for Mauthausen, and inquiries and orders may be directed to the committee's offices at 1020 Wien, Castellezgasse 35, or to the printer, Steindl-Druck, 1170 Wien, Beringgasse 15.

The history of the Auschwitz concentration and extermination camps is now also available in a single-volume English edition, a collaborative work produced by a group of Polish historians. Jozef Buszko et al., *Auschwitz: Nazi Extermination Camp*, published in a second, enlarged edition by Interpress Publishers in Warsaw, Poland, in 1985, condenses in an admirable summary the history of Auschwitz through the experience of those who were its victims.

The volume is divided into five general sections that deal with the chronology of Auschwitz's development, a profile of the prisoner population and their daily routine of suffering, an extensive description of the methods of extermination, an analysis of the inmate resistance movement that grew during the war, and a description of the liberation of the camps and the postwar prosecution of many of the SS principals responsible for the administration and operation of Auschwitz. Unfortunately, the bibliography consists almost entirely of books and documentary collections in Polish, so the volume should be consulted as an introduction to further reading in the substantial Auschwitz literature available in English.[31]

Among all the works published over the last forty years, some of the most compelling are the memoirs of the victims. The survivor literature is indispensable for anyone seriously interested in the Holocaust. Since the end of the war, a growing collection of personal accounts has become a veritable autobiographical encyclopedia, documenting in individual experiences a staggering record of persecution and inhumanity. Recorded by prisoners of virtually every nationality, these accounts offer invaluable insights into the operation of nearly every camp in the gigantic SS system of slave labor and mass murder. Three examples must serve as illustrations of this immensely important body of historical work.

Among the earliest of the survivor accounts to attract worldwide attention and establish itself as an initial classic in the field is the remarkable memoir of Eugen Kogon, *The Theory and Practice of Hell: The German Concentration Camps and the System Behind Them*. First published in English in 1950 and subsequently reissued in paperback editions beginning in 1958, Kogon's account of his six years as a prisoner at Buchenwald remains one of the most important works ever written in survivor literature. Forty years after its original publication, it still contains one of the most accurate and thorough descriptions of the organization, physical structure, and methods of SS administration and operation in any concentration camp. It is also a chilling record of camp life, unsurpassed in the authenticity of its re-creation of the atmosphere of persecution in Buchenwald. Not least important, it is extraordinary for the insights the author developed, from the restricted perspective of his confinement in one camp, of the organizational structure and purposes of the entire SS concentration-camp system. Eugen Kogon's memoir was a pioneering work, a study that exerted a direct influence upon virtually all subsequent historical inquiry into the concentration camps.

In addition to a close reading of *The Theory and Practice of Hell*, anyone seriously interested in the experiences and the will to survive among inmates in the concentration camps should consult Rudolf Vrba, *I Cannot Forgive*. First published in 1964 and reprinted in paperback in 1986, Vrba's account of his terrible odyssey through Majdanek and Auschwitz and of his incredible escape from Auschwitz-Birkenau in April 1944 ranks, in my estimation, among the greatest of the works in the literature of World War II and the Holocaust. Without any pretension, sense of self-importance, or personal bitterness, Vrba recounts his experiences in a narrative style as absorbing as it is vivid and filled with the details of horror that were commonplace to Jews deported to the death camps in Poland. Determined both to survive and remember, Rudolf Vrba transformed his consciousness into a living archive in which he preserved the most astonishing range of documentary memory any survivor managed to compile.

Confined first to Auschwitz I, then transferred to Birkenau, Vrba observed and evaluated every aspect in the operation of the giant complex, looking for weaknesses in the SS system that might improve the odds for escape. His determination to escape was as powerful as his capacity to commit to memory all he saw. The central purpose animating both his will to survive and his obsession to flee was the overpowering, self-imposed obligation to somehow warn the Jews still left in Europe, and the rest of the world, what Auschwitz was and what awaited all those deported there.

Working in Birkenau as a member of the Canada Commando, the special detail of Jewish prisoners assigned to meet the arriving trainloads of Jewish victims from all over Europe, Vrba disciplined himself to remember the dates and origins of the arriving transports in order to preserve some record of the fate of the thousands of victims who were gassed immediately upon arrival. He compiled his own statistics in an effort to keep count of the staggering numbers consumed by the machinery of industrialized murder at Auschwitz. He also became a key figure in the prisoners' underground organization in the camp.

When he learned in the early spring of 1944 that Birkenau was to be made ready to exterminate the 800,000 Jews of Hungary, the last important community remaining in Nazi-dominated Europe, he completed his long-developed plans to escape and bear witness to warn the Jewish leaders in Hungary. As the world now knows, he succeeded in the attempt, but failed in the endeavor.

The pages and chapters in *I Cannot Forgive* that recount Vrba's ingenious breakout from Birkenau, his incredible skill and luck in surviving on the run, with the entire SS and police apparatus of Nazi-occupied Europe looking for him, his return to Slovakia, and his extraordinary achievement in writing the report that would fail to convince the Hungarian Jews and President Roosevelt of their impending fate reduce to focus, in the experience of a single survivor, the great tragedy of lack of belief on the part of the then-contemporary world that still remained outside the Holocaust. The even greater tragedy, of course, was and is that in all of the postwar investigations of Auschwitz, in all the accumulation of evidence in the trials of its SS masters, and in all of the historical research and writing about Auschwitz in the four decades that followed, virtually every detail of Rudolf Vrba's original and staggering accumulation of memory in detail has remained unchallenged and uncorrected. He succeeded in recording and relating at the time what history has belatedly come to verify a thousand times over.

In addition, there is a more recent first-person compilation by a survivor of Auschwitz who has collected and edited the recollections of a large number of her fellow survivors from the largest of the Nazi death camps. Lore Shelley's *Secretaries of Death*, published in 1986 by the Shengold Publishers in New York, represents, in one sense, a new and vitally important genre of survivor literature. This is a work that assembles individual testimony and recollection to produce and present a collective view of an individual and specific area of SS administration at Auschwitz-Birkenau. Lore Shelley was a German-Jewish teenager confined to a labor camp at the time she was deported to Auschwitz in April 1943. She was assigned to the staff of prisoner clerks and secretaries in the Political Section of the SS Camp Administration of Auschwitz. This was the local Gestapo office in the camp administration. One of the main subdivisions of the Political Section was the camp registry, the SS office responsible for compiling and maintaining all of the clerical records of the camp and the individual files on all the prisoners who had been processed, tattooed, and recorded as inmates of Auschwitz.

All of the clerical work for the Political Section and for the camp registry was performed by a group of approximately sixty young Jewish women inmates, specially selected by the SS because of their secretarial skills and their knowledge of German. Shelley and the women whose accounts are included in her book all worked in this special Jewish detail during the period when Auschwitz was strained beyond full capacity as an extermination center.

In the system of record keeping devised by the SS for the concentration camps and adapted to suit the individual requirements at Auschwitz, the Jewish clerks and secretaries had to maintain and keep current two separate sets of inmate records—one set for the living and one set for the dead. Because this gave them direct access to and extensive knowledge about all of the methods of individual killing and of mass murder in Auschwitz and Auschwitz-Birkenau, the presumed certainty of death hung constantly over these young women. The commonly understood nickname they carried in Auschwitz was that of the *Himmelfahrts-kommando* (the heaven-bound squad). Like the members of the Jewish *Sonder-kommando* (special command) who worked to remove the bodies from the huge gas chambers and burn them in the giant crematoria, and who were periodically murdered by the SS and replaced by whole new gangs of Jewish prisoners, the young women who served as clerks and secretaries for the Gestapo and the camp registry were marked for liquidation because they had seen and written and recorded too much.

Though many died of disease, and others were murdered by the SS, a large number survived. In Shelley's volume, their experiences working in the camp registry and the memories they preserved offer the reader a revealing insight into the methods of administration and procedure, bureaucratic record keeping, and everyday office routine in the largest and best-organized institution of extermination in the Holocaust.

Finally, one example of memoir literature that should be studied as seriously and as carefully as any of the works in the literature of the survivors is the terrible document left by the man who built and ran Auschwitz, SS Lieutenant-Colonel Rudolf Hoess. A career SS officer in the prewar SS Death's Head units in the German concentration camps, Hoess was promoted to the assignment of building the original Auschwitz concentration camp in the spring of 1940. With the exception of brief periods late in the war, when he served as a senior staff officer in the Concentration Camp Inspectorate division of the SS Main Economic and Administrative Office in Berlin, Hoess served as the commandant of Auschwitz until its liberation by the Red Army.

Hoess's autobiography, *Commandant of Auschwitz*, was first published in Polish in 1951, subsequently in a German-language edition in 1958, and then in English translation in 1959. It has been through various editions and additional translations since it first appeared. The English edition cited here is the paperback issue released in 1960 by the World Publishing Company. In many respects, this version in English remains preferable to the earlier German translation in that it includes additional material and documentation in the form of appendixes that were not incorporated in earlier versions. These include, most importantly, Hoess's personal recollections, in the form of chapters or essays, on the Final Solution to the Jewish Question, his wartime meetings with Himmler on matters relating to Auschwitz and the Final Solution, and his biographical sketches of major figures in the SS directly involved in the extermination of the European Jews, men with whom he dealt directly and extensively: Adolf Eichmann, Heinrich Müller, Oswald Pohl, Gerhard Maurer, Odilo Globocnik, Theodor Eicke, and Richard Glücks.

*Commandant of Auschwitz* is a document of unique historical importance. What it reveals of the mind and methodology of those who ran Auschwitz, those who developed the earlier concentration-camp system, and the SS personnel who came to Auschwitz is a perspective simply unavailable in the work of anyone else who survived the war. At some point in any and every serious reader's attempt to understand Auschwitz and to comprehend the Holocaust, one simply must come to terms with the autobiography of Rudolf Hoess.

All of the works described in this chapter and those cited in the notes are different examples of literature relating to the history of the concentration camps and the extermination centers of the Third Reich. By no means do they represent a definitive or even authoritative list of suggested beginning readings in this vast and vastly complex subject. They are intended to serve only as a proven and reliable weather vane, pointing the general reader and the interested student in the direction that the prevailing winds of historical study and the best currents stirred by those winds have moved in opening a field of study that is now really only beginning. The appearance of the best and most reliable historical monographs about the concentration camps and extermination centers and the SS system to which they belonged lies ahead of us rather than behind us. In considering the works cited and described in this chapter, the reader may be fully reassured only on one point: the study and comprehension of these works represent sound preparation for engaging in the larger and more important studies yet to come.

## FURTHER RECOMMENDED READING

Among the many major reference sources and guides for further reading and study, one of the most readily available is Harry James Cargas, *The Holocaust:*

*An Annotated Bibliography* (New York: American Library Association, 1985).
The best-organized and most complete multivolume synthesis of scholarly articles
on the Holocaust is Michael R. Marrus's nine-volume collection titled *The Nazi
Holocaust: Historical Articles on the Destruction of European Jews* (Westport,
Conn.: Meckler, 1989). The published records of scholarly conferences can also
be valuable for the general reader interested in studying how the exchanges of
views among leading scholars shape the development of research and writing.
See especially *The Nazi Concentration Camps: Structure and Aims, the Image
of the Prisoner, the Jews in the Camps*, Proceedings of the Fourth Yad Vashem
International Historical Conference, January 1980 (Jerusalem: Yad Vashem,
1984). In addition, the reader should consult regularly the volumes in the *Simon
Wiesenthal Center Annual* (Los Angeles: Philosophical Library). These annual
volumes, edited by Henry Friedlander and Sybil Milton, began appearing in
1984 and are the first serial publications devoted exclusively to the wide dissemination of scholarly research articles, review essays, and other important
materials on the Holocaust prepared by leading figures in the field.

Of the scholarly single-volume histories of the Holocaust that deal with all
aspects of the subject as well as the role of the concentration camps in preparing
both the SS personnel and the Nazi infrastructure of mass murder, two texts
(Nora Levin, *The Holocaust: The Destruction of European Jewry, 1933–1945*
[New York: Crowell, 1968], and Leni Yahil, *The Holocaust: The Fate of European Jewry, 1932–1945* [New York: Oxford University Press, 1990]) can also
be recommended for the beginning student. For an excellent summary of the
history of the concentration camps and the historical literature devoted to them
at the time, see Henry Friedlander, "The Nazi Concentration Camps," in Michael D. Ryan, ed., *Human Responses to the Holocaust: Perpetrators and Victims, Bystanders and Resisters* (New York and Toronto: Edwin Mellen Press,
1981).

For additional insights into the prewar history of the SS and the development
of the various units that would become the armed SS (the Waffen-SS) in 1940,
including the SS Death's Head units that were responsible for guarding the prewar
concentration camps, see also Charles W. Sydnor, Jr., *Soldiers of Destruction:
The SS Death's Head Division, 1933–1945*, 2d ed. rev. (Princeton, N.J.: Prince-
ton University Press, 1990); Heinz Höhne, *The Order of the Death's Head: The
Story of Hitler's SS* (New York: Ballantine Books, 1971); George Stein, *The
Waffen SS: Hitler's Elite Guard at War, 1939–1945* (Ithaca, N.Y.: Cornell
University Press, 1966); Bernd Wegner, *Hitlers Politische Soldaten: Die Waffen
SS, 1933–1945* (Paderborn: Ferdinand Schöningh Verlag, 1982); and Shlomo
Aronson, *Reinhard Heydrich und die Frühgeschichte von Gestapo und SD* (Stuttgart: Deutsche Verlags-Anstalt, 1971). The standard work on the subject of the
special SS murder commandos, the units that massacred hundreds of thousands
of Jews throughout Eastern Europe and the Soviet Union, is Helmut Krausnick
and Hans-Heinrich Wilhelm, *Die Truppe des Weltanschauungskrieges: Die Einsatzgruppen der Sicherheitapolizei und des SD, 1938–1942* (Stuttgart: Deutsche

Verlags-Anstalt, 1981), which, as of this writing, has not been translated into English.

For a further examination of the process by which the SS transformed the policies of destruction from a geographically dispersed program of open-air massacres into a centralized phenomenon of continental mass murder in tightly controlled extermination centers, the reader should consult Raul Hilberg, *The Destruction of the European Jews,* 3 vols. (New York: Holmes and Meier, 1985); Gerhard Hirschfeld, ed., *The Policies of Genocide: Jews and Soviet Prisoners of War in Nazi Germany* (London: Allen and Unwin, 1986); Gerald Fleming, *Hitler and the Final Solution* (Berkeley: University of California Press, 1982); and the highly original, extremely valuable study of Ruth-Bettina Birn, *Die Höheren SS- und Polizeiführer: Himmlers Vertreter im Reich und in den besetzten Gebieten* (Düsseldorf: Droste Verlag, 1986).

On the experience of the Jewish communities trapped in the ghettos of Poland, struggling to survive until confronted with the inevitability of deportation, the following books are recommended: Lucjan Dobroszycki, ed., *The Chronicle of the Lodz Ghetto, 1941–1944* (New Haven, Conn.: Yale University Press, 1984); Alan Adelson and Robert Lapides, eds., *Lodz Ghetto: Inside a Community Under Siege* (New York: Viking Press, 1989); and Yitzhak Arad, *Ghetto in Flames: The Struggle and Destruction of the Jews in Vilna in the Holocaust* (Jerusalem: Yad Vashem, 1980).

Other volumes supply a wide range of insights into the operations of the concentration camps. Tom Segev, *Soldiers of Evil: The Commandants of the Nazi Concentration Camps* (New York: McGraw-Hill, 1987), is an important addition to the literature, offering a collection of biographical portraits of SS camp commandants whose careers were molded by Theodor Eicke in the prewar concentration-camp system. A number of excellent books have appeared in English enlarging upon the theme of the perversion of medicine by the SS and the Nazis. The best of these include Michael H. Kater, *Doctors Under Hitler* (Chapel Hill: University of North Carolina Press, 1989); Robert Jay Lifton, *The Nazi Doctors: Medical Killing and the Psychology of Genocide* (New York: Basic Books, 1976); Benno Müller-Hill, *Murderous Science: Elimination by Scientific Selection of Jews, Gypsies, and Others, Germany, 1933–1945* (New York: Oxford University Press, 1988); and Robert N. Proctor, *Racial Hygiene* (Cambridge, Mass.: Harvard University Press, 1988).

The cruelties to which women prisoners in concentration camps were subjected were, in many respects, even worse than the barbaric treatment inflicted upon men and even boys who were inmates. For a scholarly and authoritative treatment of this subject, as well as a superb historical summary of the Nazi policy in developing SS-run concentration camps for women, the reader should consult Sybil Milton, ''Women and the Holocaust: The Case of German and German-Jewish Women,'' in Renate Bridenthal, Atina Grossmann, and Marion Kaplan, eds., *When Biology Became Destiny: Women in Weimar and Nazi Germany* (New York: Monthly Review Press, 1984), pp. 297–333. See also the personal account of French resistance fighter Germaine Tillion, *Ravensbrück* (Garden City, N. Y.: Anchor Books, 1975).

## NOTES

1. This important point is graphically illustrated in the remarkable book by Gitta Sereny, *Into That Darkness: From Mercy Killing to Mass Murder* (London: Andre Deutsch, 1974). As a journalist, Gitta Sereny covered the West German trial of Franz Stangl, the SS commandant of the Treblinka extermination camp. She interviewed Stangl extensively, conducted substantial additional research, and created an extraordinary portrait of both Stangl and Treblinka.

2. Charles W. Sydnor, Jr., *Soldiers of Destruction: The SS Death's Head Division, 1933–1945,* 2d ed. rev. (Princeton, N.J.: Princeton University Press, 1990), especially pp. 8–24; Heinz Höhne, *The Order of the Death's Head: The Story of Hitler's SS* (New York: Ballantine Books, 1971), especially pp. 87–104, 225–31; and Martin Broszat, "The Concentration Camps, 1933–1945," in Helmut Krausnick and Martin Broszat, *Anatomy of the SS State* (New York: Walker, 1968), especially pp. 400–28.

3. See especially Sydnor, *Soldiers of Destruction*, pp. 7–36; and Krausnick and Broszat, *Anatomy of the SS State*.

4. An excellent summary of all the developments culminating in Hitler's appointment as chancellor and the subsequent steps taken by the Nazis to consolidate all power in a one-party dictatorship in an atmosphere of national emergency may be found in Karl-Dietrich Bracher, *The German Dictatorship: The Origins, Structure, and Effects of National Socialism* (New York: Praeger, 1970), especially pp. 199–228. The text of the Hindenburg decree, in translation, with an accompanying explanation of the circumstances that led to its drafting, may be found in Jeremy Noakes and Geoffrey Pridham, eds., *Documents on Nazism, 1919–1945* (New York: Viking Press, 1974), pp. 173–74.

5. The events that transpired between the promulgation of the Hindenburg decree on February 28, 1933, and the preparation and passage of the Enabling Act by the Reichstag on March 23, 1933, as well as a text of the Enabling Act itself, are in Noakes and Pridham, *Documents on Nazism*, pp. 175–95.

6. National Archives of the United States, Microcopy T-580: Records of the SS Wirtschafts- und Verwaltungshauptamt (the SS Economic and Administrative Main Office), Roll 49/Ordner 271, Reich Minister of the Interior, "Schutzhaft," of April 12, 1934.

7. National Archives, Microfilm Record Group T-580, Roll 49/Ordner 271, administrative circular of the Bavarian Political Police office, "Compilation of the *Schutzhaft* Decrees Currently in Force in Bavaria," dated August 1, 1936. See also the analysis of the development and use of *Schutzhaft* in relation to the development of the concentration camps in Broszat, "Concentration Camps," pp. 400–28.

8. National Archives, T-580, Roll 49/Ordner 271, Reich Minister of the Interior, "Protective Custody," dated January 25, 1938, and signed by Wilhelm Frick, the Nazi Reich minister of the interior.

9. Sydnor, *Soldiers of Destruction*, pp. 35–39; and Shlomo Aronson, *Reinhard Heydrich und die Frühgeschichte von Gestapo und SD* (Stuttgart: Deutsche Verlags-Anstalt, 1971).

10. Sydnor, *Soldiers of Destruction*, especially pp. 17–36.

11. The best treatment of the subject remains Aronson, *Reinhard Heydrich und die Frühgeschichte von Gestapo und SD*.

12. With varying degrees of emphasis, this is a general theme or conclusion found in the scholarly literature devoted to the Holocaust and the concentration camps. The best discussions are in Raul Hilberg, *The Destruction of the European Jews*, and Krausnick and Broszat, *Anatomy of the SS State*.

13. National Archives, Record Group 238, Nuremberg Document 778-PS and Nuremberg Document 1216-PS. These two documents, both promulgated by Theodor Eicke as commandant of Dachau on October 1, 1933, contain the disciplinary and punishment regulations for the prisoners in the concentration camp and the code of conduct and service regulations for the SS guards responsible for dealing with the prisoners. See also Sydnor, *Soldiers of Destruction*, especially pp. 26–30. The documents and records of persecution and destruction kept by the Nazi and SS perpetrators were assembled and evaluated by the American and Allied prosecution teams preparing for the trials of the major Nazi war criminals at Nuremberg in 1946. These documents, the trial records themselves, and a wealth of related material have been preserved, reproduced, and published in varying format and circumstances during the last forty-five years. The Nuremberg records and the Nuremberg documents, as they are generally known, are invaluable as primary source materials for the history of the concentration camps and extermination centers and the history of the Holocaust. The interested reader should consult especially the valuable reference compendium published jointly by Yad Vashem in Jerusalem and YIVO (the Institute for Jewish Research) in New York, *The Holocaust: The Nuremberg Evidence: Part One, Documents* (Jerusalem: Yad Vashem, 1976).

14. The inscriptions and the main gates still remain intact as part of the permanent memorials at Dachau in Germany and at the Auschwitz I camp in Poland.

15. Archive of the October Revolution, Moscow, Collection of Secret Publications of the Reich Security Main Office (RSHA), "Service Manual for Concentration Camps" (camp regulations), a copy of the bound publication of the RSHA for 1941, carrying the imprint of Himmler's signature. In addition, the National Archives, Record Group 242, Microcopy T-175, Roll 218, frames 2726563–2726570, is a document of the SS WVHA, Amtsgruppe D (the Concentration Camp Inspectorate), dated July 27, 1943, and entitled "Guarding the Prisoners." This is an administrative circular addressed to all the commandants in all the concentration camps, including Auschwitz and Majdanek, which was intended to serve as both a training guide and an indoctrination source for regulating the SS guards' behavior toward and treatment of the prisoners in the concentration camps.

16. The atmosphere of unrelenting cruelty that was the daily experience of the prisoners in all concentration camps is a universal theme throughout the literature written by the camp survivors who endured it. Eicke's role in establishing and in successfully imposing the SS ethos of mistreatment upon the SS camp guards and the entire concentration-camp system is verified by no less than one of his most accomplished experts, Rudolf Hoess, the commandant of Auschwitz. See, in particular, Rudolf Hoess, *Commandant of Auschwitz*, paperback ed. (New York: World Publishing, 1960), especially pp. 223–31, for Hoess's biographical profile of Eicke as inspector of concentration camps. Hoess's extraordinary memoir is described in much greater detail later in this chapter.

17. Sydnor, *Soldiers of Destruction*, especially chap. 1. See also Charles W. Sydnor, "The Selling of Adolf Hitler," *Central European History* 12, no. 2 (June 1979): 169–99, for examples of Eicke's success in operating the prewar camps without interference

from traditional German state authorities or agencies, especially in matters relating to the treatment of concentration-camp inmates.

18. Sydnor, *Soldiers of Destruction*, chap. 1.

19. Hoess, *Commandant of Auschwitz*.

20. See Sydnor, *Soldiers of Destruction*, especially pp. 326–30, 342, for a discussion of the service of Hartjenstein and Hoppe at Auschwitz, Natzweiler, and Stutthof.

21. For the concentration-camp careers of Arthur Rödel and Karl Koch, see Tom Segev, *Soldiers of Evil: The Commandants of the Nazi Concentration Camps* (New York: McGraw-Hill, 1987), especially pp. 132–38 and 142–50.

22. See Segev, *Soldiers of Evil*, pp. 115–16, 123, 185–88, for a profile of Max Kögel. See also Germaine Tillion, *Ravensbrück* (Garden City, N.Y.: Anchor Books, 1975), pp. 55–56, for an account of Kögel's personal cruelty to women prisoners at Ravensbrück.

23. Segev, *Soldiers of Evil*, pp. 10–54, is a detailed and extremely interesting biographical sketch of Josef Kramer and his service in the concentration-camp system.

24. Segev, *Soldiers of Evil*. Kramer was tried by the British after the war, convicted of murder in the deaths of thousands of inmates at Bergen-Belsen, and hanged. The published trial records and proceedings are in Raymond Phillips, ed., *The Trial of Joseph Kramer and 44 Others* (London: H.M. Stationery Office, 1949). Kramer's trial record is also available in English in *Nazi Conspiracy and Aggression*, 8 vols. (Nuremberg: International Military Tribunal, 1949). This is the published edition of war-crimes trial records and related materials commonly known as the "Red Series" of Nuremberg documents. Further information on Kramer's tenure at Bergen-Belsen is available in German in Eberhard Kolb, *Bergen-Belsen: Geschichte des "Aufenthaltslagers," 1943–1945* (Hannover: Verlag für Literatur und Zeitgeschehen, 1962).

25. The photographic evidence compiled and left by the SS perpetrators is also invaluable visual and physical evidence of how the process of destruction worked. See especially *The Auschwitz Album: A Book Based upon an Album Discovered by a Concentration Camp Survivor, Lili Meier* (New York: Random House, 1981). This remarkable compilation of photographs taken by one or more SS photographers documents visually the arrival and processing of a large transport of Hungarian Jews at Auschwitz-Birkenau in early May 1944. The photographs detail each and every step and stage of the preparations for their own destruction through which the unsuspecting victims moved. In addition, there are surviving eyewitness reports, written at the time, by an official SS visitor to Auschwitz-Birkenau and by two young Slovak Jews who escaped from the extermination camp in April 1944. SS Major Alfred Franke-Gricksch, the adjutant to the chief of the SS Personnel Office, was given a complete tour of the Birkenau killing center in May 1943 and was shown the entire process by which the victims in arriving transports were either selected for slave labor and registered into the camp or chosen for gassing and murdered shortly after arrival. Franke-Gricksch was so impressed by what he observed that he wrote a detailed memorandum, entitled "Resettlement Action of the Jews," and submitted it to his boss. An English translation of the document and a thorough description of the SS major's visit to Auschwitz are in Gerald Fleming, *Hitler and the Final Solution* (Berkeley: University of California Press, 1982), chap. 17, pp. 140–56.

An even more extraordinary contemporary document is the report written by Rudolf Vrba and Alfred Wetzler after their successful escape from Auschwitz-Birkenau and return to hiding with the Slovak underground. The Vrba-Wetzler report was so thorough and highly detailed, even to an estimate of the numbers of victims murdered at Auschwitz, as to provoke consternation and disbelief among the Allied governments when it was smuggled out through the American legation in Bern, Switzerland, to London and Washington in the spring of 1944. A complete English translation of the Vrba-Wetzler report was entered into evidence at the postwar trials at Nuremberg and survives among the Nuremberg records. See National Archives, Record Group 238, Nuremberg Document no. L-22, "The Extermination Camps of Auschwitz and Birkenau in Upper Silesia."

26. See the previously cited articles and book chapters by Henry Friedlander and Sybil Milton.

27. Michael R. Marrus, *The Holocaust in History* (Hanover, N.H., and London: University Press of New England, 1987).

28. The interested reader may also wish to consult Hilberg's other publications, in particular, Raul Hilberg, ed., *Documents of Destruction: Germany and Jewry, 1933–1945* (Chicago: Quadrangle Books, 1971); and *Sonderzuege nach Auschwitz* (Frankfurt am Main: Dumjahn, 1986).

29. Berben's history of Dachau was first published in 1968 in Belgium with the title, *Histoire du camp de concentration de Dachau, 1933–1945* (Brussels: Presses de l'Imprimerie Mondiale Pierre Wellens). The visitor who travels to the permanent Dachau museum and memorial on the site of the original camp may also obtain an English-language edition of the museum and memorial's official history of the camp, *Concentration Camp Dachau, 1933–1945*, published by the International Committee for Dachau. This is a photographic and documentary history of the camp, containing extensive records, pictures, drawings by prisoners, and other documents relating to the history of Dachau.

30. National Archives, Record Group 238, Nuremberg Document no. 1063-A-PS, Records of the Chief of the Security Police and the SD, circular to all offices of the RSHA, the Inspectorate of Concentration Camps, all Concentration Camp Commandants, "Einstufung der Konzentrationslager," dated January 2, 1941, and signed by Heydrich. An extensive, firsthand description of the site selection for Mauthausen and of the original development and enlargement of the camp, recorded by one of the SS construction engineers involved, is the sworn statement of SS Major Hubert Karl, in National Archives, Record Group 238, Nuremberg Document Number no. 4007, dated June 21, 1947.

31. Marrus, *Holocaust in History*, p. 6, notes, in citing the reference work by Vera Laska, *Nazism, Resistance, and Holocaust in World War II* (Metuchen, N.J.: Scarecrow Press, 1985), that the author lists over ten thousand publications, in many languages, on the subject of Auschwitz alone.

## SELECT BIBLIOGRAPHY

Adelson, Alan, and Robert Lapides, eds. *Lodz Ghetto: Inside a Community Under Siege.* New York: Viking Press, 1989.

Arad, Yitzhak. *Belzec, Sobibor, Treblinka: The Operation Reinhard Death Camps.* Bloomington: Indiana University Press, 1987.

————. *Ghetto in Flames: The Struggle and Destruction of the Jews in Vilna in the Holocaust.* Jerusalem: Yad Vashem, 1980.

Aronson, Shlomo. *Reinhard Heydrich und die Frühgeschichte von Gestapo und SD.* Stuttgart: Deutsche Verlags Anstalt, 1971.

*The Auschwitz Album: A Book Based upon an Album Discovered by a Concentration Camp Survivor, Lili Meier.* New York: Random House, 1981.

Berben, Paul. *Dachau, 1933–1945: The Official History.* London: Norfolk Press, 1975.

Birn, Ruth-Bettina. *Die Höheren SS und Polizeiführer: Himmlers Vertreter im Reich und in die besetzten Gebieten.* Düsseldorf: Droste Verlag, 1986.

Bridenthal, Renate, Atina Grossmann, and Marion Kaplan, eds. *When Biology Became Destiny: Women in Weimar and Nazi Germany.* New York: Monthly Review Press, 1984.

Buszko, Jozef, et al. *Auschwitz: Nazi Extermination Camp.* Warsaw: Interpress Publishers, 1985.

Dobroszycki, Lucjan, ed. *The Chronicle of the Lodz Ghetto, 1941–1944.* New Haven, Conn.: Yale University Press, 1984.

Feig, Konnilyn G. *Hitler's Death Camps: The Sanity of Madness.* New York: Holmes and Meier, 1981.

Fleming, Gerald. *Hitler and the Final Solution.* Berkeley: University of California Press, 1982.

Hilberg, Raul. *The Destruction of the European Jews.* 3 vols. New York: Holmes and Meier, 1985.

Hirschfeld, Gerhard, ed. *The Policies of Genocide: Jews and Soviet Prisoners of War in Nazi Germany.* London: Allen and Unwin, 1986.

Hoess, Rudolf. *Commandant of Auschwitz.* New York: World Publishing, 1960.

Höhne, Heinz. *The Order of the Death's Head: The Story of Hitler's SS.* New York: Ballantine Books, 1971.

Kater, Michael H. *Doctors Under Hitler.* Chapel Hill: University of North Carolina Press, 1989.

Kogon, Eugen. *The Theory and Practice of Hell: The German Concentration Camps and the System Behind Them.* New York: Farrar, Straus, Giroux, 1950.

Kolb, Eberhard. *Bergen-Belsen: Geschichte des "Aufenthaltslagers," 1943–1945.* Hannover: Verlag für Literatur und Zeitgeschehen, 1962.

Krausnick, Helmut, and Martin Broszat. *Anatomy of the SS State.* Cambridge, England: William Collins Sons, 1968.

Krausnick, Helmut, and Hans-Heinrich Wilhelm. *Die Truppe des Weltanschauungskrieges: Die Einsatzgruppen der Sicherheitapolizei und des SD, 1938–1942.* Stuttgart: Deutsche Verlags-Anstalt, 1981.

Levin, Nora. *The Holocaust: The Destruction of European Jewry, 1933–1945.* New York: Crowell, 1968.

Lifton, Robert Jay. *The Nazi Doctors: Medical Killing and the Psychology of Genocide.* New York: Basic Books, 1976.

Marrus, Michael R. *The Holocaust in History.* Hanover, N.H., and London: University Press of New England, 1987.

Maršálek, Hans. *Die Geschichte des Konzentrationslagers Mauthausen.* Vienna: Austrian Committee for Mauthausen, 1980.

Müller-Hill, Benno. *Murderous Science: Elimination by Scientific Selection of Jews, Gypsies, and Others, Germany, 1933–1945.* New York: Oxford University Press, 1988.

*The Nazi Concentration Camps: Structure and Aims, the Image of the Prisoner, the Jews in the Camps.* Proceedings of the Fourth Yad Vashem International Historical Conference, January 1980. Jerusalem: Yad Vashem, 1984.

Phillips, Raymond, ed. *The Trial of Joseph Kramer and 44 Others.* London: H.M. Stationery Office, 1949.

Proctor, Robert N. *Racial Hygiene.* Cambridge, Mass.: Harvard University Press, 1988.

Ryan, Michael D., ed. *Human Responses to the Holocaust: Perpetrators and Victims, Bystanders and Resisters.* New York and Toronto: Edwin Mellen Press, 1981.

Segev, Tom. *Soldiers of Evil: The Commandants of the Nazi Concentration Camps*. New York: McGraw-Hill, 1987.

Sereny, Gitta. *Into That Darkness: From Mercy Killing to Mass Murder*. London: Andre Deutsch, 1974.

Stein, George H. *The Waffen SS: Hitler's Elite Guard at War, 1939–1945*. Ithaca, N.Y.: Cornell University Press, 1966.

Sydnor, Charles W., Jr. *Soldiers of Destruction: The SS Death's Head Division, 1933–1945*. 2d. ed. rev. Princeton, N.J.: Princeton University Press, 1990.

Tillion, Germaine. *Ravensbrück*. Garden City, N.Y.: Anchor Books, 1975.

Vrba, Rudolf, and Alan Bestic. *I Cannot Forgive*. New York: Grove Press reprint, 1968.

Wegner, Bernd. *Hitlers Politische Soldaten: Die Waffen SS, 1933–1945*. Paderborn: Ferdinand Schöningh Verlag, 1982.

Yahil, Leni. *The Holocaust: The Fate of European Jewry, 1932–1945*. New York: Oxford University Press, 1990.

# Chapter 5

# Asking Unanswerable Questions: A Bibliographic Study of Post-Holocaust Jewish Philosophies

*Steven H. Adams*

When one undertakes the task of composing a bibliography of post-Holocaust Jewish philosophies, he or she is faced with many questions. What is Jewish philosophy as opposed to theology? Are these two disciplines mutually exclusive, or can they overlap? What makes philosophy Jewish? Is all philosophy written by Jews "Jewish"? Does it have to be written by a Jew? Having answered these questions, how does one decide which "Jewish philosophies" are relevant as a response to the Holocaust? Must post-Holocaust philosophers address the issue directly to be included in this category, or can their reactions to the Holocaust be less obvious? Finally, is the intent of the study to be all-inclusive with little depth, or is it to be a selective study considering certain works in depth?

Addressing the last question first was my primary challenge. While trying not to be overly judgmental as far as what are and what are not legitimate philosophies, I have found it necessary to limit the total number of works analyzed. Once a question, issue, or perspective has been presented by one philosopher, I have refrained from commenting on its existence in another source unless such mention would serve some worthwhile purpose. The basis of this chapter is well-known works, such as those of Rubenstein, Fackenheim, Wiesel, and Berkovits. A number of lesser-known works are mentioned in brief. All of the sources that were consulted as research are included in the Select Bibliography for the benefit of anyone wishing to pursue this topic in greater depth.

Any work that is tied to a historical event requires the setting of a context. As one who was born a decade after the end of World War II, I lack the firsthand memory of the events that is shared by those whose works are most prominent. Rather than view this fact as a liability, I consider it an asset. From the experience of the ancient Israelites in the wilderness of Sinai we learn how some distance from a historical event can be helpful. They wandered for forty years after the Exodus and their emancipation before they could truly move beyond their experience of slavery. Forty years often seems to signal an important stage in terms of our ability to view the past with some degree of emotional detachment (although no sensitive human being could help but be emotionally shaken by a horror as great as this). It is from that type of "distance" that I approach this topic.

My chronological distance from the events is part of the objectivity I can bring to this work. Nevertheless, recent events of world significance in the Middle East have displayed the importance of having good firsthand knowledge of the past. During the Persian Gulf War in early 1991 many individuals attempted to distort the history of the Israeli-Arab conflict. Dissemination of firsthand accounts was the most effective response to that situation. Yet the views expressed by the college students with whom I spoke, students born mostly after 1967, represent a different reality, one more common among young people today. Since such views, separated from the emotions many Jews felt in June 1967, are more likely to be dominant in the future, we must take them into account as we approach that topic. Similarly, I hope to provide an informed reaction to the writings of post-Holocaust Jewish philosophers, but also one that represents the perspective of my own generation.

To begin this study I have chosen to highlight a contrast. What all post-Holocaust philosophers share is fate. Living after the horrible fact has forced all to address certain realities. In certain ways the views of almost all post-Holocaust Jewish philosophers contrast sharply with the universalism and optimism expressed by Franz Rosenzweig.

Born in Germany in 1886, Franz Rosenzweig experienced the life of enlightened Western Europe. The idea of a natural religion that by reason would have universal acceptance and appeal had an impact on Rosenzweig. His works were composed mostly during the first two decades of the twentieth century, and he died in 1929. For all intents and purposes he was not influenced by the evil cloud that was approaching his homeland. Living before the storm of Nazism had a chance to affect his ideas, Rosenzweig expressed great hopes for human unity and interreligious understanding. Addressing the issue of "truth" in *The Star of Redemption*, Rosenzweig notes the incomplete understanding possessed by mortal (i.e., finite) individuals and even groups. Only through the unity of humanity and through experiences that represent such unity can we together obtain truth. Rosenzweig actually seemed to believe that such unity of the human family was possible.

The reality of the Holocaust challenges such hopes for the future. The questions of evil, posed on a greater level than ever before in the history of mankind by the events of the Holocaust, are the shared property of all post-Holocaust philosophers.

Most writing concerning the Holocaust within the first forty years was highly particularistic, dealing almost exclusively with specifically Jewish issues and concerns. This certainly suggests a withdrawal from the type of pre-Holocaust universalism that Rosenzweig espoused. During the past decade, however, the question of the Holocaust as a "human issue," a matter of concern to all humankind, has been more openly addressed. I will look at the development of post-Holocaust Jewish philosophy as a dynamic process for individual philosophers as well as in general. This will help us understand how a religious community deals with a tragedy as uniquely horrible as the Holocaust. This will also help us understand what effect the passage of time has on the process of coming to grips with such terrible events.

A final word. My main goal is that this will be used as a reference. For that reason I have limited the amount of critical comments made. My goal is to provide a general introduction to the thought and writings of the philosophers mentioned. It will be up to the reader to make his or her critical judgments after reading the primary sources. All are worth reading whether one agrees with them or not.

## RICHARD RUBENSTEIN: BREAKING THE SILENCE, CHALLENGING THE ESTABLISHMENT

For the first twenty years after World War II, there was relative silence among Jewish theologians concerning the Holocaust. As Eugene Borowitz points out in *Choices in Modern Jewish Thought*, "Not until the mid-1960's . . . did the Holocaust become a central topic in Jewish religious thought."[1] Why was there such a time lag? Borowitz suggests three reasons. First, the traumatic nature of the event made it too hard for survivors to speak. Elie Wiesel broke that silence with his book *Night* in 1960. A second factor was the guilt of not doing enough to stop the killing. This feeling was especially strong among American Jews. Finally, society was not ready to hear about the Holocaust until the 1960s. By that time the civil rights movement had forced Americans to accept the fact that they, too, could be inhumane to other people, at least to some degree. The rise in ethnic pride, along with greater self-confidence among Jews in America, made it possible for them to talk about "Jewish matters" more openly. These last two factors, along with the development of the Protestant "death-of-God" movement, created the perfect context for the writings of Richard Rubenstein.

While some of his ideas are highly controversial, Rubenstein can be credited with bringing serious discussion of the Holocaust and its religious implications to the forefront of the Jewish community. In *After Auschwitz* Rubenstein introduced the Jewish community to the concept of the "death of God." He challenges the reader to reexamine many traditional Jewish beliefs and values in light of the reality of the Holocaust. While many of his conclusions have since been disputed, the questions posed by him provide a wonderful place to begin any discussion of the Holocaust. In his later works, such as *The Cunning of History* and *Approaches to Auschwitz*, Rubenstein takes a more historical approach to the lessons of these events. In these books he considers the role that modern technology and bureaucracy played in allowing mass killings. He also asks us to consider what that means for the future of humanity.

*After Auschwitz* can be credited with opening the door to addressing serious religious issues related to living after the Holocaust. While a few others had written about the Holocaust prior to this, Rubenstein recognized the tremendous impact of the events on the Jewish community. In his introduction Rubenstein warns of the numbing shock the Holocaust holds for all Jews, those in the West as well as survivors who endured the camps.[2]

Having first warned us that many of the values we have long taken for granted are about to be challenged, Rubenstein presents his own responses to the horrible events promulgated by the Nazis. *After Auschwitz* is a collection of papers delivered by Rubenstein at various times and in different places, tied together by a few chapters written specifically for the book. The order of the chapters does not completely coincide with the order in which they were written. That would not usually be a problem, but since we are looking at the development of the author's ideas, it does pose a problem for us. I have attempted to present Rubenstein's ideas roughly in the order in which he articulated them.

Rubenstein's first issue is the impact of religion, specifically Christianity, on the Nazi mentality. He challenges the idea that the Nazis and their hatred of Jews had nothing to do with Christianity when he states, "The Nazis were religious rebels rather than genuine unbelievers."[3] From Christianity, they embraced the two-thousand-year-old tradition of the Jew as irredeemable villain.[4] To Rubenstein, the exterminationist ideology of the Nazis was a natural outgrowth of the religious beliefs of the German people. They simply took it to an extreme beyond what anyone else might have been able to imagine previously.[5]

In a later chapter Rubenstein recounts a conversation he had with Heinrich Gruber, dean of the Evangelical Church of East and West Berlin. At great personal risk Dean Gruber had opposed the Nazis on Christian religious grounds. His actions had brought him to Dachau and nearly to his death. Since the war Dean Gruber had been a leading figure in the field of reconciliation and healing. Rubenstein clearly states that Dean Gruber was not a Nazi nor an anti-Semite. That is what makes his views so troublesome. That is also why his views had such a tremendous impact on Rubenstein. Of Dean Gruber's words Rubenstein observes:

After my interview, I reached a theological point of no return—if I believed in God as the omnipotent author of the historical drama and Israel as His Chosen People, I had to accept Dean Gruber's conclusion that it was God's will that Hitler committed six million Jews to slaughter. I could not possibly believe in such a God nor could I believe in Israel as the chosen people of God after Auschwitz.[6]

Rubenstein also notes that Dean Gruber's views of Jews and Judaism as the Chosen People naturally lead to a double standard of accepted behavior. For

Gruber, the concept that Jews (whose divine function was clear) could produce scoundrels was unthinkable.[7]

Rubenstein uses these observations to point out the problems posed by many of our traditional beliefs about Judaism and God. He recognizes the strong impact that Christian ideas have on the beliefs of many Jews today. He accepts that as reality without question or challenge. It is these so-called Judeo-Christian values and their challenge to traditional Jewish beliefs that lead to his more radical theological ideas. These include the death-of-God idea.

Since the death-of-God concept as described by Rubenstein is often misunderstood, let us first consider what he seems to be suggesting in *After Auschwitz*. First, Rubenstein discusses the Reconstructionist movement in Judaism and its approach to the problem of evil. He seems to agree with the strong emphasis that is placed on peoplehood and the historical experience of the Jewish people. He also agrees with the Reconstructionist challenge to traditional views of God. But Rubenstein parts company with Reconstructionism on the need to replace the traditional view with a specific modern conception of God. Despite an existentialist approach, he states, "This does not mean that there is no God or that a God-conception is meaningless."[8] He is simply saying that God's existence is not necessarily tied to specific functions associated with the Divine.

In 1966 Rubenstein participated in a symposium on Jewish belief that was published in *Commentary* (August 1966). In his response to one of the questions posed to him he explains the relevance to Judaism of the Christian "God-is-dead" question. After noting that in some ways death-of-God theology reflects the Christian tradition of the passion of Christ, Rubenstein concludes that the terminology has a Jewish application as well. "No man can really say that God is dead. . . . Nevertheless, I am compelled to say that we live in the time of the 'death of God.' "[9]

For Rubenstein, the "death of God" refers to the absence of God as an active presence in our world. Sacred Jewish texts are traditionally viewed as portraying how God is present in our world and throughout our history. For Rubenstein, this is not a reasonable idea after the Holocaust. Alone and cold in the cosmos, he asks: "After Auschwitz, what else can a Jew say about God?"[10] On the one hand, Rubenstein is responding to the magnitude of the terrible events. On the other hand, he is reacting, like a true philosopher, to the limits of our "provable" knowledge.[11]

The death of God is a troubling concept for many Jews. However, the issues that lead Rubenstein to this concept are equally troubling. He poses questions that demand a response of some sort.

Traditional Jewish theology maintains that God is the ultimate, omnipotent actor in the historical drama. It has interpreted every major catastrophe in Jewish history as God's punishment of a sinful Israel. I fail to see how this position can be maintained without regarding Hitler and the SS as instruments of God's will. . . . To see any purpose in the death camps, the traditional believer is forced to regard the most demonic, antihuman explosion in all history as a meaningful expression of God's purposes. The idea is simply too obscene for me to accept.[12]

Actually, Rubenstein's ideas should not have seemed so unusual. As Eugene Borowitz notes, "Rubenstein's first argument, the rejection of a rigidly controlling God, was never disputed because modern Jews had not espoused it."[13] By "modern Jews" Borowitz means both the average person and philosophers such as Hermann Cohen, Leo Baeck, Mordecai Kaplan, Franz Rosenzweig, and Martin Buber.

Rubenstein's second statement is the more controversial one. Yet Borowitz observes that for many Jews it made sense. The statement that we live in a time of the "death of God" confirmed their experience.[14] As modern, rational Jews and human beings, many questioned whether God had created humankind or humankind had created God. The absence of any clear signs of God's presence during the Holocaust seemed to confirm the latter. In a strange way Rubenstein's death-of-God idea, in spite of its name, was a less radical option. Both viewpoints show how heavily our modern philosophies are influenced by a sociological perspective. In both cases the Holocaust is viewed in terms of sociological causes and its effect on society.

Rubenstein turns his attention to a clearly sociological issue as he explores further the causes of the Holocaust. In *After Auschwitz* Rubenstein writes briefly about the effect that modern technology and bureaucracy have in creating the potential for genocide. In later books he looks at that topic in more detail. In *The Cunning of History*, for example, he moves from the particulars of Jewish theology to the more general lesson of the potential for genocide made possible by our technical progress. If the Holocaust is viewed in this fashion, its lessons become more universal. This time it was primarily the Jews who suffered. Next time it could be anyone, since the mechanisms of mass destruction exist in our "modern world" and "enlightened society." Rubenstein makes this point most clearly when he states that scholars have failed to appreciate the Holocaust for what it truly was, "a thoroughly modern exercise in total domination that could only have been carried out by an advanced political community with a highly trained, tightly disciplined police and civil service bureaucracy."[15]

Rubenstein expands on this idea of the influence of the values of this century on the Holocaust. He notes that while the actions of the Nazis were the most hideous, others were not without blame. When the Allies had the opportunity to bomb the railroads to the death camps, they did not consider it worthwhile, yet as Rubenstein notes, the British demolished Dresden, a city of debatable military significance, leaving more than 80,000 civilians dead. The Jews were viewed as a superfluous population by many nations in addition to Germany. The lesson is that people are more likely to understand the Holocaust if they view it as an extreme response to some of the most profound tendencies of Western civilization in the twentieth century.[16]

In *Approaches to Auschwitz*, coauthored by Rubenstein and John K. Roth, a

Christian professor of history and Holocaust studies, all of the previously mentioned issues are presented. *Approaches to Auschwitz* is intended to be a text for
Holocaust studies. Understandably, this limits its usefulness as a forum for
Rubenstein's own views. In fact, near the end of the book, the authors present
many responses to the Holocaust. What is most significant is the attempt to
balance the uniquely Jewish aspects of the Holocaust with its meaning as a
tragedy for all people.

Richard Rubenstein is known primarily for his radical approach to Jewish
theology. He is also an important figure for his presentation of a sociological
view of the Holocaust. In spite of this, he shares with other leading thinkers the
understanding of the Holocaust as a major religious experience in the history of
Judaism. As Borowitz notes, "Rubenstein agrees . . . that Auschwitz is our
Sinai." While Rubenstein makes "its revelation about the human situation the
basis of his illusionless Judaism,"[17] others who hear the commanding voice of
Auschwitz hear a different message.

## EMIL FACKENHEIM: THE HOLOCAUST AS
## ROOT EXPERIENCE

The writings of Emil Fackenheim, viewed chronologically, show the development of his ideas in a very clear fashion. He responds to the Holocaust from
both a personal perspective and that of a Jewish theologian. Fackenheim was
one of the last men ordained a liberal rabbi in Berlin. Confined briefly at Sachsenhausen after *Kristallnacht* in 1938, he emigrated to Canada shortly before
the outbreak of war. Fackenheim taught modern philosophy at the University of
Toronto for many years prior to making *Aliyah* (emigration to Palestine) in the
mid-1980s. While his most significant works have been published since 1967,
he has been concerned with Jewish theology since younger days in Germany.
*The Jewish Thought of Emil Fackenheim: A Reader*, edited by Michael L.
Morgan, provides a sample of some previously unpublished texts that date from
that time. Morgan's work is a text that I would recommend to anyone as a good
introduction to Fackenheim's writings.

In contrast to Rubenstein's focus on God's absence from history, Fackenheim
focuses on God's presence. He is not ready to accept the position espoused by
Rosenzweig and others that religion must be rational. He uses his knowledge of
both Judaism and philosophy to respond to other reactions to the Holocaust. As
Borowitz has observed:

Fackenheim . . . utilized his considerable technical expertise to criticize the generally
accepted axiom that a modern Judaism had to be a religion of reason. He argued that all
authentic religion, certainly Judaism, is based on revelation. Religious rationalism, by
basing itself on human reason, had grossly overestimated our human powers and paid
too little attention to God's reality.[18]

Some have criticized Fackenheim as being too repetitive. His most important ideas are repeated in various books, but they are applied to different situations and set into various contexts. I will cite these ideas only once in this chapter, noting what I consider to be the source that provides the clearest explanation.

*Quest for Past and Future* is a collection of essays by Fackenheim that marks his entry into the field of post-Holocaust philosophy. In this text he reflects on the previous twenty years, providing insight into his own relationship to the horrible events of Nazi Germany. Fackenheim also makes clear his strong belief that Jewish traditional values are not so easily discarded. Yet he writes as a liberal Jew, concerned with how to reconcile Jewish traditional values and the realities of modern life. He is able to present issues such as "Can there be Judaism without revelation?" "The dilemma of autonomy in liberal Judaism," "Exposure to faith in the modern secular world," and "How to deal with God's apparent lack of presence in our modern world." The questions and issues are important, but the answers are spelled out clearly in later books.

In *God's Presence in History* Fackenheim presents the idea of root experiences. Root experiences have three conditions that set them apart from other experiences in history. First, due to a dialectical relationship between the present and the past, a root experience (from the past) can legislate to the present. In other words, while we do not actually see or experience what others saw or experienced in the past, we know what touched their lives. The Exodus from Egypt, reenacted each year at the Passover seder and at every human liberation from slavery, is an example of a root experience. The revelation at Sinai, spoken to those who were present and those who were not, which is understood to refer to future generations of Jews, is another example.

The second condition for a root experience is "its public, historical character." In addition to the two previous examples, the parting of the Red Sea was such a public event. Finally, "accessibility of the past to the present is the third and final characteristic of a root experience in Judaism."[19] The way in which these events are preserved for us and transmitted to future generations makes them accessible. I suspect that Fackenheim is also pointing to the timelessness of the event as a paradigm that makes its message accessible to our experience today. Needless to say, for Fackenheim the Holocaust is a root experience for Jews. In this way he categorizes the Holocaust as being just as important to Judaism as the examples previously mentioned. While he then describes the Holocaust as a source for divine revelation in this text, I find his explanation in *The Jewish Return into History* to be more clearly stated.

Fackenheim begins dealing with this issue by asking a question: "Can we confront the Holocaust, and yet not despair?"[20] Fackenheim often poses his questions in a most clear and concise way. This question allows him to comment on the importance of Jewish survival. As Borowitz notes:

With God withdrawn and inaccessible—no small part of the agony—and in the face of this incomparable evil, one might have expected the Jews to despair. . . . Though the

Holocaust itself discloses no transcendent meaning, Fackenheim detects a new "revelation" at the base of the Jewish people's response to it. By what logic can one explain
why the Jews did not turn their backs on life after the Holocaust?... Why... did the
survivors insist on resuming Jewish existence?... Why did they choose to be Jews in a
more self-conscious, spiritual level? They *had to do* what they did. For them to allow
the Jewish people to die would have been for themselves to complete the Holocaust. ...
Absolute evil had aroused absolute commitment.[21]

For Fackenheim, the next step follows logically. He asks the question, "Where
was God at Auschwitz?" After rejecting the applicability of Buber's image of
the "eclipse of God" in relation to Auschwitz, he continues, "Most assuredly
no *redeeming* Voice is heard from Auschwitz, or ever will be heard. However,
a *commanding* Voice is being heard, and has, however faintly, been heard from
the start." Fackenheim notes that this commanding Voice is heard by both
religious and secular Jews, as it commands that "Jews are forbidden to grant
posthumous victories to Hitler."[22]

Previously, Fackenheim has directed this charge to all Jews, whether secular
or religious. He calls it the 614th commandment.[23] By placing the Holocaust on
a level equal to the revelation at Mount Sinai he is able to make this type of
statement seem logical. Few events in Jewish history have touched the soul of
so many Jews. Seldom in the modern world do large numbers of Jews agree on
anything. The fact that almost all Jews would agree with the content of what
Fackenheim has called the 614th commandment, whether they would accept it
as divine revelation or not, is incredible. So out of the horrible deaths and
destruction comes a divine revelation. Regardless of how different they are and
how strongly opinionated they are, Jews are united in their desire to survive and
thereby refuse Hitler any posthumous victory.

Borowitz identifies three consequences of Fackenheim's "reoriented beliefs":

First, he no longer finds it useful to distinguish between religious and secular Jews.
... Any Jew, regardless of label, who helps preserve and maintain or, better, enriches
the life of the Jewish people, fulfills the supreme Jewish responsibility of our time.

The second consequence he derives from emphasizing peoplehood is a new regard for
the State of Israel. ... [This] expresses and symbolically projects the Jewish people's
rejection of death, its return to life, its willingness to face the ambiguities of history and
its insistence of remaining visibly, demonstrably, proudly Jewish. ...

Third, Fackenheim concludes that the test of good faith of gentiles who enter discussions
on Jewish matters is their willingness to face up to the Holocaust.[24]

*To Mend the World* is primarily a critical review by Fackenheim of other
philosophic views. In many ways this is a return to his writings that predate
*Quest for Past and Future*. It is inevitable, however, that some of his own ideas,
as they have developed in the intervening years, would appear in his later
writings, whatever the topic. Finally, Michael Morgan's book *The Jewish
Thought of Emil Fackenheim* provides not only some of Fackenheim's earliest

writings on the Holocaust but also some of his most recent. How his study of this topic has affected his life is described in a collection of autobiographical essays.

## ELIE WIESEL: THE STORYTELLER AS PHILOSOPHER

Elie Wiesel is generally thought of as an author of poignant novels about the Holocaust. He has recently written more nonfiction, some of it philosophical, but he is not often described as a Jewish philosopher. Nevertheless, throughout his writings he relates certain ideas and values that represent a philosophy worth mentioning, albeit briefly.

As noted earlier, Wiesel is generally credited with breaking nearly twenty years of silence about the Holocaust when his book *Night* appeared in English in 1960. In the context of a novel he is able to present a reality that was too horrible for most people at that time to have accepted as fact. If people were shocked when they realized that the truth was at least as bad as what Wiesel portrayed, then rightly they should have been. The themes that are conveyed through the story are (1) the will to survive, even when it seemed impossible, (2) the dehumanization of human beings in the camps, (3) the appropriateness of being morally outraged by these horrible events, and (4) the importance of remembering and relating what happened. For Wiesel, the last theme must have been a personal internal struggle of his own. In other novels he relates how characters take oaths of silence, yet inevitably feel that it is necessary to break such oaths. Perhaps he wonders how people will ever accept the truth of such horror, yet to keep silent is to risk repeating the atrocity in the future. In this fashion Wiesel is displaying the type of concern for the welfare of all people that he has recently expressed with regard to the threat of nuclear destruction. Wiesel is careful, however, to maintain the uniqueness (Jewish and otherwise) of the Holocaust.

In 1965 Wiesel published *One Generation After*, a nonfiction narrative of some of his personal experiences. He relates events from the time of World War II until (in later editions of the book) the Six-Day War. He confronts the relationship between the Holocaust and the founding of the State of Israel. It would be insensitive as well as morally incorrect to suggest that the Holocaust was a necessary sacrifice for the creation of a Jewish state. Instead, Wiesel suggests that the Jewish state served as consolation for the Holocaust, not just for Jews but for all people. He explains this as follows:

To pretend that without Auschwitz, there would be no Israel is to endow the latter with a share of responsibility for the former. And second, Israel cannot be an answer to the Holocaust, because the Holocaust, by its very magnitude, by its essence too, negates all answers.[25]

Wiesel is able to deal with the paradoxes surrounding the Holocaust (and life in general, for that matter) in an easy-to-understand way. He has summed up the balance between the Holocaust as a Jewish issue as opposed to a human issue through the expression of his belief in Jewish survival as an obligation. As Borowitz notes:

His quest is thoroughly universal. He wonders how anyone can affirm life after the Holocaust. He takes it for granted that if there is any proper human response to Auschwitz, it will also be true for Jews. At the same time, since no one knows human suffering better than the Jews, their wisdom is humankind's best source of insight into the mystery called existence. To Wiesel, every Jew and the Jewish people itself is holy. Promoting Jewish survival is an unshakable dogma after the Holocaust.[26]

Many of Wiesel's books are well known and readily available, so I will not list them here. Two recent books from which one can learn more about Wiesel's ideas are Elie Wiesel and John Cardinal O'Connor, *A Journey of Faith*, and Maurice Friedman, *Abraham Joshua Heschel and Elie Wiesel: You Are My Witnesses*. All of Wiesel's writing helps pose the type of questions that help guide one's exploration of matters connected to the Holocaust.

## ELIEZER BERKOVITS: THE FAITH OF EYEWITNESSES TO THE HOLOCAUST

Up to now we have considered the philosophies of those whose views, while being different from each other, are all more or less nontraditional. There are those, however, who have attempted to deal with the challenges to faith posed by the Holocaust within the framework of Jewish tradition. One such person is Eliezer Berkovits.

I have chosen to discuss the work of Berkovits because it also serves another purpose. He is not a survivor, nor does he have any close relatives who were directly associated with the terrible events during World War II. Nevertheless, he is committed to understanding the experiences and feelings of those who had "front-row tickets" to the Holocaust. He warns those of us in the same position as his:

We are not Job and we dare not speak and respond as if we were. We are only Job's brother. We must believe, because our brother Job believed; and we must question, because our brother Job so often could not believe any longer. This is not a comfortable situation; but it is our condition in this era after the holocaust. In it alone do we stand at the threshold to an adequate response to the *Shoa*—if there be one.[27]

Berkovits then explains the perspective from which he believes that a proper response should be formulated:

It must come without the desecration of the holy faith or of the holy loss of faith of the Jewish people in the European hell. And if there be no breakthrough, the honest thing is to remain at the threshold. If there is no answer, it is better to live without it than to find peace either in the sham of an insensitive faith or in the humbug of a disbelief entertained by people who have eaten their fill at the tables of a satiated society.[28]

Berkovits is impressed by the fact that even one person in the death camps could maintain his or her faith in God. That is enough to caution any ''nonsurvivor'' against the radical philosophies that deny or diminish God's existence. He asks not ''Where was God?'' but rather ''Where was Man?'' To place the onus of guilt upon God is to ignore the failings of human beings. While this point of view is interesting to consider, it does little to address the issues of good and evil and of reward and punishment. Without addressing these issues it is nearly impossible to make sense of our lives in a post-Holocaust world.

The greatest value of Berkovits's work is twofold. First, he reminds us that it is acceptable to challenge and question God. That in no way makes us less faithful. In fact, such questioning is a Jewish trait that goes back at least to the time of Abraham. The other benefit is the evidence he provides about life in the camps. In a later book, *With God in Hell,* Berkovits relies heavily on the accounts of survivors who maintained their trust in God and observance of Jewish tradition (as much as possible) to support his own position. From his perspective, Jewish suffering is a given and is a necessary part of life. It is part of the burden Jews carry by being chosen. As Borowitz notes, Berkovits is not alone. Others such as Irving Greenberg share this philosophical viewpoint, but it is not a position that is widely discussed or accepted.

## OTHER SOURCES FOR POST-HOLOCAUST JEWISH PHILOSOPHIES

In this section I will briefly note other worthwhile sources for the student of Jewish philosophy. I have grouped them by topic or style.

One of the most interesting sources of Jewish ideas in response to the Holocaust is the writings of survivors. Two texts that are worth exploring are *At the Mind's Eye* by Jean Améry and Viktor Frankl's *Man's Search For Meaning.* A study of the beliefs of Holocaust survivors is *The Faith and Doubt of Holocaust Survivors* by Reeve Robert Brenner.

Other Jewish thinkers have explored how the Holocaust has affected Jewish theological interpretations and relationship to Judaism in the modern world. These include *The Tremendum* by Arthur A. Cohen, Leonard Fein's *Where Are We?*, *How Can a Jew Speak of Faith Today?* by Eugene Borowitz, and *A Season for Healing* by Anne Roiphe. William E. Kaufman's *Contemporary Jewish Philosophies* is a study of the various people we have already considered with an interesting concluding chapter by the author.

Finally, a number of texts have collected materials from various sources. These include *The Holocaust Years*, edited by Roselle Chartock and Jack Spencer; Abraham J. Peck, *Jews and Christians After the Holocaust*; *Holocaust: Religious and Philosophical Implications*, edited by John K. Roth and Michael

Berenbaum; Albert H. Friedlander, *Out of the Whirlwind*; and *Auschwitz: Beginning of a New Era?*, edited by Eva Fleischner. These collections are ideal for use as a classroom text or any setting where the goal is to be exposed to many viewpoints at once.

As varied as are the reactions to the atrocity of the Holocaust, a few themes are common to most. First is the uniqueness of this event. The unequalled magnitude of inhumaneness creates a challenge in trying to describe and understand the Holocaust. Second is an attempt to understand what could lead people to react in the fashion the Nazis chose. The Christian roots of anti-Semitism are a recurring concern. Finally, the need to remember (or rather to "never forget") is part of a survival strategy. A Jew considers a link with eternity to be part of his or her identity. Through the process of, and a commitment to, memory, one's ties to both the past and future are secured. So too are the lessons for the survival of all. Perhaps that is the greatest revelation that one gains through a study of the Holocaust.

## NOTES

1. Eugene Borowitz, *Choices in Modern Jewish Thought* (New York: Behrman House, 1983), p. 188.

2. Richard Rubenstein, *After Auschwitz* (Indianapolis: Bobbs-Merrill, 1966), p. x.

3. Ibid., p. 3.

4. Ibid.

5. Ibid.

6. Ibid., p. 46.

7. Ibid., p. 52.

8. Ibid., p. 88.

9. Ibid., p. 151.

10. Ibid., p. 152.

11. Ibid.

12. Ibid., p. 153.

13. Borowitz, *Choices in Modern Jewish Thought*, p. 197.

14. Ibid., p. 198.

15. Richard Rubenstein, *The Cunning of History* (New York: Harper and Row, 1975), p. 4.

16. Ibid., pp. 20–21.

17. Borowitz, *Choices in Modern Jewish Thought*, p. 193.

18. Ibid., p. 200.

19. Emil Fackenheim, *God's Presence in History: Jewish Affirmations and Philosophical Reflections* (New York: New York University Press, 1970), p. 11.

20. Emil Fackenheim, *The Jewish Return into History* (New York: Schocken Books, 1978), p. 22.

21. Borowitz, *Choices in Modern Jewish Thought*, p. 202.

22. Fackenheim, *Jewish Return into History*, pp. 31–32.

23. Fackenheim is referring to the fact that according to Jewish tradition, the Torah

(received at Mount Sinai) contains 613 commandments. A new commandment of equal value and legitimacy would have to be called the 614th commandment.

24. Borowitz, *Choices in Modern Jewish Thought*, p. 203.
25. Elie Wiesel, *One Generation After* (New York: Random House, 1965), p. 166.
26. Borowitz, *Choices in Modern Jewish Thought*, pp. 192–93.
27. Eliezer Berkovits, *Faith After the Holocaust* (New York: Ktav, 1973), p. 5.
28. Ibid., pp. 5–6.

## SELECT BIBLIOGRAPHY

Améry, Jean. *At the Mind's Limits*. Translated by Sidney Rosenfeld and Stella P. Rosenfeld. New York: Schocken Books, 1986.

Berkovits, Eliezer. *Faith After the Holocaust*. New York: Ktav, 1973.

———. *With God in Hell*. New York: Sanhedrin Press, 1979.

Borowitz, Eugene B. *Choices in Modern Jewish Thought*. New York: Behrman House, 1983.

———. *How Can a Jew Speak of Faith Today?* Philadelphia: Westminster Press, 1969.

Brenner, Reeve Robert. *The Faith and Doubt of Holocaust Survivors*. New York: Free Press, 1980.

Cargas, Harry James, ed. *Responses to Elie Wiesel*. New York: Persea Books, 1978.

Chartock, Roselle, and Jack Spencer, eds. *The Holocaust Years: Society on Trial*. New York: Bantam Books, 1978.

Cohen, Arthur A. *The Tremendum*. New York: Crossroad, 1981.

Fackenheim, Emil L. *God's Presence in History*. New York: New York University Press, 1970.

———. *The Jewish Bible After The Holocaust*. Bloomington: Indiana University Press, 1991.

———. *The Jewish Return into History*. New York: Schocken Books, 1978.

———. *Quest for Past and Future*. Boston: Beacon Press, 1970.

———. *To Mend the World*. New York: Schocken Books, 1982.

Fein, Leonard. *Where Are We?* New York: Harper and Row, 1988.

Fleischner, Eva, ed. *Auschwitz: Beginning of a New Era?* New York: Ktav, 1977.

Frankl, Viktor E. *Man's Search for Meaning*. New York: Pocket Books, 1974.

Friedlander, Albert H. *Out of the Whirlwind*. Garden City, N.Y.: Doubleday, 1968.

Friedman, Maurice. *Abraham Joshua Heschel and Elie Wiesel: You Are My Witnesses*. New York: Farrar, Straus, Giroux, 1987.

Glatzer, Nahum N. *Franz Rosenzweig: His Life and Thought*. New York: Schocken Books, 1972.

Kaufman, William E. *Contemporary Jewish Philosophies*. New York: Reconstructionist Press and Behrman House, 1976.

Morgan, Michael L., ed. *The Jewish Thought of Emil Fackenheim*. Detroit: Wayne State University Press, 1987.

Peck, Abraham J. *Jews and Christians After the Holocaust*. Philadelphia: Fortress Press, 1982.

Roiphe, Anne. *A Season for Healing*. New York: Summit Books, 1988.

Rosenberg, Alan, and Gerald E. Myers, eds. *Echoes from the Holocaust*. Philadelphia: Temple University Press, 1980.

Rosenzweig, Franz. *The Star of Redemption*. Translated by William W. Hallo. Paperback ed. Boston: Beacon Press, 1972.

Roth, John K., and Michael Berenbaum, eds. *Holocaust: Religious and Philosophical Implications*. New York: Paragon House, 1989.

Rubenstein, Richard L. *After Auschwitz*. Indianapolis: Bobbs-Merrill, 1966.

———. *The Cunning of History*. New York: Harper and Row, 1975.

Rubenstein, Richard L., and John K. Roth. *Approaches to Auschwitz*. Atlanta: John Knox Press, 1987.

Ryan, Michael D., ed. *Human Responses to the Holocaust*. New York: Edwin Mellen Press, 1981.

Wiesel, Elie. *Night*. Translated by Stella Rodway. Paperback ed. New York: Avon Books, 1960.

———. *One Generation After*. Translated by Lily Edelman. New York: Random House, 1965.

Wiesel, Elie, and John Cardinal O'Connor. *A Journey of Faith*. New York: Donald I. Fine, 1990.

# Chapter 6

# The Church and the Holocaust

## David A. Rausch

In his short book, *The Sunflower*, Holocaust survivor Simon Wiesenthal poses questions about forgiveness—the ready forgiveness by the church for the Nazi perpetrators, and the refusal of a Jewish victim to grant a request for forgiveness from a dying SS killer. Beginning with the plight of a group of camp inmates slowly being worked to death as Nazi slave laborers, Wiesenthal intersperses the horrors he saw and lived in both ghetto and camp, horrors that took eighty-nine members of his own family.

Amid desperation and death, exhaustion and brutality, religious and nonreligious Jews in the concentration camp vainly groped for explanations of their plight. Wiesenthal and his friends, for example, question whether or not God was on leave. When the deeply religious Josek relates that God created humans out of a tear-soaked clod of earth, the cynic Arthur declares: "Josek, I am prepared to believe that God created a Jew out of this tear-soaked clod of earth, but do you expect me to believe He also made our camp commandant, Wilhaus, out of the same material?" "You are forgetting Cain," Josek responded. "And you are forgetting where you are," Arthur defiantly answered. "Cain slew Abel in anger, but he never tortured him. Cain had a personal attachment to his brother, but we are strangers to our murderers."[1]

Ironically, Wiesenthal was to intimately face an apparently repentant (and dying) SS murderer. Marched past a military cemetery, he was fascinated by the sunflowers planted over each German soldier's grave. "For me there would be no sunflower," he reflected in sadness. "I would be buried in a mass-grave, where corpses would be piled on top of me." That day, while on a garbage detail at a makeshift hospital, he was chosen by a Red Cross nurse to follow her to a patient's room. Left alone with a critically wounded SS soldier, whose bones almost protruded through parched skin, and whose head was completely bandaged with openings only for the nose, mouth, and ears, Wiesenthal found that he was expected to sit and hear the confession of Karl, a graduate of the Hitler Youth and a willing volunteer in Hitler's SS. Brought up as a Catholic, Karl had given his soul to the Nazis. Now, riddled with doubt and fear, he longed for that simpler time when the church and its sacrament of confession offered redemption from his sins.[2]

As the dying soldier related the horrors of his deeds, deeds for which he said he was sorry, the concentration-camp inmate had flashbacks of young, defenseless Jewish men, women, and children who had died before his eyes in previous months. Aware that he was silent, Karl pleaded for the camp inmate's response. Simon Wiesenthal wrote;

But what could I say? Here was a dying man—a murderer who did not want to be a murderer but who had been made into a murderer by a murderous ideology. He was confessing his crime to a man who perhaps tomorrow must die at the hands of these same murderers. In his confession there was true repentance, even though he did not admit it in so many words. Nor was it necessary, for the way in which he spoke and the fact that he spoke to *me* was a proof of his repentance.[3]

After reflecting on the SS soldier doomed to death and the few hours he had spent listening to his confessions and his request, Wiesenthal made up his mind. As he stood up and looked at the dying soldier, it appeared that a sunflower rested between his white, bloodless, folded hands. Wiesenthal left the room in continued silence.

Still, Simon Wiesenthal was haunted by the fact that he had failed to carry out the last wish of a dying man, in spite of the fact that even the religious Josek told him that he had no right to forgive in the name of a people who had not authorized him to do so. Miraculously surviving the Holocaust, Wiesenthal visited the SS man's mother. Viewing family pictures and hearing what a ''good boy'' and ''decent young man'' Karl was, he refused to relate what evil deeds her son had done in an effort not to destroy this mother's memory of her only son. The story ends with a question to the reader:

Was my silence at the bedside of the dying Nazi right or wrong? This is a profound moral question that challenges the conscience of the reader of this episode, just as much as it once challenged my heart and mind. There are those who can appreciate my dilemma, and so endorse my attitude, and there are others who will be ready to condemn me for refusing to ease the last moments of a repentant murderer.[4]

The last sentence of the story challenges readers to switch places with Wiesenthal and to ask what they would have done in his position. Indeed, a number of eminent Christian and Jewish scholars were invited to respond to that question, and their replies compose ''Book Two: The Symposium'' of Wiesenthal's book.

Most struggle with the question, and the responses are varied. The famed rabbi Abraham J. Heschel declared that no human could forgive others' crimes; according to Jewish tradition even God could only forgive sins against himself, not against men. It was therefore "preposterous to assume that anybody alive can extend forgiveness for the suffering of any one of the six million people who perished."[5] In contrast, noted British journalist and author Christopher Hollis suggested that a different moral imperative was delivered by Christ when he prayed on the cross for the forgiveness of "his own murderers."[6]

Generally, the Christian respondents came down on the side of forgiveness (even if just for psychological comfort to the dying Nazi), although most respected the difficulty of the situation. Few Christians in the symposium were callous toward Wiesenthal's dilemma, and they generally did not seek to judge him. But a number of the Christians in the symposium (including Edward H. Flannery, John M. Oesterreicher, and James W. Parkes) had established records of judging the Christian church for its complicity in the horror of the Holocaust. While Wiesenthal's account helps relieve the church's responsibility somewhat by declaring that the Nazi had denied the church, had left the precepts of the Christian faith, and could not regain Christian belief and assurance even on his deathbed, many of the following works in this chapter detail Christians and leaders in the church who permitted and propagated genocide while remaining "members in good standing." The church and the Holocaust, therefore, may provide the ultimate example of the breaking of God's most "absolute moral law," a travesty nearly hidden in the gaily colored silence of a sunflower.

## THE EARLY CHURCH STRUGGLE

"If it is Christian to hate the Jew, then we are all good Christians," the Catholic humanist scholar Erasmus stated at the dawn of the Reformation era. His moment of candor certainly sums up the intense struggle that the Christian church has had with anti-Semitism during its history. In the revised and updated republication of his seminal work of the 1960s, *The Anguish of the Jews: Twenty-Three Centuries of Antisemitism*, Catholic priest and scholar Edward H. Flannery underscores how the early religious anti-Semitism of the church combined with the racial anti-Semitism of the nineteenth and twentieth centuries to produce the horrid Final Solution.[7]

Flannery discusses the anti-Semitism of the ancient world, an anti-Semitism that arose in the third century B.C.E., predating the Christian church. Since the early Christian church was a Jewish church, some of the very same charges of the ancient pagan writers were applied to the new Christian religion. As Christianity spread among the pagans, however, and attempted to sever itself from its Jewish heritage, anti-Semitic rhetoric increasingly permeated the Christian fold, and a theological attack against Jews and Judaism progressively unfolded. The conflict between the church and the synagogue escalated to the point that the fine line between anti-Judaism and anti-Semitism was crossed. The critical century in this scenario was the fourth, a century when church and state were linked and religious anti-Semitism was clearly established in the church. Flannery maintains: ''No century was more fateful for Jewish-Christian relations than the fourth.''[8]

Franklin H. Littell in *The Crucifixion of the Jews* concurs, illustrating how Christian theological anti-Semitism began ''with the transfer of the base of the early church from Jewish membership to a large gentile majority.'' This led to a resentment among Gentile Christians of ''the priority of Israel'' in the Bible.[9] Like Flannery, Littell points to the early Christian literature that by the second century was labeling Jews as hypocrites and as propagators of a false religion. These books differ, however, on the extent of anti-Semitism in the early church. Flannery questions whether or not the hostile writings of the early church fathers can be categorized as anti-Semitic, while Littell believes that theological anti-Semitism was well advanced in the Apostolic Fathers of the Gentile church. Both books note that debate continues among scholars as to whether or not the Christian Testament is anti-Semitic and as to whether or not the Apostle Paul was anti-Semitic. While Flannery and Littell do not engage in this debate, *Antisemitism and the Foundations of Christianity*, edited by Alan T. Davies, contains chapters by twelve Christian theologians who debate and explore the development and dynamics of anti-Semitism within the Christian tradition, including the Christian biblical documents. Davies's volume has the horrors of the Holocaust in mind throughout its discussion.[10]

David A. Rausch in his revised and updated *A Legacy of Hatred: Why Christians Must Not Forget the Holocaust* (1990) underscores the fact that the ''Roman intrusion into Judea and the widespread acceptance of Christianity by the Gentiles complicated the history of Jewish Christianity'' and acerbated the conflict between the church and the synagogue. Rausch insists that an anti-Jewish message is evident by 250 C.E. He explains:

The foundation had been laid and the message was clear. The Jews were no longer God's chosen people. They had persecuted and killed Jesus Christ and Christians. The Jews deserved persecution and the loss of their land. The Christian church had inherited the covenant promises of God—the church was God's chosen people. The curses of the Bible were ascribed to the Jews; the blessings of the Bible to the Christians. This was religious anti-Semitism, and even Hitler would draw on this foundation.[11]

Rausch quotes excerpts from the sermons of John Chrysostom to illustrate the point that when church and state were linked in the fourth century, due initially to Emperor Constantine, Christian persecution of the Jewish people became a regular practice.

As early as 1934, James Parkes in *The Conflict of the Church and The Synagogue: A Study in the Origins of Antisemitism* illustrated such points well by recording some of the forced conversions and professions of faith required of

Jewish converts to Christianity in the ancient and medieval periods. These indicate the total separation from Judaism required by the Christian church. In 1950 Malcolm Hay's *The Foot of Pride* confronted the history of Christian anti-Semitism from its theological roots and systematic ecclesiastical formulation to its political and social manifestations in the modern period. Republished in 1981 as *The Roots of Christian Anti-Semitism,* Hay's well-written work is as powerful and lucid in the contemporary world as it was in the postwar era. Interspersing the horrors of the Holocaust throughout his historical treatment of the church's anti-Semitism, Hay underscores how the cancer of Christian anti-Semitism manifests itself in the cancer of Christian anti-Zionism. According to Hay, the hatred of Jews was so prevalent among Christians that by the time of the Holocaust "the world was now ready for the massacre."[12]

Building upon this religious anti-Semitism, Franklin Littell's *The Crucifixion of the Jews* launches into the German church struggle, 1933–45, while Edward Flannery's *The Anquish of the Jews* and David Rausch's *A Legacy of Hatred* develop the church heritage of the nineteenth century. A point understood by all of these scholars in a variety of their writings is that racial anti-Semitism was linked to religious anti-Semitism during the 1800s. The consolidation of Germany into the Second Reich on January 18, 1871, not only transformed the face of Europe, but also fed the national aspirations of the German church. Many Christians felt that God was instrumental in founding this nation, a nation they viewed as a "Christian" state. Political parties, social and economic institutions, and even some scientific societies called themselves "Christian." A civil religion developed equating "German" with "Christian." It was a religion that continued to romanticize the Germanic heritage, a heritage that was unique to the German *Volk* (common people) and *Volksgeist* (national character).

Uriel Tal's *Christians and Jews in Germany: Religion, Politics, and Ideology in the Second Reich, 1870–1914* proves that both religious and racial anti-Semitism were to be found in the Second Reich. Religious anti-Semitism insisted that a Jew could not retain a Jewish identity and demanded that a Jewish person convert and assimilate. Racial anti-Semitism treated the Jew as a parasite, a biological inferior that conversion and assimilation would not cure, a danger to the body politic. Tal points out, for example, that Friedrich Paulsen, a prominent liberal humanist and outspoken critic of racial anti-Semitism, explained in his *System of Ethics* that "to remain a complete Jew and a complete German is impossible."[13] That a liberal would construct such an obstacle for Jewish identity underscored the enormity of the problem facing the Jewish community in the very conservative Second Reich. That racial anti-Semitism was joined to the religious anti-Semitism of the early church pointed to the struggle that was to confront the German church in the twentieth century.

## THE GERMAN CHURCH STRUGGLE

In his book, *Open Thy Mouth for the Dumb! The German Evangelical Church and the Jews, 1879–1950*, Richard Gutteridge asserted that the German Church was not immune to the anti-Semitic virus as World War I ended and the era of the turbulent 1920s began. Gutteridge's lucid analysis is devastating in its portrayal of the failure of most German Protestants to meet the challenge of Nazi anti-Semitism and the lack of church officials to provide moral leadership in the face of such racist attacks. Although some Christians not only opposed the Nazis but also helped and defended the Jewish people, their numbers were so few that Gutteridge was perplexed at the minimal Christian response to racist propaganda. Church officials set up so many barriers to positive Christian response that it seemed a miracle that even a few Christians "opened their mouths for the dumb" and helped the afflicted at great personal cost. Gutteridge contended:

The ultimate failure of the Church lay not in the inability of bishops and synods to make plain and outspoken pronouncements in public, though what was most regrettably never attempted was a really united clarion call from responsible Christian leaders transcending all denominational and confessional barriers, issued on principle and irrespective as to whether it had a chance of proving acceptable or not, calling upon all, Evangelicals and Catholics alike, who took their Christianity really seriously, to raise their voices together in joint protest against what every true Christian must have known to be elementary violation of the most fundamental and manifest Divine Laws.[14]

"Most tragically of all," Gutteridge concluded about the period, "what was missing was a spontaneous outburst at any point by ordinary decent Christian folk, who certainly existed in considerable numbers."

In Gutteridge's estimation, a widespread public outburst that would have opposed anti-Semitism with the most visible righteous indignation would have had a profound effect on the Nazi leaders and at least might have curbed the most horrid excesses and brutalities. At best, such an outcry might have engendered the downfall of the Nazi tyranny. "But it never once came to that, and Adolf Hitler, despite his inability to bend the Church completely to his will, never really feared that it would," Gutteridge lamented after sifting through a mass of primary materials on the German churches. "The ghastly thing was just the fact that it was not gangsters and roughnecks, but decent, intelligent and moral people who allowed themselves to be induced to acquiesce in something deeply evil, and to serve it."

*Open Thy Mouth for the Dumb!* begins with the chapter " 'Christian' Anti-Semitism, 1879–1918." Gutteridge notes that two powerful Protestant spokesmen from the period were successful in stirring up anti-Semitic feelings: the conservative Lutheran minister from the grass roots of German society, Adolf Stoecker, who rose in 1874 to the exalted position of court and cathedral preacher in Berlin, and Heinrich von Treitschke, professor of history at the University of Berlin and editor of the prestigious *Prussian Annuals*. Charismatic and energetic, Stoecker affected lower-middle-class conservative Protestants, while Treitschke eloquently appealed to the intellectuals of Germany. As this book continues through the chapters "Anti-Jewish Sentiment in the Weimar Period," "Hitler, the Church, and the Jews, January–April 1933," "The Aryan Clause, 1933–1935," "The Nuremberg Laws and Their Effect upon the Evangelical Church, 1935–1938," "The Pogrom of November 1938, Its Aftermath, and Succour for the Afflicted, 1938–1941," " 'The Final Solution', 1941–1945," and "Conclusion," shades of Stoecker and Treitschke are ever present as Gutteridge unearths the primary religious materials from each period.

While Gutteridge lucidly conveys the personalities and publications of the era, Ernst Christian Helmreich in his monumental work, *The German Churches Under Hitler: Background, Struggle, and Epilogue*, provides a detailed analysis of the political and institutional structures of the large Protestant Land churches, the smaller Free churches, the Catholic church, and other sectarian groups. His first two chapters give an overview of Protestantism and Catholicism from the sixteenth century to 1918, while his next three chapters detail the constitutional framework of the Land churches under the Weimar Republic, Protestant church life during Weimar, and the Catholic church under Weimar. Chapters 6–20 detail the German Church Struggle (the term used to describe the complicated history of the Christian churches in Germany from 1933 to 1945, the time of National Socialist rule). The last three chapters are an epilogue describing the Protestant and Catholic churches in postwar Germany and evaluating the survey that has been presented.

Helmreich found that his detailed research into the actual workings of church institutions in Germany during the Nazi era proved beyond doubt that the churches "were slow to move, were beset by differences both among the leaders and among the ranks, and cannot be said to have won any glorious battles against Nazi activities." When Adolf Hitler took over, the large majority of Protestant churchmen wanted a more centralized and national church body. "In this they were at one with Nazi aspirations," Helmreich notes, "and there was no real objection in the churches to the drawing up of a new church constitution establishing a German Evangelical church." A glimmer of hope is found in the slow resistance and eventual creation of the Confessing church, and Helmreich suggests that one remember that there were Christians who suffered deeply for their resistance. "The names of Bonhoeffer, and Martin Niemoller, Galen and Faulhaber, and many others are known internationally," he concludes. "Perhaps the Church Struggle—actually the only real resistance by organized groups in Germany—may have begun a new trend, one away from the comfortable Volkskirche to a church much smaller in numbers but more vital."[15]

In volume 1 of his two-volume seminal work, *The Churches and the Third Reich*, Klaus Scholder details the preliminary history (1918–34) of this struggle, spending a significant amount of his first volume on the year 1933, "the year of the seizure of power." It was in this year that Hitler's early decision of the 1920s to guide his Nazi party into becoming a party of the "Christian" masses bore fruit. Scholder quotes many of Hitler's speeches to prove his assertion, including a speech Hitler gave in Passau on October 27, 1928. There Adolf Hitler declared of his Nazi movement:

This movement has gained a remarkable freedom of operation which in the supreme sense of the word allows the rejection of anything which could in any way divide the people. We are a people of different faiths, but we are one. Which faith conquers the other is not the question; the question, rather, is whether Christianity stands or falls! . . . We tolerate no one in our ranks who offends against the ideas of Christianity, who offers resistance to someone with another disposition, fights against him or acts as the arch-enemy of Christianity. This, our movement, is in fact Christian. We are filled with a desire for Catholics and Protestants to discover one another in the deep distress of our own people. We shall suppress any attempt to put religious issues on the agenda of our movement.[16]

"His success proved Hitler correct," Klaus Scholder comments on this speech. "Power could indeed be won without Christian Germany; but against Christian Germany the party had no chance." As church leaders progressively sacrificed the Jewish people on the altar of Nazi terrorism, political and administrative ecclesiastical decisions gained the upper hand over simple Christian responsibility.[17]

In a helpful shorter compendium of Klaus Scholder's essays and lectures, published posthumously in 1989 by Trinity Press International, the fact that Protestant and Catholic resistance came largely from individuals, while their church hierarchies sought to maintain the status quo with the Hitler regime, is appalling. In *A Requiem for Hitler and Other New Perspectives on the German Church Struggle*, Scholder maintained that in 1933–34 "the church struggle was exclusively concerned with the confession and church order." Sadly, "The Confessing Church had never left any doubt that otherwise it had unconditional political loyalty to Führer and Reich." "Despite its battle against the Aryan paragraph in the church, the Confessing Church which was in process of formation did not understand the significance and implications of National Socialist antisemitism," Scholder asserted, concluding, "This guilt is irrefutable."[18]

As Shelley Baranowski has shown in her *The Confessing Church, Conservative Elites, and the Nazi State*, the approximately sixteen thousand Protestant pastors in Germany had become a bureaucratic elite, a moral pillar for an authoritarian social order. "Their university training, their government-paid salaries, their political convictions and their social backgrounds (over 60 percent arose from the educated middle class) matched them with similarly qualified civil servants," Baranowski explained, "The social composition of the Protestant clergy suggests that the close ties with the state usually associated with the German Protestant Church, and often attributed to the passivity and obedience to secular rulers stressed by Lutheran orthodoxy, was maintained, rather, by the common bonds of background and training between the Protestant leadership and secular leaders." Professor Baranowski wrote:

Following Hitler's accession, the Protestant leadership supported the new government's measures with minimal reservation, convinced like other conservative elites that the suspension of civil liberties, the abrogation of federalism, the destruction of the trade unions and the political parties, and the Chancellor's increased powers were required to restore "order" against the left. Agreement with the goals of the Nazi right came easily, without regard for the dangers inherent in its methods. Churchmen rebutted foreign criticism of the Reich's actions. . . .

Similarly, the central bureaucracy of the Church Federation excused the removal of Jews from the civil service as "the first attempt at a solution of the Jewish problem." Its statement admitted acts of violence against Jews, but alleged that they were "nothing at all in comparison to the ghastly and shameful events of the 1918 revolution." The number of Jews affiliated with leftist parties, their disproportionately high numbers in public offices and their influence in journalism, the theater, scholarship and literature threatened the Christian faith, family life and culture.[19]

Arthur C. Cochrane's *The Church's Confession Under Hitler* analyzes the Barmen Declaration that was unanimously adopted by the First Confessional Synod of the German Evangelical Church on May 29–31, 1934. A storm of protest had ensued as churchmen realized that not only the Jews but also they themselves were losing freedom under the new order of "German Christians" and the Reich church government. The Barmen Confession was written under the guidance of theologian Karl Barth and pastor Martin Niemoller. It repudiated the false doctrine of the Nazi-oriented church hierarchy and questioned undivided loyalty to the state when the state attempted to usurp the role of the church. Cochrane's sixty pages of appendix documents, as well as his detailed notes, illustrate the Confessing church's penchant for freedom of conscience and doctrinal purity. Peter Matheson's useful collection of Protestant and Catholic church documents, *The Third Reich and the Christian Churches: A Documentary Account of Christian Resistance and Complicity During the Nazi Era*, also underscores this penchant. Yet, even as these pastors attacked the laws against non-Aryans in the ministry as a violation of the confessional stance of the church of Christ, and although many of these men fought for the rights of their Hebrew Christian pastors, the Confessing church failed to cry out against the violation of the civil and religious rights of the Jewish people.[20]

Dietrich Bonhoeffer, who realized in 1933 that the critical issue was the Nazi treatment of the Jews, was an exception. Niemoller, Barth, and other theologians and churchmen admitted later to fighting improperly for the Jewish cause. Franklin Littell, in assessing this history, notes:

If men of such stature, men who have worked tirelessly in the Church Struggle, can look the churches' failure in the eye and confess their own shortcomings, why should others hesitate? The reason seems to be that the same spiritual weakness that makes some men trimmers and quislings in the hour of decision makes them suppress the critical issues later. And—as the real leaders of spiritual resistance have been the first to make Christian confession—the churches did fail; most of the church leaders failed, and even the resistance largely failed to understand the signal importance of the rejection of the Jews to the malaise of Christendom.[21]

It was not until May 1936, after the Confessing church had split (the moderates left) and the infamous Nuremberg Laws had been decreed, that the remaining "radical" Confessing Christians issued a statement specifically condemning the Nazis' hatred of the Jews.[22]

Using the same skill with which he circumvented the Weimar constitution, Adolf Hitler outmaneuvered church leaders, even denying the "German Christians" leadership at the proper moment in order to incorporate them, moderate Christians, and the Confessing church under the administrative umbrella of the Reich Ministry of Church Affairs. Systematically the Nazis reduced the freedom of the German church through financial and legal intimidation. At the same time, they began promoting the Nazi party as the successor of the church. This propaganda and legal campaign was delicately balanced to retain the allegiance of devoted church members while creating a National Socialist civil religion for a younger generation and party elite. The large majority of Christians accepted the status quo, supporting the war effort with patriotic fervor. Contradicting some scholarly fundamentalist-evangelical claims that Nazi church followers were only the liberal higher critics of the Bible, David A. Rausch in *A Legacy of Hatred* has noted that even "true, Bible-believing Christians" supported Adolf Hitler, believing that Germany was on the verge of a spiritual revival. He cites documents written by a fundamentalist-evangelical pastor, Oswald J. Smith, that stated in July 1936, "Every true Christian is for Hitler. I know, for it was from the Christians I got most of my information, and right or wrong, they endorse Adolf Hitler."[23]

The Roman Catholic church also compromised with Hitler. Because of its political party and labor union, the German Catholic church was very visible. Consequently, the Nazis prepared for a wholesale attack against priests. As soon as Hitler gained power, Catholic clergymen were mistreated by the SA and arrested. Rectories were ransacked and parish schools intimidated. The laity of the Catholic church, caught up in the spirit of the New Germany, brought enormous pressure on the bishops. The Catholic church believed that it had no choice but to negotiate for the best terms possible with Hitler. On July 20, 1933, the church signed an agreement with the German government. Cardinal Eugenio Pacelli was the Vatican representative who formally affixed his signature to the document. In the spring of 1939 he became Pope Pius XII, known as a master of the language of diplomatic ambiguity. Unlike a number of priests and bishops who opposed Hitler and helped Jewish people, he refused to denounce the Nazis throughout the war and restricted his public statements about murdered Jews to mild expressions of sympathy for "the victims of injustice" (declining to say "Jew"). John F. Morley in his study *Vatican Diplomacy and the Jews During the Holocaust* concluded about the lack of spiritual direction from the Vatican:

Thus, reserve and prudence were the criterion of papal diplomacy, according to both the Pope and his secretary of state. It was a criterion that could not coexist with humanitarian concern. To avoid offending Germany, and to maintain prudent reserve, the Vatican had to act, or neglect to act, in ways that ignored the depth of suffering that was so widespread among both Christians and Jews. . . .

It must be concluded that Vatican diplomacy failed the Jews during the Holocaust by not doing all that it was possible for it to do on their behalf. It also failed itself because in neglecting the needs of the Jews, and pursuing a goal of reserve rather than humanitarian concern, it betrayed the ideals that it had set for itself. The nuncios, the secretary of state, and, most of all, the Pope share the responsibility for this dual failure.[24]

The historic anti-Semitism of the Catholic church was a definite factor in the reluctance of many German Catholics to help their Jewish neighbors. Even the debate during Vatican II in the 1960s and the failure of a strongly worded first version of a statement on the Jewish people (to "not teach anything that could give rise to hatred or contempt of the Jews") underscore the ambivalence of a number of Catholic bishops and clergy to this very day.[25]

David S. Wyman in *The Abandonment of the Jews* repeatedly proves that the American Roman Catholic church also was virtually silent, even in the critical months of 1943. While a handful of minor Christian and interfaith movements did urge rescue action in this critical period, not one of the major American Protestant denominations took a stand for the rescue of the Jewish people. William E. Nawyn in *American Protestantism's Response to Germany's Jews and Refugees, 1933–1941* explained this failure:

The fundamental reason why it received but minimal support is the failure of American Protestantism to become thoroughly aroused over the plight of the victims, Jewish or Christian, of the Nazi racial policies and, even more basically, about the moral issues involved in these policies. Latent anti-Semitism among Americans may well have played a role here. Undoubtedly, too, fears that admission of refugees would have a negative economic impact served to dampen, or outweigh, compassion. But whatever the reason, the fact remains that American Protestants did not rush forward to extend a generous welcome to the refugees from Germany—not even [to] Christian non-Aryans, much less Jews.[26]

"When human rights became endangered and the facts were clearly established," Nawyn concluded about the period, "few Protestant churchmen were ready to defend the defenseless or help the needy."

In contrast, there were individual Catholics and Protestants who gave sacrificially of themselves (some giving their lives) to help the Jewish people and to stand steadfast against a powerful Nazi regime. Those Christians that did help were more adept at actions than at broadcasting their heroic deeds. Peter Hellman found in writing his book *Avenue of the Righteous*, which details "inspiring true stories of heroic Christians and the Jews they saved from the Holocaust," that when asked why they acted as they did, most of them shrugged their shoulders and replied: "I did nothing special. Anybody would have done it."[27] Philip Friedman's *Their Brothers' Keepers* sketches scores of Christians who defied the Nazis and helped their Jewish neighbors. Protestant and Roman Catholic churches in Holland sought to save the Dutch Jews from deportation by actively protesting to the Germans and drawing up a manifesto against deportation to be read in their churches. With the exception of the Dutch Reformed congregations, all the churches read the manifesto in spite of a Nazi order that forbade its reading. Corrie Ten Boom in *The Hiding Place* relates that her family "talked often . . . about what we could do if a chance should come to help some of our Jewish friends." Caught in the act of hiding Jews, she was the only member of her family to survive their punishment in the camps as a Christian "collaborator."[28]

In the realm of Christian resistance, the Danes were an example of a nation successfully bound together to save the Jewish people. Harold Flender in *Rescue in Denmark* has documented that the citizens of Denmark saved nearly 99 percent of their seven thousand Jews. While there are a number of reasons for this, even the Christian theological and pastoral journals carried strong statements against Nazi anti-Semitism and positive statements about Jewish people. Dean Johannes Nordentoft, for example, wrote in a journal for Danish pastors: "Christians will be the first to fight this dirty anti-Semitism." He later declared that those Christians who "remain silent or disapprove by merely shrugging their shoulders" were actually Nazi collaborators.[29]

In the midst of French collaboration with the Nazis, Pastor Andre Trocme and his French Protestant community in Le Chambon saved approximately three thousand Jewish children and adults. A pacifist Huguenot, Trocme and his people knew persecution, and they had developed strong ethical standards and a keen sense of the value of human life. When philosopher Philip Hallie (dejected and disheartened by his study of the Holocaust and the evil involved) went to France to find out "why goodness occurred in Le Chambon" while the specter of evil surrounded the inhabitants of the little village, he recorded the response (as well as the story) in *Lest Innocent Blood Be Shed*: "How can you call us 'good'? We were doing what had to be done. Who else could help them? And what has all this to do with goodness? Things had to be done, that's all, and we happened to be there to do them. You must understand that it was the most natural thing in the world to help these people."[30]

Martin Niemoller, who stated in 1933 that he did not possess a "warmth of feeling" for Jews, emphasized in a sermon in 1945 what might be considered an epilogue on the German Church Struggle (and, indeed, on the response of the Christian church in general):

There were in 1933 and in the following years here in Germany 14,000 Evangelical pastors and nearly as many parishes. . . . If at the beginning of the Jewish persecutions we had seen that it was the Lord Jesus Christ Who was being persecuted, struck down and slain in "the least of these our brethren," if we had been loyal to Him and confessed Him, for all I know God would have stood by us, and then the whole sequence of events would have taken a different course. And if we had been ready to go with Him to death, the number of victims might well have been only some ten thousand.[31]

## THE MODERN CHURCH STRUGGLE

In 1931 Harry James Cargas edited *When God and Man Failed: Non-Jewish Views of the Holocaust*. This volume is basically composed of essays published in journals from 1969 to 1981 with a few new essays inserted.[32] This collection of essays is an attempt by Cargas to bring together some of the most eloquent insights by some of the finest Christian scholars of the Holocaust in the United States. These men and women are deeply troubled that the Holocaust occurred and view the Holocaust as one of the most significant Christian tragedies of history. They often refer to the failure and neglect of both the Catholic and Protestant churches during the Holocaust and give examples of Christian anti-Semitism and insensitivity during the period—illustrations that have made a profound impression upon them in their personal study of the church and the Holocaust.

For example, Eva Fleischner, professor of religion at Montclair State College in New Jersey, in her essay "The Crucial Importance of the Holocaust for Christians," relates that "not only did the churches by and large remain neutral, an attitude that in itself is reprehensible enough," but that there is "abundant evidence of strong anti-Semitism on the part of some highly placed church officials." This Catholic scholar cites the following illustration that made a deep impression upon her:

In 1942, the Nietra Rebbe went to Archbishop Kametko of Nietra to plead for Catholic intervention against the deportation of the Slovakian Jews. Tiso, the head of the Slovakian government, had been Kametko's secretary for many years and the Rebbe hoped that Kametko could persuade Tiso not to allow the deportations. Since the Rebbe did not yet know of the gas chambers, he stressed the dangers of hunger and disease especially for women, old people and children. The Archbishop replied: "It is not just a matter of deportation. You will not die there of hunger and disease. They will slaughter all of you there, old and young alike, women and children, at one. It is the punishment that you deserve for the death of our Lord and Redeemer, Jesus Christ—you have only one solution. Come over to our religion and I will work to annul this decree."[33]

"Holland, the Confessing Church of Germany, and acts of heroism on the part of individuals notwithstanding, I find it impossible to avoid the conclusion that the churches as a whole failed shamefully to speak out on behalf of Jews," Fleischner states earlier in her essay, adding: "This poses a problem for Christians today. What does being a Christian mean and demand, not only of the individual, but of the church as an institution, since it is precisely at this level that the church claims to carry on the work and mission of Christ?"[34] *When God and Man Failed* is filled with such soul-searching by Christians from divergent backgrounds. The essays are well chosen.

In 1989 Cargas published his own personal *Reflections of a Post-Auschwitz Christian*.[35] The volume begins with Cargas's agonizing attempt at self-definition:

To call myself a Roman Catholic is to describe my spiritual development incompletely. It is more honest for me to say at this time in my life that I am a post-Auschwitz Catholic, in the wider context of Western Christianity. The Holocaust event requires my response precisely as a Christian. The Holocaust is, in my judgment, the greatest tragedy for Christians since the crucifixion. In the first instance, Jesus died : in the latter, Christianity may be said to have died. In the case of Christ, the Christian believes in a resurrection. Will there be, can there be, a resurrection for Christianity? That is the question that obsesses me. Am I a part of a religious body which in fact is a fossil rather than a living entity? Can one be a Christian today, given the death camps which, in major part, were conceived, built and operated by people who called themselves Christians and some of whom—records prove, their own words prove—took pride in this work?[36]

"Thus I must conclude that to identify myself as a Roman Catholic, in the shadow of recent history, is inaccurate, incomplete, even misleading," Cargas decided after relating a brief history of the horrid complicity of Christians in the Holocaust. "Culturally, of course, I am that, but spiritually I put on the mantle of a post-Auschwitz Catholic. It is in this concept that all of my work—indeed my life—is now rooted."[37]

*Reflections of a Post-Auschwitz Christian* is interesting in that Cargas relates both the discoveries concerning the church and the Holocaust that he had made in twenty-five years and also the animosity and indifference he has encountered from members of the church. As early as 1963 Cargas had initiated publication of a booklet to defend Pope Pius XII from Rolf Hochhuth's allegations in *The Deputy*. Ironically, as Cargas began to study the history, he "became increasingly certain that Hochhuth's criticism was perhaps more valid than even he himself knew."[38] "The overwhelming evidence . . . favors those who have been critical of the papacy regarding the Holocaust, its roots and, a topic not to be gone into here, the post-Holocaust era of Jewish-Christian relations," Cargas concluded after reviewing the facts (as well as the defenses that some have given concerning Pope Pius XII's actions). "The failure to excommunicate, to interdict, to bear witness, to demand a total Catholic response, and, yes, the failure by the Vatican to this day to recognize the existence of the State of Israel, have had tragic results."

This volume also includes Cargas' plea to the Catholic church to excommunicate Adolf Hitler and to canonize the Lutheran minister and martyr, Dietrich Bonhoeffer. His letter castigating Pope John Paul II for his reception of Kurt Waldheim in 1988 and the words of praise the pope lavished upon this Nazi henchman are included in the volume. Again, the sad record of the church and the Holocaust is related, including the church in Austria. After two decades of writing and speaking of the need for the official Catholic church to make a serious gesture of repentance concerning "the role of many Catholics in the overwhelming Sin of the Holocaust and of the hierarchy's responsibility in that crime," Cargas takes it upon himself to write a suggested letter for the pope to be addressed to all of the faithful (since nothing approaching the kind of declaration he feels is necessary has been promulgated by the papacy).

Given the number of books authored by Christian scholars that are mentioned throughout this chapter, one must contend that at least a portion of Christendom is coming to grips with the Holocaust as well as the complicity and complacency of the church in the extermination of six million Jews. Much needs to be done. Much hangs in the balance. When John Roth, a Christian professor of philosophy, began to explore the religious and theological implications of the Holocaust as they were illuminated in the writings of survivor Elie Wiesel, his life was changed dramatically. As he sought in *A Consuming Fire: Encounters with Elie Wiesel and the Holocaust* to convey to other Christians the concepts that had confronted and chastened his innermost being, he related why it was imperative for the church to "take the gamble of Holocaust encounters." He explained:

*By witnessing in retrospect the worst that has befallen humanity, by facing the disillusionment and despair that such an encounter must produce—perhaps only by doing those things—we may rediscover or locate for the first time resources of heart, mind, and will without which there will be too little checking of destruction in the future.*[39]

"A risky gamble? Of course," Roth concluded. "Too risky? Not when you consider alternatives. Ignorance is *not* bliss. What is not known *can and does* hurt us."

## NOTES

1. Simon Wiesenthal, *The Sunflower* (New York: Schocken Books, 1976), p. 12. Wiesenthal adds: "Arthur's question wasn't altogether unjustified. Were we truly all made of the same stuff? If so, why were some murderers and other [*sic*] victims? Was there in fact any personal relationship between us, between the murderers and their victims, between our camp commandant, Wilhaus, and a tortured Jew?" (pp. 12–13).

2. Ibid., p. 56.

3. Ibid., pp. 56–57.

4. Ibid., pp. 98–99.

5. Ibid., p. 131.

6. Ibid., p. 134.

7. Edward H. Flannery, *The Anguish of the Jews: Twenty-Three Centuries of Anti-semitism* (New York: Paulist Press, 1985). Flannery notes in the introduction to this revised and updated edition: "The republication of this twenty year old history of anti-semitism undertaken on the initiative of a Christian publishing house is, paradoxically, a measure of both progress and failure in Jewish-Christian understanding and dialogue of the last score of years. A Christian publishing initiative taken on so self-incriminating a subject is obviously significant and encouraging. No less significant but less encouraging on the other hand is the need to republish it at all. The first objective of the original publication of the book was to acquaint Christians generally with the immense sufferings of Jews throughout the Christian era. The objective has not been realized" (p. 1).

8. Ibid., p. 47.

9. Franklin H. Littell, *The Crucifixion of the Jews* (New York: Harper and Row, 1975), p. 25.

10. Alan T. Davies, ed., *Antisemitism and the Foundation of Christianity* (New York: Paulist Press, 1979). Chapters include John C. Meagher, "As the Twig Was Bent: Antisemitism in Greco-Roman and Earliest Christian Times"; Douglas R. A. Hare, "The Rejection of the Jews in the Synoptic Gospels and Acts"; Lloyd Gaston, "Paul and Torah"; John T. Townsend, "The Gospel of John and the Jews: The Story of a Religious Divorce"; David P. Efroymson, "The Patristic Connection"; Monika K. Hellwig, "From the Jesus of Story to the Christ of Dogma"; Gregory Baum, "Catholic Dogma After Auschwitz"; John T. Pawlikowski, "The Historicizing of the Eschatological, The Spiritualizing of the Eschatological: Some Reflections"; Douglas John Hall, "Rethinking Christ"; Alan Davies, "On Religious Myths and Their Secular Translation: Some Historical Reflections"; Terence R. Anderson, "An Ethical Critique: Antisemitism and the Shape of Christian Repentance"; and Rosemary Radford Ruether, "The *Faith and Fratricide* Discussion: Old Problems and New Dimensions."

11. David A. Rausch, *A Legacy of Hatred: Why Christians Must Not Forget the Holocaust*, 2d ed. (Grand Rapids, Mich.: Baker Book House, 1990), p. 22.

12. James Parkes, *The Conflict of the Church and The Synagogue: A Study in the Origins of Antisemitism* (New York: World Publishing, 1934), pp. 334–35, 394–400; Malcolm Hay, *The Roots of Christian Anti-Semitism* (New York: Freedom Library, 1981), p. 301.

13. Uriel Tal, *Christians and Jews in Germany: Religion, Politics, and Ideology in the Second Reich, 1870–1914*, translated by Noah Jonathan Jacobs (Ithaca, N.Y.: Cornell University Press, 1975), p. 291.

14. Richard Gutteridge, *Open Thy Mouth for the Dumb! The German Evangelical Church and the Jews, 1879–1950* (Oxford: Basil Blackwell, 1976), p. 304.

15. Ernst Christian Helmreich, *The German Churches Under Hitler: Background, Struggle, and Epilogue* (Detroit: Wayne State University Press, 1979), pp. 463–69 for these quotes and his summary.

16. Klaus Scholder, *The Churches and the Third Reich*, translated by John Bowden from the German *Die Kirchen und das Dritte Reich*, vol. 1 (Philadelphia: Fortress Press, 1988), p. 98.

17. Note Klaus Scholder's chapter "The Jewish Question," ibid., pp. 254–79, which details this progressive phenomenon in the German churches in March and April of 1933. Klaus Scholder, who died in 1985, was professor of modern church history in the Evangelical Theological Faculty at the University of Tübingen and vice chairman of the German Evangelical church's commission for contemporary history.

18. Klaus Scholder, *A Requiem for Hitler and Other New Perspectives on the German Church Struggle*, translated by John Bowden from a selection of articles contained in *Die Kirchen zwischen Republik und Gewaltherrschaft* (Philadelphia: Trinity Press International, 1989), pp. 103–4.

19. Shelley Baranowski, *The Confessing Church, Conservative Elites, and the Nazi State* (Lewiston, N.Y.: Edwin Mellen Press, 1986), pp. 23–24.

20. See Arthur C. Cochrane, *The Church's Confession Under Hitler* (Philadelphia: Westminster Press, 1962). Compare Peter Matheson, ed., *The Third Reich and the Christian Churches* (Grand Rapids, Mich.: Eerdmans, 1981).

21. Littell, *Crucifixion of the Jews*, pp. 46–47.

22. See Cochrane, *Church's Confession Under Hitler*, pp. 268–79, for the complete text of this statement, which was written on May 28 and submitted to Hitler on June 4 (the date Cochrane has chosen in his appendix title).

23. See Rausch, *Legacy of Hatred*, pp. 100–103. The quote is on page 101. This book, which is used as a supplementary text in history, religion, and sociology courses on a number of university and college campuses, gives a detailed analysis of anti-Semitism and the Holocaust as a case study of the forces involved in racial and religious prejudice today. Rausch gives modern examples and case studies of this phenomenon, while delving into the mechanics of modern racist propaganda (including hate publications that call themselves "Christian").

24. John F. Morley, *Vatican Diplomacy and the Jews During the Holocaust, 1939–1943* (New York: Ktav, 1980), pp. 208–9. Compare Saul Friedlander, *Pius XII and the Third Reich: A Documentation* (New York: Octagon Books, 1980). For a portrayal of a Catholic youth caught up in the web of anti-Semitism and Nazi devotion, see Alfons Heck, *A Child of Hitler: Germany in the Days When God Wore A Swastika* (Frederick, Colo.: Renaissance House, 1981). Heck was a ranking member of the Hitler Youth, became a reporter in the United States after the war, and took years to understand the horrors of the Nazi regime.

25. See David A. Rausch and David D. Brodeur, "Catholic and Jew," *Midstream: A Monthly Jewish Review* 29 (January 1983): 14.

26. William E. Nawyn, *American Protestantism's Response to Germany's Jews and Refugees, 1933–1941* (Ann Arbor, Mich.: UMI Research Press, 1981), pp. 179–80. The following quotation is on page 183. Compare David S. Wyman, *The Abandonment of the Jews: America and the Holocaust, 1941–1945* (New York: Pantheon Books, 1984).

27. Peter Hellman, *Avenue of the Righteous* (New York: Bantam, 1980), p. viii.

28. Corrie Ten Boom, with John Sherrill and Elizabeth Sherrill, *The Hiding Place* (Washington Depot, Conn.: Chosen Books, 1971). Compare Philip Friedman, *Their Brothers' Keepers* (New York: Crown, 1957); and B. A. Sijes, "Several Observations Concerning the Position of the Jews in Occupied Holland During World War II," in *Rescue Attempts During the Holocaust*, ed. Yisrael Gutman and Efraim Zuroff (Jerusalem: Yad Vashem, 1977).

29. Harold Flender, *Rescue in Denmark* (New York: Holocaust Library, 1963), p. 69.

30. Philip P. Hallie, *Lest Innocent Blood Be Shed: The Story of the Village of Le Chambon and How Goodness Happened There* (New York: Harper and Row, 1978), pp. 20–21.

31. See *Reflections on the Holocaust: Historical, Philosophical, and Educational Dimensions*, a special volume dedicated to Holocaust studies, *Annals of the American Academy of Political and Social Science* 450 (July 1980). Note especially in this issue Heinz Kremers, "The First German Church Faces the Challenge of the Holocaust: A Report," pp. 190–201.

32. Harry James Cargas, *When God and Man Failed: Non-Jewish Views of the Holocaust* (New York: Macmillan, 1981). The essays included are (in order) Frank S. Parker, S.J., "A Visit to Majdanek"; Harry James Cargas, "Help Me to Remember: Three Personal Prayers"; Robert F. Drinan, S.J., "The Transcendental Anti-Semitism of Hitler's Third Reich"; Eva Fleischner, "The Crucial Importance of the Holocaust for Christians"; Franklin H. Littell, "Ethics After Auschwitz"; John K. Roth, "A Theodicy of Protest"; William Heyen, "A Visit to Belzec"; William Heyen, "Simple Truths"; Robert McAfee Brown, "The Holocaust as a Problem in Moral Choice"; Edward H. Flannery, "Anti-Zionism and the Christian Psyche"; Bernard Lee, S.M., "Holocaust"; W. Robert McClelland, S.T.D., "The Holocaust: A Technological Triumph"; Jack S. Boozer, "Holocaust Day, 1975"; Robert E. Willis, "Auschwitz and the Nurturing of Con-

science''; John T. Pawlikowski, "What Are They Saying About Christian-Jewish Relations?'' Harry James Cargas, "Holocaust Literature: Today's Burning Bush''; Thomas A. Idinopulos, "Art and the Inhuman: A Reflection on the Holocaust''; Harry James Cargas, "Modern World Literature and the Holocaust''; and Alice and Roy Eckardt, "How German Thinkers View the Holocaust.'' In addition to the preface and epilogue written by the editor, Cargas adds his own personal annotated bibliography (to 1981) on the Holocaust on pages 220–38.

33. Eva Fleischner, "The Crucial Importance of the Holocaust for Christians,'' in Cargas, *When God and Man Failed*, p. 31.

34. Ibid., p. 30.

35. Harry James Cargas, *Reflections of a Post-Auschwitz Christian* (Detroit: Wayne State University Press, 1989).

36. Ibid., pp. 15–16.

37. Ibid., p. 18.

38. Ibid., p. 91. The following quote is from page 105.

39. John K. Roth, *A Consuming Fire: Encounters with Elie Wiesel and the Holocaust* (Atlanta: John Knox Press, 1979), p. 10; italics in original. Elie Wiesel wrote the prologue for this book.

## SELECT BIBLIOGRAPHY

Baranowski, Shelley. *The Confessing Church, Conservative Elites, and the Nazi State*. Lewiston, N.Y.: Edwin Mellen Press, 1986.

Cargas, Harry James. *Reflections of a Post-Auschwitz Christian*. Detroit: Wayne State University Press, 1989.

———. *When God and Man Failed: Non-Jewish Views of the Holocaust*. New York: Macmillan, 1981.

Davies, Alan, ed. *Antisemitism and the Foundations of Christianity*. New York: Paulist Press, 1979.

Flannery, Edward H. *The Anguish of the Jews: Twenty-Three Centuries of Antisemitism*. Rev. ed. New York: Paulist Press, 1985.

Flender, Harold. *Rescue in Denmark*. New York: Holocaust Library, 1963.

Friedlander, Saul. *Pius XII and the Third Reich: A Documentation*. New York: Octagon Books, 1980.

Friedman, Philip. *Their Brothers' Keepers*. New York: Crown, 1957.

Gutman, Yisrael, and Efraim Zuroff, eds. *Rescue Attempts During the Holocaust*. Jerusalem: Yad Vashem, 1977.

Gutteridge, Richard. *Open Thy Mouth for the Dumb! The German Evangelical Church and the Jews, 1879–1950*. Oxford: Basil Blackwell, 1976.

Hallie, Philip. *Lest Innocent Blood Be Shed: The story of the Village of Le Chambon and How Goodness Happened There*. New York: Harper and Row, 1978.

Hay, Malcolm. *The Roots of Christian Anti-Semitism*. New York: Freedom Library, 1981.

Heck, Alfons. *A Child of Hitler: Germany in the Days When God Wore a Swastika*. Frederick, Colo.: Renaissance House, 1981.

Hellman, Peter. *Avenue of the Righteous*. New York: Bantam, 1980.

Helmreich, Ernst Christian. *The German Churches Under Hitler: Background, Struggle, and Epilogue*. Detroit: Wayne State University Press, 1979.

Littell, Franklin H. *The Crucifixion of the Jews*. New York: Harper and Row, 1975.

Matheson, Peter, ed. *The Third Reich and the Christian Churches*. Grand Rapids, Mich.: Eerdmans, 1981.

Morley, John F. *Vatican Diplomacy and the Jews During the Holocaust, 1939–1943*. New York: Ktav, 1980.

Nawyn, William. *American Protestantism's Response to Germany's Jews and Refugees, 1933–1941*. Ann Arbor, Mich.:UMI Research Press, 1981.

Parkes, James. *The Conflict of the Church and the Synagogue: A Study in the Origins of Antisemitism*. New York: World Publishing, 1934.

Rausch, David. *A Legacy of Hatred: Why Christians Must Not Forget the Holocaust*. 2d ed. Grand Rapids, Mich.: Baker Book House, 1990.

*Reflections on the Holocaust: Historical, Philosphical, and Educational Dimensions*. Special volume devoted to Holocaust studies. *Annals of the American Academy of Political and Social Science* 45 (July 1980).

Roth, John. *A Consuming Fire: Encounters with Elie Wiesel and the Holocaust*. Atlanta: John Knox Press, 1979.

Scholder, Klaus. *The Churches and the Third Reich*. Translated by John Bowden. Philadelphia: Fortress Press, 1988.

———. *A Requiem for Hitler and Other New Perspectives on The German Church Struggle*. Translated by John Bowden. Philadelphia: Trinity Press International, 1989.

Tal, Uriel. *Christians and Jews in Germany: Religion, Politics, and Ideology in the Second Reich, 1870–1914*. Translated by Noah Jonathan Jacobs. Ithaca, N.Y.: Cornell University Press, 1975.

Ten Boom, Corrie, with John Sherrill and Elizabeth Sherrill. *The Hiding Place*. Washington Depot, Conn.: Chosen Books, 1971.

Wiesenthal, Simon. *The Sunflower*. New York: Schocken Books, 1976.

# Chapter 7

# The Righteous Gentiles

*Leon W. Wells*

## FORGOTTEN HEROES

The horror of the Holocaust is of such magnitude that anything else, even the heroic actions of certain "righteous Gentiles," pales by comparison. There is nothing that one may recall from the time that may be offered as a fact mitigating, in some small way, the mass extermination of Jews in Europe. Still, we cannot ignore the heroism of the relatively few individuals who took definite steps to rescue fellow human beings.

In Jewish circles we are not to speak about "prophetic times," when only a small group spoke about "sin" and "injustice," while the majority were the sinners and perpetrators of injustice. We speak about the exceptions to the rule in evil times as "miracles." Therefore we must also speak about the "righteous Gentiles" who appeared as exceptions in this dark period of Jewish history. But first we must ask ourselves why we have not told the stories of these few heroes. Why have we not made their names and deeds known to the public at large? Even when their stories are told, they tend to be told parenthetically and not lifted up as examples of true humanity, and so they are quickly forgotten.

When the late, renowned historian Philip Friedman published his now-classic work, *Their Brothers' Keepers*,[1] he was criticized by some Jewish leaders for giving a false impression of the Holocaust, even though the work found favor with the Anti-Defamation League of B'nai B'rith. Samuel Oliner, coauthor of *The Altruistic Personality*,[2] which deals with the rescuers of Jews in Nazi Europe, mentions that several survivors believed that Friedman took away from the uniqueness of the Holocaust and, as such, did a disservice to the survivors.

Why should this be so? Certainly only a small percentage of the Gentile population could be labeled righteous, but they were no fewer in number than the Jews who took part in the Warsaw ghetto uprising. It is estimated that fewer than 50,000 Jews were involved. Perhaps 100,000 Poles risked their lives to save Jews. The Warsaw ghetto uprising has become the focal point of the Holocaust and is memorialized every year. There are kibbutzim that bear its name. Except for the Avenue of the Just at Yad Vashem in Jerusalem, and for Raoul Wallenberg, there is no similar commemoration of righteous Gentiles. Why?

One must appreciate the experience of Jewish survivors just after the end of the war. The question that was so often put to them by men of the liberating army was "Why didn't you fight?" I remember when I was liberated by Russian soldiers in 1944. Even though I looked like an invalid who was unable to walk because of nine months of hiding in a small basement with twenty-two other Jews, I was still looked upon with suspicion as being a collaborator of the Nazis. That seemed to them the only possible explanation for my having survived. They asked me why I hid and did not fight. One was supposed to fight and die for one's principles and not to hide. The Poles that hid me were even suspected of being collaborators for hiding Jews because the Russians were full of contempt for the Poles and were convinced that the Nazis were so effective in their extermination policy that survival required collaboration.

The first delegation of American Jewish representatives to come to Poland after the war was headed by Louis Segal, the secretary of the Zionist Labor movement in the United States. He put the question, "Why didn't they fight?" to Philip Friedman, who attempted to explain the predicament of Polish Jews during the Nazi occupation. Reflecting on his exchange with Segal, Friedman accounted for Segal's lack of interest in the description of the Jewish plight as a result of his failure to understand the tragedy.

Rabbi David Kahane suggests in his *Lvov Ghetto Diary* that Polish rescuers had their own reasons for not telling their story. Often they thought that they had only done what was normal and proper, and so they did not want to receive any accolades. But more often they feared the possible shunning and rebuke of their neighbors for endangering the neighborhood by their hiding of Jews, or, if their neighbors' anti-Semitism had been religiously motivated, for having betrayed God by working against the will of God to save the Jews. According to this reasoning, if God had wanted the Jews to be saved, God would have done it without any human helpers. It is therefore quite understandable that the rescuers themselves did not want any publicity, and that the story of their deeds remained an undocumented tale.

This wedding of silence on the part of both the rescued and the rescuers has been drawn out so long that now, some forty-five years after the fact, most of the rescuers are not alive and cannot be interviewed. Dennis B. Klein, editor-in-chief of *Dimensions*, a journal published by the Holocaust Center of the Anti-Defamation League of B'nai B'rith, observes that "until recently Philip Friedman's *Their Brothers' Keepers* stood alone to recount the rare instances of rescue."[3] But it is clearly the case that documented stories of rescue are much more rare than actual cases of rescue. Samuel P. Oliner and Pearl M. Oliner faced this difficulty when they began the research for their book, *The Altruistic Personality*, in 1983. The rescuer was most often a person with a family and a house, well established, so that he or she would have been at least forty years of age. In 1983 the rescuer would have been about eighty-three years old. In Poland the average life expectancy for a man is sixty-seven years and for a woman seventy years. These facts preclude any extensive interviewing of such "established" householders and intellectuals who were engaged in rescue work in the 1940s.

## RAOUL WALLENBERG

The best-known story of a righteous Gentile, one that has been the subject of several books and a television documentary, is that of the Swede, Raoul Wallenberg. Born in 1912 to a distinguished Swedish family (his grandfather had been ambassador to Japan and to Turkey; his father was a prominent banker), Wallenberg was a partner in an import-export firm and only thirty-two years old when he was recruited for a special mission to rescue Hungarian Jews facing deportation after March 19, 1944. When the situation of the Jews of Hungary became extremely precarious, Herschel Johnson, the U.S. ambassador to Stockholm, asked the Swedish Ministry of Foreign Affairs to find a prominent Swede who would be prepared to carry on rescue work in Budapest.

Wallenberg's selection may have come by sheer accident, because his partner's offices were adjacent to those of Ivar C. Olsen, who was the financial attaché at the U.S. embassy in Stockholm. Dr. Karl Laurer, the Jewish partner of Wallenberg, described him as one who was disturbed about the predicament of Hungarian Jews and who wanted to be of assistance. Wallenberg was a suitable choice, but the mission was delicate and dangerous.

In order that he might have diplomatic immunity in Budapest, he was appointed an attaché of the Swedish embassy in the Hungarian capital. He arrived on July 9, 1944, with only an attaché case containing the list of the Jews to be given rescue priority and the names of Hungarian anti-Nazis whose assistance he might seek. From 20 volunteer workers in the embassy the staff grew to 660 persons, including their families. For the most part Jewish, they enjoyed a precarious immunity as employees of the Swedish embassy. The safety of his staff was not the only concern of Wallenberg. He wanted to save as many Jews as he could. He issued hundreds of passports to Hungarian Jews with relatives or business ties in Sweden. He devised the "protective passport," a certificate emblazoned with Swedish colors, with which he protected more than a thousand Jews. In this he was also a pioneer, as other countries followed suit, including the papal nuncio and the Swiss, Portuguese, and Spanish embassies.

On one occasion Jews were assembled at the railroad station awaiting deportation. Wallenberg drove there at high speed, summoned the commander, and said, "I have it on good authority that among the people arrested by you for deportation are persons protected by the Kingdom of Sweden. This is an outrage. I demand that you instantly release them or I will complain to your superiors!"

This was 1944, and many Hungarian collaborators already saw the handwriting on the wall and wanted to be on good terms with a country like Sweden. The Germans were bewildered, and most of the Jews were released. Wallenberg also established a number of centers for children, which he placed under the protection of the Red Cross and so saved some 8,000 Jewish children. He also promised some Hungarian officials passports after the war. He bribed other officials with cash. All told, he saved from 30,000 to 100,000 Jews. There are many more stories about Wallenberg's heroic actions that deserve telling, but space does not permit. In any case, the Jews in Hungary thought of him as a modern Moses.

On January 17, 1945, shortly after the Russian army liberated Budapest, Wallenberg was taken away by an armed Russian guard, never to be heard from again. There were rumors through the years, carried by people who had been in Soviet prisons, of a prisoner fitting Wallenberg's description. One report said that he died in 1957 in a Russian prison, but others claim to have seen him in Siberia. Wallenberg became a forgotten man for the Jews. All over the world there were Jews who had been saved by Wallenberg, but the general public knew little, if anything, about him. There were no concerted efforts by Jewish organizations calling for pressure to be exerted on the Soviet Union to release him, and there were no Jewish efforts to locate him, such as were made to locate Adolf Eichmann, the war criminal who was very active in Hungary.

Finally, in 1978, some thirty-four years after he disappeared, Congressman Tom Lantos of California introduced a bill (H.J. Res. 403) to make Raoul Wallenberg an honorary citizen of the United States, so that on this basis one might begin negotiations with the Russians to find out if he still lived, and, if so, what might be done to help him. Congressman Lantos and his wife had both been saved by Wallenberg in Hungary.

What is striking is that the children of the survivors, for the most part, knew nothing of Wallenberg until the Lantoses put his name forward in 1978. Eichmann, the murderer, was better known than Wallenberg, the rescuer. Fortunately, that situation has been rectified somewhat by the appearance of a number of books, chief among which are Per Anger, *With Raoul Wallenberg in Budapest*; John Bierman, *Righteous Gentile: The Story of Raoul Wallenberg, Missing Hero of the Holocaust*; Elenore Lester, *Wallenberg, The Man in the Iron Web*; Kati Marton, *Wallenberg*; Harvey Rosenfeld, *Raoul Wallenberg, Angel of Rescue: Heroism and Torment in the Gulag*; Danny Smith, *Wallenberg: Lost Hero*; and Frederick Werbell and Thurston Clarke, *Lost Hero: The Mystery of Raoul Wallenberg*.[4]

## THE KALWINSKI FAMILY: A PERSONAL REMINISCENCE

Crypto-Jews, those who tried to pass in a Gentile society, had no choice except to find a hiding place. But the righteous Gentiles had a choice to make every day as the strains of hiding Jews threatened not only family relations, but their very existence. The penalty for hiding Jews was death. From a strictly moral standpoint, one might say that their choice was easy, but in reality it was not. Books like Kazimierz Iranek-Osmecki's *He Who Saves One Life* and *The Samaritans, Heroes of the Holocaust*, edited by Wladyslaw Bartoszewski and Zofia Lewin, and the *Anthology of Holocaust Literature*, edited by Jacob Glatstein, Israel Knox, and Samuel Margoshes, related the courage of Poles like Wanda Wnorowska, an aristocrat in Warsaw who supplied the Jews with documents to live among the ''Aryans''; a young girl, Juliana Larish, responsible for saving twenty-one Jews; Pero, a middle-aged clerk at a Polish hotel on Marskalkovska Street; and a widow, Helena Schiborowska, who sold her jewelry to obtain food for hidden Jews.

I can personally testify to the courage demonstrated by Polish Christians. On November 19, 1943, I escaped from the ''Death Brigade'' (Sonderkommando 1005) of the small concentration camp at Janowska near Lvov, Poland.[5] Our task had been to erase the signs of German atrocities. We dug up mass graves, unearthed the bodies, and burned them on a huge pyre in a pit, where old Jewish grave stones were used as the base for the flaming timbers. As the end of the grisly work drew near, we knew that we would be killed and our bodies likewise burned to eliminate the last witnesses to the atrocities, so we planned and executed a breakout from our quarters.

As I fled down a road, I met another escapee from the Brigade, a Mr. Korn, then in his early thirties. I was eighteen. He had been a horse trader before the war and knew a family, the Kalwinskis, to whom he had sold some horses. He hoped that we might find refuge with them. Although I was a complete stranger to them, without any hesitation they took me in along with Korn. When he saw me, Mr. Kalwinski simply shook his head and said in Polish, ''Why, he's only a baby,'' using the English word ''baby.'' His children overheard him and, not knowing any English words, thought that ''Baby'' was my real name, so they called me ''Baby'' throughout the nine months of my stay. After the war, one of the sons of Kalwinski came to visit me in Lvov, and arriving at my apartment building, asked where ''Baby'' lived. He was surprised to learn that it was not my real name.

We were taken to the stable and shown a small opening in the floor of the pigsty, where one or two pigs were always present. In one corner of the stable was a cow, in the other a horse. Over the top of the pigsty was a sleeping place for Kalwinski's son Kazik, who was then fifteen years old. His sleeping there was not considered unusual, for it was assumed that he was there to watch out for thieves who might steal the animals. The sounds of the pigs covered any sounds that we made, and so the sty proved to be an excellent cover for our hiding place.

We crawled through the opening and found our home for the next nine months. It was a space about ten feet wide, twelve feet long, and six feet high, dug out under the stable. We had come through the only entrance. In one corner there was a small cubicle, about three feet high, under a platform bed that stood two feet below the ceiling. The cubicle was our toilet area, with a curtain for privacy hanging in front of a pot and a bucket for emptying the pot. The only piece of furniture was a cot on one side. The rest of the floor was made into one big bed.

Twenty-one other Jews were already there. There was the Holtz family. Mr. Holtz had owned the neighborhood pub. It was not a Jewish neighborhood. His sons and daughters, already grown up, were part of this neighborhood. The Kalwinskis, like so many others, were regular customers at the pub, where they spent many an evening and Sunday afternoons. When the Germans took Lvov and started their "actions" against Jews, the Holtzes got together with their neighbors the Kalwinskis, and so the "basement" was dug. Holtz, a sixty-year-old widower, came with two sons, his married daughter and her husband, and his second daughter and her fiancé. Mr. Holtz slept on the single cot.

There were Mr. and Mrs. Herches and their daughter, and Dr. Prokoczimer and his wife, and a lawyer and his wife, Mr. and Mrs. Kessler. The Kesslers had a small daughter who was hidden with another Polish family, because a crying child might have led to the discovery of the whole group. One day the Kalwinskis came to tell us that she had been discovered and taken away to the crematorium. Of course the Kesslers were shocked, and for days they argued and fought over their tragic decision. We were so hardened by the general calamity that we never asked what had happened to the Poles who hid her. But we were in a similar danger because of the youngest of the Kalwinski boys.

One day a policeman came to the house and took a walk around the outside of the house with Mrs. Kalwinski. Staszek, then nine years old, trailed along. At one point he said within earshot of the policeman, "Mother, it seems the electric meter is running." We had a light in the basement that we would turn on briefly during the day to find our way to the toilet. To our good fortune, the policeman paid no attention to the boy. But the whole episode became a matter for a family conference that evening. It was decided to send Staszek to a farm some three hundred kilometers away. The cover story was that the boy was terrified of planes and bombing, which was not at all the case, and so was sent away for his own good. It was actually a great hardship for him and his family.

My space for my life in the basement was on the platform bed, which I shared with the Kesslers. The routine of our days was organized around the relatively "safe times" for our stirring, which meant late evening into the night. The Kalwinski children hauled away our filth at night and carried our food and clothes back and forth to Mrs. Kalwinski, who cooked for us and washed our clothes at night. The cot where Mr. Holtz slept also served as a sitting couch when any member of the Kalwinski family came to visit us. Mr. Kalwinski came down every night after eight to talk to us, passing on the news of the day and the neighborhood gossip. He was a portly man who had to be helped to squeeze through the narrow opening in the stable floor, where the pigs sometimes urinated, causing some consternation.

Every Sunday, Kalwinski's daughter Marysia came down to spend the afternoon with us, sitting on Holtz's cot and telling us stories of the neighborhood. The Holtz children were especially eager for the news. Very often we protested to her that she, as a girl in her early twenties, should be with her own companions and perhaps a boyfriend on this day. Otherwise her friends might become suspicious, wondering where she spent her Sundays.

Her answer was "How can I enjoy myself, knowing that you are sitting in this hiding place? My place is with you here." So Marysia would help her mother all week with the cooking and the washing of our underwear, which was all that we could wear under the circumstance of the heat generated by so many bodies in that small space. The cooking and washing chores included chopping wood for the wood-burning stove to heat the food and the wash water. Marysia and her mother had to go shopping for the whole group in many different places, including the black market, so as not to attract attention by the amount of food they purchased. We were fortunate that the Kalwinskis were small "city farmers" who had some vegetable crops of their own and beef to slaughter. The Germans required the registration of every animal to prevent meat being sold on the black market, but this posed no problem for the Kalwinskis, who kept the meat in the family.

February, March, and April 1944 were terrifying months for us. The German army requisitioned many rooms in the neighborhood to quarter its soldiers. It took over several rooms in the Kalwinski house for its headquarters and even put a couple of horses in the stable above our hiding place. During its stay we were fed only once a day in the dead of night.

In April twelve Jews who were hiding in the home of a nearby cattle dealer by the name of Juzefek were tragically exposed. A quarrel broke out between the parents and a sixteen-year-old daughter. In a rage at her parents, she ran out of the house screaming that they were hiding Jews. Everyone heard about it. The Germans came and found Jews in the hiding place. Juzefek and his wife were hanged publicly, and their bodies were left on the gallows for forty-eight hours as an example.

The Kalwinskis simply carried on as usual, although the execution of their friends and neighbors caused them pain and grief. For some weeks we discussed the danger to the Kalwinskis among ourselves, coming to the conclusion that we should offer to leave, since we had no right to risk their lives. When we did so, their answer was "What God wants to happen to you, it will happen to us, too." Like most Poles, the Kalwinskis were religious people. We held out for three more months until August 1944, when the Russians liberated Lvov, and we were able to don our street clothes for the first time and walk out into the sunlight.

After the war the Kalwinskis moved to Gliwice from Lvov, which became part of Russia. Marysia, their only daughter, died in childbirth in 1947. The elder Kalwinskis died of old age, the father in 1967 and the mother in 1978. Their sons are still alive.

## SURVIVORS SHARE THEIR STORIES

If Holocaust survivors could have been asked in advance what they would do, how many would have said, "I would have fought"? What percentage would have chosen to hide? What if they had been asked the following questions: "Would you kill a companion in hiding?" "Would you kill your own baby?" For many survivors, it was not moral heroism, but the ability to kill that spelled the difference between survival or death.

After liberation, I shared an apartment with a group of survivors, every one of whom had been hidden. At that point I had never met anyone who survived by fighting as a partisan. In our *kolkhoz* (commune), as we called our community of survivors, was a man by the name of Busko, who had been hidden with another man in the basement of a school by a custodian. After months of hiding in a small, dark space, the other man became claustrophobic. He finally said that he just had to get out. He did not care anymore whether he lived or died. Both the custodian and Busko felt that it was too risky, that if he left, he might be caught, tortured, and made to tell his story. In spite of their protestations, the man decided to leave one night.

When he saw him, Busko was overcome by panic, took an axe from the corner of the basement, and flailed away at the man. Blood sprayed all over the basement. All through the night and the next day until the evening, when the custodian came as usual with food, Busko, himself spattered with blood, stayed there with the corpse. He told his rescuer what had happened, and they discussed their plight. The custodian was now in double jeopardy. He could be killed by the Nazis for hiding the two Jews, and he could be placed on trial after the war as an accomplice to murder. They buried the corpse in the basement, cleaned up the area, and agreed that they would never mention it, nor ever see one another again after the liberation.

Another member of our *kolkhoz* was a pretty young woman by the name of Halina. She had survived with a group of Jews who were hidden in the sewers of Lvov by a sewer cleaner whose name was Socha. Socha had also been part of the criminal underworld before the war, a leader of a gang. Just before the war he experienced a religious conversion, becoming a "born-again" Christian. When the Germans came to Lvov and announced their anti-Jewish policy to the Poles, Socha believed that God had called him to risk his life and the lives of his wife and daughter to save the Jews, "God's beloved children." He was convinced that this was to atone for his many sins as a criminal.

Socha was able to get into the Jewish ghetto through the sewer system, and there he met a Jewish plumber who was a hunchback. There is a belief among the Polish peasantry that a hunchback brings luck. For example, one might seek out a hunchback to touch the hump before signing a contract, or just to bring luck. This hunchback was also pious, a Jew who often spoke of God, of course in the Jewish way, so everything appeared to Socha as the will of Providence. He went down every day into the city sewers through a manhole and searched through the system of pipes five feet in diameter for an appropriate hiding place. He found and prepared a place with a sleeping area, left a cache of food and candles to keep the rats away, and then commissioned the plumber to gather a group of Jews to be hidden.

The hunchback was indeed good fortune for most of the people that he collected. He found a wealthy lawyer and his wife and daughter who would be able to supply money for buying food and necessities. There was a sixty-year-old woman, a good friend of his, and Halina, to whom the hunchback may have been attracted for romantic reasons as well as pity, a barber in his late twenties, and a young market girl.

As the sewer water got higher, the little group moved from place to place in the system, always in fear of being discovered. Mrs. Weiss, the sixty-year-old, died in the sewer and was buried there. In the course of months the barber became romantically involved with the young market girl, who became pregnant and eventually gave birth to a boy right there in the sewer.

At one point, the baby would not stop crying and could not be consoled. The mother put a pillowcase over its head, and the child choked to death. The young couple lived through their grief, and she again became pregnant. About a month before the liberation she gave birth to another boy. The barber and the girl got married after the war, and the child lived to have a family of his own.

Even after the war Socha continued to care for the whole group until everyone had a place to live. He and his family moved to Katowice in western Poland, where he again found employment as a sewer man. He was killed by being run over by a truck as he was coming up through a manhole in the street. Some of the survivors who were still in Poland joined his wife and daughter in his funeral cortege.

One of our group told the story of a woman who hid a Jewish woman in her apartment. Whenever anyone came to the door, the Jewess would hide in the closet until her hostess would call out "all clear." One evening a policeman came to the door. As it was curfew, the policeman only wanted to say that light was showing through their window and that the window curtains should be drawn tighter. When the policeman left, the hostess gave the "all clear" signal. There was no answer from the closet. When she opened the door, she found that her friend had died of a heart attack. What should she do now?

She decided to go to the superintendent of the building and tell him the whole story. He suggested that they take the body up to the roof, hang her there, and in the morning give the report that someone had committed suicide on the roof. She agreed to this, so she helped him carry the body to the roof and stage the hanging. After it was reported to the police the next morning, local people started to gather on the street to catch a glimpse of the sight. There is a Polish folk belief that a rope from a hanged person brings luck. The people in the street yelled upstairs for a piece of the rope. The superintendent had the idea of cutting the rope into small pieces to sell to them, which he did. With the money he went to the local bar and became inebriated. Returning to the building, he blurted out the whole story, calling them stupid for paying him money for the pieces of rope. He and the woman were arrested forthwith. I never heard what became of them.

There were also cases where rescuers were placed in the position of having to betray some Jews in order to save others. In one Polish village a group of townspeople was enjoying a Sunday afternoon picnic of beer and kielbasa with the mayor seated at the head of the table. Two Jewish women approached the group, their faces full of fright because they were fleeing from Germans. They identified themselves as Jews and asked the mayor for a hiding place. The townspeople, hearing this, asked the mayor not to help them, as that would place the whole village in jeopardy. The Germans were well known for taking reprisals on a whole town for the "illegal acts" of its inhabitants, especially of officials. The mayor took the two women away in his horsedrawn carriage, promising them refuge. Instead, he took them to the local police station and turned them in.

The mayor became a hero to his villagers because he had not placed them in jeopardy. The German police started to think of him as a collaborator, which made the Jews whom the mayor was hiding in his own house that much safer. Had the mayor taken the two women to a hiding place, the news of it would have spread through the whole village, and the lives of all concerned would have been at stake. Was the mayor a hero? A villain? Or simply a human being with a tragic choice to make?

Other rescuers were caught in the web of their own intrigue for saving the Jews. A very close friend of mine and her sister were hidden, one in the space of a double ceiling, the other under a bed in the small apartment of the woman who cleaned their house before the war. Parysia, the cleaning woman, worked to support all three of them in a German warehouse where the clothes confiscated from the Jews of Lvov were cleaned, stored, and packaged for shipment to Germany, where they would be distributed. She would steal some items of clothing, sell them in the black market, and use the money to support herself and the two Jewish women. If anyone with whom she was dealing in the black market spotted an item as surely Jewish, she would answer "Smart aleck!" to give the impression that she was as anti-Semitic as the next person.

After the liberation the Russians suspected all Ukrainians and Poles of collaboration with the Germans, especially those who had a reputation of dealing on the black market with goods taken from Jews. The police came and searched her apartment and found a piece of velvet from a Jewish "Talit bag." This was just what the Russians needed to arrest her. Velvet was the most expensive cloth on the black market.

Parysia was taken to the railroad station to be loaded into a boxcar and shipped to Siberia. On the platform she dropped a piece of paper, a note begging the bearer to get in touch with a friend, so that she and her sister might come and prove that she worked against the Germans and not for them. The note did not reach the sisters until months later, and they were already in America and in no position to bring influence to bear upon her case. Parysia was never heard from again.

Mrs. K. was from a well-to-do Jewish family and had a law degree before the war. Her servant girl from before the war, the daughter of a prostitute, became her rescuer. She did everything that she could for Mrs. K., often risking her life, because she felt that it was the first time in her life that someone respected her and really needed her, and the one in need was from the "upper class."

The girl spoke in the language and slang of her milieu, such as, "Jews are the business people." "They are the doctors." "They stick together." "You should know. You have a Yiddish head." Such phrases were often used by Jews themselves, but when used by Poles they became "anti-Semitic." The servant often meant them with love and respect for Mrs. K., or in some cases she simply believed them. Her use of such phrases proved to be her downfall.

When the Russians crossed the old borders of Poland and were advancing westward, many people wanted to be liberated early, so they started to walk to the east to meet the Russians. Mrs. K. and her rescuer also joined them. On the road they met a young couple with a newborn baby. The mother died on the road. The young rescuer, who was nursing an infant of her own, offered to breast-feed the baby.

Some weeks later, Mrs. K. and the servant went to work for a Russian military hospital. Both had to have blood tests. The servant girl tested positive for syphilis. Mrs. K. asked her all kinds of questions about possible sexual contacts, but she swore to her that she had not been intimate with anyone lately. Another test indicated that she had got the syphilis from the feeding of the baby, who had been born with syphilis, and who had bitten her nipple. She was eventually cured and got a job in the laundry room of the hospital. There she was overheard making some of her "anti-Semitic" remarks by a Russian doctor, who happened to have been Jewish. He reported her as being a pro-Nazi and an anti-Semite. She was not only fired, but was sent to Siberia and, like so many others, was never heard of again.[6]

## EUROPEAN NEIGHBORS

Rescuers were from all walks of life. Householders and servants were prominent, but much significant rescue work was accomplished by intellectuals and priests. Philip Friedman was hidden in the apartment of Dr. Tadeusz Zaderecki, a well-known personality in Poland. Rabbi David Kahane, who became a rabbi for the Polish army after liberation, writes in his memoirs of his encounter with the Metropolitan Andreas Szeptycki, the Arch-Bishop of Lvov, who agreed to hide some Jewish children. Later Kahane himself found shelter in the Metropolitan's palace, where he worked in the library and gave Hebrew lessons to the monks.[7] Rabbi Levine was hidden by the aged Metropolitan Szeptycki in a monastery of the Fathers Studites, first as a lay worker and later as a monk.

Szeptycki told him, "I do not expect any rewards, nor do I expect you to accept my faith."[8]

In every nation of Nazi-occupied Europe there were righteous Gentiles who risked their lives to save Jews. Philip Friedman's book, *Their Brothers' Keepers*, gives an early, albeit incomplete, picture of the rescue activity. One of the ironies of the general picture is that a higher percentage of Jews were rescued in countries that formed puppet governments to administer the interests of the Third Reich, namely, France, Denmark, Hungary, and Bulgaria, than in nations such as Poland where Vichy-type governments were never considered. The delaying tactics of bureaucracies in Bulgaria, Belgium, Denmark, Norway, and even Germany have been chronicled in such diverse works as Marshall Miller's *Bulgaria During the Second World War*, Anne Somerhausen's *Written in Darkness: A Belgian Woman's Record of the Occupation, 1940–1945*, Leni Yahil's *The Rescue of Danish Jewry*, Harold Flender's *Rescue in Denmark*, Olav Riste and Berit Nokleby's *Norway, 1940–45: The Resistance Movement*, and Thomas Keneally's *Schindler's List*. In Poland the Nazis set up their own government general to carry out their policy of harvesting Jews for the death camps, which they did with characteristic efficiency, utilizing terror to secure the cooperation of the Jewish Councils that were formed to administer the ghettos and to recruit a "police force" to deliver fellow Jews for deportation.

One should not assume that the number of Jews killed in a given country was a direct reflection of the intensity of anti-Semitic prejudice. For example, in Holland, where there was little anti-Semitism, a smaller percentage of the Jewish population was saved than in other Western lands. The same was true for Czechoslovakia, which was well known for the lack of prejudice against the Jews. Many more Jews of Czechoslovakia were killed because there, as in Poland, the Germans themselves took charge of the deportations.

### Rescuers of Jewish Children

A special group of righteous Gentiles were those who gave refuge to Jewish children. While one might think that it was easier to save children, especially infants who did not speak and therefore had no Yiddish accent, as had most of the Polish Jews, there were still many obstacles to overcome.

First of all, one needed a baptismal certificate. One then had to tell the local priest that he or she had a Jewish child and thus run the risk of taking another person into one's confidence. Second, if the children were a little older, one had to work with them, instructing them so that they would not say anything to give themselves away. A boy would have to be taken to a physician or a hospital to have his prepuce drawn forward to give the appearance of being uncircumcised. For this reason it was often the case that the rescuers would only take Jewish girls. Invariably the children were raised as Christians to cover their Jewish origins.

Of course, the rearing of a Jewish child as a member of a Christian household led to strong emotional attachments, which became a problem after the war, when many Jewish parents came to claim their children. The adoptive parents often had become so attached to the children that they did not want to give them up, especially if the memory of the real parents had been erased from the child's mind. This was especially true in Holland, where of some 4,000 Jewish children who were rescued in this way, only 1,750 were returned to Jewish families. The situation was most painful when the real parents and all their relatives were killed, and other Jews came to claim the children to raise them as Jews. These children were seldom given a choice, as they found themselves caught in a tug of war between their adoptive parents and the Jews who came for them. Some of these children were kidnapped and spirited away to distant Jewish communities when the adoptive parents could not be persuaded to relinquish them. I am not aware of any case in Poland in which the rescuing family did not make an effort to return the child to its real parents. A touching story of the reunion of Jewish parents with a son who had been hidden with Polish Christians and raised as a Christian is that of Alexander Donat and his wife retrieving their son, Wlodek, at the end of the book *The Holocaust Kingdom*.[9]

In the book *The Altruistic Personality*, Samuel and Pearl Oliner, who themselves had been hidden as children in Polish Christian homes, tell the story of a rescuer and the Jewish girl who was saved. After the war she had a real baptism, and the rescuer was present for the celebration of the sacrament. They had their picture taken together. Then it was time to part.

It was decided that the girl should go to her Jewish relatives, see the place, and become acquainted with the people. If she were to become unhappy there, she could return to the rescuer, who agreed to raise her and send her to school. One month later, the rescuer received a letter from the girl, dated March 24, 1949, the last one she would receive until 1981. The girl was by then a nurse in Israel.

The rescuer was left wondering why the girl did not write in all those years. One reason may have been that she had forgotten the language, but more probably it was because she embraced her Judaism with deep conviction. The rescuer reports that she really had nothing against that. She only wanted the girl to be an honest, good nurse. It was painful to be told as a foster mother, who had adopted her officially, that although the girl and her family were grateful, they did not want her to have contact with non-Jews anymore. The rescuer grieved, feeling that hatred had been allowed to cut the human bond that was there between them before all of the religious and cultural differences.[10] While I feel that this story is an exception, it was certainly the case that when the rescued children returned to the fold of Judaism and were told the story of the crematoria and of the murder of their family and friends, there was the risk of generating hatred even for the ones that were altruistic.

## Non-Jewish Spouses

A category of righteous Gentiles that tends to be overlooked for rather obvious reasons is that consisting of the non-Jewish spouses of Jews who suddenly found themselves subject to deportation. The record of stability and loyalty of these mixed marriages was very good during the Holocaust. An American anthropologist, David Rodnick, who investigated these relationships, writes in *Postwar Germans*, "We were very much struck by the large number of German men who refused to divorce their Jewish wives and did all they could to protect them under the Nazis. . . . In all our contacts, we came across only one case of betrayal, but we heard many stories of loyalty involving great sacrifice."[11]

## Italy: The Story of the Nachts

Perhaps the most surprising story of rescue during the Holocaust, and the best one expressing a national consciousness after the Danish rescue of some 7,220 Jews in October, 1943,[12] is that of Fascist Italy. Calling Italy the "reluctant ally," Phillip Friedman documents the Italian resistance to the Nazi program of genocide. There were some 57,000 Jews in Italy, according to the census of 1938. About 40,000 of them survived the war years because the Italian government, the army, and the people simply did not share the Nazis' anti-Semitic outlook. Jews had held high public office, including a prime minister, a minister of war, and a mayor of Rome.[13] It was well known that Mussolini himself "frowned on racialism, calling it un-Italian." The Duce had said in 1924 that anti-Semitism "is an alien weed that cannot strike roots in Italy where Jews are citizens with full equality."[14]

The first anti-Jewish laws in Italy came in 1938 as a result of the Italian-German alliance. Mussolini apparently came to the realization that an Italian anti-Jewish campaign was part of the price of the alliance, and he was willing to pay it. But fortunately for Italian Jews, many government officials and the people were not willing to concur with the anti-Jewish decrees in 1938. No Italian Jews were required to wear a badge. There were no ghettos, no Italian-managed deportations to death camps.[15] Still, some 4,500 Jews converted to Christianity after the anti-Jewish laws were passed. But wherever the Italian army was in control, in southern France, Yugoslavia, and Greece, Jews were spared deportation until, toward the end of the war, the Germans took the matter into their own hands and began rounding up Jews in Italy itself.[16]

The story of a young Jewish couple from Lvov, Poland, who were studying medicine in Belgrade, Yugoslavia, when the Germans attacked Belgrade is illustrative of the experience of Jews under the Italians.[17] Mr. and Mrs. Nacht left Belgrade on April 6, 1941, when the first German bombs fell upon the city. They made their way to Montenegro, where they took a train to Split (Croatia), which was under Italian Fascist rule.

One day the Italian government made the announcement that any refugees who would like to come to Italy would be allowed to do so. There was a general fear among the refugees because of reports of hunger in Italy, and of course because of Mussolini's cooperation with Hitler's policies. The Nachts felt that hunger was not to be feared, as there was not too much food where they were, so they were among the first to register for Italy.

With a group of about two hundred they were put into railroad cars. The men were separated from the women and children and loosely handcuffed. When they arrived at the station in Trieste, the Nazis photographed the men as they were led in handcuffs from the train and gave the pictures to be published in newspapers. With the proper publicity behind them, the refugees were taken to Italian boats, where they were given wonderful treatment. They were served good food at tables properly set with white cloths.

In Italy they were transferred to trains, and the Nachts were taken with twenty-five other Jews to the small village of Crespano del Grappa near Venice and Padua. The Italians gave them eight lire a day for food and fifty lire a month for a room. Of course, food was rationed, but the Italians often sold the refugees food without ration coupons at the official prices, much lower than those of the black market. The relations between the Jewish refugees and the Italian villagers were very good, with much visiting back and forth. Most of them had never met Jews before, and they enjoyed the new social contacts very much.

One day the Nachts were informed that they would have to move from the house because the landlady's sister had come from Turino after her house was bombed. They were supposed to go to another village, but the local people did not want them to leave. The pharmacist's wife, with whom they had not been particularly close, came and offered them a beautifully furnished room in her house, which they were happy to accept. The local grocer sent them gifts of food. The Nachts lived there for two years.

Early in 1943 there was a knock at their door. An Italian girl had come to warn them, "The Germans are here!" Italian neighbors came with a car to take the Nachts to the railroad station at Bassano, some ten miles away. When they tried to pay them, they refused, saying, "When you come back, and when Mussolini will be hanged, we will drink wine together."

The Nachts kept moving toward the south, hoping to reach the Allied lines. On foot, carrying their suitcases through the countryside, they were met by a young girl who asked them where they were going. When they told her, she informed them that they were headed toward the Germans. The girl offered to help with the suitcases, even to store a couple of them until after the war, which the Nachts were happy to allow, because of their weight. The girl, who was the daughter of an Italian police commissioner, gave them her address, where they came to claim their cases after the war and found everything just as it had been.

The Nachts were indeed strangers in Italy, but the hospitality that they experienced could not have been warmer under the circumstances. They were the beneficiaries of a tradition of Italian humaneness that neither Mussolini's fascism nor Hitler's state terrorism could erase. Of course, such was also the case in France and in Belgium, Holland, and Denmark, wherever the rescue of Jews was considered an obligation that could not be avoided. The Nachts' story bears witness to the operative presence of the values of truth, justice, and human dignity in a time when barbarism reigned, and the policies of hatred and conquest by a people driven by the doctrine of "might makes right" brought chaos and destruction upon all of Europe.

## The Vatican and the Jews

The part of the Italian story that has received the most attention, and so has overshadowed the good record of the Italian people, is that of the pope during the period of the Holocaust. Rolf Hochhuth's controversial play *The Deputy* dramatized the problem of the pope's silence about the process of genocide taking place in Europe.[18] While there has been much speculation about the reasons for the pope's silence, such as that the pope's official statements would have only given the impression of papal weakness and lack of influence in international affairs, there is no doubt about the real efforts taken by the pope and the clergy to rescue Jews who lived in their territories. The chief rabbi of the Jewish community of Rome, Dr. Israel (Eugene) Zolli, was hidden by the pope during the Nazi occupation. After the war he converted to Christianity. Philip Friedman describes in detail how priests and churches helped Jews in Italy, how the pope was involved with helping Italian Jews, and how he even contributed a large sum of money to the Jewish synagogue in Rome.[19]

I must admit that the role of the pope during these years remains a riddle to me, but I suspect that much of the condemnation of the pope derives from the old religious quarrel between faith and unbelief. Anti-Catholics may be exploiting the pope's silence to question the pope's religious and moral infallibility. On the other hand, the faithful might be tempted to blame the "deputy" of God for his failure in order to turn the question away from what God was doing during the Holocaust.

The crisis of religious faith posed by the Holocaust has generated quite a discussion among Jewish and Christian theologians. Some have said that it shows that God is dead. Others have claimed that God suffered with his people in Auschwitz, and that an eleventh commandment was given there, ordering the people to fight for their survival. Others say that God went mad, and still others divide the responsibility between men and God as follows: human beings are responsible for everything bad that happened, and God is responsible for everything good that happened. A more penetrating line of inquiry in my view would be to ask about the role that religious fatalism played in the thinking of both Christians and Jews as they confronted the ineluctable forces that drew them into the killing process. How often was the statement "It is the will of God!" used as a rationale for the killing? The old Christian doctrine of the guilt of the Jews for the crucifixion of Jesus still found an echo in the thinking of many a pious Christian throughout Europe.[20] On the other hand, there were Jewish victims who came to accept the Holocaust as a punishment of God upon Jewish unfaithfulness.[21]

### Help from Anti-Semites

Another group of people who quite surprisingly appeared among the rescuers of Jews and sometimes paid with their lives were former anti-Semites. Friedman lists quite a number of them in *Their Brothers' Keepers*.[22] There was Jan Mosdorf, who before the war was the leader of the anti-Semitic youth movement in Poland. He carried letters to a woman inmate at Birkenau, where he worked, and brought food to Jews in prison. He was eventually shot by the Nazis. Stanislaw Piasecki, who had been the editor of an anti-Semitic journal, *Prosto z mostu* (Straight from the shoulder), and an outspoken admirer of Hitler, was so shocked by the events following the German invasion that he repented of his anti-Semitism. A group of Polish anti-Semitic lawyers refused, when invited by the Nazi officials, to make public statements as to their attitude toward the Jews. "Witold Rudnicki, a member of the anti-Semitic National Democratic party . . . ordered the execution of four Polish blackmailers who threatened to inform the Germans of Jews hidden in the village of Pustelnik, near Warsaw. His apartment in Warsaw eventually became a shelter for Jews who escaped from the ghetto. He was killed during the revolt in Warsaw in the autumn of 1944."[23]

Aleksander Witaszewicz, a wealthy landowner and a member of the National Democratic party, hid nine Jews for two years on his estate and helped five of them to find a hiding place in Warsaw, where he continued to supply them with food. He was assassinated on his estate in 1943. It was thought that he was the victim of an anti-Semitic guerilla unit. Friedman reports the statement of Dr. Franciszek Kowalski, a lawyer from Zakopane: "I was an anti-Semite before the war. Hitler's bestiality toward the Jews changed me. I had not imagined that human debasement as displayed by the Germans could sink to such depths."[24]

While these actions of former anti-Semites are commendable, they should force us to reflect on the nature of human prejudice and its role in generating violence. While these converts away from anti-Semitism were shocked by the violence and were made to consider the moral implications of their prejudice, there were many others, perhaps persons who were converted to anti-Semitism by some of the propaganda efforts of these leaders and publicists, who used their former statements as a rationale for the violence. If there is a lesson to be learned from all this, it is that one may not ignore any prejudicial statements or behavior on the grounds that all human beings are prejudiced in some way. The prejudicial statements and discriminatory acts of today, however bland they might appear, may very well contribute to a social process that generates violence against the discriminated tomorrow. If we take this seriously, it should lead us to the conviction, upon which we should always be willing to act, that there is no such thing as a mild or harmless statement or act of prejudice.

Perhaps the hardest thing to accept about the story of the righteous Gentiles of the period of the Holocaust is that there were, relatively speaking, so few of them. We now know that one cannot take it for granted that most people place a high value on morality and human rights. These are values that must be cultivated, taught, and reinforced by public examples and by the stories that we tell our children to prepare them for the hard decisions of life. When one considers the fact that our youth today are literally bombarded with stories of violence and vengeance in movie theaters and television, it seems that what is being reinforced today is the philosophy of force and counterforce, whether at the level of street gangs or that of international diplomacy. But shouldn't we now consider the consequences of this type of negative reinforcement and seek out and tell stories of rescuers, of persons who risked everything to save lives, and promote these stories for the purpose of cultivating a keen sense of humanity, so that our children may learn, as did the righteous of Europe during the Holocaust, to resist the prevailing barbarism of their day?

## NOTES

1. Philip Friedman, *Their Brothers' Keepers* (New York: Crown, 1957).

2. Samuel P. Oliner and Pearl M. Oliner, *The Altruistic Personality* (New York: Free Press, 1988).

3. Dennis B. Klein, *Dimensions* 3 (1988): 3.

4. Not even the breakup of the Soviet Union has resolved the mystery surrounding Wallenberg's disappearance. As late as summer 1992 the KGB still maintained it had no information on his whereabouts.

5. Leon Wells, *The Death Brigade* (New York: Holocaust Library, 1978).

6. As reported to me by Ada June Friedman.

7. Rabbi David Kahane, *Lvov Ghetto Diary* (Amherst: University of Massachusetts Press, 1990), p. 146.

8. As reported by Friedman, *Their Brothers' Keepers*, p. 136.

9. Alexander Donat, *The Holocaust Kingdom* (New York: Holt Rinehart and Winston, 1963), pp. 355–61. Wlodck, now called William, is the chairman of the Holocaust Library.

10. Oliner and Oliner, *Altruistic Personality*, pp. 234–35. Estimates on the children saved in Belgium run from 3,000 to 4,000. In France, where about 75 percent of the Jewish prewar population of 350,000 was saved, thousands of children were saved, in Paris alone some 12,000. In Poland, where there were some 921,000 Jewish children up to fourteen years of age before the war, only 5,000 were saved. See Philip Friedman, *Roads to Extinction* (Philadelphia: The Jewish Publication Society of America, 1980), pp. 415–16.

11. David Rodnick, *Postwar Germans* (New Haven: Yale University Press, 1948), pp. 121–22.

12. Jorgen Glenthoj, "The Little Dunkerque: The Danish Rescue of the Jews in October, 1943," in *Human Responses to the Holocaust*, edited by Michael D. Ryan (New York and Toronto: Edwin Mellen Press, 1981), pp. 93–119. When word leaked out that the Germans intended to deport the Jews of Denmark during the High Holy Days of 1943, a mass evacuation of Jews was organized among the Danish population, who ferried the Jews in small boats to Sweden.

13. Friedman, *Their Brothers' Keepers*, p. 72. Here Friedman identifies them as Prime Minister Luigi Luzzatti, Minister of War Giuseppe Ottolenghi, and Ernesto Nathan, who had been mayor of Rome.

14. Ibid.

15. Ibid., p. 73.

16. Friedman reports the complaint of a German Gestapo officer of the Department of Jewish Affairs, Heinz Roethke, about the situation in southern France. "The attitude of the Italians is incomprehensible. The Italian military authorities and police protect Jews. . . . The Italian zone of influence, particularly Cote d'Azur, has become the Promised Land for the Jews in France. In the last few months there has been a mass exodus of Jews from our occupation zone into the Italian zone." Ibid., p. 77.

17. Pola Nacht wrote a letter to me in which she told the story of how she and her husband, now deceased, survived in Italy.

18. In his work *The Nazi Persecution of the Churches, 1933–45* (New York: Basic Books, 1968), Canadian historian John S. Conway refers to a twenty-eight-page letter to the German government by Cardinal Maglione, the papal secretary of state, of March 1943, which Conway calls "the most forceful of all the protests" (p. 325). Surely this protest was sent with the full knowledge of the pope. It furnished explicit details of the many ways that the German government had systematically suppressed the Catholic church in the Warthegau, the region including Lodz, Gnesen, Posen, and Wladislavia in Poland, where Catholic theological seminaries existed before the Germans closed them. There had been six Roman Catholic bishops there before the war. In 1943 there was only one, and he was under house arrest. There had been some two thousand priests. In 1943 there were only a handful.

Conway does quote an address of Pius XII to the College of Cardinals of June 1945 in which the pope described the final stages of the Nazi persecution of the Catholic church and branded it "an arrogant apostasy from Jesus Christ" (p. 326). Both of these documents deal with Nazi treatment of Catholics and say nothing about the treatment of Jews and other non-Catholics.

19. Friedman, *Roads to Extinction*, p. 415.

20. The old Christian charge of the guilt of the Jewish people for the crucifixion of Jesus was even repeated in the writings of none other than the theologian and pastor Dietrich Bonhoeffer, who joined the resistance movement and was executed for it just before the end of the war. In an essay, "The Aryan Clauses," written in September 1933 for the purpose of denouncing them, Bonhoeffer wrote the following: "Now the measures of the state towards Judaism in addition stand in a quite special context for the church. The church of Christ has never lost sight of the thought that the 'chosen people', who nailed the redeemer of the world to the cross, must bear the curse for its action through a long history of suffering." *No Rusty Swords: Letters, Lectures, and Notes, 1928–1936* (New York: Harper and Row, 1965), p. 226.

21. See Leon Wells, *Who Speaks for the Vanquished?* (New York: Peter Lang Press, 1988), pp. 102–3, where the June 1941 issue of the Lubavitcher publication *Reading and Holiness* is cited. It interprets the reported suffering and travail of European Jews as a sign of the imminent coming of the Jewish Messiah. The same journal is cited as informing its readership in April 1943 that Hitler is a new Haman. "A Haman does not arise of himself, but is sent to remind the Jews that they have gone too far astray, and to force them to repent. He cannot maintain himself a single day longer than is necessary to carry out the purpose of Heaven" (pp. 174–75).

22. Friedman, *Their Brothers' Keepers*, p. 114.

23. Ibid., p. 115.

24. Ibid.

## SELECT BIBLIOGRAPHY

Anger, Per. *With Raoul Wallenberg in Budapest*. New York: Holocaust Library, 1981.

Bartoszewski, Wladyslaw, and Zofia Lewin, eds. *The Samaritans: Heroes of the Holocaust*. Translated by Alexander Jordan. New York: Twayne, 1970.

Bauminger, Aryeh. *Roll of Honor*. Tel Aviv: Menora Publishing House, 1971.

Bierman, John. *Righteous Gentile: The Story of Raoul Wallenberg, Missing Hero of the Holocaust*. New York: Viking Press, 1981.

Donat, Alexander. *The Holocaust Kingdom*. New York: Holt, Rinehart and Winston, 1963.

Flender, Harold. *Rescue in Denmark*. New York: Simon and Schuster, 1963.

Friedlander, Saul. *Pius XII and the Third Reich: A Documentation*. New York: Knopf, 1966.

Friedman, Philip. *Roads to Extinction*. Philadelphia: Jewish Publication Society of America, 1980.

————. *Their Brothers' Keepers*. New York: Crown, 1957.

Glatstein, Jacob, Israel Knox, and Samuel Margoshes, eds. *Anthology of Holocaust Literature*. Philadelphia: Jewish Publication Society of America, 1968.

Goldberger, Leo, ed. *The Rescue of the Danish Jews: Moral Courage Under Stress*. New York: New York University Press, 1987.

Grossman, Chaim. *The Underground Army*. New York: Holocaust Library, 1987.

Gutman, Yisrael, and Shmuel Krakowski. *Unequal Victims: Poles and Jews During World War II*. Translated by Ted Gorelick and Witold Jedlicki. New York: Holocaust Library, 1986.

Hallie, Philip. *Lest Innocent Blood Be Shed: The Story of the Village of Le Chambon and How Goodness Happened There*. New York: Harper and Row, 1978.

Hochhuth, Rolf. *The Deputy*. New York: Grove Press, 1964.

Iranek-Osmecki, Kazimierz. *He Who Saves One Life*. New York: Crown, 1971.

Keneally, Thomas. *Schindler's List*. New York: Simon and Schuster, 1982.

Koblik, Steven. *The Stones Cry Out: Sweden's Response to Persecution of the Jews, 1933–1945*. New York: Holocaust Library, 1988.

Latour, Anny. *The Jewish Resistance in France (1940–1944)*. New York: Holocaust Library, 1981.

Lester, Elenore. *Wallenberg, The Man in the Iron Web*. Englewood Cliffs, N.J.: Prentice-Hall, 1982.

Marton, Kati. *Wallenberg*. New York: Random House, 1982.

Meed, Vladka. *On Both Sides of the Wall*. New York: Holocaust Library, 1979.

Morley, John. *Vatican Diplomacy and the Jews During the Holocaust 1939–1943*. New York: Ktav, 1980.

Oliner, Samuel P. and Pearl M. Oliner. *The Altruistic Personality: Rescuers of Jews in Nazi Europe*. New York: Free Press, 1988.

Ramati, Alexander. *The Assisi Underground: The Priests Who Rescued Jews*. New York: Stein and Day, 1978.

Rautkallio, Hannu. *Finland and the Holocaust: The Rescue of Finland's Jews*. New York: Holocaust Library, 1987.

Riste, Olav, and Berit Nokleby. *Norway, 1940–45: The Resistance Movement*. Oslo: International Publisher, 1970.

Rodnick, David. *Postwar Germans*. New Haven: Yale University Press, 1948.

Rosenfeld, Harvey. *Raoul Wallenberg, Angel of Rescue: Heroism and Torment in the Gulag*. Buffalo: Prometheus, 1982.

Ryan, Michael D., ed. *Human Responses to the Holocaust: Perpetrators and Victims, Bystanders and Resisters*. New York and Toronto: Edwin Mellen Press, 1981.

Setemvri (State Publishing House of the People's Republic of Bulgaria). *Saving of the Jews in Bulgaria, 1941–1944*. Sofia, 1977.

Smith, Danny. *Wallenberg: Lost Hero*. Springfield, Ill.: Templegate Publisher, 1987.

Somerhausen, Anne. *Written in Darkness: A Belgian Woman's Record of the Occupation, 1940–1945*. New York: Knopf, 1946.

Steckel, Charles. *Destruction and Survival*. Los Angeles: Delmar, 1973.

Steinberg, Lucien. *The Jews Against Hitler*. London and New York: Gordon and Cremonesi, 1978.

Tec, Nechama. *When Light Pierced the Darkness: Christian Rescue of Jews in Nazi-occupied Poland*. New York: Oxford University Press, 1986.

Wells, Leon. *The Janowska Road*. New York: Macmillan, 1963.

———. *Who Speaks for the Vanquished? American Jewish Leaders and the Holocaust*. New York: Peter Lang Press, 1988.

Werbell, Frederick, and Thurston Clarke. *Lost Hero: The Mystery of Raoul Wallenberg*. New York: McGraw-Hill, 1982.

Yahil, Leni. *The Rescue of Danish Jewry*. Philadelphia: Jewish Publication Society of America, 1969.

# Chapter 8

# Understanding Motivations in
# the Holocaust

## *Eva Fogelman*

In the forty-five years since the Holocaust, scholars have examined the politics, psychology, and emotional resonances of mass murder. The task of accounting for the evil has been, and continues to be, an arduous and depressing one. But a growing number of social scientists, educators, and religious leaders are focusing on people who, during the black years of the Holocaust, acted with physical and moral courage, such as a sixteen-year-old Polish girl who had thirteen Jews in her apartment for three years; a young Dutch couple with a three-year-old girl who were caught harboring Jews in their attic (the man was brutally attacked by a Gestapo agent's German shepherd, then shot when he refused to betray their Jewish friends); and a German engineer who became known as "the Moses of Rovno" for his determined and successful efforts to lead hundreds of Jews to freedom from the Nazis.

## THE INITIAL STUDY OF RESCUERS

In the early 1960s Rabbi Harold Schulweis single-handedly began to persuade social scientists that rescuers were an invaluable resource for learning about altruism and moral courage. His dedication to this task began when, about the time of the Eichmann trial, he met several rescuers in his community. Schulweis had been struggling with the effort to impress upon children and his congregation the evil of the Holocaust, but in such a way as to avoid making them lose their trust in humanity. The rescuers' goodness struck him as "light piercing the darkness," as Nechama Tec would put it.

In an attempt to understand Nazism from a social-psychology point of view,

Schulweis contacted some leading researchers from whom the late John Slawson had commissioned work two decades earlier for the landmark study, *The Authoritarian Personality*. Almost without exception, these social scientists told him that there was nothing to be learned from interviewing rescuers. Presenting his findings in a paper titled "The Bias Against Man" at the late 1962 Rabbinical Assembly Convention in Kiamesha Lake, New York, Schulweis suggested that one reason for the silence by academics was that "evil, paradoxically, seems easier to cope with than goodness. Compared to the demonic villainy of Klaus Barbie, I am a saint. Would I act as Mengele did? I am quite sure that I would not. By contrast, goodness confronts me with a harder mirror."

When discussing the difficulty of confronting goodness, Schulweis often mentions his first contact with Herman Graebe. When the rabbi asked Graebe why he had risked his life to help Jews, he replied, "What would *you* do?"[1]

After his first encounter with a rescuer, Schulweis felt profoundly uncomfortable at, and morally challenged by, Graebe's response. He persuaded psychologist Perry London that the rescuers were worth studying. When London began work on the motivation of rescuers in the mid-1960s, there were only two books to which he could turn for background: *Their Brothers' Keepers* by historian Philip Friedman and *Die unbesungenen Helden: Menschen in Deutschlands dunklen Tagen* (The unsung heroes: people in Germany's dark days) by Kurt Grossman. Friedman's immense contribution was to record rescuer activity during the war, country by country. He also attempted to understand the rescuers' motivations in risking their lives to help strangers. In his anecdotal compilation Grossman made no effort to analyze individual acts of moral courage.

Subsequently, Perry London's essay, involving a small sample of rescuers and survivors who were aided by non-Jews, was published in 1970 (see "The Rescuers: Motivational Hypotheses About Christians Who Saved Jews from Nazis," in *Altruism and Helping Behavior*, edited by L. Macauley and L. Berkowitz). The primary question he explored was simple: "Why did they do it?" London arrived at several hypotheses about rescuers' motivations for their altruistic behavior:

1. A spirit of adventurousness
2. An intense identification with a parental model of moral conduct
3. A sense of being socially marginal[2]

## SENSE OF ADVENTURE

The first hypothesis suggested that rescuers "had not only the desire to help, but also a desire to participate in what were inherently exciting activities." But this finding was not confirmed in later studies of rescuers involving more subjects. Although the Rescuer Project (my sociopsychological study of three hundred rescuers and survivors from throughout Nazi-occupied Europe) found that more than 50 percent of the subjects reported that they were accustomed to and enjoyed adventure—not a particularly high percentage compared with other factors—this was not a motivating force for rescue activity. But it did in part explain their ability to engage in risk when confronted with life-and-death situations and affected the type of activities rescuers undertook.[3]

Samuel and Pearl Oliner, who published the results of a study commissioned by John Slawson as *The Altruistic Personality*, noted that adventurousness was not a motivating force in initiating or responding to a request for help. Rather, it affected the way in which a rescue was undertaken. Particularly adventurous rescuers tended to participate in the most risk-laden activities, such as smuggling Jews over borders, rather than in more mundane, but equally stressful acts, such as hiding Jewish families in attics or basements under the scrutiny of suspicious neighbors.

## PARENTAL ROLE MODEL

London's second observation was that most rescuers identified strongly with one parent who was a "strong moralist—not necessarily religious, but holding very firm opinions on moral issues and serving as a model of moral conduct." Larger studies have confirmed that role modeling is an important factor in shaping rescuers. According to my research, 80 percent of rescuers remembered an altruistic role model from childhood. These results were further confirmed by the Altruistic Personality Project. The Rescuer Project elaborated upon London's original hypothesis by noticing that many rescuers, in addition to having a moral role model, also participated in helping activities as children. Parents impress the importance of helping others more deeply upon their children when they enlist the youngsters' "hands-on" assistance in their own altruistic activity.

## SOCIAL MARGINALITY

London's final hypothesis, that of "social marginality" among the rescuers, opened a debate that has engaged researchers for almost twenty-five years. London hypothesized that rescuers were sympathetic to Jews because they, too, felt socially marginal. He believed that this also helped the rescuers to defy societal norms. This view of "outsiders" helping fellow "outsiders" seems to me unfortunate. Although it explains the relative rarity of rescue during the war, it also implies that altruism can only be expected from those who feel alienated from their communities. The hypothesis of social marginality suggested that rescuers possess certain characteristics that make them fundamentally different from their surroundings (e.g., being the only Catholics in a Protestant neighborhood) or, at least, make them feel different.

The question of "social marginality" is a thorny one; only recently has a consensus begun to emerge on it. A large body of evidence since London's original study suggests that the rescuers did not perceive themselves as being "out of sync" with their social milieu. True, the rescuers, by definition, were nonconformist. The question is, were they like that before they started their rescue activities? And if so, why?

Nechama Tec interviewed rescuers in Poland and Holocaust survivors who were rescued by Poles, and also engaged in extensive archival work for her book *When Light Pierced the Darkness: Christian Rescue of Jews in Nazi-occupied Poland*. Tec found that the rescuers had a sense of "individuality" or "separateness" that is somewhat akin to London's concept of "social marginality." In her study some Polish rescuers felt different from those in their community, while others were not aware of a difference. Regardless of their own feelings, the rescuers had traits that made them different from their neighbors.

While London explained that adventurousness and social marginality were separate motivating forces, Tec perceived adventuresome behavior among the rescuers as an expression of marginality. She observed that both reflect self-reliance and independence. Tec also stated that rescuers were "propelled by moral values that did not depend on the support and approval of others, but rather on their own self-approval." Both the Oliners' study and my work found that the rescuers were not socially marginal. The Oliners questioned rescuers on their childhood ability to "stand up for their own beliefs." The great majority recalled that they had acted on the basis of their principles, but that this quality had not made them isolated socially.

Clearly, there are similarities between "social marginality" and an "ability to stand up for one's beliefs." Both imply a sense of singularity within the crowd, or "separateness" in Tec's language. However, given the dangers of too easily inferring causality, especially in psychology, one cannot unequivocally claim that a sense of social marginality contributes to an ability to stand up for one's beliefs—or vice versa. Both my Rescuer Project and the Altruistic Personality Project found that although rescuers were sometimes the only Poles in a Ukrainian town, or unusually short, or noteworthy in some other way, the majority felt a sense of belonging in their social milieu. Only 14.4 percent of the rescuers in the Altruistic Personality Project responded that they felt like outsiders in their community.

## RELIGIOUSLY INSPIRED NONCONFORMITY

The Reverend Douglas Huneke, who has focused on the rescuers' distinctiveness, has coined the term *religiously inspired nonconformity*. This roughly corresponds to London's "marginality," Tec's "individuality," and my "ability to stand up for beliefs." Quoting Romans 12:2, "Be not conformed to this world, but be transformed to a new way of thinking," Huneke notes that many religious Christian rescuers justified their actions by citing the teachings of Scripture. He believes that their Christian upbringing actively fostered disobedience to malevolent earthly authorities, leading to goodness in the face of brutal, absolutist rule. Huneke found that the goodness in Christians was a rock upon which he could base his faith when it seemed to him that the Holocaust had morally bankrupted Christianity. He cited rescues by entire faith communities such as those in Le Chambon-sur-Lignon, France (see Pierre Sauvage's moving film *Weapons of the Spirit*), and Assisi, Italy, as evidence of the New Testament's power as a force for goodness in the world.[4]

Eva Fleischner, who studied Catholic rescuers in France in her paper "Can the Few Become the Many? Some Catholics in France Who Saved Jews During the Holocaust," asserts that it was a belief in "the oneness of all humanity, which was grounded . . . in Christ," that prompted some of her rescuers to act on behalf of Jews. She asked one French rescuer what had sustained her opposition to the church, which had deeply disappointed her by taking a collaborationist stance. The rescuer replied:

Christ. I come from a region of France where there are vineyards. When I read in the Gospel about Jesus' parable of the vine and the branches, I understood. I knew what a vine is, the analogy was perfect for me. Humanity is the body of Christ. I felt as if I were holding the vine and the branches in my hand . . . how could I have denied this relationship?[5]

## CLASS, GENDER, POLITICS, AND RELIGION

Beyond the question of motivation, however, there is the issue of the rescuers as people. Who were they? Were most rescuers wealthy or poor? Male or female? Politically to the Left or the Right? Catholic, Protestant, or secularist? Is there any way of classifying rescuers that significantly enhances our understanding of them?

Manfred Wolfson, a political scientist, interviewed forty rescuers and collected socioeconomic data on an additional thirty, all of whom had been active in Berlin. He found that there was little aid to Jews among blue-collar workers and that more males than females were involved in rescuing relationships. But when it came to political attitudes and religious beliefs, he could discern no pattern. Some rescuers were apolitical, others very active in various parties. Religiously, they were evenly distributed along a continuum from very religious to antireligious Catholics and Protestants.[6]

As early as 1970 researchers concluded that the classic socioeconomic variables of political affiliation, social class, gender, education, and religion were not primary factors in predicting whether a bystander would be moved to rescue. This was later confirmed by Tec's, the Oliners', and my research.

## CHILDREARING AND MORAL DEVELOPMENT

However, a great deal has been discovered about common patterns of childrearing and moral development among rescuers. Those who became rescuers were taught tolerance for differences among people. This value was found by the Oliners to be distinctly different from that of a control group of bystanders who heard much more anti-Semitic talk around their homes than had the rescuers. Similarly, Tec found only one anti-Semitic couple in her study of Polish rescuers.

Fleischner learned that most rescuers she studied either had never been exposed to the "teaching of contempt" (a triumphalist doctrine about the backwardness of the Jewish faith in comparison with Christianity; the term was coined by Jules Isaac, a French-Jewish historian) or had powerful role models who had spoken out against it. Germaine Ribiere, the rescuer who spoke of the parable of the vine when discussing her motivation for rescue, is one example of a Catholic who had never heard of the "teaching of contempt."[7]

## EXTENSIVITY

Ribiere also seems to exemplify what the Altruistic Personality Project calls "extensivity." She stated clearly that her relationship with Christ was extended to include all of humanity, indicating that she widened a close, personal bond so as to encompass a larger group. The Oliners discovered that this is quite typical. Rescuers scored very high on scales measuring their level of bonding both within the family and to society at large. The Oliners also believe that moral extensivity is learned rather than innate.

This implies that emotional attachments to both close-knit and more abstract social units are characteristics of altruism; far from being mutually exclusive, they are complementary. The rescuers were not people who cared more for a stranger than for their own children. Rather, they were able to expand their oneness of family to include people who were different from them. The Oliners state:

Those who are confined to their immediate environments alone may be wonderful family members and friends, but they are likely to perceive the rest of the world as either irrelevant or not quite worthy. Those whose attachments to others are basically abstract and generalized may have grand ideologies, but they are capable of inflicting harm because they do not relate to real people.[8]

## DISCIPLINE BY "INDUCTIVE REASONING"

Another childrearing practice typical of rescuer homes was a method of discipline known as "inductive reasoning," a term coined by psychologist Martin Hoffman, which means the consequences of children's behaviors are explained to them in terms of their impact on others' feelings and well being: "I don't want you to do that again because it makes Tom feel very sad," or "your grandmother feels less tired when you help her."[9]

The overwhelming majority of the rescuers I studied remembered at least one parent who enforced rules by "explanation" rather than "punishment." This approach might have enabled rescuers to look beyond the formal "rules" of mass murder to perceive the fundamental brutality and cruelty behind them.

## SENSE OF AGENCY

The rescuers generally had what is sometimes called a "sense of agency," a feeling of competence and independence that had been fostered by supportive parenting. This helped them to conquer their fear of torture or execution (the Nazis' punishment for engaging in rescue).

I am convinced that had more bystanders felt competent and trusting of their abilities as individuals, they would have had greater confidence that their rescue attempts would be successful. Rescuers had a capacity to master their fears that other empathic bystanders did not. Some coped by using emotional "numbing"; others were conscious of and expressed their anti-Nazi rage; while still others resorted to belief in a transcendent being or the strong human bonds of a religious or resistance network.

## EMPATHY

Most researchers have found that rescuers are unusually empathic people. Ute Klingenmann, a sociologist who compared rescuers and bystanders in Germany, found that the rescuers are still much more able to emphathize with others than those Germans who remained passive during the Third Reich.[10]

My research revealed that a significant percentage of rescuers had suffered the loss of a close relative in childhood. But they also had been raised by loving, empathic caretakers who were their role models. These early experiences may have been at the root of the rescuers' empathic responses to suffering during the war.

Huneke defines "empathic imagination" as the "ability to place oneself in the actual situation of another person and actively visualize the effect and the long-term consequences of the situation on that person." In his study of Herman "Fritz" Graebe, he credits the rescuer's mother with "one of the most sophisticated empathic imaginations" in his sample. Huneke notes, "His mother would call his attention frequently to a difficult or confusing moral situation and ask him the question, Fritz, what would you do?" (the same question Graebe later would pose to Rabbi Schulweis).[11]

## SITUATIONAL FACTORS VERSUS THE WILL TO RESCUE

One issue that has been continually raised is that of the extent to which situational factors determined the likelihood of rescue. Did people help Jews mostly because they had the opportunity to do so, or was rescue a matter of "where there's a will, there's a way"?

The Oliners, developing previous research findings, found many important differences between rescuers and bystanders. In the face of very dangerous and otherwise difficult circumstances that caused most other people to "tend their gardens," many rescuers persisted against all-but-impossible odds.[12]

Both the Oliners and I found that the great majority of rescuers were asked to help, rather than initiating the rescuing relationship themselves. In addition, many experienced an "upward curve of risk": "They began their helping activity by smuggling food or clothing into the ghetto and only gradually took the risk of sheltering persecuted Jews in their homes."

## A TYPOLOGY OF RESCUERS

I analyze rescue in terms of how an individual socialization process, personality traits, and opportunity converge in the moment of decision to risk one's life for another. I have delineated five types, based on the rescuers' values, feelings, and relationships when they initially decide to engage in rescue.

For some rescuers, the process of transformation from bystander to rescuer was directly related to gradual but increasing commitment to an anti-Nazi or religious ideology. For others, the rescue act was triggered by a sudden awareness of an imminent death of either a loved one, an acquaintance, or a total stranger.

The most prevalent were moral rescuers, who simply said, "It was the right thing to do." Morality is derived from a number of sources and finds its expression in different ways according to attitudes, beliefs, and emotions. This category can be divided into three moral types:

1. Ideological-moral rescuers are motivated by a sense of morality-based ethical behavior and justice and by moral convictions that maintain a sense of self.

2. Religious-moral rescuers are motivated by that which stems from religious beliefs and a sense of moral duty to be "thy neighbor's keeper." Some religiously motivated fundamentalist rescuers believed in the "chosenness" of the Jewish people and felt a spiritual connection with the Jews through the Bible and Jesus.

3. Emotional-moral rescuers are motivated to act humanely by feelings of pity and compassion for the victims.

Moral rescuers can be distinguished from other types by examining how their helping activity began. Moral rescuers often require a trigger event to precipitate a latent altruistic response. Most often they are led to help, or they undergo a "transforming encounter" that inspires them to actively initiate help. A transforming encounter occurs when witnessing an event so assaults one's sense of decency and humanity that one is forever disfigured. It usually involves an encounter with death, which leaves a person with indelible images as vivid today as they were forty years ago. The degree of empathy with the victim is the operative factor in the potential of a witnessed act of violence to assume transforming power.

Relational philo-Semitic rescuers all had relationships with Jews, whether spouses, relatives, close friends, acquaintances, or colleagues. In addition, these rescuers had a particular affinity toward Jews for a myriad of reasons. Some suspected that they had Jewish blood; others possessed warm memories of having been a *shabbos goy*. Some had a Jewish role model in childhood; others felt a sense of religious connectedness to Jesus, a Jew, or to the "chosenness" of Jews. Relational philo-Semitic rescuers began their activity with people they knew and sometimes moved on to helping strangers.

Next, in terms of numbers, were ideological-network rescuers, who helped Jews as part of a political or religious resistance group with intense anti-Nazi connections. Rescuers who were involved in networks were wholeheartedly immersed in anti-Nazi activities well before they aided Jews. Rescue acts escalated to meet the demands of the gradually worsening inhumane situations. Some became "professional rescuers," smuggling documents or contraband before transporting Jews. These kinds of activities became a full-time occupation.

Fourth were children and adolescents who began rescuing in obedience to their parents' wishes and then continued of their own accord. It was often safer for children to pass messages into ghettos, to bring food to people in hiding in the woods, to stand guard, and to serve as guides to bring Jews to safe houses. Until recently, this group of rescuers was almost entirely invisible, as it had been during the war.

Finally, detached professional rescuers helped Jews as part of their professional duties. Physicians, nurses, psychologists, and social workers, among others, operated both within and outside of the Nazi sphere. They maintained a kind of doctor-patient relationship with the people whose lives they saved. They were empathic while at the same time keeping a certain professional distance.

## ALTRUISM AS A JUNGIAN ARCHETYPE

In his paper "The Altruism of the Righteous Gentiles," presented in 1988 at the conference "Remembering for the Future," Mordechai Paldiel, director of Yad Vashem's Department of Righteous Among the Nations, was less concerned with classifying rescuers according to shared characteristics than with the idea of altruism itself. In an approach quite different from those taken by the psychologists, political scientists, religious leaders, and historians cited previously, Paldiel adopted a Jungian framework for understanding altruism.

Paldiel says that altruism exists as a "universal and primordial image and symbol. . . . Whether we are aware of their presence or not, [archetypes] are the centers of our psychic energy and have a 'numinous' lifelike quality." He equates the archetypes of altruism with the rabbinic concept of *hesed* (usually translated as "lovingkindness") and the Christian idea of "grace," adding:

Altruism . . . is an archetypal reality and . . . capable of momentarily wresting us from our conditioned behavior and summoning us to be at its behest. . . . However, its manifestation has all but been limited to a tolerable minimum so as not to threaten a social fabric based on ego-seeking norms and patterns, to which we are all subtly conditioned.[13]

Paldiel suggests that the rescuers responded to the question, "Why did you do it?" with surprise, less because empathy and humane behavior were "natural" for them than because an archetypal tendency has become manifest in their behavior. While the researchers mentioned earlier attempt to isolate aspects of individuals' upbringings that impelled them to engage in rescue activities, Paldiel believes that such categorization ultimately is unproductive. Altruism is at once within and beyond individual human beings, manifesting itself through human action yet existing as a force on another plane of reality.

## COMMUNAL RESCUE

Communal rescues took place in such towns as Le Chambon, France, and Nieuwlande, Holland, as well as in Italy, Bulgaria, and Denmark. Of these, it is the Danish rescue that has received the most public and scholarly attention.

Leo Goldberger, a Danish Jew who is a psychoanalyst and teacher, has devoted much time to understanding what moved his nation to defy the Nazis and smuggle almost all of its Jews to Sweden. In *The Rescue of the Danish Jews: Moral Courage Under Stress*, a collection he edited, Goldberger notes that the popular myth about King Christian—that he rode through the streets on horseback with a yellow star emblazoned on his chest—is apocryphal. But, he observes, if we "substitute the symbol of the king with the Danish people as a whole, and substitute further the wearing of a yellow star with the widespread and emphathic compassion for the Jewish plight," we will gain "the kernel of truth" behind the myth. Apparently, empathy can occur on a mass as well as an individual level, provided the "in group" has been inculcated with a tolerant, caring attitude toward the "out group."[14]

Samuel Abrahamson, a historian, in his essay in Goldberger's book, says that Denmark

had developed over the centuries what the Danes call *livkunst*, the art of living. It was a society where people *cared* about one another, where respect for individual and religious differences, self-reliance, cooperation and good humor had become hallmarks of a civilized nation. These moral, intellectual, and ethical attitudes made the Danes say: "The Jews are our fellow citizens and fellow human beings; we shall not give them up for slaughter." And they did not. . . . The diabolic plan to exterminate innocent Jews so outraged the Danish population that it *united* the nation against the Nazis and established a popular basis for the Danish resistance movement.[15]

Everyone who studies rescuers agrees on one thing: If we instruct our children to value all human life, empathize with suffering, and tolerate differences among people, we will create a society in which Auschwitz is unthinkable. These simple lessons and imperatives for moral education are no less striking for their lack of novelty, for reiterating principles and processes that we have long known.

It is vital to instill in children what Rabbi Schulweis calls "habits of virtue" and what Reverend Huneke terms "the consistency between belief, self-perception, and how one acts in life." This means that adults must not only be altruistic themselves, but should regularly engage children in helping activities.

Eva Fleischner relates a story about Germaine Ribiere. The two were walking casually down a Paris street when Germaine suddenly stopped and said, ''I'm worried about that little girl.'' Germaine thought that she might have lost her mother. Fleischner recalls:

I had noticed, vaguely, a little girl in front of us, about two years old, but I had not really *seen* her. Germaine had seen, and worried. . . . As I came to know her in the months that followed, and to learn of the extraordinary things she had done during the war, I realized how much of a piece she is. She is Germaine Ribiere because she notices a little girl who may be lost and in need of her help, in the middle of Paris in 1985, just as the Jews needed help during the war.[16]

Clearly, each rescuer was unique and must be seen in that light. But there are patterns in rescuers' upbringing that can provide us useful clues to nurturing and promoting altruistic behavior. In a world where heroes sometimes are separated from villains only by their mass-media appeal, where constant yet subtle racism periodically explodes in riots and murders, and where too many religious leaders preach the gospel of fundraising, we need all the help we can get. The rescuers can show us the way.

## EDITOR'S NOTE ON PERPETRATORS

Addressing a conference of scholars at Haifa University in 1986, Raul Hilberg noted that while much had been written about victims of the Holocaust, historians had yet to address questions relating to perpetrators. Were the Nazis so different from us? What motivated otherwise ''normal'' human beings to perpetrate inhuman acts? What moral lessons are we to draw from their behavior?

Such questions are addressed in Hilberg's comprehensive study, *Perpetrators Victims Bystanders: The Jewish Catastrophe, 1933–1945* and *''The Good Old Days'': The Holocaust as Seen by Its Perpetrators and Bystanders* (Ernst Klee, Willi Dressen and Volker Riess, eds.). Apart from excellent memoirs such as Elie Wiesel's *Night*, Alexander Donat's *The Holocaust Kingdom* (New York: Holt, Rinehart and Winston, 1963), Primo Levi's *Survival in Auschwitz* (New York: Collier, 1973), and Leon Wells's *The Janowska Road*, there are a number of collections of testimonies that address mechanisms of coping with brutality. These include Isaiah Trunk, *Jewish Responses to Nazi Persecution* (Briarcliff Manor, N.Y.: Stein and Day, 1978); Dorothy Rabinowitz, *New Lives: Survivors of the Holocaust Living in America* (New York: Knopf, 1976); and Lucy Steinitz and David Szonyi, *Living After the Holocaust: Reflections by the Post-War Generation in America* (New York: Bloch, 1976). Questions of response by victims have also been analyzed in Helen Fein, *Accounting for Genocide: National Responses and Jewish Victimization During the Holocaust* (New York: Free Press, 1979); Terrence Des Pres, *The Survivor: An Anatomy of Life in the Death Camps* (New York: Oxford University Press, 1976); and Bruno Bettelheim's *The Informed Heart: Autonomy in a Mass Age* (New York: Free Press, 1960).

Those who seek lessons in the reaction of the Jews during the Holocaust would best be advised to turn to Emil Fackenheim's *The Jewish Return into History* (New York: Schocken Books, 1978) or Viktor Frankl's *Man's Search for Meaning* (New York: Pocket Books, 1974). In a series of philosophical lectures and midrashim premised on the concept that Jews have been the target of a worldwide campaign of hostility since 1933, Fackenheim argues that there is no redeeming voice from Auschwitz, but rather a commandment, that Jews are forbidden to grant posthumous victories to Hitler. Frankl's book, most of which deals with his personal struggle to survive in a concentration camp, has meaning even for those who have no interest in the Holocaust. In discussing logotherapy, Frankl offers commonsense instruction to those who seek meaning in life. Moreover, he refutes the notion that people today are conditioned, fully determined robots. Whether men behave as swine or saints, says Frankl, "depends on decisions, but not on conditions."

Frankl's comments have relevance to the question why Nazi perpetrators did what they did. Though the answers may not satisfy Hilberg and others, the question has been addressed by a number of scholars over the years. Already in 1963 two controversial books made their appearance. Hannah Arendt's *Eichmann in Jerusalem: A Report on the Banality of Evil* (New York: Viking Press, 1963) emphasized that only a few Nazi killers were sadists. Not hatred, but bureaucratic logic dictated their behavior. At the same time, the German psychologist Konrad Lorenz in *On Aggression*, translated by Marjorie Wilson (New York: Harcourt, Brace and World, 1963), commented on the ease with which demagogues channeled the rage of frustrated peoples (what he termed *Begeisterung*) against scapegoats. Subsequently, Lorenz's colleague Irenaus Eibl-Eibesfeldt called man's ability to demonize his opponents more serious than the invention of weapons. "In the last analysis," wrote Eibl-Eibesfeldt in *Love and Hate: The Natural History of Behavior Patterns*, translated by Geoffrey Strachan (New York: Holt, Rinehart and Winston, 1971), "it is this capacity to switch off pity that makes him into a cold-blooded murderer." Virtually the same conclusions were reached by Israel Charny in his analysis of "genociders" in *Genocide: The Human Cancer* (New York: Hearst Books, 1982).

Other useful studies include Irving Horowitz, *Genocide: State Power and Mass Murder* (New Brunswick, N.J.: Transaction Books, 1976), and *Taking Lives: Genocide and State Power* (New Brunswick, N.J.: Transaction Books, 1980); Richard Rubenstein, *The Age of Triage: Fear and Hope in an Overcrowded World* (Boston: Beacon Press, 1983); Leo Kuper, *Genocide: Its Political Use in the Twentieth Century* (New Haven: Yale University Press, 1981); Alan Rosenberg and Gerald Myers, eds., *Echoes from the Holocaust: Philosophical Reflections on a Dark Time* (Philadelphia: Temple University Press, 1980); Joel Dimsdale, ed., *Survivors, Victims, and Perpetrators* (New York: Hemisphere, 1980); and Robert Abzug, *Inside the Vicious Heart: Americans and the Liberation of Nazi Concentration Camps* (New York: Oxford University Press, 1985).

Four books on the subject of the perpetrator are markedly superior to all others. Eugen Kogon's *The Theory and Practice of Hell*, translated by Heinz Norden (New York: Farrar, Strauss, Giroux, 1950), offers insight into the mentality of the prisoners and guards at Buchenwald, as well as the German people in general. Kogon's claims that many of the SS suffered from feelings of inferiority, that Germans were disoriented after the war, and that survival mechanisms for one *Häftling* (prisoner) might not work for another hold up after nearly half a century of scrutiny.

Robert Jay Lifton's *The Nazi Doctors* and Miklos Nyisali's *Auschwitz* are frightening examples of how men sworn to the preservation of life could be prompted to take "life unworthy of life." In his study of more than one hundred participants in the T4 (euthanasia) and 14f13 (*Sonderbehandlung*, extermination) programs, psychiatrist Lifton concludes that Nazi doctors who were trained to be detached in their treatment of human beings extended this concept so that Jews and other alleged "inferior" peoples became objects. Few of the doctors were sociopaths, but all engaged in the mental process of "doubling" that protected them from having to deal with their own consciences.

Committed to a racist "biocracy," the Nazis succeeded in blocking any sense of wrong, even after the war. In this, they were merely emulating the mass of Germans who, says Lifton, engaged in psychic numbing. When Germans protested that they did not know what was happening to the Jews, many were telling the truth. The villagers of Dachau did not know what went on in the concentration camps, according to Bettelheim, because they did not want to know. As for those who actually perpetrated atrocities, there was no sense of guilt because they were participating in a grand design, one where they had no choice because they were following orders.

This compelling nature of *Obrigkeit* (obedience) underlies perhaps the most chilling psychological study of the Holocaust, Stanley Milgram's *Obedience to Authority: An Experimental View* (New York: Harper and Row, 1974). As a result of tests done with Yale University students and a random sample of residents of Bridgeport, Connecticut, between 1959 and 1962, Milgram revealed that the vast majority of "normal" people (social workers, ministers, nurses, blacks, and Jews) in a free society were predisposed to follow orders, even if the orders might result in harm or death to another being. For those who thought that there was some unique flaw in the German psyche, Milgram pointed to American conduct at My Lai. There, as in the death camps, physical distance from an abused subject, the use of euphemisms and sanitized language to mask brutality, and similar behavior on the part of one's comrades all reinforced an individual's belief that what he had done was proper. *Obedience to Authority* is a humbling book that forces us to direct judgment back upon ourselves.

## NOTES

1. Harold M. Schulweis, "The Bias Against Man" (Paper presented at the Rabbinical Assembly Convention, Kiamesha Lake, New York, 1962).

2. Perry London, "The Rescuers: Motivational Hypotheses about Christians Who Saved Jews from Nazis," in *Altruism and Helping Behavior*, edited by L. Macauley and L. Berkowitz (New York: Academic Press, 1970).

3. Eva Fogelman, "The Rescuers: A Socio-Psychological Study of Altruistic Behavior During the Nazi Era" (Ph.D. diss., City University of New York [Ann Arbor, Mich.: University Microfilms International, 1987]).

4. Douglas Huneke, "Religious Community Perspectives on Rescuers" (Paper presented at a conference on "Moral Courage During the Holocaust and in the Post-Holocaust World," Woodrow Wilson School of International Affairs of Princeton University and Jewish Foundation for Christian Rescuers, Anti-Defamation League, 1990).

5. Eva Fleischner, "Can the Few Become the Many? Some Catholics in France Who Saved Jews During the Holocaust" (Paper presented at the conference "Remembering for the Future: The Impact of the Holocaust on the Contemporary World," Oxford, 1988).

6. Manfred Wolfson, "The Subculture of Freedom: Some People Will Not" (Paper presented at the Western Political Science Association Conference, 1970).

7. Fleischner, "Can the Few Become the Many?"

8. Samuel P. Oliner and Pearl M. Oliner, *The Altruistic Personality* (New York: Free Press, 1988).

9. Ibid.

10. Ute Klingenmann, "Rescuers of Jews in Berlin" (Paper presented at the International Society for Political Psychology, Washington, D.C., 1985).

11. Huneke, "Religious Community Perspectives on Rescuers."

12. Oliner and Oliner, *The Altruistic Personality*.

13. Mordecai Paldiel, "The Altruism of the Righteous Gentiles" (Paper presented at the conference "Remembering for the Future," Oxford University, 1988).

14. Leo Goldberger, ed., *The Rescue of the Danish Jews: Moral Courage Under Stress* (New York: New York University Press, 1987).

15. Samuel Abrahamsen in Goldberger, *The Rescue of the Danish Jews*, 3–11.

16. Fleischner, "Can the Few Become the Many?"

## SELECT BIBLIOGRAPHY

Adorno, T. W., E. Frenkel-Brunswik, et al. *The Authoritarian Personality*. New York: W. W. Norton, 1969.

Fleischner, Eva. "Can the Few Become the Many? Some Catholics in France Who Saved Jews During the Holocaust." Paper presented at the conference "Remembering for the Future: The Impact of the Holocaust on the Contemporary World," Oxford University. Elmsford, N.Y.: Pergamon Press, 1988.

Fogelman, Eva. "The Rescuers: A Socio-Psychological Study of Altruistic Behavior During the Nazi Era." Ph.D. diss., City University of New York. Ann Arbor, Mich.: University Microfilms International, 1987.

Friedman, Philip. *Their Brothers' Keepers*. New York: Crown, 1957.

Goldberger, L., ed. *The Rescue of the Danish Jews: Moral Courage Under Stress*. New York: New York University Press, 1987.

Grossman, Kurt R. *Die unbesungenen Helden: Menschen in Deutschlands dunklen Tagen*. Berlin: Arani Verlag, 1958.

Gutman, Y., and E. Zuroff, eds. *Rescue Attempts During the Holocaust*. Jerusalem: Yad Vashem, 1977.

Hallie, P. *Lest Innocent Blood Be Shed*. New York: Harper and Row, 1978.

Hilberg, Raul. *Perpetrators Victims Bystanders: The Jewish Catastrophe, 1933–1945*. New York: HarperCollins, 1992.

Huneke, Douglas. *The Moses of Rovno*. New York: Dodd, Mead, 1985.

―――. "Religious Community Perspectives on Rescuers." Paper presented at a conference on "Moral Courage During the Holocaust and in the Post-Holocaust World," Woodrow Wilson School of International Affairs of Princeton University and Jewish Foundation for Christian Rescuers, Anti-Defamation League, 1990.

Klee, Ernst, Willi Dressen, and Volker Riess, eds. *"The Good Old Days": The Holocaust as Seen by Its Perpetrators and Bystanders*. New York: Free Press, 1992.

Klingenmann, Ute. "Rescuers of Jews in Berlin." Paper presented at the International Society for Political Psychology, Washington, D.C., 1985.

London, Perry. "The Rescuers: Motivational Hypotheses About Christians Who Saved Jews from Nazis." In *Altruism and Helping Behavior*, edited by L. Macauley and L. Berkowitz. New York: Academic Press, 1970.

Nyiszli, Dr. Miklos. *Auschwitz: A Doctor's Eyewitness Account*. Translated by Tibere Kremer and Richard Seaver. New York: Fawcett, 1960.

Oliner, Samuel P., and Pearl M. Oliner. *The Altruistic Personality*. New York: Free Press, 1988.

Paldiel, Mordechai. "The Altruism of the Righteous Gentiles." Paper presented at the conference "Remembering for the Future," Oxford University, 1988.

Schulweis, Harold M. "The Bias Against Man." Paper presented at the Rabbinical Assembly Convention, Kiamesha Lake, New York, 1962.

―――. "The Bias Against Man." *Dimensions* 3, no. 3 (1988): 4–8.

―――. "The Fear and Suspicion of Goodness," *Dimensions* 5, no. 3 (1990): 22–25.

Tec, Nechama. *When Light Pierced the Darkness: Christian Rescue of Jews in Nazi-occupied Poland*. Oxford: Oxford University Press, 1986.

Wolfson, Manfred. "The Subculture of Freedom: Some People Will Not." Paper presented at the Western Political Science Association Conference in 1970.

Zuccotti, S. *The Italians and the Holocaust: Persecution, Rescue, and Survival*. New York: Basic Books, 1987.

# Chapter 9

# Jewish Women in the Holocaust Resistance

*Bea Stadtler*

We frequently speak about heroes and heroines in literature, in history, and even in politics. We commonly regard the hero or heroine as the one who charges into battle with a gun or knife to protect himself or herself or his or her companions. The hero is the one who defeats the evil enemy with force. This may often be the case, but not always. For heroism may be many things, many acts, many different kinds of behavior.

Are you a hero if you fight without a gun? Would that person who fights against injustice, oppression, or dictatorship, not with a gun or sword but with words, also be a hero? What if a person shares his or her last piece of bread with someone who is hungry? Can we call that person a hero? How about the one who tries to protect another from persecution, from death, though the protector knows that he or she will die if caught? The ones who shared bread and potatoes and sheltered the less fortunate who would be taken away and killed? Those people in ghettos and concentration camps who insisted on celebrating Jewish holidays and rituals, although they knew that if they were caught they would be murdered? Are these people heroes?

Today, many are critical of those whose lives hung by a thread during the Holocaust. We say that they should have fought back. But we forget that historically the Jews were a passive people. They did not believe in violence. Few had access to weapons, fewer to military training, and they were surrounded by well-fed professional soldiers armed with submachine guns, tanks, artillery, and aircraft.

Sometimes a superperson becomes a hero. Generally, it is the everyday people with whom you live, with whom you are friends, who turn out to be the real-life heroes. During the Holocaust, quite often it was the women who performed extraordinary deeds. Young girls smuggled food into the ghetto and cared for the sick. Wives lit candles or made some semblance of a holiday. In the camps women protected their mothers and accompanied their children to the gas chambers rather than abandon them. Some fought with guns and homemade weapons in the ghettos, forests, and concentration camps. The survivors tell their stories modestly.

## SOME PERSONAL INTERVIEWS

Rose Kaplowitz, born Rose Saks in Sosnowiec, Poland, was nine years old when Poland was attacked. Her brother was shot before her eyes when the Nazis marched into town. Soon after, Sosnowiec's Jews were forced into a ghetto at Shrodula. Rose's tiny hands earned her a job in a factory, painting dots on domino games. One night she came home from her job outside the ghetto and found the house empty. "I was scared," she says. "I felt as though I had been abandoned." After the third night, she heard sounds. "I discovered my family in an attic. The person who had placed furniture against the secret entry was caught by the Germans and they had no way out. They had been there three days and nights."

Life resumed what might be called a normal pace until the Nazis made a second raid. People scrambled to the hiding place in the attic bunker. This time, however, the Nazis decided to investigate what was in the attic and called for a ladder. "Once they came up, we would be lost," said Rose, "and suddenly my three-year-old niece started crying. Everyone hollered at my sister to keep the child quiet. For a few minutes, I was afraid my sister would choke her daughter and I began to cry. But luck was with us—the ladder was not long enough and they went away."

Rose's father suggested that she volunteer for work in a concentration camp, where twenty girls were needed for work in a weaving factory on a machine with tiny spindles that were never turned off. The only way to fix the machine was to stop one spindle at a time. "They weren't concerned about our fingers, but were worried the machine might break if the hands were large." The factory was at the concentration camp of Oberalstadt. Two of Rose's sisters were also in this camp.

"One girl in our barracks had epilepsy. No one knew about it except the girls in the barracks. One day at the daily count, she had an attack and that was the last we saw of her. The girls were good to each other. If someone was sick, the others covered for her. The stronger girls would help the weaker ones, even doing their cleaning and digging."[1]

Rose Braun Soloway came to Poland from Hungary when she was ten years old. As an adult, she opened a little store, fixing runners in silk stockings. When the Nazis conquered Poland, they closed her shop and sent her to work in a ghetto kitchen. One hot summer day Rose watched as a group of children, aged nine to fourteen, worked clearing rails for the Nazis. She risked her life by stealing potatoes and potato peels for the overworked, starving children. In 1942 Rose and a number of companions outfitted in wooden shoes were marched thirty miles to the concentration camp of Auschwitz. She had once been a swimmer, ice skater, and tennis player, and her athletic stamina served her well in the camp, where she was forced to dig irrigation ditches. Transferred to a factory, she worked nights at tasks "never meant for a human being." Occasionally, the Nazis placed thirty women in a circle about a pile of stones. The women were ordered to pick up the stones, carry them to another spot, then take them back to the original pile. "All day long we walked around in the circle," said Rose. "People could not survive even two hours, and many died."

From Auschwitz Rose was taken to Bergen-Belsen early in 1945. Food was distributed on a pushcart. Hoping to secure a job in the kitchen, Rose followed the help, stumbling through puddles. Confronted by an SS man, she told him she could peel potatoes, clean, and work. He pointed to a large vat of soup and said she could stay if she picked it up. "It was a joke," said Rose Soloway. "There was no way I could pick up that container. But everyone has a heart some time and this SS man had a heart. In every person there is a little bit of God, and nothing can touch you if you believe in him. Nothing has the power to hurt you because God is with you, and that is the way I survived."[2]

Ryzia Barth Frankel was a small girl when in 1939 she and her parents and grandparents fled to the Ukraine. Ryzia came from an Orthodox family. Throughout their long and bitter flight they never ate anything that was not kosher. One night Russian authorities rounded up Poles living in the Ukraine, telling them that they could only take what they could stuff into a pillowcase, and sent them to Siberia. Packed into cattle cars for nearly a month, Ryzia's family would not eat the food distributed by Communist guards because it was not kosher. They had a little money and would buy fruit, vegetables, and bread from farmers who came to the train. At great personal risk Ryzia's mother fed kosher meals to single Orthodox men, managed to have a Passover seder, and took in a fifteen-year-old boy for whom she knitted scarves and mittens.[3]

Susan Eisdorfer Beer was born in a small town in western Slovakia. Her father was a doctor. When Jews were forbidden to practice medicine, he still secretly helped people. When Susan was seventeen, she and a girlfriend left by train for the Hungarian border. The rest of her family found refuge in Budapest, living separately with friends. In 1944, hearing that one small part of Slovakia had been liberated by partisans, Susan decided to return home. There was a rumor that a regular Wehrmacht unit, disillusioned with Hitler, would take people across the border. Forty-four refugees, including Susan and her mother, were betrayed and jailed, first in Budapest, then in Birkenau. Upon their arrival in the death camp, the Germans demanded all of their valuables. Instead, Susan went into the toilets and flushed away several gold coins she had sewn into the shoulder pads of her sweater. For the duration of the war, she cared for her mother, who seemed to lose all desire to live amid the stench and reddish smoke that came from the crematoria. Susan's cousin, from Galanta, helped another old woman wash and dress. Says Susan: "For someone to be concerned about someone else at this time was really heroic. You were so involved with your own life and what was happening to you from second to second. Okay, I was involved with my mother. But it was, after all, my mother. But a stranger?"[4]

In September 1943 there was a selection at the marketplace of Chrzanow, Poland, seventeen kilometers from Auschwitz. Men were separated from women. Then women were separated into two groups, one for work, the other for what the Nazis termed *special treatment*. A survivor, Jakob Hennenberg, recalled what happened to his four sisters who took part in the selection. Sabina Hornung and Anna Wassertheil were twins and both had babies. Told to put their babies on the ground and go to the work column, they refused, knowing that they were going to their death. Ida Korngold, a third sister, who had no children, saw a crying baby on the ground, abandoned by its mother. She picked up the baby and joined her two sisters. The sisters were holding hands, and Karolla Maringer, the fourth sister, also wanted to go with them. But someone grabbed her and shoved her to the work side.[5]

Basha Rutnick Katz now lives in Bethesda, Maryland. Born in Vilna, she was the only one in a family of five children to survive the Holocaust. Basha's father was a poor cantor. In 1939 she married a childhood sweetheart from a well-to-do family, and their daughter Sheindel was born a year later. When the Germans overran Vilna in September 1941, they moved the Jews into a ghetto. "We were forced to walk out of our houses and leave everything," said Basha. "The only things I took were my daughter and a couple of personal belongings. That night, the Germans came to the Jewish houses in the ghetto and took people to jail. The next day they took the Jews to Ponary in trucks."

Ponary was a park not far from Vilna that Jews thought was being used for a labor camp. It soon became clear that those who came to Ponary never left. In a matter of days ten thousand victims were shot and buried in pits originally dug for storage of oil tanks. Once in a while a victim would pretend to drop from a bullet and in the dark of night crawl out of the mass of human bodies and return home with horrible stories generally not believed at the beginning of the German occupation. Says Basha:

The Germans came and took some of us to another ghetto, and a few days later we were rounded up to be taken to Ponary. I had a grandfather whom I loved very much. He was very religious and before he died, he blessed me and my husband. I got into the habit of "talking" to him when I was in trouble. When I realized the Nazis were going to kill me and my daughter, I began to talk to him. I heard his voice telling me to run away. We were being marched to the trucks. I noticed a wood fence surrounding a building. When I got to the fence, a boy stood there. He saw that I had a baby in my arms and had run away from the marchers. He said, "Go upstairs." Upstairs was an old woman who gave me some food. "You can't stay here," she said. "You have to go. But wait till all the people in the street go away." There were hundreds of Jews lined up in the street to be taken to Ponary. Later, I put a scarf over my Jewish star and went to the home of a Polish woman where my mother used to live. She would not let me in, but offered to take the baby. I would not give my baby up. I went to the house of another Polish woman I knew. She let me sleep there and the next day, I went back to the ghetto wall.''

Holding her child, Basha returned to the ghetto and her husband. About the same time, the Nazis summoned the elderly Jews and those with small children. Basha sought protection from a gang of Jewish toughs, the Starker, and mother, father, and daughter managed to hide during several raids. ''For three days, I hid in an oven with my daughter. When I finally came out, everyone was crying, for their children had been killed.''

Finally, Basha decided to give Sheindel to a Polish woman who promised to take care of her. The next day one of the Jews going to work saw the child sitting in the street and brought her back. That night there was another *Aktion*, and Basha and the baby hid in a bunker with about sixty other people. The smell of the bodies was oppressive, and the baby began crying. Basha recalls: ''The others wanted to kill her, but I refused to allow it. I pushed open the bunker door and went to the apartment house where I had lived and hid behind a door. A group of Germans entered and tore the place apart. They broke furniture and windows—anything they could lay their hands on. I was 'talking' to my grandfather. I know it's my imagination, but somehow they did not see us hiding.'' The next week, Basha gave Sheindel to another Polish woman, and she and her husband escaped to the forests, walking two weeks to join partisans. After the war, Basha and Chaim were able to reclaim their child. Sheindel now lives in a lovely house next door to her parents in the Washington area.[6]

Tova Markowitz Baron, known in her hometown of Lipshe Polonya as Gittel, was a young child when Hungarian Fascists occupied her region of Czechoslovakia. In May 1944 she and her family were shipped to Auschwitz. Tova remembers: ''As we came up to Mengele, he pointed with his stick that my sisters should go left. My mother, father, grandmother and I were sent to the right. I looked over the scene, saw the working camp to the left, ran from my mother's side, behind a group of people to my sisters. My mother was wringing her hands. Her baby had left. I wasn't smart. I did it on impulse.''

This was Tova's thirteenth birthday. After their hair was shaved, they showered and dressed in odd-sized clothing. When they were assigned to barracks, a woman came out to tell them the rules. Tova began crying, ''I want to go back to my mother.'' The head of the section grabbed Tova by the neck, turned her toward the smoking chimney, and said: ''You don't have a mother anymore. That smoke coming out of the chimney is your mother. You are going to live for yourself now.'' Tova stared at the smoke. She thought: ''Dear God, please let me live long enough to see these murderers punished.'' She stopped crying and did not cry again till the end of the war.[7]

## THE PROBLEM OF SOURCES

From the examples just offered, it is clear that women figured prominently in passive resistance during the Holocaust. They had small children from whom they would not part or older, ailing parents they would not forsake; they lighted candles for the Shabbat or shared food with someone less fortunate. They were also among the most active opponents of Nazism, serving as runners in the camps and ghettos, shooting guns and throwing grenades in rebellions.

It is instructive in this age of conferences focusing solely upon the role of women in the Holocaust to remember that the Nazis did not take women to ghettos, to slave labor, to camps, and to crematoria because they were women. Rather, they took them because they were Jews. They were sexually abused in some instances, but their experiences were not altogether dissimilar from those of their husbands and brothers. All were degraded, starved, beaten, placed behind barbed wire, tattooed, and gassed. The ultimate Nazi goal, *Ausrottung* or genocide, was the same for male or female Jews.

For those seeking information on the role of women in the resistance there is a dearth of published material. Until recently, there was no comprehensive study of how women behaved or where they resisted. The publication of Vera Laska's *Women in the Resistance and in the Holocaust: The Voices of Eyewitnesses* (Greenwood, 1983) helped rectify that problem, particularly from the viewpoint of inmates in camps such as Ravensbrück designed solely for women. Nevertheless, documents remain sparse, and, in some instances, unreliable.

### Official Nazi Reports

The skillful researcher should be able to cull a great deal of information from official Nazi reports, diaries of those who perished in the Holocaust, autobiographies and oral testimonies of survivors, papers delivered at academic forums, second-party biographical accounts and anthologies.

The most celebrated instance of the Nazis paying backhanded respect to Jewish women in the resistance comes from SS General Jürgen Stroop's seventy-five-page report "Es gibt keinen Jüdischen Wohnbezirk im Warschau Mehr," sent to Friedrich-Wilhelm Krüger at the conclusion of the Warsaw ghetto uprising in 1943. Whimpering at the violation of normal rules of combat, Stroop complained: "During the armed resistance, the women belonging to the battle groups were equipped the same as the men. Not infrequently, these women fired pistols with both hands. It happened time and again that they had pistols or hand grenades (Polish 'Pineapples') concealed in their bloomers up to the last moment to use against the men of the SS."[8]

In their zeal to photograph the program of extermination for Aryan posterity, the Nazis recorded further evidence of Jewish resistance. There is a photo of three girls taken by the Nazis in Warsaw that appears in many books on the

Holocaust. The only survivor was Malka Zdrojewicz Hornstein, who went to Israel in 1946. In testimony given to the Yad Vashem Historical Institute, Malka recalled how the photograph was taken. She had been working with other young people at a brush factory in the Warsaw ghetto. As the Nazis proceeded with deportations, the workers stashed whatever arms they could obtain, preparing for the inevitable clash that erupted in March 1943. Malka and other young women participated in the uprising, moving about the sewers and underground bunkers, carrying ammunition and hurling Molotov cocktails at the Germans. Crushed by superior force, some of the resistance fighters took refuge in an underground shelter where large quantities of arms were stored:

But the Germans found us and forced us out. I happened to be there with Rachela and Bluma Wyszogrodzka and that is how they took our picture. The Germans beat us and lined us up to be executed by a firing squad. Suddenly, I felt a heavy blow on my head and at the same instant heard shots. Bluma fell dead on the spot. Rachela and I, together with the others, were driven to the Umschlagplatz. They later took us to Majdanek.[9]

The photo, bearing the caption "Women of the pioneer movement, captured bearing arms," was among documents submitted at the Nuremberg War Crimes Tribunal. A Polish judge at the postwar trial noted: "This was Germany's enemy—three young Jewish girls captured in battle . . . an almost gay pride and magnificent contempt for the despicable, hated enemy are reflected in the smiling face of the first girl, who, facing death, nevertheless in mocking defiance, as it were, wears her cap at an angle."[10]

### Diaries of Those Who Did Not Survive

Standard Holocaust texts by Nora Levin, Lucy Dawidowicz, Yehuda Bauer, Leon Poliakov, Gerald Reitlinger, and Raul Hilberg and testimonies offered by Nazi commanders trying to save their lives at Nuremberg abound with complaints or indirect salutes from the Nazis about the trickery and resistance offered by desperate Jews. None is more touching than the statement of a German officer commenting on the massacre of Jews in the Ukrainian town of Dulmno. Quoted in Malcolm Hay's *Europe and the Jews*, it tells of the courage of an old, white-haired woman beside a death pit, holding a year-old baby in her arms, singing him a song and tickling him as he gurgled with pleasure.[11]

Despite Nazi efforts to eradicate every trace of Jewish life in Europe, we are fortunate to have the diaries of many individuals who understood the importance of addressing future generations. Emmanuel Ringelblum, the foremost historian of the Warsaw ghetto, hid his notes in rubberized milk bottles. He buried these bottles in the ground, and though he did not survive the war, his notes were found amid the ghetto debris in 1945. Published thirteen years later as *Notes from the Warsaw Ghetto,* the diary salutes the "indefatigable" Jewish heroines who risked death, traveling into the Aryan zones and between cities, smuggling contraband, illegal publications, false papers, food, and money. These were the "Chajkes" and "Frumkes" who brought news of the massacre in the Vilna ghetto, "the first to bring words of encouragement and moral support to the living remnant of that city." Said Ringelblum: "They undertake the mission. Nothing stands in their way. Nothing deters them." The great Jewish historian marveled at the number of times these "emissaries of the community" had looked death in the eyes and concluded: "The story of the Jewish woman will be a glorious page in the history of Jewry during the present war."[12]

Equally compelling is the diary of Hannah (or Chana) Senesh, a brave young Hungarian Jewish commando, whose story is recounted in *Hannah Senesh: Her Life and Diary*. Born in Budapest in 1921, she emigrated to Palestine at the age of eighteen. The greatest pain of that leaving was parting with her mother, who remained in Hungary. On March 13, 1944, Hannah parachuted into Yugoslavia. After several days of travel through forest and villages, her group crossed into Hungary, where they were instantly captured and imprisoned. Although Hannah was beaten on the face, hands, and feet, she would not reveal the secret radio code to the Nazis.

Said fellow prisoner Joel Nusbacher, "Even in the police wagon she raised our spirits."[13] Although she was three floors above Joel, in solitary confinement, they invented a system of "talking" to each other with mirrors. Hannah made large letters from paper that she used to form words and sentences. From morning till night, the prisoners watched Hannah's window as she "lectured" to them about Eretz Yisrael. When she was transferred to a larger cell, she conducted exercises for everyone, led discussions about the Jewish state, and taught two Polish children who had spent most of their life in prison to read and write.

When Hungary's native Fascists, the Arrow Cross, seized power in the summer of 1944, Hannah was brought to trial. Near the end, this twenty-three-year-old woman made a speech denouncing the Germans and their Hungarian collaborators, warning of the punishment that would befall them. On November 7, 1944, Hannah Senesh was sentenced to die. When she was asked if she would plead for mercy, her retort to the Hungarian prosecutor was "Mercy from you? No, I beg no mercy from the hands of hangmen." Before the firing squad, she declined a blindfold.

Hannah Senesh wanted to be a poet, and her diary is filled with many such writings about her father, pioneers in the land of Israel, and death. Perhaps her most beloved poem is one that became a rallying cry for partisans in Europe and her kibbutz comrades in Israel. "Blessed Is the Match" is a simple, four-line ode that speaks of Hannah's willingness to sacrifice herself in order to spark a greater commitment on the part of her fellow Jews.[14]

That metaphor of self-sacrifice through fire brings to mind one of Hannah's companions, Haviva Reich, in a mission to the Jews of Slovakia. The story of this level-headed woman who served as "mother" to younger parachutists is reconstructed from letters by Dorothy and Pesach Bar Adon in *Seven Who Fell*. Following the betrayal of Czechoslovakia at Munich, Reich, a Labor Zionist, fled to Palestine. At first she worked conscientiously at the Maanit kibbutz. But as the war progressed, she volunteered to return to the Carpathian Mountains. Her last letter from Slovakia before she was captured by the Nazis complains of inaccurate information and other problems. "A few days ago, they swooped down on my apartment," she wrote, "but luckily, I wasn't there that night. So I am alive. We hope that all will end well . . . but I live with only one thought— to save what is possible." After the war a group of Zionist youths paid tribute to Haviva Reich in Slovakia. In a letter, they said: "We kindled a flame on the peak of the hill—the light illuminated the whole horizon and we called it 'the flame of Haviva.' Just a narrow ridge of mountain was between us and the place where Haviva fought, fell and found eternal rest. . . . we shall remember Haviva who did not hesitate to come to our help; who sacrificed herself for our sakes. She kindled a flame in all our hearts and we shall follow in her footsteps."[15]

The proceedings of the 1968 conference on Jewish resistance held in Jerusalem and printed by Yad Vashem as *Jewish Resistance During the Holocaust* (1971) provides additional, moving epigrams and poetry from females who did not survive. Twelve-year-old Halinka Pinchonson was a pupil in Janusz Korczak's Warsaw orphanage-school. When the children were marched to the Umschlag-platz (to be shipped to the death camp of Treblinka), her mother, a nurse, tried to pull her away. The little girl refused, saying, "When things were going badly with us, you sent me to the orphanage and now you are willing for all of them to go to their death and I should live. No! My place is with them."[16] In a farewell note Fanya Barbakow, an eighteen-year-old from Druja, wrote, "We are going to our death proudly, and I am proud to die as a Jewess!"[17] Others, like Zipora Birman, a fighter in the Bialystok ghetto, called for vengeance and predicted that the Jewish people would not vanish, that "it will rise again to grow and flower as a people."[18] Another youngster, Heal Blumengraber, a pupil of the Jewish high school in Krakow, reproached her former teachers for their naivete. Her erudite teachers had unraveled the secrets of the cosmos and enchanted the pupils with the magic of words, the glory of genius, and the need to help one's fellow man. But in a world that knew no verse or song, no humanity, Jews needed instruction on how to spring from a crouch, how to strike at a forehead, how to kill while avoiding getting killed, how to shout until their suffering was heard.[19]

### Autobiographies

We are fortunate to have the complete stories of some who survived. Probably the most celebrated, Fania Fenelon's life has been published as a book, *The Musicians of Auschwitz*, and made into a television show, "Playing for Time," written by Arthur Miller and starring Vanessa Redgrave.

Fania was one of the Jewish girls who played in the orchestra at Birkenau-Auschwitz. Her specialty was "Madame Butterfly." Occasionally she would write a score for the orchestra. The musicians knew that the people for whom they played today would be dead tomorrow. Every day and twice on Sundays they played for the SS. "Hell has many faces and for us, this was one of them," said Fania. "Yet I was grateful to this musical activity for granting me a respite and also allowing me to oxygenate my brain, by working on scores and orchestrations. I was able to enjoy myself, as I was reminded of our favorite song: 'J'attendrai.' Written for those absent in 1939–40, it symbolized returning for us—theirs and ours. Every time we played the arrangement we were secretly jubilant. It was amusing to be able to sing a song of hope under their noses." Fania also defied the Nazis by arranging performances of Mendelssohn's banned Violin Concerto and transforming the Jewish folk song "Josef, Josef" into a march. "In this way, I'd seen to it that the women in the work groups marched off to the rhythm of Jewish music and some of them clearly recognized it."[20]

A second memoir, Recha Freier's *Let the Children Come*, tells of the desperate efforts of a Berlin *rebbetzin* to prepare Jewish youth for emigration to Palestine. Recha organized *hachsharot*, where youngsters were given training in agriculture. Denounced by some Jewish parents who worried that their children were being sent away forever, she was also accused by Adolf Eichmann of spreading anti-Nazi propaganda in 1938. "Eichmann threw my passport at my head and ordered me to surrender it on the morrow."[21]

At first, Henrietta Szold, who held the social welfare portfolio of the Vaad Leumi, the Jewish shadow government in Palestine, responded coolly to Freier's initiatives. Recha continued badgering the major Jewish organizations in Germany. She prepared a memo pointing out dangers Jewish youth confronted in Germany, but no Jewish journal would print it. In 1939 she managed to get 120 children to Zagreb, Yugoslavia, but Szold refused to permit them to go further because they did not hold legal immigration certificates. At her wit's end, Freier informed Szold that 90 children were already on their way and that if they returned to Germany, they would be murdered. The children were admitted to Palestine, a handful of the 10,000 saved by Recha Freier before she too fled to Palestine in 1941.

Another excellent memoir is *On Both Sides of the Wall* by Vladka Meed. After losing her family in the Warsaw ghetto, Vladka, who was fair, was assigned by the resistance to work outside the ghetto. Detained at the gate as she was leaving with a labor battalion, she was shunted into a hut, from which few emerged without a beating or worse. When the German guard was called away for a moment, she escaped into the mingling hordes of "Aryan" men and women. She managed to jump aboard a wagon rolling through the Polish streets. Assisted by a friendly Pole, she found her Jewish friends. Later, however, Vladka was captured by three blackmailers who made a business of denouncing Jews. Somehow she talked herself out of that situation and became a liaison with the ghetto, obtaining arms and dynamite for the resistance and metal files for Jews who were jailed. She smuggled illegal literature, correspondence, and money into the ghetto and also was sent to partisans in the woods to give them reports.

In the summer of 1943 Vladka was sent to Kielce to supply some isolated

Jews who had found shelter among peasants with money. Whenever she was asked for her travel permit, she relied on bribe or bluff. She was the contact person for Jews in the Czestochowa and Radom labor camps and was in the Warsaw ghetto just before the rebellion broke out. When she returned five months later, she found that "nothing was left me [sic] of my past, of my life in the ghetto—not even the grave of my father."[22]

Similar acts of heroism were performed by other women in the Warsaw ghetto. Tuvia Borzykowski writes in *Between Tumbling Walls* of her experience on the Aryan side of Warsaw. Izhak Zuckerman, one of the heroes of the ghetto rebellion, was able to escape to the woods and later brought Tuvia back to hide in the Aryan section.[23]

Zivia Lubetkin married Izhak Zuckerman and has told her story in a book (Zvi Dror, *The Dream, the Revolt, and the Vow and Lubetkin-Zuckerman (1914–1978)* and magazines ("Our Women Liaisons," *Pioneer Woman,* April 1983, and "The Last Days of the Warsaw Ghetto," *Commentary Magazine,* April 1947, pp. 401–11). Born in eastern Poland in 1914, she joined Dror, the Zionist youth movement, preparing for life in Eretz Yisrael. In 1938 she moved to Warsaw and was appointed director of a network of training groups all over the country. When war broke out in 1939, she accompanied friends on a horse-drawn cart to the Russian-occupied territory of Poland. While she was in Soviet territory, she worked rescuing Jewish youth, sending them through Romania to Palestine. In January 1940 Zivia went back to Warsaw.

Zivia tells about the women who moved from one ghetto to the other, bringing messages, illegal papers, and money. Every conceivable faction was represented by Tema Schneiderman, Havka Folman, and Rysia and Rancia Beatus from Dror; Tosia Altman from Hashomer Hatzair; Syrke Erlichman from Gordonia; and Hela Schipper from Akiva. She writes of Lonka Kozibrodska, young, beautiful and intelligent, who risked her life carrying parcels back and forth into the ghetto. She also tells of the destruction of the Warsaw ghetto, "the blazing light . . . the roar of the fire . . . the noise of falling walls." Though the Germans were firing at anything that moved, Zivia and her comrades continued to thread their way into the ghetto through the sewers until it was time to flee.[24] Sixty persons, including eighteen survivors of the catastrophe at the Mila 18 bunker, made their way through the filthy sewer water. Writes Zivia Lubetkin: "We half-walked, half-crawled like this for twenty hours, one behind the other, without stopping, without food or drink in that terrible cavern. . . . Some . . . we dragged through the water by their hands and feet. . . . More than once, one of us would fall and beg to be left lying there, but no one in all that journey was abandoned."[25]

Trucks were waiting at the sewer exits. In the daylight the grimy survivors of the Warsaw ghetto were overcome with horror at the sight of one another. Closing her account, Zivia Lubetkin says: "We thought of the mystery of the world and man. We remembered the murder of our people, the beloved dead comrades who were part of the ashes of our burned souls. The heart wondered and asked, wondered and asked . . . but there was no answer."[26]

One other biography merits special mention. Although Gisi Fleischmann did not survive the Holocaust, Abraham Fuchs's *The Unheeded Cry* reads very much like an autobiography of this extraordinary woman who worked with Rabbi Chaim Weissmandel to save the Jews of Slovakia. Gisi had sent her two daughters to Palestine in 1939, while she remained behind with her ailing mother. Chosen as chairperson of the clandestine group that called itself the "Working Group," a committee of Slovakian Jews, she negotiated with Dieter Wisliceny, the SS specialist on Jewish affairs. Arrested several times, she was also tortured. Several of her colleagues advised her to emigrate to Palestine, and while she possessed a Paraguayan passport as well, she valiantly decided to remain at her post till the end. Hailed by Rabbi Weissmandel as "that important woman of great deeds and good heart," she deterred some deportations by bribing Nazi officers. When Alois Brunner took command of the expulsions of Slovakian Jewry, she was sent to Auschwitz with a note on her file, "return not desirable." All efforts to save her were futile, and she went to the gas chambers with those she tried to save.[27]

## Anthologies

How many dramatic tales were buried with the victims of the Holocaust cannot be reckoned. Survivors, frustrated by their own literary shortcomings, are dependent upon others to tell their stories, which as a result may lack immediacy, emotion, or historicity. There are a number of sound, readable anthologies, however, that address the subject of women and resistance. Chief among these is Yuri Suhl's *They Fought Back*.

Suhl's excellent study contains numerous tales of active resistance accomplished by young girls, teenagers, and married women. Blonde, blue-eyed Sima was twelve years old when her parents were killed during the first German pogrom at Minsk in 1941. A runner to the partisans, she found no assignment too difficult. Before she started from the ghetto, she would point to a pistol sewn inside her coat and say, "Don't worry. The Fritzes will not take me alive." On cold winter nights she would sneak out through the barbed-wire fence and return through the cemetery. If she did not succeed in getting back into the ghetto, she would spend the night in a bombed-out building, waiting till dusk the next day, when she would join the column of Jews returning from work. After the war Sima was decorated for her activities against the Germans.[28]

Not so fortunate was seventeen-year-old Zofia Yamaika. Suhl tells how the daughter of a prominent Hasidic family organized soup kitchens and educational groups and staged plays for children in the Warsaw ghetto. During the mass deportations of 1942, Zofia escaped to the forests to join the partisans. Captured and placed inside a cattle car bound for Treblinka, Zofia managed to escape when the SS guards opened the doors and left her for dead. Returning to her comrades, Zofia later assassinated a German gendarme and manned a machine gun before falling in combat.[29]

Another famed commando was Nuta Teitelboim, known as "little Wanda with the braids." Twenty-four years old, very slight, with long, blonde braids and a flowered kerchief on her head that gave her the appearance of a sixteen-year-old, she made her name a legend throughout Poland. Suhl tells how she organized a woman's detachment that made contact with the Polish resistance, how they blew up railway lines, raided banks to retrieve money stolen from Jews, and bombed an exclusive cafe used by the Nazis. Her most celebrated feat came when she strolled up to Gestapo headquarters in Warsaw one day. Charming her way past guards, she was escorted to a high-ranking officer's room, where she waited alone. When the Nazi entered the room, he joked, "Do you also have here a Lorelei?" The girl did not answer. Instead, she drew her revolver from her handbag and shot the German dead. Then she left the building, smiling as she passed the guards. The Nazis placed a price of 150,000 zlotys on her head. Unfazed, Nuta told another underground worker before her death, "I am a Jew—my place is among the most active fighters against fascism in the struggle for the honor of my people, for an independent Poland and the freedom of humanity."[30]

A similar tale of courage may be found in the *Anthology of Holocaust Literature*, edited by Jacob Glatstein, Israel Knox, and Samuel Margoshes. Anna Lovskovska, known as "Sonya" or "Annushka," would appear in a village near Vilna carrying a heavy wicker basket covered with hay. Under the hay were copies of the latest issues of the partisan bulletin with an appeal to the soldiers. She was occasionally stopped, but, like Wanda, was able to charm her inquisitors with a smile. On one occasion she actually duped a garrison officer, an old Lithuanian classmate, into giving her two rifles and his own automatic. An hour later the man learned that one of his columns had been attacked with his weapons. Another time Anna and two partisan companions came under attack outside the town of Lopenko. The official German report listed 32 casualties suffered at the hands of an attacking force of 150 men.[31]

The previously cited *Jewish Resistance During the Holocaust* tells how even in the depths of the death camps, Jewish men and women offered resistance. Mala Zimetbaum was born in Brzesko, Poland, in 1920. When she was eight, her family emigrated to Belgium. A member of the wartime resistance, she was arrested in 1943 and deported to Auschwitz. There she became a runner, number 19880, moving from one section to another, risking her life carrying messages and medicine to members of separated families. She wanted to escape to tell the world what was happening in Auschwitz and in 1944 managed to accomplish this with the assistance of Edek Galinski, a Polish mechanic who had been in camp since 1940. They were free for just for a few hours. Caught and tortured, the pair was marched to the *Appellplatz* of Camp B, where their punishment was to be announced before all the prisoners. While the decree was being read, Mala cut her wrist with a hidden razor. When the head of the work detail grabbed her arm, Mala slapped his face with her bloody hand and shouted, "Murderers!

You will soon pay for our sufferings! Don't be afraid, girls. Their end is near. Remember everything they did to us.'' To quiet her, the SS taped her mouth with adhesive and took her immediately to the gas chambers.[32]

Publications of the Ghetto Fighters' House in Israel reveal how Rosa Robota, another inmate of Auschwitz, attempted to destroy the death factory. In Birkenau-Auschwitz only women, who were isolated from other prisoners, worked with explosives. Rosa agreed to supply small bundles of explosives, hidden in little match boxes, to the men of the *Sonderkommando* who were planning an armed uprising. In August 1944, when the SS tried to transfer these men to a death barracks, the revolt broke out. Crematorium 2 was blown up. A German *Kapo*, known for his cruelty, was flung alive into the furnace. Four other SS men were killed in hand-to-hand fighting. The prisoners broke through the fence, and three hundred disappeared into the surrounding area. But no help came from the outside, and most were recaptured. Subsequently, the Nazis traced the explosives back to Rosa Robota. Rosa was taken with three other girls to a bunker at Block 11 in Auschwitz I, where they were tortured. To a friend who managed to see her shortly before her death, Rosa delivered a last message. In it she promised not to betray her comrades and asked that her death be avenged. The note ended with the blessing ''hazak ve'ematz'' (be strong and courageous). A few days later a gallows was erected in the women's camp. As the four girls walked to the gallows, Rosa cried out, ''Vengeance!'' She was twenty-three years old when she was executed.[33]

Several other books offer case histories of resistance by Jewish women. Yehuda Bauer's *They Chose Life* tells how Vita Kempner, a girl of nineteen, operating with two boys, managed to plant a bomb outside Vilna, destroying a German train, the first act of sabotage in Lithuania.[34] Bernard Goldstein's *The Stars Bear Witness* tells of the efforts of Manya Wasser, Sonya Novogrodsky, a Mrs. Tiktin, and many other females who gave their time to refit cast-off clothes for the ragged children of the Warsaw ghetto.[35] Lucien Steinberg's *The Jews Against Hitler* offers the stories of Pessia Aranovitch, taken with her children to the death pits of Ponar, only to survive and become a dressmaker in the Vilna ghetto; Irina Adamowicz, who used her Girl Scout contacts to link the Jews of Warsaw, Vilna, Kovno, and Bialystok; and Charlotte Paech, a nurse and member of the underground Communist group in Germany under the leadership of Herbert Baum that disrupted Goebbels's propaganda exhibits in the middle of the war.[36]

Prominent in all these stories is the theme of people clinging steadfastly to their faith. Typical is the story of Ruszka Korczak, a member of Hashomer Hatzair and founding member of the United Partisans Organization in Vilna. Her memoir ''Shomer Pesach in the Ghetto'' is offered in *The Massacre of European Jewry* and tells how Jews made use of beet roots and potatoes to honor the Passover. Even under Nazi rule, the seder opened with the question *ma nishtanah ha layla hazeh?* (Why is this night different from all other nights?).[37]

Resistance through devotion is also the dominant theme of Irving Rosenbaum's *The Holocaust and Halakhah*. As one example, the author cites Rivka Kuper's testimony at the Eichmann trial, describing how Jewish holidays were observed at Auschwitz:

When we arrived on the 18th of January, 1943, we were put into blocks at Birkenau. They had previously been horse stables. . . . Among the first things we brought were two ends of candles. Friday night we gathered together on the top tier of our block—10 or 12 girls. . . . We lit the candles and began quietly to sing Sabbath songs. . . . we heard choked sobbing from the tiers of bunks all around us. At first we were frightened, then we understood. Jewish women who had been imprisoned months, some of them years, gathered around us, listened to the songs, and asked if they might also recite the blessings over the candles. From then on, every Shabbat we lit the candles. There was nothing to eat. But somehow we managed to get candles. And so it was on all the holidays. We fasted on Yom Kippur in Auschwitz. True, we ate no matzot on Pesach, but we traded our rations with other prisoners for potatoes, so that on Pesach we could at least fulfill the commandment of "thou shalt eat no *hametz* [leavened bread]."[38]

Even those who knew that they were doomed honored their faith to the end. On Friday evening, September 26, 1941, the Nazis beat the Jews of the Kovno ghetto out into killing fields. Among them was Ella Shmulewitz, director of a religious school for girls. Somehow she managed to take Sabbath candlesticks with her, and though she was bleeding from the blows the Germans had struck, she would not let go of the candlesticks. Standing in the fields, Ella reminded her fellow Jews that it was the Sabbath. She kindled the Sabbath candles. The people sanctified the holy day and the name of God. Then, as the sun set, they marched to their deaths at the infamous Ninth Fort, singing the traditional melody, "Lekha Dodi."[39]

It is impossible in this short space to do justice to all the heroines of the Jewish resistance: Dr. Anna Broide Heller, doctor in the Warsaw ghetto; Sonia Madejsker and Cesia Rosenberg, who came from Moscow to establish contact with the fighters of the Vilna ghetto; Rita Rosani of Verona, the first woman in Italy to fall in battle; Hella Shipper, who brought arms from Warsaw to Krakow; or Malka Zdrojewicz and Mira Fucherer of the Warsaw Hashomer Hatzair. As noted previously, it is difficult to corroborate claims. Many whose stories should have been told are dead. Many are shy or unwilling to speak. Many cannot.

There is a story about ninety-three girls from the Bais Yaakov school in Warsaw that has acquired the patina of fact over the passage of years. A copy of Haja Feldman's statement, written in Warsaw in 1942, was discovered and reprinted in Isaac Kowalski's *Anthology on Armed Jewish Resistance*. It told of ninety-three Jewish girls between the ages of fourteen and twenty-two who lived in four rooms of the Jewish school until July 27. On that day the Gestapo threw the girls and their teachers into a single darkened room. Given only water, they were sustained by the words of a former teacher who had instructed, "If you can't live according to His Will, it is an honor to give your life for His Holy Name." Haja Feldman's statement concludes:

Yesterday they led us out from the dark room to a beautiful building with large rooms and comfortable beds. They told us to take baths. They took away all our belongings, leaving us only with our underwear. They informed us that at night we would be visited by German soldiers.

Instantly we came to this decision. We swore to give our lives together. The Germans did not realize that the baths they ordered us to take would be our last undertaking before death. We prepared ourselves poison to drink when they arrived.

Not one of us is trembling before our death. We have only one wish: say *Kaddish* for our ninety-three sisters.

Only a moment and we will reunite with our mother Sara.[40]

Whether fact or fiction, this story, so reminiscent of the martyrs of Masada and Mainz, was only the tip of the iceberg. Jewish women by the hundreds and thousands were involved in some form of resistance. How would we act under such terrible circumstances? Would we become liaisons or "runners" or join uprisings in ghettos, forests, and camps? Would we light candles if we knew that we would perish if we were discovered? Would we refuse to eat bread on Pesach though we were starving? Would we crawl through filthy sewers and shoot guns, lay dynamite, and travel from village to village with false papers to give hope to others? From the security of nearly fifty years we look back upon what happened and understand that resistance comes in many forms.

## NOTES

1. Rose Kaplowitz, interview with author, 1974.
2. Rose Braun Soloway, interview with author, 1976.
3. Ryzia Barth Frankel, interview with author, 1978.
4. Susan Eisdorfer Beer, interview with author, November 1985.
5. Jakob Hennenberg, interview with author, November 1987.
6. Basha Rutnick Katz, interview with author, 1982.
7. Tova Markowitz Baron, interview with author, September 1986.
8. "The Warsaw Ghetto No Longer Exists," Report of Brigadeführer Jürgen Stroop, from *The Warsaw Ghetto Archives of Alexander Ben Bernfes* (London: Orbis Publishing, 1973), day 25.
9. M. Zdrojewicz, "I was one of the Three Fighting Girls Captured and Photographed by General Stroop's Men," *Yad Vashem Bulletin* (Jerusalem), no. 22 (May 1968): 37–39.
10. Ibid., p. 39
11. Malcolm Hay, *Europe and the Jews* (Boston: Beacon Press, 1960), p. 9.
12. Emmanuel Ringelblum, *Notes from the Warsaw Ghetto*, ed. and trans. Jacob Sloan (New York: McGraw-Hill, 1958), pp. 273–74.
13. Dorothy Bar Adon and Pesach Bar Adon, *Seven Who Fell*, Palestine Pioneer Library, no. 11 (Tel Aviv: Sefer Press, 1947), pp. 118–19.
14. Hannah Senesh, *Hannah Senesh: Her Life and Diary* (New York: Schocken Books, 1972), p. 1. See also Marie Syrkin, *Blessed Is the Match: The Story of Jewish Resistance* (Philadelphia: Jewish Publication Society of America, 1947), pp. 22–33.
15. Bar Adon, *Seven Who Fell*, pp. 141–49.

16. *Jewish Resistance During the Holocaust: Proceedings of the Conference on Manifestations of Jewish Resistance, Jerusalem, April 7–11, 1968* (Jerusalem: Yad Vashem, 1971), p. 184.

17. Ibid., p. 167.

18. Ibid., p. 193.

19. Ibid., pp. 129–30.

20. Fania Fenelon, *The Musicians of Auschwitz* (London: Sphere Books, 1976), pp. 129–30.

21. Recha Freier, *Let the Children Come* (Jerusalem: Jewish Agency, n.d.); excerpt reprinted in *Israel Digest*, no. 22 (October 24, 1975); and *Jerusalem Post,* February 6–12, 1983.

22. Vladka Meed, *On Both Sides of the Wall* (Haifa: Ghetto Fighters' House, 1973), p. 335.

23. Tuvia Borzykowski, *Between Tumbling Walls* (Haifa: Ghetto Fighters' House, 1972), pp. 115–20.

24. Zvi Dror, *The Dream, the Revolt, and the Vow and Lubetkin-Zuckerman (1914–1978)* (Israel: Histadrut and Lohamei Hagetaot, 1983), p. 27.

25. Zvia Lubetkin, ''The Last Days of the Warsaw Ghetto,'' *Commentary*, April 1947, pp. 401–11.

26. Ibid.

27. Abraham Fuchs, *The Unheeded Cry: The Story of Rabbi Weissmandel* (New York: Mesorah Publications, 1984), pp. 68–72, 76, 79, 99, 125, 132, 155.

28. Yuri Suhl, ed., *They Fought Back* (New York: Crown, 1967), pp. 241–42.

29. Ibid., pp. 77–81.

30. Ibid., pp. 51–54.

31. Jacob Glatstein, Israel Knox, and Samuel Margoshes, eds., *Anthology of Holocaust Literature* (Philadelphia: Jewish Publication Society of America, 1969), pp. 291–98.

32. *Jewish Resistance During the Holocaust*, p. 487.

33. *Extermination and Resistance: Historical Records and Source Materials*, vol. 1 (Israel: Kibbutz Lohamei Hagetaot, 1958), pp. 158–59, and Raya Kagan, ''Four Who Were Executed,'' *Yad Vashem Bulletin* (Jerusalem) (July 1958): 16.

34. Yehuda Bauer, *They Chose Life* (New York: American Jewish Committee, 1973), pp. 51–52.

35. Bernard Goldstein, *The Stars Bear Witness* (New York: Viking Press, 1949), p. 82.

36. Lucien Steinberg, *The Jews Against Hitler* (London: Saxon House, 1974), pp. 203, 229, 37–41, respectively.

37. *The Massacre of European Jewry* (Israel: Kibbutz Merchavia, 1963), pp. 191–93.

38. Irving Rosenbaum, *The Holocaust and Halakhah* (New York: Ktav, 1976), p. 97.

39. Ibid.

40. Isaac Kowalski, ed., *Anthology on Armed Jewish Resistance, 1939–1945*, vol. 3 (New York: Jewish Combatants Publishing House, 1986), p. 72.

## SELECT BIBLIOGRAPHY

Ainsztein, Reuben. *Jewish Resistance in Nazi-occupied Eastern Europe*. New York: Barnes and Noble, 1974.

Bar Adon, Dorothy, and Pesach Bar Adon. *Seven Who Fell*. Palestine Pioneer Library, no. 11. Tel Aviv: Sefer Press, 1947.

Bauer, Yehuda. *They Chose Life*. New York: American Jewish Committee, 1973.

Borzykowski, Tuvia. *Between Tumbling Walls*. Israel: Ghetto Fighters' House and Hakibbutz Hameuchad Publishing House, 1972.

Donat, Alexander. *Jewish Resistance*. New York: Waldon Press, 1964.

Dror, Zvi. *The Dream, the Revolt and the Vow and Lubetkin-Zuckerman (1914–1978)*. Israel: Histadrut and Lohamei Hagetaot, 1983.

*Extermination and Resistance: Historical Records and Source Materials*, vol. 1. Israel: Kibbutz Lohamei Hagetaot, 1958.

Fenelon, Fania. *The Musicians of Auschwitz*. London: Sphere Books, 1976.

Freier, Recha. *Let the Children Come*. Jerusalem: Jewish Agency, n.d.

Fuchs, Abraham. *The Unheeded Cry: The Story of Rabbi Weissmandel*. New York: Mesorah Publications, 1984.

Glatstein, Jacob, Israel Knox, and Samuel Margoshes, eds. *Anthology of Holocaust Literature*. Philadelphia: Jewish Publication Society of America, 1969.

Goldstein, Bernard. *The Stars Bear Witness*. New York: Viking Press, 1949.

*Jewish Resistance During the Holocaust: Proceedings of the Conference on Manifestations of Jewish Resistance, Jerusalem, April 7–11, 1968*. Jerusalem: Yad Vashem, 1971.

Kowalski, Isaac. *A Secret Press in Nazi Europe*. New York: Central Guide Publishers, 1969.

Laska, Vera, ed. *Women in the Resistance and in the Holocaust: The Voices of Eyewitnesses*. Westport: Greenwood Press, 1983.

*The Massacre of European Jewry*. Israel: Kibbutz Merchavia, 1963.

Meed, Vladka. *On Both Sides of the Wall*. Israel: Ghetto Fighters' House, 1973.

Ringelblum, Emmanuel. *Notes from the Warsaw Ghetto*. Edited and translated by Jacob Sloan. New York: McGraw-Hill, 1958.

Rosenbaum, Irving. *The Holocaust and Halakhah*. New York: Ktav, 1976.

*Hannah Senesh: Her Life and Diary*. London: Sphere Books, 1971.

Steinberg, Lucien. *The Jews Against Hitler*. London: Saxon House, 1974.

Suhl, Yuri, ed. *They Fought Back*. New York: Crown, 1967.

Syrkin, Marie. *Blessed Is the Match: The Story of Jewish Resistance*. Philadelphia: Jewish Publication Society of America, 1947.

Tenenbaum, Joseph. *Underground: The Story of a People*. New York: Philosophical Library, 1952.

Trunk, Isaiah. *Judenrat: The Jewish Councils in Eastern Europe Under Nazi Occupation*. New York: Macmillan, 1972.

Tushnet, Leonard. *To Die with Honor: The Uprising of the Jews in the Warsaw Ghetto*. New York: Citadel, 1965.

# Chapter 10

# The Relationship of Genocide to Holocaust Studies

*Nora Levin*

In recent years we have seen an increased interest in genocide and efforts to define it, to describe examples of it, and to develop studies. These efforts have been made mostly by sociologists and social scientists who have undoubtedly been stimulated in their work by the Holocaust, but who believe that the study of the Holocaust by itself is too narrow and too restrictive. Prior to 1944 the term *genocide* did not exist. It was coined in that year by the Polish legal scholar Raphael Lemkin, who was prompted by what was happening to Jews in Nazi Europe. He defined genocide as the destruction of a nation or an ethnic group, involving the destruction of its political and social institutions, culture, language, national feelings, religion, and economic existence, as well as the destruction of the personal integrity, liberty, dignity, and lives of individuals belonging to such a group. In carrying out a mandate proposed by Lemkin, the U.N. General Assembly in 1948 approved a convention on the prevention and punishment of the crime of genocide that has been ratified by many countries, most recently by the United States in 1988. However, there has been much controversy on certain sections of this convention and the impossibility of punishing perpetrators. For example, the United States itself has been charged with genocide against the American Indians, against blacks, and against Vietnamese, but these charges have been rebutted and have caused very controversial arguments. Claims of genocide have also been made with regard to the blacks in the southern Sudan, the Kurds in Iraq, the Nagas in India, Communists and Chinese in Indonesia, the Ibos in Nigeria, and Baharas in Pakistan.

The term *genocide*, it seems to me, has also become a catchword and has been misused and abused. It has been applied to a wide variety of actions: race mixing, distribution of the drug methadone, birth-control methods, medical treatment of certain groups, the closing of synagogues in the Soviet Union, and numerous other examples. In other words, when one needs a catchall to describe oppression in one form or another, one ultimately resorts to labeling it genocide, and the net result is a debasement of the concept. The term *Holocaust,* of course, also has suffered similar debasement and exploitation, practices that we have learned are difficult, but necessary to struggle against. In this chapter I try to deal with several serious and responsible thinkers on these issues and see how they confront the problems.

Helen Fein, sociologist, author of the book *Accounting for Genocide*, and director of the Institute for the Study of Genocide in New York City, proposes a theory to explain the genocide of Jews, Armenians, and Gypsies. She has sought to find certain uniformities underlying genocide, which she defines as premeditated, organized state murder requiring a myth that exalts a dominant group and identifies a victim previously defined as outside the universe of obligation of the dominant group and allegedly guilty of crimes against the dominant group. Further, she says, the dominant group in control of the state must have been reduced by defeat in war or through internal strife, requiring the murder of the victim in order to realize the state's design for a new order. Fein originally included only Jews, Gypsies, and Armenians in her roll call of twentieth-century victims of premeditated genocide, but in November 1987 she convened a conference on a more all-embracing topic, twentieth-century genocides, that covered the Holocaust, the Armenian massacres, the famine in the Ukraine in 1932–33, and mass killings in Paraguay, Cambodia, Afghanistan, East Timor, Guatemala, and Iran.

Irving Horowitz, sociologist at Rutgers University and author of a book called *Genocide: State Power and Mass Murder*, has described what he calls variables leading to what are referred to as genocidal societies. He is extremely critical of those who think that the Holocaust was unique, deserving and even requiring a treatment separate from other genocides. He argues that all too many people—Jews, Cambodians, Armenians, Paraguayans, Indians, and Ugandans—have shared the fate of victims of a mindless taking of life. He finds that it is dangerously unbecoming for victims to engage in divisive squabbles about whose holocaust is real or whose genocide is worse. Yet these divisive squabbles have become quite commonplace and, of course, distressing.

How can one sort these complexities out? Admittedly, the twentieth century has been a terrifyingly murderous century. André Malraux has called it the century that killed man. Tate Carr has tabulated the number of victims of genocide since the end of World War II, and his research has identified forty-three episodes of mass killing involving some seventy distinct communal and political groups totalling up to 16.3 million deaths of so-called ordinary people, excluding armed combatants. The data are limited to postwar episodes because studies of genocide and mass political murder have largely been neglected by scholars.

In 1987 the Institute on the Holocaust and Genocide in Jerusalem started publishing a newsletter that covers such studies and books and magazine articles in this very vast field. It is an information resource exchange aimed at "the understanding, intervention, and prevention of genocide." In 1988 the state of California mandated a program on human rights and genocide for secondary schools. A number of universities have introduced courses with titles such as "Aggression and Violence," "History and Sociology of Genocide," "Human Destructiveness and Politics," or "Genocide and Survival." Obviously, research on the history and evidence of mass killings and the monitoring of the rights of minorities around the world are vitally important. But can students and teachers intellectually or emotionally assimilate such massive doses of human slaughter? Is it not only numbing, as in the case of television violence, but possibly even hardening, instead of sensitizing? Will so much immersion in the events of mass murder blur into violations of human rights and political rights and even create pressures upon people to assimilate?

As a teacher of Holocaust history for more than twenty years, I have struggled to construct various study guides appropriate to the subject, using many sources for students and myself to ponder. This in itself is very difficult if one is not to feel swamped by the task. To go beyond these problems into dealing with other twentieth-century genocides in one course seems to me to be overwhelming. I believe that it overpowers the human capacity to understand so many human catastrophes of unimaginable magnitude, and I thus propose all-inclusive studies of genocide. Each tragic history, I believe, deserves its own study. Each will seem unique to those who identify with it and should not be in a tasteless competition for first place in uniqueness or intensity of suffering. We are not scoring points in a debate. We are trying to comprehend the shadowy histories of victimized peoples. These issues, indeed, have already caused a hardening of positions among scholars and lay people and especially intense reactions on the part of many Jews who see in the universalizing of genocide yet another attempt to dilute, distort, or diminish the syndrome of genocide before the Holocaust, a syndrome of very particular forces erupting in a very particular time in history in Germany and concentrating their lethal power singularly on Jews.

I share this feeling, because as I read the history of Nazi power in Europe, I see these forces in a certain configuration and in no other, just as, for example, the Armenian tragedy has its own configuration and its own history. Both peoples were victims, as have been other racial, national, and religious minorities. Each was alien, foreign, and hated, but in specific and differentiated ways. Each was victimized and annihilated precisely because of its particular characteristics as defined and described by the persecutor and also to be understood in a specific historical context. Without these sets of differences, we cannot understand the vehemence of the persecution and the annihilation. If there had been millions of Armenians in Europe during World War II, instead of Jews, there might well have been no Holocaust. If there had been two million Jews in Turkey in 1915–

16, instead of Armenians, then conceivably there might not have been the hideous Armenian massacres.

The uniqueness of genocidal actions simply means that each of the large number that we have experienced in the twentieth century is different from the others, as they are different from earlier genocides. The Armenian genocide was unique for its time and broke a certain threshold of permissible constraints and taboos, just as the Holocaust broke new sets of constraints and taboos. It seems to me that all these differences are important and should not be lumped into a category for the convenience of scholars and others who need labels and classification schemes. One thinks of the great political revolutions in history and may well ask what purposes are served by pushing into a single category the American, French, and Russian revolutions or the massive religious convulsions.

If the Holocaust today seems to preempt interest and attention and to make other genocides appear less terrible or less destructive, there are several possible reasons. At the same time, one may ask why there is any necessity to set up a hierarchy of mass murders, to insist upon so-called common denominators because Lemkin in 1944 coined the word and formulated the definition. The power the Holocaust has exercised over Western consciousness is partly the result of its recency and dramatization through the huge proliferation of literature, television programs, and films. There are still many survivors and their children among us, and they told us their harrowing stories. Liberators of the concentration camps have also recorded their testimony. These are phenomena we associate with the Holocaust, but they were not so fully or insistently developed in connection with other genocides, partly, at least, as a result of technological limits. Oral history testimony was rarely used during and after World War I, and tape recording was simply not available.

As fuller histories of other annihilations become available, they too will seep into public consciousness or, at the very least, enlarge our understanding of these tragic histories. Work has already been done in these fields. For example, the writer Richard Hovannisian has edited a work titled *The Armenian Genocide in Perspective,* published in 1986, and has been appointed to the first UCLA Chair on Armenian History. The Armenian Assembly of America has recently published the first teachers' resource guide on the Armenian genocide, a fifty-six-page manual for secondary schools. The Armenian National Committee of the Western Region published a handbook called *The Armenian Genocide, 1915–1923* in 1988. The Turkish government has promised that it will open up its archives on the Armenian accusations. In 1988 the Public Broadcasting System in the United States presented a one-hour documentary called ''An Armenian Journey,'' which was written and produced by Theodore Bogosian, dramatizing the killing of over a million Armenians in eastern Turkey during World War I.

In connection with the Gypsy genocide, we may say that perhaps as many as half a million Gypsies were killed during World War II, very much as Jews were. But this genocide has been largely neglected until recently. The following books have been published in recent years: Donald Kendrick's *The Destiny of Europe's Gypsies*; Ian Hancock's *The Pariah Syndrome*; and Alexander Ramati's *And the Violins Stopped Playing*. The International Romani Union now has bureaus in twenty-seven countries and since 1979 has had nongovernmental status at the United Nations. In 1987 the first Gypsy representative was appointed to the United States Holocaust Memorial Council.

There has also been a Cambodian genocide, and in 1986 Dr. Hirst Panno of the International Law Institute prepared a two hundred-page legal brief on the mass killings by the Khmer Rouge in Cambodia. These horrors were also dramatized in the film "The Killing Fields." The taping of some Cambodian survivors has already been undertaken in Oregon, California, and Chicago.

All of these corroborators are immensely valuable. Yet I still want each specific mass annihilation to be understood in its own specific context, not melded into a layer of horrors. In the case of the Holocaust, its particular history cannot be studied without analyzing and pondering centuries of Christian anti-Semitism, an uninterrupted tradition that prepared the way for the Final Solution. This intractable fact cannot be blinkered, although some have tried. Others have also tried to blur one kind of prejudice into another and universalize the dynamics of prejudice suggesting that anti-Semitism is simply sui generis. But no amount of psychosocial structure building or compulsion to classify can distort the singular facts of history, theology, and experience. As thinking men and women study the welter of documentation of Holocaust history, they are stunned by the quantity of older Christian doctrines and practices that Hitler used, knowing they would fall on fertile ground. They are also stunned to realize that he detonated hatreds, taboos, and fears, always close to the surface in Europe, and that he carried out to the literal end what earlier generations had only adumbrated.

To penetrate into such a diseased core of an ostensibly civilized continent means to lay open much more than one variation of genocide. Because other genocides have their unique and specific histories, I choose to identify those elements that differentiate genocidal historical experiences. Some sociologists apparently see more similarities than differences in the various genocides studied. However, the quest for laws or confluences, as they are called, or formations or modalities that the sociologists argue may give us a warning system, will not help us to make rational decisions, to stop the bloodletting. In this kind of building system, it seems to me, lies the great danger of concluding that history repeats itself, which it never does, and of being lulled by the illusion that creative similar structures will help us stop mass murder. Each genocide has its own etiology, the characteristic environment that fuels it, the kind of society that sanctions it. I fail to see what is gained by forcing immensely complex human experiences into tight categories except to satisfy the needs of system builders.

## NOTE

This chapter was adapted from a presentation at the Ninth Annual Kent State University Holocaust Conference, April 1989.

## SELECT BIBLIOGRAPHY

Armenian National Committee. *The Armenian Genocide, 1915–1923*. Glendale, Calif.:
    Armenian National Committee, Western Region, 1988.
Fein, Helen. *Accounting for Genocide: National Responses and Jewish Victimization
    During the Holocaust*. New York: Free Press, 1979.
Hancock, Ian. *The Pariah Syndrome*. Ann Arbor, Mich.: Karoma, 1986.
Horowitz, Irving. *Genocide: State Power and Mass Murder*. New Brunswick, N.J.:
    Transaction Books, 1976.
Hovannisian, Richard, ed. *The Armenian Genocide in Perspective*. New Brunswick, N.J.:
    Transaction Books, 1986.
Kendrick, Donald. *The Destiny of Europe's Gypsies*. London: Heinemann, 1972.
Ramati, Alexander. *And the Violins Stopped Playing*. New York: F. Watts, 1986.

# Part II

---

# Holocaust Area Studies

# Chapter 11

# Relations Between Jews and Poles During the Holocaust: New and Old Approaches in Polish Historiography

*Shmuel Krakowski*

Research on the years of the German occupation of Poland has been undertaken in many Polish historical institutes. The most important are the Historical Institute of the Academy of Science; the Central Commission for the Investigation of Nazi Crimes in Poland (which recently changed its name to Central Commission for the Investigation of Crimes Against the Polish Nation); the Institute of Military History (all of these institutes are in Warsaw); the Western Institute in Poznan; the Institute for the Study of Fascism in Wroclaw; and the museums in Auschwitz, Majdanek, and Stutthof, as well as various universities.

The most important periodicals and research collections appearing in Poland and devoted to the country's history under Nazi occupation are *Najnowsze Dzieje Polski: Materialy i Studia z Okresu Drugiej Wojny Swiatowej*; *Biuletyn Glownej Komisji Badania Zbrodni Hitlerowskich w Polsce*; *Zeszyty Oswiecimskie*; *Zeszyty Majdanka*; and *Przeglad Zachodni*. The outstanding historians engaged in research on this period include Czeslaw Madajczyk, Stanislaw Ploski, Karol Marian Pospieszalski, Czeslaw Luczak, Franciszek Ryszka, Maria Turlejska, Karol Jonca, and Alfred Konieczny.

Outside Poland the General Sikorski Historical Institute, the Polish Underground Study Trust (both in London), and the Pilsudski Institute in the United States should be noted. Many studies of the World War II period have been published in the crucial historical periodical *Zeszyty Historyczne*, which appears in Paris. Important émigré historians who wrote widely on the World War II period are Wladyslaw Pobog-Malinowski, Stefan Korbonski, and Kazimierz Iranek-Osmecki.

Polish historiography does not refrain from dealing with the fate of the Jews in occupied Poland. However, it is not free of an obvious tendentiousness and factual distortions. Recognizable differences in this treatment—in the general approach and in the presentation of the scope of the tragedy that engulfed the Jewish people—can be discerned not only by comparing various historians, but also by comparing the periods in which the research was undertaken. Generally speaking, among these it is necessary to designate the following:

1. During the years immediately following the war, most of the institutes engaged in the study of the Nazi occupation were established. The works that were published were more or less free from pressure by political forces; however, the documentation at their disposal was limited.

2. During the years 1951–56, the so-called Stalinization period in Poland, interference by the ruling party caused clearly discernible distortions in historical writings.

3. At the end of 1956, the change of leadership in the Polish Communist party wrought a certain liberalization; one of the results was a rise in the level of historical research. In these years important books appeared. One should note, in particular, the war diaries of Zygmunt Klukowski (*Dziennik z lat okupacji Zamojszczyzny, 1939–1944;* Lublin, 1958) and Ludwik Landau (*Kronika lat wojny i okupacji,* 3 volumes, Warsaw, 1962–63), which represent important strides in the documentation of the period of Nazi occupation in Poland and the Holocaust of Polish Jewry.

4. The years 1967–68 marked a wave of official government anti-Semitism in Poland that produced a series of works of pseudohistorical research, comprising defamatory and malicious falsifications regarding the Jewish people.

5. Since the end of the 1970s the quality of research has improved, and once again important research studies have appeared.

In this chapter, however, I shall limit myself to a description of the most characteristic directions of Polish historiography dealing with one subject only of the Holocaust of Polish Jewry, the relations between Poles and Jews during the Nazi occupation in Poland.

Until recent years Polish historiography did not broach the complex of problems in Jewish-Polish relations during the Holocaust years. It preferred to deal with one area only: the help extended to Jews by Poles. More has been written on this subject than on any other connected to the Holocaust of Polish Jewry. These publications are, at best, clearly one-sided and often completely distorted and based on entirely false data.

A prime example of such a distorted approach is the book written by the military historian Kazimierz Iranek-Osmecki, *Kto ratuje jedno zycie—Polacy i Zydzi, 1939–1945* (published in London in 1968; translated into English under the title *He who saves one life* [New York: Crown, 1971]). From the vast mass of archival material available, the author selected only evidence likely to support his preconceived notions. He tried to dismiss the existence of anti-Semitism among a vast part of the Polish population as the marginal attitude of an inconsequential minority. At the same time he decided to exaggerate very highly the help given by Poles to Jews during the Holocaust.

Another example is Stefan Korbonski, who has written many articles and books on the Polish underground during the years of German-Nazi occupation. In one of his book he states: "About 300,000 Jews, those who refused to go voluntarily to the ghettos and to death, and thus were saved from the Nazi waves of extermination, owe their lives to the help of the Polish population."[1] It is unnecessary to be suspicious of Korbonski, who did not know that most of the Polish Jews who were saved were those who fled to the Soviet Union. From the numerical point of view, after that group comes those who survived the concentration camps. Only a small number of those who survived had been fortunate enough to find a refuge and help from Polish families or Polish organizations.

It is strange to observe how even serious Polish researchers, historians who elsewhere pay strict attention to scientific accuracy, in dealing with the relationship with Jews permitted themselves unfounded generalizations, shocking exaggerations, and conclusions that are far from the truth. For example, Czeslaw Luczak, who undoubtedly may be counted among the most serious Polish historians, in describing the stance of the Poles on the Holocaust of Polish Jewry, wrote:

The murder of Jews in Poland deeply shocked the Polish public, which condemned it in no uncertain terms. On this matter both the underground parties and individual persons expressed their feeling. . . . Many Polish intellectuals condemned the extermination of the Jews. The common people reacted with fury. The Polish public was not satisfied with expressing its fury, but hastened, as much as its very modest opportunities allowed, to help the Jewish population in various ways, despite the danger involved. . . . This stand of the Polish public disappointed the German authorities, who had hoped for a positive reaction to their deeds. The crude and widespread anti-Semitic propaganda did not help the occupation authorities, just as the material benefits awarded to those who uncovered Jewish hiding places did not bring the desired results. . . . Only a few individuals, from society's dregs, agreed to collaborate, that is, only totally corrupt members of the underworld. The Polish public looked upon this with total abhorrence and disgust.[2]

Luczak continues:

It is impossible to measure the extent of the aid extended to Jews in occupied Poland or the number of those who benefitted from this help, principally because of its clandestine character. All that is known is that thanks to the generosity and self-sacrifice of the Polish public, more than 100,000 Jews were saved in occupied Poland.[3]

As is known, Luczak settles here on a number that is vastly exaggerated. Exaggerations of other Polish historians exceed even this figure.

Czeslaw Luczak, like most other Polish historians, completely avoids dealing in greater depth with this complex matter, the Polish attitude to the destruction of Polish Jewry. One cannot suspect that he is unfamiliar with the vast amount of data found in archives (mainly Polish) testifying to a situation far removed from the one he describes. On the one hand, we may point to the positive side of his trend of exaggerations, that is, the desire to record the help and sympathy extended to the Jews. On the other hand, there is also the opposite tendency to absolute silence about, or disavowal of, the negative side, the anti-Jewish activities of various Polish political factors during the years of the Nazi occupation, and the participation in the persecution and murder of Jews.

Since the mid-1980s Poland has been the scene of interesting developments that finally resulted in the total breakdown of the Communist regime. These developments have left their imprint also on historical research and writing. We are witnessing a development practically without precedent in the previous years. Polish intellectuals, including historians, have started openly to criticize Polish attitudes toward the annihilation of the Jewish people. This represents a significant advance over the traditional, stringently apologetic stance assumed by Polish historiography in regard to Polish-Jewish relations during the Nazi occupation.

The first openhearted discussion on the subject of Polish-Jewish relations during World War II was undertaken by the Catholic journal *Wiez* (which is published in Warsaw) in the issue for July–August 1986. Summarizing the discussion, Bogumil Luft said, "Poles were not Nazis, although they were anti-Semites to a lesser or greater extent. . . . Anti-Semitism had roots in all strata of Polish society" (page 31).

In the same journal *Wiez* in its issue for November–December 1986 an important article under the title "Z notatek" (From the notes) was published by Andrzej Szczypiorski. Here he, among others, addressed an issue that had not yet been analyzed by either Jewish or Polish historians, namely, the economic benefits reaped by many Poles following the deportation and murder of Polish Jewry. Szczypiorski wrote (page 60):

And what about the Jews? Is everything so clear-cut? Are we completely blameless in this respect? I am not even referring to such stains rising from the heinous deeds of *szmalcownicy* [individuals who turned Jews over to the Germans]—for every Nazi-occupied country had its own *szmalcownicy*, and the role of Frenchmen, Romanians, or Balts in the crime of extermination of the Jews was one incomparably larger than the collaboration of Polish scum with the Nazis. However, I would like to read an economic or sociological treatise analyzing the economic and social aspects of the transfer of property from Jewish to Polish hands. After all, the migration of thousands of residents of Warsaw, as well as other Polish cities, in connection with ghettoization surely had its effects. What about the furniture, valuables, clothing, books, paintings, capital, stores, enterprises, private practices? No doubt the Germans laid their hands on the lion's share of the loot. However, did they loot everything?

Szczypiorski goes on to launch a scathing attack on the apologetic strain in Polish contemporary historiography dealing with the period in question (page 61):

The version of the war most accepted by us portrays the Pole as a knight beyond reproach, ardent patriot, and underground fighter. This is a true portrait, but only one among many.

What about the resourceful Pole who, while giving his tacit support to the underground, during the day was busy striking lucrative business deals with the Germans? Where is the faint-hearted Pole who thought only about survival and a hundred times a day cursed the underground for allegedly exposing everyone to risk? Where is the quiet, humble Pole, burrowing himself in the dark corner of his life, who, when asked what he did during the occupation, would be likely to give the Abbe Sieyes answer: "I was staying alive"? What about the Pole in a godforsaken village, who sowed and plowed, bred hogs, complied without a murmur with the compulsory deliveries to the Third Reich and the General Government, drank illicitly distilled liquor with German gendarmes, and shopped in the city for Jewish-owned pianos, for he had to somehow invest the huge sums gained at the expense of someone else's plight?

A nationwide discussion in Poland on the subject of Jewish-Polish relations followed the article by Jan Blonski that was published in the Catholic weekly *Tygodnik Powszechny* on January 11, 1987, under the title "Biedni Polacy patrza na getto" (Poor Poles look at the ghetto). The article by Blonski and the extensive controversy that it sparked are of special interest in this context. Blonski's article provoked responses from dozens of historians and intellectuals, some of whom raised questions that either had been ignored or had attracted only limited attention on the part of Polish historians.

Anti-Semitic attitudes evident in a number of these responses indicate that anti-Semitic thinking habits die hard in Poland, not only among the Polish people in general, but also among many intellectuals and historians. However, side by side with the biased, apologetic, distortive, and anti-Semitically flavored traditional approaches, new venues have recently been opened in Polish historiography. Polish-Jewish relations during the Holocaust have become a subject of thoroughgoing study and discussions, without regard for the embarrassing, even highly disturbing, revelations they might produce.

The article by Jan Blonski was translated into English and published in *Yad Vashem Studies* 19 (Jerusalem, 1988). In the same volume appeared the English translations of the most important responses to Blonski, those in support of Blonski by Jerzy Turowicz and Teresa Prekerowa, and the sharply critical anti-Semitic response by Wladyslaw Sila-Nowicki.

Among the other most important responses to Blonski, we should mention the articles by Helena Balicka-Kozlowska and Kazimierz Dziewanowski. In the article "Kto ratowal i kogo ratowano" (Who rescued and who was rescued), which was published in the journal *Wiez*, no. 4 (1988), Balicka-Kozlowska sums up concisely two central issues: first, attitudes of the Polish underground, and second, attitudes of Polish society to rescuing Jews during the Nazi occupation. She writes, among other things:

The lack of greater involvement on the part of Poles in rescue efforts is correctly explained by an all-too-real threat of death; anti-Semitism is also, though reluctantly, cited as a factor. In my view, anti-Semitism played a part not only in the handing over of Jews [to the Germans] but also in the appalling indifference of a large part of the society and the facility with which their tragic situation was exploited. It also seems to me that anti-Semitism, so prevalent among the clergy, could, especially in the countryside, instill in the faithful an unwillingness to render any form of assistance to Jews. The whole problem was a complex one, and there were a number of closely interrelated underlying causes . . . .

Only a few considered defending Jews as one of the manifestations of the struggle against the occupier. Resistance to the Germans was universally regarded as a matter of Polish honor, and noninvolvement met with dislike and contempt. In contrast, the rescue of Jews was usually seen as a purely private matter. There were occasions when members of the underground were reproached for sheltering Jews since, so the argument went, they thereby exposed other partisans to risk and jeopardized apartments needed by the underground. . . .

There is also another, very painful issue: many more Jews could have been saved if Poles had not been afraid of other Poles. For it is not true that Jews had to be hidden only from German eyes; they were sheltered (or sheltered themselves) both from death at the hands of the Germans and from the eyes of the Poles, who were present in places beyond the reach of the Germans, or even Volksdeutschen.

Kazimierz Dziewanowski wrote one of the most interesting responses to Blonski's article. It is titled "Prosze nie mowic za mnie" (Please do not speak in my name) and was published in the weekly *Tygodnik Powszechny* of April 5, 1987. He touches upon perhaps the most important issue of all: anti-Semitism in Polish political life before the war, during the Holocaust, and in its aftermath. He writes:

The major political party before the war [the Endecja] made anti-Semitism an explicit part of its program. Proclaiming itself as a "national" party, it refused to understand that by consolidating the image of Poland in world public opinion as a country of anti-Semites, it was causing irreparable damage to Polish national interests. Examples of the body of writing from this period, whose existence Sila-Nowicki denies, can be found in every major scientific library in the country and abroad. I have them in my own library, in the writings of Roman Dmowski and statements by leaders of the ONR-Falanga and affiliated organizations. Resurgence of this line of thought nowadays is known to everyone in Warsaw who is interested in this question. Although it originates from very specific circles and fails to evoke wider response, its authors nonetheless hope that their "works" will meet with such response in the future, for this is what happened in the past.

Dziewanowski refers also to a question that has not been dealt with extensively by the students of the Holocaust, namely, expressions of anti-Semitism to be found in part of the Polish underground press during the Nazi occupation:

We also know that the Polish underground press of the occupation period was by no means free of statements to the effect that although we Poles were not collaborating in the Hitlerite Endlösung, Hitler nonetheless was performing with his own hands the task that should have been performed anyway. Historians of the occupation period can point out such passages without any effort.

Soul-searching and criticism of Polish attitudes during the Holocaust were particularly pronounced among Catholic circles. No such tendency could be observed among intellectuals and historians who were associated with, or were members of, the Communist party. Moreover, the latter tended until the final breakdown of communism in Poland to adhere to the official line established following the officially sponsored anti-Semitic campaign and upheld in the 1960s and 1970s.

One of the prominent examples of pseudohistorical, anti-Semitic publications of this period is the biased, apologetic, and superficial book by Jerzy Slaski that includes numerous slanders against Jews during the Holocaust (see Jerzy Slaski, *Polska Walczaca, 1939–1945* [Fighting Poland, 1939–1945] [Warsaw, 1986]. It is noteworthy that this dubious work by Slaski was issued in 60,000 copies. However, what was a new phenomenon in the 1980s (even before the removal of the Communists from power) was that publications like that of Slaski could be criticized. One could encounter in these years in Polish historiography a growing number of thoroughgoing analyses in response to apologetic and tendentious publications, including those misrepresenting the history of the Holocaust. For example, a strong response to the anti-Semitic slanders in the book of Slaski was published by Janusz Gaworski in the journal *Wiez* of April 1987.

Unfortunately, not all historians and writers associated with Catholic circles speak in the same voice regarding Jewish-Polish relations during the Holocaust. Many of them continue to follow the old apologetic, biased, and anti-Semitic lines. Thus, for instance, in his apologetic article ''Historical Tradition of Polish Catholicism'' Andrzej Micewski, a historian with close ties to Catholic circles, writes:

There were no Jews in postwar Poland. They were murdered by Hitler. Only a handful of them survived in the Soviet Union. After returning to Poland, these lost, luckless people made a great mistake by letting themselves be used as tools of Stalinism. For this they paid a terrible price. Polish society was free of anti-Semitism, which resurfaced in the ruling party. The party attempted, not without a measure of success, to stir up anti-Semitic feeling in order to divert attention from its blunders. Again Jews were targeted as scapegoats. The conspiratorial theory of history was reinstated. The fate that for centuries had been looming over the Jewish people manifested itself in the system, which in the view of world opinion was created mainly by Jews. It is frightening to realize that in nearly every historical stage of persecutions of Jews and militant anti-Semitism, it has always been possible to find, as in this case, objective causes of the phenomenon, which in its essence remains an evil, anti-humanistic, and, above all, anti-Christian manifestation.[4]

Micewski's statement about the absence of anti-Semitism in Poland after World War II remains puzzling. How can one then explain the Kielce pogrom in July 1946 and other, though smaller, sanguinary outbursts? Furthermore, Micewski seems to ignore the fact that in the last stage of the war and the first postwar years, right-wing political parties (and to a lesser extent the center) resorted to anti-Semitic propaganda as an important instrument in the struggle for power. At that time Poland was the scene of internecine strife, and hundreds of Jewish men, women, and children were murdered as a result of anti-Semitic propaganda. Regardless of his position and political views, the Jew was driven to the left of the political spectrum, for nowhere else could he find protection at that time. Only later did the ruling party adopt anti-Semitic positions (at first only one faction, and later most of the leadership) in the political interparty struggles.

Another example of a biased, apologetic approach with anti-Semitic overtones is the article by the priest Franciszek Stopniak, entitled "Catholic Clergy and the Jews in Poland during World War Two."[5] Stopniak writes: "Thanks to the sacrifices of Polish society over 100,000 Jews were saved. A far greater number were supplied with food, clothing, and other articles. The number of Poles who took part in rendering these acts of assistance is estimated at three million. Besides, the very fact of not speaking about a Jew's being sheltered amounted to a great deal."

This short passage is a good example of the tissue of distortions woven into many Polish historical writings. The figure of 100,000 Jews allegedly rescued by Poles remains completely unfounded, even though many Polish historians keep quoting it as a fact. Nor does the thesis about hundreds of thousands of Jews being supplied with food and clothing by Poles rest on any factual foundation. In citing the figure of three million Poles who allegedly took part in rendering aid to Jews, Stopniak draws on a mostly dubious publication by Tadeusz Bednarczyk, a person known for his inventions, which have nothing to do with historical research and historical truth.

Stopniak's article, which borrows warped quotations from Emmanuel Ringelblum's diary, provides yet another example of distortions with anti-Semitic overtones. Referring to an entry of May 18, 1942, in the diary of Ringelblum, the founder of the Warsaw Ghetto Underground Archives, Stopniak writes:

The usually well-informed local Ukrainian, Belorussian, and also [Polish] blue police reported to the Nazi authorities about acts of assistance to Jews. Many clergymen lost their lives as a result. Volksdeutschen and Reichsdeutschen insidiously came out against clergymen who helped Jews. The Jewish Order Service [Jewish police] was no better. Four hundred Jewish informers were said to operate in the Warsaw ghetto alone.

Now here is what Ringelblum wrote in the passage distorted by Stopniak:

Are there more informers and Gestapo agents among us than among others? This question gave rise to a joke: "Two Jews meet and one asked the other 'How are things?' The other one answers: 'One of us surely works for the Gestapo, which is why I won't tell you anything.' There are allegedly some 400 informers. However, I think that considering the fact that hundreds of illegal small mills are being operated in the ghetto, that there are flour depots, clandestine bakeries, workshops, a flourishing trade in leather, and all conceivable illicit merchandise, there cannot possibly be so many informers among us that one could maintain there are more of them here than among others. In any event, the underground men who arrived from the East are not afraid here of every janitor or stranger, as is the case on the other side.[6]

Another troubling phenomenon in Poland stems from the deposition in archives and submission for publication of all kinds of fictional reminiscences aimed at the falsification of various historical events, including Polish-Jewish relations during the war. Unfortunately, many of these writings are used by some historians who do not care to check their veracity. It is perhaps too early to foresee which trend will prevail in Polish historiography, the unbiased, honest, and courageous research or the apologetic pseudohistorical way of writing.

## EDITOR'S NOTE ON POLAND

The fate of Poland's three million Jews is one of the most tragic tales of the Holocaust. Once the foundation of this nation's commercial class, the Jews were all but exterminated. As Earl Vinecour notes in *Polish Jews: The Final Chapter* (New York: New York University Press, 1977), the few thousand Jews who remain in Poland are little more than a curiosity.

The English reader who seeks a broad overview of the Jewish experience in Poland should begin with Simon Dubnow's three volume *History of the Jews in Russia and Poland* (Philadelphia: Jewish Publication Society of America, 1916–20); Bernard Weinryb, *The Jews of Poland* (Philadelphia: Jewish Publication Society of America, 1973); Heinrich Graetz, *History of the Jews* (Philadelphia: Jewish Publication Society of America, 1895); Louis Greenberg, *The Jews in Russia* (New Haven, Conn.: Yale University Press, 1951); Lucy Dawidowicz, *The Golden Tradition: Jewish Life and Thought in Eastern Europe* (Boston: Beacon Press, 1967); Ismar Elbogen, *A Century of Jewish Life* (Philadelphia: Jewish Publication Society of America, 1944); and Forward Association, *Di Farshvundene Velt* (New York: Forward Association, 1947).

For more recent perspectives, the reader should consult Bernard Johnpoll's *The Politics of Futility: The General Jewish Workers Bund of Poland, 1917–1943* (Ithaca, N.Y.: Cornell University Press, 1967); Joseph Leftwich's collection of Yiddish, Hebrew and Polish poetry titled *The Golden Peacock* (New York: T. Yoseloff, 1961); and Celia Heller's incomparable study *On the Edge of Destruction: The Jews of Poland Between the Two World Wars* (New York: Columbia University Press, 1976).

During the Holocaust Polish Jews and Gentiles issued several semiofficial reports on conditions under Nazi rule. *The Black Book of Poland* (New York: Putnam's, 1942) appeared under the auspices of the Polish Ministry of Information in Exile. Its five hundred pages offered some of the first glimpses of concentration camps in Dobrzyca and Starachowice and the killing of four hundred thousand persons in the first twenty-two months of war. A year later, Jewish refugees in the United States issued one of the most depressing accounts ever written, *The Black Book of Polish Jewry*, edited by Jakob Apenszlak (New

York, 1943), focusing specifically upon the ghettoization and deportation of their kinsmen. This was followed in 1946 by the publication of *The Black Book: The Nazi Crime Against the Jewish People* (New York: Jewish Black Book Committee, 1946).

Apart from the innumerable memoirs available to the reader, scholars have also compiled studies of the Jewish tragedy in Poland. Notable among these efforts are Simon Segal's *New Order in Poland* (New York: Knopf, 1942), which reads very much like a semiofficial black book; Albert Nirenstein's *A Tower from the Enemy* (New York: Orion Press, 1959), which contains extracts of resistance in the ghettos of Bialystok and Vilna and the death camp in Sobibor; Isaiah Trunk's *Judenrat: The Jewish Councils in Eastern Europe Under Nazi Occupation* (New York: Macmillan, 1972); and Alfred Katz's *Poland's Ghettos at War* (New York: Twayne, 1970), which is probably the fairest assessment of the anguish felt by Jewish leaders as they were faced with certain death.

For what transpired in Warsaw, the essential text is Emmanuel Ringelblum's *Notes from the Warsaw Ghetto*, edited and translated by Jacob Sloan (New York: McGraw-Hill, 1958). This great historian from the Jewish Historical Institute was the founder of Warsaw's so-called Oneg Shabbat, a group of intellectuals committed to the preservation of Jewish culture in Poland. Ringelblum's diaries served as the inspiration for several later works, including John Hersey's *The Wall* and Leon Uris's *Mila 18*. Virtually forgotten, however, is another excellent work by Ringelblum that was posthumously published: *Polish-Jewish Relations During the Second World War*, edited by Joseph Kermish and Shmuel Krakowski (New York: Howard Fertig, 1976).

The historian Philip Friedman has also compiled a gripping account of the Warsaw ghetto. His *Martyrs and Fighters* (New York: Praeger, 1954) contains excerpts from German sources (including the report of SS General Jürgen Stroop on the destruction of the ghetto), survivors, and a little girl named Zosia whose statement is the most powerful supplement I have ever read. Additional insights may be obtained from *The Warsaw Diary of Chaim A. Kaplan*, translated and edited by Abraham Katsh (New York: Collier Books, 1965), *The Warsaw Diary of Adam Czerniakow* (New York: Stein and Day, 1979), and Janusz Korczak's *Ghetto Diary* (New York: Holocaust Library, 1978). The last volume, which contains a lengthy introduction by Hillel Zeitlin, offers the thoughts of the saintly doctor in Warsaw who accompanied a group of orphans to Treblinka. Korczak's tale is also told in Joseph Hyam's *A Field of Buttercups* (London: Muller, 1970).

For additional views of what transpired in Poland, see Alan Adelson and Robert Lapides's monumental *Lodz Ghetto: Inside a Community Under Siege* (New York: Viking, 1989), which is an elaboration of the earlier work by Mendel Grossman, *With a Camera in the Ghetto* (Haifa: Ghetto Fighters' House and Hakibbutz Hameuchad, 1970). See also Yitzhak Katzenelson, *The Song of the Murdered Jewish People*, translated and annotated by Noah Rosenbloom (Haifa: Ghetto Fighters' House, 1980), and *Rzeszow Jews Memorbuch* (Hebrew, Yiddish, and English) (Tel Aviv: Rzeszower Societies in Israel and the United States,

1967). Finally, for an understanding of the deep-rooted antipathy of Poles for Jews that culminated in a ritual murder pogrom at Kielce on July 4, 1946, see Yisrael Gutman and Shmuel Krakowski, *Unequal Victims: Poles and Jews During World War II*, translated by Ted Gorelick and Witold Jedlicki (New York: Holocaust Library, 1986).

## NOTES

1. Stefan Korbonski, *W imieniu Rzeczypospolitej* (Paris, 1954), p. 257.

2. Czeslaw Luczak, *Polityka ludnosciowa i ekonomiczna hitlerowskich Niemiec w okupowanej Polsce* (Poznan, 1979), pp. 95–96.

3. Ibid., p. 591.

4. Andrzej Micewski, "Tradycje historyczne katolicyzmu polskiego," *Znaki czasu: kwartalnik religijno-spoleczny* (Paris), 1986, no. 1.

5. Franciszek Stopniak, "Duchowienstwo katolickie i Zydzi w polsce w latach II wojny swiatowej," *Studia nad faszyzmem i zbrodniami hitlerowskimi* (Wroclaw) 11 (1987): 195–216.

6. Emmanuel Ringelblum, *Togbukh fun warshever geto, 1939–1942, Yiddish Bukh*, vol. 1 (Warsaw, 1961), p. 356 (published in Yiddish).

## SELECT BIBLIOGRAPHY

Adelson, Alan, and Robert Lapides. (eds.) *Lodz Ghetto: Inside a Community Under Siege.* New York: Viking, 1989.

Apenszlak, Jacob, ed. *The Black Book of Polish Jewry.* New York: Roy, 1943.

Arad, Yitzhak. *Ghetto in Flames: The Struggle and Destruction of the Jews in Vilna in the Holocaust.* Jerusalem: Yad Vashem, 1982.

Bartoszewski, Wladyslaw, and Zofia Lewin, eds. *The Samaritans: Heroes of the Holocaust.* Translated by Alexander Jordan. New York: Twayne, 1970.

Czerniakow, Adam. *The Warsaw Diary of Adam Czerniakow.* Edited by Raul Hilberg, Stanislaw Staron, and Joseph Kermisz. New York: Stein and Day, 1979.

Dawidowicz, Lucy. *The Golden Tradition: Jewish Life and Thought in Eastern Europe.* Boston: Beacon Press, 1967.

Dobroszycki, Lucjan, ed. *The Chronicle of the Lodz Ghetto, 1941–1944.* New Haven, Conn.: Yale University Press, 1984.

Dubnow, Simon. *History of the Jews in Russia and Poland.* 3 vols. Philadelphia: Jewish Publication Society of America, 1916–20.

Forward Association. *Di Farshvundene Velt.* New York: Forward Association, 1947.

Friedman, Philip. *Martyrs and Fighters: The Epic of the Warsaw Ghetto.* New York: Praeger, 1954.

Goldstein, Bernard. *The Stars Bear Witness.* New York: Viking Press, 1949.

Gutman, Yisrael. *The Jews of Warsaw, 1939–1943: Ghetto, Underground, Revolt.* Translated by Ina Friedman. Bloomington: Indiana University Press, 1982.

Gutman, Yisrael, and Shmuel Krakowski. *Unequal Victims: Poles and Jews During World War II.* Translated by Ted Gorelick and Witold Jedlicki. New York: Holocaust Library, 1986.

Heller, Celia. *On the Edge of Destruction: The Jews of Poland Between the Two World Wars*. New York: Columbia University Press, 1976.

Huberband, Shimon. *Kiddush Hashem: Jewish Religious and Cultural Life in Poland during the Holocaust*. Edited by Jeffrey Gurock and Robert Hirt, translated by David Fishman. Hoboken, N.J.: Ktav, 1987.

Hyams, Joseph. *A Field of Buttercups*. London: Muller, 1970.

Jewish Black Book Committee. *The Black Book: The Nazi Crime Against the Jewish People*. New York: Jewish Black Book Committee, 1946.

Johnpoll, Bernard. *The Politics of Futility: The General Jewish Workers Bund of Poland, 1917–1943*. Ithaca, N.Y.: Cornell University Press, 1967.

Kaplan, Chaim. *The Warsaw Diary of Chaim A. Kaplan*. Translated and edited by Abraham Katsh. New York: Collier Books, 1965.

Karski, Jan. *Story of a Secret State*. Boston: Houghton Mifflin, 1944.

Katz, Alfred. *Poland's Ghettos at War*. New York: Twayne, 1970.

Katzenelson, Yitzhak. *The Song of the Murdered Jewish People*. Translated and annotated by Noah Rosenbloom. Haifa: Ghetto Fighters' House, 1980.

Keller, Ulrich, ed. *The Warsaw Ghetto in Photographs*. New York: Dover, 1984.

Kermish, Joseph, ed. *To Live with Honor and Die with Honor: Selected Documents from the Warsaw Ghetto Underground Archives O.S. (Oneg Shabbath)*. Translated by M. Z. Prives et al. Jerusalem: Yad Vashem, 1986.

Korczak, Janusz. *Ghetto Diary*. Translated by J. Bachrach et al. New York: Holocaust Library, 1978.

Kowalski, Isaac. *A Secret Press in Nazi Europe: The Story of a Jewish United Partisan Organization*. New York: Shengold, 1969.

Krakowski, Shmuel. *The War of the Doomed: Jewish Armed Resistance in Poland, 1942–1944*. New York: Holmes and Meier, 1984.

Leftwich, Joseph. *The Golden Peacock*. New York: T. Yoseloff, 1961.

Meed, Vladka. *On Both Sides of the Wall: Memoirs from the Warsaw Ghetto*. Translated by S. Spiegel and S. Meed. New York: Holocaust Library, 1979.

Nirenstein, Albert. *A Tower from the Enemy*. New York: Orion Press, 1959.

Pankiewicz, Tadeusz. *The Cracow Ghetto Pharmacy*. Translated by H. Tilles. New York: Holocaust Library, 1987.

Pat, Jacob. *Ashes and Fire*. Translated by Leo Steinberg. New York: International Universities Press, 1947.

Polish Ministry of Information in Exile. *The Black Book of Poland*. New York: G. P. Putnam's, 1942.

Ringelblum, Emmanuel. *Notes from the Warsaw Ghetto*. Edited and translated by Jacob Sloan. New York: McGraw-Hill, 1958.

———. *Polish-Jewish Relations During the Second World War*. Edited by Joseph Kermish and Shmuel Krakowski. New York: Howard Fertig, 1976.

Rzeszower Societies in Israel and the United States. *Rzeszow Jews Memorbuch*. Tel Aviv: Rzeszower Societies, 1967.

Schoenfeld, Joachim. *Holocaust Memoirs: Jews in the Lwow Ghetto, the Janowski Concentration Camp, and as Deportees in Siberia*. New York: Ktav, 1985.

Segal, Simon. *The New Order in Poland*. New York: Knopf, 1942.

Tec, Nechama. *When Light Pierced the Darkness: Christian Rescue of Jews in Nazi-occupied Poland*. New York: Oxford University Press, 1986.

Trunk, Isaiah. *Judenrat: The Jewish Councils in Eastern Europe Under Nazi Occupation*. New York: Macmillan, 1972.

Vinecour, Earl. *Polish Jews: The Final Chapter*. New York: New York University Press, 1977.

Weinryb, Bernard. *The Jews of Poland*. Philadelphia: Jewish Publication Society of America, 1973.

Zuckerman, Isaac. *The Fighting Ghettos*. Translated by Meyer Barkai. Philadelphia: Lippincott, 1962.

# Chapter 12

# The Last Tragedy of the Shoah: The Jews of Hungary

*Asher Cohen*

## BETWEEN THE TWO WORLD WARS

From the middle of the nineteenth century, the modernization of Hungary was linked to the integration of the Jews, a process known as Magyarization. The Magyars, then part of the Austro-Hungarian Empire, enthusiastically accepted Jewish assimilation. The main advantage for the Hungarians was that the newly assimilated Jews partially counterbalanced the large number of national minorities in the country. This apparently successful process ended with World War I.

After the signing of the Treaty of Trianon in 1920, Hungary was transformed into a national state, practically without minorities. The Jewish population, which had reached 911,000 in 1910, shrank to 473,000 within the Trianon boundaries (about 6 percent of the population). This figure was further reduced by demographic decrease to 400,000 in 1941 (4.9 percent of the population). About half of the Jews lived in Budapest.

This decreasing trend in Jewish population was reversed after 1938. Some of the Jews in Transylvania, which had been annexed to Romania, and the Jews of northeastern Hungary, which had been absorbed by Czechoslovakia, as well as the Jews of Bácska (Bačka) in southern Hungary, which had been incorporated into Yugoslavia, were in 1938–41 returned to Hungarian rule and constituted a part of the Jewish population in that country during the *Shoah*. The number of Jews in Hungary then reached a total of 725,000. The approximately 100,000 "Christians of Jewish origins," as defined by the racial legislation of 1941, must be added to this figure.

Even before the Trianon Treaty was signed, Hungary underwent two revolutions, those of Mihály Károlyi in 1918 and of Béla Kun in 1919, and one counterrevolution, the latter headed by Admiral Miklós Horthy. The central elements were a group of radical rightists with extreme anti-Semitic tendencies. Violent anti-Semitism, new and completely unexpected in liberal Hungary, began with a wave of terror and murders known as the White Terror. The stabilization of the conservative right-wing government helped to moderate the violent outbreaks somewhat, but at a cost of the first anti-Jewish legislation in Europe during this period. The *numerus clausus* law of September 1920 limited the number of Jewish university students to 6 percent. The White Terror and the *numerus clausus* were cornerstones of the Horthy regime. The general attitude toward the Jews was eased somewhat under the governments headed by Prime Minister Count István Bethlen, the most prominent political figure during the 1920s.

Hungary between the two world wars was no longer overwhelmingly an agrarian nation, although agriculture still remained the main source of income, employing more wage earners than industry, mines, and communication combined. More than half of the population still lived in rural areas. Nevertheless, the relatively swift economic transformation during the last decades of the nineteenth century, in which Jewish capital and initiative played a very important part, was not accompanied by corresponding changes in the social structure. The most important social group, virtually monopolizing political power, was the aristocrats, owners of enormous and still-undivided latifundia. Awaiting reform were some three million landless peasants. That this crisis did not erupt into a dangerous social conflict was partly due to the acceptance of the landed aristocracy's social values. All classes could also unite behind rejection of the post–World War I territorial losses.

The fundamental change in the status of Hungarian Jews was primarily a result of the objective conditions created by the dissolution of the Austro-Hungarian Empire and the postwar political situation. The influence of Jews in the short-lived Communist regime of Béla Kun in 1919 was adduced as "evidence" of lack of loyalty and "failure of assimilation" of the Jews. This contention was the central theme in Hungarian nationalist propaganda between the two world wars. Conservative governments discovered that they could divert the increasing social dissatisfaction of the lower classes, both peasant and proletarian, against the Jews. This rejection of the Jews extended to cultural and literary areas. Important writers and intellectuals repeatedly maintained that the Jews did not constitute an integral part of the Hungarian nation, and that it was desirable to eliminate at least a portion of them from the national state. The assimilationist trend of the Hungarian policy was replaced by what was termed by Hungarian intellectuals as "dissimilation."

The development of the Fascist movement in Hungary toward the end of the 1930s was also an important element in the general picture. In 1937 Ferenc Szálasi, a former army major, succeeded in merging four splinter movements into one party, the Hungarian Nationalist Socialist party, better known under the name of the Arrow Cross (*Nyilaskeresztes*) party. Szálasi's theory was an

incomprehensible collection of phrases about "a farmers' state with industry."
While his nationalism and revisionism were both conventional, his plans for
agrarian reform were also vague. The only clear points in Szálasi's program
concerned the "exploiting Jews" who must be expelled from the country.

Toward the end of 1939 the Nyilas counted nearly 300,000 members. In
parliamentary elections that year the Arrow Cross won thirty-one seats, the bulk
of the forty-nine seats won by Hungarian Fascist groups. The election results
failed to dislodge Horthy's government, but the Arrow Cross emerged as the
most important opposition. Social dissatisfaction, particularly among the laboring
classes, found its most authentic expression in this Fascist movement. The weight
of the Arrow Cross members was small in those circles that determined high-
level policy, but there were many members and secret sympathizers of this party
in the low and intermediate levels of government administration, in the counties
and the cities, and in the army and the gendarmerie.

Two anti-Jewish laws, issued in 1938 and 1939, were the first results of Fascist
pressure on the legislative level. The first measure restricted activity of Jews in
intellectual occupations to about 20 percent. This alone threatened the livelihood
of about 15,000 families. The second law caused the dismissal of Jews from
virtually all the public services and created widespread unemployment. This
legislation distinguished not only between Jews and Christians, but also between
those who had converted to Christianity before August 1, 1919, and those who
had converted thereafter. In this, there was undoubtedly an element of German
racism, following its "success" in the policy of dissimilation that had been
demanded by some Hungarian intellectuals. After the second law, Jews banned
from regular army service were recruited to special Labor Service (Munkaszol-
gálat) units under army command. The first units were established immediately
after the outbreak of the war, but long before Hungary itself joined the conflict.
The Labor Service System ultimately played a significant role in the annihilation
process.

The process of eliminating Jews from any national Hungarian framework
reached a new stage with the promulgation of the third statute in August 1941.
This act explicitly forbade marriage between Jews and non-Jews. The "failure
of assimilation," incessantly proclaimed since the 1920s by Hungarian historians
and writers, was explicitly cited here as reason for the law. A Jew was defined
according to all the criteria of the Nuremberg Laws, and this included about
100,000 Christians who now fell into the category of "Jew."

Despite this clear and unmistakable development in the attitude of the Hungarians toward the Jewish problem, Hungarian Jews themselves not only continued consistently to ignore it and to deny its existence, but also to present
assimilation as a decidedly positive achievement. But assimilation is of necessity
a bilateral process, and what some leading Hungarian intellectuals called "dissimilation" was in fact a nonacceptance of assimilation by the Hungarian side.
The peculiarity of the situation lay in the fact that it was not understood as such

by the Jewish population and their leaders. They considered themselves an integral part of the Hungarian nation, and their assimilation as a fait accompli.

It should be noted that the majority of the most prominent Jewish personalities in the cultural, artistic, economic, and political life—and they were indeed many in number—were not active in Jewish affairs. Research into the special connection that nevertheless bound this elite to Judaism is still needed. At any rate, they cannot be regarded as a part of what we would call Jewish leadership. There was, of course, the leadership of the two *kehillas*, or organized communities, but a real political leadership of Hungarian Jewry did not and could not exist in the system upon which the community organization was based.

The largest and the most important *kehilla* was the Neolog, as Reform Judaism was known in Hungary. It was modern and innovative in ritual. In 1930, 65.5 percent of Hungarian Jews, most of them assimilated, were affiliated with the Neolog. Its national organization was the National Bureau of the Jews of Hungary (Magyarországi Izraeliták Országos Irodája), which was clearly dominated by the Budapest community. At the beginning of the war Samu Stern was head of both the national bureau and of the Budapest *kehilla*. The Orthodox community was a federation of smaller *kehillas*, especially in the northeastern part of the country, where the Hasidic spirit had penetrated. In 1930, 29.2 percent of Hungarian Jews were affiliated with the Orthodox community. Its national organization was known as the Central Bureau of the Autonomous Orthodox Jewish Community (Magyarországi Autonom Izraelita Hitfelekezet Központi Irodája) and was headed by Samu Kahan-Frankl. The remaining 5.3 percent of Hungarian Jews were not affiliated with either national body. The relations between the two principal communities were strained, and there was no actual cooperation between them until 1938.

Following the arrival of the first wave of refugees from post-*Anschluss* Austria, and after the passage of the first anti-Jewish law, the Orthodox and Reform organizations jointly established the Welfare Bureau of Hungarian Jews (Magyar Izraeliták Pártfogó Irodája [MIPI]), in which the local Zionist Organization also took part. Parallel to the establishment of the MIPI, a National Hungarian Jewish Assistance Campaign (Országos Magyar Zsidó Segitö Akció [OMZsA]) was set up to raise funds. For the first time some Jewish intellectuals who had hitherto distanced themselves from any activity for Jewish causes took part. The heads of the two major communities assumed leadership of OMZsA. The organization was granted formal recognition by the authorities, thus providing a legal basis for the collection of funds. Great care was taken to do nothing that might in any way be interpreted as illegal. This policy conformed with the law-abiding outlook of Hungarian Jews, but in many circumstances it severely limited the ability of the organization to help refugees.

Distinctions between the OMZsA and the MIPI were mainly theoretical. Both provided help to destitute Jews after Hungary took over Carpatho-Ruthenia early in 1939. Both provided direct relief and helped both in obtaining Hungarian citizenship and in emigration. They also provided equipment, food, and warm clothing to the Labor Service units, especially after Hungary entered the war against the Soviet Union, when Labor Service companies were dispatched to the Russian front in the Ukraine.

The Zionist Organization operated alongside the *kehillas* and was subject to their animosity. The Zionists had minimal influence on Hungarian Jewry, and even toward the end of the 1930s, when the organization began to grow, its membership was only about 5,000, including 1,200 women of the Women's International Zionist Organization (WIZO) and another 1,500 or 2,000 youth who were organized in various movements. Otto Komoly served as the head of the Zionist Organization from 1940 until he was murdered in January 1945. The Zionist movement suffered from internal problems among various factions such as Mizrahi, the General Zionists, Ihud-Mapai, and Hashomer Hatzair. The youth movements were divided along the same lines, with the addition of the Betar youth movement, associated with the militant New Zionist Organization. In the summer of 1940 the authorities banned activity of all local units except for the central office in Budapest.

The dire occurrences in Hungary on the eve of World War II weakened the status of the Jews considerably, both in economic and social terms. Yet in comparison with the condition of Jews in other European states and in North Africa, Hungarian Jewry was in a relatively good and stable condition during this period. In 1938, and especially after the *Anschluss* with Austria, there was a growing wave of refugees who sought refuge in European countries. Perhaps five thousand refugees came to Hungary. Many had family or business ties in Hungary. Some were Jews of Hungarian origin, now compelled to return to the land of their birth. Another two thousand to three thousand refugees reached Hungary from Czechoslovakia after the Germans established the Protectorate of Bohemia and Moravia in March 1939 and from Poland after the outbreak of the war in September. Provision of economic subsistence for the refugees was undertaken by MIPI, which set up improvised camps in the yards of synagogues and other Jewish institutions in Budapest.

## THE FIRST LOSSES

A fundamental change in Nazi policy toward the Jews occurred with the German invasion of the Soviet Union on June 22, 1941, an event that also dragged Hungary into the whirlpool of the war with Great Britain and the United States. That invasion marked the beginning of the mass murder by the *Einsatzgruppen*, special squads responsible for killing close to a million and a half Jews in Eastern Europe, including fourteen thousand deported from Hungary.

The expulsion from Hungary was executed in August 1941 on the initiative of the National Central Alien Control Office (Külföldieket Ellenörzö Országos Központi Hatóság [KEOKH]), a special department set up within the Hungarian police. The deportations included not only ''alien'' Jews (mainly of Polish background) but also many Jews who could not immediately prove their Hungarian citizenship. By far the greatest cruelties were committed in Carpatho-Ruthenia, where entire communities were often deported. These were handed over to the SS, supposedly to be "resettled" in Poland in homes that had been vacated by Jews who had retreated with the Soviet army. In fact, most of the deported were shot by the SS and its Ukrainian hirelings near Kamenets-Podolsk in eastern Galicia on August 27–28. Some of them managed to escape and inform the MIPI in Budapest of the mass murder. A delegation informed the minister of the interior, Ferenc Keresztes-Fischer, the only member of the council who opposed the deportation. He ordered a halt to the action and demanded that two trains nearing the border be returned.

The deportation to Kamenets-Podolsk might be regarded as a singular episode, but the same cannot be said of the policy adopted by the government and the military toward the Labor Service. When Hungary entered the war, more than fourteen thousand young Jews were taken into this paramilitary service. Early in 1942, following a mass conscription, about fifty thousand men in these units were sent to the eastern front. The men in these units did not bear arms. Living conditions were very bad, and many died of disease and exposure. Hungarian officers did not hesitate to use Jews as human minesweepers: they required the men to advance through the minefields. More than forty thousand Jewish men lost their lives in the Labor Service System, and many others perished in Soviet captivity.

The government, headed by László Bárdossy, opened the year of 1942 with a campaign of slaughter in the Bácska area in the south of the country, around the city of Ujvidék (Novi Sad). The pretext was a police operation against the partisans. In reality, it was a planned mass execution carried out by the regular Hungarian forces, and its victims were about 2,500 Serbs and some 700 Jews. The main purpose of the operation was to suppress Serbian nationalists, but the killing was random. In addition to deportations and the Labor Service System, reprisals such as this were the most ominous sign of violent anti-Semitism among the army, the police, the gendarmerie, and the general populace.

In March 1942 Horthy dismissed Bárdossy and in his place named Miklós Kállay as prime minister. Kállay was a faithful supporter of Horthy, and though there was no clear change in policy toward the Jews during his first year, this change in personnel helped clear the atmosphere. Horthy's decision indicated that he had a limit beyond which he would not go. In contrast to what was occurring in other European countries, Hungary seemed stabilized.

The date is significant, because in January 1942 Nazi leaders participated in the Wannsee Conference to coordinate and implement the Final Solution. A working paper prepared by the Foreign Ministry department headed by Hans Luther contains reference to deportation from countries falling under the rubrics of that ministry, the independent countries. The Foreign Ministry divided the countries of East Central Europe into two categories. The first included countries that were receptive to deportations: Romania, Slovakia, and Croatia. In countries

belonging to the second category—Bulgaria and Hungary—an additional stage
of racist legislation was needed. The protocol of the Wannsee Conference reveals
that Reinhard Heydrich, head of the Reich Security Main Office (RSHA), did
not anticipate difficulties from Slovakia in carrying out the Final Solution. The
roundup of Jews in Slovakia began in early March. They were told that they
were going to labor in the Reich. As a matter of fact, they became the first
victims of the gas chambers of the largest murder camp in history, Birkenau-
Auschwitz.

## REFUGEES OF THE *SHOAH* IN HUNGARY

The beginning of the deportations from Slovakia was followed by the first
great wave of refugees from that country to Hungary. Among these refugees
were also Jews from Poland who had managed to flee to Slovakia, and some
members of Zionist youth movements. Expectations of the escapees that they
would receive direct help from MIPI were often not realized because of the legal
restrictions that the relief office imposed on itself. MIPI did perform a number
of important tasks that were not always properly appreciated by the refugees.
The undertakings were for the most part connected with the camps where the
1939 refugees had been housed and that were legally approved by the authorities.
The same camps were used by the KEOKH for internment of the Jews deported
to Kamenetz-Podolsk. After these deportations ceased, the camps remained under
police supervision, but were maintained by MIPI. If new arrivals were not caught
and returned immediately to Slovakia, they were kept in these camps and could
consider themselves, at least for the time being, in a relatively safe place.
Conditions in the Budapest camps were so lenient that sometimes detainees
refused to leave, even when someone was able to bring about their release.
Political prisoners, including some members of the banned Zionist youth movements who were caught helping refugees, were also detained in camps at Garany,
Ricse, Csörgö, Sárvár, and Kistarcsa. Living conditions there were very difficult.

This arrangement for the maintenance of the detention camps by a Jewish
institution came at the initiative of KEOKH. Were it not for this, most of the
refugees arrested would have been deported at once. The refugees were uneasy
under KEOKH eyes and were convinced that no legal framework could guarantee
their lives or their continued stay in Hungary. Hungarian Jews, however, stubbornly relied on legal guarantees of their security and believed that the law that
had been assuring their existence would continue to be their salvation.

The refugees were also frustrated by their first contacts with some of the
Zionist organizations. The most important of these was the Palestine Office
directed by Moshe (Miklós) Krausz, of Mizrahi. The office dealt with *Aliyah*
(emigration to Palestine), which continued from Hungary in very small numbers.
It was in constant touch with various authorities—the Ministry of the Interior,
the police, and various diplomatic delegations—for the purpose of obtaining

safe-conduct documents necessary for emigration. Therefore, the office refrained from illegal activities that might compromise its privileged position.

When the first Zionist refugees arrived, several youth movements maintained very close relations with a number of adult activists. The more dynamic among these, and perhaps the most experienced, were those of Ihud-Mapai. These included Shmuel Springmann, Joel Brand, and Dr. Rudolph (Rezsö) Kasztner. None of the three was Hungarian. Brand was born in Transylvania, lived in Germany, and fled in 1935 to Hungary. Kasztner was also a Transylvanian, correspondent of *Uj Kelet*, the Zionist paper in Hungarian that appeared in Kolozsvár (Cluj) until it was closed in 1940 by the Hungarians. Springmann was born in Poland and was a Polish national. Unlike most Hungarian Jews, this group was prepared to operate along unconventional lines—for the most part illegal—to help refugees who were streaming into Hungary. This readiness was not based on any formal authority or prestige of any recognized leadership. At the outset its activities were marked by only a very limited political Zionist character and derived in the main from personal initiative and response to personal problems. Activists like Brand and his comrades were to be found also in other Zionist movements as well as in the Orthodox community.

## 1943: THE SITUATION EASES

The beginning of 1943 was a time of change. In Hungary the change in policy was motivated first by a worsening of the military situation for Germany. During his first year as head of the government, Kállay revealed no special affection for Jews. Anti-Jewish legislation was continued, and Jews were deprived of the right to hold farmland. The attitude of the police was generally negative. Efforts were made to prevent the entry of the refugees, and many of those who were caught were driven back. Nevertheless, Kállay's most important actions were his negative responses to German demands for deportation of the Jews. In contrast to several other countries, such as France, Slovakia, and Romania, there was no separate office representing the RSHA in Hungary, and all contacts passed through regular diplomatic channels, mainly through the Hungarian minister in Berlin, Döme Sztójay. Luther approached him for the first time on October 2, 1942, presenting a very clear demand regarding the policies the Reich wanted Hungary to pursue. Among other things, these included the elimination of the Jews from the cultural and economic life of the country, the introduction of the yellow star, and deportation to "the East." Hungarian replies were clear and unequivocal. Prime Minister Kállay repeatedly informed the Nazis that Hungary would not accommodate such requests. As his main argument, he cited the strong involvement of Jews in national industry. He maintained that orderly continuation of industrial production, 80 percent of which was diverted to Germany, was also in the Reich's interest.

Hitler was not mollified by Kállay's response. In talks held with Horthy during his visit to Schloss Klessheim on April 17, 1943, the Führer explained the meaning of transfer of Jews to Poland: "Jews who do not want to work are shot. When they can't work, they die." The German Foreign Ministry intensified pressure on Hungary to join the other European countries that had complied with the Reich's request to provide "the total solution of the Jewish question." The fact that the Hungarian Jews survived, relatively intact, as late as the beginning of 1944 is the clearest indication of Kállay's opposition to genocide.

The advance of the Red Army to Hungary's eastern border early in 1943 also gave Hungarian Jews cause for optimism. No longer were special efforts made to catch the refugees, and those who were apprehended were no longer deported. Most of the detentions at this time were a result of black-market dealings, false papers, or denouncements by informers. Refugees from Poland obtained a formal status, though as Polish Christians rather than Jews. The Polish Committee (a body recognized by the government) even supported these refugees with fixed monthly grants.

The dispatch of a delegation of Palestinian Jews to Istanbul in December 1942 decisively transformed the status of the rescue workers in Budapest. This delegation gathered information on the fate of European Jewry and sought to extend relief and rescue to the activities of the *Halutz* movements who were under Nazi rule. On both levels, the Zionists of Budapest performed a major function. The various stages of the organization of the Budapest Rescue Committee continued for about a year and a half, from the spring of 1942 until the fall of 1943. At no time was the committee ever sanctioned by Hungarian Jewry. Correspondence from Istanbul brought not only letters but money as well. From the general tone of the missives, it appears that the delegation in Istanbul was the decision-making body in rescue activities and treated its contacts in Budapest as mere executors. This subordinate role seemed natural to the workers in Budapest, perhaps because of the sense of their own weakness in the local political arena. Nevertheless, the consolidation of the relationship with Istanbul gave the committee some "international recognition" and an effective public power as a result of the funds. Thus two competitive focal points were created in the small Zionist movement in Hungary: the Palestine Office and the Rescue Committee.

The reports that streamed into Budapest, and from there to Istanbul, to Palestine, and to the Jewish world, were shocking. The general news of what was going on in Poland, and of the mass slaughter of Jews there, was already known by the end of 1942, but now reports brought by couriers sent by Springmann to Poland and the testimonies of the refugees who managed to escape in 1943 afforded the first opportunity to realize the full scale of the *Shoah*. Evidence was taken from each refugee, recorded, and passed on. In May 1943 many refugees were already telling of the destruction of entire communities. The first eyewitness report of the Warsaw ghetto revolt came in June. In July it was reported from Budapest that apparently there was no longer any Jewish community left in Poland. Most of the communication during this period was with the Krakow and Bedzin areas, but couriers also managed to get to the vicinity of Lwow and even to central Poland. The systematic annihilation was known in

Budapest immediately, though at times the details were incorrect. There is no doubt that wide knowledge of the disaster existed and was discounted in Hungary by the end of 1943.

Refugees insisted that Hungarian Jews should prepare for ghettoization, deportations, and death. When this process did indeed begin on March 19, 1944, exactly as predicted, they accused the Hungarian Jews of blindness. But the fact that their most dire forebodings came true does not at all prove that their premonitions were necessarily logical or of a high degree of reasonable expectancy in the light of the actual situation in Hungary at the time. Their absolute confidence that what had happened in Poland and in Slovakia would also transpire in Hungary grew more out of intuition than out of any objective conclusions. One can not demonstrate how many had heard the horror stories of the refugees; surely many had. How many of these thought that the information was relevant to their own future? Hardly any.

## MARCH 19, 1944

On Sunday, March 19, 1944, the German army swept into Hungary and within a few hours transformed the Jews of that land from faithful citizens into aliens condemned to death. The primary purpose of the German invasion was to intensify the economic exploitation of the country for the war effort. The implementation of the Final Solution of the Jewish problem derived from this basic reason.

The occupation, which lasted until May 5, 1945, may be divided into two periods. The first lasted to October 15, 1944, at which time Horthy was deposed after an unsuccessful attempt at negotiating a cease-fire; the second was characterized by the rule of the Arrow Cross party, headed by Ferenc Szálasi. The first period was far from monolithic. The roundup and the deportation of the Jews of the provincial cities were conducted up to the beginning of July; thereafter, the Jews of Budapest were the only ones remaining in the country.

Two days before the invasion, Regent Horthy was summoned to Germany, where he was informed of impending events by the Führer himself. Horthy returned to Hungary simultaneously with the entry of the occupying forces. During this journey he began negotiating a change of government with Edmund Veesenmayer, who had been appointed minister plenipotentiary of the German Reich (Bevollmächtigter des Grossdeutschen Reiches). Deliberations continued for three days and resulted in the designation of Döme Sztójay, a fervent supporter of the Nazi policies, as prime minister. The new government included four members of the previous government and Arrow Cross members. At the first session of the government on March 29, Sztójay was able to inform the ministers that the regent explicitly was not demanding that regulations connected with the government's policy toward the Jews be submitted for his approval. By this stand, Horthy was in effect forsaking his Jewish citizens.

The first days after the occupation were marked by a completely unforeseen development. The SS and the Gestapo, which entered Hungary with the Wehrmacht, had prepared lists of political and economic figures, journalists, government officials, and other prominent persons. Several hundred were arrested, including the former minister of the interior, Ferenc Keresztes-Fischer, his brother Lajos, the director of the regent's Military Office, Lipót Baranyai, governor of the National Bank, and József Sombor-Schweinitzer, the head of the political police and one of Horthy's protégés. All this happened without any protest on the part of the regent, not to speak of the government or public opinion. There was no protest or resistance from the anti-Nazi Christians, except one, Endre Bajcsy-Szilinszky, who drew a revolver on his captors and was himself wounded. The Gestapo also arrested a large number of Jews who just happened to be around one of the railway stations of Budapest. During the first days of the occupation, more than 3,500 Jews were arrested.

The Hungarian administrative machinery remained intact despite the occupation, and the country was perhaps more autonomous than any other land under German conquest. It was clear from the outset that the program of deportation and annihilation of Hungarian Jews by Adolf Eichmann's special department would never have been possible without both the statutory base that a legal and recognized Hungarian government could provide and the administrative facilities of the state, necessary for the execution of its policies.

Immediately following the invasion, the Gestapo assembled the leadership of the Budapest *kehillas* and demanded the establishment of a Jewish Council to serve as the sole representative for the entire country. Samu Stern, the head of the Neolog *kehilla*, was placed at the head of this council. The members of the council came from the leadership of the two communities and were more or less homogeneous in their origin and outlook. They all belonged to the upper middle class or lower aristocracy. They were all conservatives, considered themselves great Hungarian patriots, and were associated with the dominant political elite. Ernö Munkácsi, the secretary of the Neolog *kehilla*, described this leadership headed by Stern as "lacking contact with the Jewish masses and unaware of their problems."

In the first days of the occupation, everyone was in a state of shock and no one knew what to do. The leadership of the Jewish Council, as well as Ottó Komoly of the Zionist Organization and other Jewish personalities, sought to establish contact with senior government officials to clarify the situation. The appointment of the council did not set their minds at rest. The Jews did not know whether they were responsible to the new Hungarian government or to the Germans. As a result of the total prohibition against Jewish travel, and especially because of the mass arrests at the railway station from the very first day on, there was a nearly complete break in communication between the capital and the countryside. The first reaction of shock was followed by a state of paralysis.

Meanwhile, the Nazis and their Hungarian allies moved quickly. Within days László Baky and László Endre were appointed to positions in the Ministry of the Interior. On March 29 all Jews were ordered to wear the yellow badge. Jews were removed from the practice of the liberal professions, their bank accounts were frozen, and they were forbidden to engage "Aryan" household help, to travel, and to hold or use telephones, motor vehicles, and radios. The Hungarian Gestapo and a special Hungarian "Dejewification" Unit were formed at this time. Especially ominous was a decree that declared Carpatho-Ruthenia and Northern Transylvania military regions. The security status of these areas served as justification for ghettoization and then for deportation of Jewish residents to Auschwitz.

## THE DEPORTATION

Plans for ghettoization were finalized by the Ministry of the Interior and Eichmann's *Sonderkommando* on April 4. Randolph Braham summarizes the master plan in a number of distinct phases (*The Politics of Genocide*, p. 535):

- Jews in the rural communities and smaller towns were to be rounded up and temporarily transferred to synagogues and community buildings.
- Following the first round of investigation in pursuit of valuables, the Jews rounded up in rural communities and smaller towns were to be transferred to the ghettos or the larger cities in the vicinity, usually the county seat.
- In larger towns and cities the Jews were to be rounded up and transferred to a specially designated area that would serve as a ghetto, totally isolated from the other parts of the city. In some cities the ghetto was to be established in the Jewish quarter; in others, in factories, warehouses, brickyards, or under the open sky.
- Jews were to be concentrated in centers with adequate rail facilities to make possible swift entrainment and deportation.

These measures were first applied in Carpatho-Ruthenia, where "Galician" Jews might aid the approaching Red Army. The Jews of Northern Transylvania were victimized soon after. In the first area the concentration of the Jews started on April 16, the first day of Passover. As elsewhere in Hungary, the operation began with the roundup of the Jews in the villages. Wakened by the gendarmes at dawn, they were given a few minutes to pack some clothes and food and then were taken to their local synagogues. There they were robbed of their money, jewelry, and other valuables. A few days later they were marched to the nearest concentration center, normally the brickyards of the larger cities. In northeastern Hungary there were thirteen major ghettos and entrainment centers. The largest concentration was in Munkács, where some fourteen thousand rural Jews were kept in a brickyard and approximately thirteen thousand Jews of the city were ordered into a ghetto.

The leaders of the Jewish Council in Budapest, who had learned some details about the horrors perpetrated during the first ghettoization, approached Endre. He referred them to his secretary, who denied "all the horror stories." On April 27 they sent a detailed letter to the minister of the interior in which they included a very real description of the situation in the ghettos. They asked him "to take measures that the evacuated persons will receive suitable accommodations and food" and also "that you make it possible for our representatives to be deployed in the field." Another letter, dated May 3, providing additional details of horrors in the various ghettos in northeastern Hungary, was sent to Eichmann. These protests had no impact whatsoever in preventing further ghettoizations. Twelve days after the concentration of the Jews began on April 26, the government issued its ghettoization decree.

The ghettoization of the Jews of Northern Transylvania began on May 3. The Jews were to be concentrated in eleven cities. The roundups were carried out by special units composed of gendarmes, policemen, and other civil servants, including primary- and high-school teachers, under the jurisdiction of a mayoral commission. The largest ghetto in Hungary after Budapest at the end of 1944 was in Nagyvárad (Oradea). Here also there were two concentrations, one for the city's Jews, located in the neighborhood of the Orthodox synagogue, with 27,000 people, and the other, at the city grange and around a lumber yard, where some 8,000 Jews from other communities were held. In Northern Transylvania there were close to 160,000 Jews, and their ghettoization was generally completed within one week. Only a few days after the completion of the ghettoization, the Dejewification authorities turned their attention to the completion of deportation plans.

In Poland Jews remained in ghettos for several years before it was decided to send them to the death camps. In Hungary the ghetto period was very short, just enough to extort the "hidden Jewish wealth" and to arrange for transportation. It was decided to delay the process in other areas until the Jews of Carpatho-Ruthenia and Northern Transylvania had been deported. Beginning on May 15, four trains daily, each train carrying about 3,000 persons crammed into freight cars, were directed to the Slovakian border, near Kassa (Košice), where the Jews were transferred to German authorities. The deportations were carried out by the Hungarian gendarmerie and police with great brutality. The Germans even shot a "documentary" film that showed the Hungarian gendarmes beating women with rifle butts, tearing wedding rings off the helpless victims, and pressing the Jews into the freight cars like cattle. By June 7, 289,000 Jews had been deported from these two areas.

In northern Hungary, from Kassa to the German border, the concentration of some 65,000 Jews into eleven entrainment centers began on June 5, and the deportations started five days later. Then it was the south's turn, including two big cities, Szeged and Debrecen. The ghettoization began on June 16; the deportations began on June 25 and were completed four days later with the removal of more than 40,000 persons in 14 trains. Another 3,000 Jews were sent from the south, using the entrainment facilities of Nagyvárad, after the Jews of this city had already been deported.

The 30,000 Jews of Transdanubia (Dunántúl) were concentrated in the second half of June and deported before the end of that month. Then there were only the Jews of Budapest and those of the surrounding cities or suburbs of the capital. In these places, excluding Budapest proper, the Jews were concentrated in selected buildings at various dates between May 22 and June 30. Some 25,000 persons were deported from various internment camps, such as Kistarcsa, Horthyliget, Sárvár, and others. The Hungarian gendarmerie report concluded that between May 15 and July 8, 434,351 Jews were deported in 147 trains.

In all the provincial cities the operation was directed by the local mayor. The internal administration of the short-lived ghetto was entrusted to a Jewish Council consisting of the traditional leaders of the local Jewish community. These local bodies in most cases were isolated, having no contact with the outside world. Rumors spread that the transfer would be to some other locality in Hungary, most often Transdanubia. If people made contact with the Jewish Council in Budapest, they received only calming messages. In some cases the *Halutz* youth movements sent emissaries to alert the communities and the local leadership to the danger of the deportation. We know of a few dozen such undertakings. When they made contact with the local leaders, no one wanted to listen or pay heed. It should hardly be cause for surprise that well-established Jews were not prepared to listen to the stories of some youth of seventeen or twenty when the reputable leadership was announcing that no harm would come to anyone if they would only maintain law and order. Practically every Jew was still convinced that Regent Horthy would not abandon "his Jews" to deportation and destruction, especially at a time when the Red Army was so close to the Carpathians.

The ghettoization of the Jews was conducted without major incidents of resistance on the part of Jews or Christians. Many Gentiles collaborated for ideological reasons, others in expectation of quick material rewards. In practically every major community Christians denounced Jews in hiding. Very rare were those who dared to help or hide a Jew, for fear of being denounced. A notable exception was Bishop Áron Márton, who in Kolozsvár publicly warned the Hungarians not to abandon the Jews to annihilation. His warning had no effect.

Unlike the first two areas, most of the Jewish communities in Trianon Hungary had been completely Magyarized for generations, yet the attitude of the gendarmerie and the local population did not differ from that of the other areas. The heads of the churches remained silent during the deportations. Three local bishops did protest. Baron Vilmos Ápor, bishop of Győr, urged Justinian Cardinal Serédi, the primate of Hungary, to intervene. His efforts were in vain. Endre Hamvas, bishop of Csanád, also protested against the deportation of the Jews and managed to save some two hundred converted persons from deportation. The bishop of Szombathely, Sándor Kovács, also protested and succeeded in saving several Jews.

The Hungarian historian György Ránki was quite correct when he delineated the role played by the government and the administrative authorities at every level in the process of liquidating Hungarian Jewry:

Eichmann's main office was in Budapest, but within a short time he set up ten branches in the outlying towns. From the point of view of size of staff his unit seemed unimportant.

The head office in Budapest consisted of Eichmann himself, six experts, and an additional thirty people, twenty of whom were guards. In the entire country his staff was composed of about two hundred people. . . .

Obviously, the German regime could operate only if it could rely to a large extent on the Hungarian state administrative machinery. Without the assistance of various offices and the officialdom of the counties, the cities, and the towns, as well as the police, the gendarmerie, and the army, the whole Nazi occupying machine would within a few days have ground to a halt. What was unique about the German regime in Hungary was that a relatively large degree of national sovereignty was left in the hands of the Sztójay government, even more than had been done anywhere else in Europe, including Denmark. . . . The gendarmerie willingly assumed the task of organizing the deportations with the help, direct or tacit, of the administration. (*1944 marcius 19*) [My translation.]

The entire police administrative system dealing with the organization of the eviction, the ghettoization, and the deportation was handled not by the Germans but by local people. This situation went far beyond what is usually termed *collaboration*. This was a case of local initiative carrying out deportation, in some instances with enthusiasm.

As the smaller cities of Hungary were emptied of their Jews, it was evident that the same process would soon be applied to Budapest. The government's attitude became increasingly severe. In mid-June Budapest's Jews were concentrated in special buildings marked with yellow stars, yellow-star houses (*csillagos házak*). The lives of most of Budapest's Jews were spared, at least temporarily, when the deportations were suddenly halted.

The shift of policy came about as a result of mounting political pressures that finally led Horthy to intervene. News of what was happening in Hungary began to seep through to the governments and the public of neutral countries—and through them to the Allies—about the middle of April, while ghettoization was beginning. The reports increased in intensity in May, when the large transports were moving to the death camps. At the same time the Auschwitz Protocol, a detailed account by two Slovak escapees from Auschwitz, reached Switzerland and from there made its way to the West. Given to the neutral legations in Budapest, including the apostolic nuncio, Monsignor Angelo Rotta, who transmitted it to the Vatican, this report contained a full description of Auschwitz's "murder industry." The protocol was also brought to the attention of elements in the Hungarian government, including the regent and the heads of all the churches by mid-May, but remained unknown to the local Jews. At the beginning of July this protocol and details on the deportation from Hungary were published by the Swiss press as a result of efforts by Georges Mantello (Mandel), a Jew from Beszterce (Bistriţa) and then the first secretary of El Salvador's legation in Bern.

In the government the deputy foreign minister, Mihály Arnothy-Jungerth, relying on reports reaching him from Hungarian legations in neutral capitals and in Rome, persistently raised objections. Count István Bethlen, former prime minister and close friend of the regent, submitted a dramatic appeal, demanding immediate cessation of the deportations and the dismissal of the Sztójay government. In his May 15 appeal the apostolic nuncio not only requested special consideration for the converts, but warned against further deportations. An even stronger protest, accompanied by a personal letter from Pope Pius XII, was conveyed to the Hungarian government on June 27. At this time a sharp and threatening letter from American Secretary of State Cordell Hull, delivered through the Swiss legation, demanded that the Hungarians suspend at once the imprisonment of the Jews in ghettos or camps and the deportations to Poland or anywhere else. This was followed by remonstrances in a threatening tone from President Roosevelt. On June 30 the king of Sweden sent a personal cable to Horthy asking that the regent "take all necessary steps to rescue all who can be saved of this unfortunate race." Responding to these interventions and the Allied landing at Normandy, Horthy announced a halt to the deportations on June 26 (although they did not cease until July 9).

The members of the Jewish Rescue Committee, which had been trying to bring Jews into Hungary, were as surprised by the German occupation as the formal Jewish leadership and the Hungarian government. Only three days before the invasion they sent to Istanbul an assessment that foresaw an improvement in the status of the Jews in Europe as a result of negotiations.

According to Kasztner, his first contacts with Dieter Wisliceny of the SS did not take place until April 5. This meeting had been arranged by members of the German counterespionage group that maintained contact between Istanbul and the committee. Wisliceny was the most appropriate personality to conduct negotiations of this nature. Responsible for the deportation of most of the Jews from Slovakia and Greece, he had also conducted negotiations of this nature with the "working group" in Bratislava. Since these talks had begun, deportations from Slovakia had indeed ceased. Wisliceny also presented letters of recommendation from Rabbi Michael Weissmandel (of the so-called Working Group), which gave cause for great expectations.

Wisliceny reassured the committee that there would be no ghettoization or deportation from Hungary, noting that he personally had asked for a plan to be drawn calling for emigration of "at least 100,000 Jews." To continue the negotiations, Wisliceny demanded two million dollars, with an additional 10 percent as his commission. This amount was raised, most of it from the funds of the Jewish Council. While Kasztner continued to talk with other officers of Eichmann's department, Herman Krumey and Otto Hunsche, Wisliceny was busy organizing the ghettoization of the Jews in Carpatho-Ruthenia.

The Rescue Committee promised to provide six hundred certificates for admission to Palestine, which were actually available to the Palestine Office in Budapest. This gave to the negotiations the character of a Zionist operation. However, this would have been contrary to the broader, all-Jewish nature of the talks with the Germans as well as the community character of the financial sources that made the contact possible. On May 2 Krumey announced that approval had been received from Berlin for the departure of the six hundred certificate holders. He suggested adding another one hundred persons to the list, against payment of ten million pengös, even without certificates or other visas. A week earlier the deportations had begun from Kistarcsa detention camp, and word had been received from Slovakia that these deportees were being sent to Auschwitz. On May 4–5 Kasztner visited Kolozsvár, his native city, and met the leaders of the community. What he did or did not tell them about the forseeable deportation to Auschwitz is still the subject of a heated controversy, but he was given permission to select 388 Jews from the ghetto and to take them to Budapest. Some more Jews were later added from other ghettos of Transylvania.

At this point Eichmann himself presented Joel Brand with the notorious proposal, "blood for trucks." Brand left for Istanbul on May 17, arriving there in order to put the matter before the representatives of the Allies, the Zionist Organization, the Joint Distribution Committee, or any other international Jewish body. But Brand was arrested by British intelligence and detained in a Cairo prison. When it became clear in Budapest that his mission had failed and that the deportation of the Jews to Auschwitz had begun, the Rescue Committee privately began to arrange for a rescue transport.

During this period the *Halutz* resistance of the youth movements was organizing also. The integration of the refugees into the local movements altered the character and the structure of those movements. The refugees, many of whom were illegal residents, understood that for survival, not every law could be obeyed. Although the Hungarian *Halutz* youth, with their parents, believed that "it could not happen in Hungary," when their faith was shattered in March 1944, the youth were able to grasp reality better than any other Jewish element in Hungary, including the "well-informed" official leadership. The young people were able to react to the Nazi occupation and to undertake rescue techniques that had heretofore been used only for the refugees. During the first days of the occupation there were only a few dozen members of each movement in Budapest. In all, including the refugees, they totalled no more than five to six hundred persons. This number rose significantly by the end of June, after many members had succeeded in reaching the city from the provinces. Underground activity remained separate in each movement, but there was some coordination, which improved with time. The first step was to guarantee the members' lives and working possibilities by means of Aryan papers. In the second stage an attempt was made, on the one hand, to concentrate the majority in Budapest and, on the other, to send as many as possible out of the country. This was called the *tiyul* (in Hebrew a trip or excursion). Between April and August Romania became the only practicable escape route. Perhaps seven thousand young people managed to reach Romania in this fashion.

The resistance maintained close contact with the Relief and Rescue Committee. There was a clear division of tasks between the two bodies. The dealings of the committee with the SS and with the Hungarian authorities were termed the "big line" (*nagy vonal*) to distinguish them from the individual rescue activities of the resistance, which were called the "little line" (*kis vonal*). The connection between the two "lines" was constant, though not always with mutual cooperation. But up to mid-June the "big line" of the committee did not bring any result. It was only when the Jews of Budapest were concentrated, when Horthy remained silent, and when all came to the realization that Brand's mission would meet with no reaction from the Allies except a public rejection, and everything seemed lost, that Kasztner was instructed to prepare a transport to leave Hungary. This shipment was supposed to be the first step in a larger program, a sort of "goodwill gesture" on Eichmann's part. The only assurance that the train would be directed through France toward the Spanish border and not Auschwitz was to be found in Eichmann's promise to Kasztner. At the same time there was another "gesture" of Eichmann to Kasztner, in which 20,787 Jews from the Baja, Debrecen, Szeged, and Szolnok ghettos were directed to Strasshof, a camp near Vienna. Seventy-five percent of these Jews who were "laid on ice" survived the war.

To get permission to organize the goodwill train from Budapest required huge amounts of money in bribes to SS officers. Thus financial considerations were important from the start. Compiling the list took about two weeks. The Jewish leadership, which was deeply involved in the preparation of the transport, had no illusions as to the fate of those being deported. Under these circumstances a great many people placed their last remaining hope in Kasztner's project. The number of passengers constantly kept changing: 600, 700, 1,000, 1,300, and finally 1,685. The passengers were divided into three major groups. The first was composed of Zionists, including the youth of all parties. The second group comprised prominent personalities, including leaders of communities and those brought from Kolozsvár. The list also included rabbis (some of them rabid anti-Zionists), writers, journalists, professors, and intellectuals in various fields. The third group was composed of Jews who bought their places on the train by making large payments for the financing of the whole venture.

From the very outset the idea of rescue was received by many with great suspicion. The greatest objections were voiced by the refugees who refused to join any transport that came about on the initiative of Nazis. Those who favored the undertaking found it convincing and an assurance of good faith that the relatives and the children of the Komoly and Kasztner families were included. The two men remained. When the train pulled out of Budapest station on the night of June 30, no one knew for certain which way it was headed.

After a layover in Linz, the train was sent to the Bergen-Belsen concentration camp, where the Nazis maintained several special sections, including one for people scheduled to be "exchanged." Conditions were relatively bearable, and the first group of 318 people left Bergen-Belsen for Switzerland in August. The remainder followed in December.

## TENSION SLACKENS

The halting of deportations had another dimension. Subject to German approval, the Hungarian government also decided to permit the emigration of about

7,800 Jews, who would leave the country with the help of Switzerland and Sweden. The figure 7,800 was supposed to be the first step in a broader program. This proposal became known as the "Horthy offer." It came to naught on August 23 when Romania withdrew from the Axis, thus closing the emigration route. All that remained of the proposal was the principle that the Hungarian government would permit the legations of neutral states to extend their protection to Jews registered for emigration. The figure 7,800 became a magic number. The Horthy offer was thus transformed and became a basis for local rescue operations under the patronage of the neutral states. These countries began to issue various sorts of "protective pass" (*Schutzpass*).

The Swedish Foreign Ministry took the first step, even before the announcement of the Horthy offer, authorizing the issuance of a limited number of "temporary passports." The Hungarian government accepted the fiction, and holders of the documents were registered in the KEOKH, which afforded them the status of citizenship of a neutral state. Dr. Valdemar Langlet, a lecturer in Budapest, was appointed as representative of the Swedish Red Cross in Hungary. He received his appointment on July 4 and, helped by his wife, Nina, and a few local Jews, began at once to issue protective letters (*Schutzbriefe*), which did not confer Swedish nationality, only protection. On July 9 Raoul Wallenberg arrived in Budapest to conduct the operation of a special Department for Humanitarian Affairs and started to issue protective passes also.

The most comprehensive rescue operations were those of the Swiss legation and Consul Charles Lutz. From his office in the former American embassy in Szabadsag Square, Lutz worked with Jewish and non-Jewish elements preparing emigration lists for Palestine. The protective passes were distributed in a building that was a glass wholesale storehouse and thus was known as the Glass House (Üvegház).

The Spanish, the Portuguese, and the Vatican likewise began to issue protective passes in small quantities. At this time a few hundred genuine passports were also received from the El Salvador legation in Bern on the initiative of Georges Mantello. The Spanish Red Cross also offered to receive five hundred children from Hungary. Friedrich Born, who handled this offer, proposed to Ottó Komoly to use an office of the International Red Cross (IRC) to prepare the shipment of children to Spanish Tangier. This was to become Department A, of great importance in rescue activity in later months.

The departure of the Kasztner group and even more that of the *tiyul* to Romania left the *Halutz* resistance with a very limited number of members. They suffered also from arrests of activists fleeing to the border. A great number were in prison, and many were deported to Auschwitz. Like earlier Jewish resistance movements in Hungary, the *Halutz* also wavered between rescue activities and revolt. The discussions in the movements were endless, but a close study indicates a clear preference for rescue over revolt. The *tiyul* in effect provided a definitive and unequivocal response to all doubts. When this was stopped on August 23, the main effort was directed to the preparation of false papers.

During the relatively calm months of the summer of 1944, both the official Jewish leadership and Komoly renewed contacts with Hungarian political figures. The isolation of the Jews, prominent in the first months of the occupation, was less and less felt now. Both Komoly and the leaders of the Jewish Council met with the regent's son, Miklós Horthy, Jr., who headed the "extrication office" (*kiugrási iroda*) that sought ways of getting Hungary out of the war. Samu Stern, the most respected Jewish leader, was even secretly received by the regent himself.

## OCTOBER 15

After prolonged hesitations and doubts, as well as fruitless negotiations with the Soviets, the regent made the dramatic announcement on October 15 that Hungary was laying down its arms and accepting the cease-fire terms proposed by the Russians. The announcement was received by the Jews of Budapest with an outburst of joy. The illusion of salvation lasted less than a day, however. The Germans installed the Arrow Cross party in power, with Ferenc Szálasi as its head, and he at once proclaimed that the war would go on.

By removing Horthy and by placing the government in the hands of the Fascists, the Germans assured that Hungary would remain in the war at this critical time when the front was already at its borders. Early in October the Red Army penetrated into Hungary itself. Kolozsvár and Nagyvárad fell, and the battle raged around Debrecen. Its conquest would expose the Hungarian plains to the Soviets and in effect open the road to Budapest. If the Hungarians had laid down their arms, the Red Army would have swept to the Austrian border within a few days, but, unlike what had occurred in Romania two months earlier, the Germans were not caught by surprise in Hungary. Ministers in Horthy's government kept them informed of every step taken by the regent. The Nazis were willing to let Horthy continue in office only if he would refrain from openly opposing the continuation of the war. To retain what was virtually their last ally, the Germans handed rule over to Szálasi.

Szálasi's government continued to fight, and the civil administration continued to operate more or less in a normal manner. Industrial production was hardly affected. Soldiers, civil service workers, and laborers remained at their posts. All of this was a matter of supreme importance to the Germans. However, it would be a mistake to regard this regime as only the Nazis' oblique arm. Szálasi and his people had their own aspirations and were supported by a party that was itself a sociopolitical body. Although this was a coalition government, with participation of other extreme right parties, the Arrow Cross was the only one that had a broadly based mass following and was therefore able to determine the character of the regime. Immediately after Szálasi's assumption of power, armed units of the party (*pártszolgálat*) seized control of the streets of the capital and were in complete command there. The government also reorganized what was commonly known as the "Hungarian Gestapo" to deal with political foes and Jews who were hiding.

By placing the rabble in charge of the government, the Arrow Cross effected a major social revolution. Although most of the government civil servants remained at their desks—only a few were replaced by party members—the presence of armed bands was a disturbing influence on administrative procedures in Budapest. No one knew any longer what was legal and what was illegal, who had been arrested and why, and who had been freed and for how long. This took place in a city that was under almost daily aerial bombardment, with the fighting front drawing ever closer.

Even during the relatively tranquil period of July to September, the status of Budapest's 150,000 Jews was unclear. The anti-Jewish legislation had not been rescinded, and the Jews were still concentrated in the yellow-star houses, lacking mobility, economic means, and basic civil rights. More and more Hungarians, however, began to perceive that Germany had lost hope of winning the war, a realization that affected the attitude toward the Jews not only in official circles, but also among the people in the streets.

The first step of the new regime was to forbid the Jews (invalids or pregnant women) from leaving their homes. Physicians were forbidden to visit, and corpses could not be taken out for burial. This situation continued for a week. The ban on appearing on the streets was in effect when a new edict was issued calling for conscription of all Jewish males between the ages of fifteen and sixty and all females between eighteen and forty. The people were ordered to report at the race tracks, and some of them were taken from there to the brickyard outside the town. Deportations were resumed on October 21. The direction this time was Germany.

The Arrow Cross was particularly interested in securing the diplomatic recognition of the neutral states. After some initial delay, therefore, the new government ratified all the privileges that the previous regime had granted to the neutral legations in Budapest. During the first days of Arrow Cross rule, the Jewish resistance exploited confusion that reigned in the streets. The first instinctive reaction was an attempt to free its own people from the yellow-star houses. It was at this stage also that the small Glass House building of Vadasz Street began to assume major importance.

Technically under Swiss protection, the Glass House was transformed into a refuge from the renewed deportations. The number of residents grew daily. Soon family members began to appear, as well as friends, acquaintances, Jews who had fled from the Labor Service, and indeed anyone with a little pull or sharp elbows. By the beginning of November there were close to two thousand residents. At the end of November, when the number rose to over three thousand, the building next door to the Glass House was also rented. Most of the youth movement personnel were concentrated in the new building. The possibility of armed resistance, though it never materialized, was always very real. Weapons were smuggled in, and people there began to train for combat in the event the house was attacked by the Arrow Cross.

One of the most horrifyingly familiar phenomena from the ghettos of Eastern Europe was that of abandoned and hungry children dying of starvation. This did not occur in Budapest because of the short period of time and because of the effort of Komoly's Department A of the IRC and of the resistance. The *Halutzim*, who went through the yellow-star houses, were the first to pick up abandoned children and to bring them to Komoly's office. Within a few days a rumor was already circulating that the Red Cross was placing children under its patronage. People immediately came forward with youngsters. Housing for the children was obtained in various ways. In return for IRC protection many people were happy to offer their houses, their villas, or large apartments. The staff was recruited sometimes among the mothers, who thus escaped deportation, among young people who fled from the Labor Service, or among members of the resistance, who took care of organizing, furnishing, and above all feeding these houses.

The resistance never expected that it would have to become involved in the supply of food for the children's homes, for the Glass House, and later for the "protected houses" and for the ghetto. The entire program grew out of a need. At first the problem was met by members of youth movements who were able to get around with Aryan papers and Arrow Cross uniforms. But it is doubtful that they would have been able to overcome the difficulties without the aid of reliable professionals, Jews who were in the business, some of them the most important food wholesalers in the country.

Funds at the beginning came from the Rescue Committee, which had sources both in Geneva and in Istanbul. Later, when it became difficult to obtain all the money required to feed large numbers, the committee asked companies to sell them large quantities of merchandise, to be paid in dollars after the war by the American Joint Distribution Committee—a relief organization. Many manufacturers realized that the chances were poor of holding on to inventories. Warehouses either were being destroyed in the bombardments or were pillaged by the Arrow Cross. The neutral missions, and the operations carried out under their names, still commanded considerable prestige. Mention of the Swiss legation or the Red Cross was enough to open many doors. At the end of the occupation, the largest food supplies in Budapest were to be found in the storehouses of the resistance.

Alongside this successful food program, the resistance continued its production of false documents. The Swiss *Schutzpass* certified that its holder was registered in a collective passport for purpose of emigration to Palestine. The official quota, 7,800, was reached long before October. The staff began to issue passes in excess, but the procedure was regarded by the resistance as too slow and too limited. It began to create large numbers of false protective passes, most of the time of good quality. It is not possible to ascertain how many passes were circulated by the resistance. The number ranged between 100,000 and 120,000. These passes were only one of the ways by which people were saved. Perhaps another 20,000 Jews managed to survive with Aryan documents.

The new government suspected that the number of protective passes in circulation was far in excess of the number that was permitted to each legation and requested that those who held such passes be segregated into special buildings. The government edict calling for the establishment of such "protected houses" (*védett házak*) was issued on November 12. It was preceded by a meeting between Foreign Minister Gábor Kemény and representatives of the various neutral legations, who promised the minister that they would soon effect the emigration of protected Jews. The number of protective passes authorized at this time was as follows: Switzerland, 7,800; Sweden, 4,500; the Vatican, 2,500; Portugal, 700; and Spain, 100. Buildings of appropriate size were set aside, and the Jews were expected to move into them by November 15. All the "protected houses" were to be yellow-star houses. From the beginning they were flooded with thousands of Jews, including previous residents who did not possess protective passes. In addition, many thousands of Jews holding false papers also came, with the result that the congestion was dreadful. Despite the term *protected,* these houses, too, were subject to the violence of the Arrow Cross, and many Jews were taken out of them for deportation and murder.

At the beginning of November there were no more trains to transport the deportees westward. Until the complete encirclement of Budapest on December 24, Jews were herded by the Arrow Cross, the police, and the gendarmerie on a forced walk to the border town of Hegyeshalom, where they were handed over to the Germans as labor for the war industries. Not all of them reached the border station. Many died during the march or were murdered by their Hungarian escorts. Carried out in broad daylight, on open roads, for all to see, the terror-filled march covered 200 to 220 kilometers. The deportees covered this route within seven to eight days without orderly supply of food or water, without rest or shelter, and of course without medical attention.

In many cases "protected Jews" were also taken in the deportation. This fact provided the neutral representatives with the pretext to intervene in the death march for the purpose of rescuing "their" Jews. The courageous efforts of Raoul Wallenberg in defense of the "Swedish houses" have been widely described. Much less is known of a young priest named Tibor Baránszki, who conducted the protection of the Vatican. His work was carried out with devotion and with success, though on a smaller scale. Rescue attempts began at the assembly points. The tendency was to try to get people out on the grounds of foreign immunity. Representatives of various legations, diplomats and Jews, made desperate attempts in this direction. Members of the legations and of the *Halutz* resistance came to the highways with trucks to distribute food and protective passes, and on their return sometimes succeeded in concealing a few people in their vehicles. Since Szálasi had come to power, about eighty thousand Jews had been deported to Germany in one manner or another.

By mid-November the situation in the Hungarian capital had deteriorated to the point of anarchy. The city was cut off on all sides, except for the highway leading westward, toward the Reich. Roads and rail lines were at the full disposal of the military—to the extent that the constant bombardment made their use possible. The Red Army was approaching from the south and east, and the sound of the Soviet artillery could be heard in the suburbs. The population was requested to leave the city voluntarily until its "reliberation." This exodus was handicapped considerably because of a critical shortage of transport. Precedence was given to the shipment of industrial machinery, art treasures, bank reserves, and the crown, which served as the symbol of the state's independence, as well as members of Parliament and the leadership of the Arrow Cross party. Budapest was left under the control of third-rank Arrow Cross functionaries. The city was subjected to perpetual bombing and shelling, and from early December on, most of the population lived in shelters. There was only faint hope that the Germans would not try to wage a house-to-house fight in Budapest, but even this hope was quickly dissipated. Szálasi took the trouble to visit Hitler's headquarters on December 4, at which time it was made absolutely clear that the Germans would fight stubbornly within the city.

The Budapest ghetto was set up at the beginning of December and fenced around with wooden boards on the tenth of the month. Without any advance warning and with extreme brutality, the Arrow Cross government moved about 70,000 people into the ghetto. It comprised some three square kilometers out of the total area of the city's two hundred square kilometers. About 4,000 apartments with over 7,000 rooms were made available to the Jews in this area. Before the establishment of the ghetto the area consisted completely of Jewish institutions and synagogues, with 3,500 poor Orthodox Jews living there. In addition to the fearfully crowded conditions, the ghetto population was composed mainly of the elderly, children, pregnant women, and the ill. Most of those between the ages of sixteen and sixty had been sent to Germany or had gone underground.

From the moment the ghetto was constituted, the authorities demanded that the concentration should include also the children's homes. Almost daily the neutral legations and Otto Komoly, as the director of Department A of the IRC, were in touch with the authorities seeking to prevent such removal. Simultaneously, the resistance was conducting its own program to prevent removal of the children from the protected homes. These efforts were exerted not on the political-diplomatic level but on that of the street and the submachine gun. Strange to relate, most of the children's homes were unharmed. In January 1945 there were about thirty children's homes with some 3,000 to 4,000 children and 1,500 to 2,000 adults. This was a result of the combined efforts, not always coordinated in advance, of diplomatic legations, Wallenberg, Lutz, Born, and Baránszki, on the one hand, and the members of the *Halutz* resistance on the other. Komoly was the main link between the two operating levels.

Anarchy reached its peak on Christmas Eve, 1944, when the city was surrounded. One day before the siege was made complete, Eichmann and members of his staff, as well as Minister of the Interior Gábor Vajna, left the city. That day Vajna issued a warning to all the Jews in hiding to proceed to the ghetto within twenty-four hours. A special postponement until December 31 was granted only to the children's homes under the protection of the IRC and to temporary hospitals that were outside the ghetto. The order reaffirmed the existence of the "international ghetto" on condition that the population there did not exceed the quotas established. This was the last attempt by the Arrow Cross government to provide a legal framework for its policy concerning the Jews in the capital.

When it was no longer possible to get Jews out of the city, an orgy of mass murders took place on the banks of the Danube. Killing on the streets became a common occurrence. Thousands of Jews were taken, night after night, and their bodies tossed into the river. Protective passes and "protected houses" no longer had any value, and at times it appeared that the Arrow Cross gangs even singled out the "protected" Jews for their fury, leaving the others to starve in the congested ghetto, where they were suffering from illnesses, vermin, and bombing. In some cases Wallenberg or resistance members armed and dressed in one uniform or another were able to rescue Jews who were already on their way to the Danube. It is impossible to estimate how many people were massacred and how many lives were saved in these feats, nor is it possible to know how many of those saved in that way managed to survive to the end.

The Representation of Foreign Interests building at Vadász Street became the most conspicuous haven. This building, besides being a huge "bunker," was an operational base for rescue activities and a clearinghouse for all reports submitted by the activists. The fact that the water supply and the telephone lines to the Glass House were not severed was certainly a miracle. Even after some additional facilities were opened, it still provided shelter for three thousand people. On Sunday, December 31, the house was forcibly entered by policemen and Arrow Cross ruffians who shoved the inhabitants out onto the street and killed three people. Emergency phone calls were made to anyone who could be reached. Moshe Krausz sought to use his contact from the Swiss legation in Szabadság Square. An Arrow Cross unit from the Fifth District, in which the house was located, was also called upon to help. This unit had for weeks been bribed with money, food, and drink. The unit did indeed come to the building, but its intervention was not helpful. In the end, the contacts produced results. At the last moment, when all the people from the house were being lined up to march away, orders were received from higher authority, and the attackers returned the people into the "legation."

While this drama was enacted, and the people were lined up, the neighboring building remained untouched. There were members of the *Halutz* resistance who possessed about fifty or sixty rifles and considerable numbers of grenades. These young people knew very well that the next step would be the Danube, and the plan was to protect the Jews from being taken away. The commander, Sándor Nathan, decided to wait for the last possible moment, and then the Jews were returned. In his later testimony he remarked: "If we had made a hasty decision to burst out, we would have caused a catastrophe. . . . We could have become heroes in a twinkling, like the heroes of Warsaw, but dead heroes. We would have been endangering the lives of thousands of people, and perhaps even the lives of the 70,000 Jews in the ghetto'' (quoted in Asher Cohen, *The Halutz Resistance in Hungary*, pp. 238–39).

On January 17 liberation came to the ghetto, the biggest one to survive in Europe, and to the entire east bank of the Danube, on which almost all the surviving Jews of Budapest were concentrated. The survival of this big community of Jews resulted from multiple reasons, some of them independent of the Jews and some of them the results of their direct efforts. Among the latter, the most important were those of the *Halutz* resistance, but even its successes were greatly aided by objective circumstances. The entire period of October 1944 to January 1945 was marked by a combination of conditions and events. First was the relative disintegration of the central authority, which found expression in anarchy and extreme violence toward the Jews. Second was the approach of the front line, which resulted in a condition of siege or near siege shortly after the political change. Third was the creation of utterly new instruments by locally based international bodies. Finally, the entire period of the Arrow Cross rule was short.

## HISTORIOGRAPHIC NOTES

### Jews in Hungary: General Works

This chapter is based on the present state of knowledge and does not contain notes on the sources. The reader can always turn for further information to one of the following books.

First, there are three books by Jenö Lévai, *Fekete könyv* (Black book), *Szürke könyv* (Gray book), and *Fehér könyv* (White book) (Budapest: Officina, 1945–48). Lévai was a Jewish journalist, and his books were until recently the major source for the history of Hungarian Jews during the *Shoah*. These books contain no footnotes, and in most cases Lévai does not cite his sources. In numerous cases these works contain errors of fact that in part cannot now be verified. There is no doubt that the abundant materials in Lévai's books, written soon after the events, are important sources of information. Nevertheless, for the reason just mentioned, the sources should be used with caution.

Randolph L. Braham, *The Politics of Genocide: The Holocaust in Hungary* (New York: Columbia University Press, 1981), is the most extensive, comprehensive, and authoritative book on the history of the Jews during the *Shoah* in Hungary. The two volumes are rich in detailed information based on abundant sources.

Nathaniel Katzburg, *Hungary and the Jews, Policy and Legislation, 1920–1943* (Ramat Gan: Bar Ilan University Press, 1981), is a well-documented and very reliable source that brings important information on the Hungarian policies and anti-Jewish legislation. It does not pertain to the period of 1944.

The most complete bibliography, which is indispensable for research in this field, is Randolph L. Braham, *The Hungarian Jewish Catastrophe: A Selected and Annotated Bibliography* (New York: Columbia University Press, 1984).

Besides the general source books on the period, several published sources can help students of this particular subject: Randolph L. Braham, ed., *The Destruction of Hungarian Jewry: A Documentary Account* (New York: World Federation of Hungarian Jews, 1963); Ilona Benoschofsky and Elek Karsai, eds., *Vádirat a nácizmus ellen* (Indictment of Nazism) (Budapest: Magyar Izraeliták Országos Képviselete, 1958–67), three volumes covering the period up to October 1944 (a fourth volume is to be published); and György Ránki et al., eds., *A Wilhelmstrasse és Magyarország* (The Wilhelmstrasse and Hungary) (Budapest: Akadémia, 1968).

The most valuable information on the Hungarian history of the period can be found in C. A. Macartney, *October Fifteenth: A History of Modern Hungary, 1929–1945* (Edinburgh: Edinburgh University Press, 1957); and György Ránki et al., *Magyar történelem* (Hungarian history) (Budapest: Akadémia, 1976).

Two scholars have already analyzed the historiography of the *Shoah* in Hungary: Nathaniel Katzburg, "The Destruction of Hungarian Jewry in Hungarian Historiography" (till 1975), and Elek Karsai, "The Holocaust in Hungarian Literature and Arts, 1975–1983," in *The Historiography of the Holocaust Period*, edited by Yisrael Gutman and Gideon Greif (Jerusalem: Yad Vashem, 1988), pp. 369–403. Katzburg emphasizes the tendency to minimize the Jewish sufferings in Hungarian writing on the period. Karsai describes the ever-growing interest in World War II, including the persecution of the Jews, since the early 1970s. Both studies, by outstanding scholars in the field, should be consulted, and it is needless here to repeat what was only recently published. I will refer to other studies, mainly the most recent ones, assuming that those already mentioned are basic to most of the problems analyzed later. As for the publications in Hungarian, it should be noted that Braham's book *Politics of Genocide* was translated into Hungarian and published in 1988. Another important book on the *Shoah* in Hungary by Braham and Katzburg is in process of publication, in the Yad Vashem series, in Hebrew and English.

### Jews and Assimilation/Dissimilation

A thorough comprehension of the specific nature of assimilation in Hungary is a prerequisite for the proper analysis of any further event. All references to assimilation are made in the European sense, in which the term applied to primary loyalty to the nation and attachment to the culture and the language of the land, while those who were assimilated preserved their identity as Jews by religion. On the specific question of Jewish assimilation in Hungary and various approaches to the problem, see Bela Vago and George Mosse, eds., *Jews and*

*Non-Jews in Eastern Europe, 1918–1945* (New York: Wiley, 1974); and Bela Vago, ed., *Jewish Assimilation in Modern Times* (Boulder, Colo.: Westview Press/East European Monographs, 1981). In Hungarian, see Erik Molnár, István Bibó, György Száraz, and Péter Hanák, eds., *Zsidókérdés, asszimiláció, anti-szemitizmus* (The Jewish question, assimilation, anti-Semitism) (Budapest: Magvetö, 1984). The first and most important among the great number of Hungarian writers to oppose Jewish (and German) assimilation after World War I was Dezsö Szabó in his *Az elsodort falu* (The village swept away) (Budapest, 1920). The expression "dissimilation" was first used in Hungary by the famous historian Gyula Szekfü in his *Három nemzedék* (Three generations) (Budapest, 1920).

## Jews in the Economic Life of Hungary

We still have no comprehensive history of the Jews in Hungarian economic and cultural life. Most of the studies on Hungarian Jewish history deal with the *Shoah*. Katzburg's book *Hungary and the Jews, Policy and Legislation, 1920–1943*, the best on the 1920s and 1930s, emphasizes the legal situation and the development of the anti-Semitic policies. The best analysis of interwar Hungary is Iván T. Berend and György Ránki, *Underdevelopment and Economic Growth* (Budapest: Akadémia, 1978). See also Victor Karády and István Kemény, "Les Juifs dans la structure des classes en Hongrie," *Actes de la recherche en science sociales* 22 (1978): 25–29. See also the sections "Jews and Assimilation/Dissimilation" and "Anti-Jewish Legislation."

On the Arrow Cross and the Fascist movements, the most comprehensive study is Miklós Lackó, *Arrow-Cross Men, National Socialists, 1935–1944* (Budapest: Akadémia, 1969). For more recent analysis and further sources see István Deák, "The Peculiarities of Hungarian Fascism," in *The Holocaust in Hungary Forty Years Later*, edited by Randolph L. Braham and Bela Vago (New York: Columbia University Press, 1985); and Asher Cohen, "Some Socio-Political Aspects of the Arrow Cross Party in Hungary," *East European Quarterly* 21, no. 1 (1987): 369–84.

Important sources on the Labor Service System were published in Elek Karsai, *"Fegyvertelenül áltak az aknamezökön . . ."* ("Unarmed stood on the mine-fields . . . ") (Budapest: Magyar Izraeliták Országos Képviselete, 1962). The most detailed description and analysis is Randolph L. Braham, *The Hungarian Labor Service System, 1939–1945* (New York: Columbia University Press, 1977). At the moment there is no detailed research on individual units, and even more important, on the sufferings of those who were captured by the Soviets and released only several years after the war ended. Some memories of survivors should be consulted. Many were published in Hungarian and in Hebrew; see Braham, *The Hungarian Jewish Catastrophe: A Selected and Annotated Bibliography*, pp. 72–73, 196–209, 335–36. For one of the rare exceptions, a humane officer commanding Labor Service units and saving many of the Jews, see Adam

Reviczky, *Vesztes háborúk—megnyert osaták* (Wars lost—battles won) (Budapest: Magvetö, 1985) (translated into Hebrew, 1988).

### Anti-Jewish Legislation

For important information on the Hungarian policy during the interwar period, see the works cited in the previous sections. For the latest and perhaps the best elaborations on the Hungarian responsibilities, with participation of the best scholars of the field, see Braham and Vago, *The Holocaust in Hungary Forty Years Later*. The main point, that an active and aggressive anti-Jewish politic was developed in Hungary during the interwar period, is not debated (see the chapters by Katzburg, Száraz, Berend, and Juhász in Braham and Vago, pp. 3–73). However, there are different points of view on its direct application to the deportations in 1944. An important contribution to the background of this question is brought by Randolph Braham, who directs his analysis to the very source of "the *very* cordial, almost symbiotic relationship that developed between the Hungarian national and Jewish elites during the 'Golden Era' (1867–1918)" (italics in the original; Braham and Vago, p. 178). Braham's reflections are an excellent and most far-reaching background for the comprehension of the Jewish state of mind in 1944. The emphasis on Jewish ignorance and misjudgment during the interwar period was presented in my article, "Continuity in Change," *Jewish Social Studies* (New York) 46, no. 2 (1984): 131–44. For sources, see also Andrew Handler, ed., *The Holocaust in Hungary: An Anthology of Jewish Responses* (University: University of Alabama Press, 1982). See also the section "The Failure of Rescue."

### Zionism in Wartime Hungary

The only history of the Zionist movement in Hungary was published in Hebrew: Zvi Zahavi, *From Assimilation to Zionism* (in Hebrew) (Jerusalem: 1973). This book was written essentially using sources accessible in Israel. Further research in this field using documentation in Hungarian archives is needed for a more comprehensive picture. The only published and comprehensive research on the *Halutz* youth movements in Hungary is the book written by the present author, *The Halutz Resistance in Hungary, 1942–1944* (New York: Columbia University Press, 1986) (an enlarged Hebrew version was published in 1984). The studies on the resistance in Hungary systematically ignore the very existence of the Zionist movement and its contribution, for obvious political reasons. On the prewar period, see Hava Eichler, "Zionism and Youth in Hungary Between the Two World Wars" (in Hebrew), (Ph.D. thesis, Bar-Ilan University, Israel, 1982). Both Kasztner and Brand published their versions of the events, and both should be read carefully and with caution. Most of their correspondence with the delegations in Istanbul and in Geneva can be found in various archives. See especially the Central Zionist Archives, Jerusalem, and the Ghetto Fighters'

House Archives, Haifa. The only exception is Nathan Schwalb's correspondence, shamefully closed to research in the Labor Movement Archives, Tel Aviv. Further material, of varying value, was presented during the famous "Kasztner trial" in Israel, and other sources are accessible in British and German archives. Although most of the historians of the period (as well as memoirists, journalists, and other nonhistorians) wrote on the Vaad's merits or misdeeds, no professional and comprehensive history of this group exists.

### Hungarian Deportations

For the first massive roundups of Hungarian Jews see György Ránki, *1944 március 19* (March 19, 1944) (Budapest: Kossuth, 1978), pp. 159–60, 255–56. The only comprehensive and detailed study of the deportations is Braham's *The Politics of Genocide*, on which the present description is also based. The responsibility of the Hungarians for the deportation of the Jews in so late a period of the war is debated in all research dealing with the topic. On the essential role of the administration, an important contribution is Elek Karsai, "Deportation and Administration in Hungary," in *The Holocaust in Hungary Forty Years Later*, pp. 107–27. The great importance of this study is that the author is the only historian who had the opportunity to study Hungarian local archives. Two excellent scholars of the field dealt exclusively with the question of responsibility: Ránki, "The Germans and the Destruction of Hungarian Jewry," and Vago, "The Hungarians and the Destruction of the Hungarian Jews" (*The Holocaust in Hungary Forty Years Later*, pp. 77–105). There is, of course, no argument on the two responsibilities, but rather on the nuances. Vago emphasizes the responsibility of "the Hungarian society and people as a whole." For those who insist on the Hungarian preparedness for the deportation of the Jews, there remains the question why this was prevented until as late as 1944. Ránki's argument is that without the German occupation the Hungarian Holocaust would not have occurred. To this one can oppose his own and Karsai's observations on the Hungarian execution of the deportation. If there are historical problems where only the nuances are important, this is one of them. For a later interpretation and additional sources, see my articles: "Pétain, Horthy, Antonescu, and the Jews, 1942–1944," *Yad Vashem Studies* 18 (1987): 163–98; and "German Hegemony and National Independence During the Second World War," in *The Holocaust: In Answer . . .* , edited by F. H. Littell, I. G. Shur, and C. R. Foster (West Chester, Pa.: Sylvan, 1988).

We still lack a comprehensive and detailed study on the Jewish Council comparable to those on Jewish leadership in Holland, France, and many communities in Poland. The main reason is the lack of reliable sources.

### The Failure of Rescue

The most complex and the most debated question is the one that pertains to the failure to rescue the great majority of the Jews in Hungary. A historiography of this problem was published by Randolph L. Braham, "The Rescue of the Jews of Hungary in Historical Perspective," in Gutman and Grief, *The Historiography of the Holocaust Period*, pp. 447–66. This chapter was delivered as a paper in 1983 and does not contain reference to publications after this date. This question is inseparable from the fact that prior to the German occupation all the elements of the extermination policy were widely known in Hungary. This was systematically demonstrated and analyzed by Braham in his study, "What Did They Know and When?" in *The Holocaust as Historical Experience*, edited by Yehuda Bauer and Nathan Rotenstreich (London: Holmes and Meier, 1981), pp. 109–31. For the path of the Auschwitz Protocol in Hungary, see Sándor Szenes, *Befejezetlen mult: Keresztények és zsidók, sorsok* (Unfinished past: Christians and Jews, destinies) (Budapest: 1986). The most disturbing question nevertheless remains this: Was there a "conspiracy of silence" (see also Braham, *Politics of Genocide*, pp. 691–731 and chapters pertaining to the deportations) in diffusing this information among local leaders of the provincial towns and larger Jewish populations, and if so, was it the main reason for the passivity of the great majority of the Hungarian Jews?

The conclusion of most of the research, including Braham's excellent historiographic article, is that great responsibility should be attributed to Kasztner's failure to inform the Jews on the final destination of the deportations. See, for example, John S. Conway, "Frühe Augenzeugenberichte aus Auschwitz," in *Virteljahrshefte für Zeitgeschichte* 27, no. 2 (1979): 260–84. It seems to the present writer that the importance of the committee was exaggerated, and that only a professional study of all its activities after 1942 can properly place this small group in its proper historical context.

The pre-1944 information, nevertheless, remains a most complex question. Most of the survivors, in their testimonies, say that they had no notion of Auschwitz before reaching the gas chambers. These evidences cannot, of course, be disregarded. One example is Elie Wiesel, who added that in 1941 the beadle came back to his town, Sziget, from the deportation to Kamenetz-Podolsk and told the stories of the mass killing. "We didn't believe him. He was a poor beadle, a *Shamesz*. We couldn't believe him." He also said: "The information was there, but it was not transformed into consciousness" (*The Holocaust in Hungary Forty Years Later*, pp. xiii–xiv). A very similar opinion was expressed by Yehuda Bauer, *The Holocaust in Historical Perspective* (Seattle: University of Washington Press, 1978), p. 106.

The main point in this problem that should direct our analysis has to be that under the given conditions, that is, the attitude of the Hungarian administration and people and the speed of the deportation, there was no possible rescue for the Jews by their own efforts in Hungary. Nevertheless, for a number of individuals there was a possibility of rescue, and the *Halutz* resistance's activities demonstrate this limited but existing possibility. Those who insist only on the lack of the diffusion of the Auschwitz Protocol, an undeniable failure, tend to ignore the deeper reasons, specifically "the *very* cordial, almost symbiotic relationship'' that had developed not only between the Hungarian and Jewish leadership, but also between the Jews and the Hungarian people. The last point that needs a remark is the role attributed often to Kasztner and his visit in Kolozsvár. We do not know what he said or did not say on the final destination of the deportation, but we know that some Jews, among them locally prominent ones, did leave for Romania. But what is more important, Kasztner was a minor personality, except perhaps in that one town, and certainly not considered as one of the Jewish leaders in the country. His alleged or real failure has very little to do with the reaction or inaction of the Jewish population in a larger sense. The rescue led by an individual Jew, Georges Mantello, is still not sufficiently explored.

More than four hundred articles appeared in the Swiss press during the summer months of 1944 in 128 different newspapers. Some of the articles, on the front page, on three columns, give a very detailed description on the functioning of the gas chambers and the crematoria. One can assume also, on the strong basis of reports from the Hungarian consulate in Bern to Budapest, that public opinion created by the press campaign in Switzerland, which was unprecedented both in scope and in the accuracy of the information, was an important factor in staying deportations from July to October. For the most detailed descriptions of Mantello's activities, see Jenö Lévai, *Zsidósors Európában* (Jewish destiny in Europe) (Budapest: Magyar Téka, 1948).

The wider question of the handling of the information in order to create public opinion and to promote and encourage rescue certainly needs more elaborated research. For the best review of the inaction of the Allies, see Braham's historiographic article, ''The Rescue of the Jews of Hungary in Historical Perspective,'' mentioned earlier.

### Raoul Wallenberg

The personal devotion and the rescue activities of Raoul Wallenberg, important after October 1944, have been widely described, sometimes even exaggerated. On Charles Lutz only one book has been published, with important documentation: Alexander Grosman, *Nur das Gewissen: Karl Lutz und seine Budapester Aktion* (Geneva, 1986). It should also be noted that all of the rescuers, especially Lutz and the IRC, could carry out important rescue activities only thanks to local Jews. It is even more essential to remember that no rescue activities were developed by any neutral legation, and nothing was done during the deportations from the provincial towns. These rescue activities should also be considered in relation to those of the *Halutz* resistance, although there was nearly no contact in the field between the resistance and Wallenberg.

Most of the studies of Jewish resistance, especially those written in Israel up to the late 1970s, put great emphasis on armed resistance and much less on resistance to the extermination by rescue activities. A more balanced picture on the activities of the Zionist youth movements was demonstrated in a scholarly congress on "The Zionist Youth Movements in Europe during the *Shoah*" held in the Ghetto Fighters' House and University of Haifa in 1987.

## SELECT BIBLIOGRAPHY

Anger, Per. *With Raoul Wallenberg in Budapest.* Preface by Elie Wiesel. New York: Holocaust Library, 1981.

Benoschofsky, Ilona, and Elek Karsai, eds. *Vádirat a nácizmus ellen* (Indictment of Nazism). 3 vols. Budapest: Magyar Izraeliták Országos Képviselete, 1958–67.

Braham, Randolph L. *The Hungarian Jewish Catastrophe: A Selected and Annotated Bibliography.* New York: Columbia University Press, 1984.

———. *The Hungarian Labor Service System, 1939–1945.* New York: Columbia University Press, 1977.

———. *The Politics of Genocide: The Holocaust in Hungary.* 2 vols. New York: Columbia University Press, 1981.

———, ed. *The Destruction of Hungarian Jewry: A Documentary Account.* 2 vols. New York: World Federation of Hungarian Jews, 1963.

Cohen, Asher. *The Halutz Resistance in Hungary, 1942–1944.* New York: Columbia University Press, 1986.

Grosman, Alexander. *Nur das Gewissen: Karl Lutz und seine Budapester Aktion.* Geneva: 1986.

Handler, Andrew, ed. *The Holocaust in Hungary: An Anthology of Jewish Responses.* University: University of Alabama Press, 1982.

Karsai, Elek. *"Fegyvertelenül áltak az aknamezökön..."* ("Unarmed stood on the minefields..."). Budapest: Magyar Izraeliták Országos Képviselete, 1962.

Katzburg, Nathaniel. *Hungary and the Jews, Policy and Legislation, 1920–1943.* Ramat Gan: Bar Ilan University Press, 1981.

Lester, Elenore. *Wallenberg, the Man in the Iron Web.* Englewood Cliffs, N.J.: Prentice-Hall, 1982.

Lévai, Jenö, *Fehér könyv* (White book). Budapest: Officina 1948.

———. *Fekete könyv* (Black book). Budapest: Officina, 1945.

———. *Szürke könyv* (Gray book). Budapest: Officina, 1947.

Molnár, Erik, István Bibó, György Száraz, and Péter Hanák, eds. *Zsidókérdés, asszimiláció, antiszemitizmus* (The Jewish question, assimilation, anti-Semitism). Budapest: Magvetö, 1984.

Ránki, György, et al., eds. *A Wilhelmstrasse és Magyarország* (The Wilhelmstrasse and Hungary). Budapest: Akadémia, 1968.

Szenes, Sándor. *Befejezetlen mult: Keresztények és zsidók, sorsok* (Unfinished past: Christians and Jews, destinies). Budapest: 1986.

Vago, Bela, ed. *Jewish Assimilation in Modern Times.* Boulder, Colo.: Westview Press/ East European Monographs, 1981.

Vago, Bela, and Georges Mosse, eds. *Jews and Non-Jews in Eastern Europe, 1918–1945.* New York: John Wiley, 1974.

Werbell, Frederick, and Thurston Clarke. *Lost Hero: The Mystery of Raoul Wallenberg.* New York: McGraw-Hill, 1982.

Zahavi, Zvi. *From Assimilation to Zionism* (in Hebrew). Jerusalem: 1973.

# Chapter 13

# The Holocaust in Czechoslovakia: A Survey of the Literature

## *Saul S. Friedman*

### THE JEWS OF CZECHOSLOVAKIA: A RETROSPECTIVE

December, 1992. The winds of change that swept across Eastern Europe these past three years, bringing with them a spirit of optimism, have turned bitter and hostile. The Berlin Wall is gone and the Cold War is now a chapter in history books. Politburos from Lithuania to Mongolia have voted themselves out of existence and been replaced by idealists who lived under tyranny for most of this century. Yet even as the word *freedom* is chanted publicly for the first time in many languages, some people recognize the harsh realities that lie ahead. Inefficient, state-run industries in the East have had difficulty adjusting to a free market system. Populations that had been instructed as to what they might think or where they could work or shop have found themselves without employment and little food. Accordingly, old enmities have boiled over into public mayhem and civil war in this patchquilt of artificial states stitched at Versailles. As the prospect of national disintegration looms for much of Central and Eastern Europe, the remnants of once dynamic Jewish communities look on with fear and wonder at what this new order signifies for them.

Even before the Communist takeovers in the now-defunct Soviet Union and its satellites, the Jewish *Lumpenproletariat* (urban poor identified by Social Democratic theoretician Nachman Syrkin as being at the core of the battle for human rights) were the principal targets of racism and pogroms in Eastern Europe. Jews were scored by village priests and Tsars as loathsome creatures, dishonest in business, and responsible for the killing of Christ. Syrkin forecast that a change of regimes would not radically improve their lot. Under Stalin, Gomulka and Gottwald, Jewish doctors, devoted party hacks and Zionists, served as convenient scapegoats for every national failure. Now as Eastern Europe slips under the control of right-wing chauvinists, old canards against Jews are being revived. In Leningrad, the reactionary Pamiat group has tried to circulate the Protocols of the Elders of Zion. In Kiev, the ultra-nationalist Rukh movement heaps rebuke upon Jewish commissars. In Riga, the Latvian President honors the same militia that perpetrated massacres during the Holocaust. In Tashkent, Muslims, inflamed by propaganda from Iran and Afghanistan, call for Jihad against Israel.

Of all the East European republics born at Versailles, the one that seemed immune to the anti-Semitic virus, the only one that made a commitment to democracy, was Czechoslovakia. This union of Protestant urban Bohemians and Catholic rural Slovaks paid tragically for that commitment—three times—at Munich in October, 1938, when the Communists seized power in February, 1948, and again when Russian tanks suppressed a liberal, socialist revolt in the summer of 1968. Too briefly, Czechoslovakia enjoyed the post-Soviet thaw as Alexander Dubček and Václav Havel served a free Czechoslovakia as Speaker of the Parliament and Prime Minister respectively.

Yet as this chapter is written, the state is coming apart. And for the 13,000 Jews who remain in Czechoslovakia it is as if time has stood still and Hitler or Stalin were alive. In February 1990 an elderly Jewish couple from Bratislava wrote relatives in America:

Things here are not very good. In the beginning—in the first days of the revolution—it was wonderful. But after emotions subsided, the daily life began and this is very hard. Democracy has also shadowy sides. Now when everybody can say what he means, anti-Semitism is growing very fast and very open. On buildings and fences are anti-Jewish slogans and we feel as long years ago, when the persecution of Jews began and ended in concentration camps. We fear again and therefore we consider whether it wouldn't be better to emigrate. But where?! It is terrible that not even on the end of our life we have quiet.

Economics here is quite down. Opening of the borders did not bring anything good. People from the Slovak national party (fascists who are living in different parts of the world, especially in the USA and Canada) come here and propagate chauvinism and in this way support the already blooming anti-Semitism.[1]

The writers of that letter, Viera and Laci V., endured Nazi death camps and forty-five years of Soviet tyranny because Czechoslovakia was their home. Jews had played an important role in the history of Central Europe for more than a thousand years as merchants, scholars, and warriors. The region was rich in Jewish culture and tradition. In Prague stands the Altneushul, built in 1270, the oldest Jewish house of worship in the world. This simple structure allegedly is the repository of the remains of the Golem, a mute behemoth created by mystics to protect the Jews of Prague from ritual murder libels in the sixteenth century. The synagogue also contains a flag presented by the Hapsburg emperor to the city's Jews for their role in the defense of Prague during the Thirty Years' War.

The man responsible for awaking the Golem, Judah Loew, a wonder-working rabbi, is buried in the nearby Jewish cemetery amid twelve thousand teetering tombstones that date back centuries. Some commemorate notables like the astronomer-historian David Gans or the physician-physicist Josef Delmedigo. Others mark the resting places of butchers, shopkeepers, housewives, and tailors. Prague's rococo synagogues—the Klaus, Reb Maisel, High, and Spanish—are like the cemetery, quiet and empty. The names of 77,297 Jews and the concentration camps where they perished are inscribed on the walls of the Pinkas Synagogue. More than 5,000 religious objects, 24,000 prayer books, and 6,000 other items are preserved in the State Jewish Museum.[2]

Because of the shifting of borders among Poland, Hungary, and Germany after Munich, and the constant flight of refugees in the prewar period, there is no exact count for the number of Jews in Czechoslovakia before the Holocaust. A wartime report by the American Jewish Committee estimated the number in Bohemia, Moravia, Silesia, and Slovakia at 250,000.[3] Lucy Dawidowicz estimates 118,000 Jews, about one-third of all Czech Jews, in the provinces of Bohemia and Moravia, and another 135,000 in Slovakia. Virtually the same figure (315,000) is cited by both Raul Hilberg and Jacob Lestchinsky of the American Jewish Congress, although the two differ on the number of survivors (Lestchinsky claims 75,000 survivors, Hilberg only 44,000). Gerald Reitlinger agrees with the figure 315,000, but notes that the 1930 census counted 356,830 in the republic (117,551 in Bohemia and Moravia, 136,737 in Slovakia, and 102,542 in Ruthenia).[4]

Overall, the Jewish population in Czechoslovakia (less than 1.7 percent) was declining. In the west perhaps 60 percent of the Jews were in business, finance, or communications. Jews were listed on the boards of nine hundred major companies producing sugar, lumber, paper, and textiles. Most of these, including the Petschek soft coal mines (valued at $67 million and sold for $20 million), along with six thousand buildings housing Jewish enterprises, were Aryanized by the end of 1940. Like the literary giant Franz Kafka, most Jews in Bohemia were modernist; that is, they rejected traditional Judaism (there was only one kosher butcher in Prague, where 35,000 Jews resided in 1930). Stores remained open on Yom Kippur. By 1933 the intermarriage rate with Gentiles was 23 percent. This should not be taken to mean that Czechoslovakia's Jews were assimilated to the point that they rejected their religious roots or cultural identity. Like American counterparts today, most embraced the Reform or Conservative branches of Judaism. Subjected to physical attacks by Slovaks who charged them with pan-Germanism, Polonism, Magyarism, or communism, Bohemian Jews identified themselves as Jews by nationality. Two members of the Jewish party, formed in 1919, sat in the Parliament. A Jewish National Council in Prague assisted the aged, orphans, and unemployed and coordinated antidefamation activities. During the halcyon interwar years a Jew, Robert Klein (who would die in Dachau in 1942), headed a nonsectarian labor union. Jews made up 12 percent of Czechoslovakia's university students, six times their number in the general population. Before the Nazis dismissed them from their professions, Jews made up one-third of the doctors and lawyers in Bohemia.[5]

In the east there were some Jewish landed estates (fifteen thousand, valued at $42.5 million, were Aryanized after 1938). But just as in Bohemia, most Jews in Slovakia and Ruthenia clustered in towns. There the similarities ended. In the east the Jews were far poorer. Mainly small artisans, an estimated 80 percent required assistance from the Joint Distribution Committee to stave off starvation during the depression.[6] Modernism, Zionism, and socialism were practically nonexistent in a region where Orthodoxy was the rule. Forty-three percent of the Jews in the Carpathians lived in Munkács, one of the bastions of Hasidic Judaism. In a polyglot region where Hungarians, Schwabs, Slovaks, and Ukrainians despised one another, there was agreement on hatred of the Jews. An illiterate, peasant population subscribed to hoary libels of Christ killing, ritual murder, and Jews selling rotten meat or poisoned whiskey and periodically, on Easter, Christmas, or St. Nicholas's Day, attacked these outcasts. Not surprisingly, the rate of intermarriage in the east was less than 2 percent.

Despite these adversities, Czechoslovakia's Jews were optimistic about the future. The nation was ruled by Czechs, whose tradition of maverick toleration dated back to John Hus in the fourteenth century. The first president of the Republic, Thomas Masaryk, had distinguished himself as a friend in 1890 by opposing anti-Semites who charged Jews with ritual murder in the Polna case. Masaryk and his disciple Eduard Beneš were committed to the concept of honoring minority guarantees made to the peacemakers at Versailles. Masaryk had even spoken sympathetically of Zionism as a necessary moral regeneration for the Jews, and a few small Zionist societies were created in the interwar period. But in a country where Jews served on the city council of Prague and debated the merits of an eventual seven-hour work day, the thought of emigration to the dusty, war-torn Holy Land had little appeal.

Long before Hitler annexed the Sudetenland, however, there were ominous signs for the Jews of Czechoslovakia. The Slovak People's party, founded by Msgr. Andrei Hlinka, fulminated against Czechs and Jews for more than a decade. Just as in France, Romania, and Lithuania, veterans of World War I embraced the xenophobic ideology of fascism. In Czechoslovakia some joined the Svatopulk Guards, Vlajka, the Czech National Camp for Aryans, Jiri Skibrny's National Socialist party, the Agrarian party of Rudolf Beran, or Gen. Rudolf Gajda's Czech Legion. Only five members of the four-hundred-member Parliament were openly declared Fascists, but support for economic discrimination against Jews was widespread among the clergy and the masses. In February 1939 American diplomat George Kennan warned in a cable to Washington that if the Nazis attempted to bring their racial program to Czechoslovakia, they would not encounter significant resistance from the church.[7]

Five months earlier, at Munich on October 6, 1938, Britain and France yielded to Hitler's demands and returned the Sudetenland to Germany. The rest of Czechoslovakia was split into three autonomous zones ostensibly reflecting their ethnic populations, Czechia, Ruthenia, and Slovakia, none of which could ever menace Germany. On March 15, 1939, Nazi troops marched into Prague and ended the charade of an independent Czechia. Henceforth Germany would hold a protectorate over Bohemia and Moravia. Simultaneously Hungary annexed Ruthenia. The sole relic of a once-dynamic democracy was Slovakia, a Fascist puppet state ruled by Msgr. Dr. Josef Tiso.

As elsewhere in Europe, the swiftness of events left Czech Jews benumbed. Before Munich, Jews in Prague, led by social worker Marie Schmolka and the Women's International Zionist Organization (WIZO) representative Hanna Steiner, had tried to assist their kinsmen fleeing Germany and Austria. Housing, cash, and clothing had been extended to refugees, and efforts had been made to include them under some international apparatus like the Nansen Office, the League of Nations High Commissioner for Refugees from Germany, or that placebo born at the Evian Conference in July 1938, the Inter-Governmental Committee for Refugees. In late summer Jews in the Sudetenland began transferring property to the interior of Czechoslovakia. Before the end of September 1938, more than twenty thousand converged on Prague. After Munich, Czech Jews who had been so secure were immediately subjected to discrimination which had taken the Nazis six years to refine. As thousands from the Sudetenland and the Hungarian territories were dumped into empty fields along the Polish border and street attacks became common occurrences in Brno, Olomouc, and Uhersky Brod, the attitude of Czechoslovakia's Jews moved from confusion and worry to "demoralization and cynicism."[8]

The Jews had good reason for such gloom. The Nazis planned to reduce Jews economically, thereby forcing them to emigrate. For this reason Adolf Eichmann created the Zentralstelle für jüdische Auswanderung (Central Office for Jewish Emigration) in Prague in August 1939. In reality, the Zentralstelle became, like the Židovská Ústredná Úradnovňa pre Slovenskú Krajinu (Central Jewish Office for the Region of Slovakia, created in November 1938 and reformed in September 1940), the official Jewish council in Bohemia and Moravia, attempting to ameliorate the welter of decrees designed to degrade Jews.

On June 21, 1939, for example, the Nazis introduced the Nuremberg Laws to Bohemia and Moravia, defining as Jews anyone with three Jewish grandparents. This was followed in July 1941 by a law protecting racial honor and banning sexual relations between Jews and non-Jews. Over the winter of 1939–40 segregation on buses and in parks gave way to outright bans in cafes, bathhouses, gardens, barbershops, libraries, schools, and hospitals. Jewish businesses had to be clearly labeled as such. With the outbreak of war, Jews were subjected to curfew and required to turn in radio sets. Mail privileges were limited and tax exemptions for synagogues revoked. Food rationing was stricter. There were time limits for shopping, and Jews could purchase no fruit, shaving soap, or tobacco.

In April 1940 a *numerus clausus* was decreed that restricted the number of Jewish teachers, lawyers, editors, doctors, and notaries to 2 percent in each of these professions. The Nazis had been dismissing people from the civil service, banks, and the medical profession as early as October 1938. On April 30, 1941, Czech Jews were ordered to register and carry stamped identity cards with them at all times. Four months later, in September, the familiar black and yellow badge bearing the word ''Jude'' was mandated.

The pattern of persecution was actually worse in Slovakia, where Jews deluded themselves that they were essential to the vitality of the economy. In April 1939 Jews were defined as anyone with one Jewish parent. The predominantly Orthodox population was stunned when the practice of *shehitah* (kosher butchering) was banned that first summer. This was followed early in 1940 by a series of Aryanization laws compelling the ''voluntary'' transfer of land, businesses, even homes to Christians. After a meeting between Tiso and Hitler in the summer of 1940, the Slovakian Ministry of the Interior encouraged members of the Hlinka Guard and Freiwillige Schutzstaffel to pogrom activity. Meanwhile, Jewish men between the ages of eighteen and sixty were drafted into labor battalions, ostensibly for defensive work against the Russians. Thousands died while slaving in brutal road gangs or swamps. On September 9, 1941, the government consolidated its anti-Semitic activities in a single code consisting of 270 articles. The Jewish Code was actually longer than the Slovakian constitution. Included in the document was one measure requiring Jews over the age of six to wear the *Mogen David*.

The first phase of the Nazi scheme—eliminating Jews from the economic life of Czechoslovakia—worked rather well. Livia Rothkirchen estimates that $500,000,000 in property and assets were transferred to non-Jews through ''fraudulent bullying.'' Adolf Eichmann was committed to more than bankrupting Jews. He wanted them out of Europe and embraced every scheme to expedite their departure. Although the Nazis opposed Zionism, they permitted *hachsharah* centers to function and allowed three thousand pioneers to emigrate to Palestine in 1939.[9] As five hundred thousand Germans flocked to the protectorate that first year, Jews were expelled.

Responding to an order from Himmler dated October 8, 1939, Eichmann dispatched several thousand men from Ostrava and Frydek-Mistek to Nisko, a small town on the San River south of Lublin in Poland. They were to be the vanguard of more than three hundred thousand Austrian and Czech Jews destined for a ''Jewish agricultural reservation.'' Beaten by German troops and Ukrainian auxiliaries, the Jews traveled in open boxcars before reaching their destination in Poland. Lacking huts, food, water, and medical supplies, many perished in the severe winter. Poles who lived in the region opposed the use of Nisko as a dumping ground for Central Europe's Jews, as did Hans Frank, governor-general of Poland, who already had two million Jews under his control. For some Nazi leaders, the notion of a Jewish reservation somewhere, even out of Europe, had appeal. Eichmann, Hitler, Himmler, Rademacher, even Heydrich all mulled over the possibility of taking Madagascar from France for this purpose. The invasion of Russia that guaranteed a prolongation of the war rendered the question of what to do with three million more Jews moot.

Late in September 1941 Reinhard Heydrich replaced Constantin von Neurath as the protector of Bohemia and Moravia. Described by Erich Kulka as a man "who from the very beginning advocated a radical liquidation of the Jews," Heydrich, an advocate of *Kristallnacht*, the ghetto decree of September 1939, and *Einsatzgruppe* killing squads, did not wait long before acting. On October 17 he summoned a group of high-ranking SS leaders to Prague to discuss implementation of Hermann Göring's order of July 31 commanding a final solution of the Jewish question in Europe. Eichmann, SS General Karl Hermann Frank, concentration-camp specialist Colonel Gerhard Mauer, Hans Günther, Horst Bohme, and Dr. Karl Freiherr von Gregory attended what proved to be a rehearsal for the more celebrated Wannsee Conference in Berlin in January.

The minutes of this Prague meeting reveal the cold, calculated approach of Heydrich toward genocide. Initially, five thousand Jews would be shipped out to Lodz on five transports. The rest of the Jews in Bohemia and Moravia would be processed through a transit camp, possibly the fortress of Terezín, located forty miles northwest of Prague. "Von dort aus kommen die Juden nach dem Osten" (From there, the Jews would be sent to the East). Nazi authorities in Minsk and Riga had each agreed to accept fifty thousand. Heydrich advised that everything should be done in a clever manner to show the efficiency of the Germans. Czechs were to be warned that they were not to identify with Jews or interfere with the deportations, or they would share the fate of the Jews. Heydrich did not specify the true goal of this plan, mass murder, but it was evident from another sarcastic comment: "Die Juden haben sich die Wohnungen in die Erde hinab zu schaffen" (Jews will have to build their dwellings under the ground).[10]

That winter several thousand Jewish men were dispatched from Prague to renovate barracks in Terezín (renamed Theresienstadt by the Nazis). The Nazis later attempted to bilk representatives of the International Red Cross who toured this ghetto in June 1944 into believing that Terezín was a pleasant *Judensiedlung* (Jewish settlement). But far from being the idyllic *Reichsaltersheim* (showplace for the aged) intended by Heydrich at Wannsee or even a source of skilled labor fantasized by commandants Siegfried Seidl, Anton Burger, or Hans Rahm, Terezín was a place of pain and agony. Used as a prisoner-of-war facility in World War I, Terezín could accommodate 7,000 inmates. In their place, the Nazis stuffed as many as 50,000 Jews into poorly insulated attics and stables. Before liberation by the Red Army in May 1945, 33,419 died of starvation, brutality, and despair, a death toll greater even than Dachau's in its twelve years of existence. More than 130 died each day during a typhus epidemic in 1942, 3,941 in the month of September alone, a death rate thirty times higher than that of any ordinary European town of comparable size.[11]

A total of 140,000 Jews from the Reich, Czechoslovakia, Denmark, and

Holland passed through the so-called Paradise Ghetto. Some prominent persons survived, like the aged Berlin rabbi Dr. Leo Baeck. Of 86,934 persons deported to Riga, Trawniki, Treblinka, Maly Trostinec, Belsen, and Auschwitz, only 2,971 returned at the end of the war. Within Theresienstadt itself, of 15,000 children under the age of fifteen registered by the Ältestenrat in Terezín, fewer than 1 percent came back.

Reichsprotektor Heydrich was not around to observe the fruits of his labor. Four months after the Wannsee Conference, on May 29, 1942, he was assassinated while motoring to his office in Prague. Czech commandos, flown into the country by the RAF, set an ambush on the city's outskirts. Lacerated by machine-gun fire, his spine shattered, the SS leader lingered in pain for nearly a week. His death resolved little. Thirteen thousand persons were arrested in the *Grosszähmung* (dragnet) that followed. Thirteen hundred were executed, including all the males in the village of Lidice that supposedly had harbored the commandos. In Poland the roundups aimed at clearing the Warsaw ghetto, Europe's single largest concentration of Jews, were dubbed *Aktion Reinhard* in Heydrich's honor. Under his successor, SS Lt. Gen. Kurt Daluege, the deportations from Bohemia continued apace.

In Prague people were assembled at a set of dilapidated wooden shacks on the Trade Fairgrounds. In Terezín the Hamburg Kaserne, an incredibly filthy, overcrowded barracks, served as the *Schleuse* (locks). In the west, at least some Czech police were sympathetic toward the Jews. Not so in Slovakia, where Hlinka Guards beat them, destroyed passports of American citizens, and forced the doomed Jews to sign documents "voluntarily" turning property over to the state. A few pompous figures like Robert Mandler and Terezín police chief Dr. Karl Loewenstein tried to manipulate the system to their own advantage. Generally, though, Jewish leaders agonized over a process that compelled them to designate their own deportees. Survivors have expressed admiration for the actions of Jacob Edelstein, Judenältester in Terezín, his chief medical officer, Dr. Erich Munk, Dr. Erich Oesterreicher, head of the ghetto's labor department, Fredy Hirsch, a leader in Terezín's youth program, and Prague's last two community leaders, Salo Kramer and Dr. Frantisek Friedmann.

Of Slovakia's 89,000 Jews, 53,000 were gone by the end of June 1942. Failure of the rabbis to win concessions from the Tiso government resulted in the creation of a kind of shadow Jewish cabinet, the Nebenregierung (other government). Headed by Gisi Fleischmann of WIZO and Orthodox rabbi Michael Weissmandel, the so-called Working Group at first tried to soften the shock of deportation by creating synagogue groups in the transports. When escapees revealed the true nature of the Nazi extermination scheme, the Working Group offered bribes to officials in the Slovakian Ministry of the Interior and even tantalized Nazi hierarchs in 1943. Under the so-called Europa Plan, $2 million plus an unspecified amount of food and medicine would be paid to Dieter von Wisliceny, Eichmann's top aide, if the deportations would stop. Although negotiations were broken off by Eichmann, the Nazi leader revived a form of the Europa Plan in 1944 when he offered some of Hungary's Jews to Joel Brand in exchange for trucks, medical supplies, and $10 million. By that time the Working Group had convinced church leaders and moderates in Slovakia that converted Jews were also being murdered. Dissidents like Dr. Jozef Sivak, Dr. Peter Zatko, Karol Sidor, and Father Pozdech succeeded in shutting down the transports after October 1942. Until the Slovaks rose in rebellion against the Nazis in August 1944, their land was a temporary haven even for Jews fleeing Poland.

By war's end the millennium of Czech-Jewish civilization was over. Virtually all of the 350 Jewish cemeteries in the land had been desecrated, as had 315 synagogues. A few thousand Jews were in hiding in the west; perhaps another eleven thousand sickly inmates remained in Terezín. Most of the nation's Jews shared the fate of Gisi Fleischmann and Jacob Edelstein. The Nazis tantalized them with the notion of survival, as they did the five thousand Jews from Terezín who were quarantined in thirty wooden horse stables at Auschwitz in the fall of 1943. For six months the inhabitants of the "Family Camp" remained together, tried to maintain a semblance of order in their lives, and congratulated themselves on having avoided the fate of their comrades. Then, early in March 1944, they were told that they were to be removed to a new camp called Heydenbreck. Instead, all but seventy were gassed.[12]

## CZECHOSLOVAKIA IN THE MAJOR HOLOCAUST TEXTBOOKS

Researchers seeking a concise assessment of the Holocaust in Czechoslovakia in major textbooks will be disappointed. None of the major scholars devotes a separate chapter to the subject. Because the state was divided before the beginning of the war, information is diffused throughout the texts, and readers must go looking through sections labeled "Greater Germany" or "the Protectorate" to ascertain what happened in Bohemia and Moravia. Indexes help, but these are never fully comprehensive, and the reader may find himself wading through section after section in search of references to Jews in the Carpathians, Lidice, or the assassination of Heydrich.

As reported elsewhere,[13] the earliest texts, Gerald Reitlinger's *The Final Solution* and Leon Poliakov's *Harvest of Hate*, share much in common. Both offer substantial discussion on the deportation of Jews from the Reich through Theresienstadt (although Reitlinger supplies insight into the personal torment of Leo Baeck once the Berlin rabbi learned the true destinations of transports leaving the ghetto). Reitlinger devotes about ten pages (385–94) to the Slovakian tragedy, noting how the aged Premier Vojtek Tuka expressed concern about the deportations while Monsignor Tiso lied openly to representatives of the International Red Cross. Poliakov's treatment of the Europa Plan and its variants (including Joel Brand's mission from Hungary in 1944) is probably the fullest of any text, particularly as it notes the role of Haj Amin al-Husseini, the grand mufti of Jerusalem, in blocking the rescue of Jews from Europe (254–59).

There are many pluses and minuses in Raul Hilberg's mammoth *The Destruction of the European Jews*. Hilberg's fifteen pages on Slovakia (458–73) offer a chart explaining how the Nazis and Slovaks determined who was a Jew, explain the role of Dieter von Wisliceny and other officials in the Reich Security Main Office (RSHA) in covering up the truth of Auschwitz, and stress the desperation of Jews who sought refuge in the woods or accepted baptism to escape deportation. Hilberg explains that it was preferable to convert to Protestant Christianity because Catholics did not take baptism lightly. His discussion of Terezín is adequate, as is his assessment of Heydrich. But with Aryanization of the Petschek coal fields and banks mentioned in one place (61–72 passim), deportees from Prague mentioned elsewhere (177–78, 295–96), gaps on Lidice and the Europa Plan, and brief mention of postwar restitution, *The Destruction of the European Jews* is a good example of how the reader must labor to piece together a comprehensive picture of developments in Czechoslovakia.

Three celebrated texts simply are inadequate. Yehuda Bauer's *A History of the Holocaust* scatters references to Czechoslovakia through discussions of prewar diplomacy, then touches briefly upon Terezín and the rescue efforts of Gisi Fleischmann and Rabbi Weissmandel (309–12). Martin Gilbert's *The Holocaust*, not so much a text as a collection of survivors' reminiscences, is even more sporadic, offering glimpses of the Czech Family Camp at Auschwitz and negotiations for the rescue of Danish Jews, but little insight into the workings of the Hlinka Guard, Tiso, or the Europa Plan. Lucy Dawidowicz's *The War Against the Jews, 1933–1945*, dismisses the saga of Czech Jewry in a four-page synopsis (375–79) that is accurate, but overbrief.

In every way, the best text on this subject is Nora Levin's *The Holocaust*. It, too, requires perseverance on the part of the reader because of disconnected references to Czech Jews. The impact of Munich is cited (118–22), along with the restructuring of Czech society under Nazism (190–93). But Levin's substantial discussion of Jews in Slovakia (527–47) is as complete as Hilberg's. (A major plus is reference to the Salzburg Conference of July 1940.) Her treatment of negotiations between Kurt Becher and the Joint Distribution Committee in Geneva equals Poliakov's study of the Europa Plan, and her discussion of the operations of Terezín, its cultural resistance, and the end of the Family Camp surpasses those of all the other major scholars.

## THE SOCIETY FOR THE HISTORY OF CZECHOSLOVAK JEWS

Unfortunately for researchers, there is no definitive history of Czechoslovakia's Jews on the order of Jacob Presser's monumental study of Dutch Jewry or Randolph Braham's of Hungarian Jewry. A short, random list including Hana Demetz's *The House on Prague Street*, Emil Knieza's "The Resistance of Slovak Jews," in Yuri Suhl, ed., *They Fought Back*, Gerhard Jacoby's *The Common*

*Fate of Czech and Jew: Czechoslovak Jewry Past and Future*, Sheila Duff Grant's *A German Protectorate: The Czechs Under Nazi Rule*, the many oral histories preserved by the Hebrew University in Jerusalem under the title of "The Holocaust Resistance and Rescue" (Glen Rock, New Jersey, Microfilming, 1975), and the Beit Terezín Archives in Israel (Yad Vashem, 1983) demonstrates the complexities and diverse experiences of Jews in this troubled land. Those seeking information on the Pracovná Skupina (the so-called Working Group of Rabbi Weissmandel and Gisi Fleischmann) may consult Joan Campion, *In the Lion's Mouth: Gisi Fleischmann and the Jewish Fight for Survival*; Rabbi Michael Weissmandel, *Min Hameitzar* (From the depths) (New York: Emunah Press, 1960); and contrasting essays by Livia Rothkirchen, David Kranzler, and Samuel Merlin in *American Jewry During the Holocaust*, edited by Arthur Goldberg and Seymour Finger (New York: American Jewish Commission on the Holocaust, 1984).

Probably the best, most comprehensive work available in English is *The Jews of Czechoslovakia: Historical Studies and Surveys*. The product of twenty-five years of labor by the New York–based Society for the History of Czechoslovak Jews, *The Jews of Czechoslovakia* is a three-volume compendium of essays by scholars on three continents. As such, it suffers by comparison with studies developed by a single author. The latter normally possesses several advantages: clarity of style, coherence, and a sense of purpose and direction. Although onetime Czech and Israeli diplomat Avigdor Dagan (born Viktor Fischl) acted as editor-in-chief and even contributed essays, the scholarship and writing in *The Jews of Czechoslovakia* is somewhat uneven.

The first two volumes supply basic understanding of the development of Jewish economic and political freedom in the different regions of Czechoslovakia from the beginning of the nineteenth century. Joseph Pick's essay on the impact of Jews in everything from banking and mining to health spas and sugar production is especially enlightening. Some material (reference to cultural giants Franz Kafka, Franz Werfel, Gustav Mahler, and Karel Ancerl; Jewish community organization; assistance toward prewar refugees) is familiar. Other essays, like the two that focus upon the Czech-Jewish movement and the Zionists, have been amplified in Hillel Kieval's *The Making of Czech Jewry: National Conflict and Jewish Society in Bohemia, 1870–1918* and Kieval's seminal essay in *The Precious Legacy: Judaic Treasures from the Czechoslovak State Collection*, edited by David Altshuler.

Volume three is the one that will be of particular interest to students of the *Shoah*. Divided into sections ("Holocaust," "Resistance," "The Aftermath"), this volume evinces the problem of working with more than one author. This is not to criticize the choice of contributors. Haifa's Yeshayahu Jelinek, author of the essay on Jews in postwar Slovakia, has written an excellent book on Hlinka's Slovak People's party (*The Parish Republic*). Hana Volavkova, author of "The Jewish Museum of Prague," was also editor of the heart-wrenching *I Never Saw*

*Another Butterfly*. Erich Kulka, a survivor of Dachau, Neuengamme, and Auschwitz, has published *The Death Factory* and *Jews in Svoboda's Army in the Soviet Union* (Tel Aviv, 1977).

For the sake of continuity and completeness, a book by any one of these authors or Yad Vashem's resident Czech authority Livia Rothkirchen (who contributed the opening essay on Jews in Bohemia and Moravia between 1938 and 1945 and whose *Khurban Ya'hadut Slovakia* [The destruction of the Jews of Slovakia] remains to be translated into English) would have been preferable. Some of the papers, frankly, are not very good. John Lexa's cursory listing of anti-Jewish laws in the protectorate (75–103) repeats what already has been said by Professor Rothkirchen. Zdenek Lederer's assessment of Terezín (104–64) suffers by comparison with his own much more substantial volume dealing with Heydrich's Paradise Ghetto. In like manner, Ehud Avriel's brief exposition of postwar relations between Israel and Czechoslovakia offers no improvement over Peter Meyer's substantial essay in *The Jews in the Soviet Satellites*.

Three of the essays are especially noteworthy: Rothkirchen's, Ladislav Lipscher's "Jews of Slovakia, 1939–1945," and Erich Kulka's "The Annihilation of Czechoslovak Jewry." Rothkirchen has written extensively on various aspects of the Holocaust ("The Czechoslovak Government in Exile: Jewish and Palestinian Aspects in the Light of Documents," *Yad Vashem Studies* 9 [1973]: 157–99; "Czech Attitudes Toward the Jews During the Nazi Regime," *Yad Vashem Studies* 13 [1979]: 287–320; "The Defiant Jew: Jews and the Czech 'Inside Front' (1938–1942)," *Yad Vashem Studies* 14 [1981]:35–88). Here she focuses primarily upon the first few years of the Nazi occupation, noting the confusion and distress common to all of Europe's Jews once they were confronted with a Nazi occupation force. She notes sadly that thousands of Czechs subscribed to the Fascist Vlajka organization. But she also points out that the majority of Czechs "remained decent." As evidence, Rothkirchen cites university students who demonstrated against the first anti-Semitic actions; Prague's ailing Cardinal Karel Kaspar, who issued a pastoral letter denouncing Jew-baiting in 1939; and BBC broadcasts made by Jan Masaryk and Jan Stransky urging assistance to Jews as "the most wretched of the wretched."[14] Rothkirchen reserves her strongest commendation for Jewish communal leaders and organizations who attempted to cushion the suffering of their people. When Jewish refugees fled Germany after 1933, they were aided by social worker Marie Schmolka and Hanna Steiner of the WIZO. After Munich the Joint, ICA, and HIAS-HICEM tried in vain to assist congregational leaders from Dr. Emil Kafka to Dr. Frantisek Friedmann. During the terrible days of deportation, sixteen-year-old Heinz Prossnitz and his *Hechalutz* tried to buoy the spirits of the doomed.

If there is a criticism of Rothkirchen, it is that she does not pursue the matter of Nazi genocide in detail. That she leaves to Erich Kulka. At first glance, his essay seems to stray aimlessly from Czech Jews sent to Hungary in forced-labor battalions after the cessions of October 1938 to escapes from death trains leaving Slovakia in 1944. There is, however, a thread weaving through all of this. What happened to Czech Jewry is a microcosm for the entire Holocaust. The first four thousand Jews involved in the *Umsichtung* (removal of Jews from Austria and the protectorate to Nisko) were Czechs. When that so-called agricultural reservation proved a failure, the Nazis forced Jews into ghettos. Five thousand Czech Jews were sent to Lodz. A few survived the war as part of Hans Biebow's privileged corps of munitions workers. Czech Jews were killed in Minsk when the Nazis experimented with *dusegubky* (soul destroyers, vans whose exhaust pipes were connected to rear compartments). Others were murdered in the woods of Riga, Izbica, Lublin and the camps of Belzec, Chelmno, and Treblinka. Kulka describes how Jews were deceived by Eichmann before the "Czech Family Camp" at Auschwitz was eliminated in March 1944. With incredible forbearance he relates how the perpetrators—SS Sturmbannführer Fritz Lange, commander of the security police in Lithuania, SS Sturmbannführer Erwin Mere and his deputy Adolf Viks, responsible for murdering thousands at Kalegi-Liiva, Estonia, and SS Oberst Eduard Strauch, commander of the security police in Minsk— eluded punishment.

Kulka devotes separate segments of his essay to the fate of Czech Jews in Hungary (315–19) and Slovakia (302–15), but it is left to Ladislav Lipscher, author of *Die Juden im slowakischen Staat, 1939–1945*, to fully develop this subject. Like Rothkirchen, Lipscher describes the stunned reaction of Slovakian Jews to the onset of anti-Semitic legislation. Divided ideologically among Zionists and Orthodox, the Jews in the east were stripped of possessions, then deported. The few exceptions were the few thousand converts who became the object of protests by Catholic bishops and the papal nuncio. Lipscher discusses the roles of "moderate" opposition in the government, the Working Group, the Zionist Hashomer Hatzair, and even Palestinian Jews led by Haviva Reik (232), who parachuted into Slovakia to spark the uprising of August 1944. Most important, he asks crucial questions: How could a Christian state headed by a priest implement such policies? Why did Tiso, who had some influence with Himmler and Hitler, never intervene on behalf of the Jews? To those who defend Tiso by saying that he acted *ad majora mala vitanda* (to avoid greater evil), Lipscher offers the public statement of the bigot priest in August 1942: "In deporting Jews we have simply acted in accordance with the command of God: Slovak, get rid of your enemy!"[15]

Avigdor Dagan and his assistants Gertrude Hirschler and Lewis Weiner have put together a work that is meticulously annotated (even in those essays that offer little substance). There are extensive bibliographies, photographs, and lists of American congregations holding Torah scrolls from Czech synagogues. With all its intrinsic literary faults, *The Jews of Czechoslovakia* is an indispensable study of the Holocaust in Bohemia and Slovakia.

## TEREZÍN

Many people equate the saga of Czech Jewry during the Holocaust with what happened in Theresienstadt. The amount of literature available on Heydrich's

Potemkin village is astounding. Already in 1946, David Cohen had published *The Russians in Terezin*: Jacob Jacobson, *Terezin: The Daily Life, 1943–45*; and Rabbi Max Friediger of Copenhagen, *Theresienstadt* (London and Copenhagen: Clausen). There were also volumes in Czech (Mirko Toma's *Ghetto našich dnů* [the Ghetto of our time] [Prague, 1946]; Anna Aurednickova's *Tři léta v Terezíně* [Three Years in Terezin] [Prague, 1946]) and German (poetry compiled by Else Dormitzer in *Theresienstädter Bilder* [Hilversum: De Boekenvriend, 1945]; and Gerty Spies's *Theresienstadt* [Munich: Freitag Verlag, 1946]). Over the next four decades writers on three continents would be transfixed by what happened in this fortress town. There would be more reminiscences and panegyrics like Rabbi Richard Feder, *Židovská tragedie—dějství poslední* (The Jewish tragedy: the final act) (Kolin: Lusk, 1947); Karel Lagus and Josef Polák, *Město za mřížemi* (City behind bars) (Prague: Nase vojsko, 1964); Kathe Starke's excellent *Der Führer schenkt den Juden eine Stadt*; B. Čurda Lipovsky, *Terezínské katakomby* (Prague: Dielnicke nakladatelstvi, 1946); Inge Auerbacher, *I Am a Star-Child of the Holocaust* (Englewood Cliffs, N.J.: Prentice-Hall, 1968); and Ruth Bondy, *Edelshtain neged ha-zeman* (Edelstein against time) (Tel Aviv, 1981). There would be novels like Josef Bor's *Opuštěná panenka* (The deserted doll) (Prague: SNPL, 1961) and *The Terezín Requiem* (London: Heinemann, 1963); M. Jacot's *The Last Butterfly* (New York, 1974); Arnost Lustig's celebrated *Night and Hope* (Washington, D.C.: Inscape, 1978); and Ralph Oppenheim's *The Door of Death: Theresienstadt Diary* (London, 1948). There would also be quasi-official reports and compendiums like Jirmejahu Oskar Neumann's *Im Schatten des Todes: Ein Tatsachenbericht vom Schicksalskampf des Slovakischen Judentums* (In the shadow of death: A factual report of the fateful struggle of Slovak Jewry) (Tel Aviv: Olamenu, 1956); onetime Judenältester Benjamin Murmelstein's apologetic *Terezin, il ghetto modello di Eichmann* (Milan, 1961); Frantisek Ehrmann, Otta Heitlinger, and Rudolf Iltis's *Terezín* (Prague: Council of the Jewish Communities in the Czech Lands, 1965); and T. Kulisova and O. Tyl's *Terezín: Malá pevnost-ghetto* (Terezín: The little fortress ghetto) (Prague, 1960).

Some of the most powerful and moving works have been collections of art done by the prisoners of Terezín themselves. One example is *The Book of Alfred Kantor*, a volume that can only be termed brilliant. The author-artist was sent from Prague to Terezín as part of the early *Aufbaukommando* in December 1941. Kantor survived Auschwitz and the forced-labor camp of Schwarzheide outside Dresden. Upon liberation, in a displaced persons' camp at Deggendorf, Bavaria, he set down what he had seen. In simple watercolors he portrayed the incredible crowding of multitiered bunks that housed entire families in the ghetto. In both Terezín and Auschwitz old people and eighteen-year-olds, who aged instantly, stood begging for more soup from giant vats that fed the inmates. Horse-drawn carts laden with coffins trundled to the crematoria while jazz bands played in Terezín's attics. Nazi film crews recorded Terezín's embellishment for the sake of the Red Cross, but not the stacks of bodies Kantor showed being extracted from gas chambers nor Kantor's eternal light—the flame that burned day and night over the barracks in Auschwitz.

Kantor was one of a group of talented artists that had worked for the Ältestenrat in Terezin, making signs. The chief draftsman was Bedrich Fritta (Taussig), whose son Tomy was the first Jewish child born in the Terezín ghetto. Others were Norbert Troller, a young architect from Brno; a dermatologist, Dr. Karel Fleischmann; a modern artist, Petr Kien; Leo Haas, a cartoonist who subsequently was assigned the task of forging British pound sterling plates; and Otto Unger, whose last effort in Buchenwald was to try to record the misery about him on a piece of paper with a lump of coal. Unger's hands had been crushed by the Nazis because he and his comrades had tried to tell the world the reality of Terezín. Lacking cameras, they sketched the naked, the insane, and the starving workers marching out to do roadwork, their swollen eyes exaggerated by their cheekbones. The stacks of coffins and filthy, crowded barracks were drawn in black and white. But just as with Kantor's postwar watercolors, the illustrations exuded despair. Little wonder that the artists were tortured, then deported when Eichmann uncovered their scheme to inform the world in 1943.

Their story has been told twice by Gerald Green, author of *The Last Angry Man*. In 1969 Green published *The Artists of Terezin*, a superb, easily read collection of sketches and minibiographies. Nine years later Green scripted the NBC docudrama "Holocaust: The Story of the Family Weiss." This program, which incorporated substantial elements of the suffering of Terezín's artists, ran over four nights. Despite criticism of theatrics and unhistorical gaffes, Green's program, which is available on videocassette, probably did more to increase popular understanding of the Holocaust in America than all the documentaries on the Holocaust lumped together.[16] It also served to shake up several European nations. Following its broadcast in West Germany, the Reichstag debated and approved an end to the statute of limitations on war crimes.

Even more compelling than Green's work on the artists is the eighty-two-page collection of children's drawings and poems edited by Hana Volavkova titled *I Never Saw Another Butterfly*. Containing only a portion of the busywork and personal moments of Terezín's children, this may be the single most moving book of the Holocaust. Its language ("I'd like to go away alone, where there are other, nicer people, somewhere into the far unknown, there where no one kills another") is comprehensible to those of all ages. The drawings of people standing in line for potatoes, imagined butterflies, and especially five-year-old Jana Hellerova's smiling girl are all heartrending. Students have come to me in tears after reading *I Never Saw Another Butterfly*. But the pedagogic value derived is greater than the grief. *Yom ha-Shoah* programs have been based on the poetry of the Terezín children. Israeli children were encouraged to express their own reactions to war in 1967 and 1982 through art and poetry. An award-winning documentary on a Mengele twin, "Susan," has been told through the innocent drawings of American schoolchildren. A black second-grade schoolteacher in the inner city of Youngstown has constructed a five-day teaching unit on racism using this extraordinary book.[17]

The teachers who supplied lined paper, paints, and scissors to the children were part of the Jugendfürsorge headed up by Egon "Gonda" Redlich. The twenty-six-year-old Redlich came from Olmouc, where he had been a leader of the Zionist Maccabi Hatzair. Deported to Terezín in December 1941, he is remembered as the extraordinary individual responsible for giving three or four hours of instruction daily to children in Barracks L 218, 216, 318, 410, 414, or 417 who spoke German, Dutch, Czech, or Hebrew. When the Nazis ordered the suspension of formal education except songs and games, Redlich posted older students at the entry of each barrack to sound a warning if the SS approached. Redlich clamored for better housing, fuel, and food for his charges and was successful at first in preventing the deportation of children under the age of twelve.

Redlich recorded what he observed in a diary spanning nearly three years in the ghetto. Recovered from an attic in Terezín after the war, the entries are in Redlich's improving Hebrew on all days but Saturday (when, out of religious deference, he jotted his thoughts in Czech). A Hebrew version of the diary, edited by Ruth Bondy, was issued by Yad Vashem in Israel in 1982. An English version translated by Dr. Laurence Kutler and edited by this author was published in December 1992 by the University of Kentucky.

Redlich was conscious of the great issues unfolding during the war and took note of ghetto reaction to the Madagascar scheme, the assassination of Heydrich, the Nazi setback at Stalingrad, and the Allied landings in North Africa, Sicily, and Normandy. He also had no illusions about the Nazis' true intentions in Terezín. "It seems to me," he wrote, "that we will never have any peace. This apparently is the goal of the ghetto: to sap the powers of the youth, to kill the aged." As people raced about in confusion seeking exemptions from transports, Redlich noted: "Every man is a special case and there aren't enough people to send with the transports. A transport of elderly will go. Father, mother, a grandfather of people who have worked here for months. This is the reward—a ghetto in Poland. Judgment is death."

As a member of the Jewish administration, Redlich was forced to participate in the selection of deportees, and he agonized over his role:

*January 12, 1942.* My mood was pretty bad today. Being chosen to decide the fate of others is a difficult chore. It is difficult because everything depends on chance. Good news causes joy—only one transport will go. I am very tired. I am not able to exempt children.

*March 7.* The transports to Poland, the exemptions are a terrible business. Responsibility. Who has the right to free someone else from the transports or the authority to exempt the youth? The elderly? There is no answer.

*May 19.* I want to write a play on the following subject: the problems of a man who is nominated against his will for a job unfit for his personality. He reaches a point where he is forced to do something which is against his basic beliefs, one objective of which is to save some people. Others think he has abandoned his conscience and speak harshly against him and his only son opposes him. Nevertheless, the man remains resolute.

Redlich's diary is filled with touching vignettes testifying that human decency had not disappeared from the ghetto. He wrote, for example: "In the attics, a blind woman sits for many hours, without help. A small child, ten years old, helps her. A spectacle not to be believed." He told of funerals, where lines of men worked steadily and with reverence with flickering lights in the rain. He refused to cut the rations of children when someone made off with or lost margarine designated for the children's barracks. Repeatedly in his journal he paid homage to the woman who was his love, Gerta "Beczulka" Beck. It is almost embarrassing to read of his courtship, his shame over a momentary dalliance, and the risk these two young people took in marrying, then having a child in Terezín. With rare exceptions the Nazis had prohibited Jews from giving birth. In beginning a diary within a diary for his son Dan, Redlich attributed this miracle to the pity of the commandant's wife. We learn of Redlich's aspirations for his son, "for a better tomorrow, when life will be better, happier and more serene," when Jews may find refuge in their own land, Israel. "I hope that you will never have to face these degradations and insults," he wrote, "the weakness of a people on foreign soil, a people without a homeland." (Redlich's Zionist references were deleted in an early excerpt published in pre-Havel Czechoslovakia.) The last entry in Gonda Redlich's Terezín diary is dated September 6, 1944: "The families are separated in transports. On one transport, a father goes. On another a son, and on a third, the mother. Tomorrow we go, my son, we too. Hopefully, the time of our redemption is near."

Probably the most valuable (and accessible) source corroborating the diary of Gonda Redlich is Zdenek Lederer's *Ghetto Theresienstadt*. The author, a Terezín survivor, outlines the conversion of the fortress into a transit ghetto, taking the reader along with startled deportees as they arrive at the Bohusovice railway station. Lederer offers insight into the operations of the ghetto bureaucracy, describing how the Ältestenrat branched into legitimate subsidiaries, like Redlich's Youth Welfare bureau and the Labor and Cultural departments, and some whose functions were debatable, like the Jewish Police and the ghetto bank, with its worthless scrip. Jewish administrators were in the unenviable position of reconciling complaints of Czech, Austrian, and German Jews, each of whom thought themselves superior to others confined to the ghetto, nuns who were classed as Jews under Nazi racial laws, elderly Orthodox Jews upset by the noise of children, physicians lacking medicine, families separated into men's and women's barracks, *mischlings*, and assimilated Jews stunned by their sudden ostracism.

Most of all, the Ältestenrat had to yield before demands of SS commandants Seidl, Burger, and Rahm (all, coincidentally, Austrians) and their ruffian aides Rudolf Haindl, Hans Bergel, and the Czech gendarme Janetschek. The SS deliberately located its headquarters right in the middle of Terezín on the park green. In July 1943 millions of index cards from the Reich Security Main Office were transferred from Berlin to the Sudeten Barracks. With the war taking a turn for the worse in April 1944, these documents outlining tortures in dozens of different concentration camps were burned in Terezín's courtyards (92–93, 179). Earlier, in the summer of 1942, with 30 percent of the ghetto's population reporting ill, and 190 Jews dying daily, a confident Commandant Seidl had gloated, ''The clock ticks well'' (49).

Considering the overcrowding, the lack of sanitation, and epidemics, it is amazing that Terezín's death toll was not worse. Lederer describes how the Nazis allotted less than two square yards to each inhabitant, then swelled the ghetto's population to the point that a city the size of Prague would have held more than 22 million people (44–45). Water from Terezín's antiquated wells was rationed— four gallons per person per day, one-fifth the normal health standard. Lavatories barely functioned. Food consisted of black coffee, watery barley soup, and noodles or dumplings, less than eight hundred calories per day. In some of the children's barracks there was so little heat that milk stored in pots froze overnight. Small wonder that pneumonia, tuberculosis, scarlet fever, septicemia, typhoid, spotted typhus, diphtheria, dysentery, and cerebrospinal fever were endemic to Terezín (135–43).

Lederer notes how Terezín's Jews were constantly at the mercy of Nazi caprice. Originally intended as a home for the aged, the ghetto was periodically cleared of such people who could not work. Subsequently, able-bodied men and women were deported to prevent an armed uprising. Terezín's Jews were temporarily rewarded with better conditions when Hans Günther filmed the Red Cross tour of the ghetto in the summer of 1944 (119–21). They were punished on November 11, 1943, when Commandant Burger ordered everyone but the hospitalized to stand in a field from 7 AM until 11 PM and be recounted. Between two hundred and three hundred persons died during this infamous *Zählappell*.

Although not as detailed as essays by Oliva Pechova, Marie Rut Krizkova, Eva Sormova, or Milan Kuna in *Arts in Terezin, 1941–1945* or Joiza Karas in *Music in Terezin, 1941–1945*, Lederer does salute the work of artists, lecturers, doctors, and schoolteachers like Gonda Redlich who tried to maintain a semblance of cultural life and dignity (125–35). Just as Redlich's life ended with deportation, Lederer's book concludes with a long, dreary list of what happened to every transport out of Terezín (203–42). Whether to Riga, Zamosc, Rejowiece, or Lublin, the result was always the same. An early train, marked F, went to Minsk with 1,000 passengers. Eleven were liberated from Belsen. Another 1,000 Jews were placed aboard Transport Ab bound for Izbice. Three survived. Seven trains left for Maly Trostinec in September 1942. Of 12,000 Jews aboard, 5 lived. In October, 8,000 Jews left Paradise Ghetto for Treblinka. Two survived. That same month also marked the beginning of deportations of 50,000 people directly to Auschwitz.

One more book on Terezín must be mentioned: H. G. Adler's *Theresienstadt, 1941-1945: Das Antlitz einer Zwangsgemeinschaft: Geschichte, Soziologie, Psy-*

*chologie*. The most comprehensive study attempted on the fortress ghetto, this 802-page study has never been translated into English. Just as with Lederer, the reader will learn the history of Terezín, its transformation into a Jewish city at the direction of Heydrich, the amorphous makeup of the Ältestenrat, and the terrible overcrowding, disease, and death tolls. Adler's book is also highly informed with personal bias. Jewish leadership is scored for its "dictatorial authority, answerable for everything to the SS" (249). Where virtually every survivor praised Terezín's first Judenältester, Jacob Edelstein, Adler lacerates his successor, Dr. Paul Eppstein, as a theatrical, conceited poseur (116). While Lederer noted how the Nazis punished Jews who violated smoking and postal bans, Adler shows how as late as 1945 one of the Jewish judges in the ghetto was suggesting the deportation of people who stole bread (456).

Adler directs a great deal of criticism toward the *Jugendfürsorge* of Gonda Redlich. On the one hand, he writes that the children were suffering from neglect, discipline was shattered, "the rule of the horde" prevailed, schooling was "miserable" (558–59), and much of the problem stemmed from Redlich himself, a "dictatorial Zionist" who he claims was *ehrgeizig und eitel* (ambitious and conceited) (548). Leaving aside for one moment Adler's brutal assessment of Redlich, it is difficult to justify such statements. Adler concedes that in the ghetto families were destroyed. For children who received less than one-half the meat ration allotted to a heavy laborer or member of the Ältestenrat (344–47), "the future could only be a distant hope" (559). Many of the children were sick and cold, lacking pencil and paper. Yet Adler relates how they continued to study mathematics, geography, history, and physics (553). Children who spoke German and Czech were trained to speak Hebrew (567). They collected buttons, money, razor-blade wrappers, and pennants. Each children's barrack had its own soccer team, its own uniform, pennant, and anthem (553–57). Some even organized into *Jugendhilft*, volunteers who would bring meals up several flights of stairs to the aged (570).

Much of Adler's criticism, then, is too harsh. But some observations are offered in the detached language of a trained psychologist, which was Adler's profession. Some of his barbs are on target, others not. The number of attempted and successful suicides in Terezín—2 in 1941, 264 in 1942, 164 in 1943, 50 in 1944—is simply marked down as "psychologically interesting" (316). Adler offers accurate accounts for the ebb and flow of ghetto residents, including clinical descriptions of every disease treated in makeshift hospitals (565). He tells of the anxieties and mistrust among fifty men stuffed into a single room (330) and adds that the isolation and degradation of Jews was a device employed by Jew haters, justified by "scientific theories" (299). The old became irritable and the young shouted jokes and left pornographic inscriptions in filthy latrines that barely functioned (331). Adler was outraged by the actions of a small circle of "bums" that stole food parcels from the postal service and held a "scandalous" 1943 New Year's party (128). He was equally disturbed by Jews lumped together who could not renounce national antagonisms. Dutch Jewish refugees were ridiculed as indolent, Czechs as elitists, Germans as too pedantic (306). Overall, Adler's volume is an invaluable tool that may be used with caution in reconstructing events in Terezín.

## GENERAL HISTORIES

Czechs and Slovaks may share the same language, even the same territory, but as was the case in another post-Versailles state (Yugoslavia, composed of Serbs, Croatians, and Slovenes), they have no historic affection for one another. Much of this anger and frustration may be attributed to the manipulative policies of the dual monarchy that ruled the land for five hundred years. For a basic understanding of the problem, consult Henry Wickham Steed, *The Hapsburg Monarchy* (New York: Scribner's, 1913); Oscar Jaszi, *The Dissolution of the Habsburg Monarchy* (Chicago: University of Chicago Press, 1929); A. J. P. Taylor, *The Habsburg Monarchy, 1809–1918* (London: Hamilton, 1948); and several volumes by Robert Kann, including *The Multinational Empire* (New York: Columbia University Press, 1950), *The Habsburg Empire: A Study in Integration and Disintegration* (New York: Praeger, 1957), and *A History of the Habsburg Empire* (Berkeley: University of California Press, 1974).

The number of works dealing with the foundation of the Czech republic is substantial. On the eve of Hitler's rise to power, Ferdinand Peroutka's *Jací jsme?* (The way we are) (Prague: Borovy, 1934), Emanuel Chalupňy's *Nadoni filsofie československá* (Prague, 1932), Jaroslav Papousek's *The Czech Nation's Struggle for Independence* (Prague: Orbis, 1928), and Josef Borovicka's *Ten Years of Czechoslovak Politics* (Prague: Orbis, 1929) stressed the Western, humanitarian values of the emerging nation. Valuable recent studies include Dagmar Perman's *The Shaping of the Czechoslovak State* and Věra Olivona's *The Doomed Democracy*.

Three works are markedly superior: R. W. Seton-Watson's *A History of the Czechs and Slovaks* (Hamden, Conn.: Archon Books, 1965, reprint of 1943 Hutchinson edition); Josef Korbel's *Twentieth-Century Czechoslovakia: The Meaning of Its History* (New York: Columbia University Press, 1977); and *A History of the Czechoslovak Republic* by Victor Mamatey and Radomír Luža. All are meticulously documented, offering insights into crucial moments of Czech history. Seton-Watson, professor of Central European history at the University of London, quips about the ''Anabasis'' of the Czech Legion at the end of World War I. He discusses the question of Teschen, the rich coal district in north central Bohemia of which Wilson and Lloyd-George were blithely ignorant and explains the miraculous compromise at Petka where five democratic parties came together to make the Czech National Assembly workable for nearly two decades. As a supplement to forty pages that are devoted to Munich, Seton-Watson tells how he and British government leaders were duped by promises made by the ''Trojan Horse,'' Konrad Henlein (393–94). Korbel, a former Czech diplomat who became Andrew Mellon Professor of International Studies at the University of

Denver, is less polite. Fascist supporters of Gen. Rudolf Gajda, Andrei Hlinka, or the Communists are marked down as "pathological scum" (74–78). As for "the shame of Munich," Korbel concludes that the British and French bear primary responsibility. Drawing upon hitherto-unpublished memoranda, Korbel quotes Czech Chief of Staff Ludvik Krejci and three additional military commanders who urged President Beneš to resist. Korbel concludes: "The Munich dictate should have been rejected, no matter what the consequences" (148).

Munich seems to be the decisive, most traumatic moment in modern Czech history. More than the Soviet takeover in 1948 or the return of Russian tanks in the summer of 1968, historians continue to wrestle with the possibilities of late September 1938. Among the contemporary volumes on the subject of appeasement were Shiela Grant Duff, *Europe and the Czechs* (London: Penguin, 1939); George R. Gedye, *Fallen Bastions* (London: V. Gollancz, 1939); Maurice Hindus, *We Shall Live Again* (New York: Doubleday, Doran, 1939); Hubert Ripka, *Munich and After* (London: V. Gollancz, 1939); Alexander Werth, *France and Munich* (London: Hamilton, 1939); and several books by R. W. Seton-Watson, including *From Munich to Danzig* (London: Methuen, 1939) and *Munich and the Dictators* (London: Methuen, 1939). More recent scholarship includes Vaclav Kral, ed., *Die Deutschen in der Tschechoslowakei, 1933–1947* (Prague: Nakl. Ceskoslovenske akademie, 1964); R. D. G. Laffan, "The Crisis over Czechoslovakia, January to September, 1938," *Survey of International Affairs 1938*, vol. 2 (London, 1951); L. B. Namier, *Diplomatic Prelude, 1938–1939* (London: Macmillan 1948); Keith Eubank, *Munich* (Norman: University of Oklahoma Press, 1963); Jurgen Gehl, *Austria, Germany, and the Anschluss, 1931–1938* (London, 1963); Martin Gilbert and Richard Gott, *The Appeasers* (London: Weidenfeld and Nicolson, 1963); and Ronald Smelser, *The Sudeten Problem*.

I am especially impressed with J. W. Bruegel's *Czechoslovakia Before Munich: The German Minority Problem and British Appeasement Policy*. Articulate and readable, this fine study draws upon official documents from seven countries. Bruegel gives no credit to Henlein, a "comparatively primitive political confidence trickster" (xi), for the Munich catastrophe. Rather, it is clear throughout the book that Czechs as well as the Western democracies were guilty of naivete, believing that words would mean the same to their enemies as to themselves. Bruegel asks whether the old Austro-Hungarian Empire could ever have been viable and sadly concludes no. His admiration for the rapport achieved by Weimar Foreign Minister Gustav Stresemann and Eduard Beneš is apparent, as is his disapproval toward Czech leaders who failed to proclaim a nation-state in 1920, leaving the impression that Czechoslovakia was "a state of nationalities" (61).

## THE NAZI OCCUPATION AND CZECH RESISTANCE

Historians have not been particularly impressed with the behavior of Czechs under Nazi rule. Henri Michel's classic study, *The Shadow War: Resistance in*

*Europe, 1939–1945*, translated by Richard Barry (London: Andre Deutsch, 1972), makes passing reference to clandestine contacts with the British and the UVOD (the Slovakian underground), but dismisses Czech national defense as inept. Jorgen Haestrup's *European Resistance Movements, 1939–1945: A Complete History* (Westport, Conn.: Meckler, 1981) offers little more, barely six pages that note more failures (no formal alliance with the British, no military guarantees, few Free Czech troops, suppression of the Slovak uprising) than successes.

Perhaps most critical is the onetime doctoral dissertation of Vojtech Mastny that evolved into *The Czechs Under Nazi Rule: The Failure of National Resistance, 1939–1942*. Part of a select series of East Central European Studies, Mastny's work is highly critical of President Beneš (marked down as a vain man, obsessed with the urge to erase the consequences of Munich, 141–45). *The Czechs Under Nazi Rule* will not make pleasant reading for those who try to rationalize the difficult circumstances of that period. Mastny details the role of various political factions, in particular the Fascist NSM (National Solidarity Movement), ANO (Action for National Renaissance), and arch-Quisling Emanuel Moravec. In a lengthy chapter titled "Heydrich and Heydrichiada," he tells how in November 1941 the Hacha cabinet reversed itself and called for obedience to the Reich. Over that winter, acts of sabotage virtually stopped, and the Czech population contributed warm clothing for Nazi troops on the eastern front (197–206). Mastny concludes that shortly before his assassination in May 1942, Heydrich was going to take another post in France because "the very stability of Bohemia and Moravia made the country especially suitable as the showplace of the New Order" (186, 203).

Several volumes are sympathetic to the problems faced by Slovak nationalists. Not very convincing, these include Eugen Steiner, *The Slovak Dilemma* (Cambridge, England: Cambridge University Press, 1973); Joseph Mikuš, *Slovakia, A Political History: 1918–1950*, translated by Kathryn Day Wyatt and Joseph Mikus (Milwaukee: Marquette University Press, 1963); Peter Brock, *The Slovak National Awakening* (Toronto: University of Toronto Press, 1976); and Gilbert Oddo, *Slovakia and Its People* (New York: Speller, 1960). For a more critical assessment, see Tomas Pasak, "Cesky antisemitismus na počatku okupacé" (Czech anti-Semitism at the beginning of the occupation), in *Vedá a život* (Life and science) (Brno), March 1969, pp. 147–51; F. Steiner, *Tragédia slovensky Židov* (The tragedy of Slovak Jewry) (Bratislava, 1949); Vaclav Kral, ed., *Lesson from History: Documents Concerning Nazi Policies for Germanization and Extermination* (Prague: Orbis, 1961); Detlef Brandes, *Die Tschechen unter deutschem Protektorat* (Munich and Vienna: Oldenbourg, 1969); J. W. Bruegel, *Tschechen und Deutsche, 1939–1946* (Munich, 1974); Ladislav Feierabend, *Ve vlade protektorátu* (In the government of the protectorate) (New York, 1962); George Kennan, *From Prague After Munich: Diplomatic Papers, 1938–1940* (Princeton, N.J.: Princeton University Press, 1968); and Gerhard Jacoby, *Racial State* (New York: Institute of Jewish Affairs, 1944).

## THE MAJOR FIGURES

Four men dominated the history of Czechoslovakia between 1918 and 1945. For a better understanding of what happened in this period, it is essential to review the lives of Thomas Masaryk, Eduard Beneš, Reinhard Heydrich, and Msgr. Josef Tiso.

Masaryk was the elderly history professor who symbolized the potential unity of Czechs and Slovaks (he was educated in a modernist Czech-German system; his father was a Slovak, his mother a Catholic). Married to an American woman, he was one of the few East Central European leaders truly committed to bringing a form of American democracy to his people during the interwar period. Venerable biographies of the man who served as Czechoslovakia's president until his death in September 1937 include Josef Pekař, *Masarykova česká filosofie* (Prague: Historický klub, 1927); H. W. Steed, *T. G. Masaryk: The Making of a State* (New York: Frederick Stokes, 1927); D. A. Lowrie, *Masaryk of Czechoslovakia* (London: Oxford University Press, 1937); Jan Herben, *Thomas T. G. Masaryk* (Prague: Sfinx, 1947); R. W. Seton-Watson, *Masaryk in England* (London: Cambridge University Press, 1943); W. Preston Warren, *Masaryk's Democracy* (London: Allen and Unwin, 1941); and Zdenek Nejedly, *T. G. Masaryk*, 4 vols. (Prague: Melantrich, 1930–37).

Zbyněk Zeman's *The Masaryks: The Making of Czechoslovakia* is a good, readable volume on Masaryk and his son Jan. Three-quarters of the book deals with the elder Masaryk, tracing his emergence from childhood in the rural village of Hodinin to sociologist and expert on suicide at the University of Prague. For Zeman, it is clear that Masaryk was anything but an ivory-tower academician. Once the professor examined the charges against Leopold Hilsner, a Jewish vagrant charged with ritual murder in Polna in 1899, he risked public ridicule while seeking justice (51–52). He was highly critical of the repression in tsarist Russia and was personally dismayed at the great expectations and modest achievements in human liberty of Tolstoy, Lenin, and Wilson (60, 94–99, 112). Zeman offers an excellent bibliographic essay on the "philosopher king," showing how Masaryk has been misrepresented by Western partisans as Lincolnesque and in Communist polemics as a reactionary schemer. In a touch of irony, Zeman quotes Karel Čapek, the famed Czech writer, who credited Masaryk with being clever in everything in his life, even the timing of his death (145).

Zeman's book is heavily indebted to Čapek, who published several editions of personal discussions with President Masaryk. The first, *President Masaryk Tells His Story* (New York: Putnam's, 1935), reads like an oral history. The two men met frequently at Masaryk's country house in Topolčanky. After dinner Masaryk would reminisce. Then Čapek would retire to write up the details of their conversation. In this way the reader learns of the early influences upon Masaryk: his mother and three brothers and the philosophers Plato, Goethe, and Lessing. Čapek's wonderful volume offers unique glimpses of Masaryk, the man, who confesses his timidity in public speaking (200) and his doubts of his own ability (asked what he was doing in 1900–1910, between his fiftieth and sixtieth years, he replied, "Well, really nothing" [199]). Masaryk emerges as an advocate of women's rights (134), an opponent of pan-Slavism (dismissed as "empty talk"), and a biblical socialist. "My socialism," he said, "is simply love of one's neighbour, of humanity. I want to abolish poverty and enable everyone to be able to live by his work and in his work; to give everyone enough elbow-room as the Americans say" (180). His fondness for America is repeatedly expressed—in statements about the frankness of the people, the freedom of workers, even the vision that adding Ruthenia to the Czechoslovak state would serve as "a territorial bridge to the coming democratic Russia or to the Ukraine" (277–80). Masaryk, the hero of the Hilsner case, explains how, as a boy, he was afraid of Jews. The Catholic catechism he was taught was permeated with Slovak mythology and witches, and he thought that Jews used Christian blood (28–29). As a university student, however, he concluded that "the whole of Europe is still living on antiquity and Judaism" (109).

In a follow-up volume, *Masaryk on Thought and Life: Conversations with Karel Capek*, translated by M. and R. Weatherall (New York: Macmillan, 1938), the Czech president expounded at length on his theories of epistemology, religion, Jesus, science and faith, and church and state. Declaring himself "a realist in philosophy and politics" (and not a positivist, as some claimed, 57), Masaryk took his inspiration from Jesus (80). Man's basic ethic should be love of one's neighbor (100). Having reviewed the history of his Czech people from the seventh century, he argued that the best form of government was a democracy, one based on reason, love, and tolerance (192). Tolerance must be courageous and consistent (131). Finally, love of one's nation should not preclude love of humanity (212–13).

Masaryk's successor, onetime Foreign Minister Eduard Beneš, delivered the funeral oration in September 1937. In this flowery address, *Masaryk's Path and Legacy* (Prague: Orbis, 1937; reprint, New York: Arno Press, 1971), Beneš invoked images of Hugo, Rousseau, Pushkin, Byron, Washington, and Montesquieu and demonstrated the gap in leadership that existed between the first two presidents of the Czech republic. Zeman sympathizes with Beneš, confronted in 1938 with a strident Hitler, but it seems to be the consensus of historians that Beneš was the wrong leader at the wrong time. In *President Eduard Beneš: Between East and West, 1938–1948* (Stanford: Hoover Institution Press, 1981), former Czech government official and University of Texas professor Edward Tobersky credits Beneš with realistic wartime dealings with both Stalin and FDR. The essential Beneš, however, was a man haunted by a "Munich complex." Beneš's own memoir, *From Munich to New War and New Victory*, translated by Godfrey Lias (New York: Arno Press, 1972), does little to alter the impression of a man fixated with guilt. Having worked to achieve territorial stability in Europe through the Locarno pact, Beneš points accusatory fingers at others for the dismemberment of Czechoslovakia—Marshal Pilsudski's Poland, which by virtue of a nonaggression pact with Germany signed in January 1934 made possible the attacks of 1938–39 (8), the Daladier government in France and in particular Foreign Minister Georges Bonnet (38), the appeasement-bound British, and the League of Nations Council that postponed hearings on what Beneš calls the "void" Munich accord until September 1939, by which time it was too late to help (63–72).

In passing, Beneš offers an old Czech proverb that a lie has short legs. Unfortunately, this, like many other adages, is debatable. History demonstrates that it has been practically impossible to dispel the blood libel, the Protocols of the Elders of Zion, charges of Jewish plutocracy, and other canards. What a people chooses to believe is practically as important as reality. Frustrated and angry, some Arabs, Ukrainians, Romanians, and American blacks deny that they harbor any racist sentiments. Simultaneously, they lionize notorious anti-Semites like Nasser, Simon Petlura, Nicolai Codreanu, and Louis Farrakhan. Not surprisingly, Slovak nationalists also promote self-delusions. Nowhere is this more evident than in the case of Msgr. Josef Tiso, the head of the Slovakian state. Researchers should be warned that there is no scholarly/critical biography of Tiso. They will be reading propaganda, not history, should they consult Francis Vnuk, *Dr. Josef Tiso, President of the Slovak Republic* (Sydney: Association of Australian Slovaks, 1967); Milan S. Durica, *Die Slowakische Politik 1938/ 39 im Lichte der Staatslehre Tisos* (Bonn: Emil Semmel Verlag, 1967); Francois d'Orcival, *Le Danube etait noir* (Paris: La Table Ronde, 1968); J. M. Kirschbaum, *Slovakia: Nation at the Crossroads of Central Europe* (New York: Speller, 1960); Charles Murin, "Eight Fatal Days in the Life of Dr. Joseph Tiso," *Slovakia* 7 (March 1957): 13–18; J. Zubek, "Monsignor Jozef Tiso: Controversial Personality," *Slovakia* 7 (March 1957): 1–8; and Milan Durica, "Dr. Jozef Tiso and the Jewish Problem in Slovakia," *Slovakia* 8 (September–December 1957): 1–22.

The single most disreputable collection of distortions may be found in volume 22, no. 45 (1972) of the Slovak League of America's journal *Slovakia*. From an E. L. Delaney ("I Met President Tiso") we learn that the Czechs conspired to keep all industry in their part of the country (23), that after 1939 "pernicious influences" in Washington denied free Slovakia recognition (21), and that the postwar "communist regime of Eduard Benes" destroyed Czech freedom (25). There are protests against the death penalty for Tiso uttered on the floor of the U.S. House of Representatives in March 1947 by congressmen from districts with substantial Slovak constituents. For the stolid, there is also J. M. Kirschbaum's incredible apologetic, "Dr. Joseph Tiso, The Prelate-Politician Who Died on the Gallows for His People" (5–20). According to Kirschbaum, Tiso was a Slovak "patriot," a man whose ideal was "true democracy . . . Christian democracy" (9). While he may have praised the Germans, Tiso did not subscribe to the goals or methods of national socialism (10). Kirschbaum fantasizes that his "Slovak Petain" made his land a haven for Jews from Poland. He concludes that Tiso "did his best and saved many thousands of Slovak Jews" (7).

After wading through such twaddle, it is almost refreshing to cite legitimate works that make no attempt to conceal the villainy of Reinhard Heydrich. In short form, these include Joachim Fest's twelve pages in *The Face of the Third*

*Reich*, where the man who aspired to be Hitler's successor is marked down as "an unhappy man"; Andre Brissaud's *Histoire du Service Secret Nazi*, translated by Milton Waldman (New York: Norton, 1974); Shlomo Aronson's *Reinhard Heydrich und die Frügeschichte von Gestapo und SD* (Stuttgart: Deutsche Ver-lags-Anstalt, 1971); Vojtech Mastny's previously cited *The Czechs Under Nazi Rule*; and Eleanor Wheeler's forty-one-page *Lidice* (Prague: Orbis, 1962). A number of books have been published in Prague on the subject of Heydrich's assassination. Highly recommended are Čestmir Amort, *Heydrichiáda* (Prague: Nase Vojsko, 1965); Miroslav Ivanov, *Not Only Black Uniforms* (Prague: Nase Vojsko, 1964); Dusan Hamsik and Jiri Prazak, *Bomba pro Heydricha* (Prague: Mlada Fronta, 1965); and Charles Wighton, *Heydrich, Hitler's Most Evil Hench-man* (London: Odhams 1962). Callum MacDonald's *The Killing of SS Ober-gruppenführer Reinhard Heydrich* is superior in depth, range of sources, and readability to Jan Wiener's *The Assassination of Heydrich* (New York: Grossman, 1969). The latter is a personal memoir of the war years by a Czech refugee and intelligence officer grafted awkwardly upon the story of Heydrich's murder and the shootout at the Karel Boromaeus Greek Orthodox Church afterward. Wiener identifies principals in the Czech underground ("Franta," the source of classified intelligence, was really German staff officer Paul Thummel, page 61), but sup-plies only tangential glimpses of Heydrich's background.

I believe that the best volume on Heydrich is Günther Deschner's *Reinhard Heydrich: A Biography*. Written by the onetime chief political correspondent for *Die Welt* in Bonn, this book has an impressive, polyglot array of sources. From the introduction, Deschner continuously reminds his reader of what Nazi leaders and other historians had to say about Heydrich. The chapter titled "The Alleged Jew" (60–68) offers a number of possible interpretations about Hey-drich's alleged Jewish ancestry, but ends inconclusively. Whether Heydrich's grandmother or grandfather was Jewish, Deschner makes the case that he was taunted as a child because of the rumor and grew up a seething, authoritarian personality. For Joachim Fest, he was the reincarnation of Saint-Just, devoted servant of the revolution. For Werner Best, Hitler's plenipotentiary in Denmark, he was Nietzsche's "blond beast" come to life. For Nazi leaders on trial for their lives at Nuremberg, he was the mastermind for everything evil. More humbly, before his death, Heydrich referred to himself as "the chief garbage collector" of the regime. Deschner allows that there is some truth to that. Heydrich may not have been the originator of Nazi murder schemes, but this "most demonic" of the Nazi leaders (289) was the architect.

## L'ENVOI

During one of his many conversations with Thomas Masaryk in 1935, Karel Čapek quoted the president on the destiny of Czechoslovakia:

We shall always be a small minority in the world, but, when a small nation accomplishes something with its limited means, what it achieves has an immense and exceptional value, like the widow's mite. . . . it is a great thing when a small nation among great ones does not get left behind, but takes its share in the work of bettering humanity. We too want to ring the bells of the world just as the villagers of Podvorov wanted to ring the bells of Cjekovice. This is the problem of small nations; we must do more than the others, and be very clever; and if anyone tries to get the better of us by force, we must not give in. Not to give in, that is the great thing![18]

One year later Čapek offered his own comments on the potential and vulnerability of small democracies. Čapek's *Valka s Mloky* (War with the Newts) (Prague: Borovy, 1936; translated by W. Francis and G. Johnston, New York: Bantam, 1959), is one of the great books of this century. A satire in the genre of Anatole France's *Penguin Island* or George Orwell's *Animal Farm*, *War with the Newts* outlines the rise to power of a race of giant salamanders whose appetite for land is insatiable. As one nation after another is gobbled up, European leaders congregate in the mountains at Vaduz, Lichtenstein, and proudly proclaim that it cannot happen to their countries. The end comes when a newt is spotted in the waters of the Vltava (Moldau) in Prague. With prescience, months before the death of Masaryk or the Munich Conference, Čapek was warning against appeasement and the betrayal of smaller states. His advice was not heeded. The result was fifty years of terror, black and red: the annihilation of tens of thousands of Czech Jews in the Holocaust, of hundreds of "Zionist" sympathizers imprisoned in the wake of the Slansky trial of 1948, and other atrocities, leaving the few survivors, like the old, frightened couple in Bratislava, wondering whether church bells in two fragile republics signal freedom or a return to medieval terror.

## NOTES

1. Personal letter to Dr. Leonard Spiegel, Youngstown, February 11, 1990.

2. See Jiri Dolezal and Evzen Vesely, *Pamatky prazskeho ghetta* (Prague: Olympia, 1969); and David Altshuler, ed., *The Precious Legacy: Judaic Treasures from the Czechoslovak State Collection* (New York: Summit Books, 1983).

3. *The Jewish Communities of Nazi-occupied Europe* (New York: Fertig, 1972 reprint of 1944 report of the Research Institute on Peace and Postwar Problems), p. 1.

4. See Lucy Dawidowicz, *The War Against the Jews, 1933 to 1945* (New York: Holt, Rinehart, and Winston, 1975), pp. 375–76; Jacob Lestchinsky, "Balance Sheet of Extermination, 1946," *Yad Vashem Bulletin* 10 (April 1961); Raul Hilberg, *The Destruction of the European Jews* (New York: Quadrangle, 1951), p. 670; and Gerald Reitlinger, *The Final Solution* (New York: Beechhurst, 1953), p. 492.

5. See Ezra Mendelsohn, *The Jews of East Central Europe Between the World Wars* (Bloomington: Indiana University Press, 1983), pp. 145–62.

6. *The Jewish Communities of Nazi-occupied Europe*, p. 4.

7. George Kennan, *From Prague after Munich: Diplomatic Papers, 1938–1940* (Princeton, N.I.: Princeton University Press, 1968).

8. Livia Rothkirchen, "The Jews in Bohemia and Moravia, 1938–1945," in *The Jews of Czechoslovakia*, ed. Avigdor Dagan (New York: Society for the History of Czechoslovak Jews, 1984), vol. 3, pp. 14–15. See also *American Jewish Yearbook, 1939–40*, pp. 269–70.

9. *Hachsharah* centers provided training in agriculture for those youngsters who planned to emigrate to Palestine.

10. Excerpts of this crucial pre-Wannsee report appear in Avigdor Dagan, Gertrude Hirschler, and Lewis Weiner, *The Jews of Czechoslovakia*, vol. 3, p. 31.

11. Saul Friedman, "The 'Paradise Ghetto' of Theresienstadt," in *The Holocaust: In Answer*, ed. Franklin Littell, Irene Shur, and Claude Foster, (West Chester, Penn.: Sylvan, 1988), pp. 82–83.

12. Erich Kulka, "The Annihilation of Czechoslovak Jewry," in *The Jews of Czechoslovakia*, vol. 3, pp. 296–99.

13. See Saul Friedman, "The Holocaust and Its Historiography: The Major Texts," in *The Handbook of American Jewish Literature*, ed. Lewis Fried (Westport, Conn.: Greenwood Press, 1988), pp. 441–70.

14. Rothkirchen, "Jews of Bohemia and Moravia," pp. 15–17.

15. Ladislav Lipscher, "Jews of Slovakia, 1939–1945," in *The Jews of Czechoslovakia*, vol. 3, p. 240.

16. Saul Friedman, "In Defense of the Television Program 'Holocaust,' " *Jewish Frontier*, August/September 1978, pp. 7–9.

17. Mary Earnhart, "Holocaust Teaching Unit," Youngstown State Workshop, June 1989.

18. Karel Čapek, ed., *President Masaryk Tells His Story* (New York: Putnam's, 1935), p. 67.

## SELECT BIBLIOGRAPHY

Adler, H. G. *Theresienstadt, 1941-1945: Das Antlitz einer Zwangsgemeinschaft: Geschichte, Soziologie, Psychologie.* Tübingen: Mohr, 1980.

Altshuler, David, ed. *The Precious Legacy: Judaic Treasures from the Czechoslovak State Collection.* New York: Summit Books, 1983.

Auerbacher, Inge. *I Am a Star-Child of the Holocaust.* Englewood Cliffs, N.J.: Prentice-Hall, 1968.

Bondy, Ruth. *Elder of the Jews: Jacob Edelstein of Theresienstadt.* New York: Grove Press, 1989.

Bor, Josef. *The Terezin Requiem.* London: Heinemann, 1963.

Bradley, John. *Lidice: Sacrificial Village.* New York: Ballantine, 1972.

Bruegel, J. W. *Czechoslovakia Before Munich: The German Minority Problem and British Appeasement Policy.* Cambridge, England: Cambridge University Press, 1973.

Campion, Joan. *In the Lion's Mouth: Gisi Fleischmann and the Jewish Fight for Survival.* Lanham, Md.: University Press of America, 1987.

Čapek, Karel. *Valka s Mloky* (War with the newts). Prague: Borovy, 1936. Translated by W. Francis and G. Johnston. New York: Bantam, 1959.

Curda-Lipovsky, B. *Terezinske Katakomby.* Prague: Dielnicke nakladatelstvi, 1946.

Dagan, Avigdor, editor in chief. *The Jews of Czechoslovakia: Historical Studies and Surveys.* 3 vols. New York: Society for the History of Czechoslovak Jews; Philadelphia: Jewish Publication Society of America, 1984.

Demetz, Hana. *The House on Prague Street*. New York: St. Martin's Press, 1980.

Deschner, Gunther. *Reinhard Heydrich: A Biography*. Translated by Sandra Bance, Brenda Woods, and David Ball. New York: Stein and Day, 1981.

Don, Yehuda and Victor Karady, eds. *Social and Economic History of Central European Jewry*. New Brunswick: Transaction, 1990.

Dormitzer, Else. *Theresienstädter Bilder*. Hilversum: De Boekenvriend, 1945.

Fest, Joachim. *The Face of the Third Reich*. Translated by Michael Bullock. New York: Pantheon, 1970.

Friedman, Saul S. "The 'Paradise Ghetto' of Theresienstadt." In *The Holocaust: In Answer*, edited by Franklin Littell, Irene Shur, and Claude Foster, pp. 79–101. West Chester, Penn.: Sylvan, 1988.

Glas-Larson, Margarete. *Ich Will Reden*. Edited by Gerhard Botz. Vienna: Verlag Fritz Molden, 1980.

Grant, Shiela Duff. *A German Protectorate: The Czechs Under Nazi Rule*. London: F. Cass, 1970.

Green, Gerald. *The Artists of Terezin*. New York: Hawthorn Books, 1969.

Hebrew University of Jerusalem and *New York Times*. Contemporary Jewry Oral History Collection. Pt. 2. World War II. The Holocaust: Resistance and Rescue. Glen Rock, N.J.: Microfilm Corporation of America, 1975.

Jacobson, Jacob. *Terezin: The Daily Life, 1943–45*. London: Jewish Central Information Office, 1946.

Jacoby, Gerhard. *The Common Fate of Czech and Jew: Czechoslovak Jewry Past and Future*. New York: Institute of Jewish Affairs, 1943.

————. *Racial State*. New York: Institute of Jewish Affairs, 1944.

Jelinek, Yeshayahu. *The Parish Republic: Hlinka's Slovak People's Party, 1939–1945*. New York: Columbia University Press, 1976.

*The Jewish Communities of Nazi-occupied Europe*. New York: Fertig, 1972 reprint of 1944 report of the Research Institute on Peace and Postwar Problems.

Kann, Robert. *A History of the Habsburg Empire*. Berkeley: University of California Press, 1974.

Kantor, Alfred. *The Book of Alfred Kantor*. New York: McGraw-Hill, 1971.

Karas, Joiza. *Music in Terezin, 1941–1945*. New York: Pendragon, 1975.

Kennan, George. *From Prague After Munich: Diplomatic Papers, 1938–1940*. Princeton, N.J.: Princeton University Press, 1968.

Kieval, Hillel. *The Making of Czech Jewry: National Conflict and Jewish Society in Bohemia, 1870–1918*. New York: Oxford University Press, 1988.

Knieza, Emil. "The Resistance of Slovak Jews." In *They Fought Back*, edited by Yuri Suhl. New York: Crown, 1967.

Korbel, Josef. *Twentieth-Century Czechoslovakia: The Meaning of Its History*. New York: Columbia University Press, 1977.

Kral, Vaclav, ed. *Lesson from History: Documents Concerning Nazi Policies for Germanisation and Extermination*. Prague: Orbis, 1961.

Kulisova, T., and O. Tyl. *Terezín: Malá pevnost-ghetto* (Terezin: The little fort ghetto). Prague, 1960.

Kulka, Erich. "The Annihilation of Czechoslovak Jewry." In *The Jews of Czechoslovakia*, edited by Avigdor Dagan, vol. 3 (1984), pp. 262–319.

Kulka, Erich, with Ota Kraus. *The Death Factory*. Oxford: Pergamon Press, 1966.

Lederer, Zdenek. *Ghetto Theresienstadt*. New York: Howard Fertig, 1953.

Lipscher, Ladislav. "The Jews of Slovakia, 1939–1945." In *The Jews of Czechoslovakia*, edited by Avigdor Dagan, vol. 3, pp. 165–239.

———. *Die Juden im slowakischen Staat, 1939–1945*. Munich and Vienna: Oldenbourg Verlag, 1980.

Lustig, Arnost. *Night and Hope*. Washington, D.C.: Inscape, 1978.

MacDonald, Callum. *The Killing of SS Obergruppenführer Reinhard Heydrich*. London: Odhams, 1962.

Mamatey, Victor and Radomír Luža. *A History of the Czechoslovak Republic, 1918–1948*. Princeton, N.J.: Princeton University Press, 1973.

Mannheimer, Max. *From Theresienstadt to Auschwitz*. London: Jewish Central Information Office, 1945.

Mastny, Vojtech. *The Czechs Under Nazi Rule: The Failure of National Resistance, 1939–1942*. New York and London: Columbia University Press, 1971.

Mendelsohn, Ezra. *The Jews of East Central Europe Between the World Wars*. Bloomington: Indiana University Press, 1983.

Meyer, Peter. "Czechoslovakia." In *The Jews in the Soviet Satellites*, pp. 49–206. Syracuse, N.Y.: Syracuse University Press, 1953.

Olivová, Vera. *The Doomed Democracy: Czechoslovakia in a Disrupted Europe, 1914–38*. London: Sidgwick & Jackson, 1972.

Pechova, Oliva, et al. *Arts in Terezin, 1941–1945*. Translated by Hana Kvicalova. Prague: Memorial Exhibition, 1973.

Perman, Dagmar. *The Shaping of the Czechoslovak State*. 2 vols. Leiden: Brill, 1962.

Redlich, Gonda. *The Terezin Diary of Gonda Redlich*. Edited by Saul S. Friedman. Lexington: University Press of Kentucky, 1992.

Rothkirchen, Livia. "Czech Attitudes Toward the Jews During the Nazi Regime." *Yad Vashem Studies* 13 (1979): 287–320.

———. "The Czechoslovak Government in Exile: Jewish and Palestinian Aspects in the Light of Documents." *Yad Vashem Studies* 9 (1973): 157–99.

———. "The Defiant Jew: Jews and the Czech 'Inside Front' (1938–1942)." *Yad Vashem Studies* 14 [1981]: 35–88.

———. "The Jews in Bohemia and Moravia, 1938–1945." In *The Jews of Czechoslovakia*, edited by Avigdor Dagan, vol. 3, pp. 3–52.

———. *Khurban Ya'hadut Slovakia*. Jerusalem: Yad Vashem, 1961.

Skilling, H. Gordon, ed. *Czechoslovakia, 1918–88: Seventy Years of Independence*. New York: St. Martin's Press, 1991.

Smelser, Ronald. *The Sudeten Problem, 1933–1938*. Middletown, Conn.: Wesleyan University Press, 1977.

Starke, Kathe. *Der Führer schenkt den Juden eine Stadt*. Berlin: Haude und Spener, 1975.

Troller, Norbert. *Theresienstadt: Hitler's Gift to the Jews*. Chapel Hill: University of North Carolina Press, 1991.

Volavkova, Hana, ed. *I Never Saw Another Butterfly*. Translated by Jeanne Nemcova. New York: McGraw-Hill, 1964.

Zeman, Zbyněk. *The Masaryks: The Making of Czechoslovakia*. New York: Barnes and Noble, 1976.

# Chapter 14

# The Ukrainian Halychyna Division: A Case Study of Historical Revisionism

## Sol Littman

Was there really a good Waffen-SS as opposed to the bad Waffen-SS condemned as a "criminal organization" by the Nuremberg Tribunal? Were the national Waffen-SS divisions recruited in Eastern Europe essentially different in motivation and training from the SS-Totenkopfverbände that staffed concentration camps and the Leibstandarte SS Adolph Hitler that was responsible for the slaughter of American troops at Malmédy? Were the Croatian, Latvian, Estonian, and Ukrainian *Ostlegionen* any less authentically Waffen-SS than their German counterparts?

Apologists for these Eastern recruits to Himmler's armies insist that they were markedly different, that they consisted of pure fighting men concerned only with regaining their country's independence and preserving Western civilization against the onslaught of Asiatic bolshevism. As such, they harbored no anti-Semitism, guarded no extermination camps, slaughtered no Jews, and committed no crimes against humanity.

An interesting case in point is the Fourteenth Volunteer Grenadier Waffen-SS Division (Galician no. 1) formed in early March 1943 and composed almost entirely of Ukrainians recruited in that part of the western Ukraine known as Galicia. Numerous books and articles by Ukrainian nationalist authors claim that "the Ukrainian Division 'Galicia' never took part in the extermination of Jews or in the suppression of the Warsaw Ghetto uprising. It was strictly a military, front line unit of the Waffen SS and never a concentration camp guard formation."[1]

Dr. Wasyl Verhya, a veteran of the Galician Division and author of several books and articles on its history, further suggests that the division was only incidentally an SS formation and that its placement in the ranks of Himmler's legions was a superficial matter of military nomenclature without ideological significance. He makes much of the fact that "unlike the other SS units, the Galicia would have its own chaplains to feed the spiritual needs of its soldiers" and its own emblem "consisting of a golden lion resting on its haunches with three crowns, one above its head and two beneath its haunches." These factors, Verhya holds, served as impregnable barriers to Nazi ideological indoctrination and the stigma of the swastika.[2]

Nationalist Ukrainian historians also insist that the members of the division cannot be classified as either traitors or collaborators since their chief motivation was "to serve as a nucleus for an independent national Ukrainian army able to resist Communist aggression" once the Germans had been defeated and the victorious Allies initiated a further conflict against an exhausted Soviet Union.[3] Defenders of the division also delight in quoting a 1947 British report prepared by D. Haldane Porter of the Refugee Screening Commission in which the British representative stated that in his view the Ukrainians who had enlisted in the division had done so "in the hope of securing a genuinely independent Ukraine" and that "they probably were not and certainly do not now seem to be at heart pro-German."[4]

On the other hand, Soviet sources have denounced the members of the division as traitors, cutthroats, and war criminals. A stream of Soviet pamphlets, most published by Dnipro Publishers in Kiev, have denounced the blue and gold banners of Ukrainian nationalism and have accused units of the division of having engaged in a variety of death-dealing activities while still in training. "On November 6, 1943, [SS-men from the Galician Division] helped shoot some 500 Jewish inmates in a forest near the village of Dobrucow. . . . Cadets of the Halychyna Division were involved in a similar action in the forest near Wawrzice."[5]

The division is further accused of assisting in the roundup of Ukrainian youth for service in German slave-labor camps and joining in the destruction of countless towns and villages. On orders of their German masters, Galician Waffen-SS troops attacked Polish villages, shot the men in the town square, and cruelly massacred the women and children by locking them in the church and then setting it on fire. From time to time, its accusers claim, the division was called upon to reinforce the guards at concentration camps in the areas in which they were stationed.

Ukrainian nationalist historians have denounced these accusations as "lies" and have condemned the booklets published by Dnipro and other Soviet publishing houses as "Soviet propaganda" and "Soviet disinformation." Unfortunately, the tone of the booklets lends itself to such accusations. Generally, they are tendentious, angry, careless with details, and filled with slogans. Even when the Soviet writers are telling the truth, they often sound as if they are lying.

In similar fashion, the nationalist historians can be accused of historical evasion, whitewashing, and skillful manipulation of the facts. By carefully avoiding the full story, they manage to give the impression that the members of the Halychyna Division—under the command of German SS officers—did nothing but pray and fight the Red Army. There is little said in their books and articles of the division's role in antipartisan warfare, of the large number of Ukrainian police units that transferred into the division, and of the atrocities committed by many of the men in its ranks before they joined the division.

In order to sort out the truth and avoid reliance on either nationalist or Soviet historians, it is necessary to examine the ideological underpinnings of the division, to know something of the nationalist movement in Galicia, and to become familiar with the full history of the division, from its beginnings in Nazi sabotage and terrorism units, through its stages as political police engaged in cleaning out Jewish ghettos and suppressing partisan activities, to its emergence as a full-fledged national Waffen-SS division. Each period informs the other. To leave anything out is to risk serious error.

## HISTORY OF THE HALYCHYNA DIVISION

On March 24, 1943, listening posts in England intercepted a broadcast over Radio Weichsel-Donau announcing the organization of a Ukrainian Waffen-SS division "to satisfy the demand of the Ukrainian population for an active share in the struggle against the Bolsheviks." The broadcast further reported that the Germans had established a Ukrainian war committee in occupied Krakow for the purpose of enlisting recruits to fight side by side with the Germans for the salvation of Ukrainian freedom, independence, and self-determination.

The following month, on March 22, Radio Wechsel-Donau announced that the new division, named "Galician," would be distinguished by the Lion of Halycz on its badges and battle banners. This was followed by a more formal announcement on May 5 by SS Brigadier Otto Wächter, the German governor of Galicia, supported by the president of the Ukrainian Aid Committee, Professor Dr. Kubyovich, and Ing. Michael Chronovat, chairman of the Ukrainian War Committee. On May 23, the German Transocean Agency reported that sixty thousand Galician Ukrainians had applied for enrollment in the division.

German newsreel film of the period shows the volunteers of the newly formed Halychyna Division passing in review before Governor Wächter in Lviv on July 16, 1943. Still in their civilian clothes, they proudly display their SS and swastika insignia alongside the Halychyn Lion as they march by in ranks of four on their way to the railway station and boot camp. As they pass the swastika-bedecked reviewing stand, they raise their arms in the stiff-armed Nazi salute while the film's sound track intones: "One more train is departing the Fatherland with volunteers so that after training they can join the German army in defending Europe against the world Bolshevik enemy."

In a similar ceremony in Kolomyea, captured German film shows Wächter addressing the Ukrainian recruits as follows: "In joining the ranks of the volunteers you show that you are not indifferent to the struggle now taking place in Europe. . . . You wish, with arms in hand, to serve the Fatherland and the New Europe.''

For the remainder of 1943, the division was scattered from Debica to Biarritz. Two hundred and forty men were selected for officer training at German *Junkerschulen*. Others were sent to artillery and field engineering schools in Hamburg, Osnabruck, Oldenberg, and Neuhammer. A scout battalion trained at Karlsruhe and Koblenz.

Some five thousand Halychyna Division recruits—transferred from existing Ukrainian police regiments—were given further police combat training in France. While still in training, they joined other German-led troops in tracking down members of the French resistance and arresting downed Allied flyers. At swearing-in ceremonies in France in November 1943, the men of the division took an oath of absolute obedience to Hitler as Führer of the armed forces and organizer of a New Europe:

I swear by God this holy oath that in the struggle against Bolshevism I will give the C-in-C of the German armed forces, Adolf Hitler, absolute obedience, and as a fearless soldier, if it be his will, I will always be prepared to lay down my life for this oath.[6]

According to Kiev journalist-historian Valery Styrkul, subunits of the division participated in a variety of death-dealing activities while training in other sites: the execution of prisoners of war at Szebnie, the liquidation of Poles, Gypsies, and Jews in the town of Moderowka, and the reinforcement of German units guarding the concentration camp at Szebnie.[7]

By February and March 1944 the scattered units of the division had completed their training and reassembled at Neuhammer, where they began divisional maneuvers. Although the Red Army was drawing closer in its relentless drive westward, the growing strength and boldness of the Soviet partisans made it necessary to divert substantial portions of the division to the task of keeping order behind the battle lines.

In February 1944 two of the division's three regiments were organized as a special antipartisan battle-group (SS-Kampfgruppe) under the command of SS Obersturmbannführer Friedrich Beyersdorff and Battalion Commander Bristot and sent off to fight Soviet partisans in the Chelm area. "Not surprisingly, the aforementioned task force did not perform its duties well," reported the division's chief executive officer, Wolf-Dietrich Heike. "Soon after reports of the unseemly behaviour of the unit began to arrive at the Division."[8]

The Beyersdorff detachment is reported to have joined other police units in attacking the village of Kokhanivka on November 23, 1943. One hundred adults were taken for brief rides in *Gaswagens*, and twenty old people and fifty children were locked in a village house and burned to death. According to Styrkul, "Legal bodies investigating the war crimes of the Nazi occupiers estimated that the special company of the SS Halychyna Division had tortured more than 2,000 civilians to death in Poland, shipped 20,000 persons off to Germany and burned down 20 villages."[9]

By late 1943 the bulk of the Jews had been eradicated in the Ukraine through mass pogroms, mass shootings, and mass "resettlement" in concentration camps. This left the Ukrainian nationalist forces free to concentrate their attacks on the Polish villages that dotted Galicia. Since the Poles were almost entirely Roman Catholic, this meant frequent attacks on Catholic institutions and priests. On Sunday, March 4, 1944, a combined UPA (Ukrainian Partisan Army) and "SS Volunteer Ukrainian Division" rounded up some two thousand people who were hiding in the Dominican monastery in the Podkamien parish of Brody. "Altogether, they murdered 600 people in the villages of Palikrowy, Malinska, and Czernicy."[10]

Attacks on Polish villages were apparently marked by special savagery. "Entire Polish villages were wiped out, their inhabitants invariably tortured and raped before being slaughtered with knives and axes, the babies and children murdered with the same savagery as had been the fate of Jewish children."[11]

Not far from Lviv lay a triangle of Polish villages, the largest of which was Huta Pieniacka. Small bands of unarmed Jews and poorly armed partisans sometimes visited these villages in search of food and medical supplies. On cold winter nights they took shelter in the villagers' barns and sheds. German intelligence reports identified these villages as partisan havens. According to standing orders, it was required that such villages be razed to the ground and their populations murdered in such a way as to serve as a horrible example to other villages.

On February 27, 1944, a mixed force consisting of a Ukrainian police regiment, a sprinkling of Wehrmacht reserves, and a strong contingent from the SS Halychyna Division was dispatched to "pacify" Huta Pieniacka. "After firing and throwing hand grenades from the outskirts, the murderers went into the village, assembled all the farmers together with their families and locked them up in their barns. . . . Then they set fire to the entire village. . . . The village burned all day, and only at night did the murderers finally leave."[12]

## The Incorporation of Police Regiments

In the spring of 1944 five Ukrainian police regiments were incorporated into the division, police regiments 4, 5, 6, 7, and 8. The presence of these police regiments is of key importance in determining the true nature of the Halychyna Division. First, one must understand the special role of these German-recruited and German-directed police units. It was these locally recruited police groups that served as the chief executioners for the mobile killing squads known as *Einsatzgruppen*. They constituted the main force for tracking down those who fled to the forest and for wiping out entire villages suspected of sheltering partisans. Their ruthlessness and brutality were legend. In a period of eighteen months they succeeded in murdering one and a half million Jews in occupied

Soviet territory. In some cases German officers, unable to stomach their cruelty, asked that the police regiments be withdrawn from their theater of operations.

That same spring Reichsführer of the Police and the SS Heinrich Himmler visited the division at its headquarters at Neuhammer. On March 16, 1944, addressing the division's officers, he said: "Your homeland has become so much more beautiful since you have lost—on our initiative, I must say—those residents who were so often a dirty blemish on Galicia's good name, namely the Jews." In a further effort to endear himself to the men of the division, he added: "I know that if I ordered you to liquidate the Poles...I would be giving you permission to do what you are eager to do anyway." But, the Reichsführer warned them, the privilege of enforcing order on the Poles belonged solely to "the savior of Europe, Adolf Hitler, and cannot be presumed by anyone else."[13]

Within days of Himmler's visit to his Ukrainian legion, the command of the Polish resistance movement, the Armia Krajowa, or Home Army, signaled the Polish government in exile in London that units of the "SS Halychyna Division appeared recently in the county of Hrubieszow and they stepped up terrorist attacks murdering the population. Six Polish villages were burned down." A second report, dispatched on May 24, read: "The terrorist actions of the SS Halychyna Division and UPA continue in the region of Chelm." On July 7, 1944, the Home Army informed London: "The terrorist activities of the SS Halychyna Division increased in the region of Lublin."[14]

## The Battle of Brody

The Red Army's 1944 summer offensive brought the Soviet forces within reach of Lviv. To meet this threat, the Galician Division was transported from its training base at Neuhammer to the Brody area west of Lviv, where it was incorporated into the Thirteenth Corps of the Fourth Panzer Army.

On July 13 the Soviet troops launched a massive attack on a thirty-kilometer front. By July 27 the Soviets had executed a classic pincer movement that liberated Lviv and Stanislav and trapped eight Nazi divisions in a rapidly narrowing pocket. The Galician Division, called on to hold the line while the German divisions sought to break out, bore the brunt of the Soviet attack. From three-fifths to two-thirds of its officers and men were killed or captured in a week of fierce fighting. On July 21–23 the surviving remnants of the Thirteenth Corps, including three thousand men of the Galician Division, managed to slip through the battle lines and beat a retreat toward the Carpathian Mountains.

The division's German commander, General Fritz Freitag, was instructed to return with the battered remnants of his division to its former headquarters at Neuhammer. There the division was rapidly brought back to full strength in record time by the simple expedient of transferring men from a variety of Ukrainian police units that had become redundant now that there was no Ukrainian territory left for them to patrol. To these were added personnel from reinforcement and training units as well as a sprinkling of Ukrainian youngsters who had volunteered to man antiaircraft batteries now overrun by the Red Army.

In its overwhelming appetite for manpower, the division cared little whether the new recruits were Galicians or came from more easterly parts of the Ukraine. Policemen who had served in various German-formed *Schutzmannschaften* in the Kiev region and Ukrainian auxiliaries who had served in *Einsatzgruppen* were welcomed into the ranks. Former concentration-camp guards from Belzec, Treblinka, and Sobibor were thrown into the division after these camps were overrun by the Russians.[15]

Ukrainian police units that had participated in the ruthless suppression of the 1944 Warsaw uprising were later absorbed into the division, as were the members of the infamous Nachtigall and Roland formations. The former was responsible for the massacre of thousands of Jews, Poles, and democratically minded Ukrainians in the Lviv region on the heels of the German invasion; the latter assisted the *Einsatzgruppen* operating in the southern Ukraine. Together, they served as an antipartisan force in Byelorussia, where they murdered thousands of innocent villagers.

On October 1, 1944, the reconstituted Galician Division was ordered out of its barracks at Neuhammer and dispatched to Slovakia to assist in suppressing a popular, widespread revolt of the Slovak people against the puppet Tiso regime and his Nazi sponsors. The revolt was supported by important segments of the Slovak army.

Despite a spirited campaign, the Slovak forces were rapidly overpowered by vastly superior German forces. The defeated rebels fled toward the mountainous border areas, where they were readily mopped up by the Galician Division, stationed there for that purpose. Prisoners captured by the division were handed over to the Gestapo, which exacted a horrible revenge on the rebels. Czech military historians claim that the division behaved badly: "If we compare them to the regular Wehrmacht units, the way they behaved, the cruelty and pillage by the Galician Division was much worse."[16]

## Nomenclature

The Ukrainian political leaders who inspired the creation of the Halychyna Division—largely nationalists of the Melnyk faction of the Organization of Ukrainian Nationalists (OUN)—were eager to see the name "Ukrainian" emblazoned on the formation's banners and insignia. However, the Nazi occupation authorities, particularly Heinrich Himmler, were extremely reluctant to encourage nationalist notions of independence and sovereignty, insisting that the division content itself with the more provincial appellation "Galician." Himmler and the other Nazi leaders knew well that Hitler intended to ravage the Ukraine and replace the native population with *Volksdeutsche*.

Although dubbed "Police Division Galicia" by its German founders, its first formal mention in the German battle order in September 1943 shows it listed as the Fourteenth Galician SS–Volunteer Division. On October 22, 1943, it was renamed the Fourteenth Galician SS–Volunteer Infantry Division. A variety of minor changes in nomenclature followed in 1944, but it was not until November 1944 that the term ''Ukrainian'' became part of its designation as a Waffen-SS unit.

On November 1, 1944, the German high command ordered the division to move its headquarters from Neuhammer to Zilinia, in Slovakia. That same month the division received orders to change its designation to Fourteenth Waffen-SS Division (Ukrainian no. 1). The change was more cynical than real. With all of the Ukraine—including Galicia—now in Soviet hands, the issue of Ukrainian independence no longer threatened German plans to replace the bulk of the Ukrainian population. Nevertheless, in retreat on all fronts, the German high command hoped that the name change would improve the division's morale and persuade its personnel that there was still something worth fighting for.

### Transfer to Slovenia

On January 26, 1945, the division was ordered to make its way to the southern Steiermark and northern Slovenia. In the following months it vainly sought to counter Tito's partisans in a frontless battle on both sides of the Austrian border. Again, atrocities occurred. According to the division's chief executive officer, ''[any atrocities] that might have occurred took place in the course of fighting partisans, when it was often difficult to separate innocent civilians from the enemy.''[17] Heike suggests that German units sought to transfer blame for their misdeeds onto their Ukrainian comrades. Despite these efforts to disavow blame, there is little doubt that the division did commit excesses since it acted under German command and in conjunction with German police and military units.

By the time the division reached Yugoslavia, the military situation allowed little room for self-deception; the war was clearly lost and surrender at most a few months away. The division's leaders now cast about desperately to salvage whatever they could from their disastrous bargain with Hitler's Third Reich. Like thousands of other SS men, they were making preparations to lose themselves or obliterate their identification with the SS. Above all, they sought to move west to reach British and American lines to avoid surrendering to the Russians.

The division's German and Ukrainian political leaders sought to refurbish its image and rewrite its history so as to make it more acceptable in Allied eyes. In November 1944 a National Ukrainian Committee was formed under German auspices, and Colonel Pavel Shandruk, a former Petliurian officer, was appointed its head. Shandruk, who had served Skoropadsky, Petliura, and Udovychenko in the civil war and the Polish army in World War II, was appointed general of all Ukrainian forces fighting on the German side. On April 24, 1945—fifteen days before Germany's unconditional surrender—the division was renamed the First Ukrainian Division of the Ukrainian National Army. In practical terms the change in nomenclature meant little. General Fritz Freitag remained the division's commander, orders continued to be issued in German, and the men continued to be pawns in the German battle plan.

Shandruk included a number of additional German-led Ukrainian auxiliary police units in the division's ranks. Among them was the 31st SD, a Volhynia-based legion that had played a part in cruelly suppressing the 1944 Warsaw uprising. Most deadly of all were the four hundred men of the Brigade for Special Tasks under Commander T. Bulba-Borovets. This "ingathering" resulted in the division including in its ranks prior to its surrender several of the most vicious of the German-led Ukrainian formations, such as the Roland and Nachtigall battalions, the 207th and 201st Police Battalions, the 31st SD, and the Beyersdorff detachment.

On May 5 or 6 Ukrainian emissaries made contact with the British forces and begged their commander to accept the division's surrender. The British agreed, and Klagenfurt in southern Austria was appointed as the surrender site. After a brief internment in Austria, the division was moved to Rimini in Italy, where it remained for the next three years, enjoying the balmy weather and rewriting its history.

In 1948 the British government concluded a peace treaty with Germany. Now that the war was officially over, the German prisoners of war, who had become a mainstay of British agriculture during the war, were returned home. Meanwhile, full British demobilization was still a few years away as Britain continued to police its far-flung—if shrinking—empire. To meet the impending agricultural crisis, the British cabinet decided to import the bulk of the division from Italy—some sixteen thousand men—to replace the homeward-bound German POWs. The Labour Department agreed to this arrangement on condition that preparations would be made to find a new home for the Ukrainian Division members by 1950, by which time the British forces would be fully demobilized. The cabinet agreed.

The announcement of the decision in Parliament led to a number of highly critical inquiries from members who demanded to know how such an ill-reputed formation could be admitted to England. English officials defended their decision by claiming that the men had been fully screened and that no war criminals had been found among them. It was only after the defense had been publicly made in Parliament that British under secretaries realized that the men of the division had, in fact, never been screened by Allied authorities.

To avoid a possible scandal, a British team under the command of D. Haldane Porter of the Refugee Screening Commission was dispatched to Rimini. Porter's report is a welter of contradictions.[18] He admitted that he had time to interview only a small selection of the men in the camp and that these interviews were handicapped by the fact that neither he nor his staff spoke any Ukrainian. He readily admitted that the officers of the division might be lying to him and that he had no alternative but to accept what they said because he was unfamiliar with the unit's history. There were no rosters available to him, he wrote, no regimental war diaries, and no intelligence reports. It never occurred to him to ask the Russians, who were fully familiar with the division, for information. In the end he concluded that the division, whatever its history, presented no security threat to Britain and could be safely recruited for agricultural work.

In 1950 the cabinet, true to its promise, sought to rid England of its Ukrainian farm workers by seeking refuges for them in Britain's "white dominions," namely, Canada, Australia, and New Zealand. Canada initially demurred, but after being assured by the British that the men had been fully screened for war crimes, agreed to accept two thousand of them. Australia and New Zealand took similar numbers. A sizable number remained in Britain, while others managed to emigrate to the United States, Argentina, and other South American countries.

## LITERATURE ON THE HALYCHYNA DIVISION

Forty-six years have passed since the Halychyna Division laid down its arms at Klagenfurt, and in that time considerable misunderstanding has developed regarding the true nature of Himmler's Waffen-SS. An attempt has been made to rewrite history and portray the Waffen-SS as "pure fighting men" with no relation to death camps and *Einsatzgruppen.* "Since the war . . . a legend has arisen that the Germanic legions were a hand-picked body of magnificent specimens of Germanic manhood motivated by National Socialist ideals and forged into an almost superhuman fighting force by the example and know-how of a dedicated team of SS instructors."[19]

However, for a clear perspective on the SS as a criminal organization, it is necessary to consult the forty-two-volume record of the Nuremberg trials, *Trial of the Major War Criminals Before the International Military Tribunal*, in particular the volume titled "Opinion and Judgment." There, on pages 97–102, are laid out the tribunal's analysis of the SS, its condemnation as a criminal organization, and the criteria by which the individual SS man could be judged a war criminal.

From the beginning, the Nuremberg Tribunal was praised by many as a great achievement in international law and condemned by some as "victors' trials." Curiously, those Americans who had most bitterly opposed America's entry into the war against Nazism proved most vociferous in attacking the legal premises that underlay the tribunal's procedures. Bradley F. Smith, a tough-minded, generally conservative historian, documents the controversies that swirled around this first attempt by an international court to sentence a nation's leaders for war crimes and crimes against humanity. In his *Reaching Judgment at Nuremberg,* he concludes that the world has gained more by the trials than it may have lost. Bradley spells out the criteria applied by the court to determine whether the SS was, in fact, a criminal organization. According to these criteria, it is clear that a majority of the members of the Galician SS Division can be regarded as war criminals since (1) they were volunteers, (2) they were aware of the criminal purposes for which they had been recruited, and (3) they participated in acts of violence against innocent civilians.[20]

For a briefer, more popular analysis, it is useful to turn to the June 1985 edition of *Army: The Magazine of Landpower*. In a major article, this authoritative military journal forcefully describes the criminal nature of the SS as core units moved from concentration camp to death camp to front lines. The article demonstrates how long-ingrained habits of ruthlessness and terror developed in the camps found full expression on the battlefield.[21]

John Keegan's *Waffen SS: The Asphalt Soldiers* develops the same theme. Heavily illustrated and ''popularly'' written, Keegan's book is, nevertheless, based on solid scholarship.

Two American scholars who have produced highly admired, carefully researched studies of the Waffen-SS are George H. Stein, author of *The Waffen SS: Hitler's Elite Guard at War*, and Charles W. Sydnor, author of *Soldiers of Destruction: The SS Death's Head Division, 1933–1945*. The former provides a coherent, accurate history of the SS from its beginnings as an elite guard to its development as a frontline unit. The latter concentrates its analysis on the *Totenkopf* regiments that served their apprenticeship as concentration-camp guards before being sent to the front as fighting troops.

To avoid the accusation of ''American bias,'' it is necessary to turn to two German authorities on the SS, Helmut Krausnick and Martin Broszat, authors of the authoritative *Anatomy of the SS State*. While Krausnick and Broszat generally agree with Sydnor and Stein in describing the SS as a criminal organization, they do bring an important German perspective to their analysis.

On the other hand, Gerald Reitlinger, the British art critic turned student of the Holocaust, was one of the earliest and best historians of the Holocaust. Objective, insightful, and disdainful of myth, he carefully catalogs the criminal activities of the Waffen-SS in his volume, *The SS, Alibi of a Nation,* yet refuses to allow German apologists to place the blame on the SS alone.

Given the Galician Division's sorry fighting record, the formation did not attract the attention of military historians. As a result, there are few books or articles available except from those with a direct interest, either personal or political, in the unit's history. Chief among these is a volume by its chief executive officer, Wolfe-Dietrich Heike. A Wehrmacht officer assigned to provide military know-how and organization to the nonprofessional officers who staffed the unit, Heike is sometimes critical of the SS men who were in command and is largely sympathetic to the Ukrainian troops he oversaw.

Heike wrote the original text of *Sie Wollten die Freiheit: Die Geschichte der ukrainischen Division, 1943–1945* while in British custody at the war's close. While it contains many useful facts that indirectly confirm Soviet accusations, it nevertheless avoids anything that might indict the author as a war criminal holding a high office in a criminal organization. In addition, Heike did not join the division until 1944 and knew nothing or chose to know nothing of the police units that formed the unit's core. Admitting that the division had a bad reputation, he nevertheless chooses to blame others for the misdeeds of his men. Although Heike is ostensibly a ''friend of the Ukrainians,'' his description of the Ukrainians in the unit tends to be patronizing and not entirely complimentary.[22]

Appointed titular commander of the division in the last weeks of the war, General Pavel Shandruk surrendered to the Americans and emigrated to the United States early in the 1950s. His memoirs, titled *Arms of Valor,* concern themselves with the nationalist hopes of the division's leaders but avoid mention of its history as a German-commanded police force and an antipartisan brigade. It is probably true that the division under Shandruk's command had no opportunity to commit war crimes since it was too busy defending itself against Tito's triumphant partisans in the war's final stages.

Postwar Ukrainian historians are hard pressed to explain how it happened that a major Ukrainian military formation fought on the side of the Nazis. Basil Dmytryshyn, for example, in an article published in the *American Slavic and East European Review,* advances the notion that Ukrainians joined the division in the hope that it could serve as the basis of a Ukrainian army that would become effective when the German and Soviet forces had worn each other down.[23]

A similar idea is advanced by Volodymyr Kubijovyc, editor of the two-volume *Ukraine: A Concise Encyclopedia.* A principal collaborator during the German occupation of Galicia, the Ukrainian geographer was influential in persuading the Germans to form the Galician SS Division and served on its military council. Having occupied a seat in the Krakow court of German Governor-General Frank, Kubijovyc is an ardent apologist for the Ukrainian nationalist movement, the division, and the auxiliary police units that served under German command. Nevertheless, an encyclopedia requires some element of authority and fact; in reciting these facts Kubijovyc validates the data of other historians less sympathetic to the division.[24]

There are numerous military books and magazines that devote themselves to details of uniforms, insignia, and medals. One of these is by Roger James Bender and Hugh Taylor, who have produced a series of books on the *Uniforms, Organization, and History of the Waffen-SS.* Volume 4, published in 1982, devotes itself to the Galician Division. Although it is devoted primarily to the minutiae of arm stripes and collar tabs, the book is well researched and contains considerable worthwhile history and many surprising insights into the behavior of the division.

Georg Tessin, one of Germany's foremost military historians, provides a more conventional approach in his *Verbände und Truppen der deutschen Wehrmacht und Waffen SS im Zweiten Weltkrieg, 1939–1945.* Working from German records, he provides a valuable record of the division's battle order and the various police units absorbed by the division.

A veteran of the division and one of the large staff of librarians at the University of Toronto's main library, Wasyl Verhya has written numerous articles and two books on the history of the Galician Division. In ''The 'Galicia' Ukrainian

Division in Polish and Soviet Literature,'' Verhya ardently defends the reputation of the division against all comers. As can be expected, his assessment of the man accused of responsibility for pogroms during the civil war period, offered in ''General Pavlo Shandruk: An Appraisal,'' is entirely complimentary.

The Germans' purpose in organizing the division is not complicated. The losses at Stalingrad made it necessary to recruit new forces capable of patrolling the vast area behind the front lines. The growth of a partisan movement called for military units specifically trained in combatting irregulars. Motivation from the Ukrainian side is more complicated and is based on a fusion of pro-Fascist beliefs and a fanatic passion for independence. A full understanding of the division, therefore, is difficult without a full understanding of the leading Ukrainian nationalist movement, the OUN.

A spirited defense of the Galician Division is offered by Michael Yaremko's *From Separation to Unity*. However, Yaremko's work fails to illuminate many of the movement's dark corners. For example, Yaremko's claim that the German command agreed that the Galician Division would be used only on the eastern front against the Soviets and that it would never have to fight against British, French, and American forces cannot be checked. The proof, Yaremko claims, lies in documents in the Vatican Library. But the Vatican Library is closed. There are no documents, either German or Ukrainian, to substantiate the claim. In any event, even if such an agreement was made—which appears unlikely in view of the Nazis' contempt for their Ukrainian allies—it was repeatedly ignored. Ukrainian units manned defenses in Belgium and Norway. Members of the division, while training in France, joined in sweeps of the French countryside for downed British and American fliers.

Although the Soviet delegates to the United Nations have denounced the members of the Galician Division as traitors and war criminals, Western governments have consistently ignored Soviet claims. The British effort is best illustrated by the 1947 Haldane Porter report on behalf of the Refugee Screening Commission. While nationalist Ukrainian circles claim that Porter's report ''clears'' the division of any accusation of war crimes, the report itself is a welter of contradictions, as discussed earlier.

The Deschênes Commission Report fails on the same grounds. In 1984 the Canadian government appointed Justice Jules Deschênes as a one-man Royal Commission to investigate the presence or absence of Nazi war criminals in Canada. Refusing all evidence that might condemn the division, Deschênes chose to rely solely on the Haldane Porter report to conclude: ''Charges of war crimes against the Galicia Division have never been substantiated.''

The actions of the division are best understood in the context of the Holocaust in general and the role of Ukrainian auxiliary police and military units in particular. The former is best represented by Raul Hilberg's *The Destruction of the European Jews*, which is one of the most thoroughgoing, objective, and dispassionate descriptions of the Holocaust. Hilberg's classic one-volume work has been updated by a three-volume edition. However, for our purpose the one-volume edition suffices. Hilberg, working largely from German documents, describes the participation of Lithuanian, Estonian, and Ukrainian volunteers in the Nazi-organized *Einsatzgruppen* (task forces) that were responsible for the murder of one and a half million Jews on Soviet territory. Without their cooperation, Hilberg says, the Germans could not have killed so quickly and efficiently.

Szymon Datner's *Genocide, 1939–1945* presents a Polish view of events during the war years with emphasis on atrocities directed at Polish villages by auxiliary police units supported by various arms of the SS and Wehrmacht.

Not only do the Nuremberg trials remain a landmark in international jurisprudence, but the thousands of documents that served as exhibits in the various trials and the sworn statements of witnesses provide a vast data bank for contemporary historians of the Holocaust. A good review of the trials is, therefore, a necessary foundation for further research. Eugene Davidson's *The Trial of the Germans* offers a thorough and scholarly review of the most significant trials in international history. Davidson devotes some space to the crimes committed by the German forces in conjunction with their locally recruited Baltic and Ukrainian militias in the name of antipartisan warfare.

Unfortunately, there is little in either German or American military archives that bears directly on the Galician Division. The division's war diaries have been either lost, destroyed, or hidden, few of its officers were interrogated by Soviet or Allied intelligence, and the unit's survivors have been reluctant to implicate themselves in possible war-crimes charges. Nevertheless, microfilm roll T-175 at Washington's National Military Archives does contain considerable material on the organization of the Galician SS Division as an antipartisan police unit as well as a transcript of Himmler's revealing speech to the division in March 1944.[25]

Two opposite versions of the division's history are supplied by Volodymyr Kubijovyc and Valery Styrkul. The editor of *Ukraine: A Concise Encyclopedia,* Kubijovyc, chairman of the essentially collaborative Ukrainian Central Committee, boasts of the accomplishments of his committee. Among those accomplishments, the Ukrainian nationalist geographer cites the organization of a thousand-man Ukrainian auxiliary police force that served under German command.[26]

Valery Styrkul, a Soviet journalist and historian, has produced a number of propagandist booklets for Dnipro Publishers. Despite the overwrought prose employed by Styrkul in *We Accuse,* the basic facts contained in this booklet on the Galician SS Division are supported by more rigorous "western sources." He offers the most complete account of the actions of the Roland and Nachtigall, 31st SD, and other Ukrainian police formations that were incorporated into the Galician Division.[27]

### The Civil War Years

Much of what occurred in the western Ukraine during World War II can be viewed as a continuation of events and aspirations first played out during the

1917–20 civil war. There was the same futile hope of establishing an independent Ukrainian state, the same pogroms, the same reliance on foreign sponsorship to achieve political purposes, and the same betrayal by the sponsors of the nationalists' essential aims. An important difference, however, was that in World War I the Germans did not participate in the persecution of the Jews. During World War II the combination of the Ukrainian nationalist ferocity and the Nazis' thoroughness made the attack on the Jews much more deadly. The heroes of the Central Rada and the Western Ukrainian National Republic—Skoropadsky, Petliura, Melnyk, and Shandruk—became virtual and symbolic leaders of the nationalist forces during World War II.

The Ukrainian nationalists declared "Petliura Day" soon after the takeover of Galicia by the Germans in 1941 and celebrated it by killing thousands of Jews in Lviv. Melnyk and his younger rival Bandera led Nazi-organized military formations that functioned under German command. Shandruk became the general of the First Division of the Ukrainian National Army in the closing days of World War II.

The bibliographic choices are many, but *Red Victory: A History of the Russian Civil War* by W. Bruce Lincoln is not only highly readable, but a rational, objective account of the political and military forces that accounted for the ultimate Soviet victory. Orest Subtelny's political sympathies lie with the Ukrainian nationalists, making his chapter on the civil war in his *Ukraine: A History* (Toronto: University of Toronto, 1988) less illuminating than it should have been. As a historian he cannot deny nationalist-Nazi collaboration during World War II, but he seeks to minimize and rationalize it with stock nationalist arguments. Nevertheless, the York University history of the Ukraine is competent, convenient, and readable.

One of the principals among the White opponents of the Red revolution was Petr Wrangel, whose memoirs provide the freshness and immediacy that come with reading an original source written by one of the major actors of the civil war. His *Memoirs of General Wrangel* supplies considerable information lost in later accounts.

Ronald Saunders's *Shores of Refuge: A Hundred Years of Jewish Immigration* offers a compact description of the pogroms inflicted on Jews in Russia, climaxing in 1,200 incidents between December 1918 and April 1921. Poverty, political persecution, and violence led to the emigration of millions of Jews from Eastern European countries that had been their homelands for a thousand years.

## Ukrainian–Jewish Relations

A wide chasm exists between Jewish and Ukrainian historians in the interpretation of their joint history. The former emphasize the violence visited upon Jewish communities by brutal Jew-hating Ukrainians, while the latter tend to minimize the frequency and severity of the pogroms that periodically swept through the Ukraine. Even when they admit the indigenous nature of Ukrainian anti-Semitism, Ukrainian historians prefer to underline the role of Jews as middlemen for exploitive Polish nobles.

Stefan T. Possony, author of "The Ukrainian-Jewish Problem: A Historical Retrospect," *Ukrainian Quarterly* (Summer 1975): 139–51, has made consistent attempts to close the breach between Jews and Ukrainians. Possony dwells on the progressive measures enacted by the fragile Ukrainian governments that struggled and failed to maintain their independence between 1917 and 1921. He points to the creation of a Ministry of Jewish Affairs in the Directory cabinet and to Petliura's warning to his troops that the death sentence would overtake the perpetrators of pogroms. On the other hand, Saul S. Friedman, author of *Pogromchik: The Assassination of Simon Petlura,* dwells on the savagery of the pogroms and questions whether Petliura (the current Ukrainian spelling), whatever his intentions, had sufficient control over his followers to prevent the attacks on Jews.

## The Organization of Ukrainian Nationalists

The Organization of Ukrainian Nationalists (OUN), which found its greatest strength in that part of the western Ukraine known as Galicia, was founded in 1929 by Colonel Evhen Konovalets and drew its early membership from the veterans of the armies that fought to defend the short-lived Ukrainian states formed in the wake of the Russian Revolution. Possessed by an obsessive desire for self-rule, the OUN—like the Croatian Ustashi and the Romanian Iron Guard—held a mystic belief in violence and the superiority of its nation-race. Hostile to the Western democracies, antiparliamentary and anti-Semitic, the movement planned to use brute force to break out of "Greater Russian imperialism's prison of nations."

An esteemed scholar frequently cited by Ukrainian nationalist historians when it suits their purpose, David J. Dallin authored a classic analysis of Soviet power (*Soviet Espionage*) that supports the Ukrainian nationalists' vehement anti-Soviet stance. In reality, however, Dallin offers little comfort to the nationalist cause. His description of the OUN as "violently nationalistic, conspiratorial and terroristic" is far from complimentary.

Another favorite of Ukrainian nationalists, John A. Armstrong, also offers little real comfort to the nationalist cause in his most noted work, *Ukrainian Nationalism, 1939–1945*. Although he shrinks from the words "Fascist" and "Nazi" in his description of the Ukrainian nationalist movement—preferring to use the more neutral-sounding term "integrationalist"—Armstrong nevertheless describes the OUN as a Fascist movement in everything but name.

Panias Fedenko, a Ukrainian critic of the OUN and the Galician SS Division, attacks the rationalizations and the pretensions invented by the nationalists. His criticism is based on intimate knowledge of the movement. He states frankly in his article "Remarks on Modern History" that "the ideology, tactics and morals of German Nazism and Italian Fascism were adopted by the OUN."[28]

## German Recruitment of Ukrainian Nationalists

Ukrainian nationalist leaders like to pretend that whatever services they provided the Nazis were conceded at the point of a gun. History, however, tells another story. Nationalists living in exile in Austria and Germany well before the war began eagerly volunteered their services to the Germans and formed sabotage and espionage units. These German-led units were trained to demoralize Poles so as to ease the invasion of Poland. Much of this story is related in E. H. Cookridge's biography of General Reinhard Gehlen's career as a master spy (*Gehlen, Spy of the Century*). The work includes a detailed description of Admiral Wilhelm Canaris's recruitment and deployment of the OUN movement and how he played on the rivalry between Bandera and Melnyk, the movement's two paramount leaders.

Supplementing the Cookridge volume is Heinz Höhne's *Canaris* (Garden City: Doubleday, 1979). It provides a fuller description of the way in which Admiral Canaris, head of German Military Intelligence (Abwehr) recruited nationalist forces for sabotage, espionage, and political disorder.

## The Galician Pogroms, 1941

Nationalist historians prefer to describe the early days of the German invasion as a heroic period in which the nationalist movement proclaimed the independence and sovereignty of the Ukraine, only to be undone by the tyrannical Nazis. For the Jews and the Poles living in Galicia, the period was marked by savage pogroms initiated by the nationalists and directed by Bandera's Nachtigall formation, which arrived in Lviv with the advance guard of the German army.

Reuben Ainsztein's *Jewish Resistance in Nazi-occupied Eastern Europe* contains a detailed account of atrocities inflicted on the Jews, including the deaths of six thousand Jews in Lviv. Lucy Dawidowicz's *The War Against the Jews, 1939–1945* is carefully researched and splendidly written. Her major contribution to the literature of the Holocaust is her description of the role played by the Jews' Eastern European neighbors.

As the German forces retreated across the Russian steppes, numerous Soviet writers began to write accounts of the tragedy that befell their land. These accounts were collected and edited by Soviet writer (and propagandist) Ilya Ehrenburg. *The Black Book* is a highly emotional collection expressing a burning rage against the Nazi invasion written entirely from a Soviet point of view. However, this does not mean that the book is filled with falsehoods. There are some events in history whose results are so clear that even the Soviets had no need to exaggerate or lie about them.

If Ehrenburg is emotional and journalistic, Philip Friedman bends over backward to be fair and meticulously factual. A scrupulous historian, he sought to give balance to all his writings on the Holocaust despite the dramatic quality of the material. His most important work was a collection of his papers, *Roads to Extinction: Essays on the Holocaust.*

Martin Gilbert's *The Holocaust: A History of the Jews of Europe During the Second World War* is somewhat formless and lacks the tight organization and detailed chronology of other Holocaust historians. But the author of a definitive biography of Winston Churchill, a history of World War II, and numerous atlases of the Holocaust has nevertheless provided a history rich in anecdote and the direct evidence of witnesses.

Some of the most poignant histories of the period have been written by survivors who witnessed the events they describe with their own eyes. Such a history is Betti Einstein-Keshev's "The Story of Independent Ukraine," published in the Jewish volume *Fun Noenten Over* (Out of the recent past). She recalls that the Banderists (the Bandera faction of the Organization of Ukrainian Nationalists) "wanted to finish off all their enemies at once. Their method of waging war was murder and destruction with no quarter shown. . . . They distinguished themselves with extraordinary sadism which exceeded the sadism of the Germans."[29]

Another of the eyewitness books has been written by an elderly survivor of the Lviv pogroms. Joachim Schoenfeld's *Holocaust Memoirs* is a little-known but excellent book that documents events in the first days of the German invasion of Lviv.

World-famous Nazi hunter Simon Wiesenthal was also a resident of Lviv when the Germans marched in. What he observed and experienced helped formulate his determination to pursue war criminals for the rest of his life. His *Murderers Among Us* is a better book than the dramatic title suggests.

As we have previously noted, Gerald Reitlinger was one of the first and arguably one of the best historians of the Holocaust. In his volume, *The Final Solution: The Attempt to Exterminate the Jews of Europe,* Reitlinger offers not only an excellent account of the Nazis' growing determination to liquidate the Jews of Europe but also considerable material on events in Lviv in the early days of the German occupation.

Historian Orest Subtelny provides a useful article in an otherwise highly partisan nationalist volume of addresses delivered by Ukrainian spokesmen when Canada first began to investigate the presence of war criminals. Subtelny provides valuable material on Soviet atrocities but fails to explain why the nationalist movement chose to take out its revenge against the Jews.[30]

### The Ideological Underpinnings of the Nationalist Movement

OUN ideologues were deeply influenced by Fascist-leaning Ukrainian geopolitician Dmitri Dontsov, who wrote: "Every great idea is irreconcilable, uncompromisable, brutal, fanatic and amoral."[31] If Dontsov was on the far right, Michael Hanusiak is on the left. Dontsov and the Organization of Ukrainian Nationalists are among his favorite targets. His *Lest We Forget* was written with the cooperation of the Soviets, who provided him with numerous documents from their bulging archives. Hanusiak makes effective use of German records detailing the brutalities of the German-recruited Ukrainian police. His book also contains extended quotes from Dontsov.

The late Ivan Rudnitsky resisted the temptation of Ukrainian scholars to "circle the wagons" and deny any and all Ukrainian complicity with the atrocities committed against Jews, Poles, Gypsies, and fellow Ukrainians by the Nazis and their OUN allies. Somewhat reluctantly, but nevertheless honestly, Rudnitsky's collected essays (*Essays in Modern Ukrainian History*) describe the characteristics of the nationalist movement in a manner that leaves no doubts regarding its nationalist propinquities.

A little-known sidebar to Ukrainian history is the brief period of a few weeks in which the nationalists took over the government in Transcarpathia before Hitler took it away from them and assigned it to the Hungarians. Mykyta Kosakvis'kyy's description of this blip on history's screen reveals that the Ukrainian regime was marked by severe legislation against the Jews, the end of freedom of the press, the abolishment of all competing political parties, and the establishment of German-style concentration camps. The article, titled "Z Nedan 'oho Minuloho" (This was not so long ago), appeared in *Nashe Slovo Review*.[32]

### Ukrainian Formations and the Warsaw Uprisings

Ukrainian units played an important role in suppressing the Warsaw ghetto uprising in 1943 and the 1944 Warsaw resistance organized by the Polish Home Army. Care must be taken, however, to distinguish Ukrainian forces from the Kaminski Brigade and the Dirlewanger Brigade, neither of which included a significant number of Ukrainians.

Useful in this respect is Joanna K. Hanson's *The Civilian Population and the Warsaw Uprising of 1944,* as is General Jürgen Stroop's boastful account of his suppression of the 1943 Warsaw ghetto uprising. Stroop's gift to the Führer includes photographs of the Trawniki troops under his command. The Trawniki men included Balts and Ukrainians in training for concentration-camp duties who were rushed in when the ghetto uprising began.

Edward Serwanski and Irena Trawinska in their *Zbrodnia niemiecka w Warsawie, 1944* provide the Polish perspective to the same events, while Hans von Krannhals's *Der Warschauer Aufstand, 1944* offers a thoroughly German point of view. Krannhals confirms that there were Ukrainian fighting formations at Warsaw in 1944 that participated in putting down the uprising.

### "A Pledge Betrayed"

The determination of the Allies to punish Nazi war criminals evaporated as soon as the Cold War set in. Tom Bower's *Blind Eye to Murder* is an excellent, highly documented account of the retreat of the British and American governments from their determination to bring war criminals to trial.

There are, of course, numerous additional references that can be supplied that will throw light on the crimes committed by the various formations that composed the Galician Division—crimes that merit condemnation by all civilized people. Special mention should be made of the recently published *Holocaust in the Soviet Union* edited by Lucjan Dobroszycki and Jeffrey Gurock. These volumes should go far in dispelling the myths that have obscured a clear-eyed view of what transpired in the Ukraine and other parts of Stalinist Russia.

## NOTES

1. Lubomir Luciuk, "Ukraine's Wartime Unit Never Linked to War Crime," *Globe and Mail* (Toronto), March 26, 1985.

2. Wasyl Verhya, "The 'Galicia' Ukrainian Division in Polish and Soviet Literature," *Ukrainian Quarterly* 36 no. 3 (Autumn 1980): 252–70.

3. Luciuk, "Ukraine's Wartime Unit."

4. D. Haldane Porter, "Refugee Screening Commission Report on Ukrainians in SEP Camp No. 374 Italy," Public Record Office, LACAB/18rsc/RIC, February 21, 1947.

5. Valerie Styrkul, *We Accuse* (Kiev: Dnipro Publishing, 1984), pp. 246–48.

6. Roger James Bender and Hugh Taylor, *Uniforms, Organization, and History of the Waffen-SS*, vol. 4, 1st ed., 2d printing (San Jose: R. James Bender Publishing, 1982), p. 28.

7. Styrkul, *We Accuse*, pp. 134–35.

8. Wolf-Dietrich Heike, *The Ukrainian Division "Galicia," 1943–1945: A Memoir*, edited by Yuri Boshyk (Toronto: Schevchenko Society, 1988), p. 22.

9. Styrkul, *We Accuse*, p. 171.

10. Fr. Waclaw Szetelnicki, *Zapomniany Lwowski Bohater Ks. Stanislaw Frankl* (London: Polish Library, n.d., p. 132.

11. Reuben Ainsztein, "The Myth of the Fatalistic and Helpless Galician Jew," in *Jewish Resistance in Nazi-occupied Eastern Europe* (New York: Barnes and Noble, 1974), p. 254.

12. Zvi Weigler, "Two Polish Villages Razed for Extending Help to Jews and Partisans," *Yad Vashem Bulletin* (Jerusalem) 1 (April 1957): 18–20.

13. National Military Archives, Washington, D.C., File T-175-94.

14. *Armia Krajowa w dokumentach, 1939–1945*, 5 vols. (London, 1976) vol. 3, pp. 447, 458, 507.

15. *Report on the Entry of Nazi War Criminals and Collaborators into the U.K., 1945–1950*, All Party Parliamentary War Crimes Group, House of Commons, London, 1988, p. 26.

16. Interviews with Colonel Irvin Pauliak, Major V. F. Stefansky, and Dr. Pavel Simunic of the Military Historical Institute of Slovakia, Bratislava, 1984.

17. Heike, *Ukrainian Division "Galicia,"* pp. 100–101.

18. Porter, "Refugee Screening Commission."

19. Philip H. Buss and Andrew Mello, *Hitler's Germanic Legions* (London: Macdonald and Janes Publishers, 1978), p. 10.

20. Bradley F. Smith, *Reaching Judgment at Nuremberg* (New York: New American Library, 1979).

21. *Army: The Magazine of Landpower* 35, no. 6 (June 1985).

22. A Ukrainian version of Heike's book, titled *Ukräns'ska dyvisia 'Halychyna': Istoria Formuvannia i boiovykh dii u 1943–1945 rokakh*, was published in 1970. An English version, *The Ukrainian Division "Galicia," 1943–1945: A Memoir*, was published in Toronto in 1988 by the Shevchenko Society.

23. Basil Dmytryshyn, "The Nazis and the SS Volunteer Division "Galicia," *American Slavic and East European Review*, no. 15 (1956): 1–10.

24. Volodymyr Kubijovyc, "Ukraine During World War II," in *Ukraine: A Concise Encyclopedia*, 2 vols. (Toronto: University of Toronto Press, 1963–71).

25. National Military Archives, Washington, D.C., File T-175.

26. Volodymyr Kubijovyc, "The Ukrainians in German-occupied Territory," in *Ukraine: A Concise Encyclopedia*, vol. 1 (Toronto: University of Toronto Press, 1963), pp. 874–78.

27. Styrkul, *We Accuse*.

28. Panias Fedenko, "Remarks on Modern History," *Nashe Slovo* (Munich), March 1977.

29. Betti Einstein-Keshev, "The Story of Independent Ukraine," *Fun Noenten Over* (Out of the recent past), vol. 3 (New York: Central Yiddish Cultural Organization, 1957).

30. Orest Subtelny, "The Soviet Occupation of Western Ukraine, 1939–1941: An Overview," in *Ukraine During World War II: History and Its Aftermath*, ed. Yury Boshyk (Edmonton: Canadian Institute of Ukrainian Studies, 1986).

31. Dmitri Dontsov, *Nationalism* (Lemberg, 1936), and *Chrestom i meczem* (Toronto, 1967).

32. Mykyta Kosakvis'kyy, "Z Nedan'oho Minuloho," *Nashe Slovo* no. 5 (1977): 67–80.

## SELECT BIBLIOGRAPHY

Ainsztein, Reuben. *Jewish Resistance in Nazi-occupied Eastern Europe*. New York: Barnes and Noble, 1974.

Armstrong, John A. *Ukrainian Nationalism, 1939–1945*. New York: Columbia University Press, 1955.

Bender, Roger J., and Hugh Taylor. *Uniforms, Organization, and History of the Waffen-SS*. Vol. 4. San Jose: R. James Bender Publishing, 1982.

Bower, Tom. *Blind Eye to Murder*. London: Andre Deutsch, 1981.

Buss, Philip H., and Andrew Mello. *Hitler's Germanic Legions*. London: Macdonald and Janes Publishers, 1978.

Cookridge, E. H. *Gehlen, Spy of the Century*. London: Transworld, 1972.

Datner, Szymon, et al. *Genocide, 1939–1945*. Warsaw: Wydawnictwo Zachodnie, 1962.

Davidson, Eugene. *The Trial of the Germans*. New York: Macmillan, 1966.

Deschênes, Jules. *Commission of Inquiry on War Criminals*. Ottawa: Government Publications Office, 1986.

Dmytryshyn, Basil. "The Nazis and the SS Volunteer Division 'Galicia.' " *American Slavic and East European Review*, no. 15 (1956): 1–10.

Dobroszycki, Lucjan, and Jeffrey Gurock, eds. *The Holocaust in the Soviet Union*. Armonie, N.Y.: M.E. Sharpe, 1993.

Ehrenburg, Ilya, and Vasily Grossman, eds. *The Black Book*. Translated by John Glad and James Levine. New York: Holocaust Library, 1981.

Friedman, Philip. *Roads to Extinction: Essays on the Holocaust*. New York: Jewish Publication Society of America, 1980.

Friedman, Saul. *Pogromchik: The Assassination of Simon Petlura*. New York: Hart, 1976.

Hanson, Joanna K. *The Civilian Population and the Warsaw Uprising of 1944*. Cambridge, England: Cambridge University Press, 1982.

Hanusiak, Michael. *Lest We Forget*. Toronto: Progress Books, 1976.

Heike, Wolf-Dietrich. *The Ukrainian Division Galicia, 1943–1945: A Memoir*. Edited by Yury Boshyk. Toronto: Shevchenko Society, 1988.

Hilberg, Raul. *The Destruction of the European Jews*. New York: Quadrangle, 1961.

Keegan, John. *Waffen SS: The Asphalt Soldiers*. New York: Ballantine, 1970.

Krannhals, Hans von. *Der Warschauer Aufstand, 1944*. Frankfurt: Bernard und Graefe, 1964.

Krausnick, Helmut, and Martin Broszat. *The Anatomy of the SS State*. Cambridge, England: William Collins Sons, 1968.

Lincoln, W. Bruce. *Red Victory: A History of the Russian Civil War*. New York: Simon and Schuster, 1989.

Reitlinger, Gerald. *The SS, Alibi of a Nation*. London: Heinemann, 1956.

*Report on the Entry of Nazi War Criminals and Collaborators into the U.K., 1945–1950*. All Party Parliamentary War Crimes Group, House of Commons, London, 1988.

Rudnitsky, Ivan L. *Essays in Modern Ukrainian History*. Edmonton: Canadian Institute of Ukrainian Studies, 1987.

Sanders, Ronald. *Shores of Refuge: A Hundred Years of Jewish Immigration*. New York: Henry Holt, 1988.

Schoenfeld, Joachim. *Holocaust Memoirs: Jews in the Lwow Ghetto, the Janowski Concentration Camp, and as Deportees in Siberia*. New York: Ktav, 1985.

Serwanski, Edward, and Irena Trawinska. *Zbrodnia niemiecka w Warsawie, 1944*. Poznan: Wydawnictwo Institutu Zachodniego, 1946.

Shandruk, Pavlo. *Arms of Valor*. Translated by Roman Olesnicki. New York: Speller, 1959.

Smith, Bradley F. *Reaching Judgment at Nuremberg*. New York: New American Library, 1979.

Stein, George F. *The Waffen SS: Hitler's Elite Guard at War*. Ithaca, N.Y.: Cornell University Press, 1986.

Stroop, Jürgen. *The Stroop Report: The Jewish Quarter Is No More*. Edited and translated by Sybil Milton and A. Worth. New York: Pantheon, 1979.

Styrkul, Valerie. *We Accuse*. Kiev: Dnipro Publishing, 1984.

Sydnor, Charles W. *Soldiers of Destruction; The SS Death's Head Division, 1933–1945*. Princeton, N.J.: Princeton University Press, 1990.

Szetelnicki, Fr. Waclaw. *Zapomniany Lwowski Bohater Ks. Stanislaw Frankl*. London: Polish Library, n.d.

Tessin, Georg. *Verbände und Truppen der deutschen Wehrmacht und Waffen SS im Zweiten Weltkrieg, 1939–1945*. Frankfurt: Verlag E. S. Mittler und Sohh, 1974.

Wiesenthal, Simon. *The Murderers Among Us*. London: Heinemann, 1967.

Wrangel, Petr. *The Memoirs of General Wrangel*. London: Williams and Norgate, 1929.

Yaremko, Michael. *From Separation to Unity*. Toronto: Shevchenko Scientific Society, 1967.

# Chapter 15

# Approaches to the Study of the Holocaust in the Balkans

*Alexander Kitroeff*

Approximately one million of the eight million Jews that inhabited pre–World War II Europe lived in the Balkan Peninsula countries. Yet Balkan Jewry as a whole and each of the Jewish communities in the separate Balkan countries have not been accorded the place they deserve in Jewish historiography and in the study of the Holocaust.

This chapter begins with a description of the prewar status of Balkan Jews and of primary studies on Jewish life in the Balkan countries prior to World War II. Following the introductory section, the main part of the chapter reviews both the Jewish experience in each of the Balkan countries during the war and the principal studies relating to the Holocaust in those countries published in non-Balkan languages, mainly English and French, as well as a few of the most important works in Hebrew.[1] Also, the main themes and debates among scholars studying the wartime fate of the Jews in the Balkan countries are identified and analyzed. The chapter concludes by locating the work on wartime Balkan Jewry within more general trends in Holocaust historiography.

## THE JEWS IN THE PREWAR BALKANS

The Jewish population in each of the Balkan countries has failed to attract the scholarly attention that Jewish communities elsewhere in Europe have. This can be explained in part by their relatively small size. Indeed, the only Jewish community in the Balkans that has been studied with any degree of thoroughness is the Romanian, which was the third largest in prewar Europe. Other explanations for this apparent oversight include the generally peripheral status of the

Balkan countries in mainstream European historiography and the contrasts between the principally Sephardic traditions of Balkan Jewry and the Ashkenazic
traditions of most of European Jewry.

Little scholarly attention has been paid, moreover, to the study of Jews of the
Balkans as a whole. It is true that following the post–World War II establishment
of Communist regimes in Albania, Bulgaria, Romania, and Yugoslavia, most
Western scholars ceased to regard the Balkans as a common region. The period
during and preceding that war, however, was one in which several similarities
obtained among the countries of the Balkan Peninsula. These similarities were
expressed through the shared political traditions of the Balkan states, the characteristics of the dominant religion in the area, Eastern (Greek) Orthodox, and,
finally, the common traditions of the Jewish communities in these countries.

The status of minorities in the Balkan countries in the first half of the twentieth
century was strongly influenced by the shared Ottoman past of these countries.
The Ottoman Empire's system of government was one that tolerated multiethnic
cohabitation. The Ottoman policy of allowing non-Islamic minorities a degree
of autonomy, alongside the protection offered to minorities by the European
powers, helped to preserve the various ethnic cultures.

That ethnic mosaic was shattered, however, with the advent of European
nationalism in the nineteenth century and its diffusion among the Balkan
bourgeoisie and intelligentsia.[2] The subject peoples of the Ottoman Empire (and
those in the Balkan territories ruled by the Austro-Hungarian Empire) did not
embrace nationalism simultaneously; the more economically powerful and better-
educated groups were its earliest adherents. While these groups eventually succeeded in forming independent nation-states, the other less economically and
politically advanced ethnic groups lagged behind. When they did eventually
embrace nationalist doctrines, they found that they were already incorporated
into a national entity. Their challenges to the nation that had incorporated them
resulted in continual unrest and friction over disputed boundaries and territories,
with one nation often adopting the cause of a minority group of a neighboring
country. Indeed, at times, fierce intra-Balkan territorial disputes brought along
the involvement of rival European powers, earning the Balkans the name "pow-
der keg of Europe."[3]

The end of World War I brought about the final dissolution of the Ottoman
and Austro-Hungarian empires and the more or less permanent settlement of the
boundaries dividing Balkan national states. Several ethnic, linguistic, and religious groups found themselves incorporated into one or more of the six Balkan
states, Albania, Bulgaria, Greece, Romania, Turkey, and Yugoslavia.

At the same historical juncture, the newly formed League of Nations decided
to guarantee the rights of national minorities in its member countries. The observance of minority rights by states was thus made a condition of admission to
membership in the League of Nations. Those rights were guaranteed by the so-
called minority treaties signed between the Allied powers and Greece, Romania,
and the Kingdom of Serbs, Croats, and Slovenes (which was renamed Yugoslavia

in 1929), and in special provisions in the peace treaties that the Allied powers signed with Bulgaria and Turkey.

The provisions in both these treaties can be divided between those that protected a minority's common rights (what would today be described as human rights) and those designed to preserve the identity of minority populations. Common rights included the acquisition of nationality based on habitual residence or birth in the national territory of one's parents; the protection of life and liberty; the free exercise in public or private of any creed, religion, or belief; and equal access to employment opportunities. Identity rights included the right of minorities to establish charitable, religious, and social institutions and schools as well as the right to free use and instruction of language.[4]

In light of still-lingering nationalist and territorial rivalries, the Balkan states were sensitive to the possibility of a minority group within their borders playing the role of a "fifth column," acting in the interests of a neighboring country. Several minorities, therefore, occasionally faced difficulties in the use and instruction of their respective languages. But due in part to their past Ottoman experience, the Balkan states remained tolerant on matters of religious freedom. Some states had a poorer record than others in minority policies. On the whole, the policies of Bulgaria, Greece, and Yugoslavia were only mildly hostile to certain minority groups. By contrast, Romania, Turkey, and to a lesser extent Albania all reserved far harsher treatment for minority groups within their borders.

The Jews were a significant minority group in all Balkan states. The Jewish communities in the Balkan countries consisted primarily of Sephardic Jews who had been welcomed by the Ottomans after their expulsion from the Iberian Peninsula in the late fifteenth century. The large number of Sephardic Jews—over twenty thousand settled in the city of Salonika alone—joined much smaller indigenous and assimilated "Romaniot" Jewish communities. As a consequence of the Ottoman system of government that granted a degree of self-autonomy to non-Islamic religious minorities, the Sephardic communities remained self-contained and unassimilated. A greater degree of assimilation was achieved by the Ashkenazic Jews who moved from Poland and Russia to the northern Balkan regions in the nineteenth century.

The largest Jewish community in the prewar Balkans was the Romanian, amounting to about 756,930 according to the Romanian census of 1930 and comprising 4.2 percent of the population. The Jewish community in Greece numbered 79,950, equivalent to 1 percent of the population, while the Yugoslav Jewish population of 71,342 accounted for .4 percent of the population, and the roughly 50,000 Jews in Bulgaria comprised slightly under 1 percent of that country's population.

While the population of all four of these countries was primarily rural, the Jews formed an almost exclusively urban element engaged in retail trade, commerce, and handicrafts. During the interwar period the largest Jewish urban concentration was in Thessaloniki (formerly Salonika until it was incorporated into Greece in 1912), where the community made up 20 percent of the city's population. The second-largest urban concentration of Jews was in the Bulgarian capital of Sofia, where over one-half the Jewish population of the country settled. The Jews in Yugoslavia lived, for the most part, in the cities of Belgrade, Sarajevo, and Zagreb. Romania was the only exception to this pattern, its Jewish population having settled in several cities, towns, and even villages.

The Jews were among the least politically threatening ethnic groups. Other minorities, such as Armenians, Kurds, and Macedonians, had entertained notions of national self-determination at the territorial expense of the countries they inhabited. Naturally, they were an anathema to the majority population.

The Balkan Jews, however, were much less nationalistically oriented. Sephardic Jews, who comprised the majority in Albania, Bulgaria, Greece, and Turkey and about one-half of the total Jewish presence in Romania and Yugoslavia, were not particularly attracted to Zionism. Only the Bulgarian Jewry could boast of a committed Zionist movement. The indifference of most of the Sephardic and Ladino-speaking Balkan Jews toward Zionism can be explained by the primarily Ashkenazic and Yiddish-language characteristics of the early Zionist movement. Also, the Sephardic Jewry's experience with autonomy in the multiethnic Ottoman Empire strongly influenced its preference for maintaining its identity through a religious, rather than a nationalistic, consciousness.

The Jews in Bulgaria, Greece, Turkey, and Yugoslavia enjoyed the civic rights and political equality formalized in the post–World War I minority treaties. Although Jewish religious freedom was also generally respected, some obstacles were occasionally placed in the way of the use and instruction of their language. Anti-Semitism was practiced only by small, peripheral pro-Nazi groups that would become more powerful in the late 1930s.

Romania was the only Balkan country in which the state pursued anti-Semitic policies, failing to respect the minority treaty it signed and refusing to extend Romanian nationality to all Jews living in its territory. In fact, anti-Semitism manifested itself in Romania as early as the second half of the nineteenth century, its intensity paralleling the anti-Semitism that took hold across the border in imperial Russia.

What lay at the root of Romanian anti-Semitism is a matter of debate, but if one takes into account the situation in the rest of the Balkans, one can exclude political causes. Despite the intensity of nationalist rivalries in the region, the Jews did not figure prominently as objects of nationalist hostility. Moreover, religiously based anti-Semitism cannot be considered as a prime motivating force. The Eastern (Greek) Orthodox church, for instance, less concerned with doctrinal definitions than the Catholic church, preferred to ignore the relatively tiny number of non–Greek Orthodox in Southeastern Europe. But as in other aspects of the history of this region, generalizations are risky—and in stark contrast to the attitude of the church elsewhere in the Balkans, the Romanian church did condone anti-Semitic behavior.

Nonetheless, the principal causes of Romanian anti-Semitism were probably economic. Romania distinguished itself from the other Balkan countries on the issue of land tenure. The local landowning group, the boyars, was powerful enough to frustrate the attempted land reform of 1864. The Romanian peasantry thus remained subjected to a harsh quasi-feudal state of affairs, by far the worst situation experienced by peasants in the entire Balkan region. The Romanian state, however, found it more convenient to blame the peasantry's hardships on the "misdeeds" of middleman minorities in towns and villages—Jews and to a lesser extent Greeks and Armenians, many of whom had become land lease-holders through moneylending—rather than on the boyars. That strategy was successful, as evidenced by an abortive 1907 peasant revolt directed against Romanian landlords and Jewish leaseholders.

In the 1930s most European countries witnessed the rise of fascism and authoritarianism. The Balkan countries were no exception, and by the second half of the 1930s Bulgaria, Greece, Romania, and Yugoslavia were all ruled by authoritarian dictatorships. These regimes were more akin to Italian fascism than German Nazism, and they did not therefore pursue explicitly anti-Semitic policies. Moreover, the ethnic heterogeneity of the populations of the Balkan countries mitigated against the spread of Nazi theories of racial superiority that, in turn, would have contributed to the spread of anti-Semitism.[5]

The history of the Jews in the Balkans in the period preceding World War II is dealt with in the following works. The life of Jews in the Ottoman Empire is described in Abraham Galante, *Documents officiels Turcs concernant les juifs de Turquie* (Official Turkish documents concerning the Jews of Turkey), and Bernard Lewis, *The Jews of Islam*. Sephardic life is depicted in Michael Molho, *Usos y costumbres de los Sefardies de Salonica* (Habits and customs of the Sephardics in Salonica). There are no detailed studies examining prewar Balkan Jewry as a single group, only a short article that introduces such an angle by Daniel J. Elazar, "The Sunset of Balkan Jewry," *Forum* 27, no. 2 (1977): 135–41.

The main studies on the Bulgarian Jews in this period are somewhat dated. They include A. Romano, Joseph Ben, and Nisim (Buko) Levy, *Yehudut Bulgariyah* (The Jews of Bulgaria), a general history of the Bulgarian Jews from earliest times; Saul Mezan, *Les Juifs espagnols en Bulgarie* (The Spanish Jews in Bulgaria); and N. M. Gelber, "Jewish Life in Bulgaria," *Jewish Social Studies* 8 (1946): 103–26.

The standard works on the Jews of Greece are by Joseph Nehama, *Histoire des Israelites de Salonique* (History of the Jews of Salonica), and I. S. Emmanuel, *Histoire des Israelites de Salonique* (History of the Jews of Salonica). See also Leon Sciaky, *Farewell to Salonica*. For the early twentieth century, a useful article is by Rena Molho, "Venizelos and the Jewish Community of Salonika, 1912–1919." A study of Greek interwar politics by George Th. Mavrogordatos, *Stillborn Republic: Social Coalitions and Party Strategies in Greece, 1922–1936*, provides an insightful analysis of the relations between the state, the political parties, and the Jewish community in Thessaloniki.

For prewar Romania, Oskar I. Janowsky, *People at Bay: The Jewish Problem in East Central Europe*, is an early, yet extremely useful analysis of the economic roots of anti-Semitism. Ezra Mendelsohn, *The Jews of East Central Europe Between the World Wars*, offers an excellent account of the history of the Jews in the interwar period. This is one of the most important recent contributions to the immediate historical background to the Holocaust. The chapter on Romania describes the divisions between the assimilationist Jews of ''Old'' (Regat) Romania and the Zionism of the Jews in the Romanian territories to the west and north. The policies of the Romanian state toward the Jews in this period are sensitively analyzed.

The Jewish community of interwar Yugoslavia is the only one in the Balkans to have been the subject of a book-length study based on extensive archival research. Harriet Pass Freidenreich, *The Jews of Yugoslavia: A Quest for Community*, focuses on the country's three largest communities, in Belgrade, Sarajevo, and Zagreb, and analyzes the socioeconomic background of the communities, communal affairs, and issues of identity. This is by far the most thorough treatment of any of the Jewish communities in the Balkans during this period.

Finally, there are no studies on the Jews in interwar Albania and Turkey. Some information about the Jews in interwar Turkey can be gleaned from encyclopedias of Judaism and the *American Jewish Yearbook*. Neither community, however, was directly involved in the Holocaust.

## THE HOLOCAUST IN THE BALKANS

The fortunes of the Balkan countries during World War II were mixed. Greece and Yugoslavia fought against the Axis but were eventually occupied by German, Italian, and Bulgarian forces. Bulgaria and Romania sided with the Axis powers, and Romania allowed German troops to be stationed in its territory. Hitler rewarded the two collaborationist Balkan countries by allowing their troops to occupy territories that Bulgaria and Romania had either lost when the war broke out or that had formerly belonged to neighboring states. Thus Romania took over Bessarabia and Northern Bukovina, both of which had been lost to the Soviet Union, but did not recover Northern Transylvania, which the Nazis awarded to Hungary. Bulgaria occupied Western Thrace, which had formerly belonged to Greece, the Macedonian province of Yugoslavia, and the area known as Dobruja, which had belonged to Romania.

In the aftermath of their occupation of the Balkans, the Nazis did not move simultaneously against Jewish communities in each of the countries. They began rounding up Jews in occupied Yugoslavia in 1942 and Jews in occupied Greece more than a year later. The heavy-handed military control the Nazis exercised in both these countries facilitated widespread arrests of Jews, despite several efforts by the non-Jewish population to protect the community. Indeed, the rounding up of Jews in Greece was complicated by the growth of a powerful local resistance movement that successfully protected several Jewish communities. The German presence in Bulgaria and Romania was not strong enough to permit the rounding up and deportation of Jews. Moreover, the pro-Axis status of both countries made it incumbent upon Berlin to seek the prior consent, as well as the assistance, of the Bulgarian and Romanian governments. In what must surely be one of the paradoxes in Balkan wartime history, both these governments resisted Nazi pressure to deport Jews. Yet the Bulgarian and Romanian governments did themselves oversee the rounding up and deportation of Jewish communities in the peripheries of their enlarged states—Bessarabia, Northern Bukovina, Yugoslav Macedonia, and Western Thrace. In fact, the roundups by the Romanians were particularly brutal and contrasted sharply with the Romanian government's refusal to arrest the Jews in the territories in the core of Romania, known as "Old" (Regat) Romania.

There are no studies that systematically examine the unfolding of the Holocaust in the entire Balkan region. Instead, the standard works on the Holocaust in Europe normally include separate accounts of the fate of the Jews in each of the Balkan countries, and these will be examined in the following section. These accounts rely heavily on monographs that focus on the situation of the Jews in each of the Balkan countries. The issues that are addressed in each cluster of country-based monographs are those that have been central to Holocaust studies elsewhere in Europe. The earliest works were "martyrological" in nature, seeking to highlight the fate of the Jews during the war. As work on the Holocaust in Western and Eastern Europe gradually developed into new areas of inquiry such as Gentile-Jewish relations, the "passivity" of the Jews, the responsibilities of the Jewish communal leadership, the role played by pro-Nazi governments, and the response of anti-Fascist resistance movements, the church, and ordinary people, studies on the Jews in the wartime Balkans also began exploring these areas. The specific conditions that prevailed in each of the Balkan countries have determined the relative stress that scholars have placed on each of these issues.

## Bulgaria

The pro-Nazi government in Bulgaria implemented a series of anti-Semitic measures early on, but refused to comply with Nazi demands to deport the Jews. The head of state, King Boris, and members of the Sobranie (parliament) participated in the decision to resist Nazi pressure. Astonishingly, there were more Jews in Bulgaria at the end of the war than there had been when the war broke out.

A great deal of the work published on the situation of the Bulgarian Jews adopts a polemical tone in assessing the role played by the king and other officials. Nonetheless, in an effort to draw attention to the fact that there was little anti-Semitism among the population and that the small Communist resistance opposed the deportations, some other authors have chosen to stress the protection afforded the Jews by ordinary people and by the resistance movement.

The standard work in this field is Frederick B. Chary's *The Bulgarian Jews and the Final Solution, 1940–1944*, a thoroughly researched study that examines events in Bulgaria within the overall political context of the period. Chary's comprehensive study concludes that in themselves, the roles played by the king, the Sobranie, and the resistance movement were all ultimately minimal and that Jews were in fact protected only because the Bulgarian elite felt ambivalent and Nazi pressure was applied too late to be truly effective. A compromise was reached, with the Bulgarians agreeing to the deportation of the Jews in the Yugoslav and Greek territories they had occupied and the Nazis allowing the Jews of Bulgaria to be sent to that country's provinces rather than face deportation. Interestingly enough, Chary concurs with a majority of studies on Bulgaria in finding that neither the church nor the general population was anti-Semitic, a conclusion that also tallies with what has been found for neighboring Greece and Yugoslavia. Also very useful are shorter scholarly treatments of these issues: a chapter in Marshall L. Miller's *Bulgaria During the Second World War*, pages 93–106, which provides a comprehensive summary based on documentary evidence, and an article by Nissan Oren, "The Bulgarian Exception: A Reassessment of the Salvation of the Jewish Community," *Yad Vashem Studies on the European Jewish Catastrophe and Resistance* 13 (1969): 83–106. See also Frederick Chary's "The Bulgarian Writers' Protest of October 1940 Against the Introduction of Antisemitic Legislation into the Kingdom of Bulgaria," *East European Quarterly* 4 (March 1, 1970): 88–93.

Among the previously mentioned "polemical" works, which do, however, provide valuable information, are the following. Benjamin Arditi, *Yehudi Bulgariyah Bishanot Hamishpat Hanatsi, 1940–1944* (The Jews of Bulgaria during Nazi occupation, 1940–1944), is representative of the articles insisting on the central role played by the king. Articles that emphasize the role played by public opinion and the resistance movement include Vladislav Topalov, "L'Opinion publique Bulgare contre les persecutions des Juifs (Octobre 1940–9 Septembre 1944)" (Bulgarian public opinion against the persecution of the Jews), in *Etudes historiques a l'occasion du XXIIe Congrès Internationale des Sciences Historiques, 1965*; Matei Yulzari, "The Bulgarian Jews in the Resistance Movement," in *They Fought Back: The Story of the Jewish Resistance in Nazi Europe*, edited by Yuri Suhl, 275–81; Albert Koen, *Saving of the Jews in Bulgaria, 1941–1944*, which is a government publication; and Uri Oren, "A Town Called Monastir: The Heroes," in *Anthology on Armed Jewish Resistance, 1939–1945*, edited by Isaac Kowalski, a book that highlights the role of certain individuals in the resistance movement.

The destruction of the Jews in the territories occupied by Bulgaria is examined in Nadejda Slavi Vasileva, "On the Catastrophe of the Thracian Jews," and Aleksandar Matkovsky, "The Destruction of Macedonian Jewry," both in *Yad Vashem Studies on the European Castastrophe and Resistance* 3 (1959), and Hans Joachim Hoppe, "Germany, Bulgaria, Greece: Their Relations and Bulgarian Policy in Occupied Greece,'' *Journal of the Hellenic Diaspora* 11 (Fall 1984): 41–54.

## Greece

The case of neighboring Greece is different from that of Bulgaria. After a six-month war against Italy and then Germany, Greece was occupied by the Axis forces in May 1941. The Nazis, however, only retained control of several strategic points in the country, including Thessaloniki, leaving the rest to the Italians and the northeastern area of Greece to the Bulgarians. A Quisling government was installed in Athens. The harshness of the Axis occupation soon produced a Communist-led resistance movement in the mountain areas.

The Nazi authorities introduced a number of anti-Semitic measures in Thessaloniki, where the great majority of Greek Jews resided. But actual arrests and deportations were begun as late as March 1943. Nonetheless, by virtue of their military control of the area, the Nazis easily rounded up almost the entire Jewish population of the city. They were assisted in their task by the fact that they managed to persuade the community's chief rabbi of their supposed good intentions toward the Jews. Having completed the deportation of Thessaloniki's Jews by the summer of 1943, the Nazis turned their attention toward the other, smaller Jewish communities in Greece.

As most of the remaining Jewish communities were located in Italian-occupied Greece, the Nazis waited to proceed until the Italian capitulation of September 1943. Indeed, the Italians had been wholly uncooperative with their Nazi allies, steadfastly refusing to sanction anti-Jewish measures and in some cases even helping Jews avoid arrest by the Nazis. Following Italy's capitulation, however, the Germans assumed responsibility for administering the whole of occupied Greece (with the exception of the Bulgarian zone in the northeast) and moved against the remaining Jewish communities.

The Nazis were only partially successful in rounding up the remaining Jewish communities, failing to do so in towns that were accessible to the resistance movement and where Jews were more assimilated than they had been in Thessaloniki and were thus indistinguishable from the rest of the population. The majority of Jews living in the cities of Athens and Volos and on the island of Zakinthos survived largely thanks to the help proffered by the resistance movement, Greek officials, and the Orthodox church. Nonetheless, communities were totally destroyed. At the end of the war 62,573 Jews had lost their lives out of a total Jewish population of 79,950; over 46,000 of those who died were Thessaloniki Jews.

The standard, though now somewhat dated, work on the Holocaust in Greece remains the book by Michael Molho and Joseph Nehama, *In Memoriam: The Destruction of Greek Jewry* (more recent revised editions exist in French and Greek). It presents an overall picture of the Holocaust in Greece. The authors appear reluctant to underline the role played by the resistance movement. Steven Bowman, ''Jews in Wartime Greece,'' *Jewish Social Studies* 49 (Winter 1986): 45–61, offers an updated and balanced overview based on extensive research. Bowman has also published a bibliographic guide to works on the Jews in wartime Greece in *Greece in the 1940s: A Nation in Crisis*, edited by John O. Iatrides, 83–94.

Studies on the assistance proffered by the resistance movement, the church, and Greek officials include L. S. Stavrianos, ''The Jews of Greece,'' *Journal of Central European Affairs* 8 (October 1948); Avram Elmaleh, *Les Juifs de Salonique et la resistance hellenique* (The Jews of Thessaloniki and the Greek Resistance); and Alexandros Kitroeff, ''Greek Wartime Attitudes Towards the Jews in Athens,'' *Forum* 60 (Summer 1987): 41–51, where a direct link is drawn between the degree of Jewish assimilation and the effectiveness of the local resistance movement, on the one hand, and the salvation of the Jews of Athens, on the other, and ''Documents: The Jews in Greece, 1941–1944: Eyewitness Accounts,'' *Journal of the Hellenic Diaspora* 12 (Fall 1985): 5–32.

As was the case in Bulgaria and Yugoslavia, a number of Jews participated in the Greek resistance movement. A spate of recent publications in Greece on the wartime resistance contains several references on this subject. Among the non-Greek sources, see Isaac Kabelli, ''The Resistance of the Greek Jews,'' *YIVO Annual of Jewish Social Sciences* 8 (1953): 281–88; and Asher Moisses, ''Jews in the Army of Greece,'' in *Ha-Lohhem ha-Yehudi be-Seva'ot ha-'Olam* (The Jewish fighter in the armies of the world).

The reluctance of Italian forces to implement anti-Semitic measures and arrest Jews is covered in Jacques Sabille, ''Attitude of the Italians to the Jews in Occupied Greece,'' in *Jews Under the Italian Occupation*, edited by Leon Poliakov and Jacques Sabille, 151–60; and Susan Zuccotti, *The Italians and the Holocaust: Persecution, Rescue, and Survival*, 74–100, which also briefly mentions Italian policy in Croatia. The assistance of the Spanish government, which offered Sephardic Jews Spanish nationality, was another important factor contributing to the salvation of the Greek Jews. See Haim Avni, ''Spanish Nationals in Greece and Their Fate During the Holocaust,'' *Yad Vashem Studies* 8 (1970): 31–68, and his book, *Spain, Franco, and the Jews*.

The questions surrounding the role of Thessaloniki's chief rabbi, Zvi Koretz, are complicated and still unclear. The view in the standard work on the Holocaust in Greece by Molho and Nehama (*In Memoriam*, cited earlier) is that if Zvi Koretz was not a ''collaborator,'' he was at the least guilty of assisting the Germans. This view has been challenged by Nathan Eck, ''New Light on the Charges Against the Last Grand Rabbi of Salonica,'' *Yad Vashem Bulletin* 17 (1965): 9–15; and by Joseph Ben, ''Jewish Leadership in Greece During the Holocaust,'' in *Patterns of the Jewish Leadership in Nazi Europe*, edited by Yisrael Gutman and Cynthia Haft. While Eck seeks to exonerate the rabbi, Ben suggests that the rabbi was guilty of naivete rather than collaboration. For an assessment of the role of the rabbi in Ioannina, see Rachel Dalven, "The Holocaust in Jannina," *Journal of Modern Greek Studies* 2 (May 1984): 87–103.

Memoirs and eyewitness accounts of the Nazi death camps include David Benveniste, *Yehudei Saloniki be-doroth ha-aharonim* (Thessaloniki Jewry in recent generations); Albert Menasche, *Birkenau (Auschwitz II): How 72,000 Greek Jews Perished*; and Errikos Sevillias, *Athens, Auschwitz*.

## Romania

The quasi-Fascist Romanian dictatorship (1937–38) and the royal dictatorship (1939–40) were both responsible for increasing anti-Semitic measures in that country. In September 1940 Marshal Ion Antonescu became dictator, sharing power with the Fascist, terrorist Iron Guard. An office of "Romanization" was subsequently established to transfer Jewish, Greek, and Armenian property into Romanian hands; Jewish agricultural property was confiscated; and Jews employed in commerce and industry were dismissed. Forever the scapegoat for the country's problems, some 120 Jews were killed and their bodies hung in a Bucharest slaughterhouse during an Iron Guard uprising against Antonescu. Backed by the army, Antonescu soon eliminated the Iron Guard and established total control over Romania.

Worse suffering was to follow for the Jews in Bessarabia and Northern Bukovina. Falsely accusing the Jews of having welcomed the Soviets in those areas in 1940, the Antonescu regime turned against the Bessarabian and Bukovinan Jews with unprecedented brutality, even by Romanian standards. With the help of German troops, a pogrom in the town of Jassy took place in the summer of 1941. About 8,000 Jews were killed, some of them dying in closed cattle cars that were shunted from place to place. Mass shootings claimed a total of 100,000 Jewish lives.

The remaining Jews of these regions were sent to Trans-Dnistria, an area on the Romanian-Ukrainian border between the Dniester and Bug rivers. Of the 185,000 deported Bessarabian and Bukovinan Jews only about 30,000 avoided suffering a slow death in inhuman conditions that rivalled those of the Nazi death camps. All told, 380,000 Romanian Jews lost their lives in Bessarabia, Northern Bukovina, and Trans-Dnistria.

Yet despite Nazi wishes the 350,000 Jews in central Romania ("Old" or Regat Romania) were not deported. Although the Nazis did eventually reach an agreement with the Romanian regime that would have allowed deportations to begin in September 1942, ultimately these did not take place. The battle waged by Jewish community leaders in Bucharest and by the influential and proassimilationist Dr. Wilhelm Filderman bore fruit. Conditions in Trans-Dnistria were alleviated and deportations from "Old" Romania were delayed. Furthermore, the Romanian regime did not want to be regarded as merely a Nazi satellite and was thus in no hurry to comply with Nazi plans. When the Nazis began suffering setbacks in the war, the deportation plan was abandoned.

A large collection of documents relating to the Holocaust in Romania, Jean Ancel, *Documents Concerning the Fate of Romanian Jewry During the Holocaust*, provides researchers with very useful material. General overviews of events in Romania include Stephen Fischer-Galati, "Fascism, Communism, and the Jewish Question in Rumania," in *Jews and Non-Jews in Eastern Europe, 1918–1945*, edited by Bela Vago and George L. Mosse.

Most works on the plight of the Jews in wartime Romania focus on the destruction wrought in the northern areas rather than on the situation in "Old" Romania. Studies on Trans-Dnistria include Joseph B. Schechtman, "The Transdnistria Reservation," *YIVO Annual* 8 (1953): 178–96; Meier Teich, "The Jewish Self-Administration in Ghetto Shargorod (Trans-Dnistria)" *Yad Vashem Studies* 2 (1952): 219–54; Dora Litani, " 'Courier,' an Underground Newspaper in Trans-Dnistria, April–September 1943," *Yad Vashem Bulletin* 14 (March 1964): 44–48; Julius S. Fisher, *Transnistria: The Forgotten Cemetery*; and Bela Vago, "The Destruction of the Jews of Transylvania," *Hungarian Jewish Studies* 1 (1966): 171–221.

Among those works that focus on the Jewish leadership's efforts to counter anti-Semitic measures in "Old" Romania and the help offered by non-Jews, see Theodore Lavi, "Documents on the Struggle of Rumanian Jewry for Its Rights During the Second World War," *Yad Vashem Studies* 4 (1960): 274–75, "The Background to the Rescue of Romanian Jewry During the Period of the Holocaust," in *Jews and Non-Jews in Eastern Europe, 1918–1945*, edited by Bela Vago and George L. Mosse, and "The Vatican's Endeavors on Behalf of Rumanian Jewry During the Second World War," *Yad Vashem Studies* 5 (1960): 414. See also Bela Vago, "The Ambiguity of Collaborationism: The Center of the Jews in Rumania (1942–1944)," in *Patterns of the Jewish Leadership in Nazi Europe, 1939–1945: Proceedings of the Third Yad Vashem International Historical Conference*, edited by Yisrael Gutman and Cynthia J. Haft, where Vago outlines the leadership's dual role, simultaneous collaboration with the authorities and assistance to the Jews.

For the role played by the resistance movement—a factor of secondary importance in Romania—see A. Artzi, "The Underground Activities of the Pioneer Movements in Rumania During World War II," *Yad Vashem Bulletin* 12 (1962): 34–41. A very useful eyewitness account is Emil Dorian, *The Quality of Witness: A Romanian Diary, 1937–1944*, with an informative introduction by Michael Stanislawski that sketches the historical background.

The Jews of Northern Transylvania, who had suffered during the interwar period at the hands of the anti-Semitic Romanian state, found themselves under Hungarian rule during the war, since their region was transferred to Hungary by the Nazis. The bitter irony was that while the Jews had welcomed Hungarian rule, traditionally more sympathetic to the Jews than Romanian rule, they were rounded up and deported in the final stages of the war, when the Hungarians eventually relented in the face of Nazi pressures. A study by Nathaniel Katzburg, *Hungary and the Jews: Policy and Legislation, 1920–1943*, provides one of the most useful general accounts of Hungarian Jewish policy during the war. On the Northern Transylvania Jews, see R. L. Braham, ed., *Genocide and Retribution: An Aspect of the Holocaust in Hungary*, and Bela Vago, "Political and Diplomatic Activities for the Rescue of the Jews of Northern Transylvania, June 1944–February 1945," *Yad Vashem Studies* 6 (1967): 155–73. Bela Vago's "Contrasting Jewish Leadership in Wartime Hungary and Rumania" in *The Holocaust as Historical Experience*, edited by Yehuda Bauer and Nathan Rotenstreich, also provides a useful comparison between Hungarian and Romanian policies.

### Yugoslavia

Occupied by Axis forces in April 1941, Yugoslavia was partitioned and ceased to exist as a unified state. Germany occupied Slovenia, the Banat, and Serbia (the northern and central areas of the country); Italy occupied Dalmatia on the western coast and several inland regions; Hungary occupied a northeastern area of Yugoslavia; and Bulgaria occupied the southern province of Macedonia. Finally, Croatia, in the north, became an independent entity administered by the Ustasha, a Croatian Fascist organization.

As early as May 1941, preliminary measures were taken against the twelve thousand Serbian Jews. A few months later, roundups and shootings of Jews began in earnest, both in Serbia and the Banat region. Death camps were established within Serbia, and those interned were either shot or killed in gas vans. By mid–1942 the destruction of the Jews in Serbia and the Banat was completed.

In Croatia the Ustasha implemented anti-Jewish measures with a Nazi-like determination. Roundups of Croatian and Bosnian Jews began in 1941 to camps like Jasenovac. Those who did not die of hardships endured in the Croatian camps, about nine thousand, were eventually deported to Auschwitz. The eight thousand Jews living in Bulgarian-occupied territories were also deported in March 1943, while Jews in the Hungarian-occupied territories were deported by mid–1944.

Only Jews living in areas under Italian control, and those who managed to make their way to those areas, were able to avoid deportation. The Italians did not deport Jews to Germany and Poland, although they did intern Jews in those areas within their jurisdiction. As in Greece, after Italy's capitulation in September 1943, Nazi forces moved in and deported a number of Jews, but many either escaped to Italy or joined the partisan resistance movement.

The Yugoslav partisan movement was not strong enough to prevent or even frustrate deportations of Jews, as had been the case in Greece. Deportations were in fact carried out long before the Yugoslav resistance movement had time to organize. There are some works on the important role played by the Jews in the Yugoslav resistance movement. There are no studies, however, on public attitudes during the roundups, with the main bulk of work focusing on the details of the roundups and deportations in Serbia and Croatia.

Studies by Zdenko Lowenthal, ed., *The Crimes of the Fascist Occupants and Their Collaborators Against Jews in Yugoslavia*, and Jasa Romano, *Jews of Yugoslavia, 1941–1945: Victims of Genocide and Freedom Fighters*, provide an overall picture of the events in Yugoslavia, including the role that Jews played in the resistance movement. Charles W. Steckel, "Survivors and Partisans," and Uri Oren, "A Town Called Monastir," both in *Anthology on Armed Jewish Resistance, 1939–1945*, edited by Isaac Kowalski, are also worth consulting.

The fate of the Serbian Jews is accounted for in Nathan Eck, "The March of Death from Serbia to Hungary (September 1944)," *Yad Vashem Studies* 2 (1958): 255–94. The fate of the Croatian Jews is related in Yeshayahu Jelinek, "The Holocaust of Croatian Jewry: A Few reflections," *Shoah* 1 (1979): 20–23; and Edmond Paris, *Genocide in Satellite Croatia, 1941–1945: A Record of Racial and Religious Persecutions and Massacres*. Finally, Jacques Sabille's "The Attitude of the Italians to the Persecuted Jews in Croatia," in *Jews Under the Italian Occupation*, edited by Leon Poliakov and Jacques Sabille, 129–50, examines the role of the Italian forces in Croatia during the war.

## THE BALKANS AND HOLOCAUST HISTORIOGRAPHY

Eastern European Jews suffered the greatest losses during the Holocaust, and studies have thus naturally tended to focus more on Eastern than on Western Europe. But Southeastern Europe, the Balkans—with the exception of Romania, which is often considered part of Eastern Europe—has been even more neglected in Holocaust studies than Western Europe.

The most systematic treatment of the Holocaust in Balkan countries can be found in Raul Hilberg, *The Destruction of the European Jews* (originally published in 1951 and revised in 1978), pages 432–554, which also includes Hungary and Slovakia as part of the Balkans. In this masterful overview of the Holocaust in Europe, the author is primarily concerned with *how* rather than *why* questions and deals with the gruesome process of discrimination, arrest, and deportation. Hilberg outlines these processes in a detailed manner, basing his research on German documents that provide new and valuable insights on events in the Balkan countries. In addition, although only in passing, Hilberg offers some comparisons between the deportation process in the Balkan countries and that which occurred elsewhere in Europe.

Written with the intention of refuting theories of Jewish passivity, Nora Levin's *The Holocaust: The Destruction of European Jewry, 1933–1945* includes, in the second part of the book, short chapters on each of the Balkan countries. These examine wartime Jewish-Gentile relations and Jewish participation in local resistance movements and are based on several available secondary sources. The most representative work of earlier studies that have been criticized for stressing Jewish passivity is Gerald Reitlinger's *The Final Solution: The Attempt to Ex-*

*terminate the Jews of Europe, 1939–1945* (2d revised and augmented edition). Reitlinger's sections on the Balkan countries are informative—Yugoslavia, 385–98; Greece, 398–408; Bulgaria, 408–14; Romania, 425–46; and Hungarian-occupied Romania, 454–71.

Also useful is Martin Gilbert's *The Holocaust: A History of the Jews of Europe During the Second World War*, a chronological account of the Holocaust that combines archival, published, and oral sources. There are references to the fate of the Jews in each of the Balkan countries throughout this book.

Insofar as general interpretations are concerned, the explanation of the Holocaust as a preconceived Nazi plan has many adherents. The most representative general work of this so-called intentionalist school is Lucy S. Dawidowicz's *The War Against the Jews, 1933–1945* (originally published in 1975). The author suggests that the Nazis engaged in two parallel ''wars,'' one against the countries of Europe and another against the Jews, which they had systematically planned earlier on. At the end of the book Dawidowicz includes short descriptions of the fate of the Jews in each European country, including the Balkans (Romania, 383–86; Bulgaria, 386–90; Yugoslavia, 390–92; Greece, 392–94). These accounts, however, whose brevity does not permit any reference to sources, focus exclusively on measures taken against the Jews. No mention is made of parallel repressive measures against others, such as those adopted against Serbians in Croatia, or against Armenians and Greeks as well as Jews as a result of the early ''romanization of property'' legislation in Romania. Finally, the specific wartime experiences of the Balkan Jews do not furnish a great deal of evidence for Dawidowicz's main argument. Indeed, only in Yugoslavia was the Jewish question addressed early on by the Nazis. Arrests of Greek Jews began almost two years after Greece fell to the Axis, while pressure applied to the Bulgarians and Romanians to deport their Jewish populations came too late. It would seem, therefore, that not all Balkan Jewish experiences conform to the intentionalist thesis of a preplanned ''war against the Jews.''

The so-called intentionalist school has come under criticism by writers who have stressed the functional aspects of the roundups, shootings, and deportations, depicting the Third Reich as a maze of competing power groups rather than a well-oiled machine totally under Hitler's control. The arguments and debates between the two sides are more relevant to the study of Nazi wartime policy as a whole than to the study of the Holocaust per se. If indeed the Third Reich was much less a programmed, well-oiled machine than has been seen by some, it is important that Holocaust historiography take into full account the involvement of other actors involved, such as the collaborationist governments, resistance movements, and the general public. One way of assessing these other factors is by examining the issue of Gentile-Jewish relations. While underlining the importance of German anti-Semitism, Yehuda Bauer has focused on the subject of Gentile-Jewish relations in *The Holocaust in Historical Perspective*. He examines those relations in the Balkans on pages 63–67. Bauer also briefly assesses the Holocaust in Romania in *A History of the Holocaust*, pages 305–9. Bauer's conclusion, that German and Polish Jews were offered little assistance in their hour of need by ordinary people in communities where the Jews had lived in relative isolation, also holds true for Greece. The Greek public was much more helpful to the more assimilated Jewish communities than it was to the less assimilated communities. This hypothesis is one well worth pursuing in examining the cases of other Balkan countries.

The Balkan experience could also be integrated into mainstream studies of the Holocaust along the line of argumentation recently suggested by Michael Marrus's *The Holocaust in History*. The author's aim is to study the Holocaust in much the same way that other historical phenomena are studied and interpreted, without, nonetheless, denying the ''unique'' and ''humanly unimaginable'' dimensions upon which earlier works on the Holocaust have insisted. Marrus examines the whole gamut of anti-Semitic policies, arrests, shootings, deportations, and destruction of the Holocaust against the background of overall wartime Nazi strategy. He then explains why the Holocaust should not be studied in isolation from other aspects of Nazi policy during the war by furnishing ample evidence of the often-haphazard and uneven development of Nazi policy toward the Jews across occupied Europe, including the Balkans. The Balkans, in fact, offer as fertile terrain as any in which to test Marrus's approach. The Nazis adopted vastly different approaches to the Jewish question in each of the Balkan countries. General Nazi strategy differed both in the two collaborationist states of Bulgaria and Romania and in the two occupied states, Greece and Yugoslavia. These differences in Nazi policies contributed to the contrasts in the wartime experiences of the Jewish communities in the Balkan countries. Future research on the Jewish communities in the Balkans could profitably address this question, in addition to the aforementioned issue of Gentile-Jewish relations. The richness of the Jewish experiences in the Balkan countries and their similarities and contrasts provide a useful testing ground in the development and strengthening of Holocaust historiography.


**NOTES**

1. Among the various bibliographies of the Holocaust, the most useful on the Balkans is Abraham J. Edelheit and Herschel Edelheit, eds., *Bibliography on Holocaust Literature* (Boulder, Colo.: Westview Press, 1986).

2. The standard works on nineteenth-century Balkan history include L. S. Stavrianos, *The Balkans, 1815–1914* (New York: Holt, Rinehart and Winston, 1963); Peter F. Sugar and Donald W. Treadgold, eds., *A History of East Central Europe*, vols. 5 and 8 (Seattle: University of Washington Press, 1977); and Barbara Jelavich, *History of the Balkans: Eighteenth and Nineteenth Centuries* (Cambridge, England: Cambridge University Press, 1983). See also Dimitrije Djordjevic and Stephen Fischer-Galati, *The Balkan Revolutionary Tradition* (New York: Columbia University Press, 1981).

3. For the history of minorities in the Balkans, see Raymond Pearson, *National Minorities in Eastern Europe, 1848–1945* (London: Macmillan, 1983).

4. James Fawcett, *The International Protection of Minorities*, Minority Rights Group Report no. 41 (London: MRG, 1979).

5. The standard account of interwar Balkan history remains Robert Lee Wolff, *The Balkans in Our Time* (New York: W. W. Norton, 1967).

## SELECT BIBLIOGRAPHY

Ancel, Jean. *Documents Concerning the Fate of Romanian Jewry During the Holocaust.* Vols. 1–12. New York: Beate Klarsfeld Foundation, 1986.

Arditi, Benjamin. *Yehudi Bulgariyah Bishanot Hamishpat Hantasi, 1940-1944* (The Jews of Bulgaria during Nazi occupation, 1940–1944). Tel Aviv: Israel Press, 1962.

Artzi, A. "The Underground Activities of the Pioneer Movements in Rumania During World War II," *Yad Vashem Bulletin* 12 (1962): 34–41.

Avni, Haim. *Spain, Franco, and the Jews.* Translated by E. Shimon: Philadelphia: Jewish Publication Society of America, 1982.

———. "Spanish Nationals in Greece and Their Fate During the Holocaust." *Yad Vashem Studies* 8 (1970): 31–68.

Bauer, Yehuda. *A History of the Holocaust.* New York: Franklin Watts, 1982.

———. *The Holocaust in Historical Perspective.* Seattle: University of Washington Press, 1978.

Ben, Joseph. "Jewish Leadership in Greece During the Holocaust." In *Patterns of the Jewish Leadership in Nazi Europe*, edited by Yisrael Gutman and Cynthia Haft, Jerusalem: Yad Vashem, 1977.

Benveniste, David. *Yehudei Saloniki be-doroth ha-aharonim* (Thessaloniki Jewry in recent generations). Jerusalem, 1973.

Bowman, Steven. "Jews in Wartime Greece." *Jewish Social Studies* 49 (Winter 1986): 45–61.

Braham, R. L., ed. *Genocide and Retribution: An Aspect of the Holocaust in Hungary.* Boston: Kluwer-Nijhoff, 1983.

Chary, Frederick B. *The Bulgarian Jews and the Final Solution, 1940–1944.* Pittsburgh: University of Pittsburgh Press, 1972.

———. "The Bulgarian Writers' Protest of October 1940 Against the Introduction of Antisemitic Legislation into the Kingdom of Bulgaria." *East European Quarterly* 4 (March 1, 1970): 88–93.

Dalven, Rachel. "The Holocaust in Jannina." *Journal of Modern Greek Studies* 2 (May 1984): 87–103.

Dawidowicz, Lucy. *The War Against the Jews, 1933–1945.* New York: Holt, Rinehart and Winston, 1975.

Dorian, Emil. *The Quality of Witness: A Romanian Diary, 1937–1944.* Edited by Marguerite Dorian. Philadelphia: Jewish Publication Society of America. 1982.

Eck, Nathan. "The March of Death from Serbia to Hungary (September 1944)." *Yad Vashem Studies* 2 (1958): 255–94.

———. "New Light on the Charges Against the Last Grand Rabbi of Salonica." *Yad Vashem Bulletin* 17 (1965): 9–15.

Elazar, Daniel J. "The Sunset of Balkan Jewry." *Forum* 27, no. 2 (1977): 135–41.

Elmaleh, Avram. *Les Juifs de Salonique et la resistance hellenique* (The Jews of Thessaloniki and the Greek resistance). Istanbul-Thessaloniki, 1949.

Emmanuel, I. S. *Histoire des Israelites de Salonique* (History of the Jews of Salonika). Paris: Thonon, 1936.

Fischer-Galati, Stephen. "Fascism, Communism, and the Jewish Question in Rumania." In *Jews and Non-Jews in Eastern Europe, 1918–1945*, edited by Bela Vago and George L. Mosse. Jerusalem: Israel Universities Press, 1974.

Fisher, Julius S. *Transnistria: The Forgotten Cemetery*. South Brunswick: A. T. Yoseloff, 1969.

Freidenreich, Harriet Pass. *The Jews of Yugoslavia: A Quest for Community*. Philadelphia: Jewish Publication Society of America, 1979.

Galante, Abraham. *Documents officiels Turcs concernant les juifs de Turquie* (Official Turkish documents concerning the Jews of Turkey). Istanbul: Haim, Rozio, 1931.

Gelber, N. M. "Jewish Life in Bulgaria." *Jewish Social Studies* 8 (1946): 103–26.

Gilbert, Martin. *The Holocaust: A History of the Jews of Europe During the Second World War*. New York: Henry Holt, 1985.

Hilberg, Raul. *The Destruction of the European Jews*. Rev. ed. New York: Octagon Books, 1978.

Hoppe, Hans Joachim. "Germany, Bulgaria, Greece: Their Relations and Bulgarian Policy in Occupied Greece." *Journal of the Hellenic Diaspora* 11 (Fall 1984): 41–54.

Iatrides, John O., ed. *Greece in the 1940s: A Nation in Crisis*. Hanover: University Press of New England, 1981, pp. 83–94.

Janowsky, Oscar I. *People at Bay: The Jewish Problem in East Central Europe*. New York: Oxford University Press, 1938.

Jelinek, Yeshayahu. "The Holocaust of Croatian Jewry: A Few Reflections." *Shoah* 1 (1979): 20–23.

Kabelli, Isaac. "The Resistance of the Greek Jews." *YIVO Annual of Jewish Social Sciences* 8 (1953): 281–88.

Katzburg, Nathaniel. *Hungary and the Jews: Policy and Legislation, 1920–1943*. Ramat Gan: Bar Ilan University Press, 1981.

Kitroeff, Alexandros. "Documents: The Jews in Greece, 1941–1944: Eyewitness Accounts." *Journal of the Hellenic Diaspora* 12 (Fall 1985): 5–32.

———. "Greek Wartime Attitudes Towards the Jews in Athens." *Forum* 60 (Summer 1987): 41–51.

Koen, Albert. *Saving of the Jews in Bulgaria, 1941–1944*. Sofia: Setemvri, 1977.

Lavi, Theodore. "The Background to the Rescue of Romanian Jewry During the Period of the Holocaust." In *Jews and Non-Jews in Eastern Europe, 1918–1945*, edited by Bela Vago and George L. Mosse.

———. "Documents on the Struggle of Rumanian Jewry for Its Rights During the Second World War." *Yad Vashem Studies* 4 (1960): 274–75.

———. "Vatican Endeavors on Behalf of Rumanian Jewry During the Second World War." *Yad Vashem Studies* 5 (1963): 405–18.

Levin, Nora. *The Holocaust: The Destruction of European Jewry, 1933–1945*. New York: Crowell, 1968.

Lewis, Bernard. *The Jews of Islam*. London: Routledge and Kegan Paul, 1984.

Litani, Dora. " 'Courier,' an Underground Newspaper in Trans-Dnistria, April–September 1943." *Yad Vashem Bulletin* 14 (March 1964): 44–48.

Lowenthal, Zdenko, ed. *The Crimes of the Fascist Occupants and Their Collaborators Against Jews in Yugoslavia*. Belgrade: Federation of Jewish Communities, 1957.

Marrus, Michael. *The Holocaust in History*. Hanover, N. H.: University Press of New England, 1987.

Matkovsky, Aleksandar. "The Destruction of Macedonian Jewry." *Yad Vashem Studies on the European Catastrophe and Resistance* 3 (1959): 211–13.

Mavrogordatos, George Th. *Stillborn Republic: Social Coalitions and Party Strategies in Greece, 1922–1936*. Berkeley: University of California Press, 1983.

Menasche, Albert. *Birkenau (Auschwitz II): How 72,000 Greek Jews Perished*. New York, Saltiel 1947.

Mendelsohn, Ezra. *The Jews of East Central Europe Between the World Wars*. Bloomington: Indiana University Press, 1983.

Mezan, Saul. *Les Juifs espagnols en Bulgarie* (The Spanish Jews in Bulgaria). Sofia: Amiscpat, 1925.

Miller, Marshall L. *Bulgaria During the Second World War*. Stanford, Calif.: Stanford University Press, 1975.

Moisses, Asher. "Jews in the Army of Greece." In *Ha-Lohhem ha-Yehudi be-Seva'ot ha-Olam* (The Jewish fighter in the armies of the world). Tel Aviv, 1967.

Molho, Michael. *Usos y costumbres de los Sefardies de Salonica* (Habits and customs of the Sephardim in Salonika). Madrid and Barcelona: Instituto Arias Montano, Consejo Superior de Investigaciones Cientificas, 1950.

Molho, Michael, and Joseph Nehama. *In Memoriam: The Destruction of Greek Jewry*. Jerusalem: Jewish Community of Salonika, 1956.

Nehama, Joseph. *Histoire des Israelites de Salonique* (History of the Jews of Salonika). Vols. 6 and 7. Thessaloniki: Jewish Community of Thessaloniki, 1978.

Oren, Nissan. "The Bulgarian Exception: A Reassessment of the Salvation of the Jewish Community." *Yad Vashem Studies on the European Jewish Catastrophe and Resistance* 13 (1969): 83–106.

Oren, Uri. "A Town Called Monastir: The Heroes." In *Anthology on Armed Jewish Resistance, 1939–1945*, edited by Isaac Kowalski. New York: Shapolsky, 1988.

Paris, Edmond. *Genocide in Satellite Croatia, 1941–1945: A Record of Racial and Religious Persecutions and Massacres*. Chicago: American Institute for Balkan Affairs, 1961.

Reitlinger, Gerald. *The Final Solution: The Attempt to Exterminate the Jews of Europe, 1939–1945*. 2d rev. ed. N.Y.: T. Yoseloff, 1968.

Romano, A., Joseph Ben, and Nisim (Buko) Levy. *Yehudut Bulgariyah* (The Jews of Bulgaria). Jerusalem: Encyclopedia of the Jewish Diaspora Co., 1968.

Romano, Jasa. *Jews of Yugoslavia, 1941–1945: Victims of Genocide and Freedom Fighters*. Belgrade: Federation of Jewish Communities of Yugoslavia, 1982.

Sabille, Jacques. "Attitude of the Italians to the Jews in Occupied Greece." In *Jews Under the Italian Occupation*, edited by Leon Poliakov and Jacques Sabille, pp. 151–60, New York: Howard Fertig, 1983.

———. "The Attitude of the Italians to the Persecuted Jews in Croatia." In *Jews Under the Italian Occupation*, pp. 129–50.

Schechtman, Joseph. "The Transdnistria Reservation." *YIVO Annual* 8 (1953): 178–96.

Sciaky, Leon. *Farewell to Salonica*. New York: Current Books, 1946.

Sevillias, Errikos. *Athens, Auschwitz*. Translated by Nikos Stavroulakis. Athens: Lycabettus Press, 1983.

Stavrianos, L. S. "The Jews of Greece." *Journal of Central European Affairs* 8 (October 1948).

Steckel, Charles. "Survivors and Partisans." In *Anthology on Armed Jewish Resistance, 1939–1945*, edited by Isaac Kowalski, Vol. 1.

Teich, Meier. "The Jewish Self-Administration in Ghetto Shargorod (Trans-Dnistria)." *Yad Vashem Studies* 2 (1952): 219–54.

Topalov, Vladislav. "L'Opinion publique Bulgare contre les persecutions des Juifs (October 1940–9 September 1944)" (Bulgarian public opinion against the persecutions of the Jews). In *Etudes historiques a l'occasion du XXIIe Congrès Internationale des Sciences Historiques, 1965*. Sofia: BAN, 1965.

Vago, Bela. "The Ambiguity of Collaborationism: The Center of the Jews in Rumania (1942–1944)." In *Patterns of the Jewish Leadership in Nazi Europe, 1939–1945: Proceedings of the Third Yad Vashem International Historical Conference*, edited by Yisrael Gutman and Cynthia Haft.

———. "Contrasting Jewish Leadership in Wartime Hungary and Rumania." In *The Holocaust as Historical Experience*, edited by Yehuda Bauer and Nathan Rotenstreich. New York: Holmes and Meier, 1981.

———. "The Destruction of the Jews of Transylvania." *Hungarian Jewish Studies* 1 (1966): 171–221.

———. "Political and Diplomatic Activities for the Rescue of the Jews of Northern Transylvania, June 1944–February 1945." *Yad Vashem Studies* 6 (1967): 155–73.

Vasileva, Nadejda Slavi. "On the Catastrophe of the Thracian Jews." *Yad Vashem Studies on the European Catastrophe and Resistance* 2 (1959): 97.

Yulzari, Matei. "The Bulgarian Jews in the Resistance Movement." In *They Fought Back: The Story of the Jewish Resistance in Nazi Europe*, edited by Yuri Suhl, pp. 275–81. New York: Crown, 1967.

Zuccotti, Susan. *The Italians and the Holocaust: Persecution, Rescue, and Survival*. New York: Basic Books, 1987.

# Chapter 16

# The Holocaust in France

*Sanford Gutman*

In many ways France held a unique position in World War II and the Holocaust. With the exception of Italy, which was allied with Germany, France was the only Western country that had a considerable degree of autonomy and yet collaborated with Nazi authorities in defining, rounding up, and deporting its Jewish population. In Europe as a whole, France was the only country with deep democratic roots that stripped a segment of its population of its individual rights. Germany's unique treatment of France raises several important issues concerning Vichy France's treatment of its Jewish population, the role of the French population as collaborators, bystanders, or rescuers, and the responses of the Jewish population in a country Jews thought would protect them. After outlining the basic chronology of German policy toward the Jews of France, this chapter will focus on the debates that continue to rage over Vichy actions and those of the Jewish populations in occupied and unoccupied France. The chapter concludes with a look at France overseas and the aftermath of the war.

## GERMAN POLICY IN FRANCE

After its brutal conquest of Poland and several months of "phony war," Germany began the war in the West with an attack upon Denmark and Norway in early April 1940. By mid-May German troops had defeated the Netherlands and Belgium and had broken through the vaunted defenses of the French Maginot Line. In early June the French government abandoned Paris, and on June 22 French representatives signed an armistice with Germany at Compiègne.

As part of the armistice, Germany incorporated Alsace-Lorraine into the Reich.

Otherwise, German treatment of France was unique. France was divided into two zones. The Germans occupied the northern three-fifths of the country, including Paris, the entire Atlantic and channel coasts, and the more fertile regions in western, northern, and eastern France. In the south the Germans permitted an autonomous French government with a wide degree of independence. The French government, established in the southern resort town of Vichy, was to be theoretically responsible for all of France as long as its decisions did not contradict those of the Germans.

The lightning German victory brought near anarchy and panic to the French population and increased the sense of despair and defeatism that had hung over France in the last years of the Third Republic. Fearing German persecution, millions of Frenchmen, including tens of thousands of Jews, flooded the southern zone. This placed enormous economic, social, and political strain on the south. After the armistice, therefore, the Vichy government called upon Frenchmen to return to their homes. Hundreds of thousands heeded its call, but many, including most Jews, did not.

In the northern occupied zone, the Nazi style of administration encouraged an inefficient competition among agencies, with no clear chain of command. As we will see later, this administrative confusion seriously complicated the actions and responses of both the Vichy government and the French Jewish leadership.

Five different branches of the German occupation authorities controlled Jewish affairs. The German arm of the Military Administration in France (Militärbefehlshaber im Frankreich or MBF) held the highest executive authority of the German occupation. It alone was authorized to publish orders, something it did sparingly. The military commander was General Otto von Stulpnägel, but Dr. Werner W. Best of the military administration was primarily responsible for matters concerning the Jews. Stulpnägel was later replaced for being insufficiently zealous in carrying out anti-Jewish policy, and Best was later transferred to Denmark, where he helped organize the attempted roundup of Jews in October 1943.

The German embassy was responsible for cooperation with the Vichy government and for administrative problems in the occupied area. Since Vichy was allowed to promulgate laws applicable to French citizens in both parts of France, this brought the German embassy and Vichy together frequently. Otto Abetz, the German ambassador, was an early supporter of the Nazi party in Germany and was among the most eager to promote racial purification in France. Still, Abetz tried to balance his desire to win favor with Nazi ideologues with the need to restrain more aggressive anti-Semitic measures when he thought that French public opinion was not prepared for them. Abetz remained as ambassador until 1944 and played an important role in supporting the deportation first of foreign and then of French-born Jews. He was assisted by his deputy, M. Schleier, and SS Obersturmbannführer C. Zectschel, the advisor for Jewish questions.

The Security Police (the Sicherheitsdienst or SD) was a subdivision of the

RSHA (Reichssicherheitshauptamt), the gigantic Reich Security Division of Heinrich Himmler's SS. Its power and influence over the Jewish question in France was to grow significantly as the occupation continued. In France and Belgium the Security Police was headed by SS Obersturmführer Helmut Knochen. Of greater consequence was the twenty-seven-year-old SS officer Theodor Dannecker, who headed the Judenreferat, the RSHA Paris office devoted to Jewish issues. With the help of his deputy, H. Rothke, Dannecker put to effective use in France his three prior years of experience working with Adolph Eichmann in expelling Austrian Jews. While initiating and expediting anti-Jewish actions in France, Dannecker frequently confronted the wrath of other German agencies that opposed his usurpation of their authority and questioned his insensitivity to French public opinion.

Two other agencies also held some responsibility for Jewish affairs. The Einsatzstab Rosenberg, a fiefdom of Nazi theoretician Alfred Rosenberg, largely spent its time plundering French archives and the art collections of Jews and other people judged hostile to the Reich. Finally, the Armistice Commission in Wiesbaden, made up of French and German officers, diplomats, and bankers, continued to work out the details of the armistice, which included matters pertaining to the Jews.

Since the MBF held ultimate authority, all other agencies were supposed to consult with it before taking action against the Jews, but coordination among these agencies and individuals was not always smooth. They competed for bureaucratic advantage and frequently differed sharply among themselves on how to handle the Jewish question. In general, the MBF worried more than the others about breaking international law, antagonizing French public opinion, and losing the cooperation of the Vichy authorities in carrying out anti-Jewish policy.

It would be a mistake, however, to overemphasize the significance of interpersonal and interagency rivalry. Eventually, Dannecker was able to win acceptance of his policies among embassy and military officials. If not as actively hostile to the Jews, German diplomats and military officers were at best indifferent enough to their fate to allow the Judenreferat an increasingly free hand. By late February 1941 Dannecker had set up weekly meetings of all agencies involved in the Jewish question. Dannecker's success, however, was not due merely to greater drive or force of personality. The growing authority of the Gestapo and Judenreferat over the Jewish question also reflected the changing goals of the Nazis in occupied Western Europe.

Despite all these agencies, not many German troops, police, or bureaucrats were made available—fewer than three thousand civilians for occupied France in 1941. Instead, the Nazis preferred to use indigenous civil servants and police. Thus the French administration continued to function, and, though increasingly dependent on the German Security Police, French police remained the principal executive arm of German and French policy.

Michael Marrus and Robert Paxton argue that German policy toward the Jews of France, as in occupied Western Europe in general, developed in three basic stages between 1940 and 1944. The first phase lasted from the outbreak of the war in the West in April 1940 until the autumn of 1941. In this phase the Final Solution to the Jewish question was discussed but probably referred to some vast, as yet undecided, plan of mass emigration that was to await the end of the war. In the meantime, the various German occupation authorities sought to control the movement and organization of Jews, confiscate their property, count them, and sometimes concentrate them in certain regions.

The second phase began in late 1941 and ended in the summer of 1942. Because of the faltering Russian campaign, it was clear that the war was to last a long time. Therefore, the Jewish question in Western Europe needed to be dealt with more immediately. In the midst of the June 1941 invasion of Russia (Operation Barbarossa), all moral restraints were abandoned. The massive slaughter of civilians in the Soviet Union and the millions of new Jews coming under the control of Nazi authorities congealed the decision to change the definition of the Final Solution. Systematic and coordinated extermination was formally decided upon and organized in Berlin at the Wannsee Conference in January 1942.

The third and final phase began in the summer of 1942 and ended with the Allied victory in the West. During this period Nazi experts worked out the logistical arrangements for the deportations of Western Jewry to the extermination camps in the East. Especially crucial was the scheduling of sufficient trains, which had hitherto been monopolized by the Russian campaign. Only the end of the war prevented Eichmann and his representatives from exterminating all of Western Jewry.

With this background, we can now look more closely at the specific application of Nazi policy to France. In August 1940 Otto Abetz, the German ambassador to France, wired the German Foreign Office asking for permission to institute a series of anti-Semitic measures. Approved in late September by Himmler's deputy, Reinhard Heydrich, the measures banned Jews who had fled south from returning to the occupied zone; required Jews in the occupied zone to register with the local prefect and to mark their enterprises with a special placard; and appointed trustees over Jewish enterprises whose owners had fled. Jewish community leaders were required to give the necessary information to French authorities who were to carry the measures out in the occupied zone. Abetz also hoped that these measures would serve as a model for the unoccupied south.

Indeed, for reasons we will examine in the second part of this chapter, Vichy had opened its own assault on the Jews of France. On August 27, 1940, it repealed the *loi Marchandeau* which in April 1939 had banned press attacks on Jews and others because of their race or religion. On October 3, 1940, Vichy went beyond even the Abetz recommendations in the north when it passed the *Statut des Juifs*. The law defined Jews as a race and relegated all Jews to an inferior status, excluding them from top positions in the civil service, any service in the army, and from positions that influenced public opinion. Legislation of

October 4 seemed even more threatening. It authorized prefects to intern foreign Jews in special camps or to place them under police surveillance in remote villages.

Despite these measures in both zones, the early months after the armistice appeared stable and relatively unthreatening compared with what was to come. The somewhat more restrained MBF still largely controlled the Jewish agenda in France until early 1941. But by then German authorities in France were becoming increasingly concerned about the crowded refugee camps in both zones, their economic burden, and the perceived threat of the refugees to the German army's security. At the same time, Theodor Dannecker, the head of the Reich security office in Paris, pressed to gain control over Jewish policy. Envisioning a new Europe free of Jews, Dannecker argued that it was not enough to push Jews from the occupied zone to the unoccupied zone. The time had come to begin to remove all Jews from France. Dannecker convinced the MBF and the embassy to support his plan to get the French authorities to create a Central Jewish Office (Zentraljudenamt). He argued that given limited German resources in France, French help was essential in determining and carrying out anti-Jewish policy. In early March embassy officials contacted Admiral François Darlan, then prime minister of Vichy under Marshal Philippe Pétain, to discuss Dannecker's proposal. Expressing hesitations by Marshal Pétain, Darlan vacillated but eventually agreed to the proposal on the condition that the new office be extended to both zones and be placed under Vichy jurisdiction. By so doing, Vichy hoped to regain at least the pretense that it was in control of French national policy.

Thus the General Office for Jewish Affairs (Commissariat général aux questions juives, CGQJ) was created by a French law on March 29, 1941. Darlan appointed Xavier Vallat as the first commissioner of the CGQJ. Vallat was a member of the right-wing Action française and was a militantly nationalist Catholic, authoritarian and anti-Semite. Anti-German as well as anti-Jewish, however, he sought an anti-Semitism that would serve the interests of the French state and not the dictates of the Nazis.

Still defining the Final Solution in terms of expulsion, Werner Best, the top MBF civilian official in charge of Jewish affairs, explained to Vallat that the Germans were now thinking in terms of the complete "de-Judaism" of Europe. To that end he called for Vichy's help in expelling all foreign Jews from the occupied zone and the internment of three to five thousand of the least desirable Jews of all nationalities. Reflecting Vichy opposition to dumping more Jews into the unoccupied zone, Vallat argued that this expulsion and internment were not within his province. He did, however, agree to Best's third demand, the systematic application of the Vichy *Statut des Juifs* to the occupied zone.

This was accomplished by the law of July 22, 1941, which applied to French and foreign Jews alike and to the unoccupied zone as well as to the occupied zone. The new statute led to a massive purge of Jews from the liberal professions, crafts, commerce, and industry. Worried that the property confiscated from Jews would fall into German hands, Vichy also carried out an extensive policy of "Aryanization" of Jewish property.

The *Statut des Juifs* and the Aryanization of Jewish property began to have disastrous effects on Jewish life. Therefore, Dannecker sought to make the Jewish community pay for its own destitution by creating a Jewish Council or Judenrat on the model established in occupied Eastern Europe. Despite the fact that France differed markedly from Poland—there was no ghetto or large concentration of Jews in France, and the German occupation was limited to the north—Dannecker pressed on. He sought to channel the remains of Jewish wealth into the hands of those without means of support, but Dannecker may have also had in mind using a French Jewish Council for the general administration of Jewish affairs and, perhaps, even for help in later deportations.

Vallat and Vichy feared losing control over Jewish money and Jewish affairs to Dannecker. Therefore, they only agreed to establish a plan for Jewish Councils after it was decided that such a plan would be applied in both zones. The General Union of Jews of France (Union générale des Israélites de France, UGIF) was created on November 29, 1941, and was to answer to Vichy rather than to the Germans. As Vallat and Vichy were to see, however, Nazi anti-Semitism was far more dynamic than theirs. Vallat and the CGQJ would become little more than German puppets.

By the late fall of 1941 German policy toward the Jews was entering a new phase. Expulsion from the occupied north to the south, indeed expulsion as a solution, was giving way to the emerging decision to exterminate European Jewry. Partly out of coincidence and partly as a reflection of new German resolve, the major German and French officials responsible for French Jewry changed in the spring and summer of 1942. Nazi Jewish experts in France had for some time found Xavier Vallat insufficiently eager in formulating and carrying out anti-Jewish policy. Under German pressure Marshal Pétain appointed the more rabid anti-Semite and German sympathizer, Louis Darquier de Pellepoix, as Vichy general commissioner for Jewish affairs (head of the CGQJ). Darquier immediately removed the former civil servants in favor of more violent, and incompetent, personnel. Although the Aryanization of Jewish property remained the primary responsibility of the CGQJ, Darquier and his officials indulged far more in anti-Jewish propaganda, brutality, and personal enrichment than his predecessor. He and his lieutenants also worked directly with the German authorities in the later roundups and deportations of Jews. Though not a favorite of Vichy leaders, Darquier was retained in office until early 1944.

German officials were also changed. General Karl Heinrich von Stulpnägel replaced his more squeamish cousin, General Otto von Stulpnägel, as MBF commissioner. A more ominous sign for French Jews, however, was the removal of police operations from the German military command. This authority and Jewish operations in France were now placed in the hands of a deputy of SS Chief Heinrich Himmler, Carl Obrecht Olberg, who had recently arrived from directing the massacre of Jews in the East. Olberg answered only to Himmler, and his appointment signified the gathering of all police operations under Nazi party control. Consequently, Werner Best, head of the civil administration staff of the MBF, lost influence and soon left to take a higher position in Denmark. After the first large roundups in June, even Theodor Dannecker left to become Eichmann's representative, successively, in Bulgaria, Italy, and Hungary. His deputy, Heinz Röthke, assumed Dannecker's position and served actively until the end of the war. By the summer of 1942 the SS had a free hand in France.

Although the invasion of Russia in the summer of 1941 was probably the turning point in the determination of the Final Solution, the new policy of extermination was not systematized until the Wannsee Conference of January 20, 1942. There the number of Jews in France was estimated to be 165,000 in the north and a ridiculously high figure of 700,000 in the unoccupied zone. Preparations were now to be made for their deportation to the extermination camp at Auschwitz.

Roundups and internment of Jews had taken place intermittently since German troops arrived on French soil. For example, on May 14, 1941, over 3,700 foreign male Jews were asked to present themselves to the Paris Commissariat of Police. Most did and were arrested and sent to the camps at Pithiviers and Beaune-la-Rolande. After the invasion of the Soviet Union, French police sealed off the heavily Jewish eleventh *arrondissement* (district) of Paris while German police rounded up some four thousand Jews and sent them to Drancy, a camp just outside Paris.

More roundups, internments, and deportations followed direct attacks by Communist resistance groups against the occupying authorities. Massive retaliation against French hostages, including executions as well as deportation, was meted out disproportionately against Jews, Communists and non-Communists, foreign and French. Deportations to the east were announced on December 14, 1941, but were held up by the shortage of trains until March 1942.

These early actions might be seen within the context of German military concerns, especially as reprisals for attacks against German servicemen. By June 1942, however, it became clear that German Jewish policy in France had moved on to its third and final phase. On June 11 a mini–Wannsee Conference held in Berlin brought together representatives from France, Belgium, and the Hague in Eichmann's RSHA office. There the deportation to Auschwitz of an initial one hundred thousand French Jews was ordered and planned. All deportees would be stripped of their French citizenship, and the French were to bear the costs of the deportations. Back in Paris, Dannecker called on Vichy to supply half of the one hundred thousand from the unoccupied zone. The Germans did not have to bargain hard with Pierre Laval, then prime minister of Vichy, to get his approval for the deportation of "stateless" and foreign Jews.

In preparation for the deportation, Dannecker wanted to impose on French Jews in both zones the wearing of the yellow star. Vichy opposed this abridgment of its authority and worried about public opinion. The military authorities in the north also feared an adverse reaction from the French population and, in addition, needed to decide whether to impose the star on foreign Jewish nationals of the belligerent, neutral, and allied states. In the end, German officials decided to exclude the latter and to give in to Vichy's refusal to impose the star in the unoccupied south. This remained the policy in the south even after German occupation of Vichy in November 1942.

The decree ordered all Jews aged six and over to wear a yellow star, the size of a clenched fist, on the left side of their breast with the word *Juif* (Jew) or *Juive* (Jewess). The French police estimated that over 100,000 Jews were subject to the decree, but many Jews refused to obey the ordinance. After several weeks, only 83,000 had received them.

In July 1942 the MBF instituted several other measures intended to segregate Jews from the rest of the French population in preparation for deportation. Jews were prohibited from frequenting public places of entertainment and recreation and from using public telephones. In addition, they could sit only in the last car of the Paris Metro. Of most immediate hardship, Jews were limited to shopping for food during certain afternoon hours when there was usually little left.

With just three battalions of police in France—between 2,500 and 3,000 men— German occupation authorities relied heavily upon the French police for the roundup and deportation of Jews. The Jewish section of the Paris prefecture kept a remarkable card-file system listing the names, professions, locations, and nationalities of 150,000 Jews registered in the Department of the Seine. That Jewish section was also responsible for rounding up Jews in Paris and administering the concentration camps. All that remained was to make certain of the availability of trains. Dannecker and the other organizers of the deportation now turned to this complex logistical problem. Regular scheduling of trains depended on the availability of a steady stream of Jews. By 1942 Nazi policy had changed and now forbade Jewish emigration from the occupied zone except in cases expressly approved by Hitler. The somewhat more generous emigration policy in the Vichy zone also stopped in the late summer and fall of 1942 so that Vichy could produce its own quota of foreign Jews to be sent to the north for deportation. The Jewish concentration-camp population in the north and south rose in 1942 as the prefects began carrying out Vichy orders of December 10, 1941, to intern or impress into labor all foreign Jews who had come to France since 1936.

In early July 1942 German officials responsible for carrying out the Final Solution in France started planning a huge roundup of Jews. The operation was to center on Paris, but action was to take place all over France. Although the operation was nominally led by the new head of Vichy's CGQJ, Darquier de Pellepoix, Dannecker actually organized it and gained the necessary commitments from the French police and other authorities. The Germans wanted 28,000 Jews arrested in the Paris region. Twenty-two thousand of these were to be deported. The Germans targeted Jewish men and women aged sixteen to fifty. Children under sixteen would be transferred to children's homes under the care of the UGIF. Municipal police would carry out the arrests and then assemble the detainees at the Vélodrome d'hiver, a large sports arena in the south of Paris. From there, they would be transported to the French camps and then on to Auschwitz. A small German police detachment supervised the French gendarmes who guarded the deportation trains. Christened "Spring Wind" (*Vent printanier*), the operation took place on July 16 and 17, two days after the celebration of Bastille Day.

Carried out by French police, the roundups deceived and soothed the stateless and foreign Jews. Whether stunned, unbelieving, or despairing, they could not imagine what would await them at the Vél d'hiver. Although "only" 7,000 men, women, and children out of the nearly 13,000 rounded up in Paris huddled in the stadium, there was barely room to lie down. With little food or water, they remained for five days amid a malodorous stench of dysentery and diarrhea. It was too hot during the day and too cold at night. A perpetual din pervaded the hall, occasionally interrupted by howling or inexplicable hand clapping.

To the Germans, *Vent printanier* produced mixed results. They succeeded in rounding up only 12,884 Jews out of the hoped-for 28,000. Thousands had escaped the dragnet. Some French police proved unreliable, notifying Jews in advance, and many Jews hid. Many Parisians were also appalled by the wrenching scenes that took place as French gendarmes led families from their homes. Still, there were enough to fill the deportation trains, and Dannecker remained hopeful for the future.

Agreeing to the cover-up that the Jews were being sent to work camps "in the east," Vichy used census data collected in late 1941 to carry out its own roundups in the south. Against Nazi wishes, Vichy even insisted that children under sixteen be sent along with their parents. Those rounded up were sent to the detention camp in the northeastern Paris suburb of Drancy along with those who had been held at the Vél d'hiver. After a brief stay, they were sent on to Auschwitz.

The camp at Drancy holds a special place in the history of the Holocaust in France. It was the intermediate destination of Jewish transports from the unoccupied zone and the last assembly point for 67,000 of the 75,000 Jews deported from France to Auschwitz, Sobibor, and Majdanek (extermination camps in Poland). The first departure to the east took place on June 22, 1942; the transports continued until July 31, 1944.

Drancy was established in August 1941 by Dannecker and the Judenreferat as a detention center for "stateless" Jews and other undesirable foreigners. Its organization and structure were modeled after those of Nazi concentration camps. From the detainees' perspective, however, it appeared thoroughly French. French gendarmes guarded the camp until the end, and although it was under the control of the German security police, the French even administered it throughout most of the occupation. The fact that the camp administration was French until August 1943 may well have hidden from the deportees the true meaning of being sent to Drancy.

Conditions in the camp under the French were deplorable. No French agency wanted to take responsibility for the camp, so each did the minimum. The prisoners were severely undernourished, and dysentery made the inmates look like skeletons. The French administration also determined who would fill the quotas for each of the convoys, an appalling task. The administration established an elaborate table of priorities that tended to favor those most integrated into French society. Under the strain of having to fill the German deportation quotas, however, the police in charge frequently had to improvise on the spot.

There were also many other *camps de concentration*, the expression often used by French officials. In addition to Jews, they also held political prisoners and Gypsies and, in the early months after the armistice, thousands of Spanish Republicans who had fled because of Franco's victory. It is estimated that there were no less than thirty-one camps in the southern zone at the end of September 1940. A Jewish physician who worked in camps in the northern occupied zone reported that there were fifteen soon after the armistice. Since the Germans preferred larger groupings of Jews, many of these would be closed.

The major camps in the north besides Drancy were Pithiviers and Beaune-la-Rolande, both in the Loiret. The major centers in the unoccupied zone included Rivesaltes and Argeles (the latter holding mostly Spanish refugees) in the Pyr-enees Orientales; the disciplinary camp of Le Vernet in the Ariege; the women's camp Rievcros in the Lozere; Les Milles, near Aix-en-Provence, a center for those expecting to emigrate; Gurs in the Basses-Pyrenees, which held the thousands of Jewish deportees from Germany; Noe, the camp of sick and old people in the Haute Garonne; and the nearby center of Recebedou, just south of Toulouse.

Conditions at the camps that held a large number of Jews—Gurs, Rivesaltes, Le Vernet, and Les Milles—were very harsh. Sanitary arrangements were primitive. There was a shortage of water, and the detainees constantly suffered from hunger. At Gurs, the first and one of the largest detention camps in France, eight hundred detainees died of typhoid and dysentery epidemics in the winter of 1940–41. Based on the reports of Vichy Prefect André Jean-Faure, conditions were similarly severe at Rivesaltes, Le Vernet, and Les Milles.

To meet the Nazi quota of 32,000 Jews to be deported by the end of the summer of 1942, Vichy emptied the camps in the unoccupied zone of most of their Jewish internees. More Jews were needed, however, and the Nazi quota had to be met by another major roundup on August 26–28. The police knocked on doors, searched for children in convents, religious buildings, and schools, and even watched the forests where some Jews tried to live without food and shelter. Once arrested, the Jews were taken to assembly points, then to concentration camps in the unoccupied zone, then to Drancy, and, finally, to the extermination camps in Poland. At the close of 1942, 42,500 Jews had been sent from France to Auschwitz, almost one-third from the unoccupied zone.

Germany continued its policy of roundups and deportations for the next two years, but with significant changes in strategy. Increasingly, German authorities took over the tasks of directing and carrying out the roundups. More important, at the end of 1942 Germany invaded the south, and on December 10, 1942, Hitler ordered the deportation of all Jews, including French citizens.

The Vichy government was still sovereign in name, but in practical terms, "Attila," the code name for the German invasion of the unoccupied zone, radically changed the handling of the Jewish question in France. Though still dependent on the French authorities, German police powers increased drastically as the SS extended its authority to the south. Whatever former independence Vichy had, and still pretended to have, was shattered.

By late January 1943 preparations were ready for another large deportation from Drancy to Auschwitz. After several months trains were again available. Under the direction of Knochen and the SS Judenreferat, French police in the southern zone carried out another massive roundup of foreign Jews in February 1943. The French police chief, Rene Bousquet, resisted the deportation of French Jews who had been rounded up but agreed to the deportation of foreign Jews.

Although the February roundups and deportations were the largest since August 1942, the Judenreferat was dissatisfied with the total amount of Jews deported since the armistice, estimated at 49,000 by Röthke. He now envisaged a massive new program of deportations. Between early 1943 and the end of the war in France, all French Jews were at serious risk. The roundups, now frequently led by German police and French Fascist militia, were carried out with special thoroughness and brutality. Thousands more foreign and French Jews were rounded up and deported in the next year and a half. But many escaped the dragnets.

Thousands of French Jews sought refuge in the Italian-occupied zone. Allied with Germany, Italian armies occupied eight departments of southeastern France when Germany seized the rest of the southern zone. Reflecting the rather benign Italian attitude toward Jews, the Italian occupation authorities refused to carry out German and French demands for an anti-Jewish program similar to that being carried out in the rest of France. German authorities felt that they could only pressure their allies so far. For several months, therefore, Jews were safe there.

This ended tragically, however, in September 1943. Mussolini had been overthrown in July 1943, but Italian authorities continued to protect the Jews. Fearing German occupation of the Italian zone, they made plans to evacuate thirty thousand Jews to Italy and to North Africa. But on September 8 the Allies prematurely announced their armistice with Italy, several days before the evacuation plans were ready. Three days later Germany marched into Nice, where most of the Jews now resided. Although hundreds of Jews escaped, thousands more were caught up in a brutal manhunt. By now no attention was paid to whether these Jews were native-born Frenchmen, naturalized citizens, or "foreigners."

By the summer of 1943 German authorities in France were having increased difficulty in meeting their quota of Jews. As Germany's war effort continued to decline and as Germany began to deport non-Jewish Frenchmen to labor brigades in Germany, French resistance to cooperating with German authorities increased. Germans now called for the deportation of recently naturalized French citizens. To facilitate this, German authorities sought to take away French citizenship from those naturalized on or after August 10, 1927. That date was chosen because of a law passed at that time that reduced residency requirements for citizenship from ten to three years. After initial negotiations over this, Vichy refused the denaturalization of French Jews. After June 1943 deportation convoys continued at a regular, if reduced, pace until liberation. All earlier limitations on former prisoners of war, foreign volunteers for French armed forces, members of the Legion of Honor, and UGIF personnel were now abandoned. For this last chapter of the Holocaust in France, Eichmann sent one of his collaborators, SS Haupts-turmführer Alois Brunner, to speed up the deportations. Well prepared by his efficient and brutal deportation of Greek and foreign Jews in Salonika, Brunner was authorized to act independently of the German police chain of command. Using convoys of French police and French collaborators, Brunner's squads combed the countryside to arrest Jews.

By the spring of 1944 the SS was conducting the deportations practically on its own. In April Knochen ordered, and Brunner approved, the arrest and de-portation of all Jews in France, without regard for nationality. Unable to count on the local police, the SS offered bounties to local French citizens for revealing the whereabouts of Jews. Despite the intensification of the roundups, the un-derstaffed German SS was never again able to reach the numbers deported in 1942. About 33,500 Jews were sent to the east in 1943–44. What German authorities lost in numbers, however, they made up for in cruelty. One of the more famous examples was the raid on a Jewish orphanage in the closing days of the occupation. Klaus Barbie, the Gestapo chief in Lyon, brutally rounded up forty-one children and ten adults and sent them to Drancy and then on to Auschwitz.

The deportations all came to an end upon liberation in August 1944. By the end of 1944 about 75,000 Jews had been deported to killing centers in former Polish territory. Of those, only 3 percent, or 2,500, survived. Auschwitz received most of the deportees; Majdanek, Sobibor, and Buchenwald the rest. Over two-thirds were "foreign" Jewish refugees. Close to one-third were French citizens. Nearly 2,000 were under six years of age, over 6,000 were under thirteen, and 8,700 were sixty years of age or over.

These 75,000 fell far short of the 270,000 Jews that Röthke, with reasonable accuracy, had estimated there to be in France. Had German authorities had another year, they probably would have met their goal of deporting all the Jews in France. As it turned out, many Jews escaped the Nazi net because of their dispersion, insufficient German police in France, the unavailability of deportation trains, and, beginning in 1943, the increasing help of the French authorities and people. After the war, leaders of the Vichy government took credit for saving more than two-thirds of the Jews of France. Vichy's role in the Holocaust in France, however, is a source of much debate.

## VICHY FRANCE, THE FRENCH POPULATION, AND
## THE JEWS

In their important book, *Vichy France and the Jews*, Michael Marrus and
Robert Paxton assert that Vichy not only directly assisted the Germans in their
actions but also made the arrests and deportations easier by its earlier, independent
measures isolating Jews. But if the fact of Vichy's collaboration is not in doubt,
other questions remain. First, how believable is the contention of Pierre Laval,
prime minister throughout most of Vichy, that the Vichy policy of collaboration
saved most French Jews? That is, did the willingness to round up some, primarily
foreign, Jews, result in saving the many, mostly native, Jews? Second, was the
persecution of Jews by Vichy and its leaders part of a larger and deeper French
tradition of anti-Semitism and xenophobia and, therefore, not attributable only
to the immediate circumstances surrounding the Nazi occupation? Finally, at
this critical time, did the French people act more like a nation of collaborators
or more like the nation of resisters that the Gaullist myth claimed after World
War II?

France's democratic and egalitarian tradition traces its roots back to the revolution of 1789. That tradition was interrupted and challenged at several points
in the nineteenth century, but the roots of liberal democracy became firmly
planted in the Third Republic, which lasted from 1870 to the fall of France in
June 1940. This Third Republic (the First and Second having lived and died
during the revolutions of 1789 and 1848) experienced serious challenges to its
liberal political and social values during the 1880s and 1890s and again during
the hard economic times of the mid- and late 1930s. Still, most Frenchmen were
tied to the ideals of the French Revolution, and it is unlikely that the Third
Republic would have been overthrown in favor of a conservative authoritarian
regime were it not for the fall of France to the German army.

Only under the pressure of German victory did the National Assembly vote
to suspend itself and the constitutional laws of the Third Republic. In their place,
Marshal Philippe Pétain, the elderly hero of World War I, was installed as head
of state and granted full powers. Unlike the situation in other Western countries,
however, this new French government was allowed a relatively high degree of
local autonomy. Throughout the German occupation France retained an indigenous government with a French head of state, administration, and powerful
police force that, at least nominally, were responsible for all of France. Even
after the Nazi occupation of the south in November 1942, Vichy still retained
a significant amount of authority.

Many Frenchmen saw the French defeat as a failure not only of the French
military but of the liberal, democratic principles for which it had stood. After
the economic and political turbulence of the 1930s, the large immigration of the
last twenty years, and the crushing defeat by Germany, ordinary Frenchmen and
political leaders responded enthusiastically to Pétain's calls for ''national renewal'' and for bringing France back to the French.

Such as he had one, Pétain's ideology hearkened back to a mythic prerevo-lutionary France where *travail* (work), *famille* (family), and *patrie* (homeland) were respected. This was an imagined hierarchical and undemocratic France where Frenchmen were tied by mutual bonds of family, where concern for the nation outweighed greedy individualism, where piety was more important than materialism, and where authority was respected over selfish individualism and political bickering. The popular appeal of Pétain's call for a conservative, au-thoritarian "renewal" was particularly strong in the first two years of Vichy when a sense of *attentisme* (wait and see) prevailed. Most people turned inward, preferring Vichy's attempts to get the best deal from Nazi Germany rather than de Gaulle's call for open resistance. This remained true even when it became obvious that the "national revolution" included a policy of collaboration with Nazi Germany and its goals for a new Europe under Hitler's tutelage.

Vichy's willingness to collaborate included participation in the Nazi onslaught against the Jews. We have seen that Vichy took action against the Jews almost immediately. On August 27, 1940, it repealed the *loi Marchandeau* that had banned press attacks against Jews and other minorities. On October 3, 1940, Vichy gave even clearer direction to its anti-Jewish policy by passing the *Statut des Juifs*. One day later Vichy authorized prefects to intern foreign Jews in special camps. The *Statut des Juifs* even went beyond the German regulation of September 27 and was more inclusive. The German ordinance had defined Jew-ishness by religious practice and limited Jewishness to three Jewish grandparents. The Vichy *Statut* defined Jews as a race and included as Jews those with two grandparents if married to a Jew or if practicing Judaism. Marrus and Paxton conjecture that the German ordinance of September 27 may have even been precipitated by Vichy's discussions over the *Statut des Juifs*. Later, in the summer of 1941, Vichy revised the *Statut des Juifs*, resulting in the expropriation of Jewish property and thus the further pauperization of the Jewish community.

Even worse, Vichy resisted German attempts to send Jews into its zone. Well before the Germans advocated emptying France of its Jews, Vichy sought to make the unoccupied zone *Judenrein*, at least of foreign Jews. Although Vichy probably sought the forced reemigration of immigrants, not their extermination, these early policies would facilitate the later deportations to death camps.

Later Vichy agreed to the establishment of a governmental agency to direct and coordinate Jewish policy (the CGQJ) and to a unified Jewish organization to represent all racially defined Jews (the UGIF). In both cases Vichy exceeded German requests by insisting that these organizations be applied to Vichy France as well as to the occupied zone. These measures treated all Jews, French and foreign, as a category separate from Frenchmen and thereby excluded all but the most assimilated French Jews from the regenerated French family.

Vichy continued the CGQJ and its gruesome business to the very end, even after the Normandy invasion in June 1944. Except for the moderate leadership of Charles Mercier du Paty, who followed Darquier de Pellepoix, Vichy ap-pointed vicious anti-Semites as the directors of the CGQJ. Xavier Vallat may have been a more "moderate" anti-Semite, perhaps more of a "surgeon" than his successor Darquier de Pellepoix, whom Pétain described as a "butcher," but both helped to shape and carry out important steps in the process of destruction. Even as the Allies edged toward Paris, Laval appointed Joseph Antignac, a top Vichy official and virulent anti-Semite, to head the CGQJ.

Again and again, Vichy continued to take initiative in its anti-Jewish measures and to go beyond German demands. Before the roundups and deportations it stamped *Juif* on the identity cards of Jews and thus made them an easy target later. In its own unoccupied zone Vichy used census data collected in late 1941 to determine who would be rounded up and sent to Drancy. Of its own accord Vichy applied its anti-Jewish policies to French holdings in North Africa.

Vichy's role in the roundups and deportations is even more disturbing. When the roundups began in the summer of 1942, Vichy was only too willing to include its foreign Jews. To meet German quotas it suspended exit visas for Jews and thus closed the door to Jewish emigration and escape. Although the Nazis wished to exclude children under the age of sixteen from the early roundups and deportations, Vichy insisted that the children be sent along with their parents. Serge Klarsfeld, who has provided the most detailed lists of Jews deported from France, estimates that over six thousand children were sent by Vichy to their deaths in the 1942 roundups.

Vichy's room for maneuvering decreased after the German occupation of the south in November 1942, but it still retained sovereignty. Its inactions and actions cannot be explained wholly in terms of German pressure. If Vichy had the will to help Jews, Marrus and Paxton insist, now would have been the time to destroy its records and to release Jews from internment camps. With a meager police force of its own, the Nazi effort to round up Jews would have been seriously hampered. Vichy, however, was hardly motivated to help Jews. To the contrary, after Italian armies occupied eight departments in southeastern France, also in November 1942, Vichy insisted that the Vichy anti-Jewish measures be applied there and constantly complained to Italian and German authorities when they were not.

How do we explain such measures and actions, seemingly so far removed from French political tradition? Patrice Higonnet has argued that responsibility should be given to the Vichy leadership, especially Marshal Pétain, and not to the French people. Higonnet maintains that it is a mistake to blame Vichy anti-Jewish measures either on the history of French anti-Semitism or on the French population as a whole.

Although Pétain may have never publicly spoken out against Jews during Vichy, Higonnet argues that he had strong views about the place of Jews in France. Pétain supported, for example, the exclusion of Jews from the educational and judicial systems. He almost never responded to pleas from former Jewish colleagues and others to suspend the anti-Jewish measures for all, some, or even individual Jews. Higonnet also blames Pétain's friendship and support for the rabidly anti-Semitic justice minister, Raphael Alibert, who authored and pushed

Vichy's initial anti-Jewish legislation. Similarly, it was Pétain who appointed Vallat and Darquier de Pellepoix and countenanced their actions. According to this view, it is not French anti-Semitism but rather the great popularity of Pétain that explains the popular support for or acquiescence in Vichy anti-Semitic policies.

While also strongly critical of Vichy leaders, Marrus and Paxton argue that the responsibility has to be spread more widely. In the first place, neither Pétain nor his two prime ministers, Pierre Laval and Admiral François Darlan, had the ideological fervor required to initiate anti-Jewish policy. Vichy anti-Semitism was most ardently pushed by right-wing groups and fanatical individuals like Raphael Alibert and Darquier de Pellepoix, who, though appointed by Pétain, had an independent base. Pétain, on the other hand, never publicly spoke out against Jews; neither did Laval or Darlan have prior records of anti-Semitism.

But if the dynamism came from rabid anti-Semites, the support for these policies by Vichy leaders and the French population still needs explanation. Like all of Christian Europe, France had a long history of Christian anti-Semitism that culminated in the expulsion of Jews from France in the thirteenth and fourteenth centuries. During the eighteenth century Enlightenment some called for the emancipation of Jews, but at the same time *philosophes* like Voltaire also expressed their abhorrence for the backward, seemingly unassimilable Jews. During the French Revolution the National Assembly did give equal rights to Jews, but only under the condition that they give up their separate national identity and integrate rapidly into French culture. This indeed occurred, but anti-Semitism remained a problem from some elements in the Left and the Right. Some socialists charged Jews with economic exploitation, while the Right added the charge that Jews could not be truly "French." By the late nineteenth century a virulent strain of racist anti-Semitism, especially but not exclusively in the Right, had taken strong root in France.

Racist anti-Semites combined a cultural critique of modern, liberal Western civilization with the racial argument that French leadership had softened and failed through the infiltration of alien, especially Jewish, elements of lower racial standing. Jews appeared as the purveyors and main benefactors of modern French republican culture: science, industrialization, progress, and centralization, which in their train brought excessive individualism, materialism, greed, and corruption.

These views culminated in the Dreyfus affair beginning in 1895. Eduard Drumont, a journalist and publisher of the notoriously anti-Semitic newspaper *La Libre parole*, successfully combined the old anticapitalist themes of the Left with the Right's fears of moral and material decadence. The royalist, Catholic, antidemocratic, and anti-Semitic Action française became the vanguard of these views and was established in the wake of the Dreyfus affair. But as Stephen Wilson has indicated in his book *Ideology and Experience*, anti-Semitism, if in milder forms, transcended royalist and Catholic opponents of liberal, industrial society and, indeed, permeated broad reaches of French society.

There is a danger of exaggerating French anti-Jewish sentiment, however. After all, Dreyfus and republicanism won out during the affair, and Drumont's violently anti-Semitic newspaper died in 1924 for lack of readership. Even more to the point, both Stephen Wilson and Marrus and Paxton present a model of an anti-Jewish continuum, or of concentric circles, that clearly distinguishes between a broad-based social distancing, at one extreme, and a well-developed ideological and violent anti-Semitism, at the other.

Although anti-Semitism was more quiescent during World War I and into the 1920s, it regained strength in the 1930s and was promoted by some of the most important French writers of the day. This reawakening played on fears occasioned by the depression, the increasing numbers of foreigners coming into France, and the possibility that the Jewish question would force France into a war not of its choosing. Even before the war, hard-core anti-Semites in the Right called for a *Statut des Juifs* that would separate all Jews as foreigners. Though most Frenchmen, even acknowledged anti-Semites, distinguished between assimilated French Jews and recent arrivals, the distinctions themselves were riddled with anti-Semitic assumptions.

Anti-Semitism also frequently merged with a widespread xenophobia that prevailed in France in the 1930s. Part of this distrust of outsiders stemmed from the French revolutionary Jacobin influence that insisted on a rigorously unified culture. Notions of cultural pluralism never developed in France, and, therefore, immigrants were expected to absorb French culture quickly and completely. This was not easy when immigrants arrived in great numbers and tended to congregate in "ghettos" in the large cities.

During the 1920s France welcomed large numbers of foreigners, including many Jews from Eastern Europe, to help fill the population losses from World War I. Even after the depression began, however, large numbers of foreign refugees continued to arrive. Jews from Germany, Belgium, the Netherlands, and Eastern Europe came to escape the Nazi menace, but the new immigrants also included Republican Spaniards fleeing the Spanish civil war, Italians, Slavs, and non-Jewish German opponents of Hitler.

By late 1938 France was taking measures that foreshadowed later Vichy action. French officials sought to expel "undesirable foreigners," and when that did not work, to intern them in concentration camps in France until they could be deported. Some recently naturalized citizens were even stripped of their citizenship. Foreign Jews, especially, were seen as a threat to state security. Were it not for the defeat of 1940, the crisis probably would have passed without significant anti-Jewish measures or actions. Still, the stage had been set, and Vichy's actions may be seen in part as consistent with the fears and policies of the last years of the Third Republic.

Xenophobia and anti-Semitism, however, only partly explain Vichy measures. Pétain, Darlan, and Laval cared less about the fate of French Jews than about Vichy control over French administrative machinery. According to Marrus and Paxton, Vichy's leadership believed that the Germans would show their gratefulness to Vichy for pursuing its own anti-Semitic policy by granting it control over other areas of national policy. Many of Vichy's actions against the Jews can be understood in terms of this pretense to Vichy sovereignty over France. This motivation, probably more than anti-Semitism, helps explain Vichy's agreement to create the General office for Jewish Affairs (CGQJ) and the General Union of Jews of France (UGIF). Vichy's insistence that they be applied to both French zones and that Vichy supervise and control all Jewish matters was part of its pretense to sovereignty over all of France. Even the Aryanization of Jewish property by Vallat and the CGQJ and Laval's willingness to use Vichy civil servants and police to round up foreign Jews in the summer of 1942 and later can be partly explained in these terms. Better that Vichy gain the proceeds of confiscated Jewish property than the Germans, and better that French police than German carry out the roundups as a sign of France's control over its own fate.

Vichy could and did occasionally disagree with German plans in the name of its autonomy. Vichy insisted, for example, that the children of foreign Jews be rounded up and deported with their parents when, as we have seen, the Germans did not want them initially included. Vichy also opposed the forced wearing of the yellow star in its zone. Though probably more due to public opposition than an act of conscience, this did reflect Vichy "independence." Even Vichy's criticisms of Italy's refusal to apply the *Statut des Juifs* in its zone may have been more an indication of Laval's delusion of French sovereignty than of hatred for Jews.

Vichy's most notable assertion of its autonomy was its opposition to the deportation of its more culturally assimilated French Jewish citizens. In January and February of 1943 Vichy was put under increasing pressure to deport these Jews along with the foreign Jews in order to meet German quotas. Laval, Pétain, and the French police felt far less comfortable with this and offered some resistance. After initial negotiations in August 1943 to denaturalize Jews who had not been citizens before August 10, 1927 (Laval pushed for 1933), negotiations broke down, and Pétain and Laval refused the denaturalization of French citizens. This "resistance" was used after the war by Vichy leaders as evidence that Vichy had only sacrificed foreign Jews to rescue the bulk of native French Jewry. Marrus and Paxton argue, however, that there is little evidence that Vichy ever cared enough to promote such a policy, or that it ever even discussed it. More likely, Pétain and Laval opposed the deportation of a whole segment of French citizens over whom it pretended to sovereignty; and by late 1943 Vichy leaders also feared the consequences from French public opinion.

Especially in the early years between 1940 and 1942, the French civilian, military, and police administrations had few qualms about carrying out anti-Jewish legislation. Carrying out governmental policy, the administrations eliminated Jews from the civil service, limited Jewish access to educational institutions, expropriated Jewish property, policed the internment camps, and judged the anti-Jewish statutes legal and enforced them. Most agencies also worked with the anti-Semitic CGQJ. When there was friction between the CGQJ and other agencies, it was usually over boundary disputes, not over principle. One historian, Joseph Billig, has even attributed Vichy's eagerness to rid itself of foreign Jewish children under sixteen to the French administration's feeling that it would be too disruptive to its routine to keep and place these children.

There was no direct opposition to anti-Jewish laws by these civilians and military administrators, most of whom had loyally served the democratic Third Republic. Where the attitude of the local prefects and mayors was crucial, however, there was some local variation. From the beginning, a few helped Jews to escape or carried out the *Statut des Juifs* in a desultory way. But no one challenged the law. French tradition called upon civil servants to enforce the law, and immediate circumstances pressured them not to show dissent. These reasons were compounded by a shared concern over the dangers of too many foreigners in France and tolerance for some measure of anti-Semitism. Tragically, compliance with early measures built up a habit of compliance that was hard to break, even when that compliance included roundups and deportations.

After the roundups began in 1942, and especially after non-Jewish Frenchmen began to be sent to German work camps in 1943, the police and other parts of the French administration became less reliable in carrying out German policy. Nazi authorities in France began to complain that they could no longer count on the loyalty of the French police. Still, as we have shown, the deportations continued, and rarely without the help of French police.

When we move beyond the Vichy leadership and bureaucracy to the French public, it becomes far less easy to generalize. Most historians agree with Marrus and Paxton that at least during the first two years the French public stood by silently while anti-Jewish laws were being passed and even when foreign Jews were being deported. Conditioned by years of anti-Semitic and antiforeign rhetoric and now suffering the considerable privations of war and defeat, many Frenchmen accused Jews of controlling the black market, living an easy life, exploiting the rural peasantry, and being the cause of the war. Especially in the south, where French villages and cities were flooded with people escaping the occupied north, all visitors were considered outsiders or "foreigners," Jews even more so.

Even the churches and the French resistance remained silent until the summer of 1942. The French Catholic church was euphoric over Pétain and his National Revolution, which gave a prominent role to French Catholicism. There were some objections to the harsh application of the laws, especially to French citizens, but no principled or public opposition. Except for the racial aspects of the *Statut des Juifs*, the Vatican did not object and asked only that the laws be applied with "justice" and "charity." Similarly, until the deportations, neither the left-wing opposition nor the Gaullists in England spoke out against the anti-Jewish measures and Jewish suffering.

There is considerable debate whether the French public actually supported Vichy policies in general, and the anti-Semitic measures in particular, or whether most Frenchmen just acceded to that which was beyond their control. Even

Marrus and Paxton acknowledge that most Frenchmen were more indifferent than ideologically anti-Semitic. This indifference was nuanced, however; it allowed them to accept without significant protest the *Statut des Juifs*, including the expropriation of Jewish property, but not wearing a Jewish star, window smashing, anti-Semitic posters, or the roundups.

In his book *Choices in Vichy France*, John Sweets defends French public opinion. He maintains that there was neither a surge of French anti-Semitism in 1941–42 nor general support for Vichy's National Revolution. The enthusiastic acceptance of the fatherly war hero Pétain should not be confused with support for Vichy policies. If not exemplary in every respect, the actions of the French population reflected their numbness and their own preoccupations after the French defeat. According to this interpretation, as they gained their bearings and witnessed the effects of the *Statut des Juifs*, even before the deportations, the French people began to oppose Vichy policies against the Jews. Sweets also argues that the French people and the local leaders responded with a great deal of variety. Most felt powerless. Some openly expressed their anti-Semitism and sought to bar Jews from their prefectures or towns, but for every such statement there were as many calls for compassion and private acts of help.

All agree that French public opinion began to shift noticeably in the summer of 1942. Prefects reported increased opposition to the German occupation, particularly to the forced wearing of the yellow star and to the roundups in July. Even before the roundups, attempts to isolate the Jews by the wearing of the yellow star and segregating them from public facilities were seen by the French as an affront to personal dignity. Previously, persecution of Jews was hidden from the French public. Now that it was out in the open, some Frenchmen even responded by wearing yellow flowers, handkerchiefs, or bits of paper with ironic inscriptions like "Goy."

When the cruelty and violence of the roundups supplanted anti-Jewish legislation, it became impossible for the French public to claim that Jews suffered no more than others. Some of the French Catholic hierarchy in the unoccupied zone now began to speak out. The archbishop of Toulouse, Jules-Gerard Saliège, denounced the persecution and spectacle of "children, women, fathers, and mothers treated like cattle [and] members of a family separated from one another and dispatched to an unknown destination." Protestants, some veterans, and the papal nuncio, though not the pope, also protested the deportations.

If Vichy collaborated in the persecution of Jews and French public opinion was slow to respond, there were many sympathetic French individuals, families, and church institutions who courageously helped to rescue thousands of Jews. A minority themselves, and sometimes identified with Jews as "anti-France," French Protestants and Protestantism were especially sensitive to the plight of the Jews. Pastor Marc Boëgner, president of the national Protestant Federation, and René Gillouin, a Protestant traditionalist who had close ties with Pétain, spoke out early and forcefully against the *Statut des Juifs*.

More tangible help frequently came from those disenchanted with the traditionalism of Vichy. Especially in the south, where escape to Switzerland and Spain was possible, small groups of Protestants and Catholics worked to help Jews escape. Groups originating from prewar youth movements were particularly helpful in organizing relief work and clandestine assistance. The Comité d'inter-mouvement auprès des evacués (CIMADE), led by Madeline Barot and Pastor J. Delpech, was one such Protestant group. Probably the most celebrated Protestant rescue efforts were those that took place in the isolated, heavily Protestant areas of the Haute-Loire, the Hautes Alpes, and the Tarn. Chambon-sur-Lignon, its pastors André Trocme and Eduard Theis, and Trocme's wife Magda have become deservedly famous for their rescue efforts. Yet this is but the most well known of these homogeneously Protestant enclaves that hid thousands of Jews and then helped them to escape across the border.

With the courageous exception of Archbishop Saliège and a few others, the Catholic hierarchy was slower to speak out and act on behalf of Jews. Saliège, a former member of an organization of idealistic Catholic social activists, condemned doctrines of racial superiority in the first days of the regime. It took the roundups in the unoccupied zone on August 26–28, 1942, to move others in the church hierarchy to protest. Monsignor Pierre-Marie Théas, bishop of Montau-ban, Cardinal Gerlier, and Monsignor Delay, bishop of Marseilles, also publicly protested the roundups and deportations, though they frequently cloaked such denunciations in words of loyalty to the regime.

Resistance within the church, however, came more forcefully from the lower orders of the clergy and from the laity. A small group of lower clergy published the Catholic resistance publication *Témoignage chrétien*, which attacked Vichy anti-Semitism even before the deportations. Especially noteworthy in aiding the Jews were leaders of idealistic Catholic youth groups like Germaine Ribiere and the Abbé Alexandre Glasberg. Glasberg, who was born to Jewish parents, first became involved in relief work and then moved to underground activity to help rescue Jews. He joined with Father Pierre Chaillet in Amitié chrétienne, an association of priests and laity centered in Lyon and under the patronage of Cardinal Gerlier and Pastor Boëgner. They were responsible for dispersing Jewish children among a number of religious houses and refused to give them up to the police even after the arrest of Father Chaillet.

Other groups, most notably the American Friends Service Committee (Quakers), the YMCA, and the American Jewish Joint Distribution Committee, also offered essential assistance. These organizations were particularly responsible for helping several hundred Jewish children escape deportation after the August 1942 roundups. They did so against the insistent efforts of Laval to have the children stay with their parents.

Though anti-Jewish sentiment never became a significant part of either the Gaullist or left-wing resistance movements, these movements rarely focused their attention on rescuing Jews. Both the clandestine resistance journals *Franc-tireur* and *Combat* denounced Hitler's and Vichy's anti-Semitic program, but even they sometimes reflected anti-Jewish stereotypes. More important, they failed to understand the full impact of Nazi and Vichy policy against the Jews before the roundups of 1942, and even after the roundups they did little directly to aid the Jews. Seeing the occupation primarily in terms of national or class interests, they courageously worked for German defeat but lost opportunities to disrupt the roundup and deportation of Jews. For example, despite the French national railway's considerable resistance activities, not one of the eighty-five convoys of Jewish deportees was derailed or impeded in any way.

The Communist resistance was the only one to allow a special unit made up of Jews, largely immigrant. It was closely coordinated, however, with the goals of the French Communist party and was not allowed to act on behalf of specifically Jewish concerns. Some have even charged that the French Communist party (PCF) sacrificed the Jewish Communists to the Germans during the relentless Gestapo pressure against the Communist organization in 1943. Hundreds of Communists were executed and deported, but perhaps a whole Jewish unit was given up by the party as expendable because its members were "only" foreigners.

Although fewer than 25 percent of Jews living in France in 1940 were exterminated, Vichy France must be evaluated harshly for its role. At best, the government leaders held a pronounced indifference to the fate of the Jews. Despite its greater degree of autonomy than most occupied countries, France was unique among occupied Western countries in passing indigenous anti-Semitic legislation. If Nazi success depended upon the degree to which it was able to apply its power, then French aid was crucial for the roundup and deportation of Jews. Even Miklós Horthy, the leader of Hungary, offered more resistance to handing over Jews than did Laval and Pétain.

Nor can Vichy leaders hide behind the explanation that they did not know what deportation meant. Although it is true that it was difficult at that time to fully comprehend the reality of Auschwitz, there were repeated reports that informed the French government of the exterminations. More important, Vichy did not seem to want to know. Because of the refugee crisis of 1938 to 1941 and historic French anti-Semitism, Vichy seemed not to care, at least about its foreign Jews. That so many Jews survived is more a tribute to the help of many individual Frenchmen and, especially, to the resourcefulness of French Jewry.

## JEWISH RESPONSES TO PERSECUTION

Both the fate of French Jews and their responses to the Holocaust in France varied in large measure according to the degree of assimilation into French society. There were actually two very distinct communities in France on the eve of World War II. Approximately half of the Jews living in France had assimilated into French society and were either descendants of prerevolutionary French Jews or second- and third-generation children of immigrants who had come to France before World War I. The other half had immigrated to France from Eastern and Central Europe after World War I, many in the 1930s. These Jews tended to live in their own communities and were far less integrated into French society and culture.

Jewish presence in France dates at least from the first century of the common era, and by the eleventh century France had become a center of Jewish learning. In the fourteenth century, however, because of popular religious and economic opposition, French kings expelled over one hundred thousand Jews and banned them from the kingdom. Despite this ban, a small Jewish population of forty thousand, made up of Ashkenazic Jews mostly in Alsace-Lorraine and a few thousand Portuguese Jews in the south, were living in France on the eve of the French Revolution.

The French revolutionaries emancipated the Jews in stages: the more assimilated Sephardic Portuguese were given equal rights on January 28, 1790; the less assimilated Ashkenazic Jews on September 27, 1791. Both the revolutionaries and, later, Napoleon expected Jews to give up their cultural distinctiveness and autonomy in exchange for equal citizenship rights. French Jews accepted what one historian has described as this "ideology of emancipation" and pursued what another has called the "politics of assimilation."

Despite occasional anti-Semitic occurrences, French Jews had successfully integrated into French society by the 1870s. Their comfort in, and love for, France was further witnessed by the large number of Jews who came to Paris from Alsace-Lorraine after its annexation to Germany in 1870. Between 1890 and 1939, however, French Jewish life and the community's assimilationist creed was severely challenged by the rise of racist anti-Semitism and by the arrival in France of tens of thousands of Eastern European immigrants.

Few native French Jews clearly saw or believed the threat of French anti-Semitism. They emerged from the Dreyfus affair believing that their deep-seated attachment to France and French culture had been vindicated by the victory of republicanism and the exoneration of Dreyfus. That faith was again challenged in the 1930s when antiforeign and anti-Jewish sentiment resurfaced. But native French Jews convinced themselves that this xenophobia was aimed at foreign Jews, not at them, and that the new outbreak of anti-Semitism was a foreign import from Germany. Indeed, many French Jews themselves felt threatened by the massive foreign Jewish immigration that took place in the 1920s and 1930s and joined others in calling for a restrictionist immigration policy.

On the eve of World War II the native and immigrant Jewish communities remained largely separate in ideology and institutional structures. French Jews, including some of the earlier generations of immigrants, considered themselves French and felt fully accepted into the fabric of French social and political life. Their Jewish identity, such as it existed, was primarily limited to a superficial religious life organized around synagogues run by the central Consistory. The immigrants, for the most part from Poland and Romania, rejected the "politics of assimilation" as naive and self-deluding. Although they were divided among themselves as Orthodox traditionalists, Bundist socialists, Communists, varieties of Zionists, and others, they nevertheless recognized their Jewish particularism and felt threatened even in liberal, republican France. In response, the immigrants had created their own Jewish world that included a vast network of institutions and a vibrant Yiddish cultural and political life.

Despite repeated attempts over the years to unite the two separate communities, mutual suspicions kept them apart. Thus, as David Weinberg has shown in his excellent study of the Jews of Paris in the 1930s, French Jews were to face the Nazi occupation divided. If native Jews held the advantages of more integration and better political, economic, and social connections, foreign Jews were psychologically better prepared to recognize the twin threats of the German Nazis and the Vichy French.

In the summer of 1940 about 350,000 Jews lived in France, 200,000 of them in Paris. Less than half of the Jews of France, and only a quarter of the Jews in Paris, were French citizens. Most of the "foreign" Jews had come from Eastern Europe before and especially after World War I, but their numbers were augmented by refugees fleeing the expanded German Reich.

After the German invasion in May 1940, Jews felt particularly threatened and joined the millions of other Frenchmen fleeing south. Much of the Jewish lay and rabbinic leadership also fled, leaving the occupied north without organized guidance. But after the armistice in June, some 30,000 Jews believed Marshal Pétain's promise of "normalcy" and heeded his call to return north. This raised the Jewish population in the Paris region to approximately 150,000. During these same months 30,000 Jews crossed the southern border to find refuge abroad.

The tensions and substantial differences between the native Jewish community and the Eastern European Jewish immigrants resurfaced under the Nazi and Vichy threats and prevented a unified response in both the north and south. Prior to the *Statut des Juifs*, immigrant Jewish organizations in the north gradually began to reestablish themselves. Recognizing the Nazi threat, immigrant activists from the prewar Federation of Jewish Societies of France (FSJF) met and decided to pool their resources under the Amelot Committee, named after the street in Paris where they met. The committee brought together Zionists, the socialist Bund, and several fraternal organizations. Because of mutual suspicions between Jewish Communists and most Zionists, however, the Jewish Communists formed a separate underground organization known as Solidarité.

Amelot invited the leadership of the central religious organization of the native French Jewish community (Consistoire central *des* Israélites de France, or the Consistory) to join with them. The Consistory refused because it feared cooperating with "foreign" Jews at a time of intense French nationalism and xenophobia. Believing that they would be treated like other Frenchmen and would be defended by their French brethren, the Consistory and other native Jews went their own way, reopening their synagogues and reestablishing their charitable institutions.

After the passage of the Vichy and German anti-Semitic measures, Theodore Dannecker, the German's "Jewish expert," sought a unification of Jewish organizations in the occupied north to handle the ever-increasing community needs.

Both native and immigrant leaders resisted, but several months of pressure and threats ended in the establishment of the Coordinating Committee of Jewish Welfare Societies (Comité de coordination des oeuvres Israëlites de bienfaisance) in January 1941. Only the Communist organization Solidarité, also known as the Union of Jews for Resistance and Mutual Aid (Union des Juifs pour la résistance et l'entr'aide, or UJRE) refused to join.

From the beginning, Amelot was reluctant to cooperate with a committee that to them was controlled by Germans. In March 1941 Dannecker brought in two Jews from Vienna to run the committee, and in May he ordered the internment of 3,700 Jewish, mostly immigrant, men. These measures were too much for Amelot, and it resigned. This further exacerbated tensions between the native and immigrant communities. Thus, as the Aryanization of Jewish property proceeded in the summer of 1941, as Jews were interned in squalid conditions at Drancy, and as poverty deepened, the Jewish communities in France remained deeply divided.

In the occupied zone immigrant organizations connected to Amelot continued to dispense aid given them largely by the American Joint Distribution Committee; but along with Solidarité, Amelot increasingly gravitated to clandestine and illegal activity. On the other hand, the Consistory and the Coordinating Committee continued to adhere to a legalistic approach that combined respect for the law with occasional pleas and protests to Pétain and other Vichy officials. (Vichy theoretically controlled Jewish policy in both zones by then.) Native Jews continued to believe that as French citizens they would not be abandoned by the French Vichy regime.

Massive migration to the south had increased the Jewish population there to 150,000. Though the unoccupied zone was less oppressive than the north, it presented serious economic problems, especially for Jews who had fled their homes and occupations in the north. But all Jews suffered under the increasingly oppressive Vichy *Statut des Juifs*.

Congregated in the major southern cities of Lyon, Marseilles, and Toulouse and in hundreds of minor cities, native and immigrant Jews in the unoccupied zone were plagued by the same divisions as those in the north. Under the prodding of the Joint Distribution Committee's European director, Joseph Schwartz, the major Jewish relief organizations met at the end of October 1940 in Marseilles to establish the Central Commission of Jewish Relief Organizations (Commission centrale des organisations Juives d'assistance, or CCOJA). CCOJA was to coordinate all relief efforts and organizations and to act as an intermediary with governmental and public authorities. It lasted until early 1942. Mutual suspicion and the individualistic mentality of native French Jewry eventually divided the immigrant relief organizations, under the leadership of the FSJF, and the native relief agencies. Despite Vichy's anti-Semitic legislation, French Jews, including many immigrants, continued to believe that their safety would be guaranteed by the French regime in the south. Therefore, most Jews concentrated on coping with daily life rather than trying to escape. This was soon to change.

By the summer of 1941 Dannecker was looking to replace the ineffectual Coordinating Committee of the north. Nazi policy toward the Jews was changing from encouraging emigration from Nazi-controlled Europe to some as yet ill-defined "final solution." To that end, Dannecker wished to separate the Jews of France, at least in the north, and to create a Judenrat (Jewish Council) to act as a relief agency and as an intermediary with the German occupation authorities. After months of negotiations between French authorities and leaders of Jewish organizations, the General Union of Jews of France (Union générale des Israëlites de France, or UGIF) was established on November 29, 1941. As we have seen, in order to protect French sovereignty over this body and to insure that Vichy coffers gained from the expropriation of Jewish property, Vichy insisted that the UGIF be under the supervision of its General Office for Jewish Affairs (CGQJ) and that a similar organization be established in the southern, unoccupied zone.

Leaders of the native Jewish community, especially in the south, agonized long and hard over the legitimacy of such an organization. They objected to its racial definition of Jews, which separated them from their fellow Frenchmen and lumped them with foreign Jews. They also feared that the UGIF might be forced to collaborate in a policy determined by the Nazis. In the end, however, the native leadership in the north decided that there was little alternative. The economic and social needs of both native and immigrant Jews were so great that native Jewish leaders felt that they had an obligation to serve. They also believed, as did most Judenrat leaders in Eastern Europe, that it was better that they fulfill these welfare functions than the Germans. Finally, established French Jews clung to the belief that Vichy would protect at least its Jewish citizens.

From the beginning, in both the north and the south, some Jewish leaders refused officially to join the UGIF. Amelot, the leaders of the FSJF who had fled south, and Solidarité charged the UGIF leaders with collaboration and refused to join. Though Amelot retained its independence, it did cooperate with the UGIF and was occasionally helped in its own activities by the UGIF.

The central Consistory and the chief rabbi of France, representing native Jewry, also strongly opposed union. They especially rejected the racial definition of Jews but also resented the breach of their authority as the true representatives of the Jewish community. Since the spring of 1941 the Consistory had been led by Jacques Helbronner, a distinguished member of the native community and a former member of the French Council of State. Following the Consistory's long policy of obeying the law while continuing to negotiate with the authorities, Helbronner advised the Jewish community to observe the anti-Jewish legislation. At the same time, he filed numerous private protests against the legislation and frequently intervened with Marshal Pétain to help rescue individuals. In large measure these actions were of no avail.

Despite the opposition of the Consistory and the immigrant organizations, the names of nine council members for the newly created UGIF in both zones were announced on January 9, 1942. Albert Levy in the south was appointed its president and André Baur of the north its vice president. Theoretically integrated, in practice the UGIF-N and UGIF-S acted autonomously throughout most of the war.

Almost immediately UGIF-N confronted a dramatically deteriorating situation. The increased expropriation of Jewish enterprises and a billion-dollar fine imposed by the Germans on the Jewish community in December 1941 made the expanded relief and welfare work both more essential and more difficult. In March 1942 deportations began, putting the immigrant community, in particular, into a frenzied search for refuge.

From April 1942 UGIF-N was forced to undertake functions that went beyond its original charter. It complied with German demands for large quantities of goods that the Germans claimed were to be used by Jews who were being deported, ostensibly to work camps, but actually to Auschwitz. When the mass arrests of foreign Jews took place in mid-July 1942, the UGIF Council continued its compliant, legalistic response. It provided assistance to Jews herded into the Vél d'hiver sports area, cared for children whose parents had been sent to Drancy, and continued to give supplies for deportation trains. Trusting in Vichy and following German orders, the UGIF gave aid but made no attempt to alert the community about the suspected roundups.

While the UGIF-N continued to caution against illegal measures, immigrant groups advocated a bolder response. Some engaged in sabotage against German officers and institutions. Others forged papers, helped find Christian homes for Jewish children, and secreted many Jews across the border into Spain and Switzerland.

The situation continued to worsen in the occupied zone in 1943. With thirty thousand already deported, and several thousand in hiding, the Germans faced increasing difficulty in finding Jews in the north to deport. The Germans now demanded that the UGIF in the north and south give up its immigrant employees. Though UGIF-N resisted giving up many of them, others were dismissed and deported. The UGIF was now also required to take over the upkeep of Drancy and to encourage Jews to voluntarily join their relatives there. Arguing that this was beyond its scope, UGIF leaders refused. UGIF Vice President André Baur and others were deported in retaliation.

Perhaps the saddest outcome of the decision to adhere to legalism was the fate of several hundred children who were housed by the UGIF-N. As the Nazis sought more Jews for deportation, they ordered arrests in children's homes, in homes for the aged, and at the Rothschild hospital. Immigrant groups had called for the dispersal of children and the destruction of the lists of names and locations. Their advice was not taken, however, and in July 1944, just weeks before the end of the war, Alois Brunner, the SS Hauptsturmführer, ordered his troops to seize the children in the UGIF homes. Three hundred children and personnel were arrested and transported in the last major convoy to Auschwitz.

The UGIF-S did not begin to function until May 1942 and was more decentralized in organization. Like the UGIF-N, UGIF-S saw its primary function as providing relief to the community. Raymond-Raoul Lambert was its tragic leader.

Trying to balance impossible dilemmas, he provided essential aid to both native and immigrant Jews, tried to use his influence and that of Christian relief agencies to intervene with Vichy, and interceded with French administrators to avoid the deportation of certain categories of native Jews. In the end, he too was deported to Auschwitz.

Especially in the south the UGIF helped Jews to flee and worked with some representatives of immigrant welfare groups to help in the illegal evacuation of Jews from the camps. In both the north and the south some members of the UGIF also played a double game, carrying out the legal aid work of the UGIF while also helping others in illegal activities. In both zones officials of the UGIF urged resistance to anti-Jewish measures; they retained the wide-ranging welfare services of the UGIF, and they spent precious energy and time protecting the separate existence of the UGIF in each zone. The UGIF, north and south, also rejected proposals to close its offices and help disperse the Jewish population. To the very end of the German occupation, when it was very clear where the deportees were going, the UGIF in the north and south continued its work.

Toward the end of 1943 the UGIF and the Consistory began to cooperate more closely. The Consistory had already withdrawn its opposition to the UGIF after the German occupation of the south in November 1942 and the mass deportations from Marseilles in January 1943. But the major change in Consistory policy took place only after its leader, Helbronner, was deported in October 1943. Under its new president, Leon Meiss, the Consistory joined with a broad range of native and immigrant Jewish groups, including the Jewish Communists, and established the Representative Council of the Jews of France (Conseil représentatif des Juifs de France, or CRIF). Founded in January 1944, CRIF thus provided a united front against further Nazi drives and helped to ameliorate the organizational and ideological rifts between native and immigrant Jews. Under the leadership of Leon Meiss, CRIF also helped to coordinate the resistance activities of its component parts.

In recent years a lively controversy has erupted over the behavior of the native French Jewish leadership during the Holocaust. Some, like Maurice Rajsfus in *Des Juifs dans la collaboration: L'UGIF, 1941–1944*, have accused native Jewish leaders of collaborating with the Nazis in the sacrifice of foreign Jews while protecting their own French and class interests. In his far more sensitive book, *The Jews of Paris and the Final Solution*, Jacques Adler, who participated in the Jewish Communist resistance in France, has softened these charges; but he too criticizes the native community for its relative silence and inactivity on behalf of foreign Jews. Blinded by their belief in their own security, he argues, native Jews failed until near the end to warn immigrant Jews of their imminent danger and to provide the necessary solidarity with them that might have helped in rescue efforts. Born of understandable anger and despair over the loss of half of the immigrant Jews in France, this position, other historians argue, nevertheless fails to take sufficient account of the complex problems facing the native Jewish leadership.

In retrospect, it seems obvious that the native leadership's policy of legalism and bargaining with Vichy and the Germans was at best self-deceptive and at worst self-serving. Yet, as part of the bourgeois elite of the Third Republic, the Jewish leadership could not easily countenance disobeying the law, even when laws were aimed against them. The native leadership also believed that its own "Frenchness" and class origins would lead Vichy to defend the native community and that native Jews could soften the execution of anti-Jewish legislation on all Jews. When occasional crumbs were offered by Vichy, this served to reinforce the self-deceiving belief that native Jews still had some power.

In his book *The Burden of Conscience*, Richard I. Cohen defends the leaders of the UGIF. Stunned and demoralized by both the French defeat and the *Statut des Juifs*, they were at first immobilized. In his wartime diary cited by Cohen, Raymond-Raoul Lambert expresses his sense of incredulity and abandonment. "What shame! I cannot even grasp this denial of justice and scientific truth . . . this cannot last, this isn't possible . . . I cried yesterday like a man who suddenly is abandoned by a woman who is the only love of his life, the only guide of his thoughts, the only director of his acts." In the end, Lambert and other native leaders unwillingly decided to join the UGIF because they had a habit of helping and playing leadership roles.

Whatever their prejudices and blindness, the leaders of the UGIF acted only as a relief agency, not as a Judenrat. They did not pretend to represent the French Jewish community. If they provided relief to Jews in the Vél d'hiver and Drancy, instead of more actively opposing the policy that put them there, native Jews were not responsible for handing Jews over for deportations. The Germans and Vichy did that. As we have seen, some of the people working for the UGIF in fact helped those involved in clandestine rescue efforts while also carrying out the legalistic work of the agency.

In the end, like so many other Jews and non-Jews in Nazi-occupied Europe, the native leaders clung to false hopes. They did not understand what the ultimate goal of the Nazis was until it was too late. Until the end of 1942, holding on and holding out, at least for the native community, seemed to be working. Afterward, their incorrigible patriotism led them to the not-unreasonable conclusion that Germany's defeat was imminent and that, therefore, a policy of aid, comfort, and cooperation in the meantime was the right one to follow. Their prejudices and policies may have been wrong, even reprehensible at times, but, as Michael Marrus and others argue, their responses were as good as or better than the responses of other Jewish and non-Jewish leaders throughout Europe, particularly when we consider their relative powerlessness.

Although most resistance efforts were carried out by immigrant Jews, much of the more overt resistance activity of the immigrant groups was made possible by the established organs of French Jewry. For example, the UGIF provided a funnel through which hundreds of millions of francs were passed from the U.S. Joint Distribution Committee to various non-Communist Jewish groups involved in clandestine and rescue activity. The UGIF also acted as a cover for organizations that were connected with it, but whose operations were illegal. This was true of the Jewish Boy Scout movement (Eclaireurs Israélites de France), which was founded and led by a member of the UGIF, Robert Gamzon. In another example, the UGIF-S gave cover to the Oeuvre de secours aux enfants (OSE), a child-rescue organization increasingly involved in underground operations during the latter part of 1942.

Nevertheless, most direct action against German and Vichy policy against the Jews was carried out by "foreign" Jews. Having fewer illusions about the liberal heritage of France and about its beneficence to Jews, immigrant groups were better prepared to mount a unified attack against Nazi aims.

Though not politically unified, Amelot was among the earliest Jewish groups to recognize the importance of Jewish solidarity. Very early it presumed the separation of Jews from the rest of the population and, therefore, focused its resistance on aiding and rescuing Jews. Only parts of the Amelot coalition, however, participated directly in armed combat.

Adler argues that among Jewish groups the Communist Solidarité first recognized that Nazism and the German military machine, not just a lack of food or shelter, were the real enemies. Solidarité and the UJRE began active resistance the earliest (shortly after the attack on the Soviet Union in June 1941), carried out the most extensive attacks on German and Vichy targets, and in the end suffered the most for resistance actions. Supporting a collective Jewish response to persecution, Solidarité specifically formed Jewish units and encouraged other Jewish political activity.

Despite their heroic activities, however, the Jewish Communists, according to Adler, made few direct assaults on the Nazis' anti-Jewish machinery. They attacked German lines of communication but not trains taking Jews to Auschwitz; and they shot German officers but not the Judenreferenten who helped round up the Jews. Like all the Communist resistance, Solidarité identified its cause with that of the Soviet Union, and that ultimately determined its strategy. In the end, the Communist party did little to return the favor, disowning the independent Jewish line taken by the immigrant activists, yet leaving them vulnerable to the Gestapo because of the allegiance of Solidarité to the party.

The Bundist socialists and Zionist groups also formed resistance groups and were involved in independent fighting units, such as the Armée Juive, and in rescue operations connected to the Oeuvre de secours aux enfants (OSE). If less powerful than the Communists, they were more attuned to Jewish needs.

The question of the Jews in the resistance raises the general issue whether theirs was a "Jewish resistance" or a Jewish contribution to the French National Resistance. Some historians argue that Jewish organizations were part of the common struggle to free France of its German occupants. Jewish organizations, according to this view, were but a special sector of the National Resistance. This was certainly the case with many assimilated Jews like Marc Bloch, the famed historian of medieval France who was subsequently killed for his participation in the French resistance. Not looking upon Judaism as his personal point of reference, he, and others like him, refused to accept the racial and religious definitions placed on him by the Nazis and Vichy. In their view, these people participated as patriotic Frenchmen. Even a historian of the Jewish immigrant experience, David Diamant, has argued that the resistance was one and indivisible, and that the Jews were but one of the "spiritual" families that participated in it.

On the other hand, Leon Poliakov and others have presented their case for a more distinctive "Jewish" resistance. They argue that in the first place, Jews recognized far earlier than the general population the nature of the Nazi threat. Therefore, earlier than most they went underground and began to resist. In general, according to another proponent of this position, Rénee Poznanski, Jews were drawn into the resistance earlier and in significantly greater proportions than the general population. Second, the rhetoric and basic assumptions underlying the actions of those Jewish organizations involved in the resistance were deeply embedded in a historical national consciousness. All the Jewish organizations, from immigrant groups to French Judaism, sooner or later recognized that a common fate bound them together.

Unfortunately, there was little Jewish organizations and resistance groups could effectively do. Armed combat for the young and unattached provided a means for Jewish affirmation. For others, the rescue of children or giving out forged identity papers offered practical help. In the end, however, the fate of the French Jews depended mostly on others: first, on German policy, then, on Vichy, and, finally, on the willingness of the general population to help.

## SPECIALIZED JEWISH COMMUNITIES

A few specialized Jewish communities in France and Jews of North Africa and Syria and Lebanon do not fit the pattern of French Jewry already discussed and, therefore, require separate treatment.

When Germany invaded France and annexed Alsace-Lorraine, the 20,000 Jews there were left especially vulnerable. French authorities evacuated inhabitants of the border areas. Fourteen thousand Jews were among them, and they were moved to central areas of western France. After the fall of France in June 1940, some 5,000 of these Jews fled to the unoccupied south. The following month Germany expelled the remaining Jews of Alsace-Lorraine. Many Jews from Alsace-Lorraine were active in Jewish resistance organizations. Some 2,000 were killed during the Holocaust. Most of the remaining returned home and reestablished their communities after the war.

On the eve of World War II over 400,000 Jews lived in the French-dominated North African countries of Algeria, Morocco, and Tunisia. Jews had lived in North Africa since the time of the Roman Empire. In the fifteenth and sixteenth centuries the Jewish population was enhanced by the refugees from the Spanish Inquisition. More Jewish refugees, this time escaping from the ever-widening net of Nazi Germany, would come there in the wake of World War II.

Algeria's Jewish population of 120,000 was concentrated in the three large cities of Algiers, Oran, and Constantine. In 1870 the Jews of Algeria became French citizens under a law supported by Isaac Adolphe Crémieux, the Jewish French minister of justice. After gaining French citizenship, Algerian Jews improved their political and economic position considerably compared with their second-class citizenship as *dhimmis* (protected people) under the Muslims. Algerian Jews thus became very patriotic to France and, like their native French brethren, failed to recognize the danger to them from the French Vichy regime. Indicative of their patriotism, these Algerian Jews became the bulwark of Algerian resistance against the Germans.

Algeria was originally a colony and later was made part of France. Its political life was dominated by *colons*, French citizens from France who had made their home in Algeria. Threatened by the special status of Algerian Jews and concerned that French citizenship might next be given to the Muslims, the *colons* turned to right-wing, anti-Semitic movements in the late nineteenth century. There were several waves of anti-Semitic violence perpetrated by the *colons*. Most serious were those that reached their peaks in the 1890s and again from the 1920s to the end of World War II. This latter wave also affected Morocco and Tunisia, where it spread among the Arab population.

The *colons* enthusiastically welcomed Marshal Pétain when, as part of the French-German armistice agreement, Algeria became part of unoccupied Vichy France. Algeria thus came under the Vichy *Statut des Juifs*, and the Crémieux decree was repealed. By 1942 preparations were being made to establish a Jewish Council along the lines of the UGIF in France, but this ended with the Allied invasion in November 1942. Even after the Americans entered, however, Darlan, now high commissioner of North Africa, refused to abolish the anti-Jewish legislation. His assassination on December 24, 1942, only led to further harassment of Jews and the arrest of the former leaders of the Jewish underground. Pressure from the American media finally forced the U.S. government to ask Darlan's successor, General Henri Giraud, to abolish the racist laws. At the same time, however, Giraud reinstated the law that abolished the Crémieux decree. Anti-Semitic feeling among the *colons* was so strong that even when de Gaulle took over Algeria in May 1943, he let the law die quietly. It took many more months for the last vestiges of Vichy to disappear. Dozens of Jewish refugees were still imprisoned in concentration camps in late 1944, and pro-Vichy sympathizers in the Algerian administration remained even longer.

Unlike Algeria, most of Morocco was a French protectorate. Its Jewish population of 200,000 lived in numerous cities and villages throughout the country. Although the French did not change the Jews' *dhimmi* status given them by the Moslem rulers, French presence did lead to a notable legal improvement of the status of the Jewish community. Even though many of their traditional occupations were severely hurt, Jews also welcomed French modernization. In Morocco, as in Algeria and Tunisia, hostility to Jews was spread by Nazi propaganda and Arab nationalists hostile to Zionism. Unlike Algeria, however, there was no strong anti-Semitic force among the *colons*.

Moroccan Jews were also affected by Nazi and Vichy anti-Jewish policies. The Vichy *Statut des Juifs* was applied in Morocco and Tunisia, although in milder form. Jews there were defined only by religion, and, generally speaking, in Morocco the Vichy laws affected only those Jews living in urban areas who had contact with the French. Therefore, more traditional Jews, whose lives were lived in the countryside, went largely untouched during these years. When the Americans invaded North Africa, Jewish suffering in Morocco did not immediately end. French Vichy sympathizers continued their attacks until the summer of 1944, over a year after the racist laws had been abolished. Some 4,000 Jewish prisoners were interned in Moroccan labor or concentration camps, Djelfa being the largest. On the other hand, 10,000 Jewish refugees were to pass through North Africa without experiencing imprisonment in a Vichy camp.

Tunisia's 85,000 Jews were concentrated in a few places, over half in the city of Tunis. Much more than in Algeria and Morocco, Jews in Tunisia were modern and secular and were part of a vibrant ideological ferment that included Zionists, socialists, and Communists. Their experience during World War II was similar to that of Morocco until November 1942, when Germany occupied Tunisia.

Before November 1942 France applied the Vichy anti-Jewish laws in Tunisia, much to the disillusionment of the patriotic pro-French Tunisian Jews. These laws, however, were applied very mildly by the sympathetic governor-general, Vice Admiral Jean Pierre Esteva. The laws were also vitiated by the Bey Sidi Mohammed al-Mounsaf and the Italian representatives in Tunisia.

The German occupation lasted until May 1943, when the Allies liberated Tunisia. Under the occupation, 5,000 Jews were put into forced labor. Most of the labor camps where Jews were held were situated on isolated farms or open fields, and conditions were not harsh. However, the largest camp at Bizerte had a brutal regimen; Jews were worked at hard labor fourteen hours a day and were punished for the slightest transgression. Service in the forced-labor camps seems to have fallen disproportionately on the poorer Jews. As in Algeria and Morocco, very few Jews were deported to extermination camps in Europe.

The final area of French influence was in Syria Lebanon. France gained a League of Nations mandate in this area after World War I when the Middle East was divided up between Great Britain and France. Jews are thought to have lived in this region as early as the First Temple period (955 to 586 B.C.E.). By the early 1930s the Jewish population was approximately 35,000 and was concentrated in Aleppo, Damascus, and Beirut. Although Jews were well integrated into Arab society, relations between Arabs and Jews deteriorated sharply in the 1930s due to Zionism and the rise of Syrian nationalism. Nazi propaganda fell on receptive ears, and several Jews were stabbed to death by Muslim nationalists.

Vichy authorities controlled Syria and Lebanon between December 19, 1940, and July 14, 1941, when British and Free French forces occupied it. During the six months of Vichy rule, anti-Jewish legislation was issued, but there was not enough time for implementation. More serious was the economic depression that seriously affected the Jewish community after the borders between Syria and its neighbors were closed. Arab nationalists, working closely with the mufti of Jerusalem, Haj Amin al-Husseini, also posed a serious threat. These factors led to the emigration of Jews from Syria to Palestine and elsewhere even before the war was over.

## AFTERMATH

In comparison with the Jewish communities of Eastern Europe, French Jews fared well. Over 75 percent of the Jews living in France before the war survived, enough to rebuild a significant Jewish community. These numbers were reinforced by an influx of Jewish survivors fleeing displaced persons' camps. By 1950 France had the largest Jewish community on the continent outside the Soviet Union.

Still, liberation did not bring all joy and relief to French Jews. For most of the survivors, especially the immigrants, life would never be the same. Fifty thousand Parisian Jews had filled the deportation trains, thousands more had lost at least one relative, and thousands of children were orphaned. Immigrants emerged from their hiding places without homes to go to. Businesses had been dispossessed. The processes of rebuilding—of regaining rightful ownership of property, of housing the homeless, of tracing the children placed with Christian families, of placing the orphaned children in foster homes, of healing—were to become monumental tasks.

Despite the efforts of community leaders who pressed the government for restitution, French Jews met with only limited success in reclaiming the businesses, furniture, and apartments of the deportees. Orphaned children and Holocaust survivors seeking refuge in France fared better as Jewish community organizations sprang up to house and feed refugees and to place orphaned children in foster homes. The Jewish community was much less successful, however, in recovering Jewish children adopted by non-Jews during the war.

Postwar reconstruction also required the rebuilding and restructuring of Jewish communal institutions and the reconciliation of native and immigrant Jews. But despite goodwill attempts and calls for unity, native and immigrant leaders largely went their own ways. The immigrants' contempt for the UGIF and their hostility even toward the central Consistory for its xenophobia overwhelmed calls for unity. If they failed to create a unified communal structure, under the pressure of the Joint Distribution Committee French Jews were able to coordinate relief efforts. To this end, the community formed the Fondssocial Juif unifié (FSJU), which soon emerged as the central agency for fundraising and the distribution of social services. In its commitment to building a professional community service, the FSJU helped forge Jewish Communal solidarity.

Created in the last months of the German occupation, CRIF was to serve after the war as the political arm of French Jewry on a number of issues important to French Jews. Though its success depended to a large extent on the French government in power, CRIF strengthened the community by its willingness to actively assert Jewish interests.

Unfortunately, the successful philanthropic and political restructuring was not matched by an ideological transformation in regard to the historic relationship between Jews and other Frenchmen. French Jews did become more vocal in publicly demanding the banning of anti-Jewish groups and in expressing their outrage at government leniency with regard to collaboration. However, most native Jews chose to reidentify France with the heroic efforts of the resistance, rather than with the collaborators and bystanders. Even the immigrant community became caught up in the mythology of a nation of resisters. The community also failed to work out, or even seriously discuss, the meaning of the new state of Israel for French Jewish identity. Despite its successes in caring for the needy and restoring Jewish institutional life, the French Jewish community seemed to be drifting by the early 1950s. Only a fresh infusion of immigrants, this time from North Africa, would supply the dynamism and greater sense of purpose to Jewish communal and intellectual life that exists today in France.

## BIBLIOGRAPHIC NOTES

For descriptions of Nazi policy in France, see especially Michael R. Marrus and Robert O. Paxton, *Vichy France and the Jews* (New York: Schocken Books, 1981). Marrus and Paxton's book is the best account in English of German and Vichy policy in France. See also their article describing the stages of Nazi policy, "The Nazis and Jews in Occupied Western Europe, 1940–1944," *Journal of Modern History* 54 (1982): 687–714. The standard work in French, which contains several useful sketches of German leaders in France, is Joseph Billig, *La solution finale de la question juive: Essai sur ses principes dans le IIIe reich et en France sous l'occupation* (Paris: CDJC, 1977).

Other useful general accounts include that by the German historian Eberhard Jäckel, *La France dans l'Europe de Hitler*, translated by D. Meunier (Paris: Fayard, 1968); *L'étoile jaune* (Paris: Éditions du Centre, 1949) by the Polish-French Jewish historian and participant Leon Poliakov; and another older but useful work by a Polish-French Jewish historian who survived the occupation, Zosa Szajkowski, *Analytical Franco-Jewish Gazeteer, 1939–1945* (New York: Frydman, 1966). See also *Fall of France: Results*. Monographs on Europe, (Cambridge, Mass.: Center for European Studies, Harvard University, 1982).

Popular accounts include Gerald Walter, *Paris Under the Occupation*, translated by Tony White (New York: Orion Press, 1960), and David Pryce-Jones, *Paris in the Third Reich: A History of the German Occupation, 1940–1944* (New York: Holt, Rinehart and Winston, 1981). The latter contains especially interesting documentary photographs from that period.

For more specialized accounts of German policy and officials, see Christopher

Browning, *The Final Solution and the German Foreign Office* (New York: Holmes and Meier 1978), and Hans Umbreit, *Der Militärbefehlshaber im Frankreich, 1940–1944* (Boppard am Rhein, 1968).

Collections of documents and documentation include Serge Klarsfeld, *Recueil de documents des dossiers des autorités allemandes concernant la persécution des juifs en France (1940–1944)*, 8 vols. (Paris, n.d.); Henri Monneray, ed., *La persécution des juifs en France et dans les autres pays dans l'Ouest présentée par la France à Nuremberg* (Paris: Éditions du Centre, 1947); and Lucien Steinberg, *Les autorités allemandes en France occupée: Inventaire commenté de la collection de documents conservés au CDJC* (Paris, CDJC, 1966).

In addition to the works already cited, see the following for the roundups, deportations, and French concentration camps: Jean Jacques Bernard, *Le camp de la mort lente: Compiègne, 1941–1942* (Paris: Albin Michel, 1944); Andre Brissaud, *La dernière année de Vichy, 1943–1944* (Paris: Librarie Acad Émique Perrin, 1965); M. Felstiner, "Commandant of Drancy: Alois Brunner and the Jews of France," *Holocaust and Genocide Studies* 2 (1987): 21–47; Lion Feuchtwanger, *The Devil in France: My Encounter with Him in the Summer of 1940* (New York: Viking Press, 1941), the "devil" being the camp at Les Milles; Andre Fontaine, *Le Camp d'étrangers des Milles, 1939–1943 (Aix-en-Provence)* (Aix-en-Provence: Edisud, 1989), for both the text and its photographs; Serge Klarsfeld, *Le mémorial de la déportation des juifs de France* (Paris: Beate and Serge Klarsfeld, 1978); Claude Levy and Paul Tillard, *Betrayal at the Vel d'Hiv*, translated by Inea Bushnaq (New York: Hill and Wang, 1969); Donald Lowrie, *The Hunted Children* (New York: Norton, 1963); Adam Rutkowski, "Le camp d'internment de Gurs," *Monde Juif* 36, n.s. 100 (1980): 128–47, "Les déportations des Juifs de France vers Auschwitz et Sobibor," *Monde Juif* (1970): 33–75, and "Directives allemandes concernant les arrestations et les déportations des juifs de France en Avril–Aout 1944," *Monde Juif* 32, n.s. 82 (1976): 53–65; Hans Sahl, *The Few and the Many*, translated by Richard and Clara Winston (New York: Harcourt, Brace and World, 1962), a personal memoir dealing in part with his imprisonment at Les Milles; Lucien Steinberg, "Statistiques de la déportation des juifs de France d'après les dossiers de la Gestapo à Paris," *Monde Juif* (January–June 1970), pp. 35–75; Joseph Weill, *Contribution à l'histoire des camps d'internement dans l'anti-France* (Paris: Éditions du Centre, 1946); George Wellers, "Déportation des juifs en France sous l'occupation: légendes et réalités," *Monde Juif* 36, n.s. 99 (1980): 75–108, and *L'étoile jaune à l'heure de Vichy: De Drancy à Auschwitz* (Paris: Fayard, 1973).

For the Italian occupation in the south of France, see Zanfel Diamant, "Jewish Refugees on the French Riviera," *YIVO Annual of Jewish Social Sciences* 8 (1953): 264–80; Meir Michaelis, *Mussolini and the Jews: German-Italian Relations and the Jewish Question in Italy* (Oxford: Clarendon Press, 1978); Leon Poliakov and Jacques Sabille, eds., *Jews Under the Italian Occupation* (Paris: CDJC, 1955); Susan Zuccotti, *The Italians and the Holocaust: Persecution, Rescue, and Survival* (New York: Basic Books, 1987).

Marrus and Paxton's *Vichy France and the Jews* remains the best account of Vichy anti-Jewish policy. A longer and equally critical account of Vichy by a French lawyer, historian, and activist is Serge Klarsfeld, *Vichy-Auschwitz: Le rôle de Vichy dans la solution finale de la question juive en France*, 2 vols. (Paris: Fayard, 1983). Also see the important collective work of George Wellers, André Kaspi, and Serge Klarsfeld, eds., *La France et la question juive, 1940– 1944* (Paris: Éditions Sylvie Messinger, 1981). For other accounts of Vichy France that at least in part touch on the subject of the Jews, see Robert Aron, *The Vichy Regime, 1940–1944*, translated by Humphrey Hare (Boston: Beacon Press, 1969), a somewhat less critical view of Vichy; Richard Cobb, *French and Germans, Germans and French: A Personal Interpretation of France Under Two Occupations, 1914–1918/1940–1944* (Hanover, N.H.: University Press of New England, 1983); *France Under the German Occupation, 1940–1944*, 3 vols. (a collection of 292 statements of the government of Marshal Pétain and Pierre Laval), translated by Philip W. Whitcomb (Stanford: Stanford University Press for the Hoover Institute on War, Revolution, and Peace, 1958–59); Milton Dank, *The French Against the French: Collaboration and Resistance* (Philadelphia: Lippincott, 1974); Paul Farmer, *Vichy: Political Dilemma* (New York: Columbia University Press, 1955); Bertram M. Gordon, *Collaboration in France During the Second World War* (Ithaca, N.Y.: Cornell University Press, 1980); Stanley Hoffman, "Collaborationism in France During World War II," *Journal of Modern History* 40, no. 3 (September 1968): 375–95; Robert Paxton, *Vichy France: Old Guard and New Order* (New York: Columbia University Press, 1982); and John Sweets, *Choices in Vichy France: The French Under Nazi Occupation* (New York: Oxford University Press, 1986).

For Marshal Pétain, his ideology, and his collaborationism, see Herbert R. Lottman, *Pétain, Hero or Traitor: The Untold Story* (New York: William Morrow, 1984); and Robert O. Paxton, *Parades and Politics at Vichy: The French Officer Corps Under Marshal Pétain* (Princeton, N.J.: Princeton University Press, 1966).

For Pierre Laval, see René de Chambrun, *Pierre Laval: Traitor or Patriot?* translated by Elly Stein (New York: Scribner, 1984); Hubert Cole, *Laval: A Biography* (London: Heinemann, 1963); Fred Kupferman, *Pierre Laval* (Paris: Masson, 1976); Pierre Laval, *The Diary of Pierre Laval* (New York: AMS Press, 1976); and Geoffrey Warner, *Pierre Laval and the Eclipse of France, 1931– 1945* (London: Eyre and Spottiswoode, 1968).

For French fascism and its roots, see the several articles in the *Journal of Contemporary History* 1, no. 1 (January 1966): 27–74, and 11, no. 4 (October 1976): 75–128; Robert Soucy, *Fascism in France: The Case of Maurice Barrès* (Berkeley: University of California Press, 1972); Ze'ev Sternhell, *Ni droite, ni gauche: L'idéologie fasciste en France* (Paris: Éditions du Seuil, 1983); and Eugen Weber, *Action Française* (Stanford, Calif.: Stanford University Press, 1962).

For Vallat, Darquier de Pellepoix, and the General Office for Jewish Affairs

(CGQJ), see the monumental work of Joseph Billig, *Le Commissariat général aux questions juives (1941–1944)*, 3 vols. (Paris: Éditions du Centre, 1955–60); Asher Cohen, "Le peuple aryen vu par le Commissariat Général aux Questions Juives," *Revue d'Histoire de la Deuxième Guerre Mondiale et des Conflits Contemporains*, 36 (141) (1986): 45–58; and Jean Laloum, *La France antisémite de Darquier de Pellepoix* (Paris: Syros, 1979).

For the history of French anti-Semitism before Vichy, see Michael D. Biddiss *Father of Racist Ideology: The Social and Political Thought of Count Gobineau* (New York: Weybright and Talley, 1970); Robert F. Byrnes, *Antisemitism in Modern France: The Prologue to the Dreyfus Affair* (New Brunswick, N.J., Rutgers University Press, 1950); Arthur Hertzberg, *The French Enlightenment and the Jews* (New York: Columbia University Press, 1968), which argues that anti-Semitism is inherent even in the liberal tradition of the French Enlightenment; Jeffrey Mehlman, *Legacies of Anti-Semitism in France* (Minneapolis: University of Minnesota Press, 1983); Isaac Pierrard, *Juifs et catholiques français de Drumont à Jules Isaac, 1886–1945* (Paris, 1970); and Stephen Wilson, *Ideology and Experience: Antisemitism in France at the Time of the Dreyfus Affair* (Rutherford, N.J.: Fairleigh Dickinson University Press, 1982). If overly long, Wilson's book is an excellent comprehensive survey of varieties of anti-Jewish sentiment in France during that period.

For support of Marrus and Paxton's argument that anti-immigrant and anti-Jewish policy began during the interwar period, before Vichy, see Gilbert Badia, "Camps répressifs ou camps de concentration," in Gilbert Badia et al., *Les barbelés de l'éxil: Études sur l'émigration allemande et autrichienne (1938–1940)* (Grenoble, 1979), 259–332; Jean Charles Bonnet, *Les pouvoirs publics français et l'immigration dans l'entre-deux-guerres* (Lyon, 1976); Vicki Caron, "Prelude to Vichy: France and the Jewish Refugees in the Era of Appeasement," *Journal of Contemporary History* 20 (1985): 157–76; and Timothy P. Maga, "Closing the Door: The French Government and the Refugee Policy, 1933–1939," *French Historical Studies* 12 (1982): 424–42.

For a suggestive critique of Marrus and Paxton's accusations that the French public and French historical anti-Semitism were responsible for anti-Jewish policy, see Patrice Higonnet, "How Guilty Were the French?" *New York Review of Books*, December 3, 1981, 15–18.

The Vatican and the French Catholic church and churchmen, in general, either collaborated or closed their eyes to Vichy anti-Jewish policy. See Claude Langlois, "Le régime de Vichy et le clergé d'après les 'semaines religieuses des diocèses de la zone libre,' " *Revue Française de Science Politique* 22 (1972): 750–74; Leon Poliakov, "Le Vatican et le question juive," *Monde Juif*, no. 2 (December 1950): 11–14; and Wladimir Rabi, "L'église catholique sous la occupation," *Monde Juif* 33, n.s. 85 (1977): 39–40.

John Sweets's book on the French during the occupation, *Choices in Vichy France* (cited earlier), argues for a more nuanced and positive view of French public opinion and action during the occupation. For other views, see Marcel

Baudot, *L'opinion publique sous l'occupation* (Paris: Presses Universitaires de France, 1960); Samuel Osgood, "The Anti-Semitism of the French Collaborationist Press," *Wiener Library Bulletin* 23, nos. 2–3, n.s. nos. 15–16 (1969): 51–56; and Leon Poliakov, "An Opinion Poll on Anti-Jewish Measures in Vichy France," *Jewish Social Studies* 15 (1953): 135–50.

Despite the relatively dismal efforts of the French on behalf of the Jews, there were many individuals and groups who did help. For Catholic rescue, see Renée Bedarida, *Les armes de l'ésprit: Témoignage chrétien, 1941–1944* (Paris, Les Éditions/Ouvriéres 1977); *Cahiers et courriers clandestins du témoignage chrétien, 1941–1944*, 2 vols. (Paris, 1980); Jacques Duquesne, *Les catholiques français sous l'occupation* (Paris, 1966), and "Defensor Judaeorum—The French Episcopate, 1940–1944," *Wiener Library Bulletin* 21 (Spring 1967); Saul Friedlander, *When Memory Comes*, translated by Helen R. Lane (New York: Avon, 1980), a moving personal account of rescue by Catholics and the difficult decision to "leave" Catholicism at the end of the war by an Israeli-Jewish historian; Fernand Leboucher, *The Incredible Mission of Father Benoit* (London: Doubleday, 1970); Xavier de Montclos et al., "Églises et chrétiens dans la IIe guerre mondiale: La région Rhone-Alpes," *Actes du Colloque Tenu à Grenoble du 7 au 9 Octobre 1976* (Lyon, 1978); John Morley, *Vatican Diplomacy: The Jews during the Holocaust, 1939–1943* (New York: Ktav, 1980); *Un éveque français sous l'occupation: Extraits des messages de S. Ex. Mgr. Saliège, archéveque de Toulouse* (Paris, 1945).

For Protestant rescue, see Philip Hallie, *Lest Innocent Blood Be Shed: The Story of the Village of Le Chambon and How Goodness Happened There* (New York: Harper and Row, 1978). Also on Le Chambon, see Pierre Sauvage, "A Most Persistent Haven: Le Chambon-sur-Lignon," *Moment* 8, no. 9 (October 1983): 30–35; C. Rittner and S. Myers, eds., *The Courage to Care* (New York, NYU Press 1986), pp. 99–119; and Violette Mouchon et al., *Quelques actions des protestants de France en faveur des juifs persécutés sous l'occupation allemande*, 1940–1944 (Paris: CIMADE, 1945).

For miscellaneous rescue efforts in France, see Nicolas Bondy, "The Affair of the Finaly Children," *Commentary* 15, no. 6 (June 1953): 547–58; Marie M. Fourcade, *Noah's Ark: The Secret Underground* (New York: Zebra Books, 1974); Hillel Kieval, "Legality and Resistance in Vichy France: The Rescue of Jewish Children," *Proceedings of the American Philosophical Society* 124 (1980): 339–66; and Paul Vignaux, "Christian Trade Unions Fought Anti-Semitism Throughout the Period of France's Occupation," *Voice Unconquered* 3, no. 3 (March 1945): 3–6. For a personal memoir defending France during the occupation, see Jacqueline Wolf, *"Take Care of Josette": A Memoir in Defense of Occupied France* (New York: Watts, 1981).

The French resistance movements had a marginal effect on rescue efforts. For the Communist resistance, see Jacques Adler, *The Jews of Paris and the Final Solution: Communal Response and Internal Conflicts 1940–1944* (New York and Oxford: Oxford University Press, 1987); Annie Kriegel, "Résistants communistes et juifs persécutés,'' *H-Histoire* 3 (November 1970): 99–123; and Claude Levy, *Les parias de la résistance* (Paris: Calmann-Levy, 1970).

For other parts of the French Resistance, see Paul Durand, *La S.C N.F. pendant la querre: Sa résistance a l'occupant* (Paris: Presses Universitaires de France 1968); B. Ehrlich, *The French Resistance*, 1940–1945 (London: Chapman and Hall, 1966); Marie Granet and Henri Michel, *Combat: Histoire d'un mouvement de résistance* (Paris: Presses Universitaires de France 1957); Harry R. Kedward, *Resistance in Vichy France* (Oxford: Oxford University Press, 1978); Peter Leslie, *The Liberation of the Riviera: The Resistance to the Nazis in the South of France and the Story of Its Heroic Leader, Ange-Marie Miniconi* (New York: Wyndham Books, 1980); Henri Michel, *Histoire de la résistance*, 7th ed. (Paris: Presses Universitaires de France, 1975); Peter Novick, *The Resistance Versus Vichy: The Purge of Collaborators in Liberated France* (London: Chatto and Windus, 1968); David Schoenbrun, *Soldiers of the Night: The Story of the French Resistance* (New York: Dutton, 1979); John Sweets, *The Politics of Resistance in France, 1940–1944: A History of the Mouvements Unis de la Résistance* (Dekalb: Northern Illinois University Press, 1976); and Dominique Veillon, *Le Franc-Tireur: Un journal clandestin, un mouvement de résistance, 1940–1944* (Paris, 1977).

There have been several excellent works written in recent years on French Jewry in the nineteenth and twentieth centuries: Phyllis Cohen Albert, *The Modernization of French Jewry: Consistory and Community in the Nineteenth Century* (Hanover, N.H.: Brandeis University Press, 1977); Jay R. Berkovitz, *The Shaping of Jewish Identity in Nineteenth-Century France* (Detroit: Wayne State University Press, 1989); Vicki Caron, *Between France and Germany: The Jews of Alsace-Lorraine, 1871–1918* (Stanford: Stanford University Press, 1988); Nancy Green, *The Pletzl of Paris: Jewish Immigrant Workers in the Belle Epoque* (New York: Holmes and Meier, 1986); Paula Hyman, *From Dreyfus to Vichy: The Remaking of French Jewry, 1906–1939* (New York: Columbia University Press, 1979); Franz Kobler, *Napoleon and the Jews* (New York: Schocken Books, 1976); Michael Marrus, *The Politics of Assimilation: A Study of the French Jewish Community at the Time of the Dreyfus Affair* (Oxford: Clarendon Press, 1971); Michel Roblin, *Les juifs de Paris: Démographie, économie, culture* (Paris: A. et J. Picard, 1952); Charlotte Roland, *Du ghetto à l'occident: Deux générations yiddiches en France* (Paris: Éditions de Minuit, 1962); Zosa Szajkowski, *Jews and the French Revolutions of 1789, 1830, and 1848* (New York: Ktav, 1970); Rita Thalman, ''L'emigration du IIIe reich dans la France de 1933 à 1939,'' *Monde Juif* 96 (1979): 127–39; David Weinberg, *A Community on Trial: The Jews of Paris in the 1930's* (Chicago: University of Chicago Press, 1977); and Nelly Wilson, *Bernard-Lazare: Antisemitism and the Problem of Jewish Identity in Late Nineteenth-Century France* (Cambridge and New York: Cambridge University Press, 1978). Most of these works chart an increasingly assimilated French native Jewry and a separation between immigrant and native Jews. Hyman sees more interconnection by the 1930s and suggests that had it not been for the rise of Hitler, there might have been a coming together of the two communities.

I have already discussed in the text the main outlines of the debate over the appropriateness of the responses of French Jewry. For a full discussion of the issues involved, see Jacques Adler, *The Jews of Paris and the Final Solution: Communal Response and Internal Conflicts, 1940–1944*, cited earlier; Vicki Caron, *The UGIF: The Failure of the Nazis to Establish a Judenrat on the Eastern European Model*, Working Papers, no. 1 (New York: Center for Israel and Jewish Studies, Columbia University, 1977); Yerachmiel (Richard) Cohen, "A Jewish Leader in Vichy France, 1940–1943: The Diary of Raymond-Raoul Lambert," *Jewish Social Studies* 43 (1981): 291–310, and *The Burden of Conscience: French Jewish Leadership During the Holocaust* (Bloomington: Indiana University Press, 1987); Conseil Réprésentatif des Juifs de France (CRIF), *Vingt-cinq années d'activités, 1944–1969*, edited by Maurice Moch (Paris: CRIF, 1970); Robert Geissmann, "Le rabbinat consistorial sous l'occupation," *Journal des Communautées* 393 (April 28, 1967); Cynthia Haft, *The Bargain and the Bridle: The General Union of Israelites of France* (Chicago: Dialog Press, 1983); Jacob Kaplan, "French Jewry Under the Occupation," *American Jewish Yearbook* 47 (1945): 71–118; Raymond-Raoul Lambert, *Carnet d'un témoin, 1940–1943*, edited by Richard Cohen (Paris: Fayard, 1985); Michael Marrus, "Jewish Leaders and the Holocaust," *French Historical Studies* 15, no. 2 (1987): 316–31; Maurice Rajsfus, *Des Juifs dans la collaboration: L'UGIF, 1941–1944* (Paris: E.D.I., 1980), and *Sois juif et tais toi, 1930–1940: Les Français "israélites" face au nazisme* (Paris: Etudes et Documentation Internationales, 1981); Adam Rutkowski, ed., *La lutte des juifs en France a l'époque de l'occupation, 1940–44* (Paris: CDJC, 1975); Zosa Szajkowski, *Analytical Franco-Jewish Gazeteer, 1939–1945* (New York: S. Frydman, 1966), "The French Central Jewish Consistory During the Second World War," *Yad Vashem Studies* 3 (1959): 187–202, "Glimpses on the History of Jews in Occupied France," *Yad Vashem Studies* 2 (1958): 133–58, "The Growth of the Jewish Population in France," *Jewish Social Studies* 8 (1946): 179–96, and "The Organization of the UGIF in Nazi Occupied France," *Jewish Social Studies* 9 (1947): 239–56; Claudine Vegh, *Je ne lui ai pas dit au revoir: Des enfants de déportés parlent, entretiens avec Claudine Vegh* (Paris: NRF Gallimard, 1979); and Leni Yahil, "The Jewish Leadership of France," in *Patterns of the Jewish Leadership in Nazi Europe*, edited by Yisrael Gutman and Cynthia J. Haft (Jerusalem: Yad Vashem, 1977), 317–34.

For the Jewish immigrant response and the resistance movements, see Joseph Ariel (Fisher), "Jewish Self-Defense and Resistance in France During World War II," *Yad Vashem Studies* 6 (1967): 221–50; Haim Avni, "The Zionist Underground in Holland and France and the Escape to Spain," in *Rescue Attempts During the Holocaust*, edited by Yisrael Gutman and Efraim Zuroff (Jerusalem: Yad Vashem, 1977), 555–90; Marc Bloch, *Strange Defeat* (New York: Octagon Books, 1968); David Diamant, *Héros juifs de la résistance française* (Paris:

Éditions Renouveau, 1962), *Les juifs dans la résistance française, 1940–1944* (Paris: Le Pavillon, 1971), and *Le billet vert* (Paris: Éditions Renouveau, 1977), which deals with life and resistance at the French concentration camps of Pithiviers and Beaune-la-Rolande; Robert Gamzon, *Les Eaux-Claires: Journal, 1940–1944* (Paris: Éclaireurs Israelites de France, 1981); Jules Jefroykin, "L'organisation juive de Combat," *Nouveaux Cahiers* 37 (1974): 18–24; *Les juifs dans la résistance et la libération: Histoire, témoignages, débats*, edited by RHICOJ (Paris: Éditions du Scribe, 1985); Andre Kaspi, "Les juifs dans la résistance," *Histoire* 80 (1985): 38–45; David Knout, *Contribution à l'histoire de la résistance juive en France, 1940–1944* (Paris: CDJC, 1947); Gaston Laroche, *On les nommait des étrangers: Les immigrés dans la résistance* (Paris: Éditeurs Français Reunis, 1965), an especially important, if unfinished, study of the immigrant contribution to the French resistance; Anny Latour, *Jewish Resistance in France, 1940–1944*, translated by Irene R. Ilton (New York: Holocaust Library, 1981), a popular but useful study; L. Lazare, *La résistance juive en France* (Paris, 1987); Claude Levy, *Les parias de la résistance* (Paris: Calmann-Levy, 1970, which accuses the Communist resistance of sacrificing its foreign Jews; Michael Mazor, "Les juifs dans la clandestinité sous l'occupation italienne en France," *Monde Juif* (July–September 1970); Alain Michel, *Les Éclaireurs israélites de France pendant la seconde guerre mondiale* (Paris: Éditions des E.I.F., 1984); Henri Michel, "Jewish Resistance and the European Resistance Movement," *Yad Vashem Studies* 7 (1968): 7–16; *Monde Juif* 118 (April-June 1985), a special issue on Jewish resistance in France; Leon Poliakov, "Jewish Resistance in France," *YIVO Annual of Jewish Social Sciences* 8 (1953): 252–263; Rénee Poznanski, "La résistance juive en France," *Revue d'Histoire de la Deuxième Guerre Mondiale et des Conflits Contemporains* 35 (137) (1985): 3–32; Jacques Ravine, *La résistance organisée des juifs en France, 1940–1944* (Paris: Julliard, 1973); Avraham Rayski, "Les immigrés dans la résistance," *Nouveaux Cahiers* 37 (1974): 10–17, and "Diversité et unité de la résistance juive," in the previously cited *Les juifs dans la résistance et la liberation* and S. Zeitoun, *L'OSE: Du légalisme à résistance, 1940–1944* (Paris, 1988).

For "specialized" Jewish communities in France, see Asaf Atchildi, "Rescue of Jews of Bukharan, Iranian, and Afghan Origin in Occupied France, 1940–1944," *Yad Vashem Studies* 6 (1967): 257–81; Levi Eligulashvili, "How the Jews of Gruziya in Occupied France Were Saved," *Yad Vashem Studies* 6 (1967): 251–55; and Warren Green, "The Fate of Oriental Jews in Vichy France," *Wiener Library Bulletin* 32 (1979): 40–50.

For the Jews of North Africa and Syria and Lebanon during the war, see Michel Abitbol, *The Jews of North Africa During the Second World War* (Detroit: Wayne State University Press, 1989); Irit Abramski-Bligh, "The Jews of Syria and Lebanon Under Vichy Rule" (in Hebrew), *Pe'anim* 28 (1986): 131–57; M. Ansky, *Les Juifs d'Algérie du décret Crémieux à la libération* (Paris, 1963); S. Landschut, *Jewish Communities in the Muslim Countries of the Middle East*

(Westport, Conn., 1976); Jacques Sabille, *Les juifs de Tunisie sous Vichy et l'occupation* (Paris, Édition du Centre, 1954); and Zosa Szajkowski, *The Jews and the French Foreign Legion* (New York: Ktav, 1975).

For the aftermath and the meaning of the Holocaust for French Jews, see Wladimir Rabi (Rabinovitch), *Anatomie du judaïsme français* (Paris, 1962); and David Weinberg, "The French Jewish Community After World War II: The Struggle for Survival and Self-Definition," *Forum* 45 (Summer 1982): 45–54. For the debate over France's role in the Holocaust stirred by the American television film "Holocaust," which played in France in 1979, see Henri Menudier, "Holocauste en France," *Revue d'Allemagne* (France) 13 (1981): 57–88; and Marcel Tetel, "Whither the Holocaust," *Contemporary French Civilization* 6 (1981–82): 219–35. On the Klaus Barbie trial, see Ted Morgan, *An Uncertain Hour: The French, the Germans, the Jews, the Klaus Barbie Trial, and the City of Lyon, 1940–1945* (New York: Arbor House/Morrow, 1990).

## SELECT BIBLIOGRAPHY

Abitbol, Michel. *The Jews of North Africa During the Second World War*. Detroit: Wayne State University Press, 1989.

Adler, Jacques. *The Jews of Paris and the Final Solution*. New York: Oxford University Press, 1987.

Billig, Joseph. *Le Commissariat général aux questions juives, 1941–1944*. 3 vols. Paris: Éditions du Centre, 1955–60.

Cohen, Yerachmiel (Richard). *The Burden of Conscience: French Jewish Leadership During the Holocaust*. Bloomington: Indiana University Press, 1987.

Haft, Cynthia. *The Bargain and the Bridle: The General Union of Israelites of France*. Chicago: Dialog Press, 1983.

Hallie, Philip. *Lest Innocent Blood Be Shed: The Story of the Village of Le Chambon and How Goodness Happened There*. New York: Harper and Row, 1978.

Hyman, Paula. *From Dreyfus to Vichy: The Remaking of French Jewry, 1906–1939*. New York: Columbia University Press, 1979.

Klarsfeld, Serge. *Vichy-Auschwitz: Le Role le Vichy dans la solution finale de la question juive en France*. 2 vols. Paris: Fayard, 1983.

Latour, Anny. *The Jewish Resistance in France (1940–1944)*. Translated by Irene R. Ilton. New York: Holocaust Library, 1981.

Marrus, Michael R., and Robert O. Paxton. *Vichy France and the Jews*. New York: Schocken Books, 1981.

Morgan, Ted. *An Uncertain Hour: The French, the Germans, the Jews, the Klaus Barbie Trial, and the City of Lyon, 1940–1945*. New York: Arbor House/Morrow, 1990.

Sweets, John. *Choices in Vichy France: The French Under Nazi Occupation*. New York: Oxford University Press, 1986.

Weinberg, David. *A Community on Trial: The Jews of Paris in the 1930's*. Chicago: University of Chicago Press, 1977.

# Chapter 17

# Holland and the Holocaust

## Earl M. Friedman

### THE JEWS IN HOLLAND

There is a boulevard of trees along the Avenue of the Righteous at the Yad Vashem in Jerusalem. Among the hundreds of plaques are a disproportionate number dedicated to Dutch men and women who helped Jews during the Holocaust. According to Yohanan Moroz, then Israel's ambassador to Bonn, of 1,500 *Hasiday Umoth ha-Olam* (righteous Gentiles) identified by 1976, 683, fully 45 percent, were Dutch citizens.[1] It is a record no other European nation can match, an achievement that reflects the heralded Dutch courage during World War II.

This was, after all, the nation that had tried to resist the onslaught of motorized German divisions and paratroops, and that had sustained the murderous bombardment of Rotterdam in the spring of 1940. Holland's Queen Wilhelmina, like King Haakon of Norway and the heads of state of Poland, Belgium, and France, had fled to England to inspire her countrymen to resistance. For many, this may have been nothing more than pinning strips of yellow cloth or paper to their breasts as a protest against the imposition of the yellow star for Jews in Holland. Some—machinists, dockworkers, carpenters, Communists—went so far as to declare a general strike against the Nazi treatment of Jews in February 1941, the only incident of its kind in occupied Europe. Others, farmers and clerks, like Miep Gies, who assisted the family of Anne Frank, opened their homes to twenty thousand Jewish children.

Theirs was a heroic tale, one recorded in part by Philip Friedman in *Their Brothers' Keepers*. In twelve pages, eight of which are devoted to Holland, the renowned YIVO historian tells the story of the Low Countries. Unfortunately, the reader, presumably a teenager or someone interested in bettering Judeo-Christian relations, will learn mainly of the exploits of "Joop Westerville" (sic), the Dutch anarchist who helped Jewish children escape through France to Spain and Portugal before being captured and shot to death, and little else.[2]

The image of the Dutch citizen ready to sacrifice his or her life for a fellow Jew has been reinforced by a number of publications, including H. J. Boas, *Religious Resistance in Holland*; Theo Van Doren, *Orange Above London*; and the popular set of memoirs by Corrie Ten Boom, *The Hiding Place*, *A Prisoner and Yet . . .* , and *Prison Letters*. Yet the role of the Dutch is barely mentioned in some of the principal texts on the Holocaust. Save for a brief summary (pages 366–68) and a cursory reference to Calvinist church passivity, Lucy Dawidowicz glosses over events in Holland in *The War Against the Jews, 1933–1945*. The same is true for Yehuda Bauer in *A History of the Holocaust*.[3] It is surprisingly difficult to locate references to the Jews in Amsterdam, *Sperrlisten* (protected Jews), and *Onderduikers* (those with false papers) in Leon Poliakov's generally superior *Harvest of Hate*.[4]

I entered this study with many preconceptions. As a layperson, I think I shared many generalities about the Dutch people and their habits, personality, and government. "We" thought of the typical Dutch person as industrious, clean to the point of fastidiousness (clad in wooden shoes, sweeping the streets of his or her small, peaceful towns, with tulip fields and lazily rotating windmills in the background), hanging out comforters in the morning air, and, most important, not too interested in international politics, neutral, and very tolerant. After all, hadn't we seen pictures of Wilhelm II in exile peacefully tending his garden? This was the land of international peace conferences and conventions, a land that had not engaged in a European war since the days of Napoleon.

Holland was the land that offered sanctuary to Sephardic Jews fleeing Iberia in the fifteenth century. The issuance of the Union of Utrecht in 1579, which guaranteed all people, including Jews, the peaceful observance of their religion, was a landmark in the struggle for human dignity. Cecil Roth has written of the Jews' arrival and integration in his *History of the Marranos* (Philadelphia: Jewish Publication Society of America, 1932). This hospitality and friendship is also reported in Franz Landsberger's *Rembrandt, the Jews, and the Bible*, translated by Felix N. Gerson (Philadelphia: Jewish Publication Society of America, 1946), and Howard Fast's *The Jews: Story of a People* (New York: Dial Press, 1968). Notes Fast: "By 1700, there were over 10,000 Jews in Amsterdam, which made it the largest Jewish community in Western Europe. After 1815, rabbis as well as ministers were paid by the Dutch state, and in 1797, Holland became the First country In The World [Fast's emphasis] to admit Jews to its parliament and to appoint them to high public office."[5]

During the interwar period some of Holland's statesmen denounced Hitlerism and anti-Semitism. How dismaying, then, to note, as Raul Hilberg has done in his *The Destruction of the European Jews*, "Holland was the one territory of the Occupied West in which the Jews did not have an even chance to live."[6] The facts are worse. While France and Belgium both managed to save 60 percent of their Jews, even Russia (67 percent), Hungary (50 percent) and Romania (35 percent) managed to do better than urbane, tolerant Holland. More than 100,000 of the 140,000 Jews living in prewar Holland perished in the Holocaust. The perplexing question is why.

Perhaps it was because the flat Dutch terrain was devoid of forests, mountains, and other hiding places available to Jewish partisans in Carpathia or White Russia. Perhaps it was that the same treacherous waters of the North Sea that frustrated Hitler's attempts to send a flotilla of barges against England prevented Jews from rowing to safety like their kinsmen who fled from Denmark to nearby Sweden. Perhaps it was the very resistance of the Dutch, their obstinacy requiring the presence of five thousand Order Police, twice the number sent to France, that resulted in a greater crackdown in Holland. Perhaps Jews, aware of the sympathy and support of their Gentile neighbors, were lulled into a sense of false security.

But there is another dimension to all of this, and that is that the Dutch essentially are no better and no worse than other people. They may talk a great deal about the importance of freedom of thought and tolerance, but their history is stamped with the legacy of the long, bitter conflict to free themselves from the Spanish (that is, Roman Catholic) yoke. The peaceful image of a second Switzerland that they themselves have fostered is no more valid than that painted by the Swiss for themselves. History records images of the warlike Dutch sailing up the Thames to bombard London, their participation in the wars of Louis XIV and Napoleon, their entry into the race for colonies around the world, and their rating near the bottom, with the Germans and Belgians, with regard to treatment of indigenous populations.

Far from being the pugnacious opponent of Nazism, as its self-serving myth would have it, Holland acted very much like other democracies before the war. Thirty thousand Jewish refugees were admitted after 1933, a figure that compares favorably with the 120,000 allowed into the United States and 60,000 into Britain in the same period. But, as Yehuda Bauer notes, some of these, designated "undesirable" by leaders of the Dutch Jewish community, were returned to Germany.[7] The theologian Karl Barth was among those refused admission to the Netherlands. Shortly before the outbreak of World War II, Holland shut down admission to Jews altogether.

Like other European states, Holland was waffling and tremulous before Germany. Its feeble sixty-nine-year-old prime minister, D. J. de Geer, was a defeatist. In an age of tanks and pontoon bridges, de Geer placed his faith in bicycles and dikes. Even after the Nazis overran Poland, Denmark, and Norway, he refused to call up the army reserves. When, on the evening of May 9, 1940, the Dutch military attaché in Berlin (Major Sas), acting on information from a German friend, phoned The Hague to report that the Germans were about to attack Holland, de Geer's own General Staff issued no alert. When, as warned, German bombers flew over the Zuider Zee on May 10, the commander of the Bergen airfield refused to send up his best fighters. Lacking coordination, Dutch units fought valiantly for approximately one week. Not surprisingly, when de Geer issued his statement of surrender on May 20, he instructed the Dutch people to "cooperate and do nothing to disturb the normal course of life."[8]

That was precisely the course of action most followed for the next four years. As in France, the German occupation was deemed a blow to national pride, an inconvenience in housing, food, transportation, and even safety once the Allies began bombing the Low Countries in the summer of 1944. But as the three major texts that adequately chronicle the Holocaust in Holland (Nora Levin, *The Holocaust;* Gerald Reitlinger, *The Final Solution;* Raul Hilberg, *The Destruction of the European Jews)* suggest, the welfare of Jews was of low priority to Dutch Gentiles.[9] The Dutch may have been "uneasy" at first about what the Nazis were attempting to do to the Jews, but as Raul Hilberg points out, "The Dutch did fight back at first, to settle back for five years to a mixture of bureaucratic collaboration and underground sabotage."[10] Thousands of Dutch workers, domestics as well as millhands, volunteered for work in a transcendant Germany. Few Gentiles refused to sign the Aryan Attestation of October 1940 that resulted in the ouster of Jews from positions in teaching, law, medicine, journalism, even the High Court of the Netherlands. Fewer protested the deportations of Jews and non-Jews to Mauthausen and Buchenwald in 1941, or the death trains that left for Sobibor and Auschwitz in July 1942.

Fewer still resisted the impulse to participate in the looting of 29,000 Jewish dwellings and libraries that were confiscated by June 1944. Of the Einsatzstab Rosenberg that specialized in "permanent loans," Hilberg says: "In no occupied territory of the great semicircle [of destruction] from Norway to Roumania did the Germans manage in one form or another to collect so much Jewish wealth,"[11] $212,000,000, according to Nora Levin, and much of it by the Dutch themselves.[12] Notes Reitlinger: "Today many streets in the Joedenhoek quarter of Amsterdam present the appearance of bombing—but they were not bombed. These are the Jewish houses which stood empty during the terrible scarcity months of 1944 and 1945 and which were carried off bit by bit to repair the homes of neighbors."[13]

## DUTCH MEMOIRS

Slowly, incomprehensibly slowly, after more than forty years, a truer picture of what transpired in the Netherlands has emerged. Much of the problem stems from the publishing industry's preoccupation with the success of the diary of Anne Frank. The resulting spate of memoirs—Etty Hillesum's *Letters from Westerbork*, Marga Minco's *Bitter Herbs*, Jona Oberski's *Childhood*, Leesha Rose's *The Tulips Are Red*, Ernest Schnabel's *The Footsteps of Anne Frank*, and Miep Gies's *Anne Frank Remembered* (with Alison Leslie Gold)—are all moving glimpses of life under the Nazis, and they are useful for high-school instruction. Equally interesting is Malcolm MacPherson's *The Blood of His Servants*. Reading like a high-powered novel, MacPherson's book reveals interesting details of oil intrigues in the East Indies and the swirl of controversy surrounding Prince Bernhard and his relationship with I. G. Farben and his protection of the Nazi war criminal Menten. But like the other memoirs, *The Blood of His Servants* is episodic and is not an attempt to tell the complete story of what transpired during the war.[14]

Equally problematic are tomes by Jewish scholars criticizing actions taken by the Amsterdam Joodse Raad (the Jewish Council headed by Professor David Cohen and diamond merchant Abraham Asscher), rabbis, Jewish workers, and even the family of Anne Frank. The most puzzling example of focusing criticism upon the victim is found in Bruno Bettelheim's *The Informed Heart*.[15] Bettelheim claims that in order to have a better chance of survival, the family should have split up and hid separately. Yet as a psychologist he should have known that such a breakup would have been hard for a thirteen-year-old girl. The family did hide together successfully for several years, until they were betrayed. Bettelheim also suggests that the Franks should have sold their lives dearly by procuring a gun and fighting, when through the rest of the book he rationalizes that "healthy single men" (himself included) did not attempt to overpower guards they outnumbered. In short, this otherwise informative book dealing with the depersonalization of man in an industrial society trivializes Anne Frank and her plea that all men are good, dismissing the millions who have read the diary and taken hope and inspiration from it.

Over the years several legitimate critiques of Dutch behavior have appeared, usually in obscure journals favored by scholars. Among these are John Burgher, "Hitler's Quisling Dilemma," *Central European Observer* 19, no. 6 (March 20, 1942): 96; Gerhard Hirschfeld, "Collaboration and Attentism in the Netherlands, 1940–1941," *Journal of Contemporary History* 16, no. 3 (July 1981): 467–86; Rene Marcq, "Collaboration Under Enemy Occupation," *Annals of the American Academy of Political and Social Science* 247 (September 1946): 69–72; R. Schuvrsma, "Dutch Fascists' Share in Crime," *Wiener Library Bulletin* 20, no. 2 (Spring 1966): 34–37; Henry Mason, *The Purge of Dutch Quislings: Emergency Justice in the Netherlands* (The Hague: Nijhoff, 1952); Joseph Michman, "The Controversial Stand of the Joodse Raad in the Netherlands," *Yad Vashem Studies* 10 (1974): 9–49, and "The Controversy Surrounding the Jewish Council of Amsterdam," in *Patterns of the Jewish Leadership in Nazi Europe*, edited by Yisrael Gutman and Cynthia Haft (Jerusalem: Yad Vashem, 1977), 235–57; and N. W. Posthumus, ed., *The Netherlands During German Occupation*, *Annals of the American Academy of Political and Social Science* 245 (May 1946). Part of the historiographic problem derives from the fact that important works of Dutch scholars and survivors—Abel Herzberg's *Tweestroomenland* (Land of two streams, 1950), the diary of Samuel Goudsmit, the memoirs of David Cohen and K. P. L. Berkeley, Michel Riquet's *Tragédie de la déportation, 1940–1945* (Paris, 1945), Grete Salus's *Niemand nichts ein Jude*, Dr. F. W. Drees's *Van Mei tot Mei* (From May to May, 1948), H. C. Touw's *Het verzet der hervormde kerk*, and H. M. van Randwijk's "Het Grote Gebod"

(The great commandment), *Vrij Nederland*, November 10, 1951, have not been translated into English.

Only in the past two decades have works of significant scholarship appeared. Werner Warmbrunn's *The Dutch Under German Occupation, 1940–1945*,[16] and Walter Maass's *The Netherlands at War* both analyze the Nazi domination of a government labeled "sham" puppet by Reitlinger.[17] Philip Mechanicus's *Year of Fear: A Jewish Prisoner Waits for Auschwitz* and J. Boas's *Boulevard des Miseres: The Story of Transit Camp Westerbork* supply chilling glimpses of the "sluicing" operations in the onetime refugee camp on the edge of the German border.

## JACOB PRESSER'S *DESTRUCTION OF THE DUTCH JEWS*

One book, however, rises above all others in range and comprehension. As promised on its jacket, Jacob Presser's *The Destruction of the Dutch Jews* is the "definitive account of the Holocaust in the Netherlands." There are flaws in several key areas. Presser never really addresses the relationship between high-ranking members of the puppet Dutch government and Nazi Reichskommissar Artur Seyss-Inquart. His use of Latin phrases to highlight aspects of persecution (*dies irae* for the deportations from Westerbork, *morituri te salutant* as the chant of those in the boxcars, *anus mundi* for Auschwitz, and even the last word of the book, *requiescant*) is irritating and possibly inappropriate. At times, as when he describes the ouster of L. E. Visser from the Dutch High Court ("as if he were an unclean leper")[18] or chastises Jewish officials for omitting their own names from the May 1943 roundup that disposed of seven hundred of their comrades,[19] Presser permits his personal anger to intrude into his narrative.

Such controlled rage is forgivable, given the background of the author. A history professor at the University of Amsterdam, Presser endured this tragedy as a young man. His study, authorized by the Rijksinstituut voor Oorlogsdocumentatie (Netherlands State Institute for War Documentation), is necessarily punctuated with moving, personal asides. Thus we learn that Presser, a Jew, had to have his *History of the 30 Years War* published under a Gentile friend's name. Presser describes the tearful scene as youths, having just graduated from segregated Jewish schools, volunteered for "labor details" in the East. He tells how he and his wife were spared capriciously by German Security Police Commander Ferdinand Aus der Funten just minutes before two thousand other Jews were dispatched to their deaths in a roundup on August 6, 1942.[20] His reminiscences of name changes, false papers, and ever-changing hiding places are a mirror of the experiences of the Dutch Jews who did survive.

If there is a truly bothersome flaw in the structure of this translated edition, it is the absence of a handy section of source citation. For this, the author apologizes in advance, noting that a "fully documented" version of the manuscript is on deposit with the Rijksinstituut. The careful reader will quickly discern that Presser has made use of all the major works previously cited—Mechanicus,

Berkeley, Cohen, Herzberg, Goudsmit, and so on, as well as official Nazi documents, war-crimes tribunals, and postwar inquiries authorized by the Dutch government.

The virtues of this book far outweigh its flaws. A readable, straightforward narrative, *Destruction* details the process of annihilation from the moment of German entry into Holland in the spring of 1940 to the days of liberation five years later, when the handful of Jews who emerged from Terezín or Belsen— the young boy who had been hidden so long that he had forgotten how to talk, the parents who survived when their children did not—sadly realized that they had lost the war. But Presser makes it clear that the application of the term "war" to what the Jews underwent is not legitimate, for "the Germans persecuted rather than fought the Jews."[21]

Because of the disparity of forces, the actions of individuals who resisted the Nazis appear all the more heroic. Among those Presser salutes are Frans van Hasselt, president of the student council at Delft, who protested the dismissal of Jewish professors and who was subsequently sent to Buchenwald, where he died in 1942; Reverend Nanne Zwiep, whose intervention on behalf of Jews in Enschede resulted in his death in Dachau in 1942; Dr. Jacques Lobstein, director of the Jewish Mental Hospital in Apeldoorn, who died in a concentration camp a few days after Germany surrendered; Walter Susskind of the Jewish Council, who perished in Auschwitz; Dr. H. O. Ottenstein, who labored in Westerbork; and the "grandmothers . . . who consoled the dying," "the little boy, caring for your lonely baby sister," and "the mothers, who keep your children clean and healthy."[22]

By way of contrast, Presser's villains are puny figures, some of whom are barely worth mentioning, like Karel Mussert, the runty engineer who headed up the NSB (the Dutch National Socialist movement) and Artur Seyss-Inquart, an Austrian once described by Reitlinger as "a moderate party man whose part in the persecution was useful, though passive, condonation."[23] More important were Generalkommissar for Security Hans Rauter, a violent man responsible for deportations, who later denied that he knew what happened to Jews in Auschwitz; Willi Zopf, Adolf Eichmann's personal adjutant for the Jewish question in Holland; General F. C. Christiansen, Wehrmacht commander in the Netherlands, a "decent" soldier who ordered the deportation of a legless Jewish war veteran to the East in the summer of 1942, commenting, "A Jew is a Jew, legs or no legs";[24] Colonel Ferdinand Aus der Funten, the same benign figure who spared Presser, who then acted as "devil incarnate" in the brutal raid against the Apeldoorn sanitorium in January 1943; Albert Gemmeker, commandant of the Westerbork camp, a "nice man," "a gentleman crook," a "killer in kid gloves" who waved and smiled as he packed people off in cattle cars; Gertrude Slotke, a doughty spinster, described as "an old parchment bag," "an inhuman automation," "an unfeeling witch,"[25] specialist in the Zentralstelle who constantly whittled away at Jewish exemptions; and Dr. Wilhelm Harster, Friedrich Wimmer, Fritz Schmidt, and Willi Lages of the SS. All of them were earnest, devoted, zealous bureaucrats who proclaimed their innocence before postwar tribunals because they were, in Presser's words, "just forwarding agents."[26]

Perhaps as well as anyone who has ever written of the bureaucratization of the killing process (Hilberg and Hannah Arendt are the best examples), Presser understands the working of the Nazi mind. Although there was no master plan for extermination of the Jews in 1939 (Presser notes, in passing, that Hitler was wavering on sending Jews to Madagascar after the fall of France), he makes it clear that everything the Nazis did moved inexorably in that direction. Presser is almost dumbfounded at the psychological techniques employed by coarse, unsubtle men like Rauter, Harster, and Aus der Funten. "Their main object," he writes, "was to get rid of the Jews smoothly and by stages, so as to cause the minimum disruption by the victims themselves."[27] Consciously or intuitively, the Nazis achieved this by exploiting human frailties. Upon entering Holland, they reassured the Dutch of the continuity of their constitution. When the first discriminatory measures were enacted against Jews (registration, identity cards, dismissal), they were so innocuous as to arouse little outcry. When Jews were segregated into ghettos, sent to labor camps, and ultimately deported, those who did not share this experience were relieved that it was not happening to them. Even the Jews themselves, apprehensive from the first moment in May 1940, as Presser notes,[28] deceived themselves or were deceived by ill-timed promises from the Joodse Raad that what happend to twenty-five thousand stateless refugees or "less valuable" kinsmen who did not possess special certificates would not happen to them.[29] Then, as some Jews fantasized that the Communists would rise up again as they had in 1941 or the Allies would soon invade Europe, others appealed to the authorities that they were Nazi sympathizers, not Jews, still others refined their sardonic Jewish wit, and all feared the terror of the car and bell in the night, the Nazis decided in 1942, "They would have to die, all of them." Concludes Presser: "As we look back . . . we ask ourselves whether the German machine, had it consisted exclusively of sadists (which of course it did not) could have contrived with more infernal ingenuity the details of its plan to destroy a people."[30]

Ninety-three transports, carrying more than one hundred thousand persons to their doom, left Holland between July 1942 and September 1943. Presser leaves little doubt that this would have been impossible without the cooperation of Jewish leaders. His contempt for several is obvious. Jacques de Leon, the revisionist Zionist editor of the *Joodse Weekblad*, a journal that kept the general populace misinformed about their ultimate destination, even after Jacob Edelstein, a Jewish elder in the Terezín ghetto, visited Holland and issued a warning in March 1941, was one. Another was Kurt Schlesinger, the pompous Jewish refugee who enjoyed a limited reign as tyrant in the Westerbork camp. Still another was Gertrud van Tijn-Cohn, head of the so-called Jewish Emigration Office in Amsterdam. As late as November 1942 her staff was urging people to take their favorite books with them to the East.[31]

Twenty Joodse Raad leaders, especially Abraham Asscher and David Cohen, also belong in Presser's pantheon of villains. Presser allows that these men agreed to serve under duress and in good conscience, believing that they might slow the process of dehumanization. He also allows that the council was not alone in determining who would be deported. But he contrasts the behavior of Asscher and Cohen, both of whom protected family and friends, with the behavior of "the captain of the Titanic" who went down with his ship and that of M. L. Kan and I. Kisch, two Jewish leaders who resigned on principle when the council was created. Presser notes Cohen's anxiety when three children of a trusted fellow worker were about to be deported, but, in the voice of the doomed Jews, lays out a lengthy indictment, charging the leaders with arrogating power to themselves, implementing anti-Jewish measures, deceiving the Jews of Holland, and collaborating in the liquidation of Dutch Jewry. As evidence, Presser offers statements from Lages and Eichmann, calling the Joodse Raad "very easy" to work with and a Nazi report of March 20, 1943, praising it for "distinguished service during the de-Judaization of the Netherlands."[32] Citing a postwar Jewish inquiry in November 1947 that labeled the behavior of the Jewish Council "dishonorable," Presser concludes that however well intentioned their motives, the leaders became "inextricably involved in a danse macabre with Satan calling the tune."[33]

It would be wrong to suggest that Presser is turning guilt back upon Jews. However pathetic the behavior of "half-Jews" who ran about denouncing their bloodlines before the SS in the early days of the occupation or the OD Service Men (Jewish Service Police) in Westerbork, it must not be forgotten that they were all victims. Writes Presser: "Many no doubt find it more convenient to dwell upon this [the failure of Jews to resist] than on the failure of their Gentile countrymen to make any strenuous attempt to save them."[34] In almost six hundred pages of depressing reading, the singular general strike of February 1941 takes up less than three pages, the vaunted Dutch resistance less than ten.

For Presser, the true collaborators with Nazism were the Dutch people, every segment of the Dutch people: "Everyone in the vicinity, even those who had not seen the victims dragged away under cover of darkness, could but observe the furniture vans being loaded up in broad daylight."[35] In chapter after chapter he meticulously chronicles Gentiles' betrayal of their Jewish neighbors. When the Nazis imposed their "Aryan Attestation" in the fall of 1940, J. M. Kapetyn, vice chancellor at the University of Groningen, reported one of his Jewish colleagues to the authorities. Professor J. Van Dam, secretary-general of the Education Ministry, threatened parents of schoolchildren with dire consequences if they did not observe segregation orders. Even the churches were silent. According to Presser, the Roman Catholic archbishop wanted to denounce the Aryanization process, but was dissuaded under "strong pressures."[36] The Protestant clergy, who registered "profound disgust" at subsequent anti-Jewish measures (particularly those that affected converts), did nothing.[37]

Overnight, the Union of Utrecht was forgotten as every segment of Dutch society cooperated with the conquerors in the brutalization of the Jews. According to Presser, the ANP (Dutch Press Agency) was "among the first Dutch professions to allow itself to be forced to tow the Nazi line."[38] Others quickly followed. On January 15, 1941, the Census Office, having developed lists of Jewish residences that would prove helpful in the deportation process, "thanked" the Germans for measures that were saving money for the government. A few months later, J. L. Lentz, head of this office, complained that thousands of Jews were trying to elude registration, volunteered his staff's assistance in locating these felons, and even designed a special Jewish identity card for the Nazi authorities.[39]

The history of the home government abounds with moments of shame. One Dutch ministry asked German guidance in the application of the Nuremberg Laws; the Amsterdam Criminal Investigation Bureau put failure to register as a Jew on the same level as theft, embezzlement, or fraud; and H. Rodegro, commissioner for social questions, threatened to use foreign troops if Jews did not cease their escapes from Dutch forced-labor camps. The Dutch police, under threat of harm to their own families, participated in roundups in the summer of 1941 and, having lost their virginity, were less troubled when called into service during later deportations.[40] The Dutch Red Cross, with one exception (Christmas parcels to Jews in Vught in 1943), made no effort to assist Jews in wartime concentration camps or postwar displaced persons' camps. The OPK (Office of Wartime Foster Children), a postwar bureau, denied the return of at least thirty-six children to their natural parents when the Holocaust was over.[41]

There was the sleazy segment found in every society—members of the NSB and its self-proclaimed storm troopers, the WA—that sought to thrash Jews on the street, their more extreme brothers who volunteered for the SS and whose excesses forced the Nazis into closing the Ellekom transit camp, and their cowardly comrades, the Dutch "bloodhounds" who trailed Jews, threatening them with blackmail or exposure to the police.[42] There were the Dutch trainmen, about whom Eichmann rhapsodized, "the trains ran like a dream."[43] According to Presser, not a single train failed to run on schedule, not one bullet was spent on behalf of the Jews. After the war spokesmen for the Railway Board explained that no one told them not to cooperate. Amazing as it may sound, the board was correct. At no time did the Dutch government in exile issue a statement on behalf of Jews. Afterward, the postwar Jewish inquiry accused the London Committee of "crass neglect."[44]

Presser's indictment of Dutch society includes municipal officers, civil servants, teachers, judges, labor officials, bankers, trading companies, the textile bureau, and some of those nice, wooden-clogged Dutch citizens who first sheltered Jews. Many turned them in when the Jews ran out of money. Others were intimidated by threats of neighbors or SS edicts.[45] As vans of the A. Puls moving company carted off Jewish property and "to puls" became a common verb in the Dutch lexicon, Gentiles looted the homes of their onetime friends. A common lament was that nothing good was left; too much was being sent to Germany.[46] When the few Jews returned from Auschwitz and Terezín in 1945, they encountered the same surprise and animosity that greeted their brethren in anti-

Semitic Poland. Jeered the Dutch: "What a pity you are back. . . . All the good Jews are dead, only the bad returned. . . . There they are again. You can see who's got the best cameras."[47] Presser's bitter dictum sums up the behavior of the Dutch during the Holocaust: *proprium ingenii humani est odisse quem laeseris* (it is characteristic of human nature to hate whom you have wronged).[48]

## A CONVERSATION WITH A DUTCH CONSUL

In 1987 I had an opportunity to interview the Dutch consul in Buffalo, a professor of microbiology. A self-congratulatory attitude permeated his recounting of his nation's history: "No, we were not nervous about Wilhelm II seeking refuge in the Netherlands after World War I. We had been doing that sort of thing forever. We gave sanctuary to Protestants centuries before when there was trouble in France, the Spanish and Portuguese Jews in the 1500s, Paul Kruger, the first president of the South African Republic. It's a perfectly normal habit and nobody was remotely nervous about it. The Dutch are not a terribly nervous people. Holland was full of Germans between the wars because of the economic situation. All our kitchen personnel were Germans. The Dutch tradition, earlier than any country in Europe that I know of, was of total welcome to all fugitives."[49]

Asked to comment about Holland's lack of preparedness before the invasion, the consul echoed the wan apologetics of Frederic Pearson (*The Weak State in International Crisis: The Case of the Netherlands in the German Invasion Crisis of 1939–1940*, two-thirds of which consists of cybernetic theories, the gist of which is that Holland behaved in doglike fashion) and Eeko Nicolaas van Kleffens (*Juggernaut over Holland*), who offers the heroic speech of Wilhelmina as Holland's principal response to "the bolt from the blue"). "During the whole history of the kingdom," the consul said, "we had been able to defend ourselves, perhaps by flooding the countryside. 1940 was the first time it didn't work anymore."

Though he personally had participated in the underground as a sixteen-year-old and subsequently volunteered for duty in the RAF, the consul believed that the actions of his leaders in exile were absurd. "Obedience to London was ill-advisable. Directions from London were very messed up, particularly in the early part of the occupation. For a long time, there was no direction on how the Dutch should react. There were stupid people on the London side. Many of our people were arrested and shot. Afterwards, when everything cleared away, we didn't have that much respect for the government in London. We thought the things they did rather silly."

As one example, he cited how the British decided to halt all train traffic after the battle of Arnhem in September 1944. The Dutch underground was told that it must supply false papers and financial support to railway workers to protect them from arrest or deportation. "An important part of the underground was running around the countryside, its suitcases full of money. We spent two months in the province of South Holland changing identity cards. It was stupid, totally silly. In the very week they started the whole thing, no trains were running till the end of the war. Besides, the Germans were paying the workers anyway.''

The consul was more generous in his evaluation of the German occupiers. ''When they took over, they were much more clever. The anti-Jewish measures were rather gradual. They didn't amount to terribly much. We didn't notice them until about the middle of 1941.'' Reminded that the first significant act, the dismissal of High Court Justice Visser, occurred in the fall of 1940, his reply was: ''I don't think much of that gets noticed because the Germans were dismissing so many other people. I don't think that makes a big dent.'' When pressed about the Aryan Attestation, the general strike, roundups to Mauthausen and Buchenwald, and Jewish identity cards, all of which occurred before the summer of 1941, the consul was adamant: ''Measures of this sort, the whole thing, crept up.''

As for the Jews who perished, the consul's words of pity were shaded with condescension. ''There was a large Jewish proletariat in Amsterdam, maybe 60–70,000. The great majority were poor, furniture movers, cigar-makers. Holland was full of tobacco companies. Unfortunately, they were not only poor, but not terribly bright or educated. We tried to warn them when we saw things coming, but there was nothing we could do. Today there are 20–30,000 Jews in the Netherlands, virtually none from the Jewish proletariat. Quite a few of the affluent Jews survived, possibly because of luck. We saw them leaving in cars, waving, in May, 1940. My publisher was one of those. I know of a very rich relative who escaped to Portugal and then to Great Britain. They probably survived because of education. But otherwise the more educated Jews who survived did so by accident. The rich, important, university professors, doctors and lawyers, survived because they were sent to an exclusive concentration camp—Theresienstadt. The Nazis hadn't gotten around to them yet. Most who went to Terezin did not come back. The greater the background and influence they got in there [into Theresienstadt]. The rest had no chance. I wonder whether the rate of return among the poorly educated was not worse also in Poland.''

Of the ''oodles'' (one hundred thousand Dutch civilians) who went to work in Ruhr factories, the consul said only that they were ''young and stupid'' people lured by the prospect of better pay. The seventy thousand who joined the Waffen-SS or were members of the NSB, were ''boorish men, definitely with sub-100 IQs.'' Though Karel Mussert earned a degree from Delft (Holland's top engineering school), the consul maintained, ''These people were not bright. Mussert's father was not very bright.''

Neither, apparently, were most of the Dutch. While conceding that the Latin countries (Italy, Spain, and Portugal) did better by Jewish refugees (''Latin peoples are sort of color blind''), the consul noted that Jewish children fared better in the south of Holland because they could better blend in with the dark-haired population there. Reminded that hydrogen peroxide could have been used to bleach the hair coloring of Jews in the north, this Ph.D. in biochemistry replied, "We would not have known how much to use."

Those individual Dutch civilians who risked their own lives and the lives of their families to help their fellow countrymen or refugees in peril deserve our commendation. They include schoolteachers, clerks, students, village priests and ministers, housewives, and farmers. Jacob Presser has commented that it was generally the poor, not the rich, who volunteered to help the Jews. They were generally the least educated.[50] Acts of individual heroism cannot, however, justify blanket endorsement of a people. The role of the Dutch in the Nazi killing process may not be as pronounced as that played by Ukrainian, Polish, or Romanian collaborators, but Dutch denial is every bit as reprehensible. Despite the facts, the myth of Dutch generosity lives on, perpetuated by educated persons who ought to know better.

## NOTES

1. *ZINS Weekly News Bulletin*, February 27, 1976, p. 1; December 31, 1976, p. 3.

2. Philip Friedman, *Their Brothers' Keepers* (New York: Crown, 1957), pp. 60–67.

3. Yehuda Bauer, *A History of the Holocaust* (New York: Franklin Watts, 1982), pp. 240–43; and Lucy Dawidowicz, *The War against the Jews 1933–1945* (N.Y.: Holt, Rinehart and Winston, 1975).

4. Leon Poliakov, *Harvest of Hate*, (Boston: Little, Brown, 1972), pp. 170–74.

5. Howard Fast, *The Jews: Story of a People* (New York: Dial Press, 1968), pp. 248–49. Heinrich Graetz also rhapsodizes about Jewish wealth and influence in seventeenth-century Holland. See *A History of the Jews* (Philadelphia: Jewish Publication Society of America, 1956 reprint of 1894 edition), vol. 4, pp. 676–86.

6. Raul Hilberg, *The Destruction of the European Jews* (New York: Quadrangle, 1951), p. 381.

7. Bauer, *History of the Holocaust*, p. 281.

8. A. C. Roodnat and M. deKlijn, *A Tour of the Anne Frank House in Amsterdam*, trans. D. M. Balfour (Amsterdam: Anne Frank Foundation, n.d.), pp. 30–36.

9. Nora Levin, *The Holocaust* (New York: Crowell, 1968), pp. 402–22; Gerald Reitlinger, *The Final Solution* (New York: A. S. Barnes, 1953), pp. 329–41; Hilberg, *Destruction of the European Jews*, pp. 365–81.

10. Hilberg, *Destruction of the European Jews*, p. 381.

11. Ibid., p. 380.

12. Levin, *Holocaust*, p. 405.

13. Reitlinger, *Final Solution*, pp. 341–42.

14. For a contrary view on Bernhard, see the "authorized biography" of Alden Hatch, *H.R.H. Prince Bernhard of the Netherlands* (London: Harrap, 1962). Hatch contends that the German-born prince was sensitive to Dutch fears of Hitler before the war, and that Bernhard later offered patriotic addresses from an exile that was "hell" to inspire his people. Privy to Allied war plans, Bernhard warned against the Arnhem misadventure, was the principal contact with 140,000 members of the Dutch underground, and was later awarded the Militaire Willemsorde.

15. Bruno Bettelheim, *The Informed Heart* (New York: Free Press, 1960), pp. 252–54.

16. Werner Warmbrunn chastizes Party leaders Colijn and de Geer for their defeatism, then charitably describes the actions of three main secretaries-general (Hirschfeld, Frederiks, and Verwey) as characterized by "expedience." See *The Dutch Under German Occupation, 1940–1945* (Stanford: Stanford University Press, 1963), pp. 266–68.

17. Reitlinger, *Final Solution,* p. 329.

18. Jacob Presser, *The Destruction of the Dutch Jews*, trans. Arnold Pomerans (New York: Dutton, 1969, originally published in 1965), p. 27. The reader should also consult H. L. C. Jaffe, ed., *De verboden Muze: Onderdrukking van Kunst en Kultur, 1933–1945* (The forbidden muse: Suppression of art and culture) (Amsterdam: Jewish Historical Museum, 1970). This as yet untranslated work vividly portrays the Nazi wartime campaign of anti-Semitism in Dutch film, painting, and literature.

19. Presser, *Destruction of the Dutch Jews,* p. 276.

20. Ibid., pp. 154–55.

21. Ibid., p. 336.

22. Ibid., p. 520.

23. Reitlinger, *Final Solution,* p. 330.

24. Presser, *Destruction of the Dutch Jews,* p. 142.

25. Ibid., p. 309.

26. Ibid., p. 337.

27. Ibid., p. 165.

28. Ibid., p. 7.

29. Ibid., p. 165. Warmbrunn attributes the weak Jewish response to a tradition of pacifism, secularism, and fragmentation, *Dutch Under German Occupation,* p. 280.

30. Presser, *Destruction of the Dutch Jews,* p. 111.

31. Ibid., p. 252.

32. Ibid., pp. 271, 275.

33. Ibid., p. 165. Warmbrunn states that the Jewish Council tried to offer "reasonable cooperation" in the mistaken notion that this might save lives. He faults the Jewish community for "the accident of inadequate leadership," *Dutch Under German Occupation*, pp. 272, 280.

34. Presser, *Destruction of the Dutch Jews,* p. 280.

35. Ibid., p. 359.

36. Ibid., p. 22.

37. Ibid., p. 147. By way of contrast, Warmbrunn virtually gushes about the Dutch preservation of self-respect and allegiance to democratic and spiritual loyalties. He contends that the Dutch were "impervious," "uncorrupted" by the Nazi ideology, and praises the rank and file of labor, students, the medical association, and the many priests and ministers who were persecuted and lost their lives, *Dutch Under German Occupation*, pp. 283, 277, 270–71.

38. Presser, *Destruction of the Dutch Jews,* p. 41.

39. Ibid., pp. 37–39.

40. Ibid., pp. 69, 146, 168–72, 349.

41. Ibid., p. 542.

42. Ibid., p. 354.

43. Ibid., p. 457.

44. Ibid., p. 335.

45. Ibid., pp. 218, 178.
46. Ibid., p. 363.
47. Ibid., pp. 363, 404, 543.
48. Ibid., p. 545.
49. Interview with the Dutch consul, Buffalo, New York.
50. Presser, *Destruction of the Dutch Jews,* p. 387.

## SELECT BIBLIOGRAPHY

Bettelheim, Bruno. *The Informed Heart.* New York: Free Press, 1960.

Boas, H. J. *Religious Resistance in Holland.* London: Allen and Unwin, 1945.

Boas, J. *Boulevard des Miseres: The Story of Transit Camp Westerbork.* Hamden, Conn.: Archon/Shoestring Press, 1985.

Frank, Anne. *The Diary of Anne Frank.* New York: Simon and Schuster, 1963.

Friedman, Philip. *Their Brothers' Keepers.* New York: Crown, 1957.

Gies, Miep, with Alison Leslie Gold. *Anne Frank Remembered.* New York: Simon and Schuster, 1987.

Hatch, Alden. *H.R.H. Prince Bernhard of the Netherlands.* London: Harrap, 1962.

Hillesum, Etty. *Letters from Westerbork.* Translated by Arnold Pomerans. New York: Pantheon Books, 1986.

Hirschfeld, Gerhard. "Collaboration and Attentism in the Netherlands, 1940–1941." *Journal of Contemporary History* 16 (July 1981): 467–86.

Jaffe, H. L. C., ed. *De verboden Muze: Onderdrukking van Kunst en Kultur, 1933–1945* (The forbidden muse: Suppression of art and culture). Amsterdam: Jewish Historical Museum, 1970.

Maass, Walter. *The Netherlands at War.* Abelard-Schumann, 1970.

MacPherson, Malcolm. *The Blood of His Servants.* New York: Times Books, 1984.

Mechanicus, Philip. *Year of Fear: A Jewish Prisoner Waits for Auschwitz.* New York: Hawthorn Books, 1968.

Michman, Joseph. "The Controversial Stand of the Joodse Raad in the Netherlands." *Yad Vashem Studies* 10 (1974): 9–49.

———. "The Controversy Surrounding the Jewish Council of Amsterdam." In *Patterns of the Jewish Leadership in Nazi Europe*, edited by Yisrael Gutman and Cynthia Haft, pp. 235–57. Jerusalem: Yad Vashem, 1977.

Minco, Marga. *Bitter Herbs.* New York: Oxford University Press, 1960.

Oberski, Jona. *Childhood.* Garden City, N.Y.: Doubleday, 1983.

Pearson, Frederic S. *The Weak State in International Crisis: The Case of the Netherlands in the German Invasion Crisis of 1939–1940.* Washington, D.C.: University Press of America, 1981.

Posthumus, N. W., ed. *The Netherlands During German Occupation. Annals of the American Academy of Political and Social Science* 245 (May 1946).

Presser, Jacob. *The Destruction of the Dutch Jews.* Translated by Arnold Pomerans. New York: Dutton, 1969.

Rose, Leesha. *The Tulips Are Red.* New York: A. S. Barnes, 1978.

Salus, Grete. *Niemand nichts ein Jude.* Darmstadt: Darmstadter Blatter Verlag, 1981.

Schnabel, Ernest. *The Footsteps of Anne Frank.* New York: Longmans, Green, 1959.

Ten Boom, Corrie. *The Hiding Place.* New York: Bantam, 1974.

———. *Prison Letters.* New York: Bantam, 1978.

Van Doren, Theo. *Orange Above London*. Antwerp: Staples Press, 1956.

Van Kleffens, Eeko Nicolaas. *Juggernaut over Holland*. New York: Columbia University Press, 1941.

Warmbrunn, Werner. *The Dutch Under German Occupation, 1940–1945*. Stanford, Calif.: Stanford University Press, 1967.

# Chapter 18

# Italy and the Holocaust

*Alan Cassels*

## THE HISTORICAL BACKGROUND

The history of the Jews in Italy goes back a long way; evidence exists of Jewish settlement in Rome from at least the second century B.C. Originally, most of the Jewish population in Italy lived in Rome itself or in the south of the peninsula. But as a result of the expulsion of Jews from Spain and Spanish possessions in 1492 and 1542, the foci of Jewish settlement outside the Papal States shifted to the north, a circumstance that proved of some importance when the Holocaust came to Italy.

Traditional anti-Semitism, based on the myth of the Jew as "Christ killer," was disseminated from Rome throughout the whole of Italy. After a period of relative tolerance during the Renaissance, the zenith of this type of religious anti-Semitism was reached in the Counter-Reformation, which saw the introduction of the ghetto, a word of Venetian origin, and an upsurge in involuntary baptisms and forced conversions. Discrimination and persecution were fiercest in those regions under the rule of the papacy, a historical memory sometimes invoked by polemicists in the debate over the role of the pope in World War II.

It was to be the nineteenth century before Italy's Jews enjoyed emancipation, but when the process occurred, it did so with startling swiftness and completeness. The groundwork for the extension of full civil liberties was laid during the Enlightenment and then Napoleon's transitory rule in Italy, and even the restoration of "legitimacy" in 1815 was only a temporary setback. The famous Statuto whereby King Charles Albert of Sardinia-Piedmont in 1848 granted constitutional rights was extended, on the advice of his liberal advisors, to his Jewish subjects. As the Italian peninsula was progressively united under the

Piedmontese monarchy, so the provisions of the Statuto were applied to all of Italy's Jews. With the acquisition of Rome as the capital of the new kingdom in 1870, the last ghetto in Western Europe was dismantled.

Not surprisingly, the Jewish community in Italy proved to be enthusiastic supporters of the House of Savoy that had engineered their emancipation in a single generation. They felt comfortable in the secular and liberal unitary state that had been imposed on the country by a minority of middle-class northern Italians. The majority of Italian Jews were themselves middle-class northerners, and some were heroes of the *risorgimento* and unification. In the new Italy Jewish assimilation proceeded at a rapid pace. The reasons were several: Italian Jews were not numerous, a mere .1 percent of the population; unlike many Eastern European Jews, those in Italy were indistinguishable in dress and speech from the rest of the populace; and long settled in the Italian peninsula, they were regarded by their Gentile neighbors not as aliens but as Italians. In the euphoric prose of the well-known Judaic scholar Cecil Roth:

In 1848 there was no European country . . . where the restrictions placed upon [the Jews] were more galling and more humiliating. After 1870, there was no land in either hemisphere where conditions were or could be better. It was not only that disabilities were removed as happened elsewhere too during these momentous years, but that the Jews were accepted freely, naturally and spontaneously as members of the Italian people, on a footing of perfect equality with their neighbours.[1]

Jews soon began to emerge prominently in the public life of united Italy, helped in no small measure by a Jewish literacy rate far in excess of the national average. Perhaps the most notable was Luigi Luzzatti, first appointed minister of finance in 1891, who achieved the premiership in 1910. A converted Jew, Sidney Sonnino, had reached the same eminence four years earlier. Jewish loyalty to the state was reflected in a high military profile. The first Jewish general was appointed in 1888, and during World War I fifty Jews held the rank of general, while over a thousand Jews won medals for valor. Jews quickly made their mark in the professions, the arts, and business. As happened elsewhere in Europe at the turn of the century, the activities of some Jewish banks provoked a degree of prejudice to accompany the chronic anti-Semitism of the Jesuit press. More ominous for the future, though, was the fact that the Italian Nationalist Association, established in 1910, found it hard to accept Jews as patriotic Italians. In other words, anti-Semitism was not totally absent in the new Italy; after centuries of anti-Jewish feeling it could hardly be otherwise. But it was not widespread. There was no Dreyfus affair in Italy, and no Italian Karl Lueger or Adolf Stoecker made a career out of anti-Semitism. The social harmony in which Italy's Jews lived encouraged most of them to educate their children in state schools, and intermarriage followed. With the passage of time and assimilation, more and more younger Italian Jews felt themselves to be Jewish in a cultural rather than a religious way, and hardly ever in a racial sense.[2]

## ITALIAN FASCIST RACISM

At first, the relationship between Italian Jewry and fascism mirrored that between Jews and Italian society in general. No early Fascist program contained a hint of anti-Semitism, although there were a few individual anti-Semites in the Partito Nazionale Fascista (PNF). One of them, Roberto Farinacci, became party secretary in 1925 but was given no rein to vent his spleen against the Jews.[3] Many Italian Jews had no qualm about joining the PNF. Some 225 Jews participated in the March on Rome in 1922, at which point 750 were inscribed on the rolls of the Fascist and Nationalist parties (which were soon to merge); by 1928 Jewish membership in the PNF had grown to 1,770, and by 1933 to 4,819.[4] Some rose high in the Fascist hierarchy. For example, a baptized Jew, Aldo Finzi, was Mussolini's under secretary at the Ministry of the Interior in 1922–24 and later sat in the Grand Council of Fascism. In 1925, as part of the drive toward dictatorship, a Fascist rector was imposed on the University of Rome: Professor Giorgio Del Vecchio was Jewish. Of course, some Jewish intellectuals, such as the brothers Carlo and Nello Rosselli, stood out among the *fuorusciti*, anti-Fascist exiles from their homeland.[5] But within Italy Jewry found a positive advantage in at least one move to incorporate all spheres of national activity into the Fascist state. In 1930–31 legislation devised by Alfredo Rocco, the justice minister and architect of fascism's totalitarian institutions, consolidated all Jewish communities into one consortium with legal standing.[6] The arrangement was hailed by Jews and Fascists alike and accounted in part for the increase in Jewish membership in the PNF about this time.

Since the growth of the Fascist dictatorship went hand in hand with *ducismo*— that is, the unrivaled supremacy of Mussolini—relations between Italian fascism and Jewry turned increasingly on the Duce's own cast of mind. Mussolini had always associated freely with Jews. He had learned his youthful socialism from the Russian Jewess, Angelica Balabanov, and the Jewish Margherita Sarfatti was both his mistress and biographer.[7] True, he was prone to speak of international affairs in terms of race (*stirpe*), but it was clear from the context of his speeches that he equated race with nation.[8] In fact, it was Mussolini's preoccupation with nationalism and *italianità* that shaped his attitude to Italy's Jews in the 1920s.

His tolerance was circumscribed by his alarm at the rise of Zionism. He was not averse to cultivating the Zionists in order to gain advantage in the politics of Middle Eastern imperialism. For this purpose he several times entertained Chaim Weizmann, president of the World Zionist Organization, and endorsed the claim to a Jewish state. More important, however, was his concern lest Zionism wean Italy's Jews from allegiance to their native country. As a nationalist, Mussolini was hostile to most multinational bodies—the League of Nations, the Freemasons, and Judaism. Moreover, being at heart a conspirator himself, Mussolini instinctively subscribed to the notion of a worldwide Jewish conspiracy wielding vast influence. In 1928 the Fascist press launched a campaign against the Zionist danger and Jewish "separatism." Mussolini himself pronounced warningly that "one cannot be a citizen of two countries simultaneously."[9] It is quite possible that his outburst was not unconnected with Fascist overtures to the Catholic church, the ancient fount of anti-Semitism in Italy. In 1929 Mussolini achieved what had eluded liberal Italy for almost sixty years—a church-state reconciliation comprised of a concordat and the Lateran Accords. If some animosity toward the Jews would oil the wheels of a rapprochement with the Vatican, which was decidedly anti-Zionist, Mussolini would oblige.[10] Yet it is important not to exaggerate the significance of these occasional anti-Semitic comments in the 1920s. Zionism rather than Italian Jewry was attacked, and such anti-Semitism as was voiced was motivated by political opportunism. In no way were Italy's Jews characterized as racial enemies.

It was Hitler's advance toward power in 1932–33 that brought the issue of racial anti-Semitism to the fore. Mussolini, referring to the "congruent cases" of Fascist Italy and Nazi Germany, clearly expected a special relationship to develop on ideological grounds.[11] As race was central to Nazi thought, it was incumbent on the Duce to address the question whether anti-Semitism formed part of the ideological bond between Rome and Berlin. By and large, his initial response was negative. The authoritative definition of fascism in the *Enciclopedia italiana* of 1932, in whose composition Mussolini took a hand, explicitly rejected a racial interpretation of history. In a famous interview with the German writer Emil Ludwig, Mussolini stated baldly, "Antisemitism does not exist in Italy."[12] To Nahum Goldmann of the World Jewish Congress he was scathing about Hitler's anti-Semitic obsession.[13] In a nice piece of irony, the Duce's favorite emissary to the Nazis, Giuseppe Renzetti, had a Jewish wife (though Mussolini imposed his veto when his own daughter contemplated marrying a Jew). On a political plane, Mussolini instructed the Italian ambassador in Berlin to protest the Nazi boycott of Jewish shops; he urged the Austrian chancellors Dollfuss and Schuschnigg to mute their anti-Semitism; and from 1932 to 1935 the Italian Ministry of Finance was headed by the Jewish Guido Jung. On the other hand, Mussolini surprised the German ambassador by remarking that if he lived in Germany, he would be an anti-Semite. Furthermore, in March 1934, when some *fuorusciti* were caught attempting to smuggle anti-Fascist literature into Italy near the frontier town of Ponte Tresa, the captive Italian press emphasized the culprits' Jewishness. Here for the first time Italian Jews were accused, not of potential disloyalty as Zionist sympathizers, but of actual subversion.

Mussolini brought political inconsistency to a high art, and his contradictory positions on the Jewish issue can be seen as merely symptomatic. Nonetheless, a motive behind his tergiversations may be glimpsed. His jibes at Hitler's anti-Semitism were supposed to discourage the Führer, while his own anti-Jewish manipulation of the Ponte Tresa affair was a sop to Nazi prejudice. In 1934, "If Mussolini was unwilling to antagonize the Jews for the sake of Hitler, he was equally unwilling to alienate Hitler for the sake of the Jews."[14] Hence Mussolini dreamed of mediating between world Jewry and Nazi Germany; such was the proposition he put before Goldmann. However, a sinister implication lurked behind this stance. When mediation proved a chimera, as predictably it soon did, would Mussolini feel compelled to choose between friendship with Hitler and Italy's Jews? It took four years for the answer to emerge plainly and to the Jews' detriment.

Racism became official policy in Fascist Italy against a backdrop of international crises—the Italo-Ethiopian war of 1935–36 and the Spanish civil war that erupted in July 1936. The increase in the nonwhite population of the Italian Empire attendant on the conquest of Ethiopia fixed attention on race relations in the colonies, and the Fascist regime banned all sexual contact between Italians and the native peoples of East Africa. Some regard these race laws as a powerful impetus to the introduction of racism into the Italian homeland.[15] Of even greater consequence, however, was the imposition of League of Nations sanctions on Italy for its aggression against Ethiopia. Arguing that his Ethiopian campaign would liberate the Falasha Jews, Mussolini persuaded the Union of Italian Jewish Communities to use its influence to have sanctions withdrawn. When this ploy failed, he took umbrage and alleged that League sanctions were orchestrated by the world Jewish conspiracy. His sense of grievance deepened when the policy of autarchy, adopted to counter sanctions, was criticized by some Italian Jewish industrialists. But above all, the Ethiopian crisis drove a wedge between Fascist Italy and the Western democracies, and accordingly the value placed in Rome on Nazi Germany's friendship escalated.

Then, within weeks of the end of the Italo-Ethiopian war, the election of a Popular Front government in Madrid precipitated the Spanish civil war. The intervention of Italy and Germany on one side in Spain and the Soviet Union on the other made the conflict there appear to be a struggle between world fascism and world communism. Fear of communism (sometimes characterized as Jewish bolshevism) was accentuated by the success of the French Popular Front in forming an administration under the partly Jewish Léon Blum, one of Mussolini's bêtes noires. In other words, the international scene in 1936 was full of ideological overtones. Typically, the notorious Rome-Berlin Axis, announced by Mussolini on November 1, was not a political alliance, but simply an expression of common Fascist and anti-Communist affinity. By identifying the bond between the two capitals as ideological, Mussolini brought pressure on himself to conform to Hitler's ideological anti-Semitism.

Beyond any doubt, the responsibility for Fascist Italian racism must lie heavily on the Axis. The sheer physical might of Germany, which greatly impressed Mussolini on his visits there, found its counterpart in a more subtle, psychological pressure. Although Hitler made no recommendation that race laws be introduced into Italy, Mussolini seemed to feel that they were necessary to confirm his breach with the West and his link with Nazi Germany. Meir Michaelis, the leading authority on the subject, asserts unequivocally, "His sudden declaration of war on the Jews was . . . [a] precipitate attempt to bring his domestic policy in line with Italy's changed alignment in Europe."[16]

Yet this is not a completely satisfactory explanation. According to one school of thought, German influence was "more coincidental than causal."[17] Rather, anti-Semitism arose out of the very dynamism of Italian fascism. By the 1930s fascism had lost its pristine radicalism; its accommodations with Italy's traditional power structure had transformed it from a vital movement into an inert regime. Conscious of this, Mussolini between 1936 and 1938 embarked on a genuine Fascist revolution. On one level, it involved a "reform of customs": the Roman salute in place of a handshake, the abolition of the formal and polite "Lei." Mussolini's objective was to discipline and toughen the average Italian citizen in preparation for the battlefield whereon the new Roman empire was to be won. Such was the totalitarian vision of a "new man," bellicose and intolerant. A society composed of this *homo fascistus* would be the antithesis of that liberal Italy in which the Jews had found their niche. In the new garrison state the Jew, suspected of unpatriotic Zionist leanings and a lack of military ardor, was designated an outsider.[18] It is not surprising that the radical wing of the PNF that agitated for a drastic social transformation later supplied many of the most vicious Jew-baiters during the Holocaust.

The two interpretations of the onset of anti-Semitism in Italy are not incompatible; the Axis and the "revolution" of 1936–38 were complementary causes. Mussolini gambled on mutating the Italians into a nation of warriors in order to hunt with Hitler on equal terms. On both counts Italy's Jews were the losers.

Portents of the coming official anti-Semitism were not hard to find. Farinacci was restored to favor, and Mussolini commissioned an anti-Jewish diatribe by Paolo Orano.[19] On July 14, 1938, a *Manifesto degli scienziati razzisti* was published. It was compiled by ten "racial experts" whose names were kept secret for several days. The principal author was a twenty-five-year-old junior professor at the University of Rome, and there was considerable input from Mussolini. The essence of the manifesto resided in the phrases "The population and civilization of Italy today is of Aryan origin. . . . There exists a pure Italian race. . . . Jews do not belong to the Italian race."[20] At once the regime's propaganda machine went into high gear, arguing that Italian fascism had been a racist movement since its founding in 1919, and that therefore its brand of racism was quite distinct from Nazi doctrine. But no one was fooled. Mussolini himself later admitted that the race manifesto was "a conscientious German essay translated into bad Italian."[21] This widespread impression was reinforced in August 1938 with the appearance of a new journal under the editorship of Telesio Interlandi, *La difesa della razza*, which bore a distinct resemblance to the Nazi *Der Stürmer*.[22] But the exegeses on the source of Fascist racism were irrelevant; the race manifesto was no more than a device to prepare the way for anti-Jewish measures.

The immediate prelude was a census of Jews in Italy conducted in August 1938 by an office within the Ministry of the Interior, the Directorate General of Demography and Race (Demorazza). This revealed 47,200 native Italian Jews, of whom 37,200 were said to profess Judaism. The bulk lived in the large cities—some 13,000 in Rome, 10,000 in Milan, 6,000 in Trieste, and 4,000 in Turin. In addition, the number of foreign Jews in Italy had doubled between 1931 and 1938 to reach 10,000, of whom half were believed to be from Nazi Germany. In all, then, over 57,000 people stood to be affected by anti-Semitic laws, the first of which were promulgated in the fall of 1938 and barred Jews from joining all educational and artistic organizations. During the next year a host of disabilities were legislated. Jews were banned from national and municipal administration, the armed forces, and the PNF; Jewish lawyers and doctors were restricted to serving their fellow Jews; limits were set on the amount of property a Jew could own and the size of a factory he could manage; Jews were forbidden to employ non-Jewish servants; marriage between a Jew and a non-Jew was prohibited. As for the foreign Jews and Italian Jews naturalized since 1919, they were directed to leave Italy by March 12, 1939. The impact on Italian Jewry was sudden and substantial. About 200 teachers, 400 public employees, 500 in private concerns, 120 military personnel, and 2,500 in the professions lost their posts. Within two years 6,000 Italian Jews emigrated, and the Vatican recorded 4,000 conversions to Christianity.[23]

Without minimizing the distress caused by the anti-Semitic laws, it must also be noted that their effect was blunted by dozens of loopholes.[24] In the first place, the Fascist definition of a Jew was complicated and flexible. Basically, the law specified those born of two Jewish parents or of a Jewish father and foreign mother, or a child of a mixed marriage who professed Judaism. (By contrast, in Nazi Germany two Jewish grandparents or marriage to a Jew brought one within the scope of the Nuremberg Laws, and even quarter Jews suffered discrimination.) Out of deference to the church in Italy, mixed marriages were treated guardedly. Over 40 percent of Italian Jews married Gentiles, and two-thirds of the offspring of these unions were reared as Catholics. Moreover, exemption from some of the race laws was open to certain categories of Jews: among others, those who had volunteered for military service, those who had been wounded or decorated in Italy's wars, and those who had joined the PNF in times of crisis before 1922 and during 1924. By 1943 Demorazza processed 5,870 applications for exemption and granted 2,486. But as in every sphere of Fascist activity, success depended less on credentials than on influence and bribery. Particularly corrupt was a Tribuna di Razza established in 1939 and empowered arbitrarily to declare a Jew an Aryan, thus granting immunity from the race laws in toto. Over 100 petitioners obtained this certification.

The chief relief for Italy's Jews, however, stemmed from the attitude of most of the Italian people, with whom the Duce's new racial policy won little favor. At best it appeared humiliatingly subservient to Hitler, at worst morally repugnant. It was well known that even some Fascist hierarchs disapproved. The church published its distaste for Mussolini's ''Nordic'' racism and, on more self-interested grounds, protested that the ban on mixed marriages infringed clerical rights guaranteed under the concordat of 1929.[25] But Italian opinion at large was best reflected in the lax administration of the anti-Semitic regulations, nowhere better illustrated than in the case of the foreign Jews resident in Italy. The Fascist regime, bowing partly to American pressure, lifted its deadline for their expulsion, although by the outbreak of World War II 6,480 had been cowed into leaving. At the same time, however, thousands of Jewish refugees fleeing the Nazi terror found asylum in Italy.[26] Since Italy's borders were officially closed to most Central and Eastern European refugees, their arrival must be ascribed to the connivance of Italian officials who disbursed tourist and transit visas with liberality. (In five years beginning in 1938 a thousand Fascists were dismissed from the PNF for "pietism," that is, demonstrating sympathy for the Jews.) By October 1941 there were still 7,000 foreign and denationalized Jews in Italy, of which 3,000 had arrived since the promulgation of the Fascist race laws.

Because of the limits and the inchoate application of the anti-Semitic measures, the impact on some Italians seemed at first more a matter of social inconvenience than of outright persecution. For instance, in Giorgio Bassani's fictional but accurate picture of Ferrara in 1938–39, *The Garden of the Finzi-Continis*, the Jewish hero is allowed under the race laws to finish his university course, and his first exposure to the new anti-Semitism comes when he is required to resign from the town's tennis club. As long as Jewish schools and synagogues still functioned, what mattered the omission of Jewish names from the telephone directory and Jewish obituaries from the newspaper columns? Most Italian Jews felt safe from physical harm, and in the prewar circumstances their sense of security was not misplaced. Mussolini's purpose, according to Count Ciano, was "not persecution but discrimination"; his anti-Semitism, unlike Hitler's, was "tactical" and therefore knew bounds.[27] It was a question of gradations of evil.

## NONBELLIGERENCE AND INTERVENTION: ITALY IN WORLD WAR II, 1939–1943

In spite of having signed an offensive military alliance with Germany in May 1939, Italy remained neutral when war broke out, which evoked great joy among the Italian populace. But it was only under duress that Mussolini had accepted neutrality (which he preferred to call nonbelligerence), and he blamed his new scapegoat, the Jews, for the Italians' "soft-hearted" view of war. He was resolved to take his country into World War II as early as practicable. Just as the inception of the Axis had marked the start of Fascist anti-Semitism, so the prospect of fighting alongside Hitler, which became daily more certain during the spring of 1940, raised the anti-Jewish temper in Italy. The old anti-Semite, Farinacci, was foremost among those pushing for Italian intervention in the war, which he anticipated would be the opportunity "to make an end of the Jews."[28]

After Mussolini's declaration of war on June 10, 1940, the situation of Italy's Jews automatically deteriorated. Further economic penalties were imposed, and Jews allegedly hostile to the regime were arrested—about a thousand between

1940 and 1943. War propaganda against the so-called Jewish pluto-democracies prompted local Fascists to attack synagogues and Jewish shops, restaurants, and individuals. The worst of this hooliganism occurred in Trieste, whose Jewish population was four times the national average; part of the Hapsburg Empire until 1918, Trieste still exhibited a strong strain of Central European anti-Semitism. A particular grievance against Italy's Jews in wartime was that they were excluded from military service by the race laws. Some Jews wrote to the Duce asking permission to fight for their country. But the only case in which a Jew was allowed to perform a military duty concerned a former inspector-general of the Corps of Naval Engineers whose expertise was needed to raise the Italian fleet sunk at Taranto. To counter the charge that the Jews contributed nothing to the war effort, Rome decreed that male and female Jews between eighteen and fifty-five should register for forced labor. In theory, no exemptions were to be granted. But like everything else in Fascist Italy, the scheme produced few results. Although some 15,000 Jews registered, scarcely more than 2,000 actually performed any manual work. Perhaps less suffering was caused by ill treatment than by the sense of isolation felt by the majority of Jews living in their own homes but cut off from their fellow citizens and national life. "For most Italian Jews during the war, life simply went on, a little harder and a little sadder than before."[29]

It was the foreign Jews whose condition was drastically altered by Italy's entry into the war. An order was issued for their incarceration as a danger to national security. For the more fortunate this meant *confino*, a standard Fascist means of dealing with troublemakers by banishing them to a remote island or region of the Italian mainland, there to live under local police supervision. This practice has been immortalized in *Christ Stopped at Eboli* by the Jewish artist Carlo Levi, who underwent the experience in the mid-1930s. Compared to the horrors being perpetrated elsewhere in Europe, this was a mild punishment unless families were split up between one *confino* and another, as too often happened after 1940. Most of the foreign Jews in Italy were interned in fifteen camps, hastily constructed, where overcrowding and lack of amenities bred malaria and other diseases. Still, these were not concentration camps on the Nazi model. Contact was maintained with the outside world, and visits were made by the papal nuncio and by Italian rabbis. Moreover, in due course the inmates themselves took over the internal administration of the camps, some of which developed into self-contained villages behind the barbed wire with their own synagogues, schools, pharmacies, libraries, and entertainment. Fortunately, all the camps were located in southern Italy, with the consequence that the internees were liberated after the Allied landings in Italy in 1943.

Italian intervention also revived the notion of the expulsion of Jews from Italy. In fact, in further imitation of the Nazi goal of making the nation *Judenrein*, Rome adopted a plan to expel all Jews save those who had been Aryanized or converted. But this turned out to be just another Fascist gesture made without any thought to the practical difficulties, and it was eventually buried. It followed, though, that Mussolini was glad to see Jews leave Italy on their own initiative, so he tolerated the activity of the Delegazione Assistenza Emigranti Ebrei (Delasem), a relief agency founded in 1939 that directed its efforts mainly to the foreign Jews. With financial help from abroad, especially the United States, Delasem was involved in the emigration of five thousand Jews up to 1943.

Vexed by Italy's servile position in the Axis, Mussolini intended in 1940 to fight his own war, in alliance with but separate from Hitler. This "parallel war" was in no instance better illustrated than by Fascist Italy's conduct in the face of the Nazi determination to destroy the Jews throughout Europe. Until the collapse of the Italian war effort in 1943, Rome consistently refused to hand over to the Germans the Jewish refugees interned in Italy, or to permit the deportation of Italian Jews living under German rule either back to Italy or to the death camps. But much more important was Italian hindrance of Nazi attempts to round up Jews in those countries where the fortunes of war called upon Germans and Italians to cooperate in administering occupied territory. The principal areas in question were the Balkans, Greece, and France.[30]

The argumentation began in Croatia after the Axis conquest of Yugoslavia in 1941. An autonomous Croatian republic, set up under the Ustasha leader, Ante Pavelic, was in effect divided into Italian and German zones of occupation. The Ustasha launched an immediate pogrom against the Jews that was succeeded the following year by a Nazi scheme of deportations to the death camps. Pavelic yielded to the Germans in the expectation that they would overcome the obstruction of Italian military and civilian officials on the spot, nearly all of whom were revolted by Ustasha and Nazi viciousness. Naturally, as many Jews as possible fled to the haven of the Italian zone, where ultimately between 3,000 and 5,000 congregated. Mussolini, constrained to appease Berlin, wrote "nulla osta" (no objection) on the memorandum of Germany's request for Italian cooperation in deporting the Jews in Croatia eastward. This had little effect, however. Count Pietromarchi Luca, who headed the Occupied Territories Department in the Foreign Ministry, Giuseppe Bastianini, governor of Dalmatia, and General Mario Roatta, in command of Italy's Second Army in Yugoslavia, together with many others, contrived to sabotage Mussolini's instruction. Collectively, the Italians deployed their formidable gift for bureaucratic delay to thwart the Germans without doing so openly. A roundup of all Jews in the Italian zone of Croatia was followed by a slow, laborious census of the internees that held the Nazis at bay indefinitely. Finally, in the confusion of the last weeks of fascism in 1943, Italian officials in Croatia of their own accord transported some 3,000 Jews to the island of Arbe, from where most eventually found their way to safety behind Allied lines in the south of Italy.

The Italians had less chance to save the Greek Jews. Some 13,000 Jews lived in the Italian occupation zone, but there were 53,000 in Salonika alone in the German zone. When deportations began in 1943, the Italian Eleventh Army, commanded by General Carlo Geloso, like its counterparts in Croatia, declined to surrender the Jews under its control. Some Italians went further and tried to extend protection to Jews in the German zone. The Italian consulate in Salonika took the definition of Italian citizenship to lengths that would be comic if the issue had not been so grave. An Italian-sounding name, it was rumored, was sufficient to earn an Italian passport and a shield against the Nazis. Many Greek Jews were spirited into the Italian zone. Sadly, it was all in vain. With the collapse of Italian fascism and the withdrawal of Italian troops, all the Jews on the Greek mainland and islands, including 1,800 in the Italian-owned Dodecanese, were hunted down and dispatched to the gas chambers.

In France, too, Italy and Germany found themselves at cross-purposes. Propelled by the rising tide of anti-Semitism throughout Europe, thousands of Jews of different nationalities had taken refuge in France, particularly after the fall of France in 1940 in the quasi-autonomous area ruled from Vichy. But the Vichy regime put into effect race laws very similar to those in Italy and, in July 1942, acceded to what Rome steadfastly rejected—the deliverance of foreign Jews to the Nazis.[31] On November 11, after Allied landings in North Africa, Axis forces moved into Vichy France, with Italy occupying six departments east of the Rhone River. Here the Italian military immediately intervened to stop French officials handing over Jews for deportation. Within the next few months Jews crowded into the Italian zone until 50,000, about half non-French, were assembled there. The foreign Jews were subject to enforced residence, but often this meant lodging in a Riviera resort hotel. Vichy turned to Nazi Germany to put pressure on its Axis partner, and the pattern in Croatia was thus repeated.

In February 1943 Nazi Foreign Minister Joachim von Ribbentrop visited Rome; he departed believing that he had won Mussolini's collaboration in the deportations from both Croatia and France. The Italian generals, explained the Duce to the German ambassador, were guilty of "a false humanitarian twaddle which had no place in today's harsh world."[32] To back up these words, he appointed a personal acquaintance, Guido Lospinoso, a police inspector from Bari with a reputation for getting things done, to head a commissariat for Jewish affairs in Nice. In this way Italy's Ministry of the Interior, which administered the race laws at home, would bypass the squeamish generals in France—or so it seemed. But Lospinoso proved singularly elusive. For weeks his whereabouts in southern France were unknown, and he regularly missed appointments with French and German officials. The fall of Mussolini in July afforded Lospinoso a further excuse for delay as he returned to Rome for fresh instructions. Meanwhile, the Italian Fourth Army withdrew to an area around Nice, followed by 18,000 foreign Jews to add to the 5,000 French Jews in the neighborhood. An Italian Jewish businessman and accomplice of the peripatetic Lospinoso, Angelo Donati, persuaded the new government in Rome to donate four ships and the Allies to allow 30,000 Jews to sail from France to North Africa. Unfortunately, this plan was overtaken by Italy's exit from the war. The Germans at once seized almost 2,000 Jews in Nice. A thousand Jews from the truncated Italian zone crossed the mountains into Italy, only to find that they were in another Nazi-occupied country.

Their fate became merged with that of Italy's Jews in the final two years of World War II.

It is astonishing that the Italian authorities in the occupied territories were permitted to protect Jews with impunity. The explication lies partly in Berlin, partly in Rome. During 1942 Hitler showed himself reluctant to bring too much pressure to bear on Mussolini, for whom the Führer retained real affection. As Italy was still an independent nation, Italo-German relations were the preserve of the German Foreign Ministry, where Ribbentrop was Hitler's man. In other words, the main Nazi agencies of the Final Solution, the Schutzstaffel (SS) and in particular its subdepartment, the Reichssicherheitshauptamt (RSHA), were kept at arm's length. Moreover, when in 1943 Reichsführer SS Himmler prevailed upon Hitler to use his influence with the Duce, Ribbentrop was sent to Rome inadequately briefed on the full extent of Italy's obstruction of the deportations.[33] All of this served to facilitate Italian prevarication.

What motivated Fascist Italy's policy is not easy to elucidate. The Germans tried to keep from Mussolini the true nature of their Final Solution, although his subordinates were frank in telling him that deportation equaled extermination. The disobedience of Italian officials perhaps reflected no more than Mussolini's failing grip on affairs of state; Hitler called him "an old and worn-out man."[34] Yet the impression persists that those who mounted efforts to rescue Jews felt that they were not acting against the Duce's inner wishes; the lackluster application of the race laws in Italy was a yardstick by which to judge. The motives of these Fascist underlings are also less than crystal clear. After all, none had protested against, and some had even participated in, atrocities in Ethiopia and Slovenia. Why, then, did they balk at maltreatment of the Jews? It must be recognized that by the end of 1942 the writing on the wall indicated an Axis defeat, and the need to present as fair a face as possible to the Allies grew daily more urgent. An Italian diplomat in September 1943 secreted his Foreign Ministry's files on Croatia because he "thought it would be good if somebody in the future were to know that we had done something good in our lives."[35] Thus "a considerable dose of calculation in Italian policy toward the Jews" became mixed with moral considerations.[36] On the other hand, Italian noncompliance with Nazi and Ustasha persecution of the Jews antedated the turn of the tide against the Axis and swelled into blanket opposition when the full import of the Final Solution became manifest. Genocide plainly went beyond the bounds of Fascist brutality; Italian documents of the time, unlike German ones, frequently speak of the ethical aspect of the Jewish question. In maintaining some sense of right and wrong, Italians in the Axis-occupied territories foreshadowed the behavior of Italians in general when the Holocaust reached their homeland.

Ironically, on the eve of their worst trial, Italy's Jews were given reason for hope. The Axis had always been the barometer of anti-Semitism in Italy, and as defeat on the battlefield eroded its value, so in 1943 Fascist utterances about the Jews softened noticeably. On July 25 King Victor Emmanuel dismissed

Mussolini and replaced the Fascist ministry with one headed by Marshal Pietro Badoglio. The Badoglio government released a number of imprisoned anti-Fascists, some Jewish, and arrested the editor of *Difesa della razza* and also the director of Demorazza. But the office itself was not closed nor the race laws repealed; no clear instructions were issued to end forced labor and the internment camps. Thus registers of Jewish names and addresses remained in government files to await the scrutiny of an occupying force. (In fact, a number of Germans in Italy, ostensibly to plan the Axis war effort, had already had access to Jewish records.) Badoglio claimed that his inaction in the Jewish question was designed to ward off a Nazi invasion. But when, on September 8, 1943, he announced the signing of an armistice with the Anglo-Americans at Cassibile in Sicily, the Germans were poised to strike. In Operation Axis they established their military government from the Alps south to Salerno, where the Allies had begun their liberation of the Italian mainland. Within a few days most of Italy's Jews, resident in the capital and northern cities, found themselves living under the Nazi jack-boot. Few had fled during the summer. They had been lulled into a sense of security by the false calm of Badoglio's forty-five-day administration in Rome and by ignorance of the full fury of Nazi anti-Semitism.

## THE HOLOCAUST COMES TO ITALY, 1943–1945

Random murder of Jews by the SS began in Italy's picturesque northern frontier areas in September, but the first large-scale thrust of the extermination program happened in Rome. On the twelfth, Himmler ordered the deportation of as many of Rome's 12,000 Jews as could be caught:

The recent Italian events impose a final solution to the Jewish question in the territories recently occupied by the armed forces of the Reich. The Reichsführer SS therefore requests SS Obersturmbannführer [Herbert] Kappler [German security police chief in Rome] to actuate without delay all necessary preliminary measures to assure the precipitateness and the secrecy of the operations to be carried out in the territory of the city of Rome.[37]

Before executing this order, Kappler demanded of the Roman Jewish community fifty kilograms of gold. Either, as he later protested, this was to ward off deportation by demonstrating how the Jews might be exploited, for the gold was delivered in less than twenty-four hours, or, more likely, it was a tactic devised to convince the Jews that they had now purchased their immunity. Indeed, the bulk of Rome's Jews remained regrettably unapprehensive.

Yet there were warnings enough of the coming storm, mostly from German diplomats in Rome who were aware of and appalled by Himmler's order. More-over, the SS made several raids on Rome's main synagogue and seized, along with Judaic archival treasures, registers of the Jewish community. Well-informed Jews, such as the chief rabbi of Rome, dropped out of sight, and Delasem went underground. The failure to alert Rome's Jews at large, however, has spawned a vigorous controversy. Most blame has been attached to Dante Almansi, president of the national Union of Jewish Communities, and Ugo Foá, head of the Jewish community in Rome itself. It is perhaps significant that both had been high officials under fascism, the former in the police and the latter in the judiciary, before losing their positions under the race laws. They had then devoted themselves, with some success, to mitigating the harsher aspects of Fascist anti-Semitism. Having been able to achieve a sort of modus operandi with Italian fascism, they appeared to believe that they could do the same with the German Nazis. It needs to be added that many in the know, both Jews and Gentiles, expected the Vatican, which had been informed of SS plans by the German ambassador to the Holy See, Ernst von Weizsäcker, to interpose itself. But the Vatican remained silent and passive both before and after Black Sabbath.

Such is the sinister title accorded Saturday, October 16, 1943, when, beginning at dawn, the SS rounded up 1,259 victims, of whom almost 800 were women and children. A fortunate 252 were released as insufficiently Jewish. The rest, two days later, were crammed into twenty-eight railway freight cars without food, water, or sanitation. Exactly a week after Black Sabbath, they reached Auschwitz to be greeted by the celebrated Dr. Josef Mengele. Over 800 were gassed immediately; of the remainder, 15 survived the war. In Rome no word of their fate could be gleaned, though suspicion soon hardened into certainty. The shock of Black Sabbath cannot be conveyed by bare statistics. As those Jews left in Rome scrambled for safety, they now knew that the unthinkable could happen in civilized Italy.

The events of October 16 form the centerpiece in the debate over the papacy's role in the Holocaust. Most of the deportees were caught in the neighborhood of the former Roman ghetto, a mile distant from Vatican City, and the Italian Military College where they were confined for two days was even closer. As Weizsäcker put it, "The action took place, so to speak, under the Pope's windows."[38] In the evening of the sixteenth, a letter from the rector of the German Catholic church in Rome to the German military commander threatened a papal denunciation, but in fact none came. The Vatican's sole public comment was an oblique reference in *L'osservatore romano* of October 26 to papal charity knowing "neither boundaries nor nationality, neither religion nor race." We are now aware that the silence of Pope Pius XII was one side of a tacit bargain reached between Weizsäcker and Cardinal Maglione, the papal secretary of state. In return, the Germans held back from occupying the Vatican and from launching any further concerted roundup of Rome's Jews.

Nevertheless, the pope's failure to make a "flaming protest" was turned after the war into a cause célèbre, most famously by Rolf Hochhuth's vitriolic play *Der Stellvertreter*.[39] Vatican motives have been endlessly analyzed. Pius XII, it is generally agreed, was not a coward; he was prepared for martyrdom if, in his opinion, it would have served a useful purpose. He was without doubt anti-Communist, but there is absolutely no evidence that by 1943, with the Nazi armies in retreat in Russia, he regarded Hitler as a shield against bolshevism.

The papacy, it must be admitted, was mildly anti-Semitic. Pius XII may even secretly have welcomed Mussolini's race laws since they encouraged conversion, and Catholic relief work between 1938 and 1943 had concentrated heavily on baptized Jews.[40] Yet this is a far cry from condoning the Holocaust. A better view is that "in sum, Pius XII was a diplomat," which meant that he gave priority to the preservation of the Vatican as a participant in international affairs.[41] If this involved maintenance of diplomatic ties with an unchristian regime in Berlin, and even silence in the face of Nazi atrocities, so be it.

After Black Sabbath the nature of Catholic aid to the Jews changed dramatically. Whereas formerly this had concentrated on persuading Latin American states to accept Italian Jewish refugees, it now turned with more effect to sheltering the Jews from their tormentors at home. Within Rome itself the doors of religious houses were opened to some 4,000 Jews, and over 400 found safety within Vatican City. However, no directive from the pope orchestrated this activity; it arose from below rather than above. In the most spectacular instance, Father Marie Benoît, a French priest who hid 400 Polish Jews adrift in Rome for twelve months, did so almost entirely by his own ingenuity. On the other hand, it must remain moot whether Rome's religious sanctuaries would have retained the inviolability that they more often than not enjoyed had the pope spoken out against the Final Solution.

Meanwhile, the SS attempted to extend to other centers of Italian Jewry what it had begun in Rome. In this it was aided by the appearance on the scene of a final, twisted version of Italian fascism. After his fall, imprisonment in Italy, and rescue by the SS, Mussolini returned to his native country to preside over the Salò republic, so named after the village on Lake Garda whence this new regime's communiqués emanated. Perhaps Mussolini hoped to protect Italians, even the Jews, from the full rigor of Nazi occupation. But the Salò government existed only on German sufferance and by accommodation of Nazi policies, a token of which was soon offered in the Jewish question. On November 14, 1943, a Verona manifesto defined the terms of the new Fascist republic and in article 7 provided a radical new dispensation for Italy's Jews. They were now to forfeit all property and to assume the role of aliens: "Those of the Hebrew race are foreigners. While the war lasts they are deemed of enemy nationality."[42] As such, by a police order of December 1, they were made subject to internment. In the style of anti-Semitism *alla fascista*, there were exemptions on grounds of old age and sickness, and mixed families formerly exempt were simply placed under police surveillance. The Verona manifesto stopped short of endorsing deportations to the gas chambers (which was probably why the Vatican declined to condemn the document), but it served the Nazis' purpose well enough. The establishment of a huge Italian internment camp at Fossoli, near Modena, conveniently congregated all Jews in custody until such time as the Germans would step in and direct their disposal.

The Verona manifesto was testimony to the Salò republic's subservience to

Nazi Germany, but it also reflected the emergence to prominence within Italian fascism of those who had previously been fringe actors. The mainstream Fascists had broken with Mussolini on July 25, 1943, when a clear majority of the Fascist Grand Council had approved a motion of no confidence in the Duce. Therefore, those who made the odyssey to Salò were the extremists disaffected by earlier Fascist compromises, violent in method, pro-Nazi, and anti-Semitic. Mussolini, now in poor health, was forced to rely on these men. Especially notorious was one, Giovanni Preziosi, an unfrocked priest who for twenty years under Fari-nacci's protection had edited a scurrilous anti-Semitic journal. Mussolini found him "repulsive," but he won Hitler's confidence. A relentless schemer in Salò's corridors of power, he secured in March 1944 the post of inspector-general of race; his unrealistic dream was to create an Italian "racial superpolice" to match the SS.[43] Instead, 20,000 Italians enlisted in the Nazi Waffen-SS. Although engaged on the battlefront rather than in harassment of Jews at home, these were by the nature of their calling the most committed of Italy's anti-Semites.[44]

The genuine and fanatical anti-Semitism of a Preziosi or the SS was not shared by all who served Salò. Nevertheless, the chaos created by the royal dismissal of Mussolini and the subsequent armistice had let loose a host of resentful Fascist desperadoes who would hunt Jews for opportunistic reasons. Initially, semiau-tonomous squads vaguely connected with one or another Salò politician pursued anti-Fascists and Jews alike, killing, robbing, and holding for ransom. Terrorism was the raison d'être of the so-called Muti Legion in Milan and of bands led by an improbably named Major Carità in Florence and Padua and by Pietro Koch, a former German naval officer, in Rome and then Milan. When Jewish internment became official Salò policy, the Mussolini government tried, with limited suc-cess, to absorb these units into new security organizations. Finding the local police reluctant to round up Jews, Salò conjured a new political army, the Guardia Nazionale Repubblicana (GNR), out of remnants of the former Fascist militia, the *carabinieri*, and the Italian African police. In theory, this force comprised 140,000 men, but in practice its strength was probably not much more than half that figure. Conscripts and the *carabinieri* element displayed a marked lack of anti-Semitic zeal, and desertion was rampant. Hence in July 1944 the Fascist party secretary, Alessandro Pavolini, created the Brigate Nere, which, on paper, enrolled and armed all male party members between eighteen and sixty. In reality, the actual complement of 30,000 consisted heavily of military deserters, crim-inals, and teenagers. Toward anti-Fascists and Jews they behaved viciously.[45]

Neither the official GNR and Brigate Nere nor the unofficial Muti, Carità, and Koch bands could make much headway in their pogroms without the help of informers among the Italian citizenry. It is impossible to gauge how many Italians informed on their Jewish neighbors. Some did so out of anti-Semitic conviction, others out of personal spite, and others for money. Nine thousand lire was the top price offered. One or two informers were Jewish themselves and earned a sinister reputation. The most bizarre case was that of Celeste Di

Porto, an attractive eighteen-year-old Roman Jewess, who had herself lost relatives on Black Sabbath, but went on to turn in fifty of her coreligionists and win herself the sobriquet of the Black Panther.

Under Salò's jurisdiction, then, Jews lost their lives not because of official policy, but in random fashion. This, of course, was insufficient for the Nazi purpose of cold-blooded, administratively efficient genocide. Therefore, throughout the winter of 1943 the Germans tried to interfere in the Italian roundup of Jews. Guido Buffarini Guidi, Salò's minister of the interior, put up some bureaucratic resistance, but was undercut by his own police chief's instruction to his underlings to enter into "suitable arrangements with the local German authorities."[46]

SS Captain Theodor Dannecker, supervisor of the October 16 deportations from Rome and Adolf Eichmann's chief lieutenant in Italy, traveled from town to town in search of victims for the Final Solution. Some Jews were captured by the SS, but most were handed over by the Italian Fascists, and by the end of 1943 several trainloads of deportees had left Milan for Auschwitz. In February 1944 Dannecker was replaced by SS Major Friedrich Bosshammer, another of Eichmann's subordinates in the infamous Abteilung IVB of RSHA (specializing in the Final Solution). Operating from permanent headquarters in Verona, Bosshammer brought about a tight integration of German police operations, demanded full cooperation from all Italian authorities, and, most important, took over the internment camp at Fossoli. "Here we received the first blows," wrote Primo Levi, the great chronicler of the *Lager*, of his encounter with German guards at Fossoli.[47] In March Bosshammer decreed that elderly and sick Jews should henceforth be rounded up (although in recent weeks age and infirmity had not been given automatic immunity). Raids on hospitals and old peoples' homes followed. Next month the Nazi definition of Jewishness to embrace mixed families was applied to Italy's Jews. All this was wrought without prior arrangement with the Salò administration, which was by now reduced to servile assistance in providing Jews for the Nazi engine of destruction.[48]

Rome, where the Nazis had first given an earnest sign of their intentions, was liberated by the Allies in June 1944. Between Black Sabbath and Allied relief a further 800 Jews were arrested. They included 77 Jewish victims in the Ardeatine Caves massacre in March 1944 (335 Italians were executed in reprisal for a partisan attack on the SS). One was Aldo Finzi, former Fascist cabinet minister; the youngest Jew was fifteen years of age.[49] Of Italy's other cities, Milan yielded nearly 900 Jews and Turin over 400; Florence (with Siena), Fiume, Genoa (with La Spezia), and Venice each lost over 200 Jews. Fossoli became the main transit station to the death camps; some 2,600 were deported from there alone. When Allied forces drove north in July 1944, Fossoli was closed and another concentration camp opened in the Bolzano suburb of Gries. Altogether, fifteen trains with Jewish deportees left Italy in 1943–44.

Furthermore, it should be remembered that the provinces of the South Tyrol (or Alto Adige) and the Trentino, wrested from the Hapsburg Empire in 1918, had been under direct German rule since the armistice of September 1943. This had a particular impact on Trieste, which boasted the only Nazi death camp per se on Italian soil, La Risiera di San Sabba, run by "Einsatzkommando Reinhard," who had been trained in the murder of Jews in Poland.[50] Twenty-two trains carrying a mix of Italian and Balkan Jews departed Trieste for Auschwitz and other death camps, and by 1945 only 400 of the prewar population of almost 6,000 Jews remained in the town.

The anti-Jewish storm in Italy petered out with the collapse of the Nazi war effort in April 1945 in the same place as it had announced itself eighteen months earlier. As the SS and Fascist militia retreated toward Austria and Switzerland, some took delight in murdering more Jews on Italy's northern frontiers in the very last days of the war. This final slaughter coincided ironically with the capital retribution exacted of Salò's chief Jew-baiters by the victorious anti-Fascist resistance.[51]

The precise tally of total Jewish victims in Italy varies according to authority and method of calculation. The most up-to-date and reliable estimate compiled by Renzo De Felice is of 7,495 deportees, of which 610 returned from the death camps.[52] In addition, up to 300 Jews are believed to have been destroyed within Italy. In round figures, of the 45,200 Jews in Italy in September 1943, 15 percent perished in the next year and a half. These cold statistics give rise to two questions, or rather a single question framed in two ways. How could so many Jews be abstracted so suddenly from tolerant Italian society for massacre? This is the query with which Susan Zuccotti opens her study of the Holocaust in Italy, although much of her book is inevitably concerned with responding to the question in its alternate and more common form: Why was so large a proportion of Italy's Jews saved in the end, given the figures of Nazi slaughter elsewhere in Europe?[53] The answer to this latter question is itself twofold: It is to be found in a combination of Jewish resourcefulness and Gentile compassion. Both these qualities seem to have had their origin in several generations of Jewish integration into Italian society.

For a start, there was in Italy no Judenrat to cooperate with the Nazis, as so often happened in Eastern Europe. Moreover, although Italy's Jews were slow to recognize impending danger after the Cassibile armistice, they took heed of the warning inadvertently provided by the Verona manifesto. By the time the full Holocaust struck Italy in the winter of 1943, many had taken precautionary action. For some this meant simply fading into the general population, a recourse eased by the relatively small number of Italian Jews. Italy's racial legislation had never required Jews to wear the yellow Star of David, and, in view of the lack of any distinguishing physical characteristics among Italian Jewry, many Italians did not know which of their neighbors were Jewish. Yet the danger of recognition on the street remained ever present. The standard way to minimize risk was to move to another quarter of a large city or to another town altogether. In order to survive, Jews on the run had to forgo many Judaic practices, concerning diet, for example. It was necessary to avoid medical examination lest circumcision betray identity. While in relative terms it was easy for Italian Jews to hide among their fellow citizens, this was patently more difficult for the foreign Jews, as the statistics indicate. Only 12 percent of Italian Jews perished, but twice that proportion of foreign Jews were liquidated.

The Allied air raids on large Italian cities compelled many to flee to the countryside, which for the Jews was a mixed blessing. The SS and Fascist militia were less thick on the ground than in the towns, but strangers were more noticeable in a village. Peasants might be ignorant of the Jewish question but were habitually suspicious of strangers. Between 1943 and 1945, however, Italy became a land of refugees—evacuees from air raids and the battle zones, military deserters, and escaped prisoners of war. Many Jews were able to submerge themselves in this undifferentiated mass of humanity. Anywhere between 1,000 and 3,000 younger Jews joined the resistance. There the assimilation of Italian society at large was repeated; there were no distinct Jewish units, no separate Jewish underground. However, the only known female partisan to be killed was Jewish, and so too was the youngest, aged thirteen.[54]

It is incalculable how many of Italy's Jews who survived the Holocaust owed their lives to the aid rendered by non-Jewish Italians. The record of 85 percent salvation betokened far more clearly the popular Italian attitude than did the hatred of Jews by a few thousand under the Salò regime. Between 1943 and 1945 helping Jews was a hazardous business. True, it did not involve instant execution, as was the norm in Eastern Europe (though executions on the spot were known in Italy). But it invited arrest and deportation, if not to the gas chamber, at least to a Nazi camp to be worked to death. Nonetheless, countless thousands of ordinary Italians, of all classes and every political and religious persuasion, accepted the hazard.

Some Italians were by their vocation more useful than others. Priests, either on their own initiative or with the connivance of the local bishop, had access to church buildings big enough to shelter large groups of Jews, with the added attraction that the Fascist militia might respect religious sanctuary. It is estimated that 170 priests were killed and several hundred deported for anti-Fascist activities in which assisting Jews bulked large. Italy's bureaucrats, too, were of crucial importance because of their control of documentation. They might hide or destroy registers of Jews in their locality, and they had the power to issue identity papers, ration cards, and residence and travel permits to fugitive Jews. It is perhaps unfair to specify one individual out of many who performed such services, but Giovanni Palatucci, an official at police headquarters in Fiume, has won special plaudits for the number of Jews whose rescue he aided. Tragically, he perished in Dachau. Sometimes help reached the Jews from unexpected sources, even from within the Salò hierarchy. Farinacci, who had long protected his private secretary, who was Jewish, warned the Jews of Cremona of an imminent SS roundup after he himself had given the Germans a list of Jewish names.

But it was the actions of ordinary Italians without special position or privilege that spoke loudest. Again, one instance out of many must suffice. During 1941–

42 Delasem rescued ninety-two Jewish orphans from Yugoslavia and installed them in the Villa Emma, a rambling house ten kilometers from Modena. They escaped internment as required by Italy's race laws and were cared for by the local people, Jewish and non-Jewish, until the German occupation. When the Nazis arrived, Villa Emma was empty. All the orphans had been spirited away, some to the local seminary, others to nearby homes of peasants and artisans. An obliging bureaucrat furnished false identity papers, the local doctor free medical care. Everyone in the district knew of the Jewish youngsters, but no one talked, and all ninety-two were saved. In this way, all over northern Italy, some Italians risked their lives by positive acts of succor, while others served the cause more passively by keeping a discreet silence.

Besides protecting Jews within Italy, many Italians helped Jews to escape from the German-occupied areas. Delasem continued to function underground until the liberation of Rome. The anti-Fascist resistance helped some Jews to reach the Allies in the south of Italy, either by sea or across the battle lines. To the north, the neutral Swiss progressively relaxed their immigration restrictions as the Holocaust gathered pace; by the end of 1943 all Jewish refugees were admissible. Consequently, among Italy's Alpine guides and smugglers there developed a vigorous trade in taking Jews by night across the mountain tracks into Switzerland. Most of these guides were mercenary (between 5,000 and 9,000 lire per Jew conducted across the frontier), and a few were treacherous. Nevertheless, during the German occupation some 5,000 to 6,000 Jews escaped either to Switzerland or to the Allied zone to the south.

How to explain the readiness of so many Italians to obstruct the Holocaust? In the first place, of course, most Italians regarded anti-Semitism as a foreign import, a corollary of the unpopular Rome-Berlin Axis. After 1943 anti-Semitism was the creed of the hated German occupier of the homeland. Simple nationalist sentiment dictated opposition to Nazism's Jewish policy. But in addition, something deeper was undoubtedly at work. Historians are loath to refer to national character. Jonathan Steinberg typically eschews "easy generalizations about national character" and seeks "reality" in the "complex matrix of institutions, traditions, habits, customs, unspoken assumptions, conflicts both structural and personal, laws and their evasion, leadership, order and chaos"—all of which, some might say, add up to national character anyway.[55] Within this context, by whatever name it is called, Italians are deemed to possess certain "secondary vices"—disorder, disobedience, slyness, and so on—that enabled them in World War II to practice the "primary virtue" of saving human lives. (In contrast, the Germans' secondary virtues of incorruptibility and order actually fostered the primary vice of inhumanity to their fellow men.)[56] A classic example of Italian "secondary vice" is an ingrained disrespect for central authority. This attribute has been the bane of every regime to govern in Rome, but it has its uses. The truth is that Italians do not live by written law, or at least not to the degree observed in Anglo-Saxon countries. It is expected that rules will be bent regularly to allow satisfaction of a variety of tastes and interests. This makes for a sometimes venal but also humane and tolerant community. Thus Italian society operates on a series of tacit assumptions about what is or is not permissible, to which the letter of the law may or may not correspond.[57] Clearly, although anti-Semitism might be legislated by Mussolini and even imposed by Nazi brute force, it went beyond the pale of Italian custom. To oppose it was almost automatic.

Such was the sentiment expressed by Giuseppe Tiburzio, an Italian officer who sheltered a nine-year-old Jewish girl from Belgium and raised her in her own faith: ''What I did appeared then, as now, perfectly *natural*, and I believe that in my place, many others would have done the same.''[58] Modestly, he forbore to mention the self-evident courage that he and others like him displayed. It was almost as if many Italians, shamed by the vainglorious martial rhetoric of the Fascist era, deliberately sought opportunity between 1943 and 1945 to prove their mettle. Some redeemed the national honor in the resistance, others in the salvage of the majority of Italy's Jews.

## CONCLUSION

It is instructive to compare Italy's record in the Holocaust with that of certain other countries.[59] France, Denmark, and Hungary in their different ways all offer useful parallels.

France, the so-called Latin sister of Italy, might have been expected to extend the same ''Latin humanity'' to the Jews as did the Italians. There were, indeed, some similarities, but also significant differences. Possibly as many as 75,000 Jews were deported from France, almost 25 percent of those in the country at the time of the French surrender to Germany in June 1940. Admittedly, these figures owe much to the fact that the Germans occupied two-thirds of France for more than three years, as opposed to the Nazi occupation of northern Italy for eighteen months. However, the Nazis' task was facilitated enormously by French collaborationism. Months before the Germans extended their military control to the whole of France in November 1942, the Vichy government joined openly in the deportation of foreign Jews, although even under total German occupation French authorities successfully hindered mass transportation of French nationals. France thereby made a clear and odious distinction between French and other Jews. On the Italian side, Mussolini, as long as he headed an independent government, avoided all participation in the deportations. Even between 1943 and 1945 the Salò regime never officially endorsed any anti-Semitic policy beyond internment. Of course, while pretending to hold aloof from the Final Solution, Salò unleashed its GNR and Brigate Nere to hunt down Italian and foreign Jews alike. Here there was little to choose between the Fascist militia and the French Milice. Nevertheless, the willingness of the French to consign their foreign Jews to destruction remains a particularly invidious action, arguably more reprehensible than anything perpetrated by Italy's anti-Semites.

Denmark, on the other hand, withheld complicity in the Holocaust entirely and saved well over 90 percent of its 6,500 resident Jews—the only instance of a higher proportion of Jews preserved than in Italy itself. In thwarting German occupation policies so wholeheartedly, though, the Danes had certain built-in advantages. By their own racist precepts, the Nazis exercised more restraint in imposing their anti-Semitic will on the Nordic Danes than on the allegedly inferior Latins of Italy. Moreover, a geographical haven for Danish Jewry lay readier to hand than for Italy's Jews. It was much easier to cross a few miles of the Baltic to neutral Sweden than the Alpine passes to Switzerland.

Probably the fairest comparison is to be made between Italy and Hungary. Both nations fought alongside Nazi Germany in World War II. As independent allies of Germany the Mussolini government and the Horthy regime alike practiced racism at home, but refused to cooperate with the Nazi deportation policy. (From 1940 to 1943 Berlin blamed Hungarian obduracy on the Italian example.) Only with German military occupation of their countries—Italy in September 1943 and Hungary in March 1944—were the Italian and Hungarian Jews swept up in the Holocaust. While the nominal governments in Salò and Budapest turned a blind eye or were powerless to intervene, Italy's fanatical anti-Semites and the equally rabid Hungarian Arrow Cross were free, under German license, to run riot. In spite of these similarities, the net results in Italy and Hungary were strikingly different. As against the loss of 15 percent of Italy's Jews in a year and a half, about a quarter of the Jews in Hungary (over 15,000) perished in a matter of weeks. The Nazi frenzy to exterminate Jews in Italy was no less than in Hungary. The vast disparity in outcome arose from the ease of identification, and therefore capture, of Eastern European Jews as well as from the deep-rooted and pervasive strain of anti-Semitism in that part of the world. What Hungary lacked was the high degree of Jewish assimilation and the popular social tolerance—mutually reinforcing phenomena—that shielded so many Jews in Italy.

To be sure, it remains a bone of contention in Holocaust studies whether or not assimilation acts as a bar to anti-Semitism. It has been argued that in Germany and Austria, for instance, assimilation did not inhibit, but rather fueled, the growth of explicitly anti-Semitic parties; it merely lulled the Jews themselves into a false sense of security. In Italy, too, the assimilated Jews were very slow to recognize the looming danger. On the other hand, the "parallel nationalization" of Italy's Jews and Gentiles in the era of *risorgimento* and unification appeared to produce a society of genuine mutual tolerance.[60] In the Italian experience it is hard to deny the connection between Jewish assimilation and the dearth of popular anti-Semitic feeling.

Statistically, then, the Italian record in the Holocaust was a good one, certainly better than in the parallel cases of France and Hungary, and almost on a par with that of Denmark. Nevertheless, Italian society had generated a disquieting minority of accessories to the great crime. This could not be forgotten by the five out of six Jews who survived in Italy. The very unexpectedness of Italian anti-Semitism comprised for its targets a profound and unsettling shock. Things could never be quite the same again. As the Israeli scholar M. Michaelis remarks,

"The setting had disappeared."[61] In short, the Holocaust in Italy left a deeper psychological scar than the bare survival figures might suggest.

A final verdict on Italian Jewish survival, therefore, must be nuanced. In a felicitous metaphor H. Stuart Hughes remarks that Italian Jewry during the twentieth century has passed from a golden to a silver age, a decline from halcyon days to an epoch of cautious relief and recovery.[62] The Holocaust was a terrible catalyst of that transition.

## BIBLIOGRAPHIC COMMENT

The principal research institute for the Holocaust in Italy is the Centro di Documentazione Ebraica Contemporanea (CDEC) in Milan, which has issued some useful *quaderni* bearing the title *Gli ebrei in Italia durante il fascismo* and also a statistical pamphlet, *Ebrei in Italia: Deportazione, resistenza*. A further study by CDEC's director, Liliana Picciotti Fargion, "La deportazione degli ebrei dall'Italia: Indagine statistica," has for some time been scheduled for publication by Munich's Institut für Zeitgeschichte in a survey, country by country, of Holocaust victims. The most heavily documented and authoritative account of the persecution of Italian Jews is the latest edition of Renzo De Felice's *Storia degli ebrei italiani sotto il fascismo*. In the English language two titles are preeminent and complement each other nicely. Meir Michaelis, *Mussolini and the Jews: German-Italian Relations and the Jewish Question in Italy, 1922–1945*, is chiefly concerned with the *haute politique* of Fascist anti-Semitism. Susan Zuccotti's very readable *The Italians and the Holocaust: Persecution, Rescue, and Survival* draws on individual recollections at a grass-roots level and focuses more directly than does Michaelis on the years 1943–45. Italian works that concentrate on the Jewish plight during World War II include Nicola Caracciolo, *Gli ebrei e l'Italia durante la guerra, 1940–45*; Giuseppe Mayda, *Ebrei sotto Salò: La persecuzione antisemita, 1943–1945*; and Liliana Picciotti Fargion, *L'Occupazione tedesca e gli ebrei di Roma*. Serviceable but not definitive accounts of individual Fascist anti-Semites are by Harry Fornari, *Mussolini's Gadfly: Roberto Farinacci*, and, on Telesio Interlandi, by Giampiero Mughini, *A via della mercede c'era un razzista*.

Interpretations of the growth of Italian Fascist racism are advanced in several articles: Gene Bernardini, "The Origins and Development of Racial Anti-Semitism in Fascist Italy," *Journal of Modern History* 49 (1977); Michael A. Ledeen, "Evolution of Italian Fascist Antisemitism," *Jewish Social Studies* 37 (1975); and Nicholas Stigliani and Antonette Marzotto, "Fascist Antisemitism and the Italian Jews," *Wiener Library Bulletin* 28, nos. 35/36 (1975). An issue of the journal *Il Ponte* (Florence), 34, nos. 11/12 (1978), was devoted to essays— some of a memoir, others of a scholarly, nature—on Italy's encounter with anti-Semitism. Luigi Preti, *Impero fascista, africani ed ebrei*, and Esmonde M. Robertson, "Race as a Factor in Mussolini's Policy in Africa and Europe,"

*Journal of Contemporary History* 23, no. 1 (1988), find links between Fascist racism in the colonies and at home.

Consideration of the fate of Italy's Jews within the context of Nazism's overall anti-Semitic onslaught is to be found in Raul Hilberg, *The Destruction of the European Jews*; Gerald Reitlinger, *The Final Solution: The Attempt to Exterminate the Jews of Europe, 1939–45*; and Martin Gilbert, *The Holocaust*. Italian obstruction of the Nazi death machine in the Axis-occupied territories is chronicled by Jonathan Steinberg in *All or Nothing: The Axis and the Holocaust, 1941–1943*; the interpretations advanced have relevance beyond the book's temporal and geographical focus.

Regrettably few reminiscences by Italian Jews have been translated into English. Recommended are Natalia Ginzburg, *Family Sayings*; Dan Vittorio Segrè, *Memoirs of a Fortunate Jew*; and Fabio Della Seta, *The Tiber Afire*. Arguably the greatest classic to emerge from the Holocaust is Primo Levi's account of his deportation to and ordeal in Auschwitz, *If This Is a Man*, a precise rendering of the original Italian title; it has been reprinted under the title *Survival in Auschwitz* (New York: Collier, 1973). Although fiction, Giorgio Bassani's beautifully subtle *The Garden of the Finzi-Continis* relies heavily on subjective experience. H. Stuart Hughes, *Prisoners of Hope: The Silver Age of the Italian Jews, 1924–1974*, is a cultural study that analyzes the writings of, among others, Ginzburg, Levi, and Bassani.

## NOTES

1. Cecil Roth, *The History of the Jews in Italy* (Philadelphia: Jewish Publication Society of America, 1946), p. 146. For a somewhat less roseate view, see Andrew M. Canepa, "Emancipation and the Jewish Response in Mid-Nineteenth Century Italy," *European History Quarterly* 16 (1986): 403–40.

2. Meir Michaelis, *Mussolini and the Jews* (Oxford: Clarendon Press, 1978), chap. 1; Susan Zuccotti, *The Italians and the Holocaust: Persecution, Rescue, and Survival* (New York: Basic Books, 1987), chap. 2.

3. On Farinacci, see Harry Fornari, *Mussolini's Gadfly: Roberto Farinacci* (Nashville: Vanderbilt University Press, 1971).

4. In this chapter statistics and factual information on the Fascist Italian scene are drawn from Renzo De Felice, *Storia degli ebrei italiani sotto il fascismo*, 4th ed. (Turin: Einaudi, 1988), supplemented by Michaelis, *Mussolini and the Jews*, and Zuccotti, *Italians and the Holocaust*.

5. Charles F. Delzell, *Mussolini's Enemies: The Italian Anti-Fascist Resistance* (Princeton, N. J.: Princeton University Press, 1961).

6. Text in De Felice, *Storia degli ebrei italiani*, app. 2.

7. The principal English-language biography of the Duce is by Denis Mack Smith, *Mussolini* (London: Weidenfeld and Nicolson, 1982). In Italian, there is Renzo De Felice's magisterial *Mussolini*, 4 vols. in 6 parts (Turin: Einaudi, 1965–91).

8. Nicholas A. Stigliani and Antonette Marzotto, "Fascist Anti-semitism and the Italian Jews," *Wiener Library Bulletin* 28, nos. 35/36 (1975): 41–49.

9. Quoted in Michaelis, *Mussolini and the Jews*, p. 31.

10. Anthony Rhodes, *The Vatican in the Age of the Dictators, 1922–1945* (London: Hodder and Stoughton, 1973), pp. 48, 63–64.

11. MacGregor Knox, "Conquest, Foreign and Domestic, in Fascist Italy and Nazi Germany," *Journal of Modern History* 56 (1984): 1–57.

12. Emil Ludwig, *Talks with Mussolini* (London: Allen and Unwin, 1932), p. 74.

13. Nahum Goldmann, *Memories* (London: Weidenfeld and Nicolson, 1969), pp. 154–63.

14. Michaelis, *Mussolini and the Jews*, p. 49.

15. For example, Luigi Preti, *Impero fascista, africani ed ebrei* (Milan: Mursia, 1968); E. M. Robertson, "Race as a Factor in Mussolini's Policy in Africa and Europe," *Journal of Contemporary History* 23 (1988): 37–58.

16. Michaelis, *Mussolini and the Jews*, p. 164.

17. Gene Bernardini, "The Origins and Development of Racial Antisemitism in Fascist Italy," *Journal of Modern History* 49 (1977): 431–53. See also Dante Germino, *The Italian Fascist Party in Power* (Minneapolis: University of Minnesota Press, 1959).

18. Martin Clark, *Modern Italy, 1871–1982* (London: Longman, 1984), pp. 257–59; Michael A. Ledeen, "Evolution of Italian Fascist Antisemitism," *Jewish Social Studies* 37 (1975): 3–17.

19. Paolo Orano, *Gli ebrei in Italia* (Rome: Pinciana, 1937).

20. De Felice, *Storia degli ebrei italiani*, app. 16.

21. Quoted ibid., p. 254.

22. Interlandi is the central figure in Giampiero Mughini's *A via della mercede c'era un razzista* (Milan: Rizzoli, 1991). He was an urbane Sicilian and also editor of the Fascist daily, *Il Tevere* (1924–43), and his conversion to anti-Semitism appears to have been as sudden as that of the Fascist regime itself.

23. John F. Morley, *Vatican Diplomacy and the Jews During the Holocaust* (New York: Ktav, 1980), p. 169.

24. For regulations and exemptions, see De Felice, *Storia degli ebrei italiani*, app. 22.

25. Peter C. Kent, "A Tale of Two Popes: Pius XI, Pius XII, and the Rome-Berlin Axis," *Journal of Contemporary History* 23, no. 4 (1988): 589–608.

26. Klaus Voigt, "Gli emigranti in Italia dai paesi sotto la dominazione nazista: Tollerati e perseguitati, 1933–40," *Storia Contemporanea* 16 (1985): 45–87.

27. Galeazzo Ciano, July 15, 1938, *Diario, 1937–43*, ed. Renzo De Felice (Milan: Rizzoli, 1980), p. 158.

28. Quoted in Michaelis, *Mussolini and the Jews*, p. 291.

29. Zuccotti, *Italians and the Holocaust*, p. 64.

30. An authoritative account of Italo-German differences in these areas is Jonathan Steinberg's *All or Nothing: The Axis and the Holocaust, 1941–1943* (London: Routledge, 1990). See also Daniele Carpi, "Rescue of Jews in the Italian Zone of Occupied Croatia," in *Rescue Attempts During the Holocaust*, ed. Yisrael Gutman and Efraim Zuroff (New York, Ktav, 1978), pp. 465–525; Jacques Sabille, "Attitude of the Italians to the Jews in Occupied Greece," in *Jews Under the Italian Occupation*, ed. L. Poliakov and J. Sabille (Paris: Centre de Documentation Juive Contemporaine, 1955), pp. 151–60; Léon Poliakov, "Jews under Italian Occupation in France," ibid., pp. 17–44.

31. Michael Marrus and Robert Paxton, *Vichy France and the Jews* (New York: Schocken Books, 1981).

32. Quoted in Steinberg, *All or Nothing*, p. 124.

33. Christopher R. Browning, *The Final Solution and the German Foreign Office, 1940–43* (New York: Holmes and Meier, 1978).

34. Quoted in Michaelis, *Mussolini and the Jews*, p. 337.

35. Quoted in Nicola Caracciolo, *Gli ebrei e l'Italia durante la guerra, 1940–45* (Rome: Bonacci, 1986), p. 122.

36. Steinberg, *All or Nothing*, p. 169.

37. Quoted in Robert Katz, *Black Sabbath* (London: Arthur Barker, 1969), p. 48.

38. Quoted in Owen Chadwick, "Weizsäcker, the Vatican, and the Jews of Rome," *Journal of Ecclesiastical History* 28 (1977): 194. See also Leonidas E. Hill, "The Vatican Embassy of Ernst von Weizsäcker," *Journal of Modern History* 39 (1967): 138–59.

39. English-language translations of Hochhuth's play have been published as *The Representative* (London: Methuen, 1963) and *The Deputy* (New York: Samuel French, 1965).

40. Morley, *Vatican Diplomacy and the Jews*, pp. 164–78.

41. Michaelis, *Mussolini and the Jews*, p. 377.

42. Quoted in De Felice, *Storia degli ebrei italiani*, p. 446.

43. Zuccotti, *Italians and the Holocaust*, p. 176.

44. Ricciotti Lazzero, *Le SS italiane: Storia dei 20,000 che giurarono fedeltà a Hitler* (Milan: Rizzoli, 1982).

45. Ricciotti Lazzero, *Le brigate nere: Il partito armato della repubblica di Mussolini* (Milan: Rizzoli, 1983).

46. Quoted in Michaelis, *Mussolini and the Jews*, pp. 380–81.

47. Primo Levi, *If This Is a Man* (London: Orion, 1960), p. 7.

48. Enzo Collotti, *L'amministrazione tedesca dell'Italia occupata, 1943–45* (Milan: Istituto Nazionale per la Storia del Movimento di Liberazione in Italia, 1963).

49. Robert Katz, *Death in Rome* (London: Jonathan Cape, 1967).

50. Silva Bon Gherardi, "Un campo di sterminio in Italia," *Il Ponte* 34 (1978): 1440–53.

51. Preziosi, anticipating Jewish vengeance, committed suicide together with his wife on April 26, 1945, by leaping from the fifth floor of a Milanese house. Pavolini and Buffarini Guidi tried, like Mussolini, to flee to Switzerland, but were captured and summarily executed by Italian resistance fighters. Farinacci was also executed by partisans. The leaders of the Muti, Carità, and Koch bands all met a violent death in the final stages of Italy's liberation either at the hands of the Allies or the resistance. Of the Nazi anti-Semites most active in Italy, Kappler was tried by an Italian military tribunal in 1948 and sentenced to life imprisonment, but he escaped from a Roman military hospital where he was being treated for cancer in 1977 and died in West Germany the next year. The fate of Dannecker is uncertain, but he probably committed suicide in American captivity in 1945. Bosshammer was not brought to justice until 1972, when he received a life sentence from a West Berlin court; however, he was released after a few months and died, also of cancer, shortly thereafter.

52. De Felice, *Storia degli ebrei italiani*, pp. 465–66.

53. Zuccotti, *Italians and the Holocaust*, especially pp. xv–xviii, 276–85.

54. Liliana Picciotti Fargion, "La participazione ebraica alla resistenza," in Centro di Documentazione Ebraica Contemporanea, *Ebrei in Italia: Deportazione, resistenza* (Florence, 1974), pp. 43–53.

55. Steinberg, *All or Nothing*, pp. 8–9. But see also Steinberg's deference to national character, p. 229.

56. Ibid., pp. 170ff.

57. This exegesis on Italian civility is wittily and trenchantly argued by Joseph LaPalombara, *Democracy, Italian Style* (New Haven: Yale University Press, 1987).

58. Quoted in Zuccotti, *Italians and the Holocaust*, p. 94 (italics added).

59. For comparative statistics, see Raul Hilberg, *The Destruction of the European Jews*, rev. ed. (New York: Holmes and Meier, 1985), vol. 3, app. B; Gerald Reitlinger, *The Final Solution*, 2d rev. ed. (London: Vallentine, Mitchell, 1968), app. 1.

60. On the theory of "parallel nationalization," see Antonio Gramsci's posthumously published writings in *Il Risorgimento* (1949): 166–68.

61. Michaelis, *Mussolini and the Jews*, p. 414.

62. H. Stuart Hughes, *Prisoners of Hope: The Silver Age of the Italian Jews, 1924– 1974* (Cambridge, Mass.: Harvard University Press, 1983).

## SELECT BIBLIOGRAPHY

Bassani, Giorgio. *The Garden of the Finzi-Continis*. San Diego, Calif.: Harcourt Brace Jovanovich, 1977.

Bernardini, Gene. "The Origins and Development of Racial Antisemitism in Fascist Italy." *Journal of Modern History* 49 (1977): 431–53.

Caracciolo, Nicola. *Gli ebrei e l'Italia durante la guerra, 1940–45*. Rome: Bonacci, 1986.

Carpi, Daniele. "Rescue of Jews in the Italian Zone of Occupied Croatia." In *Rescue Attempts During the Holocaust*, edited by Yisrael Gutman and Efraim Zuroff, pp. 465–525. New York: Ktav, 1978.

Centro di Documentazione Ebraica Contemporanea. *Ebrei in Italia: Deportazione, resistenza*. Florence, 1974.

———. *Gli ebrei in Italia durante il fascismo*. (Quaderni). Milan, 1962–63.

Chadwick, Owen. "Weizsäcker, the Vatican, and the Jews of Rome." *Journal of Ecclesiastical History* 28 (1977): 179–99.

Collotti, Enzo. *L'amministrazione tedesca dell'Italia occupata, 1943–45*. Milan: Istituto Nazionale per la Storia del Movimento di Liberazione in Italia, 1963.

De Felice, Renzo. *Storia degli ebrei italiani sotto il fascismo*. 4th ed. Turin: Einaudi, 1988.

Della Seta, Fabio. *The Tiber Afire*. Marlboro, Vt.: Marlboro Press, 1991.

Fornari, Harry. *Mussolini's Gadfly: Roberto Farinacci*. Nashville: Vanderbilt University Press, 1971.

Ginzburg, Natalia. *Family Sayings*. New York: Carcarnet, 1984.

Hughes, H. Stuart. *Prisoners of Hope: The Silver Age of the Italian Jews, 1924–74*. Cambridge, Mass.: Harvard University Press, 1983.

Katz, Robert. *Black Sabbath*. London: Arthur Barker, 1969.

Lazzero, Ricciotti. *Le brigate nere: Il partito armato della repubblica di Mussolini*. Milan: Rizzoli, 1983.

Ledeen, Michael A. "Evolution of Italian Fascist Antisemitism." *Jewish Social Studies* 37 (1975): 3–17.

Levi, Primo. *If This Is a Man*. London: Orion, 1960.

Mayda, Giuseppe. *Ebrei sotto Salò: La persecuzione antisemita, 1943–1995*. Milan: Feltrinelli, 1978.

Michaelis, Meir. *Mussolini and the Jews: German-Italian Relations and the Jewish Question in Italy, 1922–1945*. Oxford: Clarendon Press, 1978.

Morley, John F. *Vatican Diplomacy and the Jews During the Holocaust*. New York: Ktav, 1980.

Mughini, Giampiero. *A via della mercede c'era un razzista*. Milan: Rizzoli, 1991.

Picciotti Fargion, Liliana. L'*Occupazione tedesca e gli ebrei di Roma*. Rome: Carucci, 1978.

Poliakov, Léon, and Jacques Sabille, eds. *Jews Under the Italian Occupation*. Paris: Centre de Documentation Juive Contemporaine, 1955.

*Il Ponte* (Florence) 34, nos. 11/12 (1978).

Preti, Luigi. *Impero fascista, africani ed ebrei*. Milan: Mursia, 1968.

Robertson, Esmonde M. "Race as a Factor in Mussolini's Policy in Africa and Europe." *Journal of Contemporary History* 23 (1988): 37–58.

Roth, Cecil. *The History of the Jews in Italy*. Philadelphia: Jewish Publication Society of America, 1946.

Segrè, Dan Vittorio. *Memoirs of a Fortunate Jew*. Bethesda, Md.: Adler and Adler, 1987.

Steinberg, Jonathan. *All or Nothing: The Axis and the Holocaust, 1941–1943*. London: Routledge, 1990.

Stigliani, Nicholas A., and Antonette Marzotto. "Fascist Antisemitism and the Italian Jews." *Wiener Library Bulletin*, 28, nos. 35/36 (1975): 41–49.

Voigt, Klaus. "Gli emigranti in Italia dai paesi sotto la dominazione nazista: Tollerati e perseguitati, 1933–40." *Storia Contemporanea* 16 (1985): 45–87.

Zuccotti, Susan. *The Italians and the Holocaust: Persecution, Rescue, and Survival*. New York: Basic Books, 1987.

# Chapter 19

# The Holocaust in Spain

## John Axe

The saga of Jews in Spain represents one of the more curious chapters in the history of the Holocaust. Regarded as the Golden Land for Sephardic Jews during the Middle Ages, the home of Maimonides, Ibn Gabirol, and Judah Halevi, Spain was also the site of some of the worst bigotry and brutal tortures in the fifteenth century. Its Inquisitors devised a certificate of blood dating back seven generations that served as a model for Nazi race laws. When the united forces of Castile and Aragon defeated the Moors, Jews, like Muslims, were summarily expelled in 1492. Unlike other expulsions that proved temporary in mainland Europe, this one held true until 1924, when Ferdinand's edict was formally repealed. The few Jews who returned from North Africa or France sympathized with the Republican revolution and could only be intimidated by the rise to power of General Francisco Franco during the Spanish civil war between 1936 and 1939.

Until his death in 1975, Franco ruled Spain as a Fascist tyrant. His regime owed its life to fellow dictators Adolf Hitler and Benito Mussolini. During the war years Franco offered frequent and public expressions of sympathy and respect for the Axis. Franco also managed to steer clear of joining either side in the conflict, helped avert an Allied invasion of Spain, and may also have helped forestall Operation Gisela, the German High Command's code name for a projected takeover of its Spanish flank. Such cautious diplomacy even benefitted Europe's Jews, thousands of whom escaped into Spain, where they were cared for by the American Joint Distribution Committee (JDC), the Quakers, and other interested individuals, among them American Ambassador Carlton J. H. Hayes. Until the Allied invasion of North Africa, Spain and Portugal (also ruled by a tyrant, Antonio Salazar) served as a conduit, however limited, for Jews fleeing to North Africa or the Western Hemisphere. More remarkably, before the end of World War II the Franco regime refused to turn over its own Jews and also actively intervened on behalf of Jews in Bulgaria, Macedonia and other parts of Greece, Hungary, France, and Romania who traced their lineage back to the Iberian Peninsula.

Ever since, survivors, politicians, and scholars have attempted to understand why Franco acted as he did. My own research, dating back more than twenty years, with the Ministerio de Asuntos (the Foreign Office) and the Arias Montano Institute in Madrid, the mayor's office in Valladolid (onetime administrative center of Spain), and a host of other archives leaves me wondering yet.

It requires more than police tactics to remain dictator of the Spanish people for almost forty years. Just as it is incorrect to classify all the Loyalists of the Spanish civil war as "Communists," Franco himself was not a German- or even Italian-style Fascist. On February 26, 1938, Franco's typewritten *Noticiero de España* (Spain's reporter), the weekly guide of civil-war events and his party's guide to thought and action, reported Hitler's latest speech in lyrical terms and said that he supported the Nationalist uprising as a crusade of the nation against communism. Supporters of the Republic would have cited this pamphlet as proof of Franco's Nazi nature, but his *Noticiero* of January 8 had carried an erudite and humane article on the Jews by the greatest twentieth-century Spanish novelist, Pío Baroja, who calmly and methodically refuted Hitler's anti-Semitic race theories without mentioning either Hitler or the Nazis. It was one thing to accept aid from Hitler and praise him a bit, especially when Franco knew that he would need more to win his war, but even then his regime did not care to absorb nonsensical theories about Jews and Aryans.[1]

On June 30, 1942, six weeks after President Roosevelt's newly appointed ambassador to Spain, Carlton J. H. Hayes, arrived, he reported to the president on Franco, based on personal observations:

Nor does General Franco entirely conform to the Hitler-Mussolini norm of "dictator." True, he wears a colored wool shirt and receives Fascist salutes from the faithful. But the faithful seem to be somewhat scarce and their salutes a bit perfunctory, while the wearer of the supreme shirt is strangely taciturn and untheatrical. The Papal Nuncio tells me there is an old Spanish proverb about a Galician being "as prudent as a bear, as stubborn as a mule, and as dumb as an ox," and that the proverb is particularly applicable to the Galician Franco.[2]

Later in the letter Hayes predicted a shift in the policy of the Franco regime as German fortunes might ebb and internal criticism develop within Spain. Hayes's role was to court the favor of the Spanish chief of state and to house him securely in the camp of the Allies. There were advantages for Spain also. In Hayes's October 29, 1942, letter to Roosevelt he told the president:

At Granada, the Military and Civil Governors and the Mayor all expressed appreciation of your interest in the resumption and expansion of the tourist-trade. "Turismo" has been, of course, Granada's chief industry; with its practical disappearance during the past six years, the city's economy has suffered grievously; and the prospect of eventually resuscitating it is especially alluring.[3]

Hayes told Roosevelt that there was "a crying need—and the golden opportunity—for the right kinds of propaganda" in Spain.[4] The diplomatic maneuvers of the ambassador were in the interest of winning the war for the Allies. He was not briefed on seeking aid for Jews as a priority. At that time they were being hauled away from their homes in Europe and were being "resettled" in Hitler's famous death camps. Washington had been aware for two years of the brutal deportations of Jews to concentration camps and since June 1941 had witnessed examples of Hitler's mass killings in Russia. In 1942 General Franco would have been receptive to an organized rescue plan for Jews.

## THE WOLFRAM CRISIS

In 1940 thousands of refugees began pouring over the Pyrenees into Spain, aided by paid French guides. The majority of these refugees were Jews who had had their original German, Polish, Hungarian, or other citizenship annulled by the Nazis and were without regular passports. Ambassador Hayes in Madrid recognized the urgency of their condition, which increased over the next three years, and in December 1942 set up a special "refugee and relief section" of the embassy under the direction of Niles Bond, the third secretary of the ambassador's staff. With the cooperation of the British ambassador in Madrid, Sir Samuel Hoare, arrangements were made to solicit funds and supplies to care for the refugees until they could be received elsewhere. Both Hayes and Hoare pledged to press the Spanish Foreign Office to ensure the proper reception and handling of these people and their eventual evacuation to North Africa.[5]

The Allies were at the same time attempting to free French North Africa from Axis military control, and some of the refugees were French troops who could assist in this operation. In the summer of 1943 another crisis developed, to which the State Department of the United States wanted the staff in Madrid to grant full priority to aid the Allied cause. This was the situation of wolfram ore that was being exported from Spain, which had unlimited quantities, to Germany, which required it for war production.

While Hitler was putting into motion his Final Solution for the Jews of the countries in which Panzer divisions were creating more *Lebensraum* for the Germans, Spain continued to trade with the Nazi homeland. Carlton J. H. Hayes, in *Wartime Mission in Spain*, claims that Spain did not export food products to Germany to aid the Axis powers against the Allies. The exports were in payment for imports that economically bankrupt Spain required to furnish materials that the Allies, for war reasons, were unable or unwilling to supply, such as heavy machinery, precision tools, buses and streetcars, chemicals and drugs, and seed potatoes. Spain did not export wheat to Germany, and even as late as January 1944 Germany was exporting 20,000 tons of wheat to Spain.

The greatest exportation problem confronting the ambassador was the "Wolfram crisis." The Nazis needed a supply of wolfram ore, from which steel-hardening tungsten is derived. It was in plentiful supply in the Iberian Peninsula and was not available in Germany, and Hitler was wholly dependent upon this source. From August 1943 until the end of April 1944 the project to embargo the export of wolfram ore was given more priority than saving lives in jeopardy.

A confidential staff memorandum to the ambassador on November 13, 1943, informed him of the benefits of an embargo on wolfram:

The Spanish Government has an obligation to foster the interests of the Spanish people.

It is in the interest of the Spanish people, as of all other peoples, that the war be brought to a swift conclusion.

An embargo on the export of wolfram would contribute in some degree to this end.

It is obviously in the interest of the Spanish people that economic relations between Spain and the United Nations be strengthened. The embargo would have this result.

An embargo on the export of wolfram would not be a breach of Spanish neutrality. It is within the sovereign right of the Spanish Government to impose such an embargo. The direct significance of such an embargo is purely internal and no foreign country has the right to object to it.

If the Spanish Government would object that the embargo would, in fact, be discriminatory against Germany we can point out that in 1940 and 1941 Spanish olive oil was sent to Germany and Italy while none was permitted to be exported to the United States. This was, in fact, direct discrimination against one of the belligerents in the present war. We are asking nothing like this in the case of wolfram.[6]

Another confidential memorandum on December 2, 1943, referred to a conversation between the Spanish under secretary for foreign affairs and Williard L. Beaulac, who advised Hayes:

Germany was still getting wolfram out of Spain and although we were getting the larger part of Spain's production, Germany's net purchases had not declined in any important degree. We had no use for the wolfram we purchased, and therefore Spain should contemplate the possibility that we might cease buying wolfram. The shock to Spanish economy, in that event, would be very great, as he [the minister of foreign affairs, Count Jordana] must realize.

I said that we had made a proposal which would eliminate the possibility of any such shock to Spanish economy. We were, in effect, offering Spain the opportunity to resume what amounted to normal trade with the democracies. This was an opportunity which few, if any, countries in the world had today, and we thought very seriously that Spain should take advantage of it. We proposed nothing that was not in Spain's interest; on the other hand, we were offering to Spain adequate insurance against a possible serious disruption in its economy.[7]

Through countless memoranda and much correspondence we learn the diplomatic endeavor to stop the exportation of wolfram:

> Count Jordana, the Spanish Foreign Minister, was reportedly deeply troubled over the
> matter in January of 1944 when Hayes brought it up to him. The Spanish Government
> continued to delay and failed to reply when the Ambassador's staff proposed discussions
> on the matter, and finally claimed that the delays were because of "Spanish economic
> and political matters."[8]

An embargo on wolfram to Germany would greatly affect the economy. Many
private interests involved in the production of wolfram were exerting strong
influence and were alarmed at the prospect of an embargo. The minister of
finance was likewise involved and alarmed, as was the Ministry of Industry and
Commerce, because the embargo on the one-third of wolfram production going
to Germany would affect most of the business of private interests as well as the
Spanish treasury.

At the time Spain had been actively cooperating with the Allies and had
declared neutrality, which evoked protest from Germany because of "the French
and other refugees" who were permitted to pass through Spain to safety or to
join the Allied armies in North Africa. Spain feared the large German forces
stationed on the frontier. An advisor of the ambassador informed him that if
Spain were to preserve its neutrality and stay out of the war, it had to "give to
both sides."[9] The embargo on wolfram would mean a break with Germany
because Germany would not tolerate it; and on the other hand, the Spanish
economy would suffer from such drastic action.

## SPAIN BECOMES AN "ALLY"

On the political side, all the moves that Spain had made in relation with the
Allies had been done in Spain's interest, such as accepting supplies of petroleum
from American republics. Hayes reminded Count Jordana that if the Axis powers
were in the position to, they would not hesitate to add Spain to their conquests.

At the same time the BBC in London increased the violence of its attacks
against Spain in broadcasts in several languages. The British had been attacking
Spain through radio broadcasts because of Spain's "friendly agreements" with
Germany and its exportation of products used by Germany in the war against
the Allies. The U.S. diplomatic plan did not include public pressure on Spain
and feared that attacks of the sneering and sarcastic British variety would cause
continued resistance to the requests to halt the shipment of wolfram and would
send Spain to Germany's side.[10] Hayes rushed off an urgent telegram to the
State Department in Washington to inform Cordell Hull, the secretary of state,
that the British ambassador, Sir Samuel Hoare, had promised to end the BBC
campaign and had agreed that diplomatic channels and little publicity would
have more success in halting the loadings to Germany. Hayes was afraid that

the radio attacks would cause Spain to line up with Germany because they accused Spain of harboring Nazi spies when the Spanish government knew full well that Hayes's extensive staff was heavily manned with U.S. government agents involved in espionage work. He strongly urged that the publicity concerning relations with Spain be handled through the State Department and not by radio from London.[11]

In January and February 1944 Ambassador Hayes in Spain and Secretary of State Hull in Washington exchanged a series of telegrams written in code involving the wolfram crisis. In January shipments of petroleum were delayed and were being withheld from Spain. Ambassador Cárdenas, representing Spain in Washington, complained and was reminded of the Italian ships harbored in Spain, the continuing activity of German espionage and sabotage, the Spanish Blue Division (Spanish volunteers soldiering for Germany) that was fighting in Russia, financial arrangements with Germany, the prospect of a revival of German imports, and the request for an embargo on wolfram. The Spanish ambassador was informed that if these problems were considered in earnest, the tankers would not be suspended. Hull felt that Spain should anticipate its long-term interests after the Allies had won the war, at which time there would be no market for wolfram ore. Hayes was warned to watch internal developments in Spain closely and to report them currently.[12]

The State Department requested that the American shortwave broadcasts and the BBC attacks on Spain be halted to make Count Jordana more receptive to understanding the Allied point of view. Drastic shortages in the supply of gasoline in Spain were a reminder that affected all citizens, whom Franco had to keep content. The fuel supply had been cut to 50 percent by the beginning of February. The day after Hayes dutifully reported the results of the fuel cutoff, Hull again reminded him that every ton of wolfram entering Germany was being "directly translated into terms of American casualties, and that the government was still awaiting concrete assurances from Spain respecting its desires."[13]

Hull continued to work with the Spanish ambassador in Washington. Cárdenas told him that when in 1940 Spain was unfriendly toward the United States, it continued to be kind and considerate; and that when Spain endeavored to be considerate later, the United States exercised considerable pressure. Spain claimed that it feared a German invasion if the wolfram exports were halted. Cárdenas was convinced that Russia was exerting pressure, and he feared for the 1,500 members of the Blue Division who remained on the eastern front. Russia was supposedly arousing Britain and America in order to attack the Caudillo directly.[14]

The three-month delay in solving the wolfram crisis passed more slowly in Washington than it did in Madrid, where delays are considered normal. Cárdenas promised Hull that Spain would be America's eternal friend if the United States could only exercise patience and allow Spain to remain neutral.

Hayes reached the conclusion that if Spain could be guaranteed an increase in the exportation of commodities such as fruit, fish, and cotton goods, he would be in a better position to negotiate with Count Jordana over the embargo to Germany, but Hull insisted on the discontinuation of the tanker loadings until a complete and permanent wolfram embargo had been established.[15] Hayes reported back that a demand for an embargo would violate Spanish sovereignty and that Franco and his cabinet would never accept such dictation, but if petroleum shipments would resume, they would be in a better position to drastically limit wolfram exports. Hull did not appreciate the remark made by the Spanish foreign minister that "Spain had done the United Nations a great service by not embarking on an aggression against them," which he repeated to Hayes, and declared that the United States would make no economic sacrifices to Spain until the desired embargo was completed, convincing him of neutrality.[16]

By the end of February 1944 Finland appeared interested in purchasing the wolfram in return for nickel that Spain urgently needed. This market was discovered to satisfy the Spanish economy and to avoid protests from labor and mine owners in Spain. Count Jordana then told Sir Samuel Hoare that the Spanish government was prepared to do the following things: (1) to expel the German military agents and the German Consulate from Tangier; (2) to put a drastic stop in North Africa and Spain to the espionage activities of the Germans; (3) to dissolve and repatriate Spanish units on the Russian front and not allow any new units or reliefs to leave Spain; (4) to settle the question of the Italian merchant ships on terms agreeable to the United States and the British; (5) to refer to arbitration the question of the release of Italian warships; and (6) to give every facility to assure a drastic limitation on wolfram exports to Germany.[17]

On February 28, 1944, Hayes was able to relate to Hull that Jordana had confirmed that wolfram exports to Germany would be reduced to 10 percent of the 1943 production and that the other five points promised to Hoare would be fulfilled. Spain was not losing out either. It was promised American markets for its commodities and that all arrears in capital indebtedness from American interests would be cleared. Yet Count Jordana continued to insist that the Spanish government was receiving pressure from Germany, whose spies had discovered the planned embargo, and produced a threatening note from the German embassy.[18]

The British had played no small role in all this. A final agreement was reached with the Spanish by the end of April 1944, but as late as April 25 Winston Churchill had indicated to President Roosevelt that unless the United States went along with Great Britain, "the latter would conclude an independent agreement with Spain and furnish petroleum, thereby advertising to the world a cleavage between the English-speaking Allies."[19] Portugal had already established a complete wolfram embargo, and the State Department turned its attention to the fact that Spain, now "friendly enough," was still a Fascist regime, although it had disassociated itself from the most hideous branch of fascism.[20]

## AMBASSADOR HAYES AND REFUGEES

The problem of eliciting an embargo on wolfram occupied a great deal of time and involved countless hours of work on the part of the ambassador and his staff. The embargo was essential in curtailing German war production, but it had relegated the "refugee problem" to secondary importance.

Thousands of Jews looked to the Iberian Peninsula as a place of sanctuary or a place from which to continue their journey to lands where they could escape Nazi wrath. Even the tiny state of Andorra, nestled high in the Pyrenees between Spain and France, was filled with Jewish refugees.

Tens of thousands of Jewish victims of Nazi atrocity poured into Spain in 1942 and 1943. They came from France, Holland, Belgium, Hungary, Poland, Czechoslovakia, and Austria. With no money and no food and nowhere to go, they were placed in camps, such as the one at Miranda del Ebro, which rapidly became unsanitary with overcrowding and inadequate facilities. This caused not only a financial burden on the Spanish government but diplomatic problems with the Germans, who insisted that these people would pass into Allied hands and take up arms against Germany.

Sir Samuel Hoare and members of the British embassy devoted much of their time to helping the refugees and to putting pressure on the Spanish authorities to improve conditions for them. But Hoare's version of the situation, found in *Complacent Dictator*, a memoir of his years in Spain, is inaccurate and at times deliberately incorrect. According to him, all refugees who did not seek British protection were ruthlessly herded into concentration camps where they lived under impossible and inhumane conditions and where most of the relief they received came from British charities. Hoare constantly cites the delays by the Spanish government that thwarted his own attempts to assist the refugees, but says that there were never anti-Jewish methods adopted by the Spanish government.[21]

The account of Carlton J. H. Hayes appears to be more objective. He tells in *Wartime Mission in Spain* that in the 1942 and 1943 period when the greatest number of refugees poured into Spain from France, Spain was going through a period of great shortages in food and other supplies, not having recovered from the civil war, and the delays were caused by the traditionally slow procedures of the Spanish ministers and the problem of German threats. Count Jordana promised the American ambassador, however, that Spain would resist all German pressure and threats of aggression designed to impede the release of prisoners who might be helpful to the Allied cause and that the Spanish government, and also that of Portugal, would provide transport ships to evacuate refugees to North Africa, where they could join the Allies. As for Spain not aiding the refugees, Hayes claims:

The Spanish Government had not closed its frontiers to refugees but had allowed them to enter and cross the country with considerable freedom. Their "travel documents" were not too meticulously inspected. Yet, in view of the very bad economic and food conditions in Spain in 1940–1941, the Government was reluctant to play permanent host to any large number of alien refugees.[22]

Many of the unfortunates who struggled across the Pyrenees in deep snow were homeless Jews. Allied officials at the time argued that there were Nazi agents planted among these refugees and that they should not be granted passage to Africa, but the Spanish government granted the passage to Africa, where the Allies ushered them into detention camps upon their arrival. Hoare even states that the Franco government tried to prevent the arrival of the Sephardic community from Salonika, yet we shall see how it directly intervened to save these people from the ovens of the death camps. Hayes's account of his part in helping the "stateless persons," by which he means "chiefly Jewish,"[23] although more accurate, shows that he did not do all that he might have.

From 1940 to 1942 most of the Jews who came to Spain crossed the country to Lisbon in Portugal, from where they departed to America or Britain. By 1942 there were an estimated 1,500 to 2,000 who preferred to remain in Spain or who lacked the means of going elsewhere. The care of the "stateless persons" was left entirely to "American humanitarian organizations,"[24] which consisted of the Jewish Joint Distribution Committee and the Quakers but no others, until a late time when aid was also offered by the Unitarian Service Committee and the War Relief Services of the National Catholic Welfare Conference. In addition to Jews, among the refugees were "some of France's finest military leadership and thousands of her best fighting men."[25] For this second group the State Department of the United States turned to the American Red Cross, which promptly placed $25,000 at its disposal, immediately adding another $50,000 provided by President Roosevelt. In addition, the non-Jewish refugees were treated to warm knitted garments from the "sewing circles of Mrs. Hayes," "comfort kits" from the American Catholic Bishops, and "sympathetic cooperation" from the Spanish Red Cross.[26]

From among the five thousand apparently undisturbed documents deposited at the Butler Library of Columbia University by the estate of Carlton Hayes, the earliest report on "The Refugee Problem in Spain" is dated April 21, 1942; although Hayes did not reach Madrid until May 16, 1942. Hayes was informed that at this time it was against Spanish law to form any type of Jewish organization for any purpose whatsoever, which greatly hindered the work of the JDC. The JDC had approached the wife of the previous American ambassador, Alexander Wilbourne Weddell, in January 1941. Mrs. Virginia Chase Weddell had already undertaken to represent several relief agencies in Spain and to disburse their funds, and she graciously consented to distribute the equivalents in Spanish currency from money that the JDC had deposited in her bank account in New York. Mrs. Weddell focused her principal attention on the plight of the Jews who were in the internment camp at Miranda del Ebro and on aiding the families of men who were imprisoned there. She sent food and clothing to the camp and granted cash allotments in individual cases.[27]

At the same time there were also a few hundred Jews in Spain who had entered the country earlier and who had exhausted their resources. The JDC maintained them in hotels through a representative of the JDC, as it was not possible to conduct organized relief work. The Jewish people were threatened with imprisonment because they had entered the country illegally, but they were permitted to remain in the country, costing the JDC $183,000 during 1941 and the first three months of 1942. The only other outside aid that the Jews were receiving at this time was from Protestant and Catholic groups in France, led by Dr. Marc Boëgner and Cardinal Guerlier, who provided them with supplies for their flight to Spain.[28]

In March 1943 Hayes's office was visited by Señor Baraibar, the chief of the European Section of the Ministry of Foreign Affairs, who informed the ambassador that the Spanish government would grant visas to some three hundred Jews in Germany who were of Sephardic origin if the JDC would guarantee that they would be transported elsewhere within six weeks or so. Baraibar emphasized that this information was to be entirely confidential, that it could be discussed only with the American ambassador, and that the entire project was extremely urgent, as he had information that new regulations would be applied against the Jews in Germany on April 4.[29]

From the interoffice correspondence of the American embassy in Madrid it appears that the Spanish government had made the first overtures in assisting Jews. Yet by the end of March 1943 the embassy received information that the Spanish Foreign Office planned to close the Pyrenees border frontier to all undocumented persons.[30] The Hayes office planned to inform the Spanish of the inadvisability of this scheme. By turning back refugees from the borders, Spain would appear in world opinion to be collaborating with the Germans in their effort to enslave the people of Europe; Franco was reminded that his troops were permitted to enter France during the civil war and continue their journey to Nationalist Spanish territory; there was no justification for returning escaped prisoners of war; and it was the obligation of the French and the Germans to prevent their escape, not that of Spain.

Hayes had come to Spain to influence Spain not to join the Axis, to encourage Spain to resist any Axis invasion or the threat of an invasion, and to obtain from Spain every possible facility for an Allied plan of warfare against Germany. Roosevelt had elicited a promise from Hayes that he would refrain from interference in any internal affairs in Spain, always having been cautious about making Jewish refugees a priority.[31]

On May 3, 1943, Hayes reported the situation on the "refugee problem" to the president. After November 11, 1942, when the Germans overran the previously "unoccupied" part of France, an additional fifteen thousand refugees, including many Jews, crossed the Pyrenees into Spain. Count Jordana is credited with convincing the ultracautious Caudillo and important Falangist elements to grant asylum to these persons. The Spanish government's policy involved the following points: (1) positive refusal to return any refugees to France; (2) the removal of the refugees from internment camps as soon as possible; (3) evacuation of refugees from Spain and arrangements for their transit through Portugal; (4) informal recognition of the French North African regime; (5) facilities to be extended to other Allied embassies for the care of refugees of their respective nationalities; and (6) recognition of official agents of the Joint Distribution Committee, the Quakers, and the American and British Red Cross and granting them the power to dispense relief to refugees who had to remain in Spain because they had no other place to go. Roosevelt was also informed of the help granted by the Portuguese ambassador in Madrid and by Antonio Salazar, the dictator of Portugal, in Lisbon, who permitted refugees to cross into Portugal and who granted use of Portuguese ports for transport to North Africa.[32]

Hayes did concede that all this cooperation was aided by the fact that the Allies were conducting a successful military campaign in Tunis and that there was a growing conviction in Spain that the Axis was losing the war and that the United States was winning it. He added that U.S. policy toward Spain in respecting its neutrality and territorial integrity and in supplying it with petroleum and other essential products, as well as continuing to establish friendly relations with the Spanish people, had aided this cause.

Within the ambassador's staff there were unfavorable reports about the JDC from some officials. They claimed that the JDC was only interested in aiding Jewish refugees and that its primary aim was to get the refugees to the United States, not just out of Spain. R. Brandin, who issued the report, did credit the JDC with aiding a great number of persons who had no other organization from which to elicit aid, but criticized it heavily for not discriminating "between worthy cases and unworthy ones."[33]

The same staff also calmly submitted firsthand reports from those whom the JDC aided in a Pamplona prison. A Frenchman told Percy Winner of the embassy that he had seen "many thousands of Jews" murdered in the ghetto of Lwow in Poland, and that the next month an additional 15,000 were massacred in a five-day period; he told of the three Blazquiz brothers, Basques from France, who had helped 1,500 Jews over the Pyrenees into Spain; he related the history of Jews who had escaped from the concentration camp of Ferramonti in Italy.[34]

## THE YEAR 1944

On January 4, 1944, before the formation of the War Refugee Board, Hayes had issued a telegram to the secretary of state concerning the plight of refugees. He cited the already-known fact of the "several thousand" refugees who were in Spanish concentration camps and prisons, described the great suffering they were undergoing due to an inadequacy of housing, food, medicines, heat, clothing, and sanitary facilities, and stated that the Spanish minister of the interior was hindering efforts to ease the hardships of these people. Hayes urged Secretary Hull to summon the Spanish ambassador to Washington, Cárdenas, and remind him that Spain was now being accepted as a neutral.[35]

In late June 1944 it was learned that the Jews of Hungary were to be deported to Nazi death camps, and the War Relief Board cabled Hayes to act more quickly in obtaining protection in Spain for Jewish refugees. Even Cardinal Spellman, the archbishop of New York, was quoted in the coded telegram to convince

Hayes, a practicing Catholic, that the Nazis planned to "annihilate the race from which Jesus and Mary sprang."[36] At the same time, the WRB was trying to convince Hayes that he must recognize the urgency of the situation and influence the Spaniards, whom it was always impossible to hurry, rather than be content to accept their reasoning for a lack of cooperation.

In his book *While Six Million Died*, Arthur D. Morse insists that Hayes refused to permit the assignment of a member of the War Relief Board to his embassy in Madrid, yet it seems as if this assignment would have come from the Department of State or the president if they had insisted on not considering his reasonings. A member of the WRB staff accused Hayes of an "apparent unwillingness to have private refugee organizations operate actively in Spain . . . [demonstrating] . . . a lack of understanding or sympathy." It appears that Hayes did relish such power as he had in Spain, for in May he demanded an explanation when he learned that rescue operations were being conducted without his concurrence.[37] At the same time, it must be remembered that Hayes had no real power in Spain and that ambassadors are never considered an internal matter.

Hayes answered the War Relief Board in July 1944, the time immediately after he had completed the negotiations for the much-demanded wolfram embargo. He cited how in 1942 and 1943 his office had assisted the charitable institutions in aiding refugees, this being a time before American government offices were concerned with the effort; he reiterated the cooperation of the Spanish government, which was still officially friendly with Germany; and he directly referred to the creation of the War Refugee Board on January 22, 1944, three weeks after his cable to Hull described the condition of the refugees, and told how following its policy too closely could have undermined diplomatic relations in fields more closely related to the Allied war effort (the embargo). Hayes feared interference by the Spanish government in the efforts of the groups who were actively aiding Jewish refugees and insisted that too much pressure against Franco could cause disruptions of this and the other negotiations being conducted.[38] The Spanish government was still not firmly committed to being friends with the Allies and abandoning its ally of the civil war, to whom it was still obligated and which it claimed to fear.

John Pehle, director of the Treasury Department's Division of Foreign Funds, cabled Hayes on August 24, 1944, "that in view of French victories no further efforts should be made to rescue either adults or children from France through Spain" and that the JDC was instructed to advise its Lisbon office "along these lines."[39] This decision in itself is amazing, considering that the period after August 1944 until the defeat of Germany in May 1945 was the most crucial time of all for the Jews who remained in territories under Nazi jurisdiction and that Spain was one of the few places in Europe left to receive Jews.

David Blickenstaff in Madrid issued a report to Ned Campbell of UNRRA (United Nations Relief and Rehabilitation Agency) in North Africa at the end of December 1944 to explain how the ambassador's office would aid in the transport of "stateless and other unprotected refugees" from Spain to the camp at Fedhala. It was decided that "the American Government would assemble and transport the refugees in Spain to the port of embarkation, and the British Government was to provide transportation by sea to North Africa."[40] In this report the plight, misery, and condition of the "refugees" was outlined again, and it was cited that their care was a pressing problem that demanded immediate attention. Had it not been for favorable Spanish attitudes and influence on the government, the refugees would never have entered Spain.

## SPAIN HELPS THE JEWS

Jewish leaders in Spain credit only the Spanish government and the American Joint Distribution Committee with offering aid to Jews whose lives were saved by coming to Spain. The Rabbi Benshabat of Barcelona reported that it was only through the protection of the Spanish government that the Jews who were granted asylum in Barcelona were alive.[41] Max Mazin, the president of the Hebrew Association of Spain, wrote that only the Spanish government was interested in saving lives, and despite the fact that those lives were Jewish, would have saved more if it had been able to do so.[42] Rabbis and leaders of associations were good politicians, especially in Fascist Spain, but at least in the case of Mazin there is personal knowledge of the respect given his opinions.

Granted, the Spanish government did not go all out to rescue Jews, and its acts can be attributed in part to criticism of the "Black Legend" of the fifteenth and sixteenth centuries, maneuvers to court friendship of the Allies (this is one thing they did not ask for—would it have mattered to them?), and favorable reaction to the efforts of interested persons and groups applying pressure from the outside. Nevertheless, the Spanish government intervened directly in several European countries to rescue Jews who were in danger of losing their lives at the hands of the Nazis.

### Bulgaria

On January 29, 1941, the first anti-Semitic legislation appeared in Bulgaria, affecting an estimated 28,000 Jews, the majority being of Sephardic origin, although no measures were taken against them until August 1942. At the end of 1941 Julio Palencia y Tubau, the head of the Spanish Legation in Bulgaria, formally protested to von Ribbentrop in Berlin, having received a formal protest against the anti-Semitic laws from the Bulgarian Foreign Minister. Before deportations to the work camps began in 1943, the Spanish Legation had issued 600 visas to Jews regardless of their origin. By July it was announced that all Jews who were not able to prove citizenship in other nations would be deported to the camps; those who had the proper papers would have until September 1 to leave the country. Palencia protested immediately to Vidal, the Spanish ambassador, who received permission from Madrid to issue more visas, enabling 130 Sephardic Jews to leave for Spain. During this time, León Arie, a renowned perfume manufacturer of Sofia, had the temerity as a Jew to present his case to the courts, exciting public attention regarding the deportations. The Nazis planned to make an example of this incident, and in spite of protests from the Spanish minister and Pope Pius XII, he was executed, although no Bulgarian Jews were ever deported, a unique situation among Hitler's puppet satellite governments.[43] A total of 90,000 Sephardic Jews from the other Balkan countries went to their deaths, and the situation in Bulgaria can be attributed to Spanish influence.

## Romania

Romania had a proportion of Jewish population second only to Poland, had a record of the worst treatment of Jews of all countries, and had conducted the first Jewish massacres of the entire war in 1940. In the end there was a loss of from 200,000 to 220,000 Jewish lives from a total of approximately 692,000.

In January 1939 an unknown Jewish spokesman presented himself at the embassy of the Spanish Nationalist government (this was during the Spanish civil war) to describe the plight of the Jews in Romania. He claimed that he represented 150,000 Jewish individuals who would be loyal to the Franco government and planned to convert to Catholicism and change their names to Spanish surnames. They were acting under the auspices of Cardinal Eugenio Pacelli (later Pope Pius XII), who would intervene directly with the Vatican to arrange this project of mass conversion. The spokesman said that the 50,000 Jewish families involved were financially well off and would aid the Spanish economy after the civil war. The future *bautizados* (baptized ones) claimed that arrangements could be made with the Romanian government for them to export their capital in Romanian products. The Vatican never contacted the Spanish government to aid this group and incorporate the 150,000 souls into the Catholic faith, but the situation illustrates the plight of the Jews of Romania living under the terror of the Iron Guard organization that was established in Romania in 1930.

This group of Jews contributed monetarily to the Franco government, hoping to escape the oppressive anti-Semitic legislation of Romania. The Spanish representative, Jose Rojas y Moreno, brought the situation to the attention of General Antonescu, the Romanian premier, and after long negotiations presented his undersecretaries with lists of the Jews who wished to emigrate to Spain. By the time the Franco regime had come to power in Spain, the Spanish representatives had obtained from those of Antonescu in Bucharest papers of Spanish protection that entitled 1,000 Jews to emigrate to Spain, documents of protection for 200 families who remained, and 300 certificates of protection to be exhibited over Sephardic doorways, reading, "This house belongs to a Spaniard."[44]

## Hungary

Of the 400,000 Jews of prewar Hungary, only about half survived the Holocaust. Of this 200,000, many having been officially declared "alive" when liberated from the Nazi death camps, the Spanish government claims credit for issuing 352 provisional passports, 1,898 letters of protection, and 45 passports for emigration to Spain by Sephardic Jews.[45]

## Greece

Two-thirds of all Greek Jewry from a total of about 67,200 lived in Salonika. These were the descendants of Jews expelled from Spain by the Catholic kings 452 years earlier and still spoke pure, although slightly archaic, Castilian. Spain, the first nation in the world to receive refugees from the Russian pogroms of the nineteenth century, was the nation most instrumental in saving Jews in Greece. The Franco government, following the centuries-old tradition, did not act with haste in securing safety for the Sephardic community. Its version of what happened tells part of the story:

At the beginning of 1944 we received an urgent telegram from our friends in the Jewish agency in Estambul [sic], requesting our intercession or assistance for the four-hundred Sephardite Jews of Spanish origin in the Haidari concentration camp, in Greece, who were going to be deported to Poland by the Germans. In answer to our request Don Nicholas Franco, Spanish Ambassador in Portugal and brother of General Franco, immediately contacted his government. Later, the Spanish Ambassador informed us that the Spanish government had decided to protect these Jews and that the Germans had already been informed of this decision. In this manner, the 400 Sephardite Jews in the Haidari camp were not deported. As a result of the action taken by us, the Spanish Government also decided to put under its protection all Sephardite Jews of Spanish origin in occupied countries, regardless of whether or not they were in possession of Spanish documents. More recently, the Spanish Ambassador Don Nicholas Franco, in an interview with Mr. Dextes, the representative of the War Refugees Department, and in the presence of the delegate of the World Jewish Congress in Lisbon, declared that, in accordance with information received from his government, several hundred Sephardites who had recourse to the Spanish consulates, had been recognized to be under Spanish protection and therefore had not been deported.[46]

Von Thadden of the German Foreign Office said that it was too late for Spain to repatriate Spanish Jews, as its option had been cancelled in November 1943, after five renewals. The Spanish government then consented to receive 367 Jews from the Bergen-Belsen camp on the condition that they would be transits. Those who were rescued lived in the Barcelona Jewish community and were cared for by the JDC for nine months, after which they were transferred to Palestine.[47] In April 1943 the Spanish government had opened a branch of the Falange party in Athens that was reportedly financed by Jews from Salonika. Franco had vacillated about accepting even these persons because von Thadden had warned him that "every Jew was an enemy of Germany, even if by chance he had a Spanish passport."[48] Franco defied his German allies and promised protection anyhow.

## France

Of the prewar population of 320,000 Jews in France, the best estimate of the loss is between 75,000 and 100,000. We have already seen how approximately 30,000 were saved by crossing the Pyrenees into Spain. On September 17, 1940, the Spanish Consulate in Paris informed the Spanish Ministry of Foreign Affairs that there were about 2,000 Sephardic Jews living in Paris who were subject to the same anti-Semitic regulations as all other French Jews.[49] In November Madrid sent instructions to the Spanish embassy in Vichy to inform Sephardic Jews who could claim Spanish citizenship to do so when submitting their registrations under the anti-Semitic statutes. When abuses were reported against this Sephardic group on March 7, 1942, the minister of foreign affairs in Spain cabled the embassy to "proceed to defend, in accordance with the instructions you have already received, the interests of the Sephardite Spanish subjects, demanding from French authorities the fulfillment of the Hispano-French Treaty of 1862."[50]

The Spanish government, the only one in the world that was able to persuade the German occupation authorities to do so, had the property of Spanish Jews administered by a representative of the Banco de España (the Bank of Spain), obtaining exemptions from the economic measures that threatened to destroy their means of income. The Sephardic community was even exempted from wearing the yellow star of Israel. The leaders of the Spanish Sephardim formally acknowledged the help granted by the Franco government and cited that more than 3,000 Jewish lives were saved in Paris by this gesture. Many other Sephardic Jews were granted permission to emigrate to Spain, having deposited their money in a Paris bank under the protection of the Spanish embassy, which held it for them until they were repatriated.[51]

## French Morocco

In the French territories in North Africa the French government ignored Spanish pleas to exclude Sephardic Jews from the anti-Semitic laws in spite of negotiations between the Ministry of Foreign Affairs and the French General Residency. Exclusion was finally granted to an unknown number, which was no doubt small, who had been made "honorary vice-consuls of Spain."[52]

## THE ROLE OF GENERAL FRANCO

In tangible figures the number of Jews who were directly saved by the Spanish government was small in comparison with that of all the Jews who were lost. More help was granted by permitting those who could to cross into Spanish territory without being returned, although the majority found themselves guests of concentration camps for long periods; yet the JDC and other groups were permitted to aid them. The fact remains that Spain was one of the few countries in the world, and the only one sympathetic to aspects of Nazi dogma, that directly made efforts to save human lives that happened to be Jewish.

The Spanish government claimed in 1949 that the only reason it made public documents pertaining to its rescue efforts was because it wanted to prove that it was worthy of becoming a member of the United Nations. A report was issued because Abba Eban, the Israeli delegate, had asserted:

> The United Nations arose out of the sufferings of a martyred generation, including six million Jewish dead. In the terrors of Nazism, one million of our children were thrown like useless rubbish into furnaces and gas chambers. If the history of Israel lasts for countless millennia, we shall never for a single moment allow ourselves to forget that most frightful episode of organized inhumanity. This memory is for us decisive. We do not for a moment assert that the Spanish regime had any direct part in that policy of extermination, but we do assert that it was an active and sympathetic ally of the regime which was responsible, and thus contributed to the effectiveness of the alliance as a whole.[53]

The Franco government responded:

> Spanish protection of Jewish communities during the war was not founded on cold and protocolary principles, but on a cordial and generous impulse of sympathy and friendliness towards a persecuted race, to which Spaniards feel themselves attached by traditional ties of blood and culture.[54]

This is true; so is the statement by Eban.

General Franco himself never stated his reasons for helping the Jews during World War II. It seems that the attitude of Franco toward the Jews was due in part to opportunistic reasons, as the Jews who entered Spain represented no danger to his regime. The much-professed chivalry of the Spaniards, when it involved no departure from Franco's policies, also played an important role. In Spain, where there were practically no Jews, and especially in the north, Franco's native region, where there were none, he would not have developed any personal prejudices against them.

Franco knew how to ally himself and the country with the forces that would be most beneficial. Referring to the Jews, he told the Nazi ambassador Dieckhof in 1943 that "thanks to God and the clear appreciation of the danger by our Catholic Kings, we have been relieved of that nauseating burden."[55] Franco was still pretending to be grateful for Nazi aid during the civil war. Also in 1943 Franco ordered that all discrimination against the Jewish religion be stopped. He needed grain and food products from the Allied nations, as Spain was suffering the worst droughts and starvation problems in living memory and also depended on the income from the products that Spain was able to export.

The Franco government was never anti-Jewish in its acts. The same regulations were applied to all refugees, Jewish and non-Jewish, who escaped to Spain, and were undoubtedly due to Gestapo demands. Only persons who were of military age were interned in camps, and men under eighteen and over forty and women and children were released from this ordeal.

It is not improbable that Franco himself saw the plight of the Jews, especially those who had come from Spain originally, as an unfortunate and senseless incident and was determined to exert his power and influence to assist at least some of them. Sephardic Jews were considered Spanish subjects, and he did not care to have other powers dictating to them. The professed friendliness and support that the Balkan Sephardic Jews offered Franco during the civil war would have favorably affected his attitude toward all Jews who wanted to enter Spain.

In the end, simple expedience may explain Franco's determination to exert his influence to assist some Jews. According to biographer Alan Lloyd, Franco never relished the thought of a Europe dominated by Hitler, but he thought that a democratic victory would leave the old order in a shambles with leftist powers he opposed transcendent. For that reason, on September 22, 1940, Franco wrote to Hitler offering "unchangeable and sincere adherence" both to the Führer and to the cause that he was championing.[56] Within three years, however, he was impressed by the generalship of George Patton and Omar Bradley, declaring that they would go down in history as the two greatest commanders the war had produced. Ever consistent to his principles, Franco wanted to be remembered as a man of chivalry by the winning side.

## BIBLIOGRAPHIC COMMENT

Any assessment of the Jewish experience in Iberia must begin with Abraham Neuman's *The Jews in Spain* (1942) and Cecil Roth's *The Spanish Inquisition* (1964). Neuman's two-volume study detailing the development of Jewish philosophical and economic life in Spain (including the impact of Maimonides, Nachmanides, and Kabbalists) approximates the writing of the Cambridge History series. Roth's work is more emotional, outlining a wide assortment of charges and punishments brought against innocent Christians as well as Marranos during the fifteenth century. More recent scholarship is reflected in Yitzhak Baer's *History of the Jews in Christian Spain* (1961 and 1966), R. D. Barnett's *The Sephardi Heritage: Essays on the History and Cultural Contribution of the Jews of Spain and Portugal* (1971), and Eliyahu Ashtor's *The Jews of Moslem Spain* (1973 and 1981). An interesting, if less scholarly, analysis may also be found in Simon Wiesenthal's *Sails of Hope* (1973).

Considered the best of many books chronicling events in Republican Spain between 1926 and 1939 is Hugh Thomas's *The Spanish Civil War* (1961). Thomas later contributed an essay (along with Claude Cockburn and Sheila Grant Duff) to Philip Toynbee's *The Distant Drum: Reflections on the Spanish Civil War* (1976). Ronald Fraser's *Blood of Spain: The Experience of Civil War, 1936– 1939* (1979) contains edited accounts of three hundred oral memoirs, none more poignant, however, than George Orwell's hoary, yet relevant, *Homage to Catalonia* (1952). On the Spanish dictator, General Francisco Franco, see Stanley

Payne, *Falange: A History of Spanish Fascism* (1961) and *The Franco Regime, 1936–1975* (1987); Brian Crozier, *Franco* (1967); George Hills, *Franco: The Man and His Nation* (1967); and Max Gallo, *Spain Under Franco* (1974).

Rarely, and briefly, do any of these books deal with the Holocaust. In *The Franco Regime* (page 335) Payne ascribes the safe passage of forty thousand Jews through Spain to Franco's gratitude for Jewish support when he was rallying forces in Morocco. Hills agrees in part (407–10), noting that Primo de Rivera counted the Sephardim among his earliest backers in 1923–24. For Hills, there is a more basic reason why Jews who were lumped with Franco's demons, the Socialists and Masons, did not suffer legal impairments. That is Spain's astounding tradition of religious liberty dating to the Montreux Convention of 1837.

Three books and a number of published articles deal specifically with the subject of Hitler, the Jews, and Spain. Nehemiah Robinson's *The Spain of Franco and Its Policies Toward the Jews* (1944) offers a contemporary view of Spain's much-vaunted efforts during wartime. More recently, in *Franco, Spain, the Jews, and the Holocaust* (1983) Rabbi Chaim Lipschitz offered a number of explanations for Franco's interventions. The editor of the *Jewish Press* mentions pressure from the Vatican, Franco's desire to embarrass the Allies, fear over imminent Axis defeat and his concern for his place in history, the possibility of Jewish ancestry (''not on a far limb''), gratitude for past services and the fantasy of a Jewish fifth column, neutralism for profit, and Franco's desire to play peacemaker, but after a fruitless interview with the Spanish dictator, concludes that it is impossible to answer why he behaved the way he did. Geoffrey Wigoder, editor of the prestigious *Encyclopedia Judaica*, has denounced Lipschitz for being too sympathetic to Franco in ''Franco and the Jews,'' *Midstream* 24 (January 1978): 27–32. Similar critical views of Spanish expedience are offered in Michael Kogan, ''The Jews and General Franco,'' *Ideas* 1 (Winter 1968–69): 35–43, and Perez Leshem, ''Rescue Efforts in the Iberian Peninsula,'' *Leo Baeck Institute Yearbook* 14 (1969): 231–56. Many Jewish scholars consider Haim Avni's *Spain, The Jews, and Franco* (1981), which bears the imprint of the Jewish Publication Society of America, to be the definitive work today. Drawing heavily upon oral histories done in the 1960s, Avni focuses upon Ambassador Carlton Hayes's obstreperousness and Spain's opportunism after the Battle of Britain. In forgoing the question of Franco's alleged Marrano ancestry, however, Avni leaves the door open for further research into what motivated Spanish leaders to act as they did during the Holocaust.

## NOTES

1. Brian Crozier, *Franco* (Boston: Little, Brown, 1967), p. 268.
2. Letter from Carlton J. H. Hayes to Franklin D. Roosevelt, June 30, 1942, p. 1. Carlton J. H. Hayes Papers, Special Collection, Butler Library, Columbia University,

New York. (Hereafter documents from this collection are called "Hayes Papers" if the reference is not apparent.)

3. Letter from Carlton J. H. Hayes to Franklin D. Roosevelt, October 29, 1942, p. 1.

4. Hayes to Roosevelt, June 30, 1942, p. 4.

5. Carlton J. H. Hayes, *Wartime Mission in Spain* (New York: Macmillan, 1945), pp. 112–14.

6. W. L. Beaulac, Memorandum to Ambassador Hayes, November 13, 1943, p. 1.

7. Beaulac, Memorandum to Hayes, Madrid, December 2, 1943.

8. Hayes papers, "Wolfram Embargo," January 4, 1944, p. 2.

9. Ibid., p. 3.

10. Hayes, letter to Cordell Hull, Secretary of State, January 28, 1944, no. 272, p. 1.

11. Hayes, telegram to Sec. State, January 31, 1944, no. 306.

12. Hull, telegram to Hayes, January 25, 1944, no. 204.

13. Hull, telegram to Hayes, February 3, 1944, no. 300.

14. Hull, telegram to Hayes, February 3, 1944, no. 315.

15. Hull, telegram to Hayes, February 11, 1944, no. 386.

16. Hull, telegram to Hayes, February 18, 1944, no. 458.

17. Hull, telegram to Hayes, February 24, 1944, no. 515.

18. Hayes, withheld telegram to Hull, Madrid, February 26, 1944.

19. Hayes, *Wartime Mission in Spain*, pp. 222–23.

20. Williard L. Beaulac, letter to Hayes, Washington, June 16, 1944, p. 3.

21. Sir Samuel Hoare, *Complacent Dictator* (New York: Knopf, 1946), pp. 230–34.

22. Hayes, *Wartime Mission in Spain*, pp. 112–20.

23. Ibid., p. 112.

24. Ibid. Amitié chrétienne and Boy Scout groups in France cared for Jewish children who had to be left behind as their parents fled to Spain. Their subsequent fate when their foster parents refused to return them to the Jews after the war is another chapter in Jewish suffering.

25. Ibid., p. 114.

26. Ibid., p. 115.

27. "The Refugee Problem in Spain," Hayes papers, April 21, 1942 (author unknown), pp. 1–3.

28. Donald A. Lowrie, Memorandum to Hayes, Geneva, September 19, 1942, p. 1.

29. Beaulac, Memorandum to Hayes, Madrid, March 29, 1943, p. 1.

30. Ibid., pp. 2–3; Hayes, Memorandum to Roosevelt, "The Refugee Problem in Spain," May 3, 1943.

31. Saul Friedman, *No Haven for the Oppressed* (Detroit: Wayne State University Press, 1973), pp. 167, 175, 180, 188, 189, 197, 198.

32. Hayes to Roosevelt, May 3, 1943.

33. R. Brandin, letter, Madrid, June 28, 1943, Hayes papers, p. 4.

34. Percy Winner, letters to Robert E. Sherwood, Office of War Information, Pamplona, Spain, August 29 and September 7, 1943, Hayes papers.

35. Hayes, telegram to Hull, January 4, 1944, no. 17.

36. Hull, telegram to Hayes, June 29, 1944, no. 1850, p. 2.

37. Arthur D. Morse, *While Six Million Died* (New York: Ace Publishing, 1967), pp. 268–70.

38. "N. W. B.," "Memorandum on Refugee Relief Activities of American Embassy

in Madrid, with Special Reference to Proposed Participation of War Refugee Board,"
July 7, 1944, Hayes papers, pp. 3–8.

39. "Paraphrase of Department's Telegram No. 2331, WRB 81, Dated August 24,
1944," Hayes papers.

40. Report to Ned Campbell, UNRRA, North Africa, from David Blickenstaff, Madrid, December 27, 1944, "Evacuation of Stateless Refugees to North Africa" Hayes
papers, pp. 1–7.

41. Personal letter from Rabino Revdo, Sr. Benshabat, Barcelona, Spain, May 18,
1973.

42. Federico Ysart, *España y los judíos* (Barcelona, Spain: Dopesa, 1973), p. 10. The
book by Ysart won the Essay Prize of 1973 in Spain. It includes extensive lists of many
of the Jews who were directly saved by Spain, including photocopies of their papers,
certificates pertaining to their origin, and other documents.

43. Ibid., pp. 120–21.

44. Ibid., pp. 124–32.

45. Ibid., p. 151.

46. Diplomatic Information Office, p. 24.

47. Letter from Rabino Benshabat.

48. Raul Hilberg, *The Destruction of the European Jews* (Chicago: Quadrangle, 1961)
pp. 447–48.

49. Diplomatic Information Office, p. 19.

50. Ibid., p. 20.

51. J. I. Fishbein, "Jews Under Franco," *The Sentinel,* Chicago, February 20, 1964.
Copy furnished by Embassy of Spain, Washington, D.C.

52. Diplomatic Information Office, p. 25.

53. Nehemiah Robinson, "The Spain of Franco and Its Policies Toward the Jews."
Institute of Jewish Affairs, New York, 1944, unpublished report) pp. 7–8.

54. Ibid., p. 9.

55. Ibid., p. 8

56. Alan Lloyd, *Franco* (Garden City, N.Y.: Doubleday, 1969), pp. 178–79.


## SELECT BIBLIOGRAPHY

Ashtor, Eliyahu. *The Jews of Moslem Spain*. Philadelphia: Jewish Publication Society of
America, 1973.

Avni, Haim. *Spain, Franco and the Jews*. Philadelphia: Jewish Publication Society of
America, 1982.

Baer, Yitzhak. *History of the Jews in Christian Spain*. 2 vols. Philadelphia: Jewish
Publication Society of America, 1961 and 1966.

Barnett, R. D., ed. *The Sephardi Heritage: Essays on the History and Cultural Contribution of the Jews of Spain and Portugal*. New York: Ktav, 1971.

Burdick, Charles. *Germany's Military Strategy and Spain in World War II*. Syracuse,
N.Y.: Syracuse University Press, 1968.

Crozier, Brian. *Franco*. Boston: Little, Brown, 1967.

Eshl, Shaul. "Some observations on the Place of the Sephardim in Modern Jewry." In
*Actas del Primer Simposio de Estudios Sefardies*, edited by Jacob Hassan. Madrid:
Instituto Arias Montano, 1970.

Fraser, Ronald. *Blood of Spain: The Experience of Civil War, 1936–1939*. London: Penguin, 1979.

Gallo, Max. *Spain Under Franco: A History*. Translated by J. Stewart. New York: Dutton, 1974.

Hayes, Carlton. *The United States and Spain*. New York: Sheed and Ward, 1951.

———. *Wartime Mission in Spain*. New York: Macmillan, 1945.

Hills, George. *Franco: The Man and His Nation*. New York: Macmillan, 1967.

Hoare, Sir Samuel. *Complacent Dictator*. New York: Knopf, 1946.

Lipschitz, Chaim. *Franco, Spain, the Jews, and the Holocaust*. New York: Ktav, 1983.

Lloyd, Alan. *Franco*. Garden City, N.Y.: Doubleday, 1969.

Neuman, Abraham. *The Jews in Spain*. 2 vols. Philadelphia: Jewish Publication Society of America, 1942.

Payne, Stanley. *Falange: A History of Spanish Fascism*. Stanford: Stanford University Press, 1961.

———. *The Franco Regime, 1936–1975*. Madison: University of Wisconsin Press, 1987.

Robinson, Nehemiah. *The Spain of Franco and Its Policies Toward the Jews*. New York: Institute of Jewish Affairs, 1944.

Roth, Cecil. *The Spanish Inquisition*. New York: Norton, 1964.

Thomas, Hugh. *The Spanish Civil War*. New York: Harper and Row, 1961.

Toynbee, Philip, ed. *The Distant Drum: Reflections on the Spanish Civil War*. New York: David McKay, 1976.

Whealey, Robert. *Hitler and Spain: The Nazi Role in the Spanish Civil War, 1936–1939*. Lexington: University Press of Kentucky, 1989.

Wiesenthal, Simon. *Sails of Hope*. Translated by Richard and Clara Winston. New York: Macmillan, 1973.

# Chapter 20

# Switzerland and the Holocaust

## *Herbert Hochhauser*

In February 1972 Paul Grüninger, the eighty-one-year old former chief of police for the Swiss canton St. Gallen, was laid to rest.[1] The death of a former chief of police of a Swiss canton is not exactly an event that would make world headlines. A closer look revealed that Paul Grüninger was a giant, a rare human being in a sea of inhumanity. Between the years of 1938 and 1939 he saved the lives of two thousand Jewish refugees who crossed the Swiss border from Germany and Austria. He simply overlooked the inhumane regulations imposed by the federal government of the Republic of Switzerland.[2] This led to his dismissal in the spring of 1941. He was fined three hundred Swiss francs and lost his pension rights. The dismissed police official then returned to his former vocation, that of a teacher. In 1968 efforts were under way to rehabilitate Paul Grüninger. They remained fruitless, however, and he never received his pension because he "unjustifiably" saved the lives of Jewish refugees. Subsequently the State of Israel honored this man by bestowing the Medal of the Just upon him.[3]

Paul Grüninger was part of a very small group of Swiss who opposed the role that their government played vis-à-vis Jewish refugees. Switzerland has always taken pride in being a haven for the oppressed. Anti-Semitism also found a haven in Switzerland. It was not something that had to be imported from the National Socialist state to the north.

Jews had lived in Switzerland since before it became the Helvetian Confederation.[4] In the thirteenth century Jews lived in twenty different cities and towns. They were French and German Jews who, upon payment, could live there and enjoy limited rights. Due to the Law of Usury, Jews were forced to be moneylenders. They were denied permission to engage in commerce or crafts. They could not farm because they were not permitted to own land. Blood libel accusations also surfaced in Bern and Schaffhausen in the thirteenth century. In the middle of the fourteenth century Jews were blamed for the Black Death that swept the nation. When toward the end of the fourteenth century the Law of Usury was no longer enforced, there was no need for Jews, and consequently they were expelled. Physicians were the only exception because their knowledge and skill were needed and respected.[5]

In the seventeenth century two Swiss villages gave the Jews residence permission. After substantial sums were paid, Lengnau and Oberendingen permitted them to stay for sixteen years. Thereafter, the payment had to be renewed. In 1850 there were three thousand Jews living in Switzerland. In 1930 the number of Jews stood at eighteen thousand. At that point Jews made up .44 percent of Switzerland's total population.[6] These figures hardly lend themselves to a *Verjudung* of Switzerland.

With the rise of national socialism in Germany, anti-Semitism flourished on both sides of the Rhine. In December 1930 the church newspaper of St. Peter and Paul of Zürich told its parishioners not to shop at Simon or Globus since they were storehouses for Jerusalem.[7] Anti-Semitic slogans from Martin Luther reappeared, phrases like "Don't trust a fox on the green meadow, don't trust a Jew even when he swears."[8] In German this phrase rhymes. Another of the same genre was "Purchase Swiss goods by Swiss merchants, avoid alcohol and Jews."[9]

Frequent reference was made to the quote from John 8:44–45, when Jesus supposedly said to his kinsmen, "Your father is the devil. He cannot speak the truth because the truth is not part of him. When he speaks lies, he speaks according to his own nature. He is the liar and the father of lies."[10] Even the Bible was twisted to conform to anti-Semitic viewpoints.

Anti-Semitism also found expression in the school systems. Swiss schools are organized on a cantonal basis. The reader for the third grade in the cantons of Zürich and Bern contained a poem by Friedrich Rückert. The poem deals with a tree that has golden leaves. The gist of the poem is how this tree is viewed by various individuals such as a painter, a farmer, and others. One stanza reads:

> The tree speaks
> How proud I am
> for no other tree has
> golden leaves like I.
> However, when evening approached,
> the Jew walked through the forest.
> Right away he saw the golden leaves.
> He put them in his pocket and hurried away
> and left the empty little tree behind.[11]

This poem served as reading material for nine- and ten-year-old children. There were yet other similarities between the two countries north and south of the Rhine. Long before the Nazi regime took power in Germany, Switzerland had embraced its own domestic version of anti-Semitism. According to article 25 of the Swiss Civil Code, a law enacted nearly one hundred years ago and still in effect, it is inhumane to slaughter animals according to kosher regulation. Shechitah is, therefore, unlawful. According to historian Willy Guggenheim, Switzerland is the only country in the Western world that bans the production, not importation, of kosher meat.[12] With the rise of Hitler, the Swiss emulated German racists in other ways. As late as 1944 authorities in Luzern notified refugees that they might stroll through the parks, but they could not sit down on the park benches.[13] Authorities in Zürich insisted that refugees fill out their forms by listing either Israel or Sarah as their middle name.[14] In such an atmosphere the Orell Füssli Publishing House, a well-established firm located in Zürich, revised a text by Paul de Kruif entitled *Mikroben Jäger* (Microbe hunter). Several passages in the sixth edition of this volume dealing with Dr. Paul Ehrlich, discoverer of Salvarsan (a drug effective in the early treatment of syphilis), were rewritten in a scurrilous fashion (his laboratory was described as a collection of "filthy test tubes") to suggest a medical conspiracy on the part of the Jews.[15] In 1936 that conspiracy supposedly was confirmed with the assassination of the Nazi Wilhelm Gustloff in Davos by a young Jewish medical student named David Frankfurter.[16] Although Gustloff was not a citizen of Germany, Swiss president Giuseppe Motta felt obliged to apologize to Hitler in the name of the Swiss people.[17]

Despite their carefully cultivated public image, the Swiss were anything but innocent pacifists who spent their days yodelling and/or making chocolate. As J. Christopher Herold notes in *The Swiss Without Halos* (1948; reprint, Westport, Conn.: Greenwood Press, 1979), the Swiss may not have been directly involved in war since the Napoleonic period, but, like the nonviolent Swedes, they have cynically exported weapons to belligerents. The Swiss people cheered parades and slogans of a dozen neo-Nazi movements, principally the National Front, during the 1930s. Forty thousand had joined Switzerland's version of the Hitler Youth.

Intimidated by the Nazis' presence on their onetime border with Austria and privately sharing some of the same sentiments, the Swiss were anything but receptive to the plight of the Jews before or during the war. The responsibility for the official attitude of Switzerland during these critical years rests primarily with the federal counsel, Dr. Edward von Steiger, and the chief of police, Dr. Heinrich Rothmund. It was Steiger who, in a speech in August 1942, defended Swiss policy. Speaking at the Junge Church in Zürich, Steiger referred to Switzerland as a life raft in a hostile sea. A life raft can only absorb so many people. Therefore, one must remain stolid.[18] Alfred Häsler subsequently appropriated and condemned Steiger's imagery in *Das Boot ist voll*, a collection of memoirs published in German.

Rothmund, as chief of police, saw his role as that of facilitator of racial policies from the north. He was an observer at the July 1938 Refugee Conference at Evian and noted that Switzerland could not admit more refugees because the economic resources of Swiss Jews were already exhausted.[19] Little wonder, then, that the *Völkischer Beobachter*, referring to Evian, wrote that no one wanted to have the "Mespoche" (Yiddish for "family" and meaning Jews). About the same time, Police Chief Rothmund also conferred with Dr. Hans Globke, Nazi specialist on racial laws, at the Sachsenhausen concentration camp. At this meeting the two men discussed the feasibility of stamping Jewish passports with a *J* to facilitate expulsion of Jewish refugees. (This issue is outlined in "Origins of the 'J' Passport: A Controversy in Switzerland," *Wiener Library Bulletin* 8 (May/August 1954: 20.)

During the war Switzerland did welcome three hundred thousand refugees, the overwhelming number of them Christians—political émigrés, French soldiers, Italians, and Allied POWs. Perhaps thirty thousand of the total were Jews, a figure that, incidentally, surpassed the combined total for Canada, Australia, New Zealand, and South Africa. Eight thousand of these were put to work in *Arbeitslager*, forced-labor camps for road construction, quarries, and agriculture. Twenty-three thousand were sent back.[20] The writings of Häsler (noted earlier); Werner Rings, *Schweiz im Krieg, 1933–1945* (Zürich: Kindler Verlag 1974); and Karl Ludwig, *Die Flüchtlingspolitik der Schweiz in den Jahren 1933 bis 1945* (Bern: Lang, 1957) make for depressing reading:

One morning the caretaker of the Jewish cemetery in Bern found a young Jewish couple from Belgium who had spent the night in the cemetery. In order to avoid deportation to the East, the couple had fled to Switzerland. The well-meaning caretaker took the couple to the Jewish Refugee Aid Office. The Swiss government would not permit this couple to remain. She was 19 and he was 22 when they were put across the border. He was shot and she was never heard from again.[21]

August Hirsch entered Switzerland on December 15, 1942. Four days later he was put across the border. His last known address was the French internment camp of Gurs. Most stateless Jews detained at Gurs perished in Auschwitz.[22]

Gottlieb Fuchs was a foreign correspondent for the Swiss News Service. He was arrested and spent time in Buchenwald and Dijon. He noted that everywhere he found Jewish victims who had previously been in Switzerland.[23]

For two years, Rev. A. Hubscher hid a young Jewish refugee in his rectory. The police assured the Reverend that the refugee would only spend a few days at the police station and then be returned to him. With this official assurance, Rev. Hubscher released his protege. A few days later the refugee called Rev. Hubscher from the Swiss border town of Schaffhausen to tell him that within minutes he, along with a young couple and their two-year-old child, were being deported to Germany. Nothing further has ever been heard from him.[24]

These are but a few of many documented cases. The policies of Steiger and Rothmund were carried out with the help of many, including officers of the International Committee of the Red Cross (ICRC), which is centered in Geneva and supposedly has the obligation of seeing to it that belligerents abide by so-called standards of war. Writing in the prestigious *Encyclopedia of the Holocaust*, Jean Claude Favez credits the ICRC with sending missions of inquiry to Buchenwald and Terezín. According to Favez, rector of Geneva University, the ICRC also undertook heroic efforts in Slovakia, Italy, and Hungary. Officials who sent food parcels to Russian and American POWs agonized over whether to issue public statements condemning the treatment of the Jews, but they were "helpless," as, technically, stateless Jews fell beyond the pale of protection offered by the Geneva Accords.

This assessment, which conforms to the overcautious sentiments of the *Encyclopedia*'s editors, lamentably lends credence to self-serving rationalizations offered by the ICRC in its own official publications, including *Documents sur l'activité du Comite Internationale de la Croix-Rouge en faveur des civils détenus dans les camps de concentration en Allemagne (1939–1945)* (Geneva, 1947) and *Report of the International Committee of the Red Cross on Its Activities During the Second World War, September 1, 1939–June 30, 1947* (Geneva, 1948). These documents reveal that the ICRC shied away from requests of the U.S. government to speak out on behalf of "helpless minorities" because (*a*) "every protest is a judgment"; (*b*) "the indicted party will either keep its own public in ignorance of the protest or present it in one-sided fashion, whilst the opposing side will be free to use it for purposes of propaganda"; (*c*) public protests would produce a "stiffening" of the indicted country's attitude toward the ICRC or even a "rupture"; and (*d*) such protests might be construed as a challenge to German national sovereignty. What the documents also reveal is that throughout most of the Hitlerian era the ICRC, without protest, accepted the Nazi definition that Jews, regardless of nationality and solely by virtue of birth, were classed as *Schutzhäftlinge* (common criminals) and hence beyond the protection of international convention.[25]

In a separate manuscript, *Une Mission impossible? Le ICRC, les déportations et les camps de concentration nazis* (Lausanne: Editions Playot 1988), where he was apparently unfettered by editorial constraints, Favez soundly condemned the International Committee. He faulted the ICRC for failing to issue public condemnations of the death camps in 1943 and 1944 when their existence was proven. Much responsibility for inaction may be traced back to an insensitive Swiss government. Wrote Favez: "In the use of international law, the ICRC, confronted with juridically unnamed victims who turned to it, often sought not the means to act, but on the contrary a justification for not acting, so as not to disturb the conventional missions on which, in its eyes, its very existence stood."[26] Confronted with the overwhelming evidence in Favez's book and Arieh Ben Tov's *Facing the Holocaust in Budapest* (Martinus Nijhoff, 1988), officials of the ICRC shamefacedly conceded: "The ICRC feels that the meager results yielded by the considerable efforts made at the time and in the prevailing circumstances represent the worst defeat in the history of its humanitarian mission and exemplify the failure of an entire civilization."[27]

Max Frisch, a Swiss and one of Europe's most respected dramatists, exposed Switzerland's inhumanity in his thinly veiled drama, *Andorra*. In spite of the title, no one who reads the drama would ever mistake the location of the action for the Pyrenees. The teacher is the central figure in this play. He adopts a Jewish youngster from across the border. Everyone in the town admires this deed. At the same time, all the negative traits that are supposedly inherent in Jews are observed in this youngster. The townspeople tell him that a Jew cannot be a soldier because Jews are cowardly. The youngster cannot become a carpenter because Jews cannot work with their hands. They are only good at being in business. When foreign soldiers invade the country, the town sells out its Jew. We also learn that the kindness shown to this youngster by the teacher was not an act of charity. This youngster was fathered by the teacher and a woman who also was non-Jewish. This drama depicts the Swiss attitude toward Jews as it prevailed during the war years. Other authors, notably Walter Diggelmann, have also questioned the role of Switzerland.[28]

The thirty thousand Jews who were saved owe their existence, for the most part, to a handful of Swiss who worked and spoke on their behalf. This handful of people who defied mass hysteria deserve to be recognized and remembered as true Christians. Among them was the aforementioned police chief of St. Gallen, Paul Grüninger. Another was Gottlieb Duttweiler, an influential businessman who saved many lives. The Reverend Paul Vogt did everything within his power to save Jewish refugees. It was Vogt who justified his actions by stating that a church that is not a refuge for the suffering can never be a church of Jesus Christ. Sister Anny Pfluger, a Quaker, accomplished the impossible on behalf of Jewish refugees. Other members of the clergy such as Rev. Samuel Dieterle, Rev. Walther Lüthi, and Rev. Rudolf Schwarz deserve recognition. Until Swiss censorship put an end to his writings, Professor Ragaz and his wife, Clara, wrote about conditions in the detention camps of Gurs, Rivesaltes, and Vernet. Dr. Hans Zbinden wrote a pamphlet, "The Refugee and Humanitarianism," that condemned Swiss hypocrisy. The editors and staff of *Die Neue Zürcher Zeitung* and *Die Basler Nachtrichten* also openly condemned the critical situation of the Jews.[29]

Most historians, Swiss and non-Swiss, gloss over the role that Switzerland played during World War II. Gerhart Waeger's *Die Sündenböcke der Schweiz* (Olten, Switzerland: Walter Verlag, 1971) makes no mention of the Jewish refugee question. The major textbooks on the Holocaust generally are inadequate. Yehuda Bauer's *A History of the Holocaust* (New York: Franklin Watts, 1982) and the late Lucy Dawidowicz's *The War Against the Jews, 1933–1945* (New York: Holt, Rinehart and Winston, 1975) make extremely limited references to the problem. Raul Hilberg's revised *The Destruction of the European Jews* (New York: Holmes and Meier, 1985) and Leni Yahil's *The Holocaust: The Fate of European Jewry, 1932–1945* (New York: Oxford University Press, 1990), do offer illuminating insights into Switzerland's role during the period.

Nearly half a century has passed since the demise of Germany's National

Socialist state. Has the official position of Switzerland toward Jews changed? Yes, there have been some changes. Shunned by his former friends, Dr. Heinrich Rothmund tried to atone by working on behalf of war orphans. During the first few years after the end of hostilities in Europe, nearly all of the "undesirables" left Switzerland. The United States and Israel were their principal destinations. Those who remained were mainly old and infirm, unwilling to adjust to a new setting.

Today when one searches for a scapegoat, there are many visible groups that do not fit the Swiss cultural pattern. "Guest workers" from Yugoslavia, Greece, Turkey, and Spain are the Jews of today. One must also include Gypsies, who were outsiders then and are now. Recently, a major scandal involving the highly respected Swiss charity, Pro Juventute, came to light. For years this organization has taken Gypsy children away from their natural parents and put them up for adoption. The reason given for this action has been that Gypsies are asocial and thus unfit to raise children.

Fortunately, the eighteen thousand Jews counted in the 1980 census do not face such problems today. The twelve thousand who hold citizenship (a difficult, archaic process administered by the local communes) are organized in the Schweizerische Israelitische Gemeindebund (SIG), a federation that enjoys quasi-legal status in the view of the government. Some old problems have been uneasily resolved. Rabbi Mordechai Piron has stated that with such a small market for kosher meat, domestic slaughtering would actually be more expensive than the import of meat from France and Germany.[30] Other problems remain symptomatic of the guest status of Jews in Switzerland. SIG questions why the public-school week includes a half-day session on Saturday. (Children from observant Jewish families do not have to write or take tests on that day.)[31] A nation that publicly repudiated the Protocols of the Elders of Zion in a celebrated court hearing back in 1933 now circulates all sorts of scandalous anti-Zionist and anti-Semitic literature. There is also the matter of the relationship between Mogen David Adom and the International Red Cross. Although the former has been acknowledged, even by its enemies, as the de facto Jewish health organization, the ICRC, whose headquarters are in Geneva, through the votes of third-world countries, has consistently denied Mogen David Adom membership.[32]

In Switzerland there exists great respect for Israel. This is due mainly to Israel's military accomplishments. Military advisors from Israel are frequently invited to Switzerland. Every Swiss male has to serve in the army until age fifty; thus this connection with Israel does not go unnoticed. Furthermore, many weapons used by the Swiss forces are designed and manufactured in Israel. Israeli military personnel train the Swiss in the arms purchased from Israel.[33]

Anti-Semitism still exists in Switzerland, but it is not as blatant as it was during the 1930s or 1940s. The small number of Jews who reside in the large cities pose no threat to the comfortably secure Swiss. Instead, other nationals like the Yugoslavs and Turks bear the brunt of Swiss xenophobia. Though disliked, they are necessary for menial labor. If in 1939 a Jew from Nazareth requested entry into Switzerland, he most likely would have been rebuffed. Today he would be welcomed, simply because he would carry an Israeli passport.

## NOTES

1. *Der Spiegel*, "Register," February 28, 1972.
2. Max Schmid, *Schalom* (Zürich: Eco Verlag, 1979), p. 13.
3. *Der Spiegel*, February 28, 1972.
4. Willy Guggenheim, *Juden in der Schweiz* (Küsnacht: Edition Kurz), p. 13.
5. Ibid., p. 16.
6. Schmid, *Schalom*, p. 13.
7. Ibid., p. 38.
8. Ibid.
9. Ibid., p. 93.
10. Ibid., p. 43.
11. Ibid., p. 123.
12. Willy Guggenheim, "The Jews of Switzerland," undated nine-page memo, p. 2. See also *Tages Anzeiger* (Zürich), February 8, 1972.
13. Schmid, *Schalom*, p. 206.
14. Ibid., p. 208.
15. Ibid., p. 141.
16. See Emil Ludwig, *The Davos Murder*, trans. Eden and Cedar Paul (New York: Viking Press, 1936).
17. Schmid, *Schalom*, p. 116.
18. Alfred Häsler, *Das Boot ist voll* (Zürich: Fretz und Wasmuth Verlag, 1968), p. 122.
19. Ibid., p. 329.
20. Denis Fodor, *The Neutrals* (New York: Time-Life Books, 1982), pp. 28–62.
21. Häsler, *Das Boot ist voll*, p. 214.
22. Ibid., p. 221.
23. Ibid., p. 115.
24. Ibid., p. 91.
25. Seventeenth International Red Cross Conference, *Report of the International Committee of the Red Cross on Its Activities During the Second World War (September 1, 1939–June 30, 1947)*, vol. 1 (Geneva, 1948), pp. 19, 36.
26. *Washington Post*, February 17, 1989, p. A29.
27. Ibid.
28. Max Frisch, *Andorra* (Frankfurt: Suhrkamp Verlag, 1961).
29. Häsler, *Das Boot ist voll*, p. 91.
30. Interview with Modechai Piron, Chief Rabbi of Switzerland, Jewish Community Center, Zürich, May 25, 1988.
31. Interview with Rudolf Groeflin, public-school instructor, Basel, May 25, 1988.
32. Interview with Dr. Willy Guggenheim, Secretary General of the Swiss Jewish Federation, Jewish Community Center, Zürich, May 24, 1988.
33. Interview with Guggenheim, May 25, 1988.

## SELECT BIBLIOGRAPHY

Ben-Sasson, H. H. *A History of the Jewish People*. Cambridge, Mass: Harvard, 1976.
Fodor, Denis. *The Neutrals*. New York: Time-Life Books, 1982.

Frisch, Max. *Andorra*. Frankfurt am Main: Suhrkamp Verlag, 1961.

Grayzel, Solomon. *A History of the Jews*. New York: New American Library, 1968.

Guggenheim, Willy. *Juden in der Schweiz*. Küsnacht: Edition Kurz, 1982.

Häsler, Alfred A. *Das Boot ist voll*. Zürich: Fretz und Wasmuth Verlag, 1968.

Seventeenth International Red Cross Conference. *Report of the International Committee of the Red Cross on Its Activities During the Second World War (September 1, 1939–June 30, 1947)*. Vol. 1. Geneva, 1948.

Kaufmann, Uri Robert. ''Swiss Jewry: From the 'Jewish Village' to the City, 1780–1930.'' *Leo Baeck Institute Yearbook* 30 (1985): 283–99.

Ludwig, Emil. *The Davos Murder*. Translated by Eden and Cedar Paul. New York: Viking Press, 1936.

Marcus, Jacob R. *The Jew in the Medieval World*. New York, 1975.

Milton, Sybil. *Rescue to Switzerland: The Mussy and Saly Mayer Affairs*. New York: Garland, 1982.

Schmid, Max. *Schalom*. Zürich: Eco Verlag, 1979.

# Chapter 21

# Great Britain and the Holocaust

## *Monty Noam Penkower*

On September 2, 1939, one day after Adolf Hitler's troops invaded Poland to inaugurate history's bloodiest conflagration, the ship *Tiger Hill* landed over one thousand Jews on the beach of Tel Aviv. Restrictive immigration quotas for Palestine, set down four months earlier in the White Paper of His Majesty's Government (HMG) in London, did not daunt these passengers. What matter that Great Britain, out to court Palestine's surrounding Arab countries in the face of impending global war, had sanctioned a maximum of only 75,000 entry certificates for the Promised Land in the next five years?

Aside from reneging on the 1917 Balfour Declaration and a two-decade-old mandate from the League of Nations to encourage the growth of a Jewish national home in Palestine, the barring by HMG of Jewry's most obvious shelter appeared particularly callous when alternative havens were firmly closed and the German Führer publicly forecast "the destruction of the Jewish race in Europe" in the event of world conflict. Ominous shadows then lengthening across Poland, Romania, Bulgaria, and Czechoslovakia had driven the voyagers aboard the *Tiger Hill* to leave these birthplaces and risk the illegal journey eastward. A British patrol vessel hewed to regulations, however. The first shots fired by the British government following the outbreak of World War II were aimed at the *Tiger Hill*; two Jewish men fell as their victims.

That same day British prime minister Neville Chamberlain, symbol of Western appeasement of Hitler, replied to a communiqué from Chaim Weizmann. The World Zionist Organization president had just pledged the Jewish people's fullest support "in this hour of supreme crisis" and had appealed for the political differences between the Jewish Agency for Palestine and the Mandatory Power

to give way "before the greater and more pressing necessities of the time."
Replying in noncommittal fashion, Chamberlain noted "with pleasure" the agency's promise of wholehearted cooperation, and he ended: "Your public spirited
assurances are welcome and will be kept in mind."[1]

Soon thereafter, HMG issued a memorandum concerning the Third Reich's
atrocities since 1938 against so-called German nationals. No specific reference
to Jews could be found therein.[2] To acknowledge this independent entity, London
officialdom thought, would imply the vindication of Hitler's philosophy of *das
Volk* and support German propaganda that the West was engaged in fighting a
Jewish war. Especially important, to single out Jewry might well suggest that
this unique problem demanded special attention, including a Palestine solution.
Paradoxically, Britain's rationale meant that the particular fate of European Jewry
was to be either concealed under "Poles," for example, or refused sympathy
because Jews were classified as "enemy aliens" when found in countries loyal
to the Axis. In either instance, Hitler—who thought otherwise—would secure
his primary objective.

These three instances of government policy possess an underlying unity. To
His Majesty's Government, considerations of imperial strategy at this moment
required the sacrifice of Zionism; since Jews had no choice but to hope for a
British victory, they had to approve political concessions to the Arab position
in Palestine. The support of Weizmann and other Jews could be taken for granted
during the struggle against Hitler. Lacking the ground of an autonomous state
under its feet, a powerless Jewry could command no influence in the Western
councils of war. It was far easier to mask its travail under the swastika than
grapple with the moral imperative of aiding human beings whose only crime
was their very birth. Manifest at the very start of World War II, this official
consensus in London only hardened with the passage of time.

The 1939 White Paper remained intact even as the screws tightened for the
Jews of occupied Europe. HMG persisted in bringing pressure on transit countries
along the Danube and elsewhere against facilitating unauthorized immigration
(*Aliya Bet*) to Palestine. It refused as well the Jewish Agency's request for 20,000
Polish children to enter immediately within the limited Palestine quota and in
early 1940 considerably limited Palestine land purchase by the *Yishuv* (the Jewish
community there). That February a government spokesman announced in the
House of Lords that HMG "cannot accept responsibility" for Jewish attempts
to escape "from the consequences of the well-known and deliberate policy of
the German government."[3] In December the British even deported 1,581 such
escapees who arrived in Haifa Bay to Mauritius, where they were imprisoned
until after the war. Palestine High Commissioner Harold MacMichael regularly
kept hundreds of others in the Atlit internment camp for several months on
alleged security grounds, although even the Foreign Office (with good reason)
doubted the presence of Gestapo agents aboard the illegal boats. For its part,
the Colonial Office, which on occasion seized these vessels outside Palestine's

waters in contravention of international law, doled out the precious entry permits with a penurious hand.

The *Struma* disaster well reflected the results of this stance. On February 24, 1942, all but 1 of 769 Jews who fled the Romanian Trans-Dnistria deportations died when the fifty-six-foot cattle boat *Struma* exploded outside Turkish waters; authorities in Ankara refused them entry because the British would not grant onward papers to Palestine.[4] Responding to critics at home and in the United States, the British cabinet informed the Jewish Agency in May that all who reached Palestine (but not Turkey) would be admitted henceforth. Yet, given German designs, the secret understanding meant little by then. As for agency candidate certificate lists, the relevant offices in London, Palestine, Geneva (the Swiss acting as Britain's protecting power abroad), and Ankara first had to clear these documents, followed by consulates in occupied Europe. By the end of 1942, 3,743 Jews had entered Palestine, the lowest figure for the entire war.

Fears, as confidential British memoranda regularly put it, that an "unmanageable flood" of Jewish refugees to Palestine would jeopardize the anti-Zionist policy embodied in the White Paper also lay behind London's opposition to an Allied Jewish fighting force. The Jewish Agency's offer in September 1939 of 20,000 to 40,000 Palestinian Jews to defend the Promised Land, together with a unit of volunteers from free-world Jewry to serve wherever needed, quickly roused strong War Office reservations. Winston Churchill, then first lord of the Admiralty, could not sway his cabinet colleagues, led by Colonial Secretary Malcolm MacDonald, prime architect of the White Paper. Only after Churchill assumed the reins of British power did the idea of a 10,000-man Jewish division gradually obtain cabinet acceptance in principle. Yet the choice in early 1941 of Walter Moyne to lead the Colonial Office, combined with Arabist views of Foreign Secretary Anthony Eden and British Middle East representatives, spelled the project's demise. To meet the danger of a Nazi invasion of the region, the British did secretly encourage intelligence operations and training of the Jewish Agency's Hagana defense organization. London masked, however, the *Yishuv*'s 20,000 recruits and other valuable services for the British armed forces under the rubric "Palestinian"—at the same time that the governments of Iraq, Syria, and Egypt favored the Nazi invader, and former mufti of Jerusalem Haj Amin al-Husseini took to the Axis airwaves and recruited thousands from the Balkans into Moslem units of the German Wehrmacht.

With Rommel's Afrika Korps advancing on Alexandria, Jewish Agency political director Moshe Shertok unsuccessfully implored the British Middle East commander in April 1942 to mobilize the *Yishuv*'s available manpower. If the Nazis overran the country, "an even swifter destruction" would overtake the Jews of Palestine, he added, than had fallen on "hundreds of thousands" of their fellow Jews who had perished to date in Europe.[5] Given unyielding Colonial and War Office opposition, Churchill failed to secure the appointment of ardent Zionist Orde Wingate to lead a large military force in Palestine. Separate Jewish battalions, created in August 1942, were limited to a static defensive role there. Following Britain's major victory at El Alamein two months later against Rommel, HMG reverted to the traditional position: no military cooperation with the *Yishuv* in order to frustrate Zionist hopes. Rather, HMG saw fit to select as its minister resident, Middle East, Walter Moyne, saboteur of the Jewish division, who had recently risen in Parliament to compare Zionist "aggression and domination" in Palestine with the Nazi spirit.[6]

Nor for more than two and one-half years would London permit the dispatch of medicine and food into the Jewish ghettos throughout Poland. Few in the free world grasped then that Germany had made starvation a weapon of annihilation, while public opinion believed that the blockade was the deadliest weapon in the British arsenal. "No form of relief can be devised," categorically asserted Churchill in August 1940 in the House of Commons, "which would not directly or indirectly assist the enemy's war effort."[7] One year later, pressure from the British embassy, supported by the U.S. State Department, ended food shipments by American Jewish organizations to Poland. At that same time, the Anglo-American Alliance allowed 15,000 tons of wheat and 3,000 tons of other materials through the Allied blockade to hold off starvation in Nazi-held Greece. Finally, in June 1942, the British Ministry of Economic Warfare secretly permitted the Board of Deputies of British Jews to send one-pound packages of food from neutral Portugal, up to a maximum of $12,000 per month. Washington would follow a half-year later. But the twelfth hour had already struck for Polish Jewry.

The United Kingdom itself offered but a dim beacon of hope for Jews under the Third Reich. Exaggerated fears bordering on hysteria after the fall of the Low Countries and France in mid-1940 sparked a mass internment of "friendly enemy aliens" (mostly Jews from Germany and Austria). The hasty deportation of some 8,000 such aliens to camps overseas, where they encountered anti-Semitic discrimination, eventually drew public and official criticism. The marked reversal in attitudes came after a German submarine sank the liner *Arandora Star*, taking as well the lives of bona fide refugees.

Improvement in government policy toward resident aliens did not alter a restrictionist admissions policy, however. Although preparations were said to have been made to receive up to 300,000 Dutch and Belgian refugees in the spring of 1940, the Home and Foreign offices refused admission that December to 2,000 Jews in Luxemburg facing deportation to Poland; the government's limited concession in October 1942 to admit "*de facto orphans*" from unoccupied Vichy France with near relatives in Britain came too late for implementation. Home Secretary Herbert Morrison warned that a generous entry policy might well provoke domestic anti-Semitism, then in evidence.[8] Yet no instances of serious anti-Jewish violence ever occurred, while the government did nothing to encourage that substantial element of public opinion sympathetic to Jewish refugee admission. All told, no more than 10,000 Jews entered the country during the war. As for the rest of the empire, Canada, Australia, New Zealand,

South Africa, and India combined took in fewer Jews than did the free port of Shanghai, which accepted 25,000 Jews in these same years.

Try as it might, by mid-1942 London could not entirely mute European Jewry's singular catastrophe, since known as the Holocaust. Throughout that spring press bulletins had reported the death of thousands in the Ukraine, of poison gas experiments at Mauthausen, and of slaughter in the Baltic countries and White Russia. On June 2 the BBC broadcast the gist of a detailed Bund report from Poland about "the physical extermination of the Jewish people on Polish soil," and Bundist Szmul Zygielbojm of the Polish National Council in London confirmed his comrades' figure (greatly underestimated) of 700,000 murdered in Poland. At the end of June the *London Daily Telegraph* featured the estimate of the World Jewish Congress's British Section that over 1,000,000 Jews had been killed in Europe, Hitler intending "to wipe the race from the European continent."[9] The Anglo press and the *London Jewish Chronicle* carried these and other news items throughout July. That same month Churchill (as well as Roosevelt) sent a message to a rally at Madison Square Garden, warning that all perpetrators of these atrocities would face retribution following the Allied victory. Procrastination was still the order of the day, however, even after Zygielbojm and Member of Parliament Josiah Wedgwood publicized a ghastly account by three grave diggers who had escaped from the death center at Chelmno.[10]

The Foreign Office remained skeptical about such reports of mass slaughter. In August it pondered for a week before forwarding to Member of Parliament Sidney Silverman a cable from World Jewish Congress Geneva executive Gerhart Riegner, who told of a rumor that Hitler's headquarters were contemplating a plan to murder that autumn all Jews "at one blow" in the East. The previous January Whitehall officials, having applauded a conference decision by nine democratic governments in exile not to include Nazi anti-Jewish persecutions among war crimes punishable after V-E Day, had more grounds for reserve. Some, like their State Department opposites, accepted German propaganda that Jews were being sent to Nazi labor installations. Another cable in early September, also from Jewish sources in Switzerland, which spoke of Jewish bodies being transformed into soap and artificial fertilizer, understandably recalled propaganda stories of World War I vintage. Silverman received permission to inform World Jewish Congress president Stephen Wise in New York, but was quickly cautioned that any publicity might "irritate" the Nazis and so provoke "greater excesses."[11] Additional information, including Thomas Mann's BBC broadcast on September 27, 1942, about the recent gassing of French and Polish Jews, and detailed eyewitness accounts regarding the Holocaust from individuals who had reached neutral Switzerland, did not elicit an official response.

Churchill did send a personal message to a crowd of ten thousand meeting under the auspices of the Board of Deputies in Albert Hall on October 20 that denounced the "systematic cruelties to which the Jewish people have been exposed under the Nazi regime."[12] Action only ensued, however, once the State

Department finally confirmed the substance of numerous reports from Riegner and others, survivors arrived in Palestine with harrowing testimony, and the WJC's British Section and especially the Polish government in exile convinced Whitehall to overcome its doubts.

On December 17, 1942, Great Britain, the United States, the Soviet Union, and all their allies issued the United Nations' Declaration of Jewish Massacres. Following Foreign Secretary Eden's original draft, they unanimously condemned "in the strongest terms this bestial policy of cold-blooded extermination" and resolved to bring its perpetrators to justice. The House of Commons then stood for an unprecedented two minutes of silence. Well over two million Jews had already perished, but Eden (who privately preferred the return of Jews to their former homes, rather than their settling in Palestine) immediately hinted in Parliament about the existence of unspecified "immense geographical and other difficulties." Archbishop of Canterbury William Temple, various MPs, and newspaper editorials all sought commitments of British aid, yet Parliamentary Under Secretary Richard Law had already warned a delegation from the British Council of Christians and Jews that assurance of asylum might get the government "involved in some kind of super-Balfour Declaration which would dog our footsteps forever."[13] Small wonder that mention of specific measures for rescue never found its way into the final draft. The historic declaration accomplished nothing because Great Britain and the other two major Allied powers persisted in refusing to treat Jews as a distinct ally requiring emergency help. Indeed, that document represented the only Allied pronouncement on the Holocaust throughout the war.

Mounting public pressure forced Whitehall to reconsider its formal reticence. Member of Parliament Eleanor Rathbone, the driving force behind the National Committee for Rescue from Nazi Terror, urged her government to seek Vatican intercession and to negotiate with Hitler for the mass release of Jews. The *New Statesman and Nation* and the *Manchester Guardian* took the lead in insisting that the Home Office relax immigration quotas and request neutrals Sweden and Turkey to save Jewish children.[14] The Board of Deputies sought guarantees of support to the neutral governments and the International Red Cross, as well as short-term accommodation in North Africa, the Isle of Man, Eire, and especially Palestine. Arthur Cardinal Hinsley called for "speedy deeds" to meet "the most appalling horror in recorded history," a theme that resounded through a lengthy debate in the House of Lords on March 23, 1943.[15] In that discussion the archbishop of Canterbury and like-minded individuals urged a sympathetic visa policy, ships to transport Jews to safety, an Allied commission to focus on rescue, Palestine entry, and the shipment of food and money to the neutrals for maintaining Jewish survivors. The Anglo-American Alliance's announcement that month of an exploratory conference at Ottawa to discuss the so-called refugee question struck these critics as a sign of further callousness at a time when, in Lord Rochester's acute phrase, "delay meant death."[16]

In fact, London had secured Washington's approval of that conference only after considerable diplomatic maneuvering, but the meeting would be a facade aimed at quieting calls for immediate rescue. Since Ottawa officials opposed a meeting on that territory, isolated Bermuda was chosen as the site. The Foreign Office rejected Riegner's suggestion (accepted by the World Council of Churches' Secretariat) to exchange Jews for German civilians en bloc, with Eden dismissing outright as "fantastically impossible" a proposal of American Jewry's Joint Emergency Committee that the United Nations ask Hitler publicly to release Jews or that food be sent to Jews in occupied Europe. In a more candid discussion the foreign secretary warned Secretary of State Cordell Hull in the presence of Roosevelt that acceptance of Bulgaria's threatened 60,000 to 70,000 Jews might well lead the Führer to make similar offers in Poland and Germany, and not enough ships could be had to handle these unfortunates.[17] Rather, the British Cabinet on the Reception and Accommodation of Refugees (as in the title for the Bermuda Conference on Refugees, the word "Jews" remained antiseptically absent) unanimously agreed on April 2, 1943, that Britain would undertake no commitments at Bermuda beyond transporting 5,000 Bulgarian Jews to Palestine, with the most important objective the return of Jews in "large numbers" to their own prewar countries after the Third Reich's defeat.[18]

The British delegation, headed by Richard Law, had good reason to be delighted with the Bermuda deliberations. The members found the Americans eager to accept the White Paper on Palestine; congressional immigration laws, as a quid pro quo, were also not open to question. No exchange of prisoners or lifting of the Allied blockade to bring relief to European Jewry would be permitted. The Americans even outdid the British in dismissing all possibilities of using Allied vessels for rescue, while suggestions for Santo Domingo, Angola, Madagascar, British Honduras, and Cyrenaica as refugee centers were referred to the ineffective prewar Intergovernmental Committee on Refugees. Nor did the conference discuss a Swedish offer—dependent on assurances of Anglo-American aid—to admit 20,000 Jewish children from Axis-controlled countries. A brief public statement, making no reference to Jews as such, assured the world that "a substantial number" of refugees would be aided through concrete, if secret, recommendations. In fact, the delegates recommended only the resurrection of the Intergovernmental Committee and the movement of 21,000 refugees, including an estimated 5,000 Jews, from Spain to North Africa.

British prodding secured the small joint refugee program in North Africa. Churchill, who had personally intervened in mid-April against the Spanish government's closing of the Pyrenees frontier to Jews fleeing France, sought Roosevelt's support for settling Jews in the former Italian colonies of Cyrenaica and Tripolitania. These would serve as "satellite" territories of a future large Jewish state in Palestine. State Department experts rejected the latter suggestions, however, while the U.S. Joint Chiefs of Staff strongly opposed Eden's idea that a North African center could save Allied soldiers and some Jews. Churchill finally obtained FDR's approval in early July. Ultimately, the camp that Eden so aptly characterized as a "modest suggestion" sheltered only a few hundred Jews who had the good fortune to cross General Franco's borders. The British War Office turned down Cyrenaica because of probable Arab antagonism. The government's approval—one year later—for a camp in Tripolitania to shelter 1,000 to 1,500 Jewish refugees (Whitehall was seeking to take pressure off Jewish settlement in Palestine) never materialized.

Adolf Hitler's so-called Final Solution of the Jewish problem could not be thwarted while the Western powers believed, as Eden put it to Commons in a heated debate on May 19, 1943, that "the only real solution" for Europe's Jews was "final and complete Allied victory." Rathbone, Wedgwood, and others demanded courage and speed to meet Jewry's unparalleled crisis, but these attributes could not be found in officials who feared, in Richard Law's frank phrase at Bermuda, that negotiations with Berlin might succeed, and that "would be relieving Hitler of an obligation to take care of *these useless people*."[19] Rather than risk such embarrassment, it would be far easier to sidestep the great challenge and call on the exigencies of war. Thus no help was dispatched to the defenders of the Warsaw ghetto uprising, whose heroic resistance at that same moment was conveyed to the West via radio broadcasts and newspaper bulletins. There was no acknowledgment from Churchill or Roosevelt of the death in May 1943 of Szmul Zygielbojm, whose suicide note protested "the indifference of the world which witnesses the extermination of the Jewish people without taking any steps to prevent it."[20] Half a year later, at the Moscow Conference, Churchill, Roosevelt, and Stalin issued a long statement against German barbarism, with Jewry conspicuously absent. Nor did the British and American warlords, in the course of their secret correspondence with one another, raise the possibility of rescuing the particular targets of Hitler's obsessive hatred.

Although Britain had insisted before the German *Blitzkrieg* against Poland that aid to European Jewry and the Palestine dilemma remain separate issues, these two subjects proved to be decisively linked during the Holocaust years. Thus a report, first publicized by the *New York Times* in February 1943, about Romania's offer of the remaining 70,000 Jews in Trans-Dnistria was dismissed by Whitehall as—if serious—a piece of blackmail. Romania's Marshall Ion Antonescu assured the International Red Cross of his interest in facilitating emigration (including that to Palestine), but London dragged its feet in signaling the Turkish government to approve ships and transit facilities.[21]

Privy Seal Lord Cranborne announced that the resources of His Majesty's Government to maintain "vast quantities of refugees" were greatly stretched, while Colonial Office bureaucrats privately warned against Palestine becoming inundated by Jews. The War Cabinet agreed in July 1943 to allow all Jews reaching Turkey admission to Palestine, as well as to extend the original White Paper deadline beyond April 1, 1944, yet it kept official word of this decision from the Turks. HMG showed its true intentions by torpedoing a promising scheme, arranged by some young Palestinian Jewish representatives in Istanbul, to rescue a first group of 1,000 Bulgarian Jews. In the meantime, Adolf Eichmann and the Wilhelmstrasse, prodded by the former mufti of Jerusalem, did all in their power to murder the Jews of the Balkans. A mere 526 Jews passed through Turkey in all of 1943 from Bulgaria, Hungary, and Romania, with 430 more escaping aboard small boats from Greece to Izmir and then to Palestine.[22]

Silence in the face of the Holocaust was equally reflected in a contemplated joint Anglo-American statement on Palestine, slated for issue in July 1943. Anxious about reports of impending Arab-Jewish conflict over Palestine and its potentially adverse effect on the Allied campaign in North Africa, the State Department found the Foreign Office receptive to publishing a declaration that would bar any further discussion of Palestine until after the war. British chiefs of staff and most of the War Cabinet wished to secure thereby the empire's strategic interests in the entire Middle East for an indefinite period. Only Churchill and Minister for India Leopold Amery markedly supported the *Yishuv* as Britain's one reliable ally in the Middle East, and hence the Jewish Agency's demand for a Zionist commonwealth. Owing to Churchill's insistence, the War Cabinet decided not to approve the seizure of illegal Jewish arms in Palestine. Otherwise, the joint declaration appeared headed for issue. At the last minute, in August, pressure from various American Jewish quarters halted the statement's promulgation.[23]

This development only encouraged the British Palestine authorities to sully the name of Zionism, particularly in American public opinion, and to end the contraband sale of British military equipment into Jewish hands by mounting a public trial. Although the proceedings revealed past British cooperation with the Hagana and its Palmach elite force, the eventual, severe sentences discriminated against Jews, leaving no doubt that the British sought to liquidate the Hagana. Zionist protests in Washington and London, together with the threat of a Jewish revolt throughout Palestine, halted the actions. Yet, as the agency's Moshe Shertok wrote a colleague at the time, the *Yishuv* was still being denied its request to form a separate Allied fighting force that could help conquer the Jewish "Valley of Slaughter" in Europe and save the remnants of its people.[24]

Anxieties about the Promised Land also led to Whitehall's objections concerning a revolutionary idea, first raised by Riegner, to rescue Jews, especially children, in Romania and France. The U.S. Treasury Department under Henry Morgenthau, Jr., despite strong State Department reservations, approved the scheme for blocked accounts in Swiss banks, to be paid after the war to wealthy Jews in occupied Europe who would now advance the needed sums. Consulted, Britain's Ministry of Economic Warfare expressed hesitation, despite the fact that it had quickly transferred three thousand pounds sterling to Guernsey to feed English children in the occupied Channel Islands without even asking for U.S. approval. Even when that ministry and the State Department itself finally approved the scheme, Eden cabled in January 1944 that possible "transportation and accommodation problems" that might be "embarrassing" to both governments could well ensue from the project's adoption.[25] Only days earlier, the Colonial and Foreign offices had turned down a month-old request from the American Jewish Joint Distribution Committee to set aside sufficient Palestine certificates within the White Paper quota to assure the evacuation from Switzerland of 5,000 French Jewish children after the war, although the British had been informed that this step alone would persuade the Swiss to admit these youngsters facing the gravest danger. Secretary Morgenthau appropriately termed Whitehall's politically motivated anxiety over the Riegner scheme a "Satanic combination of British chill and diplomatic double-talk: cold and correct, and adding up to a sentence of death."[26]

The Britishers' persistent worry about disposing of many Jewish refugees also explains the vexation, however absurd, of a prominent Foreign Office official on suddenly hearing of the U.S. War Refugee Board's creation that same month: "It is fundamentally all part of Zionist drive and is liable to make much trouble for us in Palestine and with our relations with America over Palestine."[27] In like vein, London registered a formal protest during March 1944 against that board's new licensing policy for private organizations to send rescue funds abroad. HMG did not set up a parallel refugee agency during the remainder of the war.

Implementation in mid-1944 of the Final Solution in Hungary, the last major Jewish community under the Nazi jackboot, did not spark a fundamental change in this persistent stance. Already in early April Britain possessed some reliable knowledge of the impending catastrophe. In mid-May, just as Eichmann commenced the massive deportation from the Hungarian provinces, the anti-Nazi Hungarian minister in Bern asked his British counterpart to have the BBC immediately warn the Hungarian people not to assist in the shipment of a targeted half-million Jews to Poland.[28] Yet nothing happened for several precious weeks.

Instead, when Joel Brand and Andor Grosz arrived in Istanbul from Budapest on May 19 with Eichmann's offer to release Jews for ten thousand trucks—to be used only on the eastern war front—and for other goods, British local intelligence arranged Brand's detention in Cairo and never returned him to Turkey and Hungary as originally promised. London warned Washington on June 5, the eve of the Normandy invasion, that acceptance of the "blackmail" proposal was "equivalent to asking the Allies to suspend essential military operations."[29] The War Cabinet also turned down a suggestion from Chief Rabbi Joseph Hertz and the Jewish Agency to recognize trapped Jews as "British protected persons," arguing that this priority would "overlook the fact that German brutality has been directed very extensively, above all in Poland, against non-Jews."[30] War Refugee Board director John Pehle obtained Roosevelt's approval to keep the Brand negotiations afloat to gain time, as the agency recommended, and the State Department sought British approval to receive Jews and others in "imminent danger of death" whom the Germans would be willing to release. This was far too late a response, for by then Rabbi Michael Weissmandel of the Bratislava Jewish underground had relayed to the West the testimony of three escapees from Auschwitz-Birkenau (two were Jews) and an account of the deportation of over 435,000 Hungarian Jews to there since May 15. Although shocked, Churchill refused any negotiation with the Germans, and on July 19

London leaked information to the press, just received from interrogation of Brand's travel companion, that high Gestapo officials were using the Brand mission to seek peace feelers with the West. So ended any hope for stalling the negotiations to save Jews.

When the press reported, that same day, Regent Horthy's order halting the deportations and his authorizing the exit of all Jewish children under the age of ten possessing a visa (with all Jews having Palestine visas allowed to emigrate there), the two major Western allies let a valuable month go by before announcing their acceptance of the offer. The British Cabinet on Refugees especially feared that a "flood" of Jews to Palestine would risk civil war in the country.[31]

Delay and callousness surfaced again over the suggestion, first advanced by Weissmandel, to bomb Auschwitz-Birkenau and/or the railway lines leading from Hungary to its gas chambers. Churchill and Eden, following receipt at the end of June of the Auschwitz escapee accounts, favored the idea. Yet Foreign Office career officers stymied this, holding back topographical data of Auschwitz (given by the Jewish Agency) from the British Air Ministry, despite the ministry's assertion that lack of such information precluded a strike operation.[32] Data on file in London and Washington could have contributed decisively to destroying the gas chambers, since the Allies controlled the skies over Poland and bombed oil refineries in the area on a regular basis with considerable success. The will to save was not there. While the War Refugee Board actually kept open the door to the negotiations suggested in Brand's mission, encouraging talks between Nazi emissaries and a Swiss representative of the Joint Distribution Committee, the British focused their attention on maintaining the prewar White Paper. From June on, Eden warned Churchill in lengthy memoranda that Middle Eastern oil and strategic communications necessitated the establishment of a state in Palestine that would satisfy the Arabs of the region. HMG finally informed Turkey— almost a full year after the cabinet's July 1943 decision—that all reaching Istanbul would be eligible for admission to the Promised Land, but London limited entry there from October onwards to 1,500 Jews per month as soon as it was threatened with waves of Jewish migration out of the liberated Balkans. In December the new Palestine high commissioner, John Gort, succeeded in having the July 1943 pledge revoked, happy, too, that cautious Russian authorities in the Balkans were reducing the potential exodus to Palestine.[33]

Only at the end of September 1944 did Great Britain establish a Jewish brigade for the Allied war effort, and this because of Churchill's strong intervention. Fearing Zionist plans in Palestine, the War Office especially had opposed all requests from the Jewish Agency, the Anglo Committee for a Jewish Army, and others for a distinctive Jewish fighting force, but the catastrophe of Hungarian Jewry deeply moved the prime minister to do something concrete at last for the Jews. Aside from supporting a cabinet proposal for Palestine's partition into Jewish and Arab states, Churchill stressed to his colleagues that the *Yishuv* should be permitted to confront the murderers of its people in battle under its own blue and white flag. Anxiety over Zionist aims had also led British officials to scale down considerably the agency's large-scale program, suggested in early 1943, of Palestinian parachutists to help endangered Jews in Europe, but over the brigade Churchill had his way.[34]

The Jewish combat group of 5,000 participated on the Adriatic front with distinction in early 1945. Still, HMG refused to bring the brigade up to its full strength of 6,000 and insisted on the unit's dispersion before its soldiers returned home. This last condition recalled the fate of the Jewish Legion after the last World War.

Yet Churchill, too, relegated the fate of European Jewry to secondary importance during the war. The Allied warlord most strongly stirred by the Nazi atrocities and most impressed with Zionist claims promised retribution only after the hour of liberation had struck in Europe. His firm support for a large Jewish postwar state in Palestine came too late for those whose traditional homelessness such a commonwealth would have ended. The assassination of Walter Moyne in November 1944 by two members of the Stern group raised serious doubts even in the prime minister's mind. "This shameful crime has shocked the world," Churchill told Commons, and he and others would have to reconsider their pro-Zionist position if that movement were to end by producing "a new set of gangsters worthy of Nazi Germany."[35] While the entire *Yishuv* was thus held culpable for the action of two youngsters, Germany's use of death factories never moved the same leader to tell Commons on any occasion that these crimes had "shocked the world." Relief and rescue were not made a major aim of his War Cabinet. As for Britain's direct complicity in closing off the most obvious refuge for Jews, after deducting some 12,000 illegals who arrived during the war, Churchill's government still had 23,000 unused permits under the White Paper when V-E Day dawned.

Great Britain discriminated in its response during World War II. Three hundred thousand Dutch and Belgian refugees might have been considered for admission to the United Kingdom, but not 2,000 Jews in Luxemburg awaiting deportation to Poland.[36] Greeks and British children in the occupied Channel Islands obtained relief to avert famine, but not Jews. The Royal Air Force successfully attacked an Amiens prison in February 1944 to free nearly 100 members of the French resistance, and a half-year later it flew in arms and supplies on hazardous night flights to Warsaw when the Polish Home Army rose against the Nazis. No such aid went to the Jewish resistance, while the crematoria and railroad lines leading to them never became prime targets. Tens of thousands of Yugoslavs and Greeks received a cordial welcome in Middle East refugee camps, but not Jews, who could prove "embarrassing" to imperial interests. Ships ferried thousands of German prisoners and Moslem pilgrims, and even once deported Jewish refugees to a Mauritius internment, but vessels could not be made available for saving innocents whose tragedy HMG persistently masked in the years 1939–45.

Anti-Semitism played some role in this sorry record. Colonial Office Permanent Under Secretary of State John Shuckburgh, who believed that Jews "hate all gentiles,'' expressed the hope to his associates at the start of the war that ''some of the sources of supply'' for illegal migration to Palestine ''may dry up''; witness too Eden's notation ''Must I?'' regarding the need to receive Weizmann and Shertok for an interview about the Hungarian transports to Auschwitz.[37]

Disbelief also hampered a response, as when the chairman of Britain's Joint Intelligence Committee, upon receiving reports in July 1943 about gas chambers, asserted: ''The Poles, and to a far greater extent the Jews, tend to exaggerate German atrocities in order to stoke us up.'' In January 1945 a Whitehall Refugee Department bureaucrat made a similar observation: ''One notable tendency in Jewish reports on this problem is to exaggerate the numbers of deportations and deaths.''[38]

Above all, political expediency reigned supreme. As Weizmann put it to South African premier Jan Smuts and Churchill in June 1944, when appealing for a Jewish state in undivided Palestine before the war's end: ''The parlous position of the Jews is due to the fact that they have no country which they can call their own.''[39] Jewish powerlessness, a bimillennial disability that made the Holocaust possible, had to undergo a radical transformation if Auschwitz-Birkenau was not to be repeated. The policy of ''rescue through Allied victory,'' alas, had proven bankrupt for a people that would never hear the bells that pealed with the joy of freedom. The *Yishuv* saw no choice after World War II but to end the curse of anonymity, bring the stateless survivors of the Holocaust home, and take up arms for sovereign independence. Inevitably, a direct collision with Great Britain loomed.

And beyond the Holocaust? When the first films of the liberated concentration camps were shown in London's Leicester Square and apparently elsewhere across the country, British and other Allied soldiers, blocking the exits, forced fleeing patrons to ''go back and face it.'' No longer could this reality be dismissed as the BBC had done when it refused to use an eyewitness account by its own correspondent in August 1944 of liberated Majdanek, thinking that detailed news story at the time a ''Russian propaganda stunt.''[40] Now the mind had to cope with absolute barbarism, as well as with the indifference exhibited by His Majesty's Government and other bystanders in the Jewish people's darkest hour. An estimated 28,000 inmates died even after the freeing of Bergen-Belsen, despite heroic British efforts at last to counter death. The tragedy, during which the free world at large deemed European Jewry expendable, would also take its toll thereafter. Other peoples became more susceptible, in time, to dehumanization and mass murder. Regrettably, the reverberations of the Holocaust are with us still.

Another Englishman, a luminary of the eighteenth century, suggested the elementary prescription for this fragile state of affairs. In words attributed to Edmund Burke: ''The only thing necessary for the triumph of evil is for enough good men to do nothing.'' Memory, unwavering vigilance, and the will to act against the cancer of bestiality are essential. We can do no other.

**BIBLIOGRAPHIC ESSAY**

For several years after World War II, the subject of British (and Allied) government response during the Holocaust escaped objective scrutiny. Studies of Anglo-American diplomacy in that period avoided the topic, such as Llewellyn Woodward's *British Foreign Policy in the Second World War* and Gabriel Kolko's *The Politics of War: The World and United States Foreign Policy, 1943– 1945* (1968). The same held true for historians of the Holocaust, including Leon Poliakov, *Harvest of Hate*; Raul Hilberg, *The Destruction of the European Jews*; Gerald Reitlinger, *The Final Solution*; and even, a decade later, Lucy Dawidowicz, *The War Against the Jews, 1933–1945*. The interested student could have begun with Hansard, *Parliamentary Debates* (5th Series) and the U.S. *Congressional Record* (1939–45), but government archives remained closed under a standard thirty-year rule. Memoirs by leading actors in the drama, including Churchill and Eden, also carried scant discussion of Great Britain's actions during the Holocaust years.

The first discussion of this subject came in attacks from Zionist sources. The Mandatory Power's restrictive Palestine immigration policy was first documented in the Jewish Agency's *Reports of the Executives Submitted to the 22nd Zionist Congress at Basle, December 1946*, then discussed in Chaim Weizmann's autobiography, *Trial and Error*. British efforts to frustrate the establishment of an Allied Jewish army, culminating in the Jewish Brigade, found analysis in books by Jacob Lifschitz, *Sefer HaBrigada HaYehudit*; Yitzchak Lamdan, *Sefer HaHitnadvut*; and Zerubavel Gilad, ed., *Magen BeSeter*. The matter of "illegal" immigration received attention in a number of memoirs, such as Moshe Basok, ed., *Sefer HaMa'apilim*; Chaim Lazar, *Af Al Pi*; Bracha Habas, *The Gate Breakers*, translated by David Segal; and Yehuda Braginski, *Am Choter El Chof*. The one official defense to these charges came in George Kirk's *Survey of International Affairs, 1939–1946: The Middle East in the War* (1952).

Related publications in this early period broadened the scope of inquiry. Henry Morgenthau, Jr.,'s "The Morgenthau Diaries, VI—The Refugee Run-Around," *Collier's* 120 (1947), indicted the British even as the former treasury secretary focused on the callousness of the U.S. State Department regarding the specific Jewish plight under Hitler. The World Jewish Congress analyzed its efforts, in the face of British and other governmental indifference, for the histories *Unity in Dispersion* (1948) and its British Section's *Outline of Activities, 1936–1946* (1948). Andrew Sharf offered a novel perspective, not followed up by other scholars, with *The British Press and the Jews Under Nazi Rule*.

Arthur Morse's popular, well-received *While Six Million Died: A Chronicle of American Apathy* provided a pioneering work in this regard. While concentrating on the U.S. government, Morse cast damning light on Great Britain as well. (An earlier hint along these lines first appeared in former Secretary of the Treasury Henry Morgenthau, Jr.,'s 1947 memoir for *Collier's* magazine.) Supplementary books by scholars of the same subject came to identical conclusions, including Henry Feingold's *The Politics of Rescue: The Roosevelt Administration and the Holocaust, 1938–1945* and Saul S. Friedman's *No Haven for the Oppressed: United States Policy Toward Jewish Refugees, 1938–1945*.

The opening in 1972 of official British archives led to fuller expositions. A. J. Sherman's *Island Refuge: Britain and Refugees from the Third Reich, 1933–1939* ably examined the far more favorable shift after 1938 in Home (but not Colonial and Foreign) Office policy toward Jews fleeing Nazi persecution. Bela Vago authored two significant articles on the Joel Brand mission and the fate of Hungarian Jewry, both drawing on these archives, for *Yad Vashem Studies* (1974) and the Yad Vashem volume *Rescue Attempts During the Holocaust* (1977). Important books on the Palestine question appeared by Gabriel Cohen, *Churchill U'Sh'eilat Eretz Yisrael, 1939–1942*; Michael J. Cohen, *Palestine, Retreat from the Mandate: The Making of British Policy, 1936–1945*; and Martin Gilbert, *Exile and Return: The Struggle for a Jewish Homeland*. Leni Yahil presented a study of selected documents on Britain's White Paper policy during 1939–40 in *Yad Vashem Studies*, and Yehuda Bauer carefully analyzed the Brand mission in its wider ramifications for an article that also appeared in his book, *The Holocaust in Historical Perspective*. John R. Fox analyzed the Jewish factor in British war-crimes policy during 1942 for the *English Historical Review*. I examined the 1943 joint Anglo-American statement on Palestine in the *Herzl Yearbook* (1978). A new approach was manifest with Meir Sampolinky's Ph.D. dissertation for Bar-Ilan University, "The Anglo-Jewish Leadership, the British Government, and the Holocaust" (1977).

In this same decade related works, although not based on British archives, appeared by Israeli historians. Worthy of note were Yehuda Bauer, *From Diplomacy to Resistance*; Yehuda Slutsky, *Sefer Toldot HaHagana* (particularly volume 3, 1972); Michael Bar-Zohar, *Ben Gurion*; Yosef Gorni, *Shutfut U'Ma'avak*; and the controversial S. B. Beit-Tsvi, *HaTsiyonut HaPost-Ugandit BeMashber HaShoa*. Valuable editions were presented as volumes 3 and 4 of Moshe Sharett's *Yoman Medini* (1974, 1979). Chaim Barlas's *HaTsala BeYemei Shoa* (1975) offered his personal perspective, as Jewish Agency representative in Istanbul, on British (and other Allied) intransigence during the unique catastrophe then befalling European Jewry. Memoirs concerning "illegal" immigration came from the pens of Ruth Aliav and Peggy Mann, *The Last Escape*; Ehud Avriel, *Open the Gates!*; and William Perl, *The Four-Front War: From the Holocaust to the Promised Land*.

With Bernard Wasserstein's volume, *Britain and the Jews of Europe, 1939–1945*, a near-definitive analysis appeared of the entire issue. Thoroughly rooted in the official British depositories at the Public Record Office (first located in London, then transferred to Kew), this study provides an exemplary discussion of practically every aspect suggested by the author's title. The book lacks interviews and the use of other related Allied (and organizational) archives. Few can argue, however, with Wasserstein's objective description of bureaucratic complacency and blindness to the specific Jewish tragedy now termed "the Holocaust."

My own work, *The Jews Were Expendable: Free World Diplomacy and the Holocaust*, presented the first overview of "the outsiders," including detailed discussion of British official policy during the Holocaust. Topics in this vein included the struggle for an Allied Jewish fighting force, the unveiling of the Final Solution, the Bermuda Conference and its aftermath, rescue from the Balkans, and the martyrdom of Hungarian Jewry. In the course of the book, I took issue with Wasserstein's defense of Churchill, a defense repeated in Martin Gilbert's *Auschwitz and the Allies*. A far stronger attack against the British warlord subsequently surfaced in chapters 7 and 8 of Michael J. Cohen's *Churchill and the Jews*.

Later studies complemented the picture. Michael Cohen's edition of the Weizmann letters for the war years, *The Letters and Papers of Chaim Weizmann* (vols. 20–21, 1979), is expertly done. Worthy of commendation is Esther Baumel's M.A. thesis for Bar-Ilan University, "The Jewish Refugee Children in Great Britain, 1938–1945" (1981), and Dalya Ofer's dissertation on "illegal immigration" in the years 1939–1942, prepared for her Ph.D. at the Hebrew University and later expanded, in book form, to cover the years 1942–44 as well. I reviewed the "Bergson boys" and their opposition to British (and Allied) apathy regarding the rescue of Jews in *American Jewish History*. Exhaustive is Yoav Gelber's four-volume treatment of Jewish efforts to raise an army in the face of British difficulties, *Toldot HaHitnadvut* (1979–84). The British angle is examined anew by Ronald Zweig, *British Policy to Palestine During the Second World War*, with the Anglo-Jewish leadership reviewed by Bernard Wasserstein in Randolph Braham, ed., *Jewish Leadership During the Nazi Era*. David Wyman's definitive book on U.S. government policy, *The Abandonment of the Jews*, bears on British responses. Haim Avni has an illuminating comparative study of British (and Allied) official reaction to Jewish and Polish refugees during 1943 in Geoffrey Wigoder, ed., *Contemporary Jewry: Studies in Honor of Moshe Davis* (1984). The Jewish leadership in Palestine during the crucial period 1942–45, including the encounter with the Mandatory Power, has been most recently evaluated by Dina Porat, *Hanhaga BeMilkod* (1986), subsequently translated into English (1990). Shabtai Tevet's biography *Ben-Gurion: The Burning Ground* is also useful in this connection. Robert Abzug's *Inside the Vicious Heart*, focusing on the reaction of American soldiers when liberating the concentration camps, has some important comments on the British response.

Yet more remains to be done. F. H. Hinsley's official discussion, *British Intelligence in the Second World War*, suggests that significant documentation still closed to scholars will reveal the extent of British knowledge of (and reaction to) the Final Solution. Students would do well to examine files regarding British propaganda policy as it related to persecuted Jews. The Ministry of Economic Warfare's records should be studied for the same end. Numerous relevant War,

Colonial, and Foreign Office files will only be opened in the next century. Additional comparative studies should be undertaken in order to analyze London's reaction to other peoples under the swastika. The papers of various Jewish agencies in England can be profitably researched further, such as the Board of Deputies, the Anglo-Jewish Association, Zionist bodies, and the Chief Rabbi's Council. Research on British intellectuals, church organizations, and labor groups concerning this topic should also be undertaken. Finally, the archives of other governments and international agencies (including the International Red Cross and the Vatican), when they are made fully accessible to scholarly inspection, will certainly prove invaluable to a fuller picture of Great Britain and the Holocaust.

## NOTES

1. Weizmann to Chamberlain, August 29, 1939, and Chamberlain to Weizmann, September 2, 1939, Weizmann Archives (hereafter WA), Rechovot, Israel.

2. Bernard Wasserstein, *Britain and the Jews of Europe, 1939–1945* (Oxford, 1979), pp. 163–65.

3. The Marques of Dufferin and Alva, February 13, 1940, cited in *New Judea*, February 1940, p. 59.

4. Wasserstein, *Britain and the Jews of Europe*, pp. 143–56.

5. Shertok to Auchinleck, April 17, 1942, Jewish Agency files, 16/3, Zionist Archives, New York.

6. Moyne in Commons, June 9, 1942, quoted in *New Judea*, May-June 1942, pp. 122–27.

7. Churchill, quoted in A. Leon Kubowitzki, "Survey of the Rescue Activities of the World Jewish Congress, 1940-44" (mimeo), file 153, World Jewish Congress Archives (hereafter WJC), New York, pp. 9–10. These archives are now stored at the American Jewish Archives, Cincinnati, Ohio.

8. Wasserstein, *Britain and the Jews of Europe*, pp. 111–13.

9. Monty Noam Penkower, *The Jews Were Expendable: Free World Diplomacy and the Holocaust* (Urbana, 1983), pp. 59–60; *London Daily Telegraph*, June 30, 1942.

10. Perlzweig to Easterman, July 23, 1942, 177a/86, WJC; Szmul Zygielbojm and Josiah Wedgwood, "Stop Them Now!" (London, 1942), Bund Archives, New York.

11. John R. Fox, "The Jewish Factor in British War Crimes Policy in 1942," *English Historical Review* 92 (January 1977): 93–94.

12. Churchill to Temple, October 29, 1942, and attachments, Premier MSS, 4, 51/7, Public Record Office (hereafter PRO), Kew, England.

13. Penkower, *Jews Were Expendable*, pp. 87–91.

14. Rathbone to Linton, December 14, 1942, Z4/14758, Central Zionist Archives (hereafter CZA), Jerusalem, Israel; *Jewish Telegraphic Agency*, December 27, 1942.

15. Hinsley, quoted in *Congress Weekly*, March 5, 1943.

16. *House of Lords*, vol. 126, March 23, 1943, cols. 811–60.

17. Penkower, *Jews Were Expendable*, pp. 106–7.

18. Cabinet Committee on Refugees meeting, March 31, 1943, and decisions, April 2, 1943, FO 371/36657, PRO.

19. *House of Commons*, May 19, 1943, cols. 1117–1204; Law, quoted (emphasis

added) in Henry Feingold, *The Politics of Rescue: The Roosevelt Administration and the Holocaust, 1938–1945* (New Brunswick, N.J., 1970), p. 199.

20. Zygielbojm to Raczkiewicz and Sikorski, May 11, 1943, 0-55, Yad Vashem Archives, Jerusalem, Israel.

21. Penkower, *Jews Were Expendable*, pp. 148–55.

22. Ibid., pp. 156–62.

23. Monty N. Penkower, "The 1943 Joint Anglo-American Statement on Palestine," *Herzl Yearbook* 8 (1978): 212–41.

24. Shertok to Locker, September 13, 1943, Z5/1217, CZA.

25. Penkower, *Jews Were Expendable*, pp. 127–33, 139–40.

26. Henry Morgenthau, Jr., "The Refugee Run-Around," *Collier's* 120 (November 1, 1947): 23ff.

27. Hankey minute, February 4, 1944, FO 371/42727, PRO.

28. Bela Vago, "The British Government and the Fate of Hungarian Jewry in 1944," in *Rescue Attempts During the Holocaust,* ed. Yisrael Gutman and Efraim Zuroff (Jerusalem, 1977), p. 208.

29. *Foreign Relations of the United States, 1944,* 1:1056–57.

30. Memorandum of Jewish Agency, June 12, 1944, Cabinet papers 65, PRO.

31. Penkower, *Jews Were Expendable*, pp. 189–99.

32. Wasserstein, *Britain and the Jews of Europe,* pp. 311–17.

33. Linton to under secretary, April 14, 1944, Correspondence files, Ben Gurion Archives, Sde Boker, Israel; Wasserstein, *Britain and the Jews of Europe,* pp. 333–34, 340.

34. Penkower, *Jews Were Expendable*, pp. 23–25.

35. *House of Commons*, vol. 404, November 17, 1944, col. 2242.

36. Wasserstein, *Britain and the Jews of Europe,* p. 354.

37. Penkower, *Jews Were Expendable*, pp. 39, 215.

38. Ibid. pp. 295–96.

39. Weizmann to Smuts (copy to Churchill), June 19, 1944, WA.

40. Alexander Werth, *Russia at War, 1941–1945* (New York, 1964), pp. 806–15.

## SELECT BIBLIOGRAPHY

Aliav (Kluger), Ruth, and Peggy Mann. *The Last Escape*. Garden City: Doubleday, 1973.

Avni, Haim. "Between Bermuda and Santa Rosa: The Allies and the Rescue of Jews During the Holocaust from a Mexican Perspective." In *Contemporary Jewry: Studies in Honor of Moshe Davis*, edited by Geoffrey Wigoder, pp. 85–115. Jerusalem, 1984.

Avriel, Ehud. *Open the Gates!* New York: Atheneum, 1975.

Barlas, Chaim. *HaTsala BeYemei Shoa*. Haifa: Lohamei Hagetaot, 1975.

Bar-Zohar, Michael. *Ben Gurion*. Vol. 1. Tel Aviv: Am Oved, 1975.

Basok, Moshe, ed. *Sefer HaMa'apilim*. Jerusalem: Histadnit, 1947.

Bauer, Yehuda. *From Diplomacy to Resistence: A History of Jewish Palestine, 1939–1945*. Philadelphia, 1970.

———. *The Holocaust in Historical Perspective*. Seattle, 1978.

Baumel, Esther. "The Jewish Refugee Children in Great Britain, 1938–1945." M.A. thesis, Bar-Ilan University, Israel, 1981.

Beit-Tsvi, S. B. *HaTsiyonut HaPost-Ugandit BeMashber HaShoa*. Tel Aviv: Bronfman, 1977.

Braginski, Yehuda. *Am Choter El Chof*. HaKibbutz HaMeuchad, 1965.

Cohen, Gabriel. *Churchill U'Sh'eilat Eretz Yisrael, 1939–1942*. Jerusalem: Yad Yitzhok Ben-Zvi, 1976.

Cohen, Michael J. *Churchill and the Jews*. London: F. Cass, 1985.

———. *Palestine, Retreat from the Mandate: The Making of British Policy, 1936–1945*. New York, 1978.

———, ed. *The Letters and Papers of Chaim Weizmann*. Vols. 20–21. Oxford, 1979.

*Congressional Record*, 1939–45.

Dawidowicz, Lucy S. *The War Against the Jews, 1933–1945*. New York, 1975.

Feingold, Henry. *The Politics of Rescue: The Roosevelt Administration and the Holocaust, 1938–1945*. New Brunswick, N.J.: Rutgers University Press, 1970.

Fox, John R. "The Jewish Factor in British War Crimes Policy in 1942." *English Historical Review* 92 (January 1977): 82–106.

Friedman, Saul S. *No Haven for the Oppressed: United States Policy Toward Jewish Refugees, 1938–1945*. Detroit: Wayne State University Press, 1973.

Gelber, Yoav. *Toldot HaHitnadvut*. 4 vols. Jerusalem: Yad Yitzhak Ben Zvi, 1979–84.

Gilad, Zerubavel, ed. *Magen BeSeter*. Jerusalem, 1952.

Gilbert, Martin. *Auschwitz and the Allies*. London: M. Joseph and Rainbird, 1981.

———. *Exile and Return: The Struggle for a Jewish Homeland*. Philadelphia: Jewish Publication Society of America, 1978.

Gorni, Yosef. *Shutfut U'Ma'avak*. Tel Aviv: Kibbutz Hameuchad, 1976.

Habas, Bracha. *The Gate Breakers*. Translated by David Segal. New York: Herzl Press, 1963.

Hilberg, Raul. *The Destruction of the European Jews*. New York: Quadrangle, 1951.

Hinsley, F. H., et al. *British Intelligence in the Second World War: Its Influence on Strategy and Operations*. Vol. 2. New York: Cambridge University Press, 1979.

Jewish Agency. *Reports of the Executives Submitted to the 22nd Zionist Congress at Basle, December 1946*. Jerusalem, 1946.

Kirk, George. *Survey of International Affairs, 1939–1946: The Middle East in the War*. London: Oxford University Press, 1952.

Kolko, Gabriel. *The Politics of War: The World and United States Foreign Policy, 1943–1945*. New York: Random House, 1968.

Lamdan, Yitzchak, ed. *Sefer HaHitnadvut*. Jerusalem: Mosad Bialik, 1949.

Lazar, Chayim. *Af Al Pi, Sefer Aliya Bet*. Tel Aviv: Mekhan Jabotinsuy, 1957.

Lifschitz, Jacob. *Sefer HaBrigada HaYehudit*. Tel Aviv: Hotsa at Yavneh, 1947.

Morgenthau, Henry, Jr. "The Morgenthau Diaries, VI—The Refugee Run-Around." *Collier's* 120 (November 1, 1947): 23ff.

Morse, Arthur. *While Six Million Died: A Chronicle of American Apathy*. New York, 1967.

Ofer Dalya. *Derech BaYam, Ahya Bet BeTekufat Hashoa*. Jerusalem, 1988. (Translated as *Escape from the Holocaust*. Oxford, 1990.)

———. "HaAliya-HaBilti Chukit LeEretz Yisrael BeTekufat Milchemet HaOlm Ha-Shniya, 1939–1942." Ph.D. diss., Hebrew University, 1981.

*Parliamentary Debates*. 5th series. House of Commons and House of Lords. London, 1939–45.

Penkower, Monty Noam. "In Dramatic Dissent: The Bergson Boys." *American Jewish History* 70 (March 1981): 281–309.

―――. *The Jews Were Expendable: Free World Diplomacy and the Holocaust*. Urbana: University of Illinois Press, 1983.

―――. "The 1943 Joint Anglo-American Statement on Palestine." *Herzl Yearbook* 8 (1978): 212–41.

Perl, William R. *The Four-Front War: From the Holocaust to the Promised Land*. New York: Crown, 1979.

Poliakov, Leon. *Harvest of Hate*. Syracuse: Syracuse University Press, 1954.

Porat, Dina. *The Blue and the Yellow Stars of David: The Zionist Leadership in Palestine and the Holocaust, 1939–1945*. Cambridge, 1990.

―――. *Hanhaga BeMilkod*. Tel Aviv, 1986.

Reitlinger, Gerald. *The Final Solution: The Attempt to Exterminate the Jews of Europe, 1939–1945*. New York: Beechhurst, 1953.

Sampolinsky, Meir. "The Anglo-Jewish Leadership, the British Government, and the Holocaust." Ph.D. diss., Bar-Ilan University, 1977.

Sharett, Moshe. *Yoman Medini*. Vols. 3–4. Tel Aviv: Am Oved, 1974, 1979.

Sharf, Andrew. *The British Press and Jews Under Nazi Rule*. London: Oxford University Press, 1964.

Sherman, A. J. *Island Refuge: Britain and Refugees from the Third Reich, 1933–1939*. London: Elek, 1973.

Slutsky, Yehuda. *Sefer Toldot HaHagana*. Vol. 3. Tel Aviv: Am Oved, 1972.

Tevet, Shabtai. *Ben-Gurion: The Burning Ground*. Vol. 1. Boston: Houghton-Mifflin, 1987.

Vago, Bela. "The British Government and the Fate of Hungarian Jewry in 1944." In *Rescue Attempts During the Holocaust*, edited by Yisrael Gutman and Efraim Zuroff, pp. 205–33. Jerusalem, 1977.

―――. "The Intelligence Aspects of the Joel Brand Mission." *Yad Vashem Studies* 10 (1974): 111–28.

Wasserstein, Bernard. *Britain and the Jews of Europe, 1939–1945*. Oxford, 1979.

Weizmann, Chaim. *Trial and Error*. New York, 1949.

Woodward, Llewellyn. *British Foreign Policy in the Second World War*. London: H. M. Stationery Office, 1962.

World Jewish Congress. *Unity in Dispersion: A History of the World Jewish Congress*. New York, 1948.

World Jewish Congress, British Section. *Outline of Activities, 1936–1946*. London, 1948.

Wyman, David. *The Abandonment of the Jews: America and the Holocaust, 1941–1945*. New York, 1984.

Yahil, Leni. "Mivchar Teudot Britiyot Al HaAliya HaBilti Legalit LeEretz Yisrael (1939–1940)." *Yad Vashem Studies* 10 (1974): 183–208.

Zweig, Ronald. *British Policy to Palestine During the Second World War*. Woodbridge, England: Royal Historical Society, 1986.

# Chapter 22

# The Politics of Collaboration: A Historiography of Arab-German Relations, 1933–1945

## Jonathan C. Friedman

In the topic of Arab-Axis collaboration, Haj Amin al-Husseini, grand mufti of Jerusalem, is the central Arab protagonist. Most analyses of German-Arab relations during the Holocaust focus upon the role of the mufti in a variety of anti-Allied efforts: the March 1940 pro-Axis coup in Iraq; pro-fascist activities in Iran the next year; Husseini's post as Berlin chief of Axis propaganda for the Levant; and his support of the Final Solution. These secondary works fall into two categories: biographies by Zionist (or pro-Zionist) authors and those by Arab (or pro-Arab) biographers.

Naturally, the trend in the Zionist realm is to portray the mufti as evil incarnate. Likewise, Arab writers minimize Husseini's Axis collaboration, stressing his indefatigable, incorruptible character. This chapter will attempt to analyze the literature in light of this historical dilemma and, for convenience, is broken down into general works, books on Axis foreign policy in the Levant, and sources concerned specifically with the grand mufti of Jerusalem.

## GENERAL EXAMINATIONS OF EUROPEAN POLICY IN THE LEVANT

For general considerations of European, specifically German/British/French, involvement in the Middle East to 1945, George Washington University professor of history Howard Sachar's *Europe Leaves the Middle East* is the best comprehensive analysis, with an exhaustive bibliography. Ian Playfair's *The Mediterranean and Middle East: Official History of the Second World War* is an older, more voluminous history of the region during World War II. Jacob Hurewitz's

*Diplomacy in the Near and Middle East: A Documentary Record, 1914–1955* serves as the basic primary source on the topic of twentieth-century Middle Eastern diplomatic history. For works on Nazi foreign policy in general, see Klaus Hildebrand's *The Foreign Policy of the Third Reich* and Gerhard L. Weinberg's *The Foreign Policy of Hitler's Germany.*

With respect to the Levant, Labor Zionist Aharon Cohen's somewhat skewed account, *Israel and the Arab World* examines the roots of the current Arab-Israeli conflict from the British mandate to 1970 but fails to cite sufficient source material usually required of histories. In *The Middle East: A Handbook*, editor Michael Adams relies on contributions from various authorities, including Arnold Toynbee, but omits a detailed citation of primary and secondary works. Finally, five often-cited books on the Palestinian conflict include Jacob Hurewitz's *Struggle for Palestine*, Christopher Sykes's *Crossroads to Israel*, John Marlowe's *Seat of Pilate: An Account of the Palestine Mandate*, Pierre van Paassen's undocumented and ardently pro-Zionist *Forgotten Ally*, and William Ziff's *The Rape of Palestine.*

## GERMANY'S ARAB POLICY

The quintessential analysis of Third Reich policy toward the Arab world in the years 1933–39 comes from Francis Nicosia's well-documented *Third Reich and the Palestine Question*. Nicosia explains that the Middle East initially provided little interest to Hitler and that German policy in the Levant before World War II was constrained by one overriding consideration, namely, Berlin's own desire to accommodate England on the basis of racial admiration and respect for the territorial integrity of the British Empire.[1] As a result, Hitler made virtually no effort to exploit Arab nationalism against Britain until the war broke out. Then, too, his hatred of Jews precluded sincere support for Zionism, even if it served the purpose of accelerating Germany's policy of *Judenreinigung*.[2]

Nicosia describes how the Arabs greeted Hitler's Reich with initial enthusiasm, and in his article, "Arab Nationalism and National Socialist Germany, 1933–1939: Ideological and Strategic Incompatibility," *International Journal of Middle Eastern Studies* 12 (1980): 351–72, he mentions that the grand mufti conveyed his support of Nazism and Hitler's anti-Jewish boycotts as early as March 1933.[3] However, the mufti coupled his support with the request that Germany halt Jewish emigration to Palestine. Between 1933 and 1935 Berlin's Consul General Wolff and German Ambassador to Iraq Fritz Grobba rejected this entreaty and numerous others from the Pan-Arab Committee in order to avoid upsetting Great Britain.

In April 1936, after several Arab attacks against Palestinian Jews (in what became known as the Arab Revolt), Germany reacted with indifference since British governance of Palestine had not been threatened.[4] However, the formation of the Rome-Berlin Axis on October 24, 1936, the failure of Hitler to secure England's cooperation in his "spheres of dominance" scheme, and recommendations of the British Peel Commission in July 1937 on the situation in Palestine prompted Germany to choose a new course without England. Hitler subsequently gave Italy predominance in the Mediterranean and Middle East against British and French interests.[5] Josef Schröder's poignant essay, "Die Beziehung der Achsenmächte zur arabischen Welt," *Zeitschrift für Politik* 18 (1971), examines this change in Nazi policy.

Even with this new change of heart, Berlin had no intention in 1938 of becoming more involved with Arab nationalists and refused assistance to most Middle Eastern states, except for Yemen, Iran, and Afghanistan, where the likelihood of running into British opposition was less.[6] Iraq also received a negligible amount of armaments by the end of 1937 after a coup in October of the previous year had brought in a regime that sought closer ties to Germany. Fritz Grobba had warned of British reprisals, but they never came.[7]

It was only after Hitler's invasion of Czechoslovakia in March 1939 and his willingness thereafter to risk war with Great Britain over Poland that the need for closer ties to the Arab world became apparent. Germany wooed Saudi Arabia through an arms deal on June 17, 1939. One month before, though, Britain's White Paper had drastically reduced Jewish immigration into Palestine and had thus neutralized Arab antipathy, guaranteeing at least tacit Arab support for England in a conflict against Berlin.[8] Both Nicosia and Josef Schröder agree that it was because of Hitler's subordination of the Middle East to his policy of *Lebensraum* in Europe and his halfhearted attempts to employ anti-British Arab sentiment against England without fully supporting the cause of Arab independence or at least paying lip service to Arab nationalism earlier that led the Middle East to become a wasted opportunity even before the war began.[9]

One of the most exhaustive studies on the subject of Nazi-Arab relations is Bernd Schröder's *Deutschland und der mittlere Osten im zweiten Weltkrieg*. Richly documented with material from the German and British Foreign offices, Schröder's book looks at Germany's wartime policy toward the Middle East through a country-by-country analysis. He asserts that after 1941 Nazi leaders directed their cooperation with Arab nationalists in such a way as to undermine British dominance without conflicting with Italian interests in the Middle East.[10]

Schröder further explains that Germany had several evanescent successes in the Middle East with respect to pro-Axis regimes, for example Iran's Reza Pahlevi, toppled by Britain in August 1941, Egypt's Ali Maher, replaced by anti-Nazi Wafd party leader Nahas Pasha in February 1942, and Iraq's Rashid Ali, overthrown in May 1941.[11] Saudi Arabia was also a fleeting success for the Nazis, as the Saudis abrogated their arms deal on September 11, 1939, and severed relations with Berlin.[12] Only Yemen, which had concluded an arms deal with the Nazis in 1937, and Palestine's grand mufti could be relied upon after 1942.

For a decent macroconsideration of developments in the Middle East during World War II, Muhammad Kemal el-Dessouki's "Hitler und der nahe Osten" (Ph. D. dissertation, Berlin, 1963) analyzes German-Arab relations by focusing specifically on events in the Levant and Egypt. Heinz Tillmann's *Deutschlands Araberpolitik im zweiten Weltkrieg* is also an essential resource in German. Regarding works in English, Lukasz Hirszowicz's *The Third Reich and the Arab East* and Robert Melka's University of Minnesota dissertation "The Axis and the Arab Middle East, 1930–1945" (1966) examine the Arab-Axis wartime collaboration in great detail but lack a sufficient consideration of prewar German-Arab relations.

Several works by Nazi authors also provide material for the analysis of propaganda techniques. Hermann Erich Seifert's especially vitriolic *Der Aufbruch in der arabischen Welt* attacks Great Britain, world Jewry, and Herzl's "pathetic essay" on a Jewish state while praising the mufti for engaging in the worldwide Nazi struggle against Judaism.[13] Fritz Grobba's *Irak* and Paul Schmitz Kairo's *Die arabische Revolution* are less polemical, but nonetheless hold high regard for Arab attacks against Jews in 1920, 1921, 1929, and 1936. Finally, the topic of Arab employment of Nazi propaganda in the Middle East is dealt with at length in Seth Arsenian's "Wartime Propaganda in the Middle East," *Middle East Journal* 2 (1948): 417–29.

## THE MUFTI

Major problems exist with books about Haj Amin Muhammad al-Husseini, grand mufti of Jerusalem. For the most part, treatment of the mufti has been less than impartial, as Zionist biographers assail his wartime collaboration with the Nazis (relying mainly on the Western press) and Arab authors praise Husseini's devotion to Palestinian nationalism.[14]

Even with this dilemma, the standard texts examining the role of the mufti as Palestinian nationalist, pan-Arabist, and Nazi collaborator have come from the Zionist realm: Maurice Pearlman's dated, hostile, and poorly documented *Mufti of Jerusalem: The Story of Haj Amin al-Husseini*, his earlier work under the pseudonym M. P. Waters, *The Mufti Over The Middle East*, Eliahu Elath's *Haj Muhammed Amin al-Husseini*, and Joseph Schechtman's less vitriolic yet equally poorly documented *The Mufti and the Fuehrer: The Rise and Fall of Haj Amin el-Husseini*. As for Arab texts, the basic source is anti-Zionist Zuhayr Mardini's *Alf Yawm ma' al-Hajj Amin* (one thousand days of Haj Amin). The most contemporary and so-called objective work on Husseini comes from Philip Mattar's article "The Mufti of Jerusalem and the Politics of Palestine," *Middle East Journal* 42 (1988): 227–40, and his book *Mufti of Jerusalem*. Asserting that he is neither pro-Arab nor anti-Zionist, Mattar attempts to present a more impartial view of the mufti, but the result is basically a thinly veiled apologetic.

Mattar, Pearlman, Elath, and Schechtman essentially agree that the mufti had political preeminence throughout Mandatory Palestine and that he played a pivotal role in the Arab struggle against Britain and Zionism.[15] Yet Mattar maintains that Haj Amin achieved his preeminence only after 1929, that he never actively incited riots against Jews in Palestine, and that his anti-British sentiment de-

veloped after 1936 with the realization that cooperation with Britain would not
curb Jewish immigration or lead to the goal of eventual Palestinian independence.[16] This is where the disagreement in historical interpretation arises.

Mattar mentions that in December 1921 Husseini was appointed grand mufti
of Jerusalem (a title that gave him sway over clerical positions and religious
institutions in Palestine) after having served as clerk in the office of the British
governor in Jerusalem.[17] Therefore, Haj Amin must have had some preeminence
before Mattar's date of 1929. Further, Mattar fails to mention the circumstances
behind his appointment as mufti, which contradict the statement that he never
instigated Arab attacks on Jews.

According to Joan Peters's *From Time Immemorial*, on April 4, 1920, during
the Muslim holiday of Nebi Musa, Husseini incited a riot in Jerusalem's Jewish
quarter that led to four days of unrestrained massacre.[18] Subsequently fleeing to
escape a ten-year sentence for instigating anti-Jewish violence, Haj Amin returned to Palestine five months later after having been granted a special pardon
by the British.[19] This was followed by his appointment as mufti and president
of the Supreme Muslim Council by British High Commander Herbert Samuel,
a Jew, whose own appointment may have sparked the anti-Jewish riots of the
previous year.[20]

With respect to the August 23, 1929, Western Wall riots that left 133 Jews
and 116 Arabs dead, Mattar insists that even though followers of Husseini
perpetrated the attacks, no solid evidence exists to implicate the mufti himself.[21]
He cites the findings of two anti-Zionist investigative bodies, the Shaw and
Hope-Simpson commissions, which had been established to study and make
inquiries about the massacre and which had placed the blame essentially on
Jewish immigration and Zionist agitation.[22]

However, British author Nicholas Bethell's *Palestine Triangle*, richly documented with Foreign Office and Colonial Office sources, charges that violence
broke out after Jews had erected a partition at the Wailing Wall to separate men
from women, a common practice among Orthodox Jews.[23] With respect to
agitation, Naomi Cohen points out in her *Year After the Riots: American Responses to the Palestinian Crisis, 1929–1930* that the British had exacerbated
anti-Jewish hatred by allowing the circulation of the anti-Semitic Protocols of
the Elders of Zion in Palestine.[24] Mattar makes no mention of this and instead
asserts that the Arabs had reason to believe that Jews planned to attack the Harem
esh-Sharif, Islam's third-holiest shrine.

First, Mattar accuses Zionists of unnecessary agitation, when it would have
been Orthodox Jews who would have erected the partition at the wall.[25] He then
maintains that the violence was spontaneous and that no one was responsible
for it.[26] Moreover, Mattar mentions that violence occurred in many towns where
the mufti's influence was weak, such as Hebron, and did not take place in many
areas where Husseini had a strong impact (no examples given).[27] This supposition
cites no source that would quantitatively reveal the "level of influence" held
by Haj Amin over certain regions. Finally, Mattar claims that Husseini's written

appeal that urged Arabs to defend the Harem esh-Sharif against a Jewish attack was probably forged.[28] Here, the only source is one of his articles, "The Role of the Mufti of Jerusalem in the Political Struggle for the Western Wall, 1928–1929," *Middle East Studies* 19 (1983): 104–18.[29]

As for the mufti's loyalty to the United Kingdom until 1936, Mattar holds steadfastly to the argument that Husseini admired the British sense of justice and thought that England's pro-Zionist policy would change when the British realized that their success in the Middle East lay with the Muslims.[30] This undocumented speculation is coupled with Mattar's citation of the mufti's approval of a proportional representation plan from MP John Philby in 1929 and only minor dissatisfaction with the withdrawal of the 1930 Passfield White Paper, which limited Jewish immigration into Palestine, to prove his thesis. However, Francis Nicosia's article "Arab Nationalism and National Socialist Germany" had already revealed that Husseini had conveyed support to Hitler as early as 1933.[31] Even the American Christian Palestinian Committee made it known in 1947 that it possessed evidence that alleged that the Jaffa Arab riots of April 1936 had been perpetrated by the mufti's following with funds from Berlin.[32]

Mattar insists that Haj Amin condemned the 1936 riots even when substantial evidence exists to support the allegation that Hussein had planned the attack to force concessions from the British vis-à-vis Jewish immigration.[33] The mufti's sudden turnaround thereafter and rejection of British pleas to help restore order as president of his newly formed Arab Higher Committee is also unexplained in Mattar's analysis. Nonetheless, Husseini's new course—without England—had been set in motion.

The Peel Commission, established to investigate the April riots, was deemed prejudicial to Arab interests by the mufti because it permitted Jews to continue to buy tracts of fertile Arab land. Furthermore, Haj Amin refused to absorb the four hundred thousand Jews already living in Palestine in order to express his newfound opposition to Britain.[34] Even the 1939 White Paper, which put severe restrictions on Jewish immigration, failed to assuage the implacable mufti. He had already found the perfect base of operation in Baghdad and the perfect ally, Nazi Germany.

Mattar's consideration minimizes Husseini's Axis collaboration, noting a lack of evidence against him. Here again, he stands *solus contra mundum*. Joseph Schechtman's *The Mufti and the Fuehrer* reveals Haj Amin's role as financial procurator of $480,000 in Nazi funds in the Iraqi political shakeup of March 3, 1940, that led to the ascension to power of pro-German Rashid Ali.[35] After Italy entered the war in June 1940, the mufti threw himself even more wholeheartedly into the anti-Allied crusade.

Historians Sachar and Hurewitz confirm that Husseini had his private secretary, Uthman Kamal Haddad, meet with Fritz Grobba on August 26, 1940, in order to elicit an unequivocal statement of support for his new cause, which had since transcended Palestinian nationalism and had been transformed into a pan-Arabist demand to become leader of an independent Arab nation.[36] Yet while Grobba asserted that Berlin had close ties to the Arab world in its struggle against Britain and world Jewry, he merely paid lip service to the mufti's demand for Arab independence. Even so, when Britain crushed Rashid Ali's movement in May 1941, Husseini fled to Teheran and continued to support Axis victories. In September of that year British and Soviet troops invaded Iran, forcing the mufti to flee again, this time to Rome and subsequently to Berlin. Historian Lukasz Hirszowicz describes the November 28 meeting between the mufti and Hitler in which unconditional Arab support for the Nazi cause was again offered.[37] For his efforts, Haj Amin was given a special office (Arabisches Büro) that was responsible for supervising Axis propaganda to the Middle East.[38]

Schechtman's account of the mufti's Axis collaboration is corroborated by Peters, Bethell, and even Simon Wiesenthal. In his *Grossmufti, Grossagent der Achsen: Tatsachenbericht*, Wiesenthal relates that the mufti had close contact with Adolf Eichmann, visited Auschwitz and Majdanek, and praised those who were particularly conscientious at their work in the crematoria.[39] Whether or not the last item is historically verifiable, the fact remains that Bethell and Peters confirm that Husseini indirectly aided the extermination process by rejecting Jewish immigration from Germany and by supporting, orally and in writing, Germany's Final Solution to the Jewish question.[40] Before the collapse of Nazi Germany, the United Nations assembled a dossier on this intimate of Himmler and Eichmann, charging him with collaboration and crimes against humanity.

In 1947 the mufti was to be tried as a war criminal in France. No formal proceeding ever took place.[41] Subsequently resettling in Egypt in 1948, he was welcomed as a hero and remained active as spokesman for the Palestinians until 1964, when he relinquished his duties to the PLO's Yasser Arafat.[42]

## EPILOGUE

Any historiographic consideration is bound to be incomplete. A full bibliographic survey on the topic of Arab-German relations would require an analysis of over two hundred books. Yet for the micro-oriented nature of this chapter, dealing specifically with the Arab-Axis collaboration, general works on the subject can be delineated while works on Germany's Arab policy and those on the mufti are dealt with in specific sections.

Regarding Nazi Germany's policy toward the Arab world, most historians, for example, Francis Nicosia and Josef Schröder, agree that the Middle East played a secondary role to Europe in Hitler's *Weltanschauung*. His policy was also constrained at first by his desire to avoid disturbing British preeminence in the region and later by a similar desire to avoid clashing with Italian interests in the Mediterranean and the Middle East.

As for works on the mufti, an historiographical conflict exists. The standard resources that paint an essentially negative picture of Husseini have been written by Zionists (Maurice Pearlman, Joseph Schechtman), whereas revisionist texts, done primarily by Arab or pro-Arab authors (Philip Mattar, Zuhayr Mardini), praise Haj Amin's devotion to Palestinian nationalism. Nevertheless, well-documented analyses from other scholars (Joan Peters, Nicholas Bethell) can be used more to support the claims of Zionist authors than those of opposing viewpoints. However, only Husseini's diaries and the documents from the British Foreign and Colonial offices can tell the full story behind the mufti's wartime collaboration with Nazi Germany.

## NOTES

1. Francis Nicosia, *The Third Reich and the Palestine Question* (London: I.B. Tauris, 1985), p. x.

2. Ibid., p. 28.

3. Francis Nicosia, "Arab Nationalism and National Socialist Germany, 1933–1939: Ideological and Strategic Incompatibility," *International Journal of Middle East Studies* 12 (1980): 352–54; also his *Third Reich and the Palestine Question*, p. 86.

4. Nicosia, *Third Reich and the Palestine Question*, p. 101.

5. Ibid., pp. 105, 108, 168; Josef Schroder, "Die Beziehung der Achsenmächte zur arabischen Welt," *Zeitschrift für Politik* 18 (1971): 82, 84.

6. This fact was due mainly to the weaker nature of British power and influence in these areas than in the rest of the Arab world. Nicosia, *Third Reich and the Palestine Question*, p. 182.

7. Ibid., p. 183.

8. Ibid., p. 189.

9. Ibid., pp. 191, 192; also J. Schröder, "Beziehung der Achsenmächte zur arabischen Welt," p. 95.

10. Bernd Schröder, *Deutschland und der mittlere Osten im zweiten Weltkrieg* (Göttingen: Musterschmidt, 1975), p. 33.

11. Ibid., pp. 36, 39, 40, 41, 42, 55.

12. Ibid., p. 40.

13. Hermann Erich Seifert, *Der Aufbruch in der arabischen Welt* (Berlin: Eher, 1941), p. 45.

14. Philip Mattar, "The Mufti of Jerusalem and the Politics of Palestine," *Middle East Journal* 42 (1988): 228.

15. Ibid., p. 228; Maurice Pearlman, *Mufti of Jerusalem: The Story of Haj Amin al-Husseini* (London: Victor Gollancz, 1947); Eliahu Elath, *Haj Mohammed Amin al-Husseini* (Jerusalem: Hebrew University Press, 1968); Joseph Schechtman, *The Mufti and the Fuehrer: The Rise and Fall of Haj Amin el-Husseini* (New York: T. Yoseloff, 1965), p. 5.

16. Mattar, "Mufti of Jerusalem," p. 232.

17. Ibid., p. 229; Nicholas Bethell, *The Palestine Triangle* (New York: Putnam, 1979), p. 23.

18. Joan Peters, *From Time Immemorial* (New York: Harper and Row, 1984), p. 360. It also must be noted that the original intent of this book was to prove that Palestinians and Jews lived together in perfect harmony before "Zionism." What Peters found, however, shed a different light on the conventional wisdom of Arab-Jewish relations before the creation of Israel.

19. Ibid.

20. Ibid.; also Paul Schmitz Kairo, *Die arabische Revolution* (Leipzig: Goldmann, 1942), p. 153.

21. Mattar, "Mufti of Jerusalem," p. 231.

22. Ibid.; Bethell, *Palestine Triangle*, p. 24.

23. Bethell, *Palestine Triangle,* p. 23.

24. Conference with British Chief Secretary, September 16, 1929, Central Zionist Archives A18/53/49; Naomi Cohen, *The Year After the Riots: American Responses to the Palestinian Crisis, 1929–1930* (Detroit: Wayne State University Press, 1988).

25. Mattar, "Mufti of Jerusalem," p. 231.

26. Ibid.

27. Ibid.

28. Ibid.

29. Mattar, "The Role of the Mufti of Jerusalem in the Political Struggle for the Western Wall, 1928–1929," *Middle East Studies* 19 (1983): 104–18.

30. Mattar, "Mufti of Jerusalem," p. 233.

31. Nicosia, "Arab Nationalism and National Socialist Germany," pp. 352–54.

32. Peters, *From Time Immemorial,* p. 360.

33. Bethell, *Palestine Triangle,* p. 26.

34. Ibid., p. 28.

35. Schechtman, *Mufti and the Fuehrer,* p. 103.

36. Howard Sachar, *Europe Leaves the Middle East* (New York: Alfred A. Knopf, 1972), p. 166; Jacob Hurewitz, *Diplomacy in the Near and Middle East: A Documentary Record, 1914–1955,* 2 vols. (New York: Van Nostrand, 1956), p. 153.

37. Lukasz Hirszowicz, *The Third Reich and the Arab East* (London: Routledge and Kegan Paul, 1966), p. 218.

38. Ibid.

39. Schechtman, *Mufti and the Fuehrer,* p. 160.

40. Foreign Office 371/45421; Bethell, *Palestine Triangle*, p. 225; Peters, *From Time Immemorial,* pp. 360–80.

41. Mattar, "Mufti of Jerusalem," pp. 239–40.

42. Ibid.

## SELECT BIBLIOGRAPHY

Arsenian, Seth. "Wartime Propaganda in the Middle East." *Middle East Journal* 2 (1948): 417–29.

Bauer, Yehuda. *From Diplomacy to Resistance: A History of Jewish Palestine, 1939–1945.* Philadelphia: Jewish Publication Society of America, 1970.

Begin, Menachem. *Revolt: Story of the Irgun.* New York: Schuman, 1951.

Bethell, Nicholas. *The Palestine Triangle.* New York: Putnam, 1979.

el-Dessouki, Muhammad Kemal. "Hitler und der nahe Osten." Ph.D. diss., Berlin, 1963.

Elath, Eliahu. *Haj Muhammad Amin al-Husseini.* Jerusalem: Hebrew University Press, 1968.

ESCO Foundation for Palestine. *Palestine: A Study of Jewish, Arab, and British Policies.* New Haven, Conn.: Yale University Press, 1947.

Gilbert, Felix. *Hitler Directs His War: The Secret Records of His Daily Military Conferences.* London: Oxford University Press, 1950.

Grobba, Fritz. *Irak*. Berlin: Junker und Dunnhaupt, 1941.

Hildebrand, Klaus. *The Foreign Policy of the Third Reich*. Berkeley: University of California Press, 1973.

Hirschmann, Ira. *Life Line to a Promised Land*. New York, 1946.

Hirszowicz, Lukasz. *The Third Reich and the Arab East*. London: Routledge and Kegan Paul, 1966.

Hurewitz, Jacob. *Diplomacy in the Near and Middle East: A Documentary Record, 1914–1955*. 2 vols. New York: Van Nostrand, 1956.

————. *The Struggle for Palestine*. New York: Greenwood Press, 1968.

Katz, Samuel. *Battleground: Fact and Fantasy in Palestine*. New York: Bantam, 1973.

————. *Days of Fire*. London: Allen, 1968.

Kimche, Jon. *Seven Fallen Pillars: The Middle East, 1915–1952*. London: Secker and Warburg, 1953.

Kirk, George. *Survey of International Affairs, 1939–1946: The Middle East in the War*. London: Oxford University Press, 1952.

Lenczowski, George. *Russia and the West in Iran, 1918–1948*. Ithaca, N.Y.: Cornell University Press, 1949.

Longrigg, Stephen. *Oil in the Middle East: Its Discovery and Development*. London: Oxford University Press, 1954.

Lugol, Jean. *Egypt and World War II*. Translated by A. G. Mitchell. Cairo: Société Orientale de Publicité, 1945.

Manuel, Frank. *The Realities of American-Palestine Relations*. Washington, D.C., 1949.

Marlowe, John. *Seat of Pilate: An Account of the Palestine Mandate*. London: Cresset Press, 1959.

Mattar, Philip. *The Mufti of Jerusalem*. New York: Columbia University Press, 1988.

Melka, Robert. "The Axis and the Arab Middle East, 1930–1945." Ph.D. diss., University of Minnesota, 1966.

Monroe, Elizabeth. *Britain's Moment in the Middle East, 1914–1956*. Baltimore, Md.: Johns Hopkins Press, 1963.

Nicosia, Francis. *The Third Reich and the Palestine Question*. London: I. B. Tauris, 1985.

Pearlman, Maurice. *Mufti of Jerusalem: The Story of Haj Amin al-Husseini*. London: Victor Gollancz, 1947.

Perl, William. *The Four-Front War: From the Holocaust to the Promised Land*. New York: Crown, 1979.

Peters, Joan. *From Time Immemorial*. New York: Harper and Row, 1984.

Playfair, Ian S. O. *The Mediterranean and Middle East: Official History of the Second World War*. 3 vols. London: H. M. Stationery Office, 1954.

Royal Institute of International Affairs. *British Security*. London, 1946.

————. *The Middle East*. London, 1943.

Sachar, Howard M. *Europe Leaves the Middle East*. New York: Knopf, 1972.

Schechtman, Joseph. *The Mufti and the Fuehrer: The Rise and Fall of Haj Amin el-Husseini*. New York: T. Yoseloff, 1965.

Schröder, Bernd. *Deutschland und der mittlers Osten im zweiten Weltkrieg*. Göttingen: Musterschmidt, 1975.

Schröder, Josef. "Die Beziehung der Achsenmächte zur arabischen Welt." *Zeitschrift fur Politik* 18 (1971).

Seifert, Hermann Erich. *Der Aufbruch in der arabischen Welt*. Berlin: Eher, 1941.

Seton-Williams, M. V. *States: A Survey of Anglo-Arab Relations, 1920–1948*. London, 1948.

Skrine, Sir Clarmont. *World War in Iran*. Washington, D.C.: U.S. Department of State, 1962.

Sykes, Christopher. *Crossroads to Israel*. London: Collins, 1963.

Thomas, Lewis V., and Richard N. Frye. *The United States and Turkey and Iran*. Cambridge, Mass.: Harvard University Press, 1951.

Tillmann, Heinz. *Deutschlands Araberpolitik im zweiten Weltkrieg*. Berlin: Deutscher Verlag für Wissenschaft, 1965.

U.S. Department of State. *Documents on German Foreign Policy, 1918–1945*. Series D. Vols. 9, 12. Washington, D.C., 1959–63.

Van Paassen, Pierre. *The Forgotten Ally*. New York: Dial Press, 1943.

Weinberg, Gerhard L. *The Foreign Policy of Hitler's Germany*. 2 vols. Chicago: University of Chicago Press, 1970, 1980.

Woodward, Llewellyn. *British Foreign Policy in the Second World War*. Vol. 1. London: H. M. Stationery office, 1962.

Ziff, William. *The Rape of Palestine*. New York: Longmans, Green, 1938.

# Chapter 23

---

# American Response to the Holocaust, 1933–1945

## *Jack Fischel*

America's response to the Nazi rise to power can be framed into two periods. The first period is 1933–38, when Hitler took power and in an incremental way segregated Jews from German society through the passage of anti-Semitic laws. This period climaxed in the violence of *Kristallnacht*, which some historians mark as the beginning of the Holocaust. During these five years anti-Semitism and isolationism intensified in the United States. As the excesses of Nazism became apparent in Europe, members of Congress, the State Department, and pressure groups warned against liberalizing the immigration laws or making special provisions for the plight of Jewish refugees fleeing Germany.

The indifference of American society to Jewish refugees only intensified a trend that had begun after World War I. Already in the 1920s the United States had begun the retreat from its past when it had provided shelter for the poor and persecuted of Europe. Starting in 1918 and through the decade of the 1920s, the U.S. Congress passed a series of immigration laws that attempted to maintain the Anglo-Saxon majority by limiting the number of immigrants from Southern and Eastern Europe. The 1924 law, known as the National Origins Act, limited Southern and Eastern European immigrants to 2 percent of the 1890 Census of Co-Nationals residing in the United States. The 1929 modification of the National Origins Act placed an annual limit of 150,000 immigrants to be allowed into the country, with 130,000 visas allocated to Northern and Western Europe and 20,000 to Eastern and Southern Europe. Although the Great Depression added to the general support for this measure, nevertheless, its racial aspect was made evident in the provision that prevented unused quotas from Western or Northern Europe from being allocated to refugees from Southern and Eastern Europe.

Although Jewish refugees escaping Nazism were supposed to be included in the overall German quota, in fact they very often fell under the quotas for Eastern and Southern Europe. Furthermore, unless they had financial assets or could prove that someone in America could guarantee them a job, German Jewish refugees were refused entry.

Throughout the decade of the 1930s the Roosevelt administration was preoccupied with fighting the depression. President Franklin Roosevelt placed relief and recovery as his highest priority. Roosevelt often formed political alliances with politicians who were racist and anti-Semitic in order to get their votes on behalf of New Deal legislation. The president was also aware of the strong isolationist sentiment that prevailed throughout the country, and voices such as those of Charles Lindbergh and Father Charles Coughlin warned the American people that Jews were attempting to take the United States into a war with Nazi Germany.

As Hitler's persecution of Jews intensified, the president found himself caught up in a crossfire of pressure between those who demanded help for Hitler's victims and those who warned the American public to oppose any relaxation of the immigration laws. For Roosevelt, it made little political sense to liberalize the immigration laws at a time when unemployment was still a national problem.

Toward the end of the 1930s, as Nazi Germany was increasingly seen by many as a threat to peace, arguments were presented both inside and out of Congress in regard to the modification of the immigration laws. The new concern centered around the fear that Nazi spies would enter the country in the guise of refugees, or that Jewish refugees would be forced to spy for Germany by the threat that harm would befall the relatives whom they had left behind.

Other factors of a less tangible nature are also part of the record. These include the attitude of those directly responsible for refugee policy, specifically in the State Department. How much did their attitude toward Jews affect their performance in implementing the immigration laws? Did personal dislike of Jews influence the rigid manner in which Under Secretary of State Breckinridge Long carried out the law? What about the president? Although Roosevelt did make a few speeches that showed concern for Nazi victims, the record seems to show that he was apathetic, if not indifferent, to the plight of Jewish refugees. Was this caused by callousness, anti-Semitism, or the weight of problems that the president deemed more important? Whatever the answer, once World War II began, all of these factors were superseded by his concern to win the war.

The second period, from 1939 to 1945, was characterized by the Allies' awareness of the Nazi plan to murder the Jews of Europe. At first, America officially showed disbelief, and many believed that these reports were a replay of the exaggerated German atrocity stories of World War I. But even after the Roosevelt administration was convinced of the authenticity of the reports, the policy of both the United States and Great Britain was not to find places of refuge for the victims, but to insist that the best way to save European Jewry was to defeat Nazi Germany. Even the creation of the War Refugee Board of

1944 was a grudging concession lest the Roosevelt administration be accused of covertly acquiescing in the murder of European Jewry. Always a cautious politician, Roosevelt was sensitive to the political risk of being accused of risking the lives of American soldiers in behalf of saving Jewish lives. Even when American flyers were only a few miles from Auschwitz, the policy to bomb specific military targets and not to bomb the railroad tracks leading to the death camp continued to be implemented.

Aside from the political concerns of the Roosevelt administration, it would appear that several other threads link both periods under consideration: the overall indifference of the American people to offering support to the idea of America as a refuge for Jews, the failure of the press to emphasize the horrors of the Holocaust, and the unwillingness of both the Protestant and Catholic churches to speak out against Nazi Germany. The historiography of both periods raises serious questions about the overall culpability of America in the face of the Holocaust. Could the United States have done more? Was the State Department and its bureaucracy guilty of impeding rescue because of their anti-Semitism, or because of the nature of bureaucrats in general, or a combination of both? How should President Roosevelt's role be evaluated? How much of the criticism leveled against Roosevelt and the State Department is hindsight history, and how much of it is a reflection of the advice the president received from anti-Semites and insecure Jewish advisors in the highest positions in government?

The most widely read and controversial books on the role of America and the Holocaust accuse the United States of being a guilty bystander who had the opportunity but failed to implement a policy of rescue. Arthur Morse's *While Six Million Died* (1967) was the first major work on the Holocaust that dealt with the role of the United States and its failure to implement a rescue policy. Written by a nonacademician, *While Six Million Died* is an impassioned indictment of the Roosevelt administration and was the first work to charge the State Department with a callousness toward Jewish life, if not with anti-Semitism. Although Morse never accuses Breckinridge Long of being an anti-Semite, he comes close to this charge and makes him the main perpetrator of a policy of inaction as peril to Jewish life increased in Europe. Morse's list of villains, in addition to Long, includes Carlton J. Hayes, Martin Dies, Robert Borden Reams, Cordell Hull, and John McCloy. The latter, as assistant secretary of war, is blamed for failing to urge the bombing of Auschwitz.

Morse is also critical of President Roosevelt for not speaking out against the persecution of Jews and for taking advantage of the disunity among Jewish leaders and organizations in their failure to present the president with a uniform plan of rescue. In all, Morse charges the United States with apathy and inaction as Nazi Germany moved closer to the Final Solution. As the murder of European Jewry gained momentum, the government and people of the United States remained bystanders. From President Roosevelt down to the State Department bureaucrats, there was a disregard for the plight of the Jews despite the abundant evidence from official and unofficial sources. Morse indicts America for going about its business unmoved and unconcerned with the fate of European Jewry.

*While Six Million Died* is an important work for two reasons. The first is that this meticulously documented book was written for a mass audience rather than for academics and thus raised the issue of America's culpability for a much wider audience than would have been the case had it been published by the academic press. Second, the book's thesis pioneered an issue that is still a subject of debate. Morse's book remains a classic of its kind and certainly influenced the later works of Henry Feingold, Saul Friedman, and David Wyman.

David Wyman's *Paper Walls* (1968) was published in the same year as Morse's work. Like Morse's more popularly read book, *Paper Walls* continues the attack on Roosevelt and the State Department bureaucracy and covers American refugee policy from 1938 to 1941. Wyman accuses the Roosevelt administration not only of failing to liberalize the immigration laws but of imposing regulations regarding existing quotas that made it difficult for refugees to enter the country within these limits. Wyman calculates that the failure to fill the German-Austrian quota led to the death of twenty thousand Jewish refugees who remained in Europe and fell prey to Hitler's program of destruction. Unlike Morse, who places the blame for failure to do more for Jewish refugees squarely on individuals such as Breckinridge Long, Wyman focuses the guilt on the American people, who, he argues, were sympathetic to Hitler's victims but refused to support measures to change the immigration laws. The recession of 1937–38, with an accompanying unemployment of ten million, did not help in creating a mood that allowed for increased immigration. *Paper Walls*, as well as *While Six Million Died*, questions the humanitarian image of the Roosevelt administration.

Arthur Morse's influence can be seen in *The Politics of Rescue* (1970) by Henry Feingold. In this book, the Morse thesis is more broadly documented and is presented less emotionally. Like Morse, Feingold accuses the Roosevelt administration of irresponsibility in regard to refugee policy. However, Feingold's cast of villains is far more extensive than that of Morse. In addition to the State Department, Feingold blames Roosevelt's advisors of Jewish extraction of being timid and fearful of an anti-Semitic backlash should Roosevelt openly call for the liberalization of the immigration laws. With the exception of Henry Morgenthau, Roosevelt's Jewish advisors, including Bernard Baruch, Samuel Rosenman, Ben Cohen, and Felix Frankfurter, did little to encourage rescue action. Similarly, with the exception of Emanuel Celler, congressional allies such as Adolph Sabath, Sol Bloom, and Samuel Dickstein remained cool to proposals to change immigration policy.

If Morse single-mindedly blames President Roosevelt and the State Department for their indifference to the suffering of European Jewry, Feingold's book emerges as a corrective to Morse's exaggerated charge. *The Politics of Rescue* sets itself apart from the Morse book by placing the president's options within the context of his limitations vis-à-vis the public's support for helping Jews. In addition, Feingold suggests possible motives for Roosevelt's relative inaction: the belief that the best way to save Jews was to win the war, skepticism about the horror stories received from Eastern Europe, the general disbelief of American policymakers about the extermination of the Jews, Roosevelt's real fear of a "fifth column," the president's fear of arousing popular prejudice toward Jews, and his reluctance to present his right-wing opponents with an opportunity to attack him if he were to urge the liberalization of the immigration laws.

Despite the wider canvas of political considerations that Feingold presents, his conclusions in regard to the Roosevelt administration are similar to those of Morse. Roosevelt emerges as having done far too little to save Jews, and Breckinridge Long's alleged anti-Semitism is far more pronounced in Feingold's work, as the under secretary of state does little, if anything, to help the refugees and has the full support of the president.

More cautious, but nevertheless as critical of the Roosevelt administration, is Saul Friedman's *No Haven for the Oppressed* (1973). Unlike Morse and Feingold, Friedman's history of refugee policy between 1933 and 1945 places blame primarily on the "faceless mass of American citizens" who never pressured Roosevelt to alter existing refugee policy in regard to Jews or to support an executive decree that would have aided Jewish refugees. In this regard, Roosevelt is accused of following public opinion in the matter of rescue, rather than taking a leadership position in mobilizing and educating the public to Nazi atrocities and urging special help for the persecuted Jewish refugees of Europe. Friedman views the Roosevelt administration's refugee policies as evolving in two stages. The first, between 1933 and 1941, was based on the president's fear of aggravating an already-difficult domestic economic situation that reached about ten million unemployed, his fear of arousing nativist and neo-Nazi feelings, and the fear of foreign agents penetrating the U.S. defense establishment should the immigration laws be relaxed. After the United States entered the war, the policy toward relief and rescue was purely one of military expediency. Like Morse, Feingold, and Wyman, Friedman notes the actions of a few anti-Semitic officials in the State Department but distributes responsibility for the overall failure of the United States to aid European Jewry. Friedman points out that Roosevelt received advice from sources other than the State Department, and these included Jewish advisors and leaders of the American Jewish community such as Stephen S. Wise and Abba Hillel Silver. But this source of advice was not unified when it came to a plan for rescue, and Roosevelt had the ability to manipulate the Jewish factions against one another.

Although Roosevelt could have ordered reprisals against German civilian populations if the Nazis continued to murder Jews, or ordered the bombing of the railway lines leading to the death camps, or supported the Wagner Bill, he did none of these things because "Roosevelt was an idol with clay feet," but one who was no hypocrite. Rather, Friedman argues, he was the archetype politician who had the ability to mesmerize personal acquaintances to believe that he was doing more for European Jews than he actually was. During this entire tragic period Roosevelt repeatedly reacted to the refugee crisis and the news of the Final Solution rather than take concrete actions that might have saved lives. Friedman concludes that Roosevelt's failure lies not with the man but with the people who deified him.

Friedman is more cautious than Morse and Feingold in dealing with Breckinridge Long. Not finding a blatant anti-Jewish statement or "smoking gun," Friedman does not label Long as anti-Semitic. Rather, he devotes pages of his text to providing the reader with a record of Long's anti-Jewish actions, which included tolerance for his anti-Semitic underlings. The reader is left to make the judgment for himself or herself with regard to the importance of these attitudes and policies on the part of the State Department in the overall failure to rescue European Jewry.

Placing the onus of the responsibility on Jewish establishment leaders as well as on the Roosevelt administration for failure to implement a plan of rescue is the thesis of Laurence Jarvik's ninety-minute documentary *Who Shall Live and Who Shall Die?* (1982). The film's protagonist, Peter Bergson, who was the head of the Emergency Committee to Save the Jewish Peoples of Europe, makes the documentary's point early on when he states that most of the victims could have been saved had the U.S. government and the American Jewish leadership been more responsive to the immediate situation, and had they been bolder and less fearful of their constituencies. The film consists of interviews with personalities such as John Pehle, executive director of the War Refugee Board, the late George Warren, a Roosevelt advisor, Josiah DuBois, and others, as well as of documentary film clips of the period under review. Roosevelt emerges as helpless in changing refugee policy because he was too busy attending to the global aims of the war, he needed to be careful in dealing with an isolationist Congress, and he was ill advised. On this last point, Bergson argues that an elitist conspiracy existed that condemned all efforts to save the refugees. The conspirators consisted of State Department advisors as well as mainstream Zionist leaders. Jarvik's film may be seen as a continuation of the bitter division that prevailed in the late 1930s and early 1940s between Stephen Wise and the mainstream Zionist leaders and those who followed Abba Hillel Silver and the Bergson group. The film takes sides but does give to the viewer a sense of the times that only newsreel clips and interviews can convey.

If Jarvik exculpates Roosevelt in regard to refugee policy, this is not the case with David Wyman's *The Abandonment of the Jews* (1984). This book continues from where Wyman had stopped in *Paper Walls*. Wyman's book is written in a judicious manner, and approaches his task by marshalling his evidence in logical constructs. Wyman maintains that in the period 1941–45 people in positions of authority regarded the news of the Holocaust as too incredible to be believed. He finds evidence of deliberate obstructionism in the State Department in regard to refugee policy as a result of the xenophobic and anti-Semitic attitude of the bureaucrats. Wyman finds that bureaucratic infighting hindered relief efforts, and he concurs with Friedman that similar infighting in the Jewish community prevented concerted pressure from being placed on the president to create additional rescue havens in America. He indicts Roosevelt for a cold indifference to the plight of the Jews in practice, in contrast to the lofty humanitarian sentiment that he proclaimed in public. He concludes that Roosevelt's refusal to do more on behalf of Jewish refugees was ''the worst failure of his presidency.''

Wyman's book also accuses the press of ignoring the news of the Holocaust, a theme that is dealt with in greater detail in Deborah Lipstadt's *Beyond Belief: The American Press and the Coming of the Holocaust, 1933–1945* (1986). Similarly, Wyman, a non-Jew, chastises the relative silence of American Christian churches and their reluctance to get involved in what was seen as a Jewish problem. This is touched on in Robert Ross's, *So It Was True: The American Protestant Press and the Nazi Persecution of the Jews* (1980).

Wyman concludes that few in Congress, whether liberal or conservative, showed much interest in saving Jews. Restrictionism was strong on Capitol Hill, and the State Department took its cue from Congress, which reflected ''the indifference of much of the non-Jewish public.'' The apathy of the public, in turn, was encouraged by the scant media coverage. Finally, Wyman argues that anti-Semitism was a constrictive influence on policymakers.

A different approach is found in *American Refugee Policy and European Jewry, 1933–1945* (1987) by Richard Breitman and Allen Kraut. Taking issue with the earlier approaches to the subject, the authors argue that American policy toward Nazi Germany and toward European Jewry must be examined in its historical and political context. They contend that on the issue of the refugees, American policy was based on four major variables: preexisting restrictive immigration laws and regulations, an entrenched State Department bureaucracy committed to a narrow interpretation of its functions and to the protection of American interests alone, American public opposition to an increase in immigration, and the reluctance of Roosevelt to accept the inherent political risks of humanitarian measures on behalf of foreign Jews.

Breitman and Kraut challenge historians, such as Morse, Feingold, and Wyman, who overestimate the influence that individual anti-Semites wielded in shaping American policy. Historians of the subject, they contend, have failed to penetrate beneath the broad social forces that encouraged restrictions. They have not adequately probed the institutional priorities of the government agencies that dealt with the refugee issue.

For Breitman and Kraut, a good part of the failure to do more in behalf of Jewish refugees had to do with a bureaucracy that followed precedent and restricted itself to its assigned tasks. Roosevelt, concerned with economic recovery and committed to protecting the United States from fascism, viewed the rescue of persecuted foreigners as being incompatible with the defense of the national interest. He sincerely believed in the danger of a fifth column and consequently refused to alter or interfere with the bureaucratic process that monitored refugee policy.

Three additional books that address the subject of this chapter, but within the context of the overall failure of the Allies to save European Jewry, should also be consulted. They include Monty Noam Penkower's *The Jews Were Expendable* (1983), *The Terrible Secret* by Walter Laqueur (1980), and Martin Gilbert's *Auschwitz and the Allies* (1981).

What all of the books discussed in this chapter have in common is an indictment of the United States in particular, and the Western world in general, as bystanders to the Holocaust. Each of the historians has attempted to explain the failure of the United States to do more to save European Jewry, and the result is a devastating portrait of the Roosevelt administration in a time of great peril. But before this picture becomes indelibly printed in Holocaust historiography, we should, in reading these works, remind ourselves of Michael Marrus's tempering words in his *Holocaust in History* (1987):

There is a strong tendency in historical writing on bystanders to the Holocaust to condemn, rather than to explain. . . . If the Holocaust was indeed unprecedented . . . then it is also true that people had no experience upon which to base their understanding at the time, and no reliable guides for action. To a degree, everyone was in the dark. Historians have quite properly combed the seamy underside of allied and Jewish policy, searching through records sometimes deliberately hidden from view. But they should take care in using such material to give contemporaries a fair hearing. (P. 157)

## SELECT BIBLIOGRAPHY

Breitman, Richard, and Allen Kraut. *American Refugee Policy and European Jewry, 1933–1945*. Bloomington: Indiana University Press, 1987.

Feingold, Henry. *The Politics of Rescue: The Roosevelt Administration and the Holocaust, 1938–1945*. New Brunswick, N.J.: Rutgers University Press, 1970.

Freidman, Saul S. *No Haven for the Oppressed: United States Policy Toward Jewish Refugees, 1938–1945*. Detroit: Wayne State University Press, 1973.

Gilbert, Martin. *Auschwitz and the Allies*. New York: Holt, Rinehart, and Winston, 1981.

Jarvik, Laurence, director. *Who Shall Live and Who Shall Die?* Kino International Corporation, 90 minutes. 1982.

Laqueur, Walter. *The Terrible Secret: Suppression of the Truth About Hitler's Final Solution*. Boston: Little, Brown, 1981.

Lipstadt, Deborah. *Beyond Belief: The American Press and the Coming of the Holocaust, 1933–1945*. New York: Free Press, 1986.

Marrus, Michael R. *The Holocaust in History*. Hanover, N.H.: University Press of New England, 1987.

Morse, Arthur. *While Six Million Died: A Chronicle of American Apathy*. New York: Random House, 1967.

Penkower, Monty Noam. *The Jews Were Expendable: Free World Diplomacy and the Holocaust*. Urbana: University of Illinois Press, 1983.

Ross, Robert. *So It Was True: The American Protestant Press and the Nazi Persecution of the Jews*. Minneapolis: University of Minnesota Press, 1980.

Wyman, David. *The Abandonment of the Jews: America and the Holocaust, 1941–1945*. New York: Pantheon, 1984.

———. *Paper Walls: America and the Refugee Crisis, 1938–1941*. Amherst: University of Massachusetts Press, 1968.

# Part III

---

# The Holocaust in Education and the Arts

# Chapter 24

# The Holocaust in the School Textbooks of the Federal Republic of Germany

*Walter Renn*

## GERMAN PARTICIPATION IN THE HOLOCAUST

There is considerable reticence among most German textbook authors in describing specifically who carried out the Holocaust.[1] Almost all of them tend to separate the German people from all aspects of its execution. Textbook authors almost never declare that Germans carried out the Holocaust, but, instead, state that Hitler and/or the SS carried it out. Karlheinz Pelzer exemplifies the alibi function provided by Hitler and the SS: "Soon after the NS revolution, Hitler began his ruthless struggle against all Jewish citizens. In the most gruesome manner, Hitler's torturers murdered more than 6 million Jews." In postwar Germany "after so many trials, we can make a picture of the inhuman gruesomeness and bestiality of the SS thugs."[2]

Other authors reveal the tendency to make Hitler and the SS solely responsible for the destruction of the European Jews. "Hitler's profound hatred" led to "criminal measures against the Jews." "The persecution of the Jews" was carried out by "the brown Dictatorship."[3] It was "Hitler's morbid anti-Semitism" that "led to the murder of nearly 6 million Jews";[4] and "the terror was carried out by the SS."[5]

This situation in the textbooks has led the Georg-Eckert-Institut für Internationale Schulbuchforschung to declare in its German-Israeli schoolbook recommendations that "while the decisive question of responsibility and coresponsibility for the persecution of the Jews is more intensively posed than in earlier textbooks, it is not clearly enough answered. In most books the persecutions are presented as the result of state measures. Moreover, they are frequently presented in connection with the use of self-styled or euphemistic terminology of the Nazi period: 'Reich Crystal Night,' 'annihilation,' 'Extermination,' 'Final Solution.' "[6]

Many authors do not mention Germans in portraying the mass murders, while others mention no agent at all for carrying out the genocide. Wolfgang Hug in his study guide asks the question: "What contributed to the fact that mass murder was organized and carried out with the participation of many?"[7] But he gives no answer in his textbook. Instead, he uses abstract formulations that leave the perpetrators anonymous and the killings taking place with mechanical autonomy: "The government of the extermination machine," he writes, "lay in the hands of the SS police power."[8] Eugen Kaier uses similar language: "Staffs of cold-blooded desk-murderers brought the victims from all the nations under German control in freight trains and trucks into huge camps." Kaier describes the mass gassings, mentions the most notorious camps, and enlarges on the mechanistic model, naming nationalities and offering an interesting assessment of attitudes and motives of those who carried out the genocide:

The millionfold murders took place according to general stafflike planning with bureaucratic precision using factorylike technology. Ukrainians, Poles, Lithuanians, and Jewish forced labor were compelled to carry out the crude activities under threat of death. The SS was placed in positions as administrative, supervisory, technical, and medical personnel. Now and then there were devilish torturers, [but] the majority were simple, upright [biedere] family fathers, correct in their private life, citizens who were obsessed with duty, and who convinced themselves that their dirty [work] was in the service of the people and the fatherland.[9]

There is no discussion of the perpetrators as part of the German people nor explanation of how traits such as service to the German people could be turned to the service of genocide. Indeed, without analysis of the Nazi manipulation of deep-seated German cultural values, Kaier's final sentence appears offensive.

The automatic quality of the killing process already noted is reiterated by Bernhardt Heinloth, who writes: "According to estimates, at least three million Jews lost their lives by means of the technical, factorylike killings in these camps."[10] Although the situation has improved in recent texts,[11] many authors still use passive sentence constructions and the impersonal "one" (German *man*) to describe the perpetrators. The passive voice allows the perpetrator of the described action to be omitted. Hans Muggenthaler, for example, in depicting the systematic denial of human rights in the course of driving the Jews out of Germany, states: "Life was made unbearable for those remaining." Who made life unbearable is ignored, as this would necessarily lead to a discussion of how German citizens could come to carry out such barbarities. In his section on the Holocaust, Muggenthaler mentions only Hitler, Himmler, Hoess, the SS, and the National Socialists; on the other hand, on the pages directly before and after the handling of the Holocaust, the terms "Germans," "Germany," and "the

German people'' are mentioned frequently, for example, as many as eleven times on the page preceding the Holocaust.[12] Hug also is most restrained in referring to Germans as perpetrators: In reporting Soviet prisoner-of-war deaths, for example, he writes, ''Of the more than 5.5 million Soviet soldiers who were prisoners of war, approximately 3.5 million died in German camps. One-seventh had to die violently; the others died through hunger and epidemics.'' In contrast, however, he refers to ''Germans'' three times in the first nine lines in the succeeding section, which describes Soviet partisan resistance to the German military: ''resistance of the population against the German occupation power''; ''partisan groups . . . tied up many German divisions;'' and ''the Warsaw rebellion, bloodily defeated by German troops.''[13]

The usual formulation for mentioning Germans in connection with the Holocaust is to state that the Jews were transported from ''German-occupied areas,'' as in Hug:

Until the fall of 1944, trains carrying Jewish men, women, and children rolled out of the German-occupied areas to the killing camps of Sobibor, Treblinka, Majdanek (near Lublin), and above all to Auschwitz-Birkenau (near Krakow).[14]

Hans Heumann uses a similar formula:

After the attack on the Soviet Union, Special Commands of the SS received the order to murder all Jews in the enormous area between the Baltic and the Black Sea. Also, from the West European countries, which had been occupied by German troops during the Second World War, the Jews were carried off to Poland and taken to killing camps where they were murdered.

. . . After the beginning of the war against the Soviet Union in 1941, Hitler ordered the ''Final Solution,'' that is, the murder of all Jews living in the German area of control.[15]

There is otherwise a tendency to link the perpetration of the mass murders with other nationalities, as, for example Kaier[16] and Hug do: ''*Einsatzgruppen* ravaged in Poland and the Soviet-occupied areas supported in part by native anti-Semitic militia units.''[17] Only one recent textbook departs significantly from the pattern. Wolfgang Mickel charges that

without the cooperation of numerous offices, for example, the German railroads, and without the assistance of countless subordinates who only did [their duty] and did not themselves murder, the realization of the [Final Solution] would not have been possible. The technical-bureaucratic organization of criminality divided responsibility and made it possible to look the other way. The official maintenance of secrecy of this unavoidable criminality, the terror and fear of becoming a victim of the machinery oneself, hindered effective resistance.[18]

Textbook authors do not deny the German origins and execution of the genocide so much as they (perhaps unconsciously) distance Germans from the events.

In this way they need not explain how the genocide could have been conceived and carried out by Germans as Germans instead of Nazis. Although all authors profess that the Holocaust is a special burden of the German people, they do not write about it as though Germans had much to do with it. Again, the SS, the Nazis, Hitler, Himmler, Heydrich, and a few others appear to have planned, ordered, and carried out these abominations single-handedly. That they held certain attitudes and views widely shared by German society and that they held such highly respected positions of German leadership in Germany are points not discussed. Specific elements and values of German culture are not compared with Nazi values and traits, nor are these characteristics analyzed in relation to carrying out the Holocaust.

By and large, the texts do not assess the German citizen's role in identifying, denouncing, registering, marshalling, guarding, or sentencing Jews; in employing, invoicing, loading, and transporting them; or in designing, engineering, fabricating, installing, operating, or repairing gas chambers, crematoria, barracks, slave-labor factories, and other camp facilities. The textbooks do not take cognizance of the fact that the roundups took place in broad daylight all over Germany and Europe and that travel was over the main lines of transport with travelers standing on the station platforms as the freight trains rolled past with their human cargo on the way to Auschwitz.

## GERMAN RESISTANCE TO THE DICTATORSHIP

Resistance to the National Socialist regime is elaborated into a complex subject and may be divided into three categories: (1) German resistance (2) foreign resistance and (3) Jewish resistance. Of these three categories, only German resistance is treated in any detail in textbooks, while foreign and Jewish resistance is usually mentioned only incidentally.

Until recently, German resistance was overemphasized in German texts for purposes of educating for democracy, presenting models of moral courage, and honoring the heroes of the German resistance. This emphasis had the effect, however, of diverting attention from the real lack of opposition among the great majority of Germans, thereby distorting reality and causing the treatment to appear apologetic. Only in the late 1970s did authors begin to take steps to present more carefully balanced accounts of the degree of German resistance.[19]

Recent study guides emphasize the obstacles to resistance. As one learning goal, Hermann Burkhardt stresses teaching "the inclination of the many weak people to subordinate themselves to the stronger, to block out the outsider and to make him into a scapegoat."[20] Joachim Hoffmann's learning goals, even more than Burkhardt's, emphasize the effects of Nazi indoctrination and intimidation, even though he is one of the few to state that "Germans" carried out the genocide.[21]

Other textbooks emphasize the danger of opposition against Hitler and the party. Kaier states, for example, that even telling political jokes denigrating

Hitler or his deputies, expressing doubt about final victory, or helping a Jew "could bring a harmless person to the scaffold." To underscore this, he reports that the number of death sentences climbed from less than 100 under the Weimar Republic to more than 16,000 under the Nazi regime between 1937 and 1944; in addition, approximately 20,000 death sentences were passed by military courts.[22]

Indeed, comparatively small acts of opposition to the regime could have dire consequences. Joachim Cornelissen tells of a retired Berliner who was sentenced to death in 1943 for writing graffiti on public restroom walls accusing Hitler of mass murder and urging his assassination to end the war. The continual threat of being placed in a concentration camp, Cornelissen notes, "was calculated to suppress opposition to the regime." He concludes that even "if broad sections of the populace viewed with outrage the injustice done to their Jewish neighbors, protests remained muted and powerless in the face of the intimidation by the Party."[23]

Even S. Grassmann, author of what is normally a progressive text, appears pessimistic about the possibility of resistance:

The entire country was soon covered with a thick network of concentration camps. Among the populace the fear of concentration camps was broadly disseminated. This was clearly expressed in a well-known saying of the time: "Dear God, make me dumb; that I might not in Dachau come." In fact, prisoners who were released from Dachau, near Munich, had to place themselves under obligation, on pain of rearrest, not to report anything of their terrible experiences, though their changed appearance due to hunger and maltreatment and their silence rather increased the fear of concentration camps, even without any knowledge of details.[24]

Pelzer is more ambiguous, on the one hand almost denying the possibility of aiding Jews by 1938, while claiming, nevertheless, that some did help: "Help for the Jews was scarcely possible since the frightened population feared the Party. Nevertheless, brave men and women, without consideration for the danger, helped the Jews to leave the country."[25]

A second group of textbooks places greater emphasis on resistance, as may be noted by the provocative questions they pose. Hug asks: "Why didn't the Germans succeed in removing the NS dictatorship?—What is the significance for us of the fact that there were German resistance groups?"[26] But Hug is more cautious in later questions: "What conflicts arise for specific social groups in cases of resistance against a dictator in one's own country?—Is resistance to be carried out even if there are no prospects for success?"[27] Only when Hug confronts the lack of public German protest or effort to rescue the Jews from their tormentors does he grasp the crucial issue. He states clearly that "little was undertaken against the persecution of the Jews," then adds, "What motives hindered the protests of our parents and grandparents?"[28]

The difficulty of resistance against a totalitarian state has led a number of textbook writers and scholars to consider a broader definition. In the narrow sense, resistance means the general aim of overthrowing the regime by such acts as sabotage, the building of underground cells, organized underground activities, the distribution of antiregime propaganda, and other attempts at direct action against the regime. However, in view of the enormous power of totalitarian dictatorships, some texts include more broadly defined actions of defiance than military, religious, labor, or political resistance. Such acts as listening to forbidden enemy radio broadcasts, telling antigovernment jokes, holding discussions with like-minded dissidents, or assisting a Jewish friend are sometimes evaluated as resistance in the context of the severity of the dictatorship. Such activities are considered acts of opposition worthy of inclusion in textbooks,[29] no doubt in order to encourage education in the right of resistance against tyranny.

Grassmann includes excellent examples that emphasize resolute defiance. He cites the courage of Carl von Ossietzky, the German pacifist and 1935 Nobel Peace Prize winner, whom Göring offered to release from confinement if he would reject his Nobel Peace Prize: "Ossietzky replied no and returned to his imprisonment."[30] Grassmann also reports Pastor Schneider's reply when he was required to sign an affidavit that he would be silent about what had happened to him in the concentration camp. His answer was that as soon as he was released, "the first curbstone will be the pulpit from which I preach your abominable crimes to the entire populace!"[31]

Grassmann includes the secret opposition represented by political jokes against the regime and its racial teachings: "There was a secret mockery even then among the public that the highest leaders, Hitler, Himmler, Goebbels, and Göring so little resembled the blond, blue-eyed ideal of the Aryan, and represented a visual contradiction to the teaching of race."[32] Grassmann is also the only general textbook author to include the sole demonstration on behalf of Jews in Germany. During the war non-Jewish spouses of Jews, mostly women, spontaneously protested outside the collection camp on Rosen Street, Berlin, until their partners were released. "The regime did not dare publicly to shoot at the protesting people. However, when the 'Aryan' partner died, the spouse was immediately deported."[33]

Thus the concept of resistance is broadened to include many acts of defiance that fell short of seeking to topple the regime, but that are no less inspiring. In an article on German worker resistance, Detlev Peukert stresses the goal of "demonstrating the conceptual significance of . . . resistance for democratic learning processes in engendering a democratic postwar spirit in the Federal Republic of Germany." He urges that "examples of civil courage and nonconformity from everyday life in the Third Reich be portrayed to give students the opportunity to identify with model personalities from democratic lines of tradition in German history."[34]

Although the principle of the right of resistance against unjust authority is not explicit in German texts, at least some emphasize acts that illustrate the vulnerability of dictatorship to attack. Hoffmann, for example, despite an emphasis on German intimidation, points out that "forward-looking traditions may be learned from the resistance to these crimes" and notes that "nations that were attacked and occupied by Germany defended themselves with great sacrifice." He concludes that the student should "understand the exceptional circumstances in which one would act according to one's conscience."[35]

While this may appear less than spectacular to the Western observer, it is useful to recall the strong tradition of law and order in the history of the German *Machtstaat*. One may also add that education in Germany is carried out under the authority of the Länder governments, and teachers are employees of the state. This adds to the difficulty of teaching resistance to state authority based on conscience, even if that authority exceeds its powers. In this respect German textbooks are only beginning to teach the right of civil disobedience and opposition to abuses of state power. The Germans, be it noted, have no historic examples—such as the Dreyfus case in France—of successful public resistance to criminal injustice, prejudice, or overweening military authority in government. Indeed, there are no examples of successful revolution against authoritarian government in German history, a fact that no doubt reflects upon German attitudes about resistance to constituted authority.

The lack of a strong opposition to the Nazi regime or of aiding German Jews may explain the weakness of textbook coverage of other countries' efforts on behalf of Jews. Only a few texts mention the efforts of other nations to rescue Jews. Hoffmann reports that the Danes succeeded in saving almost all Danish Jews by sending them to neutral Sweden.[36] Gerhart Binder and Hermann Burkhardt state that "in some lands, the annihilation actions were frustrated or rendered largely ineffective, such as in Finland, Denmark, and partly in Italy."[37]

Political science, social studies, and upper-division history texts do not include much material on the possibility of German resistance on behalf of Jews, and what little discussion is found is pessimistic about the possibility of assistance. Bernd Hey, in his teacher's manual, notes that "the populace was . . . spied upon and checked from all sides and could not rely on either a just or lawful process by the police."[38] There was, Hey states, a general reluctance among Germans to share any knowledge because of a lack of trust:

Even those who got out of a concentration camp, for the most part, feared to talk about what had happened to them for fear of being sent back. They even had to sign a declaration that obligated them to maintain complete silence about their stay in the concentration camp. The lack of comprehension and a disbelief of the reports that did leak out of the concentration camps to those outside also may have contributed to the limited instruction of the populace; this disbelief, naturally, was especially strong against the messages of the Allied broadcasts.[39]

Because listening to foreign broadcasts was severely punishable, Hey explains, those who had such information feared to pass it on. There were strong punishments for disseminating "atrocity propaganda." Hey concludes pessimistically:

Once the program of driving out and exterminating Jews was in process, it was scarcely possible any longer for anyone to do anything directly against the concentration camps or for their inmates; at best, something could have been achieved by energetic resistance at the beginning of the Third Reich.[40]

Among political science and social science texts, only Herbert Baumann indicates, by his tone at least, a tepid encouragement for the right of resistance. He asks the student, "When does the citizen have the right and duty of resistance against the government?" His book alone includes a moving inscription from the epitaph on the Berlin-Plotensee memorial to the participants in the July 20, 1944, plot to assassinate Hitler, indicative of the shame felt by many Germans:

> You do not bear the disgrace
> You defended yourselves
> You gave that great, eternal,
> wakeful sign of reversal
> Sacrificing your warm lives
> For freedom, justice and honor.[41]

The advanced history, social studies, and political science textbooks' treatment of the resistance of other countries and assistance to Jews is generally weak. Again, only Hey's teacher's manual mentions the aid of other countries to Jews. While Hey's commentary may not be taken as the norm, it is of interest for its portrayal of foreign resistance. Hey is generous to the French:

The French under the Vichy government gave the Germans considerable difficulty in deporting French Jews. Because of their great hatred of the German occupation forces, the French took their fellow Jewish citizens under their protection and tried to save them. As a result, it was mostly stateless Jews, Jewish refugees, and immigrants who had departed Germany before the war broke out who were the main victims of the Gestapo and security service forces.[42]

Hey also praises the Italian Fascist regime's resistance to German anti-Semitism. Until Italy collapsed and Mussolini was overthrown in 1943, Italy and Mussolini protected Italian Jews from the Nazis. Mussolini had implemented only halfhearted anti-Jewish measures as long as he was in power. In the occupation areas of the Balkans and Vichy France the Italian army repeatedly sought to assist persecuted Jews. "As a result of the short time they had in Italy and the worsening war situation for them, the Germans succeeded in seizing only a small part of Italy's Jewish citizens."[43] Hey's final summary is fair and insightful and could stand as a model for other texts:

In the cases of the states of France, Denmark, Italy, and Bulgaria, the states were able to save the greater part of their native Jewish citizens from extermination camps, though in most cases the Jews had to live in constant fear of their lives and had to accept the loss of their personal freedom, their property, and their positions in society and the work world.[44]

What is notable is that in most cases states sought to save only their own Jews and were more prone to sacrificing members of other states to death. On the one hand, it shows that nationalism served to cause them to commit themselves for fellow citizens of the same language, culture, and nationality; on the other hand, it is clear that they would not commit themselves for human beings who were "foreigners." In any case, what is made clear is that even the power apparatus of the Third Reich could not always get its way if it met with the opposition of the government and the people alike.

Only one additional text includes foreign national assistance to the Jews. Henning Eichberg mentions Finland's refusal to give up its Jews to its German ally; the attempts of the Netherlands to carry out a general strike on behalf of the Jews; and the resistance of French, Italian, and Greek authorities and citizens to the deportation of the Jews from their territories.[45]

Eichberg is also the only author to comment on Jewish resistance. As usual, such discussion is limited to the portrayal of events in the Warsaw ghetto. Eichberg describes the desperate Jewish resistance and war of defense against the SS, noting that "the German SS and police units attacked the ghetto with artillery support, but were repeatedly thrown back." He describes the heroic sacrifices of Jewish women and girls, the suicide missions to blow up tanks, and the fact that Jewish resistance forces were able to hold off the German military for six weeks.[46] Other authors, such as Hans-Georg Fernis and Heinrich Haverkamp, mention the "Warsaw revolt" parenthetically, in connection with descriptions of national resistance movements that sprang up to defend themselves against the Germans. Hey, usually so reliable, does not mention the Warsaw ghetto revolt, though he has a long discussion of resistance and a chronology of resistance events.

In sum, the textbook discussion of German resistance to the dictatorship is expressed in pessimistic, if not fatalistic, terms, and coverage of the foreign resistance and the Jewish resistance to the Germans, both of which were extensive, is not reflected in the textbooks.

## THE EUTHANASIA PROGRAM AND GERMAN PROTESTS

Hitler's euthanasia program, the killing of the mentally sick, incurably ill, and invalids in 1940 and 1941, though not aimed against the Jews, used methods similar to the killing processes of the Holocaust, and some of its leading personnel were later transferred to the killing centers in the East. It has been rightly considered, therefore, a prelude to the Holocaust. Binder and Burkhardt draw attention to this fact, stating that as the euthanasia project progressed, the regime "developed the methods that later would be employed in the most ghastly act of destruction in history, the 'Final Solution of the Jewish Question.' "[47] Like the killing operations of the Holocaust, the euthanasia program was officially kept secret. Nevertheless, many Germans learned of it and raised protests against the government's actions. As a result, the program was officially terminated.

Some textbooks discuss the euthanasia program, but none ask why there was not the same degree of German information and protest in response to the murder of European Jews as occurred in the euthanasia program. Franz Böhm has pointed out that the euthanasia killing program "lay under the same veil of secrecy as the destruction of the Jews,"[48] yet it soon became sufficiently known, and a few brave Germans mounted effective protests against these killings. Grassmann discusses euthanasia briefly, describing the basic events and the fact that Protestant and Catholic churches in cooperation with members of the affected families forced Hitler to halt operations for the time being.[49] Schwander also reports the religious opposition to the program:

The two great Churches defended themselves against the "killing of valueless lives." The Protestant bishop of Württemberg, D. Theodor Würm, marched bravely against the machinations of the Brown masters. . . . Pastor Friedrich von Bödelschwingh . . . declared: "The killing of the sick entrusted to me will take place over my dead body." . . . Cardinal Graf von Galen reported it as murder to the State Prosecuting Attorney. He achieved a great success. Hitler had the killing stopped for the time being.[50]

Grassmann and Schwandner leave unanswered the questions raised by their narratives about purported German powerlessness and intimidation in relation to the persecution and mass murder of the Jews.

Wilhelm Borth and Eberhard Schanbacher emphasize that "despite the greatest secrecy these murders could not be hidden. There was considerable uneasiness among the population."[51] The text then discusses the effective actions of Cardinal von Galen and Bishop Würm in halting the program without further discussion.

Hans Ulrich Rudolf and Edgar Walter note that "because of the unrest among the populace and the protests of the Churches," Hitler in August 1941 had the program stopped. Again, no connection is made between German knowledge and protest against the euthanasia program and the absence of such knowledge or concern regarding the fate of the Jews.[52]

Kaier has a relatively detailed section dealing with the "mass murder of Germans, the 'mercy killing' [euthanasia] of the incurably ill, 'according to human determination.' " He declares:

Despite the strict maintenance of secrecy, word of the dreadful events got around and aroused unrest and indignation among the populace and soldiers. Representatives of both Christian churches and other right-minded people raised protests and pressed charges. At the end of 1941, the "euthanasia" project was officially halted. In a few institutions and concentration camps, they nevertheless continued.

The alert student may wonder why relatively effective protests were made against the murder of incurable Germans, but not on behalf of German Jews. Kaier answers the question in the succeeding passage:

The murder of the sick and aged could be partially prevented because it took place in the middle of Germany. Outside the Reich area, beneath the cloak of military secrecy, and removed from the view and protests of the German population, Hitler began the extermination of the Jews that publicly he had repeatedly threatened to do.[53]

Although Kaier leaves open the question of what the Germans knew about the mass murders of Jews in the East—and whether the German people would have raised protests had they known—the inference is that they would have protested.

Regarding German public knowledge of the euthanasia program, Burkhardt notes in his teacher's manual that "the murder of these people did not remain a secret, and considerable unrest at home and among the troops made itself felt." He also cites the effective protests of Bishop Graf von Galen of Münster and Bishop Würm of Württemberg.[54] German textbooks add little to the explanation of why the euthanasia program provoked protest so that its continuance was hindered, while the genocide program aroused no protests or attempts to halt it. Some authors, such as Wanda Kampmann, Berthold Wiegand, and Wolfgang Mickel, include the euthanasia program only in the context of a long list of Nazi barbarities.[55] Other texts, for example, that of Hans-Georg Fernis and Andreas Hillgruber, point out that "prominent leaders of the Church complained and had the action partially stopped," but they, too, make no connection with the genocide.[56] Fernis and Heinrich Haverkamp treat the subject in similar fashion, but do not connect it with the Holocaust.[57]

E. D. Gallmeister's text, it may be noted, is the only one that notes that Jews were also victims in the euthanasia campaign. The purpose of the activity, he states, "was the mass murder of the helpless inmates of insane asylums and the congenitally and incurably ill as well as healthy children of Jewish or half-Jewish ancestry."[58] Gallmeister also cites details of Graf von Galen's protest sermon of August 3, 1941, describing the lawsuit brought by the bishop against the Nazi government for murder. Curiously, Gallmeister does not mention the outcome of von Galen's suit or raise the question of why the Jews were not the subject of similar initiatives.

R. H. Tenbrock and Kurt Kluxen, on the other hand, are among the few who at least raise the issue:

The success of the public condemnation of the National Socialist euthanasia crimes (from 1939 to 1941 approximately 70,000 mentally ill persons were secretly murdered) by the bishop of Münster, Graf von Galen, at least, demonstrates that occasionally there were to be found unused possibilities [for active resistance]. However, neither of the Churches condemned the policies against the Jews.[59]

Finally, Werner Ripper asks half of the question: "How may we explain that the euthanasia program of the National Socialist regime provoked the opposition of the church?"[60] The question, part of a review study section, is provocative, indeed, but no adequate answer is given in the text.

In summary, the authors of the textbooks use the protest against the euthanasia

program as an instance of courageous and effective resistance, but do not view
it as an example to teach or to encourage the necessity of resistance to inhumanity,
nor do they contrast the German response to the euthanasia campaign with that
to the genocide operation.

## SECRECY AND GERMAN WARTIME KNOWLEDGE OF
## THE HOLOCAUST

When the American NBC program "Holocaust" was first broadcast on German television in 1979, the audience was enormous and the response overwhelming. The television studio received more than thirty thousand calls from
viewers seeking additional information, wanting to provide corroborative evidence, and even turning in their spouses. German schools held discussions of
the film series, and the state of North Rhine–Westphalia distributed over one
hundred thousand fifty-six-page teaching booklets to its schools. A large majority
of viewers were shocked by the series and particularly needed to have clarified
how much the average German had known during the war about what was
happening to the Jews; what the German responsibility was today for the Nazi
crimes; and what the lessons of the Holocaust are for future generations.[61]

Questions continue to be raised about when and how much the Germans knew
about the mass murder of the European Jews. Observers have found it difficult
to imagine that the contemporary German population could have remained ignorant of the most gigantic mass-murder campaigns of modern times. Many
Germans, especially the younger generation, have been interested in this question, and the issue has long divided the German public. Frank Bahr notes in his
text that while "the NS leadership sought to keep these happenings a secret from
the German public, it is still controversial in postwar Germany today what the
individual could have known about the destruction of the Jews."[62] The division
of opinion is well summarized by Heinloth in his chapter "Mastery of the Past":
"The one side declares that the regime kept the persecution and destruction
activities a complete secret from the public so that they couldn't know anything;
others stress that the majority of Germans knew all about it, but remained
silent."[63]

In fact, no textbook takes such an extreme position as Heinloth suggests, but
most do stress the secrecy surrounding the killing operations. The consensus is
that German people knew very little about what was happening to the Jews in
the East during the war. No text takes the position that more than a handful of
Germans possessed knowledge of these events.

Some texts declare that German knowledge of the persecutions and concentration camps of the 1930s was minimal. Thus Binder and Burkhardt stress that
until the *Kristallnacht* pogrom of 1938, "all of these measures had been carried
out against the Jews step by step and still half in secret [*noch halb im geheimen
durchgeführt*]."[64] Heumann emphasizes that concentration camps were purposely
built "away from the main roads so that the public noticed them as little as

possible. Many Germans knew nothing of what went on behind the high, en-
circling, electrically charged barbed-wire fences. . . . Whoever entered there . . .
was not allowed to say anything [after release] on threat of heavy punishment."
Heumann concludes that the 1938 pogrom "would have to have opened the
people's eyes to the true character of national socialism," but that "propaganda
and terror had silenced many."[65]

Kaier's position is similar, except that he places less emphasis on the secrecy
of the camps in order to stress the purposes of intimidation they served:

The existence of the concentration camps was known in Germany as well as abroad,
though not their numbers nor the reality of the SS state, inaccessibly hidden behind the
barbed wire. The German people felt a vague dread of them that Hitler found highly
desirable. To an acquaintance he said: "I don't want retirement institutions to be made
out of the concentration camps. . . . People need a healthy fear."[66]

Some recent texts, such as that of Heinloth, place greater emphasis on German
knowledge of the camps, but only in order to substantiate the teaching that the
German people were intimidated by them:

Induction into the camp was done not all in secret; the public was supposed to learn all
about what happens to those who oppose [the regime]. "He is in Dachau!" "If you
aren't more careful about what you say, you will go to Dachau!" From 1933 onward,
such remarks—or similar ones—belonged to everyday life. In this way, the National
Socialists had achieved a second purpose: Many critics were silenced by the fear of being
hounded by the Gestapo and put in a camp without a trial for an undetermined length of
time.[67]

For the most part, authors generally minimize the extent of German civilian
wartime knowledge of the Holocaust. A significant number, however, do acknowledge that portions of the army knew about the killings. Hans Döhn informs
the student that "Armed Forces generals complained about the brutal proceedings
against the Poles and Jews" by the SS within their military domain "and demanded an end to the encroachments."[68] Helmut Kistler and Werner Stroppe
include statements by military leaders indicating their knowledge of the mass
murders taking place within their military areas,[69] and Burkhardt in his teacher's
manual emphasizes military objections.[70]

In a more recent text, Grassmann considerably broadens the scope of those
who knew about the mass killings. He reveals that "the [*Einsatzgruppen*] murders
took place partly in public and that there were eyewitness accounts of observers,
including army officers and soldiers."[71] Grassmann cites the report of the Wehrmacht major Rosler, dated January 3, 1942:

As we clambered up the earthwork there was offered . . . to our view a picture whose
gruesome horror . . . had a shocking and repulsive effect on us. Into the earth was cut an
approximately 7–8-meter-long and perhaps 4-meter-wide ditch. . . . The ditch itself was

filled with numerous . . . human bodies of all kinds and of both sexes. . . . Behind the earthen wall a *Kommando* policeman stood. . . . Numerous soldiers were standing around in a circle . . . partly in swimming trunks . . . as were numerous civilians with women and children.[72]

In addition to such eyewitness accounts of the Jewish massacres, Grassmann points out that reports by *Einsatzgruppen* killing-squad *Kommandos* have survived the war. He also includes part of the Hoess testimony that mentions that the "stink" caused by the burning of bodies in the crematoria of Auschwitz was so great that "the whole region knew that exterminations were in progress."[73] While Grassmann's presentation suggests widespread knowledge of the gassings by large numbers of Germans and others around Auschwitz, he does not discuss the issue of German public knowledge.

The most dramatic declaration of civilian knowledge of the mass killing appears in Hug, where it is stated that "indeed, although the SS police power sought as far as possible to keep their terrible deeds a secret, it could scarcely be prevented that the greater part of the German people learned of the mass murders."[74] Hug does not elaborate on this remarkable statement, but upon closer examination, it may be noted that he has not declared when the Germans learned of the Holocaust, and he could well have meant the postwar revelations of SS crimes. Hoffmann uses identical language to make the same point and also draws no conclusions, though in a review question he asks students to discuss "the question of apportioning responsibility."[75]

Other authors are more circumspect than the preceding examples. Eduard Steinbügl, for example, in an allusion to German awareness of the fate of the Jews, is brief and ambiguous: "After the outbreak of the Second World War the Hitler regime finally showed its true colors [*seine Maske fallen*] and ordered the 'Final Solution of the Jewish Question,' in other words, the extermination of the Jews in Europe."[76] Schmid's treatment uses a completely dehumanized agent to avoid reference to anyone carrying out the operations and, by stressing the secrecy of the killing operations, suggests German ignorance.[77] Some texts, such as that of Muggenthaler, seem to suggest that the German people knew nothing of the mass killing of "opponents" of the Nazi regime.[78]

Schwandner portrays the Germans as not knowing the ends to which they were being "misused," though curiously they knew enough to fear the regime, loathe its goals, and mock its official explanations for incarcerations.[79] Schwandner's second reference to German knowledge is in a section actually entitled "The Concealment of the Extermination Campaign." He clearly indicates that civilians knew nothing of the mass killings during the war and also makes the startling assertion that "Hitler himself visited Treblinka extermination camp in August 1942."[80] Schwandner thus neatly infers that the Holocaust took place without German awareness, but that Hitler had direct knowledge and was even present at one of the main killing centers. Thus Hitler bears prime responsibility.[81] What is important is the "alibi of the nation" function that Hitler serves in this passage. Not surprisingly, Schwandner's conclusion is that "only a few knew the whole truth about the camps until after the war."[82]

Hans Ebeling and Wolfgang Birkenfeld stress the remoteness of the camps and the secrecy of the operations and acknowledge that scattered information slipped out, but that it was deemed too horrible to accept.[83] This passage, however, has been deleted from the later editions of Ebeling and Birkenfeld, and this sensitive question is no longer discussed.

Tenbrock takes the view that although the Holocaust was a secret, many Germans, nonetheless, intuited what was happening, and some Germans secretly helped to save Jewish lives. It may be noted that Tenbrock stresses, however, that the Germans knew only of the deportations, and that further knowledge of the deportees' fate would have to be surmised.[84]

Rudolf and Walter declare that in September 1941, as German Jews were being shipped to Auschwitz, "no human being could have known the future that awaited these Jews." However, seven lines later on the same page, he prints Hitler's famous Reichstag speech of January 30, 1939, in which the German Führer threatened the "destruction of the Jewish race in Europe" if they "hurled the peoples of Europe once more into a world war."[85]

Otto Boeck's text reveals how the tragic fate of Jews might readily have been surmised. He refers to the stories of soldiers on leave, though he does not believe that rumors spread to many Germans:

The destruction was kept a strict secret. The participants were silent. However, reports from soldiers on leave from the East did, indeed, succeed in getting back to the homeland from time to time. [However], the German people learned the full, horrible truth only after the war when the Allied victors opened the camps, and through the great murder trials of recent years. How can human beings lend their hand to such crimes![86]

Some authors, while emphasizing the secrecy of the killing operations, point out that some Germans in the Reich did learn something of the murderous actions. In such cases, however, they conclude that the information that came into their possession was too horrifying to believe. Friedrich Lucas takes this position.[87] Lachner concurs, stating, "Even if more precise details seeped through, they were so gruesome that they were scarcely believed by the population."[88]

It is often noted that one reason why the Germans did not learn of the mass murders until war's end was because the killing camps were located outside of Germany. Heumann emphasizes the point, requiring that students learn where the killing camps were located.[89] The suggestion to the student is that such killing took place only in the East, outside the view of the German people, reinforcing the idea that Germans were ignorant of the murderous actions of their government. Thus no discussion of German reaction is necessary, nor does the issue of German complicity arise. No textbook enters into the issues of German repression and denial during the war or the horrifying implications that such knowledge would have had—that is, learning that one is led by a criminal regime, the danger of possessing such knowledge, or the shattering effect it would have on one's confidence in the regime.

Some texts challenge the consensus. Grassmann cites Walter Kempowski's book, *Haben Sie davon gewüsst? Deutsche Antworten* (Did you know about it? German answers). Kempowski's study is based on a question he asked some three hundred relatives and acquaintances: "What did you know about the Jews and about the concentration camps?" The result, Grassmann concludes, was "a very interesting book that calls into question the ignorance of contemporaries about the crimes of national socialism. Thus, for instance, one example cited: 'I had a cousin in the SS who refused to shoot Jews. This was known within the family.' "[90]

The Kempowski study, like the earlier NBC "Holocaust" television series, raises questions and tends to affirm the psychological insight that the "population during the Reich knew as much and as little as they desired to know. What they did not know they no longer wanted to know—for reasons that are understandable. To not want to know something, however, always means that one knows enough to know that one does not want to know more."[91]

Textbooks may not be expected to depart radically from the German consensus that the public knew little of the Holocaust until the end of the war. In the absence of clear evidence, the general view is that while genocide was being carried out, German contemporaries had little or no idea of the atrocities.

Wolfgang Scheffler, a foremost authority on the persecution of the Jews, has pointed out the established public views on this subject:

A number of fixed ideas have already become legends that might have been avoided had we become more precisely acquainted, for example, with the practices of ghetto evacuations in the General Government [of Poland], or the mass shootings in occupied Soviet Russia, which enormously call into question the maintenance of secrecy by which the killing measures have been characterized.[92]

Other voices have protested against the insistence on German wartime ignorance. A German educator, Eberhard Questor, a generation ago sought to admonish his fellow educators against making such claims:

It simply won't do to emphasize again and again that "only very few" knew of these things: this may be pertinent to the events in the extermination camps—although here, too, the circle of those who did know comprised significantly more persons than merely the directly participating security forces—but the unjust and brutal expulsion of Jewish citizens from the life of the community *everyone* could see, and also *did* see. Unless the clear reprimand is accepted for at least *this* political and moral failure of tolerance—for this failure to recognize inhumanity—the greater part of the recent past will remain "unmastered," and contemporary history will take on the fatal character of an apologetic.[93]

Recent German texts are more detailed in treating the Holocaust and have taken a less apologetic tone. Hug, for example, in his student workbook shows a willingness to confront the question provocatively:

After the Second World War, many Germans declared that they had known nothing of the NS crimes. Underline from the timetable of events [which students have placed in chronological order] all violations of human rights against Jewish fellow citizens that everyone in Germany had to have known about: Evacuation to work camps—''Reich Crystal Night''—boycott of Jewish businesses—destruction camps—Nuremberg Laws.[94]

Werner Grütter's advanced history text essentially acknowledges that the secret killings became known around Auschwitz when bodies were disinterred for burning: ''The burning of bodies boomeranged, however. The effects were to be sensed [spuren] in the surrounding areas, so that it was very quickly known what was really taking place in Auschwitz.''[95] But the text draws no conclusions as far as the civilian populace in Germany, or, for that matter, even in Poland. Grütter does insist that the German army was well aware of the mass execution of Jews, and he argues that the killings were decided

together with the field commandant, thus, an office of the armed forces. It can, therefore, scarcely any longer be arguably denied that the armed forces knew about the executions and protested in only a few instances against them. . . . The decision to execute was taken in agreement with the field commander. . . . Members of the Wehrmacht sought to save Jews by declaring them [economically] indispensible. [However,] Himmler soon recognized the true intent of this and put an end to the attempt.[96]

Grütter's acknowledgment bears comparison with a few similar statements found in the intermediate texts, but such statements are still rare. Most textbooks do not discuss the military's knowledge of the Holocaust, and a few, in fact, still reject the contention that even the military knew of these events: ''The fighting troops on all fronts did not know what was taking place behind the lines.''[97]

Some advanced history and political science texts emphasize the secrecy and remoteness of the killing camps without directly addressing the question of knowledge. Thus Fernis and Haverkamp emphasize that the Germans were not intended to know what was happening in the killing centers.[98] Willi and Margret Frank also blame Hitler for keeping the crimes in the East secret.[99]

Kurt Gönner and Ralph Krug in their political science text argue that the German population was ignorant of these events and add an interesting rationalization concerning the preoccupation of the Germans and the danger of resistance:

The measures within the framework of the Final Solution of the Jewish Question were to a large extent capable of being kept a secret from the German people. To this was added the fact that the events of the war caused particular concern to the German population and thus diverted [them] from the atrocities of the SS. On the other hand, anyone who turned against [the regime] would have had to reckon with forceful sanctions by the Gestapo. During the war, the National Socialist dictatorship was so strongly entrenched that a revolt against the persecution of the Jews would have meant imprisonment or even death for the individual. One would have had to defend against the discrimination against Jewish fellow citizens already in 1933 and to have opposed these things in the beginning.[100]

Gönner and Krug's apologetic is based, in part, on the assertion that the German public was largely ignorant of the Holocaust during the war. It is true that Germans were distracted by the effects of the war on their personal lives, but they were also very interested and absorbed by war news and events. What is missing in such accounts is the simple explanation that by 1941 most Germans had become indifferent to the fate of the Jews.

Many other texts accept German ignorance of the Holocaust but, unlike Gönner and Krug, are more accusatory. Elmar Krautkrämer and Eberhard Radbruch, for example, concede that German civilians knew little of the extermination scheme, but chide those who witnessed "the beginnings" for doing nothing.[101] Tenbrock and Kluxen are also critical of German moral failure during the Third Reich. In a carefully worded statement they stress the secrecy of the killing operations but are nevertheless critical.[102]

A second group of texts takes the view that even if Holocaust operations were a state secret, there were leaks. Gallmeister, for example, while remaining cautious about German knowledge of specific camps such as Auschwitz, Chelmno, Sobibor, or Treblinka, nevertheless acknowledges that "details seeped through."[103] Eichberg also takes the view that rumors of the mass killings got back to the German people:

The mass murders generally were kept a secret from the German people. However, in consequence of the participation of a large number of support personnel, a rumorlike knowledge was disseminated to a limited degree. Also, the disappearance of Jewish neighbors—as well as the public outbreaks [the 1938 pogrom] of the prewar period—was known.[104]

Gönner and Krug go further in discussing what the German people knew. In the documentation to *Politik in unseren Tag* they cite Bishop Theophil Würm's letter to Reichsminister Hans Lammers of December 20, 1943, which suggests that knowledge of the destruction of the European Jews was perhaps more widespread than is usually recognized: "I must declare, based on religious and ethical sensibilities, and in agreement with the judgment of all positive Christian peoples of Germany, that we Christians perceive this policy of destruction against Judaism [*diese Vernichtungspolitik gegen das Judentum*] as a grievious injustice, and as disastrous for the German people."[105]

Here we see a document indicating the possibility of widespread German knowledge of the destruction of the Jews and a courageous act of resistance. But Gönner and Krug do not comment on this remarkable document. Instead, they print Reichsminister Lammers's reply warning Bishop Würm to stay out of political matters and admonishing him to conduct himself with caution. The authors also ask review questions that recall the cautious attitude toward resistance: "What did Bishop Würm have to reckon with, after receiving Lammers's letter, if he made further protests?"; "What, in your opinion, would have been the situation of a lesser-known man than the bishop if he had turned against the persecution of the Jews?" Moreover, the authors entirely omit the euthanasia program and the Christian response to it.

An excellent summary of the issue is provided by Cornelissen in a section entitled "Didn't Know Anything?" Cornelissen cites Walter Laqueur's *Was niemand wissen wollte* (English version: *The Terrible Secret*):

Millions of Germans knew at the end of 1942 that the Jews had practically disappeared. Rumors traveled back to Germany by way of officers and soldiers on leave from the eastern front. . . . But the knowledge of how the Jews had been killed was limited to a few persons. And relatively few Germans were interested in the fate of the Jews, since most were concerned with a large number of problems of greater personal interest to them. The theme was unpleasant, speculation was futile, and people avoided discussion of the fate of the Jews. Consideration of this question was put aside and in the long run was repressed.[106]

One of the most ambitious analyses of German knowledge is undertaken by Bernd Hey. In his teacher's manual he emphasizes the German dread of the concentration camps, the success of the policy of secrecy, and the riskiness of obtaining further information.[107] Hey's strong emphasis in his teacher's manual on the fragmentary knowledge of the Germans is offset by the different orientation of his textbook, where he uses sources that contradict his own thesis. He cites a long passage from Eugen Kogon, *Der SS-Staat: Das System der deutschen Konzentrationslager* (The SS state: The system of German concentration camps), where Kogon massively indicts the German people. Kogon's partly ironic introductory statement does not conceal his deadly commentary on the subject of German knowledge of the murders:

What did the German know of the concentration camps? Except for the existence of the facilities, scarcely anything, since he still doesn't know anything today. The system of making the details of the terror a strictly kept secret, and the horrors remaining anonymous, making it [the system] that much more effective thus, no doubt proved itself. As I have shown, many Gestapo officials did not know about the interior of concentration camps into which they sent their prisoners; most of the inmates scarcely had any idea of the real working of the camp, or knew many details about the methods employed there. How were the German people supposed to know them? Those who were sent there were confronted with a new, incomprehensible world. This is the best proof of the universally powerful effectiveness of the principle of maintaining secrecy.[108]

And yet, writes Kogon, no Germans were unaware of the existence of concentration camps. Millions had witnessed the burning of synagogues on Kristallnacht. Policemen, judges and trainmen sent prisoners off to the camps. Civilians watched them walking to work. Industrialists profited from their labor. Doctors conducted experiments in the camps. Soldiers knew of the massacre of Russian prisoners of war. And not a few Germans learned of the operations inside the camps before war's end by listening to foreign radio broadcasts.

Kogon's cumulative indictment is supplemented with documentary evidence that the Germans knew what was taking place. Hey includes Bishop Würm's letter to Hitler of July 16, 1943, in which the bishop defends "privileged non-Aryans"—baptized Jews—who he said were "in danger of being treated in the same manner as the "non-Aryans" (Jews) who "had been removed to a great extent" from the population. Such intentions, he continued, just as those annihilation measures (*Vernichtungsmassnahmen*) undertaken against the other non-Aryans, were in sharpest contradiction to the law of God and violated the fundamentals of all Occidental thought and the God-given basic right of human existence and of human worth itself.[109]

Bishop Würm's letters, cited here, do not constitute proof of widespread knowledge of the destruction of the European Jews within Germany—Würm was in part writing to make a point—but they do suggest broader dissemination of such knowledge within the Christian community than is generally acknowledged.

A passage from Hey, cited from J. P. Stern, perhaps best summarizes the issue of awareness among the German population. Stern, an early emigrant from Czechoslovakia and later professor of German literature in London, wrote:

When it is asked, today, what was known of Hitler's Eastern policies of extermination in the Reich, various examples may be cited . . . to show that men who fought in the East or who travelled as civilians and, having access to no special or secret sources of information, knew of the extermination camps and the crimes committed there—if not exactly—then at least that they were a fact of life. Those who know the story-telling propensity of all troops, and especially those who know the German soldier, will scarcely believe that three million of them maintained a pledge of silence about what they saw on a daily basis in the East. Thus, it may be said with certainty: the population of the Reich knew as much (especially about the murder of Jehovah's Witnesses or their own [mentally-]ill fellow citizens) and as little (for example, about the murder of their Jewish fellow citizens and the gypsies) as they wanted to know. What they did not know, for understandable reasons, they did not want to know any more about. However, not to want to know something always suggests that one knows enough to know that one does not want to know *more*. And if it be asked further, whether protests by the German Aryan population would have been able to save their Jewish fellow citizens, then, one must point to the euthanasia program of the first two war years as an example whereby such protests were possible and effective—three weeks after Cardinals von Galen and Faulhaber . . . condemned the program as murder, it was stopped. It cannot be proven that similar protests in the name of the Jews would have been effective. The attempt was never made.[110]

This is by far the most accusatory statement included in a German textbook, and in the absence of a historical analysis of German society "from bottom up" that addresses the question, the inclusion of Stern's largely psychological analysis is commendable. The fact that Hey largely agrees with Stern is supported by passages in his teacher's manual. Referring to Stern's conclusions, he acknowledges that "the example of the euthanasia activities shows that where one sought to know, it was also possible to know."[111] At the same time, Hey does not speculate on the inferences suggested by his own evidence, nor does he emphasize the aspects of the question of greatest interest. Instead, like many other educators, he stresses German foreboding.[112]

Knowledge, Hey insists, is one of the prerequisites to acting. Normally when one knows an injustice has occurred, one feels obliged to try to right the situation or at least to protest. However, this was considered dangerous for the individual and scarcely possible.[113]

Another text, that of Mickel, in a section entitled "The Technique of Not Knowing," takes a position closely resembling Stern's and Kogon's. He describes the German psychology of avoidance, quoting Peter Brucker, professor of psychology at the Technical University of Hannover. Brucker wrote of his own war years in *Das Abseits als sicherer Ort* (The wayside as a secure place).

There were rumors about concentration camps and political persecutions; also of beatings, torture, shootings, and disappearances, but no reports of the life—or of the slow death—of the Jews. . . . There were endless rumors about Jewish persecutions. . . . We knew there were concentration camps and their approximate reality. However, I did not learn the names of many of them until after the war. The rumor mill was thus remarkably incomplete in this respect. . . . Among many otherwise sharp-eared people, there was a certain noticeable defense that arose against learning about certain reports of the horrors of the NS state. We avoided, fell silent, were unwilling, and forgot. I wanted to know, and what was [forgotten] made us seem unworthy. Indeed, I remember that I felt the impulse from time to time to close myself off, like an Indian monkey who saw nothing and heard nothing. Why? . . . Partly shame: Here were crimes that it would be almost unbearable to be a verbal witness to. . . . Sometimes also out of fear: I of course wanted to live and not only just survive, but laugh, fall in love, drink tea with pleasure, and write poetry, and my friends also wanted this or something similar.[114]

Whatever the final answer, Eugen Kogon, whose trenchant indictment has been cited in these pages, insists that the National Socialist terror could not have been fully comprehended before the camps were opened in 1945, and the survivors recounted their incredible stories:

In those months of 1945 during the defeat, the heroic mask that national socialism had always worn was torn from its face and the truth became visible [in] the monstrous dimensions of the terror that had been carried on during the years. It had been first carried out against Germans; from 1938 onward, in the course of Hitler's conquests, it was carried out against the peoples of those nations in the proximate area of Europe, and throughout, and worst of all against the Jews and the Slavic peoples. Taken together, its extent far exceeded in unfathomable horror the frightful events that the German people themselves encountered as a consequence: the death of soldiers on the battlefields, of civilians under the area bombardment, the misery of the millionfold flight and expulsions [from Eastern Europe].[115]

Kogon's reminder of the failure of human imagination before this glut of human destructiveness should not cause us to lose sight of Stern's comment, however, that the German people did not know in part because they did not want to know, or of Hey's and Mickel's conclusion that many Germans repressed available knowledge because they did not conceive opposition possible or because they were indifferent to the fate of the Jews.

## THE QUESTION OF GERMAN GUILT
## AND RESPONSIBILITY

The vital question of individual and collective guilt of the German people is treated only in the advanced-level history and political science texts. Among intermediate textbooks, only Hug raises the issue, in a review section, asking students to discuss "the question of the apportionment of guilt" (*Schuldanteil*) and admonishing them to note carefully "the selection of sources"[116] in the textbook. Hug's text presents the standard judgment that the Nazi leadership was to blame for everything that befell the Jews. The inference is that certain Nazis, the SS, and top leadership—Hitler, Himmler, Heydrich, Hoess, Eichmann, and a few others—bear full responsibility for the Holocaust. While the German people are not explicitly exonerated, the text does not make clear or even discuss whether they share responsibility for the infamies carried out in their name.

Generally it may be said that no textbook disclaims German guilt or responsibility for the Holocaust, but treatments differ markedly in space allocation and viewpoint. Many earlier texts exhibit signs of defensiveness and repression about the subject, while more recent texts enter into a thorough discussion of German responsibility. Recent texts also are more likely to set forth the situation of the participants and bystanders. Some texts define not only the nature and degree of German responsibility but analyze postwar repression of the subject in the Federal Republic as well.

German Minister of Education Wolfgang Bobke in 1979 examined a sampling of German history textbooks and concluded that "none of the books examined denies Germany's guilt."[117] Heinz Kremers's study of the same year reached essentially the same conclusion:

The Nazi annihilation of the Jews is described in history textbooks in recognition of historic responsibility. . . . There are no calculated omissions or gross intentional distortions. Defects are due more to mistakes in the presentation of material than to a principled intention to pass over certain aspects in silence or to downplay them.[118]

While such broad statements are difficult to evaluate, especially when authors' motives and intentions are being assessed, the judgment is probably correct for the general coverage of Jews and the Holocaust. However, this has not prevented distortions in the presentations, nor is it surprising that texts have not escaped the influence of German social and political attitudes.

The entire postwar history of guilt, shame, repression, and avoidance of the subject has been well documented,[119] and some texts, that of Grütter, for example, refer to the atmosphere of postwar shame and repression:

The [German people] felt themselves betrayed; everyone once again sought to cast off and "externalize" this dangerous idealization that had failed them. They now said: The Nazis are to blame for everything. Such a distortion of reality served . . . to protect the ego—to protect one's sense of self in the face of an abrupt devaluation.[120]

Hey notes the importance of the "demonization" of Hitler after the war to minimize the responsibility of the German nation. The demonization of an individual ("Hitler was guilty of everything") does not surface directly in the printed texts, but in the collective complex of coming to terms with the past it does represent one of the most important arguments for keeping one's own guilt at a minimum.[121]

In 1919 the German people had been told that they bore collective responsibility for the outbreak of World War I. They rejected this accusation decisively, especially since war guilt was connected with the issue of reparations. In 1945 Germans again feared that retribution would be based on the accusation of collective responsibility. This was vehemently rejected, especially since responsibility for the Holocaust would burden the Germans with an even greater guilt than the accusations of 1919. In both cases defenders of the German nation argued that it was unfair to punish a whole people for the decisions of the government executed in secret by a tiny fraction of the populace.

It was claimed that the situation would only be made worse if countries indiscriminately accused the German people collectively of having been Nazis. Textbooks of the 1950s often noted that countries of the democratic West thought that since there had been no general protest against the treatment of Jewish fellow citizens, all Germans must have accepted these crimes. In defense it was argued that Hitler's dictatorship had become so secure within a short time that open opposition "would have meant certain death."[122] The broad application of the Allied postwar policy of denazification was deemed unnecessary and was deeply resented. Some German authors felt it necessary to point out that anti-Semitism, after all, was not especially a German character trait.[123]

During the entire postwar period the accusations against the German people have led to massive repression accompanied by resentment and indignation. This repression has delayed the Germans from confronting their connection with the National Socialist past during the Third Reich and has led to a tendency to minimize the closeness many Germans felt to their government. The result has been that many Germans did not come to terms with the "need to consider the fate of the Jews as a special burden for German sensibilities."[124]

One of the earlier textbooks, that by Deuschle, illustrates this repression. Deuschle describes German postwar attitudes in a way that makes it difficult to avoid concluding that he shares these views and perhaps some anti-Semitism as well: "In addition to state, economic, and religious forces that cherish unconsciously an aversion against the 'descendants of the murderers of Christ!' . . . there is in today's Germany a certain fatigue with always hearing the same old 'refrain' of reparation and guilt ('Leave us be. We've heard enough of this old history!')."[125]

It is fair to balance this older text with another early model, that by Hannah Vogt, one of the best of the 1960s texts on the Nazi era. In contrast to Deuschle, Vogt vigorously condemns unrepentant anti-Semites[126] and chides "cowardly" people who refuse to face up to these appalling facts.[127] In her conclusion Vogt seems to be appealing over the heads of the schoolchildren to the German people:

We owe it to ourselves to examine our consciences sincerely and to face the naked truth instead of minimizing or glossing over it. This is also the only way we can regain respect in the world. Covering up or minimizing crimes will suggest that we secretly approve of them. Who will believe that we want to respect all that is human if we treat the death of nearly six million Jews as a "small error" to be forgotten after a few years?[128]

In making this appeal, Vogt was responding to the general yearning of Germans in 1945 to make a new beginning and leave behind forever the nightmare of the past.

Hey illustrates this defensive attitude, citing the "Stuttgart Declaration of Guilt" issued by the Commission of the Evangelical Church in Germany, October 19, 1945, and a second document of the conference, "A Word to Christians Abroad." The latter document has an apologetic tone. The commission document cites (1) the terrible air war that all Germans had suffered; (2) the fanaticism of the Nazis, which was not to be viewed as an "incarnation of German character"; (3) the fact that the church also had suffered atrocities and injustice at the hands of the regime; (4) the fact that the church "condemns especially the hostage murders and mass murder of the German and Polish Jews" (sic); (5) the fact that "Christians in Germany had suffered a great deal because of this, which had disgraced the German name and besmirched German honor"; (6) the fact that the church had "made no bones about this to the responsible offices, though it was very much resented;" and, finally, (7) the fact that the "lack of freedom of speech had been much worse than is imagined, and many people who had openly protested went to concentration camps."[129]

Hey uses this document to analyze the defensive and apologetic attitude of postwar Germans. He asserts that with this document, "the church sought to take the German people under its protection and justify their failure." He asks students to indicate the arguments that the church used to serve this purpose and calls attention to the "standard excuses" to be found in the Stuttgart document.[130] Hey particularly condemns the church's invocation of the suppression of freedom of speech:

Of course, a single public protest by a pastor from the pulpit would be answered with persecution; but experience also shows that the National Socialist regime was in large degree helpless in the face of public protests by especially prominent dignitaries (Galen, for example) or from the simultaneous, mass public opposition of many hundreds of pastors. Invoking the suppression of freedom of speech cannot hide the fact that church protest would also have to be made against the limiting of this basic right—for ultimately the church's preaching was thereby threatened.[131]

Mickel joins in the charge that "discrimination and persecution of the Jewish citizens in Germany was scarcely condemned by the two great churches, and only individual Christians helped persecuted Jews."[132]

On the question of collective guilt, Hey treats the subject extensively, citing the German philosopher Karl Jaspers, who after the war reflected deeply on the question. Jaspers accepted the principle of individual guilt but rejected any collective guilt of the German people.[133] Hey thinks that Jaspers rejected collective guilt because it would thereby relieve the individual of personal guilt and of the need to confront it. At the same time Jaspers accepted the principle of German collective liability:

Thus, for Jaspers all guilt is individual. On the other hand, all citizens of a state are liable for consequences of the policies of their state. Jaspers is prepared to accept this liability of the collectivity, and, indeed, one that is defined by definite citizenship in a state; such a liability does not distinguish between the guilty and the innocent, but identically affects all members of the state.[134]

Like Jaspers, most Germans reject collective responsibility for the Holocaust, but accept general collective liability "for the consequences of the policies of their state." Even in this, however, Hey expresses an uneasy dual allegiance to the claims of the Jewish victims and to the "relatively 'innocent' " Germans burdened by the deeds of the Nazis.[135]

In 1965 the German educator Eric Weniger suggested the form of collective guilt accepted by Germans willing to take responsibility for the past. Weniger does not think that Germans should accept uncritically the views of the democratic West about Germany, but he does think that German historians must accept criticism of the German people in arriving at their own judgments:

We must by our own means work through our loss of human dignity and moral self-consciousness if our own renewal is to be deep and lasting. In this effort, we must take seriously the criticisms of the world; we must examine and come to grips with every criticism. . . . This does not mean that, without reservation, we assume responsibility and guilt for the development of the most recent past because it has been forced on us by the victorious powers, but rather that we assume it for our own sake, from the deepest and most intimate need to do so, and because we want to reestablish the honor of the German name.[136]

Weniger's view entails certain consequences for German history teaching:

For the time being the German people have forfeited the moral right to sit in judgment on the rest of the world. There is no doubt that the other side also bears responsibility for what happened, and that today many things are happening that add new guilt. But as things stand now, this is not our main business, as bitter as this may be. Above all else, it does not excuse us. We must mind our own business, and we have to mind it without fouling our own nest once àgain, a task that, as is well known, we failed to do in 1918.[137]

Many significant German educators reject the concept of collective German guilt. Romano Guardini defines it because, he argues, it has contributed to the repression of the whole subject in Germany.[138] Eugen Kogon rejects it because he deems it to have been a great obstacle to coming to terms with the past: "Nothing stands more in the way of a return to humanity, both in the principle and in practice, than the fact that in the period of massive accusation of collective guilt, most of us got into the habit of doing away with these problems, complexes, and facts by shoving them aside wherever possible, or by glossing over them in silence."[139]

The textbook analyst Thomas Kremers thinks that accusations of collective guilt merely veil the real causes and culprits of the Holocaust. He suggests that the question of the guilt of the German people and the designation of those mainly responsible is "addressed in nearly all books, though with considerable differences." In the texts Kremers claims to have found "outright collective guilt theses . . . as well as differentiated analyses that designate the political responsibility of the German people and their seduction by those mainly responsible in the NSDAP, the state apparatus, the economy, and justice." At the same time, he finds that the role of justice and heavy industry in the coming to power of the Nazis has been "neglected in an irresponsible manner."[140]

Contrary to Kremers's findings, this investigator has found only one textbook that accepts "collective guilt theses," and few texts that contain "differentiated analyses that designate the political responsibility of the German people." Only Bahr, in a 1984 edition, suggests the collective guilt of the Germans. Bahr cites Margarete Mitscherlich-Mielsen, the famous coauthor of *The Inability to Mourn*, in connection with German responsibility for the genocide:

The murder of millions of defenseless, persecuted people can by no means be placed on the shoulders of the higher leadership and ultimately on Hitler. That it could come to this is the concrete result of a great many culpable decisions and actions. . . . The great mass of Germans observed or participated when the Jews were defamed and declared to be subhumans. Without this participation and agreement of the population with this judgment on the Jews, the ultimately successful mass murder of the Jews would not have been possible.[141]

In all other texts accusations of guilt are made against individual Nazi leaders, and only the smallest number of advanced texts—mainly Hey—analyze the problem of collective and individual responsibility.

Moreover, the textbook focus on individual guilt is not without complications, foremost the fact that virtually all leaders denied guilt as well. Ripper notes that the highest leader, Adolf Hitler, denied all responsibility for causing the catastrophe of World War II. Ripper uses Hitler's political testament to show repression and denial at the highest level:

He sought not only to deny responsibility (Jewry incited the war; the General Staff lost it; he himself being a victim of treason), but "obligated the leadership of the nation and his adherents to a scrupulous maintenance of the Racial Laws and pitiless resistance against the world poisoner of all peoples, international Jewry."[142]

Some texts analyze the character of the Nazi leaders responsible for the genocide. Hey notes Rudolf Hoess's extraordinary capacity for obedience and his feelings of inadequacy.[143] Hey also cites Eichmann's statement at his Jerusalem trial in 1961 that his guilt lay in his obedience and that he, too, should be deemed a victim as a means for escaping responsibility. Hey asks the student to consider Eichmann's plea that he be judged on the basis that he obeyed, and not on the basis of whom he obeyed.

In his text Hey questions whether Eichmann may be considered a victim,[144] while in his teacher's manual he denounces the victimizer who tries to pass as a victim:

Eichmann sought to pass himself off as a victim of the National Socialist leadership that misused his obedience, and for whom he now, as it were, stands as proxy before the court, in order to place himself thereby on the same footing as his Jewish victims. Naturally, this attempt to transform himself from an accomplice to a victim must be refuted; even the comparison with the real victims of the regime shows its complete lack of sense.[145]

Hey points out that Eichmann was fully in command in his position and, unlike his victims, had room to escape his situation; in reality, not only was he convinced of the rightness of his role in organizing the roundup of Jews from all over Europe and sending them to their deaths, but he was an eager and conscientious accomplice who in no way could be described as a victim under orders. Hey concludes that in the conflict between obedience and conscience Eichmann's plea indicts him further.[146]

In dealing with the responsibility of lower-ranking personnel for the Nazi-ordered killings, Hey cites Hans Buchheim's conclusions. Buchheim discusses the obligation of lower-echelon personnel to refuse to obey orders to kill concentration-camp inmates or others. He concludes that one is obligated to offer "various excuses" to avoid obeying such orders, but that one is not required to register disagreement or protest against the correctness of the order; he further adds to the ambiguity by concluding that "it cannot fairly be demanded of anyone that he conduct himself heroically or do anything that, from the outset, is without prospect."[147] Hey's conclusion is that Buchheim's advice poses the greater difficulty, Jaspers's the lesser:

Buchheim dispenses with demanding disobedience of orders, even if the order given to the recipient is an inhuman one, because he is conscious of the high risk and the futility of such conduct. For him, it is sufficient that one escape the order in one of the ways he has depicted [i.e., he is incapable of carrying it out, but does not question its legitimacy]. On the other hand, Jaspers is prepared to grant milder circumstances to a person receiving such an order because of the pressure exerted upon him and to remove his conduct from the realm of criminal guilt, but to evaluate his conduct instead within the category of moral guilt (though Jaspers calls for action to prevent crimes against other beings, including the commitment of one's own life, but failure results only in metaphysical guilt).[148]

Deuschle, who earlier has been found defensive and even anti-Semitic in his textbook treatment, sternly rejects carrying out criminal acts under orders:

Professional executioners . . . , and others who "slid in" by way of police duties, [and] unstable persons who were incapable of extricating themselves at the right time . . . cannot invoke orders from above; for anyone who was not actively prepared for this or who did not passively agree, certainly could have avoided cooperating in working in the extermination camps. Of course, the alternative was action at the front! . . .

Anyone who allowed himself to cooperate, whether in the juristic-administrative preparation of the extermination of people, or in the execution (in the truest sense of the word) itself, must, therefore, be prepared to take criminal responsibility. There is no possibility of invoking an ideology or an order. The general laws of human (humane) conduct, which must be known by all, are the decisive standard.[149]

Thus, among the texts that discuss responsibility and guilt, those that reject collective responsibility emphasize individual guilt only at the highest levels. Hey invokes Buchheim's injunction that personnel under command need only try to avoid carrying out murderous orders, but do not have the necessity of carrying out "futile heroics," such as rejecting such orders as criminal. Paradoxically, Deuschle (on the same page on which he makes anti-Semitic and seemingly pro-Nazi comments) makes the strongest imputations of the criminal responsibility of those carrying out orders to kill.

In the discussion of guilt, yet another position that some textbook authors take is to hold the German people in some way collectively responsible for what happened, whether or not they possessed knowledge of it or the power to prevent it. Such a position, expressed in 1946 by Hannah Vogt, was later adopted by her in her text:

We cannot say often and strongly enough that we may not look to the right or left in the solitude of our reflections about ourselves, but must take on the burden of the past in order to be bearers of the future. In this situation, it doesn't matter in the least how much the individual knew or did not know about this burden, or to what extent he loudly or softly protested or more or less internally distanced himself [from the regime]. The burden is upon us; we cannot shake it off. We must find the strength to bear it.[150]

The burden to be faced was the participation or acquiescence of the vast majority of Germans in injustices done to other human beings in their name during the Third Reich during peacetime and war, culminating in the Holocaust. Such texts as that by Hartwich broach the issue of "the entanglement of the greater part of the German people" in the injustices done by the government: "The tragedy of the Jewish population did not begin with the annihilation during the war, but on January 30, 1933. . . . In the entanglement of the greater part of the German people in this moral guilt lies one of the most sinister successes of the methods of Hitler's policies."[151]

The work of Fernis and Hillgruber, one of the texts that offers the heaviest indictments, concludes with a statement in support of the "collective liability" of the German people:

The terror and the crimes of the National Socialist dictatorship are unprecedented in modern history. Above all, the systematic extermination of millions of people—who neither rebelled against the ruling regime nor otherwise did anything wrong—by the National Socialist regime incriminates [belastet] the German people. Certainly, the real blind and criminal followers of Hitler comprised only a minority; [but] next to them stood the great majority made up of political opportunists and the indifferent. Only a few of those in opposition based on inner conviction found the courage and power to carry out public criticism or actual opposition. No one, however, can escape responsibility for the government of a state and the consequences of guilt that the government incurs. Without doubt a "collective liability" exists for what is done in the name of a nation by its government.[152]

In confirmation of this "collective liability," Fernis and Hillgruber cite the important German Evangelical church declaration "Solidarity in Responsibility" of October 1945: "We accuse ourselves of not having confessed with greater courage, of not having prayed with greater conviction, of not having believed more joyfully, and not having loved with greater passion."[153]

Hey reminds his readers that the Holocaust was carried out by average people who possessed typical values of the era. Citing Hans Buchheim, he notes that the average SS man was similar to Hoess and Eichmann in his attitudes about obedience, racism, nationalism, and the glorification of achievement for its own sake. Hey asks, "What warning lies therein?" In answering, Hey emphasizes that students "should reflect on their own attitudes as citizens: What [burden] must the individual share as a citizen of a state; for what can he be made coresponsible; and for what can he be made liable?" The student "should be able to discuss the problem of collective guilt and liability and the consequences for international law that follow from the history of the Third Reich and the [postwar] National Socialist trials." This process, he states, "will lead to consideration of how far and in what way the individual may codetermine and influence the political fortunes of his state." In evaluating the prosecution of the National Socialist crimes, Hey states,

it should become clear that to learn from history in the sense of strengthening and defending democracy is the best kind of "mastery" of the National Socialist past. The history of the Third Reich should teach more than anything else that the decision of the individual conscience always matters decisively, and that no one—neither by order, ideology, or propaganda—can take this away, and that disobedience and nonconformist behavior can also be appropriate.[154]

Thus, in the course of treating questions of guilt and responsibility, Hey has ended by teaching the principle of the right of resistance—"disobedience and nonconformist behavior can also be appropriate"—a rare pedagogy in German textbooks.[155]

The German word *Schuld* has connotations of both guilt and responsibility, but the concept is finely differentiated in German law and philosophy. Hey's text includes portions of Jaspers's discussion of the issue. "The individual," writes Jaspers, "bears moral responsibility even for the deeds carried out under orders, since I have moral responsibility for acts that I commit as an individual, and indeed for all of my actions, including the political and military acts that I carry out. It is never valid to simply say 'an order is an order.' . . . Rather, crimes remain crimes even if they are ordered. . . . The channel of authority is one's own conscience, the communication with friends and intimates, with loved ones and with fellow human beings who are concerned about my soul."[156]

Moral responsibility, while broadly disseminated, is limited to persons who actually carry out unjust or criminal acts. However, Jaspers defines a more broadly disseminated "metaphysical guilt" that is essentially universal:

There is a solidarity between human beings that makes us coresponsible for all injustice and all unfairness in the world, especially for crimes that occur in our presence or with our knowledge. If I do not do what I can to prevent it, I am coresponsible. If I have not engaged my life for the prevention of the murder of another, but, instead, have stood by, I feel myself guilty in a manner that is not appropriately conveyed juridically, politically, and morally. The fact that I am still alive when such things have happened lays on me an inexpiable guilt.[157]

This, according to Jaspers, is the "collective guilt" of the Germans. He conveyed the meaning of this "inexpiable" collective guilt in an address in August 1945 that sums up prevailing liberal thought immediately after the war about the meaning of what had happened in the name of the German people: "We did not go into the streets again when our Jewish friends were led away; we did not scream until we, too, were being destroyed. We preferred to stay alive on the feeble, if logical, ground that our death could not have helped anyone. . . . We are guilty of being alive." For Jaspers, this was the tragic, "ineradicable shame and disgrace" of the German people.[158]

Although moral and metaphysical guilt may be disgraceful and shameful, it nevertheless does not result in criminal guilt, which carries legal culpability and remedy. This is why the Germans more often use the word "crimes" in regard to the persecution and the murder of the Jews than they do terms of moral opprobrium that do not condemn as strongly. For while metaphysical and moral guilt may be spiritually damning, they infer no legal consequence.[159]

But if metaphysical guilt does not result in legal consequence, it is surely the pivotal point on which hinges the success of Germany's effort to take the burden of responsibility for actions by fellow Germans in its name. Gordon Craig, one of the most widely recognized contemporary U.S. historians of Germany, sees the response of young Germans as especially important as "a sign perhaps of willingness to accept a dreadful past as one's own." He cites the response of Renate Harprecht, a survivor of Auschwitz who lost her parents there, to the question of the responsibility of Germans born long after World War II: "One cannot choose one's people. In those days, I wished many a time that I was not a Jew, but then I became one in a very conscious way. Young Germans will have to accept the fact that they are Germans—this is a fate that they cannot escape."[160]

Günther van Norden summed up the situation of the first postwar generation of Germans: "The young German of the year 1969, because and so long as he is a German, is bound up in political relationships that arose from the deeds of his ancestors—as innocent as he himself may be of these deeds. Collective liability is the burden of present German policies because of the failures of the past."[161]

Perhaps the great German-Jewish philosopher Martin Buber best summed up the relationship of German youth to their past. A group of German students visited him in Israel in 1962 with their teacher, Heinz Kremers, who recounts this story: A student asked Buber provocatively: "Herr Professor, our parents want to implant in us a guilt complex in regard to your people. We defend ourselves against this because we do not feel ourselves to be accomplices to what occurred. What do you say to this?" Buber answered amicably and graciously:

Perhaps you have heard that I have always rejected and fought against the assumption of the collective guilt of your people in relation to my people. For this reason more than ever you and your generation are not guilty in my eyes of what people of your nation did to my people. You are, therefore, right to defend yourselves against the senseless attempt to produce a feeling of guilt in you about my people. You are innocent, but, as Germans, you are coresponsible for the further history of your people, which one cannot separate from past history. For that reason, I expect of you that you carefully inform yourselves about what took place and how it could come about, that you commit yourselves to the task that such a thing—or anything similar to it—can never again take place in the history of your people.[162]

Buber aptly formulates the appropriate relationship of the present generation to the past. In the final analysis, any collective guilt thesis bears a resemblance to the ancient deicide libel of collective responsibility of Jews and to the Nazi policy of making Jews collective hostages for calamities that befell Germans, ascribing all misfortunes to an "international Jewish conspiracy."

Yet, as some textbooks and German scholars have pointed out, there is an important way in which, despite a rejection of collective guilt, the German people are linked to the past. As Georg Lukacs has written:

The collective responsibility of a nation for a chapter in its development is something so abstract and intangible that it borders on absurdity. And yet a period such as that of Hitler can be regarded as over and done with in our own memory only if the intellectual and moral outlook that filled it, gave it movement, direction, and shape, has been radically overcome. Only then does it become possible for other nations to trust in the conversion and to feel that the past has truly passed.[163]

"Conversion" is perhaps too strong a term and too close to a counsel to perfection in this imperfect world. At present, one may hope that the more humane forces in Germany, maintaining the memory of the Holocaust and the sense of German responsibility for the present and future, will continue to prevail against the destructive forces at work in all societies that threaten to degrade and undermine them.

## NOTES

1. Among the best recent examinations of the subject are Chaim Schatzker, *Die Juden in dem deutschen Geschichtsbüchern* (Bonn: A. Bernecker, 1981); Heinz Kremers, "Die Darstellung der Juden in neuen Schulbüchern in der Bundesrepublik Deutschland," in *Schulbuchanalyse und Schulbuchkritik im Brennpunkt: Juden, Judentum, und Staat Israel*, ed. Gerd Stein and Horst Schallenberger (Duisburg, 1976); Dieter Schmidt-Sinns, Gernot Dallinger, and Hellmut Wettlauffer, eds., *Der Nationalsozialismus als didaktisches Problem: Beiträge zur Behandling des NS-Systems und des deutschen Widerstands im Unterricht* (Bonn: A. Bernecker, 1980); Günther van Norden, *Das Dritte Reich im Unterricht* (Frankfurt am Main: Hirschgraben, 1977); E. Horst Schallenberger and Gerd Stein, "Juden, Judentum, und Staat Israel in Deutschen Schulbüchern," *Lebendiges Zeugnis* 32, no. 21 (1977), special theme: *Judentum und Christentum*; Bundeszentrale für politische Bildung, *Beiträge zur Auseinandersetzung mit dem Nationalsozialismus* (Bonn, 1983); Peter Meyers and Dieter Riesenberger, *Der Nationalsozialismus in der historisch-politischen Bildung* (Göttingen: Vandenhoeck und Ruprecht, 1980).

2. Karlheinz Pelzer, *Geschichte für die Hauptschule: Arbeitsbuch für das 8. und 9. Schuljahr* (Donauwörth: Aver, 1974), pp. 68–69.

3. Josef Schwandner, *Geschichte 9. Jahrgangsstufe* (Munich: R. Oldenbourg, 1973), p. 111.

4. Hans Heumann, Georg Dröge, et al., *Unser Weg durch die Geschichte*, Ausgabe für Realschulen, vol. 4, *Die Welt gestern und heute* (Frankfurt am Main: Hirschgraben, 1975), p. 98.

5. Hannelore Lachner, *Geschichte für Realschulen*, vol. 4, *Neueste Zeit* (Bamberg: Buchners, 1981), p. 168.

6. Ernst Hinrich, ed., *Deutsch-israelitisch Schulbuchempfehlungen: Zur Darstellung der jüdischen Geschichte sowie der Geschichte und Geographie Israels in Schulbüchern der Bundesrepublik Deuschland—Zur Darstellung der deutschen Geschichte und der Geographie der Bundesrepublik Deutschland in israelitischen Schulbüchern*, Studien zur

internationalen Schulbuchforschung: Schriftenreihe des Georg-Eckert Instituts, vol. 45 (Braunschweig: Poppdruck, 1985), pp. 18–19.

7. Wolfgang Hug, Joachim Hoffmann, and Elmar Krautkrämer, *Lernimpulse 3: Begleitheft zum Arbeitsbuch "Geschichtliche Weltkunde,"* vol. 3 (Frankfurt am Main: Diesterweg, 1979, p. 47.

8. Wolfgang Hug, Joachim Hoffman, Elmar Krautkrämer, *Geschichtliche Weltkunde,* vol. 3, *Von der Zeit des Imperialismus bis zur Gegenwart* (Frankfurt am Main: Diesterweg, 1985), p. 163.

9. Eugen Kaier, Herbert Deissler, and Herbert Krieger, *Grundzüge der Geschichte,* Sekundarstufe 1, Gymnasium, vol. 4: *Von 1890 bis zur Gegenwart* (Frankfurt am Main: Diesterweg, 1977), pp. 221–22.

10. Bernhardt Heinloth and Helmut Kistler, *Geschichte 4* (Munich: R. Oldenbourg, 1982), p. 162.

11. See J. Dittrich and E. Dittrich-Gallmeister, *Grundriss der Geschichte* (Stuttgart, 1959), cited in Walter Stahl, ed., *Education for Democracy in West Germany: Achievements, Shortcomings, Prospects* (New York: Praeger, 1960), p. 115. The 1964 edition was improved. See also John Dornberg's examination of German history textbooks in *Schizophrenic Germany* (New York: Macmillan, 1961), pp. 215ff.

12. Hans Muggenthaler, Wolfgang Marks, and Hannah Marks, *Geschichte für Realschulen,* vol. 4, *Neueste Zeit* (Munich: Kösel-Verlag), p. 115.

13. Hug, Hoffmann, and Krautkrämer, *Von der Zeit des Imperialismus bis zur Gegenwart,* 1985, pp. 162–63.

14. Ibid., p. 162.

15. Hans Heumann, H. J. Blodom, et al., *Geschichte für den Geschichtsunterricht in der Sekundarstufe I,* vol. 4, *Zeitgeschichte* (Frankfurt am Main: Hirschgraben, 1986), pp. 73–75.

16. Kaier, Deissler, and Krieger, *Von 1890 bis zur Gegenwart,* pp. 221–22.

17. Hug, Hoffmann, and Krautkrämer, *Von der Zeit des Imperialismus bis zur Gegenwart,* p. 160.

18. Wolfgang W. Mickel, *Geschichte, Politik, und Gesellschaft: Lehr-und Arbeitsbuch für Geschichte in der gymnasium Oberstufe,* vol. 1, *Von der Französischen Revolution bis zum Ende des 2. Weltkrieges* (Frankfurt am Main: Hirschgraben, 1987), p. 360.

19. Although some progress was made during the 1970s, worker resistance and Communist resistance are still neglected, and religious resistance and military resistance are still overemphasized in the texts.

20. Hermann Burkhardt, Helmut Christmann, Gerhard Jaacks, and Fritz Klenk, *Damals und heute 5, Geschichte für Hauptschulen: Vom Ersten Weltkrieg bis heute: Lehrerbegleitheft* (Stuttgart: Ernst Klett, 1976), p. 91.

21. Joachim Hoffmann, *Spiegel der Zeiten, Lehr- und Arbeitsbuch für den Geschichtsunterricht: Lernziele und Lernschritte: Handreichung fur den Lehrer,* vol. 4, *Von der russischen Revolution bis zur Gegenwart* (Frankfurt am Main: Diesterweg, 1979), p. 55.

22. Kaier, Deissler, and Krieger, *Von 1890 bis zur Gegenwart,* p. 220.

23. Joachim Cornelissen et al., *BSV Geschichte 4N: Das 20. Jahrhundert* (Munich: Bayerischer Schulbuch-Verlag, 1986), pp. 95–97.

24. S. Grassmann, ed., *Zeitaufnahme: Geschichte für die Sekundarstufe I,* vol. 3, *Vom Ersten zum Zweiten Weltkrieg* (Braunschweig: Westermann, 1981), p. 44.

25. Pelzer, *Geschichte für die Hauptschule,* p. 68.

26. Hug, Hoffmann, and Krautkrämer, *Lernimpulse 3: Begleitheft*, p. 47.

27. Ibid., p. 47.

28. Wolfgang Hug, ed., *Geschichtliche Weltkunde*. Vol. 3. *Schulerarbeitsheft 1*. (Frankfurt: Diesterweg, 1983), p. 67.

29. See Detlev Peukert, "Der deutsche Arbeiterwiderstand, 1933–1945," and Alfred Krink, "Nationalsozialismus und Widerstand als erfahrbare Geschichte," in *Der Nationalsozialismus als didaktisches Problem*, ed. Schmidt-Sinns, Dallinger, and Wettlauffer.

30. Grassmann, *Vom Ersten zum Zweiten Weltkrieg*, p. 78.

31. Ibid.

32. Ibid., p. 56.

33. Ibid., p. 73.

34. Peukert, "Der deutsche Arbeiterwiderstand," pp. 168–69.

35. Hoffmann, *Handreichung für den Lehrer*, p. 55.

36. Joachim Hoffmann, *Spiegel der Zeiten*, vol. 4, *Von der russischen Revolution bis zur Gegenwart* (Frankfurt am Main: Diesterweg, 1978), p. 122.

37. Gerhart Binder, Hermann Burkhardt, Helmut Christmann, Alfred Jung, and Fritz Klenk, *Damals und heute 5, Geschichte für Hauptschulen: Vom Ersten Weltkrieg bis heute* (Stuttgart: Ernst Klett, 1977), p. 92.

38. Bernd Hey and Joachim Radkau, *Politische Weltkunde II, Nationalsozialismus und Faschismus: Handreichungen für den Lehrer* (Stuttgart: Ernst Klett, 1982), p. 36.

39. Ibid., p. 87.

40. Ibid.

41. Herbert Baumann, *Politische Gemeinschaftskunde*, 19 (Köln: H. Stam, 1983), 256.

42. Hey and Radkau, *Handreichungen für den Lehrer*, p. 39.

43. Ibid.

44. Ibid.

45. Henning Eichberg, *Minderheit und Mehrheit* (Braunschweig: Westermann, 1979), p. 30.

46. Ibid., p. 36.

47. Binder et al., *Vom Ersten Weltkrieg bis heute*, p. 91.

48. Franz Böhm, cited in Friedrich Minssen, Felix Messerschmid, Otto Seitzer "Unbewaltigte Vergangenheit," *Gesellschaft, Staat, Erziehung*, 1958, p. 103.

49. Grassmann, *Vom Ersten zum Zweiten Weltkrieg*, p. 73.

50. Schwandner, *Geschichte 9. Jahrgangsstufe*, p. 128.

51. Wilhelm Borth and Eberhard Schanbacher, *Zeiten und Menschen: Neue Ausgabe G*, vol. 2, *Entfaltung und Krise der modernen Welt: Vom Zeitalter der bürgerlichen Revolutionen bis zum Zweiten Weltkrieg* (Frankfurt am Main: Schöningh, Schroedel, 1986), p. 229.

52. Hans Ulrich Rudolf and Edgar Walter, *Geschichte und Gegenwart: Arbeitsbuch Geschichte, Ausgabe für Realschulen in Baden-Wurttemberg*, vol. 3, *Von der Mitte des 19. Jahrhunderts bis zum Ende des Zweiten Weltkrieges* (Frankfurt am Main: Schöningh, Schroedel, 1984), p. 181.

53. Kaier, Deissler, and Krieger, *Von 1890 bis zur Gegenwart*, p. 220.

54. Burkhardt et al., *Vom Ersten Weltkrieg bis Heute: Lehrerbegleitheft*, p. 137.

55. Wanda Kampmann, Berthold Wiegand, and Wolfgang W. Mickel, *Politik und Gesellschaft: Grundlagen und Probleme der modernen Welt: Lehr- und Arbeitsbuch für*

*den historisch-politischen Lernbereich*, Sekundarstufe II, (Frankfurt am Main: Hirschgraben, 1981), p. 176.

56. Hans-Georg Fernis and Andreas Hillgruber, *Grundzüge der Geschichte*, Sekundarstufe II, *Historisch-politisches Arbeitsbuch*, vol. 2, *Vom Zeitalter der Aufklärung bis zur Gegenwart* (Frankfurt am Main: Diesterweg, 1972), p. 187.

57. Hans-Georg Fernis and Heinrich Haverkamp, *Grundzüge der Geschichte*, Sekundarstufe II, *Von der Urzeit bis zur Gegenwart* (Frankfurt am Main: Diesterweg, 1975), p. 320.

58. E. D. Gallmeister et al., *Grundriss der Geschichte für die Oberstufe der Höheren Schulen*, vol. 3, *Von 1850 bis zur Gegenwart* (Stuttgart: Ernst Klett, 1978), p. 187.

59. Tenbrock and Kluxen, *Zeiten und Menschen, Zeitgeschichte: 1917 bis zur Gegenwart*. (Frankfurt: Schöningh, Schroedel, 1983), p. 114.

60. Werner Ripper, ed., *Weltgeschichte im Aufriss: Der europäische Faschismus und das Dritte Reich* (Frankfurt am Main: Diesterweg, 1977), p. 469.

61. Gordon Craig, *The Germans* (New York: Putnam's, 1982), p. 146.

62. Frank Bahr et al., *Grundkurse Geschichte* (Darmstadt: Winklers, 1984), p. 345.

63. Heinloth and Kistler, *Geschichte 4*, p. 163.

64. Binder et al., *Von Ersten Weltkrieg bis heute*, p. 71.

65. Heumann et al., *Unser Weg durch die Geschichte*, pp. 97, 99.

66. Kaier, Deissler, and Krieger, *Von 1890 bis zur Gegenwart*, p. 176.

67. Heinloth and Kistler, *Geschichte 4*, p. 129.

68. Hans Döhn and Fritz Sandmann, *Geschichte 3: Erkunden und erkennen* (Hannover: Hermann Schroedel, 1977), p. 130.

69. Helmut Kistler and Werner Stroppe, *Harms Arbeitsmappen Geschichte*, vol. 4, *Von 1848 bis zur Gegenwart* (Munich: List, 1980), p. 124.

70. Burkhardt et al., *Vom Ersten Weltkrieg bis heute: Lehrerbegleitheft*, p. 139.

71. Grassmann, *Von Ersten Zum Zweiten Weltkrieg*, p. 73.

72. Ibid., p. 75. Ellipses in original.

73. Grassmann, *Von Ersten zum Zweiten Weltkrieg*, p. 74.

74. Hug, Hoffmann, and Krautkrämer, *Von der Zeit des Imperialismus bis zur Gegenwart*, p. 163.

75. Hoffmann, *Von der russischen Revolution bis Zur Gegenwart*, p. 121. Martin and Eva Kolinsky in their textbook study take special note that Hoffmann stated "unequivocally that the German population had some awareness of the mass murders"; however, like Hug, Hoffmann has not stated when the German population learned of the mass murders: "The Treatment of the Holocaust in West German Textbooks" *Yad Vashem Studies on the European Jewish Catastrophe and Resistance* (Jerusalem, 1974), pp. 149–216.

76. Steinbügl, and Schreigg, p. 86.

77. Heinz Schmid, *Fragen an die Geschichte* Geschichtliches Arbeitsbuch für Sekundarstuffe I. vol. 4 Die Welt im 20 Jahrhundert (Frankfurt: Hirschgraben, 1979), p. 61.

78. Muggenthaler, Marks, and Marks, *Geschichte für Realschulen*, p. 134.

79. Schwandner, *Geschichte 9. Jahrgangsstufe*, p. 105.

80. Ibid., p. 129.

81. There is no record that Hitler ever set foot in Treblinka, nor do Holocaust scholars make this claim. Indeed, were it true, it would simplify the controversial issue about Hitler's direct knowledge of the Final Solution orders. There is, of course, other docu-

516                          In Education and the Arts

mentation implicating Hitler in the final decision-making process, and there is no doubt
about his knowledge and intentions.

82. Schwandner, *Geschichte 9. Jahrgangsstufe*, p. 125.

83. Hans Ebeling and Wolfgang Birkenfeld, *Die Reise in die Vergangenheit: Ein
Geschichtliches Arbeitsbuch* (Braunschweig: Westermann, 1982), p. 139.

84. Tenbrock and Kluxen, *Zeiten und Menschen*, p. 139; emphasis in original.

85. Rudolf and Walter, *Geschichte und Gegenwart*, p. 180.

86. Otto Boeck, Artur Dumke, Robert Hubner, Fritz Klenk, Otto Kratzert, and Eugen
Sohns, *Damals und heute 4: Geschichte für Hauptschulen* (Stuttgart: Ernst Klett, 1976),
p. 42.

87. Friedrich J. Lucas, Heinrich Bodensieck, Ernhard Rumpt, and Günter Thiele,
*Menschen in ihrer Zeit*, vol. 4, *In unserer Zeit* (Stuttgart: Ernst Klett, 1981), p. 123.

88. Lachner, *Geschichte für Realschulen*, p. 171.

89. Hans Heumann, Johannes Hampel, and Max Rieder, *Geschichte für morgen:
Arbeitsbuch für bayerische Hauptschulen*, vol. 5, *Zeitgeschichte* (9. Schuljahr) (Frankfurt
am Main: Hirschgraben, 1982), p. 74.

90. Grassmann, *Vom Ersten zum Zweiten Weltkrieg*, p. 82.

91. J. P. Stern, "Artist Hitler," cited in *Die Zeit*, no. 31 (July 28, 1978).

92. Scheffler, "Anmerkungen zum Fernsehfilm 'Holocaust,' und zu Fragen zeit-
historischer Forschung" *Antisemitismus und Judentum* (1979): 577.

93. Eberhard Quester, "Die Darstellung des Judentums im Geschichtsunterricht,"
*Die Realschule* (1963) p. 341. Emphasis in original.

94. Wolfgang Hug, ed., *Geschichtliche Weltkunde*, vol. 3, *Schulerarbeitsheft 1: Von
der Zeit des Imperialismus bis zur Nationalsozialistischen Diktatur in Deutschland* (Frankfurt am Main: Diesterweg, 1983), p. 67.

95. Werner Grütter, *Hinweise und Interpretationen*, vol. 2, *Zeiten und Menschen*
(Paderborn: Schöningh, Schroedel, 1976), p. 404.

96. Ibid., p. 400. See also the letter of Bishop Wurm to Reichsminister Hans Lammers
cited later in this chapter.

97. Friedrich Deuschle, *Du und die Politik: Lehr- und Arbeitsbuch für die politische
Bildung* (Bad Homburg von der Höhe: Max Gehlen, 1977), p. 78.

98. Fernis and Haverkamp, *Von der Urzeit bis zur Gegenwart*, 311.

99. Willi Frank and Margret Frank, *Politik heute* (Darmstadt: Winklers, 1981),
p. 196.

100. Kurt Gönner, Rolf Krug, Heinz-Theo Niephaus, and Eugen Weiss, *Politik in
unseren Tagen* (Bad Homburg vor der Höhe: Max Gehlen, 1980), p. 198.

101. Elmar Krautkrämer and Eberhard Radbruch, *Wandel der Welt* (Bad Homburg
vor der Höhe: Max Gehlen, 1975), p. 190.

102. Tenbrock and Kluxen, *Zeiten und Menschen*, p. 154.

103. Gallmeister et al., *Grundriss der Geschichte*, pp. 187–88.

104. Eichberg, *Minderheit und Mehrheit*, p. 36.

105. Gönner et al., *Politik in unseren Tagen*, p. 200.

106. Cornelissen et al., *BSV Geschichte UN*, p. 99.

107. Hey and Radkau, *Handreichungen für den Lehrer*, p. 87.

108. Bernd Hey and Joachim Radkau, *Politische Weltkunde II: Themen zur Geschichte,
Geographie, und Politik: Nationalsozialismus und Faschismus* (Stuttgart: Ernst Klett,
1983), pp. 151–52, citing Eugen Kogon *Der SS-Staat*.

109. Hey and Radkau, *Nationalsozialismus und Faschismus*, pp. 151–52.

110. Ibid., p. 153, citing J. P. Stern, "Artist Hitler."

111. Hey and Radkau, *Handreichungen für den Lehrer*, p. 88.

112. Hey and Radkau, *Nationalsozialismus und Faschismus*, p. 153.

113. Hey and Radkau, *Handreichungen für den Lehrer*, p. 87.

114. Mickel *Geschichte, Politik, und Gesellschaft*, p. 362.

115. Eugen Kogon, "Befreit durch Niederlage: Driessig Jahre deutscher Weideraufstieg," *Frankfurter Hefte* 30, no. 5 (1975): 7–8.

116. Hug, Hoffmann, and Krautkrämer, *Von der Zeit des Imperialismus bis zur Gegenwart*, p. 163.

117. Wolfgang Bobke, *Jews in West German History Textbooks*, a study commissioned by the American Jewish Committee (New York: American Jewish Committee, 1979), p. 68.

118. See Heinz Kremers, "Judentum und Holocaust in Deutschen Schulunterrecht," *Aus Politik und Zeitgeschichte*, 1979, no. 4 (January 27): 37ff.

119. See, for example, Alexander Mitscherlich and Margarete Mitscherlich, *The Inability to Mourn: Principles of Collective Behavior*.

120. Grütter, *Hinweise und Interpretationen*, p. 352.

121. Hey and Radkau, *Handreichungen für den Lehrer*, p. 86.

122. See Kolinsky and Kolinsuy, for 1950s textbooks, "The Treatment of the Holocaust in West German Textbooks," p. 185.

123. Fruhmann, "Überwindung des Antisemitismus," *Die Padagogische Provinz* (3 Ja. 1949): 47.

124. Walter Renn, "Federal Republic of Germany: Germans, Jews and Genocide," in *The Treatment of the Holocaust in Textbooks: The Federal Republic of Germany, Israel, The United States of America*, ed. Randolph Braham (New York: Institute for Holocaust Studies of the City University of New York, 1987).

125. Deuschle, *Du und die Politik*, p. 48.

126. Hannah Vogt, *Schuld oder Verhängnis? Zwölf Fragen an Deutschlands Jüngste Vergangenheit* (Frankfurt am Main: Verlag Moritz Diesterweg, 1961). The English version of this excellent text, from which the citations were taken, is Hannah Vogt, *The Burden of Guilt: A Short History of Germany, 1914–1945* (New York: Oxford University Press, 1964), p. 219.

127. Ibid., p. 230.

128. Ibid., p. 286.

129. Hey and Radkau, *Nationalsozialismus und Faschismus*, p. 154.

130. Hey and Radkau, *Handreichungen für den Lehrer*, p. 89.

131. Ibid., p. 90.

132. Mickel, *Geschichte, Politik, und Gesellschaft*, p. 340.

133. Hey and Radkau, *Handreichungen für den Lehrer*, p. 89.

134. Ibid.

135. Ibid., p. 86.

136. Erich Weniger, *Neue Wege im Geschichtsunterricht* (Frankfurt am Main: G. Schulte, Bulmke, 1965), p. 20.

137. Ibid., p. 86.

138. Romano Guardini, *Verantwortung, Gedanken zur jüdischen Frage, Geschichtswissenschaft, und Unterricht*, vol. 8 (1952), p. 458.

139. Kogon, "Befreit durch Niederlage," p. 14.

140. Thomas Kremers, "Zur Darstellung der Juden, des Judentum, und des Staates

Israel im bundesrepublikanischen Politiksschulbuch der Gegenwart,'' in Stein and Schallenberger, eds., *Schulbuch analyse und Schulbuchkritik*, p. 10.

141. Bahr et al., *Grundkurse Geschichte*, p. 345.

142. Werner Ripper and Eugen Kaier, *Weltgeschichte im Aufriss* Neubearbeitung für den historische-gesellschaftlichen Lernbereich der Sekundarestufe II, vol. 3, part 1, *Vom Ersten Weltkrieg bis 1945* (Frankfurt am Main: Diesterweg, 1979), p. 444.

143. Hey and Radkau, *Handreichungen für den Lehrer*, p. 90.

144. Hey and Radkau, *Nationalsozialismus und Faschismus*, pp. 157–58.

145. Hey and Radkau, *Handreichungen für den Lehrer*, p. 90.

146. Ibid., p. 91.

147. Hey and Radkau, *Nationalsozialismus und Faschismus*, p. 114.

148. Hey and Radkau, *Handreichungen für den Lehrer*, p. 88.

149. Friedrich Deuschle, *Du und die Politik, Lehrbuch für die politische Bildung*: *Lehrerheft* (Bad Homburg von der Höhe: Max Gehlen, 1977), p. 50.

150. Hannah Vogt, ''Zum Problem der Deutschen Jugend,'' *Die Sammlung* 1 (1945–46): 595.

151. Hans-Hermann Hartwich, ed., *Politik im 20. Jahrhundert*, (Braunschweig: Westermann, 1980), p. 146.

152. Fernis and Hillgruber, *Grundzüge der Geschichte,* p. 201.

153. Ibid. This is a self-accusation that, however redolent of phrase, remains notably silent about assessment of coresponsibility of the Christian churches of Germany for the fate of the Jews.

154. Hey and Radkau, *Handreichungen für den Lehrer*, p. 87.

155. See the section ''German Resistance to the Dictatorship'' in this chapter.

156. Hey and Radkau, *Nationalsozialismus und Faschismus*, pp. 153–54.

157. Ibid., citing Jaspers.

158. Craig, *Germans*, p. 145.

159. Hey and Radkau, *Handreichungen für den Lehrer*, p. 88.

160. Craig, *Germans*, p. 146.

161. Günther van Norden, ''Nationalsozialistische Judenverfolgung: Didaktische und methodische Überlegungen zu einem Unterrichtsproblem,'' *Geschichte in Wissenschaft und Unterricht* 21 (1970): 664.

162. Kremers, ''Judentum und Holocaust im deutschen Schulunterricht,'' p. 39.

163. Mitscherlich and Mitscherlich, *Inability to Mourn*, p. 66.

## SELECT BIBLIOGRAPHY

Altrichter, Helmut, and Hermann Glaser. *Geschichtliches Werden*. Oberstufe. Vol. 4. *Vom Zeitalter des Imperialismus bis zur Gegenwart*. Bamberg: C. C. Buchners, 1971.

Baumann, Herbert. *Politische Gemeinschaftskunde*, 19. Auflage. Köln-Porz: H. Stam, 1983.

Binder, Gerhart, Hermann Burkhardt, Helmut Christmann, Alfred Jung, and Fritz Klenk. *Damals und heute 5, Geschichte für Hauptschulen: Vom Ersten Weltkrieg bis heute*. Stuttgart: Ernst Klett, 1977.

Boeck, Otto, Artur Dumke, Robert Hubner, Fritz Klenk, Otto Kratzert, and Eugen Sohns. *Damals und heute 4: Geschichte für Hauptschulen*. Stuttgart: Ernst Klett, 1976.

Burkhardt, Hermann, Helmut Christmann, Gerhard Jaacks, and Fritz Klenk, *Damals und heute 5, Geschichte für Hauptschulen: Vom Ersten Weltkrieg bis heute: Lehrerbegleitheft*. Stuttgart: Ernst Klett, 1976.

Döhn, Hans, and Fritz Sandmann. *Geschichte 3: Erkunden und erkennen*. Hannover: Hermann Schroedel, 1977.

Eichberg, Henning. *Minderheit und Mehrheit*. Braunschweig: Westermann, 1979.

Fernis, Hans-Georg, and Heinrich Haverkamp. *Grundzüge der Geschichte*. Sekundarstufe II. *Von der Urzeit bis zur Gegenwart*. Frankfurt am Main: Diesterweg, 1975.

Fernis, Hans-Georg, and Andreas Hillgruber. *Grundzüge der Geschichte*. Sekundarstufe II. *Historisch-politisches Arbeitsbuch*. Vol. 2. *Vom Zeitalter der Aufklärung bis zur Gegenwart*. Frankfurt am Main: Diesterweg, 1972.

Frank, Willi, and Margret Frank. *Politik heute*. Darmstadt: Winklers, 1981.

Gallmeister, E. D., et al. *Grundriss der Geschichte für die Oberstufe der Höheren Schulen*. Vol. 3. *Von 1850 bis zur Gegenwart*. Stuttgart: Ernst Klett, 1978.

Gönner, Kurt, Rolf Krug, Heinz-Theo Niephaus, and Eugen Weiss. *Politik in unseren Tagen*. Bad Homburg vor der Höhe: Max Gehlen, 1980.

Grassmann, S., ed. *Zeitaufnahme: Geschichte für die Sekundarstufe I*. Vol. 3. *Vom Ersten zum Zweiten Weltkrieg*. Braunschweig: Westermann, 1981.

Grütter, Werner. *Hinweise und Interpretationen*. Vol. 2. *Zeiten und Menschen*. Paderborn: Schöningh, Schroedel, 1976.

Hartwich, Hans-Hermann, ed. *Politik im 20. Jahrhundert*. Braunschweig: Westermann, 1980.

Heinloth, Bernhardt, and Helmut Kistler. *Geschichte 4*. Munich: R. Oldenbourg, 1982.

Heumann, Hans, Georg Dröge et al. *Unser Weg durch die Geschichte*. Ausgabe für Realschulen. Vol. 4. *Die Welt gestern und heute*. Frankfurt am Main: Hirschgraben, 1975.

Hey, Bernd, and Joachim Radkau. *Politische Weltkunde II: Themen zur Geschichte, Geographie, und Politik: Nationalsozialismus und Faschismus*. Stuttgart: Ernst Klett, 1983.

Hoffmann, Joachim. *Spiegel der Zeiten*. Vol. 4. *Von der russischen Revolution bis zur Gegenwart*. Frankfurt am Main: Diesterweg, 1978.

Hug, Wolfgang, ed. *Geschichtliche Weltkunde, Quellenlesebuch*. Vol. 3. *Von der Zeit des Imperialismus bis zur Gegenwart*. Frankfurt am Main; Diesterweg, 1983.

Hug, Wolfgang, Joachim Hoffmann, and Elmar Krautkrämer. *Geschichtliche Weltkunde*. Vol. 3. *Von der Zeit des Imperialismus bis zur Gegenwart*. Frankfurt am Main: Diesterweg, 1979.

Jaacks, Gerhard, and Artur Dumke. *Damals und heute 4, Geschichte für Hauptschulen: Lehrerbegleitheft*. Stuttgart: Ernst Klett, 1980.

Kaier, Eugen, Herbert Deissler, and Herbert Krieger. *Grundzüge der Geschichte*. Sekundarstufe I, Gymnasium. Vol. 4. *Von 1890 bis zur Gegenwart*. Frankfurt am Main: Diesterweg, 1977.

Kampmann, Wanda, Berthold Wiegand, and Wolfgang W. Mickel. *Politik und Gesellschaft: Grundlagen und Probleme der modernen Welt: Lehr- und Arbeitsbuch für den historisch-politischen Lernbereich*. Sekundarstufe II. Frankfurt am Main: Hirschgraben, 1981.

Kistler, Helmut, and Werner Stroppe. *Harms Arbeitsmappen Geschichte*. Vol. 4. *Von 1848 bis zur Gegenwart*. Munich: List, 1980.

Kösthorst, Erich. *Das nationalsozialistische Regime: Geschichte, Politik, Unterrichtseinheiten für ein Curriculum: Materialheft*. Paderborn: Schöningh, 1980.

Krautkrämer, Elmar, and Eberhard Radbruch. *Wandel der Welt.* Bad Homburg vor der
    Höhe: Max Gehlen, 1975.
Lachner, Hannelore. *Geschichte für Realschulen.* Vol. 4. *Neueste Zeit.* Bamberg: Buch-
    ners, 1981.
Lucas, Friedrich J., Heinrich Bodensieck, Erhard Rumpt, and Gunter Thiele. *Menschen
    in ihrer Zeit.* Vol. 4. *In unserer Zeit.* Stuttgart: Ernst Klett, 1981.
Menzel, Karl-Heinz, and Fritz Textor. *Staatensystem und Weltpolitik.* Stuttgart: Ernst
    Klett, 1980.
Meyer, Hermann. *Probleme des Totalitarismus: Materialien für die Sekundarstufe II.*
    Hannover: Schroedel, 1980.
Muggenthaler, Hans, Wolfgang Marks, and Hannah Marks. *Geschichte für Realschulen.*
    Vol. 4. *Neueste Zeit.* Munich: Kösel-Verlag.
Ripper, Werner, ed. *Weltgeschichte im Aufriss: Der europäische Faschismus und das
    Dritte Reich.* Frankfurt am Main: Diesterweg, 1977.
————. *Weltgeschichte im Aufriss: Die nationalsozialistische Aussenpolitik und der
    Zweite Weltkrieg.* Frankfurt am Main: Diesterweg, 1977.
Ripper, Werner, and Eugen Kaier. *Weltgeschichte im Aufriss.* Neubearbeitung für den
    historische-gesellschaftlichen Lernbereich der Sekundarstufe II. Vol. 3, part 1.
    *Vom Ersten Weltkrieg bis 1945.* Frankfurt am Main: Diesterweg, 1979.
Schwandner, Josef. *Geschichte 9. Jahrgangsstufe.* Munich: R. Oldenbourg, 1973.
Steinbügl, Eduard, and Anton Schreiegg. *Geschichte.* Vol. 4. *Neueste Zeit.* Munich: R.
    Oldenbourg, 1973.
Tenbrock, R. H., and K. Kluxen. *Didaktischer Grundriss für den Geschichtsunterricht.*
    Vol. 4. *Zeiten und Menschen.* Paderborn: Schöningh, Schroedel, 1981.
————. *Zeiten und Menschen, Zeitgeschichte: 1917 bis zur Gegenwart.* Frankfurt am-
    Main: Schöningh, Schroedel, 1983.
Tenbrock, R. H., Kurt Kluxen, Erich Goerlitz, Erich Meier, Helmut Mejcher, and Kerrin
    Gräfin Schwerin. *Zeiten und Menschen.* K edition. Vol. 4. *Geschichte für Kol-
    legstufe und Grundstudium: Politik, Gesellschaft, Wirtschaft im 20. Jahrhundert.*
    Part 1. *Vom 1919 bis 1945.* Frankfurt am-Main: Schöningh, Schroedel, 1982.

# Chapter 25

# Holocaust Diaries and Memoirs

## *Laurence Kutler*

The assessing of autobiographical writing in the form of memoirs, records of oral interviews, and diaries for the period of the Holocaust is a little like sailing a boat in the fog. Without an eye on the lighthouse, one can easily be distracted and make errors in judgment causing disaster. A sailor's best rule of thumb is to have adequate maps to guide his or her approach toward a safe harbor.

The same situation confronts the historian of the Holocaust. Not enough time has elapsed for a corpus to have formed that can serve the function of history. J. Huizinga, a Dutch historian, has tried to propose a definition of history that can serve our purpose: "History is the intellectual form in which a civilization renders account to itself of the past."[1] The nature of the "intellectual form" and the accountability factor are the notions that are of the greatest concern. What did Huizinga mean by "intellectual form," and what standard could be meant? To whom are the writers of memoirs, diaries, and interviews accountable? These are some of the questions that need to be addressed before criteria can be established to identify which writings among those who survived and those who did not can be judged to have made a significant contribution to the historiography of the Holocaust.

Thus, like the sailor with maps to guide him or her to safe harbor, the historian needs a set of criteria that will serve as a guide for a proper methodology.[2] Without it, the practitioner of history will steer off course. The following statements are useful in identifying memoirs or diaries that render an account of themselves to the past and serve us as sufficiently historical:

1. Diary and memoir writing is a specific form of tradition.

2. Diaries and memoirs are not concerned primarily with the accurate reporting of events; they also involve apology and self-justification.

3. Diary writing and memoirs concern themselves with causes of events and circumstances. This could be a reflection upon events or a moralizing tendency.

4. Diary and memoir writing will incorporate or reflect upon national consciousness or fate.

Returning briefly to Huizinga's definition, I am confronted with the notion of what constitutes an "intellectual form." Diaries, memoirs, or records of oral interviews qualify as intellectual forms since they are clear forms of individual expression set to paper with the purpose of communicating ideas. The standard of such writings must be tested by the value of the information gained and the place it has in the genre.

To what degree do the writings render account to the past? In order for this question to be answered, the collections have to be assessed in terms of presentation and of judgments of events and individual behavior. But more, the manuscripts should be accountable to the facts. Diary and memoir writing as a specific form of tradition is well accounted for, especially in Jewish tradition. In the worst of times this vulnerable people has responded to oppression by recording events as they unfold in an appeal not to its contemporaries but to the judgment of history. The book of Ecclesiastes is an example from late biblical times. *The Wars of the Jews* is a written account by Josephus of the wars against Rome presented apologetically to the Roman world. The medieval period saw a continuation of this tradition. Thus we have Moses Maimonides in his *Epistle to the Yemenites* encouraging these people to remain stolid in the face of persecution, Solomon Bar Samson telling of the Kiddush ha-Shem who were massacred in Mainz in May 1096, and Nathan Hanover recounting the horrors of the Chmielnicki pogroms in his *Vale of Tears*. On the eve of World War II Polish Jewry's greatest scholar, Simon Dubnow, advised his contemporaries to record everything for posterity. Whether or not they had ever read Dubnow, countless Jews heeded his advice.

## THE DIARISTS

Personal observations may be flawed by bias, hearsay, rumor, or outright error.[3] While severe trauma may sharpen the senses momentarily, extended periods of starvation, disease, threats, and shifts from location to location can also result in confusion. As a result, some of those who experienced Elie Wiesel's "other planet" misplaced rivers and camps. Some survivors remember what they think they should remember. In retrospect, some of the jottings seem mundane—concern over food, housing, family—but none of them were unimportant. The diaries humanize the numbers. Six million people become individuals with passions and agonies that we can understand. In Holland a town clerk left a last inscription in the community notebook on December 31, 1942: "For we are left but few of many. We are counted as sheep for the slaughter, to be killed and to perish in misery and shame. May deliverance come to Jews speedily in our days."

About the time Abraham Toncman was pondering the fate of his people in Holland, a little girl who wanted to be a movie star was setting down her most personal thoughts in a journal. From 1942 to August 1944, Anne Frank complained about the crowding and discipline in the annex above her father's store in Amsterdam. But she also expressed hope when the Allies landed at Normandy. A teenager, she was falling in love, and she longed for a world without hate, where she might live as a Jew and Zionist. For many educators, *The Diary of Anne Frank* is the starting point for making the Holocaust relevant for young people.

Virtually the same aspirations are found in *Hannah Senesh: Her Life and Diary* (1972). The eleven-year journal (1933–44) of a young Jewish woman from Budapest contains some of the most moving writing on the Holocaust ever recorded. Older and more mature than Anne Frank, she expressed concern about anti-Semitism in the prewar period. Hannah Senesh steeled herself to racism by becoming an ardent Zionist and emigrating to Palestine. When her homeland was occupied by the Nazis, she volunteered to return to Hungary as a commando. There in November 1944 she was executed by a firing squad. Her poem "Blessed Is the Match" has inspired a book by the same name written by Marie Syrkin and has been incorporated into Reform Judaism's Hanukkah service. But a much more compelling statement is found in her 1941 poem "To Die" written at Nahalal, where Senesh speaks of the contrast between warm, sunny skies and the terrible consequences of war. She concludes, however, that she is willing to sacrifice herself for her home, her land, and her people.[4]

Two other journals merit special mention. Few documents are as poignant as Janusz Korczak's *Ghetto Diary* (1978). The notes of the gentle pediatrician from Warsaw were published posthumously, Korczak having accompanied 190 orphan children to death at Treblinka in the summer of 1942. Korczak (whose real name was Henryk Goldszmit) wrote of sick and abandoned children who needed to be tended, of reading stories over and over to them, of people lying on the streets dying of starvation, of his own personal torment whether to use euthanasia on his orphans, and of his hope for a world where no child would be barred from playing with any other. As if anticipating those who would deny the facts of Nazi genocide, Korczak concluded thoughtfully, "What matters is that all this did happen."[5]

Korczak, Senesh, and Anne Frank were not professional historians. But Emmanuel Ringelblum was, and his writings, recovered between 1946 and 1950 from milk jars buried during the war, constitute a conscious effort on the part of a trained historian to document what occurred in the Warsaw ghetto. A Labor Zionist who worked for the Jewish Historical Institute before the war, Ringelblum served as the model for the fictional character Noach Levinson in John Hersey's inspirational novel *The Wall*. Like Levinson, Ringelblum organized intellectual meetings in the ghetto where Peretz and Sholom Aleichem were discussed. Ringelblum's journal, however, transcends Hersey's novel because it is fact. From its masked opening in January 1940, addressed to Ringelblum's father, to the final entries posted in December 1942, *Notes from the Warsaw Ghetto* (1958) tracks the progressive dehumanization of the largest concentration of Jews in Europe. The reader learns of expedience that compromised leaders of the Judenrat who thought that they were sacrificing a few of their people to save the whole, and of the same expedience that forced overburdened families to turn a deaf ear to the whimpering of children freezing on stoops below. The reader learns how Jewish businessmen like Kohn and Heller and policemen like Jacob Leikin collaborated with the Nazis hoping to emerge richer and unscathed at war's end while volunteers at the Joint Distribution Committee, CENTOS children's aid, and TOZ medical aid worked valiantly in the most primitive conditions to help their fellow Jews. We learn what they were reading in that doomed quarter (the memoirs of Lloyd George, Napoleon, Tolstoy), how they regretted being herded into the ghetto, and how they wondered if the free world truly appreciated their plight.

Neither Ringelblum's notes nor *The Warsaw Diary of Chaim A. Kaplan* (1965) nor *The Warsaw Diary of Adam Czerniakow* (1979) cover the desperate uprising of May 1943. For that the reader should consult Philip Friedman's *Martyrs and Fighters* (1954), which includes lengthy extracts from Marek Edelman's *The Ghetto Fights* (1946), Melekh Neustadt's *Hurbn un oyfshtand fun di Yidn in Varshe* (1948), Tuvya Borzykowski's *Tsvishn falndike vent* (1949), and SS General Jürgen Stroop's report titled *Es gibt keinen judischen Wohnbezirk in Warschau mehr* (1943). Ringelblum's notes do not possess the sweep of history; no grand conclusions are offered. They are the words of a man afraid, a family man, who hoped that they would have value for posterity. Just as Anne Frank's diary has achieved epic status in literature, so too Ringelblum's notes merit a special place in historiography.

## MEMOIRS

The postwar reminiscences of Holocaust survivors form an incredibly large corpus. Ever expanding, these works may be broken into individual accounts and collections edited by professional scholars. Among the more notable memoirs that tell the tale of Jews in Poland are Alexander Donat's *The Holocaust Kingdom* (1963), Leon Wells's *The Janowska Road* (1963), Bernard Goldstein's *The Stars Bear Witness* (1949), Oscar Pinkus's *House of Ashes* (1964), Vladka Meed's *On Both Sides of the Wall* (1979), Joseph Ziemian's *The Cigarette Sellers of Three Crosses Square* (1975), Sara Zyskind's *Stolen Years* (1981), Matylda Engleman's *End of the Journey* (1980), Halina Birenbaum's *Hope Is the Last to Die* (1971), Jack Eisner's *The Survivor* (1980), Izaak Goldberg's *The Miracle*

*Versus Tyranny* (1978), George Topas's *The Iron Furnace* (1990), and Tadeusz Pankiewicz's *The Cracow Ghetto Pharmacy* (1987). The story of Jews in Hungary is told in Rudolf Vrba and Alan Bestic's *I Cannot Forgive* (1968), Georgia Gabor's *My Destiny* (1982), Livia Jackson's *Elli* (1980), and Gizelle Hersh and Peggy Mann's *Gizelle, Save the Children* (1980). For the Ukraine, see Paul Trepman's *Among Men and Beasts* (1978) and Mel Mermelstein's *By Bread Alone* (1979). For Latvia, see Gertrude Schneider's *Journey into Terror* (1980) and Frida Michelson's *I Survived Rumboli* (1982). The story of Czechoslovakia is told by Hana Demetz in *The House on Prague Street* (1980) and Saul Friedlander in *When Memory Comes* (1979). On the Jews of Holland, see Marga Minco's *Bitter Herbs* (1960), Etty Hillesum's *An Interrupted Life* (1984), and Jona Oberski's *Childhood* (1983). On France, see Joseph Joffo's *A Bag of Marbles* (1974) and Sim Kessel's *Hanged at Auschwitz* (1972). Among the more gripping concentration-camp memoirs are Filip Muller's *Eyewitness Auschwitz* (1979), Kitty Hart's *Return to Auschwitz* (1981), Eugene Heimler's *Concentration Camp* (1961), Germaine Tillion's *Ravensbrück* (1975), Fania Fenelon's *Playing for Time* (1977), Luba Gurdus's *The Death Train* (1978), Primo Levi's *Survival in Auschwitz* (1973), and Isabella Leitner's *Fragments of Isabella: A Memoir of Auschwitz* (1978). Other recommended works that have a single person's perspective include Elie Cohen's *The Abyss* (1973), William Perl's *The Four-Front War* (1979), Peter Schweifert's *The Bird Has No Wings* (1976), Ilse Koehn's *Mischling, Second Degree* (1978), Judith Strick Dribben's *A Girl Called Judith Strick* (1970), and Charlotte Delbo's *None of Us Will Return* (1968).

A second approach to memoirs is for historians, psychologists, or community leaders to interview a number of survivors for the purpose of making some sense of the Holocaust. A number of these texts stress the heroic response of Jews to the Nazis. They range from the very good (including Yuri Suhl's *They Fought Back: The Story of the Jewish Resistance in Nazi Europe* [1967], Anny Latour's *The Jewish Resistance in France (1940–1944)* [1981], Marie Syrkin's *Blessed Is the Match* [1947], and Eric Boehm's *We Survived* [1949]) to the more pedestrian (Ina Friedman's *Escape or Die* [1982], Reba Karp's *Holocaust Stories: Inspiration for Survival* [1986], and Milton Meltzer's *Never to Forget* [1976]). Some of the works have a clinical orientation, including the excellent *Survivors, Victims, and Perpetrators: Essays on the Nazi Holocaust* (1980) edited by Joel Dimsdale, Sarah Moskovitz's *Love Despite Hate: Child Survivors of the Holocaust and Their Adult Lives* (1983), Claudine Vegh's *I Didn't Say Goodbye: Interviews with Children of the Holocaust* (1984), and Shelly Lore's *Jewish Holocaust Survivors' Attitudes Toward Contemporary Beliefs About Themselves* (1984).

The late 1970s witnessed the appearance of a spate of Holocaust memoirs. For more than a quarter-century, many Holocaust survivors were disinclined to speak about their wartime experiences. They concentrated on rebuilding their lives, and raising children. Once these children were grown and out of the home, the survivors were faced with their own mortality. Now they were eager to talk, and the result was the publication of books like Dorothy Robinowitz's *New Lives: Survivors of the Holocaust Living in America* (1976), Lucy Steinitz and David Szonyi's *Living After the Holocaust: Reflections by the Post-War Generation in America* (1976), Isaiah Trunk's *Jewish Responses to Nazi Persecution* (1978), and Helen Epstein's *Children of the Holocaust* (1979).

Following along these lines in his book *The Holocaust*, Martin Gilbert attempts to gather testimony from survivors in order to constitute a record of the Holocaust. The book gives a brief historical overview of Hitler's rise to power and continues to the 1945 death marches. The book employs diary accounts to substantiate conditions throughout. Interspersed with events are also memoirs, for example, Zindel Grynzspan recalling October 27, 1938, when he and his family were expelled from Germany, or Eric Luca's account of storm troops defiling a synagogue.

Gilbert also utilizes some of the chronicles from the ghettos. For example, the Lodz chronicle is cited in his chapter "Write and Record," which were Simon Dubnow's last words before being shot in the back in December 1941. Gilbert ends his book with the following rationale: "The survivors tell their story to their children, set it down in memoirs and testimonies, relive it in nightmares. . . . Each survivor faces the past, and confronts the future with a burden which those who do not go through the torment, cannot measure. 'I may bear indelible scars in body and soul' Cordelia Edvardson has written; 'but I do not intend to reveal them to the world—least of all the Germans. That is the pride of the survivor. Hitler is dead but I am alive.' "[6]

In *Voices from the Holocaust* Sylvia Rothchild employs a tripartite system of "Life Before the Holocaust," "Life During the Holocaust," and "Life in America." As editor, Rothchild allows survivors to relate their testimonies. She edits 650 hours of conversation in a gripping fashion that conveys to the reader a feeling that he or she, too, is "a kind of survivor." Stories are told by survivors from France, Greece, Hungary, Denmark, Czechoslovakia, Poland, Holland, Yugoslavia, Germany, Austria, Italy, Russia, and the United States. Some have lived in Israel or South America. The preface gives the self-justification of the survivors "to our sons . . . may they never know the heartaches and agonies their parents suffered during those years except by reading this transcript or listening to the tapes," or "I tell you the only thing that kept me going is the burning desire to tell, to bear witness."[7]

In excerpts from "Life Before the Holocaust," Rothchild offers a precise description of the survivors' place in society. A sense of loss and nostalgia is expressed. These tapes, transcribed in written form, offer impressions of European life in much the same way as other European Jews have related them. They are accounts full of social insights. Life is simplified with statements such as "We loved each other and helped each other. And then the Germans came" or "At my job everything was normal."

The moralizing tendencies of the survivors in this volume take on important messages. "Do not hate! Do not harm! Share with others less fortunate." "Re-

member the past and learn from it." Rothchild states that they share their painful
memories of the dark places in recent history in the hope that things may never
be so dark again. Sometimes the survivors reflect upon their experiences and
feel strongly toward Israel. Their work in support of Israel may in fact bring
about a personal redemption. For Stephen Ross from Dodz, Poland, freedom in
America necessitates a state in Israel.

In *Amcha: An Oral Testament of the Holocaust*, Saul Friedman attempts to
fill a lacuna in Holocaust studies. Friedman communicates the story of the mass
of Jews who survived the Holocaust, the common folk "who lived on the
periphery of colossal events." The book is limited, for the most part, to survivors
who were acquaintances of Friedman in Youngstown.

Three themes are evinced in *Amcha* by the survivors: (1) widespread anti-
Semitism, (2) an ingenuous attitude on the part of Jews themselves, and (3)
resistance manifested in a variety of ways. The survivors' accounts include
accuracies and inaccuracies as to events and places, but these are not the important
criteria for this chapter. A search for apology and self-justification, integral
themes for our genre, do turn up. Siep Jongeling from Holland expressed the
view that "the Germans are not all bad people. I have no objections to Germans
as long as they don't want to impose their will on me."[8] Leon Lieberman
theorized on survival: "In Buchenwald, you gotta survive. When I came in they
[the Germans] noticed my number. They gave me credit for this and gave me
a better job."[9]

The book is also filled with reflections on life after the Holocaust. Morris
Weinerman, the friendly carpenter from Youngstown, expresses his feelings: "I
still have dreams. It has been a long time, and all the time I have been free.
But in the dreams right away I am surrounded. All the time I am caught again.
. . . We do not forget."[10] Optimism is expressed by Esther Bittman Shudmak:
"I don't think that anything like that would happen again. People now have
access to ammunition and guns. People protect themselves more than in those
days. I think now people care more about others in general."[11]

Isaac Kowalski's *Anthology on Armed Jewish Resistance, 1939–1945* is a
repository of accounts on Jewish resistance by partisans and underground activists. The book contains memoirs, letters, testimonies, biographies, and autobiographies of the resistance movement. This work depicts the Jew as a fighter with
a three-fold battle: fighting the Nazi invaders, facing the indigenous population
who hated him, and struggling to exist within the partisan movement.

The anthology serves the aim of an apology, that is, to explain the situation
of the partisans and their raison d'être to the Western community. To this end,
Kowalski attempts to portray the Jewish partisan as a fighting soldier. He seeks
to bury the lie that the Jew was not a fighting man. The romantic notion of
Ph.D.'s as glamorous fighting warriors, "the new chivalry," is ferreted out in
the book time and again.

The volume allows the partisans to speak for themselves, to enable the reader
to sense the tension and to recapture the moment. Jewish heroism is paraded in

Sobibor, the trenches, the ghettos, and at the front. The tendency to moralize, albeit in a grim fashion, is evinced in the book of Anthon Schmidt: "Every man must die once. One can die as a hangman or as a man helping others. I'd die for helping other men."[12]

Revenge is also a value justification. Norman Salsitz took a machine gun and fired salvo after salvo into the Germans: "Their party was over. At this moment with the gun still hot in my hands I no longer felt like a victim. I had settled my score with the *Scharffuhrer* and my pact with G-d who had let me down so many times."[13]

In Helen Fein's book *Accounting for Genocide*, the reader is asked to confront the Holocaust as an event challenging earlier notions of history. "To understand the implications of the Holocaust, the reader must grapple with its success."[14] The book's main interest to us is the part that explores the responses of Jews, drawn from first-person records in Warsaw, the Netherlands, and Hungary. She records Ringelblum's diary on the Warsaw ghetto as well as the diary of Chaim Kaplan.

The section on the Warsaw ghetto employs memoirs and diaries interspersed as a literary device within a running narrative by the author. Fein even goes so far as to use excerpts from novels. Fein's book does not lend itself to the type of literary criterion that we have posed. It is essentially a work for sociologists that uses personal accounts of the victims to reconstruct the social psychology of the camp inmates.

A literary work of merit can be found in Yaffa Eliach's *Hasidic Tales of the Holocaust*. She utilizes a long tradition of oral story telling circulating among the Hasidic communities and puts these tales and interviews down in print. The original interviews were conducted in nine languages and numerous dialects. The tales fall into four major parts reflecting four stages: ancestors and faith, friendship, the spirit alone, and the Gates of Freedom.

In the first part, "Ancestors and Faith" shows the reaction of the Jew, the innocent victim, when he encounters his executioners. Our first criterion of diary writing being a form of tradition is nowhere so exemplified as in this volume. The Hasidic tale with its themes of love, optimism, and faith in God ultimately triumphs in the world of the Holocaust.

## SUMMARY

The writing of autobiography, memoirs, and diaries is an enterprise that is essentially reflective. Not only do these authors engage in the task of writing about experience but also offer us their own thoughts of that experience. Thus different attitudes are adopted by these authors, conditioned by the momentous and monstrous experience that they all shared. They are rendering accounts about occurrences (history) while having participated in these events and in turn being shaped by these events. Thus the type of writing described here is not history but the reflective subjective passion of the participant.[15]

The authors share a burning and important question that is rarely evinced: What is this account for? For whom is it intended? The attempts to address these issues are the raison d'être of these authors and are in fact the thread that ties this type of historiography together.

The autobiographers seek an explanation; they seek self-knowledge. In their quest for this gnosis they render an account of human action so that human understanding can profit. The accounts of history in any of the forms studied here are for posterity. They are for the present readers. They make an attempt to reach out across time to an audience so that the audience can be made aware of particular and subjective events. But they are also an exercise in self-aware- ness. The tension between these two objectives gives genesis to the passion in the literature. The reader then has the task of explaining the connection between the narrative of the individuals and their reason for its rendition.

Historical research can also benefit from the memoirs and diaries cited here. These are in fact statements of eyewitnesses and, as such, contemporary with the events that they attest. Praise is due for these sources because they are not derivative. If they lack the sound judgment and interpretation of historians, they do so because there is a distinction between the two methods. Our authors do not use the tools of the modern historiographer by collecting evidence and evaluating it. Instead, they turn to personal accounts and reflect back on them. The researcher will need to avail himself or herself of the patrimony of memoirs, diaries, and other accounts in order to evaluate the history of this period.[16] This evaluation will allow a "lost" civilization to speak to new generations, render account of itself, and thereby fulfill J. Huizinga's definition of history. The researcher will then have contributed to the understanding of the period known as the Holocaust.

## NOTES

1. J. Huizinga, "A Definition of the Concept of History," in *Philosophy and History: Essays Presented to Ernst Cassiver*, ed. R. Klibansky and H. J. Patton (Oxford: Clarendon Press, 1936), pp. 1–10.

2. See the remarks of J. Van Seters, *In Search of History: Historiography in the Ancient World and The Origins of Biblical History* (New Haven, Conn.: Yale University Press, 1983), pp. 1–7, and Henry Huttenbach, "Historicity of the Holocaust: The Trans- Temporal Nature of Historical Events," Duquesne History Forum, Pittsburgh, November 1, 1974.

3. See the view of K. Y. Ball-Kaduri, "Evidence of Witnesses: Its Value and Lim- itations," *Yad Vashem Studies* (Jerusalem) 3 (1959): 79–90.

4. Hannah Senesh, *Hannah Senesh: Her Life and Diary* (New York: Schocken Books, 1972), p. 249.

5. Janusz Korczak, *Ghetto Diary* (New York: Holocaust Library, 1978), p. 185.

6. Martin Gilbert, *The Holocaust* (New York: Holt, Rinehart, and Winston, 1985), p. 824.

7. Sylvia Rothchild, ed. *Voices from the Holocaust* (New York: New American Library, 1981), p. 5.

8. Saul Friedman, *Amcha: An Oral Testament of the Holocaust* (Washington, D.C.: University Press of America, 1979), p. 175.

9. Ibid., p. 199.

10. Ibid., p. 238.

11. Ibid., p. 342.

12. Isaac Kowalski, *Anthology on Armed Jewish Resistance, 1939–1945*, vol. 1 (Brooklyn: Jewish Combatants Publishers House, 1984), p. 374.

13. Ibid., p. 484.

14. Helen Fein, *Accounting for Genocide* (New York: Free Press, 1979), p. 235.

15. This is not to say that the participant is less able to render an accounting of past events. Compare the remarks of R. G. Collingwood, *The Idea of History* (New York: Oxford University Press, 1956), pp. 2–3.

16. See A. D. Momigliano, *Studies in Historiography* (New York: Harper and Row, 1966), pp. 1–3.

## SELECT BIBLIOGRAPHY

Arad, Yitzhak. *The Partisan*. New York: ADL, 1979.

Birenbaum, Halina. *Hope Is the Last to Die*. New York: Twayne, 1971.

Boehm, Eric. *We Survived*. New Haven, Conn.: Yale University Press, 1949.

Cohen, Elie. *The Abyss*. New York: Norton, 1973.

Czerniakow, Adam. *The Warsaw Diary of Adam Czerniakow*. Edited by Raul Hilberg, Stanislaw Staron, and Joseph Kermisz. New York: Stein and Day, 1979.

Demetz, Hana. *The House on Prague Street*. New York: St. Martin's Press, 1980.

Dimsdale, Joel, ed. *Survivors, Victims, and Perpetrators: Essays on the Nazi Holocaust*. New York: Hemisphere, 1980.

Donat, Alexander. *The Holocaust Kingdom*. New York: Holt, Rinehart and Winston, 1963.

Eisner, Jack. *The Survivor*. New York: Morrow, 1980.

Eitinger, Leo. *Concentration Camp Survivors in Norway and Israel*. London: Allen and Unwin, 1964.

Eliach, Yaffa. *Hasidic Tales of the Holocaust*. New York: Oxford University Press, 1982.

Engleman, Matylda. *End of the Journey*. Los Angeles: Pinnacle, 1980.

Epstein, Helen. *Children of the Holocaust*. New York: Putnam's, 1979.

Fein, Helen. *Accounting for Genocide: National Responses and Jewish Victimization During the Holocaust*. New York: Free Press, 1979.

Fenelon, Fania. *Playing for Time*. New York: Atheneum, 1977.

Flinker, Moshe. *Young Moshe's Diary*. New York: Board of Jewish Education, 1971.

Frank, Anne. *Anne Frank: The Diary of a Young Girl*. Translated by B. M. Mooyaart. New York: Washington Square Press, 1972.

Friedlander, Saul. *When Memory Comes*. New York: Farrar, Straus, Giroux, 1979.

Friedman, Ina. *Escape or Die*. Reading, Mass.: Addison-Wesley, 1982.

Friedman, Philip. *Martyrs and Fighters*. New York: Praeger, 1954.

Friedman, Saul S. *Amcha: An Oral Testament of the Holocaust*. Washington, D.C.: University Press of America, 1979.

Gabor, Georgia. *My Destiny*. Arcadia, Calif.: Amen, 1982.

Garlinski, Jozef. *Fighting Auschwitz*. New York: Fawcett, 1975.

Gilbert, Martin. *The Holocaust*. New York: Holt, Rinehart and Winston, 1984.

Goldberg, Izaak. *The Miracles Versus Tyranny*. New York: Philosophical Library, 1978.

Gollwitzer, Helmut, Rathe Kuhn, and Reinhold Schneider, eds. *Dying We Live*. New York: Pantheon, 1956

Gurdus, Luba Krugman. *The Death Train*. New York: National Council on Art in Jewish Life, 1978.

Hart, Kitty. *Return to Auschwitz*. New York: Atheneum, 1981.

Heimler, Eugene. *Concentration Camp*. New York: Pyramid, 1961.

Hersh, Gizelle, and Peggy Mann. *Gizelle, Save the Children*. New York: Everest House, 1980.

Hillesum, Etty. *An Interrupted Life*. New York: Pantheon, 1984.

Jackson, Livia. *Elli*. New York: Times Books, 1980.

Joffo, Joseph. *A Bag of Marbles*. Boston: Houghton Mifflin, 1974.

Kessel, Sim. *Hanged at Auschwitz*. Briarcliff Manor, N.Y.: Stein and Day, 1972.

Koehn, Ilse. *Mischling, Second Degree*. New York: Bantam, 1978.

Korczak, Janusz. *Ghetto Diary*. New York: Holocaust Library, 1978.

Kowalski, Isaac. *Anthology on Armed Jewish Resistance, 1939–1945*. Brooklyn: Jewish Combatants Publishers House, 1984.

Latour, Anny. *The Jewish Resistance in France (1940–1944)*. New York: Holocaust Library, 1981.

Levi, Primo. *Survival in Auschwitz*. New York: Collier, 1973.

Lore, Shelly. *Jewish Holocaust Survivors' Attitudes Toward Contemporary Beliefs About Themselves*. Ann Arbor: UMI, 1984.

Meed, Vladka. *On Both Sides of the Wall*. New York: Holocaust Library, 1979.

Mermelstein, Mel. *By Bread Alone*. Los Angeles: Crescent, 1979.

Michelson, Frida. *I Survived Rumboli*. New York: Holocaust Library, 1982.

Miller, Judith. *One by One by One*. New York: Simon & Schuster, 1990.

Minco, Marga. *Bitter Herbs*. New York: Oxford University Press, 1960.

Moskovitz, Sarah. *Love Despite Hate: Child Survivors of the Holocaust and Their Adult Lives*. New York: Schocken Books, 1983.

Noyce, Wilfrid. *They Survived: A Study of the Will to Live*. London: Heinemann, 1962.

Oberski, Jona. *Childhood*. Garden City, N.Y.: Doubleday, 1983.

Pankiewicz, Tadeusz. *The Cracow Ghetto Pharmacy*. Translated by Henry Tilles. New York: Holocaust Library, 1987.

Perl, William. *The Four-Front War: From the Holocaust to the Promised Land*. New York: Crown, 1979.

Pinkus, Oscar. *The House of Ashes*. Cleveland: World, 1964.

Rabinowitz, Dorothy. *New Lives: Survivors of the Holocaust Living in America*. New York: Knopf, 1976.

Redlich, Gonda. *The Terezin Diary of Gonda Redlich*. Edited by Saul S. Friedman and Laurence Kutler. Lexington: University Press of Kentucky, 1992.

Ringelblum, Emmanuel. *Notes from the Warsaw Ghetto*. Edited and translated by Jacob Sloan. New York: McGraw-Hill, 1958.

Rothchild, Sylvia, ed. *Voices from the Holocaust*. New York: New American Library, 1981.

Rubinstein, Erna. *The Survivor in Us All: A Memoir of the Holocaust*. Hamden, Conn.: Archon Books, 1983.

Schneider, Gertrude. *Journey into Terror*. New York: Ark House, 1980.

Schoenfeld, Joachim. *Holocaust Memoirs: Jews in the Lwow Ghetto, the Janowski Concentration Camp, and as Deportees in Siberia*. New York: Ktav, 1985.

Schweifert, Peter. *The Bird Has No Wings*. New York: St. Martin's Press, 1976.

Senesh, Hannah. *Hannah Senesh: Her Life and Diary*. New York: Schocken Books, 1972.

Steinitz, Lucy, and David Szonyi. *Living After the Holocaust: Reflections by the Post-War Generation in America*. New York: Bloch, 1976.

Stroop, Jürgen. *The Stroop Report*. New York: Pantheon, 1979.

Suhl, Yuri, ed. *They Fought Back: The Story of the Jewish Resistance in Nazi Europe*. New York: Crown, 1967.

Syrkin, Marie. *Blessed Is the Match*. New York: Knopf, 1947.

Tillion, Germaine. *Ravensbrück*. Garden City, N.Y.: Doubleday, 1975.

Topas, George. *The Iron Furnace: A Holocaust Survivor's Story*. Lexington: University Press of Kentucky, 1990.

Trepman, Paul. *Among Men and Beasts*. New York: Barnes, 1978.

Trunk, Isaiah. *Jewish Responses to Nazi Persecution*. Briarcliff Manor, N.Y.: Stein and Day, 1978.

Vegh, Claudine. *I Didn't Say Goodbye: Interviews with Children of the Holocaust*. New York: Dutton, 1984.

Vrba, Rudolf, and Alan Bestic. *I Cannot Forgive*. New York: Bantam, 1968.

Wells, Leon. *The Janowska Road*. London: Cape, 1966.

Ziemian, Joseph. *The Cigarette Sellers of Three Crosses Square*. New York: Avon, 1975.

Zyskind, Sara. *Stolen Years*. Minneapolis: Lerner, 1981.

# Chapter 26

# The Holocaust in Fiction

### Harry James Cargas

By the very nature of the topic, Holocaust writing is often judged as either overwhelmingly moving or disappointingly ineffective; there is hardly any middle ground of response. The works of Wiesel, Sachs, Lustig, Borowski, Lind, and Schwarz-Bart have been properly praised for excellence. Gerald Green's *Holocaust*, William Styron's *Sophie's Choice*, and Leon Uris's *Mila 18* are much less successful, literately, for various reasons. Perhaps the most outstanding difference, that which appears most consistently, is that good literature reflects a certain sentiment while the lesser material is sentimental. The distinction is crucial.

Sentiment reflects a compassion, a praiseworthy reaction to someone's situation. Sentimentality, on the other hand, cheapens. It is an excess of emotion that trivializes the subject under consideration. It comes very close to writing by formula. We can imagine a group of comedy writers of the past requiring at least one mother-in-law joke per radio program because these always were good for a laugh. Jokes about death were factored into such programs for the same reason. Stock situations in books such as injured animals or missing children could be counted on to produce stock responses in unsophisticated audience members.

But good writers do not participate in such lazy habits. T. S. Eliot, in an essay on *Hamlet*, wrote that the symbol (or character) an author creates must be of sufficiently recognizable depth to be worthy of the emotion that the writer is trying to elicit. We have only to think of a young man attempting to describe his newly beloved to a friend who has never met her. If he tries to impress the friend with inadequately descriptive words about the woman such as "nice," "swell," or "pretty," he will hardly give a unique depiction of someone he finds so unique.[1] The writer of fiction, poetry, or drama always has this problem, by the very nature of writing. "How can I tell my story in a way that does justice to my subject?" Because the Holocaust is such an awesome topic, this problem is particularly troublesome for the author using the *Shoah* as a setting.

One major way that some writers have found to cope with this difficulty is to write with understatement, to write in what some critics have identified as a literature of silence. Writers in this area, especially many survivors of the death camps, feel that they must write about their experiences. Not to do so would be to betray the dead. However, to write badly about the events would also be a betrayal. It would be a cheapening, a trivialization, a sentimentalization. So the Holocaust author anguishes over what to say and how to say it with a heavy responsibility. Elie Wiesel has observed that "the act of writing is for me often nothing more than the secret or conscious desire to carve words on a tombstone: to the memory of a town forever vanished, to the memory of a childhood in exile, to the memory of all those I loved and who, before I could tell them I loved them, went away."

Wiesel is the appropriate figure with which to begin this survey of the best literary works of the Holocaust. His memoir, *Night*, while not strictly in the category of imaginative literature, sets a standard for judgment because of its style. Now about 110 pages long, this autobiographical account of the Auschwitz experience was originally published in Yiddish in over 800 pages. Wiesel cut the text to its present length but feels that "to the sensitive reader it's all still there." In a book that we wrote together, Wiesel commented on his style:

Recently I reread chronicles written by historians in the ghettos: Ringelblum, Kaplan. They were all young and became witnesses. They all felt that they had to record events for future generations, the main obsession during the war, so the tales should not be lost or wasted—the experiences should not go astray. I was amazed and astounded by the style. Such an incisive, short style; sometimes sentences of one word. When I read them I understood my own style, why I wrote in such a condensed way.

Actually, I saw myself following in their footsteps. When they began a sentence they could never tell whether they would be alive to finish it; it had to contain everything.[2]

It is with that kind of seriousness that the major Holocaust authors have approached their tasks, and they have achieved a reputation among the understanding critics in proportion to how close to the ideal they have come.

In *Night* Wiesel gives a tightly packed account of his time as a teenager in various Nazi camps, a period where he lost his parents and his baby sister. He also lost his faith in the traditional God of his people and despaired of humanity as well. To portray all of this in a few pages—in any number of pages—was an enormous undertaking that he effectively concluded. Without detailed descriptions of Nazi atrocities, Wiesel managed to convey the aura of the concentration-camp universe. One example will suffice: A starving young boy was caught by camp officials trying to steal a bowl of boiled water the Nazis called soup. The child was to be made an example. The entire camp was to witness his hanging. But the youngster was so emaciated, so light, that it took him over half an hour to strangle on the end of the rope. He died slowly in front of all of the prisoners. Wiesel's powerful comment, understated yet conveying the full burden of the event: "That night the soup tasted of corpses."[3] For some critics, *Night* is the first book to be recommended to anyone who wishes to read about the Holocaust.

Perhaps the most critically acclaimed Holocaust novel is *The Last of the Just*, Andre Schwarz-Bart's fictional tracing of the Legend of the Just Men. The world's existence depends on the fact that certain men of honor appear in history, and their piety holds God's creation together. These men are unrecognized by others, quietly living lives of integrity. The author takes liberties with the legend. Some of his characters from the twelfth century on are very aware who they might be, and, in fact, they accept persecution and disaster rather than prevent it. We read, then, of a continuum of gentle sufferers through the Middle Ages, the Renaissance, and the centuries until the present one of people whose pain was unremittingly caused by Christians, culminating in the story of the final character, Ernie Levy. As Ernie grows up in the Hitler era, he begins to feel the barbs of anti-Semitism from friends and strangers alike. After experiencing prolonged personal pain and the loss of his family, Levy decides to become what society decrees him to be: a dog. He no longer regards himself as human and humiliates himself in many ways.

However, when he realizes that he may be able to rescue certain loved ones, Ernie reinvigorates himself and goes to Paris, a city virtually rid of Jews. There he falls in love with a handicapped girl who has an engaging personality. Their night of love, of mutual affirmation, is a beautiful scene in this beautiful novel. Soon the girl disappears, and Ernie heroically goes in search of her, even to the point of entering a death camp. His deportation and moral leadership in the gas chamber bring the story to a close. It is clear that this martyred Jew, this nonresister, lived a life of moral rather than physical courage. He symbolizes that segment of victims who chose to fight violence by not participating in it, by not becoming like "them."

The narrator does not end his tale on a note of pessimism. He intuits Ernie alive today, "somewhere, I don't know where." His penultimate paragraph is a remarkable, broken prayer, but prayer nevertheless:

And praised. *Auschwitz*. Be. *Maidanek*. The Lord. *Treblinka*. And praised. *Buchenwald*. Be. *Mauthausen*. The Lord. *Belzec*. And praised. *Sobibor*. Be. *Chelmno*. The Lord. *Ponary*. And praised. *Theresienstadt*. Be. *Warsaw*. The Lord. *Vilna*. And praised. *Skarzysko*. Be. *Bergen-Belsen*. The Lord. *Janow*. And praised. *Dora*. Be. *Neungamme*. The Lord. *Pustkow*. And praised . . .[4]

A non-Jewish survivor of Auschwitz, Tadeusz Borowski, began publishing a series of short stories on the experience when he was twenty-four years old.

Some three years later he took his own life, leaving a legacy of fiction that is properly compared, in style and intensity, with the best of Ernest Hemingway. Borowski produced what one Polish novelist called "a handful of stories, which have a chance of surviving as long as Polish literature lasts, and a cemetery of broken illusions and hopes."

The impact of these short works of fiction stems, in great measure, from the author's powerful use of the technique of understatement. Without embellishment, he writes what the characters see and experience. He has no need to tell readers how to react to the everyday horrors that Auschwitz inmates live and die with. That would be to sentimentalize. Instead, he gives us the historical facts and the stark human reactions (or lack of them) to the events that are almost beyond literal presentation.

A dozen of Borowski's tales are collected in *This Way for the Gas, Ladies and Gentlemen*. The title story is about the dehumanization of the prisoners. It is, after all, the victims themselves who must remove corpses from the freight cars used to transport their human cargo. It is the prisoners who take the valuables that the newly arrived unfortunates have brought with them and that the Nazis confiscate. We read of the captive laborers who rummage through garbage to compete for decaying food in order to be less hungry for a few hours.

Everything is treated matter-of-factly. "Several other men are carrying a small girl with only one leg. They hold her by the arms and the one leg. Tears are running down her face and she whispers faintly: 'Sir, it hurts, it hurts . . . ' They throw her on the truck on top of the corpses. She will burn alive along with them."[5]

One of the prisoners has pangs of conscience because he feels no pity for other victims, people he himself is mean to on occasion because of certain tasks given him by the Nazis. He is consoled by another who insists that even their anger at other prisoners is natural and predictable—even healthy, since this is all a matter of survival.

A second story, "A Day at Harmenz," is an account of a typical camp day for an inmate, a kind of miniature *One Day in the Life of Ivan Denisovich*. Another tells of an act of resistance in which a German soldier is killed for his cruelty by a naked woman who tricked him out of his pistol. He dies unable to comprehend why he has done anything to merit such a response.

The killing of the sergeant is a well-known incident that forms the basis for a novel, *A Prayer for Katerina Horovitzova* by Arnost Lustig, one of the major figures in Holocaust fiction. This work is a tale of a modern Judith and Holofernes, a novel of innocence defeating evil. The shattering climax, in which a beauteous young Jewish woman, going to her concentration-camp death, destroys her Nazi tormentor before she is killed, is at once surprising and satisfying. The story begins in Italy, where twenty American Jews are about to be annihilated by Nazis. They try to negotiate their freedom but lose their fortunes in a cruel hoax. Among them is the young Katerina, so frightened of death, with so much

of her life before her. How she faces her end, with courage and quiet determination, is beautifully rendered.

*Diamonds of the Night* contains nine compelling stories that came out of the
author's own concentration-camp experiences. The horror of existence under the
Nazis is powerfully rendered in fiction like "The Lemon." In this story a boy
has to obtain a lemon for his dying sister who needs it for a vitamin deficiency.
To get money enough, the boy knocks the gold teeth out of his recently dead
father's corpse. The impact on the child is profoundly measured here. An old
man watches helplessly as his elderly wife dies in "The Old Ones and Death"
because medical help is not available to these victims. Lustig communicates pain
with enormous skill.

*Dita Saxova* is a powerful presentation of the lives of children who survived
the Holocaust. The exploration of life and of the impossible attempts to recover
innocence, to discard cynicism, and to learn to love are insightfully portrayed.

*The Unloved* may contain Lustig's finest writing. This tale in diary form is
about a teenager who is forced into prostitution in order to survive in Theresienstadt. Perla S. tells facts such as how many sexual encounters she had this
day and what she earned. Here is one example: "Five times. A candle. A jar
of strawberry jam. Winter socks. Twenty-five marks. Eleven marks." That is
all she notes, pitifully. This depersonalized teen finds a symbolic companion in
a rat living in her quarters, a creature that also feels sensations but is incapable
of fully human emotions and growth. The psychological destruction that occurs
in the camp is honestly rendered.

Seven short tales that might be called docustories make up *Night and Hope*.
They are based on actual records of ghetto and camp occurrences. "The Return"
is about a man who escapes from being put on a transport for Jews, but rejoins
his people after spending time on the outside alone. "Rose Street" is about the
death of a woman beaten by a Nazi and the compassion for her humanity felt
by another Nazi. "Stephen and Anne" is of two pure children who share their
first kiss, but before their love can blossom, she is removed from his life by
being put on a Nazi transport.

The novel *Darkness Casts No Shadow* is actually based on Lustig's escape,
as a teenager, from Nazi capture. He fled with a friend, and their adventures,
especially in the dark forests of Germany, are gripping. Their hunger and their
fears are delicately transmitted here.

Another sensitive work of fiction centering on the child is the less well known
novel by Merritt Linn, *A Book of Songs*. This is a beautiful first book of fiction,
telling of concentration-camp inmates struggling not to become psychologically
brutalized like their captors and finding in a violin-playing child the possibilities
of the world beyond the barbed wire and the machine-gun towers. It is unforgettable. The tension the author creates as prisoners struggle to help the boy
escape into childhood provides an artistic masterpiece, as do the episodes of
failure, the sections where Jewish inmates succumb to the pressures of hunger,

of psychological and physical terror, and of loneliness and alienation. Chapter 25, in which the prisoner/narrator, in fulfilling a promise to another Jew, approaches this other to kill him in order to put him out of misery, is a stunning triumph.

In spite of the setting, this is a tale of hope about men who encourage each other to persevere, even against apparently hopeless odds. Love and sacrifice, faith in God, heroism, and dignity in the face of betrayal and bestiality are all delineated with consummate skill. Most moving is the little boy around whom the plot revolves. He is silent and elusive, has to beg for his food to survive, and through it all remains a symbol for the other victims to take heart.

Known more for his Nazi hunting and his nonfiction works, Simon Wiesenthal has, nonetheless, contributed an excellent novel to the subgenre of writing known as Holocaust literature. Based on a true story, *Max and Helen* is a tale rooted in the concentration-camp experience. Long after the close of World War II a stranger gave Wiesenthal a tip that a man who had been a particularly brutal Nazi was now a leading business figure in Germany. Determined to bring the criminal to justice, Wiesenthal tried to find an eyewitness to the terrible acts of Hitler's henchman. Wiesenthal found such a person in Max, a Jewish medical doctor who was now the shell of his former self. Max despised the former camp commander, whom he had seen clubbing prisoners to death. Yet Max refused to testify against the clearly guilty German. A puzzled Simon Wiesenthal was impelled to investigate the reason for Max's refusal, and that is the plot line for this short, effective novel.

Max's fiancée, Helen, also chooses not to testify, and the puzzle becomes more complex. Max, a young Polish medical student, and the beautiful Helen are separated during the war, and they are reunited after their sufferings when the Axis forces are defeated. They become, as time passes, the only remaining witnesses to the commander's atrocities. Wiesenthal is unable to comprehend their reluctance to give testimony.

Eventually, however, he learns the terrible secret that would have to be revealed if a trial came to pass. For humane reasons, then, Wiesenthal does not push for prosecution. The secret is a son, forced on Helen by the murderous commander, but ignorant of his father's true identity. Max could not abide looking at the boy because he resembled his ex-Nazi father so much. Therefore he separates from Helen at the close of the novel in a heartrending ending. (Wiesenthal told me in conversation that the boy was never told who his real father was.)

One of the most significant of all creators of Holocaust fiction is certainly Aharon Appelfeld, who lives in Israel, writes in Hebrew, and is blessed with good translations into English. In answer to his own question, Appelfeld has said that there is not a danger that the Holocaust will be overtold in literature. He insists that "the Holocaust is a central event in many people's lives, but it also has become a metaphor for our century. There cannot be an end to speaking and writing about it. Besides, in Israel, everyone carries a biography deep inside him, including myself. I write about individuals more than about the Holocaust."[6]

Told in very simple language, *Badenheim 1939* is a tale of primarily nameless people. The locale is an Austrian resort town where middle-class Jews come to relax. They enjoy concerts, poetry readings, rich pastries, and detachment from the outside world. But it is 1939 and danger lurks, unknown to the patrons. From their kind of romantic existence the people are ultimately faced with four filthy freight cars that readers know, but the Jewish characters do not, will take them to destruction. They are calmed by what we realize to be the ironic line that closes the book, when the organizer of the great annual event at Badenheim, Dr. Poppenheim, remarks: "If the coaches are so dirty it must mean that we have not far to go." What the author is able to achieve here is an allegory applicable well beyond the events of the Holocaust. Except for the book's title, no date is given in the text for the plot. Hitler is never mentioned, nor is Nazism. The fate of Poland is kept from the victims at Badenheim who become increasingly aware that Poland, in fact, will be their destination. "Why not?" is their general response. These characters argue over the good and lesser aspects of Poland but never get around to asking why they are being sent there. The conclusion is powerful and convincing in this remarkable work.

Unnoticed, creeping horror in another resort town is a theme in *The Age of Wonders*, in which ten-year-old Bruno serves as Appelfeld's focus. The boy's Austrian parents, though Jews themselves, show great contempt for other Jews whose warnings of anti-Semitism are rejected by the couple. Bruno's father is a well-regarded writer, his mother a strong, charitable character. As the dangers of the Nazi era grow (this is 1937), the father's creative energy dwindles, the parents' marriage collapses, and the deportation of Bruno, his mother, and adopted sister follows. The father is spared certain horror because of remarriage to an Austrian aristocrat. The novel closes some years after these incidents. Bruno returns to his hometown, which is now completely free of Jews, to recall the past and to atone, if he can, for his father's sins. The words "Nazi," "Germany," and "Hitler" are not found in this book, which, like most other of Appelfeld's fiction, is universalized in its message. The father's blindness over the impending tragedy is frightening. His well-known actress friend is expelled from the National Theatre Company because she is Jewish; his sister-in-law abandons her own faith for the protection of Catholicism; his own writings are denounced for presenting Jewish characters who are "parasites living off the healthy Austrian tradition." Yet he is oblivious, perhaps just as we are to, say, environmental dangers of our own era. Appelfeld seems to be warning us that we may learn from the tragedy of others.

Another novel by the same author, *To the Land of the Cattails*, takes place in prewar Eastern Europe, where a thirty-four-year-old mother, Toni, and her adolescent son, Rudi, are traveling back from Austria to Toni's native territory, Bukovina (Romania). Nearly two decades ago, this Jewish woman fled from home to marry a non-Jew by whom she had Rudi. At age twenty she was already divorced and subsequently took many lovers. One of them left her a legacy that enabled her to act on an impulse to return home to see her parents, perhaps to make peace with them.

As they move closer to home, the environment becomes increasingly dangerous. Although words like "Holocaust," "Nazi," and "Germans" never appear in this novel, readers recognize the reality of what awaits the travelers. Toni becomes increasingly aware of what she perceives to be Jewish failings; Toni, after drinking and becoming unkempt, resorts to anti-Semitic slogans. Mother and son have grown apart but reconcile before she and her parents disappear. Rudi roams the countryside, never quite comprehending the evil that is happening or its magnitude.

Just as in his other novels, Appelfeld here gives us the barest of descriptive details in his own presentation of a literature of silence. He is quoted as having said that he cannot write specifically about the Holocaust because "it's just impossible to deal directly with the nakedness of the deaths. It's like looking at the naked sun on a clear summer day. You couldn't stand the temperature. You can never understand the meaning of the Holocaust. You can just come to the edges of it. If you wrote about it directly, you'd end up trivializing it."[7]

Another work of fiction by Appelfeld requires mention here: *Tzili*, subtitled *The Story of a Life*. This is the tale of a young Jewish girl, thought to be simpleminded by her family, who is left to take care of the home and goods while the rest of the members flee the Nazis. They hope that, given her dim-wittedness, she will not be harmed and their property will be preserved. But Tzili witnesses a general slaughter of Jews, herself escaping miraculously. She flees to the woods and survives for a while like an animal. She takes on the identity of a child of a known prostitute, thus passing as a Gentile and able to live, though experiencing a harsh existence at the hands of peasants with whom she lives.

Later she meets Mark, who has escaped from a prison camp though his wife and children have not. He and Tzili develop a relationship that helps each to grow spiritually. Mark dies at the hands of enemies, leaving the fifteen-year-old girl pregnant with his child. The baby dies in her womb, a symbol of the situation in which the living-dead Jews of Europe found themselves during this period. There is a sign of hope in the end as Tzili opts for settlement in Palestine, although the author does not attempt to present Zionist yearnings in any clearly romantic fashion.

As in all of his fiction, *Tzili* is written in Appelfeld's simple, understated style. In part, at least, he credits this to having written in Hebrew, which he studied before moving to Israel. "I suppose it makes a difference to use words that are acquired and not your original language," he told Herbert Mitgang. "It probably causes me to simplify my narrative voice."[8] His perfected style is universally praised by literary commentators.

One of the most controversial of Holocaust novels is Jerzy Kosinski's *The*

*Painted Bird*. The main character is a young boy, abandoned by his parents, who views certain horrors of World War II from his innocent perspective. Graphic images of violence abound in this fiction, and Kosinski insists that he had no other way to tell his story except this. The child is forced into a wandering existence, living by his wits, often escaping almost magically in times of enormous danger. He is beaten by strangers and sold to a sorceress who tortures him, but he is able to get away. He witnesses a jealous husband's vicious revenge against his wife's presumed lover, later sees a woman tortured to death at the hands of other women, and then, to escape harm at the hands of a carpenter, tricks the man into a pillbox, where he is eaten by rats. A German soldier saves the lad from execution. He has another close call with a group of villagers and witnesses the rape and murder of a Jewish woman.

After seeing and suffering additional abuse, the ten-year-old decides that only those who lived evil lives seemed to succeed; therefore, he will become like the extraordinarily successful Germans. But through it all, the child becomes morally depraved, loving revenge no matter who has to suffer, and he loses his voice. Eventually his parents reclaim him, but he arrives at the rather perverse conclusion that each man is an island and that the way to survive is to look out exclusively for oneself. Kosinski has been criticized for his graphic depiction of sadism, but his response has been that much of what he has portrayed in *The Painted Bird* is autobiographical and based on a reality that he himself had experienced.

Certain critics have insisted that Jakov Lind belongs among the top rank of writers who have chosen Holocaust literature as their genre. Lind has contributed to what has been labeled a ''literature of extremity.'' It seems as if he feels compelled to shout because he fears that most of us are unable to hear the import of his message. *Landscape in Concrete* is perhaps his finest fiction. It is a novel portraying the insanity of violence, random murder, and wild sexuality. It is set near the end of World War II. The main character, Gauthier Bachmann, is a German soldier who had gone mad while fighting on the Russian front, so he was discharged by Nazi authorities. But as he wanders through Europe, he encounters various other Nazis who manipulate him for monstrous purposes. Because Bachmann has been so successfully programmed to follow others, he willingly kills without remorse while fooling himself into thinking that all he longs for are the finer things in life. Lind's story and technique combine for a powerful indictment against Nazi values.

Another particularly moving novel, Piotr Rawicz's *Blood from the Sky*, uses an audacious symbol as a sign of the major character's destiny. Boris, the narrator, having survived the destruction of a Jewish community in the Ukraine, now lives with a group of refugees and assorted ''down-and-outers'' in Paris. These are people who feel no control over their lives—they simply allow life to impose its course on them. We learn of Boris's personal history from scraps of his journal and from some of his poetry. The remarkable symbol used by the author is Boris's penis. His circumcision is not only what ties him to his people; it is also the mark by which he is betrayed to the Nazis. It is, in addition, a signifier of Boris's connection to life.

*The Wall* is John Hersey's long, wrenching novel about the Warsaw ghetto. One of the early contributions to Holocaust literature, this story covers the period from the creation of that infamous ghetto and the further isolation caused by the wall of the title to the heroic Jewish uprising and the final destruction of the ghetto and its inhabitants by the Nazis. Based on historical evidence, this book has a devastating impact, as when a Jew has to smother a baby in order to keep its cries from revealing a hiding place to the conquerors.

*Jacob the Liar* was written by a victim of the Lodz ghetto and a number of concentration camps, Jurek Becker. From his experiences he has written a novel describing one man's personal triumph of the spirit in the midst of the Holocaust. A simple individual, Jacob Heym, communicates the will to live to an entire imprisoned community by his example. The ghetto is a lifeless place, but Jacob, unknown before the war, spreads rumors that he has invented telling of Allied combat successes, providing hope for the inmates, who are thus impelled to replace their despair with hope. A number of ghetto dwellers think that Jacob acquires his information from a contraband radio. Since this forbidden possession endangers them all, they urge him to give it up. His simple response is convincing: "Since the news reports have circulated in the ghetto, I know of no incident where anyone has taken his life." This is a very engaging tale.

Gypsies were among those marked for annihilation by the Nazis. Their sufferings are sometimes overlooked. One excellent novel on this theme is Stefan Kanfer's *The Eighth Sin*. This is the fictional narrative of Benoit, a Gypsy who survived a death camp. When the war ends, he comes to the United States as a teenager and is adopted by an American couple. Benoit is caught shoplifting and is institutionalized. He has an important skill, portrait painting, and throughout this period he develops it. He will be able to make a good living doing this, but it is not very much of a concern of his. Everything that he does and is remains haunted by his concentration-camp experiences. This is played out as Benoit seeks another Gypsy, Eleazar Jassy, who survived by carrying out the will of certain Nazis in brutalizing other Gypsies. As a child, Benoit was horrified by Jassy's willingness and ability to maim and kill; as an adult, he continues to be horrified at what he saw Jassy do. There appears to be only one way for the protagonist to purge his memory, and that is to track Jassy down and kill him. Much of the novel is based on the adventure of this search: picking up clues, finding Jassy, and then confronting him. Character drawing here is masterful, and Kanfer's sense of detail is remarkable.

Collections of poems are difficult to summarize. Here I can attempt only to give the tone of each book mentioned and to suggest its quality.

Among the most effective Holocaust poetry, and therefore the most painful to read, is that of the Nobel laureate for literature in 1966, Nelly Sachs, a German Jew who escaped to freedom in Sweden. The crematoria of the death camps are implicit in her every line. Sadness is heaped upon sadness; the ultimate tragedy is found in the deaths of the children, in all of their innocence, with always the perfect image, the perfect voice.

Charles Reznikoff's book-length poem *Holocaust* is basically a collection of verse paraphrases and quotations taken from verbatim accounts of legal records and Nazi confessions at the Nuremberg trials. There are twelve parts in this volume, ranging widely from "Deportation" (where thirteen thousand Jews are shipped from their homes, instantly) through "Invasion" (here is an account of SS men stripping and beating Jews) to "Research" (on ghastly medical experiments), ghetto atrocities, massacres, gas chambers, work camps, children, mass graves, and finally, for a few, escape. There is even a section titled "Entertainment" relating how Nazis were amused at the expense of those in their prisons.

Elie Wiesel's cantata *Ani Maamin* must be mentioned here. This work is a tremendous act of faith after Auschwitz. It is the story of Abraham, Isaac, and Jacob begging God to have mercy on the Jewish children being destroyed in World War II. God seems unmoved by the events in Europe in spite of all of the pleading. The narrator's conclusion is quietly but powerfully affirmative: "And the silence of God is God." Unknown to the three intercessors, a tear appears in God's eye, then a wash of sorrow in this poignant work of art. When the work was first performed in Carnegie Hall, the accompanying music was by Darius Milhaud.

*I Never Saw Another Butterfly* is a heart-wrenching collection of poems and drawings by children who perished in the Holocaust. As the final page of this volume notes, "A total of 15,000 children under the age of fifteen passed through Terezin. Of these, around 100 came back." Some of these children's works appear here, writing of pain, loss, loneliness, and fear. Yet through all this there is also love, hope, and a sense of beauty that emanates from the soon-to-be-lost innocence of the writers and artists. The work is edited by Hana Volavkova.

A major American poet, W. D. Snodgrass, allows his imagination to consider the last days of Hitler in all of their banality and horror in *The Führer Bunker*. In the form of a series of monologues, the author introduces the personalities who were with Hitler to his suicidal end. Included are advisor Albert Speer (hurt because he got no final handshake from his leader), Martin Bormann, the Führer's most loyal follower (a final letter to his wife), Minister of Propaganda Joseph Goebbels (concerned to the last with appearances), Eva Braun (obsessed with marrying Hitler before they die), and, of course, Hitler himself. In an afterword Snodgrass gives his rationale for some of the details rendered in this poem. He tells us that Eva Braun's favorite song was indeed "Tea for Two" and that Hitler preferred "Who's Afraid of the Big Bad Wolf?" to the opera *Lohengrin*, among other things. The author said that he wished to investigate behind the public facade. "My poems, then, must include voices they would hide from others, even from themselves."

Several other poetic works command notice. *Night of the Broken Glass* by

Emily Borenstein is written in prose-poetry form. This style seems exactly appropriate for an author who has clearly absorbed Elie Wiesel's memoir *Night* and uses several lines from that book. In this chilling volume Borenstein evokes images of starvation and torture. Agonies are rendered: a baby is strangled so as not to have its cries betray the hiding place of a group of Jews. From the despair of the Lodz ghetto, a despairing person cries out for redemption in the form of modern Maccabees.

Albrecht Haushofer was executed just before the end of World War II. His brother found his body three weeks later, with a hand clutching a manuscript under his coat. It was comprised of eighty poems published as *Moabit Sonnets*. These were written by the victim while he was awaiting death, chained hand and foot in solitary confinement. Many of these poems are of praise and love, but some are very angry, and others express sadness over the ravages of war. One sonnet even expresses compassion for the enemy.

*Erika: Poems of the Holocaust* is a major contribution to the literature by William Heyen, a German-American torn by the fact that two of his uncles met their deaths while fighting as Nazis. Heyen struggles with his emotions as his father gazes at photos of his now-dead brothers, who wore the uniform of the Third Reich. The poem "Riddle" tells of Heyen's personal angst as he tries to come to grips with images of the Belsen concentration camp.

There are not many dramas relating directly to the Holocaust, but a number of them prove extremely powerful. Rolf Hochhuth's *The Deputy* is considered as possibly the most controversial play ever to appear on the world stage. This is a thesis drama on the explosive topic of the failure of Pope Pius XII to speak out publicly against the Nazi treatment of Jews. While not great drama, it is an effective question raiser. The playwright adds an informative historical appendix to support his case. The hero is a Roman Catholic priest who argues against the Vatican's lack of involvement in the "Jewish question." His persona may seem less than credible in the scope of his relationships, but some of his arguments may be seen as effectively condemnatory of the pope.

The dramatized version of *The Diary of Anne Frank* (by Frances Goodrich and Albert Hackett) may be the best-known piece of Holocaust literature in any genre. It has been widely staged throughout the world. Audiences are drawn to the suspenseful story of the family in hiding from the Nazis and also to the characterizations drawn by the playwrights. The difficulties of living in close quarters with sometimes-cranky and less tolerant people, the romantic interest Anne has with a young boy also in hiding, and the young woman's hope-filled outlook on life despite such dismal times make for a remarkable theater experience.

*Andorra* is Max Frisch's dramatic fable about a boy who thinks, wrongly, that he is Jewish. The citizens of his community, who are anti-Semitic, also think that he is a Jew and mistreat him accordingly. Finally, they murder him because of his Jewishness, then learn the truth in this extremely powerful work of art.

Arthur Miller's *Playing for Time* is based on Fania Fenelon's memoir of the same title. Hers is the story of a women's orchestra formed in the death camp of Birkenau. The prisoner musicians were ordered to play for the pleasure of such notorious Nazis as Josef Mengele, Heinrich Himmler, and others. Fenelon tells of the eleven months she performed with the orchestra. The tensions between the victims themselves as well as with the enemy are movingly related.

*The Last Jew*, coauthored by Yaffa Eliach and Uri Assaf, is about reactions to the Holocaust by survivors and by their children. The play is set in Israel a generation after the *Shoah*. Flashbacks from the European past of some of the survivors are highly effective drama. Central to this work is the problem of how those of the younger generation are to cope with the effects of the Holocaust confronting them.

Robert Skloot has edited *The Theatre of the Holocaust*, a collection of four powerful dramas. Shimon Wincelberg's *Resort 76* is at once an inspiring and depressing effort, filled with macabre humor, yet balanced for wonderful effect. It is essentially the tale of suffering, survival, and death under the Nazis. Harold and Edith Lieberman write of betrayal of Jew by Jew in *Throne of Straw*, which centers on the Lodz ghetto's Jewish Council and its head, Mordechai Rumkowski. Surreal technique is George Tabori's style in *The Cannibals*, where characters are faced with starvation if they do not eat human flesh. Charlotte Delbo's *Who Will Carry the Word?* finds the author obsessed with the roles of witness and survivor as well as with those who do not wish to know about the horrible atrocities committed by the Nazis and their collaborators.

## NOTES

1. T. S. Eliot, *The Sacred Wood* (London: Methuen, 1960), pp. 95–103.

2. Harry James Cargas, *Harry James Cargas in Conversation with Elie Wiesel* (New York: Paulist, 1976), p. 76.

3. Elie Wiesel, *Night*, trans. Stella Rodway (New York: Hill and Wang, 1961), pp. 77–78.

4. André Schwarz-Bart, *The Last of the Just,* trans. Stephen Becker (New York: Atheneum, 1981), p. 374.

5. Tadeusz Borowski, *This Way for the Gas, Ladies and Gentlemen* (New York: Penguin, 1976), p. 46.

6. *New York Times*, November 15, 1986.

7. *New York Times Book Review*, November 2, 1986, p. 34.

8. *New York Times*, November 15, 1986.

## SELECTED BIBLIOGRAPHY

Appelfeld, Aharon. *The Age of Wonders*. Boston: Godine, 1981.
———. *Badenheim 1939*. Boston: Godine, 1980.
Arnold, Elliott. *A Night of Watching*. New York: Scribner, 1967.
Becker, Jurek. *Jacob the Liar*. New York: Harcourt Brace Jovanovich, 1976.

Borenstein, Emily. *Night of the Broken Glass*. Mason, Tex.: Timberline Press, 1981.

Borowski, Tadeusz. *This Way for the Gas, Ladies and Gentlemen*. New York: Viking, 1967.

Delbo, Charlotte. *None of Us Will Return*. Boston: Beacon, 1968.

Eliach, Yaffa. *Hasidic Tales of the Holocaust*. New York: Oxford University Press, 1982.

Eliach, Yaffa, and Uri Assaf. *The Last Jew*. New York: Smader, 1977.

Elon, Amos. *Timetable*. Garden City, N.Y.: Doubleday, 1980.

Epstein, Leslie. *King of the Jews*. New York: Avon, 1980.

Frisch, Max. *Andorra*. New York: Hill and Wang, 1964.

Goodrich, Frances, and Albert Hackett. *The Diary of Anne Frank*. New York: Random House, 1956.

Green, Gerald. *Holocaust*. New York: Bantam, 1978.

Habe, Hans. *The Mission*. New York: Coward-McCann, 1966.

Haushofer, Albrecht. *Moabit Sonnets*. New York: Norton, 1978.

Hersey, John. *The Wall*. Reprint. New York: Knopf, 1967.

Heyen, William. *Erika: Poems of the Holocaust*. New York: Vanguard, 1977.

Hochhuth, Rolf. *The Deputy*. New York: Grove Press, 1964.

Kanfer, Stefan. *The Eighth Sin*. New York: Random House, 1978.

Kosinski, Jerzy. *The Painted Bird*. New York: Pocket Books, 1966.

Kuznetsov, Anatoly. *Babi Yar*. New York: Dell, 1967.

Levin, Meyer. *Eva*. New York: Simon and Schuster, 1959.

Lind, Jakov. *Landscape in Concrete*. New York: Grove Press, 1966.

Lustig, Arnost. *Darkness Casts No Shadow*. London: Dutton, 1963.

———. *Diamonds of the Night*. Washington, D.C.: Inscape, 1978.

———. *Night and Hope*. Washington, D.C.: Inscape, 1976.

Miller, Arthur. *Playing for Time*. New York: Bantam, 1981.

Rawicz, Piotr. *Blood from the Sky*. New York: Harcourt, Brace and World, 1963.

Reznikoff, Charles. *Holocaust*. Los Angeles: Black Sparrow Press, 1975.

Sachs, Nelly. *O The Chimneys!* New York: Farrar, Straus, Giroux, 1967.

Schwarz-Bart, Andre. *The Last of the Just*. New York: Bantam, 1961.

Skloot, Robert, ed. *The Theatre of the Holocaust*. Madison: University of Wisconsin Press, 1982.

Snodgrass, W. D. *The Führer Bunker*. Brockport, N.Y.: Boa Editions, 1977.

Steiner, Jean François. *Treblinka*. New York: Simon and Schuster, 1967.

Styron, William. *Sophie's Choice*. New York: Random House, 1979.

Uris, Leon. *QB VII*. New York: Bantam, 1970.

Volavkova, Hana, ed. *I Never Saw Another Butterfly*. Translated by Jeanne Nemcova. New York: McGraw-Hill, 1964.

Wiesel, Elie. *Ani Maamin*. New York: Random House, 1973.

———. *The Gates of the Forest*. New York: Holt, Rinehart and Winston, 1966.

———. *Night*. New York: Hill and Wang, 1960.

Wiesenthal, Simon. *Max and Helen*. New York: Morrow, 1981.

# Chapter 27

# The Poetry of the Holocaust

## *Gloria Young*

The poetry of the Holocaust stems from events beyond the imagination's power to conceive, horrors unprecedented in history, horrors beyond the power of language to articulate. Stephen Spender quotes T. W. Adorno's statement that "after Auschwitz poetry can no longer be written."[1] Yet men and women and children wrote poems while in the ghettos, transports, and death camps. They wrote under conditions of starvation, torture, and epidemics, always as displaced human beings in an intellectual and cultural vacuum. For some, poetry was their last gasp before annihilation. For those who survived, poetry became their individual statements of the ordeal of surviving. For others who did not directly experience the Holocaust, writing poetry became their moral response, an obligation to tell the story as testimony to and remembrance of the victims. Tadeusz Różewicz considers it a miracle that poets of the Holocaust could write poetry and that others can still write it:

> I suspect
> they themselves don't realize
> what an unusual unexpected beautiful
> staggering ridiculous monstrous
> phenomenon they are.[2]

Stephen Spender suggests that the Jewish tradition of poetry may have contributed to this miraculous phenomenon: "In the Old Testament poetry is not an end in itself but the realization in language of a vision of life as old as the nation's history. . . . He [the Jewish poet] is the voice of the people, [his poetry]

an enduring attempt to turn ashes into an eternal light.''[3] There is a connection
between the Yiddish words *muze* (Muse) and *muz* (must). Writing was a necessity—an expression of the urge to life, a means of resistance, and a shield against
meaninglessness (see Alan Mintz's *Hurban: Responses to Catastrophe in Hebrew
Literature* for a discussion of Holocaust literature against its background of
Jewish traditions). Before readers can fully understand Holocaust poetry, they
need some background as to the conditions under which it was written, the
motivations for writing it, problems of translation, its unique aesthetic principles,
and suggestions as to how it may be read and judged.

Because poetry is often short and intense, requiring less time and materials
than other forms of writing, the poets wrote when they could on whatever they
could find. They traded food for stubs of pencils and wrote on prayer books,
prison walls, or fragments of paper. Abraham Sutzkever in the poem ''Self-
Portrait'' says:

> Once hidden in a cellar
> beside a corpse laid out like a sheet of paper
> illumined by phosphorous snow from the ceiling—
> I wrote a poem with a piece of coal
> on the paper body of my neighbour.[4]

Poetry was difficult to write and even more difficult—and dangerous—to
transmit. Nevertheless, the poetry was disseminated by underground publications, memorized and transmitted verbally, smuggled out, buried in metal cans,
found in pockets of the dead, or left on walls and bunkers. Many manuscripts,
however, were confiscated or lost at the author's death. Some were destroyed
by the author for fear of reprisal. Some were burned as buildings were burned;
others were consigned to the flames by the Nazis or the local populations. Some
have doubtless never been unearthed. Some are mere fragments. Dan Pagis
concludes the poem ''Written in Pencil in the Sealed Railway-Car'' with the
lines

> here in this carload
> with abel my son
> if you see my other son
> cain son of man
> tell him that i[5]

The lack of punctuation and the unfinished line at the end shock the reader with
the sense that the poet was unable to finish the poem because of death, discovery,
brutality, or simply because he could not continue due to the enormity of what
he was describing.

Holocaust poets wrote for many reasons. A primary reason was to give testimony to the lives and culture that were being annihilated, to bear witness as
a means of assuring some kind of immortality for those who had not even a

grave or marker to show they had once lived. Walt Whitman in his preface to *Leaves of Grass* instructs the "greatest poets" to drag "the dead out of their coffins" and stand them again on their feet. The poet must say to the past, "Rise and walk before me that I may realize you." Susan Sontag, who calls the Holocaust the "supreme tragic event of modern times," says that the "only response is to continue to hold the event in mind, to remember it." Czeslaw Milosz, Nobel Prize winner, comments in his *Nobel Lecture* that "the number of books . . . which deny that the Holocaust ever took place" indicates the "insanity" of those who write them. He adds, "Those who are alive receive a mandate from those who are silent forever. They can fulfill their duties only by trying to reconstruct precisely things as they were."[6]

Another reason for writing poetry lay in the poet's struggle to find value and meaning in a universe of pain and grief and despair. Harold Bloom in his introduction to Geoffrey Hill's poetry says that poetry became the poet's "Word, not in the sense of Logos but in the Hebraic sense of *davhar*, a word that is also an act."[7]

Some, pushed to the limits of their resources, wrote as a bulwark against the fear and loneliness of imminent death, while others used their poems as weapons in the struggle for survival, as prods to incite individual and united resistance. A few poets called for revenge, putting an entire civilization on trial and finding it guilty. Others, suffering from a loss of faith in a God who could and would allow such events to be perpetrated, battled with or turned against God, while some continued to pray to God for solace if not salvation.

Finally, poets who were neither victims nor survivors of the Holocaust felt compelled to resurrect and purify a language decimated by atrocity. Jacob Glatstein calls upon the poet to "take the faintest Yiddish speech" and "make it holy again." The poet must be "on guard" because the "wasteland calls." The poet must "sentence the entire horizon to meaning."[8] Lawrence Langer calls Nelly Sachs "a gardener in the greenhouse of our verbal and spiritual resources to express and transcend the wound of atrocity."[9]

Always there is the problem that much of the poetry is translated from other languages: Yiddish, Hebrew, German, French, and others. Nathan Ausubel agrees with Franz Werfel's remark that "translated poems are an impossibility." If they happen, it is because the translator has become a "poet in his own right. . . . Amethysts cannot be translated. Similar pressure upon another crystalline substance, however, may create a topaz."[10] The problem becomes even more difficult when the translator must move from one language family to another, as from Hungarian (Finno-Ugrian) to English (Indo-European). There are more difficulties encountered than in translating prose because of the subtlety of poetic rhythms, rhyme, connotations, allusions, and idiom. A gap always remains, an incomplete closure between the original poem and the translation, a distance never quite bridged. The translation is, finally, secondhand. In a sense this same distance is felt between the words of a survivor of the Holocaust and those of one whose experience is secondhand.

Although the aesthetic principles and literary styles of the poets vary widely, certain characteristics are pervasive. First is a subject matter that is unspeakable. The horror is so great, the deeds so unbelievable, that language is stricken with horror, disintegrated, stretched to the breaking point, shattered into syllables. Paul Celan, in the poem "Tübingen, January," powerfully illustrates this maiming of words when he calls to mind a man who wears the beard of biblical patriarchs collapsing into stuttering.[11] The reader must confront what is not said, what is not sayable. Using the image of a hooked fish, János Pilinszky advises the poet what the poem must communicate:

> Not the respiration. The gasping.
> . . . Not the gesture. Not the hysteria.
> The silence of the hook is what you must note.[12]

In the best of the poetry the diction is bare, and the word is naked, wearing no embellishments. By academic standards, some of the poetry would seem to be nonpoetry, a documentary recital of events with as little gratuitous horror as possible. Compression, ellipsis, and understatement keep the lid on what threatens to boil over into hysteria. The imagery is not literary but realistic: ovens, smoke, barbed wire, chimneys, hunger, pits, stench, cold, fire, ash, dust, grave, stone, crows, wound, blood. Often there is little evidence of poetic craft, and sometimes there is not enough distancing of the poet from his subject, but the real strength is in the mute, inarticulate level that lies just below the surface.

Frequently the poetry is written with a terrible, deadly irony, as when Irving Feldman ("The Pripet Marshes") returns the dead back "to the *shtetlach* and ghettos,"[13] restoring a people and culture now lost. In a similar vein Dan Pagis in "Draft of a Reparations Agreement" promises to return the "scream back into the throat. / The gold teeth back to the gums. / The smoke back to the chimney."[14] Another kind of irony lies in a grim imitation of the Nazis' treatment of the Jews as nonhuman objects. Ephim Fogel in "Shipment to Maidanek" lists the merchandise:

> Item: six surgeons, slightly mangled hands.
> Item: three poets, hopelessly insane.
> Item: a Russian mother and her child,
> the former with five gold teeth and usable shoes,
> the latter with seven dresses, peasant-styled.
> Item: another hundred thousand Jews:
> . . . . . . . . . . . . . . . . . . . .
> They are sorted and marked— . . .
> The books must be balanced, the disposition stated.[15]

It is difficult to read this poetry and even more difficult to judge it by ordinary literary criteria. Poetry with such a subject verges on the obscene. Still, the poems are here, like a veil between the reader and the dead, and should be read respectfully, with compassion and humility, as one would listen to a dying person's words. The best of the poets do not ask us to understand how such events could happen; they merely want us to hear and remember.

The bibliographic essay that follows is divided into three sections according to the poets' closeness to the actual events: those who did not survive, survivors, and others. Unfortunately, in a chapter of this length only a selected number of poets can be discussed. In the case of poets who did not survive, some of the poems were chosen because they were of powerful influence during the time in which they were written. Others chosen are poets whose work is strong in a literary sense and whose body of work is substantial.

## POETS WHO DID NOT SURVIVE

Poets whose poetry survived although they themselves did not include Hirsh Glik, Hannah Senesh, Miklós Radnóti, Gertrud Kolmar, Yitzhak Katzenelson, and the child-poets of Terezín. Two young poets who were killed in the Holocaust were Hirsh Glik and Hannah Senesh. Each of them is remembered primarily for one poem that stirred and inspired the Jews to resistance. Glik, who escaped from the Vilna ghetto was killed either in a German death camp (according to Ausubel) or while fighting with the partisans (according to Schmuller). He left behind the poem "We Survive!" sometimes translated as "We Are Here!" The best translation of this poem is by Ruth Rubin (Ausubel and Ausubel, *A Treasury of Jewish Poetry*, 270–71). The poem was set to music and became the most popular song to emerge from the Holocaust, translated into more than thirty continental languages. It is a stirring call to men everywhere to fight. The ballad is not great poetry, but as the battle-song of the Jewish underground, "inscribed with blood and lead," it provided a call to resistance that was heard everywhere in Europe. Hannah Senesh's poem "Blessed Is the Match" also served to ignite the "flames of underground resistance against the Nazis." Senesh escaped from Hungary to Palestine, where she joined an underground operation to rescue those in the death camps. She was parachuted into Hungary, was caught by the Nazis, and perished in a death camp. The "Blessed Match" of the title is she herself: Blessed the heart with strength to stop its beating for the sake of honor. Blessed is the match consumed in kindling flame.[16]

Miklós Radnóti, a Hungarian poet converted to Christianity, was a published poet before the Holocaust. His strongest poems, however, were found in the pockets of his trenchcoat as he lay in a mass grave at Abda, Hungary, beaten to death. The subject matter of these poems consists of almost surreal images of a world gone mad, of the past's reason falling apart, of his forthcoming death, and of the inadequacy of language to express the horrors of executions, forced marches, loss of comrades, and personal terror. He says in "The Seventh Eclogue" that he writes poems the way he lives, blind, in darkness, like a virtual animal. The title poem "Clouded Sky" makes inanimate objects animate and terrifying, with death everywhere, howling in the forest. In the poem "Only

Skin and Bones and Pain,'' the poet, who has been stripped of everything save his intellect, pleads for words not to abandon him. This is poetry in extremis.[17]

Gertrud Kolmar, a poet whose previously published work was destroyed during *Kristallnacht*, continued to write during her imprisonment in a forced-labor camp and later in Auschwitz. Born of a comfortable, middle-class family in Berlin, she had refused to leave when she might have been able to, choosing to stay with and care for her aging and sick father, who was later killed at Theresienstadt. After her death, her Holocaust poems were discovered and published in *Dark Soliloquy*. Kolmar's poetry transcends her suffering and moves toward hope. Throughout her work she writes of how the Jewish people are persecuted but continue to survive. In the poem ''The Jewish Woman'' Kolmar writes as one who endures because, she says, ''in me the altar fires ignite / Of Deborah and her tribe'' (109). In ''We Jews'' she prays to ''be the voice that echoes down the shaft of all eternity'' in remembrance of those whose ''throat is gagged,'' whose ''bleeding cry [is] suppressed'' (113–15). Her poetry changed as her sufferings increased. Gone was the strict traditional form of her earlier work. In its place was a poetic line stretched to the limit of what one can say in a breath. Her poetry became more forceful, elevated, and scriptural—even more so as she learned Hebrew and began to write in the language and tradition of the Old Testament. In her poems she expresses her desire ''to raise [her] voice to be a blazing torch,'' but she feels that she cannot. The poem concludes: ''And I can feel the fist that drags my weeping head toward the hill of ashes.''[18] With her death at Auschwitz her ''blazing torch'' was not extinguished but lives on in her poetry.

Perhaps the poems most useful to the student, teacher, or researcher of the Holocaust are those of Yitzhak Katzenelson, especially his last volume, *The Song of the Murdered Jewish People*, first published in 1945, one year after his death in the gas chambers of Auschwitz. Katzenelson and an internee who survived placed the poems in three bottles and buried them where they were concealed until after the liberation. The book, an elegiac epic chronicle in fifteen cantos, composed in an internment camp at Vittel in France, laments the slaughter of the largest Jewish community in Europe, the Warsaw Jews. Katzenelson writes firsthand of the events, having been there and having participated in the cultural and underground activities of the Warsaw ghetto. One can grasp the comprehensive historical scope of the chronicle through a brief synopsis of the cantos, which are powerfully and dramatically moving, filled with immediate details, and sustained with a compressed, understated tone.

The first two cantos (''Sing!'' and ''I Play'') introduce the poems with God's command to the poet to sing. The poet questions how he can sing in the face of such horror, but he calls for a harp (metaphor for poetry and song), and in canto 2 he plays and sings, attended by a throng greater than Ezekiel's valley of bones. ''O My Agonies'' (canto 3) describes an *Aktion*, and canto 4 deportations. Canto 5 presents ''The Meeting in the Kehillah,'' which dramatizes the agonizing dilemma of Adam Czerniakow, head of the Warsaw Judenrat, who was told that six thousand Jews for deportation were not enough; there must be ten thousand. Canto 6, "The First Ones," describes the children in the orphanages, the first to perish, while 7 and 8 deal with the Warsaw Jews, some of whom learned of the fate in store for them. Canto 9 is a meditation on heavens empty of God. Canto 10, "The Beginning of the End," describes the yellow star, the harassment, the torture, and the killing, while 11 is a charge to those remaining never to forget. The next canto, "Mila Street," states that after 350,000 from Warsaw alone had been killed or deported, all questions about the existence of God are moot. Cantos 13 and 14 describe the Warsaw ghetto uprising, and 15, "It's All Over," is an account of the end. The poet charges Gentiles who witnessed the events with collaboration and indifference.[19] There was a people, laments the poet, and now it is no more. N. H. Rosenbloom says that the "preeminence" of this poem is due to "its primeval force, unsophisticated veracity, unvarnished quality and visceral simplicity."[20] This is a poem to be included in any study of Holocaust poetry.

It is fitting to conclude this section of Holocaust poetry written by those who did not survive with a selection of poems written by children, children who lived a very little while and then were no more. The poems written by the children of Terezín, collected and saved by a teacher in one of the camp's children's homes, give the reader a simple, innocent, and moving testimony of the fact that these lives did exist. Hana Volavkova's edition, *I Never Saw Another Butterfly: Children's Drawings and Poems from Theresienstadt Concentration Camp, 1942–44*, includes an epilogue by Jirí Weil and annotated catalogs of the drawings and of the poems. The camp was established by Reinhard Heydrich in 1941 as a Jewish ghetto. The children deported there had already suffered humiliation, displacement, and loss before they arrived at Terezín. While at the camp they were forced to work from eighty to one hundred hours per week, with those over fourteen years of age working the same hours and type of work as the adults. From Terezín they were shipped further east to the death camps, usually Auschwitz. Of the fifteen thousand children under the age of fifteen who were sent to the camp, only one hundred survived.

The poems, some written by younger children in the form of nursery rhymes and all of them by children no more than sixteen, reflect the suffering of youngsters subjected to flies, bedbugs, hunger, dirt, disease, homesickness, grief at the loss of family and familiar surroundings, and shock at the imprisonment, brutality, and death that were all around them. They tell of lining up for skimpy food rations and watching as people lay dying in the streets. Images of fear fill many of the drawings that accompany the poems—fear of the Nazi commandant and his guards, fear of the night, fear of separation from mother or father, fear of the omnipresent threat of deportation. There is also hope, expressed in quatrains that speak of going away one day to lands where no one hates another, expressed also in lovely watercolors that capture the beauty of the Czech spring with its flowers and butterflies. There is also the reality, offered by Pavel Friedmann (1921–1944) in a poem titled "The Butterfly," that such beautiful creatures, like children, do not survive inside the walls of Terezín. The fifteen thousand children that passed through this transit ghetto left behind only their poems and silence, captured by this magnificent collection, which closes with the poignant drawing by nine-year-old Ruth Heinova of a little girl holding a parcel as she waits behind a barbed-wire fence. Jiri Weil says of the children's poetry: "They saw reality, but they still maintained their childish outlook, an outlook of truth."[21]

## POETS WHO SURVIVED

Of the numerous poets who survived the Holocaust years, some of the best are Paul Celan (Romania and France), Abba Kovner (Lithuania and Israel), Primo Levi (Italy), Dan Pagis (Bukovina and Israel), Tadeusz Różewicz (Poland), Nelly Sachs (Germany), Abraham Sutzkever (Lithuania and Israel), and Elie Wiesel (Romania, France and the United States). All of these poets have contributed a substantial body of work of high literary quality, having won top national and international literary prizes, including two Nobel Prizes (Sachs and Wiesel).

Paul Celan (1920–1970), pseudonym of Paul Antschel, was the son of Austrian Jews in Cernowitz, Romania. His parents were killed in an extermination camp, and Paul was sent to a labor camp. He survived the Holocaust physically but was deeply scarred emotionally, undergoing periodic bouts of deep depression, and finally committed suicide at the age of forty-nine. One of the most important poets of the Holocaust, he made original contributions to modern poetry, especially in his use of aesthetic distancing and his use of language. He compounds, splits, and leaves hanging the words he uses, creating hiatuses, silences, and dislocations. He describes his poems as "desperate dialogue" between his voice and a "receptive you."[22] He is obsessed with recreating the events of the Holocaust, using surreal images of blinding, shutting in, beating, maiming, and burning. His poetry—obscure, dense, stark, ambiguous—is difficult to read and understand. Because he believed that "existing resources of language" were inadequate to describe the Holocaust, his poetry is "close to the unutterable because it has passed through it and come out on the other side."[23] Michael Hamburger says that the poems exhibit a negative theology, due to his having to "come to grips with the experience of being God-forsaken. Negation and blasphemy were the means by which [he] could be true to that experience and yet maintain the kind of intimate dialogue with God characteristic of Jewish devotion."[24]

In *Selected Poems*, "Fugue of Death" is written in the musical form of different instruments taking up and developing a theme in succession and counterpoint. The poem begins:

Black milk of daybreak we drink it at nightfall
we drink it at noon in the morning we drink it at night

> drink it and drink it
> we are digging a grave in the sky it is ample to lie there
> A man in the house he plays with the serpents he writes
> he writes when the night falls to Germany your golden hair Margarete
> he writes it and walks from the house the stars glitter he whistles his dogs up
> he whistles his Jews out and orders a grave to be dug in the earth
> he commands us strike up for the dance

The black milk of daybreak is a reversal of the image of nourishment (milk, dawn, mother); instead, there is black milk (bitter gall or bile) that is drunk continuously. The commandant in the house writes to his golden-haired Margarete while ordering the Jews to dance as they dig their graves. The poem progresses with variations of the opening refrain and repositioning of the images. In stanza 2 the image of the Shulamith is juxtaposed with that of Margarete as the Jews "dig a grave in the sky." In the next stanza the man "grabs at the iron in his belt and swings it and blue / are his eyes" as he orders the Jews to "stab deeper your spades . . . and play on for the dancing." The last two stanzas counterpoint additional variations with "a master from Germany death comes with eyes that are blue," and the poem ends,

> your golden hair Margarete
> your ashen hair Shulamith.

Margarete, personification of blonde German ideal womanhood, is in stark contrast with the ashen-haired, cremated Jewess.[25]

Some poetry about the Holocaust is like prayer. Abba Kovner, touring the United States in 1972 and reading his poems in Hebrew, said: "When I write I am like a man praying." He went on to say that poetry is the one "place in the world without cemeteries."[26] Stephen Spender in his introduction to *Selected Poems of Abba Kovner and Nelly Sachs* commends Kovner for replacing gross fact with the "extreme agony of death-bed prayer."[27]

Kovner came from Vilna, capital of Lithuania and a leading center of Jewish culture before the Holocaust. From the Vilna ghetto Kovner wrote the first Jewish call to resistance that he was later to lead, having escaped through the sewers of Vilna into the forest. He writes of the terrible choice the escape posed for him due to the Nazis' policy of collective responsibility. Choosing to escape and fight, he knew that families and other Jews would be killed in reprisal. He survived the Holocaust and finally reached Palestine, where he edited writings by partisans. His poetry is filled with allusions to the Hebrew Old Testament and Hebrew history that the unversed reader may be unable to recognize.

Kovner tells of the young Jewish girl who crawled over thousands of bodies in the pits at Ponar and made her way back to the Vilna ghetto to tell them that forty thousand Jews were dead. Kovner is haunted by her face, and her voice is heard in his work. The "little sister" of the long poem *My Little Sister* is a composite figure of this half-crazed girl, his own younger sister, the "fragile sister'' of the Song of Songs, and all the little sisters who were killed in the Holocaust. In this work Kovner uses the *piyut* or liturgical prayer poem. The religious imagery and the intricate variations of rhyme and rhythm, revealing impressive technical skill, are extremely difficult to render in translation or in paraphrase.

Poem 2 of *My Little Sister* relates the little sister's being brought to the Dominican convent for refuge. At the outer wall the bell was rung and

> Nine sainted Sisters
> hurried to the gate. Their voices withered.
> Naked. Braids on her breast—
> my fragile sister!
> Standing at the door.[28]

Poem 10 describes the brother outside the wall looking at the statue of Christ within the wall:

> From his suffering image,
> from the feet of the cold statue,
> look, with a delicate hand
> dust is swept
> into a gold coffer—
> only my crucified memory outside the fence!
> In the court,
> in a private language, my sister plays
> with another god.[29]

The convent that gives temporary shelter is, however, out of touch with the actuality of the real world. Edward Alexander's commentary on this poem makes clear that the convent refuge was finally betrayal: ''The group that took her to the convent was itself later shot by the mobile killing units,'' and the little sister was ultimately ''turned over to the Germans by the nuns and eventually turned into ashes.''[30]

Kovner tries to bridge the world of Vilna and of Sinai, the Jews of Europe and the people of Israel, to rescue the dead by bringing about a mystic transplantation in the new land. This is the theme of the long poem *A Canopy in the Desert*, in which the canopy is that used in Jewish marriages, while the desert is where Moses led the Hebrews out of Egypt, where he made his Covenant with God, and where the State of Israel fought for its right to be. In the poem the narrator embodies all the dead of the ghettos, the partisan forests, and the Sinai desert as he takes the reader through the three most significant events in Jewish history: the Covenant of Sinai, the Holocaust, and the creation of Israel. The narrator symbolizes the people of Israel—wanderer, poet, survivor, bridegroom—and the bride is the land of Israel. Edward Alexander in *The Resonance of Dust* gives a superb summary of this poem: ''Kovner, participant in the two most important . . . events of modern . . . Jewish history, seeks to join the Holocaust and the return to the homeland by a prodigious feat of poetic imagination, which steps into the void left by the divine silence to affirm that the Jewish people shall not die, but live."[31]

Primo Levi (1919–1987), born in Turin, Italy, was a chemist and prolific writer of memoirs and autobiographical accounts of the Holocaust, as well as novels, essays, short stories, and poetry. His collected poems are in the volume *Shema*, the Hebrew imperative for "Hear!" the first word of prayer affirming God's oneness. This prayer was on the lips of many of the six million as they died. Levi was a major literary figure who won Italy's Strega Prize, the Viareggio Prize, and the Campiello Prize and shared with Saul Bellow the Kenneth B. Smilen fiction award.

In 1943 Levi quit his job and joined the Italian partisans fighting German and Italian Fascist forces. With the collapse of Mussolini's regime in 1943, he was captured and turned over to the Nazi SS, loaded into a cattle car with 650 other Jews, and taken to Auschwitz. Of these 650, only about 20 survived. Because he was healthy and strong, he was sent to slave-labor camp at Monowitz-Buna, was tattooed, had his head shaved, and was assigned to outdoor labor. Later he was transferred to the laboratory because of his scientific background. Throughout the ordeal his will to live was sustained by his determination to bear witness to what had happened, which he accomplished in *Survival in Auschwitz*, the first volume of an autobiographical trilogy. His work, without self-pity or personal bitterness, is a psychological study transformed to art. He told the *New York Times* in December 1984: "After Auschwitz, I had an absolute need to write . . . Not only as a moral duty but as a psychological need."

The poem "Shema," in the *Collected Poems of Primo Levi*, addresses the readers who are secure and well fed in their warm houses, surrounded by friendly faces.

> Who labours in the mud
> Who fights for a crust of bread
> Who dies at a yes or a no
> Consider whether this is a woman,
> Without hair or name
> With no more strength to remember
> Eyes empty and womb cold
> Consider that this has been:
> . . . Engrave them on your hearts /
> . . . Repeat them to your children."[32]

The poem "Buna" is about Levi's fellow prisoners, broken in body and in spirit: "You multitudes with dead faces . . . Another day of suffering is born." The poem describes a man reduced to nothingness:

> In your breast you carry cold, hunger, nothing.
> You have broken what's left of the courage within you.
> Colourless one, you were a strong man,

but now,

> Forsaken man who can no longer weep,
> So poor you no longer grieve,
> So tired you no longer fear.
> Quenched once-strong man.[33]

Those who have read prose accounts of the Holocaust recognize in these quiet, understated lines the plight of what was called in concentration-camp jargon the *musselman*, the man with deadened senses and deadened mind: the living dead, who no longer waited for anything, not even death.

In another poem, "Reveille," the poet describes the "brutal nights" filled with "Dense violent dreams . . . / To return; to eat; to tell the story. / Until the dawn command / Sounded brief, low: / *'Wstawac'* / And the heart cracked in the breast."[34] The word *Wstawac* means "to stand up or rise," the call to begin another brutal day, or the call to execution. The poem's second stanza takes place after the Holocaust, with the poet at home, his belly full, his story told. But he still hears "The strange command: / *'Wstawac.'* " In a poem "For Adolf Eichmann" (1960), Levi addresses Eichmann during his trial:

> What will you say now, before our assembly?
> Will you swear by a god? What god?
> . . . . . . . . . . . . . . . . . . . .
> Or will you at the end, like the industrious man
> Whose life was too brief for his long art,
> Lament your sorry work unfinished,
> The thirteen million still alive?

The final stanza curses Eichmann: "We do not wish you death. / May you live longer than anyone ever lived: / May you live sleepless five million nights," to be visited by everyone who saw "shutting behind him, the door that blocked the way back, / Saw it grow dark . . . the air fill with death."[35] Levi's poem reveals the restraint of a man who, with a terrible will, refuses to let his repressed emotions come through, who controls what is barely controllable.

In *Survival in Auschwitz* Levi describes successful and unsuccessful methods of survival. Telling the story, writing as psychological release, was his way to survive. His aesthetic of using reason and control to distance himself from the material, of understanding and compressing what is unutterable, is what makes his poetry powerful. In the afterword Levi says that he preferred the "peaceful sober speech of the witness, not the lamenting one of the victim, nor the angry one of the avenger." The poetry is not, however, "peaceful." By stifling the anger and grief, he turned his emotions inward where they became self-destructive.

Dan Pagis's *Points of Departure* is aptly titled, as it reveals many points of departure within his own life. Born in 1930 in Bukovina in a Germanized Jewish home, he remembers being hidden from the Nazis in his grandfather's study when he was nine years old. From such memoirs his poetry departs, leaving behind the "transparent wake of the past." He spent his adolescent years in a Nazi concentration camp and finally reached Palestine in 1946, where he learned Hebrew in an amazingly short time. He immediately began to write poetry in his new language, as if to cast off the German tongue with all its associations. Pagis became so thoroughly immersed in the tradition of Hebrew that, according to Robert Alter, he has become the "foremost living authority on the poetics of Hebrew literature." Alter discusses the radical displacement that governs Pagis's poetry, "from the repeated and often flaunted effects of defamiliarization in his imagery to his eerie refractions of the cataclysm that swept away European Jewry."[36]

Like other Holocaust poets, Pagis has difficulty finding language to express the inexpressible. He allows language to trail off, with the thought unfinished. He employs bitter irony along with a flat, understated tone, and he displaces his own voice into that of avatars: Abel and Cain, animals, cavemen, the creator, the murdered. In the poem "Autobiography," the narrator and first victim, the first source of grief, is Abel. Sadly, Abel multiplies even faster than Cain and Cain's legions.[37] In "Testimony" Pagis presents a powerful image of the victims' meeting with God. Both are constituted of smoke. As the victim floats up to God, there is nothing for the poet but the abyss and silence.[38]

Tadeusz Różewicz is a non-Jewish Polish poet and playwright. Born in 1921, he served during 1943–44 in the Home Army, the military underground that fought against the Germans, where he witnessed, firsthand, atrocities. His own brother was shot by the Gestapo in 1944. Różewicz became the voice of his generation. M. J. Krynski and R. A. Maguire say of Różewicz that he regards the "entire cultural heritage of the Western World as a construct of semblances and deceptions that conceals a colossal lie." Spiritual values as well as art are illusions. Man may yearn for moral, national, and religious values, but "there are no Arcadias." Różewicz expressed the principles of his poetic work in a statement he made in 1965: "I consciously gave up the privileges that accrue to poetry [the traditional resources of aesthetic principles] . . . and I returned to my rubbish heap."[39]

Instead of a privilege, Różewicz finds speech so difficult that he sometimes reverts to unintelligible stuttering. Critics have labeled this kind of poetry "naked" poetry, poetry stripped of metaphor, myth, obscurity, symbolism, logical progression, euphony, punctuation—everything that in the past was expected of poetry. What is left is an austere, groping, understated antipoetry, a poetry "for the horror-stricken."[40] Michael Hamburger says that Różewicz revolted against the fact that poetry "had survived the end of the world, as though nothing had happened."[41] The poem "For Some Time Now" suggests the futility of poetry's holding off the void: Poets "toss off / new books / in a hurry as though / they wished to stuff a hole with / paper."[42] The title poem, "The Survivor," is stark in its simplicity:

> I am twenty-four
> led to slaughter
> I survived

In view of what he has seen, he finds that labels that distinguish man and beast, light and dark, virtue and crime, truth and falsehood are empty. A teacher is needed to "once again name things and concepts." The poem ends with the repetition of the same three lines with which it began. In another poem one finds the poet desperately trying to rename ordinary people (his father and an old woman), objects (tables, windows, apples, trees), and concepts in an effort to reestablish value ("In the Midst of Life.")[43]

Nelly Sachs, winner of the Nobel Prize in 1966, published poetry in an attempt to "assimilate the Holocaust into the poetic imagination and into Jewish history."[44] Collections of her work translated into English include *O the Chimneys!* (1967), *The Seeker and Other Poems* (1970), and the posthumous *Selected Poems of Abba Kovner and Nelly Sachs* (1971). There are many excellent critical discussions of her work, especially Sidra Dekoven Ezrahi's *By Words Alone*, Lawrence L. Langer's *Versions of Survival*, Alvin H. Rosenfeld's *A Double Dying*, and Edward Alexander's *The Resonance of Dust*.

Sachs continued to write in her native German after escaping, at the last possible moment, from Germany to Sweden in 1940. Like that of the best of Holocaust poets, her work is free from excessive horror, sentimentalism, apologetic, or didacticism. Two of her strongest poems—"A Dead Child Speaks" and "Already Embraced by the Arm of Heavenly Solace"—are universal expressions of the anguish of mothers who have lost their children. Many of her poems deal with the problem of finding language to deal with death and night. Not only are the victims in their graves or in the smoke ascending, but so too (in "Glowing Enigmas II" and "Then Wrote the Scribe of the Zohar")[45] is human speech. In another poem, "And Unwrap, As Though It Were Linen Sheets," the alphabet is carefully removed from cloth, as if it were coming from a transformed chrysalis. Sachs's poetry affirms that language can be resurrected to create a new world. The last poem in *The Seeker* acknowledges the black night in chaos, but ends with hope that the word, mortally struck by silence, will bloom again.[46]

Sachs says of her work that it is "always designed to raise the unutterable to a transcendental level, so as to make it bearable and in this night of nights to give a hint of the holy darkness in which quiver and arrow are hidden," a reference to Isaiah's "The Lord puts the arrow he had used back in its quiver so that it may remain in darkness."[47] Sachs will not allow hope to replace despair, but she will not give up hoping. Although the words *death* and *night* appear frequently in her poems, so does the image of the butterfly, signifying birth and metamorphosis.

While some critics have described her work as the language of screams of expiration or as the lyrics of death, the reader cannot overlook her attempt to salvage language from silence, to rescue it from the barbed wire of the concentrationary universe.

A major Yiddish writer of the *Churban*, Abraham Sutzkever regards his poetic mission as creating a link between the living and the dead. The volume *Burnt Pearls: Ghetto Poems* serves to make fast the link, a chain of words that in the title poem of the volume he compares to burnt pearls. The persona of the poem says that it is not just because his words are like "broken hands grasping for aid" or like "teeth on the prowl in darkness" that his words are a "substitute" for his world:

> It is because your sounds
> glint like burnt pearls
> discovered in an extinguished pyre
> And no one—not even I—shredded by time
> can recognize the woman drenched in flame
> for all that remains of her now
> are these grey pearls
> smouldering in the ash—[48]

The charred pearls/teeth/words remain as objects of beauty, as memorials to the dead, among whom was his mother, who perished at the hands of the Nazis.

Sutzkever wrote his ghetto poems while he was in the Vilna ghetto and continued to write them after he escaped from the ghetto and became a leader of the partisans. After the liberation he was able to rescue many valuable documents and later was a witness at the Nuremberg trials in 1946. He settled in Palestine in 1947 and continued writing poetry as well as editing the Yiddish literary quarterly *Di goldene Keyt*.

A mark of his poetry is its insistence on poetry as redemptive, as being able to save or redeem from death. Sutzkever believed that he was giving the dead a poetic grave, an enduring memorial. The transformational character of language is symbolized in the poem "I Am Lying in This Coffin," in which the poet escapes a roundup by hiding in a coffin. The imagery of the poem converts the coffin to an ark for the muse from which speech "still moves into song."[49] The origins of the ghetto poems are concrete, factual, powerful. The poem "For a Comrade" tells the story of the poet's taking bloodstained bread from a "murdered comrade at the barbed wire," promising the comrade that he will "demand of the world a reckoning. . . . If I fall as you fell . . . let another swallow my word as I, your bread."[50]

An important poem by Sutzkever widely circulated during the war years was

"The Leaden Plates of Romm's Printing Works," in which the fighters, "dreamers who had to become soldiers," stole the lead plates of the printing works to "convert spirit of lead into bullets."

> One molten line from Babylon, another
> from Poland, flowed into the same mold.
> Jewish bravery once hidden in words
> must now strike back with shot![51]

One of the most important, prolific, and influential writers of the Holocaust is Elie Wiesel. He is primarily a novelist and essayist whose works are concerned with religious, moral, and ethical questions stemming from the Holocaust. Winner of the Nobel Peace Prize in 1986 and of the Congressional Gold Medal of Achievement from President Reagan in 1985, he has devoted his life to witnessing to what he and millions of Jews and non-Jews underwent. His entire community of Sighet was deported by the Nazis. He alone of his entire family survived Birkenau, Auschwitz, Buna, and Buchenwald concentration camps. Although not principally a poet, he is included here because the poetry in *Ani Maamin: A Song Lost and Found Again* and passages in *Night* and many of his other writings are indistinguishable from poetry in their emotional intensity, compression, and spiritual epiphanies.

*Ani Maamin* comes from one of the thirteen articles of faith of Maimonides: *Ani maamin beviat ha-Mashiah* (I believe in the coming of the Messiah). In the ghettos and camps the phrase became a song of resistance for the stubbornly pious Jews. It was the hymn of the Warsaw ghetto martyrs. Wiesel's *Ani Maamin* is a verse cantata set to music by Darius Milhaud. Its cast is a chorus, a narrator, a voice from heaven, and Abraham, Isaac, and Jacob. The three patriarchs tell God of the horrors going on in the world—Treblinka, Auschwitz, Majdanek, Belsen, Sobibor, Buchenwald, "nocturnal capitals in a strange kingdom . . . where death as sovereign [has] appropriated God's face"[52]—and they ask "Why? Why, O Lord? O Father, why?"[53] The three patriarchs narrate specific scenes of death and cruelty, "But heaven is silent, and its silence is a wall."[54] Their pleading, weeping, and anger are unheeded as God remains silent, unmoved. Then a Voice speaks: "The Master of the World / Disposes of the world. / His creatures . . . Accept his laws / Without a question,"[55] to which Abraham replies, "Have I the right to plead for Sodom— / But not for a million children, / Innocent children?" The Voice tells him that the divine thought is "unfathomable . . . blind, / Man plunges into it /Unknowing of its outcome."[56] Then Abraham asks the unanswerable question:

> But what kind of messiah
> Is a messiah
> Who demands
> Six million dead
> Before he reveals himself?[57]

and the voice of the angel rebukes him: "Does God owe you an accounting? . . . What about man? / What have you done with my creation?" The three questioners decide that they must return to the victims and tell them that "all is lost . . . insane," so that, as Jacob says, "they will die / With their eyes open, / Facing emptiness," to which Isaac adds: "They will depart this world / Repudiating it."[58] The long poem ends, however, with an assertion of belief, close to the existential assertion of Paul Tillich's belief in a God above God, of the necessity of the "courage to be . . . in spite of . . . God and man."

| Abraham: | May you be blessed |
| | Israel |
| | For your faith in God— |
| | In spite of God. |
| Isaac: | May you be blessed |
| | Israel |
| | For your faith in man— |
| | In spite of man. |
| Jacob: | May you be blessed |
| | Israel |
| | For your faith in Israel— |
| | In spite of man and God.[59] |

Wiesel's total body of work is filled with anguish and sorrow but also with hope and affirmation. Although God remains silent, as in the book of Lamentations, the sufferers move from despair to prayer. The honesty and intensity of the poetry leave the reader with an unforgettable and valuable experience.

## OTHERS

There is a large body of poetry written by onlookers, second-generation survivors, liberators, Christians, those who emigrated before the war, and others. To select from this wide range of poetry and poets is difficult, but the following selection, admittedly arbitrary, provides a sampling of its richness and variety: Uri Greenberg (1898–1981), Galicia, Austria, and Israel; Jacob Glatstein (1896–1971), Poland and the United States; William Hayen (1940–), United States; Czeslaw Milosz (1911–), Lithuania and Poland; and János Pilinszky (1921–1981), Hungary.

Uri Zvi Greenberg began as a poet writing in both Hebrew and Yiddish. After his emigration to Israel in 1924, he wrote only in Hebrew, but during and after the Holocaust years he returned to Yiddish, the common language of the millions of Jews destroyed in Europe. Greenberg was awarded the Israel Prize for Hebrew Literature in 1957. His ardent religious, mystical, prophetic view of Israel and its historical destiny is strongly evident in his poetry.[60] In 1939 Greenberg was in Poland on a mission for the Zionist Revisionist party when the war broke out. He escaped and made his way back to Palestine, although his parents were caught up and destroyed in the tide of mass murder engulfing European Jewry. He vents his wrath and anguish in *Streets of the River: The Book of Dirges and Power* (1951). Robert Alter says of *Streets of the River* that Greenberg's "vision of genocide and regeneration" is mesmeric. . . . Many of the poems have a delicate, hauntingly poignant lyricism or dazzling moments of hallucinatory power," although, as Alter mentions, there are occasional "hollow rhetorical flourishes" as well.[61] Alter discerningly points out that Greenberg speaks through two voices, the voice of the "prophet as castigator" and the voice of "an orphaned child lost in the world and aching for his parents."[62] It is this second voice that one hears in the prose poem "In the Mound of Corpses in the Snow." The poem describes the humiliation and death of Greenberg's father, who was forced to undress and stand naked, his father, who had never stood naked before except before his bed and in his bath.[63]

Jacob Glatstein, a major poet, novelist, and critic who emigrated to the United States in 1914, was in love with what he called the "joys of Yiddish," his beloved language. Ruth Whitman, translator of *The Selected Poems*, comments that Yiddish was for him a metaphor of his childhood in Lublin, the history of the Jewish people, and a personification of his vanishing race. She says that he liberated Yiddish poetry with his innovations, for example, his surrealistic juxtaposition of nonrational images, his experimentation with line lengths, speech rhythms, and diction, and his reinvention of grammatical and verbal construction.[64]

Alvin Rosenfeld in *A Double Dying* considers Glatstein a "writer of strength and sustained accomplishment" whose work has memorialized, preserved, and continued Yiddish culture and language.[65] Of the six million Jews who were destroyed in the Holocaust, at least five million spoke Yiddish, and Glatstein was obsessed with fear that the Yiddish language would be extinguished. Both this concern and fear of diminishment of the Jewish god "relate to the ancient bond of covenant, established in the revelation at Sinai." Both are of crucial thematic importance.

The covenant between God and man and the traditional covenant between the poet as prophet/priest and the people make up a powerful strand in the body of Glatstein's work. "My Holy City Lublin" recounts the history of this venerable city of Yiddish sages.[66] But "Dead Men Don't Praise God," and in this poem Glatstein contrasts the Jewish people at Sinai receiving the Torah and the Jews of Lublin perishing in gas chambers.[67] The covenant, supposedly broken by God, is repudiated by the dead. God himself is seen as a defeated, saddened, powerless human being. Sadly, the poet comforts him as a peer in "My Brother Refugee." Glatstein envisions a world where God has gone to sleep like a child, a tired émigré, no longer a deity but just another victim. In order to believe in the goodness of God, the poet has had to cease to believe in his omnipotence.[68]

Along with the diminution of God and the destruction of the Jewish people will come the extinction of language, the *mame loshen* Yiddish. "In a Ghetto" exhorts poets to save the language and revive it. It is the poet who must guard, preserve, and renew a language that has become sick unto death.[69] Glatstein, along with many other Yiddish writers, considers Yiddish to be hallowed by the millions of dead whose language it was. In resurrecting the language, Glatstein was resurrecting the dead, and both have survived. Like the burning bush from which the angel of the Lord appeared to Moses, "the bush was burning, yet it was not consumed" (Exodus 3:2).

Three powerful books of Holocaust poetry, *The Swastika Poems, Erika*, and *My Holocaust Songs*, have been written by the American poet William Heyen, born in 1940 to German parents who emigrated to the United States in 1928, leaving behind all their relatives. Heyen's memory of the war years was of not understanding why swastikas were painted on his home. He later earned a Ph.D. (1967) from Ohio University, became a poet and university professor, and read assiduously the history and accounts of the Holocaust. In 1971–72 he spent a year in Germany as a senior Fulbright lecturer in American literature. During this year he visited the camps, feeling forced to confront the history of Germany as well as his own history: Two of his father's brothers had been killed fighting for the Nazis, and his wife's father had been a Nazi.

Heyen's poetry is restrained, documentary, anguished. The poem "Numinous" traces the poet's pacing the streets of a German city watching grey smoke wafting from peaceful chimneys, just as other pillars of smoke came from crematoria. The poet seems lost in somber reverie as he imagines victims with blue numbers tattooed on their arms. Then he is jarred back to reality by an explosion of pigeons, beating the air with their wings. The transformation of the pigeons into the smoke of the chimneys is subtle and effective.

Heyen moves to lines of haunting beauty in the long prose poem "Erika." He recounts the history of Bergen-Belsen, a name that impacts upon the heart with the screech of a jet aircraft. The poem counterpoints unnatural deeds at Belsen with the natural beauty of the mounds of graves covered with Erika: Erika, bell-heather, mauve and blue blossoms, blossoms of memory, a more eloquent testimony to the inhumanity of man even than the ruins of the Cologne cathedral.[70]

Czeslaw Milosz, Roman Catholic Nobel Prize winner (1980), is a leading writer, tireless translator, and promoter of contemporary Polish poetry. Born in Lithuania, he fought with the Warsaw underground and sadly remembers "lots of Jews and synagogues in Vilna" that are no longer there.[71] Milosz was the first Slavic poet to hold the Charles Eliot Norton Professorship at Harvard and is professor emeritus of Slavic languages and literatures at the University of California, Berkeley. In *The Witness of Poetry* he states that "when an entire community is struck by misfortune . . . poetry becomes as essential as bread." "The extermination camp became a central fact of the century and barbed wire its emblem."[72] Kenneth Rexroth discusses the "subtlety and profundity" of his work "that come from an intensely humane literary sensibility . . . that has crossed the borders of language and stands in translation as amongst the very small body of truly important poetry."[73]

In "Child of Europe," a poem in eight parts, Milosz presents a chilling picture of the world after Auschwitz—the legacy of the Gentiles—and an even bleaker picture of the rationalizations this world uses to justify the events. The poem is written in the first-person plural "we." Milosz pictures himself and his generation as breathing the sweetness of air, admiring the flowering trees in spring, and enjoying all the good things of life because they have been somehow better and stronger and more worthy of survival than those who perished. Part 3 is a cynical depiction of force that calls itself "victorious justice," of power by "historical logic." Part 4 discusses the blatant lies of the post-Holocaust years, and Part 5 the words that are ambiguously used as clever weapons, because passion is better than the voice of reason. The poem continues with a warning not to love places or people because the former crumble and the latter are unreliable. The poem concludes with a warning from Milosz that it could happen again, that the world has not changed that we are always on the brink of the era of "unchained fire."[74]

Another great and authentic poet of the Holocaust is János Pilinszky, whose significant body of work includes *Selected Poems*, *Crater*, and *Scaffold in Winter*. Pilinszky, a Hungarian Catholic existentialist, was born in Budapest in 1921, was called up for military service in 1944, and was immediately imprisoned by the retreating German army to spend the last year of the war moving from prison camp to prison camp in Austria and Germany. In the world of the camps Pilinszky saw "humanity stripped of everything but the biological persistence of cells . . . savaged by primal hungers, among the odds and ends of a destroyed culture, waiting to be shot, or beaten to death, or just thrown on a refuse heap—or simply waiting in empty eternity."[75] Pilinszky, in describing the victim, presents the moral and ethical devastation of the non-Jews, those who perpetrated the horrors, or who looked the other way, or who suffered in silence. In the poem "Fish in the Net" Pilinszky describes Christians as suffocating in their guilt like fish out of water, gasping for breath and finding only the void.

> And so we atone but our atonement
> cannot appease,
> no suffering
> can redeem our hells.[76]

The victims whom the Christians are doomed to remember are delineated in language stripped to the bone. In "The French Prisoner" the poet describes a starving escapee hiding in the garden gulping a raw cattle-turnip, throwing it up, and then gulping it down again:

> Only to forget that body, those quaking shoulder blades,
> the hands shrunk to bone,
> the bare palm that crammed his mouth.
> . . . . . . . . . . . . . . . . . . . .
> And his glance—if only I could forget that!
> Though he was choking, he kept on

forcing more down his gullet—no matter what—only
to eat—anything—this—that—even himself!

The guards took the prisoner away, but never can the poet erase the memory of
the terrible hunger, the eternal hunger, "which no earthly nourishment can lessen.
/ He lives on me. And more and more hungrily! / . . . is clamouring for my
heart."[77]

The poet's despair and guilt are embedded in the poems. The roles of victim
and victimizer, murdered and murderer, are inextricably mingled and often reversed, with the victimizers being destroyed and the victims assuming a holiness,
as in the root of the word *victim*, innocence made sacred by holy burning. In
crucifying man, the murderer has crucified God and thus has condemned himself.
In the poem "Introitus" (the first variable part of the Catholic Mass), the poet
imagines the Last Judgment and asks:

> Who, now, shall open the closed book?
> Who shall make the first cut in unbroken
> time? . . . lifting the pages and letting them fall. . . . Who shall dare grope
> among the dense leaves of the sealed book?
> And how shall he dare . . . ?
> Which of us is without fear? Who would not fear
> when even God's eyes shut
> and all the angels fall flat
> and every creature darkens?
> Among us, only the Lamb has no fear.
> Him alone, the Lamb who was killed.
> . . . . . . . . . . . . . . . . . . . .
> He climbs up on to the throne. He opens the book.[78]

The poem "Apocrypha" describes a mystical revelation of the last days when
the heavens are silent and the guilty keep "vigil in banishment." The persona
of the poem faces "devastation, . . . walks without a word." Like the prodigal
son, he wants to get home, to reunite with family and God in righteousness and
forgiveness, but he cannot speak "the human speech":

> I do not understand the human speech,
> and I do not speak your language.
> My voice is more homeless than the word!
> I have no words.

And God is "nowhere" in an "empty world."[79]

Pilinszky's own words describe his poetic aesthetic: "It is some sort of lack
of language, a sort of linguistic poverty. . . . But in art even such a poor language
. . . can be redeemed. . . . Each deficiency may become a creative force. . . . I
would like to write as if I had remained silent."[80]

The statement that after Auschwitz there can be no poetry is true in the sense that there can be no more poetry that definitively asserts truth or beauty in the aesthetic forms of the past. To denote the Holocaust, a new language is needed. The poet Ted Hughes in his introduction to János Pilinszky's *Selected Poems* describes an aspect of this language: "Pilinszky's silence is the silence of that moment on the cross, after the cry. . . . In all that he writes, we hear a question: what speech is adequate for this moment? . . . The silence of artistic integrity 'after Auschwitz' is a real thing."[81] The best of the Holocaust poetry of Jews and Gentiles alike speaks of absence, of a God in whose creation the camps and modern physics are equally at home, of a world in which no adequate response is possible and authentic language is silenced. The poems seem to say that there can be no poetry. Yet something is sometimes said that is true both to the reality of the Holocaust and to the inability of language to say it. The poems seem to say that there can be no help, yet the paradox is that Holocaust poetry does help. Holocaust poetry is a body of poetry like no other, centered in a historical event like no other. Part of its reason for being lies in the hope that there will be no other.

## NOTES

1. Stephen Spender, Introduction to *Selected Poems of Abba Kovner and Nelly Sachs* trans. Shirley Kaufman and Nurit Orchan (Middlesex, England: Penguin, 1971), p.7.
2. Tadeusz Różewicz, *"The Survivor" and Other Poems*, trans. Magnus Krynski and Robert McGuire (Princeton, N.J.: Princeton University Press, 1976).
3. Spender, Introduction to *Selected Poems of Abba Kovner and Nelly Sachs*, p. viii.
4. Abraham Sutzkever, *Burnt Pearls: Ghetto Poems of Abraham Sutzkever*, trans. Seymour Mayne (Oakville, Ontario: Mosaic Press/Valley Editions, 1981), p. 50.
5. Dan Pagis, *Points of Departure*, trans. Stephen Mitchell (Philadelphia: Jewish Publication Society of America, 1981), p. 23.
6. Czeslaw Milosz, *Nobel Lecture* (New York: Farrar, Straus and Giroux, 1980), p. 22.
7. Geoffrey Hill, *Somewhere Is Such a Kingdom: Poems, 1952–1971* (Boston: Houghton Mifflin, 1975), p. xix.
8. Jacob Glatstein, *The Selected Poems of Jacob Glatstein*, trans. Ruth Whitman (New York: October House, 1972), pp. 110, 117.
9. Lawrence Langer, *Versions of Survival* (Albany: State University of New York Press, 1982), p. 219.
10. Nathan Ausubel and Maryann Ausubel, eds., *A Treasury of Jewish Poetry* (N.Y.: Crown, 1957).
11. Paul Celan, *Speech-Grille and Selected Poems*, trans. Joachim Neugroschel (New York: Dutton, 1971), p. 186.
12. János Pilinszky, *Selected Poems*, trans. Ted Hughes and Janos Csokits (New York: Persea Books, 1976), p. 9.
13. Irving Feldman, *The Pripet Marshes and Other Poems* (New York: Viking Press, 1965).
14. Pagis, *Points of Departure*, p. 27.

15. Ephim Fogel, "Shipment to Maidanek," in Ausubel and Ausubel, eds., *Treasury of Jewish Poetry*, pp. 254–55.

16. Hannah Senesh, "Blessed Is the Match," in Ausubel and Ausubel, *Treasury of Jewish Poetry*, p. 267.

17. Miklós Radnóti, *Clouded Sky*, trans. Steven Polgar, Stephen Berg, and S. J. Marks (New York: Harper and Row, 1972), pp. 88–89.

18. Gertrud Kolmar, *Dark Soliloquy: The Selected Poems of Gertrud Kolmar*, trans. Henry Smith (New York: Seabury Press, 1975), pp. 113–15.

19. Yitzhak Katzenelson, *The Song of the Murdered Jewish People*, trans. N. H. Rosenbloom (Haifa: Ghetto Fighters' House, 1980), p. 34.

20. Ibid., p. 118.

21. Hana Volavkova, ed., *I Never Saw Another Butterfly*, trans. Jeanne Nemcova (New York: McGraw-Hill, 1964), p. 60.

22. Paul Celan, *Selected Poems*, trans. Michael Hamburger and Christopher Middleton (Middlesex, England: Penguin, 1972), p. 13.

23. Ibid., p. 19.

24. Ibid., p. 17.

25. Ibid., pp. 33–48.

26. Abba Kovner, *A Canopy in the Desert*, trans. Shirley Kaufman et al. (Pittsburgh: University of Pittsburgh Press, 1973), p. xiii.

27. Abba Kovner and Nelly Sachs, *Selected Poems of Abba Kovner and Nelly Sachs*, p. 9.

28. Kovner, *Canopy in the Desert*, p. 21.

29. Ibid., p. 28.

30. Edward Alexander, *The Resonance of Dust: Essays on Holocaust Literature and Jewish Fate* (Columbus: Ohio State University Press, 1979), p. 59.

31. Ibid., p. 69.

32. Primo Levi, *Collected Poems of Primo Levi*, trans. Ruth Feldman and Brian Swann (Winchester, Mass.: Faber and Faber, 1988), p. 21.

33. Ibid., p. 17.

34. Ibid., p. 21.

35. Ibid., p. 35.

36. Pagis, *Points of Departure*, p. xi.

37. Ibid., pp. 1–3.

38. Ibid., p. 25.

39. Różewicz, *"The Survivor" and Other Poems*, pp. x, xiii, xvii.

40. Sidra DeKoven Ezrahi, *By Words Alone: The Holocaust in Literature* (Chicago: University of Chicago Press, 1980), p. 53.

41. Michael Hamburger, *The Truth of Poetry: Tensions in Modern Poetry from Baudelaire to the 1960's* (New York: Harcourt Brace Jovanovich, 1969), p. 247.

42. Różewicz, *"The Survivor" and Other Poems*, p. 89.

43. Ibid., pp. 45–47.

44. Nelly Sachs, *The Seeker and Other Poems*, trans. Ruth and Matthew Mead and Michael Hamburger (New York: Farrar, Straus and Giroux, 1970), pp. 81–82.

45. Ibid., p. 269.

46. Ezrahi, *By Words Alone*, p. 142.

47. Burghild Holzer, "Nelly Sachs and the Kabbala" (Ph.D. diss., University of California, San Diego, 1983), p. 11.

48. Sutzkever, *Burnt Pearls*, p. 38.

49. Ibid., p. 24.

50. Ibid., p. 25.

51. Ibid., p. 41.

52. Elie Wiesel, *Ani Maamin: A Song Lost and Found Again*, trans. Marion Wiesel (New York: Random House, 1973), p. 33.

53. Ibid., p. 61.

54. Ibid., p. 47.

55. Ibid., p. 65.

56. Ibid., p. 67.

57. Ibid., p. 71.

58. Ibid., p. 83.

59. Ibid., pp. 103–5.

60. Alan Mintz, *Hurban: Responses to Catastrophe in Hebrew Literature* (New York: Columbia University Press, 1984), pp. 165–202.

61. Robert Alter, *Defenses of the Imagination: Jewish Writers and Modern Historical Crisis* (Philadelphia: Jewish Publication Society of America, 1977), p. 106.

62. Ibid., pp. 110–13.

63. Uri Greenberg, *Streets of the River*, trans. Robert Friend and others (Jerusalem: Israel Universities Press, 1966), p. 259.

64. Glatstein, *Selected Poems*, p. 19.

65. Alvin H. Rosenfeld, *A Double Dying: Reflections on Holocaust Literature* (Bloomington: Indiana University Press, 1980), p. 118.

66. Jacob Glatstein, *Poems*, trans. Etta Blum (Tel Aviv: I. L. Peretz, 1970), pp. 11–12.

67. Ibid., p. 46.

68. Glatstein, *Selected Poems*, pp. 71–72.

69. Ibid., pp. 110–11.

70. William Heyen, *Erika: Poems of the Holocaust* (New York: Vanguard, 1977), pp. 57–62.

71. Milosz, *Nobel Lecture*, p. 7.

72. Czeslaw Milosz, *The Witness of Poetry* (Cambridge, Mass.: Harvard University Press, 1983), p. 51.

73. Czeslaw Milosz, *Selected Poems* (New York: Seabury Press, 1973), pp. 11–12.

74. Milosz, *Witness of Poetry*, pp. 59–64.

75. Pilinszky, *Selected Poems*, p. 9.

76. Ibid., p. 17.

77. Ibid., pp. 29–30.

78. Ibid., p. 50.

79. Ibid., pp. 38–40.

80. Ibid., p. 10.

81. Ibid., p. 103.

## HOLOCAUST POETRY BIBLIOGRAPHY

*Compiled by Deborah Murphy*

Alexander, Edward. *The Resonance of Dust: Essays on Holocaust Literature and Jewish Fate*. Columbus: Ohio State University Press, 1979.

Alter, Robert. *After the Tradition: Essays on Modern Jewish Writing.* New York: Dutton, 1969.

―――. *Defenses of the Imagination: Jewish Writers and Modern Historical Crisis.* Philadelphia: Jewish Publication Society of America, 1977.

Ausubel, Nathan, and Maryann Ausubel, eds. *A Treasury of Jewish Poetry.* New York: Crown, 1957.

Berg, Stephen, and Robert Mezey, eds. *Naked Poetry: Recent American Poetry in Open Forms.* Indianapolis: Bobbs-Merrill, 1969.

Bryks, Rachmil. *Ghetto Factory 76.* Translated by Theodor Primack and Eugen Kullman. New York: Bloch, 1967.

Cargas, Harry J. *The Holocaust: An Annotated Bibliography.* Haverford, Pa.: Catholic Library Association, 1985.

Celan, Paul. *Selected Poems.* Translated by Michael Hamburger and Christopher Middleton. Middlesex, England: Penguin, 1972.

―――. *Speech-Grille and Selected Poems.* Translated by Joachim Neugroschel. New York: Dutton, 1971.

Edelheit, Abraham J., and Herschel Edelheit. *Bibliography on Holocaust Literature.* Boulder, Colo.: Westview Press, 1986.

Ezrahi, Sidra DeKoven. *By Words Alone: The Holocaust in Literature.* Chicago: University of Chicago Press, 1980.

Fast, Howard. *Never to Forget.* New York: Jewish Peoples Fraternal Book League, 1946.

Feldman, Irving. *The Pripet Marshes and Other Poems.* New York: Viking Press, 1965.

Florsheim, Stewart J., ed. *Ghosts of the Holocaust.* Detroit: Wayne State University Press, 1981.

Gershon, Karen. *Selected Poems.* New York: Harcourt, Brace and World, 1966.

Gillon, Adam. "Here as in Jerusalem: Selected Poems of the Ghetto." *Polish Review* 10, no. 3 (1965): 22–45.

―――, ed. *Poems of the Ghetto: A Testament of Lost Men.* Edited with an Introduction by Adam Gillon, illustrated by Si Lewen. New York: Twayne, 1969.

Gillon, Adam, and Ludwik Krzyzanowski, ed. *Introduction to Modern Polish Literature: An Anthology of Fiction and Poetry.* New York: Twayne, 1964.

Glatstein, Jacob. *Poems.* Translated by Etta Blum. Tel Aviv: I. L. Peretz, 1970.

―――. *The Selected Poems of Jacob Glatstein.* Translated by Ruth Whitman. New York: October House, 1972.

Gömöri, George, and Charles Newman. *New Writing of East Europe.* Chicago: Quadrangle Books, 1968.

Greenberg, Uri Zvi. *Streets of the River.* Tel Aviv: Shukn, 1951.

Gurdus, Luba Krugman. *Painful Echoes: Poems of the Holocaust.* New York: Holocaust Library, 1985.

Hamburger, Michael. *The Truth of Poetry: Tensions in Modern Poetry from Baudelaire to the 1960's.* New York: Harcourt Brace Jovanovich, 1969.

Hecht, Anthony. *The Hard Hours.* New York: Atheneum, 1967.

―――. *Millions of Strange Shadows.* New York: Atheneum, 1978.

Heyen, William. *Erika: Poems of the Holocaust.* New York: Vanguard, 1977.

―――. *My Holocaust Songs.* Concord, N.H.: Ewert Publishers, 1980.

―――. *The Swastika Poems.* New York: Vanguard, 1977.

Hill, Geoffrey. *Somewhere Is Such a Kingdom: Poems, 1952–1971.* Boston: Houghton Mifflin, 1975.

Hirshberg, Jeffrey. "The Holocaust in Literature, 1978–9: A Bibliography." *Shoah*. 2, no. 1 (1980): 31–36.

Holzer, Burghild. "Nelly Sachs and the Kabbala." Ph.D. diss., University of California, San Diego, 1983.

Jackson, Ada. *Behold the Jew*. New York: Macmillan, 1944.

Jarrell, Randall. "A Camp in the Prussian Forests," "In the Camp There Was One Alive," and "Jews at Haifa." In *Losses*. New York: Harcourt, Brace, 1948.

Jastrun, Mieczyslaw. "Man," "Funeral," and "Here Too as in Jerusalem." In *Introduction to Modern Polish Literature: An Anthology of Fiction and Poetry*, edited by Adam Gillon and Ludwik Krzyzanowski. New York: Twayne, 1964.

Kalisch, Shoshana, and Barbara Meister. *Yes, We Sang! Songs of the Ghettos and Concentration Camps*. New York: Harper and Row, 1985.

Katzenelson, Yitzhak. *The Song of the Murdered Jewish People*. Translated by N. H. Rosenbloom, revised by Y. Tobin. Haifa, Ghetto Fighters' House, 1980.

Klein, A. M. *The Collected Poems of A. M. Klein* Toronto: McGraw-Hill, Ryerson, 1974.

Kohn, Murray J. *The Voice of My Blood Cries Out: The Holocaust as Reflected in Hebrew Poetry*. New York: Shengold, 1979.

Kolmar, Gertrud. *Dark Soliloquy: The Selected Poems of Gertrud Kolmar*. Translated by Henry A. Smith. New York: Seabury Press, 1975.

Kovner, Abba. *A Canopy in the Desert*. Translated by Shirley Kaufman et al. Pittsburgh: University of Pittsburgh Press, 1973.

Kovner, Abba, and Nelly Sachs. *Selected Poems of Abba Kovner and Nelly Sachs*. Translated by Shirley Kaufman and Nurit Orchan. Middlesex: Penguin, 1971.

Langer, Lawrence L. *Versions of Survival*. Albany: State University of New York Press, 1982.

Lask, Israel Meir. *Songs of the Ghettoes*. Tel Aviv: Eked, 1976.

Leftwich, Joseph. *The Golden Peacock: A Worldwide Treasury of Yiddish Poetry*. New York: T. Yoseloff, 1961.

———, ed. and trans. "Songs of the Death Camps: A Selection with Commentary." *Commentary* 12 (1951): 269–74.

Levertov, Denise. "During the Eichmann Trial." In *The New Modern Poetry: British and American Poetry Since World War II*, edited by M. L. Rosenthal. New York: Macmillan, 1967.

———. *The Jacob's Ladder*. New York: New Directions, 1961.

Levi, Primo. *Collected Poems of Primo Levi*. Translated by Ruth Feldman and Brian Swann. Winchester, Mass.: Faber and Faber, 1988.

Meyers, Bert. *The Dark Birds*. Garden City, N.Y.: Doubleday, 1969.

Mezey, Robert. "Theresienstadt Poems." In *Naked Poetry: Recent American Poetry in Open Forms*, edited by Stephen Berg and Robert Mezey. Indianapolis: Bobbs-Merrill, 1969.

Milosz, Czeslaw. *Nobel Lecture*. New York: Farrar, Straus, Giroux, 1980.

———. *Selected Poems*. New York: Seabury Press, 1973. Rev. ed., New York: Ecco Press, 1980.

———. *The Witness of Poetry*. Cambridge, Mass.: Harvard University Press, 1983.

Mintz, Alan. *Hurban: Responses to Catastrophe in Hebrew Literature*. New York: Columbia University Press, 1984.

Pagis, Dan. *Points of Departure*. Translated by Stephen Mitchell, introduction by Robert Alter. Philadelphia: Jewish Publication Society of America, 1981.

Penneli, S. Y., and A. Ukhmani, eds. *Anthology of Modern Hebrew Poetry*. Vol. 2. Jerusalem: Israel Universities Press, 1966.

Pilinszky, János. *Crater: Poems 1974–5*. Translated by Peter Jay. London: Anvil Press, 1978.

———. *Scaffold in Winter*. Translated by I. L. Halasz de Beky. Toronto: Vox Humana, 1982.

———. *Selected Poems*. Translated by Ted Hughes and Janos Csokits. New York: Persea Books, 1976.

Plath, Sylvia. *Ariel*. New York: Harper and Row, 1965.

Porter, Peter. "Annotations of Auschwitz." In *The New Modern Poetry: British and American Poetry Since World War II*, edited by M. L. Rosenthal. New York: Macmillan, 1967.

Radnóti, Miklós. *Clouded Sky*. Translated by Steven Polgar, Stephen Berg, and S. J. Marks. New York: Harper and Row, 1972.

Reznikoff, Charles. *Holocaust*. Los Angeles: Black Sparrow Press, 1975.

Rosenfeld, Alvin H. *A Double Dying: Reflections on Holocaust Literature*. Bloomington: Indiana University Press, 1980.

Rosensaft, Menachem Z. *Fragments: Past and Future*. New York: Shengold, 1968.

Rosenthal, M. L., ed. *The New Modern Poetry: British and American Poetry Since World War II*. New York: Macmillan, 1967.

Różewicz, Tadeusz. *Faces of Anxiety*. Translated by Adam Czerniawski. Chicago: Swallow Press, 1969.

———. "The Plains." In *Introduction to Modern Polish Literature: An Anthology of Fiction and Poetry*, edited by Adam Gillon and Ludwik Krzyzanowski. New York: Twayne, 1964.

———. *"The Survivor" and Other Poems*. Translated by Magnus J. Krynski and Robert McGuire. Princeton, N. J.: Princeton University Press, 1976.

Sachs, Nelly. *O the Chimneys!* Translated by Michael Hamburger, Ruth Mead, Matthew Mead, and Michael Roloff. New York: Farrar, Straus and Giroux, 1967.

———. *The Seeker and Other Poems*. Translated by Ruth Mead and Matthew Mead and Michael Hamburger. New York: Farrar, Straus and Giroux, 1970.

Schmuller, Aaron. *Treblinka Grass*. New York: Shulsinger Brothers, 1957.

———. *While Man Exists: A Collection of Poems and Translations from the Yiddish* Brooklyn: Parthenon, 1970.

Shapiro, Karl. *Poems of a Jew*. New York: Random House, 1958.

Siegel, Danny. *Nine Entered Paradise Alive*. New York: Town House Press, 1980.

Sklarew, Myra. *From the Backyard of the Diaspora*. Washington, D.C.: Dryad Press, 1976.

Slonimski, Antoni. "All," "He Is My Brother," and "Warsaw." In *Introduction to Modern Polish Literature: An Anthology of Fiction and Poetry*, edited by Adam Gillon and Ludwik Krzyzanowski. New York: Twayne, 1964.

Snodgrass, W. D. *The Führer Bunker*. Brockport, N.Y.: Boa Editions, 1977.

Sontag, Susan. Epigraph to *The Swastika Poems*, by William Heyen. New York: Vanguard, 1977.

Spender, Stephen. Introduction to *Selected Poems of Abba Kovner, and Nelly Sachs*. Middlesex: Penguin, 1971.

Steiner, George. *Language and Silence*. New York: Atheneum, 1967.

Sutzkever, Abraham. *Burnt Pearls: Ghetto Poems of Abraham Sutzkever*. Translated by Seymour Mayne. Oakville, Ontario: Mosaic Press/Valley Editions, 1981.

———. "Green Aquarium." Translated by Ruth Wisse. *Prooftexts: A Journal of Jewish Literary History* 2, no. 1 (January 1982): 95–121.

Szonyi, David M. *The Holocaust: An Annotated Bibliography and Resource Guide*. New York: Ktav, 1985.

Taube, Herman. *A Chain of Images*. New York: Shulsinger Brothers, 1979.

Volakova, Hana, ed. *I Never Saw Another Butterfly*. Translated by Jeanne Nemcova. New York: McGraw-Hill, 1964.

Whitman, Ruth. *The Testing of Hanna Senesh*. Historical Background by Livia Rothkirchen. Detroit: Wayne State University Press, 1986.

Wierzynski, Kazimierz. "To the Jews." In *Introduction to Modern, Polish Literature: An Anthology of Fiction and Poetry*, edited by Adam Gillon and Ludwik Krzyzanowski. New York: Twayne, 1964.

Wiesel, Elie. *Ani Maamin: A Song Lost and Found Again*. Translated by Marion Wiesel. New York: Random House, 1973.

Wolfskehl, Karl. *1933: A Poem Sequence*. Translated by Carol North Valhope and Ernst Morwitz. New York: Schocken Books, 1947.

Yevtushenko, Yevgeny. "Babi Yar." In *Selected Poems*. Translated by Robin Milner-Gulland and Peter Levi. Baltimore: Penguin, 1974.

# Chapter 28

# Juvenile and Youth Books About the Holocaust

*Bea Stadtler*

There is some controversy whether the subject of the Holocaust should be introduced to the younger child, ages nine, ten, and up. This probably depends on a number of factors, including what is discussed, read, and "taught" at home. Another is the technique of the teacher and how various topics related to the Holocaust are introduced in class. When children learn the relevance of the Holocaust to today's problems all over the world, they feel, as one fifth grader told me, "The Holocaust is not ancient history like Joseph in B.C., it's like things that are happening today."

The horror of the Holocaust should not be taught nor told to the young children of five or six years. Individual episodes from a person's life or allegorical stories may be told to them. However, the nine-, ten-, and eleven-year-olds have a remarkable sensitivity to the subject, and much more can be told to them. Still, they should be spared the unbridled horror. Children may learn about the Holocaust at different ages, sometimes even by chance. For instance, when the child goes to the bakery or butcher shop with mother and sees the bakery lady or the butcher with a funny number on the arm and asks, "Mom, what is that number?" this can be an opening to beginning a discussion on the subject and then a suggestion that the child read *The Holocaust: A History of Courage and Resistance* by Bea Stadtler as an introduction, and perhaps one of the Anne Frank books, or *I Never Saw Another Butterfly*, but first the history.

As they grow older, they can read more firsthand accounts: *The Diary of Eva Heyman*, *Young Moshe's Diary*, and others. They might also want to expand their knowledge with books like Irving Werstein's *That Denmark Might Live* and *The Uprising of the Warsaw Ghetto*, and William Shirer's *Rise and Fall of the Third Reich*, or Milton Meltzer's *Never to Forget*, published by Harper and Row.

Another reason, especially at Jewish schools, not to delay teaching about the subject is that many children drop out of Hebrew and Sunday school after bar mitzvah, and if they do not learn something about this catastrophe at ages nine, ten, eleven, and twelve, they may never learn about it. Public schools are slow to introduce this subject, and often the teacher is reluctant and sometimes not knowledgeable about the subject.

There is no dearth of Holocaust books for children, although each brings a new dimension to the complex subject. Generally, the books are divided into autobiography, history, and texts. Experiences and events surrounding the Holocaust are so unbelievable and so incomprehensible that the subject does not call for more imagination, and therefore there is little fiction in the youth books about the Holocaust. There are also a number of diaries kept by children as they went through this terrible experience. Most of those who kept the diaries perished in the Holocaust. Autobiographies are mostly a recounting of the authors' personal experiences during the years 1933–45, with a few starting earlier and some beginning later.

The age range of juvenile and youth books about the Holocaust extends from a few for the very young to more for ages eight to eleven and for ages twelve to fifteen. Books for the very young include books to read to children and those that can be read by seven-year-olds. Probably the best book that allegorically tells the story to young children is Eve Bunting's *Terrible Things*. It deals with things that come to the forest and how, group by group, the animals are taken away by them. The white rabbit's acquiescence to the acts of the terrible things bring to mind, of course, what the people said when the Jews were taken away. Also, it is probably based on Pastor Martin Niemoeller's famous statement of how each group was taken away while he kept silent, and finally when it came to his turn to be taken away, there was no one left to speak up. A similar book is David Adler's *The Number on My Grandfather's Arm*. It is illustrated with photographs. The child asks the meaning of the number on her grandfather's arm. How did it get there? The grandfather, in simple language, tells the story of what happened to him. The granddaughter, with wisdom far beyond her years, says that he should not be ashamed of the number, but rather the people who put it there should be ashamed. A third book for the very young is Gerda Klein's *Promise of a New Spring*.

Chana Byers Abells has put together a book called *The Children We Remember*. It is a touching book and a moving testimony to those children who perished in the Holocaust. The photos are from Yad Vashem archives in Jerusalem, and each black-and-white photo is accompanied by one or two sentences telling what happened to the children. While the simple text is easily read by young children, the photos are very stark and frightening and are not recommended for the very young.

In the biography category, two books about Hannah (or Chana) Senesh have been published in recent years: *In Kindling Flame*, by Linda Atkinson, and Maxine Schur's *Hannah Szenes* (her name is spelled differently in both books), published by the Jewish Publication Society. Hannah was one of the thirty-two men and women from Eretz Yisrael who parachuted into Nazi-occupied Europe, into the countries from which they originated. *In Kindling Flame* does not flow easily because of the inclusion of much history and background. Hannah's story is interrupted by these historical additions, most of which could have been incorporated into the story. The Schur book, on the other hand, tells the story with warmth and tenderness, and while it does not have quite as much historical background, it flows more smoothly. This is recommended for the eleven-to-fourteen age group, and *In Kindling Flame* for the twelve-to-fifteen age group.

Two biographies of Hitler include Ronald Gray's *Hitler and the Germans*, and *The Rise and Fall of the Third Reich* by William Shirer. Ronald Gray's book contains excellent photographs in addition to telling the history of Germany from its industrial revolution and the rise of Adolf Hitler. Language and ideas are for those thirteen to sixteen years old. William Shirer was an American correspondent in Berlin, Germany, during the early years of the war, and this book is really a firsthand description of the dictator, with the remainder of the volume based on files of secret Nazi documents captured by the Allies. Photographs enhance the book for the twelve-to-fifteen-year-old.

A biography of Rabbi Leo Baeck, published by Lodestar Books in 1986 and written by Anne E. Neimark, tells about the life of this courageous man. Though he was offered a position in America, he chose to remain with his people in Berlin. Deported to Theresienstadt, Baeck even managed to discuss philosophy with his companion while dragging wagons around the camp. This book is for those aged eleven to fourteen.

Another biography, written by Ellen Norman Stern, deals with Elie Wiesel: *Elie Wiesel: Witness for Life*. The author begins with Wiesel's childhood in Sighet, a small town in Transylvania, and continues with his bar mitzvah, the roundup of the Jews of Sighet, and the mutual attempts of his father and himself to keep each other alive. The author also incorporates short excerpts from books by Wiesel as she tells his story. This book is for those aged fifteen to adult.

*Nazi Hunter: Simon Wiesenthal*, by Iris Noble, is a biography of the tenacious Nazi hunter and tells the strange coincidences that led to the discovery of the whereabouts of Adolf Eichmann, the architect of the Final Solution, for those aged fourteen and up.

Two recent historical retellings of the Holocaust years are *A Nightmare in History: The Holocaust, 1933–1945*, by Miriam Chaikin, and *Smoke and Ashes* by Barbara Rogasky. Both books have an introductory chapter about the history of anti-Semitism, but the Rogasky book also includes minibiographies of some of the righteous Gentiles and information about how some of the small countries reacted to being conquered by Adolf Hitler. In a very interesting chapter titled "Is the Holocaust Unique?" she tells about other slaughters, ending with why, indeed, the Holocaust is unique. Another chapter is devoted to the Nuremberg trials, with a person-by-person list of what happened to those Germans who had participated in the murder of the Jews. Quotes help make *Smoke and Ashes* a more appealing book than *A Nightmare in History*. Both are for the thirteen-to-seventeen age group.

*Shadows of the Holocaust*, by Harriet Steinhorn, is a paperback presenting five short plays about the Holocaust. The author is a survivor of the Bergen-Belsen concentration camp, and while some of the dialogue is a bit forced, the book is a very worthwhile classroom tool. At the end of the book is a glossary of words and explanations of the words, as well as music and words to five Holocaust songs. Included also is a very moving reading: *At My Bar Mitzvah and His*. This is a good book for teachers to adapt to their classrooms.

There are a number of textbooks for children and youth, including David Altshuler's *Hitler's War Against the Jews*, Seymour Rossel's *The Holocaust*, and Bea Stadtler's *The Holocaust: A History of Courage and Resistance*. The book by Bea Stadtler is for the younger student from ages ten to thirteen. However, it is often used in the upper grades as well, since the information, while presented in simple language, has, at the end of each chapter, questions that present serious dilemmas in which the victims found themselves. It begins with World War I and includes a chapter about Hitler, another section on *Kristallnacht,* "The Night of the Broken Glass," and a section about all kinds of resistance. Excerpts from documents also serve to make the book an interesting and valuable text. The Rossel book, for ages fourteen and up, tells how the Nazis planned and carried out their program of extermination against the Jews, and how the Holocaust affects us today. The Altshuler book is an adaptation of historian Lucy Dawidowicz's *War Against the Jews*. Each chapter ends with a small section titled "Issues and Values." Maps and photos are included, with some dates to remember. The book is for those aged fourteen and up.

Another format for material on the Holocaust is that done by the youths themselves after studying the subject. Dr. Leatrice Rabinsky, a teacher in a secular high school, has been teaching the subject of the Holocaust for years. Frequently her students publish a booklet as they approach the end of the semester. "Journey of Conscience" is one such booklet, telling of the students' visit to various Holocaust sites in Europe on a trip that they took together with Dr. Rabinsky. The booklet was put together by Dr. Rabinsky and Mrs. Gertrude Mann and published by Collins-World.

There are many personal accounts of survivors that may be read by youth. Though the writers may have been in the same ghetto or camp, each brings his or her background and personality to this traumatic subject. Frieda Weinstein, author of *A Hidden Childhood*, spent her childhood years in a Catholic convent. She would have liked to have been baptized, but her parents objected. *Upon the Head of the Goat*, written by Aranka Siegel, is another childhood reminiscence from Hungary. Inge Auerbacher, author of *I Am a Star-Child of the Holocaust* is one of the one hundred children who survived Theresienstadt, a camp where fifteen thousand children were temporarily housed before being sent to their death in Auschwitz. Inge tells her story from the age of seven, when she was sent to Theresienstadt. Too much of the book is involved with Holocaust background material, which the children will presumably learn from other writings, and she does not start relating her own story until she is several chapters into the book. *Clara's Story*, by Clara Isaacman, is the story of a child in Antwerp, Belgium. Rose Zar, *In the Mouth of the Wolf* (1983), tells how she survived by serving as a cleaning lady for an SS German and his family, always keeping her eyes and ears open for any possibility that she would be discovered. Her father had told her that the best place to hide is in the mouth of the wolf, and that is where she hid—right in the Nazi's home. These books can be read by youths aged twelve to fifteen. *Joseph and Me*, by Judy Hoffman, is written for the younger child and tells of her and her brother's experiences during the Holocaust years, as well as her arrival in Israel.

There are also a number of published diaries that were kept by children as they went through these experiences. Best known is *The Diary of Anne Frank*. Many versions of this diary have been published, including one by Doubleday, another by Johanna Hurwitz, ed., Jewish Publication Society (1989), and one by Bookwright Press, Vanora Leigh, ed. (1986). Anne's diary relates the interaction among the people living near a secret annex in a building in Holland. Family clashes and problems of living in such a small, hidden space are very simply, but touchingly, told.

*Young Moshe's Diary* tells the experiences of a sixteen-year-old Orthodox boy day by day until he is shipped to Auschwitz. His fears, doubts, and philosophies are related on these pages. *The Diary of Eva Heyman* tells of life in a small Hungarian town under Nazi occupation until she, too, with her grandparents, is deported to Auschwitz. An especially poignant excerpt deals with her encounter with a German Nazi who wants to take her bicycle away. *Charlotte* by Charlotte Salomon tells her story in words and hundreds of pictures that she drew. These books are for those aged fifteen and up.

A classic that does not fit into any category is *I Never Saw Another Butterfly*, which incorporates children's drawings and poems from the concentration camp of Theresienstadt. Used extensively in memorial programs, it is effective with all age groups.

Another interesting and unusual book is *Through Our Eyes*, written by Itzhak Tatelbaum. It uses quotes mainly from diaries of children and adults who perished and some who survived. Black-and-white photos, some with the names of the children, illustrate the book, which is for those aged fifteen and up.

The actions against the Gypsies are described in *And The Violins Stopped Playing* by Alexander Ramati. It is based on a manuscript received by the author from a Gypsy who had survived the Holocaust. Apparent in the book is the uncaring Gypsy attitude toward the Jews. This book is for those aged fifteen and up.

The resistance by non-Jewish Germans to Hitler is told in *The Short Life of Sophie Scholl* by Herman Vinke. The book relates how Sophie and her brother gathered a group of non-Jewish German youth around them to fight against the

Nazi regime. Unfortunately, they were very idealistic and unorganized, the actions they took at the college they attended were soon discovered, and they were put to death. This book is for those aged twelve to fifteen.

Irving Werstein's *That Denmark Might Live* and *The Uprising of the Warsaw Ghetto* are both factual, interesting books for youth, with a great deal of source material incorporated into the texts for those aged twelve and up.

Erwin and Agnes Herman have written about another aspect of the Holocaust in a book for younger children, eight and up. *The Yanov Torah* tells about a Torah that was smuggled into a concentration camp, the "liberation" of the Torah, and its present use in a congregation in California.

Some of the fictionalized books have a basis in fact. One of these is Yuri Suhl's book *Uncle Misha's Partisans* about the forest fighters who fought against the Nazis. Suhl based his accounts on the experiences of a group of partisans led by the man called Uncle Misha.

Joseph Zieman's *The Cigarette Sellers of the Three Crosses Square* and Sara Neshamit's *The Children of Mapu Street* tell the stories of groups of courageous youngsters in Kovno, Lithuania, and Warsaw, Poland, also in a fictionalized format, but based on factual research. *The Boys Who Saved the Children* by Margaret Baldwin is another of these books, but the setting is the Lodz ghetto. Ben and other boys working in a fur factory in Lodz save the ghetto's children for a time by making a fur coat for a German officer's wife. *The Island on Bird Street* by Uri Orlev is pure fiction about a youngster who hides from the Nazis in the ghetto. These books are for those aged eleven to thirteen.

This is a sampling of books that have been published for children and youth, covering different age groups and different formats for presenting material on the Holocaust. The subject is endless and important for children to learn for the lessons it has for us now and in the future.


## SELECT BIBLIOGRAPHY

Abells, Chana Byers. *The Children We Remember*. New York: Greenwillow Books, 1986.

Adler, David. *The Number on My Grandfather's Arm*. New York: Union of American Congregations, 1987.

Altshuler, David. *Hitler's War Against the Jews*. West Orange, N.J.: Behrman House, 1978.

Atkinson, Linda. *In Kindling Flame*. New York: Lothrop, Lee and Shepard, 1985.

Baldwin, Margaret. *The Boys Who Saved the Children*. Englewood Cliffs, N.J.: Julian Messner, 1981.

Bunting, Eve. *Terrible Things*. New York: Harper and Row, 1980.

Chaikin, Miriam. *A Nightmare in History: The Holocaust, 1933–1945*. New York: Clarion Books, 1988.

Flinker, Moshe. *Young Moshe's Diary*. Jerusalem: Yad Vashem, 1971.

Frank, Anne. *The Diary of Anne Frank*. Reprint. Garden City, N.Y.: Doubleday, 1967.

Gray, Ronald. *Hitler and the Germans*. Minneapolis: Lerner, 1983.

Herman, Erwin, and Agnes Herman. *The Yanov Torah*. Rockville, Md.: Kar-Ben.

Heyman, Eva. *The Diary of Eva Heyman*. Jerusalem: Yad Vashem.

Hoffman, Judy. *Joseph and Me*. New York: Ktav, 1979.

Isaacman, Clara. *Clara's Story*. Philadelphia: Jewish Publication Society of America, 1984.

Kerr, Judith. *When Hitler Stole Pink Rabbitt*. New York: Coward, 1971.

Klein, Gerda. *The Promise of a New Spring*. Dallas, Tex.: Rossel Books, 1981.

Koehn, Ilse. *Mischling, Second Degree*. New York: Greenwillow, 1977.

Neshamit, Sara. *The Children of Mapu Street*. Philadelphia: Jewish Publication Society of America, 1970.

Noble, Iris. *Nazi Hunter: Simon Wiesenthal*. Englewood Cliffs, N.J.: Julian Messner, 1979.

Oborski, Jona. *Childhood*. Garden City, N.Y.: Doubleday, 1983.

Orlev, Uri. *The Island on Bird Street*. Boston: Houghton Mifflin, 1983.

Ramati, Alexander. *And The Violins Stopped Playing*. New York: Franklin Watts, 1986.

Rogasky, Barbara. *Smoke and Ashes*. New York: Holiday House, 1988.

Rossel, Seymour. *The Holocaust*. New York: Franklin Watts, 1989.

Salomon, Charlotte. *Charlotte*. New York: Harcourt, Brace and World, 1963.

Sachs, Marilyn. *A Pocket Full of Seeds*. Garden City, N.Y.: Doubleday, 1973.

Schur, Maxine. *Hannah Szenes*. Philadelphia: Jewish Publication Society of America, 1986.

Shirer, William. *The Rise and Fall of the Third Reich*. New York: Random House, 1960.

Siegel, Aranka. *Upon the Head of the Goat*. New York: Farrar, Straus and Giroux, 1981.

Stadtler, Bea. *The Holocaust: A History of Courage and Resistance*. West Orange, N.J.: Behrman House, 1973.

Steinhorn, Harriet. *Shadows of the Holocaust*. Rockville, Md.: Kar-Ben, 1983.

Stern, Ellen Norman. *Elie Wiesel: Witness for Life*. New York: Ktav and Anti-Defamation League, 1982.

Suhl, Yuri. *Uncle Misha's Partisans*. New York: Four Winds Press, 1973.

Tatelbaum, Itzhak. *Through Our Eyes*. Jerusalem: IBT, 1985.

Vinke, Herman. *The Short Life of Sophie Scholl*. New York: Harper and Row, 1984.

Volavkova, Hanna, ed. *I Never Saw Another Butterfly*. Translated by Jeanne Nemcova. New York: McGraw-Hill, 1961.

Weinstein, Frida. *A Hidden Childhood*. New York: Hill and Wang, 1985.

Werstein, Irving. *That Denmark Might Live*. Philadelphia: Marcus Smith, 1967.

————. *The Uprising of the Warsaw Ghetto*. New York: Norton, 1968.

Ziemian, Joseph. *The Cigarette Sellers of the Three Crosses Square*. Lerner, 1970.

# Chapter 29

---

# The Holocaust in Art

## Nelly Toll

Traditionally, the study of art history is based on scholarly inquiry into chronology, influences, descriptive characteristics, and stylistic evolution. A final critical analysis is based on the evidence of this accumulated research. The art of the Holocaust resists this type of study. Because of its unique roots and the circumstances under which it was executed, it does not fit the traditional demands of the discipline of other aesthetics. But despite our lack of data and our inability to trace evolutionary development of the victim artists, their fragmented works have earned an important place in the history of art.

The Holocaust artists made use of any found material, be it a stub of a pencil, a piece of coal, or some other tool. Their works have a power and simplicity of man's creative imagination. Like the artists of the cave paintings of Altamira and Lascaux and the funerary paintings of the Egyptians, who used symbols to serve the dead in the world of the hereafter and linked them with the living, thus permanently engraving their image throughout eternity, the Holocaust artists documented their existence.

Jewish intellectual and artistic expression dates back to the earliest times. Throughout the centuries Judaism has held scholarship to be most sacred and morally valuable, but during various periods of Jewish history art has been an important means of enhancing a good and ethical life.

Throughout their modern ordeal Jews have continued to find comfort in various Judaic symbols and talismans such as the menorah and the Star of David. In the same way, the artists of the Holocaust attained symbolic immortality through their canvases of the ghettos and camps. The art of the Holocaust represents only an abstraction of the cruel reality. Executed under the most deprived conditions, it cannot relate to any other suffering of this magnitude. On canvas it creates order out of chaos. Charged with power, it arouses deep emotions. In depicting an almost unimaginable odyssey of horror, this art maintains a remarkable artistic sensitivity.

These works are a response, both intellectual and intuitive, to the artists' environments. Their feelings, blood, and tears filled scraps of paper that remain symbols of integrity. The art of the Holocaust, which has survived despite the concentrated efforts of the Nazis, transcends all the barriers that divide its creators from the rest of the world.

The camp artists created order out of shambles; perceived shadows and lights; utilized line, composition, movement, and balance; and emerged to express the depths of the skeletal survival of their souls. These heroes of the ghettos and camps could not remain silent. Impelled by a sense of urgency, aware that each day might be their last, they silently recorded what went on in their world for those who were unaware of its existence. From horror they extracted and preserved images for future generations to see and, hopefully, to prevent from recurring.

Holocaust art, with its nightmarish gestures reminiscent of Bosch, Goya, and Picasso's *Guernica*, although created in secret and in widely scattered places, forms a powerful and cohesive body of work. It demonstrates the moral endurance, creative commitment, and spiritual resistance of individual artists, the few who rose like ashes in the wind and the many who were buried beneath the depths of the earth. Their work serves as a permanent reminder of the horrors that took place and bears witness to the heroism of its creators. The artists of the Holocaust testified to the belief that humans are capable of expressing their finest spirit even when pushed to the very limits of their existence.

It is my belief that if these artists of the dark days were able to see light through their creative forms amid such a profoundly dehumanizing environment, then their art must be shared by all people today and in the days to come. Although we cannot cross the barbed-wire fence that separates us from the cries and screams of their hell, the artists who perished in the gas chambers, the labor camps, and the ghettos have left us their souls on paper. This legacy expresses their last hope, the transfiguration of reality that symbolized their final embrace with life. History commands us not to forget; this art is the immortal symbol of that command.


## THE EARLY YEARS

In the late 1920s and the early 1930s, the Nazis tried to purge any art that was not propaganda. Jewish painters throughout Europe sensed the danger early on. One of the most prominent was Marc Chagall, who was influenced by Pascin, Soutine, the fauvists, and the cubists and frequently juxtaposed his Parisian existence with childhood memories of his poor Jewish-Russian background. Later he turned to spiritual and religious themes. Before escaping from occupied France to the United States in 1941, he produced an impressive series of illustrations for Gogol's *Dead Souls*.

Like many other artists, Jacques Lipchitz, a student of the Ecole des beaux-arts in Paris, came under the influence of Picasso's cubism. His massive sculpture *Prometheus Struggling with the Vulture* became a symbol of light over darkness, and his *Bull and Condor*, produced in 1932, became a prophetic depiction of German brutality. Realizing that the Nazis intended to destroy the Jews of Europe, Lipchitz and his wife hid in the hills of southern France until they, too, finally managed to escape to the United States.

George Grosz (who changed his named from Gross to Grosz, a less German-sounding name) castigated the sinister forces of the military and became actively involved in anti-Nazi propaganda. His earliest antiwar caricatures are best exemplified by *Germany, a Winter's Tale* (1917–19), which paints a kaleidoscopic portrait of Berlin, complete with the menacing expression of generals, officers, and greedy burghers. This powerful composition of broken objects and superimposed figures was probably inspired by a Heinrich Heine poem that attacked the Prussian military. George Grosz's work depicted the Nazis as instruments of hate and evil. During the 1930s he produced savage caricatures of Hitler and amassed a powerful portfolio of antiwar drawings. Grosz also used theater to express his opposition to the Nazis, creating stage designs for the controversial antiwar play *The Adventures of Good Soldier Schweik*. All this activity—but particularly the fact that Grosz was a Jew—finally made it necessary for him to flee to the United States with his wife.

Oskar Kokoschka, an artist from Vienna known for his morbid portraits, depicted his deeply felt fears and emotions in a highly expressionistic style. In 1934 Kokoschka fled from Vienna to Prague and then to London. The same year his public work was confiscated by the Nazis and termed "degenerate." Max Ernst, a leading surrealist painter who had moved to France in 1922, was also publicly humiliated and forbidden to show his work in Germany. Officially labeled a degenerate artist, like many of his compatriots, Ernst later emigrated to the United States.

The Nazi government proceeded rapidly in its "purification" of the arts, confiscating what was branded as "Jewish vermin" art and "decadent" non-Jewish modern art. Under the direction of Hitler's propagandist Joseph Goebbels, the Nazis staged exhibits that purportedly exposed "anti-Nazi" attitudes. Through these shows Nazi propagandists made a decisive attempt to blame Germany's ills on what they saw as the artistic decadence of Jews and their negative influence on society at large. In 1933 a Nazi exposition in Stuttgart called "November Spirit Art in the Service of Disintegration" was directed against Max Beckmann, Otto Dix, Chagall, and Grosz. Another exhibition, in Mannheim, focused on "cultural bolshevism" and featured Grosz's *Ecce Homo* series, which was labeled with propagandistic slogans.

Goebbels's campaign resulted in the murder of over twenty painters and the confiscation of approximately sixteen thousand works of art. Some were sold abroad to help finance Hitler's museum in Linz; others were burned or appropriated by the minister of aviation, Hermann Göring. On Hitler's personal orders, the special office of Einsatzstab Rosenberg conducted a search for valuable Jewish-owned furniture and art objects in occupied France. Once shipped from Paris to Germany, these treasures were cataloged by Rosenberg and became part of the private collections of Hitler and Göring.

## THE GHETTOS

Shortly after Germany's invasion of Poland in the fall of 1939, Jews were herded into small sections of various cities that were isolated from the non-Jewish community—the ghettos. Conditions in these areas, already overcrowded, became even worse as Jews were shipped in from other towns. The ghetto populations quickly began to suffer from hunger, disease, and exposure to the freezing temperatures. Epidemics, fed by poor sanitation, devoured the bodies of young and old alike. Terror and death reigned supreme.

Determined to let the world see the landscape of their tragedy, painters and writers feverishly recorded the doomed reality of the ghettos. By the act of documenting their life through drawings, paintings, and the written word, the artists—who often traded bread for ink, coal, paint, or paper—maintained morale within their community of friends and family. At the same time, the victims strengthened their own links with the past, fulfilling their emotional and psychological need to combat the Nazi brutality.

Just as Picasso's *Guernica* and the works of Goya, Bacon, and Daumier stir people's consciousness, so does the art that has survived the death and destruction of the ghettos. The painters of Lodz, Vilna, Warsaw, and other cities recorded their gray existence on canvas and gave their abysmal reality the permanence of written and painted images. In order to achieve this goal, the artists risked their lives.

Many of the artworks were concealed underground or smuggled out to non-Jewish friends for safekeeping. Drawn on scraps of paper, cardboard supply boxes, or any other surfaces that could be found, these works of poetry and art were tragic records of the ghetto ordeal. Unlike other ghettos, the town of Terezín in Czechoslovakia was a Nazi "showplace," but it gave only a cheap illusion of freedom. Anyone who cared to look carefully would not have been fooled. Many pieces of art from Terezín perished along with their creators; others outlived the Holocaust. When a transport left for Auschwitz with its doomed cargo, drawings that had been left behind were often hidden. After liberation, survivors turned over the cache of poems, diaries, and art to the Jewish Museum in Prague. Some of this work was edited by Hana Volavkova and published by the museum in 1962 in a volume entitled *I Never Saw Another Butterfly.*

Only a handful of the Jewish children in Terezín survived. In Lwow (Lemberg) a young girl who managed to hide with her family, Neha Zygmunt, left a collection of fifty images sewn together in little "booklets of happiness." From a window shielded with a white curtain, the little girl of seven glimpsed children playing with friends, going to school, running, and playing with puppies. Neha wanted to be with them, but was unable even to turn on the lights in the apartment of the Gentiles that hid her family. Her artwork and her diary reflected a desire to be free like the other children. *The Vacation in the Mountains with a Big Bathroom* was rooted in frightened reality, since the bathroom was used as a special hiding place during air raids. *Vaccination in School Against Scarlet Fever* represented Neha's experience with this sickness. The story of *The Friendly Village* masked the actual trauma when Neha and her mother were taunted by superstitious peasants when they hid in a forest of sunflowers. No dark colors cloud the skies of these watercolors, no black hues are emphasized. There is no isolation, no feeling of loneliness, no sign of anger or sadness. This child's view of life, despite the terrifying experiences, projects a positive outlook. (Editor's note: An exhibit of the unique works of that little girl, now known as Nelly Toll, has been touring the United States since 1991.)

## THE CONCENTRATION CAMPS

Concentration camps were a part of the Nazi reality from the first years of Hitler's rise to power. As early as 1933 there were fifty in existence, including the infamous Dachau, Sachsenhausen, Mauthausen, and Buchenwald. Supervision of the camps' terrorized slave laborers was entrusted to carefully selected Death's Head units of the SS and Ukrainian guards known for their ruthlessness and brutality.

The introduction of gassing apparatus to various concentration camps created death centers that aided the Nazis in even more rapid and efficient ways of extermination. In the spring of 1942 gas chambers appeared in Belzec, Chelmno, Sobibor, Maidanek, Treblinka, and Auschwitz. The slave laborers of other camps who somehow survived hunger, brutal beatings, raging disease, and sheer physical exhaustion were eventually deported to these and other installations. The murder of Jews had become a Nazi obsession.

The landscape of the camps transformed the surreal into the most gruesome reality. The inmates who were artists depicted their fellow prisoners with their gaunt faces and sluggishly drooped heads, moving their feet without stopping, their exhausted bodies filled with pain. Amid the cruel laughter of their tormentors, they staggered in their last funeral march. Despite their delirium, they still remained human. Unlike their captors, they did not become animals; the stronger helped the weaker. Humanity prevailed.

It seems a miracle that there should be such a strong urge to record and document the edge of death. Perhaps only through art were the victims able to overcome, even momentarily, their existence. Every scrap of paper or piece of coal or pencil stub was a treasure that, like the works of art, had to be hidden. The fragments of these compositions that remain can all too often only be labeled "artist unknown."

Despite its anonymity, this work speaks to us with its tragic desperation. The camp landscape where skeletons were turned into ashes has silently sunk into the depths of Hades, with green grass covering the sins of the past. Wildflowers spring back to life where once there was only barbed wire and death. The birds, strangers to such human suffering, fly through the blue skies, and children watch the rhythmic passage of a butterfly. Such peaceful scenes cover the black earth of the past's nightmarish reality.

The cries of these paintings and drawings, the only legacy of the dead creators, demand to be seen. Such art has never been portrayed before in the history of mankind, surpassing all the tragic events ever depicted on paper or canvas. The artists of the camps were determined to let us glimpse their last moment before descending to their deaths. Through their creativity, we can, perhaps, only for a fleeting moment become one with the victims, thus fulfilling their last wish that we shall never forget and never allow such a tragedy to happen again.

## EDITOR'S NOTE

It would be virtually impossible to offer a complete list of books that have touched upon Holocaust art in the past forty-five years. Those interested in furthering their knowledge would be well advised to begin with a glance at *The Blackwell Companion to Jewish Culture*, edited by Glenda Abramson. Apart from entries on such figures as Ben Shahn, Jacques Lipchitz, Kariel Gardosh (known for his Israeli cartoon character "Dosh"), and George Gershwin (shown working on a portrait of Arnold Schönberg), this excellent reference book contains several essays on Jewish art and even raises the question whether a people that has traveled so many continents and undergone so many disparate experiences may be said to possess its own unique art. (The philosopher Martin Buber, trained as an art historian, is quoted as advocating a need for land from which national art might spring.)

Several encyclopedic publications ought to dispel doubts about the originality or antiquity of Jewish art. Cecil Roth's *Jewish Art: An Illustrated History* contains striking photographs of ancient menorahs, Temple and synagogue architecture, medieval illuminations, and the works of modernists Max Liebermann, Leonid Pasternak, and Lesser Ury. Some of these illustrations are duplicated in the two-volume *Jewish Art and Civilization* edited by Geoffrey Wigoder of Hebrew University. Also useful is Avram Kampf's *Jewish Experience in the Art of the Twentieth Century*, which offers a broad analysis of Jewish contributions to modern art from the Ecole Juive in France through contemporary Israel. Kampf devotes a section to the Holocaust, including works by Picasso and Chagall and the smoky faces of Samuel Brak and Lasar Sagall. He also discusses constraints upon Jewish artists deriving from persecution and religion, subjects that are more thoroughly developed in Joseph Gutmann's *No Graven Images: Studies in Art and the Hebrew Bible* and David Roskies' *Against the Apocalypse: Responses to Catastrophe in Modern Jewish Culture*.

As Nelly Toll points out, a number of non-Jewish artists lashed out against Nazism before the start of World War II and continued their attacks beyond the Holocaust. *Arte e resistenza in Europa*, published after the war by the Museo Civico of Bologna, offers anti-Nazi art from Belgium (*Ça jamais* by René Magritte), Czechoslovakia (political cartoons of František Bidlo and Josef Čapek), Russia, and Italy (especially the work of Ali Sassu). The cubist styles of the faithful Communist El Lissitzky (*El Lissitzky: Life, Letters, Texts*) and Polish-born Josef Kaliszan (*The Warsaw Ghetto: Drawings by Jozef Kaliszan)* are other examples of this genre. Most compelling, however, is Herbert Bittner's salute to the woman who served as a kind of conscience for Germany through two world wars. *Kaethe Kollwitz, Drawings* is dedicated to men, women, and children, common folk who seek food and shelter. Between 1934 and 1936 she completed a number of lithographs devoted to the horrors of death. Outlawed by the Nazis, she managed to avoid detention in a concentration camp. Too late, Kollwitz's placard *Never Again War* has inspired generations of young people.

Probably the single most comprehensive volume dealing with the art of Jewish victims is a work edited by Janet Blatter and Sybil Milton. *Art of the Holocaust* is a well-produced assortment of paintings, diary illustrations, and notebook sketches, some by unknown artists. The volume is organized into sections: early anti-Nazi artists like Klee and Kollwitz; the ghettos of Bialystok, Warsaw, and Terezín; transit camps like Compiègne and Gurs; and, finally, pencil drawings from concentration camps of Stutthof and Ravensbrück. Milton has separately published *The Art of Jewish Children: Germany, 1936–1941*. The 125 drawings of Africans, Gypsies, and Orientals done under the instruction of Jules Leviln (who perished in Auschwitz) are strikingly similar to the emotional sketches collected by Hana Volavkova in *I Never Saw Another Butterfly*.

Like Volavkova's edition, Gerald Green's *The Artists of Terezin* deals with the Nazi "Paradise Ghetto," but from adults' perspectives. The story of Otto Ungar, Bedrich Fritta, Karel Fleischmann, and Leo Haas, Green's book offers stirring testimony to the valor of these underground artists. In that sense it is like a number of other collections that have been posthumously published. Yad Vashem's *Testimony Art of the Holocaust* (edited by Irit Salmon-Livne and Ilana Guri) is a bilingual catalog containing nearly one hundred pencil drawings, watercolors, and sculptures along with biographies of talented artists like Miecyzslaw Mussil and Z. Wieseniewski who vanished without a trace in the Holocaust. *Spiritual Resistance Art from Concentration Camps, 1940–1945*, edited by the Warsaw Ghetto Fighters' Kibbutz, is a brief, but helpful guide, featuring a country-by-country approach to some of the Holocaust artists. Also noteworthy are Mary Costanza's *The Living Witness: Art in the Concentration Camps and Ghettos* (the book contains powerful sketches of stacks of bodies done by concentration-camp inmates juxtaposed with photographs taken by American liberators) and Joseph Czarnecki's *Last Traces: The Lost Art of Auschwitz*. The latter contains photographs of official art (warnings about typhus), murals (children going to school), poems, and graffiti etched into the actual walls of Auschwitz barracks. Czarneck records the heroism of those who suffered torture in Block 11, including the Polish priest Maximilian Kolbe and the lovers Mala Zimetbaum and Edward Galinski.

A few artists did survive and have managed to publish their own excellent memoirs. Among these are Alfred Kantor's *The Book of Alfred Kantor*, with its primitive, yet graphic, recollections of life in Terezín, Auschwitz, and Schwarzheide; Nelly Toll's *Without Surrender: Art of the Holocaust*, with the watercolors of sunflowers and dominos painted by a young girl hiding with her mother in Lwow; Toby Fluek's *Memories of My Life in a Polish Village, 1930–1949*, with its grim similarities between Soviet and Nazi occupations; and *Gyorgy Kadar: Survivor of Death, Witness to Life*, a collection by a Hungarian-Jewish survivor whose fifty-seven prints and crayons in black and white include a hanging in Auschwitz and a woman and child being murdered on the banks of the Danube.

Special mention must be made of *The Precious Legacy: Judaic Treasures from the Czechoslovak State Collection*, edited by David Altshuler. The text includes Hillel Kieval's valuable essay on the history of Czech Jews. Photographs include pianos, violins, rings, and Torah scrolls that were confiscated in 1942 by SS Untersturmführer Karl Rahm. *The Precious Legacy* catalogs Sabbath lamps, pointers, Torah mantles, prayerbooks, dreydls, and candlesticks that were part of a traveling exhibition sponsored by the Smithsonian Institution. It is the benchmark of what a memorial volume should be, certainly far superior to Adolf Reith's *Monuments to the Victims of Tyranny*, a disappointing work that promises memorials at camps, churches, and cemeteries in Europe and supplies more photographs of Fort Brendonk than Treblinka.

Memorials in the form of sculpture are also highlighted in Vivian Thompson's *A Mission in Art: Recent Holocaust Works in America*, but these are not the works that have the greatest impact. Pittsburgh-based Bruce Carter, a Gentile, has etched a number of extraordinary woodcuts dealing with the agony of the Warsaw ghetto. The studies of Janusz Korczak, ghetto children, and the SS are evocative of some of the most emotionally wrenching Jewish art in the twentieth century, Marc Chagall's *War, 1960*, *The Haggadah* of Arthur Szyk, or *The Graphic Art of Jakob Steinhardt*.

## SELECT BIBLIOGRAPHY

Abramson, Glenda, ed. *The Blackwell Companion to Jewish Culture from the Eighteenth Century to the Present*. Oxford: Basil Blackwell, 1989.

Altshuler, David, ed. *The Precious Legacy: Judaic Treasures from the Czechoslovak State Collection*. New York: Summit Books, 1983.

*Arte e resistenza in Europa*. Bologna: Museo Civico and Artigrafiche Tamari, 1965.

Bittner, Herbert. *Kaethe Kollwitz, Drawings*. New York: Castle Books, 1959.

Blatter, Janet, and Sybil Milton. *Art of the Holocaust*. New York: Rutledge Press, 1981.

Costanza, Mary S. *The Living Witness: Art in the Concentration Camps and Ghettos*. New York: Free Press, 1982.

Czarnecki, Joseph P. *Last Traces: The Lost Art of Auschwitz.* New York: Atheneum, 1989.

Fluek, Toby Knobel. *Memories of My Life in a Polish Village, 1930–1949.* New York: Knopf, 1990.

Green, Gerald. *The Artists of Terezin.* New York: Hawthorn Books, 1969.

Gutmann, Joseph, ed. *No Graven Images: Studies in Art and the Hebrew Bible.* New York: Ktav, 1971.

*Gyorgy Kadar: Survivor of Death, Witness to Life.* Exhibition Catalog of the Vanderbilt Collection of Holocaust Art. Joel Logiudice, Curator, and Michele Douglas, Editor. Nashville: Vanderbilt University, 1988.

Kaliszan, Jozef, and Czeslaw Banasiewicz. *The Warsaw Ghetto: Drawings by Jozef Kaliszan.* New York: T. Yoseloff, 1968.

Kampf, Avram. *Jewish Experience in the Art of the Twentieth Century.* South Hadley, Mass.: Bergin and Garvey, 1984.

Kantor, Alfred. *The Book of Alfred Kantor.* New York: McGraw-Hill, 1971.

Lissitzky, El. *El Lissitzky: Life, Letters, Texts.* Translated by Helene Aldwinckle and Mary Whittall. London: Thames and Hudson, 1968.

Milton, Sybil. *The Art of Jewish Children: Germany, 1936–1941.* New York: Philosophical Library, 1989.

Rieth, Adolf. *Monuments to the Victims of Tyranny.* New York: Praeger, 1969.

Roskies, David. *Against the Apocalypse: Responses to Catastrophe in Modern Jewish Culture.* Cambridge, Mass.: Harvard University Press, 1984.

Roth, Cecil. *Jewish Art: An Illustrated History.* Rev. ed. by Bezalel Narkiss. Greenwich, Conn.: New York Graphic Society, 1971.

Salmon-Livne, Irit, and Ilana Guri, eds. *Testimony Art of the Holocaust.* Jerusalem: Yad Vashem, 1982.

*Spiritual Resistance Art from Concentration Camps, 1940–1945: Drawings and Paintings from Kibbutz Lochamei Haghettaot, Israel.* New York: Union of American Hebrew Congregations, 1978.

Steinhardt, Jakob. *The Graphic Art of Jakob Steinhardt.* With a critical appreciation by Haim Gamzu. New York and London: T.Yoseloff, 1963.

Szyk, Arthur. *The Haggadah.* Edited by Cecil Roth. Jerusalem: Massada Press, n.d.

Thompson, Vivian Alpert. *A Mission in Art: Recent Holocaust Works in America.* Macon, Ga.: Mercer University Press, 1988.

Toll, Nelly. *Without Surrender: Art of the Holocaust.* Philadelphia: Running Press, 1978.

Volavkova, Hana, ed. *I Never Saw Another Butterfly.* Translated by Jeanne Nemcova. New York: McGraw-Hill, 1964.

Wigoder, Geoffrey, ed. *Jewish Art and Civilization.* New York: Walker, 1972.

# Chapter 30

---

# Music of the Holocaust

## *Irene Heskes*

As soon as Hitler came to power in 1933, a movement for the so-called purification of German music began with a day of boycott on April 1, 1933. Joseph
Goebbels, overseer of the Ministry of Propaganda, had formed a Chamber of
Culture, with a special section for music called the Reich Chamber of Music.
That department was to supervise all musical activities and musicians and to
monitor the music that would pervade concert halls, radio programs, schools,
factories, offices, homes, and soon also the army barracks and wartime battlefields. Hitler's ideas about music, as well as all the other arts, shaped the cultural
atmosphere from the very start of his regime. In 1934 a formal ban was instituted
against Jewish music and musicians, and the next year Jews were no longer to
be employed by musical groups nor to perform publicly for general audiences.
Also strictly banned were the compositions written by Jews or by those suspected
of being pro-Jewish. With the Chamber of Music as its instrument of action,
the Gestapo took control of this "cleansing" of German culture. Following upon
the publication in 1936 of the government listings of forbidden musicians and
musical selections, the ban spread to all aspects of music and became a total
fact.

There had been precedents in Germany for such listings and for an overt anti-
Semitic movement in music. In 1869 Richard Wagner penned an infamous tract,
*Das Judentum in der Musik* (The Jews in music), a vicious and rambling diatribe
attacking Jewish influences as negative and destructive forces. Subsequently a
son-in-law of Wagner, Houston Stewart Chamberlain, also railed in print against
Jewish musicians and their works. During the 1920s and the rise of the Nazi
movement, there were several publications that underscored antipathy toward

Jews and their music. *Das Judentum in der Musik* (The Jews in music) by Heinreich Berl was published in 1926 in Berlin and Leipzig, reprinting much of Wagner's earlier work and stressing his stated opinion that anything Jewish does not belong in the Occident. Berl, an active member of the Nazi party in Stuttgart, went even further by denying any value at all to Jewish cultural expression. In Munich in 1932 Richard Eichenauer, a Nazi party member, published his book *Musik und Rasse* (Music and race), which advanced party theory that Jewish musical ideas polluted the purity of German musical expression and must therefore be erased. In fast succession there were other such publications, not only by Joseph Goebbels, but by a number of so-called music scholars: Karl Blessinger, Werner Egk, Carl Heinzen, Hans Hickmann, Hans Koeltzsch, H. W. Kulenkampff, Hans Joachim Moser, and Peter Raabe. In 1940 the first edition of a *Lexikon der Juden in der Musik* (Dictionary of Jews in music) was prepared for general distribution by the Nazis, in order to guarantee exclusion of any Judaic elements in all music. Blank pages were left in the *Lexikon* for the insertion of additional names and compositions. Its compilers, Theophil Stengel and Herbert Gerigk, worked at the Berlin central office of the NSDAP, officially known as the Workshop for Research in the Matter of the Jewish Problem.

Between the years 1933 and 1935 Jews rapidly disappeared from the ranks of orchestras and other instrumental groups, conservatories and university music departments, publishers and libraries, opera houses and concert halls, newspapers and periodicals, and radio and recording studios. Jazz music was regarded as "non-Aryan negroid" and was also banned along with most American popular music, whether by Jews or not. Richard Wagner's music was adored by Hitler, and consequently his operas were instituted as ritual events. The performances at Bayreuth assumed a particularly intense atmosphere. The music of Anton Bruckner, a disciple of Wagner, was also frequently performed at Nazi functions.

German radio broadcasts were increasingly utilized for propaganda devices, and music became a significant aspect of these programs. Suitably Nazified music was performed at mass rallies and public events. In 1938 Hitler proclaimed a National Day of Music, for which Goebbels drafted a list of "commandments" to be observed by all German musicians and included the credo: "Music is that art that deeply affects the spirit of man." Throughout Hitler's regime musicians were exempted from actual military combat service and instead were sent out to entertain soldiers in the field and workers in the factories. During the final critical months of the war, Hitler did permit the broadcasting of jazz and American popular songs to men on the front lines and encampments. However, these songs were heard only with German lyrics without any mention of their musical sources, and in that way music by Duke Ellington, Irving Berlin, George Gershwin, and Jerome Kern was enjoyed by soldiers fighting for Hitler.

To carry forward their objectives, the Nazis early on assumed the practice of adapting music, giving new texts to old favorite German songs and folk ballads. The earliest official National Socialist songbook was edited by Reinhold Zimmerman and issued in 1933 in Berlin, and music was specifically programmed for propaganda purposes up to the very last days of the regime. The rationalization among many musicians who remained active in behalf of Hitler was that good music, especially German music, could negate any evil. The anthem of the Nazi party, generally known as "Horst Wessel Lied" (Song of Horst Wessel), had been an old beer-hall ballad melody that was adapted and retitled "Die Fahne hoch" (Lift up the banner). Its newer lyrics had been set by a member of the SA Brown Shirts named Horst Wessel, who was wounded in a street brawl and died of blood poisoning. Thereupon Wessel was made a Nazi martyr, and his house in Vienna was kept as a shrine until 1945. Several Prussian marches were adapted with such lyrics as "We're marching against England" or, later in the war, "Victory and strength in battle." Parading Nazis sang out, "Wenn das Judenblut vom messer spritzt, dann gehts noch mal so gut" (When Jewish blood flows from the knife, then everything goes so well").

Apparently, music was used to create an atmosphere in which mass murder could be sung about as a justified patriotic duty and the victims as being sub-human. Such songs were created in abundance. Even the concentration camps had to have music, and all new prisoners were questioned about their musical abilities. At Auschwitz an all-female orchestra was formed, its ranks filled with other arrivals as members died of disease and starvation or were slaughtered. As early as 1938 a *Lagerskapelle* (prison-camp band) was established at Buchenwald. At Terezín many notable European Jewish musicians performed for their captors before being sent away to the crematoria.

In the concentration camps, when musicians played and sang for their captors, they did not perform music by Jewish composers, but sometimes did include parodies of Jewish selections. Musicians were relieved from work details for these performances and were often given different clothes to wear. In the early years funds were allocated for scores and instruments, but soon these music materials were only acquired as property confiscated from the inmates. Prisoner ensembles played for the health exercises and military drills of the guards, as well as for their leisure entertainment. All too frequently their musical performances accompanied the marching off to death of fellow victims. Survivors recall hearing radio broadcasts over loudspeakers, even of the Berlin Philharmonic Orchestra playing, as men, women, and children were being tortured, gassed, and burned.

During the first years of the Hitler regime German Jews, reacting to the bans, organized their own *Kulturband* (cultural organization) in many cities. Among their wide range of activities were music events at private homes, meeting halls, and synagogues. As the oppressive measures grew worse and societal isolation of Jews became almost complete, these Jewish educational and cultural groups were filled with well-known people, and for a brief time there was much creative activity. Quite soon, however, the atmosphere of oppression and human jeopardy became overwhelming, and there were desperate efforts to find some escape to another country. For notable figures this might be a feasible possibility, but only those who actually left the continent of Europe ultimately managed not to be trapped and destroyed.

Musicians who had devoted their talents to Jewish liturgical traditions were prime visible targets in every country that the Nazis occupied and thus were least able to evade capture. Their lives had been bound up with the Jewish faith in service to synagogue and temple congregants. Most *hazzanim* (precentor-cantors) went along with their local communities into the ghettos and concentration camps, where they perished. Thus ended an unbroken continuity of Judaic liturgical music traditions that had flourished throughout Europe since the early era of the Roman Empire.

Inasmuch as Hitler's deliberate endeavor was to destroy Judaism along with the Jewish people, the Nazis worked ceaselessly to denigrate and distort Jewish religion and history. The objective was to erase tangible evidence of that heritage as a viable living force in civilization, to write Jews entirely out of the chronicles of Western society. Small wonder that along with the six million human beings lost, little of substance remains from their lives, especially during the years 1933 to 1945. In terms of music, any creativity during that latter period had to be written down secretly and then zealously saved from destruction, or else had to be preserved by word of mouth and orally transmitted to the few who hopefully might not perish. As a result, some literature and simple songs are the legacy. Postwar collections of these materials shaped amidst tragic circumstances not only provide historians with a priceless remembrance but also constitute a significant form of documentary evidence describing those times and events. Some postwar collectors also have managed to gather remnants of extended vocal and instrumental works, less as works of artistry than as a sustained tribute to the greater amount of what was lost. The surviving elements of Jewish music in particular ought not to be judged by the usual rules of aesthetic evaluation. The songs are like old faded and torn photographs, dimmed and damaged likenesses from the past. They must be viewed in the context of their creative origins and circumstances of expression and as symbols of unfinished lives and shattered continuities.

Details of events during these dreadful years in Europe serve to underscore the impact upon Jewish musical expression of the time. By *Kristallnacht* in November 1938, with the shattering and looting of Jewish homes, commercial establishments, and houses of worship, Jews were in grave peril. Mass deportations to death camps had begun. As the German army entered each unlucky country, Jewish scholars and cultural leaders were the first targets. By late 1941 thousands of them were being deported to Theresienstadt (Terezín), located north of Prague in Czechoslovakia. This concentration camp had been set up in 1934 as a special holding place for those from politics and public life, as well as from the professions and the arts. It was to become the final residence of very many famous people, Jewish and Christian. For a time at that camp, the inmates were allowed to organize their own special activities, especially music, and to develop

other artistic projects. The Nazis used these activities as a deceitful instrument
of propaganda, purporting to illustrate how affluent Jews were resting and enjoying themselves while the good Germans—or the Austrians, Czechs, Poles,
and others—were laboring so hard during such difficult times.

As conditions degenerated at Terezín and became desperately impossible by
1942, ensemble and solo instrumental concerts and operatic and oratorio performances continued on. Musicians rehearsed and performed; composers wrote
and conducted; music teachers taught and lectured. That concentration camp
became a grotesque microcosm of the former flourishing European musical society. Music sustained the spirit, numbed the anguish, entertained for brief
fleeting hours, and strengthened personal resolve. Even more than that, musical
expression became a defiant act of affirmation. Over the months, starvation,
disease, and then the death transports decimated the ranks of musicians and
audience. Finally the music ended at Terezín, and that "anteroom to hell"
became merely a gathering point and stopover on the road to the gas chambers
of Auschwitz, Belsen, Buchenwald, and other death camps. In recent years
several music scholars, among them a Christian Czech (now in America) named
Joza Karas, have discovered and assembled some written scores from Terezín.
In particular there are two operas, *Brundibar,* written for children by Hans Krasa,
and *Der Kaiser von Atlantis,* composed by Viktor Ullman with a libretto by
Peter Kien. Both works have been performed in the United States, Israel, and
Czechoslovakia during recent years.

For Eastern Europe, which for centuries had been the golden area of Yiddish
culture, the artistic destruction during the Holocaust proved catastrophic. Inspired
by leaders of the nineteenth-century *haskalah* (enlightenment) movement in Judaism, who encouraged a broadening range of educational and intellectual quest,
Jewish life in that part of Europe had become remarkably productive in literature
and the arts. Much of that creativity was expressed in a distinctive Yiddish folk
medium. During the first four decades of the twentieth century, there was a
particular abundance of musical activities, both sacred and secular. It was as
though in its final urgency a burst of great expression erupted before the total
extinction.

The Ashkenazic communities of Jewish Diaspora life in Europe over many
centuries had elaborated, sanctified, and preserved the age-old religious music
traditions that illuminated their precious liturgy. For over four hundred years the
geographical area of Eastern Europe became the most productive center for
training of *hazzanim* and the other musicians at congregational rituals—the Bible
chanters, choir singers, choral directors, and liturgical composers and arrangers.
Born, bred, and trained, they went forth to serve Jews throughout Europe and
overseas to America. Synagogue music, based upon many centuries of unbroken
lyric and poetic creativity, was passed along the generations by means of personal
instruction and apprenticeship. Handed on in that process of oral dissemination
were unique cantorial styles, the techniques and nuances of devotional music
making. By the eighteenth century much of that musical repertoire had begun

to be committed to written scores and liturgical publications. As a result, by the early decades of the twentieth century, substantial libraries of liturgical music, either in the form of one-of-a-kind manuscripts or in books of liturgy, filled the sanctuaries and library shelves of European synagogues, schools, and homes. Most of this was lost or went up in flames when these buildings were desecrated and destroyed. The torch was put to Judaica as the Nazis swept through all of the Eastern European countries.

In secular music affairs, large choral groups and composer-arrangers had emerged in the decade preceding World War I, including the famous *Hazamir* choirs of Vilna, Warsaw, and Lodz. Beyond the usual folkloristic *klezmer* bands, there were musical ensembles that featured Jewish music selections in concert halls and at communal events. Yiddish musical theaters flourished, as for example the Azazel in Warsaw and the Ararat in Lodz, where general tunes were performed, along with the favorite Yiddish songs, before appreciative audiences of all types. Jews filled the performing ranks in Eastern European opera companies, light musicals, and concert-hall programs. Bridging the secular and sacred genres were the folk songs and musical expressions of social and educational societies, labor groups, and Zionist organizations. And, of course, there were the ever-popular balladeer entertainers at weddings, communal celebrations, and cabarets. Yiddish folk songs particularly reflected all aspects of life, and many balladeers also sang to their audiences about subjects of timely interest, of specific political, economic, and social concerns. Not a few warned about the dark menace further west in Europe. After World War I a new Jewish educational concept, known as *tarbuth* (culture), sought to advance the teaching of Hebrew and Yiddish through songs. A number of songbooks were published for that pedagogical method, whose ideas had spread to American shores. The children's schools proved a particularly good environment for the creation of Jewish songs. Then, too, the musical influence of centuries of the Hasidic (pietist) sects in that area of Europe had entered into the rhythms and melodies favored by all Jews. Moreover, there had always been a fluidity of musical movement between Jews and their Christian neighbors, with the elements of Slavic melos being especially adaptive between these peoples. There were Jewish popular songs much in the nature of Yiddish American songs, very many of which had found their way back from America to the general theaters and the radio programs of Eastern Europe. In all, it had been a rich musical era for Jewish music.

After 1939 musical expression persisted as Jews were herded into ghettos and then boxcars transporting them to death camps, serving as some sort of basic life force and affording a semblance of sanity in the face of the most insane of circumstances. In the shrinking ghettos adult choirs served as a last means of communication, and children's choruses became devices for the special care of orphans. Finally, into the transports went the great body of Jewish musical expression: liturgical music traditions; holiday and Sabbath chants; favorite songs of family life and community history; folk melodies from countless past generations; popular tunes and art selections; and street ditties and broadside ballads.

Rapidly added to that familiar music was a newer expression, songs and lyrics shaped and sung in reaction to the most dreadful of conditions. There can be no doubt that there was music making to the very end. It was a folk artistry wrought out of sheer necessity and old cultural habit in defiance of the Nazis and their malevolent helpers in so many European places.

In some strange way these freshly created songs traveled from ghetto to ghetto and among the various concentration camps. One was known as the chant of the *frumer Yidn* (pious Jews): "Ani Ma-amin" (I believe). The brief Hebrew verse was chanted as an affirmation of faith at the very moment of death: "I believe, with true hope and trust, in the coming of the Messiah; and though his coming be delayed, I shall never stop believing." For Judaism, this statement is a significant part of the thirteen principles of faith. In a remarkable musical reshaping, the melody combines a simplified version of a 1920s Jewish cabaret ballad with the traditional *lernshteyg* (learning chant), the age-old motival pattern intoned by rabbinical students at their studies. Although the popular *badkhen* (balladeer) Mordecai Gebirtig (1877–1943) had written his song "Es Brennt" (It is burning) as an early warning in 1938, it was sung over the next years as an ironic outcry to the outside world. "Our little town is on fire; it's burning, and you helplessly stand, watching as the flames grow wilder and higher. Who will quench the blaze, my brothers? All our world is on fire."

So many gifted musicians were lost. A few of their names now are known only because of some final musical duties, and recollection of them particularizes the enormous artistic loss. David Eisenshtadt, a noted scholar and musician, organized a symphonic ensemble and a chorus in the Warsaw ghetto. His daughter, Maryasha Eisenshtadt, was called "the nightingale of the ghetto." Both were murdered in 1942 as they tried to resist capture for deportation. Israel Faiveshes, a music educator and conservatory director, organized children's choruses in the ghettos of Warsaw, Lodz, and Vilna. Sent to Piantova concentration camp, he continued to teach youngsters to sing and perished there with them. Jacob Glatschtein had been a prolific writer of pedagogical songs and choral works for the Yiddish schools. Imprisoned at Treblinka, he gathered children together and taught them songs before they were gassed together. In the Vilna ghetto Abraham Slep, who earlier had established a leading musical institute in Vilna, led a chorus performing elegies in open defiance of the Nazis. Following an infamous massacre in April 1943 at Ponar (much like the one at Babi Yar in the Ukraine), Slep was transported to Estonia, where he was shot as a dangerous political leader.

During the final months Jewish musicians often were treated especially harshly in the camps because their music influenced the others, helped maintain bonds of relationship, or at least afforded an essence of humanity. Jewish music was used to communicate between ghettos and camps and to share information among resistance fighters. In the Vilna ghetto a music contest was held, the winning song submitted by the eleven-year-old son of a physician who had been shot. That child, Alex Volkovisky, survived and emigrated to Israel. The melody and its words were elaborated upon by many others in the camps who sang that song: "Shtiler, Shtiler" (Quiet, quiet). "Silence, quiet, make no noise; graves around us are growing. Roads lead to Ponar, but none lead back. Days are black with endless grief; hearts are frozen numb. Our crime is to be hated; who can understand why?" There also were many poetic lyrics that outlasted the melodies to which they had been sung. Some of the texts begged those who might survive never to forget what had happened to the others. There were songs and poems of those still alive mourning those who had died, of those who did not know where loved ones had gone, of pleas for help from the rest of the world. It is likely that every possible emotion was mirrored during that era. The traditional Jewish love of music had blended with a desperate will to live, if only post-humously through an artistry that might last beyond the times and tell the whole dreadful story.

Most pathetic were the ghetto and concentration-camp lullabies sung by strangers to orphans, by bereft mothers alone, and by children to each other. Among the remnants of such songs is the eloquent "S'dremlen feygel oyf di tsvaygen" (Birds are sleeping on the branches). "Sleep, poor baby, hungry baby. On the cold ground beside you, a stranger softly sings, a stranger softly weeps." Another one is an ironic refashioning of the original words of Abraham Goldfaden's widely beloved song "Rozhinkes mit mandlen" (Raisins and almonds), retitled as "Nit kayn rozhinkes, nit kayn mandlen" (No raisins nor any almonds). "Little ones, here you are all alone. Father will never bring you any sweets, and mother is also gone forever." Newer texts were constantly sung to old familiar melodies. That process of adaptation in musical contrafacta had been a general artistic phenomenon dating back to early times and was especially fruitful over the centuries among all peoples as a dynamic cultural passageway. One such example from the Holocaust songs was the deliberate textual alteration of Goldfaden's "Rozhinkes mit mandlen." Retaining the original familiar melody, newer lyrics were sung (as attributed to an Orthodox Jew from Kovno named Axelrod), and it was known as "Letste videh" (Last testament). "To my fellow Jews and all my brothers in humanity, I leave this final message. Tell your children of our grievous suffering and terrible destruction. Never forget us."

Life persisted in the ghettos and camps in constant reaffirmation of a will to live. Survivors relate how they endeavored to maintain some cultural and intellectual expression with ever more intensity as they faced death. Promises were made that those who might survive would never forget, making certain that the world would know and also remember. "Live, so you can tell what happened!" was the shriek of spiritual resistance. Ethnic folklore arose out of desperate need. Beyond comfort or communication, they wrote messages to the future, transforming the writers into real individuals, not faceless numbers. Realizing that singing afforded dignity and strength, the Nazis often shot singers on sight. Escaping from a roundup in the Vilna ghetto, a writer named Abraham Sutzkever hid in a closed box for hours. While there, he composed a poem. "Lying in this coffin, my speech still moves into song." In this manner, simple poems and songs transcended that label of folklore and passed into the realm of art as historic documentation.

Among the Jewish partisan fighters, whistles and tunes were used as signals, especially one particular song: "Zog nit keynmol az du geyst dem letsten veg" (Do not say that you go on the last road). "Do not say that this is the end of the way. Though all around is darkness and death, the time is coming soon when our footsteps will resound. Wherever our blood has red-stained the ground, from there will our courage and strength take root and blossom forth. The world will surely know that we are still here." The author of that text was Hirsh Glik (1920–1944). Born in Vilna, he organized resistance groups there and then in 1943 escaped to join partisans outside the city. Glik was captured and shipped to a camp in Estonia, where he again escaped and soon died in the woods, fighting the Nazis. He had wanted to be a journalist and wrote this poem to be sung to a well-known march tune of the time. This song became so widely popular during the last months of the war that even the Nazis were familiar with it.

Although Yiddish had rapidly become the predominant language in the ghettos and death camps, among the victims were many Sephardim (Jews of the Judeo-Spanish tradition). Before they lost their lives, they persevered in their particular cultural heritage and sang their own Ladino (Espagnol-Judaic) ballads with the various Balkan, Greek, and Turkish dialects, or inflections of Italian, French, and Flemish.

The period from the surrender of the German army in May 1945 to the formal creation of the State of Israel in May 1948 was a twilight era in Jewish history. It was a time for the full realization of the enormous crime done to six million men, women, and children, punished for being Jewish. Almost immediately, efforts were begun to salvage what was left, in terms of any human survivors as well as the legacy of all those who had been murdered. Gathered up were materials that testified to what had happened, and that process of collecting grew as a mission of verification, along with the tallying up of what had been destroyed. As a result, there emerged a body of works, consisting of timely lyrics set to older familiar tunes or newly composed melodies, and fragments of ditties or snatches of chants that had once served the needs of the martyred singers.

Fifty fully shaped song selections, original lyrics as well as melodies, are presently available in various published editions. Although their original words were in Yiddish, a language of great expressiveness, that intensity of emotion has passed readily into English translations. Along with these songs, many fragments of poetic writings have been preserved from that era, each item having its own special message. Most notable among the postwar collectors of all these materials was a concentration-camp survivor, Shmerke Kacerginsky (1908–1953), to whom lasting gratitude must be expressed for his dedication in behalf of that valuable cultural endeavor.

In reaction to the full knowledge of what happened and the consequent impact of that catastrophe, musicians and scholars have been inspired to express their reactions to the Holocaust in a wide spectrum of artistic works, studies, and musical activities. Composers especially have taken on the almost impossible burden to interpret the events and to memorialize the victims. Here, as with the legacy of Holocaust songs, the usual yardsticks of aesthetic principles ought not to be applied. Indeed, since all of this music is by no means pleasurable, performances are likely to be rare. Yet such works continue to be written. Perhaps some future musical genius will find a way to fashion an inspired masterpiece worthy of this special subject, creatively moving beyond the actual horror and anguish.

Nevertheless, some musical selections already have passed into the general repertoire. In 1962 Dmitri Shostakovich wrote his Thirteenth Symphony ("Babi Yar"), which memorializes the thousands of Ukrainian Jews murdered in 1941 at a location called Babi Yar (Old wives' ravine) outside of Kiev. Arnold Schönberg, who found refuge from the Nazis in America in 1934, composed "A Survivor from Warsaw" in 1947. Scored for speaker, male chorus, and chamber orchestra, the work was commissioned by the Serge Koussevitzky Foundation. Schönberg wrote the English text, and his brief musical work is starkly powerful, building up to an unusually dramatic chanting of *Sh'ma Yisrael,* the Jewish affirmation of faith.

Social historians cannot afford to ignore the significance of music, especially those songs created by and for the people themselves. In a special partnership with poetic expression, such songs have served mankind as a valuable form of information concerning times, places, and events, interpreting humanity, striving in the maelstrom for some verification of continuity. Viewed in these perspectives, the music related to the Holocaust era constitutes a very special documentary resource, reflective of an abiding tragedy in history. These materials truly serve to underscore that critical role of poetry and song as intrinsic to the totality of life's experience. Produced within the confines of ghettos and concentration camps, the songs constitute a unique cultural expression crafted under the worst of circumstances. In every sense, such ad hoc artistry amplifies recent history and the enormous loss suffered not only by Jewry but by all of humanity, now bequeathed a melodic portrait set within a landscape of screams.

## SELECT BIBLIOGRAPHY

### Literature

Bloch, Max. "Victor Ullman (1898–1943): A Brief Biography and Appreciation." *Journal of the Arnold Schoenberg Institute* (Los Angeles, Calif.: ASI) 3, no. 2 (1979): 150–77.

Bor, Josef. *The Terezin Requiem.* Translated from the Czech by Edith Pargeter. New York: Knopf, 1963.

Fenelon, Fania, *Playing for Time: The Musicians of Auschwitz*. Translated from the French by Judith Landry. New York: Atheneum, 1977.

Freeden, Herbert. "Jewish Theater Under the Swastika." *Leo Baeck Institute Yearbook* (London: East and West Library) 1 (1956): 142–62.

Gradenwitz, Peter. "Jews In Austrian Music." In *The Jews of Austria*, edited by Josef Fraenkel, pp. 17–24. London, England: Vallentine, Mitchell, 1966.

Heskes, Irene. "Jewish Music Resources for Holocaust Programming." In *The Holocaust: An Annotated Bibliography and Resource Guide,* edited by David Szonyi, pp. 222–51. N.Y.: Ktav, 1985.

Holde, Artur. *Jews in Music*. Revised edition prepared by Irene Heskes. New York: Bloch Publishing, 1974.

Jani, Emilio. *My Voice Saved Me: Auschwitz 180046*. Translated from the Italian by Timothy Paterson. Milan: Centauro Editrice, 1961.

Karas, Joiza. *Music in Terezin, 1941–1945*. New York: Pendragon Press, 1975.

Lederer, Zdenek. *Ghetto Theresienstadt*. London: Edward Goldston, 1953.

Nettl, Paul. "Music." In *The Jews of Czechoslovakia: Historical Studies and Surveys,* vol. 1, edited by the Publication Committee of the Society for the History of Czechoslovak Jews, pp. 539–58. Philadelphia: Jewish Publication Society of America, 1968.

Veret, Paul. "Art and Music in the Shoah (Holocaust)." In *Out of the Whirlwind: A Reader of Holocaust Literature*, pp. 259–82. New York: Doubleday, 1968.

Werner, Eric. "An Old Controversy: Aesthetics and Politics in the Writings of Mendelssohn and Wagner." In *Musicae Scientiae Collectanea: Festschrift Karl Gustav Fellerer Z, 70, Geburtstagam 7 Juli 1972*, ed. by Heinrich Hüschen, pp. 640–60. Cologne: Volk, 1973.

## Collections of Holocaust Songs

*Geto Lider aus Littland un Littauer—Songs from Lithuania and Latvia*. Compiled by Johanna Spector. Vienna: Joint Distribution Committee, 1947; 59 pages; music.

*Kedoshim—Martyrs*. Compiled and arranged by Henech Kon. New York: Machmadim Press, 1947; 32 pages; music.

*Lider fun di getos un lagern—Songs (and Poetry) from the Ghettos and Concentration Camps*. Compiled and annotated by Shmerke (Shmariah) Kacerginsky, with musical annotations by Michl Gelbart. New York: CYCO/Congress for Jewish Culture; 1948; 435 pages; text and music.

*Min Ha-metzar—Out of the Depths: From the Songs of the Ghettos*. Collected and arranged by Ernest Horvitz. Tel Aviv: Histadruth and Ha-merkav LeTarbuth, 1949; 70 pages; text and music.

Mlotek, Joseph. *Mordecai Gebirtig: Martyred Troubadour of Our People*. New York: Workmen's Circle Organization, 1970; 20 pages; text and music.

Rubin, Ruth. "Yiddish Songs of World War II." *Jewish Quarterly*, 2, no. 2 (1963): 12–17; text and music.

*Songs of the Concentration Camps*. Collected by Emma Schaver and arranged by Lazar Weiner. New York: Transcontinental Music/UAHC, 1960; 10 pages; music.

*Songs of the Ghetto*. Collected and arranged by Henech Kon. New York: CYCO Congress for Jewish Culture; vol. 1, 1960, 64 pages; vol. 2, 1972, 32 pages; music.

*Songs of the Martyrs: Hasidic Melodies of the Marmures.* Collected and arranged by Max Eisikovitz. New York: Sepher-Hermon Press, 1980; 62 pages; music.

*A Treasury of Jewish Folksong.* Compiled and annotated by Ruth Rubin. New York: Schocken Books, 1964; 212 pages; text and music.

*Twenty-Five Ghetto Songs.* Collected and arranged by Malka Gottlieb and Chana Eleanor Mlotek. New York: Workmen's Circle Organization, 1968; 54 pages; music.

*Undzer Gezang—Our Song.* Compiled by the Central Committee of Jews in Poland. Warsaw: Office of Culture and Propaganda, 1947; 15 pages; music.

*Voices of a People: The Story of Yiddish Folksong.* Compiled and annotated by Ruth Rubin. New York: McGraw-Hill, 1973; 558 pages; text and music.

*Warsaw Ghetto Memorial Program.* Prepared by Ruth Rubin. New York: Workmen's Circle Organization, 1967; 23 pages; text and music.

*We Are Here! Songs of the Holocaust.* Compiled and arranged by Eleanor Mlotek with Malke Gottlieb. New York: Workmen's Circle Organization and Hippocrene Books, 1983; 104 pages; text and music.

*Yes, We Sang! Songs of the Ghettos and Concentration Camps.* Collected and annotated by Shoshana Kalisch and arranged by Barbara Meister. New York: Harper and Row, 1985; 160 pages; text and music.

## Musical Works

### From the Legacy

(Scores are available from Holocaust organizations in the United States and Israel.)

Krasa, Hans (d. Auschwitz 1943). *Brundibar.* Children's opera composed and performed in Terezín. Libretto adapted by the composer from a folktale. Soloists, SATB chorus, and instrumental ensemble.

Ullman, Viktor (d. Auschwitz 1943). *Der Kaiser von Atlantis—The Emperor of Atlantis, or Death Abdicates.* Chamber opera composed and performed in Terezín. Libretto by Peter Kien. Soloists, SATB chorus, and instrumental ensemble.

Weber, Ilse (d. Terezín 1942). *Song Cycle.* Seven selections for soprano and piano, composed and performed at Terezín. Text by the composer.

### In Commemoration of the Holocaust

Amram, David. *The Final Ingredient: A Concentration Camp Seder.* Opera in one act, scored for male solos, chorus (TB), and chamber orchestra. Libretto by Reginald Rose. New York: C.F. Peters/Alexander Broude.

Binder, Abraham W. *Requiem-Yizkor.* Liturgical text adapted by the composer. Scored for male solo, chorus (SATB), and organ. New York: Transcontinental/Union of American Hebrew Congregations.

Cage, John. *In the Name of the Holocaust.* Music for a ballet choreographed by Merce Cunningham. Scored for instrumental ensemble. New York: Henmar Press.

Castelnuovo-Tedesco, Mario. *Lamentation and Kaddish.* Scored for organ. New York: Leeds Music.

Davidson, Charles. *I Never Saw Another Butterfly.* Cantata with text adapted by the composer from poems written by the children at Terezín. Scored for solos, boy choir (SA), and organ. Elkins Park, Pa.: Ashbourne Publishers.

Foss, Lukas. *Song of Anguish*. Cantata with text adapted by the composer from the Book of Isaiah. Scored for vocal solo and orchestra. New York: Carl Fischer.

Fromm, Herbert. *Memorial Cantata*. Text adapted by the composer from biblical passages. Scored for male solo, chorus (SATB), and organ. New York: Transcontinental/Union of American Hebrew Congregations.

Josephs, Wilfred. *Requiem: Kaddish for the Six Million*. Scored for bass solo, chorus (SATB), and orchestra. New York: G. Schirmer.

Lumsdaine, David. *Annotations of Auschwitz*. Text by Peter Porter. Scored for soprano solo and instrumental ensemble. South Hackensack, N.J.: Joseph Boonin.

Partos, Oedoen. *Yizkor: In Memoriam to the Holocaust Martyrs*. Scored for violin (or viola, or cello) and piano. Tel Aviv: Israel Music Publications.

Penderecki, Krzysztof. *Dies Irae: Oratorio in Memory of Those Who Perished at Auschwitz*. Scored for solos, chorus (SATB), and orchestra. Krakow: Polskie Wydawnictwo Muzyczne.

Ran, Shulamit. *Oh the Chimneys*. Text adapted by the composer from poetry by Nelly Sachs. Scored for female solo and instrumental ensemble. New York: Carl Fischer.

Schönberg, Arnold. *A Survivor from Warsaw*. Text by the composer. Scored for narrator, male chorus (TB), and orchestra. Los Angeles: Belmont Music Publishers.

Seter, Mordecai. *Requiem-Elegy*. Scored for clarinet (or oboe) and piano. Tel Aviv: Israel Music Institute.

Shostakovich, Dmitri. *Symphony no. 13 (Babi Yar), opus 113*. Text by Evgeny Yevtushenko. Scored for bass solo, male chorus (TB), and symphony orchestra. New York: Leeds Music.

Starer, Robert. *Elegy for Strings*. New York: MCA Music.

Waxman, Franz. *The Song of Terezin*. Text adapted by the composer from Holocaust literature. Scored for female solo, chorus (SATB), and orchestra. Bryn Mawr, Pa.: Theodore Presser.

Weisgall, Hugo. *Nine Rivers from Jordan*. Opera with libretto by Denis Johnston. Scored for solos, chorus (SATB), and orchestra. Bryn Mawr, Pa.: Theodore Presser.

Wernick, Richard. *Kaddish-Requiem*. Text by the composer. Scored for female solo and instrumental ensemble. Bryn Mawr, Pa.: Theodore Presser.

# Chapter 31

# The Holocaust as Seen in the Movies

## Morris Zyrl and Saul S. Friedman

Who would have thought that a television miniseries presented about the murder of six million Jews during World War II would create so much furor? Yet that is precisely what happened when NBC broadcast Gerald Green's "Holocaust: The Story of the Family Weiss." Despite numerous negative reviews on the part of scholars and survivors who picked apart its structural and historical flaws, "Holocaust" did something that no documentary, no motion picture dealing with genocide ever did. It reached more than one hundred million Americans of every background, awakening many to the horrors of the Final Solution. It also convinced the West German Parliament to eliminate the statute of limitations on war crimes.

Movies have come a long way since Hollywood cast Otto Preminger, Conrad Veidt, or George Sanders as scowling Nazis. Stereotypes of America's enemies in World War II have been replaced by more balanced images. With the passage of time, the outrage felt by many Americans toward Auschwitz and Buchenwald also waned. The sense that too much emphasis had been paid to a momentary aberration in history has been evidenced by America's response to commercial films on the Final Solution. Saluted for their artistry, these productions generally have been economic disasters. Morris Zyrl's experience as a movie critic has been that a typical audience includes (1) a few non-Jews who are curious about what happened, including some who just want to see shots of atrocities; (2) Jews who experienced these tragedies and their offspring; (3) a few priests or nuns; and (4) people who harbor guilt feelings about what happened. Most people simply do not go to a theater to see such films. How then do we explain the fact that television programs on the Holocaust generate excellent numbers? Is it because people feel more comfortable sitting at home, with the lights on and popcorn popping, knowing that what comes over cable anyway is make-believe, just like scenes from "Friday the 13th" and "Nightmare on Elm Street"?

Because Hollywood is now so adept in creating illusions, many people, especially teenagers, find it difficult to distinguish between what is real and what is unreal. The day the *Challenger* Shuttle exploded, Zyrl was speaking to a group of seventh graders about the Holocaust. He was relieved that they did not ask about Jewish involvement with the death of Jesus or some such medieval canard but shocked when they said that they did not believe in the Holocaust because the pictures of shrivelled human beings piled upon other human beings could not be true. Since the movies they had seen were unreal, these photos, too, had to be special effects.

Children cannot be faulted for doubting what happened in the Holocaust. More than 60 percent of this nation's population, including many adults, were born after the liberation of the concentration camps. Typical of these was an acquaintance from Florida, who, upon emerging from a screening of "The Music Box," protested, "I didn't like it. I don't believe that many people—six million—could have been killed." This was no member of the Ku Klux Klan or Institute for Historical Review speaking. This was a thirty-eight-year-old Jewish woman who had never been properly taught the reality of the Holocaust. The problem that exists is not the fault of the teachers or the movies. The problem is that not enough time is spent on the teaching of the Holocaust. Nor are the movies used as a tool to teach and be an indirect witness to history.

Films about the Holocaust may be divided into four categories: (1) American motion pictures; (2) foreign films of a commercial nature; (3) television docudramas; and (4) documentaries. Each of these, in turn, may be subdivided into those placed in the era prior to the outbreak of World War II (showing the initial phase of persecution in the Third Reich), those that focus upon wartime atrocities, those that touch tangentially upon the horrors of the Holocaust, and those that deal with postwar events. Most are currently available on videotape.

## AMERICAN MOTION PICTURES

German militarism and Adolf Hitler have always fascinated Hollywood filmmakers. The epic novels of Erich Maria Remarque (*All Quiet on the Western Front* and *Arch of Triumph*) are among numerous antiwar works that have been translated to the screen. During the war years zealous studios also churned out a host of films intended for Saturday matinees (e.g., *Background to Danger* with George Raft or *Action in Arabia* with George Sanders). Movies employing some theme of the Holocaust continue to be made. Production values range from very good to tawdry. Perhaps the best examples of this genre are those done in the black-and-white technique that lent a unique flavor to such monumental war films as *A Walk in the Sun* and *Battleground*. No list can be exhaustive. With that in mind, the following films are noteworthy.

### Films Set in the Prewar Period

*Cabaret*. Released in 1972 by Allied Artists, this Bob Fosse–directed film starred Liza Minnelli, Joel Grey, Helmut Griem, and Michael York. The signs of perverse corruption and hatred toward Jews are evident in prewar Berlin. One significant scene shows a group of Hitler Youth singing a Nazi song in an outdoor cafe. Soon virtually all the people in the cafe join the chorus, which proclaims that "the future belongs to me." Another scene shows the brutal humiliation of a wealthy Jewish family during *Kristallnacht*. This cynical film that combined the mood of Bertolt Brecht with the music of Berlin's bistros won eight Oscars, including those for best actress, best supporting actor, and best director. Highly recommended.

*Ship of Fools*. This film was released in 1956 by Columbia Pictures and was based on the Katherine Porter novel of an ocean liner bound from New York to Hamburg in 1939. Stanley Kramer directed such stars as Vivien Leigh, Oskar Werner, Lee Marvin, and Simone Signoret. Abby Mann's screenplay tells the stories of a number of individuals, much in the way of a seafaring counterpart of *Airport*.

*Voyage of the Damned*. Released in 1976 by Avco/Embassy, this is a real-life *Ship of Fools* starring Faye Dunaway, Oskar Werner, Lee Grant, and Max von Sydow. From 1933 Hitler and the Nazis taunted the world that nobody wanted the Jews. In the spring of 1939 a number of Jewish professionals and their families sailed for Cuba aboard the German-American liner *SS St. Louis*. Before their arrival, the government of Laredo Bru revoked their landing permits and demanded more money. When the U.S. government also refused haven to the passengers, the vessel was forced to return to Europe. The captain actually did consider beaching the ship on the coast of England, but not at the last moment as the film shows. The film is based on the book of the same name by Max Witt and Gordon Thomas.

### Films Set in the Wartime Period

*The Diary of Anne Frank*. George Stevens's magnificent production for 20th Century Fox in 1959. The saga of a teenaged girl penned up with her family in an Amsterdam garret is told by Millie Perkins, Shelley Winters, Ed Wynn (Oscar, supporting actor) and Lou Jacobi. The sound made by Nazi police cars as they approach the Franks' hiding place is unforgettable. Viewers interested in reading Anne Frank's diary should insist upon the complete version that tells of her growing interest in Zionism. Highly recommended.

*The Great Dictator*. A much-heralded satire by Charlie Chaplin. Released in 1940, Chaplin's first complete talkie also starred Paulette Goddard, Billy Gilbert, and Henry Daniell. Chaplin played the dual roles of Adenoid Hynkel of Tomania and his look-alike, a Jewish barber. Jack Oakie was Benzino Napaloni of Bacteria. Their scenes together, particularly where they try to adjust their respective barber chairs to higher levels, are amusing. Chaplin's concluding speech of hope and brotherhood is a testament to the naivete of people in those days before Auschwitz.

*Hanna's War.* The story of the Hungarian-Jewish heroine Hannah Senesh was directed by Menachem Golan for Cannon Films in 1988. Starring were Mersuhka Demers, Ellen Burstyn, David Warner, and Donald Pleasance. Hannah Senesh was a young woman who made *Aliyah* (emigration) to Palestine in 1939. After five years, though, she decided to risk her life by returning to occupied Hungary to help her Jewish brethren. Captured by the fascists, she was executed by a firing squad. Her four-line poem "Blessed Is the Match" has become an inspiration to Jews the world over. A strong motion picture, highly recommended.

*Me and the Colonel.* This film, released in 1958 by Columbia Pictures, has a running time of 109 minutes. Danny Kaye and Curt Jurgens star in this movie version of Franz Werfel's *Jacobowsky and the Colonel.* A Polish Jew trying to escape from Europe during World War II meets an anti-Semitic colonel who is also trying to flee. Known primarily as a comedian-dancer, Kaye was never finer than in this role, later to be performed by Joel Grey on Broadway.

*Morituri.* Also known as *Saboteur, Code Name Morituri.* A rather hokey film released in 1965 that starred Yul Brynner, Marlon Brando, Trevor Howard, and Janet Margolin. Most probably wanted to forget this melodrama of an anti-Nazi German who helps the British capture a cargo ship.

*The Pied Piper.* Monty Woolley starred as a crotchety old man who dislikes children in this 1942 potboiler from MGM. Naturally, he finds himself leading a group of them to freedom. Costars were Roddy McDowell, Anne Baxter, and the ubiquitous Otto Preminger.

*The Seventh Cross.* Released in 1944 and directed by Fred Zinneman, this film provided one of the earliest glimpses of brutality in Nazi concentration camps. It tracks the Nazi pursuit, apprehension, and hanging of Spencer Tracy and Hume Cronyn, who were among seven men who managed a temporary flight to freedom.

*Triumph of the Spirit.* Directed by Robert M. Young and starring Willem Dafoe, Robert Loggia, and Edward James Olmos, this is an unusual tale of Salamon Arouch's struggle for survival. From Salonika, Macedonia, Arouch, his family, and his friends are deported to Auschwitz, where Salamon, a world-class boxer, stays alive by beating rivals in the ring. This gripping film, with tender moments of reunion, filmed at Auschwitz, was released by Epic Films in 1989. Little seen, but highly recommended.

*War and Love.* Also released by Cannon Films, in 1985, this film had a screenplay by Abby Mann and direction by Moshe Mizrahi. Kyra Sedwick and Sebastian Keneas starred in Jack Eisner's tale of a man's survival after being separated from his family in the battle of the Warsaw ghetto. This was the first film actually to be shot on location in the Auschwitz concentration camp.

*The Young Lions.* Edward Dmytryk directed this adaptation of Irwin Shaw's novel in 1958. Stars included Dean Martin, Montgomery Clift, and Marlon

Brando. The film offers a momentary glimpse of the horrors of a Nazi labor camp.

### Postwar Films

*The Boys from Brazil.* Franklin Schaffner directed and Gregory Peck and Laurence Olivier starred in this 1978 production. Peck made a terribly sinister Josef Mengele, while Olivier (reversing roles from his insidious character in *Marathon Man*) played a frail Simon Wiesenthal type. Some parts of the plot are outlandish (it is doubtful that Hitler would have permitted any blood samples to be drawn, even if it meant cloning), but the film is still recommended.

*The Cassandra Crossing.* Avco/Embassy produced this fanciful tale in 1977, starring Richard Harris, Sophia Loren, and Lee Strasberg. The script asks the viewer to believe that a European train, filled with passengers, is being diverted to a remote camp because a plague bacillus has been loosed in one of the wagons. Naturally, the location is a concentration camp where Strasberg was once detained. Recommended only for those who savor contrived plots.

*Cast a Giant Shadow.* United Artists' 1966 paean to Colonel Mickey Marcus, onetime OSS operative and later a leader in the Israeli military. Director Mel Shavelson cast the unlikely trio of Kirk Douglas, Yul Brynner, and John Wayne. Set mainly in 1948 Israel, the film offers Wayne's reaction to seeing a concentration camp for the first time.

*The Counterfeit Traitor.* George Seaton directed this 1962 drama that starred William Holden, Lilli Palmer, and Klaus Kinski. A double agent, Holden finds himself compelled to save a Jew in hiding (Kinski). Based on a true story. Fair.

*Enemies: A Love Story.* Paul Mazursky's disturbing film of a Holocaust survivor living in Brooklyn in 1949. The 1989 20th Century Fox production stars Ron Silver, Alan King, Lena Olin, Angelica Huston, and Margaret Sophie Stein. Silver plays the lead character, a ghostwriter for a pretentious rabbi. The convoluted plot by I. B. Singer has the writer married to no less than three women at the same time: (1) his wife, who miraculously survived the death camp; (2) his onetime Polish servant, who saved his life; and (3) a girlfriend from the Bronx who ultimately commits suicide in an unforgettable scene. Silver is excellent as the pathetic roué who can never put the image of his dead children in Europe out of his mind. Three Oscar nominations make this a highly recommended film.

*Exodus.* Otto Preminger's salute to Israel (and the novel by Leon Uris) was released by United Artists in 1960, with a running time of 213 minutes. Although the film revolves around stars Paul Newman and Eva Marie Saint, central to Dalton Trumbo's screenplay are the characters of Dov Landau (Sal Mineo) and Karen (Jill Hayworth). They are among the handful of young Jewish refugees who survived the Holocaust and emigrated to Palestine. A workhorse film that has some flaws, but is still recommended after all these years.

*Judgment at Nuremberg.* Stanley Kramer's direction and a thoughtful script by Abby Mann make this 1961 United Artists film a classic dealing with the agony of war-crimes trials. Starkly photographed in black and white, the cast includes Spencer Tracy, Burt Lancaster, Richard Widmark, Marlene Dietrich, William Shatner, and Maximilian Schell (Oscar for best actor). Two especially outstanding performances as victims of Nazi atrocities were given by Judy Garland and Montgomery Clift. One of the best films of the era.

*Judith.* Paramount and Daniel Mann bear responsibility for this film released in 1966. Sophia Loren plays the unlikely role of a Holocaust survivor. Peter Finch and Jack Hawkins also star in this saga, which has as its subplot the search for a Nazi war criminal in Syria. Unbelievable.

*The Juggler.* Edward Dmytryk directed Kirk Douglas, Milly Vitale, Paul Stewart, and Alf Kjellin in this 1953 low-budget film for Columbia Pictures. The film follows an entertainer who lost his family in the camps as he emigrates to Eretz Yisrael and encounters problems adjusting. Released shortly after the Israeli army responded to terrorist attacks with a raid on a Palestinian village, *The Juggler* was denounced in some circles for suggesting that Jews did not kill. Despite some shortcomings, recommended.

*Julia.* Another film by Fred Zinneman, released by 20th Century Fox in 1977. Oscars went to Jason Roberts for best supporting actor, Alvin Sargent (screenplay), and Vanessa Redgrave (best supporting actress). The cast also included Jane Fonda and Meryl Streep (in her film debut). Based on the novella *Pentimento* by Lillian Hellman, the film harkens back to a time when the author supposedly participated in the anti-Nazi resistance. Subsequently controversial because of Redgrave's anti-Israel attack and Paddy Chayevsky's rebuttal at the Oscars.

*Lisa.* Dolores Hart is believable as a young Holocaust survivor searching for her father in Israel. The 20th Century Fox cast in 1962 included Stephen Boyd. Fair.

*The Music Box.* Released by Tri-Star Pictures in 1989, this is an underrated film starring Jessica Lange and Armin Mueller-Stahl. Joe Esterhaz's script is based loosely on the "Ivan the Terrible" (John Demjanjuk) trial in Cleveland. Here, however, the mass murderer is a onetime member of the Hungarian Arrow Cross who allegedly participated in anti-Jewish pogroms in Budapest late in 1944. Brought to trial in Chicago, he is defended against denaturalization by his lawyer-daughter. The outcome is a bit contrived, but the acting and staging are superior. Highly recommended as a bit of history.

*The Night of the Generals.* Peter O'Toole, Omar Sharif, and Tom Courtney starred in this 1967 Columbia Pictures film by Anatole Litvak. The fanciful plot involves the prosecution of a Nazi general for the killing of a prostitute twenty-five years earlier. Meanwhile, there is little sympathy expressed as the entire Warsaw ghetto is obliterated. Fair to poor.

*The Odessa File.* Based on the best-selling novel by William Forsythe, this 1974 movie starred Jon Voight, Maximilian Schell, Maria Schell, and Derek Jacobi. A young German is disturbed when he learns of the existence of an illicit organization that aids Nazi fugitives and plots to revive the old ideology. Voight's encounter with mass murderer Eduard Roschmann (Schell) is gripping. Even more so is a scene at the end of the film where he stands at the Yad Vashem in Israel and says Kaddish for someone who has no one to pray for his memory.

*Operation Eichmann.* Released by Allied Artists in 1961 in order to capitalize on publicity of the kidnap capture in Argentina of Nazi genocide specialist Adolf Eichmann. Director R. G. Springsteen's cast includes Werner Klemperer and John Banner (in pre–"Hogan's Heroes" roles). Fairly well made and acted.

*The Pawnbroker.* Sidney Lumet directed this great film, starring Rod Steiger, Thelma Oliver, Geraldine Fitzgerald, and Brock Peters, in 1965. Sol Nazerman is a Jewish pawnbroker in Harlem. A Holocaust survivor, he is haunted by memories of his lost family. In the end, even in America, he loses everything when he loses his self-respect. Nominated for an Academy Award for this role, Steiger would have to wait a year to claim an Oscar for *In the Heat of the Night.* Filmed in brooding black and white. Highly recommended.

*The Rose Garden.* Another Cannon Films picture (1989), starring Maximilian Schell, Liv Ullman, Peter Fonda, and Gila Almagor. Attorney Ullman defends an old Jew who attacked a German in an airport. The German, it develops, had specialized in killing Jewish children during the Holocaust. Among his victims were some of the Jewish survivor's relatives. Through the trial we learn of the disturbing revival of Nazism in Germany.

*The Search.* Released by MGM in 1948, this touching film by Fred Zinneman established Montgomery Clift's screen presence. An American soldier in postwar Berlin, he cares for a young concentration-camp survivor played by Ivan Jandl. At the same time, the boy's mother seeks him through displaced persons' camps that prepare Jewish children for departure to Palestine. An emotionally wrenching tale that won an Oscar for screenplay for Richard Schweitzer and David Wechsler.

*Sophie's Choice.* Meryl Streep won an Oscar for her portrayal of a Polish woman in this 1982 release from Universal Pictures. Deported to a labor camp, she is permitted to save only one of her two children. Set primarily in postwar New York, the film, based on a novel by William Styron, flashes back to scenes of "normal" home life for Nazi officers who ran the death camps. Highly recommended.

## FOREIGN FILMS

Beyond the now-defunct art theater crowds, American moviegoers have found European films to be awkward in cuts and segues, as well as overly talky and philosophical. Quite often there is surprise when, after nearly two hours of story development, a slate appears signifying "Fin." Critics, on the other hand, have been more generous toward overseas productions that have used the Holocaust as a principal theme, honoring several with Academy Awards. Most of these, as is evident from the following list, have been of a superior quality in story and direction.

*The Assault*. Released by Cannon Films in 1986, this Danish film won an Oscar for best foreign film. The lead character, a Gentile living in postwar Europe, recalls how his neighbors, a Jewish family with a twelve-year-old son, were removed and liquidated in the last days of World War II. Unevenly edited, requiring voice-over in translation.

*Au Revoir Les Enfants*. Louis Malle's 1987 film starring Gespard Manesse and Raphael Fejto. The headmaster of a Catholic boarding school shields three Jewish children from the Nazis in Occupied France. Inevitably, the boys are denounced and sent to their deaths in Auschwitz. The title words are uttered by the priest to his students as he is sent to Mauthausen. Based on an incident that occurred in the director's school when he was a youth. Highly recommended.

*Das Boot Ist Voll*. Based on the disturbing study of the same name by Alfred Hasler, this 1981 Swiss film may be fiction, but the expulsion of a handful of desperate Jewish refugees by the neutral Swiss symbolizes the world's rejection of the Levitican commandment: "Neither shalt thou stand idly by the blood of thy neighbor" (Leviticus 19:16). Highly recommended.

*Burial of Potatoes*. In the spring of 1946, an old saddler returns to his village after surviving a concentration camp. His neighbors had done nothing to prevent the arrest of his favor and now, to cover their own guilt, they reject the man who they accuse of being a Jew. A dramatic, 1991 Polish production.

*Closely Watched Trains*. A 1966 Czech release directed by Jiri Menzel. Long before Raul Hilberg focused attention on the collaboration of railworkers with the Nazis, this film told the story of a dispatcher who followed orders, did his job, and helped expedite the killing of the Jews. The winner of the best foreign film award. Recommended.

*David*. Produced in Germany and released in 1979, this fair film (starring Mario Fischel) tells of the efforts of a Jewish teenager who managed to survive the war by hiding in Berlin.

*Docteur Periot*. A 1990 French film outlining the malicious actions of a French physician who promised sanctuary to desperate Jews and killed twenty-four of them during the occupation. Director Christian de Chalonge's recreation of a true story is an allegory for the actions of the Nazis and the German people.

*Europa, Europa*. The title reflects director Agnieszka Holland's attempt to demonstrate the good and evil capabilities of twentieth century Europe. This 1991 French-German-Polish production tells the story of Salomon Perel, a Jewish youth from Germany, who managed to survive the Holocaust first by fleeing to the Russian zone of Poland, then by pretending to be an "Aryan" in the Hitler Youth. Some sequences seem unbelievable, others incredibly detached from the Holocaust. Probably more highly praised than it merits.

*The Garden of the Finzi-Continis*. Vittorio De Sica's tale of an aristocratic Italian-Jewish family that ignored the threat of fascism won an Oscar for best foreign film in 1972. Like the four thousand Jews of Florence who went about their business, unwilling to concede that the Nazis might one day deport them to their deaths (in 1943), Dominique Sanda and Fabio Teste offer portrayals of Jewish innocence. Highly recommended.

*The Inheritors.* This German film released by Island Pictures in 1985 shows the seductive method by which troubled youth in Germany today are drawn by old Nazis into the fold of the neo-Nazi movement. One particular scene has a veteran of the Hitler era showing off his lampshade made, he claims, of the skin of a Jewess.

*Jacob the Liar.* Released in 1977, this East German production stars Vlastimil Brodsky and Manuella Simon. A Polish Jew weaves tall tales in the ghetto to lift his people's spirits under Nazi occupation. Brodsky won the best actor award at the Berlin Film Festival, and *Jacob the Liar* was nominated for an Academy Award. Highly recommended.

*The Last Metro.* Directed by François Truffaut and released in 1980, this French production starred Catherine Deneuve as a Christian woman bent on protecting her Jewish husband (Gerard Depardieu) and keeping his Paris theater operating during the German occupation. Richly praised by critics, but somewhat disappointing. Recommended.

*The Lucky Star.* A little-known 1980 Canadian release starring Rod Steiger, Louise Fletcher, Lou Jacobi, and Brett Marx that must be seen. After his parents are taken away by the Nazis, a young Jewish boy is hidden by a woman on a Dutch farm. His yellow Star of David becomes his badge of courage as he detains a German colonel at gunpoint in a barn. Highly recommended.

*Mephisto.* Istvan Szabo's 1981 Hungarian film won the Academy Award for best foreign picture. Klaus Maria Brandauer starred in this film, which dealt with the efforts of an aspiring actor to ingratiate himself with the Nazis. Flawed in its arty production and also somewhat distorted in suggesting that the primary victims of the Nuremberg Laws were blacks living in Europe.

*Mr. Klein.* A French film by Joseph Losey, released in 1977 and starring Alain Delon and Jeanne Moreau. A French Catholic art dealer exploits Jews during the initial phase of Nazi occupation. Because of his name, however, he is mistakenly identified as a Jew and sent to a concentration camp himself.

*Seven Beauties.* Lina Wertmuller's 1976 Italian production of a Casanova in a concentration camp. Giancarlo Giannini gives a superb performance, but the much-ballyhooed film can only be deemed insulting to people who were trying to survive. Worth seeing and getting angry about.

*The Shop on Main Street.* Ida Kaminska's excellent film showing how an aged Jewish woman was victimized by ''Aryanization'' in Czechoslovakia. The only thing that gave meaning to her life was this tiny shop with its thread and needle supplies. The film chronicles the evolving relationship between the new caretaker and the woman, who eventually is deported. Shot in black and white, *Shop on Main Street* won an Oscar for best foreign film of 1965. Highly recommended.

*The Two of Us.* Another French film, released in 1986. Claude Berri directed Michel Simon and Alain Cohen in this tale of a Jewish boy sent to live in the country with an anti-Semitic farmer during the occupation. This warm film tracks their evolving relationship. Highly recommended.

*The Wannsee Conference.* This 1984 German film by Heinz Schick is frighteningly real because it is based on the actual protocol of Reinhard Heydrich's January 1942 meeting with high-ranking Nazis in the Berlin offices of Interpol, where the ''Final Solution of the Jewish Question'' was established. The motion picture matches the actual time of the original meeting. Highly recommended.

## TELEVISION DOCUDRAMAS

Television is perhaps the most controversial medium dealing with the Holocaust. Few can contest the good intentions of networks, producers, and writers. Generally, however, television docudramas suffer from comparison with conventional theatrical productions. This may be attributed to limited budgets that prevent large casts or elaborate sets. On occasion, the networks may employ less experienced scriptwriters or directors (although, as ''Playing for Time'' suggests, not even an Arthur Miller can redeem a script that distorts the unique persecution of the Jews). Since commercial television is aimed at a relatively unsophisticated, neutral audience, it should not surprise that its drama, generally, would be banal. Whatever the problem, no less a figure than Nobel laureate Elie Wiesel has publicly decried the ''trivialization'' of the Holocaust by some television programs.

''The Assisi Underground.'' A cable presentation of Cannon Films in 1986, this four-hour program was later released in a two-hour cassette version. The story, which stars Ben Cross, Maximilian Schell, Irene Pappas, and James Mason, tells how church leaders in Assisi, Italy, tried to rescue several hundred Jews in 1943. The effort is frustrated when the Gestapo intercepts the refugees bound for a ship in Genoa. Marginally interesting.

''Attic: The Hiding of Anne Frank.'' Presented on CBS in 1988 with a cast headed by Mary Steenburgen and Paul Scofield. The story of Anne Frank is told through the eyes of Miep Gies, the Dutch woman who hid the Frank family and others from the Germans. Based on the book *Anne Frank Remembered.* Recommended.

''The Diary of Anne Frank.'' Boris Segal's 1980 adaptation starred Melissa Gilbert, Maximilian Schell, Joan Plowright, and James Coco. A fair transcription that suffers by comparison with George Stevens's black-and-white 1959 theatrical version.

''Escape from Sobibor.'' Another underrated film from CBS in 1987. Directed by Jack Gold, this saga of one of the major death camps in Poland starred Alan Arkin, Joanna Pacula, Rutger Hauer, and Hartmut Becker. Reginald Rose's moving script tells how a small band of doomed inmates, all of them Jews, including a handful of Russian POWs sent here, destroyed the camp in an uprising in 1943. Critics have noted the emotional impact of a scene involving a young Jewish jeweler who crossed the "Path of Heaven" and witnessed a mass gassing. More powerful, though, because they are so deceiving, are the opening sequences. The *Sonderkommando* members stand at attention as incoming trains are greeted by classical music played on a loudspeaker. In the sunlight and flowers people are ushered off the trains and selected for life or death. It all takes place so quickly and efficiently, and that is what is so frightening. One of the most compelling films on the Holocaust, despite its unnecessary love subplot. Based on the stories of survivors. Highly recommended.

"Evil in Clear River." This 1985 NBC production was based on an incident in Canada where a schoolteacher was disputing the historicity of the Holocaust. Directed by Karen Arthur and starring Lindsay Wagner and Randy Quaid, the film has a few good moments. Well-intentioned.

"The Execution." If "Escape from Sobibor" is an example of television at its best, this is the opposite. This 1985 NBC melodrama starred Loretta Swit, Rip Torn, Jessica Walter, Sandy Dennis, Valerie Harper, and Barbara Barrie. Five suburban women who survived the Holocaust recognize the former Nazi doctor who experimented on them while they were in the camps. They plot his death. An example of television's trivialization of the Holocaust.

"Holocaust: The Story of the Family Weiss." Broadcast over NBC in 1978, this seven-and-one-half-hour program was nominated for sixteen Emmys and won eight. Joseph Bottoms, Tova Feldshuh, Michael Moriarity, Meryl Streep, David Warner, Fritz Weaver, and James Woods starred in this saga that covered the decade between 1935 and 1945. While the upper-middle-class Jewish family Weiss endured social ostracism, brutalization in *Kristallnacht*, expulsion, and eventual incarceration in Auschwitz and Terezín, the impoverished Dorfs moved upward through the SS hierarchy. Gerald Green's script was faulted for numerous reasons—a fanciful wedding among the partisans in the woods, the invention of Dorf, who supposedly masterminded many of Heydrich's schemes, even the robotlike killing of Jews at Babi Yar. Such sins were more than outweighed by the fact that better than one hundred million Americans watched the program, including many schoolchildren, who, with the aid of a study guide prepared by Jewish scholars, discussed the story in their classrooms. Equally important, the West German government was moved to eliminate the statute of limitations on war crimes because of notoriety generated by the film. Highly recommended.

"The House on Garibaldi Street." Produced for ABC in 1979. Director Peter Collinson attempted to tell the story of Eichmann's capture by Israeli agents with Topol, Martin Balsam, Janet Suzman, and Leo McKern in the cast. Done very much in the style of the 1945 thriller "The House on 92nd Street." Recommended.

"Inside the Third Reich." NBC's 1982 miniseries based on the autobiography of Nazi Albert Speer. Marvin Chomsky directed the four-hour show starring Rutger Hauer, Maria Schell, John Gielgud, Blythe Danner, and Mort Saul. Derek Jacobi is outstanding as Adolf Hitler. Much of the rest is self-serving bombast, like the scene in the Berlin bunker that has yes-man Speer supposedly lecturing Hitler on the conduct of the war.

"Max and Helen." Presented on TNT-Cable in 1990. Directed by Philip Saville, "Max and Helen" starred Treat Williams, Alice Krige, and Martin Landau as Simon Wiesenthal. Based on a true story of two Jewish lovers who were separated during the Holocaust. Twenty years later, through the researches of Wiesenthal, Max discovers that Helen is alive. The two are reunited, only momentarily, because she has had a child by the Nazi camp commandant that Wiesenthal is pursuing. The scenes prior to internment at the labor camp and the labor camp itself are quite powerful. Recommended.

"Miracle at Moroux." Picture Loretta Swit as a nun running a girls' school where two Jewish children are being hidden from the Nazis. That is the plot of this Disney Cable film produced in 1988. This film aims to show how the Christian children came to appreciate the Jewish dilemma, but fails to touch or educate.

"The Murderers Among Us." A 1990 presentation for HBO Cable starring Ben Kingsley and Craig T. Nelson. The story of Simon Wiesenthal is based on two books by the Nazi hunter (one with the same title and his provocative *Sunflower*). When the Americans liberated his camp of Mauthausen, Wiesenthal was little more than skin and bones. He makes a promise to hunt down the criminals who did this to him and his family. The remainder of the movie deals with his personal tribulations upon setting up his documentation center in Vienna. One particularly frustrating sequence involves the trial and acquittal of a Nazi war criminal. This program, which won an ACE Cable Award, also treats the subject of revisionism.

"Never Forget." Produced by TNT-Cable in 1991. Leonard Nimoy directed and starred as Mel Mermelstein, a survivor living in Los Angeles, who challenged revisionists at the Institute for Historical Review. Blythe Danner plays his wife, who suffered through harassment until their attorney Dabney Coleman succeeded in getting a California court to "take judicial note of the Holocaust." At 100 minutes, it seems long.

"Playing for Time." In 1980 CBS thought it was doing something right in presenting Fania Fenelon's memoir of Auschwitz. The script was written by Arthur Miller, and the cast included Vanessa Redgrave, Jane Alexander, Maude Adams, Viveca Lindfors, and Shirley Knight. The program won Emmys for Redgrave, Alexander, and Miller, but the Lord alone knows why. Fenelon was a proud Jewess who survived by enrolling in the camp orchestra that entertained the Nazis. Somehow, the specific suffering of her people was transmuted by Miller into an appeal for international brotherhood. The acting is wooden, and the selection of Redgrave is an insult. Fenelon later disassociated herself from the project. Watch it and forget it.

"Remembrance of Love." Kirk Douglas plays an aging Jew who attends a gathering of Holocaust survivors in Israel and through the miracle of computers discovers the woman he loved in the Warsaw ghetto. The show was produced for ABC in 1982 and directed by Jack Smight, with a cast including Chana Eden and Pam Dawber. Fair.

"Skokie." In 1976 the residents of Skokie, Illinois, a suburb of Chicago heavily populated with Jews, many of whom were Holocaust survivors, learned that Frank Colin's American Nazi party was planning to march through their town in full regalia. Despite warnings by civic leaders and social scientists of the "psychic scarring" this would cause, the U.S. Supreme Court stupidly upheld the right of the Nazis to march. This 1981 ABC film shows the response of the Skokie community. Herbert Wise's cast included John Rubenstein, Carl Reiner, Kim Hunter, Eli Wallach, and Lee Strasberg. Unforgettable, however, was Danny Kaye. Highly recommended.

"The Wall." CBS's disappointing 1982 adaptation of John Hersey's monumental novel was filmed entirely in Poland with a cast including Tom Conti and Lisa Eichhorn. The original book was modeled on the diary of Emmanuel Ringelblum, historian of the Warsaw ghetto. Thirty years ago George C. Scott starred in an outstanding stage production. This version suffers by all comparisons. Intended to be a salute to Jewish resistance fighters, the scripting and acting are uninspired.

"Wallenberg: A Hero's Story." Richard Chamberlain is outstanding as the Swedish diplomat who personally intervened to save the lives of more than one hundred thousand Jews in Hungary in 1944–45. The two-part NBC docudrama directed by Lamont Johnson also stars Alice Krige, Bibi Andersson, and Melanie Mayron. One particularly gripping moment comes near the end when Russian troops are approaching Budapest. A secretary in a "safe house" utters the fear of so many survivors when she says that people may not believe that all of this really happened. Instead, they will tell jokes. Wallenberg ultimately was taken into custody by the Soviets and disappeared. This Emmy-winning production is highly recommended.

"Winds of War" and "War and Remembrance." Presented as two miniseries for ABC-TV in 1983 and 1989. Directed, cowritten, and produced by Dan Curtis, the plodding script tells the story of the world through the eyes of Pug Henry (Robert Mitchum), who, we are asked to believe, was everywhere before and during the war. The connection to the Holocaust is with his daughter-in-law Natalie (played in the first program by Ali MacGraw, later by Jane Seymour) and her uncle (John Houseman, John Gielgud), who are Jewish. The sequel picks up with the two Jews trapped in Europe. They are sent to Heydrich's "Paradise Ghetto" in Theresienstadt and then to Auschwitz (in both instances filmed on location). The sequences where Jewish families are required to strip in the gas chambers of Auschwitz are among the most horrific scenes ever filmed. Paramount produced the twenty-hour programs. Recommended.

### Holocaust Documentaries

Unlike many of the major tragedies in history, the Holocaust occurred in a technological age where events could be recorded audibly and visually for posterity. Film shot of the destruction of the Warsaw ghetto by Nazi underlings was used as evidence against major war criminals at the Nuremberg Tribunal in 1945. Some twenty minutes of the special documentary staged by Hans Günther at Terezín also survives. Units of the U.S. Signal Corps and the Allied press corps offers some of the first glimpses into concentration camps like Dachau, Bergen-Belsen, Ohrdruf, Buchenwald, and Thekla. Such documentaries are available through the National Archives, Alden Films, or the National Jewish Resource Center. Because of the particularly horrific contents (the charred bodies of inmates at Thekla are still steaming, piles of corpses are bulldozed into a common trench at Belsen), viewers are advised that these films require accompanying comment by professional scholars.

*A Day in the Warsaw Ghetto: A Birthday Trip in Hell.* A short (30 minute) film by Jack Kuper combines still photographs and traditional Jewish music to give a shocking image of the Warsaw Ghetto in 1941. The photographs were taken illegally by Wehrmacht Sergeant Heinz Joest as he toured the ghetto on his forty-third birthday. Highly recommended.

*The Cross and the Star.* Beginning with the gospel of John, this hour-long documentary produced by John Michalczyk tracks anti-Semitism through Augustine, Martin Luther, and the Inquisition. Scholars and clergy agree that the roots of Nazism were planted by generations of bigots who claimed to be honoring the teachings of Jesus. Recommended.

*The Eighty-First Blow* (Haim Gouri, Israel, 1975) uses the Eichmann trial as a framework for recreating the saga of World War II. The film contains familiar, yet shocking scenes from the Warsaw ghetto and is one of three recommended documentaries produced by the Ghetto Fighters' Kibbutz, the others being *The Last Sea* and *Flames in the Ashes.*

*Genocide.* Produced by the Simon Wiesenthal Center in Los Angeles for United Artists in 1983. Narration for this Oscar-winning film was supplied by Orson Welles and Elizabeth Taylor. Through newsreels, personal testimony, and artwork, this documentary traces the roots of anti-Semitism to its ultimate end—Auschwitz. Highly recommended.

*George Stevens: A Filmmaker's Journey.* George Stevens, Jr., wrote and directed this homage to his father, the man who produced *Gunga Din, Shane, I Remember Mama, Giant,* and *The Diary of Anne Frank.* Stevens, Sr., accompanied Allied troops into Germany in the service of the U.S. Signal Corps. He was the first to capture glimpses of the liberation of concentration camps on color film. Released by Castle Hill in 1984.

*Hotel Terminus: The Life and Times of Klaus Barbie.* Released in 1988 by Samuel Goldwyn Films, this four-hour documentary is by the great French producer–director Marcel Ophuls. Barbie's capture and return from South America is a tribute to the efforts of Serge and Beate Klarsfeld. A very worthwhile movie that suggests extensive collaboration on the part of Frenchmen with the Gestapo chieftain of Lyon. Barbie also may have been protected by the American OSS after the war. Highly recommended.

*The Lodz Ghetto*. A 1990 documentary covering life in what was once the second-largest Polish city. Before Germany's attack in September 1939, perhaps two hundred thousand Jews, of every description and economic background, lived in this vibrant textile-manufacturing town. In 1940 the Nazis created the first ghetto in Poland. The film shows how the Jewish Council under Chaim Rumkowski functioned. Their ingenuous cooperation failed to deter annihilation for all but a handful. Highly recommended.

*Mein Kampf*. A Swedish documentary directed by Erwin Leiser and released through Brenner Films in 1961. This unnerving masterpiece contains some of the most graphic shots taken by Nazi filmographers of the agony of starvation and disease in the Warsaw ghetto. Probably the single most powerful documentary of the Holocaust. Highly recommended.

*Night and Fog*. François Truffaut once called this 1955 documentary "the greatest film ever made," and it certainly appears in every film bibliography on the Holocaust. Unfortunately, director Alain Resnais long ago admitted that he developed this project not so much as a protest against Nazism but as an allegory against contemporary fascism (e.g., French involvement in North Africa, America in Vietnam). Survivors find the linkage repugnant. Scholars can only wonder about a 45-minute film on the Holocaust that never once uses the word Jew, whose title focuses attention on seven thousand "Nacht und Nebel" prisoners (most of whom survived the war), and whose chronology is confusing. Recommended only if complete discussion of these issues follows.

*Olympia*. Nazi Germany's gold-medals triumph in the 1936 Olympics (heavily embellished with shots of gymnastics competition) is recorded for posterity by Leni Riefenstahl. An example of film used as propaganda. Overlong and probably overrated.

*The Partisans of Vilna*. Directed by Josh Waletzky for European Classics in 1986. This two-hour documentary is narrated by Robert Wallach and offers a comprehensive view of Vilna, once a major center of Yiddish culture. A sad telling from the prewar period through the occupation, deportations, and partisan resistance.

*Photographs to Our Children*. A gripping collection of personal testimonies and documents assembled by three producers telling of Jewish life in Budapest before and during the Nazi occupation. This 1989 Hungarian film is highly recommended.

*Shoah*. 503 minutes of repetitive interviews and translations produced by Claude Lanzmann for New Yorker Films. Some moments are chilling, particularly the tracing of railway lines into Sobibor and Treblinka and the revelations of ongoing anti-Semitism in Poland. Critics also applauded Lanzmann's decision to keep his camera set while interviewing what otherwise would be labeled "talking heads." Questions persist, however. Why is Lanzmann always on screen? Why must every question be filmed as it was framed, first in French, translated into Polish, then answered in reverse order? Probably twice as long as it should be.

*The Sorrow and the Pity*. Marcel Ophuls' 1970 film shows how most Frenchmen considered the persecution of Jews a disturbance and little more. Banned in France while De Gaulle lived, this film dispels the notion of a widespread anti-Nazi resistance in that country. Nearly four hours in length, we would like to see more. Highly recommended.

*Terezín Diary* tells the story of the fortress outside Prague that served as transit ghetto for 140,000 Jews during the Holocaust. Producers Dan Weissman and Zuzana Justman (herself a survivor) build their program around the experiences of ten survivors, written memoirs, film footage of the town today, and snippets of Nazi propaganda film made during the war.

*Triumph of the Will*. Leni Riefenstahl's salute to the Nazi party rally at Nuremberg in 1934 has been called the greatest propaganda film ever made. That distinction may be arguable, but this 1935 epic reveals the widespread support the Hitler regime enjoyed from the German people.

*The Twisted Cross*. Narrated by Alexander Scourby as part of NBC's Project Twenty Series, this program was a useful tool back in 1953. Upon closer scrutiny, the program simply does not hold up. Several scenes, such as Hitler's flight after the failed 1923 Putsch and beatings by Brown Shirts in the 1930s, are theatrical recreations and cheapen the entire production.

*The Warsaw Ghetto: Holocaust and Resistance*. Produced by the Jewish Labor Committee, this documentary also contains scenes from commercial films that are not authentic. That is unfortunate, because actual footage shot in ghettos is compelling. Recommended with caution.

*The World at War: Genocide*. One hour from the BBC's award-winning production of World War II. This program benefits from extensive archival film, masterful musical scoring, and the narration of Sir Laurence Olivier. Though much of the photography is familiar, it still is moving.

A number of good, personal testimonies have appeared in recent years. "Kitty Goes to Auschwitz" (Canadian, 1981) may have been the watershed, prompting survivors and their children to record their experiences. Others in the same genre include "A5714: Robert Clary, A Memoir of Liberation" (PBS, 1985); "Camera of My Family" (Catherine Noren, 1979); "Children in the Holocaust" (Jack Eisner and Roman Kent, 1983); "Dark Lullabies" (Canada, 1985); and "In Dark Places" (Gina Blumenfeld, 1978). Readers are also urged to consult the excellent series of documentaries produced by the National Jewish Resource Center and Kent State University Jewish Studies. The former, titled "Witness to the Holocaust," supplement documentary footage with observations of survivors. Kent's Emmy-winning productions include the Clary program already cited; "From Dust and Ashes: Scholars and Survivors Confront the Holocaust" (1983); "Susan: A Mengele Twin Remembers" (1987); "The Voice of Giants: A Century of American Zionism" (1988); "The Snow Was Red: Ukrainian-

Jewish Relations'' (1990): and "CANDLES: The Story of the Mengele Twins'' (1990).

## THE FUTURE OF FILMS DEALING WITH
## THE HOLOCAUST

It seems reasonable to assume that despite a host of problems, producers will continue to employ the tragedy that befell Europe's Jews in World War II as a central theme in films. Apart from increasing costs of productions involving large numbers in the cast, there are objections from revisionists who insist that the Holocaust did not happen, minority groups that allege that it is not relevant, and critics and audiences that supposedly have been sated with tales of genocide. We may yet reach the point where friendly governments may become so influential that they will enjoy veto power over the telling of the story, much the way the government of Turkey has blocked a film production of *The Forty Days of Musa Dagh* for nearly sixty years.

Protests to the contrary notwithstanding, there are still many important stories to be told. Somewhere there must be a talented young producer-director to recreate the agony of a young Elie Wiesel's first night in Auschwitz (*Night*), the final march of Dr. Janusz Korczak with orphan children to the Umschlagplatz of the Warsaw ghetto, or the poems and drawings of the children of the Theresienstadt ghetto. There must be someone who will finally produce a proper tribute to righteous Gentiles like the people of Denmark who rallied behind that nation's eight thousand Jews. We have yet to see a completely convincing telling of the day-to-day existence in Buchenwald or Mauthausen or a transcription of Leon Uris's *Mila 18*, Rolf Hochhuth's *The Deputy*, or Anatoly Kuznetsov's *Babi Yar*. Perhaps most important, thirty years after the publication of *The Last of the Just*, we still await the appearance on screen of Andre Schwarz-Bart's immortal Ernie Levy.

Films on the Holocaust may not make money, but producers will continue to make such films because they know that the public is fascinated by the conflict between good and evil. What transpired on the streets of Nuremberg in 1935, in the transit camp of Drancy in 1941, or behind the barbed wire of Treblinka in 1943 is the culmination of that struggle between the best and worst impulses of humanity.

## SELECT BIBLIOGRAPHY

Armour, Robert. *Film: A Reference Guide*. Westport, Conn.: Greenwood Press, 1980.
*Bowker's Complete Video Directory, 1990*. New York: Reed, 1990.
Champlin, Charles. *The Movies Grow Up, 1940–1980*. Chicago: Swallow Press, 1981.
Cowie, Peter, ed. *World Filmography*. London: Tantivy Press; South Brunswick, N.J.: Barnes, 1977.
Dyment, Alan. *The Literature of the Film: A Bibliographical Guide to the Film as Art and Entertainment, 1936–1970*. London and New York: White Lion, 1975.

Ehrlich, Evelyn. *Cinema of Paradox: French Filmmaking Under the German Occupation*. New York: Columbia University Press, 1985.

Ellis, Jack. *A History of Film*. 2nd ed. Englewood Cliffs, N.J.: Prentice-Hall, 1985.

Ellis, Jack, Charles Derry, and Sharon Kern. *The Film Book Bibliography, 1940–1975*. Metuchen, N.J.: Scarecrow Press, 1979.

Erens, Patricia. *The Jew in American Cinema*. Bloomington: Indiana University Press, 1984.

Fell, John. *A History of Films*. New York: Holt, Rinehart and Winston, 1979.

Fisher, Kim. *On the Screen: A Film, Television, and Video Research Guide*. Littleton, Colo.: Libraries Unlimited, 1986.

Fraser, George. *The Hollywood History of the World: From One Million Years* B.C. *to Apocalypse Now*. New York: Beech Tree Books, 1988.

Friedman, Lester. *Hollywood's Image of the Jew*. New York: Ungar, 1982.

Fulton, Albert. *Motion Pictures*. Norman: University of Oklahoma Press, 1970.

Hewitt, Nicholas, ed. *The Culture of Reconstruction: European Literature, Thought, and Film, 1945–50*. New York: St. Martin's Press, 1989.

Higham, Charles. *The Art of the American Film, 1900–1971*. Garden City, N.Y.: Anchor Press/Doubleday, 1973.

Hull, David. *Film in the Third Reich: A Study of the German Cinema, 1933–1945*. Berkeley: University of California Press, 1969.

Isenberg, Michael. *War on Film: The American Cinema and World War I, 1914–1941*. Rutherford, N.J.: Fairleigh Dickinson Press, 1981.

Kaes, Anton. *From Hitler to Heimat: The Return of History as Film*. Cambridge, Mass.: Harvard University Press, 1989.

Koppes, Clayton and Gregory D. Black. *Hollywood Goes to War: How Politics, Profits, and Propaganda Shaped World War II Movies*. New York: Free Press, 1987.

Leiser, Erwin. *Nazi Cinema*. Translated by Gertrud Mander and David Wilson. New York: Macmillan, 1975.

Luhr, William, ed. *World Cinema Since 1945*. New York: Ungar, 1987.

Maltin, Leonard. *TV Movies and Video Guide, 1991*. New York: Signet, 1991.

Mayer, Michael. *Foreign Films on American Screens*. New York: Arco, 1965.

Monaco, Paul. *Ribbons in Time: Movies and Society in France, Germany, Italy, and the United States Since 1945*. Bloomington: Indiana University Press, 1987.

Muffs, Judith. *The Holocaust in Books and Films*. New York: Anti-Defamation League, 1982.

Pronay, Nicholas, and D. W. Spring, eds. *Propaganda, Politics, and Film, 1918–45*. London: Macmillan, 1982.

Robinson, David. *The History of World Cinema*. New York: Stein and Day, 1973.

Rotha, Paul. *Documentary Film: The Use of the Film Medium to Interpret Creatively*. New York: Hastings House, 1952.

Shohat, Ella. *Israeli Cinema: East/West and the Politics of Representation*. Austin: University of Texas Press, 1989.

Short, K. R. M., ed. *Film and Radio Propaganda in World War II*. Knoxville: University of Tennessee Press, 1983.

Sklar, Robert, and Charles Musser, eds. *Resisting Images: Essays on Cinema and History*. Philadelphia: Temple University Press, 1990.

Stoil, Michael. *Cinema Beyond the Danube: The Camera and Politics*. Metuchen, N.J.: Scarecrow Press, 1974.

Taylor, Richard. *Film Propaganda: Soviet Russia and Nazi Germany*. London: Croom
     Helm; New York: Barnes and Noble, 1979.
Welch, David. *Propaganda and the German Cinema, 1933–1945*. New York: Oxford
     University Press, 1983.
Wollenberg, Hans. *Fifty Years of German Film*. New York: Arno Press, 1972.

# Chapter 32

---

# Resources for Holocaust Study

## Saul S. Friedman

### FOUNDATIONS OF HOLOCAUST HISTORIOGRAPHY

The field of Holocaust studies is of relatively recent origin. For that reason, readers should be wary of anyone claiming to be the first to examine a particular aspect of Nazi genocide. The probability is, however, that generations to come will still turn to seminal works authored by Raul Hilberg, Nora Levin, Leon Poliakov, Gerald Reitlinger, Lucy Dawidowicz, and Yehuda Bauer. Microcosmic analyses of the root causes of anti-Semitism may be written, but none will surpass George Mosse's *Toward the Final Solution*, Peter Pulzer's *The Rise of Anti-Semitism in Germany and Austria in the Nineteenth Century*, Norman Cohn's *Warrant for Genocide*, Joshua Trachtenberg's *The Devil and the Jews*, Maurice Samuel's *The Great Hatred*, Father Edward Flannery's *The Anguish of the Jews*, Malcolm Hay's oft-republished *The Foot of Pride*, Howard Sachar's *The Course of Modern Jewish History*, or Leon Poliakov's incomparable multivolume *History of Anti-Semitism*.

Without the preservation of documents in Europe, Israel, and the United States, serious research into the most terrible tragedy of World War II would be impossible. The special roles played by Elia Tcherikover, Philip Friedman, and Jacob Robinson in nurturing Holocaust studies in the United States have been narrated in the Preface. The fundamental bibliographic texts are also discussed there. We are also indebted, however, to a legion of academics and government historians who appreciated the need to preserve the terrible record of World War II.

## PUBLISHED DOCUMENTS

Once the Allies agreed in London in September 1943 that there must be postwar trials of Nazi leaders, multinational staffs set to work amassing evidence against these men. Their words, in speeches, publications, and orders served as the basis of the prosecution at Nuremberg in 1945–46. Published in several versions (an eight-volume edition from the U.S. Government Printing Office in 1946 titled *Nazi Conspiracy and Aggression*, and a more substantial forty-two-volume edition issued in 1947 as *The Trial of the Major War Criminals Before the International Military Tribunal at Nuremberg*), these documents are fundamental to an understanding of the Holocaust. Fortunately for the researcher, these works contain excellent indexes to their mass of material, which includes pretrial interrogations and testimony of such figures as Hermann Göring, Rudolf Hess, Franz von Papen, and Hans Frank; official communiqués from the hand of General Wilhelm Keitel, General Alfred Jodl, and Joachim Ribbentrop; and bilingual rants from the writings of Julius Streicher and Adolf Hitler.

Over the past forty years several scholars (notably Raul Hilberg in his *Documents of Destruction* and Lucy Dawidowicz in *A Holocaust Reader*) have published supplementary readers of documents designed for classroom use. These are helpful, but are, by definition, arbitrary and spotty in selection. Of much greater value is John Mendelsohn's *The Holocaust: Selected Documents*, published in 1982 by Garland Press. A specialist with the Modern Military Records, section of the National Archives, Mendelsohn offers a vital mix of German records with English translation. The eighteen volumes, which are excellent for seminars, deal in depth with such subjects as *Kristallnacht*, the Evian Conference, the St. Louis affair, activities of the *Einsatzgruppen*, medical experiments, the Wannsee Conference, the Final Solution in the camps, rescue schemes, and punishment. Equally instructive is the twenty-three-volume *Archives of the Holocaust* edited for Garland Press by Henry Friedlander and Sybil Milton and containing documents of the American Friends Services Committee, Central Zionist Archives, and United Nations War Commission. For those curious about historical methodology, Garland Press has also published a multivolume collection of the notes and research for David Wyman's *Abandonment of the Jews*.

## RESEARCH CENTERS

For those who must go to the actual sources or documents, a number of excellent libraries offer assistance. Yad Vashem in Jerusalem is probably the foremost center of Holocaust research in the world. Taking its name from a passage in Isaiah ("Even unto them will I give in my house and within my walls a monument and a memorial," 56:5), the Martyrs and Heroes Remembrance Authority was established during a two-week meeting in London in 1945. From a stark memorial building with an eternal flame, it has grown to encompass shrines to ghetto and partisan fighters and to Janusz Korczak and 1.5 million children, as well as a series of walkways scooped out of the mountainside dedicated to ravaged Jewish communities. International statesmen from Anwar Sadat to James Baker have been taken first to the museum that graphically demonstrates what happened to Jews when they were stateless. Here, next to Mt. Herzl, a staff of dedicated scholars maintains an index of victims and survivors, documenting stories, hosting conferences, and publishing the *Yad Vashem Bulletin*, *Yad Vashem Studies*, and a number of books.

There are other important research institutions in Israel. Especially recommended are Lohamei ha-Getaot, the Ghetto Fighters' Kibbutz twenty minutes north of Haifa, the Strochlitz Center for Holocaust Studies at Haifa University, the Institute for Contemporary Jewry and the Sassoon Center for the Study of Anti-Semitism at the Hebrew University of Jerusalem, and the Diaspora Center at Tel Aviv University. Researchers may face bureaucratic problems at these institutions, but generally personnel are cooperative, and some resources are unique.

Similar pluses and minuses may be encountered at any of the major documentary centers in Europe. These include the Jewish Historical Institute in Warsaw, which published an annotated bibliography of literature in Polish (*Meczenstwo i walka Zydow w latach okupacij*) in 1963; the brooding and heavily guarded Centre de Documentation Juive Contemporaine in Paris, which published a catalog of French works on the Holocaust in 1964; and the Ukrainian Academy of Arts and Sciences in Kiev, which maintains records of nationalist Ukrainian collaboration with the Nazis.

Although Germany's official archive on World War II, the Bundesarchiv, is maintained in Coblenz, the Office for Nazi War Crimes Investigations is headquartered in the southern German city of Ludwigsburg. Many of the documents (such as propaganda film taken of diseased Jews in the Warsaw ghetto) have been jealously guarded against possible abuse by contemporary anti-Semites. Despite a stated commitment to prosecution of war criminals, the Germans have not exactly distinguished themselves in a number of instances (see especially the shameful behavior of the government in the case of Bohdan Koziy, noted in Charles Ashman and Robert Wagman, *The Nazi Hunters*, pages 157–83, 266–68).

The most accessible of all of these centers is the Wiener Library, which came to London in much the way that YIVO came to New York. Founded by a number of Dutch scholars in Amsterdam in 1934, the center was transferred to London in 1939 by its director, Alfred Wiener. During and after the war the Wiener Library helped amass documents for the International Military Tribunal. Until 1965 the focus of its bimonthly *Wiener Library Bulletin* was the Holocaust. Since then, director Walter Laqueur has given the center and its associated publication, the *Journal of Contemporary History*, a broader focus.

In the United States the starting point for any serious research is the National Archives, and more specifically the Modern Military Records section in Suitland, Maryland. Materials dealing with everything from prewar immigration debates to the 1943 Bermuda Conference and postwar occupation in Bavaria are boxed and indexed. Those who think that the documents have been thoroughly exhausted may take heart from a statement offered by recently retired Raul Hilberg. Speaking to an audience of scholars in Haifa in the spring of 1986, Hilberg lamented that even after a lifetime of research, he had only begun to scratch the surface of the documents available in this one center.

In April 1993 another major institution focusing exclusively on the Holocaust opened in Washington. Planned for more than a decade (the Carter administration chartered the U.S. Holocaust Memorial Council), the U.S. Holocaust Museum is a research and teaching facility. For some time, a staff of scholars from universities in Maryland and the District of Columbia has been indexing primary documents for future researchers. Periodically, the center's education division has convened seminars and issued recommended reading lists. In September 1990 the Holocaust Memorial Council awarded its first Medal of Remembrance to Giorgio Perlasca for his efforts on behalf of Jews in Budapest. The complex, at Raoul Wallenberg Place, has been hailed for its design. Its four floors of grim testimony are intended to educate the general public. The museum's curators have been assembling oral accounts, letters, diaries, ration cards, armbands, and drawings from World War II for display in the modernistic Hall of Witness. American schoolchildren have contributed a series of ceramic tiles for a Wall of Remembrance, dedicated to the 1.5 million Jewish children who perished in the Holocaust. To make the learning experience more meaningful for young people, the museum contains a number of hands-on exhibits, including multimedia presentations, filmstrips, tapes, and a Hollerith computer machine for tracking victims.

The Holocaust Museum in Washington hopes to be the central clearinghouse for the activities of a number of research centers that have specialized in this subject. One of those, the Anti-Defamation League, was created in 1913 to respond to a variety of attacks upon the Jewish people, whether in the United States, Germany, or the Middle East. Committed to the advancement of human rights for all people, the ADL has created a number of films, pamphlets, and displays that combat bigotry toward blacks, women, Hispanics, Asians, and other minorities. Together with the American Jewish Congress, the World Jewish Congress, and the American Jewish Committee, ADL has offered up amicus curiae briefs for cases involving accused war criminals like John Demjanjuk and Fedor Federenko. From its center across from United Nations Plaza in New York City, ADL, publishes *Dimensions*, a journal that deals exclusively with the Holocaust. ADL was also responsible for devising an excellent curriculum guide, *Holocaust and Genocide,* that offers a number of role-playing activities for secondary- and primary-school teachers.

Like the ADL, the Simon Wiesenthal Center is an advocacy and research organization, but with the additional attribute of serving as a public museum. Established in Los Angeles in 1977 in honor of the celebrated Austrian Jewish

Nazi hunter, the Wiesenthal Center is committed to exposing human-rights abuses of every stripe. Although the center has published a Holocaust annual since 1984, its directors have also issued statements on terrorism and on massacres in Cambodia, Africa, and Central America. The center maintains offices in New York, Chicago, Toronto, Miami, Jerusalem, and Paris. A new $50-million complex was to open in 1992. Once completed, the center was to include offices, research archives, a 36,000-square-foot museum, and state-of-the-art multimedia training facilities. In short, the center may serve as a West Coast complement to the Holocaust Museum in Washington.

Among the many Holocaust-directed agencies in the country, several others merit special notice. The National Jewish Resource Center in New York (originally called Zachor), directed by Dr. Irving Greenberg, publishes position papers on contemporary issues that confront Jews, from violence on the streets of Brooklyn to Soviet Jewish emigration. The Center's "Witness to the Holocaust" series of fifteen-minute films based on survivors' testimonies is among the most useful tools for generating discussion in religious schools and public forums. Facing History and Ourselves, based in Brookline, Massachusetts, sponsors institutes, in-service staff development, and adult education conferences. The recipient of the U.S. Department of Education Certificate of Achievement, the organization has issued regular newsletters, an annotated bibliography on racism, and several manuals (*Holocaust and Human Behavior, Choosing to Participate*, and *Elements of Time*). Those interested in ascertaining what is available on film and video should consult The National Center for Jewish Film, based at Brandeis University, the century-old Jewish Chautauqua Society (which also supplies lecturers and scholars in residence), and the Jewish Educational Service of America (JESNA) founded in 1981.

## HOLOCAUST MEMORIAL CENTERS

Despite notoriety given to the Holocaust Museum in Washington, many people have been concerned that because of its particular location, it may not serve the purpose of educating the general public. Only those who can afford to make a pilgrimage to the nation's capital and who make a commitment to visiting the Hall of Witness may benefit from the Holocaust Museum. That was, after all, one of the considerations for establishing the museum in the first place, since even fewer Americans travel to Yad Vashem in Israel. This concern over accessibility may actually have contributed to several problems, such as competition for funds and competition for artifacts. Should a uniform from Buchenwald be given to the museum in Washington or to one in Wilmington? Where would it do the most good in terms of education?

Whether from misguided motivation or not, the result has been a multiplication of Holocaust centers beyond those already noted. Virtually every sizable Jewish population in the United States, suffering from what Hana Abells, onetime director of Yad Vashem's photographic section, labeled "an edifice complex," has felt compelled to create its own Holocaust memorial. More than just a statue or piece of sculpture, these memorials are, like the National Holocaust Museum and the Wiesenthal Center, supposed to be teaching and research facilities. Some are unpretentious, like the Holocaust Library in San Francisco, the Holocaust Awareness Institute associated with the University of Denver, the Martyrs Memorial on Wilshire Boulevard in Los Angeles, or the Southeast Florida Holocaust Memorial Center of Florida International University. Some are little more than one-person operations like the Philadelphia-based National Institute on the Holocaust. Some look good on paper and accomplish very little, like the Holocaust Center of Greater Pittsburgh and the St. Louis Holocaust Center. Some virtually overshadow the Jewish center in their towns, like the Yad Vashem replica in Detroit. Some are shunted to decaying structures, like the Holocaust Center in Cleveland that is trying to function in the old Temple of Abba Hillel Silver.

One of these facilities shows special promise. Immediately accessible to more than two million Jews in the New York and New Jersey area, the Museum of Jewish Heritage, located in Battery Park, was scheduled to open in 1992. Dedicated to the memory of the six million, the museum will offer more than just "the Holocaust." Its galleries will include "The World Before," an exhibition of the contributions made over two thousand years by the likes of Maimonides, Spinoza, and Einstein. "The Aftermath" deals with the establishment of the State of Israel. Within view of the Statue of Liberty and Ellis Island, the museum will also stress the Jewish experience in America and the contributions of people like Emma Lazarus, Henry Kissinger, and Jonas Salk in "Renewal in America." Museum personnel have already demonstrated through their computerized "Interactive Encyclopedia of Jewish Heritage," "Yad Vashem Pages of Testimony," and "Register of Jewish Genealogy" that they are on the cutting edge of research and education.

## SURVIVOR GROUPS

In the first days after the end of World War II, survivors from the death camps and those who came out of hiding returned to their hometowns, looking for loved ones. It was a natural human instinct, and when they found no one, they went on to America or Israel, leaving the memories of local animosity behind. Over the years, they made lives for themselves, but like Jews everywhere, they banded together in societies of exiles based on their old hometowns—Lodz Jews, Lwow Jews—publishing newsletters and even commemorative volumes like the impressive, trilingual *Memorbuch* published by Rszezow Jews in 1967. After years of putting their lives together, finding spouses and raising children, they realized the need for more, the need to guarantee that their story would not be forgotten or trivialized. Recognizing this, a number of oral history projects have been attempted to capture their stories before it is too late. Among the more notable were the Hebrew University oral history project of 1975, the Yale University project, and the Yaffa Eliach project directed by the Center for Holocaust Studies in Brooklyn.

As more and more of their numbers succumbed to what Simon Wiesenthal termed the biological clock, survivors also established second-generation groups, organized trips to Poland and Israel for survivors and their children, and tried to network for the purpose of locating missing friends or relatives. Along these lines, the American Red Cross has rendered vital assistance through its recently created Holocaust and War Victims Tracing Information Center in Baltimore. In its first year the center processed more than five thousand inquiries and succeeded in linking people who had not seen one another in more than forty years. The Red Cross, the Conference of Jewish Material Claims against Germany, and the Jewish Restitution Successor Organization have been helpful in processing reparations claims as well.

Among survivor groups per se, one of the more notable is CANDLES (Children of Auschwitz Nazi Deadly Laboratory Experiments, survivors of Josef Mengele's infamous experiments). Headed by Eva Mozes Kor of Terre Haute, Indiana, CANDLES has organized periodic missions for families to the concentration camps. It has pressed the American and Israeli governments for quasi-legal inquests into the whereabouts of Nazi leaders. The activities of CANDLES have been chronicled in an Emmy-winning television documentary and a 1991 book titled *Children of the Flames*.

Other noteworthy organizations in the United States include the American Federation of Jews from Central Europe, the Association of Yugoslav Jews in the U.S., and the Society for the History of Czechoslovak Jews. In Israel, survivors of the Theresienstadt transit ghetto have created the Beit Terezin Memorial, a small library-museum located outside Tel Aviv.

## STATE COUNCILS

Just as it has become de rigueur for communities to dedicate memorial statues or centers to the Holocaust, the last two decades have witnessed the creation of state councils committed to the furthering of Holocaust education. Whether self-proclaimed or chartered by state legislatures, such commissions exist in Illinois, Delaware, New Jersey, Ohio, Washington, New Hampshire, Pennsylvania, and Florida. Some of these have done creditable jobs. Although based in a particular city, the Greater Orlando Holocaust Resource and Education Center services much of the Southeast. Long before public schools anywhere were sensitizing students to racism, years before the National Endowment for the Humanities underwrote its 1989 conference on racism in Washington, D.C., the Orlando Center developed a curriculum on the subject and presented it in Tel Aviv in 1982 to an international conference on genocide. The Orlando staff merits high praise for its willingness to assist interested parties around the nation.

Even more impressive are the achievements of the Ohio Commission on Holocaust Education. Chartered by the Ohio legislature in 1984 in response to the efforts of Governor Richard Celeste and his wife Dagmar, the commission developed a five-hundred-page guide to teaching the Holocaust. *The Holocaust: Prejudice Unleashed*, edited by Leatrice Rabinsky and Carol Danks, is a comprehensive manual that should be in every school district.

A useful complement to the work of the Ohio Holocaust Commission was developed independently by Professors Zev Garber, Alan Berger, and Rabbi Richard Libovitz. Their *Methodology in the Academic Teaching of the Holocaust* (University Press of America, 1989) is a more sophisticated curriculum intended as a companion volume of *Methodology in the Academic Teaching Of Judaism* (UPA, 1987).


## SUMMARY

There are some critics of Holocaust education who complain that they have been inundated with books and documentaries on the subject. Others claim that the sources have been probed so many times that scholars are merely turning over plowed ground. Allegedly there is nothing to be learned, no more lessons to be drawn. Would that this were so. As Raul Hilberg has noted, there are still corridors of boxes in the archives of Modern Military Records that have not yet been analyzed. We need to explore historical precedents that paved the way for the Holocaust, especially in an age that sees history being rewritten in such a way as to make the Spanish Inquisition a trifle and Ferdinand and Isabella progressive monarchs. Despite momentary expressions of goodwill like those uttered by the president of the Ukrainian Republic on the fiftieth anniversary of Babi Yar, there is a need for honest soul-searching and concession on the part of Ukrainian, Lithuanian, Romanian, and Hungarian historians that many of their people did indeed welcome Nazi genocide. We need historians and teachers who do not merely mouth platitudes but who can implement programs to sensitize minorities, as well as majorities, to the pain of others.

Even if all the areas of the Holocaust had been explored, even if there were no rise of anti-Semitism in Europe, there would still be a need to continue research and publication. We live in an imperfect society, where courts have affirmed the right of self-proclaimed Nazis to chant anti-Jewish slogans in the streets of communities populated with survivors of death camps.

We live in a society that listens indifferently as congressmen rail against sinister Jewish power groups that supposedly intimidate anyone who opposes aid to Israel. We live in a society that winks at statements of anti-Zionism, considering such slander, whether uttered by a Palestinian on a radio broadcast, a LaRouchite in the Pittsburgh airport, or a Libyan at the United Nations, as an amusing tweaking of Jews. It may be a vain hope, but perhaps some good may come of reminding the world over and over that within memory all Jews on this planet were declared outlaws, that all of them were condemned to die. Perhaps the greater sensitivity shown to minorities since 1945—based on the terrible precedent that what happened to Jews could happen to others—might also be accorded to the original victims themselves.

## SELECT BIBLIOGRAPHY

*Archives of the Holocaust*. Edited by Henry Friedlander and Sybil Milton. 23 vols. Hamden, Conn.: Garland Press, 1989.

Ashman, Charles, and Robert Wagman. *The Nazi Hunters*. New York: Pharos Books, 1988.

Cargas, Harry James. *The Holocaust: An Annotated Bibliography*. Chicago and London: American Library Association, 1985.

Cohn, Norman. *Warrant for Genocide*. New York: Harper and Row, 1966.

Dawidowicz, Lucy. *A Holocaust Reader*. New York: Behrman House, 1976.

Edelheit, Abraham and Herschel Edelheit. *Bibliography on Holocaust Literature*. Boulder: Colo.: Westview Press, 1986.

*Encyclopedia of the Holocaust*. Edited by Israel Gutman. New York: Macmillan, 1989.

Flaim, Richard, and Edwin Reynolds. *The Holocaust and Genocide: A Search for Conscience*. Vineland, N.J.: ADL., 1983.

Flannery, Edward. *The Anguish of the Jews*. New York: Macmillan, 1965.

Friedman, Philip. *Martyrs and Fighters: The Epic of the Warsaw Ghetto*. New York: Praeger, 1954.

————. *Their Brothers' Keepers*. New York: Crown, 1957.

Friedman, Philip, and W. J. Gar. *Bibliography of Books in Yiddish on the Jewish Catastrophe and Heroism*. New York: YIVO, 1962.

Garber, Zev, Alan Berger, and Jeffrey Gurock, eds. *Methodology in the Academic Teaching of the Holocaust*. Lanham, Md.: University Press of America, 1988.

Hay, Malcolm. *The Foot of Pride*. Boston: Beacon Press, 1950.

Hebrew University of Jerusalem and *New York Times*. Contemporary Jewry Oral History Collection. Pt. 2. World War II. The Holocaust: Resistance and Rescue. Glen Rock, N.J.: Microfilming Corp. of America, 1975.

Hilberg, Raul. *Documents of Destruction*. New York: Quadrangle Books, 1951.

*Holocaust and Human Behavior*. Brookline, Mass.: Facing History and Ourselves, n.d.

Mark, B. *Annotated Bibliography of Literature in Polish*. Warsaw: Jewish Historical Institute, 1963.

Mendelsohn, John. *The Holocaust: Selected Documents*. New York and London: Garland, 1982.

Mosse, George. *Toward the Final Solution*. New York: Howard Fertig, 1978.

*Nazi Conspiracy and Aggression*. 8 vols. Washington, D.C.: U.S. Government Printing Office, 1946.

Poliakov, Leon. *The History of Anti-Semitism*. 4 vols. New York: Vanguard, 1965–75.

Pulzer, Peter. *The Rise of Anti-Semitism in Germany and Austria in the Nineteenth Century*. New York: Wiley, 1964.

Rabinsky, Leatrice, and Carol Danks. *The Holocaust: Prejudice Unleashed*. Columbus: Ohio Council on Holocaust Education, 1988.

Robinson, Jacob. *The Holocaust and After: Sources and Literature in English.* Jerusalem: Israel Universities Press, 1973.

Robinson, Jacob, and Philip Friedman. *Guide to Jewish History Under Nazi Impact.* New York: YIVO, 1960.

————. *Bibliography of Books in Hebrew on the Jewish Catastrophe and Heroism in Europe.* New York: YIVO, 1960.

Sachar, Howard. *The Course of Modern Jewish History.* Cleveland: World, 1958.

Samuel, Maurice. *The Great Hatred.* New York: Knopf, 1940.

Szonyi, David. *The Holocaust: An Annotated Bibliography and Resource Guide.* New York: Ktav, 1985.

Trachtenberg, Joshua. *The Devil and the Jews.* New Haven, Conn.: Yale University Press, 1943.

*Trial of the Major War Criminals Before the International Military Tribunal Nuremberg, 14 November 1945–10 October, 1946.* 42 vols. 1947. Reprint. New York: AMS Press, 1971.

U.S. Holocaust Memorial Council. *Planning Guide: Fifty Years Ago: From Terror to Systematic Murder.* Washington, D.C., 1991.

Wiener Library. Catalogue Series on Persecution and Resistance Under the Nazis. London, 1960.

# Author/Title Index

Abells, Hana, *The Children We Remember*, 576

Abitbol, Michel, *Jews of North Africa During the Second World War*, 362

Abraham, David, *Collapse of The Weimar Republic*, 58

Abramski-Bligh, Irit, "Jews of Syria and Lebanon under Vichy Rule," 362

Abramson, Glenda (ed.), *The Blackwell Companion to Jewish Culture*, 587

Abzug, Robert, *Inside the Vicious Heart*, 172

Adams, Michael (ed.), *The Middle East: A Handbook*, 460

Adelson, Alan, and Lapides, Robert (eds.), *Lodz Ghetto*, 99, 212

Adler, David, *The Number on My Grandfather's Arm*, 576

Adler, H. G., *Theresienstadt, 1941–1945*, 266–67

Adler, Jacques, *Jews of Paris and the Final Solution*, 348, 350, 359, 361

Aigner, Dietrich, *Das Ringen um England*, 63

Ainsztein, Reuben, *Jewish Resistance in Nazi-Occupied Eastern Europe*, 295

Albert, Phyllis, *Modernization of French Jewry*, 360

Aleichem, Sholom, xx

Alexander, Edward, *The Resonance of Dust*, 556, 560, 569

Altshuler, David (ed.): *Hitler's War against the Jews*, 578; *The Precious Legacy*, 259, 589

Amery, Jean, *At the Mind's Eye*, 117

Amort, Čestmír, *Heydrichiáda*, 274

Ancel, Jean, *Documents Concerning The Fate of Romanian Jewry*, 312

Anger, Per, *With Raoul Wallenberg in Budapest*, 143

Angress, Werner, *Stillborn Revolution*, 69

Apenszlak, Jakob, *Black Book of Polish Jewry*, 211

Appelfeld, Ahron, 538; *Age of Wonders*, 539; *Badenheim*, 539; *To the Land of the Cattails*, 539; *Tzili*, 540

Arad, Yitzhak, *Belzec, Sobibor, Treblinka*, 90–91; *Ghetto in Flames*, 99

Arditi, Benjamin, *Yehudi Bulgariyah Bishavot Hamishpat Hanatsi*, 308

Ariel, Joseph, "Jewish Self-Defense and Resistance in France," 361

Arendt, Hannah, xx, 4, 17n; *Eichmann in Jerusalem*, 26, 172

*Armenian Genocide, 1915–1923*, 197

Armstrong, John, *Ukrainian Nationalism*, 294

Aron, Robert, *The Vichy Regime*, 357

Aronson, Shlomo, *Reinhard Heydrich*, 98, 274

Arsenian, Seth, "Wartime Propaganda in The Middle East," 462

Artzi, A., "Underground Activities of Pioneer Movements in Rumania," 312

Ashman, Charles, and Wagman, Robert, *The Nazi Hunters*, 625

Assaf, Uri, *The Last Jew*, 545

Atkinson, Linda, *In Kindling Flame*, 577

Atler, Robert, 559, 564; *Defenses of the Imagination*, 570

Auerbacher, Inge, *I Am a Star-Child of the Holocaust*, 262, 578–79

Aurednickova, Anna, *Tři léta v Terezíně*, 261–62

*Auschwitz Album*, 102n

Ausubel, Nathan and Maryann (eds.), *A Treasury of Jewish Poetry*, 551, 568, 569

Avni, Haim: "Spain, Franco, and the Jews," 310; "Spanish Nationals in Greece," 310; "Zionist Underground in Holland and France," 361

Badia, Gilbert (ed.), *Les barbalés de l'-éxil*, 358

Bahr, Frank, *Grundkurse Geschichte*, 492, 506

Baldwin, James, xii

Baldwin, Margaret, *The Boys Who Saved the Children*, 580

Balfour, Michael, *Withstanding Hitler in Germany*, 71

Balicka-Kozlowska, Helena, *Who Rescued and Who Was Rescued*, 207

Ball-Kaduri, K. Y., "Evidence of Witnesses," 529

Bar-Adon, Dorthy and Pesach, *Seven Who Fell*, 183

Baranowski, Shelley, *The Confessing Church*, 128–29

Bartoszewski, Waldyslaw, and Lewin, Zofia, *The Samaritans*, 144

Bar-Tov, Omer, *The Eastern Front*, 68

Basani, Giorgio, *Garden of the Finzi-Continis*, 387, 612–13

Baudot, Marcel, *L'opinion publique sous l'occupation*, 359

Bauer, Yehuda: *History of the Holocaust*, xxii, 4, 6, 8, 9, 11, 14, 16, 182, 258, 315, 365, 366, 485, 623; *The Holocaust in Historical Perspective*, 246, 315; *The Holocaust as Historical Experience*, 246, 313; *They Chose Life*, 189

Baumann, Herbert, *Politische Gemeinschaftskunde*, 488, 514

Baynes, Norman, *Speeches of Adolf Hitler*, 40

Becker, Jurek, *Jacob the Liar*, 542

Bedarida, Renee, *Les armes de l'ésprit*, 359

Bekker, Cajus, *Hitler's Naval War*, 66

Bellow, Saul, 557

Ben, Joseph, "Jewish Leadership in Greece During the Holocaust," 310

Bender, Roger, and Taylor, Hugh, *Uniforms, Organization and History of the Waffen SS*, 290

Benes, Eduard: *From Munich to New War and New Victory*, 272; *Masaryk's Path and Legacy*, 272

Benoschofsky, Ilona, and Karsai, Elek (eds.), *Indictment of Nazism*, 242

Ben Tov, Arieh, *Facing the Holocaust in Budapest*, 434

Benveniste, David, "Yehudei Saloniki," 311

Berben, Paul, *Dachau*, 92

Berghahn, Volker, and Kitchen, Martin, *Germany in Age of Total War*, 65

Berkowitz, Eliezer: *Faith after the Holocaust*, 116; *With God in Hell*, 117

Bernard, Jean Jacques, *Le camp de la mort lente*, 356

Bethell, Nicholas, *Palestine Triangle*, 463

Bettelheim, Bruno, *The Informed Heart*, 171, 173, 368

Biddiss, Michal, *Father of Racist Ideology*, 358

Bierman, John, *Righteous Gentile*, 143

Billig, Joseph: *La solution finale*, 355; *Le commissariat général aux questions juives*, 358

Binder, Gerhart: *Damals und Heute 5 . . .*, 487; *Vom Ersten Weltkrieg*, 489, 492

Binion, Rudolph, *Hitler among the Germans*, 24, 44–45

Birenhaum, Halina, *Hope is the Last to Die*, 524

Birkenfeld, Wolfgang, Die Reise in die Vergangenheit, 495

Birn, Ruth-Bettina, *Die Hoheren SS und Polizeifuhrer*, 99

*Black Book: The Nazi Crime Against the Jewish People*, 212

*Black Book of Poland*, 211

Blackburn, Gilmer, *Education in the Third Reich*, 30

Blatter, Janet (ed.), *Art of the Holocaust*, 588

Bleuel, Hans Peter, *Sex and Society in Nazi Germany*, 29

Bloch, Marc, *Strange Defeat*, 361

Blonski, Jan, "Poor Poles Look at the Ghetto," 207

Boas, H. J., *Religious Resistance in Holland*, 365

Bobke, Wolfgang, *Jews in West German History Textbooks*, 502, 517

Boeck, Otto; Dumke, Artur; Hubner, Robert; Klenk, Fritz; Kratzert, Otto; and Sohns, Eugen, *Damals und Heute 4*, 495

Boehm, Eric, *We Survived*, 525

Boelcke, Willi, *Die Kosten von Hitlers Krieg*, 58

Böhm, Franz, "Unbewaltigte Vergangenheit," 490

Bonnet, Jean, *Les pouvoirs publics francais*, 358

Bor, Josef: *Opuštěná panenka*, 262; *Terezin Requiem*, 262, 600

Borenstein, Emily, *Night of Broken Glass*, 543–44

Borowitz, Eugene: *Choices in Modern Jewish Thought*, 108, 111–17; *How Can a Jew Speak of Faith Today?*, 117

Borowski, Tadeusz, 533–45; *This Way for the Gas, Ladies and Gentlemen*, 536, 545

Borth, Wilhelm, *Zeiten und Menschen*, 490, 514n

Borzykowski, Tuvia, *Between Tumbling Walls*, 186, 524

Bower, Tom, *Blind Eye to Murder*, 287

Bowman, Steven: *Greece in the 1940s*, 310; "Jews in Wartime Greece," 310

Bracher, Karl-Dietrich, *The German Dictatorship*, 26

Brady, Robert, *Spirit and Structure of German Fascism*, 59

Braham, Randolph: *Destruction of Hungarian Jewry*, 247, 258; *Genocide and Retribution*, 313; *Holocaust in Hungary Forty Years Later*, 243–45; *Hungarian Jewish Catastrophe*, 242; *Hungarian Labor Services System*, 243; *Politics of Genocide*, 227, 241, 245–46

Bramsted, Ernest, *Aristocracy and Middle-Classes in Germany*, 59

Bramwell, Anna, *Blood and Soil*, 55

Brandes, Detlef, *Die Tschenen und Deutsche*, 270

Breitman, Richard: *American Refugee Policy and European Jewry*, 476; *The Architect of Genocide*, 25

Breloer, Heinrich, *Mein Tagebuch*, 28

Brenner, Reeve, *Faith and Doubt of Holocaust Survivors*, 117

Bressel, Richard (ed.), *Life in the Third Reich*, 28, 44

Bridenthal, Renate; Grossmann, Atina; and Kaplan, Marion (eds.), *When Biology Became Destiny*, 99

Brissaud, Andre: *Historie de service secret Nazi*, 274; *La dernière année de Vichy*, 356

Broszat, Martin: *Anatomy of the SS State*, 30, 89, 90, 289; *Hitler and the Collapse of Weimar Germany*, 49; *The Hitler State*, 26

Browning, Christopher: *Fateful Months*, 67, 68; *The Final Solution*, 356

Brucker, Peter, *Das Arbeit*, 501

Bullock, Alan, *Hitler: A Study in Tyr-*

*anny*, 22, 27, 41–42, 47, 64, 66, 67, 70

Bunting, Eve, *Terrible Things*, 576

Burgher, John, "Hitler's Quisling Dilemma," 368

Burkhardt, Hermann; Christman, Helmut; Jaacks, Gerhard; Klenk, Fritz, *Damals und Heute 5 . . .* , 484, 487, 491, 492; *Vom Ersten Weltkrieg*, 489, 493

Buszko, Josef, et al, *Auschwitz*, 93–94

Byrnes, Robert, *Antisemitism in Modern France*, 358

Bytwerk, Randall, *Julius Streicher*, 26

Campion, Joan, *In the Lion's Mouth*, 259

Capek, Karel: *Masaryk on Thought and Life*, 272; *President Masayrk Tells His Story*, 271–72; *War with the Newts*, 274–75

Carell, Paul, *Hitler's War on Russia*, 63; *Scorched Earth*, 63

Cargas, Harry: *Harry James Cargas in Conversation with Elie Wiesel*, 545; *The Holocaust*, xxvii, 97–98; *Reflections of a Post-Auschwitz Christian*, 133–34; *When God and Man Failed*, 133

Caron, Vicki: *Between France and Germany*, 360; "Prelude to Vichy," 358; *The UGIF*, 361

Carr, William, *Hitler*, 25, 43

Carroll, Berenice, *Design for Total War*, 53

Cassels, Alan, *Mussolini's Early Diplomacy*, 62

Celan, Paul: "Fugue of Death," 554; *Selected Poems*, 569; *Speech-Grille and Selected Poems*, 563; "Tübingen January," 550, 568

Chaikin, Miriam, *A Nightmare in History*, 577–78

Chaplin, Charles, *The Great Dictator*, 606

Charny, Israel, *Genocide*, 69, 172

Chartock, Roselle, and Spencer, Jack, *The Holocaust Years*, 117

Chary, Frederick, *The Bulgarian Jews and the Final Solution*, 308

Childers, Thomas, *The Nazi Voter*, 49

Cobb, Richard, *French and Germans, Germans and French*, 357

Cochrane, Arthur, *The Church's Confession under Hitler*, 129

Cohen, Aharon, *Israel and the Arab World*, 460

Cohen, Asher: "Continuity in Change," 244; "German Hegemony and National Independence," 245; *The Halutz Resistance in Hungary*, 241, 244

Cohen, Elie, *The Abyss*, 525

Cohen, Naomi, *Year After the Riots*, 463

Cohen, Richard, *Burden of Conscience*, 349

Cohn, Norman, *Warrant for Genocide*, 623

Collingwood, R. G., *Idea of History*, 530

Compton, James, *The Swastika and the Eagle*, 65

Conway, John, *The Nazi Persecution of the Churches*, 158n

Cookridge, E. H., *Gehlen, Spy of the Century*, 295

Cornelissen, Joachim, *BSV Geschichte*, 485, 499

Costanza, Mary (ed.), *The Living Witness*, 588

Craig, Gordon, *The Germans*, 492, 510, 511, 515n, 518n

Curtis, Dan: "War and Remembrance," 616; "Winds of War," 616

Czarnecki, Joseph, *Last Traces*, 588

Czerniakow, Adam, *Warsaw Diary*, 212, 524

Dagan, Avidor (ed.), *The Jews of Czechoslovakia*, 259–61

Dallin, Alexander, *German Rule in Russia*, 63

Dallin, David, *Soviet Espionage*, 284

Dalven, Rachel, "The Holocaust in Jannina," 311

Dank, Milton, *The French Against the French*, 357

Datner, Szymon, *Genocide, 1939–1945*, 292

Davidson, Eugene, *The Trial of the Germans*, 292

Davies, Alan (ed.), *Antisemitism and the Foundations of Christianity*, 124

Dawidowicz, Lucy, xv, xx, xxi; *Golden Tradition*, 211; *War against the Jews*, 4, 6, 7, 8, 14, 16, 182, 251, 258, 295, 315, 365, 435, 578, 623, 624

Deakin, F. W., *The Brutal Friendship*, 62

Debo, Charlotte: *None of Us Will Return*, 525; *Who Will Carry the Word?*, 545

de Chambrun, René, *Pierre Laval: Traitor or Patriot?*, 357

Demetz, Hana, *The House on Prague Street*, 525

Deschner, Günther, *Reinhard Heydrich*, 25, 274

Des Pres, Terrence, *The Survivor*, xxi, 171

el-Dessouki, Muhammed, "Hitler und der nahe Osten," 461

Deutsch, Harold: *Conspiracy Against Hitler in the Twilight War*, 71; *Hitler and His Generals*, 65, 71

Diamant, Zanfel: Héros juifs de la résistance francaise," 362; "Le billet vert," 362; "Les juifs dans la résistance francaise," 362; "Jewish Refugees on the French Riviera," 356

Dimsdale, Joel (ed.), *Survivors, Victims, and Perpetrators*, 172, 525

Dmytryshyn, Basil, "The Nazis and the SS Volunteer Division 'Galicia,' " 290

Dobroszycki, Lucjan: *Chronicle of the Lodz Ghetto*, 99; *The Holocaust in the Soviet Union*, 298

Döhn, Hans, and Sandmann, Fritz, *Geschichte*, 493

Don, Yehuda, and Karady, Victor (eds.), *A Social and Economic History of Central European Jewry*, 277

Donat, Alexander, *The Holocaust Kingdom*, 152, 171, 524

Dontsov, Dmitri, *Nationalism*, 296–97

Dorian, Emil, *The Quality of Witness*, 312

Dorpalen, Andreas, *German History in Marxist Perspective*, 51

Döscher, Han-Jurgen, *Das Auswartige Amt im Dritten Reich*, 27

Drees, Dr. F. W., *Van Mei tot Mei*, 368

Dribben, Judith, *A Girl Called Judith Strick*, 525

Dubnow, Simon, xix, 522, 526; *History of Jews in Russia and Poland*, 211

Dubois, Josiah, *The Devil's Chemists*, 56

Dupuy, Trevor, *A Genius for War*, 65

Durand, Paul, *La S.C.N.F. pendant la guerre*, 360

Dziewanowski, Kazimierz, "Please Do Not Speak in My Name," 208

Ebeling, Hans and Birkenfeld, Wolfgang, *Die Reise in die Vergangenheit*, 495

Eck, Nathan: "The March of Death from Serbia to Hungary," 314; "New Light on the Charges Against the Last Grand Rabbi of Salonica," 310

Edelheit, Abraham and Herschel, *Bibliography on Holocaust Literature*, xxvii, 316n

Edelman, Marek, *The Ghetto Fights*, 524

Ehrenburg, Ilya, *The Black Book*, 295

Ehrlich, B., *The French Resistance*, 360

Ehrlich, Evelyn, *Cinema of Paradox*, 620

Ehrmann, Fraticek; Heitlinger, Otta; and Iltis, Rudolf, *Terezín*, 262

Eibl-Eibesfeldt, Irenaeus, *Love and Hate*, 172

Eichberg, Henning, *Minderheit und Mehrheit*, 489, 498

Eichenauer, Richard, *Musik und Rasse*, 592

Einstein-Keshev, Betti, "The Story of Independent Ukraine," 296

Eisner, Jack, *The Survivor*, 524

Elath, Eliahu, *Haj Muhammed Amin al-Husseini*, 462

Elazar, Daniel, "The Sunset of Balkan Jewry," 305

Eliach, Yaffa, 629; *Hasidic Tales of the Holocaust*, 528; *The Last Jew*, 545

Eliot, T. S., *The Sacred Wood*, 533, 545

Emaleh, Avram, *Les Juifs de Salonique et la resistance Hellenique*, 310

Emmanuel, I. S., *Histoire des Israelites de Salonique*, 310

Engelmann, Bernt, *Hitler's Germany*, 28

Engleman, Matylda, *End of the Journey*, 524

Epstein, Helen, *Children of the Holocaust*, 526

Esterhaz, Joe, *The Music Box*, 605, 609

Eubank, Keith, *Munich*, 269

Eyck, Erich, *History of the Weimar Republic*, 22

Ezrahi, Sidra, *By Words Alone*, 560, 569

Fackenheim, Emil: *God's Presence in History*, 113; *Jewish Return into History*, xxiv, 113, 114, 172; *Jewish Thought of Emil Fackenheim*, 112, 114; *Quest for Past and Future*, 113; *To Mend the World*, 114

Fast, Howard, *The Jews*, 365

Favez, Jean Claude, *Une Mission impossible?*, 434

Feig, Konnilyn, *Hitler's Death Camps*, 89

Fein, Helen, *Accounting for Genocide*, 171, 195, 528, 530

Feingold, Henry, *Politics of Rescue*, 473

Feldman, Irving, "The Pripet Marshes," 550, 568

Fenelon, Fania: *The Musicians of Auschwitz*, 184–85; "Playing for Time," 525, 545, 601, 615

Fernis, Hans-Georg, and Hillgruber, Andreas, *Grundzüge der Geschichte*, 489, 491, 497, 509

Fest, Joachim, 47, 64, 66, 67, 70; *Face of Third Reich*, 26, 273–74; *Hitler*, 23, 42

Feuchtwanger, Lion, *The Devil in France*, 356

Fischer-Galati, Stephen, "Fascism, Communism and the Jewish Question in Rumania," 312

Fisher, Julius, *Transnistria*, 312

Flannery, Edward, *The Anguish of the Jews*, 123–25, 135n, 623

Fleischner, Eva: *Auschwitz: Beginning of a New Era?*, 118; "Can the Few Become the Many?" 166; "Crucial Importance of Holocaust to Christians," 165

Fleming, Gerald, *Hitler and the Final Solution*, 69, 99

Flender, Harold, *Rescue in Denmark*, 132, 151

Flood, Charles, *The Path to Power*, 48

Fluek, Toby, *Memories of My Life in a Polish Village*, 589

Fogel, Ephim, *Shipment to Maidanek*, 550, 569

Fontaine, Andre, *Le Camp d'étrangers des Milles*, 356

Forsythe, William, *The Odessa File*, 609

Fosse, Bob, *Cabaret*, 606

Fox, J. P., *Germany and the Far Eastern Question*, 63

Franck, Norbert, *Heil Hitler, Herr Lehrer*, 29

Frank, Anne, *Diary*, 523, 544, 575, 579, 606, 613

Frank, Margret and Willi, *Politik Heute*, 497

Frankl, Viktor, *Man's Search for Meaning*, 117, 172

Freeman, Michael, *Atlas of Nazi Germany*, 32

Freidenreich, Harriet, *Jews of Yugoslavia*, 306

Freier, Recha, *Let the Children Come*, 185

Friedlander, Albert, *Out of the Whirlwind*, 118

Friedlander, Henry, 68, 98; *Archives of Holocaust*, 624

Friedländer, Saul: *Prelude to Downfall*, 64; *When Memory Comes*, 359, 524

Friedman, Maurice, *Abrahama Joshua Heschel and Elie Wiesel*, 116

Friedman, Pavel, "The Butterfly," 553

Friedman, Philip, xix-xx; *Bibliography of Books in Yiddish on Jewish Catastrophe*, xx; *Guide to Jewish History under Nazi Impact*, xx; *Martyrs and Fighters*, xx, 212, 524, 623; *Their Brothers'*

*Keepers*, xx, 131, 140, 141, 151, 153, 155, 156, 157n, 162, 364–65

Friedman, Saul: "A5714: Robert Clary, A Memoir of Liberation," 619; *Amcha*, 527, 530; *No Haven for the Oppressed*, 474–75; *Pogromchik*, 294; *Terezín Diary of Gonda Redlich*, 264

Frisch, Max, *Andorra*, 544

Fuchs, Abraham, *The Unheeded Cry*, 187

Galante, Abraham, *Documents officiels Turcs concernant les Juifs de Turquie*, 305

Gallmeister, E. D., *Grundriss der Geschichte*, 491, 498

Gallo, Max, *Night of Long Knives*, 30

Gamzon, Robert, *Les Eaux-claires*, 362

Garber, Zev; Berger, Alan; and Libowitz, Richard, *Methodology in Academic Teaching of Holocaust*, 298

Gebirtig, Mordecai, "Es Brennt," 597

Gedye, George, *Fallen Bastions*, 269

Gehl, Jurgen, *Austria, Germany and the Anschluss*, 269

Gelber, N. M., "Jewish Life in Bulgaria," 305

"Genocide," 617

Genschel, Helmut, *Die Verdrangung der Juden aus der Wirtlschaft*, 57

Gerigk, Herbert (ed.), *Lexikon den Juden in der Musik*, 592

Gies, Miep, *Anne Frank Remembered*, 367, 613

Gilbert, Martin: *The Appeasers*, 269; *Auschwitz and the Allies*, 476; *Britain and Germany between the Wars*, 63; *The Holocaust*, 3–4, 6, 8–11, 16, 296, 315, 526, 529

Gisevius, Hans, *Adolf Hitler*, 23

Glatstein, Jacob: "Dead Men Don't Praise God," 564; "In a Ghetto," 564; My Brother Refugee," 564; "My Holy City Lublin," 564; *The Selected Poems of Jacob Glatstein*, 549, 563, 570

Glatstein, Jacob; Knox, Israel; and Marsgoshes, Samuel, *Anthology of Holocaust Literature*, 144, 189

Glik, Hirsch, "Zog nit keynmol," 551, 599

Golan, Menachem, *Hanna's War*, 607

Goldberg, Arthur, and Finger, Seymour (eds.), *American Jewry During the Holocaust*, 259

Goldberg, Izaak, *Miracle versus Tyranny*, 524

Goldberger, Leo, *Rescue of the Danish Jews*, 170

Goldfaden, Abraham, "Rozhinkes mit Mandlen," 598

Goldstein, Bernard, *The Stars Bear Witness*, 189, 524

Gonner, Kurt; Krug, Rolf; Niephaus, Heinz-Theo; and Weiss, Eugen, *Politik in unseren Tagen*, 497–98

Gordon, Bertram, *Collaborationism in France*, 357

Gordon, Harold, *Hitler and the Beer Hall Putsch*, 48

Gordon, Sarah, *Hitler, Germany and the Jewish Question*, 31, 68

Gouri, Haim, *Eighty-First Blow*, 617

Grant Duff, Shiela: *Europe and the Czechs*, 269; *A German Protectorate*, 258

Grassmann, S.: *Vom Ersten zum Zweiten Weltkrieg*, 490, 493, 494, 496; *Zeitauenahme*, 485, 486

Gray, Martin, *For Those I Loved*, 5–6

Gray, Ronald, *Hitler and the Germans*, 577

Green, Gerald: *Artists of Terezin*, 263, 588; "Holocaust: Story of the Family Weise," 492, 496, 533, 604, 614

Green, Nancy, *The Pletzl of Paris*, 360

Green, Warren, "The Fate of Oriental Jews in Vichy France," 362

Greenberg, Uri: "In the Mound of Corpses," 564; *Streets of the River*, 564, 570

Grobba, Fritz, *Irak*, 462

Grosman, Alexander, *Nur das Gewissen*, 247

Grossman, Kurt, *Die unbesungenen Helden*, 162

Grossman, Mendel, *With a Camera in the Ghetto*, 212

Grunberger, Richard, *The Twelve Year Reich*, 28

Grunfeld, Frederic, *The Hitler File*, 32

Grütter, Werner, *Hinweise und Interpretationen*, 497, 503

Guardini, Romano, *Verantwortung, Gedanken zur jüdischen Frage*, 506

Guillebaud, Claude: *Economic Recovery of Nazi Germany*, 59; *Social Policy of Nazi Germany*, 59

Gurdus, Luba, *The Death Train*, 525

Guri, Ilana (ed.), *Testimony Art of Holocaust*, 588

Gutman, Joseph, *No Graven Images*, 587

Gutman, Visrael: *Patterns of Jewish Leadership in Nazi Europe*, 310, 312, 368; *Unequal Victims*, 213

Gutteridge, Richard, *Open Thy Mouth for the Dumb*, 125–26

Habe, Hans, *The Mission*, 11, 13, 19n

Habermas, Jurgen, 47, 67

Haffner, Sebastian, *Meaning of Hitler*, 43

Haft, Cynthia, *The Bargain and the Bridle*, 361

Hallgarten, George: *Hitler*, 59; *Why Dictators?*, 59

Hallie, Philip, *Lest Innocent Blood Be Shed*, 132, 359

Hamburger, Michael: "For Some Time Now," 560; "The Survivor," 569; *Truth of Poetry*, 569

Hamsik, Dusan, and Prazak, Jiri, *Bomba pro Hedricha*, 274

Hancock, Ian, *The Pariah Syndrome*, 198

Handler, Andrew (ed.), *The Holocaust in Hungary*, 244

Hanson, Joanna, *The Civilian Population and the Warsaw Uprising*, 297

Hanusiak, Michael, *Lest We Forget*, 296–97

Hart, Kitty, *Return to Auschwitz*, 525

Hartwich, Hans-Hermann, *Politik im 20. Jahrhundert*, 509

Häsler, Alfred, *Das Boot Ist voll*, 432–33, 611

Hauner, Milan, *Hitler*, 47

Haushofer, Albrecht, *Moabit Sonnets*, 544

Haverkamp, Heinrich, *Grundzüge den Geschichte*, 489, 497

Hay, Malcolm, *Foot of Pride/Roots of Christian Anti-Semitism/Europe and the Jews*, 125, 182, 623

Hayes, Carlton, *Wartime Mission in Spain*, 410

Hearnden, Patrick, *Roosevelt Confronts Hitler*, 64

Heck, Alfons, *A Child of Hitler*, 29

Heiden, Konrad, *Der Führer: Hitler's Rise to Power*, 23

Heike, Wolf-Deitrich, *Sie Wollten die Freiheit*, 289–90

Heimler, Eugene, *Concentration Camp*, 525

Heinloth, Bernhardt, and Kistler, Helmut, *Geschichte*, 482, 492, 493

Heineman, John, *Hitler's First Foreign Minister*, 27

Heinrichs, Waldo, *Threshold of War*, 65

Heller, Celia, *On the Edge of Destruction*, 211

Hellman, Peter, *Avenue of the Righteous*, 131

Helmreich, Ernst, *The German Churches under Hitler*, 127

Henke, Josef, *England in Hitlers Politischem Kalkul*, 63

Herman, Erwin, *The Yanov Torah*, 580

Herold, J. Christopher, *The Swiss without Halos*, 432

Hersey, John, *The Wall*, xxviii, 212, 524, 616

Hersh, Gizelle, and Mann, Peggy, *Gizelle, Save the Children*, 525

Herzstein, Robert, *Adolf Hitler and the Third Reich*, 27

*Heumann, Hans: Geschichte für den Gechichts-unterricht*, 483; *Geschichte r Morgen*, 516; *Unser Weg durch die Geschichte*, 492–93

Hey, Bernd, and Radkau, Joachim: *Handreichungen für der Lehrer*, 503–10;

*Nationalismus und Faschismus*, 500–2, 511; *Politische Weltkunde*, 487–89

Heyen, William: *Erika: Poems*, 544, 563, 565; *My Holocaust Songs*, 565; "Numinous," 565; "Riddle," 544; *Swastika Poems*, 563

Heyl, John, *Hitler's Economic Theory*, 51–52

Heyman, Eva, *Diary of Eva Heyman*, 579

Hiden, John, *Explaining Hitler's Germany*, 43

Higham, Charles, *Trading with the Enemy*, 56

Higonnet, Patrice, "How Guilty Were the French?," 358

Hilberg, Raul: *The Destruction of the European Jews*, xxii, 4–12, 16, 67, 69, 88, 99, 171, 182, 251, 257–58, 291–92, 314, 364–67, 435, 611, 626, 630; *Documents of Destruction*, 623–25; *Perpetrators Victims Bystanders*, 171

Hildebrand, Klaus, *The Third Reich*, 27, 460

Hill, Geoffrey, *Somewhere Is Such a Kingdom*, 549, 568

Hillesum, Etty: *An Interrupted Life*, 525; *Letters from Westerbork*, 367

Hillgruber, Andreas: *Germany and the Two World Wars*, 65; *Grundzüge der Geschichte*, 497, 509

Hirschfeld, Gerhard: "Collaboration and Attentism in the Netherlands," 368; *The Policies of Genocide*, 68, 99

Hirszowicz, Lukasz, *Third Reich and Arab East*, 462

Hitler, Adolf: *Hitler's Table Talk*, 39; *Mein Kampf*, 23, 39–40

Hochhuth, Rolf, *The Deputy*, 134, 155, 395, 405n, 544, 620

Hoess, Rudolf, *Commandant of Auschwitz*, 97

Hofer, Walther, *Die Diktatur Hitlers*, 27

Hoffman, Joachim: *Handreichung für den Lehrer*, 486–87, 499; *Spiegel dur Zeiten*, 484; *Von der Rüssischen Revolution*, 515; *Von der Zeit des Imperialismus*, 517

Hoffman, Judy, *Joseph and Me*, 579

Hoffmann, Peter, *German Resistance to Hitler*, 70

Höhne, Hans: *Canaris*, 295; *Order of the Death's Head*, 31, 48, 65, 98

Holborn, Hajo, *Republic to Reich*, 22

Holde, Artur, *Jews in Music*, 601

Holland, Agnieszka, *Europa, Europa*, 611

Holzer, Burghild, "Nelly Sachs and the Kabbala," 570

Homze, Edward: *Foreign Labor in Nazi Germany*, 57, 67; *German Military Aviation*, 66

Hoppe, Hans, "Germany, Bulgaria, Greece," 308

Horowitz, Irving: *Genocide*, 172, 195; *Taking Lives*, 172

Hovannisian, Richard, *The Armenian Genocide*, 197

Hubatsch, Walther, *Enstehung und Entwicklung*, 54

Hubner, Robert, *Damals und Heute 4 . . .*, 516

Hug, Wolfgang; Hoffman, Joachim; and Krautkrämer, Elmar: *Geschichte Weltkunde*, 483, 485, 497; *Lernimpulse*, 482; *Von der Zeit des Imperialismus*, 483, 494, 502

Hull, David, *Film in the Third Reich*, 621

Huneke, Douglas, *Religious Community Perspectives on Rescuers*, 164–65, 167, 70

Hurewitz, Jacob: *Diplomacy in Near and Middle East*, 460; *Struggle for Palestine*, 460

Huttenbach, Henry, *Historicity of the Holocaust*, 529

Hyams, Joseph, *A Field of Buttercups*, 212

Hyman, Paula, *From Dreyfus to Vichy*, 360

Iklé, Frank, *German-Japanese Relations*, 62

Iranek-Osmecki, Kazimierz, *He Who Saves One Life*, 144, 203–4

Irving, David: *Goring*, 25; *Hitler's War*, 68–69; *The War Path*, 28, 68–69

Isaacman, Clara, *Clara's Story*, 579

Ivanov, Miroslav, *Not Only Black Uniforms*, 274

Jäckel, Eberhard: *Frankreich in Hitlers Europa*, 63, 355; *Hitler's Herrschaft*, 43; *Hitler in History*, 43; *Hitler's World View*, 43

Jackson, Livia, *Elli*, 525

Jacobson, Hans-Adolf, *National-sozialistiche Aussenpolitik*, 60

Jacoby, Gerhard: *Common Fate of Czech and Jew*, 258; *Racial State*, 270

James, Harold, *The German Slump*, 56

Janowsky, Oskar, *People at Bay*, 306

Janssen, Gregor, *Das Ministerium Speer*, 56

Jarausch, Konrad, "Removing the Nazi Stain?," 47, 67, 70

Jarvik, Laurence, *Who Shall Live and Who Shall Die?* 475

Jaszi, Oscar, *Dissolution of the Habsburg Monarchy*, 362

Jefroykin, Jules, "L'organisation juive de Combat," 362

Jelinek, Yeshayahu: "Holocaust of Croatian Jewry," 314; *Parish Republic*, 259

*Jewish Resistance During the Holocaust*, 184, 189

Joffo, Joseph, *A Bag of Marbles*, 525

Johnpoll, Gerhard, *Politics of Futility*, 211

Jones, Sydney, *Hitler in Vienna*, 48

Jukes, Geoffrey, *Hitler's Stalingrad Decisions*, 64

Kabelli, Isaac, "Resistance of the Greek Jews," 310

Kadar, Gyorgy, *Gyorgy Kadar: Survivor of Death, Witness to Life*, 589

Kahane, David, *Lvov Ghetto Diary*, 141, 150

Kaier, Eugen; Deissler, Herbert; and Krieger, Herbert: *Grundzüge der Geschichte*, 482–84; *Von 1890 bis zur Gegenwart*, 490–93

Kairo, Paul Schmitz, *Die arabische Revolution*, 462

Kamenetsky, Christa, *Children's Literature in Hitler's Germany*, 30

Kaminska, Ida, *The Shop on Main Street*, 612

Kampf, Avram, *Jewish Experience in the Art of the Twentieth Century*, 587

Kanfer, Stefan, *The Eighth Sin*, 542

Kann, Robert: *The Habsburg Empire*, 268; *A History of the Habsburg Empire*, 268; *The Multinational Empire*, 268

Kantor, Alfred, *The Book of Alfred Kantor*, 589

Kaplan, Chaim, *Warsaw Diary*, 212, 534

Kaplan, Jacob, "French Jewry Under the Occupation," 361

Karas, Joiza, *Music in Terezin*, 601

Karp, Reba, *Holocaust Stories*, 525

Kaspi, Andre, "Les juifs dans la resistance," 362

Kater, Michael: *Doctors Under Hitler*, 99; *The Nazi Party*, 22, 49, 60

Katz, Alfred, *Poland's Ghettos at War*, 212

Katzburg, Nathaniel, *Hungary and the Jews*, 241, 243, 244, 313

Katzenelson, Yitzak, *The Song of the Murdered Jewish People*, 212, 552, 569

Kaufman, William, *Contemporary Jewish Philosophies*, 117

Kedward, Harry, *Resistance in Vichy France*, 360

Keegan, John, *Waffen SS*, 289

Kele, Max, *Nazis and Workers*, 23, 54

Kempowski, Walter, *Haben Sie davon gewüst?*, 496

Keneally, Thomas, *Schindler's List*, 151

Kennan, George, *From Prague after Munich*, 252, 270

Kershaw, Ian: *The Hitler Myth*, 23, 44; *Popular Opinion and Political Dissent in the Third Reich*, 30

Kessel, Sim, *Hanged at Auschwitz*, 525

Kieval, Hillel: "Legality and Resistance in Vichy France," 359, 589; *The Making of Czech Jewry*, 259

Kimmich, Chrisop, *German Foreign Policy, 1918–1945*, 60

Kirby, William, *Germany and Republican China*, 63

Kirschbaum, J. M., *Slovakia*, 273

Kitroeff, Alexandros: "Documents," 310; "Greek Wartime Attitudes Towards the Jews of Athens," 310

Klarsfeld, Serge: *Le memorial de la dé déportation des juifs de France*, 356; *Recueil de documents des dossiers des autorités allemandes concernant la persécution des juifs en France*, 356; *Vichy-Auschwitz*, 357

Klee, Ernst; Dresen, Willi; and Riess, Volker, "The Good Old Days," 171

Kleffens, Eeko van, *Juggernaut over Holland*, 374

Klein, Burton, *German Economic Preparations for the War*, 56

Klein, Dennis, *Dimensions*, 141

Klein, Gerda, *Promise of a New Spring*, 576

Kleist, Peter, *Zwischen Hitler und Stalin, 1939–1945*, 63

Klingemann, Ute, "Rescuers of Jews in Berlin," 167

Klukowski, Zygmunt, *Dziennik z lat okupagii Zamojszcyzny*, 204

Knieza, Emil, "The Resistance of Slovak Jewry," 258

Knout, David, "Contribution a'l'histoire de la resistance juive en France," 362

Knox, MacGregor, *Mussolini Unleashed, 1939–1941*, 62

Koch, H. W., *The Hitler Youth*, 29

Koelzsch, Hans, *Brundibar* 585

Koen, Albert, *Saving of the Jews in Bulgaria*, 308

Kogon, Eugen: "Befreit durch Niederiage," 517; *Der SS-Staat*, 499; *Theory and Practice of Hell*, 94, 173

Kohen, Ilse, *Mischling, Second Degree*, 525

Kolinsky and Kolinsky, "The Treatment of the Holocaust," 517

Kolmar, Gertrud: *Dark Soliloquy*, 552, 569; "The Jewish Woman," 552; "We Jews," 552

Koonz, Claudia, *Mothers in the Fatherland*, 29

Korbel, Josef, *Twentieth Century Czechs*, 268

Korbonski, Stefan, *Wimieniu Rzeczypospolitej*, 205

Korczak, Janusz, *Ghetto Diary*, xxi, 184, 212, 523, 529, 589, 620, 624

Kosakvis'kyy, Mykyta, "Z Nedan 'oho Minuloho," 297

Kosinski, Jerzy, *The Painted Bird*, 540, 541

Kovner, Abba: *A Canopy in the Desert*, 556, 569; *My Little Sister*, 555, 556

Kowalski, Isaac, *Anthology on Armed Resistance, 1939–1945*, 527, 530

Kral, Vačlav (ed.) *Die Deutschen in der Tschechoslowakei*, 269; *Lesson from History*, 270

Krannhal, Hans von, *Der Warschauer Aufstand*, 297

Kranzler, David, *Japanese, Nazis, Jews*, 73

Krausnick, Helmut: *Anatomy of the SS State*, 30, 89, 90, 289; *Die Truppe des Weltanschauungskrieges*, 98

Krug, Ralph, *Politik in unseren Tagen*, 1498

Kubijovyc, Volodymyr, "Ukraine During World War II," 290, 292

Kubizek, August, *The Young Hitler I Knew*, 23

Kuhnl, Reinhard, *Der deutsche Faschismus*, 27

Kulisova, T., and Tyl, O., *Terezín*, 262

Kulka, Erich: "Annihilation of Czechoslovak Jewry," 260; *The Death Factory*, 259; *Jews in Svoboda's Army*, 259

Kuper, Jack, *A Day in the Warsaw Ghetto*, 617

Kuper, Leo, *Genocide*, 172

Kupfermann, Fred, *Pierre Laval*, 373
Kuznetsov, Anatoly, *Babi Yar*, 620

Lachner, Hannezore, *Geschichte fur Realschulen*, 495
Lackó, Milkós, *Arrow Cross Men*, 243
Lalom, Jean, *La France antisémite de Darquier de Pellepoix*, 358
Landau, Ludwik, *Kronika*, 204
Landsberger, Franz, *Rembrandt, The Jews and the Bible*, 365
Lang, Jochen von, and Sibyl, Claus, *The Secretary: Martin Bormann*, 26
Langer, Walter, *Mind of Adolf Hitler*, 24, 44
Langlois, Claude, "Le régime de Vichy et le clergé," 358
Lanzmann, Claude, "Shoah," 618
Laqueur, Walter, *Terrible Secret*, xxi, 476, 499
Laroche, Gaston, *On les nommait des étrangers*, 362
Laska, Vera (ed.), *Women in the Resistance and the Holocaust*, 181
Latour, Anny, *Jewish Resistance in France*, 362, 525
Laval, Pierre, *Diary of Pierre Laval*, 357
Lavi, Theodore: "Background to Rescue of Romanian Jewry," 312; "Documents on Struggle of Rumanian Jewry," 312; "Vatican's Endeavors," 312
Leboucher, Fernand, *The Incredible Mission of Father Benoit*, 359
Lederer, Zedenek, *Ghetto Theresienstadt*, 260, 265–67, 601
Leftwich, Joseph (ed.), *The Golden Peacock*, 211
Leiser, Erwin: "Mein Kampf," 618; *Nazi Cinema*, 621
Leitner, Isabella, *Fragments of Isabella*, 525
Lester, Elenore, *Wallenberg*, 143
Lestchinsky, Jacob, "Balance Sheet of Extermination," 251
Lévai, Jenö: *Fehér Könyv*, 241; *Fekete Könyv*, 241; *Szürke Könyv*, 241; *Szidósors Európaban*, 247

Levi, Carlo, *Christ Stopped at Eboli*, 388
Levi, Primo: "Buna," 557; *Collected Poems*, 557; "Reveille," 558; "Shema," 557; *Shema*, 557; *Survival in Auschwitz*, 171, 525
Levin, Ira, *The Boys from Brazil*, 608
Levin, Nora: *The Holocaust*, xvi, xx–xxi, xxv, 4–9, 13–14, 98, 182, 258, 314, 367, 623, 630
Levy, Claude: *Betrayal at the Vel d'Hiv*, 356; *Les parias de la résistance*, 360, 362
Lewin, Ronald, *Hitler's Mistakes*, 43
Lieberman, Edith and Harold, *Throne of Straw*, 545
Lifton, Robert Jay, *Nazi Doctors*, 98, 173
Lind, Kakov, *Landscape in Concrete*, 533, 541
Linn, Merritt, *A Book of Songs*, 537
Lipscher, Ladislav: *Die Juden im Slowakischen Staat*, 261; "Jews of Slovakia," 260–61
Lipstadt, Deborah, xx; *Beyond Belief*, 476
Litani, Dora, "Courier," 312
Littell, Franklin, *Crucifixion of the Jews*, 124–25, 129
Lloyd, Alan, *Franco*, 425
"Lodz Ghetto," 618
London, Perry, "The Rescuers," 164
Lore, Shelly, *Jewish Holocaust Survivors' Attitudes*, 525
Lorenz, Konrad, *On Aggression*, 172
Lottman, Herbert, *Petain, Hero or Traitor*, 357
Lowenthal, Zedenko (ed.), *Crimes of Fascist Occupants and Their Collaborators against Jews in Yugoslavia*, 314
Lowrie, Donald, *The Hunted Children*, 356
Lucas, Friedrich; Bodensieck, Heinrich; Rumpt, Ernhard; and Thiele, Günter, *Menschen in Ihrer Zeit*, 495
Luczak, Czeslaw, *Polityka ludnosciowa*, 206
Ludwig, Karl, *Die Flüchtlingspolitik der Schweiz*, 433

Lumet, Sidney, *The Pawnbroker*, 610

Lustig, Arnost: "Darkness Casts No Shadows," 537; *Diamonds of the Night*, 537; *Dita Saxova*, 537; "The Lemon," 537; *Night and Hope*, 270, 537; "The Old Ones and Death," 537; *A Prayer for Katrina Horovitzova*, 533, 536; "The Return," 537; "Rose Street," 537; "Stephen and Anne," 537; *The Unloved*, 537

Maas, Walter, *Netherlands at War*, 369

Macartney, C. A., *October Fifteenth*, 242

MacDonald, Callum, *Killing of SS Obergruppenführer Heydrich*, 25, 274

McKale, Donald, *Hitler*, 45, 71

MacPherson, Henry, *The Blood of His Servants*, 367

Maga, Timothy, "Closing the Door," 358

Maier, Charles, "The Unmasterable Past," 48, 69

Malle, Louis, *Au Revoir les Enfants*, 611

Mamatey, Victor, and Luža, Radomír (eds.), *History of Czechoslovak Republic*, 268

Mann, Abby: "Judgment at Nuremberg," 608; "War and Love," 607

Manvell, Roger, and Fraenkel, Heinrich, *Himmler*, 25

Marcq, Rene, "Collaboration under Enemy Occupation," 368

Mardini, Zuhyar, *Alf Yawm ma' al-Hajj Amin*, 462

Marlowe, John, *Seat of Pilate*, 460

Marrus, Michael: *The Holocaust in History*, 67, 88, 98, 103n, 316, 477; "Jewish Leaders and Holocaust," 361; "Nazis and Jews in Occupied Western Europe," 355; *Politics of Assimilation*, 360; *Vichy France and the Jews*, 323, 333–40; 349, 355–58

Maršálek, Hans, *Geschichte des Konzentrationslagers Mauthausen*, 93

Martel, Gordon (ed.), *Origins of Second World War Reconsidered*, 61

Marton, Kati, *Wallenberg*, 143

Maser, Werner: *Adolf Hitler: Das ende der Führer Legende*, 23; *Adolf Hitler: Legend, Myth and Reality*, 23, 45

Mason, Henry, *Purge of Dutch Quislings*, 368

Mason, Herbert, *To Kill the Devil*, 71

Mason, Timothy: "Arbeiterklasse und Volksgemeinschaft," 55; "Labour in the Third Reich," 55

*Massacre of European Jewry*, 189

Mastny, Vojtech, *Czechs under Nazi Rule*, 270, 274

Matheson, Peter, *The Third Reich and Christian Churches*, 129

Matkovsky, Aleksandar, "Destruction of Macedonian Jewry," 308

Mattar, Philip: *Mufti of Jerusalem*, 462; "Mufti of Jerusalem and Politics of Palestine," 462; "Role of Mufti of Jerusalem," 464

Mavrogordatos, George, *Stillborn Republic*, 305

Mayer, Arno, *Why Did The Heavens Not Darken?*, xxiii, 69

Mazursky, Paul, "Enemies: A Love Story," 608

Mechanicus, Philip, *Year of Fear*, 369

Meed, Vladka, *On Both Sides of the Wall*, 185–86, 524

Mehlman, Jeffrey, *Legacies of Anti-Semitism in France*, 358

Melka, Robert, "The Axis and Arab Middle East," 462

Meltzer, Milton, *Never to Forget*, 525, 576

Menasche, Albert, *Birkenau*, 311

Mendelsohn, Ezra, *Jews of East Central Europe between World Wars*, 306

Mendelsoh, John, *The Holocaust*, 624

Menzel, Jiri, "Closely Watched Trains," 611

Mermelstein, Mel, *By Bread Alone*, 525

Meyers, Peter, and Riesenerger, Dieter, *Der Nationalsozialismus*, 512n

Mezan, Saul, *Les Juifs espagnols en Bulgarie*, 305

Michaelis, Meir, *Mussolini and the Jews*, 356, 384, 401–2

Michalczyk, John, *The Cross and the Star*, 617

Michel, Henri: *Histoire de la resistance*, 269, 360; "Jewish Resistance and the European Resistance Movement," 362

Michelson, Frida, *I Survived Rumboli*, 525

Michman, Joseph: "The Controversial Stand of the Joodse Raad of Amsterdam," 368; "The Controversy Surrounding the Jewish Council of Amsterdam," 368

Mickel, Wolfgang, *Geschichte, Politik, und Gesselschaft*, 483, 491, 501–2, 505

Mikus, Joseph, *Slovakia*, 270

Milgram, Stanley, *Obedience to Authority*, xxi, 6, 18n, 173

Miller, Marshall, *Bulgaria during Second World War*, 151, 308

Milosz, Czeslaw: "Child of Europe," 566; *Nobel Lecture*, 563, 566, 568; *The Witness of Poetry*, 565

Milton, Sybil: *Archives of Holocaust*, 624; *Art of Holocaust*, 588; *Art of Jewish Children*, 588; "Women and the Holocaust," 99

Milward, Alan, *The German Economy at War*, 56

Minco, Marga, *Bitter Herbs*, 367, 525

Mintz, Alan, *Hurban*, 548

Mitchell, Otis, *Nazism and the Common Man*, 28

Mitscherlich, Alexander and Margarete, *The Inability to Mourn*, 506, 517–18

Moisses, Asher, "Jews in the Army of Greece," 310

Molho, Michael: *In Memoriam: Destruction of Greek Jewry*, 309–10; "Usos y custombres de los Sefardies de Salonika," 305; "Venizelos and the Jewish Community of Salonika," 305

Molnár, Erik; Bibó, Istvan; Szráz, György; and Hanák, Péter, *Zsidokérdés asszimiláció, antiszemitizmus*, 243

Monnerary, Henri (ed.), *La Persecution des juifs en France et dans les autres pays*, 356

Morgan, Ted, *An Uncertain Hour*, 363

Morley, John, *Vatican Diplomacy and Jews during Holocaust*, 130–31, 359

Morse, Arthur, *While Six Million Died*, xxi, 419, 472

Moskowitz, Sarah, *Love Despite Hate*, 525

Mosse, George: *Germans and Jews*, 67; *Nazi Culture*, 28; *Toward the Final Solution*, 31, 623

Mouchon, Violette, et al, *Quelques actions de Protestants de France*, 359

Muffs, Judith, *Holocaust in Books and Film*, 621

Muggenthaler, Hans, and Marks, Wolfgang and Hannah; *Geschichte fur Realschulen*, 482, 494

Muller, Filip, *Eyewitness Auschwitz*, 525

Müller, Klaus-Jurgen, *Army, Politics and Society in Germany*, 65

Müller-Hill, Benno, *Murderous Science*, 99

Nawyn, William, *American Protestantism's Responses to Germany's Jews and Refugees*, 131

Nehama, Joseph, *Histoire des Israelites de Salonique*, 305

Nejedly, Zdenek, *T. G. Masaryk*, 271

Neshamit, Sara, *The Children of Mapu Street*, 580

Neumann, Franz, *Behemoth*, 59, 60

Neumann, Jirmejahu, *Im Schatten des Todes*, 262

Neustadt, Melech, *Hurbn on oyfshtand fun di Yidn in Varshe*, 524

Nirenstein, Albert, *A Tower from the Enemy*, 212

Noakes, Jeremy, and Pridham, Geoffrey, *Naziism*, 100n

Noble, Iris, *Nazi Hunter: Simon Wiesenthal*, 577

Nolte, Ernst, xiv, xxiii, 47, 48, 67, 70

Novick, Peter, *Resistance versus Vichy*, 360

Novitch, Miriam, xx

Nyiszli, Miklos, *Auschwitz*, 173

Oberski, Jona, *Childhood*, 367, 525

Oestreich, Paul, *Walter Funk*, 55

Offner, Arnold, *American Appeasement*, 64

Oliner, Samuel and Pearl, *The Altruistic Personality*, 140, 142, 152, 163, 164–68

O'Neill, Robert, *The German Army and the Nazi Party*, 65

Ophuls, Marcel: *Hotel Terminus*, 617; *The Sorrow and the Pity*, 619

Oren, Nissan, "The Bulgarian Exception," 308

Oren, Uri, "A Town Called Monastir," 308, 314

"Origins of the 'J' Passport: A Controversy in Switzerland," 433

Orlev, Uri, *The Island on Bird Street*, 580

Orlow, Dieter, *History of the Nazi Party*, 22, 49

Osgood, Samuel, "The A-S of the French Collaborationist Press," 359

Overy, R. D., *Goering, the "Iron Man"*, 25, 54

Padfield, Peter, *Himmler*, 25

Pagis, Dan: "Autobiography," 559; "Draft of a Reparations Agreement," 550; *Points of Departure*, 548, 559, 568–69; "Testimony," 559; "Written in Paenil in Sealed Railway-Car," 548

Paldiel, Morechai, *Altruism of Righteous Gentile*, 169–70

Pankiewicz, Tadeusz, *Cracow Ghetto Pharmacy*, 525

Paris, Edmond, *Genocide in Satellite Croatia*, 314

Parkes, James, *Conflict of Church and Synagogue*, 124

Paucker, Arnold; Gilchrist, Sylvia; and Suchy, Barbara, *Die Juden in Nazionalsozialistischen Deutschland*, 31

Paxton, Robert: *Parades and Politics at Vichy*, 358; *Vichy France*, 357

Payne, Robert, *Life and Death of Adolf Hitler*, 24, 43

Pearlman, Maurice, *Mufti of Jerusalem*, 462

Pearson, Frederic, *The Weak State in International Crisis*, 374

Pechova, Oliva; Krizkova, Marie Rut; Sormova, Eva; and Kuna, Milan, *Arts in Trezin*, 266

Peck, Abraham, *Jews and Christians after the Holocaust*, 117

Pelzer, Karlheinz, *Geschichte für die Haputschule*, 481, 485

Pemsel, Richard, *Hitler*, 23

Penkower, Monty N., *The Jews Were Expendable*, 477

Peretz, I. L., xx, xxvii

Perl, William, *Four-Four War*, 525

Perman, Dagmar, *Shaping of the Czechoslovak State*, 268

Peters, Joan, *From Time Immemorial*, 463, 466

Peterson, Edward, *Limits of Hitler's Power*, 27

Peuckert, Detlev and Jürgen, *Alltag im Nationalsozialismus*, 28

Picciotti Fargion, Liliana, "La deportazione degli ebrei," 402

Pierrard, Isaac, *Juifs et catholiques francais*, 358

Pilinszky, Janos: "Apocrypha," 567; *Crater*, 566; "Fish in the Net," 566; "The French Prisoner," 566; "Introitus," 567; *Scaffold in Winter*, 556; *Selected Poems*, 550, 563, 566, 568

Pinkus, Oscar, *House of Ashes*, 524

Playfair, Ian, *Mediterranean and Middle East*, 459

Poliakov, Leon: *Harvest of Hate*, 3, 6–12, 16, 182, 257, 351, 365; *History of Anti-Semitism*, 623; "Jewish Resistance in France," 359; *Jews under the Italian Occupation*, 310, 314, 356; *L'étoile jaune*, 355; "An Opinion Poll on Anti-Jewish Measures in Vichy France," 359

Porter, D. Haldane, "Refugee Screening," 280, 287, 291

Porter, Katherine, *Ship of Fools*, 606

Possony, Stefan, "The Ukrainian-Jewish Problem," 294

Posthumus, N. W. (ed.), *Netherlands during German Occupation*, 368

Prange, Gordon, *Hitler's Words*, 40

Presser, Jacob, *Destruction of the Dutch Jews*, 258, 369–74

Pridham, Geoffrey, *Hitler's Rise to Power*, 22–23

Proctor, Robert, *Racial Hygiene*, 99

Pryce-Jones, David, *Paris in the Third Reich*, 355

Pulzer, Peter, *Rise of Anti-Semitism in Germany and Austria*, 67, 623

Rabinowitz, Dorothy, *New Lives*, 171, 526

Rabinsky, Leatrice, and Danks, Carol, *The Holocaust*, 578, 630

Radbruch, Eberhard, *Wandel der Welt*, 498

Radkau, Joachim, *Politische Weltkunde*, 488, 503

Radnóti, Miklós: "Clouded Sky," 551; *Clouded Sky*, 569; "Only Skin and Bones and Pain," 551–52; "Seventh Ecologue," 551

Rajsfus, Maurice: *Des Juifs dans la Collaboration*, 348, 361; *Sois juif et tais toi*, 351

Ramati, Alexander, *And the Violins Stopped Playing*, 198, 579

Ránki, Gyorgi, et al: *A Wilhelmstrasse és Magyaroszág*, 229, 242; *1944 Március 19*, 245

Rausch, David, *Legacy of Hatred*, 124–25, 130, 137

Rauschning, Hermann, *Voice of Destruction*, 24

Ravine, Jacques, *La resistance organisée des juifs en France*, 362

Rawicz, Piotr, *Blood from the Sky*, 541

Read, Anthony, and Fisher, David, *The Deadly Embrace*, 63

Reith, Adolf, *Monuments to Victims of Tyranny*, 589

Reitlinger, Gerald: *The Final Solution*, xxii, 4, 6–12, 16, 67, 69,182, 251, 257, 296, 314–15, 367, 369, 623; *House Built on Sand*, 63; *The SS, Alibi of a Nation*, 30, 67, 289

Remarque, Erich Maria: *All Quiet on the Western Front*, 605; *Arch of Triumph*, 605

Rempel, Gerhard, *Hitler's Children*, 29

Resnais, Alain, *Night and Fog*, 618

Reviczky, Adam, *Vesztes háborúk-megnyeert osaták*, 244

Reznikoff, Charles, *Holocaust*, 543

Rich, Norman, *Hitler's War Aims*, 28, 66

Riefenstahl, Leni: *Olympia*, 618; *Triumph of the Will*, 619

Ringelblum, Emmanuel: *Notes from Warsaw Ghetto*, 182–83, 210, 212, 523–24, 528, 534; *Polish-Jewish Relations*, 212

Rings, Werner, *Schweiz im Krieg*, 433

Ripper, Werner, *Weltgeschichte im Aufriss*, 491, 507

Riquet, Michel, *Tragedie de la deportation*, 368

Riste, Olav, and Nokleby, Berit, *Norway*, 151

Ritter, Carol, and Myers, S. (eds.), *Courage to Care*, 359

Robertson, Esmonde, *Hitler's Pre-War Policy*, 60

Robinson, Jacob: *Guide to Jewish History*, xix–xx; *Holocaust and After*, xx

Roblin, Michel, *Les juifs de Paris*, 360

Rodnick, David, *Postwar Germans*, 153

Rogasky, Barbara, *Smoke and Ashes*, 577

Roland, Charlotte, *Du ghetto à l'occident*, 360

Romano, Jasa, *Jews of Yugoslavia*, 314

Rose, Leesha, *Tulips are Red*, 367

Rose, Reginald, "Escape from Sobibor," 613

Rosenbaum, Irving, *The Holocaust and Halakhah*, 190

Rosenberg, Alan, and Myers, Gerald, *Echoes from the Holocaust*, 172

Rosenfeld, Alvin, *A Double Dying*, 560, 564, 570

Rosenfeld, Harvey, *Raoul Wallenberg*, 143

Rosenhaft, Eve, *Beating the Fascists*, 69

Rosenzweig, Franz, *Star of Redemption*, 107–8, 111

Roskies, David, *Against the Apocalypse*, 587

Ross, Robert, *So It Was True*, 476

Rossel, Seymour, *The Holocaust*, 578

Roth, Cecil: *History of Jews in Italy*, 381; *History of Marranos*, 365; *Jewish Art*, 587

Roth, John, *A Consuming Fire*, 135

Rothchild, Sylvia, *Voices from the Holocaust*, 526, 527, 529

Rothkirchen, Livia: "Jews in Bohemia and Moravia," 254, 260; *Khurban Yahudat Slovakia*, 259, 266

Rozewicz, Tadeusz, *Survivor and Other Poems*, 547, 559, 568, 569

Rubenstein, Richard: *After Auschwitz*, 108–10; *Age of Triage*, 172; *Approaches to Auschwitz*, 111–12; *Cunning of History*, 108–11

Rudnitsky, Ivan, *Essays in Modern Ukrainian History*, 297

Rudolf, Hans Ulrich, and Walter, Edgar, *Geschichte und Gegewart*, 490, 495

Rutkowski, Adam: "Directives allemandes," 356; *La lutte des juifs en France*, 361; "Le camp d'internment de Gurs," 356; "Le déportations des Juifs de France vers Auschwitz et Sobibor," 356

Ryan, Michael (ed.), *Human Responses to the Holocaust*, 98Rzeszow Jews Memorbuch, 212


Sabille, Jacques: "Attitude of Italians to Jews in Occupied Greece," 310, 314; *Les juifs de Tunisie*, 363

Sachar, Howard: *Course of Modern Jewish History*, 623; *Europe Leaves the Middle East*, 459

Sachs, Nelly: "Already Embraced by the Arm of Heavenly Solace," 560; "And Unwrap, As Though It Were Linen Sheets," 560; "A Dead Child Speaks," 560; "Glowing Enigmas II," 560; *O the Chimneys!*, 560; *Seeker and Other Poems*, 560; *Selected Poems of Abba Kovner and Nelly Sachs*, 533, 542, 548, 560; "Then Wrote the Scribe of Zohar," 560

Sahl, Hans, *The Few and the Many*, 356

Salmon-Levene, Irit, *Testimony Art of Holocaust*, 588

Salomon, Charlotte, *Charlotte*, 579

Salus, Grete, *Niemand nichts ein Jude*, 368

Samuel, Maurice, *The Great Hatred*, 623

Saunders, Ronald, *Shores of Refuge*, 293

Sauvage, Pierre, "A Most Persistent Haven," 359

Schatzker, Chaim, *Juden in dem Deutschen Geschichtsbuchen*, 512

Schechtman, Joseph: *Mufti and the Führer*, 462, 464; "The Transdnistria Reservation," 313

Scheffler, Wolfgang, *Anmerkungen zum Fernsehfilm*, 496

Schick, Heinz, *The Wannsee Conference*, 613

Schmid, Heinz, *Fragen an die Geschichte*, 494

Schoenbaum, David, *Hitler's Social Revolution*, 28, 59–60

Schoenberg, Arnold, "A Survivor from Warsaw," 600

Schoenberner, Gerhard, *The Yellow Star*, xxi

Schoenbrun, David, *Soldiers of the Night*, 360

Schoenfeld, Joachim, *Holocaust Memoirs*, 296

Scholder, Klaus: *The Churches and Third Reich*, 127, 128, 135n; *A Requiem for Hitler*, 128

Schur, Maxine, *Hannah Szenes*, 577

Sciaky, Leon, *Farewell to Salonica*, 305

Schnabel, Ernest, *Footsteps of Anne Frank*, 367

Schneider, Gertrude, *Journey into Terror*, 525

Schreiber, Gerhard, *Hitler Interpretationen*, 46

Schröder, Bernd, *Deutschland und der mittlere Osten*, 461

Schröder, Josef, "Die Beziehung der Achsenmachte zur Arabischen Welt," 461

Schulweis, Rabbi Harold, "The Bias Against Man," 161–62, 167, 170

Schuvrsma, R., "Dutch Fascists' Share in Crime," 368

Schwandner, Joseph, Geschichte 9. Jahrgangsstufe, 490, 494–95, 512

Schwarz-Bart, Andre, Last of the Just, xxi, xxviii, 533, 535, 545, 620

Schwarzwaller, Wulf, The Unknown Hitler, 46

Schweifert, Peter, The Bird Has No Wings, 525

Schweitzer, Arthur, Big Business in the Third Reich, 59

Scloot, Robert, Theatre of the Holocaust, 545

Scott, William, Alliance Against Hitler, 63

Seaton, Albert, The German Army, 1933–1945, 65

Seidler, F. W., Fritz Todt, 56

Segal, Simon, New Order in Poland, 212

Segev, Tom, Soldiers of Evil, 99

Senesh, Hannah: "Blessed Is the Match," 551, 569, 576, 607; Her Life and Diary, 183, 523

Sereny, Gitta, Into That Darkness, 100

Serwanski, Edward, and Trawinska, Irena, Zbrodnia niemiecka, 397

Seton-Watson, R. W.: From Munich to Danzig, 269; History of the Czechs and Slovaks, 268; Masaryk in England, 271; Munich and the Dictators, 269

The Seventh Cross, 607

Sevillias, Errikos, Athens, Auschwitz, 311

Seward, Desmond, Napoleon and Hitler, 45

Shandruk, Pavel, Arms of Valor, 290

Shaw, Irwin, Young Lions, 607

Shelley, Lore, Secretaries of Death, 95–96

Shirer, William, The Rise and Fall of the Third Reich, 21–22, 575–77

Shostakovich, Dmitri, "Babi Yar Symphony," 600

Siefert, Hermann, Der Aufbruch in der Arabischen Welt, 462

Siegel, Aranka, Upon the Head of the Goat, 578

Skilling, H. Gordon, Czechoslovakia, 278

"Skokie," 616

Slaski, Jerzy, Fighting Poland, 209

Slawson, John, Authoritarian Personality, 162–63

Smelser, Ronald: Robert Ley, 55; The Sudeten Problem, 269

Smith, Danny, Wallenberg, 143

Smith, Denis, Mussolini, 62

Smith, Bradley: Heinrich Himmler, 25; Reaching Judgment at Nuremberg, 288–89

Snodgrass, W. D., Führer Bunker, 543

Snyder, Louis: Encyclopedia of Third Reich, xxvii; The Third Reich, 47

Somerhausen, Anne, Written in Darkness, 151

Sommer, Theo, Deutschland und Japan zwischen den Machten, 62

Songs of the Concentration Camp, 601

Songs of the Ghetto, 601

Songs of the Martyrs, 601

Sorge, Martin, The Other Price of Hitler's War, 67

Soucy, Robert, Fascism in France, 357

Speer, Albert: Inside the Third Reich, 25, 56; Spandau, 25, 56

Speier, Hans, German White-Collar Workers and Rise of Hitler, 59

Stachura, Peter: Gregor Strasser and Rise of Nazism, 52; The Nazi Machtgreifung, 27, 49; Shaping of Nazi State, 52

Stadtler, Bea, The Holocaust, 575

Starke, Kathe, Der Führer schenkt den Juden eine Stadt, 261

Steckel, Charles, "Survivors and Partisans," 314

Steed, Henry W.: Hapsburg Monarchy, 268; T. G. Masaryk, 271

Stein, George: Hitler, 42; Waffen SS, 31, 98, 289

Steinberg, Jonathan, All or Nothing, 399

Steinberg, Lucien: Les autorités alle-

*mandes en France occupeé*, 356; *Not As a Lamb*, 189; "Statistique de la déportation des juifs de France," 356

Steiner, Eugen, *The Slovak Dilemma*, 270

Steiner, George, *Portage to San Cristobal of A. H.*, xxv

Steinert, Marlis, *Hitler's Wars and the Germans*, 30

Steinetz, Lucy, and Szonyi, David, *Living after the Holocaust*, 171, 526

Steinhorn, Harriet: *At My Bar Mitzva and His*, 578; *Shadows of the Holocaust*, 578

Stengel, Theophil (ed.), *Lexikon den Juden in der Musik*, 592

Stern, Ellen, *Elie Wiesel*, 577

Stern, J. P., "Artist Hitler," 496, 500–2

Sternhell, Ze'ev, *Ni droite, ni gauche*, 357

Stevens, George, *Diary of Anne Frank, The*, 606; *Filmmaker's Journey*, 617

Stoakes, Geoffrey, *Hitler and the Quest for World Dominion*, 49, 60

Stopniak, Franciszek, "Catholic Clergy and Jews in Poland," 210

Stroop, Gen. Jurgen, *Es Gibt keinen Jüdischen Wohnbezirk in Warschau Mehr*, 181, 297, 524

Stroppe, Werner, *Harms Arbeitsmappen Geschichte*, 493

Styrkul, Valery, *We Accuse*, 282–83, 292

Styron, William, *Sophie's Choice*, 533, 610

Subtelny, Orst, *Urkaine*, 293, 296

Suhl, Yuri, *They Fought Back*, 187, 258, 308, 525, 580

Sutzkever, Abraham: *Burnt Pearls*, 561, 568; "Leaden Plates," 562; "Lying in This Coffin," 561, 598–99; "Self-Portrait," 548, 568

Sweets, John: *Choices in Vichy France*, 340, 357–58; *Politics of Resistance in France*, 360

Sydnor, Charles, 68; *Soldiers of Destruction*, 98, 289

Syrkin, Marie, xx; *Blessed Is the Match*, 523, 525

Szabó, Dezsö, *Az elsodort falu* (Village Swept Away), 243

Szajkowski, Zosa, 22; *Analytical Franco-Jewish Gazeteer*, 355, 361; *The Jews and the French Foreign Legion*, 363; *Jews and the French Revolutions*, 360

Szczypiorski, Andrzej, "Z notatek," 206

Szenes, Sandor, *Befejeztlen mult*, 246

Szonyi, David, *Holocaust: Annotated Bibliography*, xxi, xxvii

Tabori, George, *The Cannibals*, 545

Tal, Uriel, *Christians and Jews in Germany*, 125

Tatelbaum, Itzak, *Through Our Eyes*, 579

Taylor, A.J.P.: *The Hapsburg Monarchy*, 268; *1939 Revisited*, 61; *The Origins of the Second World War*, 60, 61; *The Second World War*, 61

Taylor, Telford, *Sword and Swastika*, 65

Tcherikover, Elia, xix–xx, 623

Tec, Nechama, *When Light Pierced the Darkness*, 161, 164, 165, 166

Teichert, Eckart, *Autarkie und Grossraumwirtschaft in Deutschland*, 53

Ten Boom, Corrie: *Hiding Place*, 132, 365; *A Prisoner and Yet*, 365; *Prison Letters*, 365

Tenbrock, R. H., *Zeiten und Menschen*, 491, 495, 498

*Terezin Diary*, 619

Tessin, Georg, *Verbande und Truppen der deutschen Wehrmacht und Waffen SS*, 290

Tetel, Marcel, "Whither the Holocaust," 363

Thies, Jochen, *Architekt der Weltherrschaft*, 49

Thomas, Gordon, and Witt, Max, *Voyage of the Damned*, 606

Tillion, Germaine, *Ravensbrück*, 100, 525

Tillmann, Heinz, *Deutschlands Araberpolitik im Zweiten Weltkrieg*, 462

Tobersky, Edward, *President Eduard Benes*, 272

Toland, John, *Adolf Hitler*, 23, 42, 47–48, 66, 67

Toll, Nelly, *Without Surrender*, 589

Topas, George, *Iron Furnace*, 525

Toscano, Mario, *Origins of the Pact of Steel*, 62

Touw, H. C., *Het Verzet der Hervormde Kerk*, 360

Trachtenberg, Joshua, *The Devil and the Jews*, 623

Trepman, Paul, *Among men and Beasts*, 525

Trevor-Roper, H. R.: *Hitler's War Directives*, 40; *The Last Days of Hitler*, 42, 71

*Trial of the Major War Criminals Before the International Military Tribunal at Nuremberg*, 288, 624

*Triumph of the Spirit*, 607

Trunk, Isaiah: *Jewish Responses to Nazi Persecution*, 171, 526; *Judenrat*, 212

Turner, Henry Ashby, *German Big Business and the Rise of Hitler*, 52, 56, 57, 58, 59


Ullman, Viktor, *Der Kaiser von Atlantis*, 595

Umbrelt, Hans, *Der Millitärbefehlshaber im Frankreich*, 356

Uris, Leon: *Mila 18*, 212, 533, 620; *Exodus*, 608


Vago, Bela, (ed.): "Ambiguity of Collaborationism," 312; "Contrasting Leadership in Wartime Hungary and Romania," 313; "Destruction of Jews in Transylvania," 312; *Jewish Assimilation in Modern Times*, 243; *Jews and Non-Jews in East Europe*, 242, 243; "Political and Diplomatic Activities for Rescue," 312

Van Doren, Theo, *Orange Above London*, 365

Van Paassen, Pierre, *Forgotten Ally*, 460

Vasileva, Nadejda, "On the Catastrophe of the Thracian Jews," 308

Vegh, Claudine, *I Didn't Say Goodbye*, 525

Veillon, Dominique, *La Franc-Tireur*, 360

Veret, Paul, "Art and Music in the Shoah," 601

Verhya, Wasyl, "The 'Galicia' Ukrainian Division in Polish and Soviet Literature," 290–91

Viereck, Peter, *Metapolitics*, 31

Vinecour, Earl, *Polish Jews*, 211

Vinke, Herman, *The Short Life of Sophie Scholl*, 579, 580

Vogt, Hannah: *Burden of Guilt*, 21; *Schuld oder Verhängis?*, 517 n.126; "Zum Problem der Deutschen Jugend," 518

Volavkova, Hana: *I Never Saw Another Butterfly*, 263, 543, 575, 579, 585, 588; "Jewish Museum of Prague," 259

Vrba, Rudolf, *I Cannot Forgive*, 94–95, 525


Waeger, Gerhart, *Die Sundenbocke der Schweiz*, 435

Wagener, Otto, *Hitler*, 24

Wagner, Richard, *Das Judentum in der Musik*, 588

Waite, Robert: *The Psychopathic God: Adolf Hitker*, 24, 44–45, 70, 71; *Vanguard of Nazism*, 69

"Wallenberg," 616

Warmbrunn, Werner, *The Dutch under German Occupation*, 369, 377

Warner, Geoffrey, *Laval and the Eclipse of France*, 357

Warren, W. Preston, *Masaryk's Democracy*, 271

*The Warsaw Ghetto*, 619

Warsaw Ghetto Fighters' Kibbutz, *Spiritual Resistance Art*, 588

Waters, M. P., *Mufti over the Middle East*, 462

Watt, Richard, *The Kings Depart*, 22

Weber, Eugen, *Action Francaise*, 357

Wegner, Bernd, *Hitlers Politische Soldaten*, 78

Weill, Joseph, *Contribution à l'histoire*

*des camps d'internement dans l'anti-France*, 356

Weinberg, David, 344; *A Community on Trial*, 360; "French Jewish Community After World War II," 363

Weinberg, Gerhard: *The Foreign Policy of Hitler's Germany*, 27, 60, 460; *Germany and the Soviet Union*, 63; *Hitler's Secret Book*, 39

Weinreich, Max, xix

Weinryb, Bernard, *The Jews of Poland*, 211

Weinstein, Freda, *A Hidden Childhood*, 578

Weissmandel, Rabbi Michael, *Min Hameitzar*, 258–59

Wellers, George: "Déportation des juifs en France sous l'occupation," 356; *La France et la Question juive*, 357; *L'etoile jaune à l'heure de Vichy*, 356

Wells, Leon, 144–50; *Janowska Road*, 171, 524; *Who Speaks for the Vanquished?*, 158

Weniger, Eric, *Neue Wege*, 505

Werbell, Frederick, and Clarke, Thurston, *Lost Hero*, 143

Werstein, Irving, *That Denmark Might Live*, 575, 580

Whealey, Robert, *Hitler and Spain*, 54, 57, 70

Wheeler, Elizabeth, *Lidice*, 274

Wiener, Jan, *The Assassination of Heydrich*, 274

Wiesel, Elie, xxvi, 17, 246, 522, 630; *Ani Maamin*, 54–55, 56–63; *A Journey of Faith*, 116; *Night*, 108, 115, 171, 533–35, 613, 620; *One Generation After*, 115

Wiesenthal, Simon, 5, 615, 630; *Grossmufti, Grossagent der Achsen*, 465; *Max and Helen*, 538, 615; *Murderers among Us*, 296; *Sunflower*, 121–23, 135n

Wighton, Charles, *Heydrich*, 274

Wigoder, Geoffrey (ed.), *Jewish Art and Civilization*, 587

Wilson, Stephen, *Ideology and Experience*, 336–37, 358

Witt, Max, and Thomas, Gordon, *Voyage of Damned*, xx, 606

Wolf, Jacqueline, "*Take Care of Josette,*": *A Memior in Defense of Occupied France*, 359

*The World at War: Genocide*, 619

Wyman, David, xxi; *Abandonment of the Jews*, 131, 475, 624; *Paper Walls*, 473

Yahil, Leni: *The Holocaust: The Fate of European Jewry, 1932–1945*, xx, 3–16, 98, 435; "The Jewish Leadership of France," 361; *Rescue of Danish Jewry*, 151

Zahavi, Zvi, *From Assimilation to Zionism*, 244

Zar, Rose, *In the Mouth of the Wolf*, 579

Zeitoun, S., *L'OSE*, 362

Zeman, Zbynek: *The Masaryks*, 271; *Nazi Propaganda*, 30

Ziemian, Joseph, *The Cigarette Seller of Three Crosses square*, 524, 580

Ziemke, Earl, *Stalingrad to Berlin*, 63

Ziff, William, *The Rape of Palestine*, 460

Zinneman, Fred, *The Search*, 610

Zitelman, Rainer, *Hitler*, 60

Zuccotti, Susan, *Italians and the Holocaust*, 310, 356, 397

Zygmunt, Neha: *The Friendly Village*, 586; *Vacation in the Mountains with a Big Bathroom*, 586; *Vaccination in School Against Scarlet Fever*, 586

Zyskina, Sara, *Stolen Years*, 524

# Subject Index

Abetz, Otto, 322, 324
*Action francaise*, 325, 336, 343
Albania, 302, 303, 306
Algeria, 351–52
Alibert, Raphael, 335–36
Alsace-Lorraine, 321, 343, 351
Altneuschul, 250
Amann, Max, 46
Amelot, 344, 345, 350
America: attitudes toward Jews, xiv–xv, xxiii, 470–75, 614–16, 630–31; relations with Germany, 53–58, 64–65, 471–77; during Great Depression, 50, 471; Red Cross, 416, 629; soldiers-liberators, 93, 286, 291; television productions, 613–16. *See also* Film; Roosevelt, Franklin D.; U.S. Government
American Friends Service Committee, 341, 408, 416, 418, 624
American Jewish Committee, 626
American Jewish Congress, 626
Amsterdam, 365, 367, 371, 375, 523
Andorra, 415
Anti-Defamation League, 626
Anti-Semitism, 130–32, 198; American, 470–75, 614–16, 630; Arab, 462–69, 630; Austrian, 540; British, 442, 450–51; Dzechoslovak, 252–53; East European, 483; French, 325–40, 535; general history, 123–26; German, 315, 504; Greek, 316; Hungarian, 217–41, 401; Italian, 381–95; Polish, 150, 156–67, 204–11, 213; Romanian, 304–12; Spanish, 409; Swiss, 431, 436–37; Ukrainian, 294. *See also specific nations*

Antonescu, Ion, 311, 446
Apeldoorn, 370
A. Puls Moving Company, 373
Arabs, 446–47, 459–67. *See also* al-Husseini, Haj Amin; North Africa
Armenians, xxv, 195–97, 304, 311, 315
Arrow Cross, 217–18, 225, 235–41, 401
Art of the Holocaust, 262–63, 582–590
Asscher, Abraham, 368, 371–72
Auschwitz, xix, xxiii, 81, 83–89, 97, 101n, 102n, 108–10, 115, 155, 172, 180, 187, 222, 227, 230, 232, 234, 255, 327, 342, 347, 367, 369, 370, 373, 393, 397, 433, 448–49, 451, 465, 483, 494–98, 511, 535, 547, 552, 557–58, 562, 566–68, 579, 585–86, 589, 595, 607, 610–11, 614, 617, 630; Canada, 96; crematoria, 189, 262; described, 93–95, 493–94, 533–34; ex-

termination of French, 329, 332;
Family Camp, 257–61; food, 178; holidays, 190; proposed bombing, 449,
472; resistance in, 188–89; selections,
180. *See also* Concentration Camps;
Deportations; Gassing; Genocide
"Auschwitz Protocol," 230, 246
Austria, xiv, 13, 19, 23, 48, 84, 92,
220, 235, 294, 396, 415, 526, 539

Babi Yar, xxi, 597, 600, 630
Bácska, 216, 221
Baeck, Rabbi Leo, 31, 255, 257
Baer, Commandant Richard, 84
Bagdolio, Marshal Pietro, 391
Baky, László, 226
Balfour Declaration, 439, 444
Balkans, 389, 396, 425, 441, 449, 488;
anti-Semitism, 304–5; dictatorships,
305; Greece, 309–11; Holocaust in
Bulgaria, 307–9; Jews in, 301–5; mi-
nority guarantees, 302–3; prewar pe-
riod, 310–16; Romania, 311–13;
Yugoslavia, 313–14. *See also specific
countries*
Bandera, Stefan, 293, 295–96
Baranszki, Tibor, 238, 239
Barbie, Klaus, 332, 363, 617
Bárdossy, László, 221
Baron, Tova, 180
Barot, Madeline, 341
Barth, Karl, 129, 366
Baur, Andre, 340–47
Beaune-la-Rolande, 327, 330, 362
Becher, Kurt, 258
Beckmann, Max, 584
Beer, Susan, 178
Beit Terezín Archives, 259, 629
Belgium, 151, 154, 157n, 199, 291, 323,
364, 366, 400, 415, 442, 450
Belgrade, 304, 306
Belzec, 87, 90, 261, 285, 535, 586
Beneš, Eduard, 252, 269–73
Benoit, Fr. Marie, 394
Bergen-Belsen, 85, 86, 102n, 156, 178,
222, 233, 255, 266, 422, 451, 562,
578, 595, 617
Bergson, Peter, 475

Berlin Wall, xiii–xv
Bermuda Conference, 445, 626
Bernhard, Prince, 368, 376 n.14
Bessarabia, 306–7, 309, 311
Best, Werner, 322, 325, 326
Bethlen, Count Istvan, 217, 230
Bialystok, 87, 184, 189, 212, 588
Biebow, Hans, 260
Birkenau, 84, 86, 94–96, 102n, 178,
184, 190, 448–49, 451, 483, 562. *See
also* Auschwitz
Bitburg, xxv, 31–32
Bloch, Marc, 350
Blum, Léon, 384
Böegner, Pastor Marc, 340
Bohemia, Moravia. *See* Czechoslovakia
Bonhoeffer, Pastor Dietrich, 127, 129,
134, 158n
Boris, King, 307–8
Bormann, Martin, 26, 69, 543
Brand, Joel, 4, 11, 15, 71, 223, 232,
256–57, 448–49. *See also* Great Brit-
ain; Hungary
Bratislava, 250, 448
Brecht, Bertolt, 606
Brunner, Alois, 187, 332, 347
Buber, Martin, 111, 114, 511, 587
Bucharest, 311
Buchenwald, xxiii, 82, 84, 94, 173, 332,
367, 375, 535, 562, 586, 595, 617,
620, 627
Budapest, 219, 221, 448, 523; camps,
222; conditions in ghetto, 239; film do-
cumentaries, 618, 625; murders in,
240; Rescue Committee, 224–337; re-
sistance, 241. *See also* Hungary
Bulgaria, 151, 170, 222, 327, 409, 445,
488; dictatorship, 305; Jewish resis-
tance, 446–47; Jews in, 303–4, 307;
Nazi ally, 306–7; and Spain, 421–22
Bulge, Battle of, 45
Burger, SS Commandant Anton, xxiv,
255, 265, 266
Byelorrusia, 285, 366, 443

Cambodia, 195, 198
CANDLES (Children of Nazi Deadly

Laboratory Experiments), 629. *See also* Survivors

Carpatho-Ruthenia, 221, 229, 252, 257, 284, 297, 366

Carter, Bruce, 589. *See also* Art of the Holocaust

Carto, Willis, xxii. *See also* Revisionists

Catholics and Holocaust. *See* Christians and the Holocaust∝tican

Celeste, Gov. Richard and Dagmar, 591

Celler, Rep. Emanuel, 473

CENTOS, 524

Centre de Documentation Juive Contemporaine, 12, 625. *See also* France

Chagall, Marc, 583–84, 587

Chamberlain, Houston Stewart, 591

Chamberlain, Neville, 63–64, 439–40

Chelm, 284

Chelmno, 9, 87, 261, 498, 535, 586

Children in the Holocaust: British, 447; in France, 328, 332, 335, 339, 341, 448; in Hungary, 449; in Italy, 399; Jewish mentioned, xxi, 9, 13, 150, 157n, 185, 212, 234, 255, 263–64, 267, 283; in Poland, 145–47, 151–52, 177–80, 533; in Spain, 427n; in Switzerland, 436, 444. *See also* Juvenile Literature

China, 63. *See also* Shanghai

Christian, King, 170. *See also* Denmark

Christians and the Holocaust, 8, 43, 93, 121–39; Catholics in Germany, 130–31, 498–99, 509; children and spouses of Jews, 151–53; church relations with Jews, 123–25; in Czechoslovakia, 252; in France, 336, 339, 341; German church struggle, 70, 109, 125–35; in Great Britain, 444; Greek Orthodox, 302, 304–5, 311; in Holland, 365, 372; in Hungary, 230–31; oppose euthanasia, 489–92; rescue efforts, 164–65, 167–69, 171, 347, 397; resistance, 158n; in Spain, 419; theology in poetry, 565–68; in U.S., 472. *See also* Genocide; Judaism; Rescuers; Vatican

Chrzanow, Poland, 179

Cluj, 223

Churchill, Winston: on Jewish refugees,

443–46; Middle East Policy, 441–42, 447–52. *See also* Great Britain; Palestine

Codreanu, Nicolai, 273

Cohen, Prof. David, 368, 370–72

Colons, 351

Comité d'intermouvement auprès des evacués (CIMADE), 341

Commissariat général aux questions juives (CGQJ), 325–28, 334–38, 346, 358

Concentration Camps, xviii, xx, xxii–xxv, 10, 12, 15, 57, 181, 297; atmosphere of cruelty, 101n, 536–37; bombing discussed, 449; in Budapest, 222; bureaucracy, 88; commanders, 83–86; deaths in, 483–88; described, 89–97, 493–94, 533–34, 538, 586, 607–8, 624; Dutch in, 375; extermination centers, 86–88; first created, 75–83; first in Poland, 211; French, 327–30; in Greece, 422; in Italy, 388, 395; Jasenovac, 313; liberation, 146, 255, 451; music in, 184–85; in North Africa, 353; operations, 99–100; revolts, 91; sickness and starvation, 255, 388, 483; in Spain, 415–18; SS in 121–23, 173, 279; Terezin conditions, 255–56; women's, 100, 177–91. *See also* Deportations; Genocide; Schutzstaffel; *specific camps*

Conseil Représentatif des Juifs de France (CRIF), 348, 354

Cremieux, Adolphe, 351

Crimea, 16

Croatia, 153, 221, 279, 302; atrocities, 315; and Italians, 389–91; Jews in, 314; nationalists, 291. *See also* Ustashis

Cuba, and Jews, 606

Cyrenaica, 445–46

Czechoslovakia, xxiv, 57, 66, 151, 180, 183, 217, 448–49, 500, 526, 594–95; anti-Semitism, 252, 260; conference for Final Solution, 255; current conditions, 249–50; deportations, 255; films on, 612; under Hapsburgs, 267–68; impact of Munich, 252–53, 258, 269;

independent Slovakia, 254, 256; Jews
in, 251; major leaders, 271–74; Nazi
occupation, 253–54, 269–70; Paradise
Ghetto of Terezín, 255–57, 261–67;
prewar republic, 251, 268–69; refugees, 260; resistance, 270. *See also*
Concentration Camps; Deportations;
Genocide; Terezín
Czestochowa, 186

Dachau, xix, 103n, 109, 251, 370, 398,
485; concentration camp model, 75–92;
villagers of, 173. *See also* Concentra-
tion Camps; Schutzstaffel
Daluege, SS Gen. Kurt, 256
Dannecker, SS Gen. Theodor, 323–29,
344, 346, 396
Darlan, Admiral François, 325, 336–37,
351
Darquier de Pellepoix, Louis, 326, 334,
336. *See also* France
Darre, Walther, 53–58
Debrecen, 228, 233, 235
DeGaulle, Charles, 311, 619
deGeer, D. J., 366–67
Delegazine Assistenza Emigranti Ebrei
(DELASEM), 389, 392, 399. *See also*
Italy
Demjanjuk, John, 609, 626
Denmark, 10, 14, 132, 151, 154, 157n,
170, 230, 255, 258, 321, 366, 400–
401, 487–88, 611, 620. *See also*
Rescuers
Deportations: to Auschwitz, 495, 543,
585; from Austria, 323; from Balkans,
307, 313; from Croatia, 389–91; from
Czechoslovakia, 253–57, 260–61, 265,
553; from France, 331–32, 325, 327,
329, 335, 342, 347, 390–91, 489;
from Greece, 389–90, 489; from Hungary, 180, 223, 227–33, 235–41, 245–
47, 448; from Italy, 154–56, 489, 557;
from Luxembourg, 442; from Poland,
184, 187; from Romania, 223, 441;
from Rome, 393, 396; from Slovakia,
184. *See also* Auschwitz; Concentration Camps; Genocide; Schutzstaffel
Deschenes Commission Report, 291

Diaries from the Holocaust, 522–24
Dickstein, Rep. Samuel, 473
Dirlewanger Brigade, 297
Dmowski, Roman, 208
Dora, camp, 535
Drancy, 329–31, 335, 349, 620. *See also*
France
Dreyfus Affair, 336–37, 343, 381, 487
Dubček, Alexander, 250

Eastern Europe, xxvi, 10, 13, 63–64, 66,
75, 474. *See also specific nations*
Eban, Abba, 424
Eckart, Dietrich, 70
Edelstein, Jacob, 256–57, 267, 371. *See*
*also* Terezín
Eden, Anthony, 441, 444–49, 451–52.
*See also* Great Britain
Egypt, 460
Eichmann, Adolf, xxiv, 4, 84, 97, 143,
161; artists of Terezín, 263, 323, 327;
Balkan Jews, 446–47; biographies, 26,
577; and Czech Jews, 253–54, 256;
documentaries on, 610, 614, 617; and
Dutch Jews, 370, 372; Europa Plan,
256; and Final Solution, 255, 502,
507, 558; in Hungary, 226–29, 231–
33, 239, 448; and Italian Jews, 395;
and Mufti of Jerusalem, 465; trial,
190. *See also* Genocide; Schutzstaffel;
War Crimes
Eicke, SS General Theodor, 78–84, 90,
97, 99, 101n. *See also* Concentration
Camps; Dachau; Schutzstaffel
*Einsatzgruppen*, 6, 9, 10, 12, 98, 220,
255, 283, 285, 288, 292, 494, 624.
*See also* Genocide; Schutzstaffel
*Einsatzstab Rosenberg*, 323, 367, 483
El Alamein, 442
El Lissitzky, 588
Ellekom, camp, 373
Endre, László, 226–27
Eppstein, Dr. Paul, 267
Estonia, 261, 279
Ethiopia, 384
Euphemisms, xxii, 96, 173, 179, 255
Europa Plan, 256–58
Euthanasia, xxiii, 9, 12, 173, 489–92

Evian Conference, 8, 11, 13, 243, 432–33, 624

Facing History and Ourselves, 627
Farben, I. G., 53, 56–57, 368
Farinacci, Roberto, 382, 387, 395, 398, 1403n
Fascism. *See* Hitler, Adolf; Italy; Mussolini, Benito; National Socialism; Spain
Feder, Gottfried, 52–54
Federenko, Fedor, 626
Fiction of the Holocaust, 533–46
Filderman, Dr. Wilhelm, 311
Film: documentaries and commercial of Holocaust, 604–22; in Hungary, 228; of Terezín, 262, 266; in Ukraine, 281
Finland, 414, 487, 489
Finzi, Aldo, 396
Fleischmann, Gisi, 187, 256–58, 588
Fleischmann, Dr. Karel, 263–64, 588
Florence, 396
Flossenburg, 83
Foli, camp, 396
France, xxiv, 7, 11, 16, 80, 83, 154, 171, 364, 526; anti-Semitic statutes, 324–38, 340, 345, 357–58; appeasement, 252, 272; communists, 341, 343, 348, 350; deportations, 222, 331–32, 356; detention camps, 325, 327, 329–30, 356; Ecole Juive, 583–87; films on, 611–13, 619; first Jewish arrests, 327–29; French fascists, 331; history of Jews in France, 342–44, 360; Holocaust in, 321–63; Italians in, 390, 400; Jews in Paris, 328, 343, 354; Le Chambon, 132, 165, 170, 341; legacy of French Revolution, 333–37, 343; liberation, 354; Nazi occupation, 322–23, 334–35, 355–56; North Africa, 351–53, 362–63; "Operation Attila," 331; organization of Jews, 346–47; plight of Stateless Jews, 337, 342–43, 344, 348–49, 358, 488; postwar Jewish activities, 354–55; prewar attitudes, 58, 63; rescue activities, 151; resistance, 350–51, 450; role of French police, 328–38; Spanish rescue, 423; traditional French policy on refugees,

333, 442, 447–48; Ukrainians in, 291; Vichy collaboration, 206, 333, 335, 339–40, 349. *See also* Drancy; Petain, Marshal Philippe; Union of Jews in France
Franco, Gen. Francisco, 408–9, 423–25, 446. *See also* Spain
Frank, Anne, 364, 367, 368, 523, 606, 613
Frank, Hans, 26, 254, 290, 624
Frank, Gen. Karl Hermann, 255
Friedmann, Dr. Frantisek, 256, 260
Fritta, Bedrich, 263, 588
Funk, Walther, 55
Funten, Gen. Ferdinand aus der, 369–71

Gadja, Gen. Rudolf, 252, 268
al-Gailani, Rashid Ali, 461, 464–65. *See also* Iraq
Galen, Cardinal Graf von, 490, 491, 500
Galicia, 221, 227, 229–30, 563. *See also* Halychyna Division
Gassing, xxii, 5, 9, 10, 68, 181, 189, 247, 257, 282, 313, 390, 397, 424, 443, 449, 484, 494, 543, 552, 586. *See also* Concentration Camps; Genocide
Gehlen, Gen. Reinhard, 295
Geneva Convention, 434. *See also* International Red Cross
Genocide: Allies condemn, 444; Armenians, Gypsies and Cambodians, 195–98; atrocities confessed, 543; bureaucracy, 75–86, 89–97, 99, 111, 323–24, 482, 507–8, 611; disbelief, 451, 487, 495–96, 499; in German textbooks, 481–520; guilt for, 502–12; knowledge of German people, 495–500; Nazi policy, 9–10, 74–75, 86, 181, 255, 410, 483; revelations of, 230, 443–44; secrecy of, 258, 492–502; survivor attitudes, 121–23; theories on, 172–73, 194–99, 315. *See also* Concentration Camps; Deportations; *Einsatzgruppen*; Gassing; Germany; Hitler, Adolf; National Socialism; Poland; Schutzstaffel; U.S. Government; Vatican
Germany: bureaucracy of killing, 483;

Christian inaction, 498–99; in Croatia, 389–91; euthanasia program, 489–92; films, 611–12, 615; guilt, 502–12; intelligence, 295; Jews in, xiii–xiv, 29–32, 253–54, 316; Middle East policy, 459–69; Nazi party, 21–39; non-Jewish spouses, 152–53; occupation of Czechoslovakia, 252–55; occupation of Holland, 364–65; people's knowledge of Holocaust, 484; rescue of Jews, 151, 161; resistance to Hitler, 70–71, 189, 484–92; surrender, 286, 599; textbooks, 481–520; Third Reich, 49–73; today, xiii–xvi, xix, xxiii, 510–12, 610; trade with Spain, 410, 414; war crimes, 625; Weimar period, xiii, 14, 22, 31–32, 48–49, 50–51, 58, 76, 126–27, 486, 503, 606. See also Genocide; Hitler, Adolf; National Socialism; Schutzstaffel; Wannsee Conference

Gerstein, Kurt, 9, 11

Gestapo, 77–78, 82, 84, 86, 96, 158n, 181, 188, 210, 226, 332, 424, 440, 449, 488, 497–98, 592, 613, 617. See also Himmler, Heinrich; RSHA; Schutzstaffel

Ghetto Fighters House, 189, 244, 248, 588, 617, 625

Ghettoization: Budapest, 239–41, 533–34, 588; impact upon Jews, 68, 167–68; Terezín, 255–56, 263–65; Vilna, 179–80; Warsaw, 185–87; 523–24. See also Genocide; Lodz ghetto; Warsaw ghetto

Giraud, Gen. Henri, 351

Globocnik, SS Gen. Odilo, 87, 90, 97

Glücks, Richard, 97

Goebbels, Joseph, xxiii, 25, 44, 189, 486, 543, 584–85, 592–93. See also Art of the Holocaust

Göring, Hermann, 44, 486, 585, 624; biographies, 25; Final Solution order, 255; and German economy, 52–58

Graebe, Herman, 162, 167

Great Britain, 9, 71, 220; acceptance of Ukrainian surrender, 287–88, 298; actions of troops, 102n, 286–87; ap-

peasement of Hitler, 252, 268, 272, 287; assistance to Greece, 442; condemns genocide, 444; in Depression era, 58, 60–61; domestic anti-Semitism, 442, 446–48, 450–51; disbelief in Holocaust, 451; government policies, 452–54; hostile refugee policy, 280, 366, 415, 444–45; illegal immigration, 440–41; negates bombing of concentration camps and Jewish army, 449–50; and Palestine Mandate, 429–53; prewar relations with Germany, 63, 69, 71; relations with U.S., 447–52; and Spain, 412–13; wartime appeasement of Arabs, 449–50, 459–69. See also Bermuda Conference; Brand, Joel; Churchill, Winston; al-Husseini, Haj Amin; Palestine; U.S. Government

Greece, 11, 66, 153, 231, 302, 450, 526; anti-Semitism, 315–16; deportation, 389–90; extermination, 309–11; food problems, 412; occupation, 306–9; prewar Jewish population, 303, 305; refugees, 409, 447; resistance, 489. See also Balkans

Greenberg, Rabbi Irving, 627

Grobba, Fritz, 460–64

Gross-Rosen, camp, 83–85, 87

Grosz, George, 584

Gruber, Dean Heinrich, 109–10

Grüninger, Paul, 430, 435

Günther, Hans, 255, 266, 617. See also Film; Terezín

Gurs, camp, 330, 433, 588. See also France

Gustloff, Wilhelm, 432. See also Switzerland

Gypsies, xxiv, 45, 77, 87, 93, 195, 197–98, 282, 436, 542, 579, 588. See also Concentration Camps; Genocide

Haakon, King of Norway, 364

Haas, Leo, 283, 588

Halutz, 232–247

Halychyna Division (Zionist Movements), 279–300; battle of Brody, 284–85; formation, 281–83; literature on, 280–92; massacres, 280; nomenclature, 285; as police, 283; in Slovenia, 286–88; as war criminals, 297–98. *See also* Ukraine

Hasidism, 528, 596

Haushofer, Karl, 50

Havel, Vačlav, 250, 265

Hayes, Carlton, 408–20, 426, 472. *See also* Spain

Hebrew Immigrant Aid Society (HIAS-HICEM), 260

Hebrew University, 628

Heine, Heinrich, 584

Helbronner, Jacques, 346, 348

Hennenberg, Jacob, 179

Hertz, Rabbi Joseph, 449, 455

Hess, Rudolf, 25, 39, 69, 624

Heydrich, Reinhard, 6, 90, 103n, 222, 266, 270, 271, 324, 484, 502, 552, 616; assassination, 257; biographies, 25, 273–74; and concentration camps, 78–79, 84; and Final Solution, 254–56; Nisko, 254. *See also* Czechoslovakia; Deportations; Eichmann, Adolf; Genocide; RSHA; Terezín; Wannsee Conference

Himmler, Heinrich, 14, 57, 69, 97, 254, 279, 323, 326, 391, 465, 482, 484, 486, 502, 545; biographies, 25; development of concentration camps, 85–91; in Rome, 392–93; speech of, 292; and Ukrainian SS, 284–85. *See also* Concentration Camps; Ghettoization; Schutzstaffel

Hindenburg, Paul von, 49, 59, 76–77. *See also* Germany

Hirsch, Fedy, 256

Historians: and the Holocaust, xiv–xvii, xix; in German textbooks, 481–520; intentionalists, 315; principal texts, 13–20. *See also* Resources on the Holocaust; Revisionists

Hitler, Adolf, xxii–xxv, 21–32, 110, 122, 156, 178, 432, 606; anti-Semitism inspired by church, 124, 126–28, 130, 198; biographies, 21–25, 41–46; and Communists, 69–70; creation of concentration camp system, 74–83; and death camps, 89–90, 494, 515n; eco-nomic policies, 28–29, 49–59; euthanasia policy, 489–92; foreign policy, 27–28, 60–65; and Franco, 409–11, 426; guilt of, 502–3, 507; hatred of Jews, 6, 31–32, 45, 67–69, 315, 446, 481; and Hungarians, 223–25; last days, 71, 543; Middle East policy, 459–69; and military, 65–67; and Mussolini, 383–89, 391, 606–7; Nisko, 254; orders French deportations, 331; plot to assassinate, 488; resistance to, 70–71, 498–99; in Weimar, 48–49. *See also* Concentration Camps; Genocide; Germany; National Socialism; Schutzstaffel

Hlinka, Msgr. Andrei, 252

Hlinka Guard, 254, 256, 258, 259, 268. *See also* Slovakia

Hoare, Samuel, 412, 415

Hoess, Rudolf, 26, 83–85, 96–97, 101n, 482, 502, 507. *See also* Auschwitz

Holland, 13, 80, 132, 133, 154, 170, 255, 284, 523, 526, 612; anti-Semitic laws, 371–75; children, 152; Dutch collaboration, 369, 371–73; invaded, 366–67; Jews in, 364–67; Joodse Raad, 368–69; labor camps, 374; memoirs, 367–69; Nazi occupation, 369–74; postwar attitudes, 374–76; refugees, 441, 450; resistance, 161, 370, 374, 489, 527–28, 551. *See also* Children in the Holocaust; Deportations; Frank, Anne; National Socialism; Rescuers; Resistance

Horst Wessel Lied, 593

Horthy, Admiral Miklós, 217, 221, 223–26, 230–31, 234, 342. *See also* Hungary

Hugenberg, Alfred, 52, 57

Hull, Cordell, 231, 412–14, 445, 472. *See also* U.S. Government

Hungary, 342, 410, 526–28; anti-Jewish legislation, 223, 244; Brand Mission, 4, 11, 15, 71, 231–33; children's homes, 239; deportations, 227–33; film, 612, 618; ghettoization, 225–28; Hungarian fascists, 180, 183; Jewish institutions, 219, 241–43; Jewish resis-

tance, 240–41; Jews at Auschwitz, 102; Jews massacred, 86, 95, 240–41, 589; Nazi occupation, 225–41; neutral rescue efforts, 142–43, 233–35, 245–57; protected houses, 237–38; after Russian invasion, 222–23; seizure of other territories, 252, 297, 313; Spanish rescue, 421–22, 607; survival, 366, 401, 447; between the world wars, 216–20; Zionism, 244–45. *See also* Arrow Cross; Deportations; Eichmann, Adolf; Rescuers; Wallenberg, Raoul
al-Husseini, Haj Amin (Grand Mufti of Jerusalem), 257, 354, 441, 446–47, 459, 462–67. *See also* Germany; Great Britain; Palestine

Institute for Contemporary Jewry, 625. *See also* Resources on the Holocaust
Institute for Historical Review, xxii. *See also* Revisionists
Institute on the Holocaust and Genocide, 196
Intergovernmental Committee on Refugees, 253, 445
International Law Institute, 198
International Red Cross, 8, 446, 455; in Hungary, 234, 237, 240; Swiss failure, 433–35, 536; at Terezín, 255, 257, 262, 266. *See also* Genocide; Switzerland
Iran, 459–60, 465
Iraq, 459–60, 464–65
Iron Guard, 311–12. *See also* Romania
Isaac, Jules, 166
Israel, xxii, xxv, xxvii, 14–15, 152, 182, 183, 186, 189, 526, 538, 545, 556, 599, 608–9, 614, 628; and Swiss, 430, 436; wars, xxvi, 107, 114–15. *See also* Jewish Agency in Palestine; Weizmann, Chaim; Yad Vashem; Zionism
Istanbul. *See* Turkey
Italy, 11, 13, 306, 309, 526; anti-Semitism in, 381, 385–95, 397; Black Sabbath in Rome, 155–56, 393–94; concentration camps, 388, 536–37; in Croatia, 388–89; deportations, 392–400; early history of Jews, 380, 381;

in Ethiopia, 383; fascism, 294, 382–87, 557; films, 611–13; and Germany, 60–65; under Mussolini, 153–55, 380–407; occupation of Riviera, 158n, 356, 390; reminiscences, 403; resistance, 389, 397–98, 488; return of Mussolini, 394; Saló Republic, 394–95; in Yugoslavia, 313. *See also* Deportations; Mussolini, Benito; Pius XII; Vatican
Izbice, 261, 266

Jackson, Justice Robert, xx
Janowska, camp, 144, 535
Japan, 60–65, 69–70, 142
Jasenovac, camp, 313
Jaspers, Karl, 505, 508, 510
Jassy, 311
Jehovah's Witnesses, 77, 500
Jesus, 133–34, 155, 164–65, 436. *See also* Judaism
Jewish Agency in Palestine, 441, 449. *See also* Zionism
Jewish Art, 582–83. *See also* Art, of the Holocaust
Jewish Badge, 397; Denmark, 170; France, 327–28, 340, 423; Holland, 364; Hungary, 223, 226, 230; Italy, 153; Slovakia, 254
Jewish Councils (Judenrats), 5, 7–8, 13, 256, 310, 312, 346, 368–69, 371–72, 393, 395, 524. *See also* ghettos in *Czechoslovakia, France, Holland and Poland*
Jewish Historical Institute, Warsaw, 625. *See also* Resources on the Holocaust
Jewish Philosophy. *See* Judaism
Jews. *See specific nations, cities*
Joint Distribution Committee (JDC), 232, 237, 258, 260, 341, 349, 354, 408, 416, 417, 418, 420, 423, 447, 449, 524. *See also* Rescuers
Joodse Raad, 368–69, 371
Jordana, Count, 412–17. *See also* Spain
Judaism, 141; Christians on Holocaust, 109–10; converts, 151–52; in Czechoslovakia, 251–52; death of god, 108–9, 121–23, 155; after the Holocaust, 106–21; Orthodox in Hungary, 223, 228;

poetry on God, 551, 553–55, 559; 560–64. *See also* Literature of the Holocaust; Music of the Holocaust; Poetry of the Holocaust

Juvenile Literature, 575–81. *See also* Literature of the Holocaust

Kahan-Frankl, Samu, 219

Kaliszan, Josef, 588. *See also* Art of the Holocaust

Kállay, Miklós, 221, 223–24. *See also* Hungary

Kaltenbrunner, Ernst, 25

Kamenets-Podolsk, 221, 222, 246. *See also* Poland

Kaplowitz, Rose, 177–78

Kappler, Herbert, 392, 405n. *See also* Rome

Karolyi, Mihaly, 216

Kaspar, Cardinal Karel, 260

Kasztner, Dr. Rudolph, 223, 231–34, 245, 247. *See also* Hungary

Keitel, Gen. Wilhelm, 40, 64, 624

Kemeny, Gabor, 238

Kempner, Vita, 189

Kent State University, xxvi–xxvii, 619, 630. *See also* Resources of the Holocaust

Keppler, Wilhelm, 52–54, 58

Keresztes-Fischer, Ferenc, 221, 226

Kielce, 185, 209, 213. *See also* Anti-Semitism; Poland

Klarsfeld, Beathe and Serge, 335, 630

Klein, Robert, 251

Knochen, Helmut, 323, 332

Koch, Karl, 84, 102n

Kögel, Max, 85, 86, 102n

Kokoschka, Oskar, 584. *See also* Art of the Holocaust

Kolbe, Maximilian, 589

Kollwitz, Kaethe, 588. *See also* Art of the Holocaust

Komoly, Ottó, 226, 233–39. *See also* Hungary

Konovalets, Euhen, 294. *See also* Ukraine

Kor, Eva Moses, 629

Korczak, Janusz, xxi, 184, 212, 589, 620, 624. *See also* Children in the Holocaust; Warsaw ghetto

Koretz, Rabbi Zvi, 310

Kosice, 228

Kovno, 7, 190, 580, 598. *See also* Lithuania

Krakow, 184, 190, 224, 290, 483. *See also* Poland

Kramer, Josef, 85–86, 102n

Kramer, Salo, 256

Krausz, Moshe, 222

Krejci, Ludwik, 268

*Kristallnacht*, 112, 127, 255, 470, 482, 492, 497, 499–500, 578, 594, 614, 624. *See also* Germany; National Socialism

Krumey, Hermann, 231

Krupp Family, 53, 56–57

Külföldieket Ellenörzö Országos Központi Hatóság (KEOKH/National Central Alien Control Office), 220, 222, 234. *See also* Hungary

Kun, Bela, 216–17

Lages, Willi, 370, 372. *See also* Holland

Lambert, Raymond-Raoul, 347–48

Lange, Fritz, 261. *See also* Schutzstaffel

Langlet, Dr. Valdemar, 234

Lantos, Congressman Tom, 143

Latvia, 279. *See also* Riga

Laval, Pierre, 7, 327, 333–38, 342, 357. *See also* France

Law, Richard, 444, 446. *See also* Great Britain

*Lebensraum*, 50–51, 56

Lemkin, Raphael, 194, 197. *See also* Genocide

Les Milles, camp, 330. *See also* France

Le Vernet, camp, 330

Levy, Albert, 346

Ley, Robert, 53–58. *See also* Germany; National Socialism

Lichtenburg, 82–84. *See also* Concentration Camps

Lidice, 256–58. *See also* Heydrich, Reihard

Liebermann, Max, 587. *See also* Jewish Art

Lindbergh, Charles, 471
Lipchitz, Jacques, 584, 587. *See also* Jewish Art
Lisbon, 416, 418. *See also* Portugal
Literature of the Holocaust, 521–74; diaries, 521–24; fiction, 533–46; memoirs, 524–32; poetry, 547–74. *See also* Judaism; Juvenile Literature
Lithuania, 188–90, 249, 261, 580, 630
Lodz ghetto, 7–8, 87, 255, 260, 542–45, 585, 596–97, 618, 628. *See also* Deportations; Genocide; Ghettoization; Poland
Loew, Rabbi Judah, 250
Long, Breckinridge, 471–75. *See also* U.S. Government
Lospinoso, Guido, 390
Lowenstein, Dr. Karl, 256. *See also* Tererzín
Lubetkin, Zivia, 186. *See also* Resistance
Lublin, 8, 86, 90, 261, 266, 284, 483. *See also* Majdanek
Lueger, Karl, 381
Luther, Hans, 221, 223
Luther, Martin, 431, 617. *See also* Anti-Semitism
Lutz, Charles, 234, 239, 247
Luxembourg, Jews in, 442, 450
Luzzatti, Luigi, 381
Lwow (Lvov, Lviv), 141, 144, 147, 150, 224, 283–84, 295–96, 418, 585, 628. *See also* Ghettoization; Schutzstaffel; Ukraine
Lyons, 332, 345, 617. *See also* Barbie, Klaus

MacDonald, Malcolm, 441
Madagascar, 68, 254, 371, 445
Maglione, Cardinal, 393
Magyar Izraeliták Pártfogo Irodája (MIPI/ Welfare Bureau of Hungarian Jews), 221–22. *See also* Hungary
Magyárországi Izraeliták Országos Irodája (National Bureau of Jews of Hungary), 219
Maimonides, Moses, 522
Majdanek, camp, 84–87, 94, 101n, 329, 332, 451, 465, 483, 562, 586. *See*

*also* Concentration Camps; Deportations; Schutzstaffel
Malines, camp, 11
Malmedy, 279
Malraux, Andre, 195
Maly Trostinec, 255, 266
Mandler, Robert, 256
Mann, Thomas, 443
Mantello, George, 234, 247
Marcus, Col. Mickey, 608. *See also* Israel
Márton, Bishop Aron, 229
Masaryk, Thomas, 252, 260, 271–72, 274–75. *See also* Czechoslovakia
Maurer, SS Col. Gerhard, 97, 255
Mauthausen, 83, 85, 92–93, 367, 375, 535, 586, 611, 615, 620. *See also* Concentration Camps; Schutzstaffel
Mazin, Max, 420
Medical Experiments, xxv, 10, 99, 173, 543, 624. *See also* CANDLES
Memoirs of Holocaust, 524–28. *See also* Literature of the Holocaust
Mengele, Dr. Josef, 162, 180, 393, 545, 608, 619, 629
Mercir du Paty, Charles, 334
Mermelstein, Mel, xxii, 615. *See also* Revisionists
Middle East, 459–69. *See also specific nations*
Mila 18 bunker, 186. *See also* Warsaw Conference
Milan, 386, 396
Minority Guarantees, 302–3
Minsk, 187, 255, 260, 266. *See also* Byelorrusia
Mizrahi, 220, 222. *See also* Zionism
Molotov-Ribbentrop pact, xxiv
Monowitz (Auschwitz camp), 555
Morgenthau, Henry Jr., 447–48, 452, 473. *See also* U.S. Government
Morocco, 351, 353, 423
Morrison, Herbert, 442
Moscow Conference, 446
Motion Pictures (Movies). *See* Films
Moyne, Lord Walter, 441, 442, 450. *See also* Great Britain
Müller, Heinrich, 97

Munich Conference (1938), xxiv, 183, 252–53, 260, 268–69, 272–73
Munich Putsch (1923), 48
Munk, Dr. Erich, 256
Munkács, 227, 252
Munkácsi, Ernö, 226
Music of the Holocaust, 591–603; Nazi purge, 591–95; traditional Jewish, 595–97. *See also* Yiddish
Muslims, 250, 302–3, 305, 352–53, 408, 441, 450. *See also* Anti-Semitism; Arabs; al-Husseini, Had Amin; North Africa; Zionism
Mussert, Karel, 370, 375. *See also* Holland
Mussolini, Benito, 11, 42, 43, 60–61, 70, 153, 382–400, 408, 488, 557. *See also* Deportations; Fascism; Hitler, Adolf; Italy

Nachtigall Battalion, 285, 292, 295. *See also* Ukraine
Nagyvárad, 228, 235
Nahas, Mustapha Pasha, 460
Nansen Office, 253
National Jewish Resource Center, 627. *See also* Resources on the Holocaust
National Socialism, xvi, xxiv, 57, 258, 261; anti-Semitism, 31–32; on art, 584; and Christianity, 109–10, 125–33; collaborators, 7–9, 368–69, 371–72, 393–95, 545; Euthanasia plan, 489–92; in France, 321–63; Hitler, 21–24, 39–73; in Holland, 369–74; in Italy, 382–87, 393–95; massacres of Jews, 4–7, 179–80; music, 591–95; other leaders, 25–26; in Poland, 177–80; persecution of women, 29, 99–100, 176–93; Third Reich policies, 26–31; and Ukrainians, 281–88; in Weimar Republic, 48–49. *See also* Anti-Semitism; Concentration Camps; Deportations; Genocide; Germany; Hitler, Adolf; *Kristallnacht*; Schutzstaffel; Wannsee Conference; *specific nations*
Natzweiler, camp, 83, 85, 102n
Nazis. *See* National Socialism
Netherlands. *See* Holland

Neuengamme, camp, 535
Neuhammer, camp, 282, 284, 285
Neurath, Constantine von, 254
Niemoeller, Pastor Martin, 127, 129, 132
Nietzsche, Friedrich, 274
Ninth Fort (Kovno), 190
Nisko, 254, 260
Normandy, 334, 364, 367
North Africa, 334, 351–53, 355, 390, 408, 412, 417, 420, 423, 445. *See also* Arabs; Great Britain; Muslims; Palestine
Norway, 151, 291, 321, 364, 366
Novi Sad, 221
NSB (Dutch National Socialist movement), 370, 373
*Numerus clausus*, 217, 253
Nýilas. *See* Arrow Cross

Oesterreicher, Dr. Erich, 256
Oeuvre de secours aux enfants (OSE), 350
Office of Military Government of U.S. (OMGUS), 57. *See also* Resources on the Holocaust
Olberg, Carl, 326–27
Ohrdruf, camp, 617
"Operation Barbarossa" (Russian Invasion), 66, 68–69, 324
"Operation Gisela" (Projected Invasion of Spain), 408
"Operation Reinhard" (Massacre of Jews), 87, 90, 91, 256, 397
"Operation Sea Lion" (Invasion of England), 68
Oral Histories, 628. *See also* Resources on the Holocaust
Oranienburg, camp, 82
Organization of Ukrainian Nationalists (OUN), 285–86, 291–95. *See also* Halychyna Division; Ukraine
Ossietzky, Carl von, 486
Ottoman Empire, 302, 305
Ouradour, xxiv

Pahlevi, Muhammad Rezo Shah, 460
Palestine, 9, 112, 185, 187, 222, 224, 231, 234, 237, 252, 254, 276, 354,

422, 540, 551, 559, 608; Arab and
Jews, 459–69; and British Mandate,
439–52. *See also* Bermuda; Great Brit-
ain; al-Husseini, Haj Amin; Israel;
Rescuers; U.S. Government; White Pa-
per on Palestine; Zionism
Papen, Franz von, 26, 624
Paris. *See* France
Partisans, 527–28, 580. *See also*
Resistance
Partito Nazionale Fascista (PNF), 382,
386–87. *See also* Italy
Passfield White Paper (1930), 464
Patalucci, Giovanni, 398
Patton, Gen. George, 425
Pavelic, Ante, 389. *See also* Croatia;
Ustashis
Peel Commission (1937), 464. *See also*
Palestine
Pehle, John, 419, 448, 475. *See also*
U.S. Government
Perlasca, Georgio, 625
Petain, Marshal Philippe, 325–26, 334–
40, 344, 346, 357. *See also* Concen-
tration Camps; Deportations; Fascism;
France; Laval, Pierre
Petlura, Simon, 273, 286, 293–94. *See
also* Ukraine
Photographs, 181–82, 197. *See also* Film
Pilsudski, Marshal Josef, 272. *See also*
Poland
Pithiviers, camp, 327, 330
Pius XII, 130, 134, 155, 158n, 231,
393–94, 421, 544. *See also* Genocide;
Italy; Rescuers; Rome; Vatican
Poetry of the Holocaust, 547–74. *See
also* Literature of the Holocaust
Pohl, SS Gen. Oswald, 84, 97
Poland, xx, 80, 83, 89, 294, 297, 364,
366, 410, 415, 421; aid from Allies,
440–42; anti-semitism, xxvi, 5, 7–8,
91, 150, 156–57, 204–5, 211, 313,
607; Armia Krajowa, 284, 297, 450;
chosen for extermination centers, 86–
87, 90, 330; deportations to Hungary,
220–24; deportees from Czechoslovakia, 253–54; exiled government, 294;
films, 611–12; general populace, 142,

205–11; ghettos, 15, 99; historiography, 203–15; Jewish resistance, 177–
93; Jews in, xxiii, 144–53, 524–25;
memoirs, 540–41; Nazi law, 57; Nazi
occupation, 206–8; Polish collabora-
tors, 141, 149, 206; rescuers, 141,
144–53, 161, 185, 205; Ukrainian
massacres, 280–84, 295–96. *See also*
Anti-Semitism; Auschwitz; Belzec;
Chelmno; Concentration Camps; De-
portations; Gassing; Genocide; Ghetto-
ization; Lodz ghetto; Lwow; Majdanek;
Schutzstaffel; Sobibor; Treblinka;
*Volksdeutsch*; Warsaw ghetto
Ponary, 179–80, 535, 555, 597–98
Portugal, 408, 416, 418
Prague, 250–56, 260, 585, 594. *See also*
Czechoslovakia
Preminger, Otto, 604, 608. *See also* Film
Preziosi, Giovanni, 395, 405n
Protocols of Elders of Zion, xxvi, 249,
273, 436, 463

Radom, 186
Rahm, Major Hans, xxiv, 255, 265, 589.
*See also* Terezín
Rathbone, Eleanor, 444, 446
Rauter, Hans, 370–71. *See also* Holland
Ravensbrück, camp, 83, 85, 102n, 181,
588
Reams, Robert Borden, 472
Redlich, Egon, 263–64, 267. *See also*
Terezín
Reich, Haviva, 183–84, 261
Reichstag Fire, 76
Rescuers, 131–32, 620, 624; analysis of
motives, 161–73; British, 446–51;
Denmark, 487; in France, 332, 349–
50, 447–48; Holland, 364–65, 370; in
Hungary, 233–41, 245–48; Italy, 389,
394, 399; non-Jewish spouses, 152–53;
in Poland, 140–60, 210; punishment,
167; Spain, 410, 416, 418–32, 427n;
Swiss, 433–35. *See also* Resistance
Resistance: in art, 588; in Balkans, 307;
in France, 350–51, 361–62, 450; in
Germany, 70–71, 484–92; Greece,
310; in Holland, 365, 370, 374; in

Hungary, 240–41, 247–48, 551; in Italy, 389, 397–98, 448; Jewish, 10–12, 525–27, 551, 555, 579–80; in Poland, 177–93; Romania, 311–12; in Slovakia, 251; Yugoslavia, 313–14

Resources on the Holocaust: archives, xix–xx, 624–27; memorial centers, 627–28; state councils, 629–30; study guides, 629–30; survivor groups, 628–29

Revisionists, xiv, xvi, xxi–xxiv, 32n 615

Ribbentrop, Joachim, 26, 60, 390, 391, 420, 624

Ribiere, Germaine, 171, 341

Riegner, Gerhard, 443–45, 448

Riga, 255, 261, 266

Righteous Gentiles. See Rescuers

Rijksinstituut voor Oorlogsdocumentatie, 369

Rivesaltes, camp, 330

Robota, Rosa, 189

Rödel, Arthur, 84–85

Röhm, Ernst, 26, 44, 78. See also National Socialism

Roland Battalion, 285, 292. See also Halychyna Division; Ukraine

Romania, 11, 217, 221, 223, 232, 234, 273, 539, 554; anti-Semitic collaborators, 206, 294, 304–7, 343; history of Jews, 303, 306; massacres, 311–13; offer Jews for sale, 446; and Spain, 421; survivors, 365–67. See also Deportations; Iron Guard; Trans-Dnistria

Rome, 386, 392–95. See also Italy; Vatican

Rommel, Gen. Erwin, 441

Roosevelt, Franklin D., 50, 64–65, 71, 95, 231, 409, 414, 417, 443, 445, 446, 448, 471–77. See also U.S. Government

Roschmann, Eduard, 610

Rosenberg, Alfred, 26, 64, 70, 323

Röthke, Heinz, 327, 331

Rothmund, Heinrich, 432–33, 436. See also Switzerland

Rotta, Msgr. Angelo, 230

RSHA (Reich Security Main Office), 223, 258, 265, 323, 327, 391, 396.

See also Heydrich, Reinhard; Himmler, Heinrich; Schutzstaffel

Rszezow, 638

Rukh, 250

Russia. See Soviet Union

Sachsenhausen, camp, 82, 85, 112, 533, 586

Salazar, Antonio, 409

Saliege, Archbishop Jules-Gerard, 340, 341. See also France

Saló, republic, 394–95, 400. See also Italy

Salonika, 303, 304, 309, 310, 332, 416, 422, 607. See also Greece

Sarajevo, 304, 306

Samuel, Lord Herbert, 463

Santo Domingo, 445

Schacht, Hjalmar, 53–55, 56, 58

Schirach, Baldur von, 26. See also Hitler, Adolf

Schlesinger, Kurt, 371

Schmolka, Marie, 253, 260

Scholtz-Klink, Gertrud, 29, 32n

Schroeder, Kurt von, 57

Schutzstaffel (SS): 31–32, 47, 589; camp guards, 75–83; Death's Head Division, 84, 96, 98; Economic and Administrative Office, 84; in extermination camps, 89–90, 92–93, 121–23, 173, 177, 481–83, 489, 494–97, 586; in France, 326–27, 331–32; in Holland, 370; in Hungary, 220–21, 226, 231; in Italy, 391–98; officers, 84–86. See also Concentration Camps; Deportations; Eichmann, Adolf; Einsatzgruppen; Genocide; Gestapo; Heydrich; Reinhard; Himmler, Heinrich; RSHA

Schutzhaft (Protective Custody), 77, 100n

Schwartz, Michael, xxvi

Segal, Louis, 141

Seidl, Commandant Siegfried, xxiv, 255, 265. See also Terezín

Sephardim, 302–3, 304, 343, 365, 420–23, 425, 599. See also Hungary; Spain

Serbs, 302, 313, 315

Seredi, Cardinal Justinian, 229. See also Hungary; Vatican

Seyss-Inquart, Artur, xxiv, 369–70. *See also* Holland

Shandruk, Pavel, 286–87, 290–91, 293

Shaghai, 11, 443

*Shehitah*, 254

Shertok, Moshe, 447, 451

Sicherheitsdienst (SD), 79, 322–23. *See also* Tereziaain

Silkes, Genia, xxi

Silver, Rabbi Abba Hillel, 474–75

Silverman, Sidney, 443

Skarzysko, 535

Skoropadsky, Paul, 286, 293. *See also* Ukraine

Slave labor, 177, 181, 397, 443, 482, 484, 535, 551, 554, 608; in concentration camps, 86–87, 93–94, 121–23; in France, 330; in Hungary, 221–22; in Switzerland, 433. *See also* Concentration Camps

Slep, Abraham, 597

Slotke, Gertrude, 370

Slovakia, 11, 95, 133, 178, 221, 223, 230, 231; anti-Semitic laws, 254, 257; attacks on Jews, 261, 285–86; Jews in, 187, 251; nationalists, 250, 252–53, 270; resistance in, 183–84, 257. *See also* Czechoslovakia; Deportations; Hlinka Guard; Tiso, Msgr. Josef

Slovenia, 285–88, 302, 313

Smuts, Jan, 451

Sobibor, xxii, 87, 90, 91, 212, 285, 329, 332, 367, 483, 498, 528, 535, 562, 613–14, 618. *See also* Concentration Camps; Gassing; Genocide; Resistance

Sombor-Schweinitzer, Jozef, 226

*Sonderbehandlung*, 96, 173

*Sonderkommando*, 96, 189

Sonnino, Baron Sidney, 381

Sosnowiec, 177

Soviet Union, xxiv, xxvi, 50, 51, 53, 56, 57, 71, 85, 149, 197, 286, 393, 413, 449; condemns genocide, 444; and Hungary 220, 224, 229, 235, 239; invaded, 15, 66–69, 220, 254, 541; Jewish survival, 205, 365; liberation of camps, 141, 143, 146, 255, 467; massacres of Jews, 187, 279–300, 324–27,

350; occupies Iran, 465; occupies Poland, 186; prisoners of war, 5, 91, 483, 500; relations with Hitler, 60–65, 69–70. *See also* Genocide; Halychyna Division; Stalin, Josef; Ukraine

Spain, 66, 234, 238, 303, 330, 337, 341, 347, 351, 375, 408–29; and Bulgaria, 420–21; civil war, 384, 408; expulsion of Jews, 408; and France, 423; under Franco, 409–10, 423–25; and Greece, 422; and Hungary, 142, 421–22; refugees, 414–20; relief efforts, 416–17; and Romania, 421; and US War Refugee Board, 418–20; wolfram crisis, 410–12. *See also* Sephardim, U.S. Government

Speer, Albert, 23, 25, 54, 56,, 543, 614

Spellman, Cardinal, 418

Springmann, Shmuel, 223

Stalin, Josef, xxiii, 42–44, 50, 52, 70, 249, 446. *See also* Soviet Union

Stalingrad, 66, 264, 291

Stangl, Franz, 100n

Steiger, Dr. Edward von, 432

Steiner, Hanna, 260

Stern, Samu, 226, 235

Stern Gang, 450

*St. Louis*, S.S., 606, 624

Stoecker, Adolf, 126–27, 381

Stransky, Jan, 260

Strasser, Gregor, 52

Streicher, Julius, 6, 26, 29, 624

Stresemann, Gustav von, 269

Strochlitz Center (Haifa), 625. *See also* Resources on the Holocaust

Stroop, SS, Gen. Jurgen, 181, 212

*Struma*, SS 441

Stulpnágel, Gens. Otto and Karl Heinrich von, 326

Sturmabteilung/Brown Shirts (SA), 30–31, 76, 78. *See* National Socialism

Stutthof, camp, 83, 87, 102n, 588

Sudetenland, 252–53

Survivors: attitudes, 121–23, 141–42, 171–72, 177–91; memoirs, 526; 534–45; 578, 608–10, 615, 628–29. *See also* Art of the Holocaust; Literature of the Holocaust; Poetry of the Holocaust; *specific nations*

Sweden, 10, 14, 142–43, 234, 238, 366, 445, 487, 542, 560. *See also* Rescuers

Switzerland, 11, 230, 233, 234, 240, 341, 347, 397, 399, 405n, 430–38, 443, 449, 545; anti-Semitism, 432, 436; attitudes today, 435–36; attitude toward refugees, 430–33, 435, 611; International Red Cross, 433–35; Jews in, 431; money in Swiss banks, 447–48; rescuers, 435; *Schutzpass* required, 237–38; slave labor, 433; Swiss Jewish Community (SIG), 436. *See also* Evian Conference; Genocide; International Red Cross

Syria/Lebanon, 353–54. *See also* Muslims; Palestine; Zionism

Syrkin, Nachman, 249

Szálasi, Ferenc, 217, 225, 235, 238. *See also* Hungary

Szeged, 228, 233

Szeptycki, Metropolitan Andreas, 150. *See also* Rescuers

Szold, Henrietta, 185

Sztójay, Dome, 223, 230

Teitelboim, Nuta, 88. *See also* Women and the Holocaust

*Témoignage chrétien*, 341. *See also* Rescuers.

Temple, William, Archbishop of Canterbury, 444

Terezín, xxiv, 255–56, 258, 261–67, 370, 371, 373, 375, 535, 543, 551–53, 578–79, 585, 588, 594, 614, 616–18. *See also* Art of the Holocaust; Children in the Holocaust; Czechoslovakia; Ghettoization; Literature of the Holocaust; Poetry of the Holocaust; Resistance

Thekla, camp, 617

Thyssen, Fritz, 57

*Tiger Hill* Incident, 439

Tijn-Cohn, Gertrud van, 371

Tiso, Msgr. Josef, 252–54, 257–58, 261, 271, 273. *See also* Czechoslovakia; Slovakia

Tito, Marshal Josef, 286

Todt, Fritz, 56

Trans-Dnistria, 311–12, 441, 446. *See also* Romania

Transylvania, 223, 229, 306, 312–13

Trawniki, camp, 255, 297

Trblinka, xxi, xxii, 87, 90, 91, 100n, 187, 212, 255, 261, 285, 483, 494, 498, 515n, 523, 535, 562, 586, 697, 618, 620. *See also* Concentration Camps; Deportations; Gassing; Korczak, Rabbi Zvi; Poland; Warsaw Conference

Treitschke, Heinrich von, 126–27

Trianon, Treaty of, 216, 229

Trieste, 386, 388, 396. *See also* Italy

Tripolitania, 445–46

Trocme, Pastor Andre, 132, 341

Troller, Norbert, 262

Tuka, Vojtek, 257

Tunisia, 351

Turkey, 142, 196, 224, 231–32, 302, 306, 441, 444, 446–48. *See also* Rescuers; Sephardim

Ukraine, xxiv, 91, 149, 164, 178, 182, 273, 376, 443, 482, 541, 597, 630; camp guards, 210, 254, 285, 586; civil war years, 292–93; documentaries, 619; hostility toward Jews, 252, 293–94; ideology, 280, 296–97; institutions today, 625; nationalist organizations, 294–95; period of famine, 195; pogroms, 221, 280, 295–96; police, 284–85; troops in Slovenia, 286–88; war criminals, 297–98; and Warsaw uprisings, 297. *See also* Babi Yar; Concentration Camps; *Einsatzgruppen*; Halychyna Division; Petlura, Simon; Schutzstaffel; Warsaw Conference

Ungar, Otto, 263, 588. *See also* Art of the Holocaust

Union of Jews in France (UGIF), 326, 332, 334, 338, 346–50, 354. *See also* Resistance

Union of Jews for Resistance and Mutual Aid (UJRE), 345, 350. *See also* France

Union of Utrecht, 365, 373

United Nations, 424, 444
United Nations Resolution on Genocide, 194
UNRRA (United Nations Relief and Rehabilitation Agency), 419
U.S. Government: and Axis, 220; diplomacy with British, 452; food to Europe, 442; and Italy, 389; and Jewish refugees, 355; news of genocide, 231, 444; State Department, 471–77; and Switzerland, 436; Teasury Department, 447; War Refugee Board, 418–20, 422, 448–49, 471–72, 475. *See also* America; Genocide; Great Britain; Hull, Cordell; Long, Breckingridge; Roosevelt, Franklin D.
U.S. Holocaust Memorial Council, 198, 625–28. *See also* Resources on the Holocaust
Ustashis, 313, 389–91. *See also* Croatia

Vajna, Gabor, 240
Vallat, Xavier, 325, 326, 334. *See also* France
Vatican, 11, 14, 130–31, 134, 155, 158n, 238, 291, 348, 544; activities in Slovakia, 251; appeals, 444; France, 340; confirms genocide, 230; Italy, 383, 393–94, 398; Romania, 312, 421; Spain, 408. *See also* Hungary; Pius XII; Rescuers
Versailles, 53, 252, 267
Vessenmayer, Edmund, 225
Vichy. *See* France; Laval; Petain, Marshal Philippe
Visser, L. E., 369, 375
Vittel, camp, 552
Vlajka Organization, 252, 260
*Volksdeutsch*, 208, 210, 285
Vught, camp, 373

Wachter, SS. Gen. Otto, 281
Waffen SS, 80, 279–300, 395
Wagner, Richard, 45
Waldheim, Kurt, xxiv, 134
Wallenberg, Raoul, 11, 14–43, 157n, 234, 238–40, 247–48, 616. *See also* Hungary; Rescuers

Wannsee Conference, xxii, 68, 221–22, 255–56, 276, 324, 327, 613, 624. *See also* Deportations; Genocide; Heydrich, Reinhard; Terezín
War Crimes, 100n, 101n, 261, 263, 288, 297–98, 405n, 465, 509, 609, 624, 625
Warsaw ghetto, xx, xxi, 87, 179, 190, 208, 285–97, 483, 489, 523, 542, 552, 563, 585, 588, 596–97, 615–18; uprising, xxiv, 10, 141, 181–82, 185–89, 210, 256, 279, 446. *See also* Ghettoization; Poland; Resistance
Wedgwood, Josiah (MP), 443, 446
Wehrmacht, 89, 178, 283, 322, 370, 441, 497, 500
Weimar, xiii, 14, 22, 31–32, 48–49, 50–51, 58, 76, 126–27, 485. *See also* Germany
Weissmandel, Rabbi Michael, 187, 231, 256–59, 448
Weiszäcker, Ernst von, 393
Weizmann, Chaim, 439–40, 451. *See also* Zionism
Westerbork, 369–71. *See also* Holland
White Paper on Palestine (1939), 439, 441, 445, 448, 450, 460, 464. *See also* Great Britain; al-Husseini, Haj Amin; Palestine
Wiener Library, 625. *See also* Resources
Wiesenthal Center, 68, 98, 26–27. *See also* Resources
Wilhelm II, Kaiser, 365
Wilhelmina, Queen, 364
Wingate, Orde, 441
Wise, Rabbi Stephen, 443, 474, 475
Wisliceny, Dieter, 231
Wolfram ore, 410–20. *See also* Spain
Women and the Holocaust, 29, 71, 99–100, 176–93
Women's International Zionist Organization (WIZO), 220, 253, 256–67, 260
Working Group, 231, 256–57, 259. *See also* Czechoslovakia; Fleischmann, Gisi; Weissmandel, Rabbi Michael
World Jewish Congress, 422, 443, 445, 626
Wurm, Bishop Theophil, 491, 498–500

Yad Vashem, xxi, 15, 19n, 98, 101n, 141, 182, 184, 259, 364, 576, 610, 624, 626–27. *See also* Resources

Yellow Star. *See* Jewish Badge

Yiddish: poetry, 563–64; musical compositions, 595–99, 618

YIVO (Yiddish Institute for Jewish Research), xix–xx

Zachor (Remember), xxvi, 627

Zentralstelle für jüdische Auswanderung, 253

Ziereis, Commandant Franz, 85

Zimetbaum, Mala, 188

Zionism, xxii, xxvii, 183–90, 540, 630; Anne Frank's, 606; in Balkans, 304, 306; in Czechoslovakia, 251–52, 259–60, 263–64, 275; in France, 343–44, 350; in Holland, 271, 523; in Hungary, 220–24, 226, 229, 231–33, 239–41; in Italy, 382–83, 385; and Palestine, 439–55; in Poland, 596. *See also* Great Britain; Rescuers; Resistance; U.S. Government

Zopf, Willi, 370

Zuckerman, Izhak, 186

Zwiep, Rev. Nanne, 370

Zygielbojm, Szmul, 446

# About the Contributors

STEVEN H. ADAMS served as Director of Kent State Hillel between 1988 and 1992. During that time, he chaired annual symposia on the Holocaust at the university. Rabbi Adams currently is with Temple Beth Shalom in Hudson, Ohio.

JOHN AXE is a free-lance writer who has traveled and studied extensively in Spain. Associated with the History Department of Youngstown State University, Axe has published more than thirteen books on various subjects.

HARRY JAMES CARGAS teaches literature at Webster University in St. Louis. Among his twenty-five books are *A Christian Response to the Holocaust*, *Conversations with Elie Wiesel*, *Reflections of a Post-Auschwitz Christian*, and *The Holocaust: An Annotated Bibliography*. Dr. Cargas has received humanitarian awards from the Anne Frank Institute and United Nations Association.

ALAN CASSELS is Professor of Modern European History at McMaster University, Hamilton, Ontario. One of the leading authorities on Italy under fascism, Dr. Cassels has contributed articles to *History Journal*, *The Journal of Modern History*, and *American Historical Review*. His publications include *Mussolini's Early Diplomacy* and *Italian Foreign Policy 1918–1945: A Guide to Research*.

ASHER COHEN, Senior Lecturer of Contemporary History and Research and Director of the Strochlitz Institute of Holocaust Studies at the University of Haifa, Dr. Cohen also serves as co-editor of the Hebrew annual *Studies on the*

*Holocaust*. His books include *The Halutz Resistance in Hungary, 1942–1945*, *La Shoah*, and *Persecutions et savetages*.

ANNETTE EL-HAYEK is an instructor in French and German at Youngstown State University, working toward her doctorate in History at Kent State University. Her dissertation deals with the Evian Conference of July 1938.

JACK FISCHEL is Chairman of the Millersville (Pennsylvania) University Department of History and cochairman of the annual Holocaust conference at that campus. A specialist in American History, he has published articles in *Midstream*, *Scholars*, and *The American Zionist*. Dr. Fischel co-edited *Holocaust Studies Annual* and *Jewish-American History and Culture: An Encyclopedia*.

EVA FOGELMAN is a social psychologist and psychotherapist in private practice and Senior Research Fellow at the Center for Social Research, Graduate Center, City University of New York. Dr. Fogelman is founding director of the Jewish Foundation for Christian Rescuers. She coproduced the award winning documentary "Breaking the Silence: The Generation after the Holocaust" and wrote *Doing Moral Good: Courage during the Holocaust*.

EARL M. FRIEDMAN was attached to Army intelligence and its denazification program during the five years he served in postwar Germany. Educated at the University of Maryland, University of Dayton, and Kent State University, he later served as Director of the Upper School and taught history at Park School in Buffalo before his death in 1989.

JONATHAN C. FRIEDMAN was an exchange student to Israel and a Fullbright Scholar at Kiel University before entering the Ph.D. program in German History at the University of Maryland. In 1993 he was a fellow of Leo Baeck Institute. His dissertation topic deals with Christian-Jewish relations in three Hessian communities during the Weimar and Nazi periods.

SAUL S. FRIEDMAN of Youngstown State has published nine books on Jewish affairs, among them *No Haven for the Oppressed*, *Pogromchik: The Assassination of Simon Petlura*, *The Oberammergau Passion Play*, and *Without Future: The Plight of Syrian Jewry*. Visiting Professor of Jewish History at Kent State, he has written and produced ten public television documentaries. In 1989, Dr. Friedman and colleague David Costello developed a laser disc/computer interactive program on the Holocaust for high schools.

SANFORD GUTMAN is Professor of modern European History and Coordinator of Jewish Studies at the State University of New York at Cortland. He has spent considerable time living in and doing research about France. Dr. Gutman has published several articles and book reviews on the French Revolution, nineteenth-century France, and Jews in modern France between the time of the Dreyfus affair and World War II.

IRENE HESKES attended Julliard and Eastman Schools of Music, the Jewish Theological Society, and Harvard University. She has written extensively on Jewish music. Some of her published works include *The Cantorial Art*, *The Historic Contribution of Russian Jewry to Jewish Music*, *Ernest Bloch: Creative Spirit*, and *Israeli Music*. She also contributed essays to *Encyclopedia Judaica* and *The Holocaust: An Annotated Bibliography and Resource Guide*.

HERBERT HOCHHAUSER is Director of the Ohio Council for Holocaust Education and also Director of Kent State Jewish Studies. Professor of German and Yiddish, Dr. Hochhauser was born in Berlin and survived the war years in Switzerland. A short essay of his appears in the volume *In Answer*.

ALEXANDER KITROEFF, a distinguished Balkans scholar, has taught at Haverford College and New York University. His publications include "The Jews in Greece, 1941–1944" and "The Greeks in Egypt: Ethnicity and Class" for *The Journal of Hellenic Diaspora* and *The Greeks in Egypt, 1919–1937*. Dr. Kitroeff is currently Assistant Professor for Hellenic Studies at the Onassis Center of New York University.

DENNIS KLEIN is Director of the Anti-Defamation League's Braun Center for Holocaust Studies. Founding Editor of *Dimensions*, a journal of Holocaust Studies, he is also the author of *Jewish Origins of the Psychoanalytic Movement*. Dr. Klein taught history and psychology at New York University, Harvard, and Ohio State.

REYNOLD KOPPEL is Professor of European and German History at Millersville State where he coedits the *Holocaust Studies Annual* with Jack Fischel. A founding member of the Pennsylvania State Universities Holocaust Council, Dr. Koppel cohosts the annual Millersville conference on Holocaust.

SHMUEL KRAKOWSKI is Director of the Yad Vashem Archives in Jerusalem and lecturer on Holocaust at Tel Aviv University. A member of the editorial board of the *Encyclopedia of the Holocaust*, his numerous publications include *The War of the Doomed: Jewish Armed Resistance in Poland, 1942–1945* and (with Israel Gutman) *Unequal Victims: Poles and Jews during World War II*.

LAURENCE KUTLER holds a degree in Semitic Studies from New York University. Commissioner for Jewish Education in Youngstown, Ohio, Dr. Kutler teaches Hebrew at Kent State University. He was also responsible for the recent translation of the Terezín Diary of Gonda Redlich.

NORA LEVIN was chief archivist and lecturer at Gratz College in Philadelphia for many years before her death in 1989. Her major monographs include *The Holocaust*, *While Messiah Tarried: Jewish Socialist Movements 1917–1971*, and *The Jews in the Soviet Union since 1917*.

SOL LITTMAN, sociologist turned journalist, served as Director of the Simon Wiesenthal Center in Toronto for nearly a decade. Access to European archives resulted in the publication of *War Criminal on Trial: The Helmut Rauca Case* and *Retreat from Justice*, which identifies four hundred-fifty Nazi war criminals who have found shelter in Canada.

MONTY NOAM PENKOWER holds degrees from Yeshiva and Columbia Universities. Currently Professor of History at Touro College, he has published extensively in Jewish journals. His books include *The Federal Writers Project*, *The Jews Were Expendable*, and *From Catastrophe to Sovereignty*. Dr. Penkower is currently researching a study of Palestine and the Anglo-American Alliance during World War II.

DAVID A. RAUSCH, Professor of History at Ashland University, has written over twenty books, including *Legacy of Hatred*. A prolific writer who has published nearly five hundred articles, Dr. Rausch is associated with the Ashland Theological Seminary. He has also lectured extensively about the Holocaust, Christian-Jewish relations, and anti-Semitism in this country, France, and Israel.

WALTER RENN, Chairman of the History Department of Middle Tennessee State University, has published a monumental study titled *Treatment of the Holocaust in Textbooks: The Federal Republic of Germany, Israel and the United States*. While affiliated with Wheeling College, Dr. Renn was responsible for organizing statewide observances and academic forums on the Holocaust for nearly ten years.

BEA STADTLER holds a Master of Judaic Studies degree. Once secretary to Rabbi Abba Hillel Silver, she served as registrar of the Cleveland College of Jewish Studies for twenty-three years. She has been contributing articles for Jewish publications for the past twenty-five years and is best known for her award-winning children's text *The Holocaust: A History of Courage and Resistance*.

CHARLES W. SYDNOR, JR., served until recently as President of Emory and Henry College in Virginia. The author of *Soldiers of Destruction: The SS Death's Head Division, 1933–1945*, Dr. Sydnor also developed an award-winning television documentary on Adolf Hitler. He currently is affiliated with the Public Broadcasting System.

NELLY TOLL survived the Holocaust as a child in her native Galicia. Now based in New Jersey, she lectures frequently about art and her wartime experiences. She is the author of *Without Surrender: Art of the Holocaust* and a recent volume of her own childhood drawings, *Behind the Secret Window: A Memoir of a Hidden Childhood*.

LEON W. WELLS, born in Poland in 1925, has recounted his experience during the Holocaust in *The Janowska Road*. An engineer who holds nineteen U.S. patents, Wells participated in the American Jewish Commission on the Holocaust chaired by Justice Arthur Goldberg and Dr. Seymour Finger. Wells subsequently published *Who Speaks for the Vanquished: American Jewish Leaders and the Holocaust*.

ROBERT H. WHEALEY teaches German History at Ohio University. He recently published *Hitler and Spain: The Nazi Role in the Spanish Civil War*. Dr. Whealey has also contributed essays to *Journal of Modern History, The International History Review, Diplomatic History*; *Historical Dictionary of the Spanish Civil War, The Republic and the Civil War in Spain* (edited by Raymond Carr) and *Spain in Conflict, 1931–1939: Democracy and Its Enemies* (edited by Martin Blinkhorn).

GLORIA YOUNG, Professor Emeritus of English at Kent State University, has published extensively on the works of Herman Melville and Joseph Conrad, as well as on the poetry of Howard Nemerov and Holocaust poetry. Cofounder of the annual Kent State Holocaust conferences, she served as Visiting Professor at Aristotle University in Thessaloniki in 1988–89 and Shimane University in Matsue, Japan, in 1990–91.

MORRIS ZYRL, currently a resident in Boca Raton, Florida, has been a regular radio personality, reviewing motion pictures. Cofounder of Second Generation of Holocaust Survivors in Cleveland, Zyrl has been a major force in the creation of the Cleveland Holocaust Memorial Center.